Regional Guide to International Conflict and Management from 1945 to 2003

Regional Guide to International Conflict and Management from 1945 to 2003

Jacob Bercovitch
and
Judith Fretter

University of Canterbury,

Christchurch, New Zealand

A Division of Congressional Quarterly Inc.
Washington, D.C.

CQ Press
1255 22nd Street, N.W., Suite 400
Washington, D.C. 20037

202-729-1900; toll-free: 1-866-4CQ-PRESS (1-866-427-7737)

www.cqpress.com

Cover design by Archeographics

Printed and bound in the United States of America

08 07 06 05 04 5 4 3 2 1

∞ The paper used in this publication exceeds the requirements of the American National Standard for Information Sciences—Permanence of Paper for Printed Library Materials, ANSI Z39.48-1992.

Library of Congress Cataloging-in-Publication Data

Bercovitch, Jacob.
Regional guide to international conflict and management from 1945 to 2003 / Jacob Bercovitch and Judith Fretter.
p. cm.
Rev. ed. of: International conflict. 1997.
Includes bibliographical references and index.
ISBN 1-56802-825-3 (alk. paper)
1. World politics—1945–1989—Encyclopedias. 2. World politics—1989-—Encyclopedias. 3. Conflict management—History—20th century—Encyclopedias. I. Fretter, Judith. II. Bercovitch, Jacob. International conflict. III. Title.

D842.B464 2004
909.82'5'0202—dc22 2004021954

To Gillian, Liora, and Daniella—with much love, as ever
—Jacob

To Nic and my parents, Malcolm and Valerie—for their love, constant support, and encouragement
—Judith

Summary Contents

Contents	ix
Figures, Tables, and Maps	xix
Preface	xxi
An Overview of International Conflict	1
The Nature of International Conflict	3
Understanding International Conflict Management	13
International Organizations and Regional Conflicts	34
Regional Conflicts	49
Africa: 1.1–1.97	51
Americas: 2.1–2.45	117
Asia: East Asia and the Pacific: 3.1–3.65	153
Asia: Southwest Asia: 4.1–4.39	203
Europe: 5.1–5.30	229
Middle East: 6.1–6.67	258
Appendixes	303
A. Countries and Their Regions	303
B. Chronology of Regional Conflicts	306
C. Organization Factsheets	317
References	335
Index	345

Contents

Figures, Tables, and Maps xix
Preface xxi
Acknowledgments xxii

An Overview of International Conflict 1

The Nature of International Conflict 3
Understanding International Conflict Management 13
International Organizations and Regional Conflicts 34

Regional Conflicts 49

Africa: 1.1–1.97 51

List of Conflicts 51
Countries in the Region 53
Regional Overview 54
Overview of Conflict 56
Conflict Management 57

1.1 **Madagascar–France: Nationalist Rebellion** 60
March–August 1947

1.2 **Eritrea–Ethiopia: Eritrean Nationalism and Agitation for Independence** 60
July 1949–December 1950

1.3 **Tunisia: Tunisian Independence and African Nationalism** 61
January 1952–March 1956

1.4 **Kenya–United Kingdom: Anticolonial Tribal Uprising and Mau Mau Revolt** 61
August 1952–December 1963

1.5 **Algeria: The Fight for Independence** 62
November 1954–March 1962

1.6 **Morocco–Spain: Postindependence Autonomy and the Sahara Conflict** 62
November 1957–April 1958

1.7 **France–Tunisia: Postindependence Autonomy and Military Bases Conflict** 63
February–May 1958

1.8 **France–Tunisia: French–Algerian Border Incidents** 63
February–August 1959

1.9 **Mauritania–Mali: Hodh Region Conflict** 63
Mid-1960–February 1963

1.10 **Congo (Zaire): Secession, Anarchy, Civil War, and the Belgian Congo Crisis** 64
July 1960–Mid-1964

1.11 **The African Territories–Portugal: African Nationalism and Independence Struggle** 65
1961–July 1975

1.12 **Tunisia–France: Postindependence Autonomy Dispute in Bizerte** 65
July–September 1961

1.13 **Somalia–Kenya/Ethiopia: Somali Expansionism and Separatist Insurgency** 66
November 1962–September 1967

1.14 **Sudan: Southern Separatism, Anya-Nya Terrorism, and the First Sudan Civil War** 66
September 1963–March 1972

1.15 **Morocco–Algeria: Territorial Dispute and the Tindouf War** 67
October 1963–February 1964

1.16 **Niger–Dahomey (Benin): Lete Island Dispute** 68
December 1963–June 1965

1.17 **Somalia–Ethiopia: Somali Expansionism, Separatist Guerrilla Fighting, and the First Ogaden War** 68
January–March 1964

1.18 **Rwanda–Burundi: Postindependence Ethnic Violence Between the Hutu and Tutsi** 69
January 1964–January 1965

1.19 **France–Gabon: Military Putsch, French Military Intervention, and Aubame's Coup** 69
February 1964

1.20 **Ghana–Upper Volta: Ghanaian Border Dispute** 69
June 1964–June 1966

1.21 **Eritrea–Ethiopia: Eritrean Nationalism and War of Secession** 70
1965–May 1993

1.22 **Ghana–Togo: Ghanaian Expansionism and Border Incidents** 71
January–May 1965

1.23 Uganda–Congo (Zaire): Rebel Activity and Border Incidents 71
February–March 1965

1.24 Chad–Sudan: Internal Strife, Sudanese Intervention, and the First Chad Civil War 71
November 1965–1972

1.25 Namibia: Violent Insurrection, War, and Independence Struggle 72
1966–March 1990

1.26 Ivory Coast–Guinea: Coup Plot 72
March–April 1966

1.27 Ghana–Guinea: Nkrumah's Ouster and Postcoup Tensions 73
October–November 1966

1.28 Rhodesia: African Nationalism, Guerrilla Warfare, and Zimbabwe's Struggle for Independence 73
1967–January 1980

1.29 Guinea–Ivory Coast: Regional Rivalry and Hostage Crisis 74
February–September 1967

1.30 Nigeria–Biafra: Ethnic and Regional Rivalries, Secession Attempt, and the Biafran Civil War 74
July 1967–January 1970

1.31 Congo (Zaire)–Rwanda: Regional Instability and the Mercenaries Dispute 75
August 1967–April 1968

1.32 Guinea–Portugal: PAIGC Guerrilla Warfare and the Conakry Raids 75
November 1970

1.33 Uganda–Tanzania: Postcoup Border Clashes 75
January 1971–October 1972

1.34 Equatorial Guinea–Gabon: Territorial Dispute over the Corisco Bay Islands 76
June–November 1972

1.35 Ethiopia–Somalia: Somali Expansionism, Territorial Dispute, and the Second Ogaden War 76
Mid-1972–1985

1.36 Morocco–Mauritania: Saharan Nationalism, Territorial Dispute, and the Western Saharan Conflict 77
October 1974–Ongoing

1.37 Mali–Upper Volta (Burkina Faso): Territorial and Resource Dispute 77
December 1974–June 1975

1.38 Angola–South Africa: Guerrilla Warfare in Namibia, Intervention, and Angolan Civil War 78
1975–Ongoing

1.39 Zaire–Angola: Rebel Activity and Border War 79
November 1975–February 1976

1.40 Mozambique–South Africa: African Nationalism, Intervention, and Civil War 80
1976–October 1992

1.41 Uganda–Kenya: Amin Provocations and Border Incidents 81
February–August 1976

1.42 Chad–Libya: Guerrilla Warfare, Factional Fighting, and Libyan Annexation of the Aozou Strip 81
June 1976–November 1979

1.43 Zaire–Angola: Internal Dissension, Regional Instability, and the First Invasion of Shaba 82
March–May 1977

1.44 Chad: Internal Strife, Foreign Intervention, and the Second Chad Civil War 83
January 1978–June 1982

1.45 Zaire–Angola: Regional Instability, Congolese Dissension, and the Second Invasion of Shaba 83
May 1978

1.46 Tanzania–Uganda: Cross-Border Raids, Tanzanian Invasion, and Ouster of the Amin Regime 84
October 1978–May 1979

1.47 Morocco–Algeria: Western Saharan Nationalism and Border Conflict 85
June–October 1979

1.48 Cameroon–Nigeria: Border Incident 85
May–July 1981

1.49 Uganda: Civil War 86
December 1981–1994

1.50 Zaire–Zambia: Lake Mweru Dispute 86
February–September 1982

1.51 Libya–Chad: Political Instability, Rebel Fighting, Foreign Intervention, and the Third Chad Civil War 87
Mid-1982–Ongoing

1.52 Ghana–Togo: Territorial Dispute and Border Incidents 88
August–October 1982

1.53 South Africa–Lesotho: Guerrilla Insurgency Fears and Anti-ANC Raid 88
December 1982

1.54 Sudan: Secessionist Fighting, Civil War, and the Second Sudan Civil War 89
January 1983–Ongoing

1.55 Liberia–Sierra Leone: Doe Regime Tensions 90
February–March 1983

1.56 Chad–Nigeria: Boundary/Resources Dispute and the Lake Chad Conflict 90
April–July 1983

1.57 Zaire–Zambia: Regional Tensions, Deportations, and Border Dispute 91
September 1983–January 1984

1.58 South Africa–Botswana: African Nationalism and Anti-ANC Raids 91
October 1984–May 1986

1.59 Zaire: Internal Dissent and the Third Invasion of Shaba 92
November 1984

1.60 Zaire: Internal Strife, the Fourth Invasion of Shaba, and the Collapse of the Mobutu Regime 92
June 1985

1.61 Mali–Burkina Faso: Territorial/Resource Dispute and Border War 92
December 1985–January 1986

1.62 Togo–Ghana: Regional Rivalry and Coup Attempt 93
September 1986

1.63 Zaire–People's Republic of the Congo: Regional Instability and Border Incident 93
January 1987

1.64 Ethiopia–Somalia: Somali Expansionism and the Third Ogaden War 94
February 1987–April 1988

1.65 South Africa–Zambia: African Nationalism, Insurgency Fears, and Anti-ANC Raid 94
April 1987

1.66 People's Republic of the Congo: Civil Unrest and Army Rebellion 95
September 1987–July 1988

1.67 Uganda–Kenya: Ugandan Civil War, Refugee Influx, and Border Conflict 95
December 1987

1.68 Somalia: Clan-Based Violence and the Somalian Civil War 95
May 1988–Ongoing

1.69 Burundi: Tribe-Based Communal Violence and the Hutu Conflict 97
August 1988–Ongoing

1.70 Uganda–Kenya: Border Conflict 98
March 1989

1.71 Mauritania–Senegal: Ethnic Violence and Border Incidents 98
April 1989–January 1990

1.72 Liberia: Civil War 98
December 1989–Ongoing

1.73 Guinea-Bissau–Senegal: Border Conflict 100
April–May 1990

1.74 Tuareg–Niger: Confrontation and Reprisals 100
May 1990–October 1994

1.75 Senegal: The Casamance Rebellion 100
Mid-1990–Ongoing

1.76 Tuareg–Mali: Sahel Pastoralist Rebellion and Military Coup 102
June 1990–Ongoing

1.77 Rwanda: Tribal Conflict, Genocide, and Exiles Invasion 102
September 1990–Ongoing

1.78 Liberia–Sierra Leone: Intervention, Destabilization, and the Sierra Leone Civil War 104
March 1991–Ongoing

1.79 Djibouti: Ethnic-Based Violence and Civil War 105
November 1991–July 1993

1.80 Nigeria–Cameroon: Territorial Dispute and the Diamond and Djabane Islands Dispute 105
December 1993–March 1994

1.81 Ghana–Togo: Border Incidents 106
January–February 1994

1.82 Uganda: Intervention and Democratic Movements 106
May 1995–Ongoing

1.83 Federal Republic of Grande Comoros: Coup Attempt and Anjouan and Moheli Independence 107
September 1995–Ongoing

1.84 Eritrea–Yemen: Invasion of the Hunish Islands 108
November 1995–October 1998

1.85 Congo: Independence Movements 109
October 1996–Ongoing

1.86 Uganda–Kenya: Ethnic Cross-Border Clashes 109
November 1996–July 1998

1.87 Niger: Diffa Border Insurgency 110
December 1996–April 1999

1.88 Congo–Brazzaville: Democratic Struggle 110
May 1997–Late 2000

1.89 Djibouti: Intervention and Djibouti Civil War 110
Early 1998–December 2000

1.90 Lesotho: Intervention and Military Factions 111
May 1998–March 1999

1.91 Eritrea–Ethiopia: Yirga Triangle Territorial Dispute 111
May 1998–June 1999

1.92 Guinea-Bissau: Military Factions 112
June 1998–January 2000

1.93 Ethiopia–Kenya: Ethnic Border Clashes 113
October 1998–January 1999

1.94 Liberia–Guinea: Border Dispute 113
September 1999–April 2001

1.95 Ivory Coast: Civil War 114
September 1999–Ongoing

1.96 Central African Republic–Chad: Attempted Coup, Foreign Intervention, and Territorial Occupation 115
Mid-2001–December 2002

1.97 Angola–Zambia: Civil Strife and Border Skirmishes 116
November 2001

Americas: 2.1–2.45 117

List of Conflicts 117

Countries in the Region 118

Regional Overview 118

Overview of Conflict 120

Conflict Management 121

2.1 Dominican Republic–Haiti/Cuba: Regional Aggression 123
Early 1947–December 1951

2.2 Costa Rica: Anticorruption Military Insurgency and Civil War 125
March–April 1948

2.3 Nicaragua–Costa Rica: Border Conflict 125
December 1948–February 1949

2.4 **Argentina–Chile: The Beagle Channel Border Dispute** 126
July 1952–August 1993

2.5 **Guatemala: Civil War and Insurgency** 128
June 1954–Ongoing

2.6 **Nicaragua–Costa Rica: Exiles Invasion Attempt** 129
January 1955

2.7 **Dominican Republic–Cuba/Venezuela: Dominican Republic Aggression and Exiles Conflict** 129
February 1956–January 1962

2.8 **Cuba: Communist Revolution and Cuban Civil War** 131
December 1956–January 1959

2.9 **Nicaragua–Honduras: Boundary Dispute and Mocoran Seizure** 131
April–June 1957

2.10 **Panama: Cuban-Backed Invasion and Panama Revolutionaries Conflict** 132
1958–May 1959

2.11 **Guatemala–Mexico: Mexican Shrimp Boat Incident** 132
December 1958–September 1959

2.12 **Paraguay–Argentina: Paraguayan Exiles Conflict** 133
Early 1959–December 1961

2.13 **Cuba–Haiti: Cuban-Sponsored Military Invasion and Haitian Exiles Conflict** 133
August 1959

2.14 **United States–Cuba: Anti-Castro Military Invasion—The Bay of Pigs** 134
April–May 1961

2.15 **Venezuela–Guyana (UK): Essequibo River Dispute** 134
February 1962–June 1970

2.16 **Chile–Bolivia: Lauca River Dam Dispute** 135
March 1962–1964

2.17 **United States–USSR: Cold War Dispute and the Cuban Missile Crisis** 136
September–November 1962

2.18 **Haiti–Dominican Republic: Exiles Asylum and Invasion Attempt** 137
April–September 1963

2.19 **Cuba–Venezuela: Terrorism and Invasion Attempt** 138
November 1963–May 1967

2.20 **Panama–United States: Sovereignty Dispute and the Flag Riots** 139
January–April 1964

2.21 **Colombia: Banditry and Leftist Guerrilla Insurgency** 139
1965–Ongoing

2.22 **United States–Dominican Republic: Civil War, U.S. Military Intervention, and the Constitutionalist Rebellion** 140
April 1965–September 1966

2.23 **Bolivia: Cuban-Assisted Guerrilla Insurgency** 141
November 1966–July 1970

2.24 **El Salvador–Honduras: The "Football War" Border Dispute** 141
July 1969

2.25 **Guyana–Suriname: New River Triangle Border Dispute** 142
August 1969–November 1970

2.26 **El Salvador–Honduras: Territorial Dispute and Border Incidents** 142
July 1976–October 1980

2.27 **El Salvador: Civil Conflict and the Salvadoran Civil War** 143
January 1977–Late 1992

2.28 **Ecuador–Peru: Regional Rivalry, Territorial Dispute, and the Amazon/Marañón Waterway Incidents** 143
June 1977–January 1978

2.29 **Nicaragua–Costa Rica: Regional Rivalry and Border Incidents** 144
October 1977

2.30 **Nicaragua–Costa Rica: Regional Rivalry, Cross-Border Raids, and Border Incidents** 144
September–December 1978

2.31 **Honduras–Nicaragua: Right-Wing Insurgency and the Contra War** 145
January 1980–February 1994

2.32 **Ecuador–Peru: Territorial Dispute and Border War** 145
January–April 1981

2.33 **United Kingdom–Argentina: Sovereignty Dispute and the Falklands War** 146
April–June 1982

2.34 **Guatemala–Mexico: Regional Instability, Guatemalan Civil War, and Border Incidents** 147
September 1982–January 1983

2.35 **United States–Grenada: Anti-Communist Military Invasion** 147
October–December 1983

2.36 **Ecuador–Peru: Regional Rivalry, Territorial Dispute, and Border Conflict** 148
January 1984

2.37 **Guatemala–Mexico: Regional Instability, Guatemalan Civil War, and Border Incident** 148
April 1984

2.38 **Nicaragua–Costa Rica: Regional Rivalry and Border Incidents** 148
May–June 1985

2.39 **Nicaragua–Costa Rica: Regional Rivalry and Border Incidents** 149
April 1986

2.40 **Suriname: Guerrilla Insurgency** 149
July 1986–December 1992

2.41 **United States–Panama: U.S. Anti-Noriega Military Invasion** 150
December 1989

2.42 United States–Haiti: U.S. Military Invasion and Aristide's Return from Exile 150
September 1994

2.43 Ecuador–Peru: Regional Rivalry and Cenepa Headwaters Confrontation 151
January–March 1995

2.44 Ecuador–Peru: Condor Mountain Territorial Dispute 151
January 1995–October 1998

2.45 Belize–Guatemala: Postindependence Territorial Dispute and Border Incidents 152
August 1995

Asia: East Asia and the Pacific: 3.1–3.65 153

List of Conflicts 153

Countries in the Region 155

Regional Overview 155

Overview of Conflict 157

Conflict Management 160

3.1 China: Civil War 163
1945–1949

3.2 The Netherlands–The Dutch East Indies: Indonesian Nationalism and War of Independence 164
Late 1945–November 1949

3.3 France–Indochina: Independence Struggle 165
December 1945–July 1954

3.4 United Kingdom–Malaya and Singapore: Anti-British Communist Insurgency and the Malayan Emergency 165
June 1948–July 1960

3.5 Burma: Kuomintang/People's Liberation Army Cross-Border Conflict 166
August 1948–1954

3.6 Burma (Myanmar): Karen Separatist Insurgency and Civil War 167
January 1949–Ongoing

3.7 China–Taiwan: Communist-Nationalist Conflict in the Straits of Formosa 168
October 1949–June 1953

3.8 United States–USSR: Cold War Air Incidents 168
April–October 1950

3.9 United States–North Korea: Cold War Territorial Dispute and the Korean War 169
June 1950–July 1953

3.10 China–Portugal: The Macao Territorial Conflict 169
July–August 1952

3.11 USSR–United States: Cold War Air Incidents 170
October 1952–July 1956

3.12 Cambodia–Siam (Thailand): Border Conflict and the Occupation of the Temple of Preah Vihear 170
Early 1953–May 1975

3.13 China–United States/Taiwan: The Quemoy Confrontation 171
April 1954–April 1955

3.14 Taiwan–South Vietnam: The Paracel Islands Dispute 172
June–August 1956

3.15 China–United States/Taiwan: Communist–Nationalist Territorial Dispute and Bombardment of the Quemoy Islands 172
July–December 1958

3.16 Laos: Political Anarchy and the First Laotian Civil War 173
December 1958–1962

3.17 North Vietnam–South Vietnam/United States: Communist Vietcong Insurgency, Anti-Communist U.S. Military Intervention, and Civil War 173
December 1960–May 1975

3.18 Indonesia–Malaysia: Separatist Civil Disturbances and the Borneo Conflict 174
1962–November 1965

3.19 Indonesia–The Netherlands: West Irian Administration Dispute and Separatist Insurgency 175
January–August 1962

3.20 China–Taiwan: CCP-KMT Territorial Dispute and Invasion Threat 175
March–December 1962

3.21 South Vietnam–Cambodia: Anti-Vietminh Cross-Border Raids 176
March–December 1964

3.22 North Vietnam–Laos: Political Anarchy and the Second Laotian Civil War 176
April 1964–December 1966

3.23 North Vietnam–United States: The Vietnam War 177
August 1964–May 1975

3.24 Irian Jaya–Indonesia: Territorial Dispute and Secession Insurgency 178
1965–Ongoing

3.25 North Korea–South Korea: Cold War Dispute and Border Incidents 179
Mid-1965–March 1968

3.26 North Korea–United States: USS *Pueblo* Seizure 179
January–December 1968

3.27 China–Burma: Tribal Conflicts and Border Incidents 180
January–November 1969

3.28 Cambodia (Kampuchea)–South Vietnam/United States: U.S. Bombing Campaign and Vietnam War 180
January 1970–April 1975

3.29 Mindanao–The Philippines: Communal Violence, Land Disputes, and Muslim Secessionist Insurgency 181
January 1970–Ongoing

3.30 South Vietnam–China: Territorial Dispute and the Paracel Islands 182
January 1974

3.31 North Korea–South Korea: Demilitarized Zone and Invasion Threat 182
February–July 1975

3.32 Cambodia (Kampuchea)–United States: Post–Vietnam War Tensions and the *Mayaguez* Incident 183
May 1975

3.33 Laos–Thailand: Postrevolution Exodus and Border Incidents 183
June 1975–January 1976

3.34 East Timor–Indonesia: Independence Struggle 184
October 1975–May 2002

3.35 Cambodia (Kampuchea)–Thailand: Refugee Influx, Regional Tensions, and Border Skirmishes 185
December 1975–February 1976

3.36 Thailand–Cambodia (Kampuchea): Refugee Influx, Regional Instability, and Khmer Rouge Border Incidents 185
November–December 1976

3.37 Cambodia (Kampuchea)–Thailand: Refugee Influx, Regional Instability, and Khmer Rouge Border Incidents 186
January 1977–October 1978

3.38 Cambodia (Kampuchea)–Vietnam: Border Fighting, Vietnamese Invasion, and the Cambodian Civil War 187
January 1979–Ongoing

3.39 China–Vietnam: Regional Rivalry and Border War 188
January 1979–June 1982

3.40 Cambodia (Kampuchea)–Thailand: Khmer Rouge Insurgency and Border Conflict 188
December 1979–October 1980

3.41 Espiritu Santo–Vanuatu (The New Hebrides): Secession Attempt 189
May–September 1980

3.42 Indonesia–Papua New Guinea (PNG): Secessionist Warfare, Border Incidents, and the Irian Jaya Dispute 189
May 1982–October 1984

3.43 Laos–Thailand: Territorial Dispute and Border Incidents 190
June 1982

3.44 China–Vietnam: Regional Rivalry and Border Conflict 190
April 1983

3.45 Vietnam–China: Regional Rivalry and Border Conflict 190
January 1984–March 1987

3.46 Burma–Thailand: Karen Separatist Insurgency, Counterinsurgency Raids, and Border Incidents 191
March 1984

3.47 Thailand–Laos: Boundary Dispute and Border War 191
June 1984–December 1988

3.48 North Korea–South Korea: Cold War Border Incidents 192
November 1984

3.49 Vietnam–China: Regional Rivalry, Sovereignty Dispute, and the Spratly Islands Dispute 192
March 1988

3.50 Bougainville–Papua New Guinea: Separatist Insurgency and Secession Attempt 192
October 1988–Ongoing

3.51 Burma (Myanmar)–Bangladesh: Rohingya Muslim Rebellion and Border Incidents 193
December 1991

3.52 North Korea–South Korea: Historical Enmity and Border Incident 194
May 1992

3.53 Burma (Myanmar)–Bangladesh: Border Incidents 194
March–September 1993

3.54 Burma (Myanmar)–Bangladesh: Border Incidents 194
May–August 1994

3.55 Taiwan–China: Nationalist–Communist Dispute and Shelling Incident 195
November 1994

3.56 China–The Philippines: Territorial Dispute and the Paracel and Spratly Islands Incidents 195
January–February 1995

3.57 Taiwan–Vietnam: Territorial Dispute and Spratly Islands Clash 196
March 1995

3.58 China–Taiwan: Rivalry and Military Tensions 196
January 1996–August 1999

3.59 North Korea–South Korea: Continuing Rivalry 197
September 1996–November 2000

3.60 China–The Philippines: Spratly Islands Incident 198
April 1997–July 1999

3.61 Vietnam–The Philippines: Spratly Islands Firing Incident 198
October 1999

3.62 Thailand–Laos: Mekong River Territories 199
August–September 2000

3.63 Thailand–Burma: Internal Civil Strife, Militia Activities, and Border Skirmishes 199
March–May 2001

3.64 North Korea–South Korea: Naval Incidents 200
November 2001–July 2002

3.65 Japan–North Korea: Spy Ship Incident 201
December 2001

Asia: Southwest Asia: 4.1–4.39 203

List of Conflicts 203

Countries in the Region 204

Regional Overview 204

Overview of Conflict 205

Conflict Management 207

4.1 India: Civil War, Independence, and Partition 1945–1948 207
4.2 Pakistan–India: Postpartition Separatism, First Kashmir War, and India–Pakistan Rivalry October 1947–January 1949 207
4.3 India–Hyderabad: Postpartition Separatist Violence and Secession Attempt July–September 1948 208
4.4 Afghanistan–Pakistan: Postindependence Pathan Border Conflict August 1949 208
4.5 Afghanistan–Pakistan: The Pathan Territorial Conflict June–October 1950 209
4.6 China–Tibet: Tibetan Autonomy Dispute October 1950–May 1951 209
4.7 China–Tibet: Incorporation Struggle March 1956–September 1965 210
4.8 India–Pakistan: Postpartition Border Tension and the Surma River Incidents March 1958–September 1959 210
4.9 China–Nepal: Boundary Dispute June 1959–July 1960 211
4.10 China–India: Sino–Indian Antagonism and the McMahon Line Boundary Dispute August 1959–February 1960 211
4.11 Afghanistan–Pakistan: Boundary Dispute and Pathan Conflict September 1960–May 1963 211
4.12 India–Portugal: Anti-Portuguese Territorial Dispute in Goa December 1961 212
4.13 Nepal–India: Pro-Democratic Rebellion and Border Incidents April–November 1962 212
4.14 India–China: Sino–Indian Wars and McMahon Line Border Dispute October–November 1962 212
4.15 China–USSR: Territorial Dispute over Damansky Island March 1963–September 1969 213
4.16 India–Pakistan: Border Skirmishes 1965–1970 213
4.17 India–Pakistan: Territorial Rivalry and the Second Kashmir War August–September 1965 214
4.18 China–India: Sino–Indian Wars and McMahon Line Border Incidents September 1965 214
4.19 Bangladesh–Pakistan: Secessionist Warfare and the Bangladesh War of Independence March 1971–February 1974 215
4.20 Bangladesh: Postindependence Territorial Dispute and the Chittagong Hill Tracts Conflict 1975–Ongoing 215
4.21 China–India: Territorial Dispute and McMahon Line Border Incidents October 1975 216
4.22 Bangladesh–India: Postcoup Tensions and Border Incidents April 1976 216
4.23 Pakistan–Afghanistan: Pro-Monarchist Revolt and the Peshawar Rebellion March–July 1979 217
4.24 Bangladesh–India: Boundary Dispute and Border Incidents November 1979 217
4.25 USSR–Afghanistan: Soviet Invasion and the Afghan Civil War December 1979–Ongoing 218
4.26 Pakistan–India: Regional Rivalry, Border Incidents, and India–Pakistan Wars July 1981–August 1982 219
4.27 Sri Lanka: Communal Violence, Separatist Fighting, and Tamil–Sinhalese Conflict July 1982–Ongoing 219
4.28 India–Bangladesh: Boundary Dispute and Border Conflict December 1983–June 1984 221
4.29 India–Pakistan: Territorial Dispute, India–Pakistan Rivalry, and the Siachin Glacier Dispute April 1984–September 1985 221
4.30 India–Bangladesh: Boundary Disputes and the Muhuri River Incidents February–April 1986 222
4.31 India–Pakistan: Territorial Dispute, Siachin Glacier/ Kashmir Conflict, and India–Pakistan Rivalry Late 1986–Ongoing 222
4.32 Maldives: Attempted Coup and Invasion November 1988 223
4.33 Kyrgyzstan: Uzbek and Kyrgyzis Ethnic Conflict and Post-Soviet Violence June 1990 223
4.34 Tajikistan: Post-Soviet Strife and Ethnic-Based Civil War April 1992–June 1997 224
4.35 Nepal: Intervention and Maoist Guerrilla Insurgency Mid-1998–September 1999 225
4.36 India–Bangladesh: Kushita Border Incident April–August 1999 225
4.37 Uzbekistan–Kyrgyzstan/Tajikistan: Border Insurgency August 1999–September 2000 225
4.38 Bangladesh–India: Border Incident and Seizure of Perdiwah April–July 2001 226

4.39 United States–Afghanistan: Post–September 11 "War on Terrorism," Al Qaeda Terrorist Links, and Terrorist Containment 227
September–December 2001

Europe: 5.1–5.30 229

List of Conflicts 229
Countries in the Region 230
Regional Overview 231
Overview of Conflict 231
Conflict Management 233

5.1 Greece: Antimonarchist Communist Insurgency and Civil War 236
1945–1949

5.2 Albania–United Kingdom: Corfu Channel Dispute 237
May 1946–December 1949

5.3 Yugoslavia–United States: Cold War Air Incidents 237
August 1946

5.4 USSR–Yugoslavia: Ideological Rift 238
Early 1948–December 1954

5.5 USSR–The Western Allies: The Berlin Airlift Crisis 238
June 1948–May 1949

5.6 Italy–Yugoslavia: Cold War and Trieste Territorial Dispute 239
March 1952–October 1954

5.7 Cyprus–United Kingdom: Intercommunal Violence and the Enosis Movement 239
April 1955–February 1959

5.8 USSR–Poland: Polish October 240
October 1956

5.9 USSR–Hungary: Anti-Communist Revolt, Soviet Invasion, and the Hungarian Uprising of 1956 240
October–December 1956

5.10 USSR–United States: Cold War Dispute and the Berlin Wall 241
July–November 1961

5.11 Cyprus: Intercommunal Violence and Civil War 242
December 1963–November 1967

5.12 USSR–Czechoslovakia: Liberalization Movement, the Prague Spring, and Soviet Military Invasion 242
August 1968

5.13 Iceland–United Kingdom, West Germany, and Denmark: The Cod War 243
November 1971–June 1976

5.14 Cyprus: Communal Violence, Turkish–Greek Invasions, and Partition 244
January 1974–June 1978

5.15 Poland: Internal Crisis, Solidarity Labor Movement, and the Declaration of Martial Law 244
December 1981–February 1982

5.16 Turkey–Greece: Regional Rivalry and Naval Incidents 245
March 1984–January 1988

5.17 Georgia–South Ossetia: Abkhazia Secession War 245
March 1989–Ongoing

5.18 Yugoslavia: Ethnic and Religious Warfare and the Balkans Civil War 246
Mid-1989–November 2000

5.19 USSR–Lithuania: Post-Soviet Independence Crisis 248
March 1990–Late 1991

5.20 Azerbaijan–Armenia: Nagorno–Karabakh Conflict 248
August 1990–Ongoing

5.21 Gagauzia/Dniester–Moldova: Post-Soviet Strife and Gagauzia's Struggle for Autonomy 249
October 1990–July 1992

5.22 USSR–Latvia: Post-Soviet Independence Crisis 250
January 1991

5.23 Macedonia: Civil War, Incursion, and NATO/EU Involvement 251
January 1991–Ongoing

5.24 Russia–Chechnya: Post-Soviet Strife, Separatist Fighting, Chechen and Caucasus Conflicts 252
October 1992–Ongoing

5.25 Cyprus: Ethnic-Based Tensions and Partition Incidents 253
April 1993

5.26 Greece–Albania: Border Tensions 253
April 1994

5.27 Cyprus: Partition Incidents 254
June 1996–Ongoing

5.28 Yugoslavia–Kosovo: Kosovo Conflict and Civil War 254
October 1997–Ongoing

5.29 Russia–Republic of Dagestan: The Dagestan Independence Dispute 255
May 1999

5.30 Russia–Georgia: Chechen Separatism 255
August 2000–Ongoing

Middle East: 6.1–6.67 258

List of Conflicts 258
Countries in the Region 260
Regional Overview 260
Overview of Conflict 263
Conflict Management 263

6.1 France–Levant (Syria/Lebanon): Independence Crisis 265
1945–December 1946

6.2 USSR–Iran: Pro-Communist Campaign of Secession and Azerbaijan/Kurdistan Crisis 265
August 1945–October 1947

6.3 Israel: British Decolonization, Arab–Israeli Territorial Dispute, and War of Independence 266
May 1948–January 1949

6.4 Syria–Lebanon: Syrian Exiles Dispute 266
May–August 1949

6.5 Syria–Israel: Lake Tiberias/Huleh Resource Dispute 267
April–May 1951

6.6 Egypt–United Kingdom: Suez Canal Zone Sovereignty Dispute 268
January 1952–January 1956

6.7 Saudi Arabia–Oman/United Kingdom: The Buraymī Oasis Resource Dispute 268
August 1952–October 1955

6.8 Israel–Jordan: West Bank Border Conflict 269
January 1953–December 1954

6.9 Turkey–Syria: Border Incidents 269
March 1955–1957

6.10 Syria–Israel: Lake Tiberias Dispute 270
October–December 1955

6.11 Yemen–United Kingdom: Aden Conflict 270
1956–1960

6.12 Israel–Jordan: Mt. Scopus Conflict 271
July 1956–January 1958

6.13 Egypt–United Kingdom/France: Sovereignty Dispute and Suez War 271
October–November 1956

6.14 Israel–Syria: Arab–Israeli Territorial Dispute over the Golan Heights 272
July 1957–February 1958

6.15 Egypt–Sudan: Postindependence Territorial Dispute 272
February 1958

6.16 Lebanon: Internal Strife and the First Lebanese Civil War 273
May 1958–June 1959

6.17 Syria–Iraq: Syrian-Backed Putsch, Government Suppression, and Mosul Revolt 273
March–April 1959

6.18 Kurds–Iraq: Kurdish Secession Attempt 274
March 1961–1966

6.19 Iraq–Kuwait: Territorial Dispute and the Kuwaiti Independence Crisis 274
June 1961–February 1962

6.20 Syria–Israel: Arab–Israeli Territorial Dispute over Lake Tiberias 275
February 1962–August 1963

6.21 North Yemen: Civil War and Royalist Rebellion 275
September 1962–October 1967

6.22 Syria–Israel: Arab–Israeli Dispute and Border Incidents 276
June 1964–July 1966

6.23 Israel–Jordan: Arab–Israeli Dispute and Border Incidents 276
December 1964–April 1966

6.24 Lebanon–Israel: Arab–Israeli Dispute and the Hoûla Raids 277
October 1965

6.25 Israel–Arab States: The Six-Day War 277
June 1967

6.26 Iraq–Kurds: Kurdish Struggle for Autonomy 278
October 1968–March 1970

6.27 North Yemen–Saudi Arabia: Border Conflict 278
November 1969–October 1970

6.28 The PLO–Jordan: Coup Attempt 278
February 1970–August 1971

6.29 Iraq–Iran: Border Tensions and the Shatt al-Arab Waterway Dispute 279
1971

6.30 North Yemen–South Yemen: Anti-Communist Insurgency and Border Conflict 279
October 1971–October 1972

6.31 Iran–United Arab Emirates: Tunb Islands Territorial Dispute 280
November 1971

6.32 Oman–South Yemen: Antigovernment Insurgency and Dhofar Rebellion 280
1972–August 1974

6.33 Iran–Iraq: Territorial Dispute and Border War 281
January 1972–February 1975

6.34 Syria/PLO–Israel: PLO Raids, Retaliatory Air Strikes, and the Golan Heights Conflict 281
March 1972–January 1973

6.35 Iraq–Kuwait: Territorial Dispute and Border Incidents 282
March 1973–July 1975

6.36 Israel–Egypt and Syria: Arab–Israeli Territorial Dispute, Arab–Israeli Wars, and the Yom Kippur War 282
October 1973

6.37 Kurds–Iraq: Attempted Secession and the Kurdish Rebellion 283
March 1974–July 1975

6.38 Israel–Lebanon: Arab Infiltrators and Cross-Border Attacks 283
April 1974–July 1975

6.39 Lebanon: Internal Strife, Communal Violence, and the Second Lebanese Civil War 284
February 1975–Late 1992

6.40 Syria–Iraq: Resource Dispute over the Euphrates River 284
April–Late 1975

6.41 Iran: Internal Strife, Orthodox Muslim Backlash, Iranian Civil War, and Islamic Revolution 285
1976–1980

6.42 Kurds–Iraq: Kurdish Separatist Insurgency and Kurdish Autonomy 286
May 1976–Ongoing

6.43 **Israel–Lebanon: Arab–Israeli Tensions, Christian–Muslim Factional Fighting, and Border Incidents** 287
Mid–Late 1977

6.44 **Egypt–Libya: Regional Tensions and Border War** 287
July–September 1977

6.45 **Israel–Lebanon/PLO: Arab–Israeli Tensions, PLO Incursions, and Israeli Invasion of Southern Lebanon** 288
March–June 1978

6.46 **North Yemen–South Yemen: Border War** 289
February 1979–February 1980

6.47 **Israel–Syria: Arab–Israeli Tensions and Air Incidents** 289
June 1979–February 1980

6.48 **Saudi Arabia–North Yemen: Covert Military Aid and Border Conflict** 290
August 1979–March 1980

6.49 **Iran–United States: Anti-American Sentiment, Islamic Revolution, and Hostage Crisis** 290
November 1979–January 1981

6.50 **Iran–Iraq: Regional Rivalry, Territorial Dispute, and the Iran–Iraq War** 291
February 1980–1989

6.51 **Libya–United States: Regional Instability and Air Incidents** 291
August 1981

6.52 **Israel–Lebanon: Israeli Invasion of Lebanon** 292
Early 1982–Mid-1983

6.53 **Israel–Lebanon: Arab–Israeli Hostilities, Muslim–Christian Factional Fighting, and the Security Zone** 293
Mid-1983–Ongoing

6.54 **Kurds–Turkey: Kurdish Secession Struggle** 293
August 1984–Ongoing

6.55 **United States–Libya: International Terrorism Fears and Naval Incidents** 295
January–April 1986

6.56 **Qatar–Bahrain: Sovereignty Dispute and the Hawar Islands Dispute** 295
April 1986

6.57 **United States–Libya: Rabat Chemical Plant Tensions and Mediterranean Air Incident** 295
January 1989

6.58 **Iraq–Kuwait/Coalition Forces: Territorial Dispute, Iraqi Expansionism, and the Gulf War** 296
August 1990–May 1991

6.59 **Iran–United Arab Emirates/Egypt: Abu Musa and Tunb Islands Territorial Dispute** 297
April 1992

6.60 **Saudi Arabia–Qatar: Post–Gulf War Tensions and Border Incidents** 297
September–October 1992

6.61 **Egypt–Sudan: Territorial/Resource Dispute and Halaib Dispute** 297
December 1992

6.62 **Iraq–Coalition Forces: Post–Gulf War Incidents** 298
December 1992–July 1993

6.63 **Yemen: Unification Difficulties and Yemen Civil War** 298
November 1993–July 1994

6.64 **Iraq–Coalition Forces: Post–Gulf War Tensions and Kuwaiti Border Incidents** 299
October 1994

6.65 **Saudi Arabia–Yemen: Post–Gulf War Border Conflict** 299
December 1994

6.66 **Iran–Iraq: Regional Rivalry and Border Incidents** 300
September 1997

6.67 **Israel–Syria: Border Clashes** 300
February 2001–Ongoing

Appendixes 303

A. Countries and Their Regions 303
B. Chronology of Regional Conflicts 306
C. Organization Factsheets 317

References 335

Index 345

Figures, Tables, and Maps

Figures

1 Linkages between mediation and other methods of international conflict management 20
2 Method of conflict management 29
3 Conflict management by organizations 30

Tables

1 Characteristics of international conflicts 8
2 Incidence of conflict by geopolitical region 9
3 Conflict type and duration 9
4 Fatality levels and conflict type 10
5 Core conflict issue by geopolitical region 10
6 Conflict type and outcome 11
7 Method of conflict management and outcome 29
8 Organizations and conflict management outcome 30
9 United Nations involvement by decade 31
10 Geopolitical regions and regional organizations 45
11 Comparative overview of regional characteristics 46

Maps

1 Africa today 54
2 Africa in 1945 55
3 The Americas 119
4 East Asia and the Pacific 156
5 Indochina 157
6 Southwest Asia 205
7 Europe 230
7A The Caucasus 231
8 Soviet expansion in Europe, 1939–1991 232
9 The Middle East 260
10 Israel and Occupied Territories 261
World map (see end pages)

Preface

Regional Guide to International Conflict and Management from 1945 to 2003 summarizes and analyzes international conflicts since World War II to provide readers with a deeper understanding of international conflict, what characterizes conflict in the major regions of the world, and how conflict is managed.

This book is a product of the International Conflict Management project begun more than fifteen years ago at the University of Canterbury in New Zealand. The project was designed to accumulate as much reliable information as possible on international conflict management from 1945 to the present. To that extent, we can honestly say the book represents the culmination of many years of work.

The intellectual origins of the project owe much to J. David Singer's Correlates of War project. We wanted to explore conflict management with the same systematic rigor that Singer and his associates brought to their study of conflict and war. In keeping pace with more recent conflicts and in offering fuller information on each of them, the scope of the project has expanded considerably since it began. The project spawned numerous publications for scholars and policymakers. The goal of this volume is to present a comprehensive chronological account of international conflict from 1945 to 2003 for the six main regions of the world and to shed some light on the occurrence, patterns, and management of international conflict.

This work is a thoroughly revised and reorganized successor edition to the 1997 book *International Conflict: A Chronological Encyclopedia of Conflicts and Their Management 1945–1995*. The new edition's regional organization and regional context allow readers to gain a better perspective of the interrelation of conflicts and countries than they would gather if only presented with a time frame in which the conflicts took place.

Plan of the Book

Regional Guide to International Conflict and Management begins with two introductory chapters that examine the basic elements, issues, and techniques in international conflict and conflict management. A third introductory chapter looks at the constraints and conditions that affect conflict management efforts by international organizations. Tables and figures enable readers to see patterns and trends.

Each of the six sections on regional conflicts—the heart of the book—begins with a chronology of conflicts in the region, a list of countries in the region, and maps to guide the reader. An overview analyzes conflict in that particular region, the external and internal influences that have led to conflict, and how conflict is being managed in that part of the world. Each section continues with descriptions, in chronological order, of the conflicts that have occurred from 1945 to 2003.

In all, the book covers 343 conflicts, examining the history, issues, circumstances, players, management, and outcomes. Extensive cross-references enable readers to trace related conflicts. The appendix also serves as a useful reference tool, providing an alphabetical listing of countries and their regions, a master chronology incorporating all conflicts, and detailed factsheets on major conflict management organizations. Selected references, divided by region, offer the reader a way to explore the subject further.

Criteria for Inclusion of Conflicts

Some explanation of the criteria we used in choosing to include (or not to include) certain conflicts may be helpful in understanding how we arrived at the 343 conflicts that appear in the book. We began by identifying all interstate armed conflicts, internationalized civil wars, and militarized disputes since 1945. Although we have strived to include the most recent events, our comprehensive approach to analyzing conflicts has meant that much of the information we need to synthesize was not available for conflicts that began in 2003, although ongoing conflicts have been updated through the end of that year. One of the most important international conflicts of recent years is, of course, the 2003 Iraq War (March 19, 2003–Ongoing). It is not included here as one of the 343 conflicts. However, we have included information about the issues and actors involved and the direction of the war that was available as the book went to press (*see* pp. 6 and 263). We hope to deal with the conflict fully in future editions of the book.

The task of identifying these conflicts involved synthesizing past studies on war and carefully examining such primary data sources as the *New York Times Index, Keesing's Record of World Events,* and newspaper accounts from the *New York Times,* the *Times* (London), and Reuters Online Service for the period in question.

Each conflict was then examined to see whether it conformed to a strict set of specifications. First, we included conflicts between states that involved actual military hostilities or *significant* shows of force, such as large troop mobilizations along borders, occupations of disputed territory, or the firing of warning shots. This criterion allowed us to include cases such as the Cuban Missile Crisis (*see* conflict 2.17), which, although it caused no direct combat deaths, posed a grave threat to international peace and security, and had political effects and ramifications equal to that of any major war. The defining criterion here was the crossover from the use of diplomatic or political means of addressing conflict to the use of *credibly threatening* force. The decision to use force is the critical moment that turns a conflict into an *armed* international conflict or militarized dispute. It is a crucial moment, because the decision to use force is the final step along the path to putting at risk the political survival of an opposing state or, at the very least, threatening its territorial integrity.

Second, for internationalized civil conflicts, we included only those instances with *verifiable* and *significant* international aspects, such as the use of foreign troops, the use of foreign territory to launch attacks, large-scale efforts at agitation and subversion, or logistical and military support to internal groups by outside states. For example, the United States gave significant logistical support to the contra rebels in their insurgency against the leftist government of Nicaragua. It also provided advisers to train the contras and even mined Nicaraguan ports. We have therefore included the 1980–1994 war in Nicaragua (*see* conflict 2.31), although it was primarily a civil conflict. The above standards also explain why such internal civil conflicts as that in Northern Ireland have been omitted.

In addition, we included cases of secession or attempted secession in which the seceding party had been accorded international recognition, even if it had failed to win full independence. This decision permitted us to include conflicts such as the war in Biafra, which lasted from 1967 to 1970 (*see* conflict 1.30); the conflict between East Timor and Indonesia, which began in 1975 (*see* conflict 3.34); and the ongoing war in Chechnya, which started in 1992 (*see* conflict 5.24). All of these conflicts were regarded as major threats to international peace and security, and the international community made efforts to resolve them peacefully. For example, the British Commonwealth sought to mediate in the Biafran war, and the Organization for Security and Cooperation in Europe has actively tried to mediate the Chechen war since 1994.

Third, we included militarized disputes that had the potential for wider and more serious conflict because of the threat they posed to international peace and security. Most militarized disputes occur in unstable regions. That is, armed border incidents between traditionally hostile neighbors—for example, Israel and Lebanon, Peru and Ecuador—were included because of their great potential for escalation. In contrast, political incidents pose no real threat to the territorial integrity of the opposing state or to its physical survival. The threat to international peace and security is low and occurs in the context of otherwise friendly relations, so political incidents were excluded.

Once selected based on one of the above criteria, each case was scrutinized to identify the issues leading to conflict, which parties were involved, what course hostilities took, how many fatalities resulted, what the outcome entailed, and how the conflict was managed. The aim throughout was to discover patterns and variables that would shed light on how international conflicts can be better managed to minimize their destructive aspects.

Names and Dates of Conflicts

Our method of naming and dating the conflicts may require some explanation. Each conflict summary begins with a number identifying the conflict according to its region and time period, the principal country or countries involved, and a brief description of the fighting, such as territorial dispute, ethnic-based violence, secessionist warfare, and so on. This information is followed by the dates of the conflict. For example:

> **2.4 Argentina–Chile: The Beagle Channel Border Dispute**
> **July 1952–August 1993**

The dates represent the first and last occurrences of *identifiable* violence directly related to the conflict. The corresponding description, however, focuses on major incidents that best foster an understanding of the dispute.

Acknowledgments

This book has been a monumental project that involved many people over many years. Much of the work was done at the University of Canterbury, but we owe a great debt of gratitude to many others who have been working on different aspects of the project for some time. The collation of material is the combined result of individual research projects and a constant updating of recent conflict events. The project has grown over the years, with a loyal group of researchers painstakingly collating new data.

They have made this project possible. Jacob Bercovitch thanks coauthor Judith Fretter, who worked so diligently to bring the project to completion. We also thank Victoria Andrews, Debbie Dwan, Dya Fadel, Sue Fitzmaurice, Jon Foulkes, Anita Hackett, Andrew Hampton, Richard Jackson, Jim Lamare, Jeff Langley, David Miller, Andrew Moore, Janine Ogg, Mikio Oishi, Tamsin Quinn, Pat Regan, Michael Ross, Simon Tucker, and Gareth Upton. We gratefully acknowledge Richard Jackson, coauthor of the 1997 edition, for his substantial earlier contribution to the overall completion of this project. Allison Houston has been with us from the beginning and deserves our special thanks. She has been responsible for so many aspects of the project. Her computer and programming skills are much appreciated. Robert Trappl, of the University of Vienna, has been a close friend and supporter of this project for many years. His financial support for various aspects of the project and way of thinking about and presenting information on social phenomena inspired us to keep on, even when the will to do so became weak. To Jill Dolby we extend heartfelt thanks for all her secretarial and social help.

We are grateful to Robert Litwak of the Woodrow Wilson Center; Frederic Pearson of the Center for Peace and Conflict Studies, Wayne State University; and Randolph Siverson of the University of California, Davis, who carefully read through and reviewed drafts of the original manuscript for the 1997 edition; and Valerie Fretter, who carefully read through and reviewed drafts of this original manuscript. All of them offered useful suggestions, many of which we sought to incorporate. They are not responsible, however, for any errors or shortcomings that might remain.

Shana Wagger and the CQ Press team of Carolyn Goldinger, January Layman-Wood, Gwenda Larsen, and Olu Davis deserve our thanks for their support and professionalism and the meticulous care they brought to bear on the project. Their suggestions and advice made it possible for us to conceive of better ways to organize and present our information and produced, we have no doubt, a much better book.

The library staff at the University of Canterbury has been most helpful with our many requests for interlibrary loans, online searches, and access to primary sources vital to our preparation of this volume. We also express our gratitude to the University of Canterbury (Research Grant 2202062) and the Department of Internal Affairs, Peace and Disarmament Educational Trust for providing the financial assistance that allowed us to undertake and complete this project.

Our greatest debts, however, are acknowledged in the dedications.

Regional Guide to International Conflict and Management from 1945 to 2003

An Overview of
International Conflict

The Nature of International Conflict

Of all the social processes, conflict is perhaps the most universal and potentially the most dangerous. A feature of every society and every form of relationship, conflict can be found at all levels of human interaction, from sibling rivalry to genocidal warfare. We all face conflicting emotions and impulses as we respond daily to situations of conflict in our personal relationships. The groups we belong to—schools, clubs, companies, churches, associations, unions—continually undergo conflict. Some conflicts are internal, such as the infighting between old and new members of an association; some are external, such as disputes with other groups, which might include strikes by unions against employers or environmental groups remonstrating with oil companies. The largest human group—the state, or nation—also encounters conflict. At times the conflict is internal, as when different groups oppose the government or its policies, and at times the conflict is external, as when two states go to war.

Conflict is not only universal but also normal and necessary in the sense that every person and every group has needs, expectations, and ways of behaving that it regards as appropriate. Given this diversity, and given that we live in a world of limited resources and opportunities, it is not surprising that conflict is a normal part of life. In fact, we could argue that conflict is necessary for our growth, both as individuals and as groups. It is only through conflict and its resolution in productive and creative ways that new ideas emerge, higher levels of understanding are reached, and obstacles are surmounted.

In other words, conflict should not be viewed as a wholly negative phenomenon. Individuals face a myriad of conflicts every day, and, for the most part, these problems are settled in a positive manner or at least in a way that is not harmful. It is only when people use coercion or violence—physical or psychological—that conflict devolves into something negative and destructive. Although this result is relatively rare in terms of the total number of conflicts that occur every day, it is frequent and destructive enough to warrant careful study.

We recognize that conflicts, unless properly understood, may pose the greatest threat to the international environment, and we see this book as part of an effort to generate socially useful knowledge, in particular, knowledge about international conflict—its scope, patterns, outcomes, and management. We do not presume that such knowledge will enable us to move apparently intractable conflicts toward a solution; rather, we believe that a lack of knowledge about international conflict may preclude its successful management.

Conceptual clarity and a measure of verbal precision are preconditions for understanding conflict. If we seek to describe a range of behavior, we must begin by distinguishing it from related phenomena. Doing so is particularly necessary with conflict, which is a ubiquitous process and easily confused with other processes, such as aggression, violence, coercion, and so forth.

What Is Conflict?

In everyday language, conflict denotes overt, coercive interactions in which two or more contending parties seek to impose their will on one another. *Fights, violence,* and *hostility* are the terms customarily used to describe a conflict relationship. The range of conflict phenomena is, however, much wider than that. The term *conflict* is used to describe inconsistencies as well as the process of trying to solve them; it has physical and moral implications; it embraces opinions as well as situations and a wide range of behavior. For the most part, the conventional usage of the term does not fully capture the range of conflict phenomena.

Conflict is defined as a process of interaction between two or more parties that seek to thwart, injure, or destroy their opponent because they perceive they have incompatible interests or goals. The conflict relationship is characterized by a specific set of attitudes and behaviors, and the conflict process implies a level of interdependence and dynamism between the parties. Conflict attitudes engender conflict behaviors which in turn foster a further hardening of attitudes in a cyclical fashion.

The different components of a conflict relationship may be thought of in terms of three interrelated elements: (1) a specific conflict situation; (2) motives and the parties' cognitive structure; and (3) the behavioral-attitudinal dynamics of a conflict process. These elements can be considered jointly or separately. A *conflict situation* refers to a circumstance that generates incompatible goals or values among different parties. *Conflict attitudes* consist of the psychological and cognitive processes that engender conflict or are subsequent to it. And *conflict behavior* consists of actual, observed activities undertaken by one party and that are designed to injure, thwart, or eliminate its opponent.

International relations can be defined as the interaction or behavior and interdependence among actors, in this case, nations. And the interdependence we refer to is among nations. Their organization determines the configuration of the international system and the extent and intensity of conflict within that system. Interdependence can be negative—for example, the relationship between Greece and Turkey, or positive—for example, the United States and Canada. *Negative interdependence* implies a preponderance of competitive interests in the relationship, resulting in suspicious and hostile attitudes that define conflict as a win-lose situation. *Positive interdependence,* on the other hand, is characterized by largely cooperative interests.

International conflict, like peace, is a process rather than an end state. It is active and dynamic rather than passive and static. Its behavior consists of one nation's organized and collective effort to influence, control, or destroy the persons and property of another nation. International conflict is also a multicausal and multifaceted phenomenon. Unless it is violent, its occurrence should not be taken as an interruption of "normal" interactions, but as a natural and probable consequence of the existence of actors with different values and interests. Given a system with fairly autonomous and diverse units, linked in a relationship both competitive and cooperative, the potential for conflict is unbounded. This does not mean that every relationship displays conflict. International conflict depends on a diffuse set of structures, attitudes, and feelings.

Although other kinds of conflict may be annoying or disruptive—such as public transport strikes at the municipal level—they rarely produce extensive violence or numerous casualties. Moreover, the parties themselves or legal authorities can resolve such conflicts. In other words, they are regulated. The same is not true of states, which exist in an anarchical environment without enforceable laws or norms, where conflicts are unregulated and can quickly spiral out of control. In such an environment, some conflicts will inevitably escalate into large-scale violence or war. Most international conflicts, however, are resolved peacefully and constructively through regular channels of diplomacy and international forums such as the United Nations. Very few conflicts escalate to the point of war. Here we want to examine the almost sixty years since the end of World War II not only to ascertain the pattern, characteristics, and descriptions of conflict, but also to determine how conflict was managed.

International Conflict, 1945–2003

Since 1945 somewhere between 25 million and 30 million people have been killed as a result of war-related violence or by the famine and disease brought on by war. Most of those deaths have occurred in the eighty or so major conflicts in Africa, Asia, and the Middle East. The wars in Korea (1950–1953), Sudan (1963–1972, 1983–), Vietnam (1964–1975), Bangladesh (1971–1974), Mozambique (1975–1992), Afghanistan (1980–), and Iran and Iraq (1980–1989) each killed more than a million people. Others, like the genocidal ethnic conflict in Rwanda (September 1990–Ongoing) and the Angolan civil war (1975–1995), each resulted in at least half a million deaths. On top of this, more than 200 other armed conflicts between states have been recorded. Although many of these did not result in extensive casualties, they had other destructive effects such as economic and environmental dislocation, political instability, tension, ethnic hatred, food crises, and the creation of vast refugee populations.

A total of 343 international conflicts occurred over the period from 1945 to 2003. These 343 international conflicts have for the most part been related to the two main fault-lines of the postwar period—namely, the East–West conflict, which divided states into the Communist Eastern bloc and the democratic Western camp, and the North–South conflict, which divided the advanced industrial countries of the North from the developing world of the South.

The Cold War

The cold war split the world into two hostile camps, or spheres of influence, after the late 1940s, with each sphere dominated by one of the superpowers—the United States or the Soviet Union (USSR). Both countries vied for influence in zones outside their control, and many of the conflicts from 1950 to 1989 reflect this competition. In the Vietnam War (1964–1975), U.S. forces fought directly against Communist forces supported by the USSR. In the Afghanistan conflict (1980–), the Soviets fought directly against U.S.-backed mujahideen rebels.

Other conflicts that exhibit signs of this rivalry include the Korean War (1950–1953), the wars between Ethiopia and Somalia (1972–1985), the civil wars in Angola (1975–1995), Mozambique (1975–1992), and the Cambodian conflict (1979), and many of the conflicts in

Central America, such as Guatemala (1954–1995), El Salvador (1977–1992), and Nicaragua (1980–1994). In each case, one or both superpowers intervened with a significant show of force, producing a crisis with a high potential for escalation.

Decolonization

The other major postwar fault line, the North-South divide, produced a series of conflicts related to decolonization. In some cases, the conflicts were essentially wars of independence from European colonial powers like Britain, France, the Netherlands, and Portugal. Algerian nationalists fought a particularly vicious war of independence from France in the 1950s and 1960s, and other wars of independence were fought in British colonial India (1945–1948); in the Portuguese African territories of Mozambique (1961–July 1975) and Angola (1961–July 1975), in Rhodesia/Zimbabwe (1967–January 1980), South West Africa/Namibia (1966–March 1990), French Indochina (December 1945–July 1954), the Dutch East Indies (1945–November 1949), and Malaya/Malaysia (June 1948–July 1960).

In other cases, war broke out when new states emerged from colonial domination and upset local power balances. Israel's war of independence (May 1948–January 1949) and subsequent conflicts with its neighbors resulted directly from British decolonization. In other cases, conflicts grew out of colonial policies that failed to consider local sensibilities and conditions. The ethnic violence between the Hutu and Tutsi tribes, which has plagued Rwanda and Burundi since their independence, can be directly linked to Belgium's colonial policies, which not only exploited tribal animosities but also drew boundaries for the new nations without regard for tribal land settlements. The intense violence between India and Pakistan following independence was largely caused by the haphazard boundary demarcations during the 1947 partition of the Indian Subcontinent.

The end of the cold war in the late 1980s quelled a number of conflicts. The Soviets withdrew from Afghanistan, and the Americans stopped aiding the mujahideen rebels. The United States and Soviet Union both withdrew support from the warring parties in Angola and Mozambique and forced them to the negotiating table. Wars ended in Cambodia, El Salvador, and Nicaragua, and the U.S.-led Coalition forces forced Iraq out of Kuwait in the Gulf War (August 1990–March 1991). It seemed as if a new era of peace had begun, especially because the threat of global nuclear annihilation was gone.

Ethnic Conflict

The collapse of the Soviet Union and the end of superpower rivalry, however, did not produce the tranquility envisioned at the end of the cold war. In fact, the breakup of the Soviet Union unleashed a whole host of conflicts in the 1990s, which can be largely characterized as wars of nationalism or ethnic-based conflict. The war in the former Yugoslavia (1989–November 2000) involving Serbs, Croats, and Bosnians is the most vivid example of this, but similar wars in Georgia (March 1989–Ongoing), Armenia (August 1990–Ongoing), Tajikistan (May 1992–June 1997), and Chechnya (October 1992–Ongoing) are also examples. In each case, ethnic groups vie for power and resources in a spiral of violence laced with hatreds and grievances that often go back centuries. Other ethnically based conflicts are Sudan's civil war (January 1983–) being waged between the Muslim Arabic northerners and the black African Christians and animists in the south, the Philippines (January 1970–Ongoing), Burundi (August 1988–Ongoing), Bougainville (October 1988–Ongoing), Liberia (December 1989–Ongoing), Rwanda (September 1990–Ongoing), and Moldova (October 1990–July 1992).

Another characteristic of post–cold war conflicts is that they take place largely within, not between, states. As such, they are called *civil conflicts.* The fighting in the former Yugoslavia erupted when Serb militias sought to prevent Croatia and Bosnia-Herzegovina from seceding from the federation and becoming new states. All the fighting took place within the borders of what used to be Yugoslavia, although at times it threatened to spill over into neighboring states, and the conflict involved many outside powers in the search for a settlement.

Terrorism

September 11, 2001, marked a major turning point in contemporary international relations. The well-orchestrated terrorist attacks against the United States changed perceptions of conflict and conflict prevention. Terrorist attacks had occurred previously, but nothing on the scale or the sophisticated planning, which involved hijacking four commercial aircraft, had ever been seen before. Two of the planes crashed into the twin towers of the World Trade Center in New York City; another flew into the Pentagon, which is just outside of Washington, D.C. The fourth plane, its target still unknown, crashed in Pennsylvania when the passengers apparently overcame the hijackers. A total of 3,056 people died as a result of these synchronized terrorist attacks, and many more were injured. The casualties were predominantly civilian.

As television cameras captured both the horrific events as they unfolded and the worldwide condemnation for the premeditated acts of terrorism, the events of September 11 drastically changed commonly held perceptions of international security. The events also provided the momentum for many states to introduce sweeping changes in strategic and defense policy, including the idea of a preemptive war to prevent future such attacks.

Two more decisive international events occurred in direct response to the events of September 11: the war on terrorism in Afghanistan (*see* conflict 4.39) and the war on Iraq (*see* pp. xxi and 263).

The United States launched a retaliatory war, the so-called war on terrorism, beginning with "Operation Enduring Freedom" in Afghanistan.[1] A full-scale military intervention by the United States and a coalition of states, including Britain and, by 2002, more than sixty-seven other nations, aimed to seek out and destroy the terrorist network al Qaeda and its leader, Osama bin Laden. Substantial evidence indicated that this group was responsible for the attacks on the World Trade Center and the Pentagon.

With counterterrorist operations ongoing in Afghanistan, the U.S. government asserted that clear links existed between bin Laden and Iraqi leader Saddam Hussein and his weapons of mass destruction (WMD) capabilities. These allegations culminated in a U.S.-led war in Iraq, labeled "Operation Iraqi Freedom." The United States assembled a "coalition of the willing": thirty states that agreed to support—militarily, diplomatically, politically, and economically—a possible U.S.-led invasion of Iraq.[2]

After the initial victory, Iraqi insurgents began a continuing resistance with an average of twenty-six attacks against coalition forces occurring daily. As of July 16, 2004, there had been 1,012 coalition combat deaths in Iraq, including 892 Americans, 60 Britons, 6 Bulgarians, 1 Dane, 1 Dutch, 1 Estonian, 1 Hungarian, 19 Italians, 1 Latvian, 6 Poles, 1 Salvadoran, 3 Slovakians, 11 Spaniards, 2 Thai, and 7 Ukrainians. The number of wounded and civilian deaths as a result of the war has been estimated at somewhere between 8,700 and 10,000. As yet the military has found no conclusive evidence of weapons of mass destruction, but Saddam Hussein has been captured and is to by tried by the Iraqi interim government.

The first problem in dealing with terrorism is to define what it means. U.S. law defines terrorism in Title 22 of the U.S. Code, Section 2656f (d), which states: "the term *terrorism* means premeditated, politically motivated violence perpetrated against non-combatant targets by subnational groups or clandestine agents, usually intended to influence an audience. The term *international terrorism* means terrorism involving the territory or the citizens of more than one country. The term *terrorist group* means any group that practices, or has significant sub-groups that practice, international terrorism." Over the period from January 1967 to September 11, 2001, a total of 11,300 terrorist incidents were recorded, some causing substantial loss of life and extensive damage and others registering no significant damage. Since September 11, several additional acts of terrorism have rocked the world, and it appeared that the type of attack was aimed at achieving the maximum possible impact. The bombing incidents in Bali in October 2002 (killing 182) and Madrid in March 2004 (killing 190) demonstrated that the United States was no longer the only terrorist target. The matter of utmost concern to all governments in the post–September 11 environment is the potential for terrorists to use chemical, biological, radiological, or nuclear (CBRN) weapons to devastating ends.

The second problem facing counterterrorism efforts is to identify the terrorist. Under current classifications, separatist, secessionist, and independence movements that resort to violence as a means of political influence are also classified as terrorists. Indeed, one of the main criticisms of the war on terror rests on the difficulty associated with identifying and targeting the terrorist: little distinction is made between the freedom fighter, who employs nonconventional guerrilla warfare, and the terrorist, who also employs methods of nonconventional warfare. To illustrate the dilemma, Nobel Peace Prize winners Nelson Mandela (1993), Sean McBride (1974), Menachem Begin (1978), and Yasser Arafat (1994) were all labeled terrorists before each was awarded this international honor (Jackson 2002).

The third issue, formulating counterterrorism measures, becomes an uncertain business of trying to identify the terrorists, understand the complexity of the terrorists' aims, and evaluate their actions with a level of detached clarity and perspective. What counterterrorist measures are most effective in different situations? Are conventional methods of warfare effective against unconventional forms? In the end, terrorism is an effective but deadly tool: effective because it generally achieves its main aim, creating a level of fear that is often disproportionate to the terrorist attack, and deadly because fatalities usually result. And, because terrorism is invariably a tool used to elicit an emotional response, dealing with it objectively becomes difficult.

---

1. "Operation Enduring Freedom was initially to have been called Operation Infinite Justice but this name is believed to have been changed following concerns that this might offend the Muslim community as Islam teaches that Allah is the only one who can provide Infinite Justice." See http://www.globalsecurity.org/military/ops/enduring-freedom.htm (accessed April 1, 2004).

2. In March 2003, U.S. Secretary of State Colin Powell named the following countries as members of the coalition of the willing: Afghanistan, Albania, Australia, Azerbaijan, Bulgaria, Colombia, the Czech Republic, Denmark, El Salvador, Eritrea, Estonia, Ethiopia, Georgia, Hungary, Italy, Japan, Latvia, Lithuania, Macedonia, the Netherlands, Nicaragua, the Philippines, Poland, Romania, Slovakia, South Korea, Spain, Turkey, the United Kingdom, and Uzbekistan. Of these original members of the coalition, the Netherlands, the Philippines, and Spain withdrew their troops and/or personnel from Iraq in 2004.

Types of International Conflict

International conflicts can be categorized in various ways. Here we divide them into four main types, which help to explain their causes and the form they take. The four types are (1) conflicts between states, or interstate conflict; (2) internationalized civil conflicts; (3) militarized conflicts; and (4) political incidents. The following discussion will help us distinguish among these different kinds of conflicts.

Interstate Conflict

Interstate conflicts usually involve territory held in conflict by contiguous states. Somalia and Ethiopia, for example, have gone to war several times (1964, 1972–1985, 1987–1988) over the Ogaden region, an area ruled by Ethiopia but inhabited by Somali tribes. The coveted area lies on their mutual border, and Somalia has long claimed it. Very few wars are fought by states situated a long distance apart, although the Falklands war (1982) between Britain and Argentina is an exception. Great Britain spends millions of pounds every day to maintain a military presence on these distant islands.

In some cases, states will go to war when they have competing ideologies, or when they feel insecure. In 1980 opposition to Iran's brand of Islamic fundamentalism was one reason why Iraq attacked its Shiite neighbor in what became one of the world's bloodiest conflicts. Occasionally, interstate conflicts can escalate and bring in other states, resulting in a regional conflict that affects many countries in a given geographical area. This was the case in Indochina in the 1960s and 1970s, southern Africa in the 1980s, and the Middle East since 1948.

Interstate conflicts may also arise from rivalries in which states feel threatened or intimidated by their opponents. They may engage in a dangerous cat-and-mouse game of provocation and escalation that often results in armed conflict. In these cases, a pair of rivals might have four or more wars over a twenty-year period and many lesser incidents and periods of tension. India and Pakistan have been rivals since their independence in 1948 and have gone to war more than six times since then. Ecuador and Peru are rivals that regularly clash over a piece of territory in the Amazon. Israel and its neighbors have constantly maneuvered against each other since the Jewish state was founded in 1948. Other bitter historical rivals include Iran and Iraq, Greece and Turkey, China and Vietnam, Somalia and Ethiopia, and Chile and Argentina.

Internationalized Civil Conflict

The second type of international conflict occurs when another state becomes involved in a violent civil conflict, either directly by invasion or indirectly by actively supporting a faction in the other country. Examples of direct intervention in a civil conflict include Saudi Arabia's invasion of Yemen on the side of the royalists and Egypt's invasion on the side of the republicans in Yemen's 1962–1970 civil war. Also, in 1965 the United States invaded the Dominican Republic on the side of the government, which was then fighting a civil war against the constitutionalists, who wanted to restore to power Juan Bosch, a former president ousted in a military coup.

Indirect support, on the other hand, takes many forms. It may involve sending arms and providing training and advisers for one faction in the conflict, such as the U.S aid to the contra rebels fighting the Nicaraguan government (1980–1994). It may also involve allowing rebels to use territory from which to launch attacks. Zambia supported the Rhodesian rebels by allowing the Zimbabwe African People's Union (ZAPU)—one of the African nationalist factions that fought Rhodesia's white minority government in the war of independence (1967–1980)—to have bases and training camps on Zambian territory. ZAPU guerrillas would launch attacks across the Zambezi border into Rhodesia and then cross back into the relative safety of Zambia.

In extreme cases, superpower rivals can fight "proxy" wars by supporting opposing factions in a civil conflict. For example, the United States supported Jonas Savimbi's National Union for the Total Independence of Angola (UNITA) guerrilla group in Angola, while the Soviets backed the governing Movimento Popular de Libertação de Angola (MPLA). This way, the superpowers could strike at each other indirectly without risking all-out war. A similar conflict took place in El Salvador (January 1977–late 1992), but here the United States supported the government, and Cuba and the Soviet Union backed the left-wing rebels.

Some civil conflicts last for decades and take the form of guerrilla insurgencies. Often the guerrillas live in dense forest in border areas and move across borders at will, attacking government targets and then disappearing into the jungle again. The insurgencies in Burma (1949–) by ethnic Karen guerrillas and in Colombia (1965–) by Marxist insurgents have gone on for decades because neither side has the ability to completely defeat the other. Other civil conflicts result from attempts by particular ethnic groups living in one area to break away, or secede, and form their own state. The Biafran war (1967–1970), the 1975 invasion of East Timor by Indonesia, and Western Sahara's efforts to resist Morocco's territorial claims since 1974 are examples of this type of conflict. In each case, states outside the conflict gave their recognition and support to the seceding party, and some even provided military aid.

For the most part, civil conflicts result from different ideologies, such as the Communist insurgents in Guatemala who opposed the right-wing government and its policies, or from ethnic factors, such as many of the conflicts in the former Soviet republics, where Abkhazians, Chechens, ethnic Russians, and Ukrainians coexist in close quarters. In all cases, they became international conflicts when a second or third state intervened in a significant way and threatened international peace and security. In contrast, although the civil conflicts in Peru, in the Basque region of Spain, and in Northern Ireland have involved fighting, other states have not mounted a significant intervention. These conflicts do not, therefore, pose the same risk as internationalized civil conflicts.

Militarized Conflicts

The third type of international conflict is the militarized conflict, which occurs when two states face off militarily, escalating a crisis or sparking an incident. Such face-offs may not result in all-out wars, but they create the potential for serious conflict and threaten international peace and security. In most cases, people are killed.

A famous example of a militarized conflict was the Cuban Missile Crisis of 1962, when the Soviet Union tried to station medium-range nuclear missiles in Cuba and the U.S. Navy threatened to sink any Soviet ships that entered the waters around Cuba. This crisis did not result in direct military conflict. It nevertheless took the world to the brink of nuclear war. The persistent tension between the Soviet Union and the United States produced a number of air incidents in the 1950s in which Soviet and U.S. jets shot each other down. With the threat of escalation, such incidents were diffused only by exercising deterrence.

Militarized conflicts, which occur in the context of a tense and hostile relationship, are almost always preceded by a history of violence and contain a very real risk of escalation into all-out war. Relations between rival states are usually characterized by numerous militarized conflicts. Other important militarized conflicts have occurred between states such as Zambia and Zaire (1982, 1983–1984), the United States and Cambodia (the *Mayaguez* incident in 1975), and Guatemala and Mexico (1982–1983, 1984).

Political Incidents

The fourth and final type of international conflict is the political incident, which can be defined as an interstate conflict that escalates beyond the normal day-to-day conflicts between states, such as disputes over trade, visas, diplomatic etiquette, and so forth. Political incidents usually involve verbal and political demonstrations, such as denunciations, propaganda, name-calling, diplomatic insults, and maybe even threats and ultimatums. In a very few cases, armed incidents may occur. Political incidents happen, however, between states that are normally friendly. Furthermore, the disputants tend to be democracies, and there is no history of violence or the likelihood that the conflict will escalate into a war.

Examples of what we consider to be a political incident include the Anglo-Icelandic fishing conflict, which occurred over 1972 and 1973. This event involved several acrimonious verbal and political demonstrations, as well as the use of naval vessels to prevent boats from fishing in conflicted waters. Although force was used in this case, no real threat of war was in the air, and the conflict took place in the context of otherwise friendly relations between two democracies. In recent years, similar fishing conflicts between Canada and Spain and Britain and Spain have also escalated into political incidents. We exclude them from the book because, in our view, they posed no threat to international peace and security and do not qualify as true armed international conflicts.

Patterns of International Conflict, 1945–2003

Our survey of the period from 1945 to 2003 found 343 international conflicts that conformed to these four categories—interstate conflicts, internationalized civil conflicts, militarized conflicts, or political incidents. Further analysis of these conflicts revealed some important facts. For example, the majority of conflicts took place from 1956 to 1985, during the era of decolonization and superpower confrontation (*see* Table 1). Another feature of these conflicts is that both Europe and North America remained relatively free from conflict while the developing world was extricating itself from colonial ties and becoming prey to cold war adventurism. It is also clear that many post–cold war conflicts

Table 1. Characteristics of international conflicts

Decade	Total conflicts	Type of conflict		UN involvement
		Interstate	Intrastate (civil)	
1945–1955	47 (13.7%)	35 (10.2%)	12 (3.5%)	20 (5.8%)
1956–1965	77 (22.4%)	52 (15.2%)	25 (7.3%)	33 (9.6%)
1966–1975	54 (15.7%)	35 (10.2%)	19 (5.5%)	23 (6.7%)
1976–1985	72 (21.0%)	52 (15.2%)	20 (5.8%)	21 (6.1%)
1986–1995	64 (18.7%)	39 (11.4%)	25 (7.3%)	17 (5.0%)
1996–2003	29 (8.4%)	15 (4.4%)	14 (4.1%)	7 (2.0%)
TOTAL	343 (100.0%)	228 (66.5%)	115 (33.5%)	121 (35.3%)

Table 2. Incidence of conflict by geopolitical region

Geopolitical region	Frequency	Percentage
Africa	97	28.3%
Americas	45	13.1
Asia: East Asia and Pacific	65	19.0
Asia: SW Asia	39	11.4
Europe	30	8.7
Middle East	67	19.5
TOTAL	343	100.0

arose from the disintegration of the Soviet Union and the consequent collapse of Europe's cold war structures. While it lasted, therefore, the cold war kept the peace in Europe. It did not, however, prevent war elsewhere; nor did it guarantee a tranquil Europe in the twenty-first century—indeed, it was not designed to.

Another noteworthy pattern during the 1945–2003 period is that, although the absolute number of conflicts has risen, the number of conflicts *in progress* has been declining since the mid-1980s. The number of conflicts initiated dropped dramatically in the late 1980s, when the Soviet Union was collapsing and commentators were quick to declare a new age of international peace. The years from 1991 to 1995, however, saw a sharp rise in new conflicts, as fragile states collapsed in Africa and as ethnic and nationalist rivalries sparked into war across Eastern Europe and throughout what had been Soviet Asia. Since 1996 the incidence of conflict, both intrastate and interstate, has decreased significantly with only twenty-nine conflicts occurring over the period to 2003. Since 2001 many states have been preoccupied with terrorism and have been united to a greater degree in a common cause. Efforts to stabilize otherwise unstable states have been given greater priority, and more effort has been made to engage in conflict prevention rather than wait until conflicts intensify.

Most conflicts flared in the traditional hot spots of Africa and the Middle East (*see* Table 2). While Africa attempted to throw off colonial oppression, the Middle East played host to the superpower rivalry and tried to cope with the destabilizing effects of the establishment of the state of Israel. Our research shows that war is being used less and less, at least relative to the number of new states joining the international system. That is, while the absolute amount of war may go up (or down), this is "normal" in the sense that the more states there are in the international system, the greater potential there is for conflict.

Although the potential for conflict is greater, this is not the same as saying that states are now more willing to use war as an instrument of foreign policy. Many of the conflicts in Africa in the 1970s and 1980s occurred between states that did not exist in the international system before the 1960s, and the wars in Eastern Europe and what was formerly Soviet Asia are all between states that have only just joined international society.

When we look at the types of international conflicts (civil conflicts and interstate conflicts) in the context of their system periods, it becomes clear how important interstate conflicts became during the cold war. The cold war had the effect of suppressing many civil conflicts, except those exploited by the superpowers. It was only after the collapse of the Soviet Union in 1991 that many civil conflicts once again emerged.

In regional terms, Africa has suffered by far the most (*see* Table 2), which is not surprising, because colonial policies in Africa often placed historically hostile ethnic groups together in a single state. The civil war in Chad (1982–) between Arabic Muslim northerners and black African Christian southerners is a direct result of a colonial boundary that placed rival groups in the same country. Rwanda and Burundi were both deeply affected by colonial policies that favored one tribe over another, leading to postindependence rivalry and, eventually, genocidal conflict.

Similarly, the Middle East has suffered more interstate conflicts than any other region, despite the fact that, with only seventeen countries, it has the second-fewest states of any region. This can be accounted for by the establishment of the state of Israel after 1948, which upset regional power balances and injected a great deal of instability into the region. Israel has been involved in more than twenty conflicts since 1948. In addition, the region's oil reserves and the Suez Canal make the Middle East strategically important—with a great deal of superpower maneuvering and intrigue being the result.

As for duration, international conflicts tend to be either short and quickly resolved or long and drawn out (*see* Table 3). Few will last more than a year or two before being resolved one way or the other. Either they are caught early on and resolved peacefully, or they go on for many years with horrendous costs. The war in the former Yugoslavia demonstrates this clearly. Most observers believe the drawn-out war of attrition might have been avoided altogether had the Western powers, working in concert with the United Nations, tried harder to force a settlement at the outset. Without an early resolution, states begin to feel they have invested too much

Table 3. Conflict type and duration

Duration (months)	Type of conflict: Civil	Type of conflict: Interstate	Total
0–1	12 (3.5%)	64 (18.7%)	76 (22.2%)
1–3	9 (2.6%)	25 (7.3%)	34 (9.9%)
4–6	2 (0.6%)	27 (7.9%)	29 (8.5%)
7–12	7 (2.0%)	36 (10.5%)	43 (12.5%)
13–24	14 (4.1%)	20 (5.8%)	34 (9.9%)
25–36	9 (2.6%)	14 (4.1%)	23 (6.7%)
36+	62 (18.1%)	42 (12.2%)	104 (30.3%)
TOTAL	115 (33.5%)	228 (66.5%)	343 (100.0%)

Table 4. Fatality levels and conflict type

Fatality levels	Type of conflict: Civil	Interstate	Total
0–500	42 (12.2%)	166 (48.4%)	208 (60.6%)
501–1,000	8 (2.3%)	16 (4.7%)	24 (7.0%)
1,001–5,000	16 (4.6%)	21 (6.1%)	37 (10.7%)
5,001–10,000	5 (1.5%)	4 (1.2%)	9 (2.7%)
10,000+	44 (12.9%)	21 (6.1%)	65 (19.0%)
TOTAL	115 (33.5%)	228 (66.5%)	343 (100.0%)

blood and treasure to give in or that they can still win and decide to press on.

These considerations were at work in Iran and Iraq's decision to pursue a long and costly war (1980–1989) after Iraq failed to reach its objective soon after invading the Shattal Arab Waterway. Similarly, the conflict between Indonesia and the Netherlands over West Irian (1962) could have resulted in a long and costly war of liberation, but the UN's quick and effective mediation prevented such an outcome, and the conflict was resolved in a few months.

States that do not resolve their conflicts early on tend to invest a great deal in their effort to win, and, in the end, these conflicts prove costly in terms of human life. Most conflicts resolve themselves before thousands of fatalities occur, but, when conflicts go unchecked, fatalities may reach huge proportions (*see* Table 4). Since 1945, sixty international armed conflicts have resulted in the loss of more than 10,000 lives. The Korean War, the Vietnam War, the Bangladesh war of independence, the Sudan and Mozambique conflicts, Cambodia, and Afghanistan each cost more than 1 million lives. Most of the dead were civilians, who were seen as legitimate targets, and many more died of disease and starvation brought about by war conditions.

When we look at why states resort to war, we see that territory and sovereignty are by far the most potent motivating factors (*see* Table 5). The fundamental basis of every state is its territory and the control it has over that land. This makes it a most compelling issue whenever it is in conflict. States will go further in defending their territory than they will over defending access to resources, for example. For this reason, most international conflicts that reach the point of armed confrontation are about territory. Even when the territory has little strategic or economic value, its symbolic value is sufficiently powerful to motivate states to go to war.

The Siachen Glacier conflict between India and Pakistan (1984–) is a case in point. The area under conflict is remote, barren, and difficult to reach. Many of the soldiers sent there die of the cold, avalanches, and accidents in the snow and ice. Despite the conditions and the unlikelihood of either side gaining a significant advantage, both sides have invested vast amounts of resources and troops to continue fighting. In contrast, no states went to war over the 1973 oil shocks, which involved access to vast supplies of essential resources.

The second most common reason a state gets involved in military conflicts is a threat to its security by interference from a rival state, or states, or from a group from within its own borders. Israel and South Africa have both launched attacks on other states because they felt their security was threatened. Israel attacked Lebanon in 1982 to protect its northern borders from Palestinian infiltrators, and South Africa launched raids into Botswana (1984–1986), Zambia (1987), and Lesotho (1982) to attack African National Congress (ANC) bases.

Most conflicts, however, stemmed from more than one cause. Nearly all the conflicts we surveyed had multiple issues, especially those persisting for more than three years and involving large loss of life. Over time, conflicts become reframed by the warring parties so that multiple interlocking issues are seen to be at stake, and the struggle becomes freighted with powerful symbolic meaning. The single-issue conflicts tend to be militarized conflicts that were over quickly and involved few fatalities. For example, the *Mayaguez* incident between Cambodia and the United States (1975), the shelling incident between Taiwan and China (1994), and the Belize-Guatemala border incidents (1995) were all fairly simple conflicts in that they concerned single events that involved few fatalities.

Most states that resort to hostilities do so after a period of conflict that culminates in armed conflict. Few states that are friendly or that have few points of contact will end up in armed conflict with each other. International

Table 5. Core conflict issue by geopolitical region

Geopolitical region	Core conflict issue: Territory	Ideology	Security	Independence	Resources	Ethnicity	Total
Africa	16 (4.7%)	22 (6.4%)	16 (4.7%)	11 (3.3%)	2 (0.5%)	30 (8.7%)	97 (28.3%)
Americas	13 (3.8%)	18 (5.2%)	11 (3.3%)	1 (0.3%)	1 (0.3%)	1 (0.3%)	45 (13.1%)
Asia: East Asia and Pacific	19 (5.5%)	7 (2.1%)	25 (7.3%)	3 (0.8%)	1 (0.3%)	10 (3.0%)	65 (19.0%)
Asia: SW Asia	11 (3.3%)	3 (0.8%)	9 (2.6%)	3 (0.8%)	0 (0.0%)	13 (3.8%)	39 (11.4%)
Europe	2 (0.5%)	5 (1.5%)	11 (3.3%)	2 (0.5%)	1 (0.3%)	9 (2.6%)	30 (8.7%)
Middle East	17 (4.9%)	8 (2.4%)	23 (6.5%)	4 (1.3%)	3 (0.8%)	12 (3.5%)	67 (19.5%)
TOTAL	78 (22.7%)	63 (18.4%)	95 (27.7%)	24 (7.0%)	8 (2.3%)	75 (21.9%)	343 (100.0%)

armed conflicts represent a process that includes a relationship of conflict or rivalry that under certain conditions can lead to armed confrontation. Conflicts do not happen in a vacuum, and the roots of any war can almost always be traced back to a long history of antagonistic competition. Nearly all the conflicts were preceded either by antagonistic relations between the parties, or by actual violence. For example, Peru and Ecuador have long disputed a piece of territory in the Amazon, and their relations are characterized by frequent armed clashes over it. Other rivals have been India and China, India and Pakistan, the United States and the Soviet Union, Ethiopia and Somalia, Vietnam and China, Uganda and Tanzania, and Iran and Iraq.

It is noteworthy that, of the 343 conflicts, only about 50 resulted in victories for one side or the other (*see* Table 6). In other words, although the likelihood of victory is fairly remote (at least based on these statistics), states are still willing to initiate hostilities in pursuit of their goals. Of the few conflicts that did produce victory for one side, that side generally had a massive advantage over the other, for example, the U.S. invasions of Grenada, Haiti, and Panama and China's invasion of the Spratly Islands.

For the most part, however, the usual pattern is for states to go to war, for a stalemate to develop either immediately or after a long campaign, and for negotiations to begin with the goal of ending the conflict. A case in point: the war being waged by the Polisario (Frente Popular para la Liberatión de Saguia el-Hamra y Rio de Oro) to free the Western Sahara from Moroccan control (1974–) has resulted in an impasse, despite Mauritania's support for the rebels. After thirty years of fighting, the United Nations is still trying to resolve the conflict.

Also of interest here is that nearly a third of these conflicts were at least partly settled through conflict management techniques such as mediation and negotiation. This is a significant achievement given the high number of international armed conflicts and their potential and real capacity for destruction. Of more pressing concern at present are the forty-two ongoing conflicts, of which many—such as Afghanistan, Angola, Cambodia, East Timor, Mindanao, and Western Sahara—have been persistent and destructive. Furthermore, some conflicts have

Table 6. Conflict type and outcome

Conflict outcome	Type of conflict		
	Civil	Interstate	Total
Ongoing	35 (10.2%)	7 (2.0%)	42 (12.2%)
Lapse	13 (3.8%)	38 (11.1%)	51 (14.9%)
Victory	26 (7.6%)	22 (6.4%)	48 (14.0%)
Abated	16 (4.7%)	77 (22.4%)	93 (27.1%)
Partially settled	8 (2.3%)	29 (8.5%)	37 (10.8%)
Full settlement	17 (5.0%)	55 (16.0%)	72 (21.0%)
TOTAL	115 (33.5%)	228 (66.5%)	343 (100.0%)

merely abated, making them potential flashpoints. Many of India's conflicts with its neighbors and Israel's with the surrounding Arab states fit into this category; it takes only a minor crisis to spark a major war. The war in Angola was thought to be over when elections were held in 1992, but UNITA's failure at the polls proved to be a flashpoint for further vicious fighting.

A comparison of conflict outcome with conflict type reveals the striking fact that nearly every ongoing conflict is civil (*see* Table 6), many of them brought on by the collapse of the Soviet Union. Also of concern are the many conflicts that have simply abated for the time being. These represent unresolved conflicts that no longer involve military hostilities. Many of these "rivalry relationships"—such as those between the Arabs and Israel, Ecuador and Peru, China and Vietnam, and others—are ripe for renewed military confrontation given the right circumstances.

The Need for Conflict Management

International conflicts can be very costly, particularly if they are not managed early on. We have already mentioned the millions of people, mainly civilians, who die because of fighting between states; other millions die as a result of starvation, disease, and exposure to the elements. War also produces refugee populations—vast numbers of people on the move to escape the violence, without adequate food or shelter, who have to be cared for by neighboring countries and aid agencies. In 2004 the UN estimated that there were some 21 million refugees worldwide. The war in Mozambique uprooted 1.7 million people, 1 million of whom fled to Malawi, one of the world's poorest countries that can hardly feed its own population.

Another cost of international conflict is the environmental damage caused by modern weapons. Dozens of Kuwaiti oil wells were blown up by retreating Iraqi forces in 1991, polluting the air; devastating oil slicks ran up onto Persian Gulf beaches. In Cambodia, the Khmer Rouge forces have strip-mined vast areas under their control to finance their insurgency with emeralds. In the 1970s the United States defoliated Vietnamese forests using the powerful herbicide, Agent Orange.

Conflicts are also expensive. It costs a great deal of money to finance armies and their offensives. War diverts resources from education, health care, and infrastructure development. For example, it cost around $40 billion to finance the U.S.-led Coalition forces that defeated Iraq in the Gulf War (1990–1991). The cost of the war on terrorism in Iraq is estimated to be around $50 billion to $60 billion with an additional budget of $87 billion approved by the U.S. Congress in November 2003. The postwar costs of reconstruction are also enormous, especially in the poorer countries of Africa, Asia, and Latin America, where instability and insecurity have led to the financing of large armies at the expense of the poor.

States also lose out in trade opportunities if neighbors close their borders and refuse any exchange. Even minor conflicts can result in millions of dollars in losses as states have to reroute goods through other countries. For example, in the late 1960s, Zambia routed nearly all its copper exports through white-dominated Rhodesia (Zimbabwe). When Zimbabwean nationalist guerrillas waged their war of independence (1967–1980), Zambian support for the rebel forces led to the closure of the then-Rhodesian-Zambian border. Zambia was therefore forced to devote vast sums to reroute its copper through other countries.

Finally, the international community usually has to donate millions or even billions of dollars toward emergency aid for postwar reconstruction. For example, more than $1 billion has been pledged to rebuild the successor states of the former Yugoslavia.

Costs are also felt on the political level. Conflicts lead to tension, instability, and the threat of escalation. Routine governance becomes exceedingly difficult. The Middle East is an unstable region because the persistent, sporadic wars mean that politics can consist of little more than maintaining peace and security. In Africa, the social and political instability brought on by war erodes human rights and produces epidemics and famine. As a result, international companies are loath to invest in the region, and organizations like the African Union (AU) are unable to resolve conflicts.

Furthermore, armed conflicts represent the failure of international organizations, like the United Nations, and international policies to maintain peace. These failures may exacerbate the instability because states then feel that, if the United Nations cannot solve their conflicts, they must take matters into their own hands.

These problems are further complicated by the proliferation of nuclear weapons. Although the threat of global nuclear war has evaporated with the end of the cold war, responsible nations rightly fear the emergence of unstable countries, and even terrorist organizations, with access to nuclear weapons. India and Pakistan came to the brink of nuclear confrontation over Kashmir in 1990, and it was only forceful intervention by the United States that averted further escalation. Iraq's attempts to acquire nuclear weapons were well known and made the country a target of the war on terrorism.

These dangers underscore the urgent need to manage international conflict peacefully. As we have seen, it is not inevitable that conflicts between states escalate into long, drawn-out wars that are hugely destructive. If conflicts can be caught early on and managed effectively, they can be contained. In an attempt to do this, states and international organizations like the United Nations have developed a number of procedures and mechanisms to deal with conflicts. They include direct negotiations, the use of mediators, arbitration by appointed international judges, conciliation by an investigating panel, or the help of international organizations like the United Nations, the Organization of American States (OAS), and the African Union. The next chapter discusses these methods.

References

CIA. *Terrorism: Frequently Asked Questions Sheet.* http://www.cia.gov/terrorism/faqs.html. March 28, 2004.

Jackson, R. D. W. 2002. "The Discourses in Terrorism: Myths and Misconceptions." *NZ International Review* 27 (March/April): 2–5.

Understanding International Conflict Management

International conflict is an immutable feature of international relations, with both good and bad corollaries. Its drawbacks—the staggering human and economic costs that threaten the order, stability, and very viability of international society—are obvious enough. At times, conflict has even threatened the existence of the international system, as with the Cuban Missile Crisis in 1962, when the superpowers came to the brink of nuclear war. But conflict can also bring about beneficial change. One example is the guerrilla war waged by the South West Africa People's Organization (SWAPO), which eventually freed Namibia from South Africa's illegal and oppressive occupation (1966–1990). Conflict can also curb expansionist states, as with the Gulf War (1990–1991), which frustrated Saddam Hussein's designs not only on Kuwait but also on other states in the Persian Gulf region.

Three postwar developments, however, caused a shift in opinion about conflict: (1) the decolonization of the 1960s, when both the number of states and the potential for conflict proliferated; (2) the spread of nuclear weapons; and (3) the increasing destructiveness of conventional weapons. Whereas conflict used to be an instrument of policy—one of the many ways by which an individual state might achieve its objectives—it was now viewed in a wholly negative light. The international system nevertheless had to find a functional equivalent to conflict—one that did not involve force (Claude 1964).

War, then, has come to be seen as having such grave consequences that the international community has proscribed it until every other option has been exhausted (Claude 1964). Even when states resort to war, their behavior is governed by certain norms. For example, only sovereign states possess the right to wage war, and traditional rules of war designate acceptable weapons, forbid the targeting of civilians, and dictate the treatment of prisoners of war (POWs). In addition, the legitimacy of resorting to war in the first place is reserved for "just causes," and, once war has broken out, laws of neutrality contain its spread (Bull 1977).

All social systems have established mechanisms for limiting and regulating conflict. Families have norms and informal rules; groups have customs and traditions; and states have legal and normative systems. Unregulated conflict is destructive and antithetical to the orderly functioning of social life. Without conflict-mitigating mechanisms, social systems break down into violence and anarchy and cease to function. The international system is no different. What methods, processes, or institutional arrangements are therefore available to states (or nonstate international actors such as ethnic groups or national liberation movements) that want to manage their conflicts without resort to violence? Just how effective are they?

In a section titled, "Pacific Settlement of Disputes," Article 33(1) of the UN Charter, states: "The parties to any dispute, the continuance of which is likely to endanger the maintenance of international peace and security, shall, first of all, seek a solution by:

1. negotiation,
2. enquiry,
3. mediation,
4. conciliation,
5. arbitration,
6. judicial settlement,
7. resort to regional agencies or arrangements, or by other peaceful means of their own choice."

This chapter considers these methods.

Dealing with International Conflict

Conflict management is often confused with *conflict prevention* or *conflict control.* This confusion is regrettable because conflict cannot be prevented or controlled; it can only be managed or resolved. To say that conflicts can be managed presupposes that conflicts are dynamic social processes that move from an incipient, latent stage to maturity and termination. It also suggests that conflicts have certain consequences for the parties involved as well as for the environment in which they occur.

The primary purpose of conflict management is to arrest the escalation of violence and to create conditions that permit benefits to accrue to adversaries who are considering peace. The proper concern of conflict management, therefore, is to increase values and benefits and decrease costs and harm. Conflict management is an attempt to inject some learning into the process of conflict, learning that can make it more productive and less costly. Naturally, many factors influence conflict and its management. Among the most important of these are (1) the characteristics of the conflict parties; (2) the nature of the issues at stake; (3) the strategy and tactics each party employs; and (4) the presence and activities of disinterested third parties.

Social systems have various procedures built into their structure for managing conflicts. Conflicts can be managed by institutional methods such as collective bargaining, social norms, or social roles, for example, third parties. Of these, legal regulation and bargaining and negotiation are perhaps the best-known methods. The international system has its own conflict-management procedures.

A conflict can be considered *settled* when hostile attitudes have been ameliorated and destructive behavior curtailed. A conflict is said to be *resolved* when the basic structure of the situation that originally gave rise to hostile attitudes and destructive behavior has been reevaluated or perceived anew by the parties in conflict. Conflict management can therefore be directed toward either conflict settlement or the more complex and durable outcome—conflict resolution.

When states have a conflict, they can either resort to violence—war or armed conflict—or employ one or more of the many peaceful methods of conflict management advocated by the United Nations. This is not to say that warring states have forfeited their ability to use peaceful methods. Often states will attempt violence first, only to realize that either the costs are too high for the potential benefits or that peaceful methods are a better way to achieve their goals.

Adversaries have three basic choices: they can *manage* their conflict peacefully, *confront* each other violently, or *withdraw* from the conflict altogether. Hans Morgenthau expressed these options as "diplomacy, war, and renunciation" (quoted in Sawyer and Guetzkow 1965). Democratic states usually resolve their conflicts in a peaceful manner. Either that or they voluntarily withdraw from the conflict and renounce those actions that instigated the conflict. Such responses are common among friendly, democratic states like Britain and France.

Alternatively, a state can go to war in an effort to physically overwhelm its opponent. The United States pursued this option in 1983 when it invaded Grenada without ever broaching a peaceful solution. In the face of such attempts or threats of violence, states can simply submit. Haitian military leaders did so in 1994, acceding to UN and U.S. demands when the country was threatened with invasion by a much superior force.

States may also, as noted above, withdraw from the conflict and renounce their claims. This choice is often useful if the costs of pursuing the conflict are higher than the expected gains of winning or compromising. In 1988 China took over the Spratly Islands after expelling the Vietnamese troops stationed there. Although Vietnam could have counterattacked, the potential costs of starting an all-out war with China would have been too high. Vietnam contented itself with lodging a diplomatic protest.

Once states are in conflict—whether or not they have resorted to violence—they can peacefully manage the conflict in only two ways. First, they can try to solve their differences directly, or bilaterally, which will require them to negotiate, either openly or in secret. Second, they can enlist the support of a third party. Mediation, conciliation, adjudication, and referral to the United Nations are all examples of third-party intervention.

Another way to view peaceful conflict-management methods is to differentiate between legal and political conflicts. In other words, some conflicts lend themselves to a legal solution, while others require political settlement. For example, when Iran nationalized its oil industry in 1951, the International Court of Justice (ICJ) was asked to rule on the legality of this move under international law. (The ICJ's response on July 22, 1952, was that it had no jurisdiction in the matter.) For those conflicts that cannot be settled by legal or quasi-legal procedures, a political solution is required. Distinguishing between political and legal issues in international conflicts is important, as the distinction bears directly on the effectiveness of legal methods of conflict management.

Methods and Types of Conflict Management

There are three approaches to conflict management. The first, which is advocated and pursued largely by states themselves, seeks to maintain the primacy of states in the international system through the use of bilateral negotiations. These negotiations keep the conflict-management process and outcome solely in the states' hands. Negotiation, mediation, and inquiry fulfill this need and are therefore the most commonly used methods under the first approach. The parties in nearly all the 343 conflicts described in this book resorted to negotiation or mediation or both. States do not like to submit their conflicts to an outside power.

The second approach, advocated both by individuals concerned for international peace and order and by international lawyers, sees the establishment of international law as the panacea for international conflict. If states could be convinced or forced to submit their conflicts to international courts or tribunals, the thinking goes, the peaceful rule of law would prevail. This approach is at odds with the state-centered, bilateral approach, as arbitration and judicial settlement take away a great deal of control from states during the conflict-management process. This factor alone has made the legal approach unpopular. In most cases, states do not even consider such methods. Out of the hundreds of conflicts between states every year, the ICJ considers only a handful. Even then, when a state gets a judgment it believes unfavorable, it will ignore the ruling. When the ICJ ruled in favor of Chile in the Beagle Channel dispute (1952–1968), Argentina simply ignored the ruling and pressed its claims militarily.

The third, or "functionalist," approach sees the establishment of international organizations with specialized roles, such as the United Nations, as the most promising means of achieving peace and order in international relations. If states can cooperate in international organizations and use their peaceful settlement mechanisms, the organizations might eventually perform functions like those of national governments and national legal systems, providing order in international society. Again, however, states are reluctant to relinquish any sovereignty to a body they cannot directly control. One example is Morocco, which has been fighting the Saharan nationalist group, Polisario, for control over the Western Sahara since 1974 and impeding UN attempts to hold a referendum there since 1992. Fearing the outcome of a UN-sponsored event, Morocco wants to run the referendum on its own terms.

These three approaches are mirrored in peaceful conflict-management methods: *diplomatic, legal,* and *political* (Merrills 1991). The list of diplomatic methods is extensive and includes traditional diplomacy, bargaining and negotiation, mediation, observation and fact-finding missions, peacekeeping, good offices and shuttle diplomacy, referrals, international forums for airing conflict issues, conciliation, and inquiry; and all are determined and controlled entirely by the disputing states. Legal methods include arbitration and adjudication, forms of judicial settlement. Although the states sometimes negotiate the terms, methods, interpretation of outcomes, and so on, it is out of their hands once the legal method is under way. Political methods of conflict management are used by international organizations, such as the United Nations, or a regional group, such as the European Union (EU) or the African Union (AU). The following section examines these methods in more detail, focusing on their conceptual aspects, history, actual use in international relations, and their limitations.

Diplomatic Methods of Conflict Management

Diplomatic methods of conflict management may be thought of as a continuum in which adversaries first try to solve their differences through normal diplomatic channels. If this fails, they may then progress to direct negotiations in a neutral environment. If unsuccessful there, they may then call in a third party to mediate, engage in conciliation, or hold an inquiry. In reality, however, states may choose to use one or all of these methods in any order, or even all at once. They may immediately negotiate, or a mediator may offer its services as soon as the conflict erupts.

Traditional Diplomacy

Traditional diplomacy refers to the official relationship between sovereign states and can be defined in the widest sense as the conduct of relations between states and other international actors by official agents and by peaceful means. Sir Ernest Satow defined it more specifically as "the application of intelligence and tact to the conduct of official relations between the Governments of independent states. . . . [Traditional diplomacy is] the conduct of business between states by peaceful means" (quoted in Schuman 1969).

Diplomacy became established in the seventeenth century when the international system was in its infancy. As interaction among emerging political units grew more intense, the need for permanent missions became obvious. Such missions were first established in Renaissance Italy and by the eighteenth century had become common throughout western Europe. Today, most states have permanent diplomatic missions in the countries with which they have many interactions. Professional diplomats reside in the host country and are a link between the two states.

In a general sense, traditional diplomacy has several important functions. It eases both the negotiation of agreements and routine communication between the political leaders of states and other internationally recognized bodies. Diplomatic missions can also be used to gather intelligence, to reduce the effects of friction in international relations, and to symbolize the existence of the international society (Bull 1977).

"Diplomacy is the continuing method of avoiding disputes" (Suter 1986). Indeed, reducing friction and managing conflict is diplomacy's main function. When a conflict breaks out between two states, the senior diplomat, usually the ambassador or chargé d'affaires, is often expected to remain in close communication with the host government. These traditional diplomatic channels are then used to transmit messages between the disputing states in the search for a peaceful settlement.

Although traditional diplomacy is used every day to manage minor conflicts and misunderstandings, such as trade disputes, it is less well suited for managing violent conflicts. In fact, historically speaking, the onset of war usually meant breaking off diplomatic relations (Frankel 1969). The practice continues to this day: a conflict escalates through several stages before all-out war is reached. An early stage involves expelling all the diplomats of the opposing country to signal the seriousness of the conflict. In this situation, traditional diplomacy is of little use in managing conflict because no diplomats are in place to talk with each other.

Other developments in contemporary international relations have also limited the usefulness of diplomacy for conflict management. First, ambassadors and resident diplomats are often unnecessary when heads of government can simply fly to another capital or talk directly with their counterparts. Modern transport and communications have made diplomats somewhat redundant. Second, states meet all the time in organizations such as the United Nations and do not need to arrange special bilateral meetings. Many important diplomatic questions are now addressed in a multilateral context. Third, technical experts have replaced diplomats in negotiating agreements, and intelligence-gathering organizations have overtaken the diplomats' former function of gathering information and intelligence.

In addition, the rules and conventions of diplomatic institutions have deteriorated in the postwar period. Diplomats are often vulnerable to physical attacks, surveillance, and other abuse (Bull 1977). For example, the U.S.-Iran hostage crisis (1979–1981) began when the Iranian government allowed radical students to ignore the traditional sanctity of embassies and to seize the diplomatic staff in complete violation of international agreements. Incidents involving the mistreatment of diplomats by host countries are now commonplace.

Bargaining and Negotiation

All these developments severely constrain the usefulness of traditional diplomacy in managing conflicts. As a result, states are often forced to turn to direct negotiation. In reality, negotiation is the principal means of handling all international disputes, including economic and trade disputes, and is employed more frequently than all other methods of conflict management put together (Merrills 1991)—although this does not mean that negotiation is the most successful method of managing conflict. Negotiation is the process by which states exchange proposals in an attempt to agree about a point of conflict. It has been used for conflict management since relations between states began and has always been the primary method of attempting to solve disputes. As Suter (1986) observed:

> Direct negotiation between sides in a dispute is the ideal way to resolve conflict on all levels. It is the most efficient method because it requires the least formality, eliminates the expense of third parties and helps avoid adversary proceedings which often aggravate hostility. The complexity of the communication problem may be reduced. . . . Privacy of discussion allows for flexibility and candor so important issues can be discussed with fewer risks. One of the major advantages of bilateral negotiations is that they can be more binding. Mutual consent to a resolution gives it legitimacy.

This is not to say that negotiation is the perfect conflict-management method. Its record of failure in preventing, managing, or resolving many recent international conflicts is a testament to that. Most of the conflicts between 1945 and 1995 included negotiation at some point, but many of these efforts did not succeed. In fact, negotiation has its limitations. For example, negotiations cannot even take place if the disputing parties have broken off diplomatic contact and refuse to have anything to do with each other, or do not even recognize each other officially. A case in point is the conflict between Israel and the Palestine Liberation Organization (PLO), which for years refused to recognize each other or to speak officially. This prevented any attempts at conflict management until the two sides commenced secret negotiations in Norway in 1993.

Also, negotiations are of little use when the states in conflict have few or no common interests and their respective positions are wildly divergent, as was true with the United States and North Vietnam during the Vietnam War (1964–1975). Despite many years of negotiations in Paris, they were unable to reach any accommodation. Negotiations need a strong motivation, a basic trust, and an overlapping field of interest. Further, the failure of negotiations can encourage the use of force by seeming to eliminate all other alternatives (Merrills 1991). In the war in Chechnya, which began in October 1992, the breakdown of talks between Russian and Chechen officials usually signals the resumption of fierce fighting.

Mediation

When states reach an impasse in their negotiations or cannot begin them (because no communication channels exist or few areas of mutual interest are found), they often resort to mediation. Mediation can be defined as a conflict-management method in which an outside party helps adversaries to solve their differences peacefully. Outside parties can be individuals such as former U.S. president Jimmy Carter, representatives of international organizations such as UN Secretary-General Kofi Annan, or state officials such as Madeleine Albright, the former U.S. secretary of state. Essentially, mediation is the injection of a third party into negotiations designed to help the disputants find an acceptable solution.

> Like negotiation, mediation has been employed by states for conflict management since states began to have conflicts; the method is widely used in international relations. Typically, the role of a mediator is to take the thread of negotiations into his own hands; to discuss with the parties, jointly and/or separately, their proposals for ending the dispute; to act . . . as a channel of communication between the parties if necessary; to suggest proposals of his own; to play an active role in narrowing the gap between the two sides; and possibly even to serve as the guarantor of the settlement ultimately reached, if any. (Northedge and Donelan 1971)

For example, Cyrus Vance and Lord Owen, mediating in the Balkans conflict (1989–1995), would typically take the various faction leaders to a house in a neutral country like Switzerland. They would then give them carefully thought out proposals for ending the conflict. When appropriate, the Vance-Owen team would also separate the leaders into different rooms and shuttle messages between them. When the faction leaders were intransigent, Vance and Owen sought to win them over with promises of material aid or to intimidate them with threats of air strikes and sanctions.

For mediation to occur at all, however, willing mediators must step forward, and disputants must accept the mediation and the mediators. In most instances, mediation occurs when (1) conflicts are long, complex, and drawn out; (2) conflict-management attempts have failed; (3) both sides are eager to limit further costs and escalation; and (4) the disputants have a degree of willingness to cooperate and seek a peaceful solution (Bercovitch 1984).

It is often said that "mediation is more likely to be successful [than negotiation] in international politics because it retains the flexibility and control over the conflict management process, while adding extra resources and creativity. That is, mediation can break negotiation deadlocks, re-open channels of communication, provide face-saving for concessions, propose creative solutions, etc." (Jackson 1998). Most commonly, organization mediators can act as go-betweens who promote the conditions required for a settlement—arranging meetings or maintaining a distance between the disputants, organizing appropriate settings for discussion, and producing information required by disputants for informed decision making. To increase conflict management success, the peace process must be analyzed by considering more closely the various organization officials' mediation efforts. The UN secretary-general's use of good offices has increased the importance of formal mediation as a conflict management strategy despite mediation's otherwise low public profile.

Mediation is crucial to UN and regional organization conflict management. It is a flexible, cost-effective strategy and exhibits a high level of complementarity with other methods of conflict management. Mediation offers disputants the opportunity to move toward "official" resolution and is "also widely seen as an extension of the disputants' own bargaining and negotiation efforts" (Bercovitch and Lamare 1993; Wall 1981). Despite this, mediation is often overlooked as an integral element of the overall peace process because peacekeeping missions have a higher profile and wider involvement, and they more readily capture public interest. Unfortunately, the separation of disputants in a buffer zone, a typical function of peacekeeping, does not ensure a durable settlement, and the underlying conflict issues often remain unresolved. "The role of the peacekeeping force is not . . . military, but rather supervisory and related to the provisions of an agreed, not an imposed, truce. These peacekeeping operations result in no real resolution of conflicts" (Baehr and Gordenker 1984). Mediation, however, can be used simultaneously with peacekeeping efforts and can gradually address the resolution of conflict issues. Indeed, the UN often mediates simultaneously during peacekeeping operations.

Observer and Fact-Finding Missions

The most passive organizational role is that of the observer. Observer and fact-finding missions perform a purely supervisory role, allowing the UN and regional organizations to unobtrusively and impartially observe, investigate, and monitor conflict developments "from the inside." Fetherston (1993) includes the role of observer as a function of peacekeeping missions. Although disputant consent is required for both peacekeeping and observer missions, there is one distinct difference in the functions and capabilities of these roles. Observer missions do not engage in enforcement measures; they observe cease-fires but do not intervene to enforce them.

Observers are charged with monitoring cease-fires, observing conflict circumstances, and investigating the facts of conflict situations. For most of the organizations, the power to perform this role is inherent in their founding documents or at least implied to some degree. Observer and fact-finding missions are recognized by Article 34 of the UN Charter, which states: "The Security Council may investigate any dispute, or any situation which might lead to international friction or give rise to a dispute, in order to determine whether the continuance of the dispute or situation is likely to endanger the maintenance of international peace and security." Over the 1945–2003 period, the UN engaged several observer or fact-finding missions during which it also conducted simultaneous mediation attempts. Many of these missions were mandated to observe cease-fires and report on alleged violations. This was the task of the first UN mission, the Peace Observation Commission in the Balkans (1951–1954), established to report on frontier violations on Greece's northern borders. Additional UN "verification" missions have been created to supervise elections, democratic transitions, or self-determination referendums. Examples include the UN Observer Mission in South Africa (UNOMSA) in 1992, the UN Mission in Haiti (UNMIH) in 1993, and the UN Angola Verification Mission (UNAVEM II) in 1991 (McCoubrey and White 1995).

Regional organizations have frequently initiated observer missions. Article 6 of the 1947 Organization of American States (OAS) Inter-American Treaty of Reciprocal Assistance permits foreign ministers in the Organ of Consultation to "deal with any fact or situation that might endanger the peace of America" (McCoubrey and White 1995). The OAS has dispatched observer groups or OAS investigation committees in twelve conflicts. In addition to creating observer groups, the OAS also used investigation and mediation mechanisms such as the Contadora Group and the Inter-American Peace Committee (IAPC). The Contadora Group, established by several South American states in 1983 to promote regional peace, has provided support for the OAS and has conducted mediation under the aegis of the organization (Ramsbotham and Woodhouse 1999). The OAS established the IAPC in 1940 (Zacher 1979). This specialized OAS body had five member states and was initially mandated only to observe, investigate, and offer advice, although the role expanded to include mediating as well as peacebuilding functions.

In July 1992 the African Union (AU) sent a large team of observers to assess the scope of the Hutu and Tutsi tribal conflict involving Uganda and Tanzania. The first mission, the Neutral Military Observer Group (NMOG I), had fifty members. A year later the mission, renamed NMOG II, was more than doubled in size to 130 members. NMOG II was eventually incorporated in the UN monitoring group, United Nations Assistance Mission for Rwanda (UNAMIR). In addition to sending a peacekeeping mission to Chad, the AU also established the Neutral AU Force in Chad to oversee and maintain cease-fire arrangements, restore law and order, ensure civilians freedom of movement during a disarmament program, and assist in the training and organizing of an integrated armed force (Gioia 1997). The Arab League (AL) has also used observer and fact-finding missions, although these roles are not specifically mentioned in Arab League documents. A fact-finding role is implied in Article 5 of the 1945 Arab League Pact, stating that "the Council shall mediate in all differences which threaten to lead to war between two member states, or a member state and a third state, with a view to bringing about their reconciliation" (McCoubrey and White 1995). An Arab Observer Cease-fire Mission was established to supervise troop withdrawals and demilitarization in Amman after hostilities between the Palestine Liberation Organization and Jordan.[1] A joint monitoring commission (JMC), involving delegates from the United Nations, African Union, Arab League, and Organization of Islamic Conference (OIC), was engaged as an observer mission in Somalia in 1992.

The council of the Organization for Security and Co-operation in Europe (OSCE), formerly the Commission on Security and Co-operation in Europe (CSCE), granted the Consultative Committee and the Committee of Senior Officials the authority to establish fact-finding and observer missions. In 1992 the capability of these OSCE missions expanded, allowing them the use of "good offices," conciliation, and diplomatic conflict management strategies (McCoubrey and White 1995). OSCE long-term missions are sometimes referred to as observer missions, although this usage depends largely on the mandate. Tasks of the OSCE long-term mission to Tajikistan, established in 1993, are more characteristic of an observer mission than a peacekeeping mission. The participants were instructed "to maintain contact with and facilitate dialogue and confidence-building between regionalist and political forces in the country; to actively promote respect for human rights; to promote and monitor adherence to OSCE norms and principles, and; to promote ways and means for the OSCE to assist in the development of legal and democratic political institutions and processes" (OSCE December 19, 1997). Similar OSCE missions were engaged in Abkhazia, Albania, Belarus, Bosnia and Herzegovina, Chechnya, and Nagorno-Karabakh (OSCE 1998). The OSCE has also used small preliminary fact-finding missions to report on conflict conditions and assess the viability of initiating more comprehensive intervention. Occasionally, regional organizations have cooperatively engaged monitoring groups; for example, in 1991 the European Community (EC) joined with the OSCE in a verification and observation mission to Yugoslavia.

The EC acknowledged its potential to engage in fact-finding in the 1987 Single European Act (McCoubrey and White 1995). An EC preventive initiative in the former Yugoslavia saw the formation of the European Community Monitoring Mission (ECMM) in July 1991. Launched to assist in peace treaty negotiations between Croatia and Serbia, the ECMM was to monitor the cease-fire and provide support for other locally negotiated military settlements. It was the first external involvement in the Balkans, operating ten months prior to UN peacekeeping. Early intervention by the ECMM failed to prevent the escalation to war, however, with "many feeling that the European initiative had failed because the EC was unable to back up its position with the capability to use force to maintain cease-fires and enforce a settlement between Serbia and Croatia" (Ramsbotham and Woodhouse 1999). The EC, which became the European Union (EU) in 1993, also sent observers to Bosnia, Croatia, and Macedonia. In general, observer and fact-finding missions are preliminary interventions, investigating and assessing the conflict "in the field" before other management strategies, such as peacekeeping, are employed (McCoubrey and White 1995).

Peacekeeping

Peacekeeping was spawned from the statutes in Chapter VI of the UN Charter and evolved as a means of resolving international conflicts. As a by-product of the

1. This was not the Arab League's first fact-finding mission. The council established an ad hoc Commission of Investigation in February 1948 to assess the situation in Yemen after the monarch, Imam Yahya Mohammed Hamid el Din, was assassinated in a coup d'état in Sanaa. This crisis does not fulfil the international dispute coding criteria used in this study and is therefore excluded. The Arab League conducted no mediation during this crisis (Hassouna 1975).

first cold war era, 1948–1960, peacekeeping was an important improvisation for the UN (Falk, Kim, and Mendlovitz 1991). The epitome of compromise, the improvised peacekeeping approach allowed UN decisions to be implemented despite continuing ideological stalemates in the Security Council. Often "it proved impossible even to agree on a definition of aggression, and it was seldom that the members of the Council could be persuaded to vote together on a particular conflict situation. . . . The Council tended instead to take the more tentative path of conciliation" with an emphasis on allowing governments face-saving opportunities (Urquhart 1989). The need for these innovations stems from the restrictions placed on the resort to force and the obligations of members to seek resolution through the peaceful means of settlement outlined in Article 33/1 and Article 34. Although Chapter VII of the UN Charter leaves no doubt about the use of forceful measures, the "Council more often takes the path of conciliatory conflict management, aiming to reach cease-fire agreements, promoting the cooperation of disputing governments and utilizing the strategies of mediation and good offices" (Urquhart 1989). As it is generally thought that compromise and cooperation are more likely to provide a lasting and constructive resolution, international conflict management has developed a reliance on pacific methods of conflict settlement.

Current peacekeeping missions operate under a blueprint of "peacekeeper conduct" established by the first *multilateral* peacekeeping mission in 1956[2] (Väyrynen 1991). UN peacekeeping is often described as the thin blue line between pacific settlement and enforcement. Peacekeepers are bound to use force only as an act of self-defense. The peacekeeper must be seen to be impartial, a third party who holds no leverage over either party in the conflict. The practice of peacekeeping follows four basic principles:

1. consent of the parties to the dispute;
2. impartiality and neutrality of the peacekeeper and perceptions of the impartiality of a peacekeeping mission as a whole;
3. the voluntary and international composition of a peacekeeping mission; and
4. Nonuse of force except in self-defense (Fetherston 1993; Knight and Yamashita 1993; Wiseman 1990).

As with any third-party mediation role, the perception of a peacekeeper's impartiality is crucial. Dealings with all parties to the dispute must be "seen" to be handled in the same way. Impartiality, however, is not necessarily conducive to the smooth execution of some aspects of the peacekeeper's agenda, activities such as the creation of positive peace or peacebuilding. Positive peace or peacebuilding recognizes the facilitative role of the peacekeeper in encouraging constructive interaction and social development, although peacekeepers can perform several roles (Fetherston 1993).

Peacekeeping can be divided into several categories based on levels of activity and function. Diehl (1994) and Diehl et al. (1998) have developed a comprehensive classification of peacekeeping activities, identifying twelve mission categories:

1. "traditional peacekeeping to ensure cease-fire conditions are maintained and to promote an environment conducive to dispute resolution;
2. observation or monitoring of cease-fires or human rights and the collection of information;
3. collective enforcement via multi-dimensional missions;
4. election supervision and support;
5. humanitarian assistance;
6. state or nation building following the absence or transfer of government power;
7. pacification to quell civil disruption;
8. preventive diplomacy to create a buffer zone between the disputants;
9. arms control verification and the identification, collection, custody and/or destruction of weapons;
10. use of protective services in the creation of safe-havens or 'no fly' zones;
11. military intervention in support of legitimate and democratic government; and,
12. sanctions enforcement" (Berdal 1993; Diehl 1994; Diehl et al. 1998; Fetherston 1993; Lennane and Newton 1994; Mackinlay and Chopra 1992; United Nations 2000).

The importance of peacekeeping as a strategy should not be considered above the other strategies of peacemaking, peacebuilding, and enforcement in a priority listing of strategies at the disposal of the UN. If better recognition were given to the brewing stages of a dispute

2. The first *multilateral* peacekeeping mission refers to the UN operation in the Suez Crisis of 1956. Some argue that the first UN peacekeeping operation occurred during the Korean War. Although this mission was authorized by the UN Security Council (June 25, 1950), authorization deviated significantly from UN Charter provisions. Peacekeeping was not conducted by national units permanently assigned to the UN, nor was the operation under the command of the UN Security Council as required by Article 42 and Article 43 of the UN Charter. Instead, the operation was controlled by a U.S. command structure. Authorization for this force was obtained in the Security Council in the absence of the Soviet Union and was clearly a *unilateral* mission—a mission involving no other countries' troops.

and more preemptive, preventive strategies employed, then perhaps fewer conflicts would escalate to the point where peacekeeper deployment was necessary.

Peacekeeping often operates in conjunction with a number of other strategies. The whole process of attaining a peaceful settlement appears to be an incremental process involving one or more of these strategies in succession, or a combination of each, to achieve a successful result. The complementarity of these strategies is evident in Figure 1. The strategies are not mutually exclusive. For example, an independent mediation attempt can occur at the same time as a peacekeeping operation. Likewise, observer missions and peacekeeping forces can be deployed in the same conflict. The deployment of peacekeeping troops merely highlights the fact that other, more preemptive, strategies have failed or were not engaged early enough or at all. When this is the situation, the conflict has deteriorated beyond the point where the other three strategies are entirely effective.

The United Nations has conducted fifty-seven peacekeeping operations since 1948, and fourteen are currently active (United Nations 2004). Many of these missions have been instrumental in separating disputants by enforcing buffer zones, easing the imminent threat of hostilities, and providing a safer environment for mediators to restart dialogue between the disputants. Mediation and peacekeeping are often theoretically associated, but some have recognized a need to infuse this link in the development of a more comprehensive UN approach. "Effective peacekeeping presupposes long-term efforts to mediate the conflict in question. . . . This linkage was urged by the Palme Commission in its Delhi Statement on 19 January, 1986" (Väyrynen 1987). Mediation is frequently used in conjunction with peacekeeping and is used in entrenched conflicts often with overenthusiastic expectations of success.

Regional organizations have established several independent peacekeeping missions as well as contributing to those of the UN. In 1965, for example, the OAS Inter-American Peace Force (IAPF) mobilized a six-member multinational force with the task of "co-operating in the restoration of normal conditions in the Dominican Republic, maintaining the security of its inhabitants and the inviolability of human rights, and establishing an atmosphere of peace and conciliation in which democratic institutions will be able to function" (Gioia 1997). The IAPF was far from being as comprehensive as a UN peacekeeping force, but it did make multilateral what would have otherwise been a unilateral intervention by the United States (Nye 1971). An "improved" body, the Committee on Peaceful Settlement, replaced the IAPC in 1967. The new committee was a "subsidiary organ of the Council and could take up conflicts only at the request of the parties or the Council chairman. If requested by one party, the Committee can also be asked by the Council to offer its 'good offices' to conduct an investigation and to seek a settlement—but only with the other party's consent" (Zacher 1979). Although it can now offer disputants its good offices, mediate, and perform a range of procedural peacebuilding tasks, the strength of the IAPC lies in its multilateral composition, an asset allowing it to maintain a regional approach.

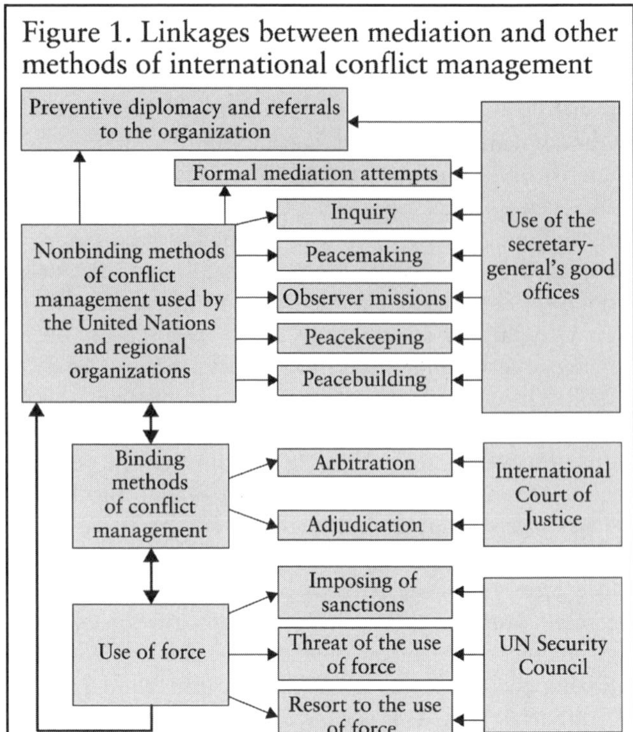

Figure 1. Linkages between mediation and other methods of international conflict management

African heads of state soured toward external involvement after the UN Operation in the Congo (UNOC) in 1964 failed to quiet the civil war.[3] The resulting dissatisfaction left the AU seeking to assert its regional conflict management role. The AU dispatched a peacekeeping force of 3,500, the Inter-African Force (IAF), to Chad in 1981 (Ramsbotham and Woodhouse 1999; Lall 1982). The AU's decision to send a peacekeeping force to Chad was indicative of its concerns for the region and its aim to stem any further possible escalation (Väyrynen, 1985a). The implementation of the pan-African peacekeeping force was, however, fraught with problems. Despite the

3. In 1960 the UN was intensely divided over the direction of UNOC's mandate amid continuing civil strife in the Congo. After a Security Council resolution supported a return to constitutional government, a new central government was formed under Prime Minister Cyrille Adoula in August 1961. The Katangese refused to accept the new government, and the UN conducted two unsuccessful military operations in Katanga in September and December 1961 in an effort to deal with Katangese secessionism (Zacher 1979). "By the end of June 1964, when the last batch of the UN troops were withdrawn from the Congo, a crisis was booming large" with fighting spreading to four provinces: Kwilu, Katanga, Orientale, and Kivu (Oluo 1982, Andemicael 1976).

organization's commitment to the peacekeeping plan, there were obvious deficiencies. Among the problems, the parties to the conflict were not so committed; the logistics of running a peacekeeping operation via AU channels were not as easily orchestrated as a peacekeeping operation run under the auspices of the UN; and the means and resources needed to run such an operation were not readily available to AU members.[4] The IAF failed to achieve its mission objectives and was withdrawn in 1982. This failure discouraged member state support for future AU peacekeeping proposals (Ramsbotham and Woodhouse 1999, 188).

Similarly, membership disagreement has marred Arab League attempts at independent peacekeeping. The AL has contributed to UN peacekeeping missions, but its attempts to initiate independent peacekeeping have failed (Ramsbotham and Woodhouse 1999). The league tried to mobilize peacekeeping operations during Kuwait's independence crisis, even though Kuwait was not a league member at the time. Many AL members felt strongly about the potential for serious hostilities in this conflict. The league's secretary-general, Abdel Khaliq Hassounah, tried to resolve the situation, and, after continued discussion under the aegis of the league, Kuwait agreed to allow Arab League forces to replace the withdrawing British forces. Kuwait became a league member over the course of these meetings, even after Iraq voiced its objections. The AL force arrived in Kuwait on September 10, 1961, and by October 19 all of the British forces had withdrawn. After Iraq relaxed its claims over the territory, the Arab League force was reduced on December 6, and by February 1962 had left Kuwait. The initiation of the Arab League force was arranged in the same manner as a UN mission, gaining written agreement with the Kuwaiti government on the terms of engagement (Ramsbotham and Woodhouse 1999).

The Arab League attempted another peacekeeping mission during Lebanon's second civil war, which began in early 1975. The league established a "symbolic" peacekeeping force and a mediation commission. The peacekeeping force consisted of mostly Syrian troops, with several units from Libya, Saudi Arabia, and the Sudan. The mediation commission was unable to secure a peaceful solution, and, without the parties adhering to cease-fire conditions, the peacekeeping force was left with the unenviable task of maintaining a line of partition between the hostile parties. By October 18, 1976, the league had approved the formation of a deterrent force under a new comprehensive peace plan. The heads of state of Egypt, Kuwait, Lebanon, Saudi Arabia, and Syria signed the plan in Riyadh. About 20,000 to 30,000 Syrian troops were assigned to serve in a multilateral operation called the Arab Deterrence Force (ADF) (Merrills 1991). "Once again the size, composition, and deployment of an Arab League Peacekeeping Force was the subject of disagreement. The Palestinians objected to the Syrian presence, the Syrians objected to the inclusion of the Palestinians, and Egypt walked out on the whole mission" (Ramsbotham and Woodhouse 1999). At a league summit meeting, held October 25–26, 1976, nineteen of the members accepted the Riyadh Plan, with only Iraq and Libya voicing their opposition. In November the ADF moved to Beirut and consolidated positions throughout Lebanon. The Syrian occupation of many strategic sites in Lebanon eventually helped to force a cessation of hostilities. The Arab League efforts were later dwarfed by the UN Interim Force in Lebanon (UNIFIL) in 1978. The ADF mission ended unsuccessfully in September 1982, with Syria and Israel impervious to ADF efforts to bring about reconciliation (Merrills 1991).

As yet, the OSCE has not officially deployed independent peacekeeping missions, even though Chapter III of the Helsinki Document (1992) provides for the organization to authorize them. The OSCE has participated in peacekeeping missions initiated by other organizations but has found that implementing independent peacekeeping is problematic because it has no military personnel at its disposal. In 1994 the OSCE almost authorized a peacekeeping force of 3,000 multinational troops during the conflict over the status of Nagorno-Karabakh, but the proposal did not find favor with Russia, which wanted to maintain regional dominance and did not welcome the international community's full involvement. The possibility of engaging an OSCE multinational force dwindled in unison with the international community's unwillingness to become committed to another potentially drawn-out conflict. Experiences in Bosnia and Chechnya acted as a deterrent to becoming deeply involved in the Nagorno-Karabakh conflict (Ellingwood 1997). Instead of traditional peacekeeping, the OSCE has independently engaged eleven long-term missions to Bosnia and Herzegovina, Croatia, Estonia, Georgia, Kosovo, Latvia, Moldova, Sanjak and Vojvodina, Sarajevo, Skopje, Tajikistan, and Ukraine (OSCE 1998). These long-term missions perform a range of functions, such as fact-finding, monitoring troop withdrawals, promoting

4. In some cases, perceptions of AU interference have discouraged disputants from using the organization's dispute-management capabilities. The AU's charter specifies noninterference in the internal affairs of a member state and respects an undeniable right to independence (Article 3, Paragraphs II and III). But perceptions of AU complicity in the internal affairs of member states have complicated its efforts at dispute management. An example is the AU's involvement in the Congo's postindependence struggle (July 1960–mid-1964). During another dispute, the Nigerian/Biafran Civil War, the two charter paragraphs were put into interpretative conflict, with one disputant claiming rights of independence, and the other arguing "noninterference in internal affairs" (Oluo 1982). Selective interpretation of these two charter principles has weakened the AU's ability to intervene effectively, highlighting an ambiguity the organization needs to repair.

observance of human rights, providing expertise in developing legal and democratic institutions, and state-building. In addition, the OSCE has dispatched personal representatives and assistance groups and has also established negotiation forums, such as the Minsk Group, which was formed to address the Nagorno-Karabakh conflict, under the OSCE umbrella.

Like UN peacekeeping, OSCE long-term operations cannot use enforcement strategies unless authorized by the UN Security Council, but compliance with the civilian composition regulations in the Helsinki Document has given OSCE missions a different character from the military composition of UN peacekeeping missions. OSCE long-term mission civilian operatives use a range of strategies including good offices, monitoring, and fact-finding (Ronzitti 1997). Curiously, the Helsinki Document has no provisions for funding long-term missions, yet financial provisions for possible OSCE peacekeeping missions are well addressed. "The main characteristic of peacekeeping operations is that they have a sound legal basis in the Helsinki Document, unlike long-term missions which have evolved from OSCE practice. Moreover, a peacekeeping operation requires a diffused presence on the ground, while this is not necessary for a long-term mission" (Ronzitti 1997). Although OSCE long-term missions are distinct from peacekeeping roles, it is evident that long-term missions complement more traditional peacekeeping, allowing the organization to maintain a visible presence while continuing peacebuilding and encouraging further dialogue, as was the case in Bosnia and Herzegovina.

Further explanation of peacebuilding, preventive diplomacy, and peacemaking is appropriate here as a peacekeeping role often transforms to include these functions as conflict circumstances evolve. Secretary-General Boutros Boutros-Ghali clarified the scope of these roles in terms of the UN in conflict management in his 1993 report, *An Agenda for Peace*. Boutros-Ghali emphasized preemptive strategies as well as management strategies, detailing four types of UN missions: preventive diplomacy, peacemaking, peacekeeping, and peacebuilding. Formalized mediation complements Boutros-Ghali's four initiatives and can be employed simultaneously with each strategy. Primarily, what is used to differentiate the initiatives is the timing of their application.

> *Preventive diplomacy* is action to prevent conflicts from arising between parties, to prevent existing conflicts from escalating into major conflicts, and to limit the spread of the latter when they occur.
>
> *Peacemaking* is action to bring hostile parties to agreement, essentially through such peaceful means as those foreseen in Chapter VI of the Charter of the United Nations.
>
> *Peacekeeping* is the deployment of a United Nations presence in the field, hitherto with the consent of all the parties concerned, normally involving United Nations military and/or police personnel and frequently civilians as well. Peacekeeping is a technique that expands the possibilities for both the prevention of conflict and the making of peace.
>
> *Peacebuilding* is an action to identify and support structures that will tend to strengthen and solidify peace in order to avoid a relapse into conflict (Boutros-Ghali 1993).

Some of Diehl's categories are also considered characteristic of traditional preventive diplomacy, specifically, peacekeeping, observation, pacification, preventive diplomacy, and initiation of protective services (Diehl 1994; Diehl et al. 1998; Plano and Riggs 1967). Although it is generally assumed that preventive diplomacy occurs prior to hostilities, it also encompasses attributes normally associated with peacekeeping. "Preventive diplomacy is complementary to peaceful settlement in that both seek to ease tensions in a conflict, both need the consent of the state or states involved, and both have the objective of achieving a stabilization of the situation" (Plano and Riggs 1967). The OSCE's use of confidence and security-building measures (CSBMs) can also be identified as preventive strategies.

The peacemaking phase occurs after the conflict has already begun, while peacekeeping is engaged during the conflict in an effort to contain or control the conflict. Although peacebuilding is commonly associated with the process of rebuilding trust and confidence between the parties after a conflict, its application is by no means limited to the postconflict period (Boutros-Ghali 1993). "Peacebuilding underpins the work of peacemaking and peacekeeping by addressing structural issues and the long-term relationships between conflictants . . ." and ". . . tries to overcome the contradictions which lie at the root of the conflict" (Galtung 1976; Miall et al. 1999). Current research is often separated into these simplified categories, despite the difficulty in identifying distinctive conflict phases (Sherman 1987, 1994). Boutros-Ghali's address reflects the importance of early conflict identification as one of the most urgent concerns facing the development of international conflict management. The complementarity of mediation with these strategies, "with its perceived impartiality and fairness, informality and flexibility, and lack of hidden agenda . . . can strengthen international capacity for preventing deadly conflicts" (Bercovitch 1997).

Good Offices and Shuttle Diplomacy

Good offices is a passive form of mediation and is often described as a diplomatic method of conflict management (*see* Figure 1). This strategy does not accord third parties the full range of active mediation techniques. The mediator acts as a facilitator or go-between but does not persuade or press disputants to reach a resolution (Yarrow 1978). The third party here can only offer a channel of communications, relay information (shuttle diplomacy), or arrange facilities and meeting places for the disputants. By strict definition, the use of good offices does not allow third parties to offer suggestions for the terms of settlement. "By providing a neutral ground for the negotiation or by offering to carry messages between the disputants, the third party displays a friendly desire to promote a settlement without getting involved in the issues at stake" (Bennett 1988). Although not listed in Article 33 of the UN Charter with the other seven methods of conflict management, good offices is a traditional mediation strategy and is frequently used in conjunction with all of the other nonbinding diplomatic strategies. The Good Offices Committee was an early mode of UN field operations and intervened only in the Netherlands/Dutch East Indies–Indonesian independence dispute of late 1945 to November 1949 (Critchley 1994). Subsequent mediation committees have engaged in other strategies besides the use of good offices.

Fetherston describes this possible exchange and flexibility between strategies as a potential of complementarity (Fetherston 1993). Indeed, the potential for complementarity is substantial. Good offices has the hallmarks of diplomacy, and it is not unusual for a good offices role to expand into broader mediation roles in subsequent contacts. Mediator initiative and adaptability are imperative given the evolving nature of conflicts. A mediator's experience has been seen as a significant determinant of mediation success (Carnevale and Pegnetter 1985; Kolb 1983, 1985). Expertise, experience, flexibility, a favorable disputant/mediator background, diplomatic skill, credibility of the office and the individual, personality, knowledge of the conflict and disputants, a level of impartiality, and well-developed interpersonal skills all help to establish a level of trust and confidence and can increase mediation success. The secretary-general's use of good offices as an effective stand-alone strategy exemplifies the importance of many of these factors. This mediation strategy relies a great deal on the disputants' perception of the secretary-general, both as an individual and as a representative of the organization, although the position is more visible as a highest level interaction amongst state officials (Tunnicliff 1984; Skjelsbæk 1991). It is also evident, however, that competency in the role as secretary-general depends on the person who holds the office and that individual's particular operational style (Skjelsbæk and Fermann 1996).

Organizational representatives have experienced mixed success when using shuttle diplomacy. During the Namibian independence struggle, the UN secretary-general acted as a go-between in negotiations during November 1984. Secretary-General Javier Pérez de Cuéllar received letters and proposals from both South Africa and Angola, although neither party accepted the other's proposals. The UN's mediation attempts in the Yom Kippur War (October 1973), aided greatly by the shuttle diplomacy of Henry Kissinger, the U.S. secretary of state, were on the whole very successful. UNEF II provided logistical and technical assistance throughout the conflict, acting as a buffer zone and an observer team, as well as a facilitator in troop redeployment.

Shuttle diplomacy is not always beneficial to the resolution of a conflict. Shuttle diplomacy by the OSCE-initiated Minsk Group inadvertently eliminated much of the implied legitimacy that the involvement of the United States and Russia lent to the group's mediation attempts. During the Nagorno-Karabakh conflict, the OSCE brought together the Minsk Group comprising high-level representatives from Armenia, Azerbaijan, Finland, France, Germany, Hungary, Italy, Russia, Switzerland, Turkey, and the United States. Nagorno-Karabakh representatives attended the meetings as an interested third party. The membership of the Minsk Group altered after 1992 but the main actors, Armenia, Azerbaijan, France, Russia, Turkey, and the United States, continued to function within the group. The changing membership of the Minsk Group has been cited as one of the problems faced by the OSCE. With each change—and there were four rotations of chairmanship—the dynamics of the mediator-disputant relationship also changed. Evidence of the problem can be seen in the marginalized role of the United States in the Minsk Group after 1993 (Ellingwood 1997). Marginalizing such an important actor decreased the perceived legitimacy of the group and undoubtedly affected its mediation efforts.

The successful use of good offices, shuttle diplomacy, and mediation strategies in general frequently rests on the timing of intervention. Regional organizations are better positioned to provide timely intervention and can often persist with simple mediation strategies in conflicts where the logistics of travel would hinder immediate UN preventive diplomacy. For example, the AU established an ad hoc commission as a mechanism to provide good offices to the disputants during a border conflict between Algeria and Morocco. The "provision of good offices over a long duration allowed the AU to successfully resolve the border conflict between Algeria and Morocco in 1963 and eventually restore diplomatic relations between the disputants" (Merrills 1991). Regional organization timeliness is exemplified in two conflicts. The AU's secretary-general, Eteki Mboumosa, made one timely mediation in a territorial conflict between Uganda and Kenya. President Idi Amin of Uganda had appealed to both the UN and AU secretaries-general to initiate an investigatory mission to assess the situation, stating that Uganda was prepared to take further action if it was not resolved. The parties indicated their willingness to resolve their conflict and resume normal relations prior to making a final settlement under the guidance of the AU secretary-general. "Same day" action by the OAS quelled a border conflict between Costa Rica and Nicaragua. On October 15, 1977, Gauzalo

Facio, Costa Rica's foreign minister, protested to the government of Nicaragua about incursions into Costa Rican territory and airspace. The same day, an OAS team mediated between the parties in Nicaragua and achieved a full settlement, with OAS observers being stationed along the border as a precautionary measure. After this intervention, the conflict abated. Like most mediation strategies, good offices and shuttle diplomacy can be implemented speedily and may prevent a complete break down in disputant dialogue.

International Organizations as Forums for Airing Conflict Issues

Both the United Nations and regional organizations provide a valuable forum for airing disputant grievances and issues. The organizations' forums provide disputants with (1) an arena for informal and formal discussion; (2) a neutral environment; (3) an opportunity to internationalize or localize their conflict; and (4) accessibility to mediation or more informal negotiation.

Once a referral is made to the UN and a conflict is under consideration, the Security Council must evaluate the extent of the conflict and decide upon an appropriate course of action. The Security Council debating chamber becomes the hub of discussions between the disputants and UN representatives in an effort to obtain a peaceful solution. The working role of the UN as a forum is best described by a former president of the UN Security Council:

> The most striking feature of the Council's working procedures was the careful and prudent preparation by way of extensive informal consultations . . . members were in contact almost daily. The methods of consultation ranged from daily informal, bilateral contacts . . . to full, informal consultations in the President's office in the presence of permanent representatives, assisted by their own staffs, and senior Secretariat officials, normally including the Secretary-General himself. Formal meetings were called for two reasons: (a) to give the parties an opportunity to present their case formally and officially; (b) to record any agreement or decision reached during the consultations. No substantial negotiations took place during the formal meetings. They were, rather, the end-product of a long process (Riggs and Plano 1989).

Agreements can appear piecemeal at first, but discussions in the Security Council chamber are part of an incremental process. "Quick agreement on a solution to the underlying substantive conflict is uncommon, but an understanding is frequently reached as to the appropriate limits of Security Council action" (Riggs and Plano 1989). What begins as an agreement to dispatch a special representative in an investigatory capacity often leads to acceptance of active mediation.

UN-initiated summit meetings are another formal variation of the forum environment. Superpower dialogue in this low-pressure environment allowed parties to discuss arms-control negotiations more than before and fostered the establishment of a fresh framework for multilateral consultation to improve interstate relations (Väyrynen, 1985b). The ease of détente dialogue determined the extent of reliance on the UN as a universal forum. Where bilateral blockages occurred in communications, often the UN offered an alternative to a complete breakdown in relations. "The Security Council is not obligated to discuss every complaint that a state chooses to submit to it, and potentially inflammatory debate may sometimes be avoided by prior consultation and informal decision not to place an item before the Council" (Riggs and Plano 1989). Thirteen of the conflicts we consider in this book have noticeably shown the value of the UN as a forum, with the UN General Assembly providing a forum in two conflicts.

Regional organizations also provide a useful forum for the discussion of disputants' concerns in existing or potential conflicts. Taking a conflict issue to a regional organization can bring the matter to public attention in a formal environment, but it can also allow the disputants the opportunity to negotiate informally during the course of their contact or meeting (Merrills 1991). The airing of a conflict in the AU forum was instrumental in resolving a border conflict between Mali and Upper Volta (Burkina Faso). The AU forum aided disputant dialogue in four conflicts. Alternatively, OAS experience as a forum was received poorly by disputants who expected the organization to take a stronger role in resolving the territorial conflict over the Lauca River Dam. The fact that the OAS acted only as a forum for the disputants to air their grievances frustrated Bolivia to the point that it temporarily withdrew from the organization in June 1963 and withdrew again in September 1963 in protest at the lack of OAS action.

Most studies are primarily concerned with mediation, but it is important to note that the organizations' role is broader than just providing a mediation environment: Organizations allow disputants the freedom to conduct their own negotiation in a private setting. If disputants are willing to engage in dialogue, the organizations' broader forum provides an informal, neutral environment where contact is perhaps made easier and more accessible.

Referrals

A *referral* is simply an action whereby a disputant or concerned party requests that an international organization consider a conflict—its issues and implications—with the desire that the organization become involved in the conflict's management. Referrals fall within the spectrum of techniques available to mediators, which range from the ostensibly passive role, such as acting as a go-between, to the more active role, in which mediators can impart persuasive techniques and offer settlement incentives to disputants (Bercovitch 1996). By their nature, referrals are indirect acts of negotiation involving a third party. Referrals can involve third parties in a persuasive role even though they may not always engage in face-to-face negotiation and may provide nonbinding decisions.

Both the UN and regional organizations can receive referrals. In the case of the UN, a referral brings a conflict to the Security Council's attention and places it on the international agenda as a matter of importance. The referral is evidence of the UN's unique position of leverage and power in its international role, achieving a result even before the Security Council has considered the conflict. In his 1986 study of collective international conflict management, Haas did not consider referrals in his analysis, saying that a "referral was purely symbolic [and that] circumstances made any real organizational impact impossible" (Haas 1986). Here we refute Haas's assumption that a referral is purely symbolic. When a referral is brought to the Security Council, it is an indication of the seriousness with which the international community views the situation. It also indicates an organization's intention to deal with a conflict, possibly with weightier treatment if the disputants do not make a greater effort to come to an agreement. The prospect of increased external involvement in the internal affairs of a state can often be a persuasive tool in its own right. Certainly, the unpredictability of judicial settlements is a deterrent for the same reason (Riggs and Plano 1989). Disputants are reluctant to engage in a conflict management process if there is a greater possibility that it will end unfavorably.

Conciliation

If the disputants are inflexible and unwilling to mediate, conciliation may be employed. Conciliation has been described as "an attempt to induce negotiations" (Bailey 1982). It may be described more formally as "a method for the settlement of international conflicts of any nature according to which a commission set up by the parties, either on a permanent basis or an ad hoc basis to deal with a conflict, proceeds to the impartial examination of the conflict and attempts to define the terms of a settlement" (Merrills 1991). That is, two states in conflict nominate officials to sit on a panel. The panel then gathers all relevant information on the conflict, examines it, and suggests ways to settle it. Another way to conceive of conciliation is to think of it as "institutionalized negotiation" (Merrills 1991).

Theoretically, the line between conciliation and mediation is difficult to draw. Suffice it to say that conciliation formalizes the third-party intervention, institutionalizing it to a greater degree (Merrills 1991). It is usually instituted by treaty. The conciliator's role is to propose either the rules governing the settlement—that is, the means by which the parties shall come to agreement—or the terms of the settlement itself (Suter 1986). Historically, conciliation emerged out of treaty practice in Europe and reached its height between 1925 and World War II, when nearly 200 treaties involving conciliation were concluded (Merrills 1991). Since then, it has declined. In fact, when compared with other methods of conflict management, conciliation has never been widely used. Of the thousands of conflicts over the past seventy years, fewer than twenty cases of formal conciliation have been heard (Merrills 1991). Informal conciliation through international organizations is used only slightly more often.

There are several reasons for the relative inutility of conciliation. First, many bilateral treaties restrict the categories of conflicts open for conciliation to a small area of relatively unimportant issues. Areas of political concern, where conflicts are most likely to occur and most likely to be violent, are not covered by the treaties. Second, the expense and difficulties involved in convening and operating a conciliation meeting often make other procedures more attractive. Third, conciliation is too elaborate for many minor conflicts but lacks the political authority for major conflicts. In short, conciliation has demonstrated some success only for conflicts that were strictly legal and of minor importance (Merrills 1991).

Inquiry

Another conflict-management method resembling conciliation is inquiry, "a specific institutional arrangement which states may select in preference to arbitration or other techniques because they desire to have some disputed issue independently investigated. In its institutional sense, then, inquiry refers to a particular type of international tribunal, known as the commission of inquiry" (Merrills 1991). In other words, inquiry is the attempt by a third party to "establish the relevant facts and to elucidate those aspects of the dispute where incomplete or misleading information has been an unnecessary cause of contention" (Bailey 1982).

Like conciliation, inquiry is a fairly recent and little-used addition to the range of conflict-management methods. The reason is that it is designed only for dealing with conflicts that revolve around disputed facts or information. Only four inquiries were conducted between 1905 and 1922. Another took place in 1962 and none since then (Merrills 1991). Although international organizations make much more use of it than suggested by these figures, the inquiry remains a relatively unimportant method of conflict management in international relations.

Legal Methods of Conflict Management

As has been mentioned, legal methods of conflict management represent the attempt to establish international law as the primary means of maintaining order in international society. A discussion of international law is necessary if we are to examine its two methods, arbitration and adjudication. When we talk about law, we are referring to a "general rule which covers a specific class of cases, and which is backed by a probable sanction, stated in advance and widely accepted as legitimate" (Deutsch 1978). International law, then, may be conceived of as "a body of rules which binds states and other agents in world politics in their relations with one another and is considered to have the status of law" (Bull 1977). As we shall see, however, the status of international law differs from that of domestic law.

International law has four functions. First, international law regulates interaction and interrelations in such a way that they can proceed in an orderly and efficient manner. For example, international law regulates the treatment of diplomats and the keeping of treaties. Second, international law fosters orderly change in the society of nations, permitting the system to adapt itself to changing circumstances without being violently disrupted. Third, it functions to limit and control the destructive or disorderly effects of conflict on the system; that is, it provides conflict-resolution mechanisms. Fourth, and from a more sociological perspective, international law functions to identify and embody the idea of a society of sovereign states (Delbruck 1987; Bull 1977) in much the same way that domestic law provides a sense of identity and nationhood.

Because rules are so vital to the existence of society—no society can exist without them—the history of international law is as old as the international system itself. Among the many elements contributing to the development of international law, the most fundamental are the need to limit the use of force and the need for cooperation (Fawcett 1971). After the medieval feudal system disintegrated and the first European states emerged, states cooperated or fought as they saw fit. Although the international system of the seventeenth and eighteenth centuries has therefore been called anarchic despite the reign of sovereign monarchs, certain basic rules of conduct, or rules of international law, were developed and observed. These were formulated primarily to regulate mutual relations in peace and conflict.

In the nineteenth century, when the idea of the state took hold, international rules of law developed at a fast pace. The Act of the Vienna Congress, the Treaty of Paris of 1856 ending the Crimean War, the Acts of the Berlin Congress (1875, 1888), and the Act of the Brussels Congress (1890) were all important steps in codifying international relations. Furthermore, international rules of law provided criteria for settling disputes (Delbruck 1987). International law was refined and developed even further in the twentieth century. Most important, from the pioneering of the League of Nations following World War I to the establishment of the United Nations in 1945, international law has sought to create centralized, authoritative mechanisms for regulating state relations and resolving conflict.

Contemporary international law, therefore, attempts to prohibit states from engaging in activities that are likely to disturb international peace and security. It also attempts to encourage those activities that are conducive to establishing a peaceful order, such as the regulation of economic, social, communications, and environmental matters (Delbruck 1987; Bull 1977).

Arbitration

International law provides two basic mechanisms for managing conflict—arbitration and adjudication. The Hague Convention for the Pacific Settlement of International Disputes (1907) offers the following definition: "International arbitration has for its object the settlement of disputes between states by judges of their own choice, and on the basis of respect for law. Recourse to arbitration implies an engagement to submit in good faith to the award" (quoted in Schuman 1969). In other words, states in conflict agree to turn their dispute over to arbitrators who will decide between them on the basis of international law.

For example, when Chile and Argentina began to dispute the ownership of the Beagle Channel after World War II, they both submitted their claims to the ICJ. The ICJ judges investigated the relevant information and treaties and ruled that, on the basis of international law, Chile was the rightful owner. Argentina later repudiated this ruling.

Arbitrators may use four sources of law to decide a dispute: (1) international conventions that have established rules recognized by the states; (2) international custom, as evidence of a general practice accepted as law; (3) the general principles of law recognized by civilized nations; and (4) judicial decisions and teachings by recognized experts (Bull 1977). Furthermore, arbitration may proceed by means of ad hoc tribunals or individual arbitrators. For example, in some cases, the states may establish a commission. In other cases, they may refer to a foreign head of state or specially qualified individual, or they may use a tribunal or collegiate body (Merrills 1991). Normal practice is to have an odd number of judges, with each party having at least one of their own representatives on the panel.

The use of arbitration can be traced back to classical Greece, and during the Middle Ages the pope often served as arbitrator. Interestingly, the pope also mediated the Beagle Channel conflict (1977–1984) between Argentina and Chile after Argentina rejected the ICJ's ruling and pressed its claims militarily. Although the arbitration system fell into disuse with the rise of the state system, it was revived in the nineteenth and early twentieth centuries (Suter 1986). Even at its height, however, in comparison to other forms of conflict management, arbitration was never used to any great degree.

Adjudication

Like arbitration, adjudication (or judicial settlement) has also been little used by states. Adjudication refers to "the reference of a dispute to the World Court or some other standing tribunal, such as the European Court of Human Rights" (Merrills 1991). In other words, the only essential difference between arbitration and adjudication is the manner in which the judges are chosen. They are identical in all other respects. In arbitration, states choose judges themselves, whereas in adjudication, states refer to established courts. The Permanent Court of International Justice (PCIJ), established by the League of Nations as the first such permanent court, heard only thirty-three contentious cases. Its successor, the ICJ, established in 1945, has heard little more than one case for every year of its existence (Northedge and Donelan 1971).

Despite this sorry record, legal methods do have some advantages. In a general sense, legal methods supply a rational, orderly, and authoritative way of settling disputes. More specifically, the binding, impartial decisions handed down by arbitrators and adjudicators not only allow for states under domestic pressure to save face but also legitimize the successful party's claim in the eyes of the international community. Litigation is a good way to dispose of troublesome issues, and it gives states confidence in the process when they can choose judges. Permanent tribunals also relieve states of the need to set up new tribunals for every new dispute. In a general sense, legal methods discourage unreasonable behavior by reminding states that there are alternatives to violence. Moreover, arbitral awards are usually observed (Merrills 1991).

The Limitations of International Law

Nevertheless, the legal methods of conflict management have serious limitations, and these are especially evident in three regards: enforcement, judicial scope, and the advent of nonstate actors.

International law differs from the domestic law of nations because it has no enforcement machinery. If a state is determined to violate international law, no central authority or coercive machinery exists to prevent or punish that state. In other words,

> The difference between international law and the domestic law of countries lie[s] not in their character as law or in the kind of order they are designed to support, but in the actual distribution of power in the countries they serve, and in the degree to which that distribution has itself been reduced to order. A national community is one in which there is a very large number of weak units of power, so that sanctions against breaches of the law are normally effective and easy to maintain. . . . The international community is one in which there is a small number of units of power, of which some are enormous, most are considerable, and none are negligible (Fawcett 1971).

This problem strikes at the very heart of international law and means that observance of international law is based on considerations other than the threat of coercion. In international relations, self-enforcement is the basis for the observance of international law, and this self-enforcement proceeds from calculations that states make regarding their self-interest. The first calculation is that the costs and benefits of observing international law make observance a better option. For example, both Iran and Iraq suffered greatly from the international community's sanctions when they flouted international laws. Iran was sanctioned when it violated the U.S. embassy in 1979, and Iraq for its 1990 invasion of Kuwait. Obedience to international law is obtained by the threat of coercion and negative world and/or domestic opinion.

States also obey international law because they have an interest in reciprocal action by others—action that would not be forthcoming if they were to scorn international rules of behavior (Bull 1977; Deutsch 1978). If a state were to ignore some treaty obligations, it might find its treaties with other states likewise spurned.

A second shortcoming of the legal methods of conflict management concerns judicial scope. Legal methods do not adequately address political questions. Inasmuch as few disputes relate purely to legal questions, litigation is suitable for very few international conflicts. It can even be argued that, because states are political entities, even strictly legal questions are never truly divorced from political considerations. Most states are therefore reluctant to use judicial methods where political interests are involved (Merrills 1991), which excludes nearly every armed conflict in modern times.

The third limitation is that law is a very conservative creature that does not adjust easily to change. The many changes in the nature and make-up of the international system have not been matched by appropriate changes in international law. The main body of current international law originated in the European state system and therefore has little relevance for many new African and Asian states, which have no cultural affinity with it. Also, most international law sees only the state as a valid subject of law, whereas the contemporary international system contains a multitude of significant nonstate actors, such as international organizations, ethnic groups, liberation movements, and powerful multinational companies. Many of the actors involved in internal conflicts do not qualify as states and, therefore, have no recourse to international law.

For example, the Kurdish minorities fighting for independence in both Iraq and Turkey have no legal standing in the international community, as they do not constitute a state. Even if they were to submit their dispute to an international court, the court would be unable to make a ruling because the Kurds are not a legally recognized member of the international community. The Iraqi Kurds frequently appealed to the United Nations, alleging state-sanctioned genocide, but the world body has so far ignored them. This situation could change if the war in Iraq becomes an internationalized civil conflict.

Political Methods of Conflict Management

Political methods of conflict management originate in the functionalist theory of international relations. More specifically,

> The theory of functionalism in international relations is based on the hope that more and more common tasks will be delegated to such specific functional organizations and that each of these organizations will become in time supranational; that is, superior to its member governments in power and authority. In this way, according to the theory, the world's nations will gradually become integrated into a single community within which war will be impossible (Deutsch 1978).

These *international organizations*, or *intergovernmental organizations* (IGOs), usually have a dual task. They work to encourage intergovernmental cooperation in many areas, such as air traffic control, the international postal system, and global environmental controls. They also provide mechanisms and forums for settling international disputes. Examples include the Universal Postal Union (UPU), founded in 1874; the International Telecommunication Union (ITU), founded in 1932; the International Civil Aviation Organization (ICAO), founded in 1947; the International Labor Organization (ILO), founded in 1919; the Food and Agriculture Organization (FAO), founded in 1945; and the World Health Organization (WHO), founded in 1948.

Regional Organizations

The United Nations encourages states to refer their conflicts to regional organizations before coming to the world body. Regional organizations are agencies created by treaty among states in a recognizable geographical area. There are two main kinds of regional organizations: collective defense organizations like the North Atlantic Treaty Organization (NATO) and regional arrangements or agencies like the African Union (AU).

The most important regional organizations include the AU, the Organization of American States (OAS), the Arab League (AL), the Association of South-East Asian Nations (ASEAN), the European Union (EU), the Organization of Security and Cooperation in Europe (OSCE), and the Pacific Islands Forum (PIF). Most of these groups originated in the postwar period and, like the UN, all have built-in mechanisms of conflict management. In fact, for these regional organizations, conflict management among member states is their primary purpose. Most regional organizations effectively use mediation, conciliation, fact-finding, arbitration, and good offices in attempting to settle disputes. In other words, this represents conflict management *through* rather than *by* regional organizations (Merrills 1991). Furthermore, regional agencies have addressed many conflicts since 1945 and, in several important cases, successfully.

The Limitations of Regional Organizations

Like the United Nations, however, regional organizations have several limitations. They are restricted to intraregional disputes and have little to offer the multitude of interregional conflicts (Merrills 1991). For example, the OAS was of little use during the Falklands War (1982) between Argentina and Great Britain. Principles of state sovereignty and noninterference in another state's affairs, basic tenets governing organization behavior, do not aid intraregional conflict management. Furthermore, like the UN, regional agencies are limited by problems of enforcement, political constraints, lack of resources, dependence on the political will of member states for action, and an inherent inability to involve themselves in internal disputes. Again, this usually means that states will attempt to resolve their conflicts bilaterally before submitting to a regional agency.

Patterns of Conflict Management, 1945–2003

In our study of international conflicts from 1945 to 2003, we paid close attention to the way each conflict was managed. When adversaries spurned outside help or refused to discuss their differences, we coded these disputes as having no conflict management. Frequently, one side was much stronger than the other and simply overwhelmed the weaker party; the stronger side saw no need to negotiate an agreement. The U.S. invasion of Grenada in 1983 is a case in point.

If, on the other hand, the parties bargained with each other or accepted outside assistance, we coded these conflicts as having undertaken negotiation, mediation, arbitration, referral to an international organization, or in a few cases, multilateral conference. Multilateral conferences occurred in complex conflicts involving several important disputants, such as the Trieste conflict (1952–1954), in which

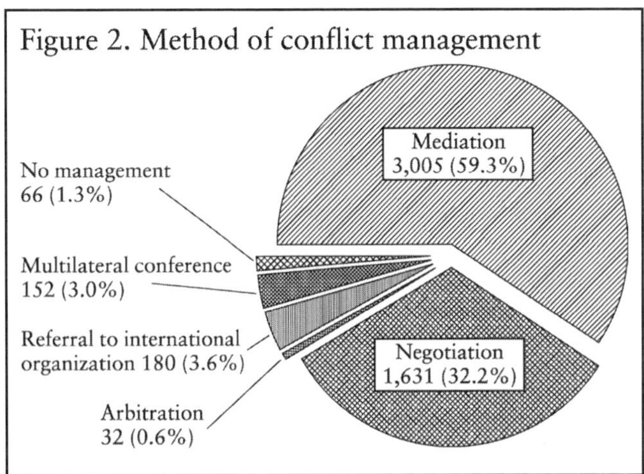

Figure 2. Method of conflict management

Italy, Yugoslavia, and several Allied nations met in London in an effort to find a permanent solution.

Each case of conflict management was coded separately by determining the beginning and end dates of an effort and identifying the individuals involved. This way, for example, we could say that Lord Owen and Cyrus Vance undertook more than twenty mediations during the Balkans conflict (1989–1995) and that China and Vietnam negotiated twelve times over the Spratly Islands (1988). Of the 343 registered conflicts, a number were not managed at all (*see* Figure 2). In all, however, more than three-quarters of the disputants engaged in some form of peaceful conflict management. Most of the unmanaged conflicts occurred during the cold war period (1956–1985), when many organizations, especially the United Nations, were prevented from intervening in certain conflicts because of competing superpower interests.

The data in Table 7 highlight the states' preference for diplomatic methods of conflict management (mediation and negotiation), which maximize state control. States rarely allow international organizations or tribunals to settle a conflict, an unwillingness that reflects the perceived limitations of these methods.

When we look at the effectiveness of each type of conflict management in Table 7, we once again see the states' reluctance to use international organizations, as the organizations appear to be far less effective at settling conflicts. By way of contrast, mediation and negotiation seem to offer a relatively high chance of success, while allowing states to maintain control over the process. The lack of success enjoyed by referral to an international organization is explained by the small number of cases involved and the fact that few conflicts that reach the stage of armed confrontation are influenced simply by the possibility of international embarrassment. An unlikely "winner" here is arbitration, where it has traditionally been assumed that disputants are less amenable to a purely legal settlement. Arbitration, however, remains best suited to conflicts over points of law that have not been complicated by violence or other political considerations, and arbitration here is less likely to occur in serious conflict situations.

States, then, prefer diplomatic methods of managing their conflicts, and, indeed, negotiation is a highly successful form of conflict management. Nearly half of all negotiations end in a settlement or cease-fire. This compares well with the other diplomatic method, mediation, where the rate of success is only around 26 percent. Nondiplomatic methods are relatively successful but used far less frequently.

When armed conflicts break out, however, the first response is often to expel the opposing country's diplomats and break off all contacts. Once states take this step, negotiation becomes difficult, if not impossible. Mediation, then, becomes the preferred method of conflict management, as its flexibility allows the disputants to bargain without relinquishing control over the peace process and, if necessary, without having to face each other at a table. More than a third of all mediations are successful in achieving either a cease-fire, or a partial or full settlement (*see* Table 7).

Most often, states themselves act as mediators, as they may have interests in the conflict, or they may be closely aligned with one or both sides. This alignment gives them both an obligation and an opportunity for fruitful intervention, especially for large states, which often have wide-ranging interests and a stake in the outcome of many conflicts. The United States, for example, has been actively mediating in the Middle East since the 1960s, not only because it has strategic interests in the region but also because it is closely aligned with Israel and is therefore in a stronger position to exert some leverage when pressing for concessions.

Table 7. Method of conflict management and outcome

	Method of conflict management						
Conflict management outcome	Mediation	Negotiation	Arbitration	Referral to international organization	Multilateral conference	No management	Total
Success	26.3%	16.4%	0.3%	0.7%	1.6%	0.0%	45.3%
Failure	33.0%	15.8%	0.3%	2.9%	1.4%	1.3%	54.7%
TOTAL	59.3%	32.2%	0.6%	3.6%	3.0%	1.3%	100.0%

Figure 3. Conflict management by organizations

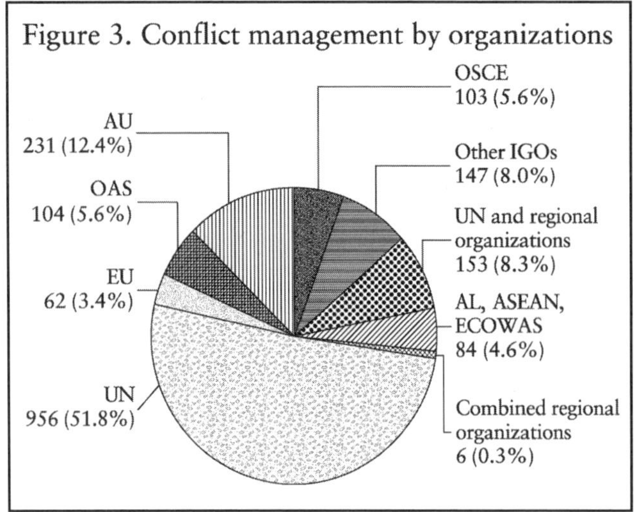

Comparatively speaking, international organizations do little mediating (*see* Figure 3). The reason is partly that adversaries are encouraged to take their disputes to regional organizations first and, only if this fails, to proceed to the United Nations. Regional organizations, furthermore, are especially equipped to deal with conflicts in their locale. The OAS has actively attempted to mediate in nearly every conflict involving its members, and the AU has conflict management as one of its primary functions. The Economic Community of West African States (ECOWAS), a West African regional organization, has been the principal mediator in the Liberian civil war since it broke out in December 1989; it has even sent peacekeeping forces.

Most mediation efforts have focused on African and Middle Eastern conflicts because these regions have experienced the most postwar conflict overall. Europe has experienced relatively few conflicts compared with the Middle East, although it has received nearly as many mediation efforts. This disparity is mostly explained by the war in the Balkans (1989–1995), which roused fears of a wider European war and therefore garnered a great deal of diplomatic attention. More than 150 mediation attempts were made in the Balkans war before a settlement was reached in Dayton, Ohio, in November 1995.

Regional organizations appear to make the best, if not the most active, mediators (*see* Table 8). Their success and failure rates are almost equal. States and international organizations are not always as successful as the regional bodies. Mixed groups of mediators, such as the Vance-Owen team in the Yugoslav war, also had respectable success rates. In cases mediated by mixed groups, separate members of the team can resort to different types of resources and use their different relationships with the parties to push for a settlement.

Although states have been the primary actors in managing international conflict, the United Nations has also played an important role. Its involvement in international conflict management has several interesting features. First, on the whole, the UN has been more involved in interstate conflicts than in civil conflicts. The reason is not just because the number of interstate conflicts is higher than the number of civil conflicts, but because the UN is designed primarily to deal with states and their affairs. Civil conflicts usually involve groups that do not belong to the UN, such as the Kurds in Iraq and Turkey, who cannot make use of the UN's conflict-management resources. The UN is also prevented in principle from interfering in the domestic affairs of member states.

UN involvement is fairly low, however, as a proportion of interventions in all interstate disputes (*see* Table 1), which reflects states' preference for managing their own conflicts. Also interesting here is that quite a high proportion of the civil disputes do end up at the UN's doorstep. The reason is that civil disputes are often the most intractable, and, as a result, states eventually give up and

Table 8. Organizations and conflict management outcome

	Conflict management outcome		
Organizations	Success	Failure	Total
UN	398 (21.6%)	558 (30.2%)	956 (51.8%)
AL	25 (1.4%)	30 (1.6%)	55 (3.0%)
EU	31 (1.7%)	31 (1.7%)	62 (3.4%)
OAS	58 (3.1%)	46 (2.5%)	104 (5.6%)
AU	99 (5.3%)	132 (7.1%)	231 (12.4%)
OSCE	34 (1.9%)	69 (3.7%)	103 (5.6%)
ASEAN	2 (0.1%)	2 (0.1%)	4 (0.2%)
Other IGOs	63 (3.4%)	84 (4.6%)	147 (8.0%)
ECOWAS	13 (0.7%)	12 (0.7%)	25 (1.4%)
UN and regional organizations (cooperative management)	71 (3.9%)	82 (4.4%)	153 (8.3%)
Combined regional organizations (cooperative management)	4 (0.2%)	2 (0.1%)	6 (0.3%)
TOTAL	798 (43.3%)	1,048 (56.7%)	1,846 (100.0%)

ask the UN to intervene, even though the world organization is the least well equipped to do so. Since 1974 the UN has become involved in civil conflicts in Afghanistan, Angola, Cambodia, Somalia, Tajikistan, Western Sahara, the former Yugoslavia, and, belatedly, Rwanda and Burundi. Each of these cases has defied attempts by interested states to manage the conflict peacefully.

As we have seen, UN mediations are less likely to succeed than mediation by states or regional organizations. Although this discrepancy is partly explained by the UN's increasing involvement in protracted civil conflicts that are almost impossible to manage effectively—for example, the Western Saharan conflict (1974–)—it is also a function of states' distrust of international organizations and their preference for managing conflicts bilaterally or with mediators of their own choosing.

Looking closer at UN involvement, we are able to observe a historical decline in UN involvement from 1956 onward (*see* Table 9). The decline is clearly the result of cold war inertia, when the UN became captive to the rivalry between the superpowers and their veto power in the Security Council. During these years, the UN was often confined to sending out fact-finding teams to the world's trouble spots and then withdrawing to let the major powers take over. After 1990 UN involvement in world conflicts rose slightly, as the liberation of Kuwait by U.S.-led coalition forces during the Gulf War (1990–1991) raised hopes for an expanded and empowered UN role in managing world conflicts. The rise of ethnic civil conflicts in the wake of the Soviet Union's collapse, however, simply highlighted the UN's inability to deal effectively with civil conflicts, despite the new international environment.

Although international conflict is widespread and destructive, the situation is not totally hopeless. States in conflict have a wide range of mechanisms and opportunities for solving their differences without resorting to bloodshed. The three approaches discussed in this chapter can be distinguished by the degree to which states or nonstate international actors maintain control over the conflict-management process. Diplomatic approaches—negotiation, mediation, conciliation, and inquiry—give states the greatest control, and this accounts for their popularity. Negotiation and mediation are noted especially for their flexibility and creativity and therefore their level of success.

Table 9. United Nations involvement by decade

	UN Involvement		
Decade	UN involved	UN not involved	Total
1945–1955	20 (5.8%)	27 (7.9%)	47 (13.7%)
1956–1965	33 (9.6%)	44 (12.8%)	77 (22.4%)
1966–1975	23 (6.7%)	31 (9.0%)	54 (15.7%)
1976–1985	21 (6.1%)	51 (14.9%)	72 (21.0%)
1986–1995	17 (5.0%)	47 (13.7%)	64 (18.7%)
1996–2003	7 (2.0%)	22 (6.4%)	29 (8.4%)
TOTAL	121 (35.3%)	222 (64.7%)	343 (100.0%)

In contrast, legal approaches—arbitration and adjudication—provide states with the least degree of control and have limited applicability to complex, drawn-out political conflicts. Similarly, international organizations—universal and regional—lack the control, flexibility, and inventiveness of negotiation and mediation. For this reason, most states prefer to manage their conflicts bilaterally and usually refer to bodies like the United Nations only when their own efforts have failed or when they can see a definite advantage in submitting to the machinery of the organization.

As our survey has shown, international conflict-management methods can be effective and are used in most conflicts, often successfully. In most cases, the only element that prevented a peaceful conclusion to the conflict was the lack of political will. What is clear is that without negotiation, mediation, and efforts by organizations like the OAS and the United Nations, many more international conflicts would spiral out of control and end in unprecedented levels of destruction.

References

Andemicael, B. 1976. *The OAU and the UN: Relations Between The Organization of African Unity and the United Nations.* UNITAR Regional Study No. 2, United Nations Institute for Training and Research. New York: Africana Publishing Company.

Baehr, P.R., and L. Gordenker. 1984. *The United Nations: Reality and Ideal.* New York: Praeger.

Bailey, S.D. 1982. *How Wars End—United Nations and the Termination of Armed Conflict, 1946–1964.* Vol. 1. Oxford: Clarendon Press Ltd.

Bennett, P.G. 1988. *International Organizations—Principles and Issues.* 4th edition. Englewood Cliffs, N.J.: Prentice Hall.

Bercovitch, J. 1984. "Problems and Approaches in the Study of Bargaining and Negotiation." *Political Science* 36, No. 2: 125–144.

———. 1996. "The United Nations and the Mediation of International Disputes." In *The United Nations at Fifty—Retrospect and Prospect.* Thakur, R., editor. Dunedin, New Zealand: Otago Foreign Policy School Symposium, Otago University Press, 73–87.

———.1997. "Preventing Deadly Conflicts: The Contribution of International Mediation." In *Preventing Violent Conflicts: Past Record and Future Challenges,* Report No. 48. Wallensteen, P., editor. Uppsala, Sweden: Department of Peace and Conflict Research, Uppsala University, 231–248.

Bercovitch, J., and J.W. Lamare. 1993. "The Process of International Mediation: An Analysis of the Determinants of Successful and Unsuccessful Outcomes." *Australian Journal of Political Science* 28 (December): 290–305.

Berdal, M.R. 1993. "Whither UN Peacekeeping?—An Analysis of the Changing Military Requirements of UN Peacekeeping with Proposals for its Enhancement." *Adelphi Paper 281*. London: The International Institute for Strategic Studies (October): 1–88.

Boutros-Ghali, B. 1993. *An Agenda For Peace*. New York: United Nations Department of Public Information.

Bull, H. 1977. *The Anarchical Society: A Study of Order in World Politics*. London: MacMillan Press.

Carnevale, P. J.D., and R. Pegnetter. 1985. "The Selection of Mediation Tactics in Public Sector Disputes: A Contingency Analysis." *Journal of Social Issues* 41, No. 2: 65–81.

Claude, I.L. Jr. 1964. *Swords into Plowshares—The Problems and Progress of International Organization*. 3d edition. Reprinted in 1966. New York: Random House.

Critchley, T. 1994. "Mediation—The United Nations Role in Indonesia, 1947–1950." Chapter 10 of *Building International Community—Cooperating for Peace Case Studies*. Clements, K., and R. Ward, editors. St. Leonards, NSW, Australia: Allen & Unwin Australia Pty. Ltd., in association with the Peace Research Centre, Research School of Pacific and Asian Studies, Australian National University, Canberra, ACT, Australia, 243–249.

Delbruck, J. 1987. "Peace Through Emerging Law." In *The Quest for Peace: Transcending Collective Violence and War Among Societies, Cultures and States*. Väyrynen, R., editor. London: Sage Publications.

Deutsch, K.W. 1978. *The Analysis of International Relations*. 2d edition. Englewood Cliffs, N.J.: Prentice Hall.

Diehl, P.F. 1994. "Operations Other than War (OOTW): Mission Types and Dimensions—Taxonomy of Mission Types,"http://www.ccsr.uiuc.edu/People/gmk/Projects/UNCMCW/Documents/OOTW.html (August 18).

Diehl, P.F., D. Druckman, and J. Wall. 1998. "International Peacekeeping and Conflict Resolution: A Taxonomic Analysis with Implications." *The Journal of Conflict Resolution* 42 (February): 33–55.

Ellingwood, S. 1997. "At the Crossroads: Nagorno-Karabakh." Chapter 8 of *Breaking the Cycle: A Framework for Conflict Intervention*. Von Lipsey, R., editor. New York: St. Martin's Press, 215–228.

Falk, R.A., S.S. Kim, and S.H. Mendlovitz, editors. 1991. *The United Nations and a Just World Order*. Studies on a Just World Order, No. 3. Boulder: Westview.

Fawcett, J.E. 1971. *The Law of Nations*. Harmondsworth, Middlesex: Penguin.

Fetherston, A.B. 1993. "Making United Nations Peacekeeping More Peaceful: Relating Concepts of 'Success' to Field Reality." *Working Paper 139*. Canberra, Australia: The Australian National University Research School of Pacific Studies, Peace Research Centre, 1–26.

Frankel, J. 1969. *International Politics: Conflict and Harmony*. London: Allen Lane, Penguin Press.

Galtung, J. 1976. *Peace, War and Defense—Essays in Peace Research*. Vol. II. Copenhagen: Christian Ejlers Forlag.

Gioia, A. 1997. "The United Nations and Regional Organisations in the Maintenance of Peace and Security." Chapter 7 of *The OSCE in the Maintenance of Peace and Security—Conflict Prevention, Crisis Management and Peaceful Settlement of Disputes*. Bothe, M., N. Ronzitti, and A. Rosas, editors. The Hague, Netherlands: Kluwer Law International, 191–236.

Haas, E.B. 1986. "Why We Still Need the United Nations—The Collective Management of International Conflict, 1945–1984." *Policy Papers in International Affairs, No. 26*. Berkeley: University of California, Institute of International Studies, 1–104.

Hassouna, H. A. 1975. *The League of Arab States and Regional Disputes—A Study of Middle East Conflicts*. Dobbs Ferry, N.Y.: Oceana Publications.

Jackson, R.D.W. 1998. *Negotiation Versus Mediation in International Conflict: Deciding How to Manage Violent Conflicts*. Doctoral dissertation, University of Canterbury, Christchurch, New Zealand.

Knight, W.A., and M. Yamashita. 1993. "The United Nations' Contribution to International Peace and Security." Chapter 12 of *Building a New Global Order: Emerging Trends in International Security*. Dewitt, D.B., D.G. Haglund, and J.J. Kirton, editors. Toronto, New York: Oxford University Press, 284–312.

Kolb, D.M. 1983. *The Mediators*. Cambridge: MIT Press.

———. 1985. "To Be a Mediator: Expressive Tactics in Mediation." *Journal of Social Issues* 41, No. 2: 11–26.

Lall, B.G. 1982. "Disarmament and International Security." In *Alternative Methods for International Security*. Stephenson, C.M., editor. Lanham, Md.: University Press of America, 95–101.

Lennane, R., and R. Newton. 1994. "Traditional Peacekeeping: United Nations Truce Supervision Organisation and the Multinational Force and Observers." Chapter 15 of *Building International Community—Cooperating for Peace Case Studies*. Clements, K., and R. Ward, editors. St. Leonards, NSW, Australia: Allen & Unwin, in association with the Peace Research Centre, Research School of Pacific and Asian Studies, Australian National University, Canberra, ACT, Australia; 280–287.

Mackinlay, J., and J. Chopra. 1992. "Second Generation Multinational Operations." *The Washington Quarterly*. 15 (summer): 113–134.

Merrills, J.G. 1991. *International Dispute Settlement*. 2d edition. Cambridge, England: Grotius Publications Ltd.

McCoubrey, H., and N.D. White. 1995. *International Organisations and Civil Wars*. Hants, England: Dartmouth Publishing Company Ltd.

Miall, H., O. Ramsbotham, and T. Woodhouse. 1999. *Contemporary Conflict Resolution—The Prevention, Management and Transformation of Deadly Conflicts*. Malden, Mass.: Polity Press, published by Blackwell Publishers.

Northedge, F., and M. Donelan. 1971. *International Disputes: The Political Aspects*. London: Europa Publications.

Nye, J.S. Jr. 1971. *Peace in Parts: Integration and Conflict in Regional Organization*. Perspectives on International Relations Series. Written under the auspices of the Center for International Affairs at Harvard University. Boston: Little, Brown and Company.

Oluo, S. L. O. 1982. *Conflict Management of the OAU in Intra-African Conflicts, 1963–1980.* Ann Arbor, Mich.: University Microfilms International.

Organization for Security and Co-Operation in Europe (OSCE). 1998. www.osce.org.

Plano, J.C., and R.E. Riggs. 1967. *Forging World Order—The Politics of International Organization.* New York: Macmillan.

Ramsbotham, O., and T. Woodhouse. 1999. *Encyclopedia of International Peacekeeping Operations.* Santa Barbara, Calif.: ABC-CLIO.

Riggs, R.E., and J.C. Plano. 1989. *The United Nations—International Organization and World Politics.* Chicago: Dorsey Press.

Ronzitti, N. 1997. "OSCE Peacekeeping." Chapter 8 of *The OSCE in the Maintenance of Peace and Security—Conflict Prevention, Crisis Management and Peaceful Settlement of Disputes.* Bothe, M., N. Ronzitti, and A. Rosas, editors. The Hague, Netherlands: Kluwer Law International, 237–255.

Sawyer, J., and H. Guetzkow. 1965. "Bargaining and Negotiation in International Relations." Chapter 13 of *International Behavior: A Social-Psychological Analysis.* Kelman, H., editor. New York: Holt, Rinehart and Winston, 466–520.

Schuman, F.L. 1969. *International Politics: Anarchy and Order in the World Society.* 7th edition. New York: McGraw-Hill.

Sherman, F.L. 1987. *Partway to Peace: The United Nations and the Road to Nowhere?* Doctoral dissertation. University Park: Pennsylvania State University. Sherman has created an extensive data set dividing the cases of conflict into phases of severity for analysis. The SHERFAC's data set is a comprehensive coverage of disputes and is based on the contingency theory of conflict research.

———. 1994. "SHERFACS: A Cross-Paradigm, Hierarchical and Contextually Sensitive Conflict Management Data Set." *International Interactions. Special Issue: New Directions in Event Data Analysis* 20. Duffy, G., editor. Nos. 1–2: 79–100.

Skjelsbæk, K. 1991. "The UN Secretary-General and the Mediation of International Disputes." *Journal of Peace Research* 28, No. 1: 99–115.

Skjelsbæk, K., and G. Fermann. 1996. "The UN Secretary-General and the Mediation of International Disputes." Chapter 4 of *Resolving International Conflicts—The Theory and Practice of Mediation.* Bercovitch, J., editor. Boulder: Lynne Rienner, 75–104.

Suter, K.D. 1986. *Alternatives to War: Conflict Resolution and the Peaceful Settlement of International Disputes,* 2d edition. Sydney: Women's International League for Peace and Freedom.

Tunnicliff, K.H. 1984. *The United Nations and the Mediation of International Conflict.* Doctoral dissertation. Ames: University of Iowa. Reprinted 1987 by University Microfilms International, Ann Arbor, Michigan.

United Nations. 2000. *Comprehensive Review of the Whole Question of Peacekeeping Operations in All Their Aspects.* United Nations General Assembly, Fifty-Fifth Session, Item 87 of the Provisional Agenda, A/55/305—S/2000/809, August 21.

———. 2004. United Nations Homepage, www.un.org.

Urquhart, B. 1989. "Problems and Prospect of the United Nations." *International Journal* 44, No. 4 (autumn): 803–822.

Väyrynen, R. 1985a. "Focus On: Is There a Role for the United Nations in Conflict Resolution?" *Journal of Peace Research* 22, No. 3: 189–196.

———. 1985b. "The United Nations and the Resolution of International Conflicts." *Cooperation and Conflict* 20: 141–171.

———. 1987. "Third Parties in the Resolution of Regional Conflicts." *Bulletin of Peace Proposals* 18, No. 3: 293–308.

———. 1991. "The United Nations and the Resolution of International Conflicts. In *The United Nations and a Just World Order:* Studies on a Just World Order, No. 3. Falk, R.A., S.S. Kim, and S.H. Mendlovitz, editors. Boulder: Westview, 222–239.

Wall, J.A. 1981. "Mediation: An Analysis, Review and Proposed Research." *Journal of Conflict Resolution* 25: 157–180.

Wiseman, H. 1990. "Peacekeeping in the International Political Context: Historical Analysis and Future Directions." In *The United Nations and Peacekeeping—Results, Limitations and Prospects: The Lessons of 40 Years of Experience.* Rikhye, I.J., and K. Skjelsbæk, editors. London: MacMillan, 32–51.

Yarrow, C.H.M. 1978. *Quaker Experiences in International Conciliation.* New Haven: Yale University Press.

Zacher, M.W. 1979. *International Conflicts and Collective Security, 1946–1977: The United Nations, Organization of American States, Organization of African Unity, and Arab League.* New York: Praeger.

International Organizations and Regional Conflicts

The most important international governmental organization (IGO) today is the United Nations, which was established in 1945 as a successor to the League of Nations. Both the League of Nations and the UN were born out of the chaos of a world war, and both reflected the hope that functionalism and collective security could guarantee peace and order in the international system. To accomplish this goal, both organizations had built-in mechanisms for conflict settlement. Currently, states in conflict can settle their differences through the UN by submitting the dispute to the UN Security Council, which then recommends a course of action. But, unlike other conflict managers, the Security Council does not need the disputing parties' consent to intervene: under the UN Charter, the council has the right to consider any conflict that might pose a threat to international peace and stability.

The Security Council can also appoint mediators or mediating committees; it can instruct the secretary-general to use his "good offices"; it can refer the dispute to regional organizations or other specialist agencies; or it can itself promote quiet negotiation between the disputants (Merrills 1991). In addition, the Security Council can, theoretically at least, enforce its decisions "by any means." Usually, the means include sanctions and/or military intervention. The UN can also initiate peacekeeping operations to keep disputant forces apart while a negotiated settlement is sought.

In a typical case, such as the first Kashmir war between India and Pakistan in 1947, the UN would appeal for a cease-fire when the fighting flared. It would then send a mediator or mediation committee to gather information and bring the parties together. In 1948 the world body sent the UN Kashmir Commission to India and Pakistan on such a mission. Following this, and with the parties' permission, the UN might send peacekeeping troops to separate the warring factions and monitor a cease-fire.

Since the UN's inception, states in conflict have used the world organization to manage their disputes. The UN has been involved to some extent in almost every armed conflict since 1945, whether it be direct consideration in the Security Council, the sending of a fact-finding mission to the area of conflict, or mediation by UN personnel. Even the short-lived League of Nations, which was founded after World War I and collapsed at the onset of World War II, considered sixty-six political disputes. Again, however, in comparison with negotiation and mediation, disputants have generally avoided conflict management by IGOs—realizing, perhaps, the limitations of IGOs in addressing international conflicts.

Conflict Management: Responsibilities, Roles, and Constraints

In terms of its role in international conflict management, the United Nations is truly unique: it is the only organization to be charged with a primary objective to uphold *international* peace and security. Replacing its ineffective predecessor, the League of Nations, the UN was born into an environment reeling from the devastation of World War II (Baehr and Gordenker 1999; Plano and Riggs 1967). Fifty states formally agreed to uphold principles of international peace and security, ratifying the UN Charter on June 25, 1945. Provisions for "maintaining international peace and security" are stated in Chapter VI of the UN Charter, "Pacific Settlement of Conflicts," but three basic functions spelled out in the charter shape the organization's conflict-management role. The charter "sets out the structures of the UN and their interrelationships; it establishes a set of rules and principles which form the legal framework and justification of the UN's action in the international sphere; and it sets out norms for behavior between states" (Fetherston 1994). Indeed, obligations are set out in Chapter VI requiring disputing parties to show some responsibility for conflict settlement. If a conflict's continuation is likely to threaten international peace and security, disputants are obliged "to seek a solution by negotiation, inquiry, mediation, conciliation, arbitration, judicial settlement, resort to regional agencies or arrangements, or other peaceful means of their own choice" (Article 33/1).

In 2004 the UN membership numbered 191 states. Ironically, universal membership, one of the organization's crowning assets, also creates one of its main problems, weak membership cohesion. Many critics suggest that the success of UN conflict management relies, to a great degree, on the support and commitment of its members. In fact, it is aptly observed that the UN can be nothing more than the sum of its members (Roberts and Kingsbury 1988). "Critics charge that states tend to abandon to the UN 'orphan conflicts' for which states lack either political will or resources [or both] to resolve. However, the UN's effectiveness depends on the political will and resources of its member states; alone it lacks leverage, and increasingly, also credibility" (Leatherman and Väyrynen 1995). Having no standing army of its own to engage in conflict management strategies, the UN must rely solely on the support of its members to give its resolutions credibility and its actions strength. The fact that UN membership and participation is voluntary is central to why those who wrote the charter were reluctant to include watertight provisions for the application and limitation of UN pacific settlement practices. They were "not ready to commit their governments to any radical departure from established practices. The sovereignty of states and the protection of the prerogatives of the major powers were the basic conditions around which all other features of the Charter had to fit" (Bennett 1988). Consequently, member states are committed only as much as they want to be.

The Security Council

The UN Charter established four organs, the Security Council, the secretary-general, the General Assembly, and the Court on Conciliation and Arbitration, to handle conflict management. The Security Council, the main decision-making body, has the "primary responsibility" for the maintenance of international peace and security (Article 24). "The Council is required, 'when it deems necessary,' to call upon the parties to a conflict likely to endanger the maintenance of international peace and security to settle it by peaceful means [Article 33/2]. The Council is also authorized by the Charter to recommend appropriate procedures for settling such conflicts [Article 36/2]" (Murphy 1983). It is the Security Council's responsibility to determine what constitutes a "threat to the peace, breach of the peace, or act of aggression" (Article 39) and decide what measures to take to maintain or restore international peace and security (Articles 41 and 42). Most commonly, the Security Council handles conflict referrals and authorizes the initiation of UN management strategies.

Early in its development "the permanent members of the Security Council had to sanction all action; their failure to agree meant inaction" (Haas 1986). Inaction caused by internal disagreement has been extremely costly to the UN in terms of leverage and reputation. As a result of dissension between the two voting bodies, the Security Council and General Assembly, and between the leading members of the Security Council, the UN is often seen as an ineffective conflict manager. Hesitancy in Bosnia, Haiti, Rwanda, and Somalia reflects neither legal constraints nor the organization's inability to determine or agree on issues of international law; rather, it reflects a lack of decisive will in the Security Council to follow through with the resources for such ventures (Evans 1994a). On rare occasions when the use of vetoes has hamstrung Security Council action, the General Assembly has voted to initiate conflict management (*see* conflict 5.9, October–December 1956). Conflicts are rarely brought to the General Assembly, and only three are documented in this study (*see* conflict 1.3, January 1952–March 1956; conflict 2.30, September–December 1978; and conflict 5.9). The Court on Conciliation and Arbitration can make recommendations on UN action, but this body has not been used extensively. Conflicts requiring legal determination, conflicts involving territorial issues, for example, are generally referred to the International Court of Justice (ICJ) for a legal solution (Article 36/2).

The Secretary-General

When the Security Council is unable to come to a decision, the secretary-general can intervene on his own initiative.[1] The secretary-general, who is on the whole constrained by the will of the Security Council, needs the council's visible support to attempt any mediation with the hope of achieving a successful resolution (Skjelsbæk and Fermann 1996; Tunnicliff 1984). Unfortunately, any lack of consensus, indecision in the Security Council, or semblance of disunity severely undermines the perceived legitimacy of the secretary-general's position (Tunnicliff 1984). As the figurehead representative of an organization, the secretary-general is supposed to epitomize the unified voice of the organization. The secretary-general's position carries with it the aura of legitimacy, the support and authority of the UN organization, and usually some recognition of the personal attributes and diplomatic expertise of the person elected to the job.[2] Kolb points out that some mediators' authority is derived referentially, but others derive theirs from expertise and their reputation as mediators (Kolb 1985). The secretary-general derives authority from his position as spokesman of a global body. Membership support and confidence in the incumbent secretary-general is "a

1. Masculine pronouns are used because, to date, the seven appointees to the position of UN secretary-general have been men.
2. It is widely recognized that "personality" is also an important factor in the UN secretary-general's ability to provide effective leadership. "A dynamic Secretary-General (e.g. Hammarskjöld, Pérez de Cuéllar) enhances the performance of the organization, whereas an ineffectual Secretary-General (e.g. Waldheim) diminishes it" (Falk et al. 1991).

precondition for satisfactory performance" (Skjelsbæk and Fermann 1996). In turn, the secretary-general can act effectively only if the UN has the semblance of a cohesive entity or, at least, of an organization in one voice on its conflict management objectives (Touval 1994).

The secretary-general's organizational position is a political role involving administrative responsibility as well as diplomacy. According to Tunnicliff (1984), Skjelsbæk (1991), and Skjelsbæk and Fermann (1996), the role of the secretary-general is increasingly hindered by the duality of the position. It requires more time and skill to balance the pressures of administration, financial constraints, and organizational bureaucracy and allows less time for conducting mediation and performing the tasks involved with good offices, a function that requires visible commitment. On the whole, the secretary-general's role has certain operating considerations:

Resource constraints: With few physical resources at his disposal, the secretary-general's ability to offer carrots or wield sticks is limited.

Modus operandi: The secretary-general has the choice to rigidly expound UN Charter principles or deliberately refrain from giving open political criticism and maintain a semblance of impartiality. These stances have the potential to jeopardize or enhance the secretary-general's skills as a mediator but, more often, the general political environment governs the choice of stance.

Constituency support: Confidence in the neutrality of the secretary-general can affect how much support UN members are willing to give. A lack of confidence, particularly by the five permanent members of the Security Council, can render the secretary-general's actions ineffective. Membership approval for the secretary-general plays an important part in determining how much support he garners. The secretary-general is wise to maintain a broad constituency of support rather than focus on the concerns of one ideological group or geographic region at the expense of others.

Organizational position: As a principal organ of the UN, the secretary-general can take independent initiatives, but he is also responsible to the General Assembly, the Security Council, and three other UN councils (UN Charter, Article 98). A flexible relationship exists between the secretary-general and the other organs. The relationship can be one in which the secretary-general takes a leadership role or, alternately, is dependent on another organ. Most commonly, the secretary-general interacts with the Security Council, maintaining an open line of communication about his activities using his good offices.

Personal skills: Some character traits are particularly desirable in a secretary-general. He must possess the following: the ability to alter his style to suit circumstances; competency in organizational, financial, and diplomatic matters; the ability to maintain neutrality or uphold organizational principles under pressure; an even temperament; a nonjudgmental attitude; a strong notion of duty; expertise in "quiet diplomacy"; and good communication skills. A strongly independent secretary-general, however, risks admonishment from the powerful Security Council members (Skjelsbæk and Fermann 1996).

Although it is "very difficult, if not impossible, to measure the influence of the secretary-general in specific situations," this analysis attempts to assess the validity of this criticism by specifically examining the secretary-general's mediation role in comparison with other organization mediators (Skjelsbæk and Fermann 1996).

Constraints on the United Nations

The success or failure of international mediation relies heavily on the *leverage* of the third party, whether it is the UN or another IGO. When the UN is able to authorize collective action with consensus, the organization's position of leverage is strong. Unfortunately, collective action is sometimes questioned by member states, and any apparent incohesiveness in the organization devalues its leverage. Support of its membership is essential for the running and perceived stature of the world organization. "Some of the UN leverage derives from its institutional standing and the kind of norms it exemplifies, but beyond that UN mediation is hampered considerably by *lack of resources*" (Bercovitch 1996). In recent times members have demonstrated a growing reluctance to commit themselves to deteriorating conflicts. This diminished level of commitment among member states is reflected in the extent of overdue annual financial contributions. The United States, for example, is the UN's biggest financial contributor as well as its principal debtor, owing approximately two-thirds of the total $305 million due from seventy-two member states in 2003 (Rosbalt News Agency 2003). A general lack of commitment is also reflected in members' reluctance to provide military personnel and equipment, one of the most visible ways the organization can add substance to otherwise symbolic Security Council mandates.

Cold war complications have also emphasized the importance of membership cohesiveness. The view that UN strength is derived from its membership is more evident when members take ideological positions and show minimal solidarity in the authorization of conflict-management. The ideological agendas of major powers, primarily the Soviet Union and the United States frequently prevented decisive and cooperative action in the Security Council. As a result, much-needed conflict management was employed only "in a later phase of the conflict when it had already broken into open hostilities and threatened regional and/or global stability. However, when great powers co-operated, the results tended to be visible as the Near Eastern crisis of 1973 shows" (Leatherman and Väyrynen 1995). Even when cold war ideological alignments have almost disappeared, consensus is still difficult to reach with new North-South alignments emerging to fill the vacuum (Kim and Russett 1996). Clearly, cooperation between member states is not essential to operations, but it has distinct advantages, allowing the UN to act decisively and project an aura of legitimate authority.

The perception of legitimacy is crucial to UN leverage. UN mediators derive much of their power from the organization's status and the support of its "universal" membership. Some UN mediation success can be attributed, in part, to its position as an international organization and its international backing. What is clear is that UN objectives must be laid out plainly and coherently to intervene with the most appropriate strategy, one that is amenable to success. Vague secretariat objectives often result in unclear organizational policies and insufficiently defined mandates (Diehl 1997). Ambiguous Security Council mandates or rapidly changing mission objectives, such as those of the United Nations Operation in Somalia (UNOSOM), are extremely problematic for delivering effective field operations (Weinberger 1995). Even when the UN intervenes successfully in intrastate conflicts, little credit is given to the completion of its mandates. "Amidst all the distortion and misunderstanding surrounding the UN mission in Bosnia, it is often forgotten that its mandate was simply to sustain the people of that country in the midst of civil war, and to try and bring about the conditions necessary for a peaceful resolution of that war . . . that mandate, by the end of 1994 had, by and large, been fulfilled" (Rose 1996).

The UN Protection Force to Yugoslavia (UNPROFOR) was one of fifty-seven peacekeeping operations active from 1948 to 2004. The reality of UN mediation indicates that it is often a complementary method, used in conjunction with peacekeeping as a last-ditch method of conflict management. Achieving a settlement after such a long period of hostilities seems virtually impossible from any international organization and it appears that, as yet, UN mediation attempts have not struck that optimum moment of resolution. This conclusion highlights the need to study UN mediation attempts more closely to predict when the organization's attempts have a greater chance of success and when they are more likely to fail. If the current emphasis on preventive methods and early intervention are to become effective, offering mediation in earlier conflict phases becomes crucial.

The UN operates under a number of constraints in its exercise of leverage. Indeed, while performing its role as a third-party mediator, the UN faces more roadblocks than regional organizations, nongovernmental organizations (NGOs), or private individuals. These constraints come mainly from the UN's position as a "global" organization because, regardless of its official status, it remains the product of "an institutionalized response" (Falk et al. 1991). Systemic pressures, resource availability, and membership commitment are inextricably linked to the UN's role as an international mediator. As an international organization, it must operate within the bounds of the international convention regarding state sovereignty, a constraint that often allows conflicts to become entrenched before international assistance is sought or internationally condoned.

UN conflict management can be impeded by seven operational constraints:

1. Voluntary participation: Member states participate only as much as they wish, choosing or refusing to participate. The fact that the UN cannot force members to participate presents a major stumbling block in UN conflict management.

2. Level of membership commitment: Membership commitment affects the level of financial support and the availability of personnel and equipment. The perceived level of commitment enhances the perception of UN strength and leverage in mediation situations. The UN generally lacks resources of its own, and the support of its members lends credibility for its actions. UN indecision over intervention in Bosnia, Haiti, Rwanda, and Somalia was mainly due to a lack of political will in the Security Council rather than any systemic constraints (Evans 1994b).

3. Level of membership cooperation: Disagreement can promote inaction and hesitancy, with sluggish responses unlikely to result in a quick outcome. Disunity and a lack of consensus within the organization reflects unfavorably on a mediator who is assigned to represent the organization as a whole. A mediator's position can be undermined if organization support for the mediation effort is divided. UN cohesion enhances the leverage position of the UN mediator.

4. "Strategic voting" in UN organs: Issues put to the Security Council have caused ideological division in the General Assembly and the council itself, resulting in bloc voting. The use of the veto by the members of the Security Council can be seen as an indicator of the UN's resolve to deal with conflicts (Junn 1983). South Africa's exclusion in 1974 and the matter of Palestine Liberation Organization (PLO) observer status clearly show that the disagreement between the two voting bodies makes decisive collective action almost impossible (Väyrynen 1991). France and Britain used the veto to offset their interventions in the Suez crisis in 1956 and left the matter in the hands of the General Assembly. Both Security Council members eventually acquiesced on their decisions after the General Assembly called for an immediate cease-fire and foreign party withdrawal (Roberts and

Kingsbury 1988). This example is one of the few in which the decisions of the General Assembly brought about an alteration in the veto stance.

5. Systemic constraints: Principles of state sovereignty, conventions of international relations, state motivations, and bloc alignments all impede decisive UN action. Prioritizing national interests over UN directives presents a common predicament for the organization. "If the major powers employ international organizations chiefly as public relations vehicles and fail to supply them with the means to get the job done, then the credibility of those organizations, and that of collective norms and decisions, will suffer" (Luck 1992–1993).
6. Explicit operating principles set out in the UN Charter: The charter's binding prescriptions and procedures denote the UN's international position and primary responsibility. The charter sets out restrictions on the UN's use of force and expresses its obligation to use peaceful means of conflict settlement, where possible, before forceful measures are engaged.
7. Consensual decision-making procedures: The UN system is based on consensual decision making. Achieving the required vote approval and the general bureaucratic process itself can hinder a quick response in a crisis situation.

When entering into a conflict, the UN relies on its international status as a global organization, the legitimacy it acquires from this status, its credibility as an international actor, the cohesiveness of its membership, and its mediators' experience and persuasiveness. With little resources of its own, the organization is limited in its ability to offer inducements or threaten penalties. Invariably, the UN relies on its international status to give its resolutions the weight to be taken seriously. It is clear that the UN's international status can be the organization's strength or its handicap.

The Limitations of the United Nations

The facts of international politics limit what the United Nations can accomplish. First, states will not submit their disputes to the UN unless they see some advantage in doing so. Although the UN can consider a dispute without a state's permission, the world body has little hope of peacefully managing the conflict without it. In other words, the UN has scant power apart from that exercised by its members, meaning that, by itself, the UN can do little to enforce the process or outcome of peaceful conflict management (Claude 1964). For example, the UN worked frantically to bring about a cease-fire and to separate the warring parties in the Balkans conflict of 1989 to 1995, but it was for the most part simply ignored and could do nothing to force the factions to the negotiating table.

Second, the UN is limited by the composition of its membership. Nonstate actors, such as liberation movements and rebel groups, cannot be members and are therefore unable to avail themselves of the UN's machinery. On the other hand, the UN principle of noninterference in a country's internal affairs gives many states and nonstate actors a powerful tool—either to suppress internal unrest or to foment rebellion without fear of UN intervention. Internal conflicts, which are the most intractable kind to resolve, have overtaken interstate violence as the most common conflict in the international system since the end of the cold war. The UN's failure to prevent the carnage in Rwanda that began in 1990 is a dramatic example of the organization's powerlessness in the face of civil conflicts.

Third, political factors severely constrain the UN, so much so that "the field of dispute settlement with which the United Nations has been concerned has been defined by the major political forces of the post-1945 period. . . . The tension between the United States and the Soviet Union has excluded a major group of disputes from the organization, while permitting or requiring its involvement in others" (Merrills 1991). In other words, the UN could not tackle conflicts that involved superpower interests because either the United States or the Soviet Union would simply veto any action the UN might want to take. The UN's involvement in the Korean War occurred only because the Soviet Union was not at the meeting to cast its veto when the vote was taken.

Fourth, conflict management is not the UN's strong point. Touval (1994) argues that the world organization does not serve well as an authoritative channel of communication: it has little political leverage; its threats and promises lack credibility; and it is incapable of pursuing coherent, flexible, and dynamic negotiations guided by an effective strategy. For these and other reasons, states tend to turn to the UN as a last resort (Suter 1986; Touval 1994). This further damages the UN's reputation because conflicts that states have been unable to solve become associated instead with UN failure. For example, the UN was called in after regional actors failed to resolve the civil war in Somalia (1988–). By this time, the conflict was intractable, and the UN was forced to pull out in humiliating failure.

Differentiating Between the UN and Regional Organizations

The term *international organization* describes the United Nations, but it can also be loosely applied to treaty arrangements, such as the North Atlantic Treaty Organization (NATO) and the South East Asia Treaty Organization (SEATO), and groups formed to promote economic and political cooperation among member states, such as the Organization for Economic Cooperation and Development (OECD) and even the British Commonwealth. To distinguish between types of international and regional organizations, we consider four different characteristics: organization objectives, organizational function, scope, and membership.

The UN's universality as an international organization and the limited scope of the regional organizations is most commonly used to distinguish them. The obvious difference between regional organizations and the UN is the regional groups' "absence of intention to become universalistic in scope. Although the reasons for the limited membership of these associations may vary widely, in general, it is safe to assume that these reasons are historical in nature, the product of perceived political, cultural, economic, or military ties" (Miller 1970). The UN Charter recognizes the potential role of regional arrangements in the management of local conflicts and provides for the coexistence of regional organizations with the UN in the pursuit of peace and security but with certain limitations on the use of enforcement actions. Entitled *Regional Requirements,* Chapter VIII specifically refers to the arrangements and operations of regional organizations:

> Article 52 (1) Nothing in the present Charter precludes the existence of regional arrangements or agencies for dealing with such matters relating to the maintenance of international peace and security as are appropriate for regional action, provided that such arrangements or agencies and their activities are consistent with the purposes and principles of the United Nations.
>
> Article 52 (2) The Members of the United Nations entering into such arrangements or constituting such agencies shall make every effort to achieve pacific settlement of local disputes through such regional agencies before referring them to the Security Council.
>
> Article 52 (3) The Security Council shall encourage the development of pacific settlement of local disputes through such regional arrangements or by such regional agencies either on the initiative of the states concerned or by reference from the Security Council.
>
> Article 53 (1) The Security Council shall, where appropriate, utilize such regional arrangements or agencies for enforcement action under its authority. But no enforcement action shall be taken under regional arrangements or by regional agencies without the authorization of the Security Council, with the exception of measures against any enemy state. . . .
>
> Article 54 The Security Council shall at all times be kept fully informed of activities undertaken or in contemplation under regional arrangements or by agencies for the maintenance of international peace and security.

These articles bore specific reference to the utilization and development of conflict management activities by "regional arrangements," namely with the Arab League (AL) and the Organization of American States (OAS), the only active regional organizations at the time of the UN's conception (Padelford 1954).

As an IGO, the United Nations provides a cooperative forum in which governments can negotiate, lobbied by NGOs and other interest groups. It operates within a set mandate, has voluntary membership, and must conform to implicit norms operating in the international "system," most significantly, the recognition of state sovereignty. The UN is not a supranational organization with "the power to make decisions binding on the members whether they have participated in the decision or not" (Taylor and Groom 1978). The UN performs specific functions on behalf of its members, but it cannot impose binding decisions on them. It is acknowledged, however, that the UN is "supreme" when compared to regional organizations.

Although the differences between regional organizations and the UN may seem insignificant, they are not just a matter of definitive nuance. The differences between the organizations are reflected in the disputants' choice to engage one organization or another by making a conscious decision to regionalize or internationalize their conflict's management.

The Decision to Regionalize or Internationalize Conflict Management

Disputants and mediators both can potentially find advantages in the decision to bring a dispute to a regional organization or to the world body. Engaging a regional organization can ensure the localization of conflict management, keeping it a regional affair. Seeking UN involvement expands the conflict's management to an international level. Internationalization of a conflict can have five main effects:

> legitimizing the efforts of the regional organizations or other mediators (Burci 1997; Bercovitch and Rubin 1992);
>
> setting the conflict on the international political agenda, which can raise international interest and, perhaps, political embarrassment for the disputants involved;
>
> helping to balance the power parity between weak and strong disputants by empowerment of the weaker party and/or legitimization of a weaker party and its claims—for example, UN intervention in conflict 5.1, 1945 to 1949; and conflict 5.11, December 1963–November 1967;
>
> reducing fear of interference in the conflict by neighboring states;

presenting timely temporary intervention or prolonged extraneous intervention in the sovereign affairs of a disputant state (Nye 1971; Richmond 1998).

Regional organization involvement can have a legitimizing effect for external multilateral intervention or, additionally, can enhance the credibility, legitimacy, and authority of another third party. Enhancement of third-party intervention was apparent in conflict 1.18, the Hutu and Tutsi conflict between Rwanda and Burundi from January 1964 to January 1965. The African Union (AU) Council asked that President Mobutu Sésé Séko of the Congo (Kinshasa) mediate between members from Burundi and Rwanda. He conducted three meetings and successfully secured the free movement of refugees. In this conflict the AU was seen by the parties to be an impartial third party whose assistance was welcomed. There is little doubt that AU backing and support for Mobutu's mediation attempts helped to legitimize his involvement.

In some cases, localization of a conflict is preferred and the UN is merely informed of the regional organization's approach and progress. In the Dominican Republic's constitutionalist rebellion, the OAS played an important part in the conflict by "multilateralizing" the unilateral intervention by the United States, thereby legitimizing the intervention attempt. The OAS Meeting of Consultation of Foreign Ministers put to the vote the degree of OAS involvement and created the OAS Inter-American Peace Force.[3]

Inviting mediation to address inequity in the disputants' power is not always desirable to the stronger party. Intrastate conflicts often involve disparate groups with diverse demands. "It must be remembered that disputants are rarely a coherent group. . . . The difficulties in accepting a mediator for the stronger party in a conflict lie in their perception of the possibility of acceptance leading to direct or indirect recognition of their adversaries' claims, or of the rebel party" (Richmond 1998). In this way, mediator involvement tends to legitimate the status of minor disputants, a result sometimes not welcomed by stronger disputants. An example of internationalization providing disputant empowerment can be seen in Cyprus, where "the issue of internationalization has been vital for both sides as it is in the interests of both sides to bring in a third party that will strengthen their position" (Richmond 1998). (*See* conflict 5.11, December 1963–November 1967, and conflict 5.14, January 1974–June 1978.) The effects of internationalization are clear in the account of the confrontation over Quemoy (*see* conflict 3.13, April 1954 to April 1955). Although the UN took little action in this territorial conflict involving China, the United States, and Taiwan, the international attention paid to the matter via the UN forum helped to minimize the possibility of escalation.

The effectiveness of regional organizations in the settlement of localized conflicts has been argued on two fronts. Some assert that the geographical homogeneity of regional organizations, and therefore the proximity of its members to a specific conflict, acts as an impediment to its settlement. The goals of actors in regional organizations can come into question, as did the motivations of the member states of the Organization for Security and Cooperation in Europe's (OSCE) Minsk Group in their mediation role over the status of Nagorno-Karabakh territory (*see* conflict 5.20, August 1990–Ongoing). A series of mediation attempts illustrated Russia's vested interest in the resource-rich territory, and by 1994 the OSCE was seriously questioning Russia's impartiality. After Russian mediation continued without OSCE consultation, the OSCE Budapest Summit Meeting eliminated Russian unauthorized mediation in a declaration (Dehdashti 1997). "Regional organizations, to the extent that they are dominated by a single power, are functionally equivalent to spheres of influence. Most regional organizations that are moderately effective have a small group of states that are willing to contribute disproportionately to the 'collective' enterprise. In some instances they might be acting as an agent of the regional community, but in others such an agency is tied to self-interest" (Barnett 1998). Alternatively, it is argued that shared regional history and mutual associations can be regarded as a beneficial element of regional organization involvement rather than a hindrance in its role.

Regional organization conflict management can also be considered preferable to UN management. Regionalization or localization of conflict management can be considered advantageous in four ways (Ramsbotham and Woodhouse 1999):

1. Geopolitical knowledge: It is recognized that "regional states and arrangements can have superior knowledge of the dynamics of local conflicts and strong incentives to resolve them and, by definition, they have staying power" (Bennett 1998). This was the case in a recurring border conflict between Tanzania and Uganda from October 1978 to May 1979 (*see* conflict 1.46). The initial proposal of UN involvement in this conflict found disfavor with the African nations that wanted the African Union to handle it, which the AU did, along with officials from Kenya, Libya, Nigeria, and Zambia. The AU kept the UN informed of its progress. In Lebanon, during the second phase of its civil war from February 1975 to late 1992, the Arab League took on an active mediating role (*see* conflict 6.39). Although the UN was heavily committed—deploying the UN Interim Force in Lebanon (UNIFIL)—it was the Arab League that conducted extensive mediation to try to resolve the conflict.

---

3. Troops numbering approximately 2,000 from Brazil, Costa Rica, Honduras, Nicaragua, and Paraguay joined U.S. troops stationed in the Dominican Republic by the end of May 1965 (*see* conflict 2.22, April 1965–September 1966).

2. Proximity to the conflict: Coupled with the benefit of regional knowledge is the capability of a regional organization to act on potential conflicts before hostilities begin. "Certain regional and ideological associations have an advantage over the UN. As a means of preventing or settling conflicts, talking is more productive and certainly easier, the greater the general feeling of sympathy and friendship among the participants" (Nye 1971). The proximity of regional organizations to potential flash points allows the organization to react faster to assess a conflict situation and engage preventive diplomacy or initiate a speedy intervention. For example, border clashes between Uganda and Tanzania lasted for more than a year, but during September and October 1972, a timely mediation effort by the AU secretary-general, Nzo Ekangaki of Cameroon, paved the way for a later joint mediation attempt by him and President Siyad Barreh of Somalia. The result was a peace agreement and full resolution between the disputants only a month after a flare-up in fighting occurred (*see* conflict 1.33).

3. Providing a forum for dialogue and cooperation: Regional organizations can provide a formal or informal discussion environment for disputants. The importance of this role can be seen in several conflicts handled by the AU (*see* conflicts 1.15, October 1963–February 1964; 1.20, June 1964–June 1966; 1.35, Mid-1972–1985; 1.37, December 1974–June 1975) and by the OAS (*see* conflict 2.16, March 1962–1964), where the organizations provided a forum for formal and informal discussion.

4. Homogeneity of membership and shared culture: The level of cultural and regional knowledge displayed in UN interventions has sometimes impeded UN efforts to smooth disputant relations. UN peacekeeping in Somalia suffered because of a lack of knowledge about local culture and society. It can also be noted that the membership homogeneity of regional organizations can be advantageous in conflict management decision making. "Regional organizations can advance consensus, make intervention more acceptable to the disputants, and provide greater insight into local problems and the root causes of conflict" (Ramsbotham and Woodhouse 1999).

Although no criteria exist for determining whether the UN or a particular regional organization should handle a conflict, Haas found no definitive patterns of selectivity based on regional expertise and that the UN and regional organizations were really competing conflict managers (Haas 1986). In his comparison of UN and regional organization conflict management success, Haas concluded that the regional organizations are no more capable than the UN in achieving a workable solution and that they operate in a relationship of complementarity. "The regional record of success excels that of the United Nations in some of the contextual categories in which UN performance has been weak, but on the whole, with the exception of the period 1971–75, regional organizations dealt with cases that were far less intense than those the United Nations addressed" (Haas 1986). Haas explains that the majority of disputes referred to regional organizations rarely involved warfare and these disputes were smaller state disputes. In contrast, "before 1955 the typical regional dispute tended to be of low intensity, between small and middle powers, with minimal armed conflict. Since then, regional organizations have entertained a range of disputes not much different from those handled by the UN, and referral to one or the other hinges on the political circumstances of each case" (Riggs and Plano 1989).

Complementarity and Cooperation: Organizations Managing Conflicts Together

The degree of complementarity between the organizations is evident in both their rhetoric and their conflict management practices. When the drafting of the UN Charter took place, the OAS and Arab League, the only active regional organizations at the time, assisted in the formulation of the UN provisions for regional arrangements (Padelford 1954). As discussed earlier, the UN Charter provides for the coexistence of regional organizations in the pursuit of peace and security but with certain limitations on the use of enforcement actions. Chapter VIII, entitled Regional Requirements, specifically refers to the arrangements and operations of regional organizations.

The UN Charter acknowledges the gradual expansion of regionalism but is a compromise at best in its provisions for cooperating with regional organizations (Sutterlin 1995). In Claude's view:

> The finished Charter conferred general approval upon existing and anticipated regional organizations, but contained provisions indicating the purpose of making them serve as adjuncts to the United Nations and subjecting them in considerable measure to the direction and control of the central organization. The Charter reflected the premise that the United Nations should be supreme, and accepted regionalism conditionally, with evidence of anxious concern that lesser agencies should be subordinated to and harmonized with the United Nations (Claude 1964).

Chapter VIII of the UN Charter implies that all nations would be best served by joining a regional group, regardless of their bloc alignment (Waters 1967). Overall, the charter welcomes regional dispute management with the provision "that such arrangements or agencies and their activities are consistent with the purposes and principles of the United Nations" (Article 52/1). The apparent clarity of the charter articles does not always translate into a clear interpretation of interorganizational relations. Interpretations vacillate between considering the limitations of regional organization authority in maintaining international peace and security and deciding if the exhaustion of regional dispute management efforts is necessary before a dispute is brought to the Security Council (Merrills 1991).

Constitutional consistency is recognized in many of the regional organizations' founding documents. The OAS Charter's provisions for cooperation (Article 20) indicate the regional organization's legal obligations to the UN for the referral of difficult disputes (Claude 1973). The UN Charter states: "Within the United Nations, the Organization of American States is a regional agency" (UN Charter, Chapter 1, Article 1). The African Union's constitutional consistency is captured in Article 2 of the AU Charter, which declares that its members will promote international cooperation, respecting the principles of the UN Charter and the Universal Declaration of Human Rights. ASEAN consistency is detailed in Chapter IV (Article 17) of the Treaty of Amity and Cooperation in Southeast Asia, 1976:

> Nothing in this Treaty shall preclude recourse to the modes of peaceful settlement contained in Article 33 [1] of the Charter of the United Nations. The High Contracting Parties which are parties to a dispute should be encouraged to take initiatives to solve it by friendly negotiations before resorting to the other procedures provided for in the Charter of the United Nations (ASEAN 2000).

The OSCE took the unusual step of declaring that it was a regional arrangement as recognized by Chapter VII of the UN Charter (Sutterlin 1995). The Treaty on European Union sets out the European Union's responsibility "to preserve peace and strengthen international security, in accordance with the principles of the United Nations Charter as well as the principles of the Helsinki Final Act and the objectives of the Paris Charter" in Article J.1 (Barbour 1996). Generally, regional organizations are bound by charter obligations to notify the UN of any issues of concern. Conflicts often come to the notice of the UN after a regional organization has exhausted its own lines of dispute management or after a regional organization has referred the disputants' situation directly to the UN for consideration. An immediate referral to the UN is generally made when the regional organization has neither the resources nor its member states' commitment to provide a speedy dispute management strategy.

The Arab League is the only organization not to write an explicit commitment to cooperate with the UN in its charter. Article 2 of the Arab League Pact (1945) states:

> The League has as its purpose the strengthening of the relations between the member-states, the coordination of their policies in order to achieve cooperation between them and to safeguard their independence and sovereignty; and a general concern with the affairs and interests of the Arab countries.

The reason for this exclusion is a simple chronological fact. The pact was signed before the UN had officially come into existence. The Arab League anticipated the formation of the UN, charging the council with the "task to decide upon the means by which the League is to cooperate with the international bodies to be created in the future" (Article 3). But essentially, the pact focused on promoting closer cooperation between AL members. The pact fostered cooperation both within the organization and between individual member states in matters of finance, commerce, communication, culture, nationality, social affairs, and health issues (Article 3). A relationship of cooperation between the UN and the AL has since been recognized. In December 1960 the Memorandum on Cooperation and Liaison was released, detailing unofficial agreement on increased interorganization cooperation between UN Secretary-General Dag Hammarskjöld and Abdel Khalik Hassouna, the Arab League's secretary-general. The memorandum envisaged cooperation to include "mutual consultation, joint action, exchange of information and documentation, exchange of representation and other arrangements for liaison" (Hassouna 1975).

The UN has formally defined interorganizational relations with some regional organizations, but provisions for cooperation are general. Clearer lines of definition and formulated procedures are needed to allow the organizations to work effectively together. In several cases, regional organizations have entered into supplementary formal agreements with the UN; for example, the OAS and UN came to an unofficial agreement in 1995 (Sutterlin 1995), and the OSCE chairman-in-office drew up an agreement with the UN secretary-general in May 1993 (Klein 1998). In his comparison of the performance of the EU and the OSCE with the performance of the UN in Yugoslavia, Sutterlin (1995) discusses in detail the potential of UN and regional organization cooperation. Sutterlin concludes that regional organizations certainly have dispute management potential, but the cooperative nature of operations needs development and empirical analysis. Developing regional dispute management is clearly important considering that "the regional effects are both outwards—'spill-over,' 'contagion,' 'diffusion'—and inwards—'influence,' 'interference,' 'intervention'" (Miall et al. 1999). Regional organizations are better able to provide early warning for potential disputes, up-to-date local information, and effective peacebuilding and confidence-building measures (Sutterlin 1995).

UN dispute management practice falls short of fully exercising the charter's principles of regionalism (Claude 1964). Article 52/3 categorically states that "the Security Council shall encourage the development of pacific settlement of local disputes through such regional arrangements or by such regional agencies either on the initiative of the states concerned or by reference from the Security Council." It seems, however, that one of the fundamental problems facing international dispute management has been the lack of cooperation and coordination among the United Nations, regional organizations, and ad hoc multilateral coalitions of "willing states" (Bennett 1988). Claude recognizes that, although present legal arrangements between the UN and regional organizations are a far cry from achieving a constitutional balance, their founding documents certainly display elements of complementarity. Weighing universalism and regionalism is, perhaps as Claude suggests, more a matter of *managing* the problem rather than *solving* it (Claude 1964).

Recognition of levels of interorganizational cooperation came in 1995 with the release of the UN's *Report of the Secretary-General on the Work of the Organization* (Ramsbotham and Woodhouse 1999; UN Document, Part I/16). In the document, Boutros Boutros-Ghali identified five different forms of cooperation between the UN and regional organizations:

1. Consultation: Affirmations of increased cooperation between the organizations are formalized. Examples include the unofficial agreement between the OAS and UN in 1995 (Sutterlin 1995); the official agreement between the chairman-in-office of the OSCE and the UN secretary-general in May 1993 (Klein 1998); and the Memorandum on Cooperation and Liaison between the UN and Arab League in December 1960 (Hassouna 1975).
2. Diplomatic support: Provision of technical or local information; for example, the OSCE "local knowledge" assisted the UN's involvement in the Abkhazian Secession War and its counsel on the implementation of an OSCE mission in Nagorno-Karabakh.
3. Operational support: Provision of logistical support to improve an organization's chance of success, for example, the UN Security Council's authorization of NATO air support to defend so-called safe areas in Bosnia and Herzegovina (Klein 1998).
4. Co-deployment: Regional organization and UN peacekeeping or observer missions operate simultaneously. For example, the UN Observer Mission in Liberia (UNOMIL) coordinated efforts with the Economic Community of West African States Military Observer Group (ECOMOG) during Liberia's civil war.
5. Joint operations: UN and regional organization missions are combined under one command presenting a unified approach. In Rwanda the AU Neutral Military Observer Group (NMOG II) was absorbed into the United Nations Assistance Mission for Rwanda (UNAMIR), and the International Conference on the Former Yugoslavia (ICFY) was jointly chaired by a UN and EU steering committee.

The UN has also taken steps to develop closer cooperation during peacekeeping operations. A UN document, *Cooperation Between the United Nations and Regional Organizations/Arrangements in a Peacekeeping Environment—Suggested Principles and Mechanisms,* puts forth some cooperative operating procedures to improve joint peacekeeping missions and eliminate the ad hoc nature of current practices (1999). Although this document focuses on peacekeeping practices, it reiterates the underlying principle of UN supremacy in the development of more cooperative conflict management practices.

Regional Organizations: Origins and Functions

Most geopolitical regions sustain a regional organization, the purpose of which includes the management of regional conflict. In fact, the desire for regional security is one of the most powerful incentives for establishing and participating in cooperative regional organizations (Padelford 1954; Miller 1970, 1973). In addition to a basic focus on security issues, regional organizations can also derive a regional identity from one or a combination of three sources.

The first source is the geographical proximity of its membership. The second is the organization's function, such as mutual defense, the need for cooperative relations to promote the settlement of conflicts between members, or economic cooperation. Defensive organizations include the North Atlantic Treaty Organization (NATO), and cooperative groups include the Arab League. The economic groups include the Organization of Petroleum Exporting Countries (OPEC), the Council for Mutual Economic Assistance (COMECON), and the Latin American Free Trade Association (LAFTA). The third source of regional identity is the origin of the organization. Either it was established explicitly for the maintenance of regional security and for the promotion of regional integration (Macdonald 1965) or it developed from integrating economic structures, where increased cooperation between the membership provided a platform for additional security-oriented functions. Clearly, *strong* regional organizations require a geographically proximate membership, a common purpose, and shared history of organizational evolution.

Synonymous with regional organization is the notion of a regionally defined geographic identity, a geopolitical region. Geopolitical regions are identified by five characteristics: social and cultural homogeneity, shared or similar attitudes and external behavior, political interdependence, economic interdependence, and geographic proximity (Archer 1992; Waters 1967; Yalem 1973). A regional organization's strength or weakness is often gauged on the presence and intensity of these features. The extent of membership determines an organization's universalism or regionalism (Archer

1992). In addition to describing shared regional characteristics, the term *regionalism* is used to convey the nature of integration—in simple terms, the propensity of states to join and tackle problems at a regional level (Taylor 1993). Regionalism, in this sense, is international organization based on geographic proximity. Regional association is recognized by a common language, cultural or defense ties linking inhabitants of a particular geographic region. Miller points out that limited association, where membership is geographically concentrated to a particular region, is the main distinguishing characteristic of a regional organization (Miller 1970).

Regional organizations, however, are not defined only by the geographic proximity of their membership. Archer argues that "it is far better to refer to organizations with limited membership [and one of the limits may be geography] as opposed to organizations with more open or extensive membership" (Archer 1992). The nature of the British Commonwealth as an association has also been described as regional in reference to its sense of community, even though its membership is far from geographically distinct. It is clearly not appropriate to classify a regional organization solely on the presence of this attribute. A combination of geographic proximity and shared characteristics is fundamental to regional organization. As with international organizations, states have incentives for joining and developing ties with regional organizations. Increased regional cooperation can be advantageous to states wanting to strengthen collective security or maximize on economic solidarity. Regardless of the functional focus or geographic congruity of the regional organization, the founding principle of cooperation governs the interactions between the member states. When relations are tense between member states or member states are involved in a conflict, the real level of cooperation becomes more evident in their collective security, economic, or defense arrangements (Miller 1970).

Cooperative regional organizations have a more permanent make-up than do the alliance and functional groups. They are committed to the maintenance of peace, as most of them have declared in their charters, and "their raison d'être springs from territorial unity, which itself may contribute to an ethnic or ideological common ground" (Miller 1970).

Alliance organizations generally originate from the perception of a common threat. An alliance organization's response to controlling conflict is directed only to external sources of concern. Aside from the occasional verbal condemnation of member activities, alliance organizations have no mandate to regulate or intervene in their members' affairs for matters of conflict resolution. Instead of using the alliance organization as medium for collective action, individual member states deal with conflicts on their own. Many of these alliance associations are regional in scope, aim to promote regional collective security, and control the spread of international violence. Classic examples of alliance organizations include NATO, the South East Asia Treaty Organization (SEATO), and the Australia-New Zealand-United States Defense Agreement (ANZUS).

Alliance organizations are structurally insubstantial and are generally bound by defense agreements, but they too perform a function in the provision of collective security arrangements. NATO has been heavily involved with the maintenance of peace and security, but, as was pointed out earlier, this organization is generally classified as a security arrangement and cannot rightly be classified as a cooperative regional organization (Plano and Riggs 1967). NATO has acted in support of the UN, EU and OSCE, most notably in the former Yugoslavia (*see* Conflict 5.18, mid-1989 to November 2000). As a security organization, its strength lies in its military capabilities, an asset for peacekeeping that none of the organizations studied here physically possess. The Western European Union (WEU), the European equivalent of NATO, is designed, in part, to provide military logistical support for EU peacekeeping operations. So far, the WEU has failed to provide the necessary means for effective peacekeeping. It has no readily available troops, no command structure, and no agreement within the organization itself on peacekeeping initiation and objectives (Sutterlin 1995). Neither of these security organizations has official representation at the UN, nor do they have interorganizational agreements based on constitutional consistency with the UN, EU, or OSCE. "This was a distinct disadvantage when NATO agreed to undertake military enforcement action in behalf of the UN in Bosnia. Rules of engagement were agreed to only after different and sometimes acrimonious negotiations" (Sutterlin 1995).

Not every regional organization neatly fits the typology. The Commonwealth of Independent States (CIS) combines the characteristics of both a cooperative and functional organization and, moreover, is territorially diffused. The predominantly Russian composition of CIS peacekeeping forces has led to questions of its level of regional representation. Despite Russian requests for funding assistance, the UN has been reluctant to bestow official recognition and financial backing for CIS peacekeeping operations, "not wishing to authorize action that might prove inconsistent with the UN Charter. However, the Security Council eventually endorsed the CIS operations as legitimate peacekeeping. The UN did not extend financial support" (Sutterlin 1995). Although the CIS and NATO are both capable of providing adequate logistical support for peacekeeping, neither organization fulfils the criteria for classification as a true cooperative organization.

ASEAN is indicative of an organization primarily established to ensure regional economic growth and development. It began to exercise its mandate to promote regional peace and security in 1979 in regard to the Spratly Island dispute and continued to attempt to reach a settlement (*see* conflicts 3.38, January 1979–Ongoing; 3.40, December 1979–October 1980; 3.60, April 1997–July 1999; and 3.61, October 1999). The EU is also a product of the second phenomena. With its role broadened to include the role of collective security, the EU now acts as a regional organization in the management of conflicts between its member states as well as continuing its political and economic functions.

Reasons for the formation of an organization can provide clues about the level of regional homogeneity within it. Members of the Arab League and the African Union hold in common the experiences and cultural developments of an imperial history. A shared historical development in this respect has acted as a unifying factor for the members, reinforcing their sense of regional identity and focusing their attention on security issues, both internal and external. For globally dispersed regional organizations, homogeneity is assumed by means other than just geographic proximity. Homogeneity from common political or economic goals, experiences, shared cultural backgrounds, language, ethnic composition, and religious values can affect the responsiveness and cohesiveness of the organization, particularly in moments of crisis. Although a level of organizational homogeneity is desirable, the notion of a world environment based on the clustering of regionally homogeneous security organizations is not yet conducive to increased global cooperation (Farer 1993). And, despite the level of homogeneity in the regional organization, "regional solidarity cannot be assumed, especially if substantial interests are at stake" (Merrills 1991). AU problems have stemmed from ethnic differences within its membership, so regional proximity is not always a reliable indicator of organizational cohesiveness.

The development of regional mechanisms for conflict prevention reflects the current emphasis of conflict management: prevention rather than containment and management of a hostile situation. (*See* Table 10.) Many of the regional organizations have already established preventive mechanisms for conflict management: ASEAN's Regional Security Forum (RSF); ECOWAS's Mechanism for Conflict Prevention, Management, Resolution and Security; the EU's European Community Monitoring Mission (ECMM); the AU's Mechanism for Conflict Prevention, Management and Resolution (MCPMR); and the OSCE's Conflict Prevention Centre (CPC).

Despite the benefits that a regional composition and a common history can afford, these regional organizations operate under many of the same organizational constraints and resource limitations as the UN. They are charged with the responsibility for managing conflicts in their region, and they all have (1) stated obligations to pursue the peaceful settlement of conflicts in their respective regions; (2) formulated organizational objectives conducive to the principles outlined in the UN Charter (Chapter VIII); (3) agreed to regulate member state behavior in a manner consistent with constitutional requirements in the UN Charter; and (4) been recognized specifically by the UN Charter because of their central function, regional conflict management. "The UN Charter is not concerned with all regional organizations; rather, only those dealing 'with such matters relating to the maintenance of international peace and security as are appropriate for regional action'" (Sutterlin 1995).

Table 10. Geopolitical regions and regional organizations

Geopolitical region	Regional organization
Africa	African Union (AU) Economic Community of West African States (ECOWAS)
Americas	Organization of American States (OAS)
Asia: East Asia and the Pacific	Association of Southeast Asian Nations (ASEAN) Pacific Islands Forum (PIF)
Asia: SW Asia	–
Europe	Organization for Security and Co-operation in Europe (OSCE) European Union (EU)
Middle East	Arab League (AL)

Six Regions of Conflict

The six major geopolitical regions—Africa, the Americas, East Asia and the Pacific, Southwest Asia, Europe, and the Middle East—their conflicts from 1945 to 2003, and conflict management in these regions are the subjects of the rest of this book (*see* Table 11). If a conflict cannot be clearly identified in a single region, the location of the most serious action or region in which the conflict was initiated determines the region in which it is listed.

The only substantial geographic region omitted is the Antarctic, the area south of 60° South latitude. This is not to say that the Antarctic region has been devoid of conflict, but incidents of armed conflict there are rare (Bertram 1958). In fact, "the first and only shots so far fired in anger *in Antarctica* were in February 1952, when Argentines attempted to affright a British party at Hope Bay in [our] Falkland Island Dependencies, which we [Britain] have continually occupied since 1943" (McDonigal and Woodworth 2001). After the ratification of the Antarctic Treaty in 1961, several conflicts occurred within the region. The most serious armed conflict, which had the potential to spill over into Antarctic territory, was the April–June 1982 war between Argentina and Britain over the contested sovereignty of the

Table 11. Comparative overview of regional characteristics

Regional characteristics (by frequency and percentage of total conflict count)	Geopolitical region					
	Africa	Americas	Asia: East Asia and Pacific	Asia: SW Asia	Europe	Middle East
Total number of conflicts	97 (28.3%)	45 (13.1%)	65 (19.0%)	39 (11.4%)	30 (8.7%)	67 (19.5%)
Intrastate conflicts	45 (13.1%)	14 (4.1%)	13 (3.8%)	12 (3.5%)	11 (3.2%)	20 (5.8%)
Interstate conflicts	50 (14.6%)	30 (8.7%)	52 (15.2%)	27 (7.9%)	16 (4.6%)	53 (15.5%)
Ethnic conflict	48 (34.3%)	4 (2.9%)	12 (8.6%)	15 (10.7%)	12 (8.6%)	21 (15.0%)
Enduring rivalries	4 (1.2%)	13 (3.8)	16 (4.7%)	18 (5.3%)	6 (1.8%)	26 (7.6%)
Superpower involvement: either as disputant, ally, or mediator	31 (9.9%)	34 (9.9%)	29 (8.5%)	13 (3.8%)	25 (7.3%)	48 (14.0%)
Most common core conflict issue	Ethnic and cultural: 30 (8.7%)	Ideology and political: 18 (5.2%)	Security and military: 25 (7.3%)	Ethnic and cultural: 13 (3.8%)	Security and military: 11 (3.2%)	Security and military: 23 (6.7%)
Intensity level exceeding 501 fatalities per month	19 (5.7%)	3 (0.9%)	11 (3.3%)	10 (3.0%)	5 (1.5%)	12 (3.6%)
Entrenched conflicts: more than 36 months in duration	30 (8.7%)	13 (3.8%)	25 (7.3%)	8 (2.3%)	12 (3.5%)	16 (4.7%)
Most common level of hostilities	War: 65 (19.0%)	War: 24 (7.0%)	Use of force: 30 (8.7%)	War: 22 (6.4%)	War: 12 (3.5%)	War: 43 (12.5%)
Reciprocity between disputants	87 (25.4%)	42 (12.2%)	55 (16.0%)	36 (10.5%)	23 (6.7%)	65 (19.0%)
Most frequent system periods when conflict occurred	1976–1985: 22 (6.4%) 1986–1995: 23 (6.7%)	1956–1965: 16 (4.7%) 1976–1985: 13 (3.8%)	1945–1955: 13 (3.8%) 1976–1985: 13 (3.8%)	1956–1965: 12 (3.5%)	1945–1955: 7 (2.0%) 1986–1995: 10 (2.9%)	1956–1965: 14 (4.1%) 1966–1975: 16 (4.7%) 1976–1985: 14 (4.1%)
Previous disputants' relationship	Antagonism: 34 (9.9%)	Antagonism: 17 (5.0%)	More than 1 previous conflict: 21 (6.1%)	More than 1 previous conflict: 16 (4.7%)	Antagonism: 11 (3.2%)	More than 1 previous conflict: 24 (7.0%)
UN involvement	32 (9.3%)	13 (3.8%)	20 (5.8%)	5 (1.5%)	13 (3.8%)	38 (11.1%)
Ongoing conflicts	17 (5.0%)	1 (0.3%)	8 (2.3%)	3 (0.9%)	8 (2.3%)	5 (1.5%)

Falkland/Malvina Islands (*see* conflict 2.33). This war took place on South Georgia and the Falkland Islands, just outside the Antarctic Treaty area (Beck 1983, 1990, 1994, 1995; Dodds 1993, 1996, 2000; Fox 1985).

The task of making peaceful conflict management more effective requires the careful study of international conflicts—its causes, patterns, outcomes, and management. The aim of this book is to aid in this task by providing a reference to international conflict from 1945 to 2003. The summary descriptions in the regional conflict sections shed light on the causes, outcomes, and conflict-management efforts of each case.

The following sections each present a brief overview of each region, maps to enhance understanding, and a description of the conflicts the region has experienced. Emphasis is placed on conflict management and its success or failure.

References

Archer, C. 1992. *International Organisations.* 2d edition. London: Routledge.

Association of Southeast Asian Nations (ASEAN). 2000. www.geocities.com/Athens/1058/asean.html.

Baehr, P.R., and L. Gordenker. 1999. *The United Nations at the End of the 1990s.* 3d edition. New York: St. Martin's Press.

Barbour, P., editor. 1996. *The European Union Handbook.* Chicago: Fitzroy Dearborn.

Barnett, M.N. 1998. "The Limits of Peacekeeping, Spheres of Influence, and the Future of the United Nations." Chapter 4 of *Collective Conflict Management and Changing World Politics.* Lepgold, J., and T.G. Weiss, editors. Albany: State University of New York Press, 83–103.

Beck, P. 1983. "The Anglo-Argentine Dispute over Title to the Falkland Islands: Changing British Perceptions on

Sovereignty since 1910." *Millennium: Journal of International Studies* 12: 6–24.

———. 1990. "International Relations in Antarctica: Argentina, Chile and the Great Powers." In *Great Power Relations in Argentina, Chile and Antarctica.* Morris, M., editor. New York: St. Martin's Press, 101–130.

———. 1994. "Looking at the Falkland Islands from Antarctica: The Broader Regional Perspective." *Polar Record* 30: 167–180.

———. 1995. "History and Policy Makers in Argentina and Britain." In *Two Worlds of International Relations.* Hill, C., and P. Beshoff, editors. London: Routledge.

Bennett, P.G. 1988. *International Organizations—Principles and Issues.* 4th edition. Englewood Cliffs, N.J.: Prentice Hall.

Bercovitch, J. 1996. "The United Nations and the Mediation of International Disputes." In *The United Nations at Fifty—Retrospect and Prospect.* Thakur, R., editor. Dunedin, New Zealand: Otago Foreign Policy School Symposium, Otago University Press, 73–87.

Bercovitch, J., and J.Z. Rubin, editors. 1992. *Mediation in International Relations: Multiple Approaches to Conflict Management.* New York: St. Martin's Press.

Bertram, C. 1958. *Arctic and Antarctic—Prospect of the Polar Regions.* Cambridge, England: W. Heffer and Sons Ltd.

Burci, G. 1997. "Division of Labour Between the UN and the OSCE in Connection with Peacekeeping." Chapter 11 of *The OSCE in the Maintenance of Peace and Security—Conflict Prevention, Crisis Management and Peaceful Settlement of Disputes.* Bothe, M., N. Ronzitti, and A. Rosas, editors. The Hague, Netherlands: Kluwer Law International, 289–313.

Claude, I.L. Jr. 1964. *Swords into Plowshares—The Problems and Progress of International Organization.* 3d edition. New York: Random House. Reprinted in 1966.

———. 1973. "The OAS, the UN, and the United States." In *Regional Politics and World Order.* Falk, R.A., and S. Mendlovitz, editors. San Francisco: W.H. Freeman.

Dehdashti, R. 1997. "Nagorno-Karabakh: A Case Study of OSCE Conflict Settlement." Chapter 18 of *The OSCE in the Maintenance of Peace and Security—Conflict Prevention, Crisis Management and Peaceful Settlement of Disputes.* Bothe, M., N. Ronzitti, and A. Rosas, editors. The Hague, Netherlands: Kluwer Law International, 459–478.

Diehl, P.F. 1997. "The Conditions for Success in Peacekeeping Operations." Chapter 9 of *The Politics of Global Governance—International Organizations in an Interdependent World.* Diehl, P.F., editor. Boulder: Lynne Rienner, 159–173.

Dodds K. 1993. "War Stories: British Elite Narratives of the 1982 Falklands/Malvinas War." *Society and Space* 11: 619–640.

———. 1996. "The End of a Polar Empire? The Falkland Islands Dependencies and Commonwealth Reactions to British Polar Policy 1945–1961." *Journal of Imperial and Commonwealth History* 24: 392–421.

———. 2000. "Geopolitics and the Geographical Imagination of Argentina." In *Contested Traditions of Geopolitical Thought.* Dodds, K., and D. Atkinson, editors. London: Routledge.

Evans, G. 1994a. "Cooperative Security and Intrastate Conflict." *Foreign Policy* 96 (fall): 3–20.

———. 1994b. *Cooperating for Peace—The Global Agenda for the 1990s and Beyond.* St. Leonard's, New South Wales: Allen Unwin Ltd.

Falk, R.A., S.S. Kim, and S.H. Mendlovitz, editors. 1991. *The United Nations and a Just World Order.* Studies on a Just World Order, No. 3. Boulder: Westview.

Farer, T.J. 1993. "The Role of Regional Collective Security Arrangements." In *Collective Security in a Changing World.* A World Peace Foundation Study. Weiss, T.G., editor. Boulder: Lynne Rienner, 153–186.

Fetherston, A.B. 1994. *Towards a Theory of United Nations Peacekeeping.* New York: St. Martin's Press; London: Macmillan.

Fox, R. 1985. *Antarctica and the South Atlantic: Discovery, Development and Dispute.* London: British Broadcasting Corporation.

Haas, E.B. 1986. "Why We Still Need the United Nations—The Collective Management of International Conflict, 1945–1984." *Policy Papers in International Affairs, No. 26.* Berkeley: Institute of International Studies, University of California, 1–104.

Hassouna, H.A. 1975. *The League of Arab States and Regional Disputes—A Study of Middle East Conflicts.* Dobbs Ferry, N.Y.: Oceana Publications.

Junn, R.S. 1983. "Voting in the United Nations Security Council." *International Interactions.* 9, No. 4.

Kim, S.Y., and B. Russett. 1996. "The New Politics of Voting Alignments in the United Nations General Assembly." *International Organization* 50, No. 4 (autumn): 629–652.

Klein, J. 1998. "Interface Between NATO/WEU and UN/OSCE." Chapter 8 of *NATO and Collective Security.* Brenner, M., editor. London: Macmillan, 249–277.

Kolb, D.M. 1985. "To Be a Mediator: Expressive Tactics in Mediation." *Journal of Social Issues* 41: 11–26.

Leatherman, J., and R. Väyrynen. 1995. "Conflict Theory and Conflict Resolution—New Directions for Collaborative Research Policy." *Cooperation and Conflict* 30, No. 1: 53–82.

Luck, E.C., 1992–1993. "Making Peace." *Foreign Policy* 89 (winter): 137–155.

Macdonald, R.W. 1965. *The League of Arab States—A Study in the Dynamics of Regional Organization.* Princeton: Princeton University Press.

McDonigal, D., and L. Woodworth. 2001. *The Complete Story: Antarctica.* Auckland, New Zealand: Random House.

Merrills, J.G. 1991. *International Dispute Settlement.* 2d edition. Cambridge, England: Grotius Publications Ltd.

Miall, H., O. Ramsbotham, and T. Woodhouse. 1999. *Contemporary Conflict Resolution—The Prevention, Management and Transformation of Deadly Conflicts.* Malden, Mass.: Polity Press, published by Blackwell Publishers.

Miller, L.H. 1970. "Regional Organizations and Subordinate Systems." In *The International Politics of Regions—A Comparative Approach*. Cantori, L.J., and S.L. Spiegel, editors. Englewood Cliffs, N.J.: Prentice Hall, 357–409.

———. 1973. "Regional Organizations and Subordinate Systems." In *Regional Politics and World Order*. Falk, R.A., and S.A. Mendlovitz, editors. San Francisco: W.H. Freeman, 412–431.

Murphy, J.F. 1983. *The United Nations and the Control of International Violence: A Legal and Political Analysis*. Manchester, England: Manchester University Press.

Nye, J.S. Jr. 1971. *Peace in Parts: Integration and Conflict in Regional Organization*. Perspectives on International Relations Series. Written under the auspices of the Center for International Affairs at Harvard University. Boston: Little, Brown and Company.

Padelford, N.J., 1954. "Regional Organization and the United Nations." *International Organization* 8, No. 2 (May): 203–216.

Plano, J.C., and R.E. Riggs. 1967. *Forging World Order—The Politics of International Organization*. New York: Macmillan.

Ramsbotham, O., and T. Woodhouse. 1999. *Encyclopedia of International Peacekeeping Operations*. Santa Barbara: Calif.: ABC-CLIO.

Richmond, O.P. 1998. *Mediating in Cyprus—The Cypriot Communities and the United Nations*. London: Frank Cass Publishers.

Riggs, R.E., and J.C. Plano. 1989. *The United Nations—International Organization and World Politics*. Chicago: Dorsey Press.

Roberts, A., and B. Kingsbury, editors. 1988. *United Nations in a Divided World—The UN's Roles in International Relations*. Oxford, England: Clarendon Press.

Rosbalt News Agency. 2003. "US Largest Debtor Nation to UN." http://www.rosbalt.ru/2003/05/10/62484.html (accessed May 10, 2003).

Rose, M. 1996. "The Bosnia Experience." In *The United Nations at Fifty—Retrospect and Prospect*. Thakur, R., editor. Dunedin, New Zealand: Otago Foreign Policy School Symposium, Otago University Press, 167–178.

Skjelsbæk, K. 1991. "The UN Secretary-General and the Mediation of International Disputes." *Journal of Peace Research* 28, No. 1: 99–115.

Skjelsbæk, K., and G. Fermann. 1996. "The UN Secretary-General and the Mediation of International Disputes." Chapter 4 of *Resolving International Conflicts—The Theory and Practice of Mediation*. Bercovitch, J., editor. Boulder: Lynne Rienner, 75–104.

Suter, K.D. 1986. *Alternatives to War: Conflict Resolution and the Peaceful Settlement of International Disputes*. 2d edition. Sydney: Women's International League for Peace and Freedom.

Sutterlin, J.S. 1995. "The Potential of Regional Organizations." Chapter 7 of *The United Nations and the Maintenance of International Security—A Challenge To Be Met*. Sutterlin, J.S., editor. Westport, Conn.: Praeger, 93–111.

Taylor, P.G. 1993. "The Role of the United Nations in Global Security in the Early 1990s: How Far Forward?" Chapter 9 of *International Organisation in the Modern World—The Regional and Global Process*. London: Pinter Publishers, 205–249.

Taylor, P., and A.J.R. Groom, editors. 1978. *International Organization—A Conceptual Approach*. London: Frances Pinter.

Touval, S., 1994, "Why the UN Fails." *Foreign Affairs* 73, No. 5 (September/October): 44–57.

Tunnicliff, K.H. 1984. *The United Nations and the Mediation of International Conflict*. Doctoral dissertation. Ames: University of Iowa. Reprinted 1987 by University Microfilms International, Ann Arbor, Michigan.

Väyrynen, R. 1991. "The United Nations and the Resolution of International Conflicts." In *The United Nations and a Just World Order. Studies on a Just World Order, No. 3*. Falk, R.A., S.S. Kim, and S.H. Mendlovitz, editors. Boulder: Westview, 222–239.

Waters, M. 1967. *The United Nations—International Organization and Administration*. New York: Macmillan.

Weinberger, N. 1995. "How Peacekeeping Becomes Intervention: Lessons from the Lebanese Experience." Chapter 6 of *International Organizations and Ethnic Conflict*. Esman, M.J., and S. Telhami, editors. Ithaca, N.Y.: Cornell University Press, 148–175.

Yalem, R. 1973. "Theories of Regionalism. In *Regional Politics and World Order*. Falk, R.A., and S.A. Mendlovitz, editors. San Francisco: W.H. Freeman, 218–231.

Regional Conflicts

Africa

List of Conflicts

1.1 Madagascar–France: Nationalist Rebellion 60
March–August 1947

1.2 Eritrea–Ethiopia: Eritrean Nationalism and Agitation for Independence 60
July 1949–December 1950

1.3 Tunisia: Tunisian Independence and African Nationalism 61
January 1952–March 1956

1.4 Kenya–United Kingdom: Anticolonial Tribal Uprising and Mau Mau Revolt 61
August 1952–December 1963

1.5 Algeria: The Fight for Independence 62
November 1954–March 1962

1.6 Morocco–Spain: Postindependence Autonomy and the Sahara Conflict 62
November 1957–April 1958

1.7 France–Tunisia: Postindependence Autonomy and Military Bases Conflict 63
February–May 1958

1.8 France–Tunisia: French–Algerian Border Incidents 63
February–August 1959

1.9 Mauritania–Mali: Hodh Region Conflict 63
Mid-1960–February 1963

1.10 Congo (Zaire): Secession, Anarchy, Civil War, and the Belgian Congo Crisis 64
July 1960–Mid-1964

1.11 The African Territories–Portugal: African Nationalism and Independence Struggle 65
1961–July 1975

1.12 Tunisia–France: Postindependence Autonomy Dispute in Bizerte 65
July–September 1961

1.13 Somalia–Kenya/Ethiopia: Somali Expansionism and Separatist Insurgency 66
November 1962–September 1967

1.14 Sudan: Southern Separatism, Anya-Nya Terrorism, and the First Sudan Civil War 66
September 1963–March 1972

1.15 Morocco–Algeria: Territorial Dispute and the Tindouf War 67
October 1963–February 1964

1.16 Niger–Dahomey (Benin): Lete Island Dispute 68
December 1963–June 1965

1.17 Somalia–Ethiopia: Somali Expansionism, Separatist Guerrilla Fighting, and the First Ogaden War 68
January–March 1964

1.18 Rwanda–Burundi: Postindependence Ethnic Violence Between the Hutu and Tutsi 69
January 1964–January 1965

1.19 France–Gabon: Military Putsch, French Military Intervention, and Aubame's Coup 69
February 1964

1.20 Ghana–Upper Volta: Ghanaian Border Dispute 69
June 1964–June 1966

1.21 Eritrea–Ethiopia: Eritrean Nationalism and War of Secession 70
1965–May 1993

1.22 Ghana–Togo: Ghanaian Expansionism and Border Incidents 71
January–May 1965

1.23 Uganda–Congo (Zaire): Rebel Activity and Border Incidents 71
February–March 1965

1.24 Chad–Sudan: Internal Strife, Sudanese Intervention, and the First Chad Civil War 71
November 1965–1972

1.25 Namibia: Violent Insurrection, War, and Independence Struggle 72
1966–March 1990

1.26 Ivory Coast–Guinea: Coup Plot 72
March–April 1966

1.27 Ghana–Guinea: Nkrumah's Ouster and Postcoup Tensions 73
October–November 1966

1.28 Rhodesia: African Nationalism, Guerrilla Warfare, and Zimbabwe's Struggle for Independence 73
1967–January 1980

1.29 Guinea–Ivory Coast: Regional Rivalry and Hostage Crisis 74
February–September 1967

1.30 Nigeria–Biafra: Ethnic and Regional Rivalries, Secession Attempt, and the Biafran Civil War 74
July 1967–January 1970

1.31 Congo (Zaire)–Rwanda: Regional Instability and the Mercenaries Dispute 75
August 1967–April 1968

1.32 Guinea–Portugal: PAIGC Guerrilla Warfare and the Conakry Raids 75
November 1970

1.33 Uganda–Tanzania: Postcoup Border Clashes 75
January 1971–October 1972

1.34 Equatorial Guinea–Gabon: Territorial Dispute over the Corisco Bay Islands 76
June–November 1972

1.35 Ethiopia–Somalia: Somali Expansionism, Territorial Dispute, and the Second Ogaden War 76
Mid-1972–1985

1.36 Morocco–Mauritania: Saharan Nationalism, Territorial Dispute, and the Western Saharan Conflict 77
October 1974–Ongoing

1.37 Mali–Upper Volta (Burkina Faso): Territorial and Resource Dispute 77
December 1974–June 1975

1.38 Angola–South Africa: Guerrilla Warfare in Namibia, Intervention, and Angolan Civil War 78
1975–Ongoing

1.39 Zaire–Angola: Rebel Activity and Border War 79
November 1975–February 1976

1.40 Mozambique–South Africa: African Nationalism, Intervention, and Civil War 80
1976–October 1992

1.41 Uganda–Kenya: Amin Provocations and Border Incidents 81
February–August 1976

1.42 Chad–Libya: Guerrilla Warfare, Factional Fighting, and Libyan Annexation of the Aozou Strip 81
June 1976–November 1979

1.43 Zaire–Angola: Internal Dissension, Regional Instability, and the First Invasion of Shaba 82
March–May 1977

1.44 Chad: Internal Strife, Foreign Intervention, and the Second Chad Civil War 83
January 1978–June 1982

1.45 Zaire–Angola: Regional Instability, Congolese Dissension, and the Second Invasion of Shaba 83
May 1978

1.46 Tanzania–Uganda: Cross-Border Raids, Tanzanian Invasion, and Ouster of the Amin Regime 84
October 1978–May 1979

1.47 Morocco–Algeria: Western Saharan Nationalism and Border Conflict 85
June–October 1979

1.48 Cameroon–Nigeria: Border Incident 85
May–July 1981

1.49 Uganda: Civil War 86
December 1981–1994

1.50 Zaire–Zambia: Lake Mweru Dispute 86
February–September 1982

1.51 Libya–Chad: Political Instability, Rebel Fighting, Foreign Intervention, and the Third Chad Civil War 87
Mid-1982–Ongoing

1.52 Ghana–Togo: Territorial Dispute and Border Incidents 88
August–October 1982

1.53 South Africa–Lesotho: Guerrilla Insurgency Fears and Anti-ANC Raid 88
December 1982

1.54 Sudan: Secessionist Fighting, Civil War, and the Second Sudan Civil War 89
January 1983–Ongoing

1.55 Liberia–Sierra Leone: Doe Regime Tensions 90
February–March 1983

1.56 Chad–Nigeria: Boundary/Resources Dispute and the Lake Chad Conflict 90
April–July 1983

1.57 Zaire–Zambia: Regional Tensions, Deportations, and Border Dispute 91
September 1983–January 1984

1.58 South Africa–Botswana: African Nationalism and Anti-ANC Raids 91
October 1984–May 1986

1.59 Zaire: Internal Dissent and the Third Invasion of Shaba 92
November 1984

1.60 Zaire: Internal Strife, the Fourth Invasion of Shaba, and the Collapse of the Mobutu Regime 92
June 1985

1.61 Mali–Burkina Faso: Territorial/Resource Dispute and Border War 92
December 1985–January 1986

1.62 Togo–Ghana: Regional Rivalry and Coup Attempt 93
September 1986

1.63 Zaire–People's Republic of the Congo: Regional Instability and Border Incident 93
January 1987

1.64 Ethiopia–Somalia: Somali Expansionism and the Third Ogaden War 94
February 1987–April 1988

1.65 South Africa–Zambia: African Nationalism, Insurgency Fears, and Anti-ANC Raid 94
April 1987

1.66 People's Republic of the Congo: Civil Unrest and Army Rebellion 95
September 1987–July 1988

1.67 Uganda–Kenya: Ugandan Civil War, Refugee Influx, and Border Conflict 95
December 1987

1.68 **Somalia: Clan-Based Violence and the Somalian Civil War** 95
May 1988–Ongoing

1.69 **Burundi: Tribe-Based Communal Violence and the Hutu Conflict** 97
August 1988–Ongoing

1.70 **Uganda–Kenya: Border Conflict** 98
March 1989

1.71 **Mauritania–Senegal: Ethnic Violence and Border Incidents** 98
April 1989–January 1990

1.72 **Liberia: Civil War** 98
December 1989–Ongoing

1.73 **Guinea-Bissau–Senegal: Border Conflict** 100
April–May 1990

1.74 **Tuareg–Niger: Confrontation and Reprisals** 100
May 1990–October 1994

1.75 **Senegal: The Casamance Rebellion** 100
Mid-1990–Ongoing

1.76 **Tuareg–Mali: Sahel Pastoralist Rebellion and Military Coup** 102
June 1990–Ongoing

1.77 **Rwanda: Tribal Conflict, Genocide, and Exiles Invasion** 102
September 1990–Ongoing

1.78 **Liberia–Sierra Leone: Intervention, Destabilization, and the Sierra Leone Civil War** 104
March 1991–Ongoing

1.79 **Djibouti: Ethnic-Based Violence and Civil War** 105
November 1991–July 1993

1.80 **Nigeria–Cameroon: Territorial Dispute and the Diamond and Djabane Islands Dispute** 105
December 1993–March 1994

1.81 **Ghana–Togo: Border Incidents** 106
January–February 1994

1.82 **Uganda: Intervention and Democratic Movements** 106
May 1995–Ongoing

1.83 **Federal Republic of Grande Comoros: Coup Attempt and Anjouan and Moheli Independence** 107
September 1995–Ongoing

1.84 **Eritrea–Yemen: Invasion of the Hunish Islands** 108
November 1995–October 1998

1.85 **Congo: Independence Movements** 109
October 1996–Ongoing

1.86 **Uganda–Kenya: Ethnic Cross-Border Clashes** 109
November 1996–July 1998

1.87 **Niger: Diffa Border Insurgency** 110
December 1996–April 1999

1.88 **Congo–Brazzaville: Democratic Struggle** 110
May 1997–Late 2000

1.89 **Djibouti: Intervention and Djibouti Civil War** 110
Early 1998–December 2000

1.90 **Lesotho: Intervention and Military Factions** 111
May 1998–March 1999

1.91 **Eritrea–Ethiopia: Yirga Triangle Territorial Dispute** 111
May 1998–June 1999

1.92 **Guinea-Bissau: Military Factions** 112
June 1998–January 2000

1.93 **Ethiopia–Kenya: Ethnic Border Clashes** 113
October 1998–January 1999

1.94 **Liberia–Guinea: Border Dispute** 113
September 1999–April 2001

1.95 **Ivory Coast: Civil War** 114
September 1999–Ongoing

1.96 **Central African Republic–Chad: Attempted Coup, Foreign Intervention, and Territorial Occupation** 115
Mid-2001–December 2002

1.97 **Angola–Zambia: Civil Strife and Border Skirmishes** 116
November 2001

Countries in the Region

Countries included in this region are:

- Algeria
- Angola
- Benin
- Botswana
- Burkina Faso
- Burundi
- Cameroon
- Cape Verde
- Central African Republic
- Chad
- Comoros
- Congo
- Democratic Republic of the Congo
- Djibouti
- Equatorial Guinea
- Eritrea
- Ethiopia
- Gabon
- Gambia
- Ghana
- Guinea
- Guinea-Bissau
- Ivory Coast
- Kenya
- Lesotho
- Liberia
- Libya
- Madagascar
- Malawi
- Mali
- Mauritania
- Mauritius
- Morocco
- Mozambique
- Namibia
- Niger
- Nigeria
- Rwanda
- São Tomé and Principe
- Senegal
- Seychelles
- Sierra Leone
- Somalia
- South Africa
- Sudan
- Swaziland
- Tanzania
- Togo
- Tunisia
- Uganda
- Western Sahara
- Zambia
- Zimbabwe

Map 1. Africa today

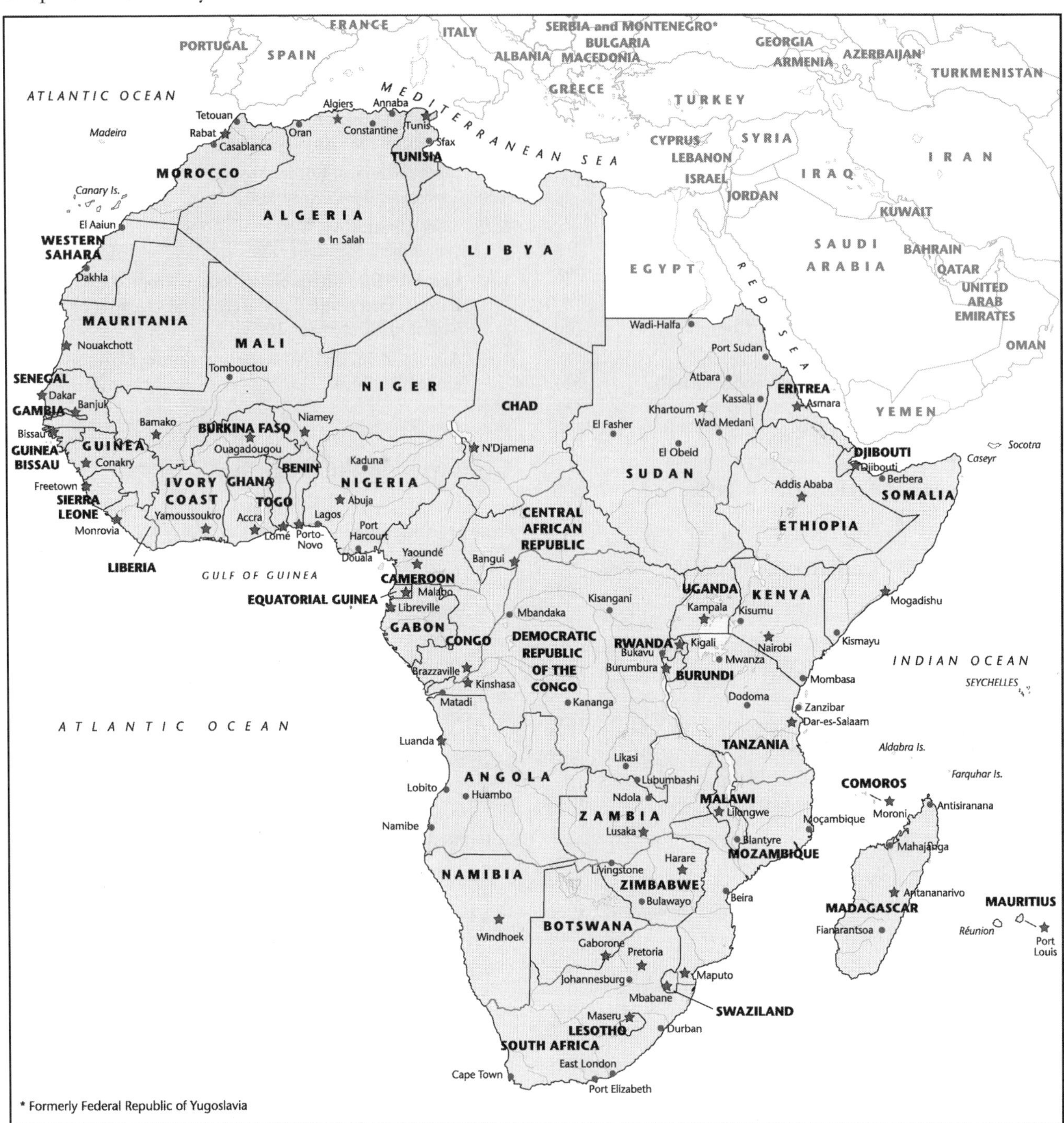

Regional Overview

In the face of rising nationalism in the 1950s and 1960s, most European powers granted independence to their colonies in Africa. Most of the colonies made smooth transitions to independence, but some engaged in war before and during the transition period. In the Portuguese colonies, the battles were particularly lengthy and bitter. Wars of independence were fought in Angola, Eritrea, Guinea Bissau, Mozambique, Namibia, and Zimbabwe. Once independence was granted, the absence of the colonial powers often left a power vacuum, which led to fighting over the orientation of the new state and among domestic groups over control of the process; examples are Angola, Namibia, Sahara, and Zimbabwe. Following independence, it became apparent that there was a lack of unity among the people within a state. Once the colonial powers had gone, the Africans no longer had a common enemy that united them.

The apportionment of areas and peoples into political states by colonizing nations probably had the greatest impact on African conflict. These states were based on little more than the location of natural resources that the colonial powers wanted to exploit and the amount of land over which they could maintain control. The unsatisfactory nature of these artificial state borders is a

Map 2. Africa in 1945

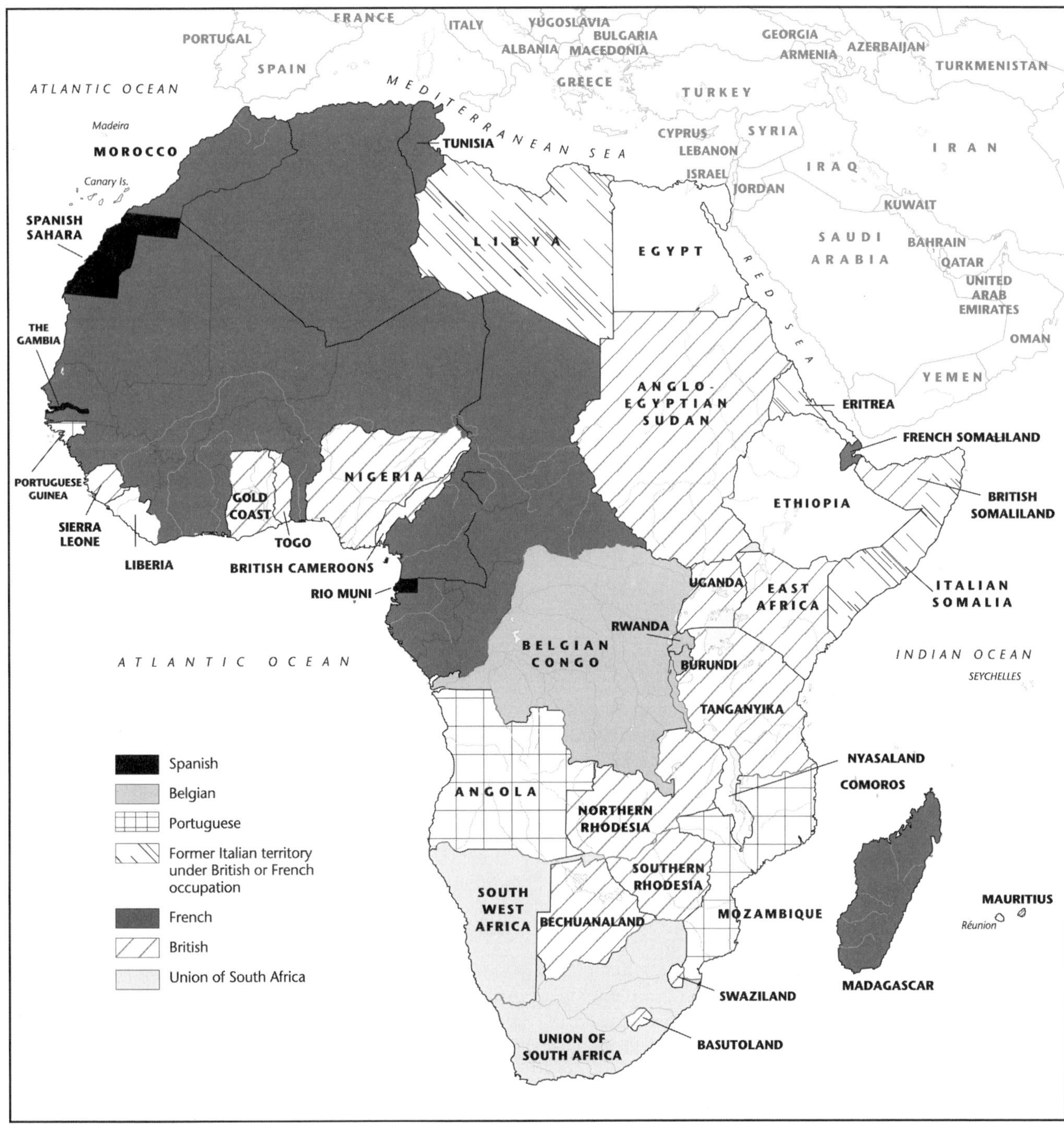

Source: Steven W. Hook and John Spanier, *American Foreign Policy Since World War II*, 16th edition (Washington, D.C.: CQ Press, 2004), 88.

common feature of many African conflicts. It has led to interstate conflict over specific territorial claims, for example, the wars between Chad and Libya and between Malawi and Tanzania, and also to conflict between different groups within state boundaries. The doctrine of the Organization of African Unity, established in 1963, has been to maintain the existing borders, mainly because one of the group's principal tenets is noninterference in a member state's internal affairs.

The ruling classes in Africa during the colonial period were European, and, when they pulled out, those left behind to rule did not have sufficient experience to carry out the task effectively. The burgeoning nations were modeled on the constitutions and structures of the European states. Systems that had taken centuries to evolve in Europe were thrust upon the Africans, who lacked the cultural, institutional, or economic experience to run them.

Conflicts in Africa have led to an increase in refugees; the spread of disease, malnutrition, and starvation; and the decline of the economy and social institutions. These factors in turn aggravate and intensify conflicts in the region. Many intrastate conflicts in Africa have become regionalized. The spillover effect of intrastate conflicts into neighboring countries adds complications. In west, central, and southern Africa, civil wars have had significant consequences for the neighboring countries, particularly through the influx of refugees. Huge numbers of refugees can destabilize the host state and contribute to civil war, as was the case in Sierra Leone. The presence of refugees heightens ethnic tensions by creating new minority groups within the host country. Africa's refugees make up more than half of the world's refugee population.

During the cold war, many African nations formed alliances either with the Soviet Union or the United States in order to receive aid. This resulted in the overthrow of many democratic governments and the installation of military regimes and one-party governments supported by one superpower or the other. A number of client states emerged. The Horn of Africa and southern Africa were of particular geostrategic importance to the superpowers, who were actively involved in military training in these subregions, which were the recipients of dramatic arm flows and military expenditure. Where belligerents relied on their own military resources, hostilities rarely escalated into full-scale conflicts: the one exception is South Africa, which has its own armament manufacturing capabilities.

In particular, Angola, Ethiopia, Liberia, Mozambique, Somalia, and Zaire depended heavily on superpower patronage. With the end of the cold war and the consequent decline in geostrategic significance of Africa in the eyes of the Western countries, these countries deteriorated rapidly. The breakdown of the bipolar cold war mindset and alliances unleashed ethnic, religious, and political conflicts that had previously been hidden behind superpower rivalries and strong nationalist governments. After the cold war, the major powers adopted a policy of "benign neglect" toward Africa, and in the 1990s the number of conflicts and their intensity increased. Africa became the most conflict-affected region in the world.

While old conflicts continued in Liberia, Somalia, and Sudan, new conflicts erupted in other countries, following a pattern in the early 1990s of democracy movements linked to the demands of civil society. These developments pitted ruling elites against democratic movements and resulted in violent civil conflict. Some countries—Angola, Ethiopia, Mozambique, Namibia, and South Africa—made peaceful transitions to democracy. But between 1996 and 1998, a large number of military coups took place. Examples include Burundi, Congo, the Democratic Republic of the Congo (formerly Zaire), and Sierra Leone.

Violent conflict in Africa increased dramatically in intensity and scale throughout the 1990s. A characteristic of the conflict is the use of extreme violence that deliberately targets the civilian population. In Angola, Mozambique, Rwanda, Sierra Leone, Sudan, and Uganda, warring groups have used horrific forms of warfare, including mass rape, torture, ritualistic violence, mutilation, and the use of knives and machetes on the civilian population, including women and children. Since 1960 more than 8 million people have died from war-related deaths in Africa; 5.5 million were civilians.

In addition, genocidal and ethnically based conflict reappeared in Africa in the 1990s. The political exploitation of ethnic differences is common in Africa, resulting in severe levels of violence aimed at particular ethnic groups and in genocide in Burundi and Rwanda. Ethnicity is not a root cause of conflict, but is used as a means of aggravating and sustaining it. The increasing poverty and marginalization of the poor in Africa, and the unequal access to power and resources associated with this, allow the elite to play the ethnic card as a way of sustaining power. Internal conflicts rapidly escalated into serious crises, humanitarian disasters, and collapsed states, as was the case in Liberia, Rwanda, Sierra Leone, and Somalia.

The political systems that developed in postcolonial Africa were dominated by one-party or military governments. The process of nation building was carried out by elites who often adopted a model of national unity through ethnic hegemony in the new state. The governments of the newly independent African states were not democratic and consequently lacked accountability; these governments were characterized by corruption and favoritism. Corrupt political practice in Africa along with economic stagnation and social dislocation, made worse by the economic recession of the 1980s, aggravated political conflicts. With no legitimate means of venting discontent or frustration over conditions of adverse poverty and government corruption, the majority of Africans have suffered crises of government that adversely affect the region's stability.

Overview of Conflict

African nations have fought civil wars since they began attaining independence, beginning with Sudan in 1956. Causes of conflict in the region can be traced back to colonial rule, acute underdevelopment, land shortages, resource scarcity, ethnic rivalry, and the colonial legacy of artificial borders, which do not reflect demographic and ethnic realities. Domestic leaders have exploited and manipulated cultural and ethnic differences, thereby intensifying them.

Wars have also been fought over natural resources, either their scarcity or abundance. On the one hand, large areas of Africa are unusable because of the shortage of water or the presence of disease; any natural disaster, such as prolonged drought, increases pressure on already scarce resources. On the other hand, rare and precious metals and gemstones are abundant in Africa's ancient geology. Most of the world's diamonds are found there, including Sierra Leone's alluvial diamonds that do not need mining to remove. Some of Africa's worst conflicts and gravest humanitarian emergencies are associated with diamonds. In countries with an abundance of natural resources and few primary exports, conflict over the natural resource is an emerging pattern. Four countries in the region are associated with "conflict" diamonds: Angola, the Democratic Republic of the Congo, Liberia, and Sierra Leone. Government forces, rebel groups, and mercenaries hired by diamond prospectors are all fighting each other, and these nations' militaries have developed their own commercial companies. Wars become self-financing, self-sustaining, and therefore less open to mediation, as diamond revenues are used to fund the conflicts. Since 1989, hundreds of thousands have died directly and indirectly in the wars over diamonds. Sierra Leone and Angola are developing a fragile peace process, but conflict continues in the other two countries.

Conflict Management

As the strategic importance of the region to the main global powers declined and the great powers were no longer prepared to intervene, it became apparent that intervention and resolution would have to come from within the continent.

The Organization of African Unity (OAU) developed greater responsibility as a conflict manager in the region with the establishment of the Mechanism for Conflict Prevention, Management and Resolution in 1993. The unwillingness to intervene within the internal affairs of African states and the desire to protect state sovereignty were weaknesses in the organization and limited its ability to be an effective mediator; this changed with the end of the cold war. The group later changed its name to the African Union (AU), and it played a prominent role in mediation efforts in Rwanda.

Subregional economic organizations are the main structures involved in Africa's conflict resolution. Organizations such as the Economic Community of Western States, the Southern African Development Community, and the intergovernmental Authority on Development in East Africa, which were founded to promote economic development, have been required to play a role in conflict management. All three have been involved as mediators. The countries in the region cannot afford to establish organizations with the sole purpose of conflict resolution. Conflicts in the region are interlinked; therefore, neighbors have an interest in peace and stability in each other's countries. Regional powers, such as South Africa in the south and Nigeria in the west, have acted as mediators.

Individuals have also acted as mediators in the region. Former U.S. president Jimmy Carter and South Africa's Nelson Mandela were involved in mediating civil wars in Burundi, Ethiopia, Greater Horn sub-region, Liberia, Rwanda, Sudan, and the African Great Lakes region.[1]

The African Union

After rapid decolonization had taken its toll in Africa during the late 1950s and early 1960s, many of the newly independent states saw the need for some regional integration and looked to the creation of a pan-African organization. The newly independent states held common concerns regarding the effects of decolonization; social and economic development; regional defense; racial discrimination, namely South Africa's policy of apartheid; and a desire for increased regional cooperation (Taylor 1984). The OAU was formed from a desire to coordinate African common interests, not a need to provide a means for regional conflict settlement (Merrills 1991). The culmination of almost six years of discussion resulted in the creation of the OAU on May 25, 1963, in Addis Ababa (Wallerstein 1966). The first Council of Ministers meeting was held in August 1963, followed by meetings of the Assembly of Heads of State and Government and the Permanent Secretariat in 1964. In 1965 the Committee of Five—later the Committee of Nine or the Liberation Committee—was created to assist nationalist movements (Taylor 1984).

On July 9, 2002, the organization officially changed its name to the African Union (AU), following through on a decision the leaders had made the year before.[2] The recognition of the sovereign rights of states, a fundamental principle in the AU charter, has served as a serious impediment in its conflict management role. Unlike the Organization of American States (OAS), the AU has a loose interpretation of organizational obligations, basing its decisions more on questions of morality rather than adhering to a stricter legal interpretation of the charter provisions.[3] The AU's emphasis on respect for a member's national sovereignty is illustrated in the level of power given to its four main organizational bodies (Merrills 1991). Member states are committed to the "peaceful settlement of conflicts by negotiation, mediation, conciliation or arbitration" (Article 3), while Article 19 provides that member states settle all conflicts among themselves by peaceful means or via the AU Commission of Mediation, Conciliation and Arbitration established for this purpose.

The organizational structure of the AU has four main echelons. The Assembly of Heads of State and

---

1. The African Great Lakes region is in East Central Africa and includes Lake Victoria, Lake Tanganyika, Lake Nayasa, and many smaller lakes.

2. See http://www.worldstatesmen.org/International_Organizations.html#African%20Union.

3. It is worth noting that a former OAS representative and Chilean diplomat assisted the emperor of Ethiopia in the drafting of the AU Charter (Nye 1971).

Government is the primary organ of the AU. It meets annually and can debate matters and pass resolutions, but it has no power to enforce them. Its resolutions are basically "only recommendations to the completely sovereign member states," and this weakness is highlighted by the fact that it cannot expel any of its members for noncompliance (Meyers 1974). The Council of Ministers meets twice a year and is the organ that is designed to implement the decisions of the assembly. Answerable to the assembly, it also coordinates and promotes the cooperation of the African members. The general secretariat of the AU performs the administrative functions of the organization. The secretary-general heads this body, but, compared to the roles played by the secretaries-general of other organizations, the AU secretary-general is weak. The founders of the AU were fully aware of the scope of the UN secretary-general's power and the independence of the individual elected to that position. The AU founders envisioned the secretary-general's job as administrative, with the real power remaining with the Assembly of Heads of State and Government. To reinforce the difference between the AU secretary-general and counterparts in other organizations, the official title of the AU secretary-general was altered in Article 16 of the AU charter to read, "Administrative Secretary-General" (Meyers 1976). This problem has since been addressed.

The AU's official channel for conflict management is the Commission of Mediation, Conciliation and Arbitration. The commission was established in 1964 and was to operate with a panel of twenty-one elected assembly members. The action of the commission was made reliant on the consent of the parties to the conflict. The commission cannot order member states to appear before it. In addition, it lacks the authority to give its own legal interpretation of the AU charter, a privilege reserved for the Assembly of Heads of State and Government, and it has no means to enforce its decisions. Compared to other organizational arbitration arenas, the World Court and the International Court of Justice (ICJ), the AU Commission of Mediation, Conciliation and Arbitration is virtually powerless (Meyers 1974). As a result of these binding limitations on what was to be its main forum for conflict management, the AU has allowed its other organizational arms to become more functional than had previously been planned. "The AU introduced the African Mechanism Apparatus for Preventing, Managing and Resolving African Crises[4] at its 1993 summit; the procedure allows the AU Secretary-General to undertake mediation and fact-finding missions and to send special envoys" (Miall et al. 1999). Thus, the role of the administrative secretary-general has evolved to a more active role than was originally envisaged in the charter (Merrills 1991).

Along with the minimalist interpretation of the AU charter provisions, the organization's lack of homogeneity has been cited as another intrinsic weakness (Wild 1971). With the inclusion of some Arab states on Africa's northern frontiers, the organization was no longer African in membership composition. The AU's "unity is 'paper thin'. As is still true of the Arab League (AL), a central strand of the rope binding together the AU's disparate parts in an association of symbols and rhetoric was a bête noir [South Africa] linked with a collectively recalled experience of humiliating domination by Europe's imperial states" (Farer 1993). Exacerbating the lack of unity is the persistence of nationalism among the African states. Assertion of nationalism has meant that many states have refused to relinquish any sovereignty to assist AU missions. The whole principle of "nonintervention," as expressed in the AU charter, has virtually paralyzed AU action to prevent or stem the abuse of human rights. Ironically, the charter's firm acknowledgment of distinct territorial boundaries has not precluded border conflicts between its members (Taylor 1984).

Lack of membership homogeneity is not the only weakness in the African Union. The inclusion of developed states in an organization enhances its ability to provide adequate resources and leadership for effective conflict management mobilization, but neither the AU nor the AL has sufficient access to resources and funds. The AU has only a few developed states in its membership and so struggles to provide resources and leadership for conflict management efforts. The organization was suffering a $2.5 million (U.S. dollars) debt only two years after its foundation (Nye 1971). "The AU's feeble attempt in Chad in the early 1980s unraveled because of internal political tensions and a lack of financing" (Farer 1993). The AU has consistently suffered from a lack of trained staff, technical expertise, and funding.

To summarize, the AU's weaknesses lie in the organization's:

1. Lack of homogeneity: Disparate membership has broad differences over issues.
2. Lack of resources: Personnel, technical expertise, material, and financial resources are often scarce.
3. Historical legacy of colonialism: Many AU members are still dealing with the remnants of colonialism.
4. Weak charter provisions: The members are concerned with moral obligations rather than legal obligations. The voluntary nature of membership and the overriding principle of state sovereignty make conflict prevention and management difficult.

4. Also known as the Mechanism for Conflict Prevention, Management and Resolution (MCPMR). The organization assisted in establishing the Cairo Center for African Crisis Solving within the MCPMR framework, an initiative designed to train "specialized African corps in predicting, managing, and solving crisis in Africa" (Ramsbotham and Woodhouse 1999).

5. Limited authority of AU organs: Member states cannot be compelled to appear before the AU commission. The commission also lacks the authority to interpret the AU charter and has no authority to enforce decisions or expel members for noncompliance. The role of the AU secretary-general, previously limited to administrative functions, has only just evolved to allow more active mediation.
6. Major power absence: The AU is the only regional organization without a major power as a member. This weakness can also be argued as an organizational strength, allowing the AU to avoid a strong country to become involved in regional conflicts (Merrills 1991; Meyers 1974).

Despite these organizational weaknesses, the AU has mediated in more than thirty conflicts; ten of these interventions have been cooperative attempts with the UN, and two have involved action with the UN and AL. In February 1964 with the encouragement of the UN, the AU employed its first independent mediation effort in a border conflict between Kenya and Somalia (*see* conflict 1.13). Since then, the organization has provided a useful informal forum for it members to resolve their conflicts peacefully (*see* conflicts 1.15; 1.20; 1.35; 1.37), but it was unsuccessful in expanding its methods of conflict management to peacekeeping (*see* conflict 1.44), and has frequently used the secretary-general's good offices (*see* conflicts 1.33; 1.34; 1.36; 1.38; 1.41; 1.44; 1.48; 1.51; 1.62; 1.68; 1.69; 1.77; 1.80; 1.84).

Economic Community of West African States

The Economic Community of West African States (ECOWAS) was initially conceived in 1964 by President William Tubman of Liberia, who argued the value of a West African organization to peacefully settle conflicts in the region. Guinea, Ivory Coast (Côte d'Ivoire), Liberia, and Sierra Leone signed an agreement in February 1965, but it was not until April 1972 that General Yakubu Gowon of Nigeria and General Gnassingbé Eyadéma of Togo became motivated to bring other regional players into agreement on the plan. A meeting was then called at Lomé, Togo, from December 10–15, 1973, which led to several subsequent meetings. On May 28, 1975, fifteen West African countries signed the Treaty of Lagos to create the Economic Community of West African States. ECOWAS was officially launched in Lomé on November 5, 1976.

ECOWAS seeks to control and manage conflicts, promote cooperation and security, and further political and economic development. A later development within the organization established stronger mechanisms for conflict management. The ECOWAS summit of December 1999 agreed on the Protocol for the Establishment of a Mechanism for Conflict Prevention, Management and Resolution, Peace and Security. The mechanism has a Council of Elders, as well as a Security and Mediation Council. The ten members of the latter are the foreign ministers of the following states: Benin, Gambia, Ghana, Guinea, Ivory Coast, Liberia, Mali (which acts as chair), Nigeria, Senegal, and Togo.

The organization became a principal mediator in these conflicts: Liberian Civil War (December 1989–Ongoing); Liberia–Sierra Leone: Intervention, Destabilization, and the Sierra Leone Civil War (March 1991–Ongoing); Guinea-Bissau: Military Factions (June 1998–January 2000); Liberia–Guinea: Border Dispute (September 1999–April 2001); and the Ivory Coast: Civil War (1999–Ongoing). In Liberia, ECOWAS undertook several initiatives aimed at a peaceful settlement. These included the creation in 1990 of a military arm, the Military Observer Group of ECOWAS (ECOMOG). ECOWAS-led talks concluded a peace agreement among warring Liberian factions in Cotonou, Benin, in 1993. During Sierra Leone's civil war ECOWAS brokered the 1997 Conakry Accord, which provided that ECOMOG would disarm all factions and reorganize Sierra Leone's army. The disarmament did not occur as agreed, however. In the conflict between Guinea and Bissau, initial mediation efforts by Portugal and Angola were conducted under the auspices of the Community of Portuguese-Speaking Countries (CPLP) and ECOWAS, resulting in a ceasefire. When serious fighting broke out again in 1999, ECOMOG troops were subsequently withdrawn.

In the border conflict between Liberia and Guinea, ECOWAS undertook numerous conflict management efforts, but had only minimal impact on deteriorating relations between the states. This territorial dispute eventually prompted ECOWAS to prepare for the deployment of 1,600 peacekeepers to patrol the border between Liberia and Guinea. Violence persisted, and further conflict management by the United Nations, ECOWAS, and the Organization of African Unity could only contain, but not settle the conflict.

The ongoing civil war in Ivory Coast prompted an emergency summit meeting of ECOWAS to determine what action to take. ECOWAS called for the army to return immediately to its barracks, but offers to mediate between the government and rebels failed. Representatives from ECOWAS also cooperated with the African Union and the United Nations in a bid to mediate between the government and the rebels. A ceasefire was signed on October 3, 2002, but lasted only three days until the rebels began a new offensive. On October 25 army chiefs from fifteen ECOWAS states met to discuss deployment of a regional force to monitor the ceasefire. Further talks collapsed amid accusations by the rebels that Ghana had agreed to let the Ivorian government use its territory from which to launch attacks and to hire mercenaries. This conflict continues with sporadic but serious fighting between the parties.

References

Farer, T.J. 1993. "The Role of Regional Collective Security Arrangements." In *Collective Security in a Changing World.* A World Peace Foundation Study. Weiss, T.G., ed. Boulder: Lynne Rienner, 153–186.

Merrills, J.G. 1991. *International Dispute Settlement.* 2d Edition. Cambridge, England: Grotius Publications Ltd.

Meyers, D.B. 1974. "Intra-Regional Conflict Management by the Organisation of African Unity." *International Organisation* 28, No. 3 (summer): 345–373.

———. 1976. "The OAU's Administrative Secretary-General." *International Organisation* 30, No. 3 (summer): 509–520.

Miall, H., O. Ramsbotham, and T. Woodhouse. 1999. *Contemporary Conflict Resolution—The Prevention, Management and Transformation of Deadly Conflicts.* Malden, Mass.: Polity Press, published by Blackwell Publishers.

Nye, J.S. Jr. 1971. *Peace in Parts: Integration and Conflict in Regional Organization.* Perspectives on International Relations Series. Written under the auspices of the Center for International Affairs at Harvard University. Boston: Little, Brown and Company.

Ramsbotham, O., and T. Woodhouse. 1999. *Encyclopedia of International Peacekeeping Operations.* Santa Barbara: Calif.: ABC-CLIO.

Taylor, P. 1984. *Non State Actors in International Politics: From Transregional to Substate Organisations.* Boulder: Westview, Special Studies in International Relations.

Wallerstein, I. 1966. "The Early Years of the OAU: The Search for Organisational Pre-eminence." *International Organisation* 20, No. 4 (autumn): 774–787.

Wild, P.B. 1971. "Radicals and Moderates in the OAU: Origins of Conflict and Bases for Coexistence." In *Regional International Organisations/Structures and Functions.* Tharp, R.A., ed. New York: St. Martin's Press, 36–50.

1.1 Madagascar–France: Nationalist Rebellion March–August 1947

France gained control over Madagascar and its associated islands between the seventeenth and nineteenth centuries. At the end of World War II Madagascan nationalists, represented by the Mouvement Démocratique de la Rénovation Malagache (MDRM), demanded independence from France. Rebels claiming to represent the MDRM attacked French military strongholds on March 29, 1947, on the main island of Madagascar. The French authorities responded with violent repression, and by December 1947, French troops had crushed the main rebel bands. Sporadic resistance continued after this date in the form of a guerrilla insurgency; the rebellion was declared officially over on December 1, 1948. Additional French Senegalese and Foreign Legion troops helped to crush the rebellion.

Approximately 350 French soldiers were killed, and official French figures put Madagascan deaths at 11,000. Many of the casualties were civilians who died from starvation and disease after being driven from their homes. At no time did either side attempt to resolve the conflict peacefully. Madagascar achieved independence in 1960.

References

Andereggen, A. 1994. *France's Relationship with Sub-Saharan Africa.* Westport, Conn.: Praeger.

Carmoy, G. de. 1970. *The Foreign Policies of France, 1944–1968.* Chicago: University of Chicago Press.

Paret, P. 1964. *French Revolutionary Warfare from Indochina to Algeria: The Analysis of a Political and Military Doctrine.* London: Centre for International Studies.

Somerville, K. 1990. *Foreign Military Intervention in Africa.* London: Pinter.

Tillema, H.K. 1991. *International Armed Conflict Since 1945: A Bibliographic Handbook of Wars and Military Interventions.* Boulder: Westview.

1.2 Eritrea–Ethiopia: Eritrean Nationalism and Agitation for Independence July 1949–December 1950

Italy acquired Eritrea in the nineteenth century and in 1936 added it to Italian East Africa, consisting of Italian Somaliland and Ethiopia. After World War II Italy was forced to give up its colonial territories in Africa, and British troops occupied the area. The status of Eritrea was disputed: the Eritreans requested independence, but Sudan and Ethiopia both claimed sovereignty over the territory. Eritrean nationalists agitated for independence, resorting to terrorism and attacks on foreign nationals, especially Italian residents. In January 1950 Britain used troops to quell the insurrection. Military activities were halted in July, and no British fatalities were reported.

In early 1950 a UN commission investigated the Eritrean case, and, on the basis of its recommendations, Ethiopia was officially awarded a mandate to rule the region. Eritrea's union with Ethiopia was completed in 1962 when Haile Selassie annexed the territory. About 150 people lost their lives in the conflict, which foreshadowed a much graver conflict starting in 1965 and ending with Ethiopian defeat and Eritrean independence in 1993 (*see* conflict 1.21).

References

Brogan, P. 1989. *World Conflicts: Why and Where They Are Happening.* London: Bloomsbury.

Day, A., ed. 1987. *Border and Territorial Disputes.* 2d edition. Burnt Mill, Harlow (Essex), England: Longman.

Doornbos, M.B., ed. 1992. *Beyond Conflict in the Horn: Prospects for Peace, Recovery, and Development in Ethiopia, Somalia, and the Sudan.* Trenton, N.J.: Red Sea.

Erlikh, H. 1983. *The Struggle over Eritrea, 1962–1978: War and Revolution in the Horn of Africa.* Stanford, Calif.: Hoover.

Farer, T. 1979. *War Clouds on the Horn of Africa: The Widening Storm.* 2d revised edition. New York: Carnegie Endowment for International Peace.

Fukin, K., and J. Markakis, eds. 1994. *Ethnicity and Conflict in the Horn of Africa.* Athens: Ohio University Press.

Gorman, R. 1981. *Political Conflict on the Horn of Africa.* New York: Praeger.

Minority Rights Group. 1983. *Eritrea and Tigray.* London: Minority Rights Group.

Tillema, H.K. 1991. *International Armed Conflict Since 1945: A Bibliographic Handbook of Wars and Military Interventions.* Boulder: Westview.

1.3 Tunisia: Tunisian Independence and African Nationalism January 1952–March 1956

France obtained Tunisia as a protectorate in the late nineteenth century. Active resistance to French rule, organized around Habib Bourguiba's Neo-Déstour Party, began in 1934 and became more ferocious after World War II. Guerrilla activity began in January 1952, and French troops were quickly mobilized for a crackdown. The French authorities outlawed not only Neo-Déstour trade unions but also women's and youth movements.

Preliminary bilateral negotiations between French and Tunisian representatives were unproductive, and the violence continued until December 1954, when France conceded independence to the territory in principle. The ban on the Neo-Déstour was lifted, and the party was included in independence negotiations, which led to internal autonomy in September 1955 and full independence in March 1956. About 2,000 people were killed during this conflict, and France retained large military installations in Tunisia after independence, leading to a series of violent conflicts later on (*see* conflicts 1.7; 1.8; 1.12). A faction opposing the continuing French military presence was put down in late 1955 to mid-1956.

References

Andereggen, A. 1994. *France's Relationship with Sub-Saharan Africa.* Westport, Conn.: Praeger.

Carmoy, G. de. 1970. *The Foreign Policies of France, 1944–1968.* Chicago: University of Chicago Press.

Ling, D. 1967. *Tunisia: From Protectorate to Republic.* Bloomington: Indiana University Press.

Tillema, H.K. 1991. *International Armed Conflict Since 1945: A Bibliographic Handbook of Wars and Military Interventions.* Boulder: Westview.

1.4 Kenya–United Kingdom: Anticolonial Tribal Uprising and Mau Mau Revolt August 1952–December 1963

Kenya became a British protectorate in the late nineteenth century. British settlers established farms in areas formerly designated as tribal reserves. Land-ownership disputes after World War II led to the formation of opposition groups, some of which demanded independence. Known as the Mau Mau revolt, the tribal uprising by the Kikuyu tribe began in August 1952 as a campaign of guerrilla warfare against the colonial government in Kenya. British farms and police stations were attacked, and the government declared a state of emergency.

Heavy fighting continued for the next four years, during which 21,000 paramilitary police, thousands of Kenyan army units, and a division of the British army with support from the Royal Air Force, sought to contain the rebellion. The bulk of the Mau Mau forces were defeated by 1956, but sporadic fighting continued until 1960 when the state of emergency was lifted. The Mau Mau were defeated by superior arms and a counterterrorist strategy that relied heavily on paramilitary units comprising locally recruited Kikuyu.

Only two attempts were made to engage the rebels in peaceful dialogue, and both failed. The brutality of the uprising led to political pressure on the British government to grant Kenya independence, which was formally attained in 1963. In all, more than 45,000 people were killed during the course of the revolt, including 60 British soldiers.

References

Berman, B., and J. Lonsdale. 1992. *Unhappy Valley: Conflict in Kenya and Africa.* London: J. Currey.

Clayton, A. 1984. *Counter-Insurgency in Kenya: A Study of Military Operations Against the Mau Mau.* Manhattan, Kans.: Sunflower University Press.

Cloete, S. 1956. *Storm Over Africa: A Study of the Mau Mau Rebellion, Its Causes, Effects, and Implications in Africa South of the Sahara.* Cape Town: Culemborg.

Edgerton, R. 1989. *Mau Mau: An African Crucible.* New York: Free Press.

Rosberg, C., and J. Nottingham. 1966. *The Myth of the "Mau Mau": Nationalism in Kenya.* New York: Praeger.

Tillema, H.K. 1991. *International Armed Conflict Since 1945: A Bibliographic Handbook of Wars and Military Interventions.* Boulder: Westview.

Venys, L. 1970. *A History of the Mau Mau Movement in Kenya.* Prague: Charles University.

1.5 Algeria: The Fight for Independence November 1954–March 1962

France acquired Algeria from the Ottoman Empire in the nineteenth century, and large numbers of French citizens settled there. Along with Tunisia and Morocco, Algeria began to seek independence from France in the period after World War II. At first, nationalists lobbied the French government, but, when independence appeared not to be forthcoming, the nationalists began a covert campaign to organize an armed force. The National Liberation Front (FLN) and the National Liberation Army (ALN) initiated a rebellion on November 1, 1954, which then settled into a protracted guerrilla and terrorist war.

Violence broke out in Algeria, spreading across the border into Tunisia and Morocco. Amid news of the terrible casualties suffered by French military units and revelations of the use of torture on suspected guerrillas, the French government collapsed in 1958. General Charles de Gaulle, a World War II hero, became president of France and in 1959 began to discuss Algerian independence. By the end of that year the French military had gained a greater degree of control over the country, and the nationalist guerrillas were on the defensive. The climate became more amenable to a political settlement, and negotiations got under way.

France and Algeria held a series of referendums on the independence issue in 1961, and they returned a positive response. Negotiations that had begun in 1960 were therefore continued, despite ongoing guerrilla activities. During this time, however, mutinous elements of the French army in Algeria formed a group known as the Secret Army Organization (SAO).* The SAO was committed to keeping Algeria in French hands, and made terrorist attacks on French and Algerian targets alike. It even staged an unsuccessful coup to derail the peace process. Loyal French forces suppressed the organization in March 1962.

On April 8, 1962, a final referendum in France produced an overwhelming vote for independence, which was subsequently granted on July 1. Fifteen thousand French troops had died during the conflict, and tens of thousands of civilians, most of them Algerian, were killed in terrorist attacks and reprisals. After Algeria gained independence, many French settlers returned to France.

* To avoid possible confusion, the acronym for the Secret Army Organization will read as SAO rather than OAS.

References

Andereggen, A. 1994. *France's Relationship with Sub-Saharan Africa.* Westport, Conn.: Praeger.

Andrews, W.G. 1962. *French Politics and Algeria: The Process of Policy Formations, 1954–1962.* New York: Appleton-Century-Crofts.

Carmoy, G. de. 1970. *The Foreign Policies of France, 1944–1968.* Chicago: University of Chicago Press.

Clark, M. 1960. *Algeria in Turmoil—The Rebellion: Its Causes, Its Effects, Its Future.* New York: Grosset and Dunlap.

Gillespie, J. 1960. *Algeria, Rebellion, and Revolution.* New York: Praeger.

Henissart, P. 1971. *Wolves in the City: The Death of French Algeria.* London: Hart-Davis.

Horne, A. 1987. *A Savage War of Peace: Algeria, 1954–1962.* Revised edition. New York: Penguin.

O'Ballance, E. 1967. *The Algerian Insurrection, 1954–1962.* Hamden, Conn.: Archon.

Tillema, H.K. 1991. *International Armed Conflict Since 1945: A Bibliographic Handbook of Wars and Military Interventions.* Boulder: Westview.

1.6 Morocco–Spain: Postindependence Autonomy and the Sahara Conflict November 1957–April 1958

After Moroccan independence in 1956, Spain maintained military bases and a protectorate in southern Morocco. This arrangement rankled the newly independent Morocco, which wanted sovereignty over the entire territory. An army of 12,000 guerrillas, fighting under the name "The Army of Liberation for the Sahara" (AOL), began harassing the Spanish forces stationed in the southern protectorate and French forces, which were then fighting Algerian nationalists (*see* conflict 1.5).

Serious guerrilla attacks on the Spanish forces began in November 1957. Morocco moved its regular troops into the area and surrounded the Spanish enclave, ostensibly for the purposes of containing the fighting and preventing Spanish incursions.

The fighting died down in 1958 following large-scale Spanish operations and Spanish threats to take the war into Agadir, an important Moroccan port. In February 1958 a joint French-Spanish military operation pushed the AOL back into Moroccan territory. Morocco deescalated the conflict from this point and sought negotiations. U.S. mediation helped to push the negotiations toward agreement. Approximately 1,000 fatalities were recorded during this conflict. Spain ceded its southern protectorate to Morocco on April 7, 1958, but remained in possession of other Saharan territories. Morocco continued to press for all of Spain's territories in North Africa (*see* conflict 1.36).

References

Day, A., ed. 1987. *Border and Territorial Disputes.* 2d edition. Burnt Mill, Harlow (Essex), England: Longman.

Tillema, H.K. 1991. *International Armed Conflict Since 1945: A Bibliographic Handbook of Wars and Military Interventions.* Boulder: Westview.

Trout, F. 1969. *Morocco's Saharan Frontiers.* Geneva: Droz.

1.7 France–Tunisia: Postindependence Autonomy and Military Bases Conflict February–May 1958

After Tunisian independence in 1956, France retained substantial military installations within Tunisia. Rebels opposed to the French presence began attacks on the French military, and France alleged Tunisian government complicity. A counterinsurgency operation was launched, and on February 8, 1958, French military aircraft bombed Sakiet-Sidi-Youssef, a town on the Tunisian border. The Tunisian army responded by surrounding the French military installations and on February 13 lodged a complaint about French activities to the United Nations.

Negotiations arranged by the UN secretary-general, Dag Hammarskjöld, succeeded, and the siege was partially lifted. An Anglo-American good offices committee then began to mediate a more permanent solution to the crisis. The French created a buffer zone on the Algerian border, but this action did not prevent incidents. Tensions flared with the arrest on February 20 of a number of Tunisians in retaliation for a mine explosion that killed two French soldiers. The situation appeared to ease somewhat until May 1958, when serious fighting broke out at Remada and Gabes, causing more than 300 casualties. Negotiations continued despite the fighting, and in June an agreement was reached under which all French troops, excepting a force of 12,000 stationed at Bizerte, would be withdrawn. The conflict did not end here, however, and fighting broke out again in 1959 and 1961 (*see* conflicts 1.8; 1.12).

References

Andereggen, A. 1994. *France's Relationship With Sub-Saharan Africa.* Westport, Conn.: Praeger.

Carmoy, G. de. 1970. *The Foreign Policies of France, 1944–1968.* Chicago: University of Chicago Press.

Ling, D. 1967. *Tunisia: From Protectorate to Republic.* Bloomington: Indiana University Press.

Paret, P. 1964. *French Revolutionary Warfare from Indochina to Algeria: The Analysis of a Political and Military Doctrine.* London: Centre for International Studies.

Tillema, H.K. 1991. *International Armed Conflict Since 1945: A Bibliographic Handbook of Wars and Military Interventions.* Boulder: Westview.

1.8 France–Tunisia: French-Algerian Border Incidents February–August 1959

From 1954 to 1962 French troops were engaged in a brutal war against Algerian nationalists. The fighting often spilled over into bordering countries, including Tunisia, one of France's former colonies. Tunisia itself had engaged in a number of armed conflicts with France from 1952 to 1956 and in 1958 (*see* conflicts 1.3; 1.7).

On February 14, 1959, Tunisia alleged that French fighter aircraft had crossed the border and attacked a group of Tunisians, causing three deaths and several casualties. Further sorties by French troops across the Tunisian border were reported on February 9 and again in April. France alleged a Tunisian incursion on May 26 in which six French troops were killed. Incidents were reported in July and August, but the conflict gradually abated. Neither side attempted to settle the conflict by peaceful means, and the continued French presence in the region led to armed conflict in 1961 (*see* conflict 1.12).

References

Andereggen, A. 1994. *France's Relationship with Sub-Saharan Africa.* Westport, Conn.: Praeger.

Carmoy, G. de. 1970. *The Foreign Policies of France, 1944–1968.* Chicago: University of Chicago Press.

Clark, M. 1960. *Algeria in Turmoil—The Rebellion: Its Causes, Its Effects, Its Future.* New York: Grosset and Dunlap.

Ling, D. 1967. *Tunisia: From Protectorate to Republic.* Bloomington: Indiana University Press.

Paret, P. 1964. *French Revolutionary Warfare from Indochina to Algeria: The Analysis of a Political and Military Doctrine.* London: Centre for International Studies.

Tillema, H.K. 1991. *International Armed Conflict Since 1945: A Bibliographic Handbook of Wars and Military Interventions.* Boulder: Westview.

1.9 Mauritania–Mali: Hodh Region Conflict Mid-1960–February 1963

In 1904 the areas now known as Mali and Mauritania were incorporated into the colonial territory of French West Africa. The boundaries of Mauritania and of the French Soudan (Mali) were set by a decree of the French government on April 23, 1913. On July 5, 1944, a decree by the governor general of French West Africa transferred the eastern Hodh region to Mauritania. At the crux of this boundary dispute is the subsequent and contradictory demarcation set out in an order by the governor-general on October 28, 1944. The order effectively transferred about 5,000 square kilometers of French Soudanese territory to Mauritania. Although the July decree should have taken precedence over the October order, it did not, in turn becoming the catalyst for the boundary dispute.

Mauritanian rulers had considered the Hodh region to be Mauritanian territory and its people, Mauritanian subjects. Mauritania therefore viewed the new demarcation as the reinstatement of a previously ignored historical claim. Mali, on the other hand, felt it was the aggrieved party, unfairly denied jurisdiction over the territory, which was rich in water wells. In an area where rainfall rarely exceeds ten inches a year in the southwest and less than four inches a year to the east, wells are a valuable resource.

Prior to both countries gaining independence, talks were held to discuss the future of the boundaries, but the talks ceased once independence was granted, and relations deteriorated rapidly. Exacerbating the situation further was a series of violent incidents between the tribespeople who lived on either side of the border. It was alleged that guerrillas operating along the border were based in Mali and received Moroccan support. Several assassination attempts of Mauritanian officials were also reported.

The conflict escalated when six people were accused of murdering French officers stationed at Nama in eastern Mauritania on March 29, 1962. Mali was accused of harboring the guerrilla group whose aim it was to oust the French from Mauritania and support Moroccan territorial claims in the region. President Moktar Ould Daddah of Mauritania declared on April 6 that no violation of his country's integrity would be tolerated. The UN representative for Mauritania made an official complaint to the United Nations on June 7, alleging that Morocco was supporting the Mali-based terrorists in their border raids on Mauritania.

Heads of state met in early February 1963 and, after prolonged negotiations, reached a settlement that President Daddah and President Modibo Keiti of Mali signed at Kayes on February 16. The Treaty of Delimitation of the Frontiers between the Islamic Republic of Mauritania and the Republic of Mali or the Treaty of Kayes, "in effect, has settled the disputed Mali-Mauritania boundary to the advantage of both states. Mauritania has obtained full title to the western Hodh area which it has administered since 1944. Mali has not only retained the villages of Diandioume, Gourdian, Gouguel, and Boulouli, but has also obtained important wells in the southeastern sector of the frontier" (The Geographer 1963). Although the settlement was more in favor of Mali than Mauritania, this compromise appears to have held.

References

Brecher, M., J. Wilkenfeld, and S. Moser. 1988. *Crises in the Twentieth Century*. New York: Pergamon.

Butterworth, R.L. 1976. *Managing Interstate Conflict, 1945–1974*. Pittsburgh: Center for International Studies, University of Pittsburgh.

The Geographer. 1963. *International Boundary Study No. 23: Mali-Mauritania Boundary*. Washington, D.C.: Department of State, Office of Research in Economics and Science, Bureau of Intelligence and Research. http://www.law.fsu.edu/library/collection/LimitsinSeas/IBS023.pdf. (Released December 16, 1963; accessed February 16, 2004.)

1.10 Congo (Zaire): Secession, Anarchy, Civil War, and the Belgian Congo Crisis July 1960–Mid-1964

Nationalists in the Belgian Congo, most notably Patrice Lumumba and Joseph Kasavubu, began agitating for independence from Belgium in the 1950s. Although plagued by intertribal fighting and civil disorder, the country was granted independence on June 30, 1960, with Lumumba as prime minister and Kasavubu as president. But on July 5, less than a week after the country was granted independence, Congolese troops mutinied and began attacking Belgian nationals. Belgium sent in troops to quell the rebellion without Congolese permission.

Six days later a second crisis developed when the mineral-rich province of Katanga (now called Shaba) was declared independent by Moisé Tshombé, who worked closely with foreign mining interests. Tshombé bolstered his army with large numbers of foreign mercenaries. Fearing that Belgium would regain control over Katanga, Lumumba appealed for UN assistance to quell the rebellion and reestablish civil order. The United Nations formed a special operation, the UN Operation in the Congo (UNOC), and called for the withdrawal of Belgian troops. By August 1960 UN troops had replaced Belgian troops but refused to take Katanga by force. In September the government split into three factions, one under Prime Minister Lumumba, another under President Kasavubu, and still another under army chief of staff Lieutenant General Joseph Désiré Mobutu (later Mobutu Sésé Séko, president of Zaire from 1965 to 1997).

These three factions and the secessionist regime in Katanga then engaged in a year of unlimited civil war. The UNOC supported the Kasavubu faction, while the Soviet Union began supplying the Lumumba faction. The United States backed Mobutu. Throughout this period, the United Nations tried desperately to mediate a peaceful solution, but without success. Lumumba was taken to Katanga and murdered in January 1961, and his faction was defeated in early 1962. A government of national unity was gradually established. Following inconclusive talks with the Katangan separatists, the breakaway province was invaded in December 1962. By January 1963 the rebels had been defeated and Katanga reincorporated into the country. But Katanga (Shaba) separatism would continue to plague Congo culminating in four subsequent conflicts (*see* conflicts 1.43; 1.45; 1.59; 1.60).

With the war winding down, the UNOC began to disband in February 1963. The fighting had always been intense, and more than 110,000 people were killed, including 50 Belgian soldiers and 126 UN peacekeepers. UN efforts at mediation were largely ineffective in the many-sided conflict, and the UN secretary-general himself was killed in a plane crash during one of the peace missions. Mobutu took power from Kasavubu in a 1965 military coup.

The civil war caused massive upheaval in Congo (which Mobutu renamed Zaire in 1971), and military pacification efforts continued for several decades. The Mobutu regime recruited mercenaries in its initial drive to establish control over a country as large as the United States east of the Mississippi, and these initial pacification efforts led to conflict with Uganda, Congo's northern neighbor. A surge in rebel activity in 1996 eventually saw the complete collapse of the Mobutu regime in 1997, leading to instability throughout Central Africa. Soon after Mobutu's ouster, the country was renamed Democratic Republic of the Congo (*see* conflicts 1.23; 1.31; 1.39; 1.43; 1.50; 1.57; 1.63).

References

Abi-Saab, G. 1978. *The U.N. Operation in the Congo, 1960–1964.* Oxford: Oxford University Press.

Biebuyck, D., and M. Douglas. 1961. *Congo Tribes and Parties.* London: Royal Anthropological Institute.

Epstein, H., ed. 1965. *Revolt in Congo, 1960–1964.* New York: Facts on File.

Kalb, M. 1982. *The Congo Crisis: The Cold War in Africa from Eisenhower to Kennedy.* New York: Macmillan.

Tillema, H.K. 1991. *International Armed Conflict Since 1945: A Bibliographic Handbook of Wars and Military Interventions.* Boulder: Westview.

1.11 The African Territories–Portugal: African Nationalism and Independence Struggle 1961–July 1975

Portugal's colonial holdings in Africa date back to the sixteenth century. By the middle of the twentieth century, its African territories included Angola, Cape Verde Islands, Guinea-Bissau, Mozambique, and São Tomé and Principe. Portuguese rule was generally harsh, and the colonial administration did little to prepare the territories for independence.

Beginning with armed revolt in Angola in 1961, these territories began to press for independence. In February 1961 the Union of Angolan People (UPA) began to make terrorist attacks against European settlers. The conflict expanded significantly in March when the Marxist Movimento Popular de Libertação de Angola (MPLA) merged with the UPA and precipitated total guerrilla warfare. Protracted, bloody conflict went on for thirteen years and was immediately followed by civil war.

Similar armed struggles for independence began in Guinea-Bissau in 1963 and in Mozambique in 1964. Nationalist parties took up arms in a guerrilla war to liberate their countries from the oppressive Portuguese rule. Throughout the conflict, rebels received aid from independent frontline states, such as Zambia, from which they also launched attacks. On the other side, Portugal received significant aid from South Africa and what was then Southern Rhodesia (now Zambia) in its attempts to contain the fighting. Portugal also employed mercenaries, most notably in an effort to destabilize Zaire (Congo), which was actively supporting the Frente Nacional de Libertação de Angola (FNLA) guerrilla movement. Typically, small guerrilla bands would attack Portuguese targets and then vanish into the bushland. Portuguese troops and mercenary forces would take repressive measures and periodically mount operations to flush out the rebels.

Neither side was able to get the upper hand, but Portuguese casualties were mounting and the costs becoming unbearably high. The intransigence of the Portuguese government and the unwinnable nature of the war led to a military coup in Lisbon on April 25, 1974. The new military government implemented a unilateral cease-fire and offered independence to all the territories on July 27. Guinea-Bissau formally gained independence on September 10. Mozambique completed the transition to independence on June 25, 1975, and Angola on November 11, 1975. More than 100,000 people were killed during the struggle for independence, including large numbers of civilians and as many as 5,000 Portuguese troops. The only negotiations undertaken were those that led to independence at the end of the conflict. Like Angola, Mozambique splintered and plunged into civil war upon gaining independence (*see* conflict 1.40).

References

Birmingham, D. 1992. *Frontline Nationalism in Angola and Mozambique.* London: J. Currey.

Bruce, N. 1975. *Portugal: The Last Empire.* New York: Wiley.

Burchett, W. 1978. *Southern Africa Stands Up: The Revolutions in Angola, Mozambique, Zimbabwe, Namibia, and South Africa.* New York: Urizen Books.

Hanlon, J. 1984. *Mozambique: The Revolution Under Fire.* London: Zed.

Harsch, E., and T. Thomas. 1976. *Angola: The Hidden History of Washington's War.* New York: Pathfinder.

Humbaraci, A., and N. Muchnik. 1974. *Portugal's African Wars: Angola, Guinea-Bissau, Mozambique.* New York: Third Press.

Tillema, H.K. 1991. *International Armed Conflict Since 1945: A Bibliographic Handbook of Wars and Military Interventions.* Boulder: Westview.

1.12 Tunisia–France: Postindependence Autonomy Dispute in Bizerte July–September 1961

Fighting between France and Tunisia had occurred from 1952 to 1956, in 1958, and again in 1959 (*see* conflicts

1.3; 1.7; 1.8). The 1959 conflict emerged out of France's continued military presence at a base at Bizerte, despite protracted negotiations aimed at a complete French withdrawal from Tunisia.

When France sought to extend the runway at Bizerte to accommodate more modern aircraft, Tunisia intensified its efforts to gain an immediate withdrawal of French units. It issued political demands to France, and on July 19, 1961, instituted a military blockade of the base. Tunisia announced it would open fire on any French aircraft attempting to land at the base. A French helicopter and some reconnaissance aircraft were shot at, and the French responded by strafing Tunisian troops.

On July 20 French troops opened fire on Tunisian demonstrators surrounding the base. French troops then tried to take the town of Bizerte, and over the ensuing two days, hundreds of Tunisians and several French soldiers were killed. Tunisia protested to the United Nations and broke off all diplomatic ties with France. UN Secretary-General Dag Hammarskjöld sought to mediate the conflict, but his efforts were unsuccessful, although a cease-fire was arranged. A stand-off ensued for the next several weeks, but in September tensions eased somewhat when both sides expressed interest in negotiating an eventual French pull-out. Withdrawal was completed on October 15, 1963. About 1,000 people were killed during the conflict.

References

Andereggen, A. 1994. *France's Relationship with Sub-Saharan Africa.* Westport, Conn.: Praeger.

Carmoy, G. de. 1970. *The Foreign Policies of France, 1944–1968.* Chicago: University of Chicago Press.

Ling, D. 1967. *Tunisia: From Protectorate to Republic.* Bloomington: Indiana University Press.

Paret, P. 1964. *French Revolutionary Warfare from Indochina to Algeria: The Analysis of a Political and Military Doctrine.* London: Centre for International Studies.

Tillema, H.K. 1991. *International Armed Conflict Since 1945: A Bibliographic Handbook of Wars and Military Interventions.* Boulder: Westview.

1.13 Somalia–Kenya/Ethiopia: Somali Expansionism and Separatist Insurgency November 1962–September 1967

Somalia gained independence in 1960 and immediately announced its intention of uniting all the Somali tribes under a single state. Such an aim involved making territorial claims on Ethiopia and Kenya, both of which had significant numbers of Somalis living within their borders. In 1962 Somali tribes living in northern Kenya declared their wish to join the new Somali republic and initiated guerrilla attacks on Kenyan government targets to reinforce their claims. A few border incidents occurred between Kenyan and Somali troops. The violence was halted in March 1964, when the Somali tribes declared their acceptance of Kenyan rule. Somali tribes in the Ogaden region of Ethiopia also began a campaign during this period, and Kenya and Ethiopia allied themselves against Somalia.

In the autumn of 1965 relations between Kenya and Somalia degenerated once again when serious fighting resumed in the border areas. The Organization of African Unity (OAU) made several unsuccessful attempts to settle the conflict peacefully. The conflict deescalated in late 1967 when Somalia began to adopt a policy of disengagement in favor of negotiations over its territorial claims. Negotiations from 1967 led to an understanding in 1969, and relations between Somalia and Kenya were normalized. The issues were never fully resolved, however, and a number of similar conflicts reemerged in later years (*see* conflicts 1.17; 1.35; 1.64). The fighting cost at least 4,200 lives.

References

Doornbos, M.B., ed. 1992. *Beyond Conflict in the Horn: Prospects for Peace, Recovery, and Development in Ethiopia, Somalia, and the Sudan.* Trenton, N.J.: Red Sea.

Farer, T. 1979. *War Clouds on the Horn of Africa: The Widening Storm.* 2d revised edition. New York: Carnegie Endowment for International Peace.

Fukin, K., and J. Markakis, eds. 1994. *Ethnicity and Conflict in the Horn of Africa.* Athens: Ohio University Press.

Gorman, R. 1981. *Political Conflict on the Horn of Africa.* New York: Praeger.

Hoskyns, C., ed. 1969. *The Ethiopian-Somalia-Kenya Dispute, 1960–1967.* Dar es Salaam, Tanzania: Oxford University Press/Institute of Public Administration, University College, Tanzania.

Nzongola-Ntalaja, G., ed. 1991. *Conflict in the Horn of Africa.* Atlanta: African Studies Association Press.

Tharp, P.A. 1971. *Regional International Organizations: Structures and Functions.* New York: St. Martin's.

Tillema, H.K. 1991. *International Armed Conflict Since 1945: A Bibliographic Handbook of Wars and Military Interventions.* Boulder: Westview.

1.14 Sudan: Southern Separatism, Anya-Nya Terrorism, and the First Sudan Civil War September 1963–March 1972

Egypt and Britain had ruled Sudan since the nineteenth century. The protracted Sudanese civil war had its roots in the British decision, prior to Sudanese independence in

1955, to combine northern and southern Sudan instead of implementing the favored alternative, which had southern Sudan joining Uganda. Uganda and southern Sudan shared a similar ethnic and religious composition of black African animists, whereas northern Sudan was largely Arabic and Muslim.

Following independence, the more economically and socially advanced north ruled from Khartoum with an iron fist. It sought to expand missionary activity in the south and began a program of imposing Islamic culture and Arabic language. Those who resisted were harshly repressed, and many southern Sudanese were driven into neighboring countries: the Central African Republic, Ethiopia, Kenya, and Uganda. Rebel organizations emerged with the express aim of attaining independence for southern Sudan. Attacks were often launched from bases in these countries.

Resistance arose in southern Sudan in 1963, with the Anya-Nya terrorists, who began attacking the government in September 1963 and continued until 1972. Most of the rebels operated under the umbrella of the Sudan Africa National Union (SANU) organization. Although SANU and the government met for talks on more than one occasion, they were unable to resolve their differences.

The conflict was internationalized from 1966, when the Sudanese government of Sadiq al-Mahdi was aided by Milton Obote's Ugandan army operating in Uganda to crush rebel activities in the border areas. Ugandan involvement continued until an Ethiopian-mediated cease-fire ended military hostilities on March 12, 1972. As many as 700,000 people were killed during the course of the war, many of them civilians killed by government troops in reprisals. Others died from starvation and disease. The issue of race and religion was never fully resolved, however, and this conflict presaged another civil war (*see* conflict 1.54).

References

Albino, O. 1970. *The Sudan: A Southern Viewpoint.* London: Institute of Race Relations, Oxford University.

Alport, C.J.M. 1965. *The Sudden Assignment: Being a Record of Service in Central Africa During the Last Controversial Years of the Federation of Rhodesia and Nyasaland, 1961–1963.* London: Hodder and Stoughton.

Assefa, H. 1987. *Mediation of Civil Wars: Approaches and Strategies—The Sudan Conflict.* Boulder: Westview.

Beshir, M.O. 1968. *The Southern Sudan: Background to Conflict.* New York: Praeger.

———. 1974. *Revolution and Nationalism in the Sudan.* London: Rex Collings.

Eprile, C. 1974. *War and Peace in the Sudan.* London: David and Charles.

Johnson, D.H. 1988. *The Southern Sudan.* Minority Rights Group Report #78. London: Minority Rights Group.

O'Ballance, E. 1977. *The Secret War in the Sudan, 1955–1972.* Hamden, Conn.: Archon.

Tillema, H.K. 1991. *International Armed Conflict Since 1945: A Bibliographic Handbook of Wars and Military Interventions.* Boulder: Westview.

Verney, P. 1995. *Sudan: Conflict and Minorities.* London: Minority Rights Group.

Wai, D. 1981. *The African-Arab Conflict in the Sudan.* New York: Africana.

1.15 Morocco–Algeria: Territorial Dispute and the Tindouf War
October 1963–February 1964

Morocco and Algeria had both been ruled by France, which in 1952 assigned a mineral-rich zone including Bechar and Tindouf to Algeria. Morocco tried to reclaim the area after it gained independence in 1956. Following Algerian independence in 1962, Morocco made a number of hostile moves in the disputed territory, raising tensions between the two states considerably.

In September 1963 Morocco sent troops into the area and attempted to occupy it forcibly. Algeria launched a counterattack in October and repulsed the invading troops. War broke out, and Morocco recaptured the towns on October 14. The intense fighting spread to other border areas. Algeria gained military support, including tanks and troops, from Cuba on October 27.

A mediation attempt by Haile Selassie of Ethiopia succeeded in securing a cease-fire on November 4, 1963, and a demilitarized zone was established in the disputed area in February 1964. There were thought to be as many as 1,000 fatalities during the conflict. Relations between the two states remained strained, and they came into indirect conflict during the Western Sahara war and direct confrontation in 1979 (*see* conflict 1.47).

References

Clark, M. 1960. *Algeria in Turmoil—The Rebellion: Its Causes, Its Effects, Its Future.* New York: Grosset and Dunlap.

Day, A., ed. 1987. *Border and Territorial Disputes.* 2d edition. Burnt Mill, Harlow (Essex), England: Longman.

Gillespie, J. 1960. *Algeria, Rebellion, and Revolution.* New York: Praeger.

Henissart, P. 1971. *Wolves in the City: The Death of French Algeria.* London: Hart-Davis.

Horne, A. 1987. *A Savage War of Peace: Algeria, 1954–1962.* Revised edition. New York: Penguin.

O'Ballance, E. 1967. *The Algerian Insurrection, 1954–1962.* Hamden, Conn.: Archon.

Tillema, H.K. 1991. *International Armed Conflict Since 1945: A Bibliographic Handbook of Wars and Military Interventions.* Boulder: Westview.

1.16 Niger–Dahomey (Benin): Lete Island Dispute December 1963–June 1965

Dahomey, now called Benin, and Niger had a long-standing border conflict over Lete Island, strategically located in the Niger River, which is a significant part of the boundary separating the two territories. The disagreement over who had exclusive jurisdiction over the island dates back to colonial times and reemerged in the 1960s when both territories were about to become independent states. Talks to determine the island's status were held after independence, but the talks broke down in 1963.

Following a period of civil disorder, a military coup ousted President Coutoucou Hubert Maga of Dahomey. The commander of the army, Colonel Christophe Soglo, set up a provisional government on October 29, 1963. This development had a profound effect on Niger–Dahomey relations, as Maga, the ousted president, had been a close friend and ally of Niger's authoritarian president, Hamani Diori. President Diori and his government suspected that Dahomey's new regime was supported by the Sawaba, Niger's outlawed opposition party, and its leader, Djibo Bakary. With these suspicions came the fear that Dahomeyans living in Niger, who had supported Maga, would "infect" Niger with Maga's more liberal ideology.

On December 20, 1963, the government of Niger dismissed all Dahomeyan civil servants from its administration and ordered the expulsion of 16,000 Dahomeyan residents by January 1964. The conflict escalated on December 21, when the National Assembly of Niger, alleging that Dahomey was preparing to send troops to occupy Lete Island, sent its own troops to occupy it first. Niger justified its actions by saying it was retaliation for the deaths of three of Niger's citizens that occurred in Dahomey's October riots. President Soglo of Dahomey sent troops to defend the island and ordered the closure of Dahomey's road and rail routes to landlocked Niger, effectively cutting off Niger's access to Dahomey's main port, Cotonou. Troops from both sides were mobilized along the border. At this time, Dahomey lodged a complaint with the United Nations, but the organization took no formal action to manage the conflict.

Negotiations from 1960 to 1963 all ended in deadlock, amid accusations of subversion and growing distrust. On January 4, 1964, delegations from both sides engaged in a series of meetings on the border. The meetings involved arbitration by the Union Africaine et Malgache (UAM) and five mediation attempts by parties including the UAM, the Counceil de l'Entente (CDE), President Maurice Yameogo of Upper Volta, and other West African heads of state. As a result, a joint communiqué was issued on June 15, 1965, allowing the reopening of road and rail routes and announcing the withdrawal of military forces from the border. Although the specifics of the bilateral agreement remain secret, the negotiations did reveal that nationals of both countries would be allowed to remain on Lete Island until a final solution could be reached and compensation was agreed upon for those Dahomeyans who had been expelled from Niger. No further dispute has erupted over the control of Lete Island.

References

Brecher, M., J. Wilkenfeld, and S. Moser. 1988. *Crises in the Twentieth Century*. New York: Pergamon.

Butterworth, R.L. 1976. *Managing Interstate Conflict, 1945–1974*. Pittsburgh: Center for International Studies, University of Pittsburgh.

1.17 Somalia–Ethiopia: Somali Expansionism, Separatist Guerrilla Fighting, and the First Ogaden War January–March 1964

When Somalia became independent from Britain in 1960, the new government began to lay claim to territory in surrounding states. This practice had already brought Somalia into armed conflict with Kenya from 1962 to 1967 (*see* conflict 1.13). Somalia's strongest claim, however, was to the Ogaden region of Ethiopia, which was inhabited by Somali tribes people. Somalia asserted that the region should be united with Somalia or allowed to pursue self-determination. Ethiopia was totally opposed to this notion, and relations between the two states became strained.

With some Somali agitation, an insurrection by the Somali tribes in the Ogaden in 1960 and 1961 led to serious fighting with the Ethiopian army. When Somali soldiers began supporting Ogaden tribes in their guerrilla activities in November 1963, both states moved major units to the border. Ethiopia launched air attacks against Somalia in mid-January 1964, followed by an invasion of Somali territory in February. Fighting ended in March, following Sudanese mediation, but guerrilla attacks continued until April. As many as 700 people were killed in the fighting, which foreshadowed a much graver conflict in the 1970s and 1980s (*see* conflicts 1.35; 1.64).

References

Doornbos, M.B., ed. 1992. *Beyond Conflict in the Horn: Prospects for Peace, Recovery, and Development in Ethiopia, Somalia, and the Sudan*. Trenton, N.J.: Red Sea.

Farer, T. 1979. *War Clouds on the Horn of Africa: The Widening Storm*. 2d revised edition. New York: Carnegie Endowment for International Peace.

Fukin, K., and J. Markakis, eds. 1994. *Ethnicity and Conflict in the Horn of Africa*. Athens: Ohio University Press.

Gorman, R. 1981. *Political Conflict on the Horn of Africa*. New York: Praeger.

Legum, C., and T. Hodges. 1978. *After Angola: The War over Southern Africa*. 2d edition. New York: Africana.

Nzongola-Ntalaja, G., ed. 1991. *Conflict in the Horn of Africa.* Atlanta: African Studies Association Press.

Tillema, H.K. 1991. *International Armed Conflict Since 1945: A Bibliographic Handbook of Wars and Military Interventions.* Boulder: Westview.

Talbott, J. 1980. *The War Without a Name: France in Algeria, 1954–1962.* New York: Knopf.

Tillema, H.K. 1991. *International Armed Conflict Since 1945: A Bibliographic Handbook of Wars and Military Interventions.* Boulder: Westview.

1.18 Rwanda–Burundi: Postindependence Ethnic Violence Between the Hutu and Tutsi January 1964–January 1965

Rwanda and Burundi, ruled by Belgium as a single territory, obtained independence as separate states in July 1962. Both countries contained a mix of Hutu and Tutsi tribes people. The Belgian colonial policy of promoting Hutu to positions of prominence in Rwanda and Tutsi to positions of prominence in Burundi had already led to serious ethnic violence from 1959 to 1962. This violence had caused large numbers of Tutsi to flee from Rwanda into Burundi and other surrounding states.

An organization known as the Union Nationale Rwandaise (UNAR) sought to promote the interests of the Tutsi within Rwanda, but began military operations against the Hutu-dominated Rwandan government on November 25, 1963. The UNAR launched guerrilla operations from Burundi and other surrounding states. A second attack was launched on December 21, 1963. The Rwandan authorities countered with severe repression of Tutsi within Rwanda, killing thousands in massacres. Most of the invading force was also killed, but some attacks continued.

Relations between Rwanda and Burundi deteriorated rapidly as Rwanda accused Burundi of supporting the Tutsi guerrillas. The conflict escalated even further when Rwandan troops raided Tutsi refugee camps located inside Burundi territory. The fighting eventually abated, but not before approximately 15,000 people, mainly Tutsi, had been killed. The African Union (AU) Council asked that President Mobutu Sésé Séko (Congo-Kinshasa) mediate between members from Burundi and Rwanda. He conducted three meetings and successfully secured the free movement of refugees. The parties in this conflict saw the AU as an impartial third party and welcomed its assistance. This ethnic conflict, however, was the beginning of a cycle of violence that thirty years later produced the genocidal wars in Burundi (*see* conflict 1.69, 1988–Ongoing) and Rwanda (*see* conflict 1.77, 1990–Ongoing).

References

Lemarchand, R. 1970. *Rwanda and Burundi.* New York: Praeger.

Melady, T. 1974. *Burundi: The Tragic Years.* Maryknoll, N.Y.: Orbis.

Reyntjens, F. 1995. *Burundi: Breaking the Cycle of Violence.* London: Minority Rights Group.

1.19 France–Gabon: Military Putsch, French Military Intervention, and Aubame's Coup February 1964

After Gabon gained independence from France in 1960, a coalition government under the leadership of Léon M'Ba of the Democratic Bloc Party took control of the nation's affairs. Beginning in February 1963 M'Ba undertook to form a one-party state—a move the opposition Democratic and Social Union Party, which was led by Jean-Hilaire Aubame, was against.

On February 17, 1964, Gabonese armed forces officers staged a bloodless coup, detained M'Ba, and installed Aubame as president. M'Ba loyalists immediately requested assistance from France under existing security arrangements, and French troops entered Gabon and reinstated M'Ba as president on February 20. French troops remained in country and were slowly withdrawn during April 1967. The dispute lapsed after this point. An estimated thirty people were killed during the restoration moves, including two French soldiers.

References

Andereggen, A. 1994. *France's Relationship with Sub-Saharan Africa.* Westport, Conn.: Praeger.

Carmoy, G. de. 1970. *The Foreign Policies of France, 1944–1968.* Chicago: University of Chicago Press.

Clayton, A. 1988. *France, Soldiers, and Africa.* London: Brassey's.

Paret, P. 1964. *French Revolutionary Warfare from Indochina to Algeria: The Analysis of a Political and Military Doctrine.* London: Centre for International Studies.

Tillema, H.K. 1991. *International Armed Conflict Since 1945: A Bibliographic Handbook of Wars and Military Interventions.* Boulder: Westview.

1.20 Ghana–Upper Volta: Ghanaian Border Dispute June 1964–June 1966

Relations between Upper Volta and Ghana became strained in 1963, when Ghanaian prime minister Kwame Nkrumah and his government were disturbed by Upper Volta's pursuit of closer ties with Ivory Coast. At the same time Upper Volta's government suspected that Ghana was secretly supporting the subversive activities of rebels within its borders. The dispute focused on the border issues, but other residual antagonisms fuelled the disputants' reactions. In 1963 Ghanaian troops were occupying a fifty-mile strip of territory previously controlled by Upper Volta. Upper Volta formally denounced the occupation in 1963 but waited until July 1964 to refer the matter to the Organization of African Unity (OAU). In addition to the occupation, Ghana had closed its borders with Upper Volta without warning in June 1964 and had begun building a school in the disputed territory.

Upper Volta lodged its formal complaint at the OAU Assembly Summit Conference, which was held in Cairo July 13–July 17, 1964. The OAU Assembly passed a resolution that approved the maintenance of current border demarcation in Africa. Ghana acknowledged a willingness to withdraw its occupation forces and begin negotiations with Upper Volta with a view to settling the border issue. The OAU Assembly passed a resolution in favor of immediate negotiations between the two states to settle the dispute. Ghana, however, did not comply with the resolution, and the matter was reintroduced at an OAU Council forum in June 1965. Discussion at the OAU Council forum centered on complaints of Ghanaian subversion against neighboring states and on the threat of a number of French-speaking West African states boycotting a meeting to be held in Accra in August 1965.

Upper Volta raised the matter at the Accra OAU meeting, and Ghana restated its willingness to withdraw from the territory to resolve the dispute. This time, the Ghanaian government adhered to its stated intentions and withdrew from the territory. The dispute ended peacefully.

References

Butterworth, R.L. 1976. *Managing Interstate Conflict, 1945–1974.* Pittsburgh: Center for International Studies, University of Pittsburgh.

Central Intelligence Agency. 1998. *CIA World Factbook 1998.* http://www.odci.gov/cia/publications/factbook/uv.html; http://www.odci.gov/cia/publications/factbook/gh.html.

Fretter, J.M. 2001. *Effective Mediation in International Disputes: A Comparative Analysis of Mediation by the United Nations and Regional Organizations 1945–1995.* Doctoral dissertation, Vol. II: Appendices. University of Canterbury, Christchurch, New Zealand.

Political Leaders 1945–1999. http://web.jet.es/ziaorarr/ghana.htm; http://web.jet.es/ziaorarrPurkina.htm.

Zacher, M.W. 1979. *International Conflicts and Collective Security, 1946–1977.* New York: Praeger.

1.21 Eritrea–Ethiopia: Eritrean Nationalism and War of Secession 1965–May 1993

Part of ancient Ethiopia, Eritrea was taken over by the Italian government in 1882 and in 1936 made part of Italian East Africa along with Italian Somaliland and Ethiopia. Following a short-lived war of independence (1949–1950), Eritrea became federated with Ethiopia until 1962, when Ethiopia annexed the territory and made it an Ethiopian province. Eritrean nationalists, however, had not given up hope of gaining full independence, and since 1956 the Eritrean Democratic Front (EDF) had been agitating to reach that goal. The EDF initiated armed resistance under the banner of the Eritrean Liberation Front (ELF) soon after Ethiopia's annexation of Eritrea.

The conflict then entered a stage of steady escalation, culminating in an unrestricted guerrilla war in 1967. ELF expanded its operations with large-scale military support from Cuba, Egypt, and the People's Republic of China. The conflict often spilled into Sudan, as Ethiopian troops pursued Eritrean rebels across the border between the two countries. Following the 1974 ouster of Emperor Haile Selassie in Ethiopia, Sudan offered increased support for the rebels, resulting in repeated clashes between the two countries in the border area.

The war continued throughout the 1980s, with neither side able to win complete victory. At various times, the Eritrean rebels held vast areas under their control. A severe drought, combined with the effects of the war, created a massive famine in 1985, which was partly relieved by worldwide humanitarian aid. In the 1990s, under pressure from several devastating famines and a similar rebellion in the Tigre province, the Ethiopian government was unable to maintain effective control and fell in May 1991 after a concerted offensive by several rebel groups.

Following a period of instability and, at times, factional violence, a referendum in the province overwhelmingly voted for independence. With a relatively stable government in place, Ethiopia was beginning to recover at the end of 1995, while Eritrea was rebuilding and establishing its independence. The fighting throughout the conflict was often intense and brutal, and 200,000 people are estimated to have been killed as a result. Many of these were civilians killed in reprisal attacks, and many more died as a result of war-induced famine.

References

Brogan, P. 1989. *World Conflicts: Why and Where They Are Happening.* London: Bloomsbury.

Day, A., ed. 1987. *Border and Territorial Disputes.* 2d edition. Burnt Mill, Harlow (Essex), England: Longman.

Doornbos, M.B., ed. 1992. *Beyond Conflict in the Horn: Prospects for Peace, Recovery, and Development in Ethiopia, Somalia, and the Sudan.* Trenton, N.J.: Red Sea.

Erlikh, H. 1983. *The Struggle over Eritrea, 1962–1978: War and Revolution in the Horn of Africa.* Stanford, Calif.: Hoover.

Farer, T. 1979. *War Clouds on the Horn of Africa: The Widening Storm.* 2d revised edition. New York: Carnegie Endowment for International Peace.

Fukin, K., and J. Markakis, eds. 1994. *Ethnicity and Conflict in the Horn of Africa.* Athens: Ohio University Press.

Gorman, R. 1981. *Political Conflict on the Horn of Africa.* New York: Praeger.

Minority Rights Group. 1983. *Eritrea and Tigray.* London: Minority Rights Group.

Tillema, H.K. 1991. *International Armed Conflict Since 1945: A Bibliographic Handbook of Wars and Military Interventions.* Boulder: Westview.

1.22 Ghana–Togo: Ghanaian Expansionism and Border Incidents January–May 1965

Relations between Ghana and Togo were strained because colonial boundaries had split the Ewe tribe between the two states, and Ewe organizations were campaigning for reunification. Togo was also suspicious of Ghana's president, Kwame Nkrumah, who was committed to expansionist policies and regularly sought to undermine his neighbors by supporting dissident movements and military subversion.

From January to May 1965 a number of border incidents between Ghana and Togo were reported, in which Ghanaian police crossed the border into Togo. During one such sortie, a member of the Togolese security forces was killed. Similar allegations and complaints of interference were made against Ghana by Ivory Coast, Niger, and Upper Volta, and these three states brought Ghana's actions to the attention of the Organization of African Unity (OAU). Togo did not formally take part in this action for fear of further intimidation by Ghana. The OAU passed a broad resolution condemning involvement in neighboring states' internal affairs, although it did not mention Ghana directly. This state of relations led to further armed conflicts in 1982, 1986, and 1994 (*see* conflicts 1.52; 1.62; 1.81).

References

Awoonor, K. 1990. *Ghana: A Political History from Pre-European to Modern Times.* Accra: Sedco.

Butterworth, R.L. 1976. *Managing Interstate Conflict, 1945–1974.* Pittsburgh: Center for International Studies, University of Pittsburgh.

Carmichael, J. 1993. *African Eldorado: Gold Coast to Ghana.* London: Duckworth.

Tillema, H.K. 1991. *International Armed Conflict Since 1945: A Bibliographic Handbook of Wars and Military Interventions.* Boulder: Westview.

1.23 Uganda–Congo (Zaire): Rebel Activity and Border Incidents February–March 1965

Bands of rebels still roamed Congo's frontiers following years of bloody civil war and secessionist warfare in Katanga province.* Government efforts to pacify the country were initially aided by foreign mercenaries and involved the pursuit of rebels along Zaire's northern border with Uganda. Some evidence suggests that Uganda may have been supporting the northern rebels. In any event, the military activity strained relations between these two Central African nations.

In February 1965 Uganda accused Zaire of bombing Ugandan villages while in pursuit of the rebels; Zairean and Ugandan troops also engaged in a number of clashes. The conflict began to intensify when the countries closed their mutual border and sent troop reinforcements to the area. The conflict quickly died down, however. Although no formal attempts were made at peaceful conflict management as such, the border was soon reopened and relations resumed later that year.

* Following its independence in 1960, the Belgian Congo was renamed the Democratic Republic of the Congo. President Mobutu Sésé Séko, who ruled the Central African nation from 1965 to 1997, changed the country's name to Zaire in 1971. The name reverted to the Democratic Republic of the Congo when Laurent Kabila came to power in May 1997.

References

Avirgan, T., and M. Honey. 1982. *War in Uganda: The Legacy of Idi Amin.* Westport, Conn.: Lawrence Hill.

Hooper, E., and L. Pirouet. 1989. *Uganda.* Minority Rights Group Report #66. London: Minority Rights Group.

Smith, G. 1980. *Ghosts of Kampala.* New York: St. Martin's.

1.24 Chad–Sudan: Internal Strife, Sudanese Intervention, and First Chad Civil War November 1965–1972

Chad had been riven by dissension between the politically dominant black south and the largely Muslim north since its independence from France in 1960. Ngarta Tombolbaye, a southerner, served as Chad's president when the nation gained independence. Controlled by Christians from the south, his regime was deeply resented by Muslims in the east and north. Matters worsened in 1963, when Tombolbaye sought to establish a one-party state.

Opposition groups responded by organizing the Front de Libération Nationale du Tchad (FROLINAT) with the aim of deposing Tombolbaye and instituting an Islamic state. A new military regime in neighboring Sudan permitted various exile groups to operate in the country. FROLINAT set up headquarters in Sudan's capital, Khartoum, which led to serious tensions between Chad and Sudan.

A rebellion was instigated in the eastern province of Ouadai, and fighting began on the border between Chad and Sudan in November 1965. Chadian armed forces pursued the rebels throughout 1966, undertaking frequent cross-border incursions. For the next two years, however, the war was largely confined to Chadian territory.

In August 1968 French troops were sent to help the government forces. By April 1969, 2,000 French troops were in Chad, and by May 1970 most of the rebel-held territory had been recaptured and returned to government hands. Sporadic fighting continued until late 1972, when the rebellion collapsed. The conflict cost as many as 3,500 lives, including 50 French soldiers. Chad again fell into civil war in 1978, when Libya became involved (*see* conflict 1.44).

References

Decalo, S. 1976. *Coups and Army Rule in Africa: Studies in Military Style.* New Haven: Yale University Press.

Johnson, D.H. 1988. *The Southern Sudan.* Minority Rights Group Report #78. London: Minority Rights Group.

Thompson, V.B., and R. Adloff. 1981. *Conflict in Chad.* Berkeley: Institute of International Studies, University of California.

Tillema, H.K. 1991. *International Armed Conflict Since 1945: A Bibliographic Handbook of Wars and Military Interventions.* Boulder: Westview.

Whiteman, K. 1988. *Chad.* Minority Rights Group Report #80. London: Minority Rights Group.

1.25 Namibia: Violent Insurrection, War, and Independence Struggle 1966–March 1990

From the 1880s until World War I, South West Africa (Namibia) was a German colony and subject to a harsh regime. In 1908 German forces suppressed a Namibian revolt, and nearly 85,000 black Africans lost their lives. South Africa took over the administration of the territory during World War I and then governed it under a League of Nations mandate.

Asked to surrender its mandate in 1945 and place the country under a UN trusteeship, South Africa refused. In the meantime, Namibians had begun to agitate for independence. The South West Africa People's Organization (SWAPO), working primarily out of neighboring Angola, lobbied the United Nations for Namibian independence.

In 1966 the world body complied, passing a resolution condemning continued South African administration of the territory. SWAPO began a simultaneous campaign of violent insurrection, sabotage, and low-level guerrilla warfare. Despite an International Court of Justice (ICJ) ruling in 1971 that South Africa withdraw from Namibia, South Africa continued to govern the territory. During this period, police actions were sufficient to contain SWAPO-inspired violence. More serious violence erupted after a general strike in December 1971, and Portuguese troops from Angola joined South African units in suppressing rebel activities. An intense guerrilla war between SWAPO and South African defense forces began in February 1972 and persisted continuously until the late 1980s.

Between 1978 and 1980 the war expanded into Zambia, where SWAPO had set up training bases, and it later spread to Botswana and Angola. By the 1980s Angola (independent since 1975) and its Cuban allies had increased their involvement in SWAPO's struggle, providing significant support. The United States and the Soviet Union initiated peace overtures in the Angolan civil war, linking any progress to the end of Angolan support for SWAPO. A series of UN-sponsored mediations by U.S. negotiator Chester Crocker led to a settlement signed on December 22, 1988, providing for the withdrawal of South African troops from Namibia. The withdrawal was completed by November 23, 1989, and UN-supervised elections were held in 1990. The elections brought SWAPO's guerrilla leader, Sam Nujoma, to power with 57 percent of the vote; he was reelected in 1994. More than 13,000 people were killed during the course of the conflict, many of them civilians. Large numbers of South African troops were killed in the fighting, as well as a number of Portuguese and Zairean soldiers. Namibia made a successful transition to independence and has been rebuilding its economy.

References

Burchett, W. 1978. *Southern Africa Stands Up: The Revolutions in Angola, Mozambique, Zimbabwe, Namibia, and South Africa.* New York: Urizen Books.

Cliffe, L., and R. Bush. 1994. *The Transition to Independence in Namibia.* Boulder: Lynne Rienner.

Fraenkkel, P.J. 1978. *The Namibians of South West Africa.* Minority Rights Group Report #19. London: Minority Rights Group.

Herbstein, D., and J.A. Evenson. 1989. *The Devils Are Among Us: The War for Namibia.* London: Atlantic Highlands.

Jaster, R.S. 1985. *South Africa in Namibia: The Botha Strategy.* Lanham, Md.: University Press of America.

———. 1990. *The 1988 Peace Accords and the Future of South-Western Africa.* Adelphi Papers #253. London: Brassey's.

Katjavivi, P. 1988. *A History of Resistance in Namibia.* Paris: UNESCO Press.

Koig, B. 1983. *Namibia, The Ravages of War: South Africa's Onslaught on the Namibian People.* London: International Defence and Aid Fund for Southern Africa.

Tillema, H.K. 1991. *International Armed Conflict Since 1945: A Bibliographic Handbook of Wars and Military Interventions.* Boulder: Westview.

1.26 Ivory Coast–Guinea: Coup Plot March–April 1966

Guinea had been ruled by President Sékou Touré since its independence. His regime had steadily moved Guinea in a Marxist direction, creating considerable domestic turmoil, and large numbers of exiles who fled to Senegal, Ivory Coast, and France. Touré's radical stance isolated Guinea and caused considerable friction between the country and its more moderate neighbors.

In late 1965 Guinea announced that it had foiled a plot to overthrow Touré's regime. Tensions grew between Guinea and Ivory Coast, as Guinea accused Ivory Coast of aiding rebels opposed to the new regime. Some evidence supported this charge, and Guinea broke off all relations with Ivory Coast. Although some observers feared an outbreak of war, no fatalities occurred. No attempts at peaceful conflict management were tried. Eventually, the dispute lapsed altogether, although a much more serious conflict broke out again in February 1967 (*see* conflict 1.29).

References

Africa Contemporary Record. Annual. 1968/1969– .

African Recorder. Weekly. 1962– .

Butterworth, R.L. 1976. *Managing Interstate Conflict, 1945–1974*. Pittsburgh: Center for International Studies, University of Pittsburgh.

Chan, S. 1992. *Kaunda and Southern Africa: Image and Reality in Foreign Policy*. London: British Academic Press.

1.27 Ghana–Guinea: Nkrumah's Ouster and Postcoup Tensions October–November 1966

Relations between Ghana and Guinea had been good since the countries gained their independence in the late 1950s. Kwame Nkrumah had ruled Ghana since its independence in 1957. Following his ouster in a 1966 military coup, Nkrumah sought refuge in Guinea, which led to a rapid deterioration in relations between Guinea and the new Ghanaian regime.

On October 30, 1966, nineteen Guineans were removed from a Pan American flight while on stopover in Ghana. Ghana announced that the detainees were being held in retaliation for Guinea's aggressive stance. Furthermore, they would not be released until Guinea freed Ghanaians who, the government claimed, were being held in Guinea. Guinea denounced Ghana's actions and accused the United States of complicity, detaining the U.S. ambassador and Pan Am representatives. Many feared the conflict would escalate.

Ethiopia sent its minister of justice to mediate the dispute, and on October 31, 1966, an Organization of African Unity (OAU) mediation team was appointed. Guinea freed the U.S. ambassador that same day, and Ghana released the nineteen Guineans on November 5. The Ghanaians who were alleged to have been detained in Guinea said they wished to remain where they were. A last-minute crisis was averted when Ghana dropped its demands for their return.

References

Africa Contemporary Record. Annual. 1968/1969– .

African Recorder. Weekly. 1962– .

Butterworth, R.L. 1976. *Managing Interstate Conflict, 1945–1974*. Pittsburgh: Center for International Studies, University of Pittsburgh.

1.28 Rhodesia: African Nationalism, Guerrilla Warfare, and Zimbabwe's Struggle for Independence 1967–January 1980

Rhodesia had been a self-ruling British Crown colony since 1923. In November 1965 the Rhodesian government, under staunch conservative Ian Smith, declared unilateral independence from Britain, an act the British denounced as a rebellion. Although Rhodesia's white-ruled government developed the country, the benefits of prosperity were not shared with the majority black population. Denied the franchise by the new republic, black African nationalists initiated a two-pronged uprising through the Zimbabwe African People's Organization (ZAPO) and the Zimbabwe African National Union (ZANU).

South Africa came to the aid of Rhodesian security forces in 1967, sending large quantities of arms and advisers. At this stage, the fighting was confined to small-scale terrorist attacks, sabotage, and guerrilla warfare that targeted isolated white-owned farms.

The liberation of Angola and Mozambique from Portuguese rule in 1975 greatly aided the guerrillas, for the new African regimes gave them sanctuary. The conflict heightened in intensity in 1976, when ZAPO and ZANU were joined in alliance with the African National Congress of South Africa (ANC) in what was called the Patriotic Front. The rebels gained formal support from neighboring black African states in August 1977, when Botswana, Mozambique, Tanzania, and Zambia formed the frontline states. As a result, fighting regularly spilled across the borders of these states, as the Rhodesian security forces pursued guerrillas and raided training camps.

On May 3, 1979, Abel Muzorewa became prime minister in an ill-fated internal settlement proposed by Smith. This move solved none of the issues, as the white minority still wielded the real power. The fighting intensified. In September Lord Harrington undertook a mediation effort at Lancaster House in London. It produced a cease-fire that was to begin on December 5, 1979, and a plan for elections and independence that came into effect in January 1980.

More than 30,000 people were killed during the conflict, despite numerous mediation attempts by Britain and the United States. The transition to independence was smooth, and Zimbabwe began to rebuild in the following years. Zimbabwean troops were later involved in conflicts 1.40 and 1.85.

References

Burchett, W. 1978. *Southern Africa Stands Up: The Revolutions in Angola, Mozambique, Zimbabwe, Namibia, and South Africa.* New York: Urizen Books.

Charlton, M. 1990. *The Last Colony in Africa: Diplomacy and the Independence of Rhodesia.* Oxford: B. Blackwell.

Cilliers, J. 1985. *Counter-Insurgency in Rhodesia.* London: Croom Helm.

Gann, L., and T. Hendriksen. 1981. *The Struggle for Zimbabwe: Battle in the Bush.* New York: Praeger.

Henderson, W. 1967. *The Rhodesian-U.K. Conflict: The Constitutional Issue.* Klemzig, South Australia: South Australia-Rhodesia Association.

International Defence and Aid Fund. 1973. *The Rhodesia-Zambia Border Closure, January–February 1973.* London: International Defence and Aid Fund.

Jaster, R.S. 1986. *South Africa and Its Neighbours: The Dynamics of Regional Conflict.* Adelphi Papers #209. London: IISS/Jane's.

Loey, M. 1975. *Rhodesia: White Racism and Imperial Response.* Harmondsworth (Middlesex), England: Penguin.

Ranger, T.O. 1985. *Peasant Consciousness and Guerrilla War in Zimbabwe: A Comparative Study.* London: J. Currey.

1.29 Guinea–Ivory Coast: Regional Rivalry and Hostage Crisis February–September 1967

Regional rivalry between Guinea and Ivory Coast had created simmering tensions between the two West African states since 1965. Opponents of Sékou Touré's one-party Socialist regime in Guinea conducted a campaign against their government from Ivory Coast and were therefore a source of antagonism between the two states.

A crisis erupted on February 19, 1967, when Guinea captured a fishing vessel from Ivory Coast, claiming the boat had violated Guinean territorial waters and was conducting covert operations. The Guinean action followed an earlier incident in January, when Ivory Coast exiled students who were participating in antigovernment demonstrations. The students were subsequently invited to reside in Guinea, and Ivory Coast regarded the offer as a diplomatic snub. The worsening diplomatic situation elicited an attempted mediation by Liberian vice president William Richard Tolbert Jr. in March, but nothing came of his efforts.

The crisis escalated alarmingly on June 26, when Ivory Coast removed the Guinean foreign minister and the country's UN ambassador from an international flight on stopover in Abidjan. Ivory Coast announced the officials would be released only when the crew of the fishing vessel was returned. The conflict threatened to escalate into war at this point.

Diplomatic representations to the United Nations and the Organization of African Unity (OAU) by both sides led to peaceful intervention by UN Secretary-General U Thant and President William V.S. Tubman of Liberia. Tubman's continued mediation led to Guinea freeing the fishing vessel crew on September 21 and the release of the diplomats four days later.

References

Africa Contemporary Record. Annual. 1968/1969– .

African Recorder. Weekly. 1962– .

Butterworth, R.L. 1976. *Managing Interstate Conflict, 1945–1974.* Pittsburgh: Center for International Studies, University of Pittsburgh.

Cohen, M.A. 1974. *Arab Policy and Political Conflict in Africa: A Study of the Ivory Coast.* Chicago: University of Chicago Press.

1.30 Nigeria–Biafra: Ethnic and Regional Rivalries, Secession Attempt, and the Biafran Civil War July 1967–January 1970

A period of civil instability followed Nigerian independence in 1960, caused in the main by regional differences and resistance to northern domination. Ethnic rivalries ultimately led to a military coup in January 1966, through which a Biafran military commander, Major General Aguiyi Ironsi, gained power. Ironsi was toppled by another coup in July 1966, led by Lieutenant General Yakubu Gowon. The new regime then took revenge on Biafrans in a program of violent repression. Numerous massacres caused Biafrans to flee to their tribal lands in eastern Nigeria and provoked Biafran leader Colonel Chukwuemeka Odumegwu Ojukwa into declaring Biafran secession and independence on May 30, 1967.

Initially, Gowon sought a peaceful solution to the crisis, but in the face of Biafran refusals to negotiate on the issue of sovereignty, Nigeria launched an invasion on July 6, 1967, beginning a protracted and bloody war. Although a number of African states recognized Biafran independence, a complete blockade of the territory prevented any outside assistance from reaching the beleaguered Biafrans. Several mediation efforts by the Organization of African Unity (OAU), the papal nuncio, and the Commonwealth secretary-general, among others, were unsuccessful, and, apart from short Biafran offensives, Nigeria slowly took control of Biafra in heavy fighting. Biafran forces surrendered on January 15, 1970, and Ojukwa went into exile. The war and the

Nigerian blockade of Biafra caused a famine that killed hundreds of thousands of people. In all, more than 1 million people, many of them civilians, died as a result of the conflict.

References

Ekwe-Ekwe, H. 1990. *Conflict and Intervention in Africa: Nigeria, Angola, Zaire.* Basingstoke (Hants), England: Macmillan.

Nafziger, E.W. 1983. *The Economics of Political Instability: The Nigerian-Biafran War.* Boulder: Westview.

Niven, R. 1970. *The War of Nigerian Unity, 1967–1970.* Ibadan, Nigeria: Evans Brothers.

Oluleye, J. 1985. *Military Leadership in Nigeria, 1966–1979.* Ibadan, Nigeria: Ibadan University Press.

Stremlai, J. 1977. *The International Politics of the Nigerian Civil War.* Princeton, N.J.: Princeton University Press.

Tillema, H.K. 1991. *International Armed Conflict Since 1945: A Bibliographic Handbook of Wars and Military Interventions.* Boulder: Westview.

1.31 Congo (Zaire)–Rwanda: Regional Instability and the Mercenaries Dispute August 1967–April 1968

Since its independence in 1960, Congo (renamed Zaire in 1971) had experienced massive civil unrest. The separatist fighting in the copper-rich southern province of Katanga involved numerous foreign mercenaries. In fact, their numbers in Central Africa grew so large that they became the source of some instability. Mercenaries were employed not only by the Congolese government in its intensive pacification efforts but also by Portugal to destabilize the regime of President Mobutu Sésé Séko, which was actively supporting Angolan rebels.

In August 1967 a large contingent of Portuguese-backed mercenaries took refuge in Rwanda after losing to Congolese troops at the town of Bukavu. Mobutu demanded their immediate extradition, and Rwanda intended to repatriate them. In January 1968 Congo closed its border with Rwanda and broke off all relations. A tense war of words followed, leading to fears of an escalation to conflict. After mediation, however, the conflict was settled and the mercenaries were all repatriated. In the initial fighting, nearly 2,000 people were killed.

References

Africa Contemporary Record. Annual. 1968/1969– .

African Recorder. Weekly. 1962– .

Clayton, A. 1984. *Counter-Insurgency in Kenya: A Study of Military Operations Against the Mau Mau.* Manhattan, Kan.: Sunflower University Press.

Thomas, G. 1985. *Mercenary Troops in Modern Africa.* Boulder: Westview.

Tillema, H.K. 1991. *International Armed Conflict Since 1945: A Bibliographic Handbook of Wars and Military Interventions.* Boulder: Westview.

1.32 Guinea–Portugal: PAIGC Guerrilla Warfare and the Conakry Raids November 1970

The Partido Africano da Indepēndencia da Guinée Cabo Verde (PAIGC) in Guinea-Bissau waged a guerrilla war of independence against the Portuguese. Along with a number of other states neighboring Guinea-Bissau, Guinea granted diplomatic recognition to the PAIGC, which strained its own relations with Portugal. Furthermore, Guinea allowed the PAIGC to operate from within its frontiers.

From the beginning of the 1961 uprising in Guinea-Bissau, Portuguese counterinsurgency operations were concentrated along the borders of Guinea and Senegal, both of which frequently charged that Portuguese forces were making unauthorized incursions into their territory. In November 1970 a group of mercenaries invaded Guinea from Guinea-Bissau, and fighting broke out in Conakry, Guinea's capital. The fighting lasted for several days, causing several hundred fatalities. Guinean forces eventually repulsed the invaders.

A UN fact-finding mission later revealed that Portugal had sponsored the invasion, which was aimed at ousting President Sékou Touré's regime. The conflict lapsed in 1975, when Portugal withdrew altogether from its African territories following the military overthrow of its government in 1974.

References

Bruce, N. 1975. *Portugal: The Last Empire.* New York: Wiley.

Burchett, W. 1978. *Southern Africa Stands Up: The Revolutions in Angola, Mozambique, Zimbabwe, Namibia, and South Africa.* New York: Urizen Books.

Tillema, H.K. 1991. *International Armed Conflict Since 1945: A Bibliographic Handbook of Wars and Military Interventions.* Boulder: Westview.

1.33 Uganda–Tanzania: Postcoup Border Clashes January 1971–October 1972

In January 1971 Major General Idi Amin ousted A. Milton Obote in a military coup. Obote had been Uganda's leader since its independence from Britain in 1962. During Amin's subsequent reign of terror, about 300,000 Ugandans were killed, and the country's Asian community of about 80,000 was expelled. Obote and his supporters fled to Tanzania and with that country's compliance conducted cross-border raids in an effort to destabilize Amin's new government. Tanzania refused to recognize the Amin regime altogether. Starting in August 1971 Tanzanian regulars participated in these cross-border raids, and Uganda retaliated. Both states closed their borders and conducted a number of air strikes on each other's territory.

Intensive mediation efforts by Kenya led to a resumption in diplomatic communications between the two countries in November 1971, and the conflict was considered settled. As many as 200 Ugandan and Tanzanian military personnel are reported to have died in the fighting. This conflict was a precursor to more grievous wars later on (*see* conflicts 1.41; 1.46; 1.49).

References

Avirgan, T., and M. Honey. 1982. *War in Uganda: The Legacy of Idi Amin.* Westport, Conn.: Lawrence Hill.

Hooper, E., and L. Pirouet. 1989. *Uganda.* Minority Rights Group Report #66. London: Minority Rights Group.

Mittleman, J. 1975. *Ideology and Politics in Uganda.* Ithaca, N.Y.: Cornell University Press.

Nnoli, O. 1978. *Self-Reliance and Foreign Policy in Tanzania: The Dynamics of the Diplomacy of a New State, 1961 to 1971.* New York: NOK.

Smith, G. 1980. *Ghosts of Kampala.* New York: St. Martin's.

Tillema, H.K. 1991. *International Armed Conflict Since 1945: A Bibliographic Handbook of Wars and Military Interventions.* Boulder: Westview.

1.34 Equatorial Guinea–Gabon: Territorial Dispute over the Corisco Bay Islands June–November 1972

In 1900 France and Spain, the colonial powers, respectively, of Gabon and Equatorial Guinea, signed a treaty assigning the small islands in Corisco Bay to Equatorial Guinea. Neither country had established an official presence on the islands; nor had they ever worried over issues of sovereignty. Following Gabon's independence in 1960, Gabonese fishermen frequently used the islands for shelter.

This situation changed in 1972, however, when traces of oil were found in the area. In an effort to preempt Gabonese actions, Equatorial Guinea, then on the eve of achieving full independence from Spain, asserted its claims to the islands. Its military units began attacking the Gabonese fishing camps in September 1972, and Gabon referred the issue to the United Nations. Equatorial Guinea responded that Gabon had invaded the islands.

A propaganda war began, as did a number of serious firing incidents. President Mobutu Sésé Séko of Zaire and President Marien Ngouabi of Congo sought to mediate the dispute in September, finally gaining agreement between the parties on November 13, 1972. The two sides agreed to "neutralize" the disputed islands, but tensions abated only gradually. Approximately twenty fatalities were reported during the conflict.

References

Africa Contemporary Record. Annual. 1968/1969– .

African Recorder. Weekly. 1962– .

Day, A., ed. 1987. *Border and Territorial Disputes.* 2d edition. Burnt Mill, Harlow (Essex), England: Longman.

1.35 Ethiopia–Somalia: Somali Expansionism, Territorial Dispute, and the Second Ogaden War Mid-1972–1985

Successive Somali regimes claimed territory that was occupied by Somali tribes but belonged to other states—a practice that had already led to armed conflict with Kenya in 1962–1967 and a war with Ethiopia over the Ogaden region in 1964 (*see* conflicts 1.13; 1.17).

The second Ogaden war began in mid-1972, when Somali tribesmen in the region resumed their revolt. At the same time Somali regulars again began to fight alongside the rebels, and a low-intensity conflict began. The war escalated in June 1972, when Somalia launched combat operations, a precursor to invasion the following month. The fighting was fierce, but Somalia began to make headway. Five years later, by October 1977, it had occupied the entire Ogaden area.

With the aid of Soviet military hardware and troop support from Cuba and South Yemen, Ethiopia launched a massive counterattack and by March 1978 had retaken the region. Intermittent border clashes occurred in the ensuing years, but the conflict did not escalate again to the level seen in 1977 and 1978. Upwards of 30,000 people died in the conflict, and, when fighting died down in 1985, the territorial dispute still had not been fully addressed. Tensions between the two states remained high, and armed conflict over the Ogaden region broke out again in 1987–1988 (*see* conflict 1.64).

References

Doornbos, M.B., ed. 1992. *Beyond Conflict in the Horn: Prospects for Peace, Recovery, and Development in Ethiopia, Somalia, and the Sudan.* Trenton, N.J.: Red Sea.

Farer, T. 1979. *War Clouds on the Horn of Africa: The Widening Storm.* 2d revised edition. New York: Carnegie Endowment for International Peace.

Fukin, K., and J. Markakis, eds. 1994. *Ethnicity and Conflict in the Horn of Africa.* Athens: Ohio University Press.

Gorman, R. 1981. *Political Conflict on the Horn of Africa.* New York: Praeger.

Nzongola-Ntalaja, G., ed. 1991. *Conflict in the Horn of Africa.* Atlanta: African Studies Association Press.

Tillema, H.K. 1991. *International Armed Conflict Since 1945: A Bibliographic Handbook of Wars and Military Interventions.* Boulder: Westview.

1.36 Morocco–Mauritania: Saharan Nationalism, Territorial Dispute, and the Western Saharan Conflict October 1974–Ongoing

Since independence in 1956, Morocco claimed the large expanse of desert to its south. Spain had controlled the territory, known as Western Sahara, since the nineteenth century, and, when it decided to withdraw in 1975, it conceded the area to Morocco and Mauritania for partition despite an International Court of Justice (ICJ) ruling that neither state possessed an enforceable claim to the area. While Spanish troops withdrew, both states occupied the area militarily.

The indigenous Saharan nationalist organization, Polisario (Frente Popular para la Liberatión de Saguia el-Hamra y Rio de Oro), which was initially formed to resist Spanish rule, promptly began attacking Moroccan and Mauritanian forces. Polisario was backed by Algeria, and Algerian troops intervened in the conflict in January 1976, clashing with Moroccan troops. Morocco had to deploy thousands of troops to Mauritania in July 1977, when Polisario began attacking targets within Mauritanian territory. France increased its military aid to Morocco and even engaged in air attacks against Polisario bases in Mauritania in December 1977.

In 1979 Mauritania abandoned the territory it held in Western Sahara because of the heavy costs involved in maintaining a presence there, and Morocco attempted to occupy the entire area. Serious fighting continued in the region throughout the 1980s. Despite Moroccan attempts to prevent infiltration across the Algerian frontier, the conflict often spilled into neighboring states because Moroccan forces pursued the rebels into Mauritania and Algeria. Polisario also began attacking targets in Moroccan territory.

Neither side has been able to achieve a significant advantage, and tens of thousands of deaths have occurred throughout the conflict; by 1989 Morocco had sustained nearly 10,000 military fatalities. Dozens of mediation attempts and numerous negotiations have addressed this conflict, but no lasting solution has been found. An agreement to hold a referendum on the status of the area in 1992 under UN auspices was postponed several times because of disagreements between Morocco and Polisario and problems with the UN voter identification operation. The level of fighting abated due to an agreement signed in 1991.

Because of the continuing disagreement between the parties regarding voter eligibility, the UN-sponsored peace process practically came to a halt, and the voter registration process for the proposed referendum was formally suspended in May 1996. In 1997 new peace talks between the two parties resulted in a series of agreements over criteria for voter eligibility, and a new deadline for the referendum was set. The lack of progress in drawing up a voters' list for the referendum has, however, resulted in widespread pessimism regarding the peace process.

Morocco's continuing demands have been interpreted as a lack of sincerity in its commitment to grant the right to self-determination to the original inhabitants of the Western Sahara. In spite of Morocco's stated support of the peace process and the high financial costs of its military deployment in the territory, it seems to hold to its position that the Western Sahara is historically part of its territory, and Polisario is seen as an illegitimate group of secessionist terrorists. Public statements by Moroccan officials, including King Muhammad VI, stressing that Morocco will never surrender the Western Sahara, cast further doubts over the kingdom's intention to let a referendum determine the final status of the territory.

Consequently, Polisario has repeatedly stated its disappointment with the peace process and indirectly threatened to resume its armed struggle "to defend [the Sahrawis'] right to self-determination and independence" should Morocco ultimately fail to carry out its commitments under the agreements it has signed. There is little optimism about the future of the current negotiations. The continuing failure to hold a free and fair referendum increases the likelihood that armed conflict will resume. Victims of the conflict include 120,000 Sahrawi refugees that remain trapped in the camps of Tindouf in Algeria and Moroccan prisoners of war held in Sahrawi prisons.

References

Day, A., ed. 1987. *Border and Territorial Disputes.* 2d edition. Burnt Mill, Harlow (Essex), England: Longman.

Gillespie, J. 1960. *Algeria, Rebellion, and Revolution.* New York: Praeger.

Leenders, Reinoud. 2002. *European Platform for Conflict Prevention and Transformation Online.* Country Surveys: www.euconflict.org/euconflict/guides/surveys.htm (March 9, 2002).

Tillema, H.K. 1991. *International Armed Conflict Since 1945: A Bibliographic Handbook of Wars and Military Interventions.* Boulder: Westview.

Trout, F. 1969. *Morocco's Saharan Frontiers.* Geneva: Droz.

1.37 Mali–Upper Volta (Burkina Faso): Territorial and Resource Dispute December 1974–June 1975

Mali and Upper Volta (after 1984, Burkina Faso or "Land of the Upright People") gained their independence in 1960. France's 1919 demarcation of the colony of Upper Volta was overturned in 1932 and reinstated in

1947, which led to a dispute over the border area with Mali. The contested area contained a chain of pools through which flowed the Belì River—the region's only source of fresh water. Regular talks on the disputed territory since 1961 failed to resolve the issue, leading to tensions between the two states.

A crisis in relations occurred in December 1974, when armed clashes broke out. A Malian patrol attacked Upper Voltan troops on December 14, 1974, near the village of Gasselago in Upper Volta. This incident was followed by further hostilities and arrests, and military operations intensified from December 1974 to June 1975. Few fatalities resulted from these encounters, but tensions were extremely high.

Ivory Coast, Senegal, and Guinea attempted to mediate the conflict. This effort failed, but an appeal to the president of the Organization of African Unity (OAU) resulted in the establishment of a mediation commission consisting of Guinea, Niger, Senegal, and Togo to guarantee safety in the disputed territory and supervise troop withdrawal. A final agreement to the border dispute was achieved in Lomé on June 18, 1975, mediated by the presidents of the commission nations and the OAU. The agreement recommended an independent demarcation of the common frontier. This recommendation did not resolve the issue, and a more serious armed conflict broke out in 1985–1986 (*see* conflict 1.61).

References

Brownlie, I. 1963. *African Boundaries: A Legal and Diplomatic Encyclopedia.* Berkeley and Los Angeles: University of California Press.

Day, A., ed. 1987. *Border and Territorial Disputes.* 2d edition. Burnt Mill, Harlow (Essex), England: Longman.

Folz, W.J. 1965. *From French West Africa to the Mali Federation.* New Haven: Yale University Press.

LeVine, V.T. 1967. *Political Leadership in Africa: Postindependence Generational Conflict in Upper Volta, Senegal, Niger, Dahomey, and the Central African Republic.* Stanford, Calif.: Hoover.

Sankara, T. 1988. *Thomas Sankara Speaks: The Burkina Faso Revolution, 1983–1987.* Translated by S. Anderson. New York: Pathfinder.

Talbott, J. 1980. *The War Without a Name: France in Algeria, 1954–1962.* New York: Knopf.

1.38 Angola–South Africa: Guerrilla Warfare in Namibia, Intervention, and Angolan Civil War 1975–Ongoing

The conflict between Angola and South Africa, provoked in the main by Angolan government support for Namibian independence, represented an extension of the conflict that had engulfed the region since the early 1960s. During Portugal's withdrawal from Angola in 1975, civil war erupted among the three rival nationalist organizations that had earlier been fighting for Angolan independence. These were the União Nacional para a Independência Total de Angola or UNITA (Union for the Total Independence of Angola), which was supported by South Africa and the United States and in control of most of southern Angola; the Soviet-backed Movimento Popular de Libertação de Angola (MPLA), which held the capital, Luanda, and parts of the south; and the Frente Nacional de Libertação de Angola (FNLA), backed by Zaire (Congo) and in control of the north.

The FNLA and UNITA both launched offensives in 1975 in an attempt to gain control of Luanda. By October of that year, the pressure on the MPLA brought Cuban troops into the war at the instigation of the Soviet Union. The MPLA soon gained enough of an advantage to declare itself the sole government of Angola. The FNLA was defeated, and the UNITA forces retreated and began a long-term guerrilla war against the MPLA government.

Angola came into direct fighting with South Africa in 1976 after it joined Zambia in declaring support for the South West African People's Organization (SWAPO), which was fighting a guerrilla war of independence in Namibia. For the next decade Angola and South Africa clashed regularly when the apartheid government lent support to UNITA, or pursued SWAPO guerrillas into their bases in Angola.

In 1987 and 1988 the war escalated when South Africa invaded Angola, and Angola counterattacked with Cuban troop support. In June 1987 MPLA and Cuban forces surrounded a large South African force within Angola. South Africa was subsequently forced to agree to remove its forces from Angola by mid-1988, and UN mediation efforts, which had punctuated the entire conflict, achieved a cease-fire on August 22, 1988. Subsequent negotiations led to an agreement providing for Namibian independence and South Africa's withdrawal from Angola.

The civil war in Angola continued until the 1990s, however, when mediation secured an agreement to hold multiparty elections and to lay down arms. UNITA lost the 1992 elections by narrow margins and immediately went back to war. The fighting was so intense and vicious in 1993 that the United Nations declared it the worst war then being waged, estimating that 1,000 people per day were dying as a direct result of the conflict.

The fighting continued throughout 1994, despite desperate diplomatic efforts by the United Nations and states in the region. In November 1994 government forces took Huambo, UNITA's headquarters and center of support. At the same time, a new peace process began, culminating in the signing of the Lusaka Protocol in Lusaka, Zambia. The agreement covered (among other issues) mutual troop withdrawal and quartering, making the country safe for ordinary citizens, and reconciliation. The United Nations made intense efforts throughout

1995 to consolidate the Lusaka agreement. Although meetings between UNITA leader Jonas Savimbi and President José Eduardo dos Santos suggested the war was over, the peace was still extremely fragile. Throughout the process, it was frequently alleged that UNITA was intent on stalling the peace process, withholding troops, and stockpiling arms. UNITA incurred the wrath of the United Nations, which imposed sanctions in October 1997. Meanwhile, the MPLA-dominated government went on an arms-buying spree, mortgaging its future oil revenues to pay its arms suppliers and seriously compromising Angola's future development. Cease-fire violations continued throughout this period.

Between 1996 and late 1998, the continuous unraveling of the peace process reached its inevitable conclusion. The government attempted to isolate UNITA militarily, politically, and diplomatically. In addition, it became clear that UNITA had been lying about its compliance with the terms of the Lusaka Protocol. By June 1998 fighting had already seriously intensified in several provinces, displacing tens of thousands of people. Violent recruitment by both parties resurfaced, sending thousands more across Angola's borders. UNITA recaptured territory it had previously returned to the government, and the Angolan army launched a number of heavy attacks on UNITA positions. Roads and other areas were re-mined. In December 1998 the Angolan army launched a major offensive in the center of the country, marking the beginning of the third civil war.

Since then the war has moved from a series of all-out conventional battles to another bush war. In early 1999 UNITA laid siege to several provincial centers and conducted a rural depopulation campaign, committing terrible atrocities against "their own people" in Central Angola. An estimated 1 million people were forcibly removed. They fled to the cities, turning them into death traps as a result of food shortages, disease, and UNITA shelling. In the second half of 1999, the situation changed. The government, fueled by another round of arms buying and supported by new allies Great Britain and the United States, reversed UNITA's initial gains, and in October it took hold of rebel strongholds in the highlands. UNITA has been in considerable disarray ever since, although it continues to wreak havoc.

The war also began to spread to Angola's neighbors. Areas inside the Democratic Republic of Congo—the former Zaire—had always been drawn into the Angola conflict, but in early 2000 it became clear that Namibia was also becoming part of the war zone. The Namibian government had allowed Angolan government forces to operate from its territory, prompting UNITA to declare Namibian collaborators legitimate targets. In January 2000 the world's attention was drawn to the violence in Namibia when three French tourists were killed there.

The prospects for resolution of the conflict in Angola are poor; the war is likely to drag on with no apparent benefit to anyone. The humanitarian disaster continues unabated. The renewed hostilities have displaced large numbers of people, and at the end of 2000 an estimated 400,000 Angolans were refugees in neighboring countries, while 5,000 sought asylum in Europe. Between 1 million and 3.5 million people are internally displaced in Angola, according to various estimates. Up to 1.5 million lives may have been lost during the last quarter century of fighting, many of them civilians.

References

Bender, G.J. 1978. *Angola Under the Portuguese: The Myth and the Reality.* London: Heinemann.

Birmingham, D. 1992. *Frontline Nationalism in Angola and Mozambique.* London: J. Currey.

Bruce, N. 1975. *Portugal: The Last Empire.* New York: Wiley.

Burchett, W. 1978. *Southern Africa Stands Up: The Revolutions in Angola, Mozambique, Zimbabwe, Namibia, and South Africa.* New York: Urizen Books.

Harsch, E., and T. Thomas. 1976. *Angola: The Hidden History of Washington's War.* New York: Pathfinder.

Humbaraci, A., and N. Muchnik. 1974. *Portugal's African Wars: Angola, Guinea-Bissau, Mozambique.* New York: Third Press.

Kitchen, H.A., ed. 1987. *Angola, Mozambique, and the West.* Washington Papers #130. New York: CSIS/Praeger.

Posthumus, B. 2000. *European Platform for Conflict Prevention and Transformation Online.* Country Surveys: www.euconflict.org/euconflict/guides/surveys.htm (March 9, 2002).

Tillema, H.K. 1991. *International Armed Conflict Since 1945: A Bibliographic Handbook of Wars and Military Interventions.* Boulder: Westview.

1.39 Zaire–Angola: Rebel Activity and Border War
November 1975–February 1976

This particular conflict grew out of Angola's civil war, which broke out on the eve of that country's independence from Portugal in November 1975. The fighting was primarily between the Soviet-backed Movimento Popular de Libertação de Angola (MPLA) government and right-wing rebel factions, including the Union for the Total Independence of Angola (UNITA) and the Frente Nacional de Libertação de Angola (FNLA). President Mobutu Sésé Séko of Zaire had been supporting the right-wing factions for some time—mostly in a cold war gambit to secure Western aid (*see* conflict 1.38).

Once civil war erupted, Zaire openly sided with FNLA-UNITA forces, and substantial U.S. aid began flowing into FNLA coffers through Zaire. By November 6, 1975, at least two battalions of regular Zairean troops were supporting FNLA forces advancing on Luanda.

Fighting was also fierce near Angola's oil-rich coastal enclave of Cabinda, near the mouth of the Congo River. Zairean troops began massing on the border. As a result of the continuing hostilities and foreign aid (especially through Zaire), Mobutu, Emperor Jean-Bédel Bokassa of Central African Republic, and President Idi Amin of Uganda met in Bangui on January 1, 1976. This meeting called for the formation of a government of national unity in Angola to prevent foreign troops from passing through their countries to Angola and to end the international intervention in the civil war.

By mid-January Zaire threatened to declare open war on the MPLA after claiming that it had attacked Zairean border positions. It lodged a protest with the United Nations, alleging that Cuban troops had been involved in the MPLA bombing of the Zairean border town of Dilolo. The United States and the Organization of African Unity (OAU) made mediation attempts, but they ended in deadlock, as Zaire continued to refuse to recognize the MPLA government in Angola. Also, calls for a cease-fire were rejected because the MPLA claimed its aim was to drive the FNLA back into Zaire.

By February Zaire still refused to recognize the MPLA government, despite OAU recognition. Eventually, mediation by Congo produced a settlement. The fighting subsided, and relations were soon normalized. An estimated 500 fatalities occurred during the fighting. Further armed conflict broke out again in 1978 as a result of Zairean support for Angolan rebels and ongoing tensions between the two states (*see* conflict 1.45).

References

Biebuyck, D., and M. Douglas. 1961. *Congo Tribes and Parties*. London: Royal Anthropological Institute.

Birmingham, D. 1992. *Frontline Nationalism in Angola and Mozambique*. London: J. Currey.

Epstein, H., ed. 1965. *Revolt in Congo, 1960–1964*. New York: Facts on File.

Harsch, E., and T. Thomas. 1976. *Angola: The Hidden History of Washington's War*. New York: Pathfinder.

Kalb, M. 1982. *The Congo Crisis: The Cold War in Africa from Eisenhower to Kennedy*. New York: Macmillan.

Tillema, H.K. 1991. *International Armed Conflict Since 1945: A Bibliographic Handbook of Wars and Military Interventions*. Boulder: Westview.

1.40 Mozambique–South Africa: African Nationalism, Intervention, and Civil War 1976–October 1992

Mozambique, on the southeastern coast of Africa, was one of Portugal's overseas territories. Rebels launched a war of independence in 1964, and by the 1970s guerrilla forces controlled much of the country. Mozambique gained its independence following the 1974 overthrow of the Portuguese government. By this time Mozambican nationalists had split into two main groups—the Soviet-backed Mozambique Liberation Front (Frelimo), operating in the north, and the right-wing Mozambique National Resistance Movement (Renamo), controlling the south. Samora Moïses Machel, Frelimo's leader, assumed control of the country as president of the Marxist regime, nationalized the land, and supervised the departure of the country's 220,000 whites. Frelimo's efforts to integrate Renamo into the new government failed.

In 1976 full-scale civil war broke out between the new regime and the Renamo rebels. South Africa assisted the rebels, and the Frelimo government returned the favor by joining forces with its newly independent neighbors—Botswana, Tanzania, and Zambia—to form the so-called frontline states, which were devoted to overturning white rule in the region. Mozambique therefore served as a base of operations for rebels from the ANC (African National Congress) and ZANU (Zimbabwe African People's Organization) fighting white rule in South Africa and Rhodesia.

Although South Africa provided only covert support for Renamo in the early years of the war, open warfare between the two countries became more common in the 1980s. In the early 1980s Zimbabwe committed thousands of troops to fight the South African-backed Renamo rebels, as did Tanzania and Malawi. South Africa invaded and bombed ANC camps in Mozambique on a number of occasions, and there were numerous border incidents. Despite a 1984 nonaggression pact (the Nkomati accord) between South Africa and Mozambique, Mozambique continued to allege South African support for Renamo, and fighting flared periodically into the late 1980s.

The fighting was intense throughout the war, and beginning in the early 1980s Renamo began to target Mozambique's economic infrastructure. This led directly to a number of serious famines beginning in 1985. The collapse of the Soviet Union and the subsequent loss of aid to the Frelimo government created pressure for a settlement. From 1989 to the end of 1991 numerous mediation attempts led to some short-lived cease-fires and various settlements. In March 1991 a protocol was signed paving the way for multiparty elections.

The fighting ceased at the end of 1992, and the parties made tentative moves to end the war and hold elections, although the situation remained tense. Further talks into 1994 saw a peaceful, but strained, transition and successful elections in which Frelimo won a majority. It is thought that the war cost almost 1 million lives, many of them civilians who fell to hunger and disease because of Renamo's deliberate policies of economic and infrastructural destruction. In the 1990s the United Nations ranked Mozambique as one of the poorest countries in the world.

References

Birmingham, D. 1992. *Frontline Nationalism in Angola and Mozambique.* London: J. Currey.

Bruce, N. 1975. *Portugal: The Last Empire.* New York: Wiley.

Burchett, W. 1978. *Southern Africa Stands Up: The Revolutions in Angola, Mozambique, Zimbabwe, Namibia, and South Africa.* New York: Urizen Books.

Hanlon, J. 1984. *Mozambique: The Revolution Under Fire.* London: Zed.

Humbaraci, A., and N. Muchnik. 1974. *Portugal's African Wars: Angola, Guinea-Bissau, Mozambique.* New York: Third Press.

Kitchen, H. A., ed. 1987. *Angola, Mozambique, and the West.* Washington Papers #130. New York: CSIS/Praeger.

Tillema, H. K. 1991. *International Armed Conflict Since 1945: A Bibliographic Handbook of Wars and Military Interventions.* Boulder: Westview.

1.41 Uganda–Kenya: Amin Provocations and Border Incidents February–August 1976

In 1971 Major General Idi Amin led a military coup that ousted Ugandan president A. Milton Obote, setting the stage for a brutal and unpredictable regime that by 1977 had led to the deaths of 300,000 Ugandans and the deportation of the country's Asian community. In addition to plunging his own nation into chaos, Amin destabilized the entire region (*see* conflict 1.33).

This particular conflict began in February 1976, when Amin claimed that part of Kenya (and Sudan) was historically Ugandan territory. He demanded an explanation from the British government about areas of Uganda "illegally" transferred to Kenya from 1894 to 1902, further stating he did not want to go to war with Kenya, but would fight to protect Uganda's access to the sea.

Incidents over the next few months included Ugandan raids on Kenyan villages in border areas. An increase in anti-Kenyan propaganda broadcasts, expulsions, and political killings led to a rapid deterioration in relations between the two states. The situation worsened with word that the United States and Britain were providing Kenya with military aid; Libya was said to be assisting Uganda. There were also reports of the massing of troops on the borders.

The dispute intensified on July 8, 1976, when it was announced that Uganda would have to use Kenyan currency at the port of Mombasa, the principal gateway for Ugandan trade. Calling this action a deliberate economic blockade, Amin cut off supplies of electricity to Kenya. Tensions were high, and observers feared that Amin might do something desperate.

The dispute was settled through negotiations between government ministers of Kenya and Uganda in the presence of Eteki Mboumosa, secretary-general of the Organization of African Unity (OAU). A statement was issued on August 6, 1976, in Nairobi, and approved by Amin and Kenyan president Jomo Kenyatta on August 7. More than forty people were killed during the incidents. Fighting recurred between Uganda and Kenya in 1987 and 1989 (*see* conflicts 1.67; 1.70).

References

Avirgan, T., and M. Honey. 1982. *War in Uganda: The Legacy of Idi Amin.* Westport, Conn.: Lawrence Hill.

Hooper, E., and L. Pirouet. 1989. *Uganda.* Minority Rights Group Report #66. London: Minority Rights Group.

Mittleman, J. 1975. *Ideology and Politics in Uganda.* Ithaca, N.Y.: Cornell University Press.

Smith, G. 1980. *Ghosts of Kampala.* New York: St. Martin's.

1.42 Chad–Libya: Guerrilla Warfare, Factional Fighting, and Libyan Annexation of the Aozou Strip June 1976–November 1979

Tensions between Chad and Libya along their common border had existed for a number of years. Libya's active support for the Muslim factions in northern Chad greatly exacerbated friction between the Muslim Arab north and the politically dominant black African south. The population in the south consisted of Kirdi, or pagan people. (*Pagan* is a broad, collective name for a number of groups living in northern Cameroon, southeastern Nigeria, and southwestern Chad. At one time, all of these groups were truly pagan. Today, some of them are Muslim, Christian, or animist.) On October 10, 1976, Chad closed its border with Libya, citing Libya's "equivocal attitude" toward the Front de Libération Nationale du Tchad (FROLINAT), a rebel group operating in northern Chad under the leadership of Dr. Abba Sidick.

In fact, Libya had been actively supporting FROLINAT, and its September 1976 annexation of the uranium-rich Aozou strip in northern Chad further fueled the conflict. President Félix Malloum of Chad declared there would be no cooperation with Libya until it had withdrawn from the Aozou strip. Hostilities were reported in June 1977 between Libyan and Chadian forces in northern Chad; it was also alleged that Libya had armed and aided rebels in the region with the intention of setting up a puppet state. Chad appealed to the Organization of African Unity (OAU) to use its authority to restore Chad's rights in the Aozou strip. An early 1978 cease-fire between Chad troops and the rebels failed, and Chad and Libya suspended diplomatic relations in February 1978.

Relations between the two countries improved later that month as a result of Sudanese mediation, when a cease-fire was reached and diplomatic relations resumed.

In March France sent 1,000 troops to Chad, allegedly on training exercises but in reality to prevent a Libyan invasion. In June Chad stated that Libya had invaded in the north, advancing all the way down to the central provinces of Kanem, Batha, and Ouadai. Other Libyan offensives were reported in April and June 1979, but the Libyan troops were repulsed and retreated after heavy fighting. At this time, the Chadian rebel groups that Muammar Qaddafi had been supporting turned against Libya and demanded the return of the Aozou strip.

Libya continued to intervene periodically on the side of various Chadian rebels in the civil war, but from late 1979, the new Chadian government and Libya had friendly relations, and the conflict abated. Approximately 250 people were killed in the fighting. Libya took a close interest in Chadian affairs, however, and once again intervened after a change of government and a renewed outbreak of fighting in 1982 (*see* conflict 1.51).

References

Atlapedia. 2004. "Countries A to Z: Chad." http://www.atlapedia.com/online/countries/chad.htm.

Bethany World Prayer Center. 2004. "The Unreached People's Prayer Profiles: Prayer Profile—The Kirdi of North Central Africa, a cluster of 11 closely related groups in 3 countries." http://www.ksafe.com/profiles/clusters/8047.html.

Day, A., ed. 1987. *Border and Territorial Disputes.* 2d edition. Burnt Mill, Harlow (Essex), England: Longman.

Decalo, S. 1976. *Coups and Army Rule in Africa: Studies in Military Style.* New Haven: Yale University Press.

Kelley, M. 1986. *A State in Disarray: Conditions of Chad's Survival.* Boulder: Westview.

Thompson, V.B., and R. Adloff. 1981. *Conflict in Chad.* Berkeley: Institute of International Studies, University of California.

Tillema, H.K. 1991. *International Armed Conflict Since 1945: A Bibliographic Handbook of Wars and Military Interventions.* Boulder: Westview.

Whiteman, K. 1988. *Chad.* Minority Rights Group Report #80. London: Minority Rights Group.

World Flags. 2004. "Chad." http://world-flags.info/Africa/chad.html.

1.43 Zaire–Angola: Internal Dissension, Regional Instability, and the First Invasion of Shaba
March–May 1977

Civil war broke out in Angola immediately upon independence in 1975, as rival factions vied for control of the government. The Soviet-backed Movimento Popular de Libertação de Angola (MPLA), supported by Cuban troops, emerged victorious after a year of fighting. Zaire's right-wing regime immediately started to support factions fighting Angola's Communist government, straining relations between the two countries.

Relations between Zaire and Angola were normalized in January 1977 when Zaire offered formal recognition of President António Agostinho Neto's government. They agreed that no military activities would be permitted against each other in their territories. Angola repeated allegations, however, that Frente Nacional de Libertação de Angola (FNLA) rebels were training in Zaire for war against the government. Zaire claimed these people were only refugees.

Tensions came to a head on March 8, 1977, when a rebel army led by Lieutenant General Nathanael Mbumba invaded Shaba (formerly Katanga) from Angolan territory. Mbumba, a Katangan rebel, claimed the aim of the invasion was not to sabotage Zaire's mineral production (the southern province was rich in cobalt and copper mines) but to depose President Mobutu Sésé Séko and form a government of national unity. Zaire accused Angola of being a Cuban-Soviet pawn by aiding the invasion force, but Angola denied any involvement. On March 11 the Congolese National Liberation Front (FLNC)—an opposition group made up of the remnants of Katangan (Shaba) rebels who fled Zaire after the civil war—claimed responsibility for the invasion, saying it was a popular national uprising.

Exercising his penchant for using outside forces to put down revolts, Mobutu immediately called for assistance from other African states and the United States and Belgium, which resulted in the stationing of 1,500 Moroccan troops in Zaire. In March and April, Nigeria attempted to reconcile differences between the two countries and end the invasion. Meanwhile, suspicions of Cuban and Soviet involvement in the invasion continued. As a result of rebel advances into Zaire, Mobutu appealed to the Organization of African Unity (OAU) for help in driving the Socialist invaders out of Zaire. A joint Zairean-Moroccan force was approved and, with the diplomatic backing of other countries (Egypt, Saudi Arabia, Sudan, Togo, and Uganda), gradually advanced in the face of the retreating rebels, with few fatalities.

In May 1977 the rebel forces retreated farther into Angola, and Zairean and Moroccan troops recaptured lost territory and ended the invasion. In early June all foreign forces, having completed their mission, returned to their countries. About 1,000 people were killed during the invasion. Identical invasions by Zairean rebels operating from foreign territory recurred in 1978, 1984, and 1985 (*see* conflicts 1.45; 1.59; 1.60).

References

Birmingham, D. 1992. *Frontline Nationalism in Angola and Mozambique.* London: J. Currey.

Harsch, E., and T. Thomas. 1976. *Angola: The Hidden History of Washington's War.* New York: Pathfinder.

Tillema, H.K. 1991. *International Armed Conflict Since 1945: A Bibliographic Handbook of Wars and Military Interventions.* Boulder: Westview.

1.44 Chad: Internal Strife, Foreign Intervention, and the Second Chad Civil War January 1978–June 1982

Following Chad's independence from France in 1960, fighting broke out between the Muslim north and the politically dominant south, which was primarily black Christian. Tensions grew throughout the 1960s and 1970s, with Libya and the Chadian government having already been involved in an armed conflict in 1976 (*see* conflict 1.42). On January 28–29, 1978, armed conflict erupted when the Front de Libération Nationale du Tchad (FROLINAT), a Libyan-backed rebel group, attacked government troops in the town of Faya-Largeau. Hostilities continued through February, and all sides ignored calls for a cease-fire. Renewed tensions between Libya and Chad hampered mediation efforts, and a number of negotiations between some of the warring parties failed.

March and April 1978 brought French military involvement in support of the Chadian government. This move was partly a response to fears of a Libyan invasion. Government troops and rebels engaged in sporadic fighting, and France stepped up its intervention in central and east Chad, while Libya increased its support for the northern rebels. Talks on national unity broke down in early July 1978, and, despite the formation in August of an interim government, hostilities continued with increasing severity.

The remainder of 1978 and early 1979 saw a deterioration in relations between Chadian president Félix Malloum N'Gakoutou and his prime minister Hissène Habré, a former rebel leader, as well as dissent among different rebel factions. Fighting in the north was predominantly between Muslim Arab guerrilla forces and troops of the national army, the Forces armées tchadiennes (FAT), loyal to President Malloum, who represented black Christian or animist southerners.

In February 1979 renewed hostilities between the president's troops and rebel groups engulfed Ndjamena, the capital of Chad. Neighboring countries attempted to reconcile the opposing sides in a series of meetings in Nigeria. In late August the parties signed the Lagos accord, which established a transitional government of national unity comprising all eleven factions under the leadership of Goukouni Oueddei, a former rebel from the north; Malloum and Habré had resigned their posts in March 1979. The 1979 accord broke down in March 1980, with the onset of fierce fighting in Ndjamena.

Previous conflict in the civil war had been along religious and regional lines, but it now involved rival northern groups struggling for supremacy in the new government. The main protagonists were Oueddei's rebel group, Forces armées populaires (FAP), and Habré's faction, Forces armées du nord (FAN). Fighting continued throughout 1980 with 5,000 to 6,000 deaths and severe infrastructural damage. The Organization of African Unity (OAU) made many unsuccessful attempts to reconcile the rival factions. The situation changed in late 1980 with large-scale Libyan intervention. Together with Libyan and OAU support, President Oueddei's FAP forced FAN to retreat. By this stage France was withdrawing its troops from the country.

Early in 1981 Chad and Libya announced their intention to merge the two countries, but mounting internal opposition to Libyan troops in Chad resulted in their withdrawal by November. In an attempt to contain internal strife and encourage stability, the OAU sent in a peacekeeping force in November and December 1981, but it was completely ineffectual. The coalition government was too fragile. Habré's FAN took the capital in June 1982. Despite this defeat, hostilities persisted, and further OAU proposals for a cease-fire, draft constitution, and elections were disrupted by continued fighting between government and FAN forces.

After Libya withdrew from areas in Chad, FAN progressively gained control of regions in eastern and northern Chad. Habré became head of state on June 19, 1982, and formed a new government. For the time, the opposition was defeated. As many as 9,000 people were killed during the conflict, including more than 300 Libyan troops and 9 French military personnel. Peace did not last long, however, and war broke out again almost immediately (*see* conflict 1.51).

References

Decalo, S. 1976. *Coups and Army Rule in Africa: Studies in Military Style.* New Haven: Yale University Press.

Kelley, M. 1986. *A State in Disarray: Conditions of Chad's Survival.* Boulder: Westview.

Somerville, K. 1990. *Foreign Military Intervention in Africa.* London: Pinter.

Thompson, V.B., and R. Adloff. 1981. *Conflict in Chad.* Berkeley: Institute of International Studies, University of California.

Tillema, H.K. 1991. *International Armed Conflict Since 1945: A Bibliographic Handbook of Wars and Military Interventions.* Boulder: Westview.

Whiteman, K. 1988. *Chad.* Minority Rights Group Report #80. London: Minority Rights Group.

1.45 Zaire–Angola: Regional Instability, Congolese Dissension, and the Second Invasion of Shaba May 1978

Relations between Zaire and Angola had been hostile for some time. President Mobutu Sésé Séko of Zaire opposed

Angola's Communist government, run by the Movimento Popular de Libertação de Angola (MPLA), and therefore permitted Angolan rebels to operate from his territory. In 1977 Angola returned the favor by supporting dissident Zairean forces in their invasion of Shaba province; at the time, this copper-rich southern province accounted for two-thirds of Zaire's foreign earnings. Shaba province had also figured prominently in the Congo crisis, when for several years powerful secessionist forces waged war against the central government (*see* conflict 1.10).

In May 1978 an invasion force of 4,000 rebels again entered the Shaba province from Angolan territory, this time in an attempt to gain control of the strategic copper- and cobalt-mining area and bring down the Mobutu government. The rebels, including many members of the local Lunda tribe, were again led by General Nathanael Mbumba and directed by the Congolese National Liberation Front (FLNC) (*see* conflict 1.43).

The invasion force reached the town of Kolwezi on May 11–12, 1978. Over the next ten days the rebels and uncontrolled Zairean army troops killed 200 French and Belgian nationals; 500 troops and civilians also died in the fighting. It was alleged that Algeria, Cuba, Libya, and the Soviet Union had met in Havana and Algiers to plan and support the rebel operation, code-named "Operation Dove." The parties involved later denied these allegations, even though Cuban troops did participate in the fighting in the town of Mutshatsha on May 14 against the Zairean army.

On May 14, 1978, the Zairean foreign minister asked the ambassadors of Belgium, China, France, Morocco, and the United States for assistance. Foreign nationals were then evacuated from Zaire, and the United States provided the country with fuel, equipment, and financial aid, but no personnel. On May 19 the French government sent a paratroop regiment of 800 from the Foreign Legion, along with Belgium paratroopers, to rescue trapped Europeans, and alongside the Zairean army, they took back the town of Kolwezi from the rebels.

The evacuation of foreign nationals was completed by May 22, and was followed by the withdrawal of the foreign troops, but rebel fighting continued. On May 27 the rebels were reported to have recaptured the town of Mutshatsha. In June the Angolan government ordered the disarming of the rebels and the pulling back of the FLNC rebels from the border area. The rebellion dissipated after this.

In late May, Mobutu, the European Community's Léo Tindemans, and French president Valéry Giscard d'Estaing proposed the formation of an "African corps," composed entirely of African troops, to keep peace in African countries. Mobutu, with Morocco's King Hassan II, set up the provision of troops to keep the peace in Shaba province starting in June 1978. There were no attempts at peaceful conflict management during the conflict. Approximately 1,000 people were killed in the fighting, many of them civilians. This conflict led to other invasions in 1984 and 1985 (*see* conflicts 1.59; 1.60).

References

Biebuyck, D., and M. Douglas. 1961. *Congo Tribes and Parties*. London: Royal Anthropological Institute.

Birmingham, D. 1992. *Frontline Nationalism in Angola and Mozambique*. London: J. Currey.

Harsch, E. 1978. *The Ethiopian Revolution*. New York: Pathfinder.

Kalb, M. 1982. *The Congo Crisis: The Cold War in Africa from Eisenhower to Kennedy*. New York: Macmillan.

Tillema, H.K. 1991. *International Armed Conflict Since 1945: A Bibliographic Handbook of Wars and Military Interventions*. Boulder: Westview.

1.46 Tanzania–Uganda: Cross-Border Raids, Tanzanian Invasion, and Ouster of the Amin Regime October 1978–May 1979

Relations between Tanzania and Uganda had been strained ever since General Idi Amin seized power from President A. Milton Obote in a 1971 military coup. Amin had repeatedly accused Tanzania of planning to invade the country to reinstate the former president. Indeed, after his ouster, Obote fled to Tanzania, where he started a destabilization campaign against the Amin regime. Furthermore, Tanzania had initially refused to recognize the Amin government.

This particular conflict began in early October 1978 with small Ugandan cross-border raids. In late October Ugandan troops occupied the "Kagera salient," an area between the Ugandan-Tanzanian border and the Kagera River. Tanzania viewed this move as tantamount to a declaration of war and staged a massive counterattack involving Tanzanian troops and exiled Ugandans opposed to Amin's regime. The cross-border fighting and bombing went on until late January 1979, when Tanzania launched a full-scale invasion deep into Uganda. By the end of March, fighting was focused on the capital, Entebbe, and even the dispatch of several hundred Libyan troops to aid Amin could not prevent the fall of the capital in April 1979.

The Amin regime and some surrounding states had appealed to the Organization of African Unity (OAU), the United Nations, and the Arab League, but to no avail. In November 1978 Kenya, Libya, and the OAU all extended offers of mediation, which were rejected. Attempts at negotiations and offers of withdrawals were similarly unsuccessful during December 1978 and January 1979. An OAU ad hoc committee on interstate conflict met on February 22, 1979, and suggested a cease-fire, but no agreement was reached. The OAU was subsequently asked to refrain from interfering in Ugandan affairs.

The anti-Amin Ugandan National Liberation Front (UNLF), an umbrella organization of Ugandan exiles, took control of Uganda after Entebbe fell and Amin fled the country. Tanzania officially recognized the new Ugandan government on April 12, and other African countries extended recognition on April 15. An estimated 3,500 people were killed during the conflict, including 1,000 Tanzanian military fatalities and at least 200 Libyan soldiers. Amin went to Saudi Arabia, and in late 1981 Uganda fell into total civil war (*see* conflict 1.49).

References

Avirgan, T., and M. Honey. 1982. *War in Uganda: The Legacy of Idi Amin.* Westport, Conn.: Lawrence Hill.

Hooper, E., and L. Pirouet. 1989. *Uganda.* Minority Rights Group Report #66. London: Minority Rights Group.

Mittleman, J. 1975. *Ideology and Politics in Uganda.* Ithaca, N.Y.: Cornell University Press.

Nnoli, O. 1978. *Self-Reliance and Foreign Policy in Tanzania: The Dynamics of the Diplomacy of a New State, 1961 to 1971.* New York: NOK.

Smith, G. 1980. *Ghosts of Kampala.* New York: St. Martin's.

Tillema, H.K. 1991. *International Armed Conflict Since 1945: A Bibliographic Handbook of Wars and Military Interventions.* Boulder: Westview.

1.47 Morocco–Algeria: Western Saharan Nationalism and Border Conflict June–October 1979

In 1979 Algeria and Morocco came into direct conflict over the issue of Western Sahara, which Morocco had claimed since 1974 (*see* conflict 1.36). Algerian-backed Western Saharan nationalists, calling themselves the Polisario Front (Frente Popular para la Liberatión de Saguia el-Hamra y Rio de Oro), had started a guerrilla war to gain independence for the territory. Beginning in June 1979, Polisario began attacking Moroccan territory itself, and Morocco threatened to attack Algeria in retaliation. Algeria warned against any violations of its border, and war seemed imminent.

Border incidents continued and, following a massive attack by Polisario in which 792 Moroccan troops were killed, Morocco began attacking Algerian territory. In September 1979 the conflict threatened to escalate when Egypt began shipping arms to Morocco and offered its full support. Although the conflict was referred to the Organization of African Unity (OAU), the group could do little to resolve the fighting. Algeria rejected Tunisia's offer to hold a summit on the issue. After October 1979 the fighting waned, and the conflict eventually subsided. Fighting in the Western Sahara continued without respite, however, into the 1990s. The status of Western Sahara has yet to be resolved.

References

Day, A., ed. 1987. *Border and Territorial Disputes.* 2d edition. Burnt Mill, Harlow (Essex), England: Longman.

Gillespie, J. 1960. *Algeria, Rebellion, and Revolution.* New York: Praeger.

Horne, A. 1987. *A Savage War of Peace: Algeria, 1954–1962.* Revised edition. New York: Penguin.

Tillema, H.K. 1991. *International Armed Conflict Since 1945: A Bibliographic Handbook of Wars and Military Interventions.* Boulder: Westview.

Trout, F. 1969. *Morocco's Saharan Frontiers.* Geneva: Droz.

1.48 Cameroon–Nigeria: Border Incident May–July 1981

A plebiscite in 1961 transferred parts of Cameroon's northern territories to Nigeria. Cameroon had never pressed any claim on the area. Another plebiscite gave to western Cameroon territory with Nigerian tribes living in it, despite some opposition from the tribes. Relations between Cameroon and Nigeria steadily deteriorated in early 1981 over these territorial issues, culminating in a border incident on May 15, when five Nigerian soldiers were killed and three wounded after a Cameroon patrol boat attacked the border area of the Akpa Yafi River. Nigeria called for effective military action against Cameroon and rejected the Cameroon government's apology and peace proposal. Nigeria demanded full reparations and spurned the suggestion of a joint commission of inquiry, preferring instead to seek international arbitration.

Over this period, Nigeria continued to call for military action against Cameroon, and each side accused the other of troop buildups. In mid-July 1981 Kenyan president Daniel arap Moi, who was the sitting president of the Organization of African Unity (OAU), successfully mediated an agreement between the parties. The agreement called for full compensation to the families of the Nigerian soldiers killed in the fighting and for the establishment of an international arbitration panel to examine the border question and to avoid further disputes. The panel failed to resolve the outstanding issues, however, and minor incidents and tensions continued to plague relations between Nigeria and Cameroon in later years (*see* conflict 1.80).

References

Brownlie, I. 1963. *African Boundaries: A Legal and Diplomatic Encyclopedia.* Berkeley and Los Angeles: University of California Press.

Day, A., ed. 1987. *Border and Territorial Disputes.* 2d edition. Burnt Mill, Harlow (Essex), England: Longman.

Touval, S. 1972. *The Boundary Politics of Independent Africa*. Cambridge: Harvard University Press.

1.49 Uganda: Civil War December 1981–1994

The 1971 military coup by Major General Idi Amin that ousted Ugandan president A. Milton Obote set the stage for a brutal and unpredictable regime that by 1977 had led to the deaths of 300,000 Ugandans and the expulsion of the country's entire Asian population (*see* conflict 1.33). In addition to plunging his own nation into chaos, Amin also managed to destabilize most of Central Africa.

Exiled opposition groups united under the banner of Obote's Ugandan National Liberation Front (UNLF). Backed by the Tanzanian army, Obote's group invaded Uganda in 1979 and deposed Amin, who then fled to Saudi Arabia to live in exile. As the Tanzanian army withdrew and the new Obote government began to establish itself, a number of disaffected groups undertook an antigovernment insurgency. Especially important was Yoweri Museveni's Uganda Patriotic Movement (UPM), later called the National Resistance Army (NRA). Many of these groups had been defeated in the national elections held after Amin's ouster. Moreover, claims of extensive human rights violations were made against the Obote government.

Within a few months, the country was engulfed in civil war. The fighting was intense, with rebel attacks on the military, police, government patrols, and industrial installations, in addition to assassinations and bombings. After mid-1983 the war reverted to an insurgency, although at various times the rebels maintained effective control over portions of the countryside and claimed to have established "administrations." This was especially true for Museveni's NRA, which by this time had become the strongest and most significant rebel group.

Throughout the fighting, reports persisted that Libya was providing aid to the rebels. Meanwhile, the Ugandan government remained in power with the help of Tanzanian and North Korean troops. The conflict was further complicated by the intervention of Amin loyalists backed by Zairean troops.

On July 27, 1985, Obote was deposed in a coup led by Bazilio Okello, the commander of the army's northern region. The new military government, headed by Okello, initiated negotiations in August 1985, and in December a power-sharing agreement was signed in Nairobi, Kenya. The agreement provided for an end to the civil war and the holding of elections.

The agreement was never implemented, however, and within weeks fighting broke out again. On January 26, 1986, Kampala fell to the NRA, and on January 29 Museveni was sworn in as president. The National Resistance Council (NRC) was then established to govern the country. By the end of March 1986 Museveni claimed to have established control over the whole country through an intensive military campaign.

By August 1986 a guerrilla war once again flared, fueled by a whole gamut of rebel groups and factions, including supporters of deposed presidents Amin, Obote, and Okello, in addition to alienated NRA members. The most important rebel group was the Ugandan People's Democratic Army (UPDA). Throughout 1986 and 1987, however, the rebels sustained several major setbacks, including the defeat of Alice Lekwana's "Holy Spirit" movement in November 1987.* Over the next few years, the government gradually established greater control over the countryside and, through negotiations and amnesties, obtained the surrender and absorption of numerous rebel groups.

Although rebel activities continue on a relatively small scale, they do not appear to directly threaten Museveni's government. Throughout the course of the civil war, it is thought that more than 500,000 people lost their lives as a direct result of the conflict.

* The Holy Spirit movement emerged in 1986 with Lekwana claiming to be possessed by a spirit that guided her as protector and advocate of the Acholi people. Her moral and religious-based movement was defeated but resurrected in 1987 by her cousin, Joseph Kony, who also claimed to act under spiritual guidance. Kony's movement was to become the Lord's Resistance Army (LRA), which gained notoriety for committing atrocities on civilians and conscripting children into its armed service.

References

Avirgan, T., and M. Honey. 1982. *War in Uganda: The Legacy of Idi Amin*. Westport, Conn.: Lawrence Hill.

Hooper, E., and L. Pirouet. 1989. *Uganda*. Minority Rights Group Report #66. London: Minority Rights Group.

IRIN Web Special on Life in Northern Uganda. 2004."When the Sun Sets, We Start to Worry. . . ." http://www.plusnews.org/webspecials/northernuganda/overview.asp.

Mittleman, J. 1975. *Ideology and Politics in Uganda*. Ithaca, N.Y.: Cornell University Press.

Project Ploughshares. 2004. *Armed Conflicts Report 2003*. "Uganda (1987–First Combat Deaths)." Institute of Waterloo, Ontario: Peace and Conflict Studies, Conrad Grebel College. http://www.ploughshares.ca/content/ACR/ACRBriefs/ACRBrief-Uganda.html (accessed May 20, 2004).

Smith, G. 1980. *Ghosts of Kampala*. New York: St. Martin's.

Tillema, H.K. 1991. *International Armed Conflict Since 1945: A Bibliographic Handbook of Wars and Military Interventions*. Boulder: Westview.

1.50 Zaire–Zambia: Lake Mweru Dispute February–September 1982

Beginning in 1979, Zaire and Zambia maintained a running border dispute concerning the Lake Mweru region on Zambia's northern border. Zambia claimed that Zaire had set up border posts in the Kaputa district, nearly 30 kilometers inside its territory. On February 28, 1982, an exchange of fire and the seizure of Zambian troops led to large numbers of refugees and the closure of the border.

Following talks by a joint commission in April 1982, both sides agreed to exchange prisoners. Zaire continued to establish border posts within Zambian territory, however, and the abductions of Zambian citizens continued. Zaire agreed to withdraw its troops only after talks between President Kenneth Kaunda of Zambia and President Mobutu Sésé Séko of Zaire and further sessions of the joint commission in September 1982. The conflict lapsed after the talks, and tensions eased. The dispute was not fully resolved, however, and more fighting broke out in September 1983 (*see* conflict 1.57).

References

Aluko, O., and T. Shaw, eds. 1985. *Southern Africa in the 1980s*. London: Allen and Unwin.

Chan, S. 1992. *Kaunda and Southern Africa: Image and Reality in Foreign Policy*. London: British Academic Press.

Jaster, R.S. 1986. *South Africa and Its Neighbours: The Dynamics of Regional Conflict*. Adelphi Papers #209. London: IISS/Jane's.

Pettman, J. 1974. *Zambia: Security and Conflict*. Lewes (Sussex), England: J. Friedman.

Touval, S. 1972. *The Boundary Politics of Independent Africa*. Cambridge: Harvard University Press.

1.51 Libya–Chad: Political Instability, Rebel Fighting, Foreign Intervention, and the Third Chad Civil War
Mid-1982–Ongoing

Chad had been torn by civil conflict and foreign interventions since its independence from France in 1960. In the previous round of violence, Hissène Habré's Forces armées du nord (FAN) ousted President Goukouni Oueddei. After Habrè was named president, he attempted to reconcile with the other Chadian factions while consolidating his position. He was unsuccessful, however, and low-level fighting continued (*see* conflict 1.44).

In October 1982, with Libyan support, former president Oueddei established a rival "national peace government" in the northern town of Bardaí. In mid-1983 Oueddei's forces advanced southward with Libyan troop support, but they were driven back in a successful government counterattack. With the aid of Libyan air power, the rebels recaptured the town of Faya-Largeau in early August and again marched south. The fighting subsided only after French and Zairean forces, invited in by President Habré, assisted government forces in establishing a series of strong points across the country.

Fighting and famine continued into 1984, with increased French and Libyan involvement and the arrival of more Zairean troops. Growing numbers of French fatalities fueled diplomatic efforts to end the war, but these were unsuccessful. Despite a September 1984 agreement providing for the withdrawal of all foreign troops from Chad, Libyan troops remained and continued to clash with government forces. The government consolidated its position in central and southern Chad in 1985, often resorting to repressive tactics, but the north remained under rebel control. Drought and famine continued to plague the country.

Fighting continued without letup throughout 1986 and 1987, with U.S. support and renewed French involvement on the side of the Habré regime and Libyan defeats in the north. Neither side managed to defeat the other, and fortunes fluctuated. In 1988 the Chadian government signed agreements with both Libya and the forces armées tchadiennes (FAT) rebels, but other factions, including Oueddei's forces (GUNT, or Transitional Government of National Unity), continued to fight. The government survived a coup attempt in April 1989, but on December 1, 1990, the Habré regime fell to the rebel Patriotic Salvation Movement (MPS) under the leadership of Colonel Idriss Déby, who had been in exile since the 1989 coup attempt. Based in Sudan, the MPS had launched a series of offensives from the northern Darfur province.

In late 1991 forces loyal to former president Habré began actions in the Tibesti region of northern Chad. Rebel attacks began in earnest in December 1991 and included an invasion from the Lake Chad region, which was repulsed only with the aid of French paratroopers. Despite peace agreements signed throughout the 1992–1995 period with various rebel factions, the Chadian government remained vulnerable, and rebel activities continued. Starting in 1994 Déby's regime committed itself to national reconciliation and a timetable for democratic elections. Agreements were signed with several main rebel factions, but low-level fighting continued into late 1995. Also, in 1995 the International Court of Justice (ICJ) ruled in favor of Chad's sovereignty over the Aozou strip, a disputed territory on the Chad-Libyan border that Libya had seized in 1973. Approximately 25,000 people died during this conflict, including 2,000 Libyan and 9 French.

The scale and intensity of the fighting in the late 1990s did not reach the catastrophic levels of the 1970s and 1980s. Nevertheless, serious human rights abuses, including mass executions, rapes, and beatings, were reported, especially in the south. Déby, the current leader, faced coup attempts, and at least five armed opposition groups operated at any one time in the west, east, and south. The biggest challenge to the Déby government was posed by the Armed Forces for a Federal Republic (FARF). In May 1998 FARF surrendered to the government and its leader, Laokein Barde, reportedly fled the country. Peace, concluded in 1996, continued to be hampered by low-intensity insurgency.

In early 1999 another rebellion started in the northern Borkou-Ennedi-Tibesti (BET) region, led by a disgruntled former minister in the Déby government. In August 1999 Déby sent a delegation to the BET to open talks with the rebels who called themselves Mouvement pour la Démocratie et la Justice au Tschad (MDJT). No settlement was reached, and fighting continued to be reported throughout the rest of 1999 and into 2000, with the government and rebels both claiming success.

References

Davidson, B. 1972. *In the Eye of the Storm: Angola's People.* London: Longman.

Decalo, S. 1976. *Coups and Army Rule in Africa: Studies in Military Style.* New Haven: Yale University Press.

Kelley, M. 1986. *A State in Disarray: Conditions of Chad's Survival.* Boulder: Westview.

Posthumus, B. 2000. *European Platform for Conflict Prevention and Transformation Online.* Country Surveys: www.euconflict.org/euconflict/guides/surveys.htm (March 9, 2002).

Thompson, V.B., and R. Adloff. 1981. *Conflict in Chad.* Berkeley: Institute of International Studies, University of California.

Tillema, H.K. 1991. *International Armed Conflict Since 1945: A Bibliographic Handbook of Wars and Military Interventions.* Boulder: Westview.

Whiteman, K. 1988. *Chad.* Minority Rights Group Report #80. London: Minority Rights Group.

1.52 Ghana–Togo: Territorial Dispute and Border Incidents August–October 1982

Relations between Ghana and Togo had been strained ever since colonial boundaries split Ewe tribal lands between the two countries, giving rise to an ongoing reunification campaign. Ghana's expansive policies had also caused regional instability, bringing about an armed conflict between Ghana and Togo in 1965 (*see* conflict 1.22).

Tensions rose dramatically in August 1982, when each side accused the other of harboring rebels. Several violations of airspace and a number of border incidents occurred. One such incident left six people dead and several injured and resulted in the closure of the Ghana-Togo border. No peaceful conflict-management attempts were made during the dispute, and, although the allegations and recriminations continued into 1983, the conflict lapsed. The underlying hostility remained, however, and there were further armed conflicts in 1986 and 1994 (*see* conflicts 1.62; 1.81).

References

Awoonor, K. 1990. *Ghana: A Political History from Pre-European to Modern Times.* Accra: Sedco.

Butterworth, R.L. 1976. *Managing Interstate Conflict, 1945–1974.* Pittsburgh: Center for International Studies, University of Pittsburgh.

Carmichael, J. 1993. *African Eldorado: Gold Coast to Ghana.* London: Duckworth.

Tillema, H.K. 1991. *International Armed Conflict Since 1945: A Bibliographic Handbook of Wars and Military Interventions.* Boulder: Westview.

1.53 South Africa–Lesotho: Guerrilla Insurgency Fears and Anti-ANC Raid December 1982

Lesotho, a small enclave within the Republic of South Africa, became an independent state in 1966. Although relations between these two states were generally cordial, they became strained in mid-1982 following a number of border incidents. Lesotho alleged that South Africa was supporting the rebel Lesotho Liberation Army (LLA) in its armed struggle against the government. Anxious about guerrilla infiltration, South Africa responded that Lesotho was serving as a base for African National Congress (ANC) guerrillas planning terrorist attacks against the apartheid regime.

On December 9, 1982, South African commandos launched a raid on alleged ANC members in residential areas of Maseru, Lesotho's capital, which resulted in forty-two deaths. It was reported that sixty-four South African commandos were trapped in Lesotho for a few hours and had to be airlifted out. South African military commanders are said to have warned Lesotho security forces of massive retaliation if they interfered with the withdrawal. South Africa conducted similar raids against ANC bases in Botswana from 1984 to 1986 and Zambia in 1987 (*see* conflicts 1.58; 1.65).

The international community widely condemned the attack against Lesotho, but made no attempts at peaceful conflict management during the conflict. Although South Africa put Lesotho under increasing economic and political pressure, and allegations and recriminations continued, the conflict abated after the end of 1982.

References

Aluko, O., and T. Shaw, eds. 1985. *Southern Africa in the 1980s.* London: Allen and Unwin.

Bardill, J., and H. Cobbe. 1985. *Lesotho: Dilemmas of Dependence in Southern Africa.* Boulder: Westview.

Burchett, W. 1978. *Southern Africa Stands Up: The Revolutions in Angola, Mozambique, Zimbabwe, Namibia, and South Africa.* New York: Urizen Books.

Cawthra, G. 1986. *Brutal Force: The Apartheid War Machine.* London: International Defence and Aid Fund for Southern Africa.

Heitman, H. 1985. *South African War Machine.* Novato, Calif.: Presidio.

Jaster, R.S. 1989. *The Defence of White Power: South African Foreign Policy Under Pressure.* New York: St. Martin's.

Tillema, H.K. 1991. *International Armed Conflict Since 1945: A Bibliographic Handbook of Wars and Military Interventions.* Boulder: Westview.

1.54 Sudan: Secessionist Fighting, Civil War, and the Second Sudan Civil War January 1983–Ongoing

Sudan's predominantly Arab Muslim northern provinces had controlled the central government since the country's independence from Britain in 1956. As a consequence, the three southern provinces, populated largely by black Christians and animists, engaged in secessionist warfare from the early 1960s to 1972 (*see* conflict 1.14). Secessionist sentiment resurfaced in January 1983, when the southern rebels began attacking police stations and army patrols; southern army units began to stage mutinies.

The conflict escalated after President Gaafar Mohammed Numeiry announced the redivision of southern Sudan and the imposition of Islamic law (Shari'a) there, effectively rendering the southerners second-class citizens. Colonel John Garang led the primary rebel group, the Sudan People's Liberation Army (SPLA), which attacked towns and government patrols and engaged in hijackings, sabotage, and other terrorist activities. Despite offensives by both sides and several peace initiatives, the war continued unabated into 1985. In 1985–1986 another rebel movement, Anya-Nya II, began to act as a progovernment militia, hampering the rebels' efforts to consolidate their successes.

Khartoum's brand of militant Islam hampered efforts to bring a peaceful end to the civil war. Persistent government moves to impose Shari'a in the south finally split the coalition government and ended numerous peace initiatives, including a number of signed agreements. The fighting continued in a cyclical fashion from 1987 to 1989. Typically, both sides would launch offensives during the dry season and consolidate their gains when the rains came. On June 30, 1989, the civilian government of Prime Minister Sadiq al-Mahdi was overthrown in a bloodless military coup. Negotiations were immediately opened with the SPLA, but these were unsuccessful.

Mediation by former U.S. president Jimmy Carter in December 1989 also failed—negotiations again broke down over the issue of Shari'a law. Fighting erupted anew in January 1990 and continued without letup for the rest of the year. Both sides claimed victories, but in reality, neither side was able to gain the advantage. Beset by drought and famine that had claimed the lives of close to 300,000 people, Sudan also had to deal with numerous coup attempts. In late 1991 the SPLA leadership split over the issue of southern secession, and intrafactional fighting broke out, which hampered both rebel efforts and the recently revived peace initiatives. The government launched a major offensive in late February 1992 that caused the United Nations to suspend aid to the south. In 1993 the Khartoum government was cited for gross human rights violations and "ethnic cleansing" against the southern Nuba people.

Between 1993 and 1994 a major mediation effort took place, at various stages involving Carter and the Inter-Governmental Authority on Drought and Development (IGADD), led by Kenya and fellow member states from the region (Eritrea, Ethiopia, and Uganda). IGADD's first peace initiative led to an agreement between the Sudanese government and the two SPLA factions for talks later that year. This said, reports surfaced alleging Eritrean, Ethiopian, Kenyan, and Ugandan support for the rebels based on these countries' distaste for Khartoum's militant Islam. Renewed talks began in May 1994, but ended in deadlock in September, when the Sudanese government rejected the rebel-sponsored "Declaration of Principles." The toll from the conflict at this stage was thought to be as many as 500,000, many of whom died from war-induced famine and disease. The Khartoum government's economic blockade of the south was particularly devastating. Mediation efforts over this time met with no real success, and agreements that were reached did not hold.

A series of cease-fires in 1995 bought some respite, but negotiations to end the fighting failed to get off the ground, and fierce fighting continued in a similar, cyclical fashion until the end of 1995. In the same year, neighboring Eritrea opened its doors to the Sudanese opposition, providing an outlet for the resistance.

In April 1996 the government of Sudan entered into a political charter with six southern rebel groups. Under the accord, the north and south would remain in a unitary state and the Shari'a Islamic law and local customs would become the main sources of law. Several leaders of rebel groups were rewarded with government posts. At the end of 1996, however, the National Democrat Alliance (NDA) became co-belligerents of the SPLA. Their coordinated attacks posed the most serious threat to the government since it came to power. The neighboring countries of Ethiopia, Eritrea, and Uganda openly supported the coalition, and the Sudanese conflict evolved into a multifront war with dangerous regional implications.

In 1997 the combined Sudanese opposition launched several attacks in the areas bordering Eritrea and Ethiopia as well as Uganda, resulting in significant advances. Sudanese government officials alleged that the armed forces of the three neighboring countries led the campaigns. In January 1998 the government's situation worsened when rebel group leader, Kerubino Bol, defected from the government side, realigned with the SPLA forces, and launched a number of surprise attacks on government forces in the Bahr al Ghazal province.

In May 1998 war broke out between Eritea and Ethiopia, and these countries withdrew their support for the rebels and made peace overtures to Sudan (*see* conflict 1.91). Sudan's government seized this opportunity and launched fresh attacks against the rebel movement. In the meantime, the humanitarian situation deteriorated even further and hundreds of thousands of people died in the subsequent famine. In response, the SPLA announced a three-month cease-fire in July. The government then implemented a one-month truce, which was later extended to April 1999.

The Sudanese civil war remains unresolved, and the casualties continue to mount. Since 1999 direct confrontations between government and rebel forces have been largely avoided, except with regard to the security of a new 1,600 kilometer oil pipeline from the Helig area to the Red Sea port. Government forces continue their stranglehold on the well-being of the south, keeping most southerners in perpetual humanitarian crisis. The government has made several overtures that indicate a willingness to consider reconciliation, but its actions are viewed with skepticism due to a history of similar, unfulfilled promises. After thirty years of fighting, no end to the conflict is in sight. The government and the SPLA have settled into a brutal routine of accepting limited cease-fires that "buy time" for both sides, despite the increase in international pressure on the parties to resolve the crisis.

The massive loss of life caused by the war in Sudan far surpasses that of any civil war being waged elsewhere in the world, and all parties to the conflict have committed war crimes. The Sudanese government has engaged in indiscriminate aerial bombardments and used policies of torture, disappearance, and summary execution to quell civilian resistance. The southern rebel groups abduct civilians, use starvation as a means of combat, and deploy children as soldiers on a massive scale. Since the conflict began, it is estimated that 1.9 million people have died as a direct result of civil war or war-induced famine and disease. A further 4 million, predominantly southern Sudanese, have been internally displaced or have fled as refugees, making this conflict one of the most devastating in history.

References

Albino, O. 1970. *The Sudan: A Southern Viewpoint*. London: Institute of Race Relations, Oxford University.

Assefa, H. 1987. *Mediation of Civil Wars: Approaches and Strategies—The Sudan Conflict*. Boulder: Westview.

Beshir, M.O. 1974. *Revolution and Nationalism in the Sudan*. London: Rex Collings.

Eprile, C. 1974. *War and Peace in the Sudan*. Newton Abbot: David and Charles.

Gurr, T., M. Marshall, and D. Khosla. 2000. *Peace and Conflict 2001: A Global Survey of Conflicts, Self-Determination Movements, and Democracy*. College Park: Center for International Development and Conflict Management, University of Maryland.

Johnson, D.H. 1988. *The Southern Sudan*. Minority Rights Group Report #78. London: Minority Rights Group.

Tillema, H.K. 1991. *International Armed Conflict Since 1945: A Bibliographic Handbook of Wars and Military Interventions*. Boulder: Westview.

van de Veen, H. 2002. *European Platform for Conflict Prevention and Transformation Online*. www.euconflict.org/euconflict/guides/surveys.htm (February 1, 2002).

Verney, P. 1995. *Sudan: Conflict and Minorities*. London: Minority Rights Group.

Wai, D. 1981. *The African-Arab Conflict in the Sudan*. New York: Africana.

1.55 Liberia–Sierra Leone: Doe Regime Tensions February–March 1983

Liberia, a West African state founded in 1822 by freed American slaves, had been independent since 1847 and had enjoyed a fairly peaceful existence until a bloody military coup in 1980 installed Master Sergeant Samuel K. Doe as head of state. Surrounding states had qualms about Doe's brutal regime, which were borne out after a story published in Sierra Leone claimed that Doe had personally shot and killed his wife for taking part in an abortive coup. Relations between Sierra Leone and Liberia underwent a serious deterioration after this report. Doe recalled the Liberian ambassador to Sierra Leone, closed the border with that country and, in a significant show of force, deployed 3,500 troops along the border.

Tensions were extremely high, but after an offer of mediation by Guinean President Ahmed Sékou Touré on February 26, 1983, and negotiations March 7–12, the conflict was resolved. Doe's regime continued to cause concern, however, and in 1989 Sierra Leone allowed a rebel force to invade Liberia from its territory in the start of what was to become civil war in Liberia (*see* conflict 1.72).

References

Africa Contemporary Record. Annual. 1968/1969– .

African Recorder. Weekly. 1962– .

Clapham, C.S. 1976. *Liberia and Sierra Leone: Essay in Comparative Politics*. Cambridge: Cambridge University Press.

1.56 Chad–Nigeria: Boundary/Resources Dispute and the Lake Chad Conflict April–July 1983

Chad and Nigeria achieved independence in 1960, and relations between the two states were generally good during the 1960s and 1970s. Although both countries accepted colonial boundaries, areas of Lake Chad had not been demarcated, and a number of small islands became the focus of ownership disputes. The conflict escalated in the late 1970s and early 1980s when oil exploration in the region began. In addition, civil war in Chad had resulted in Nigerian troops being stationed in Chad as part of an Organization of African Unity (OAU) peacekeeping force. When the Nigerian troops were forced out of Chad by a military coup, tensions were at an all-time high.

The focus of conflict moved to the Lake Chad islands, and a number of minor incidents escalated into a series of serious military clashes from April to July 1983. More than 370 soldiers are thought to have been killed in the fighting. Despite an agreement to end hostilities, which was signed in Lagos, Nigeria, on May 17, Chadian soldiers engaged in a major offensive backed by French mercenaries. Nigeria responded by bombing Chadian lakeside villages with MiG jet fighters. Negotiations between the two countries' presidents in July 1983 and early 1984 led to an end to the fighting and the reopening of the border, which had been closed for several months.

In August 2000 Chad and Nigeria decided to move forward on security matters in the area around Lake Chad, where the remnants of rebel groups were reportedly engaged in acts of banditry, a problem that the two countries want to eradicate.

References

Brownlie, I. 1963. *African Boundaries: A Legal and Diplomatic Encyclopedia.* Berkeley and Los Angeles: University of California Press.

Day, A., ed. 1987. *Border and Territorial Disputes.* 2d edition. Burnt Mill, Harlow (Essex), England: Longman.

Tillema, H.K. 1991. *International Armed Conflict Since 1945: A Bibliographic Handbook of Wars and Military Interventions.* Boulder: Westview.

Touval, S. 1972. *The Boundary Politics of Independent Africa.* Cambridge: Harvard University Press.

1.57 Zaire–Zambia: Regional Tensions, Deportations, and Border Dispute September 1983–January 1984

Following a 1982 Zaire–Zambia border conflict over Zambia's Lake Mweru region (*see* conflict 1.50), tensions were heightened dramatically in September 1983, when Zairean troops killed two Zambians in an ambush near the southwestern border town of Mufulira. Zambia deployed troops in the area, claiming the need to control widespread smuggling and banditry. A number of other border incidents followed.

Tensions rose again when Zambia announced it would deport thousands of Zairean nationals in July 1984. Zaire responded by deporting large numbers of Zambians living in Shaba province. Relations between the two countries improved in 1986 following talks between the two presidents, Kenneth Kaunda and Mobutu Sésé Séko, and the dispute lapsed.

References

Aluko, O., and T. Shaw, eds. 1985. *Southern Africa in the 1980s.* London: Allen and Unwin.

Chan, S. 1992. *Kaunda and Southern Africa: Image and Reality in Foreign Policy.* London: British Academic Press.

Jaster, R.S. 1986. *South Africa and Its Neighbours: The Dynamics of Regional Conflict.* Adelphi Papers #209. London: IISS/Jane's.

Pettman, J. 1974. *Zambia: Security and Conflict.* Lewes (Sussex), England: J. Friedman.

Touval, S. 1972. *The Boundary Politics of Independent Africa.* Cambridge: Harvard University Press.

1.58 South Africa–Botswana: African Nationalism and Anti-ANC Raids October 1984–May 1986

South Africa's white-minority government was fighting a guerrilla insurgency led by the African National Congress (ANC), whose leader, Nelson Mandela, had been sentenced in 1964 to life imprisonment. With a goal of establishing a majority-ruled state, the ANC guerrillas were aided by neighboring frontline states—Botswana, Mozambique, Tanzania, and Zambia. These countries allowed the guerrillas to operate from their territories and provided refuge for exiled ANC leaders. Support for the ANC made relations between South Africa and its neighbors very tense. South African commandos had already made raids into Lesotho in pursuit of ANC activists in 1982 (*see* conflict 1.53). Economic reprisals were also common practice by the South African regime.

This particular conflict began with an incident on the Botswana-Namibian border. The resulting tension escalated after South Africa alleged that ANC fighters were using Botswana as an infiltration route into South Africa. South Africa threatened to invade Botswana if the infiltration was not stopped, and great pressure was put on Botswana to sign a nonaggression and security pact with South Africa, similar to the Nkomati accord signed with Mozambique (*see* conflict 1.40).

On June 14, 1985, seventy South African commando troops raided targets in Gaborone, killing twelve people in a firefight. The international community condemned the raid, which targeted ANC centers of activity, as an act of aggression. Another such raid on Gaborone in May 1986 killed another person. Apart from unsuccessful negotiations in December 1984, February 1985, and September 1985, no other conflict-management efforts were undertaken, and the fighting eventually lapsed. A similar conflict involving a South African raid on ANC bases in Zambia occurred in 1987 (*see* conflict 1.65).

References

Aluko, O., and T. Shaw, eds. 1985. *Southern Africa in the 1980s.* London: Allen and Unwin.

Burchett, W. 1978. *Southern Africa Stands Up: The Revolutions in Angola, Mozambique, Zimbabwe, Namibia, and South Africa.* New York: Urizen Books.

Carmichael, J. 1993. *African Eldorado: Gold Coast to Ghana.* London: Duckworth.

Heitman, H. 1985. *South African War Machine.* Novato, Calif.: Presidio.

Jaster, R.S. 1989. *The Defence of White Power: South African Foreign Policy Under Pressure.* New York: St. Martin's.

Tillema, H.K. 1991. *International Armed Conflict Since 1945: A Bibliographic Handbook of Wars and Military Interventions.* Boulder: Westview.

1.59 Zaire: Internal Dissent and the Third Invasion of Shaba
November 1984

The corrupt and authoritarian regime of President Mobutu Sésé Séko, in power since a 1965 military coup, had aroused not only the dissent of Zaireans but also the resentment of neighboring countries. Dissatisfaction with the Mobutu regime was most effectively expressed with invasions of Shaba (formerly known as Katanga), the mineral-rich southern province that accounted for two-thirds of Zaire's foreign earnings. The Mobutu regime prospered on graft skimmed off mining profits.

In the most serious disturbances in the province since the 1977 and 1978 invasions (*see* conflicts 1.43; 1.45), rebels launched an invasion from Tanzanian territory and captured the town of Moba, 380 miles northeast of Lubumbashi, on November 13, 1984. The government counterattacked the same day, and by November 15 the town was recaptured. At least 125 people were killed during the fighting. There were no attempts at managing the conflict peacefully, and another invasion was attempted in June 1985 (*see* conflict 1.60).

References

Biebuyck, D., and M. Douglas. 1961. *Congo Tribes and Parties.* London: Royal Anthropological Institute.

Birmingham, D. 1992. *Frontline Nationalism in Angola and Mozambique.* London: J. Currey.

Epstein, H., ed. 1965. *Revolt in Congo, 1960–1964.* New York: Facts on File.

Kalb, M. 1982. *The Congo Crisis: The Cold War in Africa From Eisenhower to Kennedy.* New York: Macmillan.

Tillema, H.K. 1991. *International Armed Conflict Since 1945: A Bibliographic Handbook of Wars and Military Interventions.* Boulder: Westview.

1.60 Zaire: Internal Strife, the Fourth Invasion of Shaba, and the Collapse of the Mobutu Regime
June 1985

Zaire, the third largest country in Africa, had been wracked by civil unrest since its independence from Belgium in 1960. The regime of President Mobutu Sésé Séko, brought to power through a 1965 military coup, had spawned dissident movements, incessant rebellions, invasions, mercenary revolts, and trouble in most of the nine bordering nations. Most of the invasions involved the cobalt- and copper-rich Shaba province (*see* conflicts 1.43; 1.45; 1.59).

In this particular conflict, a dissident group of exiles launched an attack on the town of Moba in Shaba on June 16–17, 1985, the second such attack in less than a year (*see* conflict 1.59). Invading from Tanzanian territory, the rebels were routed after five hours of fighting. Approximately fifty people were killed during the conflict, which was not considered as serious as the previous invasion. There were no attempts at peaceful conflict management during the conflict, and opposition to the government and civil unrest continued to plague the area. Relations with Tanzania were not greatly affected, but underlying tensions remained. Civil unrest in Zaire itself continued into the 1990s. In 1996 a rebel alliance led by Laurent Kabila began attacking government forces with the backing of Rwanda. Within a few months Mobutu's regime collapsed entirely, and Kabila took control of the country, which was renamed Democratic Republic of the Congo (*see* conflict 1.85).

References

Biebuyck, D., and M. Douglas. 1961. *Congo Tribes and Parties.* London: Royal Anthropological Institute.

Birmingham, D. 1992. *Frontline Nationalism in Angola and Mozambique.* London: J. Currey.

Epstein, H., ed. 1965. *Revolt in Congo, 1960–1964.* New York: Facts on File.

Kalb, M. 1982. *The Congo Crisis: The Cold War in Africa From Eisenhower to Kennedy.* New York: Macmillan.

Tillema, H.K. 1991. *International Armed Conflict Since 1945: A Bibliographic Handbook of Wars and Military Interventions.* Boulder: Westview.

1.61 Mali–Burkina Faso: Territorial/Resource Dispute and Border War
December 1985–January 1986

Mali and Burkina Faso both claimed a border area that contained a chain of pools through which flowed the Belí River, the only source of fresh water in the region. Mali claimed it was geographically and ethnically part of Mali, but Burkina Faso claimed the French colonial authorities had included it in Burkinabe territory. The dispute had already led to fighting in 1974 (*see* conflict 1.37).

Several months before the conflict erupted in December 1985, Burkina had expelled Drissa Keita, the Malian secretary-general of the francophone West African Economic Community (CEAO). Burkina's attempts to carry out a census led to an outbreak of fighting on December 25 in the disputed Agacher border area. The fighting quickly escalated to all-out war. Air attacks and ground battles spread, and the fighting continued for five days. A cease-fire was arranged by members of the Non-Aggression and Defense Aid Agreement (ANAD) on December 31, and troops were withdrawn.

ANAD undertook further mediation in January 1986. The dispute was submitted to the International Court of Justice (ICJ) border commission in January 1986. The ICJ produced a settlement ending the conflict on January 18. As many as 400 people were killed during the four days of fighting, many of them civilians.

References

Brownlie, I. 1963. *African Boundaries: A Legal and Diplomatic Encyclopedia.* Berkeley and Los Angeles: University of California Press.

Day, A., ed. 1987. *Border and Territorial Disputes.* 2d edition. Burnt Mill, Harlow (Essex), England: Longman.

Folz, W.J. 1965. *From French West Africa to the Mali Federation.* New Haven: Yale University Press.

Sankara, T. 1988. *Thomas Sankara Speaks: The Burkina Faso Revolution, 1983–1987.* Translated by S. Anderson. New York: Pathfinder.

Touval, S. 1972. *The Boundary Politics of Independent Africa.* Cambridge: Harvard University Press.

1.62 Togo–Ghana: Regional Rivalry and Coup Attempt
September 1986

Togo and Ghana had been rivals ever since the division of Togoland prior to its independence. Ghana absorbed the western part of the country (British Togoland), and the eastern half (French Togoland) became independent Togo. The partition split Ewe tribal lands between the two countries, giving rise to an ongoing and destabilizing unification campaign. Ghanaian leaders for decades laid claim to Togo in an effort to reunite the two countries, and these efforts led to constant friction. Ghana attempted to undermine Togo, leading to armed conflict in 1965 and 1982 (*see* conflicts 1.22; 1.52). Tensions simmered in the months preceding the 1986 conflict, with Togo accusing Ghana of harboring subversives.

On September 23, 1986, an armed commando unit of about sixty soldiers entered Togo from neighboring Ghana with the aim of overthrowing the regime of President Gnassingbé Eyadéma. By September 28 the commandos had been defeated, but only after France had sent in 150 paratroopers backed by a minesweeper and a Jaguar jet fighter, plus 350 Zairean troops. The borders with Ghana and Burkina Faso were closed. Togo claimed the attack was launched from Ghana, that Ghana had trained the insurgents, and that both Ghana and Burkina Faso had massed troops on the Togo border in preparation for supporting the coup. Ghana and Burkina Faso denied the allegations.

Up to thirty people are thought to have been killed in the conflict, and minor border incidents with Ghana continued for some time. On November 26, 1986, Ide Oumarou, secretary-general of the Organization of African Unity (OAU), attempted unsuccessfully to mediate the conflict, and President Félix Houphouët-Boigny of Ivory Coast attempted mediation in early January 1987. Although the conflict eased for some years, fighting broke out again in 1994 (*see* conflict 1.81).

References

Awoonor, K. 1990. *Ghana: A Political History from Pre-European to Modern Times.* Accra: Sedco.

Carmichael, J. 1993. *African Eldorado: Gold Coast to Ghana.* London: Duckworth.

Tillema, H.K. 1991. *International Armed Conflict Since 1945: A Bibliographic Handbook of Wars and Military Interventions.* Boulder: Westview.

1.63 Zaire–People's Republic of the Congo: Regional Instability and Border Incident
January 1987

Zaire (later called Congo and then the Democratic Republic of the Congo) and People's Republic of the Congo (formerly Middle Congo) both attained independence in 1960 and since that time were plagued by civil conflict and internal instability. Zaire in particular engaged in numerous armed conflicts with its neighbors (*see* conflicts 1.23; 1.31; 1.39; 1.43; 1.45; 1.50; 1.57; 1.59; 1.60). Only four months after Zaire and the People's Republic of Congo agreed on measures to promote peace in the region, a conflict over security and territorial sovereignty erupted in January 1987.

Fighting between the two countries broke out in the Mindouli region of the Congo, southwest of Brazzaville, when Zairean troops crossed the Zaire-Congo border and entered the village of Ngombe. At least three people were killed in the clash. No attempts were made to settle the dispute peacefully, and relations normalized within a few months. Given the ongoing instability in the region, the conflict had the potential to escalate seriously.

References

Africa Contemporary Record. Annual. 1968/1969– .

African Recorder. Weekly. 1962– .

Great Britain Central Office of Information, Reference Division. 1961. *Congo, Gabon, Central African Republic, and Chad*. London: (n. p.).

Legum, C., and T. Hodges. 1978. *After Angola: The War over Southern Africa*. 2d edition. New York: Africana.

Nzongola-Ntalaja, G., ed. 1991. *Conflict in the Horn of Africa*. Atlanta: African Studies Association Press.

Tillema, H.K. 1991. *International Armed Conflict Since 1945: A Bibliographic Handbook of Wars and Military Interventions*. Boulder: Westview.

1.64 Ethiopia–Somalia: Somali Expansionism and the Third Ogaden War February 1987–April 1988

When Somalia became independent from Britain in 1960, the new government began to claim the existence of a "Greater Somalia" owing to the presence of some 350,000 Somali tribes people in surrounding states. Such expansionist statements brought Somalia into armed conflict with Kenya from 1962 to 1967 (*see* conflict 1.13). Somalia's strongest claim, however, was to the vast Ogaden region of eastern Ethiopia inhabited primarily by Somalis. Earlier Somali efforts to take the region had led to war with Ethiopia in 1964 and again from 1972 to 1985 (*see* conflicts 1.17; 1.35). Somalia continued to foment separatist passions among Ogaden tribesmen, arming and supplying them to attack Ethiopian targets.

Despite ongoing negotiations over the issue, tensions remained high, and the situation deteriorated in early 1987. On February 12 Ethiopian troops launched an air and ground attack on Somali positions. Intense fighting resulted in heavy casualties, and there were reports of earthen ramparts being erected on either side of the border, apparently in preparation for further offensives. Somali National Movement (SNM) rebels, who were opposed to the Somali government, operated jointly with the Ethiopian forces. The conflict lost some of its intensity, and only minor incidents occurred from this time until April 1988, when, as a result of numerous negotiations between President Mengistu Haile Mariam of Ethiopia and President Muhammad Siad Barre of Somalia, who had attained the presidency in 1976, a settlement was reached, and both sides withdrew. More than 300 people are thought to have been killed during the fighting.

References

Doornbos, M.B., ed. 1992. *Beyond Conflict in the Horn: Prospects for Peace, Recovery, and Development in Ethiopia, Somalia, and the Sudan*. Trenton, N.J.: Red Sea.

Farer, T. 1979. *War Clouds on the Horn of Africa: The Widening Storm*. 2d revised edition. New York: Carnegie Endowment for International Peace.

Fukin, K., and J. Markakis, eds. 1994. *Ethnicity and Conflict in the Horn of Africa*. Athens: Ohio University Press.

Gorman, R. 1981. *Political Conflict on the Horn of Africa*. New York: Praeger.

1.65 South Africa–Zambia: African Nationalism, Insurgency Fears, and Anti-ANC Raid April 1987

The white minority government in South Africa tried hard to protect its borders from attacks by African National Congress (ANC) guerrillas fighting for a majority-ruled South Africa. The frontline states—Angola, Botswana, Lesotho, Malawi, Mozambique, Swaziland, Tanzania, and Zambia—provided the ANC with military training and bases from which to operate. South African forces had already made raids into Lesotho in 1982 and Botswana in 1984–1986 to attack ANC bases and safehouses (*see* conflicts 1.53; 1.58).

On April 25, 1987, a South African commando raid on Livingstone in southern Zambia, launched from northern Namibia, resulted in five fatalities. South Africa claimed that the dead were all ANC "terrorists," but Zambia claimed they were Zambian citizens. The South African government's motive for the raid was thought to be an attempt to win right-wing votes in the forthcoming whites-only elections, although the South African Defence Forces (SADF) claimed it was only an "armed reconnaissance" mission. Neither side attempted to resolve their differences peacefully, and the conflict gradually lapsed. Reforms in South Africa eventually led to the release of Nelson Mandela, the legalization of the ANC, a new constitution, and a majority-elected ANC government.

References

Aluko, O., and T. Shaw, eds. 1985. *Southern Africa in the 1980s*. London: Allen and Unwin.

Burchett, W. 1978. *Southern Africa Stands Up: The Revolutions in Angola, Mozambique, Zimbabwe, Namibia, and South Africa*. New York: Urizen Books.

Cawthra, G. 1986. *Brutal Force: The Apartheid War Machine*. London: International Defence and Aid Fund for Southern Africa.

Heitman, H. 1985. *South African War Machine*. Novato, Calif.: Presidio.

Jaster, R.S. 1989. *The Defence of White Power: South African Foreign Policy Under Pressure*. New York: St. Martin's.

Tillema, H.K. 1991. *International Armed Conflict Since 1945: A Bibliographic Handbook of Wars and Military Interventions*. Boulder: Westview.

1.66 People's Republic of the Congo: Civil Unrest and Army Rebellion
September 1987–July 1988

People's Republic of the Congo gained independence from France in 1960, and its postindependence history is a litany of coups and civil unrest. The army was the source of much instability. In early September 1987 fighting broke out in the northern region of Curette between government troops and supporters of a former army officer, Captain Pierre Anga, who had escaped to the region and taken up arms after refusing to be questioned as part of an inquiry into an antigovernment plot.

French army forces based in Gabon were sent to maintain order in the region after government troops failed to quell the uprising. Former military leader Joachim Yhombi-Opango, a close friend of Captain Anga, was arrested and brought to Brazzaville, the capital of the Congo, on September 8, 1987, in a government bid to suppress the rebellion. Intermittent clashes continued for several months, as Anga eluded capture.

No attempts at peaceful conflict management were made, and it was estimated that fifty lives were lost during the fighting. The rebellion ended on July 4, 1988, when Anga was killed during a clash with an army detachment near his hometown of Owando. His supporters fled or surrendered, and the French troops were withdrawn.

References

Africa Contemporary Record. Annual. 1968/1969– .

African Recorder. Weekly. 1962– .

Andereggen, A. 1994. *France's Relationship With Sub-Saharan Africa.* Westport, Conn.: Praeger.

Carter, G.M., ed. 1964. *Five African States: Responses to Diversity: The Congo, Dahomey, the Cameroon Federal Republic, the Rhodesias, and Nyasaland, South Africa.* London: Pall Mall.

Great Britain Central Office of Information, Reference Division. 1961. *Congo, Gabon, Central African Republic, and Chad.* London: (n. p.).

Somerville, K. 1990. *Foreign Military Intervention in Africa.* London: Pinter.

1.67 Uganda–Kenya: Ugandan Civil War, Refugee Influx, and Border Conflict
December 1987

Strained relations on the Kenya–Uganda border were heightened by the arrival of refugees fleeing the civil war in Uganda. Both sides accused each other of harboring rebels and trying to undermine each other's regime. Alarmed by the large numbers of Ugandan troops stationed close to the Kenyan border in November 1987, the Kenyan government threatened to retaliate if Ugandan troops attempted to pursue rebels into its territory.

After numerous incidents in early December, a serious outbreak of fighting December 14–16 near the border at Busia in Kenya left at least fifteen dead. Libyans were also thought to have been involved on the Ugandan side. The Organization of African Unity (OAU) president, Zambian president Kenneth Kaunda, offered to mediate the dispute, but his offer was rejected. Negotiations between President Daniel arap Moi of Kenya and President Yoweri Museveni of Uganda on December 28, 1987, led to an easing of tensions. Mutual suspicion remained, however, and another armed conflict broke out in 1989 (*see* conflict 1.70).

References

Avirgan, T., and M. Honey. 1982. *War in Uganda: The Legacy of Idi Amin.* Westport, Conn.: Lawrence Hill.

Hooper, E., and L. Pirouet. 1989. *Uganda.* Minority Rights Group Report #66. London: Minority Rights Group.

Mittleman, J. 1975. *Ideology and Politics in Uganda.* Ithaca, New York: Cornell University Press.

Smith, G. 1980. *Ghosts of Kampala.* New York: St. Martin's.

1.68 Somalia: Clan-Based Violence and the Somalian Civil War
May 1988–Ongoing

Somalia, which gained its independence in 1960, is composed of many tribal clans and factions. In 1977 the Socialist state broke its ties with the USSR over the issue of Soviet aid to Ethiopia and expelled more than 6,000 Soviet advisers. Following the Soviet withdrawal, the loose alliance that constituted the government began to unravel. In May 1988 the Somali National Movement (SNM), based in the northern, Issa-dominated region, launched a rebellion against the despotic regime of President Muhammad Siad Barre, a former major general who became president in 1976. The attack came after an Ethiopian–Somali agreement isolated the SNM, previously supported by Ethiopia. The SNM quickly took control of several important towns. A counterattack by the army took back the towns, but the rebels continued to control most of the countryside, engaging in guerrilla activities throughout 1988 and the first part of 1989. The initial fighting was intense, killing approximately 50,000 people—many of them in army reprisals.

Throughout 1989 the Somali army was beset with mutinies, and in July antigovernment disturbances in the capital, Mogadishu, led to 400 deaths. The SNM made significant gains in December 1989, although the army continued its violent repression. In August 1990 the SNM joined a number of other guerrilla groups, and by the end of 1990 they controlled most of the countryside, while the government controlled only Mogadishu and its immediate surroundings. In December 1990 the United Somali Congress (USC), which was based in central Somalia and dominated by the Hawiye clan, also launched an assault on the Barre regime. By the end of January 1991 Barre had fled, Mogadishu had fallen, and the USC had installed an interim government. In the north, the SNM had taken the regional capital.

The USC immediately began fighting other southern, clan-based groups as well as Barre supporters, while the SNM in the north set up a rival administration in April 1991; the north seceded in May. Calling itself Somaliland, the new entity essentially partitioned the country, but received no international recognition. In Mogadishu thousands were killed in September and November 1991, because of clan-based fighting within the USC between President Ali Mohammed and General Mohammed Farah Aidid. The fighting continued through 1992 and, combined with the general state of anarchy, led to the threat of mass starvation. Armed gangs looted supplies of food and other aid, and by August 1992, 2,000 people were reported dying each day of starvation, while hundreds were being killed in factional fighting.

The state of the country and the failure of numerous peace initiatives to resolve the conflict led to UN military intervention beginning in July 1992. This culminated in a full-scale U.S.-led invasion in December 1992 by 28,000 U.S. troops with the mission to restore law and order and protect aid convoys and food distribution. But unclear U.S. objectives, the reluctance of Somali clan leaders to negotiate, and intractable clan-based fighting meant that, after nearly two years, anarchy still reigned in Somalia with no end to the fighting in sight. Rising UN fatalities, especially among the U.S. forces, and the failure of UN mediation ended in the complete failure of the mission in late 1994; the United Nations was forced to withdraw. The last UN forces left in March 1995, and the country returned to full-scale clan-based fighting led by General Mohammed Said Hirsi (a son-in-law of the former dictator, Barre) and Mohammed Haji Aden. Aidid was killed in 1996. Deaths from the civil war and resulting famine were in the hundreds of thousands.

In December 1997, an agreement was signed by several of the rival factions, including Mohammed Farah Aidid's United Somali Congress/Somali National Alliance (USC-SNA) and Cali Mahdi Mohammed's Somali National Salvation Council. Called the Cairo Declaration, the agreement called for cease-fire and the establishment of an interim government for a three-year transition period that could be extended an additional two years with the approval of the 189-member Constituent Assembly. Subsequently, national elections would be held. Provisions for a cessation of military operations and the reopening of Mogadishu's airport and seaport were to take effect immediately.

In January 1998 it was announced that a national reconciliation conference would be held in Baidoa in February, but the conference was postponed several times. In July the three most powerful faction leaders, Hussein Mohammed Farah Aidid (taking over the USC-SNA faction after his father's death), Cali Mahdi Mohammed, and Osman Hassan Ali (dubbed "Atto") of the Rahanwein Resistance Army (RRA), signed a peace agreement to form a joint administration of Mogadishu to start in August. Atto immediately boycotted it. In December 1999, five of the main factions reached a five-point agreement under which an administration was to be set up for southern Somalia. However, Muse Sidi Yalahow, who controlled territory in the area, refused to participate. In February 1999 the RRA announced that Hussein Aidid's USC-SNA faction had killed sixty civilians in Baidoa and Daynunay that week.

In December 1999 the Oromo Liberation Front, an Ethiopian rebel group, began to withdraw after an October agreement between Aidid and the Ethiopian government. In exchange, Ethiopian troops were to be withdrawn. The agreement also called for joint cooperation in fighting Al Itihad, previously called the Western Somali Liberation Front (WSLF), a group wanting the unification of the Ogaden region in Ethiopia with Somalia.

At the end of 2000, the conflict remained unresolved. The south and central regions of Somalia continue to be torn by factional fighting among rival clans and warlords, despite sixteen peace initiatives. No central government has operated in Somalia since the collapse of the Barre regime in 1991. A new parliament was formed in September 2000, as a result of negotiations among Somali clan and political leaders held in neighboring Djibouti. Some clans have vowed to resist the reestablishment of central governance.

References

Doornbos, M.B., ed. 1992. *Beyond Conflict in the Horn: Prospects for Peace, Recovery, and Development in Ethiopia, Somalia, and the Sudan.* Trenton, N.J.: Red Sea.

Fukin, K., and J. Markakis, eds. 1994. *Ethnicity and Conflict in the Horn of Africa.* Athens: Ohio University Press.

Gorman, R. 1981. *Political Conflict on the Horn of Africa.* New York: Praeger.

Gurr, T., M. Marshall, and D. Khosla. 2000. *Peace and Conflict 2001: A Global Survey of Conflicts, Self-Determination Movements, and Democracy.* College Park: Center for International Development and Conflict Management, University of Maryland.

Legum, C., and T. Hodges. 1978. *After Angola: The War over Southern Africa.* 2d edition. New York: Africana.

Nzongola-Ntalaja, G., ed. 1991. *Conflict in the Horn of Africa.* Atlanta: African Studies Association Press.

Parker, K., A. Heindel, and A. Branch. 2000. *Armed Conflict in the World Today: A Country by Country Review.* Humanitarian Law Project: http://www.hri.ca/doccenter/docs/cpr/armedconflict2000.shtml# (accessed March 20, 2002).

Tillema, H.K. 1991. *International Armed Conflict Since 1945: A Bibliographic Handbook of Wars and Military Interventions*. Boulder: Westview.

1.69 Burundi: Tribe-Based Communal Violence and the Hutu Conflict August 1988–Ongoing

Although the immediate causes of this conflict remain unclear, they are rooted in Burundian society and history. The Tutsi tribe in Burundi makes up only 15 percent of the population, yet Tutsis dominate the country's political, economic, and social institutions. This dominance was the result of deliberate colonial policies and led to a bitter history of ethnic rivalry. Previous conflict between the Tutsi and the majority Hutu in 1972 had caused more than 100,000 deaths, and in 1964 it had involved neighboring Rwanda in war (*see* conflict 1.18).

In August 1988 Hutu began attacking local Tutsis in the northern districts, killing some 2,000 people. The Tutsi-dominated army was sent in, and, in a series of reprisal attacks, the army killed another 3,000, mainly Hutu villagers. More than 50,000 Hutus then took refuge in southern Rwanda. It was suggested that the initial attacks were made from Rwandan territory. Although the government of Burundi took measures to defuse the situation and heal the rift between the two communities, none succeeded. A number of killings and police operations continued throughout 1991, until another major rebellion took place between November and December 1991. Between 500 and 3,000 people are thought to have been killed in this instance.

In another coup attempt and period of turmoil in 1992 and 1993, about 100,000 people (most of them civilians and refugees) were killed in fighting between the Tutsi-dominated military and Hutu rebels. The conflict continued throughout 1994, and the international community feared bloodletting on the scale that was witnessed in Rwanda. To prevent this, the Organization of African Unity (OAU) proposed sending in a peacekeeping force. No attempts at peaceful conflict management were ever undertaken owing largely to the ethnic-based nature of the fighting. The Hutu majority had few recognized leaders with whom the government could negotiate. In 1995 the ethnic violence claimed between 10,000 and 15,000 lives and created large numbers of refugees in the region. The United Nations stepped up efforts to reconcile the two communities, and the OAU threatened to intervene militarily. A proposal to create two separate, ethnically based states—effectively a Hutuland and a Tutsiland—was rejected by all sides, and the conflict remained unresolved at the end of 1995, with continuing acts of violence occurring almost daily.

A short-lived peace pact that divided power between a Hutu president and a Tutsi prime minister ended when President Sylvestre Ntibantuganya, a Hutu, was removed from power by the military in July 1996 and replaced by a Tutsi, Pierre Buyoya, who continues to hold the office. Fighting immediately began between the Hutu rebels, known as the National Council for the Defence of Democracy (CNDD), and the Tutsi-dominated army. Tens of thousands of civilians fled to refugee camps in Zaire, now the Democratic Republic of the Congo (DRC). In October 1996 the then-rebel force in the DRC dispersed the camps on the Burundi/Rwanda borders where Hutu rebels from both countries had been based. More than 100,000 civilian Hutu refugees who had fled attacks by Burundi's army were also forced back over the border. There were numerous reports of disappearances of returning refugees and confirmed accounts of refugee massacres in Burundi and the DRC.

The fighting continued throughout 1997 and 1998 but intensified in 1998 with an attack near Bujumbura's airport that killed about 300. Both the CNDD and the government denied responsibility. The attack left as many as 15,000 people newly homeless, joining the tens of thousands of people already displaced. The CNDD has accused the army of killing almost 40,000 civilians since its 1996 coup, while the Burundian officials accuse the rebels of massacres.

As of 2003 at least three different groups were fighting in Burundi, primarily the Party for the Liberation of the Hutu People (Palipehutu) and its military wing the National Liberation Forces (NLF), the Front for National Liberation (FROLINA), and the CNDD and its military wing, the Forces for the Defense of Democracy (FDD). There are reports that these groups use bases inside the DRC. Reliable information supports accusations of mass killings of unarmed civilians by all parties. The Burundian army is said to target Hutu civilians in reprisal for opposition-armed attacks. The army has been accused of rape, torture, and killing detainees. Opposition groups have been accused of attacking refugees.

About 600,000 people (one-tenth of the population) are internally displaced, and with considerable forced relocation of Hutu civilians into widely condemned "regroupment" camps. The dispossessed are forced to deal with the destruction of their homes and crops, and the squalor of the regroupment camps has contributed to many more deaths. A cease-fire has been in effect since July 1998, although numerous clashes continue. In 1999 Nelson Mandela agreed to mediate, but fighting continued to intensify. In June 2000 Mandela reached an agreement with President Buyoya on two major points: (1) army restructuring along ethnically equal lines and (2) the closure of the Hutu regroupment camps. Intense international pressure to negotiate a settlement resulted in the signing of the Arusha Accords in August 2000, but the refusal of the two main rebel groups to accept the terms leaves the settlement in doubt. Civil war continues.

References

Gurr, T., M. Marshall, and D. Khosla. 2000. *Peace and Conflict 2001: A Global Survey of Conflicts, Self-Determination Movements, and Democracy.* College Park: Center for International Development and Conflict Management, University of Maryland.

Lemarchand, R. 1970. *Rwanda and Burundi.* New York: Praeger.

Melady, T. 1974. *Burundi: The Tragic Years.* Maryknoll, New York: Orbis.

Parker, K., A. Heindel, and A. Branch. 2000. *Armed Conflict in the World Today: A Country by Country Review.* Humanitarian Law Project: http://www.hri.ca/doccenter/docs/cpr/armedconflict2000.shtml# (accessed March 20, 2002).

Reyntjens, F. 1995. *Burundi: Breaking the Cycle of Violence.* London: Minority Rights Group.

Tillema, H.K. 1991. *International Armed Conflict Since 1945: A Bibliographic Handbook of Wars and Military Interventions.* Boulder: Westview.

1.70 Uganda–Kenya: Border Conflict March 1989

Uganda's persistent civil war (1981–1995) had led to strained border relations with Kenya, which played host to a steady flow of war-weary Ugandan refugees. The situation had already led to military conflict fourteen months earlier (*see* conflict 1.67), and each side regularly accused the other of harboring rebels.

Relations deteriorated still further when 400 heavily armed men in military uniform were reported to have invaded Kenya's West Pokot area on March 2, 1989. Serious fighting ensued, and more than seventy people were killed in the battle. Kenya protested vigorously, but Uganda blamed Karamojong cattle rustlers. On March 7 the Kenyan border town of Lokichokio was bombed and five people killed. Kenya again blamed Uganda and its collaborators, Sudan and Libya, for the attack and claimed Uganda was massing troops in the region. Relations eased in the following months, even though no attempts were made to resolve the conflict peacefully.

References

Avirgan, T., and M. Honey. 1982. *War in Uganda: The Legacy of Idi Amin.* Westport, Conn.: Lawrence Hill.

Hooper, E., and L. Pirouet. 1989. *Uganda.* Minority Rights Group Report #66. London: Minority Rights Group.

Mittleman, J. 1975. *Ideology and Politics in Uganda.* Ithaca, N.Y.: Cornell University Press.

Smith, G. 1980. *Ghosts of Kampala.* New York: St. Martin's.

1.71 Mauritania–Senegal: Ethnic Violence and Border Incidents April 1989–January 1990

Relations between these two West African countries were complicated by the many Senegalese nationals living and working in Mauritania and the numerous Mauritanians doing the same in Senegal. Mauritania, populated mostly by Arab Berbers, also suspected Senegal of harboring black African opponents of its regime. The conflict began with the death of two individuals in a dispute on April 9, 1989, over competing claims to farming rights on the common border, the Senegal River. Both sides reinforced troops along the border, and two more fatal shootings occurred a few days later. This violence was followed by ethnically motivated rioting and attacks in both countries. Despite a declared state of emergency, the attacks continued. An airlift and repatriation exercise was undertaken in early May to deal with the crisis. Thousands had to be flown back to their country of origin, most leaving all their possessions behind.

A steady deterioration in relations between the two countries followed the interethnic violence, with hostile diplomatic moves, troop buildups along the border, and reports of expulsions and forced repatriations. Mediations by the Maghreb Union and the Organization of African Unity (OAU), plus a number of negotiations, failed to resolve the crisis. In January 1990 the conflict escalated with an exchange of heavy artillery fire across the Senegal River. The fighting subsided, however, and negotiations in July 1991 brought about a partial settlement to the conflict, although relations remained tense. In all, up to 500 people are thought to have been killed during the conflict, most of these in the ethnic violence.

References

Africa Contemporary Record. Annual. 1968/1969– .

African Recorder. Weekly. 1962– .

Folz, W.J. 1965. *From French West Africa to the Mali Federation.* New Haven: Yale University Press.

LeVine, V.T. 1967. *Political Leadership in Africa: Postindependence Generational Conflict in Upper Volta, Senegal, Niger, Dahomey, and the Central African Republic.* Stanford, California: Hoover.

1.72 Liberia: Civil War December 1989–Ongoing

This conflict began in December 1989, when Charles Taylor led the previously unknown National Patriotic Front of Liberia (NPFL) in an attack on government forces, launching the assault in northeastern Liberia from bases in Sierra Leone. A former government employee charged with theft, Taylor had escaped custody in the United States. The NPFL was composed of political dissidents and ex-soldiers who fled Liberia after a 1985 putsch failed to unseat President Samuel Doe; Libya and Burkina Faso had backed the coup attempt.

The fighting turned into a full-scale revolt against Doe's regime when government troops began to exact brutal punishment against local villagers. By May 1990 the rebels were moving south, and by mid-July fighting had moved into the capital, Monrovia. Doe's government was close to collapse. A splinter group from the NPFL emerged at this time led by Prince Yormie Johnson, who was opposed to both Taylor and President Doe. Many atrocities and revenge attacks on civilians occurred during the fighting, including a massacre of 500 refugees in a church on July 29, 1990, by government troops. U.S. mediation in September 1990 failed to halt the bloodshed.

The Economic Community of West African States (ECOWAS) emerged as the primary peace broker. It sent a peacekeeping force, the ECOWAS Monitoring Group (ECOMOG), to Liberia in August 1990 to stop the war and oversee a cease-fire. ECOMOG arranged a meeting between Doe and Johnson in September 1990, but fighting broke out at the meeting, and Doe was killed. In October 1990 ECOMOG forces launched an offensive to separate the warring factions, which was largely successful. A cease-fire in November 1990 led to a wider peace agreement in February 1991.

By this point, four main factions claimed leadership of the country: Brigadier General David Nimley, who was Doe's successor; Charles Taylor; Prince Johnson; and Amos Sawyer, an academic and lawyer who was the head of an ECOWAS-installed interim government. In November 1991 another group called the United Liberation Movement of Liberia for Democracy (ULIMO), made up of Doe supporters and based in Sierra Leone, also joined the war, attacking the NPFL.

Throughout 1991 and early 1992, the peace agreement was partially successful, but it stumbled on the intransigence of Taylor, who refused to disarm or join the interim government. Numerous incidents and atrocities continued, until full-scale fighting broke out between ULIMO and NPFL forces in August 1992. In October 1992 the NPFL attacked ECOMOG forces in Monrovia in an attempt to seize the capital. ECOMOG responded with massive air attacks. Over 1993 and 1994 ULIMO and ECOMOG made significant gains against Taylor's NPFL, but not enough to dislodge him completely. In June 1993 a massacre of 450 refugees briefly focused world attention on the conflict. The United Nations sent an envoy but left the conflict largely in the hands of ECOWAS. In September Nigeria decided to withdraw its troops from ECOMOG, weakening it greatly and negating its gains. Despite numerous conflict management attempts, none of the underlying issues had been resolved by 1994. No side had either the ability to achieve a significant advantage nor the willpower to make any real concessions in the interest of peace. Many of the dead were civilians killed in grisly massacres, reprisals, or by starvation and disease. A cease-fire in December 1994 held until April 1995, when another brutal massacre claimed the lives of sixty-two people, mainly women and children. By this stage, the war had cost upward of 150,000 lives, and peace remained elusive.

In August 1995 the end of the war appeared to be imminent with the signing of a peace accord in Abuja, the new Nigerian capital. In September, a transitional government was formed; elections were planned for 1996; and all the warlords went to Monrovia to take their places in the transitional government. Under the agreement, ECOMOG was charged with disarming an estimated 60,000 rebels, but fighting in April 1996 over the attempted arrest of Roosevelt Johnson, leader of the Liberation Movement for Democracy in Liberia (ULIMO-J), prolonged the conflict throughout the summer. Within days, the capital was engulfed in anarchy and factional fighting.

Charles Taylor was elected president in May 1997. An ECOWAS-brokered peace agreement in August 1997 largely ended the civil war in Liberia but did not lead to reconciliation among all warring factions. Fighting erupted in Monrovia in 1998, and another outbreak was recorded in northern Lofa Country in August 1999. Throughout 1999, there were reports of widespread human rights abuses by the government's military forces and paramilitary forces, primarily former NPFL combatants and 10,000 former non-NPFL combatants. These troops were ostensibly deployed to prevent attacks from insurgents in the border area. Armed rebels of the ethnic Krahn-based ULIMO headed by Roosevelt Johnson continued to oppose Taylor's government. Incursions by rebels based in Guinea increased tensions between Liberia and Guinea.

Liberia has 2.7 million people, and half of them became refugees within their own country. More than 250,000 people were killed, most of them civilians. On July 6, 2003, Taylor accepted an offer of asylum from Nigeria's president, and on August 11 he stepped down as president, handed over power to Vice President Moses Blah, and left Liberia.

References

Africa Contemporary Record. Annual. 1968/1969– .

African Recorder. Weekly. 1962– .

Clapham, C.S. 1976. *Liberia and Sierra Leone: Essay in Comparative Politics*. Cambridge: Cambridge University Press.

Gurr, T., M. Marshall, and D. Khosla. 2000. *Peace and Conflict 2001: A Global Survey of Conflicts, Self-Determination Movements, and Democracy*. College Park: Center for International Development and Conflict Management, University of Maryland.

Parker, K., A. Heindel, and A. Branch. 2000. *Armed Conflict in the World Today: A Country by Country Review.* Humanitarian Law Project: http://www.hri.ca/doccenter/docs/cpr/armedconflict2000.shtml# (accessed March 20, 2002).

1.73 Guinea-Bissau–Senegal: Border Conflict
April–May 1990

Relations between the West African states of Senegal and Guinea-Bissau had been tense for some time. In addition to a long-standing dispute over the demarcation of the maritime border, each side accused the other of harboring subversives. Serious border clashes in April and May 1990 and an exchange of artillery fire between border troops resulted in seventeen deaths. Pressures were extremely high, and there were fears of more serious conflict. But, as neither side wanted to go to war, they sought a peaceful solution to the conflict.

Following emergency talks in Paris and negotiations in São Domingo, Guinea-Bissau, the two sides agreed to maintain border troops at a reasonable distance, strengthen military cooperation, and refrain from harboring each other's rebels. Relations stabilized after this point.

References

Africa Contemporary Record. Annual. 1968/1969– .

African Recorder. Weekly. 1962– .

Folz, W.J. 1965. *From French West Africa to the Mali Federation.* New Haven: Yale University Press.

LeVine, V.T. 1967. *Political Leadership in Africa: Postindependence Generational Conflict in Upper Volta, Senegal, Niger, Dahomey, and the Central African Republic.* Stanford, Calif.: Hoover.

Touval, S. 1972. *The Boundary Politics of Independent Africa.* Cambridge: Harvard University Press.

1.74 Tuareg–Niger: Confrontation and Reprisals
May 1990–October 1994

The Tuareg, a Muslim nomadic tribe spread out over the Sahel region of north-central Africa, had a long history of grievances against the Niger government. These included overzealous army reprisals, development policies aimed primarily at urbanized inhabitants and settled agriculturalists, government neglect, broken promises regarding resettlement aid, and so forth. In May 1990 Tuareg nomads, recruited and trained in Libya, attacked a gendarmerie in the region of Tchin-Tabaradene in Niger. The Tuareg were returning refugees, and the fighting soon took on a separatist tone, as the Tuareg blamed the government for failing to keep its promises. The death toll reached several hundred, and government troops were blamed for reprisal killings. The Tuareg were organized into the Liberation Front of Air and Azawad (FLAA).

Although the conflict was fairly low level during 1991, attacks continued, and in early 1992 the new government was determined to find a solution without partitioning the country. In February the government closed the border with Algeria, possibly to stop the infiltration of arms to the Tuareg. In May peace initiatives resulted in a truce and the agreement to pursue further talks. In September, however, some elements of the army took unauthorized reprisals against the Tuareg, and the conflict flared again. At the end of 1992 the government had released Tuareg taken prisoner by rebellious army troops, and the peace process resumed.

Peace efforts continued into 1993 and 1994, with intermittent clashes and outbreaks of fighting. Efforts by Algeria, Burkina Faso, and France led to a full settlement of the conflict in October 1994. At times throughout the conflict, the fighting was intense, and more than 400 people were killed, many of them civilians in reprisals.

References

Africa Contemporary Record. Annual. 1968/1969– .

African Recorder. Weekly. 1962– .

Folz, W.J. 1965. *From French West Africa to the Mali Federation.* New Haven: Yale University Press.

LeVine, V.T. 1967. *Political Leadership in Africa: Postindependence Generational Conflict in Upper Volta, Senegal, Niger, Dahomey, and the Central African Republic.* Stanford, Calif.: Hoover.

1.75 Senegal: The Casamance Rebellion
Mid-1990–Ongoing

Casamance province in southern Senegal is nearly cut off from the rest of the country by Gambia, an independent state that forms an elongated "enclave" within Senegal, along the Gambia River. In 1982, complaining of government neglect, the people of Casamance organized the Movement of Democratic Forces of Casamance (MFDC) to voice their demands for better treatment. When MFDC demonstrations turned violent in 1982 and 1983, a brutal government crackdown on the protesters garnered more sympathy and support for the movement. As a consequence, the organization began to adopt secessionist aims. Low-level agitation continued for the next few years.

In mid-1990 the MFDC launched a full-scale secessionist insurrection with a series of attacks on civilian and army personnel. The government responded by reinforcing troops in the Casamance, and a vicious guerrilla war ensued. Largely made up of members of the

Diola tribe, the MFDC often targeted Muslim Madingos and Fulanis. In mid-1992 the conflict featured widespread ethnic violence, which the government had difficulty containing. The violence continued into 1995, with spectacular MFDC attacks and brutal government counterattacks, including reported disappearances, summary executions, and other human rights abuses.

The fighting led to thousands of refugees seeking safety in Gambia. The war threatened to escalate in December 1992, when Senegalese infantry forces bombarded MFDC rebel bases near São Domingo, Guinea-Bissau. A number of Guinean civilians were killed in the attack, and the Guinea-Bissau government protested. Senegalese aircraft also bombed targets in Guinea-Bissau in February 1995, despite Guinean protestations that they were not aiding the rebels. Also in 1995 international attention was focused on the region when the rebels began kidnapping foreign nationals.

In all, several hundred people lost their lives, and, despite a government peace commission set up in 1990, the fighting continued. Mediation by Guinea-Bissau led to a number of short-lived cease-fires, but the underlying issues remained unresolved. The conflict was complicated in mid-1992 when the MFDC split, and a new faction emerged that opposed the peace process.

Renewed clashes in August 1997 led to further deaths. The situation worsened in September when an army offensive was launched against secessionist rebels in Senegal in response to a wave of assassinations and kidnappings. These clashes coincided with unsuccessful peace talks. In January 1998 the Guinea-Bissau army, which had deployed reinforcements along the border of southern Casamance, killed ten MFDC members and captured forty. The leader of the MFDC, Augustine Diamacoune Senghor, called for his followers to cease hostilities, which led to a notable reduction in violence. Attacks and confrontations between the army and MFDC forces continued, however. It soon became apparent that the aging MFDC leader was losing influence with the rebel movement, which splintered further into gangs of armed bandits. Rebels in northern Casamance were favorably disposed toward negotiations with the government, but the militiamen of the south remained committed to armed struggle. Clashes continued into May 1998.

Throughout 1998 the economic and ecological wellbeing of Casamance was under serious threat. Tourism seriously declined, and deforestation increased. The civilian population had been subjected to arbitrary detention, murder, rape, extortion, and intimidation from both sides throughout the conflict, but in 1998 their plight worsened with a rise in violent armed robberies, the introduction by rebels of landmines into the conflict, and Senegalese intervention in the civil war in Guinea-Bissau. Tens of thousands of Bissau-Guineans and Casamancais found themselves trapped between two vicious conflicts.

The violence continued in 1999, with rogue rebel elements hindering any progress in the peace process, despite attempts at dialogue. In the face of increased military activity, talks opened in June among separatist factions in the Casamance region seeking to establish a united front before reopening negotiations with the Senegalese government. Government talks with MFDC forces produced a December 1999 cease-fire, and peace talks were held in January 2000 in accordance with the cease-fire agreement. Even with the moves toward negotiation, sporadic fighting continued through January and February of that year. Achieving peace in Casamance was a priority for newly elected President Abdeulaye Wade soon after he took office in March 2000, but the situation began to deteriorate rapidly. Minor clashes by rebels based in Guinea-Bissau were reported in April. In October the Gambian government withdrew from its role as mediator in the conflict.

Now in its eighteenth year, the Casamance problem, which began as a contest between a single-issue independence movement and the Senegalese authorities, has grown in complexity. The independence movement has fragmented, while neighboring countries—especially Guinea-Bissau—have become more deeply enmeshed in the conflict. Signals are contradictory: the consistently hard line of the Senegalese government does not prevent it from attending peace negotiations, and, while one part of the rebel movement escalates its violence, another talks peace. The outcome of the conflict remains unclear. The civilian population, meanwhile, remains the principal victim.

References

Africa Contemporary Record. Annual. 1968/1969– .

African Recorder. Weekly. 1962– .

Folz, W.J. 1965. *From French West Africa to the Mali Federation*. New Haven: Yale University Press.

Gurr, T., M. Marshall, and D. Khosla. 2000. *Peace and Conflict 2001: A Global Survey of Conflicts, Self-Determination Movements, and Democracy*. College Park: Center for International Development and Conflict Management, University of Maryland.

Keesing's Record of World Events: K43781, K43349, K42258, K41993, K41803.

LeVine, V.T. 1967. *Political Leadership in Africa: Postindependence Generational Conflict in Upper Volta, Senegal, Niger, Dahomey, and the Central African Republic*. Stanford, California: Hoover.

Middle East Intelligence Wire, August 10, 1997.

Posthumus, B. 2002. *European Platform for Conflict Prevention and Transformation Online*. Country Surveys: www.euconflict.org/euconflict/guides/surveys.htm (February 8, 2002).

Reuters Online New Service. April 9, 1997.

Touval, S. 1972. *The Boundary Politics of Independent Africa*. Cambridge: Harvard University Press.

1.76 Tuareg–Mali: Sahel Pastoralist Rebellion and Military Coup June 1990–Ongoing

A pastoral tribe inhabiting the Sahel region in north-central Africa, the Tuareg had nursed some long-standing grievances against their central governments of Mali and Niger. Prompted by the Tuareg fighting in Niger, Tuareg in Mali launched an attack in 1990 at Menaka in the north, in which some twenty people died (*see* conflict 1.74). The government declared a state of emergency and carried out reprisal attacks in July and August. In this case, it appeared that the Tuareg nomads were attempting to overthrow the government rather than simply secede. After Algerian mediation, a peace agreement was signed in January 1991, but there were reports of fighting again in May.

The government of Mali was overthrown in March 1991 by a popular revolution and replaced by a transitional government. At this point, the Tuareg rebellion erupted in earnest, with rebel attacks and government reprisals. The renewed fighting caused refugees to flee into neighboring Algeria, worsening the strains between those two countries; there was also speculation about Libyan and French involvement in the rebellion. In addition, the refugees were thought to have established bases and launched attacks from Algerian territory.

The conflict was partly settled after an all-party conference in December 1991 and negotiations in January 1992, which produced a cease-fire. Another agreement was signed in March, but an attack on the Tuareg in May underlined the fragility of the peace agreement. The Tuareg responded with fresh rebel activity in July. At the end of 1992 the implementation of the agreement was going ahead, albeit with delays and continued strains. Tension and occasional violence were still present in 1993 and 1994, and, despite negotiations leading to a number of minor agreements, the conflict remained unresolved at the end of 1994. In all, more than 300 people were killed.

The conflict went through a final phase of escalation before peace could prevail, with widespread killings by rebel groups and revenge killings by the armed forces. The violence receded during 1995. A series of locally mediated agreements that fed into a national process of reducing violence and building peace resulted in considerable improvements. In early 1996 former Tuareg rebels were integrated into the national army and paramilitary services to help consolidate the peace process. In March of that year, the Tuareg Unified Movements, the Fronts of Azawad, and the Ghanda Koy Movement announced their "irreversible dissolution." A ceremonial burning of 3,000 firearms (known as the "Flames of Peace") took place in March 1996 to mark the end of the five-year conflict. In June 1999 the United Nations Commission of Human Rights ended its repatriation and resettlement program for people who fled northern Mali after the Tuareg rebellion broke out in 1990. The basic problems that underpin the conflict, however, remain.

References

Africa Contemporary Record. Annual. 1968/1969– .

African News Service. Reuters June 29, 1999.

African Recorder. Weekly. 1962– .

Folz, W.J. 1965. *From French West Africa to the Mali Federation.* New Haven: Yale University Press.

Keesing's Record of World Events: K40892, K40942, K40983.

Posthumus, B. 2002. *European Platform for Conflict Prevention and Transformation Online.* Country Surveys: www.euconflict.org/euconflict/guides/surveys.htm (February 8, 2002).

1.77 Rwanda: Tribal Conflict, Genocide, and Exiles Invasion September 1990–Ongoing

Intense tribal animosities between the Tutsi and Hutu people are at the root of this conflict. These animosities deepened after a bloody 1959 coup ousted a Tutsi government and increased even further after bloodshed in 1963 and 1973 sent Tutsi Rwandans flooding into neighboring countries. At present, more than 70,000 Tutsi refugees reside in Uganda, and estimates put the number of refugees at 1 million worldwide. Successive Rwandan governments have refused to acknowledge them as Rwandan nationals.

On the night of September 30, 1990, the Tutsi-dominated Rwandan Patriotic Front (RPF) invaded Rwanda from Uganda seeking to overthrow President Juvénal Habyarimana's regime and to repatriate all the refugees. The invasion was launched in the Mutara region in the north and was contained only after thousands of French, Belgium, and Zairean troops were dispatched. Hundreds of troops were killed in the initial clashes, which were intense. Diplomatic efforts by Organization of African Unity (OAU) and Belgian mediators failed to stop the fighting in the second half of October, and by the end of the month the government was claiming victory.

But RPF forces continued to invade from Uganda and engage government troops, particularly throughout December 1990 and January 1991. There were many fatalities. Fighting continued into March, despite peace initiatives, until Zairean President Mobutu Sésé Séko secured a shaky cease-fire on March 18. This soon collapsed, and low-level guerrilla fighting continued throughout the year. Numerous peace efforts during this period also failed. The formation of a transitional government in Rwanda in April 1992 saw the beginning of serious peace initiatives by the government, although fighting intensified again in May and June.

In July 1992 the government and the RPF began serious peace negotiations in Arusha, Tanzania. Despite continuous accusations of cease-fire violations, the two parties made progress. In October they signed a power-sharing agreement and agreed to end the war, but there was opposition to this, and sporadic ethnic violence was still evident at the end of 1992.

In early 1993 the RPF launched another major offensive after Hutu extremists killed fifty-three Tutsi. France sent in troops to protect its nationals. Peace talks continued. The parties signed a settlement in August 1993, but it never took hold. On April 6, 1994, the presidents of Rwanda and Burundi were killed in a suspicious plane crash. At this point, Hutu militias launch a well-organized and systematic massacre of Tutsi civilians and opposition members.

The RPF resumed its offensive in earnest and made significant gains, but it could not prevent the massacres of up to 500,000 Tutsi and Hutu opposition members by the gangs. Although the United Nations had observers on the ground and intelligence to suggest that the Hutu were waging a genocidal campaign, the world body vacillated, eventually doing nothing to stop the mass killings. The RPF captured the whole country by mid-July 1994, and its victory caused more than 1 million Rwandans to flee the country, mainly ethnic Hutus who feared reprisals at the hands of the Tutsi-dominated rebels.

The repatriation of Rwandan refugees continued to vex the region throughout 1995, especially after a moderate Hutu political leader was assassinated in May in Kigali. The former Hutu government and its extremist militias also began to receive arms and organize for guerrilla warfare in 1995, and there were a number of clashes in border areas, culminating in an RPF government attack on a rebel training camp at Lake Kivu that left 141 rebels dead.

In all, as many as 1 million Rwandans were killed in this phase of the conflict—mainly Tutsis by Hutu militias and Hutu colleagues and neighbors. Continued violence and animosity in refugee camps made the situation there extremely volatile. Despite frantic mediation efforts by the UN, the OAU, and Tanzanian officials during the worst of the fighting, no issues were resolved, and nothing could stop the violence. French troops in Rwanda were only partially successful in protecting civilians.

In July 1994 the Tutsi-dominated RPF captured the capital. The Hutu factions responsible for the 1994 genocide, the Interahamwe (the former governments militia), were driven and pursued into neighboring regions, mainly Uganda and the DRC (Democratic Republic of Congo, formerly Zaire).

More than 1 million Hutu refugees have lived in refugee camps in the DRC, Tanzania, Burundi, and Uganda as a result of the killings. The Interahamwe militiamen (literally, "those who work together," but, in this case, "those who fight together") from the northwest based themselves in border areas and refugee camps, intimidating refugees not to return and conducting raids into the country. They also joined in attacks with Burundian Hutu rebels.

An estimated 15,000 Hutu rebels of the Army for the Liberation of Rwanda (ALIR) began advocating the destruction of the Tutsi minority, publishing racist literature, and broadcasting hate messages from a clandestine radio station in Democratic Republic of the Congo (DRC). The ALIR reportedly assassinated local officials and freed hundreds of genocide suspects. RPF counterinsurgency campaigns resulted in the deaths of thousands of Hutu civilians, increasing support for the ALIR in its areas.

In December 1997 at least 271 people were hacked to death at Mudende camp, following an attack four months earlier. In early January 1998 the ALIR entered Rwanda from Congolese bases and killed and maimed Tutsi civilians. The Hutu army is said to have had one goal—to kill as many Tutsi as possible in Rwanda, Burundi, and the DRC. Rwanda's army had troops in the DRC since DRC's President Laurent Kabila's May 1997 victory. Hundreds of thousands of Rwandan Hutu refugees began returning home after their camps were raided and dispersed by Zairian rebels led by Kabila, acting with the assistance of the RPF. The RPF has been accused of massacring thousands of Hutu refugees during these joint operations.

In July 1998 Kabila asked the Rwandan army to leave the DRC, and in August 1998, citing Kabila's inability to secure their common border, the RPF began supporting the new rebel movement there. Kabila's forces fought the Congolese rebels with significant support from those considered responsible for the Rwandan genocide: the former Rwandan Armed Forces (FAR) and the Interahamwe militias. As many as 40,000 Hutu Rwandan rebel troops were thought to be active in the DRC, from where they carried out raids into Rwanda as part of a campaign to eliminate Tutsi and overthrow the Tutsi government. The Rwandan government promised to withdraw its troops from the DRC under the 1999 Lusaka agreement, but wanted its security concerns addressed beforehand. Kabila himself was assassinated in January 2001, allegedly by one of his bodyguards.

Since the end of the genocide in 1994, tens of thousands of people have been murdered in Rwanda and at least 5,000 killed in massacres by Hutu militias. Much of the violence in centered in Gisenyi and Ruhengeri provinces in the north where some 600,000 displaced people live. The RPF have been accused of large-scale disappearances. The Rwandan government is still holding more than 100,000 people accused of participating in the genocide. Approximately 1,500 people have been tried, and in April 1998, twenty-two convicted persons were executed.

On June 19, 2002, the traditional courts or *gacaca* were established by Rwandan authorities to begin to try the alleged perpetrators of the 1994 genocide. More than 100,000 people were expected to appear before these courts in 2003, including several journalists. "At least 25 journalists were in prison in Rwanda at the end of 2002. All were accused of participating, in one form or another, in the 1994 genocide." From the evidence presented so far, only two of these cases constituted press freedom violations and the justification for imprisonment of the other journalists is inconclusive. Freedom of the press in Rwanda remains tenuous.

In 2003 a European Union Election Observer Mission (EOM) was deployed in Rwanda to observe the referendum on the new constitution held on May 26. The EU has decided to extend EOM's mandate to the forthcoming presidential and parliamentary elections scheduled for August 25 and September 29, 2004, respectively. The satisfactory completion of these events is expected to strengthen the foundations of democratic and sustainable institutions in Rwanda.

After its experience of war and genocide, Rwanda is now taking a more active role in regional and international conflict management. In July 2003 Patrick Mazimhaka, Rwanda's presidential special envoy for the Great Lakes, was elected deputy chairperson of the ten-person African Union Commission, and President Paul Kagame was elected as the first vice-chairman of the African Union. Rwanda also participates in the UN and presided over the Security Council during part of 1995. "The UN assistance mission in Rwanda (UNAMIR), a UN Chapter Six peacekeeping operation, involved personnel from more than a dozen countries. Most of the UN development and humanitarian agencies have had a large presence in Rwanda."

References

Gurr, T., M. Marshall, and D. Khosla. 2000. *Peace and Conflict 2001: A Global Survey of Conflicts, Self-Determination Movements, and Democracy.* College Park: Center for International Development and Conflict Management, University of Maryland.

Lemarchand, R. 1970. *Rwanda and Burundi.* New York: Praeger.

Parker, K., A. Heindel, and A. Branch. 2000. *Armed Conflict in the World Today: A Country by Country Review.* Humanitarian Law Project: http://www.hri.ca/doccenter/docs/cpr/armedconflict2000.shtml# (accessed March 20, 2002).

Segal, A. 1964. *Massacre in Rwanda.* Fabian Research Series #240. London: Fabian Society.

Tillema, H.K. 1991. *International Armed Conflict Since 1945: A Bibliographic Handbook of Wars and Military Interventions.* Boulder: Westview.

1.78 Liberia–Sierra Leone: Intervention, Destabilization, and the Sierra Leone Civil War March 1991–Ongoing

While Liberia settled into an uneasy peace and tried to negotiate an end to its civil war, members of Charles Taylor's National Patriotic Front of Liberia (NPFL) began cross-border raids into Sierra Leone in March 1991, killing numerous civilians. The NPFL wanted to destabilize Sierra Leone and take control of mineral-rich areas close to the Liberian border in order to finance its war in Liberia. By mid-April Sierra Leone forces were pursuing the raiders inside NPFL-held Liberian territory. Meanwhile, NPFL troops with heavy weapons were advancing into Sierra Leone, aided by a heavily armed Sierra Leone guerrilla movement, the Revolutionary United Front (RUF), led by Foday Sankoh. Although its specific aims were unclear, the RUF was opposed to the Sierra Leone government. The fighting was intense, and both sides claimed successes.

In May 1991 Nigerian and Guinean troops were deployed in border areas to help Sierra Leone. By this stage, NPFL troops had advanced some 150 kilometers into Sierra Leone territory. Burkinabe troops may also have been fighting for Taylor's group. The NPFL continued to fight alongside the Sierra Leone guerrillas for some time, partly because the Sierra Leone government had backed a rival Liberian faction that had invaded NPFL territory from Sierra Leone in September 1991.

Fighting continued until April 1992, when a coup in Sierra Leone led to renewed peace efforts by the new government. Although these overtures did not succeed, the surge in fighting in Liberia itself compelled NPFL forces to shift their focus away from Sierra Leone. The RUF, however, continued to fight the government, leading to a general state of civil war. By this stage, the RUF's only discernible aim was to rid the country of foreign troops. Nigerian and Guinean peacekeepers began to take mounting casualties, as the government was unable to contain rebel activities.

Fighting was intense throughout the conflict, with more than 4,600 people killed, many in grisly massacres. No attempts at peaceful conflict management took place, even though Sierra Leone's government had offered negotiations. The United Nations sent a mediator, but this envoy was unable to make contact with rebel leaders. Sierra Leone was in a general state of anarchy by the end of 1995, with inter- and intrafactional fighting complicating the conflict. Since the outbreak of civil war in 1991, more than 100,000 people have been killed. The 1.2 million internal refugees suffered malnutrition, and severe security problems emptied the countryside. Banditry was common. In 1995 the rebels started kidnapping foreign nationals, which got the attention of the international community.

In February 1996 Sierra Leone held its first multiparty election in three decades, electing Ahmed Tejan Kabbah president. In April 1995 Executive Outcomes, a South African-based company specializing in mercenary activities, trained the Republic of Sierra Leone Military Force (RSLMF) units and participated in attacks against the RUF. The attacks took a serious toll on the rebels, and in March 1996 a cease-fire was announced. By the end of the year, the Abidjan Accord was in place. In May 1997, however, the president was overthrown by a military junta calling itself the Armed Forces Revolutionary Council (AFRC) led by Major Johnny Paul Koromah. The coup led to peace between the new regime and the

RUF, but desultory fighting continued against the Kamajors, a Mende ethnic militia led by Hinga Norman, architect of an earlier coup in 1967. This militia was armed and trained by the Nigerians.

The 1997 Conakry Accord, brokered by the Economic Community of West African States (ECOWAS) provided that ECOMOG, the ECOWAS military force, would disarm all factions and reorganize Sierra Leone's army. Disarmament did not occur as agreed, and Koromah indicated he probably would not meet the deadline for transfer of power. The UN and Nigeria imposed sanctions. In February 1998 Nigerian forces captured Freetown, and in the following week the Kamajors occupied Bo and Kenema. The junta leaders fled, and Kabbah was reinstated as president. The remaining rebel forces, including remnants of the AFRC, continued sporadic but violent attacks against civilians, many of whom had their hands hacked off. Several hundred thousand began streaming into government-controlled areas.

In June 1999 the warring factions signed the Lome Agreement, but many RUF forces refused to disarm and continued to control the interior, including diamond mines. Numerous clashes have been reported since the peace agreement was implemented and serious fighting was renewed in early 2000. Spillover effects have led to increased tensions in neighboring Guinea and clashes involving Guinean and Liberian forces. Since the civil war began in 1991, between 15,000 and 50,000 people have died, and more than 30 percent of the population has been displaced, with 400,000 refugees living in Guinea.

References

Africa Contemporary Record. Annual. 1968/1969– .

African Recorder. Weekly. 1962– .

Assefa, H. 1987. *Mediation of Civil Wars: Approaches and Strategies—The Sudan Conflict.* Boulder: Westview.

Avirgan, T. and M. Honey. 1982. *War in Uganda: The Legacy of Idi Amin.* Westport, Conn.: Lawrence Hill.

Gurr, T., M. Marshall, and D. Khosla. 2000. *Peace and Conflict 2001: A Global Survey of Conflicts, Self-Determination Movements, and Democracy.* College Park: Center for International Development and Conflict Management, University of Maryland.

Parker, K., A. Heindel, and A. Branch. 2000. *Armed Conflict in the World Today: A Country by Country Review.* Humanitarian Law Project: http://www.hri.ca/doccenter/docs/cpr/armedconflict2000.shtml# (accessed March 20, 2002).

1.79 Djibouti: Ethnic-Based Violence and Civil War
November 1991–July 1993

The Djibouti civil war began in early November 1991 as a revolt by the Front for the Restoration of Unity and Democracy (FRUD) against the Issa-dominated central government (the Issas are ethnically related to Somalis). The Afaris, who have strong ethnic ties to the Ethiopians, make up 35 percent of the Djibouti population and had long been mistreated by the majority Issas. Ethiopia assisted the Afari rebel movement by providing training and support, and Afaris living in Ethiopia and Somalia joined the guerrilla group as fighters. The Djibouti government claimed early on that FRUD was a foreign invasion force.

The rebels' aim was to replace "the tribalist regime of President Hassan Gouled Aptidon with a government of national unity that represents equally the Issas, the Afaris, and other communities." Fighting centered on the northern coastal towns of Tadjoura and Obock and was intense during late November and December 1991. Despite several French attempts at mediation, fighting continued into January 1992.

French diplomatic efforts produced a cease-fire and moves toward a negotiated end to the conflict in February 1992, as well as the deployment of a French peacekeeping force. The cease-fire broke down in mid-June, and high civilian casualties began to result from a government blockade of the rebel areas in the north, leading to starvation and disease. The fighting continued into 1993, but ended in July when negotiations between government ministers and FRUD leaders resulted in a full settlement of the conflict. FRUD joined the political process, and the Afar fighters were integrated into the army. Approximately fifty fatalities were directly attributed to the conflict. Ethnically based civil war resumed in 1998 (*see* conflict 1.89).

References

Africa Contemporary Record. Annual. 1968/1969– .

African Recorder. Weekly. 1962– .

Andereggen, A. 1994. *France's Relationship With Sub-Saharan Africa.* Westport, Conn.: Praeger.

Clayton, A. 1988. *France, Soldiers, and Africa.* London: Brassey's.

1.80 Nigeria–Cameroon: Territorial Dispute and the Diamond and Djabane Islands Dispute
December 1993–March 1994

Following a long history of border disputes, the Diamond and Djabane Islands in the Gulf of Guinea, off the coast of West Africa, became the source of serious conflict in late 1993. These areas provided good fishing grounds and were thought to contain oil deposits. On December 30, 1993, 500 Nigerian troops invaded and occupied the islands and killed six Cameroon soldiers. Cameroon responded with a number of incursions, and there was a serious battle on February 19, 1994, on the Bakassi peninsula, where up to twenty soldiers were killed.

The conflict escalated even further when France sent troops and a frigate to bolster Cameroon's forces in late February. Numerous negotiations failed to stop the conflict, but following mediation by African leaders from the region and the Organization of African Unity (OAU), the dispute abated beginning in March. French forces were withdrawn, and troops maintained separation. Cameroon attempted to have the dispute submitted to the International Court of Justice (ICJ) in April, but Nigeria refused, and the basic issues remained unresolved.

References

Brownlie, I. 1963. *African Boundaries: A Legal and Diplomatic Encyclopedia*. Berkeley and Los Angeles: University of California Press.

Day, A., ed. 1987. *Border and Territorial Disputes*. 2d edition. Burnt Mill, Harlow (Essex), England: Longman.

Touval, S. 1972. *The Boundary Politics of Independent Africa*. Cambridge: Harvard University Press.

1.81 Ghana–Togo: Border Incidents January–February 1994

Relations between Ghana and Togo had been strained for some time. After armed conflict between these two West African states in 1982, Ghana backed a 1986 coup attempt against the Togolese government. The two regimes constantly traded accusations of harboring each other's rebels.

Armed conflict broke out in January 1994, when government forces and an armed group engaged in serious fighting in Lomé, Togo's capital. Nearly 100 people were killed. Claiming that Ghana had trained and then infiltrated Togolese rebels into the capital, Togo responded by shelling Ghana across the border. Evidence supported the claim that Ghana was backing Togolese opposition forces. A number of serious border incidents occurred in the following days, and the situation was complicated by an outbreak of ethnic-based fighting in northern Ghana in February, which left 1,000 dead. More than 6,000 refugees fled to Togo. Although no intensive conflict management attempts were made, the fighting stopped. After a few months, relations returned to a state of nonviolent antagonism.

References

Awoonor, K. 1990. *Ghana: A Political History from Pre-European to Modern Times*. Accra: Sedco.

Carmichael, J. 1993. *African Eldorado: Gold Coast to Ghana*. London: Duckworth.

Tillema, H.K. 1991. *International Armed Conflict Since 1945: A Bibliographic Handbook of Wars and Military Interventions*. Boulder: Westview.

1.82 Uganda: Intervention and Democratic Movements May 1995–Ongoing

The situation in Uganda involves at least two civil wars, as well as military actions against Rwanda carried out in the Democratic Republic of the Congo (DRC) (*see* conflicts 1.49; 1.67; 1.77). Several rebel groups are fighting in Uganda. The Ugandan government has been fighting the Lord's Resistance Army (LRA) since the current president, Yoweri Museveni, took power in 1986. To bolster its forces, the LRA uses abducted children as combatants. Based on the border with Sudan, its aim is to replace the current government with one based on the biblical Ten Commandments. The LRA engages in military action against the Sudanese People's Liberation Army (SPLA) in Sudan due to its belief that the SPLA receives support from the Ugandan government.

In May 1995 the Kakwa-dominated West Nile Bank Front (WNBF) began fighting with the aim of returning Idi Amin, the former dictator, to power. The Allied Democratic Front (ADF), based on Uganda's border with the Democratic Republic of the Congo, has been fighting government forces since November 1996. Senior officials in the opposition Democratic Party (DP) formed the Federal Democratic Army (FDA), also in November 1996, to fight for the establishment of federalism. The National Army for the Liberation of Uganda (NALU), the National Democratic Alliance (NDA), and the Ninth October Movement in the east are smaller groups that also have been fighting the government.

In May 1996 approximately 2,000 WNBF soldiers invaded Uganda from Sudan, but were beaten back by the Uganda People's Defense Forces (UPDF). Then, in September, 800 WNBF rebels, suspected to have been trained by the Sudanese military, again invaded from Sudan. The rebels attacked a refugee camp where southern Sudanese were living. Throughout 1996 the WNBF and the LRA attacked camps in Uganda, killing hundreds of Sudanese refugees. In early January 1997 fierce fighting was reported between government soldiers and the LRA. Human rights groups accused the LRA and the WNBF of killing hundreds of civilians, engaging in atrocities, and abducting school children. In January 1997 the United Nations began a relief effort for more than 40,000 displaced people in the north of the country. At the beginning of 1997 the LRA and the WNBF together controlled the northern third of the country and had formed an alliance against the government. Uganda accused Sudan of supporting the rebels, and Sudan in turn accused Uganda of assisting the SPLA. The two countries broke off diplomatic relations in 1995.

In October 1997 President Museveni offered amnesty to the LRA and its leaders. The LRA and the WNBF reportedly disbanded, but violence continued into 1998. In

June the ADF attacked the Kichwamba National Institute, burning close to 100 students and abducting another 100. In August 1999 the ADF carried out a number of raids and in September attacked a UPDF base. The UPDF counterattacked and overran seventeen ADF hideouts. Uganda accused Rwanda of helping the ADF, which Rwandan authorities vehemently denied. In November 1999 the UPDF deployed 6,000 soldiers against the ADF in the Ruwenzori Mountains in a move thought to have dealt a serious blow to the ADF. In December, however, the ADF abducted 365 inmates in the Ruwenzori area and massacred 90 of them.

In December 1999 Sudan and Uganda agreed to reestablish diplomatic relations and to stop providing support to each other's rebel groups (the Nairobi Accords). Since then, the ADF has increased its attacks in Western Uganda. Uganda passed a bill giving rebels six months to stop fighting in exchange for amnesty from prosecution. In February 2000 Uganda began negotiations with Sudan for the extradition of LRA leader Joseph Kony.

Twenty terrorist-related incidents have occurred in Uganda since 1997, with 50 people killed and more than 200 injured. Both the ADF and the LRA are suspected to have been involved. The NALU has claimed responsibility for several of the attacks. Approximately 100,000 Sudanese refugees are in Uganda, and the fighting has displaced at least 300,000 Ugandans. Food convoys headed for Sudan have been attacked in Uganda. In April 1999 several humanitarian agencies, including the World Food Program, were forced to leave Western Uganda due to security concerns.

The UPDF in the Democratic Republic of the Congo carried out sporadic actions against the Rwandan forces also in the DRC throughout 1999. In June 2000 a major battle between Uganda and Rwanda in Kisangani caused severe damage to the city before a UN-brokered peace was established. The UPDF is fighting in the DRC with the aim of preventing the ADF from crossing into Uganda to attack civilians. Kenya also accuses the UPDF of entering Kenya. So far, the estimates of the death toll are in the region of 500 fatalities.

References

Gurr, T., M. Marshall, and D. Khosla. 2000. *Peace and Conflict 2001: A Global Survey of Conflicts, Self-Determination Movements, and Democracy.* College Park: Center for International Development and Conflict Management, University of Maryland.

Parker, K., A. Heindel, and A. Branch. 2000. *Armed Conflict in the World Today: A Country by Country Review.* Humanitarian Law Project: http://www.hri.ca/doccenter/docs/cpr/armedconflict2000.shtml# (accessed March 20, 2002).

Project Ploughshares. 2004. *Armed Conflicts Report 2003.* "Uganda (1987–First Combat Deaths)." Waterloo, Ontario: Institute of Peace and Conflict Studies, Conrad Grebel College. http://www.ploughshares.ca/content/ACR/ACRBriefs/ACRBrief-Uganda.html (accessed May 20, 2004).

1.83 Federal Republic of Grande Comoros: Coup Attempt and Anjouan and Moheli Independence
September 1995–Ongoing

The Comoros Islands (Anjouan, Mayotte, Moheli, and Moroni), off the Mozambican coast of Africa, became French protectorates at the end of the nineteenth century. They were granted independence in 1975. The Comoros had been wracked by political instability since independence—withstanding eighteen coup attempts. France continued to play a political role, with the French intelligence service frequently supplying mercenaries to the coup perpetrators. In 1989 President Ahmed Abdallah was assassinated and his government overthrown with the help of mercenaries led by Bob Dénard, who had fought in many African conflicts.

In late September 1995 the previously unknown Captain Ayouba Combo staged a coup to overthrow the regime of President Said Mohammed Djohar, ostensibly to restore the conditions for a return to democracy. Dénard and a force of mercenaries aided the rebels. In fierce fighting, they managed to capture the presidential palace and disarm government troops. The coup collapsed, however, when France sent in 900 antiterrorist troops, which surrounded Dénard and his men in October 1995. Dénard surrendered without resistance and was flown to France to stand trial.

In all, two Comoran soldiers and one civilian were killed. Following the coup, some confusion and political uncertainty prevailed about who was actually in control of the government. Negotiations throughout the rest of the year led to the return of President Djohar in early 1996.

In August 1997 conflict resurfaced when separatists from the islands of Anjouan and Moheli declared their independence from the Federal Republic of Grande Comoros. This declaration gave rise to considerable political instability and resulted in the deaths of hundreds of military and civilian personnel. It also created a disastrous humanitarian situation on both islands. The Anjouan and Moheli desire for independence from Comoros was driven by the mix of chronic political instability and extreme poverty. The leaders of both islands stated that they wanted a return to French rule with a similar status to Mayotte, the only island that voted to retain French rule in 1975. France is not interested in any new colonial alliance with the two islands, although they continue to ask the French government for help.

Each island has a different response to the situation. The Mohelis condemned the use of force and tried to seek a solution through a dialogue with the federal government and the Organization of African Unity (OAU). In contrast, the political groups of Anjouan attempted to secure independence by military force. In August 1997, in response to the declaration of independence from Anjouan, President Mohamed Taki sent central government troops to Anjouan to restore order. The subsequent fighting with separatists resulted in the deaths of forty people. More skirmishes with fatalities were reported after August.

President Taki and the OAU made various attempts to seek a solution to the conflict, but these proved unsuccessful. Further violence erupted on Anjouan in early December 1998. More than sixty casualties and displacement of the population were reported. On this occasion the fighting was primarily between the two separatist camps, that of Fonndi Abdallah Ibrahim's party, whose main goal was to achieve recognition for his independent state, and that of Said Omar Chamassi, whose supporters demanded a state constitutionally linked to France.

On December 15, 1998, the two secessionist parties signed a forty-eight-hour cease-fire agreement. A subsequent OAU-mediated interisland conference was held in Madagascar, and several of the parties signed the Antananarivo Accords on April 23, 1999. The agreement did not grant independence but gave the islands greater autonomy. The Anjouan delegation failed to sign the accord, leading to violence on Grande Comore that targeted people of Anjouan descent. This violence resulted in a military coup in April 1999, in which the army claimed to have intervened to "restore order." In August 2000 the separatists and the military government negotiated an agreement, the Fomboni Declaration, for national reconciliation and a loose federation. The OAU and various Comoran and Anjouan opposition groups rejected the declaration, wanting the conflict settled within the framework of the earlier Antananarivo Accords. Low-intensity conflict continued at the end of 2000. It is very likely that economic development is a prerequisite for a solution to the conflict.

References

Africa Contemporary Record. Annual. 1968/1969– .

African Recorder. Weekly. 1962– .

Andereggen, A. 1994. *France's Relationship with Sub-Saharan Africa.* Westport: Praeger.

Clayton, A. 1988. *France, Soldiers, and Africa.* London: Brassey's.

Factiva References for 1999, 2000.

Galama, A. 2002. *European Platform for Conflict Prevention and Transformation Online.* Country Surveys: www.euconflict.org/euconflict/guides/surveys.htm (accessed February 21, 2002).

Somerville, K. 1990. *Foreign Military Intervention in Africa.* London: Pinter.

Thomas, G. 1985. *Mercenary Troops in Modern Africa.* Boulder: Westview.

1.84 Eritrea–Yemen: Invasion of the Hunish Islands November 1995–October 1998

After a long and bloody war that ended in 1993 (*see* conflict 1.21), Eritrea won its independence from Ethiopia and promptly laid claim to the three Hunish Islands in the Red Sea on the historical basis that they had been variously owned by the Ottoman Empire, Italy, Britain, and Ethiopia. The islands were strategically situated near important shipping lanes. Yemen disputed Eritrea's claims, and a Yemeni fishing community occupied one of the islands. Negotiations failed to find any solution.

Following a Yemeni attempt to build tourist facilities on one of the islands, Eritrean troops invaded the islands in early November 1995. Eritrea demanded Yemen's withdrawal. Yemen responded by reinforcing its troops, and the conflict escalated. On December 15, Eritrean forces attacked Yemeni positions, and a full-scale battle erupted, with both sides using aircraft, battleships, and troops. After three days of fierce fighting, Eritrea seized the Greater Hunish Island and took 2,000 Yemeni soldiers prisoner.

Frantic mediation efforts by Algeria, Egypt, Ethiopia, the Organization of African Unity (OAU), and UN Secretary-General Boutros Boutros-Ghali managed to secure a cease-fire. The conflict ended when Yemen agreed to remove its troops from the islands and submit to international arbitration. In all, twelve soldiers were killed in the fighting.

The discovery of possible oil reserves in the Red Sea made the islands more desirable than ever, and border issues became intertwined with future economic gains from tourism and oil. In early January 1996 international efforts attempted to break the deadlock between the two nations. Boutros-Ghali held extensive talks with the parties and secured demonstrations of good will from both sides. Subsequent Ethiopian mediation resulted in a document for a peaceful resolution within the framework of international and maritime law, but an enduring solution was not achieved. At the end of January, Eritera expelled the Yemeni ambassador, and tensions rose once more.

Later in 1996 the two parties agreed to allow the Permanent Court for Arbitration to craft a solution. The court reached its decision in October 1998, when it awarded some of the islands to Yemen and others to Eritrea. The two parties reconciled themselves to the decision. French diplomats played a crucial role in the mediation process.

References

Africa Contemporary Record. Annual. 1968/1969– .

African Recorder. Weekly. 1962– .

Andereggen, A. 1994. *France's Relationship with Sub-Saharan Africa.* Westport, Conn.: Praeger.

Van Beurden, J. 2000. *European Platform for Conflict Prevention and Transformation Online.* Country Surveys:

www.euconflict.org/euconflict/guides/surveys.htm (accessed February 8, 2002).

1.85 Congo: Independence Movements October 1996–Ongoing

The situation in the Democratic Republic of the Congo (DRC), formerly Zaire, is a civil war with international aspects. In October 1996 Zairean "Banyamulenge" rebels led by Laurent Kabila (and supported by Rwanda) launched an offensive against the government and quickly captured large sections of the country. The Banyamulenge are mainly Tutsis of Rwandan origin who have lived in the eastern parts of the Congo for hundreds of years. They originally came to Zaire from Rwanda toward the end of the eighteenth century and now fought the indigenous Zairians for the land that they claimed was rightfully theirs. Numbering about 2,000, the Banyamulenge fighters revolted when local officials attempted to engineer their expulsion at the behest of Rwandan and Burundian Hutu rebel groups based in the country. Kabila's Banyamulenge rebels appear to have merged with rebel forces from the north and south, forming a group called the Alliance of Democratic Forces for the Liberation of Congo-Democratic Republic of the Congo (ADFL). This group helped to overthrow the thirty-year government of President Mobutu Sésé Séko in May 1997 and install Kabila as president.

Kabila's forces emptied the rebel Hutu-controlled Rwandan refugee camps on the border and dislodged Burundian Hutu rebels with the assistance of the Rwandan government. In June 1998 a UN report claimed that Kabila's forces and the Rwandan army were responsible for murdering thousands of Hutus. Soldiers from Angola and Uganda were also reportedly fighting alongside Kabila's ADFL. Kabila renamed Zaire the Democratic Republic of the Congo (DRC), banned all political activity, and announced multiparty elections in two years. Opposition political leaders, journalists, and some human rights activists were arrested.

In late June 1998 there was a clash with Bernard Mizele's secessionist Bakango group. In August Tutsi rebel forces turned against Kabila and began a military drive in eastern DRC. The United Nations brokered an agreement in Paris in the fall of 1998, but military operations continued, with Kabila's government gaining support from the militaries of Zimbabwe and Namibia. Rwanda and Uganda backed the rebel factions. Rebels from Angola, Burundi, Rwanda, and Uganda continue to operate out of Congolese territory. As many as 30,000 foreign troops are stationed in the country.

The Lusaka Peace Accord was signed in August 1999 by Kabila and his allies, as well as all the main rebel factions. Under its terms, foreign soldiers and rebel militias such as the Burundian CNDD-FDD and Rwandan Interahamwe were supposed to be disarmed, and democratic elections held within three years. Fighting continued in many areas of eastern DRC despite the accord, and most issues of disagreement remained unresolved. The most serious violence in 2000 involved Ugandan and Rwandan forces fighting for control of the Kisangani diamond trade. The territory under central government authority continues to dwindle.

Called "Africa's World War," the fighting in the DRC is said to have resulted in 1.7 million casualties in twenty-two months (not counting casualties from the latest fighting). Of those, 700,000 are direct war casualties, and 1 million casualties resulted from war-related disease and hunger. An estimated 600,000 people have been displaced by the fighting. Kabila was assassinated in January 2001 and was succeeded in office by his son.

References

Gurr, T., M. Marshall, and D. Khosla. 2000. *Peace and Conflict 2001: A Global Survey of Conflicts, Self-Determination Movements, and Democracy.* College Park: Center for International Development and Conflict Management, University of Maryland.

Parker, K., A. Heindel, and A. Branch. 2000. *Armed Conflict in the World Today: A Country by Country Review.* Humanitarian Law Project: http://www.hri.ca/doccenter/docs/cpr/armedconflict2000.shtml# (accessed March 20, 2002).

1.86 Uganda–Kenya: Ethnic Cross-Border Clashes November 1996–July 1998

Cattle-rustling tribes in Kenya and Uganda have a history of cross-border raids. The pastoralist Pokot and Marakwet communities have shared the same region in northwest Kenya for a long time and have sometimes fought with each other. In June 1996 several high-level government officials and politicians from Kenya organized meetings with the Ugandan authorities to try and resolve the conflict between Kenyan pastoral groups and the Ugandan Karamojong. A second meeting was held in November 1996. It was attended by Pokot from Uganda, Kenya, Sabiny, and Turkana. The meeting was intended to develop the basis for regular meetings and to coordinate regional planning in these areas.

In April 1998, however, 500 Marakwet attacked a police post in West Pokot's Lelan division. Two policemen were killed and three injured. Hundreds of cattle were stolen or maimed. A few weeks later the violence spilled over into an area of northeastern Uganda inhabited by the Karamojong, a people closely related to the Pokots. In July 1998 the Pokot and Uganda's Karamojong clashed over cattle. At least eighty-four people were killed.

References

Global IDP Database. OCHA, October 7, 2000. *Uganda.* http://www.db.idpproject.org/Sites/IdpProjectDb/idpSurvey.nsf/wViewCountries/ (accessed April 1, 2002).

1.87 Niger: Diffa Border Insurgency December 1996–April 1999

A peace accord in 1994 between the government and several Tuareg-dominated rebel groups ended the conflict in Niger (*see* conflict 1.74). Although punctuated by incidents, the peace process remained largely on track, and a few hundred refugees have returned. Despite this progress, signs of another rebellion appeared in the south-eastern Diffa region, bordering Chad. A Toubou rebel group, which continued its activities in the east, was reported to have attacked a village in July 1998, but barely a month later it was said to have signed a cease-fire with the government.

A Toubou group calling itself the Democratic Front of Renewal (FDR), which appears to have ties with Chadian rebel groups, leads the nascent Toubou rebellion. Massacres in the Diffa region, in which almost 200 people were reportedly killed by the Nigerian army in October 1998, and violence in March and April 1999, increased tensions in the area. Many Toubou have fled to Nigeria and refuse to return. The continued availability of small arms in the entire region remains a destabilizing factor. Low-intensity fighting continues, both between government and rebels and among various local groups.

References

Posthumus, B. 2002. *Niger: A Long History, a Brief Conflict, and Open Future.* European Platform for Conflict Prevention and Transformation Online. Country Surveys: www.euconflict.org/euconflict/guides/surveys.htm (accessed October 9, 2001).

1.88 Congo–Brazzaville: Democratic Struggle May 1997–Late 2000

Tensions rose in the Republic of Congo during the spring of 1997 as the country prepared for elections. President Pascal Lissouba, elected in 1992 amid accusations of voting irregularities, and former president Denis Sassou-Nguesso, the current opposition leader, vied for control of the capital, Brazzaville. Civil war broke out in June 1997, when the army of the Republic of Congo attacked the Brazzaville residence of Sassou-Nguesso, claiming to be searching for arms. Rebel forces backing Sassou-Nguesso (the Cobra militia, reportedly supported by Angola, Rwanda, and Uganda) seized Brazzaville in mid-October 1997 and several days later took Pointe-Noire, the second-largest city and economic capital. Sassou-Nguesso gained control of the government, announcing a three-year transition period leading to new presidential elections.

In December 1987 the militias of Bernard Kolela (the former Brazzaville mayor) and Lissouba resumed fighting. An estimated 6,000 people were killed, mostly civilians. With Angolan backing, the government launched a major offensive in May 1999 and claimed to capture all rebel bases in the center of the country. The Pointe-Noire Peace Agreement was signed on November 16, 1999, by Ninja, Cobra, and Southern Resistance groups. The negotiated cease-fire has been respected by all parties, and national reconciliation talks were planned for late 2000 to seek a permanent settlement.

Hundreds of thousands of people have been displaced by the conflict in the Congo, and an estimated 10,000 have died. Both sides have been accused of perpetrating massive violence against civilians, and it is reported that 250,000 refugees in the Pool region have been subject to summary executions, rape, and looting.

References

Gurr, T., M. Marshall, and D. Khosla. 2000. *Peace and Conflict 2001: A Global Survey of Conflicts, Self-Determination Movements, and Democracy.* College Park: Center for International Development and Conflict Management, University of Maryland.

Parker, K., A. Heindel, and A. Branch. 2000. *Armed Conflict in the World Today: A Country by Country Review.* Humanitarian Law Project: http://www.hri.ca/doccenter/docs/cpr/armedconflict2000.shtml# (accessed March 20, 2002).

1.89 Djibouti: Intervention and Djibouti Civil War Early 1998–December 2000

The small North African state of Djibouti, a former French colony, has continually been affected by the conflicts in neighboring countries, most notably in Eritrea, Ethiopia, and Somaliland (*see* conflict 1.79). In recent years this pattern has continued. Despite earlier peace agreements ending the civil war of 1991–1993, distrust of the Issa-dominated government, led by President Gouled Aptidon, remained deep-seated. The Afari-led Front for the Restoration of Unity and Democracy (FRUD) launched several small-scale attacks in the first months of 1998, but these proved to be no real threat to the government, and casualties were limited.

In the second half of 1998, the Ethiopian-Eritrean border conflict heightened traditional ethnic tensions and intensified the conflict in Djibouti. Since 1996 Ethiopia and Djibouti had been covertly intensifying their relationship, culminating in the stationing of Ethiopian troops inside Djibouti in mid-1998. It is highly likely that Ethiopia wanted to dissuade Eritrea from making use of the armed FRUD resistance in Djibouti. As the cooperation between Djibouti and Ethiopia increased, relations between Djibouti and Eritrea steadily deteriorated. In June 1998 Djibouti deployed its army to the north, where FRUD units were based, to patrol its borders with Eritrea and prevent any incursion. Some French army units joined the Djibouti troops, officially to participate in a demining program. In late 1998 Eritrea accused Djibouti of allowing Ethiopia to use its port for importing military equipment for use in the border conflict. Djibouti immediately severed its relations with Eritrea and recalled its ambassador. Relations worsened in early 1999, when the French provided Djibouti with a frigate to patrol the coast and prevent any foreign troops from landing. Attempts to mediate failed, and tensions rose to the point that war seemed imminent.

In the presidential elections of April 1999, Ismael Omar Guelleh was elected as the new leader of Djibouti, and efforts to end the tensions intensified. Negotiations began between the government and the armed wing of FRUD, and in February 2000 a seven-point agreement for reform and civil concord, including a cease-fire agreement, was signed in Paris. In May the first steps toward disarmament, rehabilitation, and reintegration of ex-fighters and the strengthening of the democratic process were taken. In April Djibouti and Eritrea restored their diplomatic and commercial relations. The peace agreement signed between Ethiopia and Eritrea in December 2000 should increase stability in Djibouti.

The damage resulting from the civil war and unrest in Djibouti is serious. Trade and services have deteriorated, resulting in the destruction of livestock, water resources, and education and health facilities. Djibouti's humanitarian requirements have increased significantly since the first outbreak of civil war in 1991.

References

Bercovitch, J., and R. Jackson. 1997. *International Conflict: A Chronological Encyclopedia of Conflicts and their Management 1945–1995.* Washington, D.C.: Congressional Quarterly.

van Beurden, J. 2002. *European Platform for Conflict Prevention and Transformation Online.* Country Surveys: www.euconflict.org/euconflict/guides/surveys.htm (accessed February 13, 2002).

1.90 Lesotho: Intervention and Military Factions May 1998–March 1999

Lesotho is a small sovereign nation in central Africa. King Letsie III and a democratically elected government govern the country. This conflict was a result of mass protests in the wake of controversial elections in May 1998. The electoral process was declared free, fair, and transparent, but there were obvious irregularities. The Basotho Congress Party, an opposition party, alleged that the election was rigged, and tensions began to rise. In accordance with the election results, the leader of the Lesotho Congress for Democracy (LCD), Bethuel Pakalitha Mosisili, was appointed prime minister, but the opposition party continued to believe the election results were fraudulent. The court of appeal ruled that only the king had the right to overrule the decisions of an election. In response, the opposition began mass protests at the palace in which at least four people were killed.

An independent group of experts, convened to investigate the claims of the opposition, established that the election had been mishandled. Violence intensified in September, when government officials and military officers joined the protesters and there was an attempted mutiny within the armed forces. The king, along with South African president Nelson Mandela, appealed to the crowds to disperse. Central authority failed, and South African troops intervened to impose order. More than 100 people were killed in one day of violence. The capital was looted and the damage was estimated to be $1 million (U.S.).

The South African Development Community (SADC) brokered talks between the opposition parties and the LCD, resulting in an agreement to hold a fresh round of elections in March 1999. The elections were delayed because of strong disagreements over future arrangements. In December 1998 an interim political authority was sworn in, the culmination of peace efforts by the SADC, King Letsie III, and the South African government. In 1999 the SADC removed its troops and an advisory team replaced them.

References

Gurr, T., M. Marshall, and D. Khosla. 2000. *Peace and Conflict 2001: A Global Survey of Conflicts, Self-Determination Movements, and Democracy.* College Park: Center for International Development and Conflict Management, University of Maryland.

1.91 Eritrea–Ethiopia: Yirga Triangle Territorial Dispute May 1998–June 1999

A simmering border dispute between Eritrea and Ethiopia erupted into interstate warfare in May 1998 and intensified dramatically in early 1999 and again in May 2000. The Ethiopian government accused Eritrea of occupying areas in the northwest, and Eritrea said it was reacting to border violations by Ethiopia. High-intensity fighting ebbed in June, after thousands were killed, but frequent shelling continued. Fighting began again in February 1999 after seven months of international diplomacy, especially by the Organization of African Unity (OAU), failed to resolve the conflict. Most observers blamed Eritrea for rejecting the OAU plan, the only proposal on the table. Air strikes resumed in breach of a June 1998 moratorium.

Fighting in February and March 1999 resulted in up to 60,000 killed. The violence continued sporadically for the remainder of 1999, with Ethiopia regaining some territory. The fighting intensified in April and May 2000, and Ethiopia made substantial military gains. In June Eritrea accepted a new OAU peace plan (nearly identical to the earlier plan) worked out in Algiers, and subsequently approved by Ethiopia. Under this plan both sides would retreat to positions held in May 1998, and UN forces would monitor a fifteen-mile-wide buffer zone on Eritrean border territory while UN mediators worked out a line of demarcation between the two countries.

Both sides accuse each other of forcibly deporting each other's nationals. There are an estimated 600,000 refugees from the fighting, including 150,000 Eritreans, living in temporary camps along the Ethiopian border with little shelter. Almost 70,000 Eritreans, including nationals of Eritrean origin, were illegally expelled by Ethiopia after their property was confiscated. Several Somali factions have accused Eritrea and Ethiopia of arming them to fight against each other. Somali groups have also accused Eritrea of training Ethiopian rebel groups in southern Somalia.

References

Gurr, T., M. Marshall, and D. Khosla. 2000. *Peace and Conflict 2001: A Global Survey of Conflicts, Self-Determination Movements, and Democracy*. College Park: Center for International Development and Conflict Management, University of Maryland.

Parker, K., A. Heindel, and A. Branch. 2000. *Armed Conflict in the World Today: A Country by Country Review*. Humanitarian Law Project: http://www.hri.ca/doccenter/docs/cpr/armedconflict2000. shtml# (accessed March 20, 2002).

1.92 Guinea-Bissau: Military Factions June 1998–January 2000

This conflict began in June 1998, when the Guinea-Bissau army, led by General Ansumane Mané, mutinied, announced the formation of a "transitional government," and demanded the resignation of President Joao Bernardo Vieira. Opposition groups and the media had criticized Vieira for undemocratic actions, such as postponing proposed elections and allowing himself to be reelected to the presidency of his party in contravention of the constitution. Strong dissatisfaction with corrupt presidential power and the harsh conditions of life led many people in Guinea-Bissau to side with the military junta.

The army denied that it was instigating a coup, calling instead for elections to be held without delay. Government forces immediately counterattacked, drawing on military support from Senegal and Guinea-Conakry. The capital city, Bissau, was subjected to intense bombardment with heavy artillery. Despite this, the rebels maintained control over strategic bases in the capital. Thousands of people were evacuated as the country plunged into civil war.

Mediation efforts began in July 1998, led by Portugal and Angola under the auspices of the Community of Portuguese-Speaking Countries (CPLP) and the Economic Community of West African States (ECOWAS). A cease-fire agreement was signed at the end of August 1998. Fresh fighting erupted in October, precipitated by rebel objections to the army's use of Senegalese and Guinean troops. The rebels gained control of most of the country. President Vieira declared a unilateral cease-fire in mid-October, calling for talks. In response, the rebels also declared a cease-fire. At this time, the conflict was in a deadlock with the president holding the capital's center and General Mané controlling the rest of the country.

By November 1998 another peace agreement had been formulated. It agreed to the withdrawal of foreign troops, a reaffirmation of the cease-fire, and presidential elections by the end of March 1999. This cease-fire lasted until February 1999, when renewed fighting killed at least thirty-five people. Further peace talks occurred in mid-February, and Vieira and Mané agreed, in the spirit of national reconciliation, to work together to guarantee peace. The conflict deescalated after the Vieira government was overthrown by Mané and his troops in May 1999. Serious clashes were again reported in September 1999, but new elections took place in late 1999 without serious disruption. ECOWAS Monitoring Group (ECOMOG) troops were subsequently withdrawn.

Although no serious fighting was reported in 2000, economic recovery presented a daunting challenge for the newly elected president, Koumba Iala. In November 2000 General Mané was shot dead by government troops, a week after it was alleged that he had led an unsuccessful coup attempt.

References

Gurr, T., M. Marshall, and D. Khosla. 2000. *Peace and Conflict 2001: A Global Survey of Conflicts, Self-Determination Movements, and Democracy*. College Park: Center for International Development and Conflict Management, University of Maryland.

Keesing's Record of World Events: K42323, K42381, K42430, K2542, K42601, K42827, K42924, K42986, K43344, K43893.

Mekenkamp, M. 2002. *European Platform for Conflict Prevention and Transformation Online.* Country Surveys: www.euconflict.org/euconflict/guides/surveys.htm (accessed February 13, 2002).

1.93 Ethiopia–Kenya: Ethnic Border Clashes October 1998–January 1999

Although Kenya appears to epitomize stability in comparison with its neighbors, it is confronted with a range of mostly low-intensity conflicts, most of which have an ethnic dimension. In early 1998 the Kenyan government moved forcefully to keep out a massive wave of refugees fleeing drought in Somalia. Once this flow of potential refugees was halted, the government invited the UN High Commission for Refugees (UNHCR) and other humanitarian organizations to provide assistance. Subsequently, guerrilla activity was reported from the Ethiopian border, and the refugees were subjected to armed raids by bandits. In October 1998 a large group, mostly Borana, raided several settlements in Kenya inhabited by the ethnic Somali Degodia clan, killing at least 142 and abducting around 50 people. An estimated 17,500 cattle were stolen. Government officials said that the majority of the attackers came from the Oromo Liberation Front (OLF), an Ethiopian rebel group. Survivors and witnesses, however, maintained that the attackers were Borana acting with Ethiopian backing.

Following a new incident in January 1999, Kenya lodged a formal protest with the Ethiopian government, claiming that Ethiopian army troops had entered the country searching for fleeing OLF rebels. Cattle-rustling and cross-border guerrilla activity continue to be sources of conflict in Kenya.

Reference

van Beurden, J. 2001. "Kenya: Small Scale Conflicts Could Have Major Repercussions." *European Platform for Conflict Prevention and Transformation Online.* Country Surveys: www.euconflict.org/euconflict/guides/surveys.htm (accessed October 9, 2001).

1.94 Liberia–Guinea: Border Dispute September 1999–April 2001

Long and bloody civil wars in Liberia (1983, 1989–) and Sierra Leone (1991–) have contributed to ongoing instability in West Africa (*see* conflicts 1.55; 1.72; 1.78). Despite the supposed conclusion of the Liberian conflict, that country's continued involvement with rebel groups fighting in Guinea and Sierra Leone has served to exacerbate tensions in the region. Numerous conflict management efforts, most notably by the Economic Community of West African States (ECOWAS), have had only minimal impact on deteriorating relations among the three states. Continued support by Guinea and Liberia for rebels working to destabilize each other have drawn these two nations into conflict.

This territorial dispute occurred after cross-border attacks into Liberia by a rebel group, the Joint Forces for the Liberation of Liberia (JFFL), stationed in neighboring Guinea. In response, Liberia closed its border with Guinea. Several towns in northwestern Liberia were held by the JFFL. Liberian troops were mobilized into the border area, and a state of regional emergency was declared. In September 1999 Liberian security forces counterattacked the rebels, a move that Guinea repulsed. Following this, the leaders of seven West African nations met in Ajuna on September 16, 1999, to discuss the incident. The talks revealed that Guinea was not controlling the actions of the JFFL, and, as a result, Liberia and Guinea reached a rapprochement.

The conflict flared up again in September 2000, however, when Liberian-based rebels led incursions into Guinea, prompting Guinean artillery attacks on the Liberian border town of Zorzor. Further strife occurred in December with attacks on the Guinean town of Gueckedou that resulted in a considerable number of fatalities (conflicting sources report the deaths from approximately fifty to several hundred). This prompted ECOWAS to prepare for the deployment of 1,600 peacekeepers to patrol the border. Violence persisted, however, and ten people died as fighters staged in Liberia launched another attack on Gueckedou in January 2001. Liberia claimed that Guinean artillery bombardments of Liberian villages in preceding days had served as a catalyst for the attacks and promptly withdrew its ambassador from Guinea. This escalation of conflict was a cause of considerable concern among organizations responsible for monitoring the welfare of the more than 250,000 refugees sheltering in Guinea to escape the violence of Sierra Leone and Liberia.

Claims and counterclaims set the tone in the following months, with each side accusing the other of sponsoring attacks on its territory. During February, Liberia issued a full military call-up in response to fears that Guinea was massing troops near the border. Relations were further strained in March when the Guinean ambassador was deemed persona non grata. An agreement to hold presidential talks suggested a thaw in diplomatic relations and was followed in April by an ECOWAS summit to address relations among Guinea, Liberia, and Sierra Leone. Although this meeting succeeded in staving off a full-blown war between Guinea and Liberia and established a committee to monitor relations, the conflict persisted with more rebel incursions and claims of government complicity originating from both sides. Further efforts and conflict management by the United Nations, ECOWAS, and the Organization of African Unity (OAU) have contained, but not settled, the conflict.

References

Economist. 2001. May 19, page 4.

The Europa World Year Book. 2002. London: Europa Publications.

Keesing's Record of World Events: K43737, K43892, K43933, K43984, K44042, K44093.

KOSIMO. *Conflict Barometer 1999*. Annual Publication from the Heidelberg Institute for International Conflict Research: http://www.hiik.de.

1.95 Ivory Coast: Civil War
September 1999–Ongoing

Fighting broke out between government forces and rebel soldiers on September 19, 2002, over reports that the government was planning to force large numbers of soldiers to retire. This fighting was led on the rebel side by General Robert Guei, who, in 1999, had been installed as head of a military junta following the December 19 coup against former president Henri Konan Bédié over army pay. This first coup had crumbled in October 2000, and the military government was replaced by a civilian one led by President Laurent Gbagbo. General Guei had repeatedly criticized Gbagbo's government for mismanagement and the arbitrary arresting of civilian and military personal. During the September 19 fighting, General Guei was killed, as was Emile Boga Doudou, the Ivorian interior and decentralization minister.

The fighting carried on through the day, and by evening the government claimed control of the commercial capital Abidjan, but fighting continued in the central city of Bouake and the northern city of Karogho. Three main rebel groups were involved in this conflict: the Popular Ivorian Movement for the Far West (MPIGO), the Patriotic Movement of the Ivory Coast (MPCI), and the Movement for Justice and Peace (MJP).

Claiming the need to protect French nationals and other western ex-patriots, the French government, on September 23, 2002, sent three helicopters and an additional 100 troops and equipment to bolster the existing garrison of 500 troops. They set up a base outside the political capital Yamoussoukro. Following President Gbagbo's claim of Burkina Faso's support of the rebel soldiers on September 29, the French were obliged to enact a defense treaty and come to the government's aid. Citing a lack of evidence of Burkina Faso's involvement, the French, however, restricted its aid to "logistical support" at this point.

The United States also had a military presence of around 200 troops, but the troops' mission was to airlift westerners out of the country, especially from the western city of Bouake.

On September 25 Nigeria sent an advance force of three jet fighters to aid the Ivorian government. By September 29 an emergency summit meeting of the Economic Community of West African States (ECOWAS) was called to decide on a course of action in regard to the conflict. The summit called for the army to immediately return to its barracks and promised to send a military force if talks between the government and rebels, to be mediated by ECOWAS, failed. The seriousness of the conflict and its perceived likelihood and consequences of escalation were highlighted by the presence of President Thabo Mbeki of South Africa at the summit meeting.

Representatives from ECOWAS, the African Union, and the United Nations met in Abidjan on October 2, 2002, in a bid to mediate between the government and the rebels. The mediators traveled to Bouake the following day to meet the rebel commanders. A cease-fire was signed on October 3, but only lasted three days when a fresh rebel offensive was launched. On October 14 rebels suspended negotiations, claiming Angolan soldiers had arrived to bolster government troops. The rebels were demanding "national stability and equal treatment for all the country's people."

On October 17 President Abdoulaye Wade of Senegal proposed a peace plan that was agreed to by the rebels and signed that same day. Although the government was not represented, mediators claimed the government had accepted the proposed cease-fire. French troops set up a buffer zone to monitor the cease-fire on October 20.

On October 25 army chiefs from fifteen ECOWAS states met to discuss the deployment of a regional force to monitor the cease-fire, and on October 30 ECOWAS hosted talks in Togo between the government of the Ivory Coast and the MPCI. The talks continued sporadically with varying levels of representation but faltered around November 19 amid accusation by the rebels that Ghana had agreed to let the Ivorian government use its territory to launch attacks. Ghana and the Ivory Coast strongly denied this. On November 28 the government's mercenaries (mainly of Israeli and South African origin) advanced on rebel positions effectively ending the peace talks.

At this point, the French sent in hundreds of additional troops, bringing the total number of French troops in Ivory Coast to around 2,500. The French reported sporadic fighting with rebels, mainly from the MPIGO group. French-mediated talks involving both sides were scheduled for December 30, 2002. At the start of 2003 there was continued fighting, various efforts at mediation and negotiation, increases in the number of foreign troops, particularly French, and a generally worsening situation.

References

Keesing's Record of World Events: 44968, 45026, 45027, 45079, 45131, 45175.

Lee, R.A. (2002). *New and Recent Wars and Conflicts of the World*. The History Guy Web site, page 3. http://www.historyguy.com/current_conflicts/Index.htm (accessed April 30, 2003).

Lloyd's List Casualty Report, December 31, 2002. http://www.factiva.com (accessed June 25, 2003).

New York Times. December 31, 2002. http://www.factiva.com (accessed June 25, 2003).

Reuters News Service. September 24, 26, 30, 2002; November 25, 2002; December 16, 17, 31, 2002. http://www.factiva.com (accessed June 25, 2003).

1.96 Central African Republic–Chad: Attempted Coup, Foreign Intervention, and Territorial Occupation Mid-2001–December 2002

Following its independence from France in 1960, the Central African Republic (CAR) underwent decades of political upheaval and misrule, largely at the hands of the military, until the establishment of a civilian government in 1993 under President Ange-Félix Patassé. The new government could not ensure long-term stability, however, with former leaders and opposition parties harshly critical of Patassé's leadership and dubious of the ballot that reelected him in 1999. In mid-2001 this discontent led to an attempted coup that ultimately drew the CAR into conflict with Chad and peripherally involved the Democratic Republic of Congo (DRC), Libya, and Rwanda. The conflict began in late May when attackers attempted to storm the presidential palace in Banguit. The immediate result was some twenty fatalities, including the director general of the gendarmerie. The ensuing battle lasted for several days and resulted in a further 300 dead, including several members of a Libyan contingent sent to support the government and a number of Congolese fighters associated with the rebellion. The initial attack, meanwhile, was eventually accredited to Rwandan mercenaries, and apparently masterminded by General André Kolingba, who fled to his home village of Kembe.

Although the fighting had died out, one immediate result of the failed coup and subsequent accusations against Kolingba was an outbreak of ethnic unrest, causing members of Kolingba's southern Yakoma ethnic group to flee from members of Patassé's northern Kaba group. The situation developed further in September, when Defense Minister Jean-Jacques Defamouth was detained in connection with the coup and ultimately implicated the chief of general staff, Francois Bozize, who was dismissed from service in early November. This lead to further fighting, with troops loyal to Bozize putting up resistance in northern Bangui and prompting the deployment of 100 Libyan troops to assist the government. Bozize fled to Chad, eventually surrendering himself to that country's government. Chadian officials met with Bozize, but they refused to extradite him, causing tension between Chad and the CAR.

Early in December 2001 some attempts were made to diffuse the situation, as Patassé met first with representatives from Libya, Sudan, and Zambia regarding the establishment of a peacekeeping force to monitor the situation in the Central African Republic. He then travelled to Libreville for talks with his Chadian counterpart, Idriss Déby, under the auspices of the Economic and Monetary Community of the Central African States (CEMAC). A commission was also created to arrange for Patassé, Bozize, and Kolingba to meet. The situation was inflamed, however, just prior to Christmas, with the CAR complaining to the United Nations about Chad's occupation of the far north. Charges against Bozize were dropped shortly thereafter.

Chad's refusal to extradite Bozize, however was essentially the starting point for a marked increase in tensions between the CAR and Chad that found expression in a border incident, another attempted coup, and the exchange of verbal reprimands and mutual recriminations. Tension in the region was such that on February 1, 2002, the Organization of African Unity (OAU) requested that the UN Security Council redeploy a peacekeeping force to help consolidate peace in the CAR. On August 6, 2002, a border skirmish in the CAR village of Sido took the lives of two Chadian and twenty CAR citizens. Abdoulaye Miskine, whom Chad considers to be a rebel Chadian, leads the CAR's forces responsible for the northern border with Chad. He reported that the CAR has trouble with banditry on and around the border and that every time he tries to deal with it Chad sends its military in to fight him. Chad denies this accusation. Chad also denies having any connection with the skirmish in Sido that was almost certainly fought by troops loyal to the deposed Bozize. The CAR considers that Chad is at least partially responsible by rearming and probably reinforcing the rebel troops with Chadian troops.

On August 14, 2002, on the sidelines of the inauguration ceremony of Congolese president Denis Sassou Nguesso, a summit meeting was held to find a diplomatic solution to the crisis under the auspices of CEMAC, which replaced the OAU in July 2002. At this meeting the presidents of the CAR and Chad agreed to find a peaceful solution, and CEMAC established a mission to assist them. The president of Gabon, Omar Bongo, led the mission and acted as mediator throughout. Another summit meeting took place October 2, 2002, at which CEMAC agreed to send in a mixed force of about 350 peacekeepers from the various African nations involved (Cameroon, Congo, Gabon, Equatorial Guinea, and Mali) with the double objective of protecting President Patassé and patrolling the CAR-Chad border. It was also decided to remove two of the main protagonists, Bozize and Miskine, with the former to go to France and the latter to Togo.

Before the deployment of the subregional force took place, however, there was another attempt to topple Patassé, the seventh such attempt since May 1993. Rebels occupied the north of the CAR capital, Bangui, for five days before being forced to withdraw by the Libyan Expeditionary Force stationed there. (The Libyans had been there to protect Patassé in a deal that further damaged Patassé's popularity. The agreement was that the Libyans would protect his position in return for exclusive rights to the extraction of the CAR's rich diamond, gold, and other mineral resources for the next ninety-nine years. Patassé signed this deal without consulting anyone else, including his own parliament.) After the failure of this coup attempt, Chad claimed that the CAR had massacred 150 Chadians living in Bangui and called for an international enquiry. The CAR denied the massacre, but it seems likely it did occur, although establishing the facts is difficult. In a counterclaim, the CAR charged that Chad had been behind the coup attempt and displayed copies of Chadian documentation to journalists taken from fleeing rebels as they headed north toward the Chadian border.

The first contingent of the subregional force arrived in Bangui on December 4, 2002, with the full force expected to follow soon after. By December 28, 2002, the subregional force had replaced the Libyans who were providing security to the presidential residence. At this point order appears to have been restored and the conflict abated.

References

Agence France-Presse. 2002. August 15, 24; October 2; November 1, 4, 5; December 28. Downloaded from www.factiva.com July 23, 2003.

BBC Monitoring Service. 2002. December 4, 6. Downloaded from www.factiva.com on July 23, 2003.

CIA World Fact Book. 2002. http://www.cia.gov/cia/publications/factbook/.

The Economist. 2002. "No Pay, No Peace: Yet Another Coup Attempt in the CAR." November 2, page 50.

The Europa World Year Book. 2002. London: Europa Publications.

Keesing's Record of World Events: K44142, K44199, K44255, K44331, K44439, K44494, K44715.

Panafrican News Agency (PANA). October 25, 2002. www.factiva.com (accessed July 23, 2003).

World Markets Research Centre Ltd. *Daily Analysis*. 2002. November 5. www.factiva.com (accessed July 23, 2003).

1.97 Angola–Zambia: Civil Strife and Border Skirmishes November 2001

An unfortunate side effect of Angola's ongoing civil strife, specifically as regards the government's struggle with the União Nacional para a Independência Total de Angola (UNITA), has been increased tension with bordering Zambia. Angola has repeatedly accused Zambia of supporting UNITA forces, and Zambia, which is home to tens of thousands of Angolan refugees, has in turn protested Angola's willingness to take its fight with UNITA into Zambian territory.

Efforts to stabilize relations with a joint security committee for dealing with border matters served as a step toward addressing these concerns. The simmering dispute, however, deteriorated into armed conflict in November 2001, when Angolan troops abducted 103 Zambian villagers, killing seven, during an incursion into the Shang Omba district of Zambia in pursuit of fleeing UNITA rebels. This raid placed a severe strain on relations and, although attempts were made to address the situation, Zambia responded just over a week later, killing ten Angolan soldiers in a border skirmish. Angolan president José Eduardo dos Santos denied the initial allegations against his country, but he moved to control the situation, sending a special envoy to Zambia for talks. Zambia also dispatched a number of military officers to Angola for bilateral talks. The brief conflict ultimately subsided, although many of the issues at its root remain unresolved.

References

Keesing's Record of World Events: K44437.

Xinhua News Agency. 2001. August 30; November 15, 30.

Americas

List of Conflicts

2.1 Dominican Republic–Haiti/Cuba: Regional Aggression 123
Early 1947–December 1951

2.2 Costa Rica: Anticorruption Military Insurgency and Civil War 125
March–April 1948

2.3 Nicaragua–Costa Rica: Border Conflict 125
December 1948–February 1949

2.4 Argentina–Chile: The Beagle Channel Border Dispute 126
July 1952–August 1993

2.5 Guatemala: Civil War and Insurgency 128
June 1954–Ongoing

2.6 Nicaragua–Costa Rica: Exiles Invasion Attempt 129
January 1955

2.7 Dominican Republic–Cuba/Venezuela: Dominican Republic Aggression and Exiles Conflict 129
February 1956–January 1962

2.8 Cuba: Communist Revolution and Cuban Civil War 131
December 1956–January 1959

2.9 Nicaragua–Honduras: Boundary Dispute and Mocoran Seizure 131
April–June 1957

2.10 Panama: Cuban-Backed Invasion and Panama Revolutionaries Conflict 132
1958–May 1959

2.11 Guatemala–Mexico: Mexican Shrimp Boat Incident 132
December 1958–September 1959

2.12 Paraguay–Argentina: Paraguayan Exiles Conflict 133
Early 1959–December 1961

2.13 Cuba–Haiti: Cuban-Sponsored Military Invasion and Haitian Exiles Conflict 133
August 1959

2.14 United States–Cuba: Anti-Castro Military Invasion—The Bay of Pigs 134
April–May 1961

2.15 Venezuela–Guyana (UK): Essequibo River Dispute 134
February 1962–June 1970

2.16 Chile–Bolivia: Lauca River Dam Dispute 135
March 1962–1964

2.17 United States–USSR: Cold War Dispute and the Cuban Missile Crisis 136
September–November 1962

2.18 Haiti–Dominican Republic: Exiles Asylum and Invasion Attempt 137
April–September 1963

2.19 Cuba–Venezuela: Terrorism and Invasion Attempt 138
November 1963–May 1967

2.20 Panama–United States: Sovereignty Dispute and the Flag Riots 139
January–April 1964

2.21 Colombia: Banditry and Leftist Guerrilla Insurgency 139
1965–Ongoing

2.22 United States–Dominican Republic: Civil War, U.S. Military Intervention, and the Constitutionalist Rebellion 140
April 1965–September 1966

2.23 Bolivia: Cuban-Assisted Guerrilla Insurgency 141
November 1966–July 1970

2.24 El Salvador–Honduras: The “Football War” Border Dispute 141
July 1969

2.25 Guyana–Suriname: New River Triangle Border Dispute 142
August 1969–November 1970

2.26 El Salvador–Honduras: Territorial Dispute and Border Incidents 142
July 1976–October 1980

2.27 El Salvador: Civil Conflict and the Salvadoran Civil War 143
January 1977–Late 1992

2.28 Ecuador–Peru: Regional Rivalry, Territorial Dispute, and the Amazon/Marañón Waterway Incidents 143
June 1977–January 1978

2.29 **Nicaragua–Costa Rica: Regional Rivalry and Border Incidents** 144
October 1977

2.30 **Nicaragua–Costa Rica: Regional Rivalry, Cross-Border Raids, and Border Incidents** 144
September–December 1978

2.31 **Honduras–Nicaragua: Right-Wing Insurgency and the Contra War** 145
January 1980–February 1994

2.32 **Ecuador–Peru: Territorial Dispute and Border War** 145
January–April 1981

2.33 **United Kingdom–Argentina: Sovereignty Dispute and the Falklands War** 146
April–June 1982

2.34 **Guatemala–Mexico: Regional Instability, Guatemalan Civil War, and Border Incidents** 147
September 1982–January 1983

2.35 **United States–Grenada: Anti-Communist Military Invasion** 147
October–December 1983

2.36 **Ecuador–Peru: Regional Rivalry, Territorial Dispute, and Border Conflict** 148
January 1984

2.37 **Guatemala–Mexico: Regional Instability, Guatemalan Civil War, and Border Incident** 148
April 1984

2.38 **Nicaragua–Costa Rica: Regional Rivalry and Border Incidents** 148
May–June 1985

2.39 **Nicaragua–Costa Rica: Regional Rivalry and Border Incidents** 149
April 1986

2.40 **Suriname: Guerrilla Insurgency** 149
July 1986–December 1992

2.41 **United States–Panama: U.S. Anti-Noriega Military Invasion** 150
December 1989

2.42 **United States–Haiti: U.S. Military Invasion and Aristide's Return from Exile** 150
September 1994

2.43 **Ecuador–Peru: Regional Rivalry and Cenepa Headwaters Confrontation** 151
January–March 1995

2.44 **Ecuador–Peru: Condor Mountain Territorial Dispute** 151
January 1995–October 1998

2.45 **Belize–Guatemala: Postindependence Territorial Dispute and Border Incidents** 152
August 1995

Countries in the Region

Countries included in this region are:

- Antigua and Barbuda
- Argentina
- Aruba
- Bahamas
- Barbados
- Belize
- Bermuda
- Bolivia
- Brazil
- Canada
- Chile
- Colombia
- Costa Rica
- Cuba
- Dominica
- Dominican Republic
- Ecuador
- El Salvador
- Falkland Islands
- French Guiana
- Grenada
- Guatemala
- Guyana
- Haiti
- Honduras
- Jamaica
- Mexico
- Montserrat
- Nicaragua
- Panama
- Paraguay
- Peru
- Puerto Rico
- Saint Kitts and Nevis
- Saint Lucia
- Saint Vincent and the Grenadines
- Suriname
- Trinidad and Tobago
- United States of America
- Uruguay
- Venezuela
- Virgin Islands

Regional Overview

Although not as prone to civil war as some other areas of the world, Latin America—as the former colonies of France, Portugal, and Spain in the Western Hemisphere are called—has endured some extremely violent and destabilizing intrastate conflicts. Political turmoil and economic decline characterized the early years of most of the new nations. By the mid-nineteenth century, conservative dictators dominated much of the region. Postindependence progress was limited, and poverty grew worse for the vast majority of inhabitants. Inequality and a closed political arena with limited voting rights created discontent among many Latin Americans.

After 1959 the number of conflicts in the Americas increased. Throughout the 1960s and 1970s conflict in Latin America was characterized by suppression of human rights, revolution for social change, and resistance to this change. It was a period of Socialist- or Communist-inspired uprisings and revolutions, direct military rule, state terrorism, insurgent violence, and civil war. The armed forces took over to deal with what was perceived as a serious internal threat. The region developed a reputation for political violence, assassinations, military coups, and human rights abuses.

The Socialist revolution in Cuba led to a complete restructuring of Cuban society and altered Cuba's international alliances. Cuba became a Communist state under Fidel Castro. The revolution in Cuba had wide-ranging consequences for the rest of the region. It posed a serious threat, real or imagined, to the elites of other Latin American countries and to the regional system. It inspired a following of guerrilla movements in other states of the region throughout the 1960s. The Nicaraguan revolution brought the Marxist-oriented

Map 3. The Americas

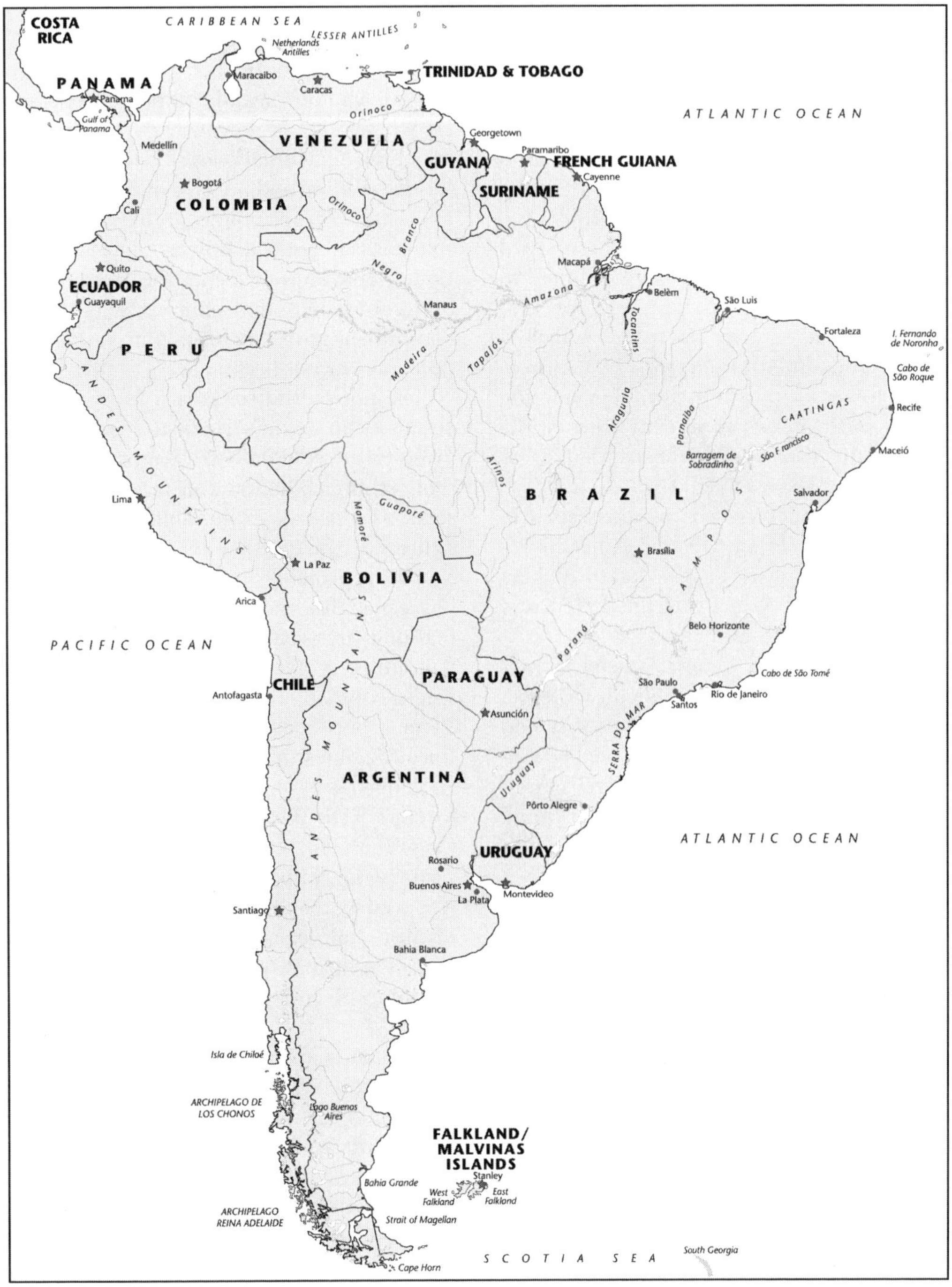

Sandinistas to power. Bolivia, Chile, and Peru attempted their own Latin American forms of socialism.

Movements in Colombia, Guatemala, and Venezuela were organized with Cuban support. Most were short-lived due to the merciless counterinsurgency campaigns by local elites with backing from the United States. In response to these developments, the United States and local governments and elites wanted to prevent further revolutions and stop those already under way. Central America and South America were and continue to be of strategic importance to the United States because of their geographical proximity. The U.S. involvement was justified by the East/West confrontation of the cold war. The United States supported dictatorships in the hope that they would destroy socialism in the region. One result is that displaced populations and refugees from Latin America became a problem for the American government, as illegal immigrants living in the United States numbered approximately 7 million in 2003.[1]

In the Southern Cone countries of South America a pattern of repressive state terrorism emerged. Between 1973 and 1976 the military took power in Argentina, Chile, and Uruguay, three of the most highly developed Latin American countries at the time. They attempted to restructure society completely, justifying these developments under the "national security doctrine," which is also called bureaucratic authoritarianism. The dictatorships implemented forms of state terrorism. By depicting greater numbers of their citizens as security threats, the regimes suppressed the threat with means that grew harsher and more comprehensive.

Many parts of South America began to industrialize in the 1930s, but the countries of Central America remained agrarian, with highly stratified societies. A characteristic of strife in Central America in the 1970s was class conflict between landlords and peasants.

Although the history of Latin America since the mid-1950s is characterized by internal political violence, military coups, dictatorships, social revolutions, and counterinsurgency campaigns, the region is comparatively peaceful in terms of interstate wars. Two significant interstate wars have been fought: the 1969 Football War between Honduras and El Salvador and the Falklands War of 1982 between Britain and Argentina. On a smaller scale, the United States invaded Panama in 1989; Ecuador and Peru engaged in military disputes in 1941, 1981, and 1995; Argentina and Chile have contested the Beagle Channel; and military attacks have taken place on the Colombian and Venezuelan border.

Overview of Conflict

Given the history of military intervention in Latin America, it is striking that today no country in the region is under military rule. Military dictatorships have generally given way to democratically elected governments, and countries such as Mexico, Nicaragua, and Panama now allow foreign observers to monitor their elections. The collapse of the Soviet Union led to the cessation of its support of leftist insurgencies around the world. This in turn weakened many insurgent movements in Latin America and removed one of the serious threats for the region's militaries. Moreover, the impetus for economic reform across the region puts pressure on civilian governments to reduce the size of their armed forces and free up budget funds that are desperately needed elsewhere.

The success of popularly elected governments, however, does not diminish the continuing political importance of the military in many Latin American countries. Elected governments still tend to support their own interests or those of elite groups. In many places suffrage and voter turnout are not true indicators of democracy, and the poor are worse off than they were in the 1970s—not what they voted for. Charismatic local leaders have been able to use the desperation and poverty of the people, government neglect, and corrupt politics to initiate protests. Faced with challenges to political power, many governments turned to brutal repression to silence the voice of protest. The issue of accountability and human rights violations from past and present governments continues to mar the reconciliation and peace process.

The illicit drug trade is a serious problem for many countries in Latin America, especially Colombia. The drugs create conflicts between drug lords fighting to keep their stranglehold on the trade. The drug lords often serve as a source of funding for rebel guerrilla groups fighting against the government.

The protracted armed conflict in Colombia, which has raged for more than forty years, is the only remaining large-scale conflict in the region. The fighting in Colombia is complex and cannot be described as a single conflict because it involves petty and organized crime groups, contract killers, drug lords, as well as political disputes involving the army, police, paramilitary, guerrillas, and legally recognized private rural security forces. With more than 25,000 deaths each year, Colombia has the highest murder rate in the world. The country is riddled with institutional corruption and wracked by the failure to resolve social conflicts through institutional legitimate means. Despite the many attempts at mediation and peacemaking, the peace process continues to collapse.

The Peruvian Sendero Luminoso or Shining Path movement is a Maoist revolutionary group dedicated to the creation of a classless society. Its ideology makes violence an integral part of this goal. Shining Path appealed to peasants and college students angered by Peru's racial and class divisions. Between 1970 and 1992 guerrilla groups carried out a campaign of sabotage, bombings, and murders that damaged billions of dollars worth of property and left 25,000 dead. In response, the Peruvian

1. See http://www.cnn.com/2003/US/01/31/illegal.immigration.

government imposed military rule and suspended civil liberties. Although the terrorism abated substantially with the capture of Shining Path leader Abimael Guzmán in September 1992, the group's loyalists remain active.

Throughout the 1960s the mechanisms of the Central American Common Market (CACM) worked to the advantage of the more highly developed economies of the region, particularly those of Guatemala and El Salvador. El Salvador is a small country with a rapidly growing population and a severely limited amount of available land. Honduras is larger but has a smaller population and a less-developed economy than El Salvador. The growth of Salvadoran-owned businesses in Honduras underscored for Hondurans the relative economic disparity between the two countries. In addition, by 1969 some 300,000 Salvadorans had drifted over the border and taken up residence in Honduras. Most of these Salvadorans were squatters, technically illegal immigrants whose sole claim to the land they worked was their physical presence on it. Hondurans feared the Salvadorans would overrun their country. The issue of the Salvadoran squatters, despite its lack of real economic significance, became a nationalistic sore point for Honduras, a question of adding territorial insult to perceived economic injury.

Tensions increased along the border during the two years preceding the outbreak of hostilities. The incident that provoked active hostilities—and lent the conflict its popular designation as the Football War—took place in San Salvador in June 1969 (*see* conflict 2.24). During and after a soccer match between the Honduran and Salvadoran national teams, Salvadoran fans vilified and harassed the Honduran team. Media coverage of this incident brought matters to a fever pitch. Tension between the two countries was inflamed by rioting during the second qualifying round for the 1970 Football World Cup. On July 14, 1969, the Salvadoran army launched an attack against Honduras. The Organization of American States (OAS) negotiated a cease-fire that took effect on July 20, and the Salvadoran troops withdrew in early August. The two nations signed a treaty on October 30, 1980, to put the border dispute before the International Court of Justice (ICJ).

Since the early 1800s colonial period, Chile and Argentina had contested possession of three islands in the Beagle Channel—Lennox, Nueva, and Picton. Also at stake were their congruent maritime extensions, some 30,000 square miles, with fishing and mineral, especially oil, rights, and possible Antarctic rights. Often negotiated, the issue went to the ICJ in 1971; the court ruled for Chile on May 2, 1977. Argentina disputed the decision and sought bilateral negotiations. In July each side protested territorial buoys placed by the other. Argentina repeatedly violated Chilean air and maritime space. Bilateral negotiations failed, and, on January 25, 1978, Argentina declared the court's award "fundamentally null."

Tensions increased, and two bilateral commissions seeking a solution accomplished little. Chile asked for ICJ mediation; Argentina sought continued negotiation. On December 9, 1978, Argentina sent a naval squadron to the Beagle Channel region, and Chile followed suit. With both countries prepared for war, on December 11 Pope John Paul II sent a personal message to their presidents urging a peaceful solution. War preparations continued as did diplomatic efforts to avert hostilities. Argentina complained to the United Nations; Chile asked the OAS to convene. On December 21 Chile accepted the pope's mediation, as did Argentina the next day. On January 9, 1979, the Act of Montevideo was signed, pledging both sides to a peaceful solution and a return to the military situation of early 1977. No significant reduction in tensions occurred until the democratic government of Raul Alfonsin took office in Argentina in December 1983. On January 23, 1984, Argentina and Chile signed the Treaty of Peace and Friendship.

After 80 percent of the Argentine electorate voted to accept the Vatican-mediated compromise, a protocol of agreement to a treaty was signed on October 18, 1984. The Treaty of Peace and Friendship was signed in Rome on November 29. Argentina officially ratified it on March 14, 1985, and Chile did so on April 12. At the Vatican, Chile and Argentina signed a treaty giving the islands to Chile but most maritime rights to Argentina.

Conflict Management

The Organization of American States is the oldest regional organization. It was established in 1890 for commercial purposes as the international Union of American Republics and became the OAS in 1948. The group currently has thirty-five members. Cuba is a member, although its present government has been excluded from participation since 1962 for incompatibility with the principles of the OAS charter. The main purposes of the OAS are to strengthen peace and security in the region; promote representative democracy; ensure the peaceful settlement of disputes among members; provide common action in the event of aggression; and promote economic, social, and cultural development. The OAS is the principal instrument of conflict resolution in the region, but, because of its moral authority over the region's large Catholic population, the Vatican has on occasion also acted as mediator (*see* conflict 2.4).

The OAS was officially established by the 1948 charter of the Bogotá Treaty, for all intents and purposes, the OAS charter. The American Treaty on Pacific Settlement established a legal framework, and the Pact of Bogotá of 1948 elaborated on conflict management mechanisms, recommending a number of peaceful strategies, namely mediation, inquiry, conciliation, arbitration, and adjudication. However, "the system envisioned is relatively uncoordinated and none of the provisions are compulsory" (Taylor 1984). The chief weakness of the OAS is also one of its treaty's fundamental principles: "No state or group of states has the right to intervene in any way, directly or indirectly, for any reason whatever, in the internal or external affairs of any other state" (Article XIII).

Ostensibly, the OAS was reinvented to curtail hostilities between its members and encourage the peaceful settlement of their conflicts, but one of most beneficial aspects of OAS conflict management for Latin American states has been the reduction of U.S. interference in the region. Obsessed by the need to eliminate and contain communism in South America, the United States was initially reluctant to adhere to the principle of nonintervention and actually sponsored covert interventions in Guatemala (*see* conflict 2.5) and in Cuba (*see* conflict 2.14; 2.17).[2] "By the late 1960's, the United States could no longer command the weighted majority in the OAS required for authorizing coercive action by its members.... So after successfully if narrowly securing post facto ratification by the OAS of its invasion of the Dominican Republic in 1965, the United States did not again seek legitimation for its coercive initiatives in the hemisphere" (Farer 1993). It is unclear whether the level of U.S. satisfaction with OAS conflict management grew in the 1970s; it is, however, evident that a spate of leftist uprisings in the 1980s once again challenged U.S. adherence to the principle of nonintervention and pitted it against most of the OAS's Latin American members (Farer 1993; Taylor 1984).

The OAS functions through five mains bodies: the Inter-American Conference, the General Assembly, the Meeting of Consultation of Ministers of Foreign Affairs, the Permanent Council, and the secretariat and secretary-general. The Permanent Council, secretary-general, and a specialist body, the Inter-American Committee on Peaceful Settlement, usually handle conflict management. The original role of the secretary-general, specified in Article 116 of the OAS charter, was limited to administrative duties. Prior to 1985, the secretary-general merely acted "with voice but without vote in all meetings of the Organization" under Article 110 of the charter. The Protocol of Cartagena de Indias (1985), Article 116, expanded the role of the secretary-general, bringing it parallel to that of the UN secretary-general.

The OAS secretary-general is now instructed to alert the General Assembly or Permanent Council to "any matter which in his opinion might threaten the peace and security of the Hemisphere or the development of the Member States" (Merrills 1991). This amendment has allowed the secretary-general to perform a more active role in conflict management. The UN has delegated responsibility for conflict management in Central America to the OAS secretary-general on several occasions. Cooperative efforts by the UN and OAS secretaries-general assisted the OAS-affiliated Contadora Group (Merrills 1991; Ramsbotham and Woodhouse 1999).

The OAS is unique among regional organizations because it is the only one that "challenges" the supremacy of the UN in the role of conflict management (Claude 1968). A resolution passed in 1954 pressured members to "Try OAS First" before referring a conflict to the UN (Claude 1968, 1973; Taylor 1984). This doctrine was considered quite radical and came to mean "that American states are bound to treat the OAS as the international agency of first resort and that the organs of the UN are obligated to respect the jurisdictional priority" (Claude 1973). "Preferential management" became apparent in ten conflicts until the policy was eventually abandoned after 1964 (*see* conflicts 2.5; 2.6; 2.7; 2.9; 2.10; 2.13; 2.16; 2.18; 2.19; 2.20). The OAS never managed to stem conflicts between its member states, but the policy did minimize the influence of the UN Security Council over OAS conflict management efforts in routine cases and thereby minimized superpower involvement in the region (Claude 1973). The organization was largely unwilling to see anti-Communist sentiment reduce the region to an ideological battlefield.[3] A study by Haas and Nye concluded that OAS conflict management success was twice that of the African Union (AU) and almost four times more successful than attempts by the Arab League (AL) over the same period (Taylor 1984).

Some OAS success can be attributed to its resource capabilities. Of the earliest established organizations (AL, AU, and OAS), the OAS has the greatest amount of material resources at its disposal. Its membership consists predominantly of developed states, with the United

---

2. In relation to the OAS's pattern of anti-Communist intervention (also intervention aimed at authoritarian regimes) over the 1950s and 1960s, Drier posits that "the outright failures of the regional collective security system ... have been those concerned not with truly inter-American conflicts but with broader power conflicts, essentially those of the Cold War, which lie outside the competence of a regional system as such. Such was the case of Guatemala in 1954 and of Cuba since 1960" (Zacher 1979).

3. The U.S.-sponsored invasion of Cuba by Cuban exiles in 1961 and the subsequent Cuban Missile Crisis of 1962 are the clear exception to this unwritten OAS goal. These instances illustrate that, at least where Cuba was concerned, OAS members willingly supported the U.S. anti-Communist stance. In 1961 Cuba did not even bother to protest to the OAS about U.S. interference, preferring to go directly to the UN with its concerns. "Cuba probably recognised that most OAS members were strongly prejudiced against it" (Zacher 1979). And, when the United States made threats of military invasion during the Cuban Missile Crisis, "not only did the Latin American states fail to support Cuba, but they supported a U.S.-backed resolution calling on all OAS members to take action to prevent Cuba from receiving missiles to ensure that the weapons did not become a threat to the hemisphere" (Zacher 1979).

States its largest proponent, initially providing two-thirds of the organization's budget (Nye 1971). Although no formal restrictions were imposed on Canada's joining, it has not become an active member, but offers support for the organization's principles (Goodspeed 1967). In addition to general funding, the OAS is better able than similar groups to provide the personnel, resources, and leadership needed to mobilize conflict management. Indeed, the organization's effectiveness derives mainly from its ability to provide adequate resources and the strength of its membership, especially because the United States is acutely concerned about regional issues in Central America. Much of the organization's power comes from U.S. participation and support, even though the OAS comprises mainly developed states within its geographically defined region.

Operational limitations affecting OAS conflict management are:

1. Policy of nonintervention: Charter provisions demonstrate a traditional unwillingness to become involved in the domestic affairs of other states.
2. Ideological stances: Fears that the OAS was being used as a vehicle for U.S.-sponsored anti-Communist intervention strained membership relations in eight conflicts, particularly those involving the Dominican Republic and Cuba (Goodspeed 1967). These conflicts were Dominican Republic–Haiti/Cuba: Regional Aggression (Early 1947–December 1951); Dominican Republic–Cuba/Venezuela: Dominican Republic Aggression (February 1956–January 1962); Cuba–Haiti: Cuban-Sponsored Military Invasion and Haitian Exiles Conflict (August 1959); United States–Cuba: Anti-Castro Military Invasion—The Bay of Pigs (April–May 1961); United States–USSR: Cold War Dispute and the Cuban Missile Crisis (September–November 1962); Cuba–Venezuela: Terrorism and Invasion Attempt (November 1963–May 1967); Bolivia: Cuban-Assisted Guerrilla Insurgency (November 1966–July 1970); and Honduras–Nicaragua: Right-Wing Insurgency and the Contra War (January 1980–February 1994).

Overall, OAS observer missions conducted investigations and mediation in twenty-seven conflicts. The OAS has not employed a comprehensive peacekeeping force but the Inter-American Peace Committee (IAPC) aided settlement in five conflicts.

References

Claude, I.L. Jr. 1968. "The OAS, the UN and the United States." In *International Regionalism: Readings*. Nye, J.S., ed. Written under the auspices of the Center for International Affairs at Harvard University, Boston: Little, Brown: 3–21.

———. 1973. "The OAS, the UN, and the United States." In *Regional Politics and World Order*. Falk, R.A., and S.A. Mendlovitz, eds. San Francisco: W.H. Freeman, 269–307.

Farer, T.J. 1993. "The Role of Regional Collective Security Arrangements." In *Collective Security in a Changing World*. A World Peace Foundation Study. Weiss, T.G., ed. Boulder: Lynne Rienner, 153–186.

Goodspeed, S.S., 1967. *The Nature and Function of International Organisation*. Oxford, England: Oxford University Press.

Merrills, J.G. 1991. *International Dispute Settlement*. 2d edition. Cambridge, England: Grotius Publications Ltd.

Nye, J.S. Jr. 1971. *Peace in Parts: Integration and Conflict in Regional Organization*. Perspectives on International Relations Series. Written under the auspices of the Center for International Affairs at Harvard University. Boston: Little, Brown.

Ramsbotham, O., and T. Woodhouse. 1999. *Encyclopedia of International Peacekeeping Operations*. Santa Barbara: Calif.: ABC-CLIO.

Taylor, P. 1984. *Nonstate Actors in International Politics: From Transregional to Substate Organizations*. Boulder: Westview.

Zacher, M.W. 1979. *International Conflicts and Collective Security, 1946–1977: The United Nations, Organization of American States, Organization of African Unity, and Arab League*. New York: Praeger.

2.1 Dominican Republic–Haiti/Cuba: Regional Aggression Early 1947–December 1951

Although all sides in this conflict alleged conspiracies and claimed potential invasions, the rule of dictator Rafael Leónidas Trujillo Molina in the Dominican Republic became the focus of regional tension involving the Dominican Republic, Haiti, Cuba, and Guatemala. Generalissimo Trujillo's controversial rule (1942–1952; 1961) lasted in the Dominican Republic until his assassination in 1961. The initial phase of this dispute began in 1947 and reemerged in 1949 in another guise.

Early in 1947 a force of approximately 1,000 men began training in Cuba for an invasion of the Dominican Republic. The Cuban government denied complicity in these preparations and the subsequent invasion, but a later investigation by the Special Committee on the Caribbean of the Organization of American States (OAS) from April 8, 1950, to May 14, 1951, confirmed that Cuban officials had been involved in the invasion preparations. When the Dominican Republic learned of the invasion plans, it lodged a complaint with the Cuban government on July 23, 1947. The Cuban government did not react to the complaint until September 28, arresting the conspirators and confiscating their arms. The conspirators who remained at large formed the "Caribbean legion," a group opposed to dictators. The Cuban government dealt with the conspiring Cuban officials, as did the Dominican Republic with those citizens it suspected of involvement in the invasion plot.

During their invasion preparations, the Cuban conspirators had captured a Dominican ship in international waters. The Dominican Republic tried to secure the release of the detained ship but to no avail. The Dominican Republic then appealed to the Inter-American Peace Committee (IAPC) to assist in the return of the vessel (August 1948). After initial negotiations with the parties, the IAPC decided that the parties should settle the dispute through bilateral negotiations. Both parties agreed to negotiate, and the tension between the Dominican Republic and Cuba abated.

In 1949 it was reported that the remaining conspirators from the 1947 invasion attempt had reorganized in Guatemala and Nicaragua with the assistance of both governments. In early February 1949 the Haitian government lodged a formal complaint with the OAS, alleging that the Dominican Republic was supporting a rebel Haitian army colonel, Astrel Roland, who had been implicated in an attempt to overthrow Haiti's government the previous month. The OAS Council decided that the parties should settle the matter, and, recognizing a potential for the dispute to be settled without outside interference, the OAS decided not to engage any dispute management strategy (February 25, 1949). Haiti, dissatisfied with the OAS decision, referred the matter on to the IAPC on March 24. The IAPC visited both countries to conduct talks, and the Dominican Republic and Haiti signed a joint declaration on June 10, in which they agreed to settle future disagreements peacefully. The agreement lasted only six days. Fighting and antagonistic propaganda between Haiti and the Dominican Republic intensified in November and December 1949 and into January 1950.

On another front, the Dominican Republic announced on June 20, 1949, that the invasion potential from Cuba had been dealt with and was no longer considered a threat. The invasion threat would probably have been far greater if Mexico the day before had not confiscated two aircraft carrying considerable arms supplies to the rebels based in Cuba.

On June 21, 1949, the Dominican Republic publicly objected to Cuba's support for anti-Trujillo activists. In response to the Dominican Republic's complaint, the United States asked the IAPC to investigate the situation. By September 14 the IAPC had reiterated a previous OAS Council resolution calling for regional states to deal with conspirators in their respective jurisdictions. The Dominican Republic continued to protest about Cuba harboring conspirators, particularly those allegedly planning an invasion from the l'Amelie region in eastern Cuba. A Cuban invitation to the IAPC for further investigation was not accepted, with the IAPC accepting Cuba's guarantees. At the end of December 1949, the Dominican Republic legislature had officially granted Trujillo the power to declare war on any country supporting conspiracies against the Dominican government.

Haiti appealed to the OAS Council on January 3, 1950, renewing its complaint against the Dominican Republic. At this point, Haitian fears were aroused again by the discovery of arms supplies making their way to the Dominican Republic and Trujillo's assumption of special war powers. On January 6 the Dominican Republic also registered a complaint with the OAS Council over its issues with Haiti and Cuba. With continuing concerns over the alleged involvement of Guatemala, Cuba, and Haiti in conspiracies against the Dominican Republic, and concerns over retaliatory Dominican Republic plots, the OAS Council met on January 6. The OAS Council established the Special Committee on the Caribbean to investigate all complaints and allot blame for the various incidents according to their findings (April 8, 1950). The OAS Council called for negotiations to begin between Haiti and the Dominican Republic and referred the parties to the terms of their previous joint declaration of 1949. In addition, the OAS Council condemned the special war powers Trujillo had assumed.

Problems between Haiti and the Dominican Republic had all but dissipated by the time the Special Committee on the Caribbean began its investigation. A coup d'état in Haiti had replaced President Dumarsais Estimé (August 16, 1946–May 10, 1950) with Franck Lavaud (May 10–December 6, 1950), who proved to be a more affable ally for Trujillo. The Dominican Republic legislature repealed the war powers act by April 1950. The Special Committee on the Caribbean continued its fact-finding in the region until it issued a full report on May 14, 1951. In its final observations, the committee noted that all parties had complied with the OAS resolutions. Relations between the Dominican Republic and Haiti remained relatively stable after April 1950, but the same cannot be said for relations between Cuba and the Dominican Republic.

In July 1951 tensions between Cuba and the Dominican Republic reignited. The Dominican Republic's navy detained a Guatemalan vessel, the *Quetzal,* as it was making its way to Cuba. Alleging that the crew was an invasion force, the Dominican Republic accused it of "subversive plotting." Of the fourteen crewmen captured and sentenced to thirty years in prison, five were Cuban. Cuba lodged a formal protest with the IAPC on behalf of its citizens, and Guatemala acknowledged that it would act on behalf of the imprisoned Guatemalan crewmen. The IAPC notified the Dominican Republic of the complaints, and the Dominican Republic responded by asking for the IAPC's assistance in resolving the matter. The foreign ministers of Cuba and the Dominican Republic participated in a series of meetings arranged by the IAPC in Washington in 1951. By December 25 the IAPC meetings had proved a success, with the parties signing a joint declaration to avoid interference in each others' internal affairs and to refrain from propaganda warfare. As a result of the IAPC mediation, the prisoners were pardoned and released.

References

Brecher, M., J. Wilkenfeld, and S. Moser. 1988. *Crises in the Twentieth Century*. New York: Pergamon.

Butterworth, R.L. 1976. *Managing Interstate Conflict, 1945–1974*. Pittsburgh: Center for International Studies, University of Pittsburgh.

Fretter, J.M. 2001. *Effective Mediation in International Disputes: A Comparative Analysis of Mediation by the United Nations and Regional Organizations 1945–1995*. Doctoral dissertation, Vol. II: Appendices. University of Canterbury, Christchurch, New Zealand.

"Political Leaders." http://web.jet.es/ziaorarr/domin-re.htm (accessed April 9, 1999).

Zacher, M.W. 1979. *International Conflicts and Collective Security, 1946–1977*. New York: Praeger.

2.2 Costa Rica: Anticorruption Military Insurgency and Civil War March–April 1948

The roots of the Costa Rican civil war go back to 1942, when José Figueres Ferrer publicly denounced corruption within the government of Rafael Calderón Guardia. Forced into exile in Mexico, Figueres continued to agitate for reform and to organize opposition, first against the Calderón government and then against its successor under Teodoro Picado Michalski, who assumed power in 1944.

In 1947, with the support of Guatemalan president Juan José Arevalo, Figueres and other revolutionary exiles signed the Caribbean Pact, which called for the overthrow of all dictatorial regimes in Central America and the Caribbean, including Costa Rica's. Following the presidential elections in Costa Rica in February 1948, won by opposition leader Otilio Ulate Blanco, President Picado delayed the transfer of power at the instigation of his predecessor, Calderón.

On March 11, 1948, Figueres, heading a national liberation army, invaded Costa Rica from bases in Guatemala. Full-scale civil war erupted. Figueres reached the capital, San José, by April 13 and called for Picado's unconditional surrender. The national liberation army controlled most of the surrounding country. At this point, the papal nuncio and ambassadors from Argentina, Mexico, Panama, and the United States attempted to broker a peace agreement, but without success.

On April 17 the war escalated further with the movement of Nicaraguan troops into Costa Rica to support Picado. Nicaragua, also targeted by the Caribbean Pact, had been supporting Picado since the start of the conflict with arms and "volunteers." But Picado surrendered to Figueres on April 19. Nicaraguan forces withdrew on April 21, and Figueres established a new government on April 24, 1948. Total fatalities for the war were estimated at approximately 1,000, with no Nicaraguan troops killed.

References

Bell, J. 1971. *Crisis in Costa Rica: The 1948 Revolution*. Austin: University of Texas Press.

Bird, L.A. 1984. *Costa Rica, the Unarmed Democracy*. London: Sheppard.

Earley, S. 1982. *Arms and Politics in Costa Rica and Nicaragua, 1948–1981*. Albuquerque: Latin American Institute/University of New Mexico Press.

Tillema, H.K. 1991. *International Armed Conflict Since 1945: A Bibliographic Handbook of Wars and Military Interventions*. Boulder: Westview.

2.3 Nicaragua–Costa Rica: Border Conflict December 1948–February 1949

The conflict between Costa Rica and Nicaragua emerged directly out of the Costa Rican civil war (*see* conflict 2.2). Nicaragua had supported the regime of Teodoro Picado Michalski during the civil war by sending troops and supplies. Supporters of the deposed Picado fled to Nicaragua and set up bases there with the intention of overthrowing the new Figueres regime in Costa Rica. Such moves led to a number of serious border incidents and a deterioration in relations between the two countries.

On December 10, 1948, armed rebels invaded Costa Rica from Nicaragua. Costa Rica charged Nicaragua with support for the rebels and protested to the Organization of American States (OAS). The OAS set up an investigating committee on December 14, which began to mediate the dispute. Costa Rican airplanes then attacked rebel bases within Nicaraguan territory on December 20.

OAS representatives met with the parties in Washington, and a cessation of hostilities was agreed to and signed on February 21, 1949. Approximately fifty people were killed during the course of the conflict. The issues were never fully resolved, and the two sides fought in 1955, 1977, 1978, and during the contra war (*see* conflicts 2.6; 2.29; 2.30; 2.31).

References

Bell, J. 1971. *Crisis in Costa Rica: The 1948 Revolution*. Austin: University of Texas Press.

Bird, L.A. 1984. *Costa Rica, the Unarmed Democracy*. London: Sheppard.

Butterworth, R.L. 1978. *Moderation from Management: International Organizations and Peace*. Pittsburgh: Center for International Studies, University of Pittsburgh.

Crawley, E. 1984. *Nicaragua in Perspective*. Revised edition. New York: St. Martin's.

Earley, S. 1982. *Arms and Politics in Costa Rica and Nicaragua, 1948–1981*. Albuquerque: Latin American Institute/University of New Mexico Press.

Tillema, H.K. 1991. *International Armed Conflict Since 1945: A Bibliographic Handbook of Wars and Military Interventions*. Boulder: Westview.

2.4 Argentina–Chile: The Beagle Channel Border Dispute July 1952–August 1993

Argentina and Chile share a history peppered with border disputes. One such recurring dispute, which began in the nineteenth century, concerned the contested ownership of Lennox, Nueva, and Picton, three small islands at the eastern entrance of the Beagle Channel, and the rights to the waterway itself (some 150 miles in length and 3 to 8 miles wide, at the southernmost tip of South America). In the 1970s "the islands were inhabited by Chilean shepherds and patrolled by Argentinean torpedo boats" (Brecher et al. 1988, 327). Both the waterway and the islands situated at its eastern mouth are regarded as strategically important and provide a vital route to potential resources in the South Atlantic and Antarctic regions.

An 1881 border treaty divided Tierra del Fuego, awarding half of the territory to Chile and the other half to Argentina. The treaty also awarded the islands south of the Beagle Channel, including Cape Horn, to Chile. Problems over territorial possession were exacerbated by the fact that treaty "cartographic errors placed the Channel as running north of the islands of Lennox, Nueva and Picton; when it was discovered that its actual position was south of those islands, Argentina raised a claim to them" (Butterworth, 1976, 236). The Beagle Channel provides Argentina access to the Atlantic and its Antarctic bases as well as separating Tierra del Fuego, Argentinean territory, from Navarino Island, Chilean territory. Chile was concerned that if Argentina controlled the channel, Argentina could also control Chile's trade routes and strengthen Argentina's claims to jointly contested Antarctic territories.

In July 1952 Argentina ignored a ruling by the International Court of Justice (ICJ) that the Beagle Channel and islands belonged to Chile. Levels of civilian and military occupation of the islands continued to be a source of contention from 1952 to 1972. The United Kingdom brought the issue of the Beagle Channel to the ICJ for consideration on May 4, 1955. The UK claimed that Argentina and Chile had encroached on its territorial sovereign rights over the area, "relying on Article 36 (1) of the ICJ Statue for the Court's jurisdiction" (Allesbrook, 1986, 118). Objection letters were received from both parties: from Chile on July 15, 1955, and from Argentina on August 8, 1955, even though Argentina had refused to recognize the Court's jurisdiction on August 1. The ICJ reached a contentious decision on March 16, 1956, resulting in the removal of the matter from ICJ lists.

Tension mounted in 1958 when Chile constructed a lighthouse on Snipe Island, which is located in the Beagle Channel area. Marines from the Argentinean navy destroyed the lighthouse, and Chile built another to replace it. Argentinean forces destroyed this lighthouse and occupied the island. A diplomatic solution was reached whereby the parties agreed to restore the pre-1958 situation on the island. Border conflicts continued to occur along the channel, specifically in the Palena district, a territory about forty-five miles long on the north-south Andean border. Provisional agreements were reached in 1960, but Chile revoked them in 1963, claiming that Argentina had too much freedom in Chilean waters. No fatalities were reported in this phase of the dispute, which lapsed until the territorial question was raised again in 1964. Deliberating from 1964 to December 14, 1966, the British Court of Arbitration ruled that the Palena border region be divided between the two states.

In 1964 both parties agreed that the ICJ should decide possession of the Beagle Channel. In October 1965 Argentina and Chile took steps to refrain from provocative actions in two other inflammatory regions: Palena and Laguna del Desierto, an area along the southern side of the Andean frontier. After a Chilean police officer died in border skirmishes in the Laguna region, the parties' earlier accord ended with each side accusing the other of border violations. The two countries eventually agreed to continue diplomatic efforts to resolve rights to the Laguna region. On December 11, 1964, a Joint Border Commission was established to set out new border landmarks in the Palena and Laguna del Desierto regions. Despite progress on these territorial issues, none was made in resolving the Beagle Channel question, which arose again in 1967.

In August 1967 an Argentinean fishing vessel on route in the channel met with Chilean warships. Although there was no military response, the incident had repercussions in Chile, fermenting accusations of Argentinean expansionism. In late November 1967 a Chilean patrol boat passed within two miles of Argentina's naval base at Ushuaia. This provocation was answered by warning fire from Argentinean air and naval forces. Argentina rejected a Chilean proposal to allow UK arbitration on December 23, 1967, citing a UK bias in favor of Chile (tension between Argentina and the United Kingdom over the territorial question of the Falkland Islands, already evident, would not become violent until the 1982 Falklands War; *see* conflict 2.33). By 1968 the threat of war had intensified. Argentina reinforced its military base at Ushuaia with aircraft, an aircraft carrier, a submarine, three cruisers, and a patrol boat. Chile also strengthened its bases in the vicinity. Chilean diplomacy during 1969 left Argentina quite isolated in terms of continental politics. A rapprochement was reached between President Alejandro Lanusse of Argentina and President Salvador Allende's Socialist government in Chile. On July 22, 1971, the parties decided that "the Channel border would be established by the Queen of England on the basis of a technical decision by a five-man arbitration court drawn from the ICJ" (Butterworth 1976, 237).

Chile's foreign minister, Dr. Clodomiro Almeyda, and Argentina's foreign minister, Dr. Luis de Pardo, held three meetings in March, April, and July 1972 to resolve the matter. Argentina's concerns over a UK bias in favor of Chile appeared to fade at this point, and the parties reached a ten-year arbitration agreement providing for ICJ involvement in deciding the matter (December 1972). President Isabel Martinez de Person of Argentina and General Augusto Pinochet of Chile met at Moron Airbase outside Buenos Aires on April 18, 1975, and reached a partial agreement.

On May 2, 1977, the ICJ awarded the islands to Chile. In July Chilean and Argentinean naval forces clashed in the channel, and both sides strengthened their presence in the area. On December 5 Argentina's government issued a formal note objecting to the May ruling of the ICJ. Negotiators from both countries met December 28, but achieved no solution. On January 5, 1978, Pinochet announced that Chile would be pursuing a more pragmatic and aggressive foreign policy. Militaries of both states were promptly mobilized in preparedness. Argentina moved naval vessels to the Beagle Channel area on January 8. Unspecified negotiators from the United States offered to mediate on January 10, but the offer was not accepted. Negotiations held January 19 in Mendoza, Argentina, between Pinochet and President Jorge Rafael Videla of Argentina were unsuccessful. A presidents' meeting in Puerto Montt, Chile, on February 20 ended with a partial settlement, the Act of Puerto Montt, which established a negotiating committee and allotted 180 days to resolve the dispute. The United States tried to persuade the parties to resolve the matter through talks. Senior officials from Argentina and Chile negotiated from March until August 16, 1978. A partial agreement was reached over September 13–November 2, but on October 16 minor clashes were reported along the border as Argentinean troops moved into position. This provocation drew more concern with Argentina calling up 50,000 reserves. On October 24, 1978, Chile deployed additional border forces and withdrew from scheduled naval exercises with the United States and Peru, fearing that Argentina would invade the channel while Chile's navy was at sea. As the agreement deadline to the 180-day moratorium drew closer, Argentina began to ready military forces. With the deadline reached on November 2, 1978, both states announced that they had agreed to the joint development of the Beagle Channel region. The designation of maritime zones, however, had not been resolved. On December 11 senior officials from Argentina and Chile again held talks, this time deciding to allow the Vatican to assist them.

On December 16 the Vatican agreed to mediate, but the same day Chile placed 45,000 troops, stationed on the borders, on full alert. Argentina complained about Chile's troop deployment to the UN Security Council on December 21, but the Security Council took no further action. Also on December 21 Chile requested an urgent meeting of the Organization of American States (OAS) to deter Argentina from attacking the islands. Despite further U.S. and Chilean requests for OAS involvement, the organization offered no assistance. On December 26 the parties acknowledged their acceptance of mediation by the Vatican in the Declaration of Montevideo. Cardinal Antonio Samore, a papal envoy, mediated over the course of six years achieving only limited success (December 21, 1978–January 8, 1979; April 23, 1979–November 1980; December 12, 1980–March 25, 1981; February 1, 1982–April 1982; December 1983–January 23, 1984). In early October 1984, the dispute intensified when Argentinean forces shelled Chilean positions; Argentina claimed that the shelling was the act of a dissident officer. Finally, on October 18, 1984, Cardinal Samore brought about a full settlement between senior Chilean and Argentinean negotiators, resulting in the signing of the Treaty of Peace and Friendship in Rome on November 29. The treaty awarded Chile sovereignty over the islands in the Beagle Channel, but restricted its maritime rights to the Pacific waters. Argentina was granted rights over the waters on the Atlantic side of the channel.

After a meeting of foreign ministers in August 1991, both parties resolved almost all of their contentions over Palena, leaving ownership of only a small section of Laguna del Desierto undecided. Both countries submitted the question of the remaining territory to an OAS panel of judges in August 1993. An official decision from the panel was reported to be still pending in 1994, but in effect, the OAS panel of judges had mediated a resolution to the conflict.

References

Allsebrook, M. 1986. *Prototypes of Peacemaking: The First Forty Years of the United Nations.* Harlow (Essex) England: Longman Group UK Limited.

Bercovitch, J., and R. Jackson. 1997. *International Conflict: A Chronological Encyclopedia of Conflicts and Their Management 1945–1995.* Washington, D.C.: Congressional Quarterly.

Brecher, M., J. Wilkenfeld, and S. Moser. 1988. *Crises in the Twentieth Century.* New York: Pergamon.

Butterworth, R.L. 1976. *Managing Interstate Conflict, 1945–1974.* Pittsburgh: Center for International Studies, University of Pittsburgh.

Day, A., ed. 1987. *Border and Territorial Disputes.* 2d edition. Burnt Mill, Harlow (Essex), England: Longman.

Fretter, J.M. 2001. *Effective Mediation in International Disputes: A Comparative Analysis of Mediation by the United Nations and Regional Organizations 1945–1995.* Doctoral dissertation, Vol. II: Appendices. University of Canterbury, Christchurch, New Zealand.

Huth, P.K. 1996. *Standing Your Ground: Territorial Disputes and International Conflict.* Ann Arbor: Michigan University Press.

Tillema, H.K. 1991. *International Armed Conflict Since 1945: A Bibliographic Handbook of Wars and Military Interventions*. Boulder: Westview.

2.5 Guatemala: Civil War and Insurgency June 1954–Ongoing

In June 1954 Guatemala's democratic regime was ousted in a coup d'état backed by the U.S. Central Intelligence Agency (CIA) and United Fruit, a U.S. multinational company and the principal foreign interest in Guatemala. Carlos Castillo Armas was installed as Guatemala's leader. This event inaugurated a period of political strife and civil war that was to endure for more than thirty years.

Armas was assassinated in July 1957. Elections were held under the supervision of a military junta that resulted in victory for General Miguel Ydigoras Fuentes. Ydigoras acquiesced in the United States' disastrous Bay of Pigs invasion of Cuba, even allowing the invasion force to conduct training exercises in Guatemala. His involvement in the invasion led to discontent in the army, and a military revolt broke out on November 13, 1960. It was rapidly crushed with U.S. assistance.

In the aftermath of the failed revolt, a left-wing guerrilla insurrection took shape. Made up of various opposition groups that formally united as the Rebel Armed Forces (FAR) in February 1962, this group of guerrillas was joined by the October 20 Front, led by the former defense minister in the democratic regime ousted in 1954. Massive rioting broke out in Guatemala City in March 1962, costing at least twenty lives and increasing the tensions between government and insurgency forces. In support of the government, the United States moved counterinsurgency forces into Guatemala, halting the insurrection.

In 1963 the army, with U.S. support, removed Ydigoras from office and replaced him with the minister of defense, Enrique Peralta Azurdia, who continued the fight against the guerrillas. Elections held in 1966 installed Julio César Mendez Montenegro as a puppet president. Following the defeat of the FAR in 1970, army strongman Colonel Manuel Arana Osorio replaced Mendez as president. His leadership was marked by brutal repression resulting in thousands of disappearances. The 1974 presidential elections changed little, as the results were annulled when a dissident army general won.

In the wake of the annulled election, a number of guerrilla groups reemerged. At first they operated independently, but in 1982 they formed an alliance called the Guatemalan National Revolutionary Unity (URNG). The civil war entered a new phase in that year, as the Reagan administration actively sought to promote democracy in Central America to resist the influence of communism. Another coup brought President José Efraín Ríos Montt to power in 1982. He intensified the fight against the URNG by organizing peasants into militias and feeding and equipping them. The aim of the militias was to eradicate all opposition at the grassroots level. The campaign hampered the guerrillas but did not end their campaign.

With U.S. approval, another coup in 1983 replaced Montt with General Oscar Humberto Mejia, who set about a reconstruction plan with the help of renewed U.S. aid. It is estimated that in excess of 120,000 people died during the course of the civil war. Actions against suspected guerrilla targets continued throughout the 1980s, including a number of raids into neighboring Mexico. In early 1995 there were numerous allegations of CIA involvement in the civil war, and an official inquiry was launched.

An arduous peace process brokered by the United Nations began with direct negotiations between the government and the URNG in 1991. Meeting in Mexico, Roldolfo Toruno, a Roman Catholic bishop, and Jean Arnault, a UN mediator, engaged in more than twenty separate mediation attempts up to the end of 1994. Armed conflict ended with a negotiated settlement in December 1996, and President Alvaro Arzú fulfilled his promise to have a definitive peace treaty signed by the end of the year. The treaty, signed on December 29, provided for a one-third cut in the size of the army, the return of URNG fighters to civilian life, and the strengthening of the rights of the majority Indian population—the main victims of the conflict. The World Bank promised to make loans of $100 million each year from 1997 to 1999 to help the country implement the treaty.

Despite the peace agreement, a climate of intimidation continued. In May 1999 Guatemalans voted to reject constitutional reforms that were aimed at rectifying some of the underlying causes of the war by guaranteeing equal rights for the country's Maya Indian majority and curbing the powerful Guatemalan army. Elections took place in November 1999, followed by a second round for the presidency in December 1999. Alfonso Portillo of the far-right Guatemalan Republican Front (FRG) emerged as the country's new leader. Civil society groups strongly criticized the FRG because of its ongoing relationship with Ríos Montt, who presided over the period of worst human rights violations in the country's history. Montt was elected president of the National Congress. Under the new leadership, peasant organizers and human rights campaigners continue to experience threats, intimidation, and abductions.

References

Gleijeses, P. 1978. *The Dominican Crisis: The 1965 Constitutionalist Revolt and American Intervention*. Translated by L. Lipson. Baltimore: Johns Hopkins University Press.

Gurr, T., M. Marshall, and D. Khosla. 2000. *Peace and Conflict 2001: A Global Survey of Conflicts, Self-Determination Movements, and Democracy*. College Park:

Center for International Development and Conflict Management, University of Maryland.

Immerman, R.H. 1982. *The CIA in Guatemala: The Foreign Policy of Intervention.* Austin: University of Texas Press.

LaFeber, W. 1993. *Inevitable Revolutions: The United States in Central America.* 2d edition. New York: Norton.

Melville, T., and M. Melville. 1971. *Guatemala—Another Vietnam?* Harmondsworth (Middlesex), England: Penguin.

Reuters Alert Net. 2001. "Guatemala" Country Profile: http://www.alertnet.org/thefacts/countryprofiles/ (accessed March 9, 2002).

Schlesinger, S.C., and S. Kinzer. 1982. *Bitter Fruit: The Untold Story of the American Coup in Guatemala.* Garden City, N.Y.: Doubleday.

Tillema, H.K. 1991. *International Armed Conflict Since 1945: A Bibliographic Handbook of Wars and Military Interventions.* Boulder: Westview.

2.6 Nicaragua–Costa Rica: Exiles Invasion Attempt January 1955

In a reprise of the conflict between these Central American countries following the Costa Rican civil war, the two states traded accusations of harboring each other's exiled rebels with the aim of overthrowing their respective governments (*see* conflict 2.3). In fact, on January 11, 1955, exiled opposition groups invaded Costa Rica with support from Nicaraguan troops. The fighting was intense, and Costa Rica's small army was unable to stem the rebels' advance.

Costa Rica immediately appealed for intervention by the Organization of American States (OAS), which formed an investigatory committee that recommended OAS air support for the beleaguered country. The United States was the only OAS country to respond, dispatching aircraft on January 16, 1955. The border conflict rapidly subsided after this.

The OAS asked both sides to reaffirm their commitment to the 1949 Amity Agreement, which they did on February 24, 1955. Approximately 1,000 people were killed during the fighting. Relations between the two states improved only gradually after this time.

References

Bell, J. 1971. *Crisis in Costa Rica: The 1948 Revolution.* Austin: University of Texas Press.

Bird, L.A. 1984. *Costa Rica, the Unarmed Democracy.* London: Sheppard.

Crawley, E. 1984. *Nicaragua in Perspective.* Revised edition. New York: St. Martin's.

Earley, S. 1982. *Arms and Politics in Costa Rica and Nicaragua, 1948–1981.* Albuquerque: Latin American Institute/University of New Mexico Press.

Tillema, H.K. 1991. *International Armed Conflict Since 1945: A Bibliographic Handbook of Wars and Military Interventions.* Boulder: Westview.

2.7 Dominican Republic–Cuba/Venezuela: Dominican Republic Aggression and Exiles Conflict February 1956–January 1962

Cuba charged the Dominican Republic with planning aggressive strategies against it on February 27, 1956. The Cuban government appealed to the Inter-American Peace Committee (IAPC) for assistance in settling the potential threat posed by the Dominican Republic's dictator, General Rafael Leónidas Trujillo Molina. In response, the Dominican Republic made countercharges, accusing Cuba's government of sending arms supplies to support an abortive revolution in the Dominican Republic. Cuba denied the allegations and requested that the IAPC investigate its claims. Cuba had stated that its internal security was threatened in a related incident after it had given sanctuary to an exiled former Dominican Republic police chief. It was later revealed that the exiled police chief had returned to the Dominican Republic and had merely been sent on a military intelligence gathering mission. Cuba also voiced suspicions about Dominican Republic involvement with Cuban dissidents who were plotting to assassinate Cuban dictator, Fulgencio Batista y Zaldívar, who had come to power March 10, 1952.

The IAPC announced its decision on April 20, 1956, requesting that the parties seek a resolution via bilateral negotiations, but announcing no particular findings. The dispute continued unresolved. Cuba renewed charges of Dominican Republic interference in its internal affairs on November 29, 1956, claiming that the Dominican Republic was financing and training Cuban rebels. On January 1, 1959, Cuban revolutionaries overthrew Batista.

On June 12, 1959, Venezuela broke off diplomatic relations with the Dominican Republic. In February 1960 the antagonism between Venezuela and the Dominican Republic continued, with Venezuela accusing the Dominican Republic of human rights violations and lodging a complaint with the Organization of American States (OAS) on February 17. The IAPC was active in the region investigating claims of human rights violations as well as keeping a watchful eye on the potential for interstate conflict. In November 1959 an airplane, registered in the United States, was preparing to drop revolutionary propaganda over Venezuela. Pilot error resulted in the pamphlets being dropped accidentally over the island of Curaçao on November 19, and, compounding the pilots' dilemma, the plane ran low on fuel and was forced to land on Aruba. Venezuela lodged a formal complaint against the Dominican Republic with the IAPC on November 25, alleging Dominican Republic involvement in the fiasco.

The IAPC findings confirmed the Venezuelan suspicions, and the Dominican Republic authorities were charged with "connivance" in the affair (Butterworth, 1976: 266)

In April 1960 an exiled Venezuelan general, Castro León, and a number of his followers, invaded Venezuela from encampments in Colombia. The invasion mission seized full control of a border town, San Cristobal, and then declared over the local radio station that they had overthrown Venezuelan president Rómulo Betancourt. The Venezuelan exiles were dealt with by force, and the situation was brought under control in a matter of days.

Relations continued to deteriorate, and on June 24, 1960, there was an assassination attempt on Betancourt, when explosives were detonated close to his car. Betancourt survived the attempt with serious burns, but one of his aides was more grievously injured. The Venezuelan government suspected the Dominican Republic's complicity in the incident and discovered that those responsible for the assassination attempt were Venezuelan exiles living in the Dominican Republic. The fact that a radio station in the Dominican Republic reported the attempt only fifteen minutes after it happened did not allay Venezuelan authorities' suspicions. On June 25 Venezuela formally accused Trujillo, the Dominican Republican leader, of initiating the assassination attempt. The Dominican Republic denied the allegations and, fearing a Venezuelan attack, placed troops on stand-by alert.

Venezuela also placed its forces on alert and made another formal accusation against the Dominican Republic. On June 30 Venezuela declared a state of emergency after Trujillo charged Venezuela with making war preparations.

On July 1, 1960, the Venezuelan government called for an emergency meeting of the OAS, requesting the implementation of sanctions against the Dominican Republic. Betancourt issued an ultimatum saying that if the OAS took no action against Trujillo's regime Venezuela would be forced to act unilaterally. On July 8 the OAS formed a committee to investigate the situation. The committee returned its findings, and on August 20 the OAS passed a resolution condemning the Dominican Republic's "acts of aggression and intervention." The OAS committee found that the Dominican Republic had furnished passports to León and his followers, so that they could gain entry to Colombia. The committee also found that the Dominican Republic had actively supported the assassination conspirators, from supplying the explosives to instructing the would-be assassins on how to use them. The OAS called upon its members to break diplomatic relations with the Dominican Republic and to enforce a strict arms embargo and partial trade sanctions.

Over the course of the OAS debate on the matter, the United States initially tried to get a more lenient resolution passed, but eventually complied with the implementation of sanctions and the severing of diplomatic relations. The OAS established a special committee to oversee the sanctions. Later in August 1960, the OAS informed the United Nations that it was about to impose economic and diplomatic sanctions against the Dominican Republic for its acts of aggression and intervention against Venezuela. The UN Security Council notified the OAS that its approval was not necessary and that the sanctions did not constitute an enforcement action. The OAS cancelled the sanctions on January 4, 1962, when it considered that the Dominican Republic no longer posed a threat to Venezuela.

Dominican Republic opposition leaders had taken refuge in Cuba during Trujillo's dictatorship, and Cuban interference in the internal affairs of the Dominican Republic can be traced back to this group of political exiles. The approximately 200 rebel exiles actively pursued the overthrow of Trujillo's regime. In June and July 1959, they began a series of small air and sea invasions against the Dominican Republic with the support of Cuba and Venezuela. The Dominican Republic army was able to repel the exiles' invasion attempts. Although not completely successful, the invasion attempts were instrumental in exposing the problems within the Trujillo regime. Some army units sent to repel the exiles defected and joined their struggle. Trujillo referred the matter to the OAS in July 1959, but the OAS took no action, and no other dispute management strategy was attempted.

On September 5, 1960, a UN Security Council meeting was called to discuss the situation, and the Soviet Union requested a resolution to deal with OAS sanctions, but the resolution was not passed. This phase of the dispute dissipated after September 1960, when the threat to Venezuela had been alleviated by OAS action. The OAS special sanctions committee reported that the Dominican Republic had not fulfilled any of the OAS demands of August 1960. As a result, the OAS Council imposed additional economic sanctions on the Dominican Republic on January 4, 1961. In April 1961 the IAPC concluded that there was a direct relationship between the interstate tensions and Trujillo.

The OAS was also involved in the Dominican Republic later in 1961; it was active in promoting democratic elections following Trujillo's assassination May 30. After a coup d'état overthrew the new democratic leader, President Joaquin Balaguer, in November, the OAS showed minimal interest with only a brief council debate on the matter.

Referrals to the OAS in this border dispute were on the whole ineffective. The OAS body, the IAPC, was asked to help resolve a potential threat to Cuban internal affairs posed by exiles. OAS investigations and sanctions did help Venezuela to cope better with the presence of constant Dominican Republic aggression. The OAS cancelled its sanctions on January 4, 1962, once it was perceived that the Dominican Republic no longer posed a threat to regional security.

References

Allsebrook, M. 1986. *Prototypes of Peacemaking: The First Forty Years of the United Nations.* Harlow (Essex) England: Longman Group UK Limited.

Bercovitch, J., and R. Jackson. 1997. *International Conflict: A Chronological Encyclopedia of Conflicts and Their Management 1945–1995.* Washington, D.C.: Congressional Quarterly.

Brecher, M., J. Wilkenfeld, and S. Moser. 1988. *Crises in the Twentieth Century.* New York: Pergamon.

Butterworth, R.L. 1976. *Managing Interstate Conflict, 1945–1974.* Pittsburgh: Center for International Studies, University of Pittsburgh.

Fretter, J.M. 2001. *Effective Mediation in International Disputes: A Comparative Analysis of Mediation by the United Nations and Regional Organizations 1945–1995.* Doctoral dissertation, Vol. II: Appendices. University of Canterbury, Christchurch, New Zealand.

"Political Leaders": http://web.jet.es/ziaorarr/domin-re.htm (accessed April 9, 1999).

Tillema, H.K. 1991. *International Armed Conflict Since 1945: A Bibliographic Handbook of Wars and Military Interventions.* Boulder: Westview.

Zacher, M.W. 1979. *International Conflicts and Collective Security, 1946–1977.* New York: Praeger.

2.8 Cuba: Communist Revolution and Cuban Civil War December 1956–January 1959

In 1954 Fulgencio Batista y Zaldívar sought a democratic mandate for his control of Cuba, which he had seized in a March 1952 coup. Batista won the election, but opposition groups contested the result. In May 1955 political prisoners were released from prison; among them was Fidel Castro, who promptly left Cuba for Mexico City to organize a revolutionary force to oust Batista. Opposition groups began a terrorist campaign against the government in late 1955.

In the autumn of 1956 the Dominican Republic began to support Castro's force, training and equipping it in preparation for an invasion of Cuba. The revolutionary force launched their invasion in November 1956, but the Cuban army quickly defeated it in early December. Severely weakened, the revolutionary force had to hide out in the jungle and limit its activities to small-scale terrorist attacks against government outposts. Throughout 1957 and 1958 popular support for the Batista regime evaporated, guerrilla activities intensified, and the United States moved to restore confidence in the regime.

Batista called elections in November 1958, but army support for his regime diminished and he was forced into exile in the Dominican Republic on January 1, 1959, causing a power vacuum. The civil war continued, and within a week Castro's forces prevailed. Castro entered Havana on January 8, 1959, to assume power.

At least 5,000 people were killed during the war, and neither side sought to resolve the conflict peacefully. Upon his accession to power, Castro set about to establish a Communist state and export revolution. In this latter respect particularly, Cuba became the locus of international conflict for a number of years. Cuba mounted invasion attempts and insurgency operations against Panama in April 1959, Dominican Republic in June 1959, Haiti in August 1959, Bolivia in November 1966, and Venezuela in April 1967 (*see* conflicts 2.10; 2.13; 2.19; 2.23).

References

Baloyra, E.A., and J.A. Morris, eds. 1993. *Conflict and Change in Cuba.* Albuquerque: University of New Mexico Press.

Benjamin, J.R. 1970. *The United States and the Origins of the Cuban Revolution: An Empire of Liberty in an Age of National Liberation.* Princeton, N.J.: Princeton University Press.

Blasier, C., and C. Mesa-Lago, eds. 1979. *Cuba in the World.* Pittsburgh: University of Pittsburgh Press.

Bonachea, R.L., and M. San Martin. 1974. *The Cuban Insurrection, 1952–1959.* New Brunswick, N.J.: Transaction.

Bonsal, P.W. 1971. *Cuba, Castro, and the United States.* Pittsburgh: University of Pittsburgh Press.

Butterworth, R.L. 1976. *Managing Interstate Conflict, 1945–1974.* Pittsburgh: Center for International Studies, University of Pittsburgh.

Del Aguila, J.M. 1984. *Cuba: Dilemmas of a Revolution.* Boulder: Westview.

Gonzalez, E. 1974. *Cuba Under Castro: The Limits of Charisma.* Boston: Houghton Mifflin.

Halebsky, S., and J.M. Kirk, eds. 1985. *Cuba: 25 Years of Revolution, 1959–1984.* New York: Praeger.

Tillema, H.K. 1991. *International Armed Conflict Since 1945: A Bibliographic Handbook of Wars and Military Interventions.* Boulder: Westview.

2.9 Nicaragua–Honduras: Boundary Dispute and Mocoran Seizure April–June 1957

Honduras and Nicaragua had disputed a section of the border between the two countries since the nineteenth century. Honduras was awarded the area in a 1906 arbitration decision rendered by the King of Spain. Nicaragua rejected this decision, however, and kept a small military force stationed in the disputed region. Honduras reasserted its claim in 1947.

On April 18, 1957, Nicaraguan forces moved to take control of the disputed border region, including the town of Mocoran. The Honduran army counterattacked with air and ground forces, and sustained fighting went on until May. The Organization of American States (OAS) brokered a cease-fire by mediation, and a month later Honduras and Nicaragua agreed to submit their dispute to the International Court of Justice (ICJ). In November 1960 the ICJ ruled in favor of Honduras, and in 1961 the boundary was redrawn and residents relocated. An estimated 1,000 people were killed during this conflict, and a much graver conflict broke out again in 1980 following the Sandinista revolution in Nicaragua (*see* conflict 2.31).

References

Butterworth, R.L. 1976. *Managing Interstate Conflict, 1945–1974.* Pittsburgh: Center for International Studies, University of Pittsburgh.

Crawley, E. 1984. *Nicaragua in Perspective.* Revised edition. New York: St. Martin's.

Day, A., ed. 1987. *Border and Territorial Disputes.* 2d edition. Burnt Mill, Harlow (Essex), England: Longman.

Morris, J.A. 1984. *Honduras: Caudillo Politics and Military Rulers.* Boulder: Westview.

2.10 Panama: Cuban-Backed Invasion and Panama Revolutionaries Conflict 1958–May 1959

The immediate cause of this conflict was a political feud between Panamanian president Ernesto de la Guardia and the wealthy Arias family in 1950. After Arias-owned newspapers criticized the president, Finance Minister Gilberto Arias and diplomat Roberto Arias were dismissed from their posts. On his return to Panama from his diplomatic post in London, Roberto Arias began plotting to overthrow the Guardia regime. Cuba was supporting destabilization efforts in the entire region at the time, so the Ariases recruited an invasion force in Cuba, and in late April 1959 the force landed in Panama.

Panama immediately appealed to the Organization of American States (OAS) for support, and Ecuador, Guatemala, and Peru sent planes, gunships, and troops. An OAS committee persuaded the rebels to surrender, and Roberto Arias fled into exile in Brazil. Cuba was exonerated, even though the invaders had been recruited there. Approximately twenty fatalities were reported during the fighting.

References

Butterworth, R.L. 1976. *Managing Interstate Conflict, 1945–1974.* Pittsburgh: Center for International Studies, University of Pittsburgh.

Dubois, J. 1964. *Danger in Panama.* Indianapolis: Bobbs-Merrill.

Farnsworth, D.N., and J.W. McKenney. 1983. *U.S.-Panama Relations, 1903–1978: A Study in Linkage Politics.* Boulder: Westview.

Kitchel, D. 1978. *The Truth About the Panama Canal.* New Rochelle, N.Y.: Arlington House.

Liss, S. 1967. *The Canal: Aspects of United States-Panamanian Relations.* South Bend, Ind.: University of Notre Dame Press.

Tillema, H.K. 1991. *International Armed Conflict Since 1945: A Bibliographic Handbook of Wars and Military Interventions.* Boulder: Westview.

2.11 Guatemala–Mexico: Mexican Shrimp Boat Incident December 1958–September 1959

The president of Guatemala spoke about his observations of a Mexican economic threat on December 29, 1958. At the same time, he warned Mexican fishermen of the dangers of encroaching into Guatemalan territorial waters. On December 31, 1958, Guatemalan air force planes attacked three Mexican shrimp boats fishing near the Pacific coast of Guatemala near Champanico. Three Mexicans died in the attack, and a number of others were wounded. The dispute escalated over the course of nine months, as growing Mexican nationalism and Guatemalan accusations of Mexican-incited subversive activities in Guatemala became more frequent. Guatemala also made frequent accusations of Mexican violations of the 12-mile Guatemalan territorial limit and issued several warnings to Mexican authorities. Guatemala had ordered Mexican crews to disembark and acknowledged that incidents of violence occurred when Mexican shrimp boats refused to comply. Guatemala claimed that its purpose in searching and detaining the shrimp boats and their crews was to control smuggling of arms and drugs.

For its part, Mexico claimed that the fishing boats had been in its territorial waters and on January 3, 1959, asked Guatemala for a formal apology and reparations for the parties involved in the incident. Under public pressure, Mexico broke diplomatic relations with Guatemala on January 23. Mexico had already made efforts to have the matter dealt with by the International Court of Justice (ICJ) and the Organization of American States (OAS), but in both cases, Guatemala had refused to participate. Guatemala claimed that Mexico had established a strong military presence along Guatemala's borders. Guatemala instigated conciliatory measures to prevent a rapid escalation of the crisis and withdrew its border guards fifteen kilometers from its borders. Its diplomats remained in Mexico for eight days, and on January 24 the Guatemalan government brought the matter of Mexican military build-up to the UN Security Council, but no action was taken.

On January 26 it was reported that Mexico had taken action against some of its Guatemalan residents and frozen their assets. On January 29 a bridge was destroyed in anti-Mexican demonstrations in a Guatemalan border town, and Guatemalan aircraft made threatening aerial maneuvers over Mexican territory. It was reported that Mexicans had looted a Guatemalan village at gun-point and, on January 30 Guatemala announced that it was considering severing diplomatic relations with Mexico. Further demonstrations occurred, but the dispute was resolved peacefully on September 15, 1959, after Mexico resumed diplomatic ties with Guatemala.

References

Brecher, M., J. Wilkenfeld, and S. Moser. 1988. *Crises in the Twentieth Century.* New York: Pergamon.

Butterworth, R.L. 1976. *Managing Interstate Conflict, 1945–1974.* Pittsburgh: Center for International Studies, University of Pittsburgh.

Fretter, J.M. 2001. *Effective Mediation in International Disputes: A Comparative Analysis of Mediation by the United Nations and Regional Organizations 1945–1995.* Doctoral dissertation, Vol. II: Appendices. University of Canterbury, Christchurch, New Zealand.

2.12 Paraguay–Argentina: Paraguayan Exiles Conflict
Early 1959–December 1961

In 1954 the chief of the Paraguayan army, General Alfredo Stroessner, assumed the presidency. His repressive regime drove many Paraguayans into exile, with substantial numbers fleeing to Buenos Aires, Argentina. From 1954 to the early 1960s, cordial relations between Paraguay and Argentina fluctuated, as did Argentinean support for the Paraguayan exiles. Stroessner reacted to demonstrations against him in May 1959 by placing Paraguay in a stage of siege. Fearful of returning exiles who would support his removal from office, he closed the Paraguay-Argentine border.

In December 1959 there were reports that an attempted invasion by Paraguayan exiles had been repulsed by Paraguayan border patrols. Paraguay accused Argentina of aiding and abetting the exiles. Cross-border clashes were common occurrences with Paraguayan troops trying to repel the Argentine-based exiles. One Argentinean was reported dead from crossfire. This type of border activity continued throughout 1960, with Paraguay claiming that it had repulsed several rebel invasion attempts in April and December 1960. Stroessner accused Argentina, Cuba, and Venezuela of collusion with the rebels, and, each time a rebel attempt was made, he used it to justify tighter controls in Paraguay. Although political unrest continued in Paraguay, there were no reported raids or guerrilla attacks in 1961: cross-border rebel activity appeared to have ceased.

In November 1962 a small unit of Argentine troops occupied Remansito Paraguayo on the Pilcomayo River with Paraguay. The group withdrew after a few days. The implications of this situation de-escalated when the Paraguayan government explained the incident away, recognizing it only as a logistical error made by the Argentinean commander. No injuries were reported in the incident, and the problem of Paraguayan exiles abated.

References

Brecher, M., J. Wilkenfeld, and S. Moser. 1988. *Crises in the Twentieth Century.* New York: Pergamon.

Butterworth, R.L. 1976. *Managing Interstate Conflict, 1945–1974.* Pittsburgh: Center for International Studies, University of Pittsburgh.

2.13 Cuba–Haiti: Cuban-Sponsored Military Invasion and Haitian Exiles Conflict
August 1959

In February 1959 a revolutionary force of Haitian exiles was formed in Cuba. Its aim was to invade Haiti and depose Haiti's hated dictator, François "Papa Doc" Duvalier. Cuba's official policy at the time was to refrain from supporting revolutionary groups based in Cuba. In April the Cuban coast guard blocked the exiles' attempt to invade Haiti from Cuba.

The continued presence of Haitian exiles in Cuba strained relations between the two countries. Haiti appealed for international aid to prevent invasion. The United States sent large amounts of military and economic aid to the Haitian military, while the Dominican Republic mobilized its coastal forces as a joint defense exercise with Haiti.

On August 15, 1959, a small invasion was once again launched from Cuba. A group of thirty armed exiles invaded and were promptly repelled. Haitian reports of the rebels recruiting approximately 200 Haitians to join their forces were unsubstantiated, and only five of the original thirty ring-leaders were captured alive. Haiti lodged a formal complaint against Cuba at the Organization of American States (OAS) Conference of Foreign Ministers meeting in Santiago, Chile. "Evidence gathered by a subsequent OAS probe together with other sources suggests that the rebels were an autonomous group; although they were based in Cuba, they received neither aid nor support from Fidel Castro's government" (Butterworth, 1976, 259).

On August 31 Haiti requested an investigation by the Inter-American Peace Committee (IAPC). Haiti made no direct accusations of Cuban responsibility for the invasion, but the Haitian appeal to the OAS implied that Haiti suspected Cuban complicity in the whole affair. Cuba was refused entry to the IAPC. A seven-man investigating subcommittee of the IAPC visited Haiti and confirmed the circumstances of the invasion but took no further action.

On September 5 the Haitian government announced that the invasion force had completely surrendered. No further invasion attempts were launched from Cuba into Haiti. Twenty-six people were killed during the conflict, and no efforts were made to settle the conflict peacefully.

References

Baloyra, E.A., and J.A. Morris, eds. 1993. *Conflict and Change in Cuba.* Albuquerque: University of New Mexico Press.

Blasier, C., and C. Mesa-Lago, eds. 1979. *Cuba in the World.* Pittsburgh: University of Pittsburgh Press.

Butterworth, R.L. 1976. *Managing Interstate Conflict, 1945–1974.* Pittsburgh: Center for International Studies, University of Pittsburgh.

Goldenberg, B. 1965. *The Cuban Revolution and Latin America.* London: Allen and Unwin.

Halebsky, S., and J.M. Kirk, eds. 1985. *Cuba: 25 Years of Revolution, 1959–1984.* New York: Praeger.

Heinl, R.D., and N.G. Heinl. 1978. *Written in Blood: The Story of the Haitian People, 1492–1971.* Boston: Houghton Mifflin.

Tillema, H.K. 1991. *International Armed Conflict Since 1945: A Bibliographic Handbook of Wars and Military Interventions.* Boulder: Westview.

2.14 United States–Cuba: Anti-Castro Military Invasion—The Bay of Pigs April–May 1961

After the Cuban civil war ousted the U.S.-backed Batista regime in 1959, the United States began to investigate the possibilities for overthrowing Fidel Castro's new Communist state. It was the height of the cold war, and the United States was worried about Cuba's role in fomenting Communist insurgencies in the region.

With U.S. Central Intelligence Agency (CIA) encouragement, the new administration of President John F. Kennedy adopted a plan to equip and train anti-Castro Cuban exiles as an invasion force. Having recently installed a friendly regime in Guatemala, the CIA used that country to train Cuban exiles it had recruited in the United States.

On April 17, 1961, 1,500 exiles launched the invasion by landing at Cuba's Bay of Pigs. Covert U.S. air strikes failed to knock out Cuban air superiority, and the invasion force was quickly pinned down on the beaches. The exiles were forced to surrender on April 20. Those who escaped were to establish guerrilla bases in the Cuban highlands, but all remaining invaders were hunted down and caught by early May.

The Bay of Pigs operation was a humiliating embarrassment for the new U.S. administration and to its foreign policy. In the ensuing months, tensions between Cuba and the United States remained extremely high. There were hijackings of planes and boats by both sides, and numerous other such incidents. In all, approximately 300 people were killed in the failed invasion. This conflict was the precursor to a far more serious confrontation in 1962, when the Soviet Union attempted to station nuclear missiles in Cuba (*see* conflict 2.17).

References

Blasier, C., and C. Mesa-Lago, eds. 1979. *Cuba in the World.* Pittsburgh: University of Pittsburgh Press.

Bonsal, P.W. 1971. *Cuba, Castro, and the United States.* Pittsburgh: University of Pittsburgh Press.

Butterworth, R.L. 1976. *Managing Interstate Conflict, 1945–1974.* Pittsburgh: Center for International Studies, University of Pittsburgh.

Goldenberg, B. 1965. *The Cuban Revolution and Latin America.* London: Allen and Unwin.

Halebsky, S., and J.M. Kirk, eds. 1985. *Cuba: 25 Years of Revolution, 1959–1984.* New York: Praeger.

Higgins, T. 1987. *The Perfect Failure: Kennedy, Eisenhower, and the CIA at the Bay of Pigs.* New York: Norton.

Tillema, H.K. 1991. *International Armed Conflict Since 1945: A Bibliographic Handbook of Wars and Military Interventions.* Boulder: Westview.

2.15 Venezuela–Guyana (UK): Essequibo River Dispute February 1962–June 1970

In 1831 Great Britain merged three Dutch colonies that had existed on the territory that is now Guyana to form a single colony known as British Guiana. In 1899 an arbitration tribunal awarded Britain approximately 94 percent of disputed territory bordering Venezuela. This decision incorporated into British Guiana the region west of the Essequibo River, a region rich in mineral deposits, particularly gold. Both sides initially agreed that the findings of the arbitration tribunal would be accepted as a "full, perfect, and final settlement," and, after a lengthy U.S.-led arbitration, the boundary was demarcated in 1905. In 1962, however, Venezuela restated claims over the territory when documents emerged alleging that the arbiters of the 1899 decision had been subjected to coercion. Venezuela brought the matter before the UN General Assembly in February 1962. It was alleged that Venezuela raised the claims at the United Nations at this time only to preempt territorial settlements before Britain granted Guyana its independence. Venezuela initially acknowledged support for the existing boundaries. Following the Venezuelan appeal to the UN, the parties agreed to discuss the documentation relating to the boundary. They met in London November 5–7, 1963, but were unable to reach an agreement.

The Essequibo territory dispute abated until May 1965, when Venezuela declared that oil concessions for the Essequibo region, granted by British Guiana were invalid. After Guyana's independence was declared in 1966, Venezuela began to make claims on territory amounting to approximately 62 percent of Guyana's territory. Gold had recently been discovered in the disputed territory. By February 17, 1966, a multiparty commission of British, Venezuelan, and Guyanese representatives came together to investigate claims and seek a peaceful solution to the border dispute. The parties signed an accord, and Venezuela seemed content to allow the multiparty commission to conduct a four-year boundary study without pressing its claims further until the study was completed. Venezuelan patience did not last four years. On October 14, 1966, Venezuela took the island of Ankokoin in the Guyuni River and occupied territory originally awarded to British Guiana.

President Raúl Leoni of Venezuela annexed the territorial waters off the coast of Guyana Essequibo on July 9, 1968. These waters extended from three to twelve miles off the coastline. Venezuelan naval vessels were reported patrolling the area just outside the three-mile zone. Guyana lodged a complaint with UN Secretary-General U Thant. Other UN members also protested Venezuela's actions but did not intervene. The United States appealed to the Venezuelan government to retract the annexation policy. Guyana's government announced that the annexation was based on claims that were null and illegal and that it would resist Venezuelan invasion attempts. Venezuela then withdrew its representatives from the multiparty boundary commission. By August 1968 this phase in the dispute had dissipated. Secretary-General U Thant had offered his good offices to help the parties come to a peaceful resolution, but the parties did not accept his offer, and the UN took no action.

In January 1969 the Essequibo dispute resurfaced during a small rebellion in the Rapununi district, situated in the Essequibo region. As the Guyanese government took measures to capture the secessionist rebels, the rebels sought refuge in Venezuela. Venezuela denied any involvement in the rebellion, but Guyana accused Venezuela of supplying the rebels with arms and training. The rebellion was quashed by January 12. Spasmodic clashes continued to occur in February 1970 and led to direct mortar attacks between Guyanese and Venezuelan border troops on March 22. Further similar incidents were narrowly avoided. The multiparty boundary commission ended its mandate in 1970. Venezuela and Guyana negotiated between themselves to defer settlement of the Essequibo border for twelve years, as was agreed in the Protocol of Trinidad, signed in Port-au-Prince on June 18, 1970.

The Protocol of Trinidad expired in June 1982, and Venezuela made it clear the agreement would not be renewed. Both parties and the United Kingdom were obligated, under the Geneva Agreement of February 17, 1966, to negotiate a peaceful settlement to the dispute. Unable to reach an agreement themselves, the parties approached Secretary-General Javier Pérez de Cuéllar for advice. He said he would fulfill his responsibilities under the Geneva Agreement and dispatched Under-Secretary-General Diego Cordovez to assess the situation. Cordovez visited Venezuela and Guyana from August 21 to August 26, 1983, to assess the border situation. The conflict has not recurred.

References

Allsebrook, M. 1986. *Prototypes of Peacemaking: The First Forty Years of the United Nations.* Harlow (Essex) England: Longman Group UK Limited.

Brecher, M., J. Wilkenfeld, and S. Moser. 1988. *Crises in the Twentieth Century.* New York: Pergamon.

Butterworth, R.L. 1976. *Managing Interstate Conflict, 1945–1974.* Pittsburgh: Center for International Studies, University of Pittsburgh.

Davies, J. 2002. "Venezuela-Guyana Border Dispute: Inter- and Intra-State Conflict in Latin America and Resolution Strategies." Summary updated June 6. Preliminary draft concept paper by John Davies of CIDCM http://www.inform.umd.edu/LAS/InfoStudent/Courses/GVPT309P/GuyanaVenezuela.htm (accessed May 20, 2004). College Park: Latin American Studies Center, University of Maryland.

Fretter, J.M. 2001. *Effective Mediation in International Disputes: A Comparative Analysis of Mediation by the United Nations and Regional Organizations 1945–1995.* Doctoral dissertation, Vol. II: Appendices. University of Canterbury, Christchurch, New Zealand.

Huth, P.K. 1996. *Standing Your Ground: Territorial Disputes and International Conflict.* Ann Arbor: Michigan University Press.

Tillema, H.K. 1991. *International Armed Conflict Since 1945: A Bibliographic Handbook of Wars and Military Interventions.* Boulder: Westview.

Zarate's Political Collections (ZPC). "World Political Leaders 1945–2004": http://www.terra.es/personal2/monolith/home.htm (accessed April 9, 1999).

2.16 Chile–Bolivia: Lauca River Dam Dispute March 1962–1964

In 1962 Chile made it known that it had drawn up plans for the construction of a dam on the Lauca River. Diverting the Lauca River would increase water flow to Chile, but it was also predicted that it would reduce Bolivia's irrigation reserves considerably. Bolivia threatened that the diversion of the river would be regarded as an act of aggression. Bolivia severed diplomatic ties with Chile and called for the Organization of American States (OAS) Council to consider the matter in April 1962.

The dispute escalated after three people were killed at the Chilean Embassy in Bolivia during a student demonstration in April 1962. In response the Chilean government authorized the mobilization of 100 armed police to patrol the border region to prevent the entry of Bolivian saboteurs.

Bolivia reiterated its charges against Chile at an OAS Council meeting on April 20, 1962, stating that Chile was acting aggressively and did not have the legal right to disturb the flow of the Lauca River. At the time no international legal precedents existed to determine a ruling on the flow of rivers from a high altitude state to a lower altitude state. Chile presented its own arguments for rights to divert the river. Bolivia presented its case again at an OAS meeting on May 24. Bolivia also suggested that several states in the region (Brazil, Costa Rica, Ecuador, Uruguay, and Venezuela) could act as mediators in resolving the dispute. Chile rejected Bolivia's proposal for mediation, stating that the dispute was more a matter of legal rights than a political disagreement. Chile proposed that the dispute be referred officially to the International Court of Justice (ICJ). This proposal was not initiated. The OAS took no direct action on the matter except to pass a resolution calling for the parties to settle the dispute peacefully, but at its May 24 meeting the OAS also offered its good offices to assist the parties in achieving a settlement.

In 1963 the Lauca Dam was near completion. Bolivia was so frustrated by the lack of action from the OAS that it temporarily withdrew from the organization on June 12, 1963. Informal negotiation began between the disputants and the mediators (Brazil, Honduras, Mexico, United States, and Venezuela) on August 1, 1963. The talks deadlocked soon after they had started because in 1964 Bolivia extended its territorial claims to include access to Chilean ports on the Pacific Ocean. Bolivia withdrew from the OAS a second time on September 3, 1964, alleging that Chile had plans to also divert water from the Caquena River. Bolivia resumed participation in the OAS a few weeks after it had withdrawn, based on assurances that the OAS would act to resolve the matter. This dispute dissipated after 1964, and by 1970 relations between Bolivia and Chile had improved after the implementation of a joint economic plan, the Andean Development Corporation (1968).

References

Butterworth, R.L. 1976. *Managing Interstate Conflict, 1945–1974.* Pittsburgh: Center for International Studies, University of Pittsburgh.

Fretter, J.M. 2001. *Effective Mediation in International Disputes: A Comparative Analysis of Mediation by the United Nations and Regional Organizations 1945–1995.* Doctoral dissertation, Vol. II: Appendices. University of Canterbury, Christchurch, New Zealand.

Huth, P.K. 1996. *Standing Your Ground: Territorial Disputes and International Conflict.* Ann Arbor: Michigan University Press.

Tillema, H.K. 1991. *International Armed Conflict Since 1945: A Bibliographic Handbook of Wars and Military Interventions.* Boulder: Westview.

2.17 United States–USSR: Cold War Dispute and the Cuban Missile Crisis September–November 1962

As a result of its poor relationship with the United States following the failed Bay of Pigs invasion attempt in 1961 (*see* conflict 2.14), Cuba allied itself closely with the Soviet Union, which supplied it substantial military support. In mid-1962 the Soviet Union began to station nuclear-capable missiles on Cuba. The United States became aware of this through spy satellite photos in mid-October 1962. On October 22, President John F. Kennedy demanded their removal and declared that a naval blockade of Cuba would begin on October 24. The United States said that any attacks by Cuba would result in retaliation against the Soviet Union. The Soviet Union refused to acknowledge the stationing of the missiles on Cuba but on October 26 offered to reach an understanding with the United States on the issue.

Meanwhile, Soviet ships carrying nuclear weapons continued to steam toward Cuba, heightening the possibility of nuclear confrontation. UN efforts to resolve the crisis were unsuccessful. Tensions were extremely high, especially when a U.S. spy plane was shot down over Cuba on October 27. Some believed that the United States might invade Cuba to prevent the stationing of missiles there, thus provoking direct confrontation between the superpowers. Despite the downing of the spy plane, a U.S.-Soviet agreement was reached that day, with the Soviet Union saying it would remove the missiles in exchange for U.S. assurances that it would not invade Cuba. This was the superpowers' first game of nuclear brinkmanship, and, although there were no fatalities, the world had come to the very threshold of catastrophe. Relations between the superpowers remained extremely strained, as did those between Cuba and the United States.

References

Allison, G.T. 1971. *Essence of Decision: Explaining the Cuban Missile Crisis.* Boston: Little, Brown.

Baloyra, E.A., and J.A. Morris, eds. 1993. *Conflict and Change in Cuba.* Albuquerque: University of New Mexico Press.

Blasier, C., and C. Mesa-Lago, eds. 1979. *Cuba in the World.* Pittsburgh: University of Pittsburgh Press.

Bonsal, P.W. 1971. *Cuba, Castro, and the United States.* Pittsburgh: University of Pittsburgh Press.

Butterworth, R.L. 1976. *Managing Interstate Conflict, 1945–1974.* Pittsburgh: Center for International Studies, University of Pittsburgh.

Gonzalez, E. 1974. *Cuba Under Castro: The Limits of Charisma*. Boston: Houghton Mifflin.

Griffiths, J., and P. Griffiths, eds. 1979. *Cuba: The Second Decade*. London: Writers and Readers Publishing Cooperative.

Tillema, H.K. 1991. *International Armed Conflict Since 1945: A Bibliographic Handbook of Wars and Military Interventions*. Boulder: Westview.

2.18 Haiti–Dominican Republic: Exiles Asylum and Invasion Attempt April–September 1963

The election of a democratic government, under Juan Bosch Gaviño, in the Dominican Republic in 1962 exacerbated the already strained relations between the Dominican Republic and the Haitian dictator, François "Papa Doc" Duvalier, who ruled from October 22, 1957, to April 21, 1971 (*see* conflict 2.1). Growing antagonism between the two countries led to both supporting the others' exiles and their revolutionary aims. Bosch feared that the relatives of the Dominican Republic's former dictator, Rafael Leónidas Trujillo Molina, would organize a coup against him. Reacting to these fears, he escalated what was a minor incident to a serious attempt to overthrow Duvalier.

On April 26, 1963, Haitian police officers forcibly entered the Dominican Republic Embassy in Port-au-Prince and conducted a search of the premises. The embassy was allegedly harboring a large number of opponents to the Haitian regime, who had entered the premises seeking asylum. The Dominican Republic threatened to retaliate and appealed to the Organization of American States (OAS) for assistance. The United States supported the Dominican Republic's referral to the OAS. The OAS voted unanimously to form an OAS investigation committee to assess the complaint. Haiti severed diplomatic relations with the Dominican Republic on April 28. The next day the Dominican Republic mobilized troops along the Haitian border, but the OAS investigation committee did not consider this act to be a threat because it had received assurances from Haiti that it would cease harassing embassies and would take measures to cope with refugees leaving the country. The OAS investigation committee began its mission on April 30; the committee was able to alleviate the crisis a little during its visits to both countries, but it did not look to resolve any underlying causes for the continued tension. It managed to arrange the evacuation of the Dominican Republic's diplomats in Haiti and the transfer to other embassies of those seeking asylum. The committee left Haiti satisfied by these assurances, but as soon as the committee members left the country, Haiti resumed its earlier policies. As a result, the Dominican Republic continued to build up its military presence along the Haitian border. On May 5, 1963, Haiti announced that any invasion would result in heavy fatalities, especially among foreigners in Haiti. The United States took a serious view of this threat and dispatched a naval task force to the region. On May 8 the OAS authorized its investigation committee to return to the region to resume its investigation and to offer its good offices to the parties.

Dispute management was left in the hands of the OAS peace mission. Haiti lodged a formal complaint with the UN Security Council on May 8, 1963, alleging that the Dominican Republic had threatened to invade Haiti. Haiti felt that many of the OAS member states despised the Haitian regime and so perceived that a more balanced decision would come from the UN. In response, the Dominican Republic claimed that, by attacking its embassy, Haiti was provoking the Dominican Republic to retaliate. The UN Security Council met to discuss the issue May 8 and May 9. The OAS committee was already investigating the matter, and the parties and the Security Council agreed that no further UN action would be taken until the OAS had concluded its investigation.

The five-nation OAS committee resumed its investigation in the Dominican Republic and Haiti on May 13 and continued until May 23. On May 13 the Dominican Republic withdrew its troops, and Haiti allowed most of the Haitian refugees who sought asylum a safe passage. The OAS issued its final report on June 3. The report allotted blame for the incident with both of the parties and recommended no further OAS action. With the OAS not acting against Duvalier, the United States gradually reestablished "normal" diplomatic relations with Haiti and withdrew its military forces from the area.

Tensions between the Dominican Republic and Haiti flared up again on August 5, 1963, when a group of Haitian exiles entered the Dominican Republic and occupied a small area. Haiti accused the Dominican Republic of complicity in the invasion and requested that the OAS consider the matter and secure the removal of the exile force. The OAS investigation committee attempted to get the parties to accept a conciliation plan in Washington in August. This mediation attempt was unsuccessful, and, after a second invasion force was reported entering Haiti on August 12, 1963, the OAS ordered that the investigation committee return to Haiti to further assess the situation. Haiti asked the OAS to arrange an OAS border patrol. In addition, Haiti called for the organization's condemnation of the Dominican Republic's action and requested that limits be placed on the number of Haitian exiles absorbed into the Dominican Republic.

The investigation committee arrived in Haiti on August 23, 1963. The committee spent a number of days looking into the matter, but could find no proof of the Dominican Republic's complicity in the exile invasion. "Its judgement on this matter was almost certainly wrong" (Zacher, 1979, 248). Despite this ruling, the presence of the OAS investigation committee helped to deter further interventions and to bring the parties to some agreement on the exile problems both countries were experiencing (September 1963). OAS mediation failed after Haiti withdrew from the talks and took the matter to the UN. The dispute seemed to end when a new military junta, under Emilio de los Santos, seized power in the Dominican Republic on September 25.

References

Allsebrook, M. 1986. *Prototypes of Peacemaking: The First Forty Years of the United Nations.* Harlow (Essex) England: Longman Group UK Limited.

Brecher, M., J. Wilkenfeld, and S. Moser. 1988. *Crises in the Twentieth Century.* New York: Pergamon.

Butterworth, R.L. 1976. *Managing Interstate Conflict, 1945–1974.* Pittsburgh: Center for International Studies, University of Pittsburgh.

Fretter, J.M. 2001. *Effective Mediation in International Disputes: A Comparative Analysis of Mediation by the United Nations and Regional Organizations 1945–1995.* Doctoral dissertation, Vol. II: Appendices. University of Canterbury, Christchurch, New Zealand.

Zacher, M.W. 1979. *International Conflicts and Collective Security, 1946–1977.* New York: Praeger.

Zarate's Political Collections (ZPC). "World Political Leaders 1945–2004": http://www.terra.es/personal2/monolith/home.htm (accessed April 9, 1999).

2.19 Cuba–Venezuela: Terrorism and Invasion Attempt November 1963–May 1967

Following the Cuban revolution and the establishment of Fidel Castro's Communist regime, Cuba attempted to export the Communist revolution to other Latin American states. Cuba's ambitions often led to regional conflict: Cuba had already interfered in the Dominican Republic in 1959, in Haiti in 1959, and in Bolivia from 1966 to 1970 (*see* conflicts 2.7; 2.13; 2.23).

Venezuela was on the brink of civil war in 1963 with increasing Communist guerrilla activity in Caracas. Venezuelan president, Rómulo Ernesto Betancourt Bello, who was in office from February 13, 1959, to March 11, 1964, and again in 1981, ordered a crackdown on Communist and left-wing parties operating in Caracas. Many Communists were arrested following an assassination attempt on Betancourt in November 1963. In his foreign policy, Betancourt made no secret of his desire to isolate Cuba. He had requested that the Organization of American States (OAS) impose sanctions against the Castro regime. In November 1962 Betancourt complained to the OAS about suspected Cuban subversive activities, but he did not request any action. The Armed Forces for National Liberation (FALN), the National Liberation Front (FLN), and the Venezuelan Communist Party wanted to oust Betancourt and install a strong dictatorship. The Communist guerrillas intensified their efforts to prevent Betancourt's reelection in the December 1963 elections.

On November 1, 1963, the Venezuelan government laid a serious complaint about a large shipment of arms that had been landed on the secluded Paraguana Peninsula. On November 29 an OAS investigation committee confirmed the complicity of the Cuban government in the arms shipment, and Venezuela complained officially to the OAS in December. The planned presidential elections went ahead unimpeded on December 1, and Venezuelans elected a new president. On December 3 the OAS Council decided to allow an investigation committee to look further into the allegations. It was discovered that the arms supplies had been landed with Cuban assistance, and a guerrilla plot to capture Caracas and halt the elections was also revealed.

With its charges against Cuba verified, Venezuela requested that the OAS impose more severe sanctions on Cuba. The OAS did not initiate more substantial sanctions after other Latin American states voiced some opposition to the proposal. Harsher sanctions were imposed only after a military coup d'état in Brazil in April 1964 aligned Brazil with the anti-Cuban OAS member states and further OAS action was then considered feasible. But by the time the OAS acted on sanctions in July 1964, Cuba was no longer a member of the organization. On July 26 the OAS severed all remaining diplomatic ties with Cuba. The effect of the trade and diplomatic sanctions was weak.

The FALN and the FLN reorganized and regrouped in 1965. The guerrilla movements became distinctly revolutionary and intensified their activities in 1966 after the Venezuelan government began counteroffensive strategies. The FALN and the FLN initiated "Operation Bolivar" on July 24, 1966, landing a group of trained guerrillas led by Luben Petkoff onto Margarita Island, off the north coast of Venezuela. The guerrilla commandos attacked the mainland and joined forces with the remaining guerrilla forces of the Venezuelan Communist Party, led by Douglas Bravo. The Venezuelan Communist Party had previously split, with one group pursuing legal lines of political opposition and the other group developing as a guerrilla force that pursued its goals through terrorist activities. When the guerrilla forces renewed their attacks, the politically active Venezuelan Communist Party started a propaganda attack against the FLN and FALN guerrillas. Tension and antagonism persisted and resulted in a Cuban invasion attempt in the early months of 1967.

The Communist effort to overthrow the Venezuelan regime immediately led to an escalation of tensions between Venezuela and Cuba over Cuba's support for the Venezuelan rebels. The propaganda attack by the Venezuelan Communist Party prompted condemnation from Fidel Castro and led to direct Cuban intervention on Venezuelan territory. On May 8, 1967, four Cuban guerrillas and several Cuban-trained Venezuelan guerrillas landed in Miranda state in northern Venezuela. The Venezuelan government announced that a guerrilla force originating from Cuba and led by Cuban army officers had landed 90 miles from Caracas. It later reported that the invasion force had been repulsed and some of the guerrillas captured alive. Although there were only two reported fatalities from the invasion attempt, tensions remained high for some time. Neither side attempted to settle the conflict peacefully, and it eventually lapsed altogether.

Venezuela lodged a complaint with the OAS in June 1967, and the OAS authorized a fact-finding committee to visit Venezuela to assess the situation. The OAS investigative committee reported in August 1967 that the Venezuelan claims of Cuban subversion were substantiated and that Cuba had participated in training and arming the guerrillas. The OAS condemned Cuba's actions and called on member states to refrain from supplying any fuel or port facilities to vessels transporting goods to and from Cuba, reiterating its previous sanctions on Cuba. Guerrilla activity continued, but ineffectively, and to a much lesser degree than the events of 1967.

References

Bercovitch, J., and R. Jackson. 1997. *International Conflict: A Chronological Encyclopedia of Conflicts and Their Management 1945–1995.* Washington, D.C.: Congressional Quarterly.

Brecher, M., J. Wilkenfeld, and S. Moser. 1988. *Crises in the Twentieth Century.* New York: Pergamon.

Butterworth, R.L. 1976. *Managing Interstate Conflict, 1945–1974.* Pittsburgh: Center for International Studies, University of Pittsburgh.

Fretter, J.M. 2001. *Effective Mediation in International Disputes: A Comparative Analysis of Mediation by the United Nations and Regional Organizations 1945–1995.* Doctoral dissertation, Vol. II: Appendices. University of Canterbury, Christchurch, New Zealand.

Zacher, M.W. 1979. *International Conflicts and Collective Security, 1946–1977: The United Nations, Organization of American States, Organization of African Unity, and Arab League.* New York: Praeger.

Zarate's Political Collections (ZPC). "World Political Leaders 1945–2004": http://www.terra.es/personal2/monolith/home.htm (accessed April 9, 1999).

2.20 Panama–United States: Sovereignty Dispute and the Flag Riots January–April 1964

The Panama Canal was vital to U.S. shipping interests. After a sovereignty dispute in 1959, the United States reached a compromise with Panamanian authorities in 1963 that provided for the flying of both the U.S. and Panamanian flags within the Canal Zone. On January 9, 1964, riots broke out in the Canal Zone after hundreds of Panamanians attempted to raise a Panamanian flag over a school at which American students had raised a U.S. flag on January 7.

In an effort to quell the riots, U.S. troops took control of the Canal Zone, but disturbances along the border with Panama continued for several days. A number of serious cross-border sniping incidents occurred, and tensions were high. The situation eased on January 16, when Panamanian civil authorities cleared the border area. The dispute was later settled without further violence. There were twenty-four fatalities during the conflict, four of them U.S. servicemen.

References

Butterworth, R.L. 1976. *Managing Interstate Conflict, 1945–1974.* Pittsburgh: Center for International Studies, University of Pittsburgh.

Dubois, J. 1964. *Danger in Panama.* Indianapolis: Bobbs-Merrill.

Farnsworth, D.N., and J.W. McKenney. 1983. *U.S.-Panama Relations, 1903–1978: A Study in Linkage Politics.* Boulder: Westview.

Kitchel, D. 1978. *The Truth About the Panama Canal.* New Rochelle, N.Y.: Arlington House.

Liss, S. 1967. *The Canal: Aspects of United States–Panamanian Relations.* South Bend, Ind.: University of Notre Dame Press.

Tillema, H.K. 1991. *International Armed Conflict Since 1945: A Bibliographic Handbook of Wars and Military Interventions.* Boulder: Westview.

2.21 Colombia: Banditry and Leftist Guerrilla Insurgency 1965–Ongoing

Colombia had a problem with banditry for many years, but in 1965 some bandits linked up with left-wing political movements in an attempt to overthrow the government. The left-wing guerrillas consisted originally of two groups, the Ejército de Liberación Nacional (ELN) and the Fuerzas Armadas Revolucionarias de Colombia (FARC). They were motivated by a desire for greater social justice and supported by many priests, peasants, students, and workers. Guerrilla-led ambushes, assassinations, kidnapping, bombings, and attacks on villages began to claim hundreds of lives every year from this time. A move by the government to undermine peasant support for the guerrillas through a program of land reform failed to make any headway. In 1976 a new guerrilla group called M19 emerged, and in 1978 the Workers' Self-Defense Movement also joined the guerrilla groups in their war against the government.

In 1980 Colombia accused Cuba of aiding the guerrillas and broke off diplomatic relations. By 1984 it was thought that between 6,000 and 15,000 guerrillas were operating in Colombia, and the government seriously pursued efforts to find a negotiated settlement with them. The ELN also began operating closely with Venezuelan, Peruvian, Ecuadoran, and Salvadoran guerrilla groups in this period.

Despite various truces and agreements with the guerrilla groups, including the surrender and incorporation of the M19 group into the government, the peace process never took hold, and the fighting continued. By the end of 1995 the conflict still had no end in sight, and relations with Venezuela had deteriorated seriously as a result of cross-border raids in pursuit of rebels. There were also allegations of Venezuelan aid to the rebels. Evidence also emerged that FARC was collaborating with the Calí drug cartel, complicating the conflict even further. Peace efforts continued intermittently but futilely. In late 1998 Andrés Pastrana of the Conservative Party won the presidential election with a promise to end the decades-long conflict that had by then claimed an estimated 40,000 lives, many of them civilians. Following a number of fierce rebel attacks in November and December 1998, Pastrana received the full support of political leaders and members of Congress to pursue peace negotiations with the various guerrilla movements, grant presidential pardons to rebels, and offer them guarantees for their return to society. In November 1998 Pastrana pulled some 2,000 government troops out of a 16,000-square-mile (42,000 square kilometers) area of southeast Colombia to make way for the release of troops held prisoner by FARC.

FARC insisted that Pastrana crack down on illegal right-wing death squads, which it accused of fighting a "dirty war" with the help of the armed forces against leftist sympathizers. Right-wing paramilitary groups numbered an estimated 5,000 to 7,000 and have been accused of widespread human rights abuses. The paramilitaries have also been accused of deliberately displacing civilians, often to benefit wealthy patrons. Peace talks began again in January 1999, but stalled in the same month. Guerrillas increased their use of kidnapping that year as a way of raising funds. Paramilitaries and guerrillas alike are reported to rely on growing and selling coca to finance their operations.

President Pastrana persisted in long-term negotiations to reach a political settlement with FARC, but with little success. The violence continues. It is estimated that 10,000 rebels remain active in various areas. At the end of 2000, an estimated 2.1 million Colombians were internally displaced. The number of Colombians seeking refuge abroad was also on the increase in neighboring countries and in North America and Europe. Approximately 8,000 refugees applied for asylum in the United States, Europe, Costa Rica, and Canada in 2000. More than 226,000 remained abroad after their visas expired, and more than 80,000 were living in refugee-like circumstances in neighboring countries, primarily Venezuela and Ecuador.

References

Gurr, T., M. Marshall, and D. Khosla. 2000. *Peace and Conflict 2001: A Global Survey of Conflicts, Self-Determination Movements, and Democracy*. College Park: Center for International Development and Conflict Management, University of Maryland.

Hartlyn, J. 1988. *The Politics of Coalition Rule in Colombia*. Cambridge: Cambridge University Press.

LaFeber, W. 1993. *Inevitable Revolutions: The United States in Central America*. 2d edition. New York: Norton.

Levine, D.H. ed. 1986. *Religion and Political Conflict in Latin America*. Chapel Hill: University of North Carolina Press.

Reuters Alert Net 2001. "Colombia" Country Profile. http://www.alertnet.org/thefacts/countryprofiles/ (accessed March 9, 2002).

2.22 United States–Dominican Republic: Civil War, U.S. Military Intervention, and the Constitutionalist Rebellion April 1965–September 1966

After the brutal Trujillo regime was toppled in 1961, the Dominican Republic was beset by civil unrest and political violence. A rebellion began on April 24, 1965, when a group calling themselves the Constitutionalists ousted the civilian regime led by Donald J. Reid Cabral. The rebels were mostly supporters of Juan Bosch, who had been president until his ouster in a military coup in September 1963.

The pro- and anti-Bosch forces engaged in heavy fighting in Santo Domingo over control of strategic positions. U.S. forces intervened on April 28, 1965, on the side of Colonel Pedro Bartolene Benoit, who wanted to form a new government with the anti-Bosch faction. Fearing a Constitutionalist victory would lead to a pro-Communist government, the United States was eager to support Benoit. U.S. troops quickly seized the Constitutionalist-controlled areas of Santo Domingo, although there was heavy fighting.

On May 23, 1965, the Organization of American States (OAS) deployed a peacekeeping force to the Dominican Republic, and domestic opinion in the United States turned against the intervention. Negotiations led to the formation of an interim government led by Hector Garcia Godoy. There were some isolated acts of political violence. In OAS-supervised elections held in June 1966, Joaquín Balaguer defeated Bosch and served as the country's president until 1978 and again from 1986 to 1996, bringing a new measure of economic security to the nation. U.S. troops pulled out on September 21,

1966. As many as 3,500 people were killed in the fighting, including 30 American soldiers.

References

Butterworth, R.L. 1976. *Managing Interstate Conflict, 1945–1974.* Pittsburgh: Center for International Studies, University of Pittsburgh.

Curry, E.R. 1979. *Hoover's Dominican Diplomacy and the Origins of the Good Neighbor Policy.* New York: Garland.

Gleijeses, P. 1978. *The Dominican Crisis: The 1965 Constitutionalist Revolt and American Intervention.* Translated by L. Lipson. Baltimore: Johns Hopkins University Press.

Gutierrez, C.M. 1972. *The Dominican Republic: Rebellion and Repression.* Translated by R.E. Edwards. New York: Monthly Review Press.

Lowenthal, A.F. 1972. *The Dominican Intervention.* Cambridge: Harvard University Press.

Mansback, R.W. 1971. *Dominican Crisis, 1965.* New York: Facts on File.

Martin, J.B. 1966. *Overtaken by Events: The Dominican Crisis from the Fall of Trujillo to the Civil War.* Garden City, N.Y.: Doubleday.

Nelson, W.J. 1990. *Almost a Territory: America's Attempt to Annex the Dominican Republic.* Newark: University of Delaware Press.

Palmer, B. 1989. *Intervention in the Caribbean: The Dominican Crisis of 1965.* Lexington: University Press of Kentucky.

Tillema, H.K. 1991. *International Armed Conflict Since 1945: A Bibliographic Handbook of Wars and Military Interventions.* Boulder: Westview.

2.23 Bolivia: Cuban-Assisted Guerrilla Insurgency November 1966–July 1970

This conflict was precipitated by the woeful state of Bolivian society and by Cuba's wish to export its Communist revolution to other Latin American countries. In late 1966 Cuban revolutionary leader Ché Guevara entered Bolivia with the aim of establishing a rural guerrilla movement that would oust the government in a Cuban-style revolution. At least ten other high-ranking Cuban officers were involved with the operation, and Fidel Castro maintained contact with them by radio and courier. The insurgents received supplies smuggled in from Argentina, Brazil, and Paraguay.

The revolutionaries failed to win popular support, however, and the guerrilla training camp was soon pinpointed by the Bolivian authorities, who mounted a counterinsurgency operation with U.S. assistance. Skirmishes continued for months, and the guerrillas had to go on the defensive. On October 7, 1967, Guevara was captured and subsequently killed. By the end of the year the guerrilla movement had been completely eradicated. Some guerrillas escaped to Chile, and attempts by Bolivia to extradite them led to strained relations between the two countries. Fatalities caused by the conflict were reported at 138. Conflict-management attempts did not succeed.

References

Baloyra, E.A., and J.A. Morris, eds. 1993. *Conflict and Change in Cuba.* Albuquerque: University of New Mexico Press.

Blasier, C., and C. Mesa-Lago, eds. 1979. *Cuba in the World.* Pittsburgh: University of Pittsburgh Press.

Butterworth, R.L. 1976. *Managing Interstate Conflict, 1945–1974.* Pittsburgh: Center for International Studies, University of Pittsburgh.

Dunkerley, J. 1984. *Rebellion in the Veins: Political Struggle in Bolivia, 1952–1982.* New York and London: Verso.

Goldenberg, B. 1965. *The Cuban Revolution and Latin America.* London: Allen and Unwin.

Malloy, J.M. 1970. Bolivia: *The Uncompleted Revolution.* Pittsburgh: University of Pittsburgh Press.

Malloy, J.M., and E. Gramarra. 1988. *Revolution and Reaction: Bolivia, 1964–1985.* New Brunswick, N.J.: Transaction.

Malloy, J.M., and R.S. Thorn, eds. 1971. *Beyond the Revolution: Bolivia Since 1952.* Pittsburgh: University of Pittsburgh Press.

Tillema, H.K. 1991. *International Armed Conflict Since 1945: A Bibliographic Handbook of Wars and Military Interventions.* Boulder: Westview.

2.24 El Salvador–Honduras: The "Football War" Border Dispute July 1969

El Salvador and Honduras had disputed territory on their common border since the early 1800s. Several agreements had failed to resolve the issue, which became a major source of contention. Relations had also been complicated by the migration of thousands of Salvadorans to Honduras, where they cultivated land. The Honduran government began an agrarian reform program in early 1969, which left thousands of Salvadorans without land and facing deportation. Relations between the two states became extremely strained.

In June 1969 the two countries' teams were in qualifying matches for the soccer World Cup. The games ended in serious rioting that led to a diplomatic crisis. Relations were severed on June 27, and on July 8 Salvadoran troops began cross-border raids. On July 14 El Salvador invaded Honduras, and heavy fighting continued. Honduras engaged in retaliatory air attacks on Salvadoran cities until the Organization of American States (OAS) brokered a cease-fire on July 18.

Further mediations ultimately led to a full settlement on July 30 under which Salvadoran troops were to withdraw from Honduran territory. Known as the "football war," this conflict resulted in the deaths of 5,000 people, mainly civilians. Continuing contacts in following years led to a treaty in 1976, but fighting again broke out before the treaty could be implemented (*see* conflict 2.26).

References

Anderson, T. 1981. *The War of the Dispossessed: Honduras and El Salvador, 1969.* Lincoln: University of Nebraska Press.

Baloyra, E.A. 1982. *El Salvador in Transition.* Chapel Hill: University of North Carolina Press.

Didion, J. 1982. *Salvador.* New York: Simon and Schuster.

Diskin, M., and K. Sharpe. 1986. *The Impact of U.S. Policy in El Salvador, 1979–1985.* Berkeley: Institute of International Studies, University of California.

Durham, W.H. 1979. *Scarcity and Survival in Central America: Ecological Origins of the Soccer War.* Stanford, Calif.: Stanford University Press.

Morris, J.A. 1984. *Honduras: Caudillo Politics and Military Rulers.* Boulder: Westview.

Tillema, H.K. 1991. *International Armed Conflict Since 1945: A Bibliographic Handbook of Wars and Military Interventions.* Boulder: Westview.

2.25 Guyana–Suriname: New River Triangle Border Dispute
August 1969–November 1970

Neighbors on the northeastern coast of South America, Guyana (formerly British Guiana) and Suriname (then under Dutch colonial control) had contested sovereignty over the New River triangle of the Corantijn River since its discovery in the late 1800s. The disputed area was then part of the territory administered by Guyana and had been the source of some tension. Following Guyana's independence from Britain in 1966, Suriname reasserted its claim to the region. Talks in London failed to resolve the issue.

In December 1967 Suriname sent a survey party into the triangle to conduct a survey for a hydroelectric power plant. Guyana claimed the men were armed and sought to expel them. Suriname then claimed that Guyana had occupied a Surinamese airstrip in retaliation. A few other minor incidents occurred, but with no reported fatalities. Tensions remained high until the parties resumed negotiations in an attempt to find a peaceful solution to the conflict. Talks continued intermittently for decades, and relations remained cordial.

References

Day, A., ed. 1987. *Border and Territorial Disputes.* 2d edition. Burnt Mill, Harlow (Essex), England: Longman.

Jeffrey, H., and C. Baber. 1986. *Guyana: Politics, Economics, and Society.* London: Pinter.

Manley, R. 1979. *Guyana Emergent: The Postindependence Struggle for Nondependent Development.* Boston: G.K. Hall.

2.26 El Salvador–Honduras: Territorial Dispute and Border Incidents
July 1976–October 1980

Relations between El Salvador and Honduras were strained because of an ongoing territorial dispute and the large numbers of Salvadorans living in Honduras. On June 14, 1976, following years of negotiations, the presidents of El Salvador and Honduras signed a treaty resolving the 1969 "football war" (*see* conflict 2.24). Provisions of the San José plan included the conditions of withdrawal of military forces from a demilitarized zone along their common frontier. Despite this, fighting broke out again on July 13, when Honduran troops clashed with Salvadoran soldiers in the Za Zalapar sector of the frontier.

A cease-fire agreement was reached on July 25, 1976, placing the frontier zones under direct military control to prevent further incidents. The Organization of American States (OAS) also sent an investigation team to the border, and Costa Rica, Guatemala, and Nicaragua, the guarantors of the San José agreement, held talks with the presidents of Honduras and El Salvador in late July. Despite an improvement in relations between the two presidents, border hostilities continued. By October 6 an agreement was signed placing the long-standing border dispute in the hands of a mediator.

After four years of negotiations mediated by a former president of Peru, José Luis Bustamente y Rivero, and the International Court of Justice (ICJ) in the Hague, a peace treaty was signed on October 30, 1980. The treaty reopened a newly demarcated border, provided for OAS supervision of the border area, and arranged for future discussions on disputed areas. The state of war that had existed since the 1969 conflict was over. Approximately 150 fatalities had resulted from the border clashes.

References

Anderson, T. 1981. *The War of the Dispossessed: Honduras and El Salvador, 1969.* Lincoln: University of Nebraska Press.

Baloyra, E.A. 1982. *El Salvador in Transition.* Chapel Hill: University of North Carolina Press.

Didion, J. 1982. *Salvador.* New York: Simon and Schuster.

Diskin, M., and K. Sharpe. 1986. *The Impact of U.S. Policy in El Salvador, 1979–1985.* Berkeley: Institute of International Studies, University of California.

Durham, W.H. 1979. *Scarcity and Survival in Central America: Ecological Origins of the Soccer War.* Stanford, Calif.: Stanford University Press.

Morris, J.A. 1984. *Honduras: Caudillo Politics and Military Rulers*. Boulder: Westview.

Tillema, H.K. 1991. *International Armed Conflict Since 1945: A Bibliographic Handbook of Wars and Military Interventions*. Boulder: Westview.

2.27 El Salvador: Civil Conflict and the Salvadoran Civil War January 1977–Late 1992

The El Salvador civil war is rooted in the country's vast number of landless peasants; the dominance of a small, landed oligarchy; and a succession of authoritarian military dictatorships. In the 1970s numerous small guerrilla groups representing various leftist tendencies emerged; they began mounting serious armed challenges in 1977. Right-wing terrorist squads, commonly known as death squads, were developed as counterpoise. The death squads often included members of El Salvador's military establishment.

Fighting in eastern and western areas led to large numbers of refugees attempting to flee into Honduras. In 1980 Honduran soldiers forced 600 refugees back across the border river, where they were immediately massacred by the Salvadoran army. In 1981 several left-wing guerrilla groups combined to form the Farabundo Martí National Liberation Front (FMLN), the most important group from this time. The FMLN made serious inroads in a number of offensives, but the Salvadoran army's counteroffensives always succeeded in winning back lost territory.

Beginning in the 1970s the United States provided heavy weapons and logistical support to the Salvadoran army; without such aid the government may not have been able to control the situation. Committed to fighting Communist forces in Latin America, especially under the Reagan administration, the United States was also actively helping the contras in their war against the Socialist government in neighboring Nicaragua (*see* conflict 2.31) and aiding the Guatemalan army in its fight against Communist guerrillas.

The Salvadoran army often engaged in cross-border raids into Honduras in pursuit of rebel forces, sometimes provoking formal Honduran protests. Nevertheless, the two countries cooperated in a ten-day joint operation against the rebels in 1982, involving more than 2,000 Honduran troops operating in Salvadoran and Honduran territory.

The Salvadoran conflict is estimated to have cost more than 75,000 lives, most of them civilian. Numerous mediation attempts, especially by the United Nations, ended the fighting in late 1992 after decades of low-level guerrilla warfare and civil terror. There followed an uneasy period of demobilization by the FMLN, the FMLN's transition to a political party, a purge of the military, and the resettlement of the former guerrillas. The United Nations oversaw the entire operation, which was considered one of its most successful peacemaking efforts.

References

Baloyra, E.A. 1982. *El Salvador in Transition*. Chapel Hill: University of North Carolina Press.

Didion, J. 1982. *Salvador*. New York: Simon and Schuster.

Diskin, M., and K. Sharpe. 1986. *The Impact of U.S. Policy in El Salvador, 1979–1985*. Berkeley: Institute of International Studies, University of California.

Hadar, A. 1981. *The United States and El Salvador: Political and Military Involvement*. Berkeley: U.S.-El Salvador Research and Information Center.

LaFeber, W. 1993. *Inevitable Revolutions: The United States in Central America*. 2d edition. New York: Norton.

McClintock, M. 1985. *State Terror and Popular Resistance in El Salvador*. Vol. 1 of *The American Connection*. London: Zed.

Montgomery, T. 1982. *Revolution in El Salvador: Origins and Evolution*. Boulder: Westview.

2.28 Ecuador–Peru: Regional Rivalry, Territorial Dispute, and the Amazon/Marañón Waterway Incidents June 1977–January 1978

Ecuador has claimed the Loreto area in northern Peru for more than 150 years—ever since a territorial reorganization under Spanish colonial rule assigned it to Peru. This disputed area left Ecuador without access to the Amazon or the Marañón River, but negotiations in 1942 settled the issue in Peru's favor.

In the 1970s, however, Ecuador began to claim that the 1942 border peace treaty, the protocol of Río de Janeiro, had been forced on Ecuador. Both sides raised this issue at the United Nations during 1976, but no action was taken. Between June 1977 and January 1978, tensions increased because the Peruvian government claimed Ecuador had on several occasions attacked Peruvian posts in the disputed area. Ecuador blamed Peru for the incidents.

The tension was defused after talks between the countries' top military commanders on January 19 and 20, 1978. No other peaceful conflict-management efforts were undertaken, and the matter appeared settled. There were about ten fatalities during the actual fighting. This conflict, however, was merely a precursor to much graver conflicts in 1981 and 1984 (*see* conflicts 2.32; 2.36)

References

Butterworth, R.L. 1976. *Managing Interstate Conflict, 1945–1974*. Pittsburgh: Center for International Studies, University of Pittsburgh.

Day, A., ed. 1987. *Border and Territorial Disputes*. 2d edition. Burnt Mill, Harlow (Essex), England: Longman.

Fitch, J.S. 1977. *The Military Coup d'État as a Political Process: Ecuador, 1948–1966*. Baltimore: Johns Hopkins University Press.

Schodt, D.W. 1987. *Ecuador: An Andean Enigma*. Boulder: Westview.

Tillema, H.K. 1991. *International Armed Conflict Since 1945: A Bibliographic Handbook of Wars and Military Interventions*. Boulder: Westview.

2.29 Nicaragua–Costa Rica: Regional Rivalry and Border Incidents October 1977

Relations between Nicaragua and Costa Rica had been cool since the 1948 Costa Rican revolution, and armed conflict had occurred in 1955 (*see* conflict 2.6). Matters worsened in 1977 over accusations that Costa Rica was harboring Sandinista guerrillas, then fighting the Nicaraguan regime. Relations were further strained on October 14, 1977, when a Nicaraguan aircraft strafed three boats on Costa Rica's side of the border on the Frio River. One of the boats was carrying the Costa Rican minister of public security, and he was detained on the Nicaraguan side for several hours.

After the minister's release, Costa Rican president Daniel Oduber Quiros ordered units to avoid any confrontations with the Nicaraguan army. It was suggested that the incident was a case of mistaken identity, as the presence of the boats in the area had not been announced, and they could have held Sandinista guerrillas. But Costa Rica's foreign minister, Gauzalo Facio, protested the incident on October 15, 1977, requesting that Nicaraguan aircraft refrain from flying into Costa Rican airspace without permission. This request was ignored by Nicaragua, which continued to violate Costa Rican airspace in its search for Sandinista guerrillas.

The same day, an Organization of American States (OAS) team was sent to investigate Nicaragua's complaints that Costa Rica and Honduras were harboring Sandinistas and allowing them to operate from their territory. Nicaragua also accused Cuba of funding the Sandinistas. At Costa Rica's request, the OAS stationed observers along the border as a security measure. There were forty fatalities because of the conflict, and the OAS action settled it for the time being. In 1978 similar fighting broke out again (*see* conflict 2.30).

References

Bird, L.A. 1984. *Costa Rica, the Unarmed Democracy*. London: Sheppard.

Crawley, E. 1984. *Nicaragua in Perspective*. Revised edition. New York: St. Martin's.

Earley, S. 1982. *Arms and Politics in Costa Rica and Nicaragua, 1948–1981*. Albuquerque: Latin American Institute/University of New Mexico Press.

Tillema, H.K. 1991. *International Armed Conflict Since 1945: A Bibliographic Handbook of Wars and Military Interventions*. Boulder: Westview.

2.30 Nicaragua–Costa Rica: Regional Rivalry, Cross-Border Raids, and Border Incidents September–December 1978

Mutual hostility and armed conflict had marked relations between Nicaragua and Costa Rica since 1948, mostly over exiled opposition groups forming rebel armies and staging cross-border attacks (*see* conflict 2.3). The dictatorial Somoza regime had ruled Nicaragua since 1937, and General Anastasio Somoza Debayle had been president off and on since 1967. In December 1974 he imposed martial law after Sandinista guerrillas kidnapped some government officials, an action that sparked intense opposition culminating in nationwide antigovernment strikes in 1978 and a virtual civil war. Of particular concern to the regime was the Sandinistas' burgeoning Marxist guerrilla insurgency.

This particular conflict began on September 12, 1978, when Costa Rica's government, which had no military forces of its own, accused Nicaragua of bombarding its territory near the frontier and pursuing Sandinista rebels across the border. Nicaragua defended its actions, claiming that many rebel attacks had been launched from Costa Rican soil. The Somoza regime's problems worsened on September 14 when Venezuela sent military aircraft, along with support from the government of Panama, to the Sandinista rebels. The Nicaraguan government reacted by recalling its ambassadors from Costa Rica, Panama, and Venezuela.

An Organization of American States (OAS) foreign ministers meeting was held September 21–23, 1978, in Washington, D.C., to discuss events in Central America. The ministers agreed to provide only humanitarian aid and to abstain from direct intervention in Nicaragua. Although the foreign ministers' negotiations with Somoza and the Nicaraguan Broad Opposition Front (FAO) failed, the OAS sent an investigation team to examine the alleged border violations. On November 21, following further clashes between Nicaraguan troops and the Costa Rican civil guard, Costa Rica severed diplomatic relations with Nicaragua and called for its expulsion from the OAS.

On December 15, 1978, a UN General Assembly resolution (33/76) demanded a halt to the military hostilities between Nicaragua and Costa Rica. Nicaragua closed its mutual border with Costa Rica on December 27 and threatened invasion if Sandinista guerrillas continued their attacks from Costa Rica. About ten fatalities resulted from the fighting, and eventually the dispute abated. The fall of the Somoza regime to the Sandinistas on July 19, 1979, kindled further conflict in the region (*see* conflicts 2.31; 2.38; 2.39).

References

Bird, L.A. 1984. *Costa Rica, the Unarmed Democracy.* London: Sheppard.

Christian, S. 1985. *Nicaragua: Revolution in the Family.* New York: Random House.

Cockburn, L. 1987. *Out of Control: The Story of the Reagan Administration's Secret War in Nicaragua.* New York: Atlantic Monthly Press.

Crawley, E. 1984. *Nicaragua in Perspective.* Revised edition. New York: St. Martin's.

Earley, S. 1982. *Arms and Politics in Costa Rica and Nicaragua, 1948–1981.* Albuquerque: Latin American Institute/University of New Mexico Press.

Tillema, H.K. 1991. *International Armed Conflict Since 1945: A Bibliographic Handbook of Wars and Military Interventions.* Boulder: Westview.

2.31 Honduras–Nicaragua: Right-Wing Insurgency and the Contra War January 1980–February 1994

The right-wing, U.S.-backed Somoza regime had ruled Nicaragua from 1937 to 1979, until it was overthrown by the leftist guerrillas belonging to the Frente Sandinista de Liberación Nacional (FSLN, named for Augusto César Sandino, an early Nicaraguan patriot). Many Somoza supporters and members of the National Guards fled to Honduras. Beginning in January 1980, these exiled antigovernment forces began an insurgency from bases in Honduras, increasing their activities after 1981, when the United States began to give them massive military and economic support with Honduran cooperation. The recently elected Reagan administration in the United States was violently opposed to the new FSLN government, seeing it as a Communist threat. In one operation, the United States mined Nicaraguan harbors, sinking many ships. Commonly known as contras, the right-wing insurgents were formed into an army that frequently invaded Nicaragua from Honduras with the aim of ousting the Socialist FSLN regime.

The contras' activities led to numerous armed clashes on the Honduras-Nicaraguan border throughout the 1980s. In addition, heavy U.S. support for the contras through the U.S. Central Intelligence Agency (CIA) led to a number of domestic scandals for the U.S. administration. In August 1987 the Arias peace plan, named for President Oscar Arias Sanchez of Costa Rica, who proposed it, led to direct negotiations between the FSLN and the contras, and a number of cease-fires were arranged. Over the next few years the FSLN government made many concessions, including the holding of free elections, which the government lost. At the end of 1992 the war as such was over, but the defeated Sandinistas underwent a serious division, and the contras were proving difficult to demobilize. These tensions threatened to escalate into serious civil conflict. In 1993 some fighting broke out between disgruntled right-wing and left-wing rebel factions and the government, but after mediation by the Organization of American States (OAS), their grievances were settled and the fighting ended.

More than 25,000 lives were lost because of the war, most of them civilian fatalities. The war also devastated the Nicaraguan economy, as the contras and the CIA targeted many of the country's economic facilities.

References

Black, G. 1981. *Triumph of the People: The Sandinista Revolution in Nicaragua.* London: Zed.

Christian, S. 1985. *Nicaragua: Revolution in the Family.* New York: Random House.

Cockburn, L. 1987. *Out of Control: The Story of the Reagan Administration's Secret War in Nicaragua.* New York: Atlantic Monthly Press.

Crawley, E. 1984. *Nicaragua in Perspective.* Revised edition. New York: St. Martin's.

Gutman, R. 1988. *Banana Diplomacy: The Making of American Policy in Nicaragua, 1981–1987.* New York: Simon and Schuster.

LaFeber, W. 1993. *Inevitable Revolutions: The United States in Central America.* 2d edition. New York: Norton.

Morris, J.A. 1984. *Honduras: Caudillo Politics and Military Rulers.* Boulder: Westview.

Tillema, H.K. 1991. *International Armed Conflict Since 1945: A Bibliographic Handbook of Wars and Military Interventions.* Boulder: Westview.

2.32 Ecuador–Peru: Territorial Dispute and Border War January–April 1981

In early January 1981 fighting erupted over disputed territory in the Loreto area of northern Peru—a remote jungle region in the Condor mountain range that had been the scene of previous Ecuador–Peru clashes in 1977 (*see* conflict 2.28). Ecuador had been claiming this area for more than 150 years, ever since a territorial reorganization under Spanish colonial rule that left Ecuador without access to the Amazon River or the Marañón waterway. Although Peru regarded the dispute as settled under the 1942 protocol of Río de Janeiro, Ecuador claimed the treaty was imposed and challenged its validity.

Fighting erupted on January 28, 1981, the eve of the thirty-ninth anniversary of the protocol, following Ecuador's accusations that Peru had violated its airspace and fired on a military outpost. President Jaime Roldós Aguilera of Ecuador declared a state of emergency and imposed a press blackout on news from the border. The border was immediately closed and troops mobilized on both sides. Peru rejected offers of mediation from Colombia, Venezuela, and the Organization of American States (OAS). Fighting continued, and Peru retook its military posts. On January 31 the guarantor nations of the protocol, Argentina, Brazil, Chile, and the United States, mediated discussions between the warring states in Brasilía, resulting in a cease-fire and acceptance of observers to supervise the disputed area.

In early February 1981 the OAS adopted a resolution calling for peace in the border area, which was supported by the four guarantor nations. In late February, however, hostilities recurred in the border area, and Peru declared that any further infiltration by Ecuador into the region would be regarded as "an act of war." The two countries sealed their mutual border on February 23, but then agreed to proposals by the guarantor nations to withdraw their troops from either side of the border. A series of meetings of OAS countries and the guarantor nations from February to March 1981 resulted in a firm commitment on the withdrawal of troops by both parties. On April 2, 1981, the border was reopened. About ten fatalities were reported during the fighting. Tense relations led to renewed fighting in 1984 and 1995 (*see* conflicts 2.36; 2.44).

References

Butterworth, R.L. 1976. *Managing Interstate Conflict, 1945–1974.* Pittsburgh: Center for International Studies, University of Pittsburgh.

Day, A., ed. 1987. *Border and Territorial Disputes.* 2d edition. Burnt Mill, Harlow (Essex), England: Longman.

Fitch, J.S. 1977. *The Military Coup d'État as a Political Process: Ecuador, 1948–1966.* Baltimore: Johns Hopkins University Press.

Schooley, H. 1987. *Conflict in Central America.* Burnt Mill, Harlow (Essex), England: Longman.

Tillema, H.K. 1991. *International Armed Conflict Since 1945: A Bibliographic Handbook of Wars and Military Interventions.* Boulder: Westview.

2.33 United Kingdom–Argentina: Sovereignty Dispute and the Falklands War April–June 1982

The Falkland Islands, together with dependencies, the South Georgia and South Sandwich Islands, have been a British crown colony since the 1830s. Calling them the Islas Malvinas, Argentina had disputed British sovereignty ever since Britain asserted its claim to the islands by establishing a naval garrison there in 1833, and Argentina continued to pursue a long-term policy of establishing its sovereignty over the islands. As a consequence, a number of incidents occurred concerning the Falklands, which lie 600 kilometers off the Argentinean coast in the South Atlantic Ocean. Inconclusive negotiations over the issue had been going on for years.

The conflict began to escalate after bilateral negotiations broke down in February 1982. On March 21, after the hard-line Argentinean government issued some particularly bellicose statements, a group of about sixty Argentineans, said to be scrap merchants, landed illegally at Leth Harbor, on the island of South Georgia. Tensions escalated steadily amid repeated Argentinean claims to the islands and the buildup of naval and military hardware. Intense diplomatic activity and repeated warnings from Britain and the United Nations did nothing to defuse the situation.

On April 2, 1982, Argentinean troops invaded and took control of the Falkland Islands, overwhelming the seventy Royal Marines stationed there. By April 12 Argentina's troops numbered a reported 10,000. The invasion was widely condemned by the United States, the European Community (now the European Union), and the United Nations. Great Britain quickly dispatched a naval task force composed of nearly 6,000 troops, almost seventy destroyers, carriers, frigates, and submarines, in addition to air support. Both nations then declared maritime exclusion zones around the islands and off the Argentinean coast.

Tensions heightened despite a Peruvian truce proposal and diplomatic initiatives by the United Nations and the U.S. secretary of state, Alexander Haig. On April 24 Great Britain announced its readiness to retake the islands, and the following day British marines, landing by helicopter, recaptured South Georgia. On April 30 Britain announced a total exclusion zone of 200 nautical miles around the Falklands, which further escalated the conflict.

War began on May 1, 1982, with British air attacks on Port Stanley on East Falkland, and major naval engagements, bombardments, and attacks on installations. Diplomatic initiatives by the United States, Peru, and the United Nations failed to stop the fighting, and on May 21, 1982, 5,000 British troops landed on East Falkland and around Port San Carlos, establishing a bridgehead. Heavy ground, air, and sea fighting ensued, but British forces made steady advances, and on June 14–15 Argentina surrendered the islands to Britain. Prisoners were returned, and British troops and naval ships began to leave for home in the following months.

Throughout the conflict more than 1,200 troops and civilians were killed, hundreds of planes were destroyed, and many ships were sunk. Despite the British victory, the dispute over sovereignty of the islands continued. British forces remain on the island, at great cost, while negotiations continue on resolving the sovereignty debate.

References

Brown, J., and W.P. Snyder, eds. 1985. *The Regionalization of Warfare: The Falklands/Malvinas, Lebanon, and the Iran-Iraq Conflicts.* New Brunswick, N.J.: Transaction.

Calvert, P. 1982. *The Falklands Crisis: The Rights and the Wrongs*. London: Pinter.

Coll, A.R., and A.C. Arend, eds. 1985. *The Falklands War: Lessons for Strategy, Diplomacy, and International Law*. Boston: Allen and Unwin.

Dabat, A. 1984. *Argentina, the Malvinas, and the End of Military Rule*. Translated by R. Johnstone. New York and London: Verso.

Danchev, A. 1992. *International Perspective on the Falklands Conflict: Matter of Life and Death*. Basingstoke (Hants), England: Macmillan.

Day, A., ed. 1987. *Border and Territorial Disputes*. 2d edition. Burnt Mill, Harlow (Essex), England: Longman.

Dillon, G. 1989. *The Falklands, Politics, and War*. New York: St. Martin's.

Eddy, P., and M. Linklater, eds. 1982. *The Falklands War*. London: André Deutsch.

Freedman, L. 1991. *Signals of War: The Falkland Conflict of 1982*. Princeton, N.J.: Princeton University Press.

Freedman, L., and O. Gamba-Stonehouse. 1991. *Signals of War: The Falklands Conflict of 1982*. Princeton, N.J.: Princeton University Press.

Tillema, H.K. 1991. *International Armed Conflict Since 1945: A Bibliographic Handbook of Wars and Military Interventions*. Boulder: Westview.

2.34 Guatemala–Mexico: Regional Instability, Guatemalan Civil War, and Border Incidents
September 1982–January 1983

Various guerrilla insurgencies throughout Latin America made the region unstable in the 1980s. Guatemala's brutal civil war in particular, which began in 1961, led not only to massive civilian casualties (100,000 dead, 40,000 missing) and refugee populations. It also led to a number of border incidents with surrounding states, as Guatemalan forces pursued leftist guerrillas, called the Guatemalan National Revolutionary Unity (URNG), across national boundaries (*see* conflicts 2.5; 2.11).

With the outbreak of renewed fighting in 1982, thousands of Guatemalan refugees crossed into the Mexican border state of Chiapas. From September 1982 to January 1983, Guatemalan troops made frequent incursions into Mexican territory to harass, kill, or abduct refugees, purportedly in pursuit of URNG rebels. Mexico protested and then began to move the refugee camps farther away from the border area. No attempts at peaceful conflict management were made during the dispute, and it soon lapsed. Although Guatemalan and Mexican troops had not engaged in direct fighting, the regional instability made the incidents serious. Another such armed conflict arose in 1984, when Guatemalan troops again crossed the border into Mexico (*see* conflict 2.37).

References

Fried, J.L., ed. 1983. *Guatemala in Rebellion: Unfinished History*. New York: Grove.

Gleijeses, P. 1991. *Shattered Hope: The Guatemalan Revolution and the United States, 1944–1954*. Princeton, N.J.: Princeton University Press.

Immerman, R.H. 1982. *The CIA in Guatemala: The Foreign Policy of Intervention*. Austin: University of Texas Press.

Melville, T., and M. Melville. 1971. *Guatemala—Another Vietnam?* Harmondsworth (Middlesex), England: Penguin.

Schlesinger, S.C., and S. Kinzer. 1982. *Bitter Fruit: The Untold Story of the American Coup in Guatemala*. Garden City, N.Y.: Doubleday.

Tillema, H.K. 1991. *International Armed Conflict Since 1945: A Bibliographic Handbook of Wars and Military Interventions*. Boulder: Westview.

2.35 United States–Grenada: Anti-Communist Military Invasion
October–December 1983

The election of Ronald Reagan to the U.S. presidency in 1980 led to an intensification of the cold war. The new U.S. administration was particularly sensitive to Soviet forays into the Caribbean. Relations between the United States and the small island nation of Grenada deteriorated in early 1983 because of Cuban participation in the construction of an airport on the island. The United States saw the airport as a potential military base, and Reagan referred to it as part of the "Soviet-Cuban militarization of Grenada."

On October 25, 1983, on the heels of a Cuban-backed military coup in which Maurice Bishop, the prime minister of Grenada, and many civilians were killed, the United States invaded the island with substantial force. The huge U.S. contingent established control of Grenada after a few days of fighting, although fierce resistance occurred in some isolated areas. A contingent of 300 soldiers from Antigua, Barbados, Dominica, the Grenadines, Jamaica, and St. Lucia and St. Vincent landed around the same time.

More than 250 people were estimated to have been killed in the invasion, including 42 U.S. soldiers and up to 70 Cubans. The coup leaders were subsequently arrested and imprisoned and the legitimate government restored. International criticism of the action was strong from some quarters. The U.S. troops withdrew in December 1983, but the Caribbean troops remained for some time after. No peaceful conflict-management attempts were made during the conflict, and life for the island nation soon returned to normal.

References

Burrowes, R. 1988. *Revolution and Rescue in Grenada: An Account of the U.S.-Caribbean Invasion*. New York: Greenwood.

Davidson, S. 1987. *Grenada: A Study in Politics and the Limits of International Law*. Aldershot (Hants), England: Gower.

Lewis, G. 1987. *Grenada: The Jewel Despoiled*. Baltimore: Johns Hopkins University Press.

O'Shaughnessy, H. 1984. *Grenada: An Eyewitness Account of the U.S. Invasion and the Caribbean History that Provoked It*. New York: Dodd, Mead.

———. 1984. *Grenada: Revolution, Invasion, and Aftermath*. London: Hamilton/The Observer.

Schoenhals, K.P., and R.A. Melanson. 1985. *Revolution and Intervention in Grenada: The New Jewel Movement, the United States, and the Caribbean*. Boulder: Westview.

Thorndike, T. 1985. *Grenada: Politics, Economics, and Society*. Boulder: Lynne Rienner.

2.36 Ecuador–Peru: Regional Rivalry, Territorial Dispute, and Border Conflict
January 1984

Ecuador and Peru had been rivals since a long-standing border dispute erupted into armed conflict in 1977 and 1981 (*see* conflicts 2.28; 2.32). The disputed territory in the Loreto region of northern Peru had been in contention for more than 150 years. Although Peru's claim was validated in a 1942 treaty, Ecuador maintained it had been forced into signing the treaty.

Tensions between the two states were still high in the early 1980s. On January 15, 1984, fighting broke out at a frontier post on the Corrientes River (400 kilometers southeast of Quito); one Ecuadoran soldier was killed. Given the history of armed conflict between the two sides, the incident could easily have escalated into all-out war. The conflict eventually subsided, even though neither side attempted any peaceful conflict management. Another conflict over the same piece of territory erupted in 1995, with more serious consequences (*see* conflict 2.44).

References

Butterworth, R.L. 1976. *Managing Interstate Conflict, 1945–1974*. Pittsburgh: Center for International Studies, University of Pittsburgh.

Day, A., ed. 1987. *Border and Territorial Disputes*. 2d edition. Burnt Mill, Harlow (Essex), England: Longman.

Fitch, J.S. 1977. *The Military Coup d'État as a Political Process: Ecuador, 1948–1966*. Baltimore: Johns Hopkins University Press.

Schodt, D.W. 1987. *Ecuador: An Andean Enigma*. Boulder: Westview.

Tillema, H.K. 1991. *International Armed Conflict Since 1945: A Bibliographic Handbook of Wars and Military Interventions*. Boulder: Westview.

2.37 Guatemala–Mexico: Regional Instability, Guatemalan Civil War, and Border Incident
April 1984

Guatemala's brutal civil war, which began in June 1954 and is still ongoing (*see* conflict 2.5), not only created huge numbers of refugees; it also led to regional tensions, as Guatemalan troops pursued rebels from the Guatemalan National Revolutionary Unity (URNG) over national boundaries.

In April 1984 an armed Guatemalan group crossed into Mexico and attacked a refugee camp, killing six people. The Mexican government protested and relocated its refugee camps farther away from the border. No attempts at peaceful conflict management were undertaken, and the dispute soon lapsed. Although direct fighting between Guatemala and Mexico had been avoided, the incident had given cause for alarm, given the general instability in Central America at the time.

References

Fried, J.L., ed. 1983. *Guatemala in Rebellion: Unfinished History*. New York: Grove.

Gleijeses, P. 1991. *Shattered Hope: The Guatemalan Revolution and the United States, 1944–1954*. Princeton, N.J.: Princeton University Press.

Immerman, R.H. 1982. *The CIA in Guatemala: The Foreign Policy of Intervention*. Austin: University of Texas Press.

Melville, T., and M. Melville. 1971. *Guatemala—Another Vietnam?* Harmondsworth (Middlesex), England: Penguin.

Schlesinger, S.C., and S. Kinzer. 1982. *Bitter Fruit: The Untold Story of the American Coup in Guatemala*. Garden City, N.Y.: Doubleday.

Tillema, H.K. 1991. *International Armed Conflict Since 1945: A Bibliographic Handbook of Wars and Military Interventions*. Boulder: Westview.

2.38 Nicaragua–Costa Rica: Regional Rivalry and Border Incidents
May–June 1985

Nicaragua and Costa Rica had been rivals since 1948, when Nicaragua intervened in the Costa Rican civil war. Since then the neighbors had engaged in four militarized conflicts. Tensions were high in 1985 as the war between Nicaragua's left-wing Sandinista government and the U.S.-backed right-wing contra rebels spread to surrounding states.

The immediate context of this conflict was a diplomatic dispute concerning a Nicaraguan student who had taken refuge in the Costa Rican Embassy in Managua but was subsequently arrested. Relations between the two countries were then seriously strained following a number of border incidents and violations of airspace, including the killing of two Costa Rican Civil Guards on May 31, 1985, for which Nicaragua took responsibility. Following hostile diplomatic moves, the conflict was partially resolved after mediation by the Contadora Group (the foreign ministers of Colombia, Mexico, Panama, and Venezuela) on February 24, 1986. Costa Rica rejected the suggestion of the creation of a demilitarized zone between the two countries, though, and fighting broke out again in 1986 (*see* conflict 2.39).

References

Bird, L.A. 1984. *Costa Rica, the Unarmed Democracy.* London: Sheppard.

Black, G. 1981. *Triumph of the People: The Sandinista Revolution in Nicaragua.* London: Zed.

Christian, S. 1985. *Nicaragua: Revolution in the Family.* New York: Random House.

Cockburn, L. 1987. *Out of Control: The Story of the Reagan Administration's Secret War in Nicaragua.* New York: Atlantic Monthly Press.

Crawley, E. 1984. *Nicaragua in Perspective.* Revised edition. New York: St. Martin's.

Earley, S. 1982. *Arms and Politics in Costa Rica and Nicaragua, 1948–1981.* Albuquerque: Latin American Institute/University of New Mexico Press.

Tillema, H.K. 1991. *International Armed Conflict Since 1945: A Bibliographic Handbook of Wars and Military Interventions.* Boulder: Westview.

2.39 Nicaragua–Costa Rica: Regional Rivalry and Border Incidents April 1986

Nicaragua and Costa Rica had been rivals for decades, starting disputes in 1948, 1955, 1977, 1978, and 1985 (*see* conflicts 2.3; 2.6; 2.29; 2.30; 2.38). During the contra war in Nicaragua, Costa Rica had allowed the right-wing contra rebels to operate from its territory. With the support of the United States, the contras were fighting a guerrilla insurgency to overthrow the Sandinista government in Nicaragua.

Despite some recent improvement in relations, a Nicaraguan incursion into Costa Rican territory at the border post of Los Chiles on April 16, 1986, resulted in armed clashes. The incident was not considered as serious as the conflict in May 1985, but the history of hostility between the two states heightened the potential for escalation. Although neither side attempted to settle the conflict peacefully, it subsided in the following months. In the 1990s the contra war ended, and relations improved between Nicaragua and Costa Rica.

References

Bird, L.A. 1984. *Costa Rica, the Unarmed Democracy.* London: Sheppard.

Black, G. 1981. *Triumph of the People: The Sandinista Revolution in Nicaragua.* London: Zed.

Christian, S. 1985. *Nicaragua: Revolution in the Family.* New York: Random House.

Cockburn, L. 1987. *Out of Control: The Story of the Reagan Administration's Secret War in Nicaragua.* New York: Atlantic Monthly Press.

Crawley, E. 1984. *Nicaragua in Perspective.* Revised edition. New York: St. Martin's.

Earley, S. 1982. *Arms and Politics in Costa Rica and Nicaragua, 1948–1981.* Albuquerque: Latin American Institute/University of New Mexico Press.

Tillema, H.K. 1991. *International Armed Conflict Since 1945: A Bibliographic Handbook of Wars and Military Interventions.* Boulder: Westview.

2.40 Suriname: Guerrilla Insurgency July 1986–December 1992

Suriname, on the northeastern coast of South America, gained its independence from the Netherlands in 1975 and since that time had experienced civil unrest and a number of coups. The initial cause of this particular conflict was opposition to government plans to move thousands of so-called boschnegers out of the rainforests and into towns.* The boschnegers violently resisted the government's plan, and the rebellion soon took on a general opposition to Suriname's military regime. In July 1986 the boschneger-based Surinamese Liberation Army (SLA), led by Ronnie Brunswijk, attacked military bases in eastern Suriname and launched a guerrilla war. Initial army desertions to the rebels resulted in early successes, but army counterattacks led to fluctuating fortunes for the rebels from July 1986 to 1992.

From the beginning of the conflict, the SLA received massive financial and logistical support from the Amsterdam-based Movement for the Liberation of Suriname, which paid for British mercenaries to fight with the rebels. Beginning in December 1986 it became obvious that French Guyana was also aiding the rebels, allowing them to operate from French Guyanan territory. In July 1987 the conflict escalated when the French sent troop reinforcements to the border areas, warning Suriname not to pursue rebels into French territory.

In 1987 former president Hendrick R. Chin A Sen joined the SLA, and in April of that year the SLA declared a rival government administration in the territory it held. The army fueled the conflict by committing massive human rights violations. A peace accord with the SLA in August 1989 led to the outbreak of another insurgency in western Suriname among the Tucayana tribe.

The Tucayana Amazonicas rebel group, led by Thomas Sabajo, opposed the peace accord. The fighting continued until May 1992, when both sides suspended their rebel activities. A peace agreement was signed in July 1992, but by the end of the year it had not been fully implemented, primarily because the rebels were refusing to disarm. The fighting ceased by December 1992, however, and the peace process moved forward.

The few attempts at peaceful conflict management failed to resolve any of the underlying issues. Several hundred people were killed during the fighting. Although the insurgency was over by December 1992, civil unrest and instability continued to plague the country.

* The boschnegers, or bush Negroes, are the descendants of escaped slaves. Since the 1760 treaties signed with the Dutch colonial authorities, the boschnegers have lived an autonomous existence in the rain forests, developing a unique tribal society with its own language, rituals, and political structure. With a population of 50,000, they make up 15 percent of the total population of Suriname.

References

Davies, J. 2002. "Venezuela-Guyana Border Dispute: Inter- and Intra-State Conflict in Latin America and Resolution Strategies." Summary updated June 6. Preliminary draft concept paper by John Davies of CIDCM http://www.inform.umd.edu/LAS/InfoStudent/Courses/GVPT309P/GuyanaVenezuela.htm (accessed May 20, 2004). College Park: Latin American Studies Center, University of Maryland.

Gurr, T.R. 1993. *Minorities at Risk: A Global View of Ethnopolitical Conflicts.* Washington, D.C.: U.S. Institute of Peace Press.

Jeffrey, H., and C. Baber. 1986. *Guyana: Politics, Economics, and Society.* London: Pinter.

Tillema, H.K. 1991. *International Armed Conflict Since 1945: A Bibliographic Handbook of Wars and Military Interventions.* Boulder: Westview.

2.41 United States–Panama: U.S. Anti-Noriega Military Invasion December 1989

Panama occupies a strategic place in the U.S. economy, as much shipping passes through the Panama Canal. It has therefore been important to the United States to maintain good relations with the Panamanian government. Armed conflicts had soured U.S.-Panamanian relations in 1964. The relationship between the United States and Panamanian strongman, General Manuel Antonio Noriega, had been severely strained for two years, despite Noriega's having once been on the payroll of U.S. intelligence organizations. Noriega's human rights abuses angered the U.S. State Department. In addition, two U.S. federal grand juries had indicted him on drug charges.

Tensions rose significantly after Panamanian voters went to the polls to elect a new president in May 1989. Although international observers declared an overwhelming victory for the opposition party, the government voided the elections. When Noriega announced a "state of war" with the United States, the United States responded on December 20, 1989, by invading Panama with 23,000 troops backed by massive air support. The primary military objective was to capture Noriega and overthrow his regime. The resistance to the invasion was strong, and more than 550 people were killed in the fighting, including 26 U.S. soldiers and a number of civilians. The invasion was completed by December 23. Noriega took refuge in the Vatican diplomatic mission on December 24 and did not surrender until January 3, 1990. The general was then taken to the United States to stand trial. He was convicted on eight counts of racketeering and drug trafficking in 1992.

President George H.W. Bush (1989–1993) said the reasons for the invasion were to restore democracy, to protect the Panama Canal, to safeguard U.S. citizens in Panama, and to bring Noriega to trial, but the international community widely condemned the action. Neither side had sought to manage the conflict peacefully. U.S. troops began to withdraw in January 1990, when the U.S.-installed regime stabilized.

References

Dubois, J. 1964. *Danger in Panama.* Indianapolis: Bobbs-Merrill.

Farnsworth, D.N., and J.W. McKenney. 1983. *U.S.-Panama Relations, 1903–1978: A Study in Linkage Politics.* Boulder: Westview.

Kitchel, D. 1978. *The Truth About the Panama Canal.* New Rochelle, N.Y.: Arlington House.

Liss, S. 1967. *The Canal: Aspects of United States–Panamanian Relations.* South Bend, Ind.: University of Notre Dame Press.

2.42 United States–Haiti: U.S. Military Invasion and Aristide's Return from Exile September 1994

In December 1990 Jean-Bertrand Aristide, a Roman Catholic priest, became Haiti's first democratically elected president. He was forced into exile after a September 1991 military coup. Amid concerns over human rights abuses and alarm about Haitian refugees trying to reach U.S. waters by boat, the United States and the United Nations began pressuring the Haitian military junta to step down and allow Aristide to return to office. The United Nations declared a worldwide oil, arms, and financial embargo on Haiti and dispatched human rights monitors. After a tense standoff with Haiti's military leaders, the UN gave the go-ahead for restoring democracy in Haiti using "all necessary means."

In early September 1994 the United States built up an invasion force of some 20,000 troops and twenty naval vessels in the area. A "last chance" mission to Haiti led by former U.S. president Jimmy Carter on September 18 produced a compromise agreement whereby the military leader agreed to step down. U.S. troops entered Haiti on September 19 unopposed by the military. In subsequent weeks the UN sanctions were lifted, Aristide was restored to the presidency, and more troops were deployed. By September 27 there were 15,700 U.S. troops in Haiti. The apparent suicide of a U.S. soldier on guard duty was the only U.S. fatality in the operation.

After the invasion, violence between the police and pro-Aristide supporters led to dozens of deaths, while efforts to disarm paramilitary and police groups by civilians and U.S. soldiers also resulted in numerous fatalities. Policing remained in the hands of U.S. troops in the following months. Aristide attempted to rebuild the country's economy and its shattered democratic institutions, but his prime minister and the United States wanted him to pursue different policies, which led to further strife after Aristide was reelected in 2000.

References

Fagen, R. 1987. *Forging Peace: The Challenge of Central America.* New York: B. Blackwell.

Heinl, R.D., and N.G. Heinl. 1978. *Written in Blood: The Story of the Haitian People, 1492–1971.* Boston: Houghton Mifflin.

2.43 Ecuador–Peru: Regional Rivalry and Cenepa Headwaters Confrontation January–March 1995

Ecuador and Peru had been rivals since 1977, when a long-standing territorial dispute over the Loreto region of northern Peru erupted into armed conflict. Skirmishes in 1981 and 1984 had created a tense and hostile border situation (*see* conflicts 2.28; 2.32; 2.36). Although a 1942 treaty had validated Peru's sovereignty over the region, Ecuador maintained it had been forced into signing the agreement.

In early January 1995 fighting erupted once again in the Loreto region when Ecuadoran helicopters attacked and destroyed a Peruvian border post. Both sides quickly called up reserves and mobilized their forces in the area. A virulent propaganda war ensued, and each side threatened total war. This escalation of tensions flared into full-scale offensives involving tanks and air support in late January. Heavy fighting continued into February, and several planes were shot down.

Neighboring states and the guarantor nations of the 1942 treaty sought a peaceful resolution to the fighting, and their efforts produced a cease-fire in February 1995. Despite the cease-fire, skirmishes continued into March. In April both sides agreed to end the fighting and withdraw their forces from the area. In all, an estimated 100 troops were killed in the fighting, and efforts to resolve the underlying dispute continued throughout the rest of the year.

References

Butterworth, R.L. 1976. *Managing Interstate Conflict, 1945–1974.* Pittsburgh: Center for International Studies, University of Pittsburgh.

Day, A., ed. 1987. *Border and Territorial Disputes.* 2d edition. Burnt Mill, Harlow (Essex), England: Longman.

Fitch, J.S. 1977. *The Military Coup d'État as a Political Process: Ecuador, 1948–1966.* Baltimore: Johns Hopkins University Press.

Schodt, D.W. 1987. *Ecuador: An Andean Enigma.* Boulder: Westview.

Tillema, H.K. 1991. *International Armed Conflict Since 1945: A Bibliographic Handbook of Wars and Military Interventions.* Boulder: Westview.

2.44 Ecuador–Peru: Condor Mountain Territorial Dispute January 1995–October 1998

The 1942 Río de Janeiro Treaty gave Peru 173,500 square kilometers of potentially oil-rich Ecuadorian territory. Ecuador refused to recognize the treaty, and several clashes occurred along this ill-defined border (*see* conflicts 2.28; 2.32; 2.36; 2.43). In January 1995 a war with Peru erupted in the small remote Condor Mountain region where the boundary prescribed by the 1942 Río Protocol was in dispute. Peru launched military raids, and Ecuador defended and held its positions. Ecuador called for a cease-fire and diplomatic negotiations.

In February 1995 the two countries held negotiations to achieve a cease-fire. The negotiations took place in Brazil with the assistance of the guarantor countries: Argentina, Brazil, Chile, and the United States. On February 17 the Declaración de Itamaraty was signed. In addition to a cease-fire, the agreement included a separation of the armed forces, the demilitarization of the conflict zone under the supervision of military observers from the guarantor countries, and the determination to solve all pending "impasses" between Ecuador and Peru. The Mission of Military Observers Ecuador–Peru (MOMEP) was implemented and oversaw the separation of forces and the demilitarization of the zone.

On October 25, 1998, the conflict was settled permanently by the signing of another peace treaty. The existing status quo was to a large extent acknowledged: Peru was awarded the disputed area, but in return Ecuador was granted commercial rights and maritime law on the Amazon River, as well as the private and economic use of a large area (20 square kilometers) in the Tiwinza Ravine. To prevent future military clashes, the peace treaty obliged both parties to establish a national park along their borders, in which no troops may be stationed.

References

Embassy of Ecuador. 2002. "Ecuador–Peru Peace Process: History of the Dispute": http://www.ecuador.org/ecuadorperu.html (accessed March 24, 2002).

KOSIMO. 1998. "Conflict Barometer." Annual publication from the Heidelberg Institute for International Conflict Research. http://www.hiik.de.

Reuters Alert Net. 2001. "Ecuador." Country Profile: http://www.alertnet.org/thefacts/countryprofiles/ (accessed March 24, 2002).

2.45 Belize–Guatemala: Postindependence Territorial Dispute and Border Incidents August 1995

A British colony in the nineteenth century, the tiny Central American country of Belize became fully independent in 1981. Guatemala had long claimed Belize as part of its own territory, but pre-independence negotiations had never resolved the issue. Britain had agreed to guarantee Belize's security immediately following the country's independence and had left a military force there. Belize took over full responsibility for its own defense in 1990.

Friendly relations between Belize and Guatemala were hindered by a poorly demarcated border and Guatemala's refusal to recognize Belize's independence. Tensions escalated alarmingly in August 1995, when Belizean army units crossed the border into Guatemala and began harassing local villagers. Guatemala promptly reinforced its troops in border areas and threatened a strong retaliation if any further territorial violations occurred. Tensions remained high, and many feared war would break out. There were no further incidents, however, and the conflict lapsed.

References

Child, J. 1985. *Geopolitics and Conflict in South America: Quarrels Among Neighbors.* New York: Praeger.

Day, A., ed. 1987. *Border and Territorial Disputes.* 2d edition. Burnt Mill, Harlow (Essex), England: Longman.

Asia: East Asia and the Pacific

List of Conflicts

3.1 China: Civil War 163
1945–1949

3.2 The Netherlands–The Dutch East Indies: Indonesian Nationalism and War of Independence 164
Late 1945–November 1949

3.3 France–Indochina: Independence Struggle 165
December 1945–July 1954

3.4 United Kingdom–Malaya and Singapore: Anti-British Communist Insurgency and the Malayan Emergency 165
June 1948–July 1960

3.5 Burma: Kuomintang/People's Liberation Army Cross-Border Conflict 166
August 1948–1954

3.6 Burma (Myanmar): Karen Separatist Insurgency and Civil War 167
January 1949–Ongoing

3.7 China–Taiwan: Communist-Nationalist Conflict in the Straits of Formosa 168
October 1949–June 1953

3.8 United States–USSR: Cold War Air Incidents 168
April–October 1950

3.9 United States–North Korea: Cold War Territorial Dispute and the Korean War 169
June 1950–July 1953

3.10 China–Portugal: The Macao Territorial Conflict 169
July–August 1952

3.11 USSR–United States: Cold War Air Incidents 170
October 1952–July 1956

3.12 Cambodia–Siam (Thailand): Border Conflict and the Occupation of the Temple of Preah Vihear 170
Early 1953–May 1975

3.13 China–United States/Taiwan: The Quemoy Confrontation 171
April 1954–April 1955

3.14 Taiwan–South Vietnam: The Paracel Islands Dispute 172
June–August 1956

3.15 China–United States/Taiwan: Communist-Nationalist Territorial Dispute and Bombardment of the Quemoy Islands 172
July–December 1958

3.16 Laos: Political Anarchy and the First Laotian Civil War 173
December 1958–1962

3.17 North Vietnam–South Vietnam/United States: Communist Vietcong Insurgency, Anti-communist U.S. Military Intervention, and Civil War 173
December 1960–May 1975

3.18 Indonesia–Malaysia: Separatist Civil Disturbances and the Borneo Conflict 174
1962–November 1965

3.19 Indonesia–The Netherlands: West Irian Administration Dispute and Separatist Insurgency 175
January–August 1962

3.20 China–Taiwan: CCP-KMT Territorial Dispute and Invasion Threat 175
March–December 1962

3.21 South Vietnam–Cambodia: Anti-Vietminh Cross-Border Raids 176
March–December 1964

3.22 North Vietnam–Laos: Political Anarchy and the Second Laotian Civil War 176
April 1964–December 1966

3.23 North Vietnam–United States: The Vietnam War 177
August 1964–May 1975

3.24 Irian Jaya–Indonesia: Territorial Dispute and Secession Insurgency 178
1965–Ongoing

3.25 North Korea–South Korea: Cold War Dispute and Border Incidents 179
Mid-1965–March 1968

3.26 North Korea–United States: USS *Pueblo* Seizure 179
January–December 1968

3.27 China–Burma: Tribal Conflicts and Border Incidents 180
January–November 1969

3.28 Cambodia (Kampuchea)–South Vietnam/United States: U.S. Bombing Campaign and Vietnam War 180
January 1970–April 1975

3.29 Mindanao–The Philippines: Communal Violence, Land Disputes, and Muslim Secessionist Insurgency 181
January 1970–Ongoing

3.30 South Vietnam–China: Territorial Dispute and the Paracel Islands 182
January 1974

3.31 North Korea–South Korea: Demilitarized Zone and Invasion Threat 182
February–July 1975

3.32 Cambodia (Kampuchea)–United States: Post–Vietnam War Tensions and the *Mayaguez* Incident 183
May 1975

3.33 Laos–Thailand: Postrevolution Exodus and Border Incidents 183
June 1975–January 1976

3.34 East Timor–Indonesia: Independence Struggle 184
October 1975–May 2002

3.35 Cambodia (Kampuchea)–Thailand: Refugee Influx, Regional Tensions, and Border Skirmishes 185
December 1975–February 1976

3.36 Thailand–Cambodia (Kampuchea): Refugee Influx, Regional Instability, and Khmer Rouge Border Incidents 185
November–December 1976

3.37 Cambodia (Kampuchea)–Thailand: Refugee Influx, Regional Instability, and Khmer Rouge Border Incidents 186
January 1977–October 1978

3.38 Cambodia (Kampuchea)–Vietnam: Border Fighting, Vietnamese Invasion, and the Cambodian Civil War 187
January 1979–Ongoing

3.39 China–Vietnam: Regional Rivalry and Border War 188
January 1979–June 1982

3.40 Cambodia (Kampuchea)–Thailand: Khmer Rouge Insurgency and Border Conflict 188
December 1979–October 1980

3.41 Espiritu Santo–Vanuatu (The New Hebrides): Secession Attempt 189
May–September 1980

3.42 Indonesia–Papua New Guinea (PNG): Secessionist Warfare, Border Incidents, and the Irian Jaya Dispute 189
May 1982–October 1984

3.43 Laos–Thailand: Territorial Dispute and Border Incidents 190
June 1982

3.44 China–Vietnam: Regional Rivalry and Border Conflict 190
April 1983

3.45 Vietnam–China: Regional Rivalry and Border Conflict 190
January 1984–March 1987

3.46 Burma–Thailand: Karen Separatist Insurgency, Counterinsurgency Raids, and Border Incidents 191
March 1984

3.47 Thailand–Laos: Boundary Dispute and Border War 191
June 1984–December 1988

3.48 North Korea–South Korea: Cold War Border Incidents 192
November 1984

3.49 Vietnam–China: Regional Rivalry, Sovereignty Dispute, and the Spratly Islands Dispute 192
March 1988

3.50 Bougainville–Papua New Guinea: Separatist Insurgency and Secession Attempt 192
October 1988–Ongoing

3.51 Burma (Myanmar)–Bangladesh: Rohingya Muslim Rebellion and Border Incidents 193
December 1991

3.52 North Korea–South Korea: Historical Enmity and Border Incident 194
May 1992

3.53 Burma (Myanmar)–Bangladesh: Border Incidents 194
March–September 1993

3.54 Burma (Myanmar)–Bangladesh: Border Incidents 194
May–August 1994

3.55 Taiwan–China: Nationalist-Communist Dispute and Shelling Incident 195
November 1994

3.56 China–The Philippines: Territorial Dispute and the Paracel and Spratly Islands Incidents 195
January–February 1995

3.57 Taiwan–Vietnam: Territorial Dispute and Spratly Islands Clash 196
March 1995

3.58 China–Taiwan: Rivalry and Military Tensions 196
January 1996–August 1999

3.59 North Korea–South Korea: Continuing Rivalry 197
September 1996–November 2000

3.60 China–The Philippines: Spratly Islands Incident 198
April 1997–July 1999

3.61 Vietnam–The Philippines: Spratly Islands Firing Incident 198
October 1999

3.62 Thailand–Laos: Mekong River Territories 199
August–September 2000

3.63 Thailand–Burma: Internal Civil Strife, Militia Activities, and Border Skirmishes 199
March–May 2001

3.64 North Korea–South Korea: Naval Incidents 200
November 2001–July 2002

3.65 Japan–North Korea: Spy Ship Incident 201
December 2001

Countries in the Region

Countries included in this region are:

- American Samoa
- Australia
- Brunei
- Burma (Myanmar)
- Cambodia (Kampuchea)
- China (including Hong Kong, Macau, and Tibet)
- Cook Islands
- East Timor
- Federated States of Micronesia
- Fiji
- Indonesia
- Japan
- Kiribati
- Laos
- Malaysia
- Marshall Islands
- Nauru
- New Zealand
- Niue
- North Korea (Democratic People's Republic of Korea)
- Palau
- Papua New Guinea
- The Philippines
- Samoa
- Singapore
- Solomon Islands
- South Korea (Republic of Korea)
- Spratly Islands
- Taiwan
- Thailand
- Tokelau
- Tonga
- Tuvalu
- Vanuatu
- Vietnam

Regional Overview

After World War II many of the countries of East Asia became independent nations. At first they were plagued by political turmoil, weak economies, ethnic strife, and social inequities, but in the 1980s and 1990s the situation improved for some, but not all, of them. A broad, seemingly incompatible, array of political institutions govern the region.

In Burma, also called Myanmar, a hard-line antidemocratic government has fostered political isolation and caused the economy to stagnate. The government is severe in its treatment of the opposition. In contrast, Cambodia held free elections under the United Nations following a peace agreement in 1991, and the Philippines' system of government, after it survived the corrupt regime of Ferdinand Marcos, is similar to that of the United States. Indonesia is a constitutional republic with an elected president, an elected parliament, and an appointed judiciary.

Malaysia, which gained independence from Britain in 1957, is a constitutional monarchy. In 1963 it joined together with Singapore, Sabah, and Sarawak to form the Federation of Malaya. Singapore then withdrew, became an independent republic in 1965, and is now a parliamentary democracy. Although other political parties exist, the same party has been in power since Singapore's independence in 1965. The government exercises tight control on the population, but the people enjoy a high standard of living and a robust economy.

Prior to French control, Vietnam was an imperial country based on the Chinese system. Modern Vietnam has a unitary system of government with a strong central government; exclusive power resides with the Vietnamese Communist Party, the sole legal party in the state. Laos is also a Communist state, established in 1975, when the Communist Pathet Lao took control of the government and ended six centuries of monarchy.

Secessionist movements create instability in the region. For example, Indonesia's population of approximately 235 million is ethnically diverse and spread out over the country's thousands of islands where many of the inhabitants want to form their own states. The first to secede was East Timor (*see* conflict 3.34). Its transition to independence was a long and bloody one in which the UN eventually intervened. Several other areas are also seeking independence from Indonesia, namely Aceh, Papua, and parts of the Moluccas.

A high level of economic disparity exists in the region, and several economic factors can be considered potential causes of conflict. The Cambodian economy is still trying to recover from the decades of war that damaged much of the country's infrastructure. Laos is one of the poorest countries in the world, with 80 percent of the population living in the countryside. Opium poppies are one of the main agricultural products in the golden triangle (Laos, Myanmar, and Thailand) and are used to finance insurgent groups.

Thailand's transition to a newly industrializing country (NIC) encouraged people to move from the countryside to the cities to seek new opportunities. Many who could find adequate employment ended up living in large slums. In 1997 an economic crisis began in Thailand, spread quickly through Southeast Asia, and affected economies worldwide. The crisis began with the collapse of the currency market in Southeast Asia. Foreign companies were less willing to invest in the region, and nonperformance of many loans and contracts exacerbated the economic downturn. Since then, the economies of these nations have recovered. The results of the collapse were most severe in Indonesia, which underwent economic, political, and social turmoil in the late 1990s.

Some countries did not suffer from the 1997 Asian financial crisis. Brunei, which has been ruled by a sultan since gaining independence from Britain in 1984, is a wealthy country with a small population and considerable oil reserves. Malaysia, too, had one of the world's fastest-growing economies during the mid-1970s to mid-1990s, mainly due to rapid industrialization. Because of Singapore's sound fiscal policies and diversified trading partners, its economy was not affected too harshly by the economic downturn. Vietnam has significant mineral deposits. It is self-sufficient in oil, which is an important part of its export earnings.

Map 4. East Asia and the Pacific

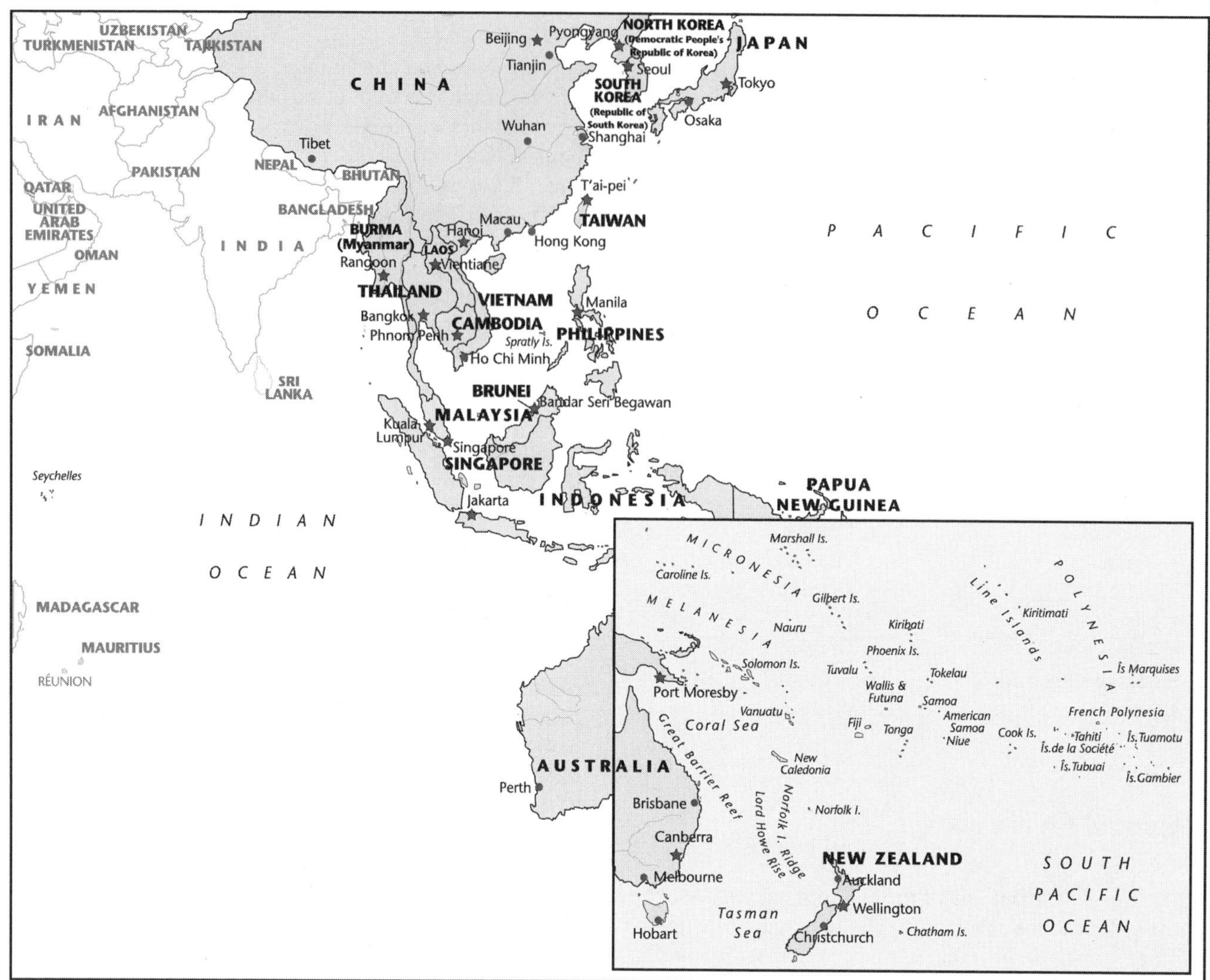

After partition in 1954, North Vietnam operated under a highly centralized, planned economy, while the South maintained a mostly free-market system with some government involvement. Vietnam's economy performed disastrously in the first decade after the 1960–1975 war (*see* conflict 3.17) because of excessive government controls, lack of managerial experience, limited capital resources, and the absence of a profit incentive. To combat these conditions, in 1986 the government launched a reform program called *doi moi* (economic renovation) to reduce government interference in the economy and develop a market-based approach to increase productivity. In the years since the *doi moi* reforms were launched, Vietnam's economic growth has accelerated.

The Pacific region is characterized by vast diversity of populations and large geographical differences between countries and between islands belonging to the same country. Because of the geographical differences, conflicts in the region are localized, are rarely interrelated, and do not have the same spillover effect into neighboring states as is the case in other regions, such as Africa and the Middle East. Nevertheless, common characteristics are apparent in the causes and dynamics of the conflicts. Compared to other developing countries, the Pacific Islands are comparatively well off, with abundant natural resources. Bougainville is rich in copper and gold, Papua New Guinea (PNG) in coffee and timber, the Solomon Islands in palm oil and gold, Fiji in timber and sugar, and New Caledonia in nickel. In all of these countries, the benefits from these resources are unevenly distributed. Export revenues go to a small economic and political elite, creating widespread ethnic and social disparity. Tension is common between the richer, Western-influenced cities, usually the capital, and the poorer, more traditional rural areas. The concentration of wealth has created a sense of injustice among many groups in society and is a source of conflict. Another source of tension is the inadequate opportunity for secondary education, which results in high unemployment and a resentful youth that can be mobilized for rebellion. A large number of those who fought in the Bougainville Revolutionary Army were unemployed youth, as were those who violently supported the coups in Fiji.

The promotion of good governance and regime stability is central to conflict prevention in the region. In general, the independent nations have replaced hereditary chiefs of the past with constitutions providing for executives and legislatures, but with varying degrees of success. In several instances, the hereditary chiefs have been incorporated into the role of government. An exception is Tonga, where a hereditary king controls politics. Corruption and nepotism are rampant in many nations of the Pacific and have led to the economic ruin of a number of nations such as Nauru (Pleasant Island).

To complicate matters further, environmental change threatens many Pacific states with extinction. Global warming is of paramount importance in the Pacific—especially to the low-lying atoll states such as Kiribati. Some of these territories rise a maximum of only five meters above sea level. A significant rise in sea level could leave these islands under water and create a refugee problem for other nations in the Pacific, most likely New Zealand and Australia. Other environmental problems include loss of ocean resources such as fish and coral reefs, the potential continuation of nuclear testing and its aftermath, loss of forest cover and other natural vegetation and animals, and natural hazards, especially destructive tropical storms.

Overview of Conflict

Since the end of World War II the countries of East Asia, particularly Southeast Asia, have been plagued by political turmoil, weak economies, ethnic strife, and social inequities, although the situation for most of these countries improved in the 1980s and 1990s. Massacres and severe human rights violations in some nations have shared the headlines with incredible economic growth in others. Ideological struggles, military coups, separatist insurgencies, and wars of independence are characteristic of the conflict environment in Southeast Asia since 1945.

For several countries in the region the transition to independence from colonial rule was bloodless, while others involved violent armed conflict that claimed many lives. One of the bloodiest battles for independence was fought in Vietnam between the French and the Vietminh, a nationalist Communist movement. The war that began in 1946 ended with the defeat of the French in 1954 and resulted in the loss of 92,000 French troops and an estimated 200,000 Vietnamese. Indonesian independence from the Netherlands was achieved through armed conflict. The Dutch were reluctant to give up Indonesia, but after several battles they agreed to independence in 1950.

Because of its position between Japan and India, and the shipping routes that traverse it, Southeast Asia was strategically important to both the Allied and Japanese forces during World War II. The region was the scene of some of the bloodiest battles of the war, and the violence continued into the cold war, with proxy wars fought on behalf of the superpowers. The superpowers could not risk a direct confrontation, so, each hoping to see its ideology triumph, they supported opposing sides in different parts of the world. The geopolitical cold war scenario was particularly apparent in the Indochinese states. The Vietnam War, which raged for twenty years, became the test case for the battle between revolutionary Communist nationalism and the American capitalist economic and political order. The Communist north was supported financially by China and the USSR, and the South by the United States. The intervention of the United States in Indochina's conflicts transformed them, determining both the longevity and destruction of the fighting. More than 58,000 American soldiers were killed, and around 2 million Vietnamese died as consequence of the war.

Map 5. Indochina

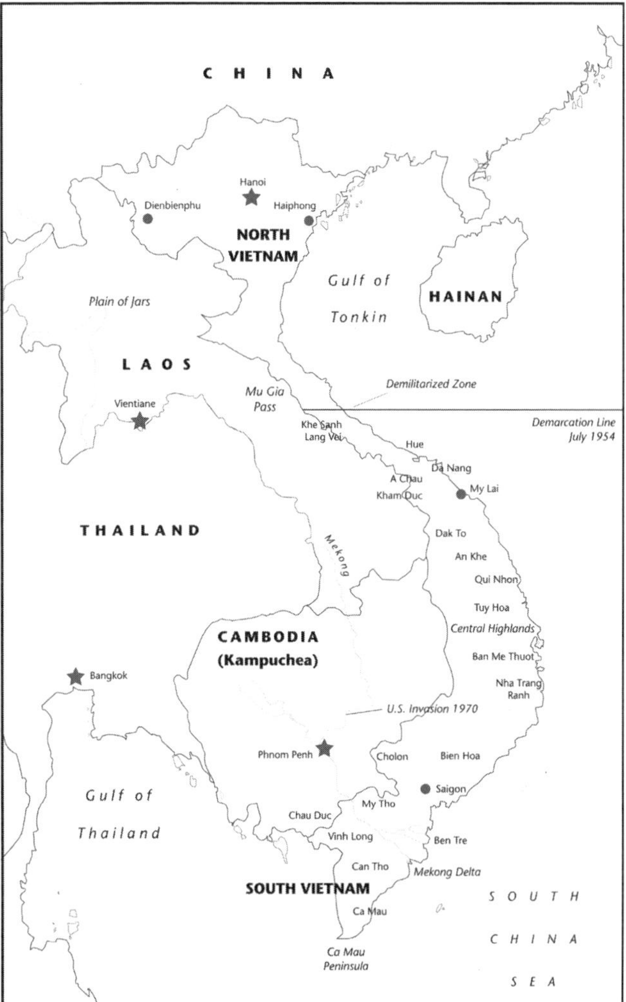

The number of conflicts initiated by East Asian countries since World War II (65) is third highest overall, after 97 for Africa and 67 for the Middle East (*see* Table 2, p. 9). The United States-Vietnam war (*see* conflict 3.23) is perhaps the best-known conflict to grip the region, but disputes involving Laos, Thailand, Cambodia (now Kampuchea), among other nations, have been similarly devastating.

In 1970 a bloody civil war began in Cambodia that ended in 1975 after the victory of Pol Pot and the Communist Khmer Rouge (*see* conflict 3.38). Pol Pot then unleashed a reign of terror that resulted in the deaths of more than 2 million Cambodians—about a quarter of the country's population at the time. Vietnamese troops invaded Cambodia in 1978, which resulted in the overthrow of Pol Pot and a civil war (*see* conflict 3.38).

Ideological and political domination played an important part in the Indonesian massacres in the mid-1960s. General Suharto came to power in 1966 after suppressing a Communist coup in which six other top military generals were killed. The subsequent crackdown, between December 1965 and early 1966, killed an estimated 500,000 to 1 million people; the worst hit areas were Central and East Java and Bali. In Bali, with a population of just under 2 million, 80,000 people were massacred. The main targets were alleged members and supporters of the Communist parties (the PKI in Bali and the BTI in the rest of Indonesia). Over his nearly twenty years as president, Suharto managed to concentrate a large slice of Indonesia's wealth in the hands of his family and their associates. Although opposition to Suharto was growing in the late 1980s and 1990s, it took a failing economy to bring him down. In the Asian financial crisis of 1997, Indonesia's currency plummeted and the economy weakened significantly, causing widespread unrest and riots. In May 1998 Suharto was forced to step down as president.

Although ethnic plurality is common in many Southeast Asian countries, it is not regarded the same way everywhere. In Malaysia and Singapore, ethnic conflict exists without recurrent ethnic violence, and ethnic minorities are accommodated within the political systems. In Burma, Indonesia, and the Philippines, however, ethnic conflict has led to violence and secessionist demands. It is helpful to understand the nature of the postcolonial states in Southeast Asia in order to comprehend the protracted ethnic conflicts that plague the region. The elites who undertook the nation-building process emphasized homogeneity and a uniform sense of national identity. This idea resulted in policies of forced assimilation and repression that became a cause of conflict. Absent was any provincial or regional autonomy or a pluralist sense of national identity.

Indonesia is a typical example. Its huge population is spread over many islands and numerous ethnic groups, some of which want to form their own state. The first area to achieve independence was East Timor, but not without a fight. When the Portuguese withdrew from East Timor in 1975, the territory was annexed by Indonesia against its will, and the Timorese people began a guerrilla war to gain their freedom. In 1999 Indonesia allowed the Timorese to vote on whether they wanted independence or to remain autonomous within Indonesia. They voted overwhelmingly for independence. At this point, Indonesian and pro-autonomy Timorese militia groups went on a violent rampage throughout the country, destroying much of the infrastructure, murdering pro-independence supporters, and forcing large numbers of East Timorese to flee (*see* conflict 3.34). After weeks of bloodshed, a UN peacekeeping mission intervened to stabilize the region.

Several other areas in Indonesia are seeking independence, including Aceh, Papua, and parts of the Moluccas. Since 1976 a civil war has simmered between the local rebel army and the Indonesian military in the northern tip of Sumatra over the future of the province of Aceh, a small but resource-rich piece of land. It is estimated that 10,000 people have died in the conflict.

In the Philippines various Muslim guerrilla groups are fighting for secession or autonomy of the Mindanao-Sulu region. Intense communal conflicts between Philippine Muslims and Catholics had by 1999 killed more than 120,000 people (*see* conflict 3.29). The Muslims, who are known as the Moros, constitute 6 percent of the population and are territorially concentrated in Mindanao-Sulu, in the southern region. Extremist Moros have engaged in terrorist activities in an effort to create an independent Islamic nation. Following the Philippines' independence from the United States, the Muslims in the south had hoped they would become a separate nation. The U.S. colonial policy of integration and assimilation of the Muslims instead sowed the seeds for the separatist conflict. After independence, the group continued to suffer from deliberate social, economic, and political deprivations that still provoke violence. The movement has been successful in achieving partial autonomy; in 1996 the Philippine government and Muslim rebel groups signed a peace accord. Fighting persisted, however, and intensified in 1999. Since the terrorist attacks on the United States on September 11, 2001, American troops have been sent to the Philippines.

Burma is an ethnically diverse country where minorities are treated appallingly; in fact, many are slave laborers. Non-Burmese ethnic groups, such as the Karen, Karenni, Mon, Rohingya, and Shan, are conducting wars of resistance against the state's severe oppression and domination. The civil wars and human rights violations have resulted in a large number of Burmese refugees fleeing to Thailand. The Burmese army are known to attack, kill, and rape refugees in the camps in Thailand, creating border tensions between the two countries (*see* conflict 3.46).

Another form of opposition against the military dictatorship is the pro-democracy movement, which is led by Aung San Suu Kyi. Her father, Aung San, gained the country's independence from Britain. Aung San Suu Kyi has become the face for the democracy struggle in Burma. She won the Nobel Peace Prize in 1991 and has been imprisoned or placed under house arrest numerous times. In 1988 pro-democracy protests reached an unprecedented level. They were brutally suppressed resulting in a civilian death toll of an estimated 10,000.

Thailand did not want to be taken over by colonial powers and so played the European powers off against each other, which meant that Siam, as it was known then, did not succumb to colonization. Although Thailand has been spared many of the conflict issues common to the process of decolonization, it has been involved in repeated conflicts with its neighbors, including four conflicts with Laos (*see* conflicts 3.33; 3.43; 3.47; 3.62), five conflicts with Cambodia (*see* conflicts 3.12; 3.35; 3.36; 3.37; 3.40), and two conflicts with Myanmar/Burma (*see* conflicts 3.46; 3.63).

In 1946, after more than 300 years under foreign rule, first by Spain and then by the United States, the Philippines became an independent democratic republic. In 1972 Philippine president Marcos imposed martial law, suspending democratic institutions and restricting civil rights. His corrupt regime introduced what came to be labeled "crony capitalism," under which Marcos created state-mandated monopolies and awarded the rights to friends and associates. The regime was toppled in 1986, and a new constitution based on democratic principles was ratified the following year. In the South various Muslim guerrilla groups are fighting either for secession or more autonomy. By 1999 more than 120,000 people had been killed in this violence (*see* conflict 3.29).

First colonized by the Dutch, Indonesia was invaded by the Japanese during World War II and gained its independence from the Netherlands in 1950 (*see* conflict 3.2). General Suharto came to power in 1966 after he put down a Communist coup. The subsequent crackdown on Communists killed between 300,000 and 1 million people. After Suharto's corrupt regime was removed from power, the conflicts in Indonesia have been predominantly secessionist struggles in various Indonesian provinces, namely Irian Jaya and East Timor (*see* conflicts 3.19; 3.24; 3.34).

Singapore became part of the British Empire in the 1820s. Britain developed Singapore into a major international trade center, and the local Malay population soon swelled with immigrants from China and India. Its strategic location on the Singapore Strait and its deep natural harbor made it an important port for British trade. The Japanese captured and occupied Singapore during World War II, and Britain reclaimed it when the war ended. Singapore gained independence in 1965 and has since developed a very successful economy and one of the world's highest standards of living. It is one of the few countries in Southeast Asia not to have experienced a succession of conflicts (*see* conflict 3.4).

France invaded Vietnam in the late nineteenth century. The French joined Vietnam with Cambodia and Laos into French Indochina and exploited Vietnamese resources to benefit France. Ho Chi Minh established the Vietminh in the face of the failure of the French to repel the Japanese during World War II. At the end of the war the Vietminh declared an independent republic, which the French refused to recognize. War broke out in 1946 when the two sides failed to reach an agreement. In 1954 the Vietminh defeated the French at the Battle of Dien Bien Phu. Later that year, the Geneva accords were signed between the Vietminh and the French, despite the United States urging France to continue the fight. The accords called for the withdrawal of French troops and a temporary division of the country into two separate zones. The Communists would withdraw to North Vietnam, and the non-Communists would move into South Vietnam (*see* conflict 3.17).

For the next twenty years the war in Vietnam raged, with the United States supporting the government in the South against the Communist North (*see* conflict 3.23). The U.S. military found it difficult to fight the Vietminh guerrillas in the jungles of Vietnam. Many of the Vietnamese lived underground in an extensive network of tunnels, which made them difficult to locate. The United States withdrew in 1973, and South Vietnam fell to a Communist offensive two years later. In 1976 a unified Communist state was established with its capital at Hanoi.

The supply route of the Vietminh, known as the Ho Chi Minh Trail, ran the length of the country and through the neighboring countries of Laos and Cambodia. As a result, the United States bombed Cambodia and Laos, killing thousands and destroying infrastructure and farmland. A great deal of unexploded ordnance remains in the countryside and still endangers the inhabitants. Chemical weapons, such as Agent Orange, used during the conflict, have resulted in birth defects and made large tracts of land barren. Following the defeat of the anti-Communist forces in Vietnam, the Pathet Lao (the Lao Communists) overthrew the monarchy and established the People's Democratic Republic of Laos (*see* conflicts 3.16; 3.22).

During World War I Japan gained control of Germany's possessions in the Pacific islands of Micronesia. After the war the League of Nations divided the islands among Japan, Australia, and New Zealand. During World War II Japan turned these islands into a battleground as it sought to expand its empire. On December 7, 1941, Japan opened the Pacific phase of the war by bombing Pearl Harbor, a large U.S. naval base in Hawaii. Japan swept across the Pacific in late 1941 and early 1942. By mid-1942, the peak of the Japanese advance, nearly the entire Pacific north of Australia was under Japanese control. Allied forces fought bloody battles to regain Japanese-held islands.

Since World War II the Pacific has been spared any large outbreaks of armed conflict. Some countries, in particular the Melanesian subregion, have, however, experienced a variety of violent conflicts and deterioration of law and order. Although the damage and loss of life in the Pacific conflicts seem small on a global scale, they have had severe consequences on the economic prosperity, social stability, and development of these small island states.

The areas most affected by violent conflict are Papua New Guinea and its Bougainville province, the Solomon Islands, Fiji, and, to a lesser degree, Vanuatu and New Caledonia. Civil wars in the Solomon Islands and Bougainville, a violent coup d'état against the elected government in Fiji, and continuing instability in PNG are all illustrative of what is often termed the Melanesian "arc of instability."

The longest and most violent conflict in the region is between the armed forces of the central government of PNG, supported by a local resistance force, and the Bougainville Revolutionary Army, which wants secession (*see* conflict 3.50). Bougainville is the most distant from the mainland capital of Port Moresby. PNG is a country of immense ethnic diversity, with more than 800 distinct languages. Bougainvilleans share a strong sense of ethnic identity with the neighboring Solomon Islands. Grievances exist among Bougainvilleans about the imposition of colonial boundaries and significant economic inequality. Many blamed the new economic inequalities on the mine operator, BCL, and the influx of non-Bougainvilleans who work in the mine. Another grievance is that the revenue from the Panguna copper mine has not benefited Bougainville while it has detrimental effects on the environment and the people.

These factors led to a separatist war, which raged from 1988 to 1997, resulting in an estimated 10,000 deaths and 60,000 displaced persons. In 1998 the war in Bougainville was to a certain degree ended and a process of postconflict reconstruction, reconciliation, and peacebuilding began. The Bougainville conflict has had international repercussions, affecting PNG's relations with its neighbors, especially the Solomon Islands and Australia, and involving the region in several attempts at conflict resolution. In addition, election violence in 2002 resulted in dozens of deaths and property destruction.

Since 1960 an independence war has been fought in West Papaya/Irian Jaya between the Indonesian government and different factions of the OPM, fighting for independence from Indonesia. The area is on the border of Southeast Asia and the Pacific. Since 2000 the war has intensified, and the Indonesian government, fearing a repeat of East Timor, has hardened its position.

The decolonization process in the Pacific was relatively peaceful, compared to Africa or Asia. In New Caledonia, however, violent clashes occurred between 1984 and 1988 between security forces, local Europeans, and the FLNKS, the independence movement of the indigenous Kanak population. The nickel mining project has also led to violence in New Caledonia.

Throughout the 1980s and 1990s, Vanuatu suffered from instability, riots, and police revolts. The conflict often relates to the Anglophone and Francophone differences from the colonial period (*see* conflict 3.41).

Fiji has experienced three military coups since 1987. The coups are related to unequal economic opportunities and political participation between indigenous Fijians and between indigenous Fijians and Indo-Fijians. The coups have caused many Indo-Fijians to flee the persecution and leave the country. Inter- and intra-ethnic tensions persist, exacerbated by a coup in May 2000. The indigenous population, fearing a loss of cultural identity and acquired privileges, sought to secure its dominance in politics and the economy, especially land ownership, but often sacrificing the rule of law, democracy, and human rights.

Decolonization of the Pacific islands changed the region's power dynamic and challenged the pattern of these countries as an exclusive sphere of Western influence. The Pacific, which had been regarded as a placid ANZUS (Australia, New Zealand, and the United States) lake, had not been considered of much strategic importance since World War II. The newly independent states were now in charge of their own foreign policy, and this had serious implications for New Zealand and Australia, particularly as the Soviet Union and China were showing interest in the region. In the 1970s and the 1980s some island states developed relations with China, Libya, the Soviet Union, and Vietnam, but no proxy wars were fought in the Pacific. The two cold war camps used aid to gain influence, but cold war politics had no significant impact on regional conflict.

Libya's presence in the Pacific in the mid- to late 1980s was, however, a serious concern to Australia. Libya established diplomatic relations with Vanuatu, and Vanuatu dissidents and members of the militant Kanak United Liberation Front were trained in Libya. Australia increased its aid to Vanuatu from $3 million (Australian) in 1984 to $8.7 million in 1987, which was the period of Libyan and Soviet diplomatic relations and commercial and political interest.

In 2000 the Solomon Islands experienced an incident of internal conflict between the people from the island of Malaita and those from the island of Guadalcanal. The violence destroyed the Solomons' infrastructure and economy. An Australian-led peacekeeping mission began its operation to stop the violence on July 24. The opposition movement, the Malaita Eagle Force (MEF), was mainly lead by warlord Harold Keke, who surrendered not long after the coalition moved in. With the rebel groups agreeing to disarm, the peacekeeping forces declared the mission a success on October 29.

Conflict Management

In 1967 Indonesia, Malaysia, the Philippines, Singapore, and Thailand created the Association of Southeast Asian Nations (ASEAN) to promote regional economic growth, political stability, social progress, and cultural development. Since then, Brunei (1984), Vietnam (1995), Laos (1997), and Myanmar and Cambodia (1999) have joined ASEAN. The association and the concept of a zone of peace, freedom, and neutrality illustrate these countries' attempt to maintain peace and security through regional mechanisms.

Association of Southeast Asian Nations

In the beginning, ASEAN's concerns were primarily economic, and, although regional security was a major motivation for the founding states in 1967, it was not addressed as such. "It was contemplated in practical terms as a by-product of institutionalized regional reconciliation. To that end, the five founding governments hoped in time to attract to their ranks all of the states of Southeast Asia" (Leifer 1989). Most important, ASEAN members expressed a strong organizational commitment to the peaceful settlement of conflicts in its region. To achieve this goal, ASEAN's members have focused more on providing a "collective political defense" rather than providing any form of military defense. ASEAN is geographically homogenous and has a resource-rich membership, but the organization has lacked cohesiveness where security issues have involved member states (Grinter and Kihl 1987). "In corporate decision-making, ASEAN has abided by the principle of consensus which has meant that policy initiatives can arise only on the basis of a common denominator" (Leifer 1989).

ASEAN has taken time to develop into a multilevel organization, from the first declaration in 1967 to the Treaty of Amity and Cooperation in Southeast Asia, signed in Indonesia on February 24, 1976. In its first decade the organization utilized only the annual ministerial meeting (AMM), but now it has four structures responsible for promoting "habits of dialogue and functional cooperation among its members" (Khong 1997). In addition to the AMM, ASEAN's structures for dialogue and conflict management include summit meetings of the heads of government, the secretariat and secretary-general, and specialist ad hoc bodies. Heads of government summit meetings, however, are so infrequent that the AMM has effectively become the primary decision-making body of the organization (Wah 1995). The AMM is a plenary body of foreign ministers and can meet more than once a year. According to the treaty, member states were committed to settle conflicts through regional processes, namely, through an established High Council. The High Council was to "take cognizance of the conflict or the situation and recommend to the parties in conflict appropriate means of settlement such as good offices, mediation, inquiry or conciliation. The High Council could however offer its good offices, or upon agreement of the parties in conflict, constitute itself into a committee of mediation, inquiry or conciliation" (Article 15). Although the treaty specified this conflict management mechanism, it has never been activated (Haas 1989).

The secretariat was not established until 1982, and its head was described as "Secretary-General of the ASEAN Secretariat and *not* of ASEAN" (Leifer 1989). The position's scope did not surpass the authority of national secretariats. Moreover, the secretary-general was not an active mediator. Appointed by the ASEAN heads of government with the advice of the AMM, the secretary-general's office was critically referred to as a "glorified post office," operating within a minimal budget, few staff, and short-term tenure (Wah 1995). In 1993, however, the role was enhanced: "to initiate, advise, coordinate and implement ASEAN activities and the status of the Secretariat, the Secretary-General is now re-designated as the secretary-general of ASEAN and given ministerial [as opposed to the previously ambassadorial] status" (Wah 1995). The secretary-general provides an important functional link between the AMM and economic institutions, but so far the role has not been used for mediation.

Since 1990 ASEAN has undergone a series of institution-building measures, broadening its capacity to promote regional cooperation and security, but it still has no permanent body specifically mandated to deal with conflict management. Instead, ASEAN uses a relatively new conflict management mechanism, an ad hoc body of mediators. The group was "established as a legal mechanism for the peaceful settlement of conflicts. ASEAN members are legally bound to seek its help before turning elsewhere for assistance in the event of a conflict. Members so far have not needed to make use of this facility" (Sutterlin 1995). Open discussions on ASEAN peacekeeping and peacemaking roles were held in 1996 between ASEAN representatives and UN Secretary-General Boutros Boutros-Ghali (Alley 1998). At present, ASEAN has no mechanism for conducting peacekeeping, but contributed extensively to the UN Transitional Authority in Cambodia (UNTAC) (Alley 1998). Ministerial and civil service cooperation with the UN is fostered through the ASEAN Regional Forum (ARF) established in 1994 (Alley 1998; Khong 1997; Ramsbotham and Woodhouse 1999). Indeed, the founding of ARF was a response to Boutros-Ghali's recommendation for an integrated approach to conflict management in his 1992 report, *An Agenda for Peace* (Alley 1998).

A prevention mechanism, ASEAN's Regional Security Forum (RSF), aims to maintain the consensus of Southeast Asian nations and prevent regional conflicts, operating with the central principle of noninterference in internal state matters (Miall et al. 1999). ASEAN is only beginning to take its position as a regional conflict manager and may define its role as it increases its activity. Alley, however, predicts that the extent of ASEAN's cooperation with the UN in a broader conflict management role will depend on "unresolved North/South asymmetries" (Alley 1998). Greater cooperation between the UN and ASEAN also depends on UN Security Council reform, allowing a greater regional representation and small state presence.

In practice, ASEAN has conducted mediation in two conflicts, having minimal impact (*see* conflicts 3.38; 3.39). ASEAN made its first appearance in the arena of international conflict mediation in the Cambodian Civil War (January 1979–Ongoing). ASEAN offered to mediate between the parties, but the offer was not accepted. This conflict has been intense, resulting in approximately 500,000 fatalities to date. ASEAN's ability to resolve it was directly affected by the presence of competing foreign interests in Southeast Asia and their potential to cause serious regional instability.[1] Even though ASEAN's offers to mediate were refused, the organization provided a valuable forum for discussions between members of the ad hoc committee and ASEAN foreign ministers at Kuala Lumpur (July 6–8, 1985). Overall, ASEAN's performance during Cambodia's civil war bolstered the organization's political solidarity (Sutterlin 1995).

Any strengthening of organizational cohesiveness gained after ASEAN's effort in Cambodia was not particularly evident during the border war between China and Vietnam (January 1979–June 1982). ASEAN offered assistance, but generally its response was to maintain an air of neutrality. ASEAN appeared divided over how seriously to approach the Chinese acts of aggression. Malaysia and Indonesia viewed the action more seriously than did Thailand and Singapore. The neutral response from ASEAN was symbolic of its unwillingness to take sides. It appeared that regional actors feared Vietnamese supremacy in the region as much as they feared the growth of Chinese Communist influence. After the Chinese seventeen-day invasion, ASEAN leaders engaged in a number of visits and talks. On March 4, 1979, after meeting in Jogjakarta, the heads of government of Indonesia and Malaysia decided to open communications with Vietnam and China. This offer was met by Vietnam pointing out that ASEAN states should refrain from intervention. The evidence of ASEAN practice suggests that, although the organization has a strong degree of regional solidarity, it was able to act only symbolically when conflicts involved member states. Further evidence of this weakness can be seen in the organization's approach to the status of Myanmar. ASEAN states, who "as a group, have strongly resisted calls for the application of sanctions against Myanmar," have done so despite the ongoing nature of this complex ideological conflict (Farer 1993).

So far, ASEAN has mediated twice (independently) and once with the UN (cooperatively). The infrequency of ASEAN mediation may be due to the fact that because of its alliance origins, it does not possess the necessary machinery to control the use of force between its members. It does, however, possess distinct regional organization characteristics: organizational institutions, constitutional consistency with the UN Charter, and cooperative organizational obligations and objectives.

This said, there is good reason to recognize the organization's potential role in the Asia-Pacific region. With the development of ARF, ASEAN has become a new "player in the regional security network by creating opportunities to enter dialogue with the adversaries" (Sum 1996). ARF comprises ASEAN foreign ministers and ASEAN dialogue partners—Australia, Canada, the European Union, Japan, New Zealand, South Korea, and the United States. For broader regional security discussions, six other regional actors can participate: Cambodia, China, Laos, Papua New Guinea, Russia, and Vietnam (Khong 1997).

In this regard, one can argue that ASEAN is seeking to serve as regional security balancer or mediator (Sum 1996). With the so-called arc of instability stretching from Melanesia through the Pacific to Asia, the need to develop a more active conflict management presence in the region is paramount and it appears that ASEAN is poised to take up this challenge.

The Pacific area has adopted a regional approach to conflict prevention and management. As the two major players in the Pacific, Australia and New Zealand are expected to and often live up to their role as overseers of peace and security in the region. The nations of Asia are showing greater interest in the Pacific region, in particular China, Japan, Korea, and Taiwan. The Pacific Islands Forum and its Regional Security Committee are mechanisms for debating and pursuing regional security issues.

In the Solomon Islands, Australia and New Zealand facilitated a cease-fire between warring ethnic groups on August 5, 2000, followed by the Townsville Peace Agreement on October 15, and the Marau Peace Agreement on February 7, 2001. The agreements, however, have not brought about sustainable peace in the Solomons, as fighting continues.

New Zealand and Australia each has its own perception of and relationship with the Pacific. New Zealand has a large Pacific Island community, which makes up almost 20 percent of its population, and New Zealand Maori have a unique perspective of the Pacific. New Zealand forsook the ANZUS alliance, an action unthinkable for Australia, and instead adopted an antinuclear stance in line with its Pacific island neighbors. Australia lacks the geographic isolation of New Zealand and therefore has a heightened sense of strategic insecurity. New Zealand is known for a more culturally sensitive approach and has been favored over Australia as conflict manager in the region. Instability in the Pacific Islands has become a real concern for New Zealand and Australia, as it increases crime and money laundering, creates refugee flows, and heightens the threat of terrorism.

Pacific Islands Forum

The South Pacific Forum (SPF) was established August 5, 1971, providing Pacific Island nations with a forum "to discuss regional issues and present collective views to the international community" (34th PIF Communiqué 2003). On October 27, 2000, the organization changed its name to Pacific Islands Forum (PIF). Its membership is regionally homogenous, but comprises the most geographically dispersed region of the world; it covers an oceanic area that makes up approximately 18 percent of the globe.

1. For example, ASEAN proposed a resolution for the cessation of hostilities in Southeast Asia in February 1979 but the USSR rejected it.

The forum has evolved to become proactive in the maintenance of peace and security in the region, although its involvement in conflict management is in its infancy. The forum has focused on several issues that could potentially undermine regional stability: international terrorism; the war in Bougainville (1988–1997); the coups and continuing instability in Fiji (1987 and 2000–Ongoing); and internal instability in the Solomon Islands (1999–Ongoing).

The Thirty-third Pacific Islands Forum Communiqué (August 15–17, 2002) reinforced the forum's commitment to the Biketawa Declaration signed at Biketawa, Kiribati, on October 28, 2000. This declaration engaged the forum's first observer mission, the Forum Elections Observer Mission, established to observe the 2001 Solomon Islands elections and to support the implementation of a democratic process. This "signals an increasingly proactive role by the Forum in maintaining peace and stability in the region" (PIFS 2003).

One of the primary concerns of the organization is the promotion of good governance and stability in the region, that is, a focus on preventive measures to reduce the likelihood of conflict. Like most of the organizations discussed here, PIF relies on its member states to provide the resources to prevent, manage, and resolve conflicts. Unfortunately, much of the responsibility falls on the organization's two most powerful regional players, Australia and New Zealand. Although reliant on these two member states for logistical support, military personnel, and expertise, PIF maintains a strong multilateral presence in the make up of PIF task forces.

References

Alley, R. 1998. *The United Nations in Southeast Asia and the South Pacific.* International Political Economy Series. London: Macmillan.

Farer, T. J. 1993. "The Role of Regional Collective Security Arrangements." In *Collective Security in a Changing World.* A World Peace Foundation Study. Weiss, T.G., ed. Boulder: Lynne Rienner, 153–186.

Grinter, L.E., and Y.W. Kihl, eds. 1987. *East Asian Conflict Zones: Prospects for Regional Stability and Deescalation.* New York: St. Martin's.

Haas, M. 1989. "ASEAN: A Spirit of Cooperation to be Emulated." Chapter 7 of *The Asian Way to Peace—A Story of Regional Cooperation.* New York: Praeger, 124–148.

Khong, Y.F. 1997. "ASEAN and the Southeast Asian Security Complex." Chapter 14 of *Regional Orders—Building Security in a New World.* Lake, D.A., and P.M. Morgan, eds. University Park: Pennsylvania State University Press, 318–339.

Leifer, M. 1989. *ASEAN and the Security of South-East Asia.* London: Routledge.

Miall, H., O. Ramsbotham, and T. Woodhouse. 1999. *Contemporary Conflict Resolution—The Prevention, Management and Transformation of Deadly Conflicts.* Malden, Mass.: Polity Press, published by Blackwell Publishers.

Pacific Islands Forum Secretariat (PIFS). 2003. "34th Pacific Islands Forum Communiqué 2003." PIFS (03)11. Auckland, New Zealand, August 14–16, 2003. http://www.forumsec.org.fj/ (accessed July 14, 2004).

Pacific Islands Forum Secretariat (PIFS). 2002. "33rd Pacific Islands Forum Communiqué 2002." Suva, Fiji Islands. August 15–17, 2002. PIFS(02)8. http://www.forumsec.org.fj/ (accessed July 14, 2004).

Pacific Islands Forum Secretariat (PIFS). 2000. "31st Pacific Islands Forum Communiqué 2000. Includes Attachment 1: Biketawa Declaration, signed October 28, 2000. Tarawa, Republic of Kiribati, October 27–30, 2000. http://www.forumsec.org.fj/ (accessed July 14, 2004).

Ramsbotham, O., and T. Woodhouse. 1999. *Encyclopedia of International Peacekeeping Operations.* Santa Barbara: Calif.: ABC-CLIO.

Sum, Ngai-Ling. 1996. "The Newly Industrial Countries (NICs) and Competing Strategies of East Asian Regionalism." Chapter 7 of *Regionalism and World Order.* Gamble, A., and A. Payne, eds. London: Macmillan, 207–245.

Sutterlin, J.S. 1995. "The Potential of Regional Organizations." Chapter 7 of *The United Nations and the Maintenance of International Security—A Challenge To Be Met.* Sutterlin, J.S., ed. Westport, Conn.: Praeger, 93–111.

Wah, C.K. 1995. "ASEAN: Consolidation and Institutional Change." *Pacific Review* 8, No. 3: 424–439.

3.1 China: Civil War 1945–1949

The roots of the Chinese civil war go back to 1927, when Chiang Kai-shek, leader of the Kuomintang (KMT), or Nationalists, ousted the Chinese warlords with the help of his Communist allies. Chiang then seized Shanghai in an effort to eliminate all Chinese Communist Party (CCP) members and their sympathizers. At least 10,000 people were slaughtered in the process.

The Communists fled to southern and central China, where they rebuilt the party among the peasantry. Constantly harassed by KMT troops and facing incredible barriers, the Red Army under Mao Zedong undertook the fabled Long March in 1934 and 1935, in which 90,000 men and women marched west to Guizhou province and then to Shaanxi province in the north; more than half the marchers died during this one-year trek of some 9,660 kilometers (6,200 miles).

Believing the Red Army to be defeated, Chiang turned his attention to the Japanese, who had invaded China in 1937 prior to World War II. Mao's troops joined the Nationalists in the war against the Japanese, but, following Japan's surrender in 1945, the CCP immediately began operations against Chiang's army for control of the country.

From about 1937 until the end of World War II, the United States sought to broker a political settlement between the two parties. In the months preceding the civil war, the Soviet Union also became involved in a minor way. U.S. Special Envoy George C. Marshall undertook to mediate between the parties from December 23, 1945, to January 10, 1946, managing to secure a cease-fire lasting until April 1946, but fighting broke out again in Manchuria.

Throughout the course of the conflict, the United States gave extensive military aid to the Nationalists. Despite the U.S. aid, the Communists steadily gained battlefield dominance, culminating in victory over the Nationalists in January 1949. The CCP declared the mainland to be the People's Republic of China on October 1, 1949. The fighting was often intense, and an estimated 100,000 people died. Following their military defeat, the Nationalists fled to Formosa (Taiwan) in the Formosa Strait, where their presence continued to be the source of friction and armed conflict (*see* conflicts 3.7; 3.13; 3.15; 3.20; 3.55; 3.58).

Although the Soviet Union immediately recognized Mao's new republic, the United States insisted that Chiang Kai-shek's regime was China's true government. This state of affairs lasted into the 1970s, when China was admitted to the United Nations. China remains committed to reuniting the Formosa islands, especially Taiwan, with the mainland. The rise of the People's Republic caused a major upheaval in Asia and frequent conflicts (*see* conflicts 3.10; 3.27; 3.30; 3.39; 3.44; 3.45; 3.49; 3.56; 3.60).

References

Brogan, P. 1989. *World Conflicts: Why and Where They Are Happening.* London: Bloomsbury.

Butterworth, R.L. 1978. *Moderation from Management: International Organizations and Peace.* Pittsburgh: Center for International Studies, University of Pittsburgh.

Chiu, H., ed. 1979. *China and the Taiwan Issue.* New York: Praeger.

Fairbank, J.K. 1971. *The United States and China.* Cambridge: Harvard University Press.

Gurtov, M., and B. Hwang. 1980. *China Under Threat: The Politics of Strategy and Diplomacy.* Baltimore: Johns Hopkins University Press.

Hinton, H.C. 1966. *Communist China in World Politics.* New York: Houghton Mifflin.

Li, S. 1971. *The Ageless Chinese: A History.* New York: Charles Scribner and Sons.

Tillema, H.K. 1991. *International Armed Conflict Since 1945: A Bibliographic Handbook of Wars and Military Interventions.* Boulder: Westview.

Watson, F. 1966. *The Frontiers of China.* New York: Praeger.

3.2 The Netherlands–The Dutch East Indies: Indonesian Nationalism and War of Independence Late 1945–November 1949

The Netherlands acquired control over the Dutch East Indies between the seventeenth and early nineteenth centuries. Japan seized the islands in 1942. Two days after Japan's surrender at the end of World War II, on August 16, 1945, Indonesian nationalists led by Ahmed Sukarno declared independence. Armed with Japanese weapons, the nationalists resisted attempts by British and Australian troops to take control of the East Indies and to facilitate the Japanese surrender. The first Dutch troops arrived in October 1945, with the clear aim of regaining colonial control over their former possession; they were also forcefully resisted. At this stage the fighting was mainly confined to Java and Sumatra.

Early mediation efforts failed to forge a political solution to the war. Britain exerted diplomatic pressure on the nationalists and the Dutch to negotiate before withdrawing British troops in late 1946. The United States threatened to cut off Marshall Plan aid if the Dutch did not grant independence. Negotiations and guerrilla warfare proceeded simultaneously for the next three years, and full-scale conflict was limited to two Dutch "police actions." Although the Dutch were fairly successful in reducing the territory under the nationalists' control, they had no allies and were under great pressure from the international community.

Britain, the United States, and the United Nations all attempted to mediate; in all, seventeen different mediation attempts and numerous negotiation efforts took place. The breakthrough came when the UN Commission for Indonesia (UNCI) convened two conferences. The first ran from April 14 to August 1, 1948, and produced an agreement facilitating the withdrawal of Dutch troops and a cessation of hostilities on August 10. A second conference, held from August to November 1949, formalized Indonesian independence, which was duly declared in December 1949.

Throughout the course of the conflict, tens of thousands of Indonesians died; Dutch and British losses were put at 400 and 600, respectively. Although the Dutch retained control of West New Guinea, later renamed Irian Jaya, their presence produced protracted fighting in later years (*see* conflict 3.19).

References

Dahm, B. 1971. *History of Indonesia in the Twentieth Century.* Translated by P.S. Falla. New York: Praeger.

Jones, H. 1971. *Indonesia: The Possible Dream.* New York: Harcourt, Brace, Jovanovich.

Lijphart, A. 1966. *The Trauma of Decolonization: The Dutch and West New Guinea.* New Haven: Yale University Press.

Suter, K.D. 1979. *West Irian, East Timor, and Indonesia.* London: Minority Rights Group.

Tillema, H.K. 1991. *International Armed Conflict Since 1945: A Bibliographic Handbook of Wars and Military Interventions.* Boulder: Westview.

Wehl, D. 1948. *The Birth of Indonesia.* London: Allen and Unwin.

3.3 France–Indochina: Independence Struggle December 1945–July 1954

France acquired protectorates in Cambodia, Laos, and Vietnam—known as French Indochina—in the nineteenth century and lost them to Japan in World War II. French Indochina's struggle for independence grew out of France's postwar attempts to reassert control over the region in the wake of Japan's capitulation and the subsequent supervision of the Japanese surrender by British and Chinese forces.

By March 1946 France had regained control over Indochina, despite violent resistance from local nationalist forces, which had declared independence with Japanese encouragement. France and Vietnam began negotiations, but the talks ceased with the eruption of more serious fighting after the French bombardment of Haiphong in November 1946, in retaliation for continued guerrilla attacks on French forces.

In the period up to 1949, Vietnamese guerrilla forces eroded French dominance throughout much of Vietnam. The position of the French worsened in the wake of the Chinese civil war, when Communist China began providing military support for the Vietnamese guerrillas.

Concurrent with the conflict in Vietnam, guerrilla action against the French was taking place in Laos and Cambodia. Thailand was drawn into the conflict when it sent forces to protect territories in Laos and Cambodia that were seized with Japanese acquiescence in 1941. Thai military involvement ended in December 1946, in the wake of repeated French incursions into Thai territory. Successful resistance from the Lao Issara (Free Lao) in Laos and the Khmer Issarak (Free Cambodia) in Cambodia resulted in their gaining independence in late 1953.

The end of French military involvement in Laos and Cambodia allowed France to devote its full attention to the worsening situation in Vietnam, where Vietminh forces controlled most of the country and parts of Cambodia and Laos. The Vietminh were Communist forces led by Ho Chi Minh, who had begun a liberation movement in the 1920s, was driven underground, and returned to Vietnam during World War II to fight the Japanese. The army he raised upon his return, the Vietminh, attacked the French forces concentrated at Dienbienphu in March 1954. This was the climactic battle of the war, and it ended with the French surrendering on May 7, 1954. In July France accepted a negotiated settlement providing for full French withdrawal, the independence of Laos and Cambodia, and the partition of North and South Vietnam.

The war cost at least 500,000 lives, including approximately 90,000 French fatalities and about 40 British troops. There were no outside attempts at peaceful conflict management, despite numerous negotiations. This was not the end of conflict in Indochina, however; a much more destructive conflict, the Vietnam War, began in 1960 (*see* conflict 3.17).

References

Caldwell, M., and L. Tan. 1973. *Cambodia in the Southeast Asian War.* New York: Monthly Review Press.

Chandler, D.P. 1991. *The Tragedy of Cambodian History: Politics, War, and Revolution Since 1945.* New Haven: Yale University Press.

Davidson, P. 1988. *Vietnam at War: The History, 1946–1975.* Novato, Calif.: Presidio.

Deane, H. 1963. *The War in Vietnam.* New York: Monthly Review Press.

Devillers, P., and J. Lacouture. 1969. *End of a War: Indochina 1954.* London: Pall Mall.

Georges, A. 1974. *Charles de Gaulle et la guerre d'Indochine.* Paris: Nouvelles Editions Latines.

Karnow, S. 1983. *Vietnam: A History.* New York: Viking.

Kelly, G.A. 1965. *Lost Soldiers: The French Army and Empire in Crisis, 1947–1962.* Cambridge: MIT Press.

Kiernan, B., and C. Boua. 1982. *Peasants and Politics in Kampuchea, 1942–1981.* London: Zed.

Lancaster, D. 1961. *The Emancipation of French Indochina.* New York: Oxford University Press.

O'Ballance, E. 1964. *The Indo-China War, 1945–1954: A Study in Guerrilla Warfare.* London: Faber and Faber.

———. 1981. *The Wars in Vietnam, 1954–1980.* New enlarged edition. New York: Hippocrene.

Tillema, H.K. 1991. *International Armed Conflict Since 1945: A Bibliographic Handbook of Wars and Military Interventions.* Boulder: Westview.

3.4 United Kingdom–Malaya and Singapore: Anti-British Communist Insurgency and the Malayan Emergency June 1948–July 1960

Britain gained control of the Malay Peninsula in the nineteenth century but lost it to the Japanese after the defeat of Singapore early in World War II. After the war

Britain resumed control and reformulated the prewar colonial arrangements to include Singapore. The new entity, called the Union of Malaya, signified a loss of some autonomy to local rulers, and opposition to British control grew as a consequence.

In 1948 the Communist Malayan People's Anti-British Army (MPABA) was formed and undertook a campaign of guerrilla warfare and economic sabotage against the British-controlled government. Members were recruited almost entirely from the Chinese community in Malaya and represented the continuation of wartime resistance. The British initiated military actions in June 1948, following attacks on government posts and police and military patrols. Australian aircraft were deployed in August 1950 to provide air support for British troops, and in October 1955, Australian and New Zealand ground forces joined counterinsurgency operations.

The fighting involved small engagements in Malaya's vast jungles, which Britain's highly trained guerrilla warfare units almost always won. The insurgency gradually lost its momentum and virtually disappeared by mid-1960, owing in great part to the British army's tactic of creating "new villages" under government control. This approach to the insurgency cut the Communists off from their popular base and dried up the "sea" in which they could, according to Maoist doctrine, "swim."

More than 10,000 fatalities were reported during the course of the conflict, including 525 British soldiers and 50 New Zealand and Australian troops. The last traces of the Communist insurrection disappeared in December 1989, when the Communist Party of Malaya surrendered, although their actions had been inconsequential since the end of the emergency. Two minor attempts at conflict management took place in 1955, but neither was successful.

References

Allen, R. 1968. *Malaysia—Prospect and Retrospect: The Impact and Aftermath of Colonial Rule.* New York: Oxford University Press.

Butterworth, R.L. 1976. *Managing Interstate Conflict, 1945–1974.* Pittsburgh: Center for International Studies, University of Pittsburgh.

Clutterbuck, R. 1985. *Conflict and Violence in Singapore and Malaysia, 1945–1983.* Boulder: Westview.

O'Ballance, E. 1966. *Malaya: The Communist Insurgent War, 1948–1960.* Hamden, Conn.: Archon.

Short, A. 1975. *The Communist Insurrection in Malaya, 1948–1960.* New York: Crane, Russak.

Thompson, R. 1966. *Defeating Communist Insurgency: Experiences from Malaya and Vietnam.* London: Chatto and Windus.

Tillema, H.K. 1991. *International Armed Conflict Since 1945: A Bibliographic Handbook of Wars and Military Interventions.* Boulder: Westview.

3.5 Burma: Kuomintang/People's Liberation Army Cross-Border Conflict August 1948–1954

Following its defeat in the Chinese civil war (1945–1949), a 12,000-man Kuomintang (KMT) army known as the Yunnan Anti-Communist and National Salvation Army (YANSA), under General Li Mi, fled into Burma. It occupied part of the Shan state on the eastern border, and from its base there launched attacks against the People's Liberation Army (PLA) of China. Taiwan and the United States supported the YANSA.

The KMT army forcefully resisted Burmese troops, which tried to take control of the area, and actively supported guerrilla movements trying to overthrow the Burmese government. The Burmese government attempted to pacify the area through bombing raids, which often spilled into neighboring Thailand, sparking conflict between these two states.

After repeatedly asking Taiwan and the United States to facilitate the withdrawal of Li Mi's army, Burma took the issue to the United Nations in 1953. The U.S. military attaché in Siam, Colonel R.V. Palmer, subsequently sought to mediate the dispute. At a conference held in Rangoon and attended by Burma, Taiwan, Thailand, and the United States, an agreement was reached under which the YANSA would be removed to Taiwan. An airlift of the KMT army was undertaken in late 1953 and 1954. More than 1,000 people were estimated to have been killed during the conflict.

References

Cady, J. 1958. *A History of Modern Burma.* Ithaca, New York: Cornell University Press.

Collis, M. 1975. *Trials in Burma.* New York: AMS.

Lintner, B. 1990. *Land of Jade: A Journey Through Insurgent Burma.* Bangkok: White Lotus.

———. 1990. *The Rise and Fall of the Communist Party of Burma (CPB).* Ithaca, New York: South East Asian Program, Cornell University.

Lissak, M. 1976. *Military Roles in Modernization: Civil-Military Relations in Thailand and Burma.* Beverly Hills: Sage.

Pettman, R.H. 1973. *China in Burma's Foreign Policy.* Canberra: Australian National University Press.

Silverstein, J. 1977. *Burma: Military Rule and the Politics of Stagnation.* Ithaca, New York: Cornell University Press.

Taylor, R.H. 1973. *Foreign and Domestic Consequences of the KMT Intervention in Burma.* Ithaca, N.Y.: Southeast Asian Program, Department of Asian Studies, Cornell University.

Tillema, H.K. 1991. *International Armed Conflict Since 1945: A Bibliographic Handbook of Wars and Military Interventions.* Boulder: Westview.

3.6 Burma (Myanmar): Karen Separatist Insurgency and Civil War January 1949–Ongoing

Britain annexed Burma in the nineteenth century as part of its conquest of the Indian Subcontinent. In light of the partition of India and Burmese agitation for independence, Britain signed a treaty in October 1947 granting independence to Burma. As with the other newly independent South Asian nations, Burma immediately fractured, and a revolt staged by the Karen tribal group led to all-out civil war in the first six months of 1949. Complicating the conflict were remnants of Kuomintang armies, which had been driven out of China by Chinese Communist Party (CCP) troops and taken refuge in northern Burma. Various Communist and tribal groups also opposed the Burmese government.

The fighting was at first bitter, but no side ever achieved a decisive victory. Despite numerous campaigns, the war dragged on, eventually taking on the character of a guerrilla insurgency. There were periodic government campaigns to rid rebel areas of insurgents, while the rebels ambushed government posts and then disappeared into the dense jungle.

The war became international when the Chinese supported tribal insurgents at various times. In November 1969 Chinese soldiers actually skirmished with Burmese troops within Burma. Also, Karen insurgents were especially active along the Thai border, and Burmese attempts to quell them often carried across the border. On March 12, 1984, 200 Burmese troops crossed the Thai border in pursuit of rebels. Fifteen Burmese troops were killed in this incident when they encountered Thai border police. There were very few serious attempts at conflict management during these years, especially by outside mediators. Negotiations with some of the groups involved occasionally produced cease-fires, but the real political issues were never resolved.

From 1992 on, there were many such cross-border skirmishes, and in 1994 the Karens began to suffer some heavy defeats, culminating in the fall of Karen National Unity (KNU) headquarters at Manerplaw to government troops in early 1995. Also during this time, serious negotiations got under way between the Karen insurgents and the military government, but they proved fruitless in the long run. By the end of 1995 it was estimated that as many as 140,000 people had lost their lives, many of them civilians.

Since 1995 the military regime, the State Law and Order Restoration Council (SLORC), has shown no sign of accepting greater civilian rule, ethnic accommodation, or power-sharing. Armed opposition to the regime has weakened considerably since government offensives overran Karen strongholds in 1995 and forced the Shan-dominated Mong Tai Army to surrender in 1996. In 1997 the failure of peace negotiations led to renewed fighting between the SLORC and the KNU, and the United States imposed economic sanctions against Burma in response to the "severe repression" of the political opposition. It was reported that 10,000 Karen refugees fled to Thailand in 1997. Further incidents occurred in 1998, including another Burmese incursion into Thai territory in pursuit of Shan State National Army (SSNA) guerrillas and fleeing refugees.

Since then, confrontations have largely been avoided except when government forces enter ethnic enclaves. Nearly two years after the imposition of sanctions, and despite the government's easing of some restrictions on opposition parties, summary executions, arbitrary detentions, and forced labor still occur. Fighting also continues between Myanmar and Thailand over a border claimed by both countries, and Myanmar has accused Thai troops of aiding ethnic rebels (*see* conflicts 3.46; 3.63). In late 2000 secret talks, brokered by the United Nations, began between the government and the National League for Democracy (NLD), Myanmar's main political party. Since then the government has released dozens of political prisoners and allowed the NLD to reopen some offices. However, it is still estimated that Burma holds more than 1,500 political prisoners, at least 50,000 child soldiers, and some 800,000 people who are subjected to forced labor. Among those periodically held in house arrest is Aung San Suu Kyi, who was awarded the 1991 Nobel Peace Prize for leading a nonviolent movement to secure human rights in Myanmar.

References

Cady, J. 1958. *A History of Modern Burma.* Ithaca, N.Y.: Cornell University Press.

Collis, M. 1975. *Trials in Burma.* New York: AMS.

Gurr, T., M. Marshall, and D. Khosla. 2000. *Peace and Conflict 2001: A Global Survey of Conflicts, Self-Determination Movements, and Democracy.* College Park: Center for International Development and Conflict Management, University of Maryland.

Hinton, H.C. 1972. *China's Relations with Burma and Vietnam: A Brief Survey.* Ann Arbor, Mich.: University Microfilms.

Lintner, B. 1990. *Land of Jade: A Journey Through Insurgent Burma.* Bangkok: White Lotus.

———. 1990. *The Rise and Fall of the Communist Party of Burma (CPB).* Ithaca, N.Y.: South East Asian Program, Cornell University.

———. 1994. *Burma in Revolution: Opium and Insurgency Since 1948.* Boulder: Westview.

Lissak, M. 1976. *Military Roles in Modernization: Civil-Military Relations in Thailand and Burma.* Beverly Hills: Sage.

Reuters Alert Net. 2001. "Myanmar (formerly Burma)" Country Profile: http://www.alertnet.org/thefacts/countryprofiles/ (accessed March 2, 2002).

Silverstein, J. 1977. *Burma: Military Rule and the Politics of Stagnation.* Ithaca, N.Y.: Cornell University Press.

Smith, M. 1991. *Burma: Insurgency and the Politics of Ethnicity*. London: Atlantic Highlands.

Taylor, R.H. 1988. *The State in Burma*. Honolulu: University of Hawaii Press.

3.7 China–Taiwan: Communist-Nationalist Conflict in the Straits of Formosa October 1949–June 1953

After Chiang Kai-shek's Kuomintang (Nationalists) suffered defeat on the mainland in the Chinese civil war (*see* conflict 3.1), the KMT continued to fight from bases on Taiwan (Formosa), other offshore islands (Quemoy and Matsu), Burma, and pockets on the mainland. Immediately after proclaiming the People's Republic of China, the victorious Chinese Communist Party (CCP) was committed to a united China and therefore tried to eradicate the remaining Nationalist positions by shelling islands in Amoy (Xiamen) harbor in October 1949.* Amphibious assaults on Nationalist-held islands followed, including an unsuccessful attempt on Quemoy (Kinmen) in late October and the conquest of Hainan Island in May 1950. Small, retaliatory raids by the Nationalists and persistent bombings by the Communists continued until late 1952. A Chinese invasion of Taiwan was averted in June 1950, when the United States sent the Seventh Fleet to the Taiwan Strait.

The United States began training Taiwanese military units for large, amphibious operations in early 1952, and in October the Nationalists launched a successful amphibious attack against Communist-held Nanri Island; other, smaller assaults were made on other positions until June 1953. The Communists continued to bomb Nationalist-held islands throughout this time. The conflict cost thousands of lives—mostly military—on both sides, and no attempts were made at peaceful conflict management. Because the issues were never resolved, fighting broke out again from 1954 to 1955 and in 1958 (*see* conflicts 3.13; 3.15). Nationalist issues remain central to continuing tension between China and Taiwan, as China remains committed to uniting Taiwan with the mainland and has not ruled out using force to achieve this end (*see* conflict 3.55).

* China and Taiwan use different transliteration systems for romanizing Chinese ideographs. The Taiwanese employ the Wade-Giles system (hence, Kuomintang, Mao Tse-tung, Teng Hsiao-ping, Peking, Amoy, and so forth), while the Chinese use pinyin, resulting in much different spellings, for example, Guomindang, Mao Zedong, Deng Xioaping, Beijing, and Xinmen.

References

Chiu, H., ed. 1979. *China and the Taiwan Issue*. New York: Praeger.

Kerr, G. 1965. *Formosa Betrayed*. Boston: Houghton Mifflin.

Stolper, T. 1985. *China, Taiwan, and the Offshore Islands*. Armonk, N.Y.: M.E. Sharpe.

Tillema, H.K. 1991. *International Armed Conflict Since 1945: A Bibliographic Handbook of Wars and Military Interventions*. Boulder: Westview.

Tsou, T. 1959. *The Embroilment over Quemoy: Mao, Chiang, and Dulles*. Salt Lake City: Institute of International Studies, University of Utah.

Watson, F. 1966. *The Frontiers of China*. New York: Praeger.

3.8 United States–USSR: Cold War Air Incidents April–October 1950

Following the Berlin airlift crisis of 1948–1949, relations between the United States and the Soviet Union worsened. All across Europe and the Far East, the armed forces of the two superpowers engaged in an uneasy standoff. On April 11, 1950, the Soviet Union alleged that two days previously, a U.S. plane had flown over the Soviet republic of Latvia. When the U.S. plane failed to land on request, Soviet aircraft opened fire and shot it down. The United States then announced that on the previous day it had lost an unarmed reconnaissance plane over the Baltic Sea. Further investigations revealed that the two incidents were related and that Soviet actions had violated international law. The United States demanded that the Soviet Union investigate the incident and issue instructions to the Soviet air force not to repeat its actions. The Soviets, in reply, reiterated their earlier allegations and did not address U.S. demands. Relations continued to be tense.

On September 4, 1950, U.S. fighters allegedly shot down a Soviet aircraft off the west coast of Korea. On September 6 the Soviet Union asserted that the plane had been within Soviet airspace and warned the United States of the consequences of such an attack. The United States referred the incident to the UN Security Council, but no action was taken. In the third air incident of 1950, the Soviet Union alleged that on October 8 two U.S. aircraft strafed and bombed the Soviet airfield of Sukhaya Rechka, near the Korean border. The Soviet Union sought the strict punishment of those responsible. The United States admitted the incident on October 19 and offered to pay compensation.

Although few fatalities occurred, the growing intensity of the cold war and the increase in aggressive moves by each state to extend its areas of influence, such as in Korea, made these disputes serious. Further incidents occurred throughout the 1950s, and in 1962 the Cuban Missile Crisis brought the world to the brink of nuclear confrontation (*see* conflict 2.17).

References

Bartlett, C.J. 1994. *The Global Conflict: The International Rivalry of Great Powers, 1880–1990*. 2d edition. London: Longman.

Cimbala, S.J., and S.R. Waldman, eds. 1992. *Controlling and Ending Conflict: Issues Before and After the Cold War.* New York: Greenwood.

Gablentz, O.M. van der. 1964. *The Berlin Question in Its Relations to World Politics, 1944–1963.* Munich: Oldenbourg.

3.9 United States–North Korea: Cold War Territorial Dispute and the Korean War June 1950–July 1953

Korea was taken over by Japan in 1905 following the Russo-Japanese war. After World War II the Soviet Union and the United States accepted Japan's surrender on either side of the 38th parallel, effectively partitioning Korea. In mid-1949 Soviet and U.S. forces were withdrawn from the demarcation line, and North Korea and South Korea were left to supervise their own borders. From this point on frequent border incidents occurred, as the two governments had become implacable enemies: North Korea was a Communist state, and South Korea was pro-Western.

On June 24, 1950, North Korea invaded South Korea, quickly overwhelming the forces and surrounding Seoul, South Korea's capital. At South Korea's urgent request, the United States began military actions in aid of the South Korean forces on June 27. The UN Security Council, with the Soviet Union absent, passed a resolution requesting UN members to come to the aid of South Korea. Britain entered the war on June 28, and Australia on July 4. From September 1950 to June 1951 forces from Belgium, Canada, Colombia, Ethiopia, France, Greece, Luxembourg, the Netherlands, New Zealand, the Philippines, South Africa, Thailand, and Turkey joined the UN force.

After the loss of Seoul, UN forces landed behind the North Korean front line at Inchon and began to push from the south, quickly overwhelming the North Korean forces and regaining Seoul. In late September and early October 1950 the UN forces entered North Korean territory, thus fulfilling the original aims of the UN resolution. At the behest of General Douglas MacArthur, its commander, the UN force continued to advance toward North Korea's border with China, provoking a large-scale deployment of Chinese forces. First contact with the Chinese troops was made in late October. In November China launched a major invasion that eventually led to the recapture of Seoul. The UN force counterattacked, retaking Seoul and reaching the 38th parallel in March 1951. At this point fighting stalemated and the front line changed little, despite continued efforts by both sides to break through.

In July 1951, after indications that both sides were amenable to a restoration of borders along the 38th parallel, negotiations were initiated in search of a cease-fire and peace settlement. Talks at Panmunjom, a neutral village in no-man's land, produced a truce based on battle lines existing at the end of fighting, and a formal peace agreement was signed on July 27, 1953. An early agreement was delayed by the problems associated with the return of prisoners. India played a crucial role in these negotiations.

Total fatalities during the war amounted to approximately 3 million killed. China suffered 1 million deaths, and North and South Korea each lost half a million people. The United States lost 50,000 troops, and the other members of the UN force suffered 7,000 fatalities. North and South Korea remained divided, and a number of smaller armed conflicts have continued to plague their relations (*see* conflicts 3.25; 3.31; 3.48; 3.52; 3.59; 3.64).

References

Baldwin, F. 1974. *Without Parallel: The American-Korean Relationship Since 1945.* New York: Pantheon.

Barnds, W.J. 1976. *The Two Koreas in East Asian Affairs.* New York: New York University Press.

Cumings, B. 1981. *Liberation and the Emergence of Separate Regimes.* Vol. 1 of *The Origins of the Korean War.* Princeton, N.J.: Princeton University Press.

———. 1990. *The Roaring of the Cataract.* Vol. 2 of *The Origins of the Korean War.* Princeton, N.J.: Princeton University Press.

Foot, R. 1985. *The Wrong War: American Policy and the Dimensions of the Korean Conflict, 1950–1953.* Ithaca, N.Y.: Cornell University Press.

Matray, J.I. 1985. *The Reluctant Crusade: American Foreign Policy in Korea, 1941–1950.* Honolulu: University of Hawaii Press.

O'Ballance, E. 1969. *Korea: 1950–1953.* Hamden, Conn.: Archon.

Polomka, P. 1986. *The Two Koreas: Catalyst for Conflict in East-Asia?* Adelphi Papers #208. London: IISS.

Rees, D. 1964. *Korea: The Limited War.* New York: St. Martin's.

Srivastava, M.P. 1982. *The Korean Conflict: Search for Unification.* New Delhi: Prentice Hall of India.

Tillema, H.K. 1991. *International Armed Conflict Since 1945: A Bibliographic Handbook of Wars and Military Interventions.* Boulder: Westview.

3.10 China–Portugal: The Macao Territorial Conflict July–August 1952

Portugal had controlled Macao, a tiny peninsula on the coast of southeast China, since 1557, but Macao was not recognized as Portuguese territory until the 1887 Treaty of Peking. Macao became an important port for Chinese international trade, even after the UN trade embargo against the Communist country during the Korean War.

In 1952, however, Portugal sought to restrict Chinese access to the port in an attempt to halt smuggling. Both nations moved significant numbers of troops to the border, and a minor border conflict ensued. Exchanges of fire took place on July 25 and 26. On July 29 and 30 a battle ensued involving mortars and a gunboat. Portugal later accepted responsibility for the battle and paid compensation. There were five Portuguese deaths and forty Chinese casualties. The two sides met in Hong Kong in August 1952, and a full settlement of the matter was reached.

References

Day, A., ed. 1987. *Border and Territorial Disputes.* 2d edition. Burnt Mill, Harlow (Essex), England: Longman.

Rao, R. 1963. *Portuguese Rule in Goa, 1510–1961.* New York: Asia Publishing.

Tillema, H.K. 1991. *International Armed Conflict Since 1945: A Bibliographic Handbook of Wars and Military Interventions.* Boulder: Westview.

3.11 USSR–United States: Cold War Air Incidents October 1952–July 1956

The increasing chill of the cold war, the aftermath of the Korean War, and previous air incidents led to an expanding disquiet between the superpowers (*see* conflict 3.8). Matters were complicated in Europe, which was now partitioned into three blocs: Western, Communist, and neutral. Germany and Austria were divided into American, British, French, and Soviet occupation zones with their corresponding airspace. As the enmity between the superpowers grew, so did their need for intelligence. As a consequence, the United States and the Soviet Union undertook more air reconnaissance missions (and incurred more airspace violations) at the margins of the superpowers' spheres of influence.

On February 16, 1952, two Soviet aircraft were intercepted by U.S. jet fighters, which opened fire. One Soviet aircraft was damaged when the U.S. planes broke off the engagement. On October 7, 1952, an American B-29 Superfortress had, according to Soviet authorities, entered Soviet airspace in the vicinity of Yuri Island. This island is part of the Kuril Islands, which lie just north of Japan, but are Soviet territory. After refusing to land at the Soviet's request, the bomber was shot down and the crew killed. The United States denied charges that the aircraft had been in Soviet airspace and demanded compensation for the loss of the bomber and crew. The Soviet Union refused to pay, and the matter lapsed.

On March 10, 1953, two Czechoslovak MiG-15 jets attacked two U.S. F-84 Thunderjets over Bavaria, shooting one down. On March 12 Soviet jet fighters shot down a British bomber that had been flying over the British zone in Germany, killing seven airmen. Two days after this incident, a Soviet fighter fired on a U.S. reconnaissance aircraft off the Kamchatka Peninsula. The American plane returned fire, but neither plane was damaged. Later, in July, the Soviet Union alleged that four U.S. jet fighters had downed a Soviet passenger aircraft, resulting in the loss of twenty-one passengers and crew. The Soviet Union demanded that the United States take action against those who orchestrated the attack and reserved the right to seek compensation.

On July 31, 1953, the United States accused the Soviet Union of shooting down a U.S. B-50 Superfortress over the Sea of Japan. One survivor of the attack was rescued by a U.S. vessel, and the United States alleged that Soviet vessels had picked up the remaining survivors. The United States demanded information on the status of these crew members. The Soviet Union had earlier released a statement asserting that the U.S. bomber had entered Soviet territory near Vladivostok and had opened fire when two Soviet fighters approached. On August 4 the Soviet Union denied holding the remaining crew members.

A two-year hiatus in hostilities ended June 23, 1955, when Soviet fighters downed a U.S. plane over the Bering Strait. Announcing its regret for the incident, the Soviet Union acknowledged the possibility that an error may have occurred and offered to pay 50 percent compensation for the loss of the plane. The United States accepted the offer on July 7. In all, fifty-four military personnel were killed in these air incidents.

The cold war rendered these air incidents extremely dangerous, inasmuch as the superpowers were beginning to defy each other all over the world. Direct, armed confrontation could have spelled global catastrophe.

References

Bartlett, C.J. 1994. *The Global Conflict: The International Rivalry of Great Powers, 1880–1990.* 2d edition. London: Longman.

Cimbala, S.J., and S.R. Waldman, eds. 1992. *Controlling and Ending Conflict: Issues Before and After the Cold War.* New York: Greenwood.

Gablentz, O.M. van der. 1964. *The Berlin Question in Its Relations to World Politics, 1944–1963.* Munich: Oldenbourg.

Rabel, R.G. 1988. *Between East and West: Trieste, the United States, and the Cold War, 1941–1954.* Durham, N.C.: Duke University Press.

3.12 Cambodia–Siam (Thailand): Border Conflict and the Occupation of the Temple of Preah Vihear Early 1953–May 1975

Siam (Thailand) and Cambodia had been traditional enemies for centuries. Relations between the two states deteriorated following Cambodia's recognition of the

People's Republic of China (PRC) at the end of the Chinese civil war (*see* conflict 3.1). The Siamese government moved troops to the frontier as security against potential Communist insurgency operations into Siam.

As border tensions increased in 1954, Thailand requested that the UN Security Council consider the threat posed by the ongoing fighting by Vietminh forces in neighboring Laos and Cambodia. The USSR vetoed proposed UN Security Council action in this dispute. At the Conference of Foreign Ministers held in Geneva in June 1954, it was evident that UN action was directed toward containing the dispute in Indochina and limiting the spread of Communist-based insurgency across borders. Thailand voiced its concerns to the UN Security Council again in June 1954, submitting a draft resolution that requested a peace observation commission visit Thailand to assess the situation. The USSR vetoed the draft resolution on June 18. Thai concerns were somewhat alleviated by the Geneva Agreement of July 1954.

After Cambodia gained independence from France in 1956, Thai fears were further awakened with the neighboring Communist presence. As a precautionary measure, Thailand moved troops into the border region. Border tensions between the two countries flared on November 24, 1958, when Cambodia severed diplomatic relations with Thailand. Thailand responded by sealing off the border between them, and the situation suddenly became very tense.

On November 29, 1958, Cambodia informed UN Secretary-General Dag Hammarskjöld that Thailand was occupying the Temple of Preah Vihear, which is in Cambodia near the Thai border. Both governments requested that the secretary-general send a special representative to assess the situation. Baron Johan Bech-Friis was appointed as the secretary-general's special representative and visited the area from January 20, 1959, to February 23, 1959. While the special representative was visiting, normal relations between the states were restored with the return of the respective ambassadors to their posts on February 6. Bech-Friis managed to secure the release of thirty-two Thai prisoners who were under arrest in Cambodia on charges of border violation. Cambodia approached the International Court of Justice (ICJ) on October 6, 1959, to resolve the issue of ownership over the Temple of Preah Vihear. The ICJ returned a judgment in favor of Cambodia and stated that Thailand should cease its occupation.

On October 19, 1962, UN Secretary-General U Thant advised the Security Council that the two states were accusing each other of aggression and had requested a second visit by a special representative. The secretary-general appointed Nils Gussing to the position, and he remained in the region until the mission withdrew in December 1964. Both countries lodged similar complaints of border insurgency in 1966. The secretary-general consulted with the parties and August 16, 1966, appointed a new special representative, Herbert de Ribbing, to investigate and propose ways of settling the border dispute. De Ribbing continued in this capacity until February 16, 1968.

References

Allsebrook, M. 1986. *Prototypes of Peacemaking, The First Forty Years of the United Nations.* Harlow (Essex) England: Longman Group UK Limited.

Bercovitch, J., and R. Jackson. 1997. *International Conflict: A Chronological Encyclopedia of Conflicts and Their Management 1945–1995.* Washington, D.C.: Congressional Quarterly.

Brecher, M., J. Wilkenfeld, and S. Moser. 1988. *Crises in the Twentieth Century.* New York: Pergamon.

Butterworth, R.L. 1976. *Managing Interstate Conflict, 1945–1974.* Pittsburgh: Center for International Studies, University of Pittsburgh.

Fretter, J.M. 2001. *Effective Mediation in International Disputes: A Comparative Analysis of Mediation by the United Nations and Regional Organizations 1945–1995.* Doctoral dissertation, Vol. II: Appendices. University of Canterbury, Christchurch, New Zealand.

Tillema, H.K. 1991. *International Armed Conflict Since 1945: A Bibliographic Handbook of Wars and Military Interventions.* Boulder: Westview.

3.13 China–United States/Taiwan: The Quemoy Confrontation April 1954–April 1955

After the formation of the People's Republic of China in 1949, the Chinese Communist Party (CCP) laid claim to the offshore islands still controlled by the Nationalists (Kuomintang, or KMT) and tried to take them by force. In 1954 China declared its intention to liberate these islands, including Taiwan. The United States expressed its support for the Kuomintang and warned that the Seventh Fleet would stand in the way of any invasion attempt. Nevertheless, on September 3, 1954, China began a massive bombardment of Quemoy Island (called Kinmen by the Chinese), which continued intermittently for several weeks. During this period the United States refrained from any active intervention. In January 1955 Chinese forces began to move onto the Tachen islands. The United States promptly evacuated U.S. and KMT forces, leaving the islands to China.

Although the conflict deescalated when the Chinese halted its bombardment, a solution was not reached. U.S. forces remained in the region to supervise the situation. Both U Nu, the Burmese prime minister, and UN Secretary-General Dag Hammarskjöld, attempted to mediate, but without success. There were few fatalities, but the conflict had brought two superpowers to the brink of war. Conflict in the same region broke out again in 1958 (*see* conflict 3.15).

References

Chiu, H., ed. 1979. *China and the Taiwan Issue.* New York: Praeger.

Fairbank, J.K. 1971. *The United States and China.* Cambridge: Harvard University Press.

Kerr, G. 1965. *Formosa Betrayed.* Boston: Houghton Mifflin.

Stolper, T. 1985. *China, Taiwan, and the Offshore Islands.* Armonk, N.Y.: M.E. Sharpe.

Tillema, H.K. 1991. *International Armed Conflict Since 1945: A Bibliographic Handbook of Wars and Military Interventions.* Boulder: Westview.

Tsou, T. 1959. *The Embroilment over Quemoy: Mao, Chiang, and Dulles.* Salt Lake City: Institute of International Studies, University of Utah.

Watson, F. 1966. *The Frontiers of China.* New York: Praeger.

3.14 Taiwan–South Vietnam: The Paracel Islands Dispute June–August 1956

The Paracel Islands in the South China Sea have been claimed by Brunei, China, the Philippines, South Vietnam, and Taiwan. It was thought the area had valuable mineral deposits. South Vietnam placed a small garrison on one of the islands for some time. In June 1956 Taiwan sent a naval force that hoisted the Taiwan flag with the intent of taking possession of the islands.

A month later, on July 11, Taiwan sent armed forces to the Spratly Islands, some 600 miles south of the Paracel Islands, and raised its flag there, too.* South Vietnam responded by sending its own force to the area and raising its flag on one of the islands in August 1956. The conflict gradually abated, although it set the stage for much more serious conflicts in 1974, 1988, and 1995 (*see* conflicts 3.30; 3.49; 3.57). Although there were no armed clashes, the tensions caused by the incidents, and subsequent armed clashes, made it a serious dispute. None of the parties involved attempted to settle the conflict peacefully, and none of the issues involved were ever resolved.

* The Spratly Islands are also known as the Spratleys.

References

Day, A., ed. 1987. *Border and Territorial Disputes.* 2d edition. Burnt Mill, Harlow (Essex), England: Longman.

Tillema, H.K. 1991. *International Armed Conflict Since 1945: A Bibliographic Handbook of Wars and Military Interventions.* Boulder: Westview.

Valencia, M.J. 1995. *China and the South China Sea Disputes.* Adelphi Papers #298. London: IISS.

3.15 China–United States/Taiwan: Communist–Nationalist Territorial Dispute and Bombardment of the Quemoy Islands July–December 1958

Control over Taiwan and other offshore islands by the exiled Kuomintang (KMT) or Nationalists continued to rankle the Chinese Communist Party (CCP) leadership a decade after the Communists had taken power on mainland China. The persistent dispute had produced a number of assaults and bombardments of the Nationalist-held islands, and, in an effort to protect Taiwan from invasion, the United States had stationed part of the Seventh Fleet in the Taiwan Strait (*see* conflict 3.7). Sino-U.S. negotiations were held throughout this period in an attempt to reach an understanding about the Taiwan issue.

On August 23, 1958, however, the Chinese resumed their bombardment of Quemoy. On September 4 China announced it was extending its territorial limit from 3 miles to 12 miles, which would bring Quemoy within its jurisdiction. On September 7, U.S. warships were deployed to escort Taiwanese supply convoys into Quemoy. On October 6 the Chinese halted the bombardment on the condition that U.S. ships refrain from conducting escort duties, but the bombardment resumed on October 20 amid allegations that the United States had infringed these conditions. Bombardments were restricted to alternate days after October 25, thus allowing supply convoys safe passage. The shelling stopped altogether in December 1958. About 1,500 people were killed during the intense bombardment.

The United States and China conducted ambassadorial-level talks in Warsaw, but these ended inconclusively. Once again, the United States had narrowly avoided being dragged into a direct military confrontation with China.

References

Chiu, H., ed. 1979. *China and the Taiwan Issue.* New York: Praeger.

Fairbank, J.K. 1971. *The United States and China.* Cambridge: Harvard University Press.

Kerr, G. 1965. *Formosa Betrayed.* Boston: Houghton Mifflin.

Stolper, T. 1985. *China, Taiwan, and the Offshore Islands.* Armonk, N.Y.: M.E. Sharpe.

Tillema, H.K. 1991. *International Armed Conflict Since 1945: A Bibliographic Handbook of Wars and Military Interventions.* Boulder: Westview.

Tsou, T. 1959. *The Embroilment over Quemoy: Mao, Chiang, and Dulles.* Salt Lake City: Institute of International Studies, University of Utah.

Watson, F. 1966. *The Frontiers of China*. New York: Praeger.

Toye, H. 1968. *Laos: Buffer State or Battleground?* London: Oxford University Press.

3.16 Laos: Political Anarchy and the First Laotian Civil War December 1958–1962

The 1954 Geneva Conventions signed at the end of the French-Indochina War attempted to unite Laos under a single government. By 1958 the coalition government of national reconciliation had overcome numerous obstacles and integrated the country's various factions. The International Control Commission (ICC), which was overseeing the transition to Laotian rule, was adjourned. The United States wanted a friendly government in Laos and began to undermine the government of unity while supporting right-wing factions.

Fighting broke out in December 1958, and by 1959 Laos was in the midst of full-blown civil war. The government had split into left- and right-wing factions. The United States alleged North Vietnamese involvement, and a French investigation revealed that North Vietnam was training and equipping left-wing Pathet Lao forces. The United States began stepping up its support for the conservatives, and the conflict became embroiled in cold war politics. By 1961 the Soviet Union was airlifting supplies to the Pathet Lao, and the United States was sending troops to support the government. North Vietnamese forces also became actively involved, fighting for the Pathet Lao.

The United Nations failed to solve the conflict, and another Geneva conference was convened in June 1961. After months of talks, agreements were reached that led to the withdrawal of all foreign troops from Laos and the establishment of a new coalition government. By late 1962 Laos was again neutral. The Geneva agreements did not last, however, and civil war again broke out in 1964 (*see* conflict 3.22). The exact number of casualties is not known for this conflict but is thought to be in the thousands.

References

Butterworth, R.L. 1976. *Managing Interstate Conflict, 1945–1974*. Pittsburgh: Center for International Studies, University of Pittsburgh.

Dommen, A.J. 1971. *Conflict in Laos*. Revised edition. New York: Praeger.

Gunn, G.C. 1990. *Rebellion in Laos: Peasant and Politics in a Colonial Backwater*. Boulder: Westview.

Kirk, D. 1971. *Wider War: The Struggle for Cambodia, Thailand, and Laos*. New York: Praeger.

Stuart-Fox, M. 1986. *Laos: Politics, Economics, and Society*. Boulder: Lynne Rienner.

Tillema, H.K. 1991. *International Armed Conflict Since 1945: A Bibliographic Handbook of Wars and Military Interventions*. Boulder: Westview.

3.17 North Vietnam–South Vietnam/United States: Communist Vietcong Insurgency, Anti-communist U.S. Military Intervention, and Civil War December 1960–May 1975

After the French-Indochina war ended in 1954 with the defeat of France, Vietnam was divided into the Socialist Republic of Vietnam (North Vietnam) and the Republic of Vietnam (South Vietnam). Acting with the support of North Vietnam, Communist rebels, called the Vietcong, began a campaign of terrorism in South Vietnam in 1957. The rebels opposed to the U.S.-backed military regime in the South and wanted to unite the country as a Communist state.

In its early years, the war was largely restricted to insurgent attacks on South Vietnam from rebel camps in North Vietnam, Laos, and Cambodia. South Vietnamese army units conducted counterinsurgency operations in these countries in an effort to stamp out the rebels.

American military involvement began in 1961, when large numbers of advisers and aircraft were sent to aid South Vietnam. Despite frequent allegations of North Vietnamese battle support for the Vietcong, full-scale hostilities between the United States and North Vietnam did not begin until August 2, 1964, after the Gulf of Tonkin incident. The United States claimed that North Vietnamese torpedo boats attacked a U.S. destroyer in retaliation for U.S. support of South Vietnamese attacks against North Vietnamese targets in the gulf area. On August 4, after allegations that North Vietnam attacked a U.S. naval vessel, the U.S. initiated bombing raids of North Vietnamese military facilities along the gulf. Attempts by UN Secretary-General U Thant to bring the two sides together to seek a peaceful settlement failed, as did similar efforts by Soviet foreign minister Aleksey Kosygin.

The United States initiated repeated bombing raids against North Vietnamese and Vietcong bases in Laos following the Gulf of Tonkin incident. These raids were expanded in 1966 to include Cambodia. U.S. ground troops were engaged in a combat role in March 1965, after the Vietcong attacked a U.S. military base at Pleiku. International involvement in the war expanded in mid-1965, when Australia, New Zealand, and South Korea contributed forces to the conflict. In subsequent years, Thailand and the Philippines also entered the war.

The Tet offensive of 1968 changed the course of the war. Backed by North Vietnamese troops, the Vietcong won a series of battles that brought serious fighting close to South Vietnam's capital, Saigon (now Ho Chi Minh City). Although the United States quickly regained the lost territory, it sought to scale down its involvement and step up negotiations. The United States ended its bombings of North Vietnam on November 1, 1968. At the same time, representatives of the Vietcong were admitted to the peace talks.

U.S. troop withdrawals began in 1969, and negotiations continued until a peace agreement was signed in January 1973, providing for a cease-fire, a withdrawal of all U.S. troops, a joint military commission, and an international commission for control and supervision to oversee the implementation of the peace agreement. Australia, New Zealand, and Thailand withdrew their forces in 1972. South Vietnam and the Vietcong continued to fight until the government in South Vietnam was toppled in April 1975.

The war was particularly brutal and cost the lives of an estimated 1.8 million people, including almost 60,000 U.S. troops and 4,000 South Korean troops. Thailand and Australia each lost 500 troops, but civilians made up the greatest number of fatalities by far. Hundreds of thousands of civilians were killed in indiscriminate bombing raids. The war polarized U.S. public opinion and had a profound effect on subsequent U.S. foreign policy. The now-united Vietnam began to flex its powers in the region, posturing that saw the emergence of five subsequent conflicts (*see* conflicts 3.38; 3.39; 3.44; 3.45; 3.49).

References

Burchett, W.G. 1970. *The Second Indo-China War: Cambodia and Laos.* New York: International Publishers.

Cao, V., and D. Khuyen. 1980. *Reflections on the Vietnam War.* Washington, D.C.: U.S. Army Center of Military History.

Davidson, P. 1988. *Vietnam at War: The History, 1946–1975.* Novato, Calif.: Presidio.

Deane, H. 1963. *The War in Vietnam.* New York: Monthly Review Press.

Evans, G., and K. Rowley. 1984. *Red Brotherhood at War: Indochina Since the Fall of Saigon.* London: Verso.

Falk, R.A., ed. 1976. *The Vietnam War and International Law.* Princeton, N.J.: Princeton University Press.

Hess, G.R. 1990. *Vietnam and the United States: Origins and Legacy of War.* Boston: Wayne.

Huxley, T. 1983. *Indochina and the Insurgency in the ASEAN States, 1975–1981.* Working Paper #67. Canberra: Strategic and Defence Studies Center, Australian National University.

Isaacs, A. 1983. *Without Honor: Defeat in Vietnam and Cambodia.* Baltimore: Johns Hopkins University Press.

Karnow, S. 1983. *Vietnam: A History.* New York: Viking.

Tillema, H.K. 1991. *International Armed Conflict Since 1945: A Bibliographic Handbook of Wars and Military Interventions.* Boulder: Westview.

3.18 Indonesia–Malaysia: Separatist Civil Disturbances and the Borneo Conflict 1962–November 1965

Before World War II the island of Borneo was divided between Britain and the Netherlands. Britain controlled Brunei, Sarawak, and Sabah, and the rest of the island was a Dutch colonial territory, which Indonesia incorporated at its independence in 1949. In 1961 Britain declared its wish to federate the British protectorates on Borneo with Malaya. The Philippines and Indonesia protested, as it infringed on their own territorial claims to Borneo.

In the period immediately before the granting of independence to Sabah and Sarawak, Indonesia actively supported opposition groups in the British territories, including the Sarawak United People's Party (SUPP), the Sarawak Advanced Youth's Association (SAYA), and the National Army of North Borneo (TMKU). These organizations sometimes engaged in guerrilla activities against colonial targets, forcing British troops to be deployed.

Sabah and Sarawak were granted independence on September 16, 1963, and they subsequently joined the Federation of Malaysia. Indonesia refused to recognize the incorporation of Sabah and Sarawak into Malaysia and, starting in January 1964, began military operations on the border with Malaysia Borneo. British troops were brought in to contain Indonesian activities in the border area. The conflict escalated dangerously in August 1964, when Indonesia began to attack from the air and sea. New Zealand and Australian troops subsequently assisted British and Malaysian forces in repelling the attacks.

Several states in the region attempted to mediate, including Cambodia, the Philippines, and Thailand. The United Nations and the British Commonwealth also tried to facilitate dialogue, with varying degrees of success. As it was, the conflict deescalated rapidly after October 1965, when civil unrest in Indonesia undermined President Ahmed Sukarno's powers. Britain scaled down its deployment from November 1965, and the conflict evaporated completely in March 1966, when Sukarno was forced to resign. Perhaps as many as 1,000 people were killed during the conflict, including 75 British soldiers and 600 Indonesian military personnel.

References

Allen, R. 1968. *Malaysia—Prospect and Retrospect: The Impact and Aftermath of Colonial Rule.* New York: Oxford University Press.

Dahm, B. 1971. *History of Indonesia in the Twentieth Century.* Translated by P.S. Falla. New York: Praeger.

Jones, H. 1971. *Indonesia: The Possible Dream.* New York: Harcourt, Brace, Jovanovich.

Mackle, J. 1974. *Konfrontasi: The Indonesia-Malaysia Dispute, 1963–1966.* New York: Oxford University Press.

Suter, K.D. 1979. *West Irian, East Timor, and Indonesia.* London: Minority Rights Group.

Tillema, H.K. 1991. *International Armed Conflict Since 1945: A Bibliographic Handbook of Wars and Military Interventions.* Boulder: Westview.

3.19 Indonesia–The Netherlands: West Irian Administration Dispute and Separatist Insurgency January–August 1962

The status of the western part of the island of New Guinea, known as West Irian (now Irian Jaya), remained unresolved after Indonesia was granted independence in 1949. The Netherlands retained control over the region, despite talks aimed at incorporating the territory into Indonesia. In an effort to remove the Netherlands from West Irian, Indonesia initiated a full mobilization of its armed forces and began a series of small raids into the region.

Following a number of serious troop and naval clashes, the United Nations intervened in a desperate attempt to restrict the spread of the conflict. UN Secretary-General U Thant arranged talks in January 1962. U.S. ambassador Ellsworth Bunker, U Thant's representative, took over in March, and on July 31, 1962, he secured an agreement. Both sides would withdraw their troops, and UN troops would administer the territory until May 1, 1963, at which time Indonesia would take possession. This all took place according to the agreement, and the last violence associated with this conflict occurred in August 1962, when the Netherlands transferred the territory to Indonesia under UN supervision. A condition of the agreement, however, was that Indonesia implement a program leading to West Irian self-determination by 1969. Indonesia never carried out this program, and a guerrilla movement emerged in 1965 aimed at Irian independence; this movement still plagues Indonesia (*see* conflict 3.24).

Much of the fighting involved guerrilla warfare and fomenting violence among the local population. It is possible that as many as 30,000 people were killed in the disturbances, including 100 Indonesian military personnel, mostly at the hands of the police.

References

Dahm, B. 1971. *History of Indonesia in the Twentieth Century.* Translated by P.S. Falla. New York: Praeger.

Henderson, W. 1973. *West New Guinea: The Dispute and Its Settlement.* South Orange, N.J.: Seton Hall University/American-Asian Educational Exchange.

Jones, H. 1971. *Indonesia: The Possible Dream.* New York: Harcourt, Brace, Jovanovich.

Lagerberg, K. 1979. *West Irian and Jakarta Imperialism.* New York: St. Martin's.

Lijphart, A. 1966. *The Trauma of Decolonization: The Dutch and West New Guinea.* New Haven: Yale University Press.

Savage, P. 1978. *The National Liberation Struggle in West Irian: From Millenarianism to Socialist Revolution.* Wellington, N.Z.: South Pacific Action Network.

Suter, K.D. 1979. *West Irian, East Timor, and Indonesia.* London: Minority Rights Group.

Tillema, H.K. 1991. *International Armed Conflict Since 1945: A Bibliographic Handbook of Wars and Military Interventions.* Boulder: Westview.

3.20 China–Taiwan: CCP-KMT Territorial Dispute and Invasion Threat March–December 1962

Following the Nationalists' defeat on mainland China in 1949, conflict between China and Taiwan broke into open warfare from 1949 to 1953, from 1954 to 1955, and again in 1958 (*see* conflicts 3.7; 3.13; 3.15). China remained committed to reuniting all the territories that had once been part of mainland China, and this caused a constant state of alarm in Taiwan. Starting in December 1958, however, tensions had eased somewhat, but conflict broke out again from March to December 1962, when China moved major army units near Nationalist-controlled islands in the Taiwan Strait. The troop concentrations were thought to be greater than at any other time, and Taiwan went on alert, anticipating an invasion.

At the same time, Nationalist leaders in Taiwan made bellicose statements about a "return to the mainland," meaning a military invasion of China, implying that the United States would back any invasion attempt. Conscription was increased and new taxes levied. Following U.S. statements indicating the United States would not back a Taiwanese invasion of mainland China but would defend Taiwan against invasion, the conflict abated, although tensions remained extremely high because no conflict-management attempts had been made. China gradually reduced troop concentrations near the islands but did not renounce its aim to unite all of China.

References

Chiu, H., ed. 1979. *China and the Taiwan Issue.* New York: Praeger.

Fairbank, J.K. 1971. *The United States and China.* Cambridge: Harvard University Press.

Kerr, G. 1965. *Formosa Betrayed.* Boston: Houghton Mifflin.

Stolper, T. 1985. *China, Taiwan, and the Offshore Islands.* Armonk, N.Y.: M.E. Sharpe.

Tillema, H.K. 1991. *International Armed Conflict Since 1945: A Bibliographic Handbook of Wars and Military Interventions.* Boulder: Westview.

Tsou, T. 1959. *The Embroilment over Quemoy: Mao, Chiang, and Dulles*. Salt Lake City: Institute of International Studies, University of Utah.

Watson, F. 1966. *The Frontiers of China*. New York: Praeger.

3.21 South Vietnam–Cambodia: Anti-Vietminh Cross-Border Raids March–December 1964

Beginning in 1957 sympathizers with North Vietnam, known as the Vietcong, conducted terrorist operations in South Vietnam with the aim of destabilizing the government. North Vietnam was a Communist state supported by the Soviet Union, and South Vietnam was supported by the United States. Beginning in 1960 South Vietnamese forces began to conduct intermittent cross-border operations into Cambodia on the pretext of pursuing the Vietminh, the forces of North Vietnam. The raids intensified in March 1964, after Cambodia continued to resist U.S. and South Vietnamese pressure to take action against the insurgents.

In April 1964 Cambodia lodged a complaint with the UN Security Council, which passed a resolution calling for a halt to the border violations. A UN fact-finding mission recommended a remarcation of the border between Cambodia and South Vietnam. Cambodia rejected this suggestion, however, because it feared it would lose territory to South Vietnam. The dispute remained unresolved and gradually abated. About 100 fatalities resulted from the conflict. Beginning in 1965, with North Vietnam's large-scale troop infiltrations into South Vietnam, the conflict grew into all-out war involving the United States and North Vietnam. At various times during the Vietnam War, the fighting spilled over into Cambodia (*see* conflict 3.28).

References

Burchett, W.G. 1970. *The Second Indo-China War: Cambodia and Laos*. New York: International Publishers.

Caldwell, M., and L. Tan. 1973. *Cambodia in the Southeast Asian War*. New York: Monthly Review Press.

Chandler, D.P. 1991. *The Tragedy of Cambodian History: Politics, War, and Revolution Since 1945*. New Haven: Yale University Press.

Davidson, P. 1988. *Vietnam at War: The History, 1946–1975*. Novato, Calif.: Presidio.

Deane, H. 1963. *The War in Vietnam*. New York: Monthly Review Press.

Haas, M. 1991. *Cambodia, Pol Pot, and the United States: The Faustian Pact*. New York: Praeger.

Heder, S.R. 1991. *Reflections on Cambodian Political History: Background to Recent Developments*. Canberra: Strategic and Defence Studies Center, Australian National University.

Isaacs, A. 1983. *Without Honor: Defeat in Vietnam and Cambodia*. Baltimore: Johns Hopkins University Press.

Karnow, S. 1983. *Vietnam: A History*. New York: Viking.

Kiernan, B., and C. Boua. 1982. *Peasants and Politics in Kampuchea, 1942–1981*. London: Zed.

3.22 North Vietnam–Laos: Political Anarchy and the Second Laotian Civil War April 1964–December 1966

Although the 1962 Geneva Agreements brought the first Laotian civil war to an end (1958–1962), the second civil war grew directly out of the failure of these agreements to provide a basis for lasting peace. The Geneva-prescribed coalition government was headed by neutralist Prince Souvanna Phouma and had representatives from neutralist, Communist, and conservative factions.

But the political struggle among the factions led the Pathet Lao, a Communist organization supported by North Vietnam, to withdraw from the coalition. A military coup in April 1964 was followed by the almost immediate resumption of the civil war between the U.S.-supported conservative forces and the Pathet Lao. South Vietnam and Thailand also sent troops and equipment to the rightists. From 1964 to 1970 the war followed a consistent pattern, with the Pathet Lao and Vietminh forces launching offensives between October and May and the rightists countering in the middle months of the year, supported by U.S. air strikes.

Discussions between Prince Souvanna Phouma and Prince Souphanouvong, leader of the Pathet Lao, began in 1970 in an attempt to end the conflict, but these talks were unsuccessful, and the fighting continued. By 1972 the Pathet Lao had made some gains and controlled two-thirds of Laos.

Concessions by both sides led to a peace conference in Paris in February 1973. These talks led to the formation of a provisional government that equally represented both parties. By 1975 the Pathet Lao had de facto control over the government and large numbers of right-wing supporters began to flee the country. Thousands are thought to have been killed during this war.

References

Butterworth, R.L. 1976. *Managing Interstate Conflict, 1945–1974*. Pittsburgh: Center for International Studies, University of Pittsburgh.

Duiker, W. 1986. *China and Vietnam: The Roots of Conflict*. Berkeley: Institute of East Asian Studies, University of California.

Gunn, G.C. 1990. *Rebellion in Laos: Peasant and Politics in a Colonial Backwater*. Boulder: Westview.

Kirk, D. 1971. *Wider War: The Struggle for Cambodia, Thailand, and Laos*. New York: Praeger.

Stuart-Fox, M. 1986. *Laos: Politics, Economics, and Society*. Boulder: Lynne Rienner.

Tillema, H.K. 1991. *International Armed Conflict Since 1945: A Bibliographic Handbook of Wars and Military Interventions*. Boulder: Westview.

Toye, H. 1968. *Laos: Buffer State or Battleground?* London: Oxford University Press.

3.23 North Vietnam–United States: The Vietnam War August 1964–May 1975

The reasons for U.S. involvement in this dispute had developed earlier, and its support militarily and logistically was already firmly committed to the South Vietnamese government (*see* conflict 3.17). The focus of U.S. support for South Vietnam against the Vietcong rebels along the Cambodian border was broadened in scope and commitment in 1964.

On August 2, 1964, the United States charged that North Vietnam had attacked the U.S. destroyer *Maddox* in the Gulf of Tonkin. North Vietnam claimed the attack was retaliatory, for previous attacks made by South Vietnamese vessels as they traveled under covert protection of U.S. destroyers. By August 4 a second complaint by the United States alleged North Vietnamese attacks on two U.S. destroyers. Despite North Vietnamese denials of the attacks, the U.S. began air strikes as an immediate response. Consequently, the U.S. Congress authorized U.S. forces to use all necessary force to repel any armed attacks. The United States notified the UN Security Council of its actions on August 4, stating that U.S. vessels had been in territorial waters at the time and that the North Vietnamese attacks were unprovoked. The UN asked North Vietnam and South Vietnam to submit their accounts of the incident. The accounts from each of the parties were placed on the agenda, along with an accumulation of past grievances and violations of the 1954 Geneva Agreements. The UN took no action on the complaints, however, because the United States had not called for its intervention, and neither of the parties requested assistance. The United States merely used the UN as an international platform for clarifying the "defensive" nature of its actions.

Following the Gulf of Tonkin incidents, UN Secretary-General U Thant promoted a round of negotiations between the United States and North Vietnam in Rangoon, Burma. North Vietnam accepted the idea, but the United States postponed its involvement until after the domestic elections had finished. The negotiations never took place despite continued attempts to get the parties to the table during 1965. A stronger attempt at resolution was made on December 24, 1965, when the United States halted air strikes on North Vietnamese targets in the hope that negotiations could begin. A three-point bulletin issued by North Vietnam set out some preconditions for any U.S. negotiations, all of which were unacceptable to the United States.

The United States brought the matter to the attention of the Security Council again on January 31, 1966. Before the meeting of the Security Council took place, the United States tried a number initiatives, including calls for an end to the fighting and the international supervision of a cease-fire. The item made it on the Security Council agenda on February 2, 1966, despite the Soviet Union's disapproval. Private, informal debates on the issue were held at the request of the president of the Security Council, but not much was achieved by these means. The Security Council also discussed the matter openly in session between September 1966 and December 1966, but no further action was taken.

During this period U Thant made successive attempts to reconvene the Geneva Conference in an effort to draw the parties back into negotiations. His efforts were not fruitful, although he met with North Vietnamese officials in Burma in March 1967 to restate the conditions of his own three-point proposal for rekindling the negotiation process. U Thant had further meetings throughout 1968. He met with the Consul-General of North Vietnam while attending the United Nations Conference on Trade and Development (UNCTAD) conference in India, and with other leaders in Delhi, London, Paris, Moscow, and Washington.

Serious and sustained land and air offensives occurred from 1966 to 1968. After an announcement by U.S. President Lyndon Johnson detailing a limitation of air strike zones for U.S. bombers and new offers of negotiation, North Vietnam agreed to begin fresh discussions on April 3, 1968. The secretary-general twice urged the parties to decide on a venue for the talks. North Vietnam agreed to engage in peace talks in Paris and they started in early May 1968. In October 1968 the United States announced that it would halt all hostilities, and this was achieved by November 1, 1968.

The inflexibility of the disputants' positions meant that the negotiations dragged on over a three-year period, and the United States, in particular its negotiator, Henry Kissinger, and North Vietnam, represented by Le Duc Tho, also conducted secret bilateral talks before a full settlement could be agreed upon.

UN Secretary-General Kurt Waldheim offered his good offices in April 1972, but none of the parties accepted his offer. On May 9 Waldheim stated that all the UN machinery should be used to put an end to the hostilities and help the parties to come to a settlement. On May 11 the secretary-general sent a memorandum to the president of the Security Council. The report detailed suggestions on how to move the parties to further talks on cessation of hostilities. In early 1972 the peace talks in Paris had still not come to a satisfactory conclusion, and frustration saw an outbreak of bombing against the North. The talks were suspended from May 4 to July 12, 1972. The United States reported details of its "collective defense" operation to Waldheim on May 8. Even though

Waldheim supported initiating more active UN participation in resolving the dispute, none of the Security Council members agreed. After this small skirmish abated in June 1972, the parties decided to return to negotiations. Extensive negotiations culminated in Paris on January 27, 1973, in the signing of the Final Agreement on Ending the War and Restoring Peace in Vietnam. Continued peace talks were held at a conference from February 26 to March 2, 1973, with the secretary-general in attendance. Fighting persisted intermittently until 1975.

The United Nations was not involved in the final peace settlement, but UN groups such as the United Nations Children's Fund (UNICEF), the United Nations High Commissioner for Refugees (UNHCR), and the Food and Agriculture Organization of the United Nations (FAO) were active in humanitarian relief efforts during the dispute.

References

Allsebrook, M. 1986. *Prototypes of Peacemaking, The First Forty Years of the United Nations.* Harlow (Essex) England: Longman Group UK Limited.

Bercovitch, J., and R. Jackson. 1997. *International Conflict: A Chronological Encyclopedia of Conflicts and Their Management 1945–1995.* Washington, D.C.: Congressional Quarterly.

Brecher, M., J. Wilkenfeld, and S. Moser. 1988. *Crises in the Twentieth Century.* New York: Pergamon.

Butterworth, R.L. 1976. *Managing Interstate Conflict, 1945–1974.* Pittsburgh: Center for International Studies, University of Pittsburgh.

Fretter, J.M. 2001. *Effective Mediation in International Disputes: A Comparative Analysis of Mediation by the United Nations and Regional Organizations 1945–1995.* Doctoral dissertation, Vol. II: Appendices. University of Canterbury, Christchurch, New Zealand.

Huth, P.K. 1996. *Standing Your Ground: Territorial Disputes and International Conflict.* Ann Arbor: University of Michigan Press.

Zacher, M.W. 1979. *International Conflict and Collective Security, 1946–1977.* New York: Praeger.

3.24 Irian Jaya–Indonesia: Territorial Dispute and Secession Insurgency 1965–Ongoing

The Netherlands granted independence to Indonesia in 1949 following a bloody war, but retained control over West Irian (Irian Jaya), which occupies the western half of the island of New Guinea. Following another war between Indonesia and the Netherlands in 1962, the Netherlands ceded the territory to Indonesia on the condition that it would implement a program leading to Irian independence (*see* conflicts 3.2; 3.19). West Irian was inhabited by Papuans, who are ethnically closer to Papua New Guineans.

Once Indonesia gained control of the area, it reneged on its promise to grant independence and, beginning in 1965, instead tried to pacify West Irian. Ethnic Papuans in particular forcefully resisted these efforts. The separatist Organisasi Papua Mendeka (OPM) fomented violence in the region, particularly along the ill-defined Indonesian-Papua New Guinean border. The conflict grew more serious in the 1970s, when Indonesia was forced to commit a regular army battalion to the area and engaged in repression and reprisals against villagers. A pattern of attacks by the OPM, followed by reprisals by Indonesian troops continued into the 1990s.

The conflict was internationalized when Indonesian troops began crossing the Papua New Guinea border in pursuit of rebels, who had a natural sanctuary among Papuans. Tensions associated with the OPM insurgency became a feature of relations between Papua New Guinea and Indonesia throughout the 1980s and 1990s. No attempts at conflict management were made. With the apparent shrinking of the rebel army, the OPM offered talks with the government in 1995, but received no response. Perhaps as many as 10,000 people were killed in the conflict up to this point, and in 1995 foreign governments began to raise questions about Indonesia's human rights record in the territory. Also, the OPM gained international attention when it kidnapped a number of foreign nationals.

When President Suharto of Indonesia was forced from power in May 1998, many of the long-repressed sentiments of the people of Irian Jaya were made public for the first time. In September 1998 Indonesia revoked Irian Jaya's status as a "military operation zone" following the conclusion of a cease-fire agreement with the OPM. Local leaders reacted to the cease-fire with some doubt because it was not accompanied by the withdrawal of nonlocal forces.

In 1998 a broad-based and well-organized West Papuan independence movement began to emerge, holding provincewide congresses and petitioning the Indonesian leadership to hold a popular referendum on independence. The strength of pro-independence sentiment was unmistakable in February 1999, when 100 leading Papuan leaders met with President B.J. Habibie to initiate what was being hailed as a "national dialogue" on Papuan concerns. The leaders demanded independence, thus displeasing the government, which had encouraged the national dialogue up to then, and the process was soon suspended.

In April 1999 the government reverted to the methods used during the Suharto era, attempting to round up independence supporters and censor discussion of the subject. The crackdown included bans on expression, assembly, and association; arbitrary arrests; and widespread intimidation of independence supporters. With demands for democratization still mounting across Indonesia, however, the opposition was not easily silenced. Papuan leaders continued to assert their right to advocate Papuan independence.

Following democratic elections in October 1999, a new government took office in Indonesia under President Abdurrahman Wahid and promptly initiated a number of reforms. Openly acknowledging the errors of the past, the new administration moved quickly to allow greater freedom and to permit the open expression of pro-independence views. Peaceful Papuan flag raisings, which had been broken up under Suharto and Habibie, were now permitted and were held without police interference in at least a dozen places in Papua in December 1999. Not all such ceremonies were peaceful, however, with several people killed and many injured. Other clashes between civilians and security forces occurred in February, March, and August 1999.

Tensions rose further in October 2000, when Indonesia banned the "Morning Star" flag, emblem of the pro-independence movement. This marked a dramatic turnaround from more tolerant policies in effect for the past year, and from President Wahid's promise that the peaceful expression of pro-independence views would not be punished. In a number of cases, forcible removal of the flag led to bloody clashes in which more than twenty-five people were killed, most of them non-Papuan migrants killed by a Papuan mob. The secession conflict continued into 2004 with sporadic fighting between the Indonesian government and the OPM.

References

Dahm, B. 1971. *History of Indonesia in the Twentieth Century.* Translated by P.S. Falla. New York: Praeger.

Human Rights Watch. 2000. *World Report 2000.* "Indonesia Urged To Call Off Papua Ultimatum." http://www.hrw.org/press/2000/10/indo1017.htm. October 17.

Jones, H. 1971. *Indonesia: The Possible Dream.* New York: Harcourt, Brace, Jovanovich.

Lagerberg, K. 1979. *West Irian and Jakarta Imperialism.* New York: St. Martin's.

Suter, K.D. 1979. *West Irian, East Timor, and Indonesia.* London: Minority Rights Group.

Tillema, H.K. 1991. *International Armed Conflict Since 1945: A Bibliographic Handbook of Wars and Military Interventions.* Boulder: Westview.

3.25 North Korea–South Korea: Cold War Dispute and Border Incidents Mid-1965–March 1968

Following the Korean War of 1950 to 1953 (*see* conflict 3.9), relations between the two Koreas were extremely volatile. The 38th parallel was heavily reinforced with troops, and each side waged a virulent propaganda war against the other. The tensions erupted into a serious border conflict in October 1965, when North Korea began cross-border commando raids. In November 1965 U.S. troops clashed with North Korean troops; these skirmishes continued periodically until September 1971. South Korean artillery and other small ground forces also retaliated.

Eventually, the conflict abated. Fighting broke out again, however, in 1968, 1975, 1984, and 1992 (*see* conflicts 3.26; 3.31; 3.48; 3.52).

References

Baldwin, F. 1974. *Without Parallel: The American-Korean Relationship Since 1945.* New York: Pantheon.

Barnds, W.J. 1976. *The Two Koreas in East Asian Affairs.* New York: New York University Press.

Foot, R. 1985. *The Wrong War: American Policy and the Dimensions of the Korean Conflict, 1950–1953.* Ithaca, N.Y.: Cornell University Press.

O'Ballance, E. 1969. *Korea: 1950–1953.* Hamden, Conn.: Archon.

Polomka, P. 1986. *The Two Koreas: Catalyst for Conflict in East-Asia?* Adelphi Papers #208. London: IISS.

Srivastava, M.P. 1982. *The Korean Conflict: Search for Unification.* New Delhi: Prentice Hall of India.

Tillema, H.K. 1991. *International Armed Conflict Since 1945: A Bibliographic Handbook of Wars and Military Interventions.* Boulder: Westview.

3.26 North Korea–United States: USS *Pueblo* Seizure January–December 1968

The United Nations had little success in moderating this dispute over North Korea's detention of a U.S. research vessel. A referral to the organization provided only a forum for airing the dispute.

After the parties signed a truce ending the Korean War, border skirmishes continued between the Republic of Korea (South Korea) and the Democratic People's Republic of Korea (North Korea) from 1965 to 1971 (*see* conflict 3.25). North Korea tried to infiltrate the UN-policed demilitarized zone over the 1962–1963 period, launched cross-border attacks from 1965 to1971, and attempted to invade the South Korean coast from the sea, using naval and air support.

North Korean (PDRK) patrol boats seized and detained a U.S. naval intelligence ship, the *Pueblo,* on January 22, 1968. On the same day the USS *Enterprise,* an aircraft carrier operating in the region, was diverted from its patrol around the North Vietnam coast to the Sea of Japan. The U.S. government called for the return of the *Pueblo* and its eighty-three-man crew at the Panmunjom Armistice Talks. The PDRK claimed that the vessel was inside North Korean waters, in the Wonsan region, but the U.S. authorities denied this. A number of diplomatic efforts were made to secure the release of the vessel; these initial efforts proved fruitless. On January 25, 1968, the U.S. ambassador in Moscow called on the USSR to use its good offices to broker the release of the vessel. At the same time, the United States called up its air force and army reservists. On January 26, the USSR sent a trawler to watch over the activities of the *Enterprise*. After U.S. ambassador Llewellyn E. "Tommy" Thompson made a second request for USSR assistance, which was bluntly refused, the U.S. government on January 28 called an urgent meeting of the UN Security Council. The United States accused the North Korean government of seizing the unarmed *Pueblo* in an orchestrated attack. The United States requested that the UN Security Council secure the return of the vessel and the release of its crew, and resume the conditions agreed to in the Korean Armistice accords.

On February 3, 1968, the United States and North Korea reached an agreement, including placing the *Pueblo* seizure on the agenda of the continuing Panmunjom talks. Subsequently, the United States withdrew the *Enterprise* from the region, diminishing the threat of armed retaliation. The USSR still maintained that the vessel was engaged in spying activities within the PDRK's territorial waters. Ethiopia proposed that the Security Council investigate the dispute, but no action was taken. The commander of the *Pueblo* admitted to involvement in spying activities on December 16, 1968. The admission was broadcast the same day over North Korean airwaves. The U.S. government denied that the vessel engaged in espionage, but continued negotiations.

After ten months of negotiation, the United States and North Korean officials reached an agreement on December 23, 1968. Major General Gilbert H. Woodward of the United States, signed a proclamation apologizing for the American vessel's presence in North Korean waters. The proclamation acknowledged the statement of the *Pueblo*'s commander and some of the crew as genuine. Before signing the proclamation however, Woodward read a statement revoking the apology. North Korea released the ship's crew, but retained the vessel.

References

Allsebrook, M. 1986. *Prototypes of Peacemaking, The First Forty Years of the United Nations*. Harlow (Essex) England: Longman Group UK Limited.

Brecher, M., J. Wilkenfeld, and S. Moser. 1988. *Crises in the Twentieth Century*. New York: Pergamon.

Butterworth, R.L. 1976. *Managing Interstate Conflict, 1945–1974*. Pittsburgh: Center for International Studies, University of Pittsburgh.

Fretter, J.M. 2001. *Effective Mediation in International Disputes: A Comparative Analysis of Mediation by the United Nations and Regional Organizations 1945–1995*. Doctoral dissertation, Vol. II: Appendices. University of Canterbury, Christchurch, New Zealand.

Tillema, H.K. 1991. *International Armed Conflict Since 1945: A Bibliographic Handbook of Wars and Military Interventions*. Boulder: Westview.

3.27 China–Burma: Tribal Conflicts and Border Incidents January–November 1969

China and Burma signed a friendship treaty in 1960 that resolved some lingering territorial disputes. Despite the treaty, the two countries continued to vie for control over tribal groups—the Kachins and the Shans—that lived along their mutual border and had long resisted government efforts to absorb them. In fact, these tribes did not intrinsically identify with either China or Burma.

A conflict erupted in 1969, when Burma launched a military campaign to assert control over these tribes. At the time, Chinese road construction near the border was straining relations and causing security concerns, which China compounded by providing military assistance to some of the tribes. Between May and October 1969, Burmese units occasionally clashed with Chinese troops operating within Burma; as many as 300 fatalities resulted from these skirmishes. Only one negotiation attempt was made, but it failed. The dispute eventually lapsed altogether, as Burma focused its attention on a continuing guerrilla insurgency.

References

Cady, J. 1958. *A History of Modern Burma*. Ithaca, N.Y.: Cornell University Press.

Collis, M. 1975. *Trials in Burma*. New York: AMS.

Hinton, H.C. 1972. *China's Relations with Burma and Vietnam: A Brief Survey*. Ann Arbor, Mich.: University Microfilms.

Lintner, B. 1990. *The Rise and Fall of the Communist Party of Burma (CPB)*. Ithaca, N.Y.: South East Asian Program, Cornell University.

Lissak, M. 1976. *Military Roles in Modernization: Civil-Military Relations in Thailand and Burma*. Beverly Hills: Sage.

Pettman, R.H. 1973. *China in Burma's Foreign Policy*. Canberra: Australian National University Press.

Silverstein, J. 1977. *Burma: Military Rule and the Politics of Stagnation*. Ithaca, N.Y.: Cornell University Press.

3.28 Cambodia (Kampuchea)–South Vietnam/United States: U.S. Bombing Campaign and Vietnam War January 1970–April 1975

Cambodia was a major battlefield during the Vietnam War. Vietcong and North Vietnamese troops used the country as a transit area and supply line to the fighting in South Vietnam, and the United States responded to the traffic with punishing air strikes.

Cambodia's ruler at the time was Prince Norodom Sihanouk. He was ousted in a 1970 military coup led by Lon Nol, a South Vietnamese army general. Lon Nol then took control of Cambodia, hoping to curb North Vietnam's military onslaughts. But the North Vietnamese simply stepped up their incursions into the south. By April 1970 U.S. ground troops were fighting in Cambodia.

Although the bulk of U.S. troops were withdrawn from Cambodia in June 1970, three months later, the United States was still providing logistical support to South Vietnamese troops there. The United States made heavy bombing runs until 1973, causing thousands of fatalities. The U.S. bombing campaign turned many rural Cambodians into ardent supporters of the Communist Khmer Rouge rebellion, which deposed the Lon Nol regime in 1975.

Aside from a U.S. commando raid into Cambodia in 1975, all U.S. involvement in Cambodia ended with the signing of the Paris Peace Accords in January 1973. North Vietnamese and South Vietnamese troops continued operations in Cambodia until the fall of South Vietnam in 1975. Only two attempts were made at negotiation, and both failed. It is estimated that perhaps as many as 300,000 people lost their lives in Cambodia during this period of fighting.

References

Burchett, W.G. 1970. *The Second Indo-China War: Cambodia and Laos.* New York: International Publishers.

Caldwell, M., and L. Tan. 1973. *Cambodia in the Southeast Asian War.* New York: Monthly Review Press.

Chandler, D.P. 1991. *The Tragedy of Cambodian History: Politics, War, and Revolution Since 1945.* New Haven: Yale University Press.

Davidson, P. 1988. *Vietnam at War: The History, 1946–1975.* Novato, Calif.: Presidio.

Deane, H. 1963. *The War in Vietnam.* New York: Monthly Review Press.

Haas, M. 1991. *Cambodia, Pol Pot, and the United States: The Faustian Pact.* New York: Praeger.

Heder, S.R. 1991. *Reflections on Cambodian Political History: Background to Recent Developments.* Canberra: Strategic and Defence Studies Center, Australian National University.

Hildebrand, G.C., and G. Porter. 1976. *Cambodia: Starvation and Revolution.* New York: Monthly Review Press.

Isaacs, A. 1983. *Without Honor: Defeat in Vietnam and Cambodia.* Baltimore: Johns Hopkins University Press.

Karnow, S. 1983. *Vietnam: A History.* New York: Viking.

Kiernan, B., and C. Boua. 1982. *Peasants and Politics in Kampuchea, 1942–1981.* London: Zed.

White, M. 2004. "Death Tolls for the Major Wars and Atrocities of the Twentieth Century." *20th Century Atlas—Alphabetical List of War, Massacre, Tyranny and Genocide.* http://users.erols.com/mwhite28/warstat2.htm#Cambodia. (Last updated February 2004; accessed May 24, 2004.)

3.29 Mindanao–The Philippines: Communal Violence, Land Disputes, and Muslim Secessionist Insurgency January 1970–Ongoing

An archipelago nation of more than 7,000 islands, the Philippines was administered for 400 years by the Spanish, who in 1898 lost control of their possession to the United States during the Spanish-American War. Mindanao, the country's southernmost and second-largest island, is home to a sizable Muslim minority population, a disenfranchised and oppressed group.

This conflict began when a militant movement known as the Blackshirts staged acts of violence against new Christian settlers arriving from the northern islands. The Blackshirts were made up of Moros, as members of the Muslim minority were known, many of whom had never recognized the legitimacy of the Manila government. Fearing secession, the government immediately sent in troops.

In the first year of the conflict, more than 1,000 people lost their lives in violent clashes. In 1971 the conflict took on the aspect of a religious war, when Christians began attacking Muslims, and Muslims attempted to drive Christians off land they considered their own. In 1973 the conflict changed to an intense, organized struggle for secession by the Moros, who organized themselves into the Moro National Liberation Front (MNLF) in the mid-1970s. Thousands were being killed every year. The conflict was internationalized as Muslim countries such as Afghanistan, Egypt, Libya, Pakistan, and Saudi Arabia began to aid the Moros, including sending arms through Malaysia. Malaysian-Philippine relations were strained when it was alleged that Malaysia was arming and training the Muslim insurgents.

By the early 1980s as many as 10,000 government troops alone had been killed. The conflict was further complicated in the mid-1980s by a split in the MNLF. Despite numerous negotiations between the government and the MNLF, and mediation attempts by Muslim nations and the Islamic Conference Organization (ICO), no solution to the conflict was found. The Moro Islamic Liberation Front (MILF), the MNLF's main rival, remained outside the peace talks and continued to fight without respite.

The government reached a number of agreements and cease-fires with the MNLF and made efforts to improve the lives of the Muslims, but these measures led to only temporary lulls in the fighting. In early 1995 large-scale fighting broke out when the rebels attacked a Christian town and more than fifty civilians were killed. Approximately 60,000 people had lost their lives in the conflict by this time.

In April 1996 the government and MILF agreed to an interim cease-fire, although more than a year later clashes continued. A peace agreement between the government and the MNLF in September 1996 created an autonomous region in Muslim Mindanao (ARMM) and ended twenty-four years of rebellion that left more than 120,000 people dead. Despite the agreement, the MILF splinter group vowed to continue the fight for independence. The MILF, which wants to establish an Islamic state, was covered by the government cease-fire but was not a party to the peace talks with the MNLF. Peace talks were scheduled for October 1999, but renewed demands for independence in the wake of an East Timor referendum led to increased tensions and the postponement of elections in the ARMM. A spate of kidnapping by the Abu Sayaff faction triggered a major government offensive in late 2000.

The activities of the Communist New People's Army (NPA) added a further dimension to this conflict. The NPA, which maintains a presence in eastern Mindanao, central Philippines, and in parts of northern Luzon, also signed a cease-fire agreement with the government in December 1993. Nevertheless, hostilities increased between the NPA and the Philippine government since ongoing peace talks were terminated in May 1999. The NPA then centered its activities in northern Mindanao. Since June 2000 reports have surfaced of cooperation between the NPA and the Moro Islamic Liberation Front.

References

Brogan, P. 1989. *World Conflicts: Why and Where They Are Happening*. London: Bloomsbury.

Gurr, T., M. Marshall, and D. Khosla. 2000. *Peace and Conflict 2001: A Global Survey of Conflicts, Self-Determination Movements, and Democracy*. College Park: Center for International Development and Conflict Management, University of Maryland.

Reuters Alert Net. 2001. "Phillipines" Country Profile: http://www.alertnet.org/thefacts/countryprofiles/.

Tan, S.K. 1989. *Decolonization and Filipino Muslim Identity*. Quezon City, Philippines: Diliman.

Turner, M.M., R.J. May, and L. Turner. 1992. *Mindanao: Land of Unfulfilled Promise*. Quezon City, Philippines: New Day.

3.30 South Vietnam–China: Territorial Dispute and the Paracel Islands January 1974

At the end of World War II Japan renounced its claims to the Paracel Islands in the South China Sea. Since then, Brunei, China, Malaysia, the Philippines, and South Vietnam have disputed possession of these islands, as well as the Spratly Islands. The islands were thought to contain oil deposits, although no independent evidence had confirmed this information.

In January 1974 South Vietnam formally incorporated the Paracel Islands into its Phuoc Tuy province and began granting contracts for oil exploration. China rigorously objected to this de facto assertion of ownership. South Vietnam then sent naval patrols to the area to bolster its claims, and a number of naval clashes occurred. The conflict escalated when both sides sent in troops and land fighting broke out. The Chinese held the Paracel Islands, taking the Vietnamese inhabitants prisoner, while South Vietnam reinforced its garrisons on the Spratly Islands. There were twenty to thirty fatalities, and, although the dispute lapsed after this, China took the Spratly Islands in an armed encounter in 1988 (*see* conflict 3.49). No serious attempts at peaceful conflict management took place during this conflict.

References

Day, A., ed. 1987. *Border and Territorial Disputes*. 2d edition. Burnt Mill, Harlow (Essex), England: Longman.

Tillema, H.K. 1991. *International Armed Conflict Since 1945: A Bibliographic Handbook of Wars and Military Interventions*. Boulder: Westview.

Valencia, M.J. 1995. *China and the South China Sea Disputes*. Adelphi Papers #298. London: IISS.

3.31 North Korea–South Korea: Demilitarized Zone and Invasion Threat February–July 1975

North and South Korea had been implacable enemies since the Korean War (1950–1953). The constant strain produced border incidents in 1965 and a continuous state of alert (*see* conflict 3.25). Talks aimed at normalizing relations had been going on since 1972 without success, and tensions escalated again in early 1972 following the discovery of tunnels under the demilitarized zone (DMZ). The Communist victories in Cambodia and Vietnam, combined with stepped-up contacts between Pyongyang and Beijing, served only to heighten tensions, prompting South Korean allegations of an imminent invasion by North Korea. U.S. warnings against such an invasion included the threat of using tactical nuclear weapons.

During May and June 1975, North Korean leader Kim Il Sung railed against the United Nations' North-South, or "two Koreas," plan. Both sides alleged military buildups in the border areas, published propaganda, and staged hostile incidents in the DMZ. No attempts at peaceful conflict management were made, and the dispute gradually abated. Armed conflict broke out again in 1984 and 1992 (*see* conflicts 3.48; 3.52).

References

Baldwin, F. 1974. *Without Parallel: The American-Korean Relationship Since 1945.* New York: Pantheon.

Barnds, W.J. 1976. *The Two Koreas in East Asian Affairs.* New York: New York University Press.

Foot, R. 1985. *The Wrong War: American Policy and the Dimensions of the Korean Conflict, 1950–1953.* Ithaca, N.Y.: Cornell University Press.

O'Ballance, E. 1969. *Korea: 1950–1953.* Hamden, Conn.: Archon.

Polomka, P. 1986. *The Two Koreas: Catalyst for Conflict in East-Asia?* Adelphi Papers #208. London: IISS.

Srivastava, M.P. 1982. *The Korean Conflict: Search for Unification.* New Delhi: Prentice Hall of India.

Tillema, H.K. 1991. *International Armed Conflict Since 1945: A Bibliographic Handbook of Wars and Military Interventions.* Boulder: Westview.

3.32 Cambodia (Kampuchea)–United States: Post–Vietnam War Tensions and the *Mayaguez* Incident May 1975

Cambodia served as a major battlefield and transit area during the Vietnam War and was subjected to a massive aerial bombardment by the United States (*see* conflict 3.28). As a consequence, U.S.-Cambodian relations were quite strained in 1975. This particular incident began when a U.S. merchant ship, the *Mayaguez,* was stopped and boarded by Cambodian forces near the island of Poulowai, which Cambodia and South Vietnam both claimed. The ship was seized in international waters, and, on charges of spying and carrying military cargo, the crew was detained and interrogated. The United States called the seizure an act of "piracy" and responded with aerial actions against the boat carrying the U.S. crew. The conflict escalated when the United States landed marines near the Cambodian coast and began bombing raids on the Cambodian mainland, using Thailand as a military base for these operations, without Thai permission.

The United States used a Chinese liaison to demand the release of the crew members, without success, and on May 14, 1975, appealed to UN Secretary-General Kurt Waldheim to secure their release. On May 15 the Cambodian authorities released the ship and crew, but the United States continued its air assaults on Cambodian targets with numerous Cambodian casualties. Offensive U.S. operations stopped on May 20, and the dispute eventually lapsed. About fifty people were killed during the conflict, and tensions remained high for some time.

References

Caldwell, M., and L. Tan. 1973. *Cambodia in the Southeast Asian War.* New York: Monthly Review Press.

Chandler, D.P. 1991. *The Tragedy of Cambodian History: Politics, War, and Revolution Since 1945.* New Haven: Yale University Press.

Chen, K. 1987. *China's War with Vietnam, 1979: Issues, Decisions, and Implications.* Stanford, Calif.: Hoover.

Haas, M. 1991. *Cambodia, Pol Pot, and the United States: The Faustian Pact.* New York: Praeger.

Heder, S.R. 1991. *Reflections on Cambodian Political History: Background to Recent Developments.* Canberra: Strategic and Defence Studies Center, Australian National University.

Kiernan, B., and C. Boua. 1982. *Peasants and Politics in Kampuchea, 1942–1981.* London: Zed.

Shawcross, W. 1979. *Sideshow: Kissinger, Nixon, and the Destruction of Cambodia.* London: André Deutsch.

3.33 Laos–Thailand: Postrevolution Exodus and Border Incidents June 1975–January 1976

When the leftist Pathet Lao came to power in 1975 following years of civil war, Laotians, most of them from the professional and commercial classes, began flooding into neighboring Thailand. The presence of these exiles, plus a number of unresolved border disputes, greatly strained relations between Laos and Thailand in the period leading up to this conflict. It escalated when both sides broke off diplomatic relations and closed their common borders.

Beginning in June 1975 daily skirmishes on the frontier led to casualties, and on August 5 Laos arrested two Thai military attachés. Relations improved slightly after the attachés were released on August 15, and, in a conciliatory gesture, Thailand expelled leaders of the Meo tribes people (54,000 Meo refugees were encamped in Thailand, and their leaders were engaging in anti-Pathet Lao activities). Unsuccessful negotiations and border clashes continued until early 1976, when the conflict abated. The unresolved issues led to a recurrence of fighting in 1982, and a war that lasted from 1984 to 1988 (*see* conflicts 3.43; 3.47).

References

Alagappa, M. 1987. *The National Security of Developing States: Lessons from Thailand.* Dover: Auburn House.

Dommen, A.J. 1971. *Conflict in Laos.* Revised edition. New York: Praeger.

Gunn, G.C. 1990. *Rebellion in Laos: Peasant and Politics in a Colonial Backwater.* Boulder: Westview.

Kirk, D. 1971. *Wider War: The Struggle for Cambodia, Thailand, and Laos.* New York: Praeger.

Lissak, M. 1976. *Military Roles in Modernization: Civil-Military Relations in Thailand and Burma.* Beverly Hills: Sage.

Stuart-Fox, M. 1986. *Laos: Politics, Economics, and Society.* Boulder: Lynne Rienner.

Toye, H. 1968. *Laos: Buffer State or Battleground?* London: Oxford University Press.

Turton, A., J. Fast, and M. Caldwell, eds. 1978. *Thailand: Roots of Conflict.* Nottingham: Spokesman Books.

3.34 East Timor–Indonesia: Independence Struggle October 1975–May 2002

Portugal had ruled the eastern half of Timor, an island in the Lesser Sundas, which forms the southeastern portion of the Malay archipelago, since the sixteenth century. Japan took over the island during World War II, but Portugal regained control after Japan's defeat. In 1949 Indonesia assumed control over West Timor, which had been ruled by the Dutch.

In 1959 an East Timor revolt against Portuguese rule was put down. Following the 1974 coup in Lisbon and Portugal's loss of its African territories, Portugal allowed political organizations to form in East Timor. Several parties emerged: the pro-independence Frente Revolutionario de Este Timor Independente (Fretilin); the Partido Democratico (PDU), which favored federation with Portugal; and the Associacão da Populaca Democratica de Timor (Apodeti), which advocated union with Indonesia and which Indonesia supported.

Fighting among these factions broke out in October 1974, but ended in January 1975. In mid-September 1975 small-scale Indonesian military units began operating in East Timor on behalf of Apodeti, and by October civil war had broken out. Fretilin proclaimed independence from Portugal at the end of November, and on December 7, 1975, Indonesia began a full invasion of the island. Fighting was intense, and it is thought that as many as 100,000 people were killed during this period. In July 1976 Indonesia formally annexed East Timor and sent in more than 20,000 Indonesian troops. Fretilin supporters continued to fight on.

Hostilities continued in East Timor, with heavy casualties. In April 1977 an Australian fact-finding team found that Indonesia's incorporation of East Timor had become an irreversible fact. Despite this, during the late 1970s and into the 1980s the United Nations repeatedly reaffirmed East Timor's right to self-determination and continued to regard it as a Portuguese-administered colony. Along with the Red Cross, the UN continually called for Indonesian troops to cease human rights violations.

Guerrilla activity continued in the early 1980s, despite Indonesian military offensives, a program of "Jawanization" and resettlement, development funds, and amnesties for Fretilin guerrillas who surrendered. The first half of 1983 was relatively peaceful, but fighting broke out in August with an Indonesian offensive that lasted well into 1984. The United Nations, Australia, and the United States continued to pressure Indonesia to find a solution to the conflict.

By December 1988 Fretilin was no longer perceived as a security threat in East Timor, and Indonesia lifted a thirteen-year closed-territory status that had limited information on the situation there. In 1990 reports emerged, however, of violent suppressions of student-led demonstrations, continued unrest, and government refusals to negotiate with Fretilin. Persistent reports of human rights abuses against pro-independence activists continued in 1991.

On November 12, 1991, Indonesian troops opened fire on demonstrators in Dili, the capital of East Timor, killing as many as 180 people; the troops blamed the demonstrators for provoking the attack. The protest was to coincide with a visit from a Portuguese parliamentary delegation, which Indonesia subsequently canceled. As a result of international pressure over the incident, senior army officers were punished for their role in the massacre. This event marked an upsurge in pro-independence activities in the area, and hostilities persisted. Xanana, Fretilin's leader was captured in December 1992 and subsequently tried and imprisoned. The UN sponsored a number of high-level talks between Indonesia and Portugal in 1995, but the meetings failed to resolve any of the substantive issues, and human rights abuses, riots, and pro-independence activities continued.

In 1998 President Suharto of Indonesia was forced from power amid an economic crisis. His successor, B. J. Habibie, abruptly changed policy in early 1999, stating that East Timor could have independence if it voted to reject autonomy within Indonesia. In the lead-up to the independence referendum in August 1999, pro-Jakarta militias backed by the Indonesian military embarked on a wave of terror that killed dozens. On August 30, more than 450,000 East Timorese voted against autonomous status within Indonesia, favoring independence. Large-scale violence, mostly carried out by the pro-Jakarta militias, ensued. An estimated 400,000 to 500,000 people were driven from their homes, and the UN—with government agreement—dispatched an Australian-led multinational force to restore peace.

Indonesia recognized East Timor's right to independence in October 1999, leaving it under UN administration en route to full independence. Despite progress in East Timor, pro-Indonesia militias continued to operate and terrorize refugees in camps in neighboring West Timor. The militias forced thousands of people into West Timor, where nongovernmental organizations (NGOs) said they were unable to operate because of the danger to staff. About 90,000 East Timorese refugees were estimated to be in Indonesian territory.

In East Timor, peacekeepers found massive destruction of infrastructure. The United Nations Transitional Authority for East Timor had the responsibility for overseeing the initial reconstruction process and laying the foundation for democratic self-rule, although these efforts were hampered by militia attacks. Peacekeepers remained in the territory temporarily despite the announcement and international recognition of East Timor's independence in May 2002. Overall, it is thought that as many as 200,000 people were killed in the conflict, including many civilians who died from disease, starvation, and in reprisals.

References

Amnesty International. 1985. *East Timor: Violations of Human Rights: Extrajudicial Executions, "Disappearances," Torture, and Political Imprisonment, 1975–1984.* London: Amnesty International.

Budiardjo, C., and L. Liong. 1984. *The War Against East Timor.* London: Zed.

Dahm, B. 1971. *History of Indonesia in the Twentieth Century.* Translated by P.S. Falla. New York: Praeger.

Gurr, T., M. Marshall, and D. Khosla. 2000. *Peace and Conflict 2001: A Global Survey of Conflicts, Self-Determination Movements, and Democracy.* College Park: Center for International Development and Conflict Management, University of Maryland.

Jolliffe, J. 1978. *East Timor: Nationalism and Colonialism.* St. Lucia, Australia: University of Queensland Press.

Jones, H. 1971. *Indonesia: The Possible Dream.* New York: Harcourt, Brace, Jovanovich.

Reuters Alert Net. 2001. "East Timor" Country Profile: http://www.alertnet.org/thefacts/countryprofiles/ (February 25, 2002).

Suter, K.D. 1979. *West Irian, East Timor, and Indonesia.* London: Minority Rights Group.

Tillema, H.K. 1991. *International Armed Conflict Since 1945: A Bibliographic Handbook of Wars and Military Interventions.* Boulder: Westview.

U.S. Agency for International Development, Asia and the Near East. 2002. "East Timor." Country Overviews: http://www.usaid.gov/regions/ane/newpages/one_pagers/india01a.htm (March 2, 2002).

3.35 Cambodia (Kampuchea)–Thailand: Refugee Influx, Regional Tensions, and Border Skirmishes December 1975–February 1976

In 1975 Cambodia fell to the Communist Khmer Rouge, whose brutal collectivization drives and massive purges caused many Cambodians to flee to surrounding states, primarily Thailand. The new regime, which renamed the country Democratic Kampuchea, was hostile to foreigners, and relations with surrounding states were tense. In December 1975 a number of incidents took place along the Thai-Cambodian border and in the Gulf of Thailand.

From December 12 to 15 Thai border police clashed with Khmer Rouge troops in the Ta Phraya district east of Bangkok, resulting in several fatalities. There were also reports of Khmer troops crossing the border into Thailand and of activities by Cambodian guerrillas opposed to the Khmer regime, commanded by former prime minister In Tam. The Thai government responded by expelling In Tam from Thailand on December 22; he fled to France. Other incidents included the sinking of two vessels—an armed Cambodian fishing boat and a Thai fishing boat—in the Gulf of Thailand on February 20, 1976.

On January 22, 1976, the foreign ministers of Thailand and Cambodia agreed to meet for talks on February 27, but on February 22 the discussions were postponed at the request of the Cambodian government, which gave no reason. Four days later, however, the Khmer government alleged that a U.S. aircraft had dropped bombs on Siem Reap, which caused fatalities and heavy damage, and that these aircraft were based in Thailand. Thai premier Kukrit Pramoj denied the allegations, stating that no U.S. combat troops were stationed in Thailand. No other attempts at peaceful conflict management took place, and the dispute eventually lapsed. This was not the end of hostilities between the two regimes, however, with further armed incidents in 1976, 1977, and 1979 (*see* conflicts 3.36; 3.37; 3.40).

References

Caldwell, M., and L. Tan. 1973. *Cambodia in the Southeast Asian War.* New York: Monthly Review Press.

Chandler, D.P. 1991. *The Tragedy of Cambodian History: Politics, War, and Revolution Since 1945.* New Haven: Yale University Press.

Haas, M. 1991. *Cambodia, Pol Pot, and the United States: The Faustian Pact.* New York: Praeger.

Heder, S.R. 1991. *Reflections on Cambodian Political History: Background to Recent Developments.* Canberra: Strategic and Defence Studies Center, Australian National University.

Kiernan, B. 1985. *How Pol Pot Came to Power: A History of Communism in Kampuchea, 1930–1975.* London: Verso.

Shawcross, W. 1979. *Sideshow: Kissinger, Nixon, and the Destruction of Cambodia.* London: André Deutsch.

3.36 Thailand–Cambodia (Kampuchea): Refugee Influx, Regional Instability, and Khmer Rouge Border Incidents November–December 1976

The Khmer Rouge took control of Cambodia in 1975. Renaming it Democratic Kampuchea, the Khmer Rouge launched a vicious collectivization drive that sent many

Cambodians fleeing to Thailand. By 1978 perhaps as many as 1 million Cambodians had been killed or died from the enforced hardships. The massive numbers of refugees strained border relations between Thailand and Cambodia, and armed conflict erupted almost immediately (*see* conflict 3.35).

Relations between the two countries improved during 1976, however, with increasing diplomatic contacts, agreement on border markings in June, the reopening of their mutual frontier for trade (which had been closed since April 1975), and notably few incidents along the disputed frontier areas.

But tensions rose again when, on November 22, 1976, fighting broke out in the Thai coastal province of Trat. Cambodian troops and Thai border police exchanged fire, and both sides sustained fatalities. The hostilities increased when gunboats from both sides joined in the fighting and one of them sank. On December 24 more fighting occurred between the two countries' navies. The dispute eventually lapsed without any attempt at peaceful conflict management. Only three fatalities were reported, but the tensions caused by this conflict and the general instability in the region owing to the brutality of Pol Pot's regime led to armed conflict again in 1977 and 1979 (*see* conflicts 3.37; 3.40).

References

Chandler, D.P. 1991. *The Tragedy of Cambodian History: Politics, War, and Revolution Since 1945.* New Haven: Yale University Press.

Chang, P. 1985. *Kampuchea Between China and Vietnam.* Singapore: Singapore University Press.

Haas, M. 1991. *Cambodia, Pol Pot, and the United States: The Faustian Pact.* New York: Praeger.

Heder, S.R. 1991. *Reflections on Cambodian Political History: Background to Recent Developments.* Canberra: Strategic and Defence Studies Center, Australian National University.

Jackson, K., ed. 1989. *Cambodia, 1975–1978: Rendezvous with Death.* Princeton, N.J.: Princeton University Press.

Kiernan, B. 1985. *How Pol Pot Came to Power: A History of Communism in Kampuchea, 1930–1975.* London: Verso.

Shawcross, W. 1979. *Sideshow: Kissinger, Nixon, and the Destruction of Cambodia.* London: André Deutsch.

3.37 Cambodia (Kampuchea)–Thailand: Refugee Influx, Regional Instability, and Khmer Rouge Border Incidents January 1977–October 1978

The enforced hardships and brutality of Pol Pot's rural collectivization program in Cambodia, which the Khmer Rouge renamed Democratic Kampuchea, had caused the deaths of approximately 1 million Cambodians by 1978, a massive influx of refugees into Thailand, and regional instability, which particularly affected Thai-Cambodian border relations. The strained relations between Thailand and Cambodia in 1976 were marked by several border incidents (*see* conflicts 3.35; 3.36).

Relations worsened in late January 1977, when 300 Khmer Rouge soldiers crossed the border and raided three villages in the Prachin Buri province, east of Bangkok, which resulted in severe damage, a number of fatalities, and more refugees. The raids were followed by a clash with border police in the disputed border area. A major source of friction was the "Free Khmers," supporters of the former Lon Nol regime in Cambodia whose border raids were aimed at discrediting Pol Pot's regime. As a result of the January incursion, the border at Ban Aranyaprathet was closed on January 29, 1977.

Border incidents continued throughout 1977 between Thai, Khmer Rouge, and Cambodian rebel forces. On February 25 the Cambodian government alleged that Thai forces were responsible for several serious incidents over the past months and were aiding the Cambodian rebels. A major reason for the 1977 incidents was that the two neighbors were consulting different maps to determine the border. The Khmer Rouge were using maps based on a 1909 Thai-French border agreement, and the Thai authorities were using a U.S. military map prepared in 1954. Moreover, the 420-mile boundary was designated by only seventy-three markers, and some of the disputed areas were claimed by Thailand, when in fact the majority of the inhabitants were ethnic Khmers (Cambodians).

As clashes and incidents continued throughout the year, it was feared that Thailand would take full-scale military action. By January 1978 Cambodian troops were being reinforced along the Thai border because of fears that Thailand would use the border fighting as an excuse to launch retaliatory attacks.

Despite an agreement in February by the new Thai government to normalize relations with Cambodia, raids by Pol Pot's troops and small groups of Thai Communist guerrillas continued into 1978, including frequent attacks on Thai villages that caused damage and numerous fatalities. Thai military officials indicated that 111 border incidents had occurred in the first half of 1978 and that strong retaliatory action had been taken after each one.

Incidents continued until October 1978, when Cambodian troops were redeployed to the Vietnamese border. No attempts at peaceful conflict management occurred, and the dispute eventually lapsed. About 120 fatalities resulted from this conflict, a number of them civilian. Armed conflict broke out again in 1979 (*see* conflict 3.40).

References

Chandler, D.P. 1991. *The Tragedy of Cambodian History: Politics, War, and Revolution Since 1945.* New Haven: Yale University Press.

Chang, P. 1985. *Kampuchea Between China and Vietnam.* Singapore: Singapore University Press.

Haas, M. 1991. *Cambodia, Pol Pot, and the United States: The Faustian Pact.* New York: Praeger.

Heder, S.R. 1991. *Reflections on Cambodian Political History: Background to Recent Developments.* Canberra: Strategic and Defence Studies Center, Australian National University.

Jackson, K., ed. 1989. *Cambodia, 1975–1978: Rendezvous with Death.* Princeton, N.J.: Princeton University Press.

Shawcross, W. 1979. *Sideshow: Kissinger, Nixon, and the Destruction of Cambodia.* London: André Deutsch.

3.38 Cambodia (Kampuchea)–Vietnam: Border Fighting, Vietnamese Invasion, and the Cambodian Civil War January 1979–Ongoing

Pol Pot's Khmer Rouge guerrillas had taken control of Cambodia in 1975. Renaming the country Democratic Kampuchea, the Khmer Rouge launched a program of violent domestic repression in which an estimated 1 million Cambodians lost their lives. Violently xenophobic, Khmer Rouge troops also targeted the many ethnic Vietnamese residing in Cambodia, causing as many as 10,000 deaths. In the late 1970s Pol Pot's forces began a brutal purge of eastern Cambodia, which led to cross-border attacks on Vietnam in pursuit of refugees.

The many Vietnamese fatalities and border violations led to the formation of a Vietnamese-backed army of dissident Cambodians. In 1978 this army staged a full-scale invasion of Cambodia that by January 8, 1979, succeeded in capturing Phnom Penh. The Vietnamese then installed a puppet government under Heng Samrin. The new Vietnamese-backed regime then set about driving the Khmer Rouge out of Cambodia.

Although the rebel Communist regime staged major offensives throughout the 1980s against the Khmer Rouge forces, it was never totally successful. The Khmer Rouge were given sanctuary and aid in Thailand and China, and they also received aid from the United States and other Western states, despite their appalling human rights record. Prince Norodom Sihanouk, the former Cambodian premier, and Son Sann, the non-Communist leader, joined with the Khmer Rouge in an anti-Vietnamese alliance, but they were unable to drive out the Vietnamese army. The war ebbed and flowed with many fatalities throughout the 1980s.

In the late 1980s the Soviet Union pressured Vietnam to begin negotiating a withdrawal. A period of intense diplomatic activity ensued, producing a Vietnamese withdrawal in 1989 and UN-sponsored elections in 1993. The Khmer Rouge refused to disarm, however, and threatened to boycott the elections and resume full-scale civil war. They engaged in many provocative incidents throughout 1992.

True to their word, the Khmer Rouge boycotted the 1993 elections and resumed a limited, but at times intense, guerrilla war against the coalition government. Despite massive defections in 1994 and 1995, Khmer Rouge strength was estimated to be 5,000 to 10,000 dedicated guerrillas who fought regular battles with government troops in Khmer-controlled areas. The government was unable to defeat the rebel army, and the attacks continued, while in other areas of the country, a slow rebuilding process got under way. Attempts at finding a formula for including the Khmer Rouge in the Cambodian government and halting the fighting were unsuccessful.

The violence continued into the late 1990s. At least sixteen people were killed in March 1997 when grenades were thrown into an antigovernment rally, and two days of fighting were reported in Phnom Penh in July. The Khmer Rouge, which had begun to fracture in August 1996, suffered a further blow in March 1997, when many remaining troops mutinied and seized their headquarters at Anlong Veng. Khmer Rouge chief Pol Pot, purged in July 1979, died near the Thai border in April 1998.

Although remnants of the Khmer Rouge have resisted UN-sponsored reconciliation, government forces have reestablished control over the borderlands. A new coalition government, involving the main rivals for state power, formed in November 1998 after a 1997 coup and signaled a willingness to stabilize the country in its recovery from years of devastating armed conflict and violence. Two of the three remaining senior leaders of the Khmer Rouge surrendered late in December 1998, and the last of the rebel fighters formally joined the Cambodian army in February 1999.

Most peaceful conflict-management attempts failed to solve the basic problems presented by the presence of several well-armed and ideologically opposed factions. This war was particularly brutal—500,000 people are thought to have died, many of them civilians. The Vietnamese army is estimated to have lost more than 50,000 personnel.

References

Caldwell, M., and L. Tan. 1973. *Cambodia in the Southeast Asian War.* New York: Monthly Review Press.

Chandler, D.P. 1991. *The Tragedy of Cambodian History: Politics, War, and Revolution Since 1945.* New Haven: Yale University Press.

Chang, P. 1985. *Kampuchea Between China and Vietnam.* Singapore: Singapore University Press.

Chen, M. 1992. *The Strategic Triangle and Regional Conflicts: Lessons From the Indochina Wars.* Boulder: Lynne Rienner.

Evans, G., and K. Rowley. 1984. *Red Brotherhood at War: Indochina Since the Fall of Saigon*. London: Verso.

Gurr, T., M. Marshall, and D. Khosla. 2000. *Peace and Conflict 2001: A Global Survey of Conflicts, Self-Determination Movements, and Democracy*. College Park: Center for International Development and Conflict Management, University of Maryland.

Haas, M. 1991. *Cambodia, Pol Pot, and the United States: The Faustian Pact*. New York: Praeger.

Heder, S.R. 1991. *Reflections on Cambodian Political History: Background to Recent Developments*. Canberra: Strategic and Defence Studies Center, Australian National University.

Hildebrand, G.C., and G. Porter. 1976. *Cambodia: Starvation and Revolution*. New York: Monthly Review Press.

Jackson, K., ed. 1989. *Cambodia, 1975–1978: Rendezvous with Death*. Princeton, N.J.: Princeton University Press.

Kiernan, B., and C. Boua. 1982. *Peasants and Politics in Kampuchea, 1942–1981*. London: Zed.

Reuters Alert Net. 2001. "Cambodia" Country Profile: http://www.alertnet.org/thefacts/countryprofiles/ (February 25, 2002).

Shawcross, W. 1979. *Sideshow: Kissinger, Nixon, and the Destruction of Cambodia*. London: André Deutsch.

White, M. 2004. "Death Tolls for the Major Wars and Atrocities of the Twentieth Century." *20th Century Atlas—Alphabetical List of War, Massacre, Tyranny and Genocide*. http://users.erols.com/mwhite28/warstat2.htm#Cambodia. (Last updated February 2004; accessed May 24, 2004.)

3.39 China–Vietnam: Regional Rivalry and Border War
January 1979–June 1982

Sino-Vietnamese relations had been troubled since the unification of Vietnam at the end of the Vietnam War (*see* conflict 3.23). Chinese support for the Khmer Rouge in Cambodia, who were slaughtering ethnic Vietnamese people and violating Vietnam's borders, and the ongoing dispute over the Spratly and Paracel Islands led to a high level of tension between these two nations. Vietnam was also closely allied to the Soviet Union, which had become China's bitter enemy.

Tensions were raised to the breaking point in 1978 after a number of incidents in poorly demarcated border areas. China suspended all technical and economic aid to Vietnam, and Vietnam responded by persecuting and expelling thousands of Chinese. Vietnam's invasion of Cambodia proved to be the final straw for China, and it began to prepare for war.

In January 1979 a number of serious border incidents occurred, and in February 75,000 Chinese troops invaded Vietnam along the entire length of their mutual border. After capturing five provincial capitals by sheer weight of numbers, China was forced to pull back from a fierce Vietnamese counterattack. China announced its withdrawal from Vietnam in March 1979, following heavy defeats, but fighting continued in some border areas. It was a total defeat for China, and the initial fighting was thought to have cost China and Vietnam more than 50,000 troops. Fighting along the border, which was at times serious, continued until 1982, when both sides agreed to repatriate prisoners. China and Vietnam attempted a number of bilateral negotiations, but the talks failed to fully resolve the issues in dispute, and this conflict was a precursor to more fighting in 1983, 1984–1987, and 1988 (*see* conflicts 3.44; 3.45; 3.49).

References

Chang, P. 1986. *The Sino-Vietnamese Territorial Dispute*. Washington Papers #118. New York: CSIS/Praeger.

Chen, K. 1987. *China's War With Vietnam, 1979: Issues, Decisions, and Implications*. Stanford, Calif.: Hoover.

Duiker, W. 1986. *China and Vietnam: The Roots of Conflict*. Berkeley: Institute of East Asian Studies, University of California.

Hinton, H.C. 1966. *Communist China in World Politics*. New York: Houghton Mifflin.

Tillema, H.K. 1991. *International Armed Conflict Since 1945: A Bibliographic Handbook of Wars and Military Interventions*. Boulder: Westview.

Watson, F. 1966. *The Frontiers of China*. New York: Praeger.

3.40 Cambodia (Kampuchea)–Thailand: Khmer Rouge Insurgency and Border Conflict
December 1979–October 1980

Vietnam deposed Cambodian dictator Pol Pot's brutal regime in 1979, but fighting continued between the newly installed Heng Samrin regime and insurgent Khmer Rouge forces. The new regime in Phnom Penh renamed the country the People's Republic of Kampuchea (PRK). Beginning in December 1979, Thai-Cambodian relations deteriorated because of PRK military offensives against Khmer Rouge strongholds on the Thai border. The PRK accused Thailand of harboring the Khmer Rouge and Cambodian non-Communist resistance forces, allowing them to train and rest. During this period rival groups fought over black-market food supplies along the Thai border, resulting in more than 200 casualties.

In June 1980 the repatriation of refugees from Thailand prompted fears in the Vietnamese-backed PRK regime that Khmer Rouge forces would be strengthened; the act was said to demonstrate Thailand's hostile attitude to the PRK. On June 23 and 24 serious fighting occurred along the Thai border between Thai units and PRK forces. The Thai government protested the incident to the Vietnamese government and the UN secretary-general, appealing for the restoration of peace and security. Meetings of the Association of Southeast Asian Nations (ASEAN) in late June reinforced ASEAN and UN support for peace and backed recognition of the new PRK government. The United States also strengthened its military support for Thailand. From July to December 1980 Cambodia and Thailand made repeated accusations of border violations and the fighting between border troops continued.

ASEAN countries offered peace proposals that brought a partial settlement and cessation of hostilities in early August 1980, largely through the mediation of UN Secretary-General Kurt Waldheim. The two states then had further discussions in September and October at the United Nations that led to the resolution of additional issues. The fighting between Thai and PRK troops resulted in approximately 300 fatalities.

References

Chandler, D.P. 1991. *The Tragedy of Cambodian History: Politics, War, and Revolution Since 1945.* New Haven: Yale University Press.

Chang, P. 1985. *Kampuchea Between China and Vietnam.* Singapore: Singapore University Press.

Haas, M. 1991. *Cambodia, Pol Pot, and the United States: The Faustian Pact.* New York: Praeger.

Heder, S.R. 1991. *Reflections on Cambodian Political History: Background to Recent Developments.* Canberra: Strategic and Defence Studies Center, Australian National University.

Jackson, K., ed. 1989. *Cambodia, 1975–1978: Rendezvous with Death.* Princeton, N.J.: Princeton University Press.

Kiernan, B. 1985. *How Pol Pot Came to Power: A History of Communism in Kampuchea, 1930–1975.* London: Verso.

Shawcross, W. 1979. *Sideshow: Kissinger, Nixon, and the Destruction of Cambodia.* London: André Deutsch.

3.41 Espiritu Santo–Vanuatu (The New Hebrides): Secession Attempt May–September 1980

The eighty-three South Pacific islands that make up the New Hebrides Islands had been a jointly administered British and French Condominium since 1906. During the late 1970s, as the islands moved toward independence, various groups, including some that wanted to secede, stirred up a great deal of political turbulence. The islands became independent as the Republic of Vanuatu on July 30, 1980, but even before independence was official, secessionist movements erupted—primarily on the island of Espiritu Santo, but also on Aoba, Malakula, and Tanna—and were supported by numbers of local French-speaking residents.

On May 28, 1980, members of the Nagriamel movement, which was led by Jimmy Stevens, took control of Santo town and proclaimed a provisional government. In June and July negotiations between the secessionists and Vanuatu, French, and British officials failed, leading to the armed intervention involving 200 British and French troops, that took control of Santo on July 24 with only light resistance. Similar incidents took place on the island of Aoba. The Anglo-French joint force was replaced on August 18 by 150 Papua New Guinean (PNG) troops. It is believed that three people were killed in clashes between the PNG troops and secessionists, but by September 24, 1980, most of the rebels had been arrested and imprisoned.

References

Beasant, J. 1984. *The Santo Rebellion: An Empirical Reckoning.* Richmond (Victoria), Australia: Heinemann.

Tillema, H.K. 1991. *International Armed Conflict Since 1945: A Bibliographic Handbook of Wars and Military Interventions.* Boulder: Westview.

3.42 Indonesia–Papua New Guinea (PNG): Secessionist Warfare, Border Incidents, and the Irian Jaya Dispute May 1982–October 1984

The status of Irian Jaya (formerly West Irian) has long vexed Indonesia. In 1962 it went to war with the Netherlands in an effort to oust the former colonial power from the region, which makes up the western half of the island of New Guinea, and gain control over its abundant natural resources. A UN intervention in 1962 secured an end to the fighting and granted Indonesia possession of the territory (*see* conflict 3.19). There was one condition: Indonesia would have to effect a program leading Irian Jayan self-determination by 1969. This plan was never implemented.

An armed secessionist movement took shape in Irian Jaya by 1965 after it became clear to the ethnic Papuan inhabitants that Indonesia had no intention of granting them independence. The rebels often operated from Papua New Guinean (PNG) territory, on the eastern half of the island, where the local population provided them with sympathy and support (*see* conflict 3.24). Relations between Indonesia and the PNG deteriorated in early 1982. By May 1982 Indonesian troops had begun crossing into the PNG in pursuit of insurgents, provoking protest and troop buildups in the border area. Relations between the two countries were further strained by border incidents and the alleged infringement of PNG airspace by Indonesian military aircraft. The dispute was resolved after a new five-year border agreement was signed in October 1984, replacing a similar agreement signed in 1979. Five fatalities were reported in connection with these incidents.

The agreement did not prevent the Irian Jayan rebels from continuing their activities.

References

Dahm, B. 1971. *History of Indonesia in the Twentieth Century*. Translated by P.S. Falla. New York: Praeger.

Day, A., ed. 1987. *Border and Territorial Disputes*. 2d edition. Burnt Mill, Harlow (Essex), England: Longman.

Premdas, R. 1978. "Papua New Guinea in 1977: Elections and Relations With Indonesia." *Asian Survey* 18 (January): 58–67.

Suter, K.D. 1979. *West Irian, East Timor, and Indonesia*. London: Minority Rights Group.

Tillema, H.K. 1991. *International Armed Conflict Since 1945: A Bibliographic Handbook of Wars and Military Interventions*. Boulder: Westview.

3.43 Laos–Thailand: Territorial Dispute and Border Incidents June 1982

Relations between Laos and Thailand were complicated by an ill-defined and dense jungle border and a number of unresolved disputes over territorial boundaries. Relations were further strained after the Pathet Lao came to power in 1975, following years of civil war. Large numbers of Laotians, most of them from the professional and commercial classes, flooded into Thailand seeking refuge. The problems had already led to armed border clashes in 1975–1976 (*see* conflict 3.33) but, despite a number of incidents along the Thai-Laos border in early 1982, relations between the two countries had generally been improving with the help of reciprocal ministerial visits.

This particular conflict began on June 16, 1982, when it was reported that Lao troops on the island of Don Sangkhi in the Mekong River had opened fire on the Thai village of Ban Mae, killing two villagers. The following day, when Thai patrol boats passed the island, they were shelled; one sank, and another ran aground, killing two crew members. After additional shootings on June 22, the Thai ambassador to Laos made an official protest about the incidents, and the border was closed. No peaceful conflict management was attempted during the dispute, which eventually faded. Fighting broke out again in June 1984 (*see* conflict 3.47).

References

Alagappa, M. 1987. *The National Security of Developing States: Lessons from Thailand*. Dover: Auburn House.

Dommen, A.J. 1971. *Conflict in Laos*. Revised edition. New York: Praeger.

Gunn, G.C. 1990. *Rebellion in Laos: Peasant and Politics in a Colonial Backwater*. Boulder: Westview.

Kirk, D. 1971. *Wider War: The Struggle for Cambodia, Thailand, and Laos*. New York: Praeger.

Lissak, M. 1976. *Military Roles in Modernization: Civil-Military Relations in Thailand and Burma*. Beverly Hills: Sage.

Stuart-Fox, M. 1986. *Laos: Politics, Economics, and Society*. Boulder: Lynne Rienner.

Toye, H. 1968. *Laos: Buffer State or Battleground?* London: Oxford University Press.

Turton, A., J. Fast, and M. Caldwell, eds. 1978. *Thailand: Roots of Conflict*. Nottingham: Spokesman Books.

3.44 China–Vietnam: Regional Rivalry and Border Conflict April 1983

Sino-Vietnamese relations had been extremely hostile ever since a costly war in 1979 (*see* conflict 3.39). In Cambodia, the Vietnamese-backed Heng Samrin regime fought a running battle with Khmer Rouge guerrillas, which were supported by China. Troops engaged in a tense standoff on the Sino-Vietnam border, shelling each other's positions.

Repeated allegations of incursions and provocations by both sides escalated into fighting in April 1983. On April 16 Chinese soldiers in Guangxi Zhuangzu Autonomous Region shelled Vietnamese border positions; artillery bombardments and clashes spread to a second region on the border of Yunnan province the following day.

The fighting caused heavy casualties and coincided with a renewed Vietnamese offensive in Cambodia. No serious attempts at peaceful conflict management took place during the conflict, although Vietnam did adopt a conciliatory attitude toward China, apparently in response to pressure from the Soviet Union. The dispute gradually subsided in the following months but broke out into serious fighting again in January 1984 (*see* conflict 3.45).

References

Duiker, W. 1986. *China and Vietnam: The Roots of Conflict*. Berkeley: Institute of East Asian Studies, University of California.

Hinton, H.C. 1966. *Communist China in World Politics*. New York: Houghton Mifflin.

Watson, F. 1966. *The Frontiers of China*. New York: Praeger.

3.45 Vietnam–China: Regional Rivalry and Border Conflict January 1984–March 1987

China and Vietnam had been rivals since Vietnam was reunified at the end of the Vietnam War. They had fought an extremely bloody war in 1979 and in 1983 engaged in more fighting (*see* conflicts 3.39; 3.44). Strains increased in late 1983 after relations between China and the United States eased and Vietnam launched an offensive in Cambodia against the Chinese-backed Khmer Rouge. China and Vietnam also had a number of disputes over border demarcations.

From January to March 1984 many serious border incidents occurred, with shellings and incursions by both sides. These occasions were merely precursors to a major intensification of the fighting to come in April, when attempts to take the high ground meant massive shelling attacks and some serious incursions. In May the Chinese began to build up their troop concentrations along the border, causing tensions to rise.

Clashes continued along the border until March 1987, with particularly heavy fighting in October 1986 and January 1987. Although China threatened to mount a serious attack on Vietnam, these threats never materialized. Most of the Chinese offensives coincided with Vietnamese offensives in Cambodia, and China insisted that any peace talks between the two countries could take place only after a Vietnamese withdrawal from Cambodia. Because of this precondition, no attempts at peaceful conflict management took place, despite Vietnamese willingness. As many as 3,000 died in the conflict, most of them Chinese. The hostilities tapered off after 1987.

References

Butterworth, R.L. 1976. *Managing Interstate Conflict, 1945–1974.* Pittsburgh: Center for International Studies, University of Pittsburgh.

Day, A., ed. 1987. *Border and Territorial Disputes.* 2d edition. Burnt Mill, Harlow (Essex), England: Longman.

Tillema, H.K. 1991. *International Armed Conflict Since 1945: A Bibliographic Handbook of Wars and Military Interventions.* Boulder: Westview.

3.46 Burma–Thailand: Karen Separatist Insurgency, Counterinsurgency Raids, and Border Incidents March 1984

Burma had been fighting the separatist Karen guerrillas since 1949 in what has become the longest-running guerrilla insurgency in the world (*see* conflict 3.6). Occupying positions on the Thai border, the Karen rebels would attack Burmese targets and then withdraw across the border into the dense jungle. Relations between Burma and Thailand were quite strained because Burma suspected that the Thai government was actively aiding the rebels.

In March 1984 Burmese troops crossed the Moei River into Thailand to attack Karen rebel positions. Fighting broke out when the Burmese soldiers encountered a unit of Thai border police; two Thai border police were killed. The Burmese troops withdrew before Thai reinforcements could arrive and the conflict could escalate any further. There were no attempts at peaceful conflict management, and the dispute soon lapsed. More serious conflict had only narrowly been averted but did occur in 2001 (*see* conflict 3.63).

References

Cady, J. 1958. *A History of Modern Burma.* Ithaca, N.Y.: Cornell University Press.

Collis, M. 1975. *Trials in Burma.* New York: AMS.

Lintner, B. 1994. *Burma in Revolution: Opium and Insurgency Since 1948.* Boulder: Westview.

Silverstein, J. 1977. *Burma: Military Rule and the Politics of Stagnation.* Ithaca, N.Y.: Cornell University Press.

Smith, M. 1991. *Burma: Insurgency and the Politics of Ethnicity.* London: Atlantic Highlands.

Taylor, R.H. 1973. *Foreign and Domestic Consequences of the KMT Intervention in Burma.* Ithaca, N.Y.: Southeast Asian Program, Department of Asian Studies, Cornell University.

3.47 Thailand–Laos: Boundary Dispute and Border War June 1984–December 1988

Thailand and Laos had a history of armed conflict going back to 1975, when the Pathet Lao's victory sent a flood of Laotians, most of them from the professional and commercial classes, across the border into Thailand. Relations were also complicated by an ill-defined border and the consequent territorial disputes (*see* conflicts 3.33; 3.43).

Following a number of border incidents earlier in the year, a serious Lao-Thai clash occurred in June 1984 over a proposed road through villages on the Thai border that Laos claimed as its own. Small-scale clashes continued in the area, despite ongoing bilateral negotiations, until 1986, when the fighting became more serious. The fighting intensified in late 1987, and in the early part of 1988 the conflict threatened to escalate into all-out war, with air attacks and the use of heavy weaponry. Negotiations in February 1988 led to a cease-fire, and the conflict was over by December. In all, more than 700 military personnel died in the fighting.

References

Alagappa, M. 1987. *The National Security of Developing States: Lessons from Thailand.* Dover: Auburn House.

Dommen, A.J. 1971. *Conflict in Laos.* Revised edition. New York: Praeger.

Gunn, G.C. 1990. *Rebellion in Laos: Peasant and Politics in a Colonial Backwater.* Boulder: Westview.

Kirk, D. 1971. *Wider War: The Struggle for Cambodia, Thailand, and Laos.* New York: Praeger.

Lissak, M. 1976. *Military Roles in Modernization: Civil-Military Relations in Thailand and Burma.* Beverly Hills: Sage.

Stuart-Fox, M. 1986. *Laos: Politics, Economics, and Society.* Boulder: Lynne Rienner.

Toye, H. 1968. *Laos: Buffer State or Battleground?* London: Oxford University Press.

Turton, A., J. Fast, and M. Caldwell, eds. 1978. *Thailand: Roots of Conflict.* Nottingham: Spokesman Books.

3.48 North Korea–South Korea: Cold War Border Incidents November 1984

Following World War II two separate regimes were established on the Korean peninsula: the Communist Democratic People's Republic in the north, and the Republic of Korea in the south. Since the Korean War of 1950–1953, North Korean and South Korean troops had faced each other along the 38th parallel in an intensely hostile standoff that had given rise to a number of armed conflicts from 1950–1953, 1965 to 1968, and in 1975 (*see* conflicts 3.9; 3.25; 3.31).

This particular incident threatened to destroy a gradual improvement in relations. On November 23, 1984, shooting broke out between North Korean and South Korean units when a Soviet citizen crossed the border at Panmunjom in an attempt to defect; three soldiers from the north and one from the south were killed in the fighting. The potential for serious escalation was always present in conflicts between these two states. No attempts were made to settle the conflict peacefully, and fighting broke out again in 1992 (*see* conflict 3.52).

References

Baldwin, F. 1974. *Without Parallel: The American–Korean Relationship Since 1945.* New York: Pantheon.

Barnds, W.J. 1976. *The Two Koreas in East Asian Affairs.* New York: New York University Press.

Foot, R. 1985. *The Wrong War: American Policy and the Dimensions of the Korean Conflict, 1950–1953.* Ithaca, N.Y.: Cornell University Press.

O'Ballance, E. 1969. *Korea: 1950–1953.* Hamden, Conn.: Archon.

Polomka, P. 1986. *The Two Koreas: Catalyst for Conflict in East-Asia?* Adelphi Papers #208. London: IISS.

Srivastava, M.P. 1982. *The Korean Conflict: Search for Unification.* New Delhi: Prentice Hall of India.

Tillema, H.K. 1991. *International Armed Conflict Since 1945: A Bibliographic Handbook of Wars and Military Interventions.* Boulder: Westview.

3.49 Vietnam–China: Regional Rivalry, Sovereignty Dispute, and the Spratly Islands Dispute March 1988

China and Vietnam had been rivals in the region since the Vietnam War, when North Vietnam was closely allied with the Soviet Union. They fought a bloody war in 1979 and had disputed the ownership of the Paracel and Spratly Islands chains for decades. Both sides maintained that extensive oil reserves existed in the area, although this claim has never been proven. The real issue relates to their regional rivalry, and the dispute had simmered since the Vietnamese occupied the islands in 1975 (*see* conflicts 3.39; 3.44; 3.45).

In early 1988 a Chinese military force went ashore on the Spratly Islands, and not long afterward Chinese naval vessels sank a Vietnamese gunboat, killing more than seventy soldiers. Vietnam responded by sending naval reinforcements to the area, and the situation remained tense. Eventually, Vietnam withdrew unilaterally, and the conflict lapsed. The islands remain in dispute, however, and some minor attempts at conflict management have failed to make any progress. China's aggressive actions caused a great deal of concern to other states in the region who feared Chinese expansionist designs. Further armed conflicts over the islands took place in 1995 between China and the Philippines and between Taiwan and Vietnam (*see* conflicts 3.56; 3.57).

References

Chang, P. 1986. *The Sino-Vietnamese Territorial Dispute.* Washington Papers #118. New York: CSIS/Praeger.

Chen, K. 1987. *China's War With Vietnam, 1979: Issues, Decisions, and Implications.* Stanford, Calif.: Hoover.

Duiker, W. 1986. *China and Vietnam: The Roots of Conflict.* Berkeley: Institute of East Asian Studies, University of California.

Hinton, H.C. 1972. *China's Relations with Burma and Vietnam: A Brief Survey.* Ann Arbor, Michigan: University Microfilms.

Ross, R. 1988. *The Indochina Tangle: China's Vietnam Policy, 1975–1979.* New York: Columbia University Press.

Valencia, M.J. 1995. *China and the South China Sea Disputes.* Adelphi Papers #298. London: IISS.

Watson, F. 1966. *The Frontiers of China.* New York: Praeger.

3.50 Bougainville–Papua New Guinea: Separatist Insurgency and Secession Attempt October 1988–Ongoing

An island nation in the South Pacific, Papua New Guinea (PNG) comprises the eastern half of the mountainous island of New Guinea, in addition to the Bismarck archipelago, which includes New Britain and New Ireland; Bougainville and Buka, which form part of the West Solomon Islands; and other islands. PNG gained its independence from Australia in 1975 and is sometimes described as "a mountain of gold floating in a sea of oil" because of its abundant natural resources.

This particular conflict flared after years of anger over the seizure of a Bougainville copper mine by an Australian firm. The Panguna mine, one of the world's largest copper mines, had accounted for about a third of PNG's income. But the Australian owners had not compensated the Bougainville landowners. Led by Francis Ona, a former mine employee, the landowners incited insurgency and embarked on a sabotage campaign that led to several deaths and the deployment of the PNG army to quell the disturbances.

In May 1989 sabotage and violence closed the mine, and in July the government declared a state of emergency on Bougainville and withdrew government services. The government's brutal campaign to put down the rebellion actually redounded to the rebels' advantage. They called themselves the Bougainville Revolutionary Army (BRA), and the rebellion took on greater secessionist overtones. After failing to stop the rebellion, government forces withdrew from the island in March 1990, as a prelude to peace talks. In May 1990 the BRA declared independence for Bougainville, and PNG's government responded with a total blockade of the island. No other states recognized Bougainville's independence. Although a number of agreements were signed between the protagonists, they inevitably broke down over the issue of independence. Government troops returned to Bougainville in September 1990, April 1991, and May 1992. In October 1992 PNG forces launched a major offensive and began making large gains against Bougainville.

Although it refused to send troops, Australia provided helicopters and matériel to the PNG government starting in 1990. In late 1991 it became clear that the rebels were using the Solomon Islands not only as a base but also as a source of aid. This discovery led to PNG raids on Solomon territory in March and September 1992. The Solomons responded by protesting and deploying troops in the region. The conflict continued in a similar manner throughout 1993 and 1994.

In April 1995 successful talks led to the establishment of the Bougainville Transitional Government. The terrain and the indigenous roots of the rebellion prevented either side from gaining any significant advantage, and the issue of Bougainville independence proved to be the main stumbling block to gaining a resolution. A surge in rebel activities in late 1995 led to the abandonment of the Bougainville peace negotiations and a new round of hostilities. By the end of 1995, several hundred people had been killed as a direct result of the fighting, and up to 3,000 had died as a consequence of the economic and medical blockade.

Further negotiations with Sir Julius Chan, PNG's prime minister, continued into 1996. These and other negotiation efforts contributed to a more successful peace process that began in mid-1997. Since a July 1997 meeting of Bougainvillean groups at Burnham military barracks, New Zealand, the peace process has contributed to remarkable changes in Bougainville. The opposing armed elements have ceased fighting. Most of the tens of thousands of Bougainvillean refugees have left the camps in Bougainville and the Solomon Islands and returned home. All over Bougainville, individuals and communities are beginning to reconcile over the differences that contributed to and arose during the conflict. Support for peace is nearly universal among Bougainvilleans, but Ona, the BRA's leader, did not participate in the final peace accord.

Some sources of tension that contributed to the conflict remain unresolved, and new tensions have arisen. Basic law and order problems are increasing in some areas, and violent conflict erupted between the BRA elements in one area late in 1998. Bougainville's future political status and its path toward economic development remain uncertain.

References

Australian Department of Foreign Affairs and Trade. 2000. *Country Information, Papua New Guinea: Bougainville.* Background Notes: http://www.dfat.gov.au/geo/png/bougainville/png_bg.html (February 25, 2002).

Boucher, J., D. Landis, and K.A. Clark, eds. 1987. *Ethnic Conflict: International Perspectives.* Newbury Park, Calif.: Sage.

Brogan, P. 1990. *The Fighting Never Stopped: A Comprehensive Guide to World Conflicts Since 1945.* New York: Vintage.

Conner, W. 1994. *Ethnonationalism: The Quest for Understanding.* Princeton, N.J.: Princeton University Press.

Gurr, T.R. 1993. *Minorities at Risk: A Global View of Ethnopolitical Conflicts.* Washington, D.C.: U.S. Institute of Peace Press.

Regan, A. 1999. "Bougainville: The Peace Process and Beyond": http://rspas.anu.edu.au/melanesia/ajregan2.htm (accessed February 25, 2002).

3.51 Burma (Myanmar)–Bangladesh: Rohingya Muslim Rebellion and Border Incidents
December 1991

The Burmese government had been fighting Rohingya Muslim rebels in the province of Arakan for years. A brutal offensive against the rebels in late 1991 caused more than 60,000 civilian refugees to cross into neighboring Bangladesh. Border relations became strained as a result, culminating in an incident on December 21, 1991. Burmese border guards fired on a Bangladesh Rifles camp near Ukhia Upazila, killing one soldier and wounding seven others. Both countries then began massing troops in the region.

The dispute subsided in the following months, however, and agreement was reached on several important issues after negotiations in December 1991 and January and April 1992. The border in the region was ill-defined and frequently used by smugglers, and the continued presence of numerous refugees led to similar armed conflicts in 1993 and 1994 (*see* conflicts 3.53; 3.54).

References

Cady, J. 1958. *A History of Modern Burma.* Ithaca, N.Y.: Cornell University Press.

Collis, M. 1975. *Trials in Burma.* New York: AMS.

Lintner, B. 1994. *Burma in Revolution: Opium and Insurgency Since 1948.* Boulder: Westview.

Silverstein, J. 1977. *Burma: Military Rule and the Politics of Stagnation.* Ithaca, N.Y.: Cornell University Press.

Smith, M. 1991. *Burma: Insurgency and the Politics of Ethnicity.* London: Atlantic Highlands.

3.52 North Korea–South Korea: Historical Enmity and Border Incident May 1992

Relations between North Korea and South Korea were in a constant state of hostility. This conflict was the most serious border incident in several years and followed the pattern of earlier conflicts between the two countries since the Korean War (*see* conflicts 3.9; 3.25; 3.31; 3.48).

A heavily armed North Korean patrol was said to have infiltrated the demilitarized zone, where it encountered a South Korean unit. Three North Koreans were killed in the ensuing skirmish, and two South Korean soldiers were wounded. No attempts at peaceful conflict management were undertaken, and in the following months the conflict lapsed without any great concern. Given the history of conflict between the two states, however, this incident could easily have escalated into serious fighting.

References

Baldwin, F. 1974. *Without Parallel: The American–Korean Relationship Since 1945.* New York: Pantheon.

Barnds, W.J. 1976. *The Two Koreas in East Asian Affairs.* New York: New York University Press.

Foot, R. 1985. *The Wrong War: American Policy and the Dimensions of the Korean Conflict, 1950–1953.* Ithaca, New York: Cornell University Press.

O'Ballance, E. 1969. *Korea: 1950–1953.* Hamden, Conn.: Archon.

Polomka, P. 1986. *The Two Koreas: Catalyst for Conflict in East-Asia?* Adelphi Papers #208. London: IISS.

Srivastava, M.P. 1982. *The Korean Conflict: Search for Unification.* New Delhi: Prentice Hall of India.

Tillema, H.K. 1991. *International Armed Conflict Since 1945: A Bibliographic Handbook of Wars and Military Interventions.* Boulder: Westview.

3.53 Burma (Myanmar)–Bangladesh: Border Incidents March–September 1993

On March 21, 1993, Burmese border guards infiltrated Bangladeshi territory and attacked a number of villages, killing one person and wounding five others. Bangladesh responded to the incident with a storm of protest. The enormous Burmese refugee population in Bangladesh (some estimates put the number as high as 288,000) was already straining relations between the two countries, and the border incidents only made matters worse. Burma, called Myanmar by the military regime that came to power in 1988, then accused Bangladesh of allowing Burmese rebels to operate from its territory. Tensions remained high throughout April and May, especially after Burmese troops abducted a number of Bangladeshi fishermen and refused to release them.

The conflict escalated alarmingly in July, when Bangladesh began deploying large numbers of troops along the border with Burma after the country refused to release Bangladeshi smugglers it had taken into custody. Burma responded by reinforcing its troops in the area as well. In early September, Burmese border guards fired on a group of Bangladeshi fishermen, killing one and wounding four others. The conflict dissipated after this time. No attempts at peaceful conflict management took place, and a similar conflict broke out in 1994 (*see* conflict 3.54).

References

Cady, J. 1958. *A History of Modern Burma.* Ithaca, N.Y.: Cornell University Press.

Collis, M. 1975. *Trials in Burma.* New York: AMS.

Lintner, B. 1994. *Burma in Revolution: Opium and Insurgency Since 1948.* Boulder: Westview.

Silverstein, J. 1977. *Burma: Military Rule and the Politics of Stagnation.* Ithaca, N.Y.: Cornell University Press.

Smith, M. 1991. *Burma: Insurgency and the Politics of Ethnicity.* London: Atlantic Highlands.

Taylor, R.H. 1988. *The State in Burma.* Honolulu: University of Hawaii Press.

3.54 Burma (Myanmar)–Bangladesh: Border Incidents May–August 1994

Like earlier fighting between Burma and Bangladesh (*see* conflict 3.53), this conflict began when Burmese border guards abducted a number of Bangladeshi fishermen. Ill-defined and densely vegetated, the border between the two countries was used extensively by fishermen and smugglers. Tensions were high between the two states because of the large numbers of Burmese refugees who had fled to Bangladesh to escape the military junta. Burma, which was renamed Myanmar by the State Law and Order Restoration Council (SLORC), as the junta called itself, often accused Bangladesh of allowing Burmese rebels to operate from its territory.

In May 1994 Bangladeshi border guards fired on Burmese border guards. The conflict escalated with a troop buildup in the area and the reinforcement of border garrisons. Further incidents in June and August—including the killing of a Bangladeshi fisherman and the laying of mines on Bangladeshi territory by Burmese troops—kept the tension high. No serious attempts were made to manage the conflict peacefully, and the dispute eventually faded.

References

Cady, J. 1958. *A History of Modern Burma.* Ithaca, N.Y.: Cornell University Press.

Collis, M. 1975. *Trials in Burma.* New York: AMS.

Lintner, B. 1994. *Burma in Revolution: Opium and Insurgency Since 1948.* Boulder: Westview.

Silverstein, J. 1977. *Burma: Military Rule and the Politics of Stagnation.* Ithaca, N.Y.: Cornell University Press.

Smith, M. 1991. *Burma: Insurgency and the Politics of Ethnicity.* London: Atlantic Highlands.

Taylor, R.H. 1988. *The State in Burma.* Honolulu: University of Hawaii Press.

3.55 Taiwan–China: Nationalist–Communist Dispute and Shelling Incident November 1994

A series of dangerous conflicts had plagued Taiwanese-Chinese relations since the 1940s (*see* conflicts 3.7; 3.13; 3.15; 3.20). China had repeatedly expressed its intention to unite all the offshore islands, including Taiwan, with the mainland. Tensions between the two countries rose when twenty-four Taiwanese tourists were murdered in China in March 1994.

In mid-November Taiwanese troops stationed in Lesser Quemoy, an island less than 2 kilometers off the Chinese mainland, fired at least a dozen shells into a suburb of Xiamen. Several people were injured, and China put its forces on alert. There were grave fears of Chinese retaliation and a major escalation of the conflict. The Taiwanese government quickly apologized for the incident, however, claiming it was an accident, and offered to pay compensation to the victims. Although tensions remained high for a time, the conflict gradually eased. No other attempts at conflict management took place. Although only a few casualties occurred in this incident, the history of bloodshed between the two states meant a strong likelihood of future conflict.

References

Chiu, H., ed. 1979. *China and the Taiwan Issue.* New York: Praeger.

Fairbank, J.K. 1971. *The United States and China.* Cambridge: Harvard University Press.

Stolper, T. 1985. *China, Taiwan, and the Offshore Islands.* Armonk, N.Y.: M.E. Sharpe.

Tillema, H.K. 1991. *International Armed Conflict Since 1945: A Bibliographic Handbook of Wars and Military Interventions.* Boulder: Westview.

Tsou, T. 1959. *The Embroilment over Quemoy: Mao, Chiang, and Dulles.* Salt Lake City: Institute of International Studies, University of Utah.

Watson, F. 1966. *The Frontiers of China.* New York: Praeger.

3.56 China–The Philippines: Territorial Dispute and the Paracel and Spratly Islands Incidents January–February 1995

Brunei, China, Malaysia, the Philippines, Taiwan, and Vietnam for decades all claimed the Paracel and Spratly Island groups, which lie in the South China Sea. Thought to contain valuable mineral deposits, these islands were the source of armed conflict in 1956, 1974, and 1988 (*see* conflicts 3.14; 3.30; 3.49). Ongoing discussions among the claimants had resolved none of the issues, and ownership of the islands was a constant source of tension in the region.

In late January 1995 Chinese troops, supported by eight naval ships, occupied Mischief Reef, which was only 200 kilometers from the Philippine island of Palawan. The Philippines lodged a formal protest and began to step up its patrols in the area. Philippine troops reinforced other islands already held by the Philippines in the event of further Chinese attacks, and tensions remained high.

In March 1995 Philippine patrols arrested more than sixty Chinese fishermen and detained a number of Chinese vessels said to be violating Philippine waters. The conflict escalated even further when Philippine patrols began to destroy Chinese territorial markers in the area. The conflict died down after this, but another armed clash between Spratly Island claimants occurred in March 1995 (*see* conflict 3.57).

References

Day, A., ed. 1987. *Border and Territorial Disputes.* 2d edition. Burnt Mill, Harlow (Essex), England: Longman.

Tillema, H.K. 1991. *International Armed Conflict Since 1945: A Bibliographic Handbook of Wars and Military Interventions*. Boulder: Westview.

Valencia, M.J. 1995. *China and the South China Sea Disputes*. Adelphi Papers #298. London: IISS.

3.57 Taiwan–Vietnam: Territorial Dispute and Spratly Islands Clash March 1995

Chinese-Philippine fighting over the disputed Spratly Islands chain in January 1995 led to a heightened state of tension in the area (*see* conflict 3.56). The islands were claimed in whole or in part by Brunei, China, Malaysia, the Philippines, Taiwan, and Vietnam. Armed conflict had broken out over either the Spratly Islands or the other disputed island chain in the region, the Paracel Islands, in 1956, 1974 and 1988 (*see* conflicts 3.14; 3.30; 3.49). Although it was never proven, the island chain was thought to contain valuable mineral deposits.

The territorial dispute heated up in early 1995, when Taiwan started building outposts on the disputed Ban Than island. Vietnam claimed Ban Than, but Taiwan announced plans to rename it Taiping. On March 25 Taiwanese troops fired on a Chinese freighter as it passed the island. Vietnam protested the incident and demanded the withdrawal of Taiwan from Ban Than, while also reinforcing its presence in the area.

Tensions remained high, especially after Vietnam reasserted its claim to the islands in mid-April, but, with no further incidents, the conflict eased. The islands remained a potential flashpoint in the region throughout the rest of 1995.

References

Day, A., ed. 1987. *Border and Territorial Disputes*. 2d edition. Burnt Mill, Harlow (Essex), England: Longman.

Tillema, H.K. 1991. *International Armed Conflict Since 1945: A Bibliographic Handbook of Wars and Military Interventions*. Boulder: Westview.

Valencia, M.J. 1995. *China and the South China Sea Disputes*. Adelphi Papers #298. London: IISS.

3.58 China–Taiwan: Rivalry and Military Tensions January 1996–August 1999

The dispute between China and Taiwan revolves around the very existence of Taiwan as an autonomous entity. Initially a place of refuge for Chiang Kai-shek's Kuomintang (Nationalists), Taiwan developed, with support from the United States, into a Nationalist stronghold with its own government and bureaucratic systems, even though mainland China claimed it as part of the nation. Despite the fact that both sides maintained policies promoting the reunification of China as one nation, differing ideologies have led to no resolution of the situation and the recurring outbreak of conflict in 1949–1953, 1954–1955, 1958, and 1962 (*see* conflicts 3.7; 3.13; 3.15; 3.20).

This particular conflict was born out of a Chinese desire to influence Taiwan's first direct presidential election, scheduled for March 26, 1996. At the heart of Chinese concerns was that election favorite Lee Teng Hui, a Taiwan native running on a pro-democracy platform, was seen as likely to promote independence upon victory. In the months preceding the election China performed an array of troop exercises and missile tests, with the *New York Times* reporting possible Chinese plans for a post-election missile attack. During this time, Chinese premier Li Peng announced that China favored peaceful means of reunification, but would not rule out the use of force. In late February 1996 China amassed some 150,000 troops in southeast Fujian (facing Taiwan), ostensibly to practice amphibious landings. At this point, Taiwan placed its military on alert and began to encourage the United States to use its influence to alleviate tensions in the region. The United States perceived no real threat of invasion, but raised concerns about the possibility of a "mistake" by either party leading to an escalation of the situation.

In the build-up to the election, China undertook a concerted policy of intimidation, demonstrating its ability to blockade Taiwan while also carrying out naval exercises and an array of missile tests directed toward it. During this time, the United States moved two aircraft carriers into the region and agreed to sell Stinger missiles to Taiwan. China's tactics ultimately failed, and Lee achieved a clear victory in the election. It has been suggested that Chinese actions may have even strengthened Lee's support, although the Taiwanese economy was undoubtedly damaged by the affair.

Subsequent to Lee's victory, tensions began to ease. China stepped back from its intimidatory stance, and the United States withdrew. In April Taiwan announced that it still wanted a peaceful dialogue on reunification. The statement was qualified, however, by indications a reunion could take place only on the basis of freedom, democracy, and the equitable distribution of wealth. Conciliatory gestures continued into May, and, although no real progress was made, the conflict did start to fade.

The conflict resurfaced in July 1999. President Lee stated that China and Taiwan should hold nation-to-nation talks, implying a shift away from the traditional "one nation" policy, which was reinforced by Taiwan's later announcement that it intended to pursue full United Nations membership. China condemned this apparent policy shift and returned to the tactics of 1996. Throughout July, August, and September China undertook a series of military exercises and threatened invasion of Taiwan, as well as seizing a Taiwanese supply ship. The conflict gradually deescalated although the issues at its heart remain.

References

Bercovitch, J., and Jackson, R. 1997. *International Conflict: A Chronological Encyclopedia of Conflicts and their Management 1945–1995*. Washington D.C.: Congressional Quarterly.

Keesing's Record of World Events: K40904, K40953, K40996, K41049, K41099, K43103-4, K43149.

3.59 North Korea–South Korea: Continuing Rivalry September 1996–November 2000

Since a major war between North Korea and South Korea from 1950 to 1953, four subsequent incidents have occurred between the two countries, and their rivalry continues to be the source of regional tension (*see* conflicts 3.25; 3.31; 3.48; 3.52). In September 1996 North Korean troops infiltrated South Korea by submarine. This move strained bilateral relations and was the most significant military intrusion into South Korea since 1968. North Korea later apologized in talks brokered by the United States. Several additional skirmishes occurred in 1996 and 1997, most notably at the border's demilitarized zone where several North Korean soldiers were injured and guard posts destroyed.

In March 1998 North Korea announced a "war mobilization" against a military build-up by South Korea, which claimed it was conducting a routine military exercise. Tensions rose higher with evidence of another North Korean submarine incursion into South Korean waters in June. On August 31, 1998, North Korea test-fired an alleged long-range ballistic missile, which flew over Japan and landed in the Pacific Ocean. This action added to growing concern over North Korea's nuclear capability and its development and alleged transfer of missile technology to Iran, Iraq, Pakistan, and Syria. The conflict escalated in September, when a U.S. spy satellite indicated that a second "missile" was to be launched. Both South Korea and Japan put their air force and warships on emergency alert, and the United States moved six strategic bombers to its base on Guam in a show of support.

Talks between North Korea and the United States in October 1998 attempted to defuse the situation, but no lasting agreement was reached. North Korea went on war alert in December, accusing the United States of bringing the country to the "brink of war" and citing U.S. President Bill Clinton's speech about the military danger on the Korean peninsula as evidence that the United States intended to invade North Korea. These events occurred in the midst of further allegations that North Korea was continuing its attempts to infiltrate South Korea.

In March 1999 the regional repercussions of the conflict became evident, as Japan responded aggressively to two suspected North Korean spy vessels that had intruded into Japanese waters in the Sea of Japan. Japanese patrol boats fired ammunition, and Maritime Self-Defence Force destroyers were deployed in pursuit of the vessels. Also in March, the United States refused to ease trade sanctions or establish diplomatic ties with North Korea until its leaders abandoned their ballistic missile development program and halted missile exports. A week-long naval confrontation between North Korea and South Korea occurred in June, allegedly an attempt by North Korea's military to sabotage upcoming talks. Tensions remained high throughout the following months in the midst of the continual threat of another North Korean missile launch.

The conflict escalated once again in September 1999, when North Korea announced that it was unilaterally extending its territorial waters 65 kilometers further south of the Northern Line Limit (NLL), a maritime border established at the end of the 1950–1953 war. In response, South Korea issued a warning that its armed forces would defend the NLL against any violations by the North Korean navy. Worsening the situation, U.S. satellite photos revealed in November that South Korea had been secretly developing long-range missiles able to strike the whole of North Korea.

In 2000 the situation began to improve. North Korea launched a diplomatic offensive that restored relations with Australia and Italy and held a series of talks on normalizing ties with the United States and Japan. Kim Jong-il made a surprise visit to Beijing, his first known overseas trip since becoming leader of North Korea. The burst of diplomacy led to a summit in Pyongyang in June between Kim and South Korea's president, Kim Dae-jung, the first face-to-face meeting between rival Korean leaders. They signed an agreement pledging economic cooperation, steps toward building mutual trust, and "to resolve the issues of reunification independently and through the joint efforts of the Korean people." In October Madeleine Albright, the U.S. secretary of state, paid a visit to North Korea that symbolized the promise of change on one of the world's last cold war frontiers.

In November 2000 talks between North Korea and the United States on North Korea's missile programs stalled, and talks between Japan and North Korea on establishing normal diplomatic relations also ended in failure. Relations between North Korea and South Korea, however, continued to improve through low-level military talks. At the end of 2000, the signs looked promising for future relations between the two countries, although the situation remains fragile and could regress at any stage.

References

Bercovitch, J., and R. Jackson. 1997. *International Conflict: A Chronological Encyclopedia of Conflicts and Their Management 1945–1995*. Washington, D.C.: Congressional Quarterly.

Reuters Alert Net. 2001. "North Korea" Country Profile: http://www.alertnet.org/thefacts/countryprofiles/ (accessed March 2, 2002).

Reuters Online: 41272-73, 41407, 41737, 41817, 41863, 42333, 42466, 42502, 42671-72, 42842, 42335, 42843, 43003, 43150, 43209-10, 43861-2.

3.60 China–The Philippines: Spratly Islands Incident April 1997–July 1999

The Spratly Islands have been at the center of a number of conflicts in the South China Sea region (*see* conflicts 3.49; 3.56). Brunei, China, Malaysia, the Philippines, Taiwan, and Vietnam have claimed the islands in part or in their entirety because they are thought to be rich in resources. This particular dispute, between China and the Philippines, involved the Chinese occupation of Mischief Reef in 1995 (*see* conflict 3.57).

In April 1997 Chinese naval vessels were present in the disputed area. Although the vessels in question left after protests from the Philippine foreign minister, another vessel was forcibly removed from the Scarborough Shoals region. Chinese nationals had previously raised a flag in the region. The Chinese flag was subsequently replaced by Filipino fishermen, resulting in Chinese protests. Another incident occurred in May, when twenty-one Chinese fishermen were arrested and their boats impounded for illegal entry into Philippine territory. Attempts to ease the tension began in June, and in bilateral talks each party agreed to inform the other of intended actions in the disputed region.

The issue remained contentious, however, and in November 1998 the conflict escalated, when the Chinese built developments on Mischief Reef and the Philippines seized another Chinese fishing vessel. At the end of November the two countries reached an agreement regarding the sharing of resources on Mischief Reef. Days later another twenty Chinese fishermen were seized, and Philippine president Joseph Estrada insisted that they be charged, rather than simply held and released, as this pattern had only exacerbated matters.

In January 1999 the Philippine National Security Council met with Estrada and former presidents Corazon Aquino and Fidel Ramos to discuss the Spratly situation. They expressed a desire to pursue the matter through bilateral and multilateral talks, although a decision to authorize modernization of the Philippine armed forces underpinned the talk of peacemaking. Talks between the two countries took place in March and resulted in an agreement to exercise "joint restraint," but little substantive progress resulted. China offered Philippine fishermen access to the developments on Mischief Reef but opposed any mediation of the conflict.

The conflict took a new twist in May 1999 with the sinking of a Chinese fishing boat and the loss of its crew, apparently because of an accidental collision with a Philippine navy vessel in rough seas. A similar incident occurred soon after, prompting the United States to express concern at the escalating situation. Also in May some progress was made in resolving the conflict. The Association of Southeast Asian Nations (ASEAN) endorsed a code of conduct for the Spratly Islands, drafted by the Philippines, and the code was approved in late November. Although opposed to the code of conduct, China attempted to reassure ASEAN that it did not seek hegemony in the Spratly Island region.

References

Bercovitch, J., and R. Jackson. 1997. *International Conflict: A Chronological Encyclopedia of Conflicts and Their Management 1945–1995*. Washington, D.C.: Congressional Quarterly.

Keesing's Record of World Events: K41645, K41686, K42622, K42679-80, K42731, K42835, K42946, K43068, K43263.

3.61 Vietnam–The Philippines: Spratly Islands Firing Incident October 1999

The Spratly Islands are a group of some 250 islands in the South China Sea that have long been a focal point of regional conflict. Situated along strategic shipping lines and believed to be rich in natural gas and oil, the Spratly Islands have been claimed by Brunei, China, Malaysia, the Philippines, Taiwan, and Vietnam. The result of such a number of competing claims is a plethora of confrontations of varying intensity between various parings of disputants. Vietnam was involved in disputes with both China in 1988 and Taiwan in 1995, and the Philippines have had conflicts with China in 1995 and 1997–1999 (*see* conflicts 3.49; 3.56; 3.57; 3.60).

On October 13, 1999, tensions flared between Vietnam and the Philippines after Vietnamese troops fired at, but did not hit, a Philippine plane flying over Vietnamese developments on the Tennent Reef. Vietnam claimed the low altitude reconnaissance flight to be a violation of their sovereignty. They also justified the shooting on the basis that such a flight pattern was suggestive of a bombing run. The Philippines, meanwhile, protested both the shooting and the increased Vietnamese development on islands considered to fall within the Philippines' exclusive economic zone.

Tensions eventually deescalated. Vietnam admitted the plane fired upon had not in fact been a direct threat, and the Philippines acknowledged that the fly-over had been lower than general protocol allowed. Vietnam also began promoting the idea of a code of conduct for parties involved in the disputed region, in keeping with an initiative of the sixth Association of Southeast Asian Nations (ASEAN) summit, although the issue remains largely unresolved.

References

Bercovitch, J., and R. Jackson. 1997. *International Conflict: A Chronological Encyclopedia of Conflicts and Their Management 1945–1995*. Washington, D.C.: Congressional Quarterly.

Keesing's Record of World Events: K43205.

Reuters Online: October 28, October 30, 1999.

Straits Times. October 30, 1999. http://straitstimes.asia1.com.sg/.

Vietnam News Agency. October 31, 1999. www.vnagency.com.vn/.

3.62 Thailand–Laos: Mekong River Territories August–September 2000

Territorial disputes have long been a source of tension between Laos and Thailand. A 1926 Siam-French treaty that poorly demarcated the borders, coupled with concerns arising from the flow of refugees into Thailand following the Laotian civil war, led to clashes between the two states in 1975–1976, 1982, and 1984 (*see* conflicts 3.33; 3.43; 3.47).

In August 2000 another flare-up occurred when Laotian troops seized two islands on the Mekong River, evicting forty-eight Thai farming families. Laos claimed sovereignty under the 1926 treaty and suggested that the presence of the Thai farmers was courtesy of Laotian magnanimity. Laos also claimed that the Mekong River islands had served as a refuge for antigovernment forces operating out of Thailand. Thai officials protested the occupation, requested a full withdrawal, and argued that a return to the status quo was necessary if talks on demarcation were to bear fruit. Such talks had been going on since 1996 and included an agreement to use the 1926 treaty to demarcate the Mekong River territory. The parties held talks in early September 2000 and resolved the matter September 13.

References

Bercovitch, J., and R. Jackson. 1997. *International Conflict: A Chronological Encyclopedia of Conflicts and Their Management 1945–1995*. Washington, D.C.: Congressional Quarterly.

Keesing's Record of World Events: K43146.

The Nation. August 26, September 8, 14, 2000. http://www.nation.com.pk/.

3.63 Thailand–Burma: Internal Civil Strife, Militia Activities, and Border Skirmishes March–May 2001

One side effect of Burma's ongoing civil strife and struggle against separatist insurgency was strained relations with Thailand. The poor state of relations was particularly evident in a series of border incidents sparked by Burma's suspicion of Thai complicity in Karen insurgencies that resulted in an armed skirmish between Burmese troops and Thai border police in 1984 (*see* conflict 3.46). Making matters worse were contentions regarding drug trafficking in the so-called "golden triangle" region encapsulating the border region of Burma, Laos, and Thailand, where several different militia groups control the trade.

In early March 2001 relations between Burma and Thailand again flared into conflict, as 200 Burmese troops crossed into Thailand. They were in pursuit of fleeing Shan State Army (SSA) rebels, a conglomerate force formed in 1995 by the three Shan groups that continued their resistance following the 1996 surrender of drug lord Khun Sa's Mong Tai army. Burma's actions were symptomatic of several months of growing tension in the region and continued suspicion that rebel forces were receiving Thai support. Two villagers in the Mae Sai district of Northern Chiang Rai province died during the incursion. Thailand's initial response was a heavy artillery bombardment that the Thai government claimed was responsible for the deaths of 100 Burmese. Burma placed the deaths at a more modest fourteen.

The month before a cease-fire had closed the border, but tensions remained. Local level talks broke down later that month, and Thai authorities detained forty Burmese nationals on suspicion of spying. Drug trafficking was allegedly at the heart of the dispute: Burma claimed that the SSA was smuggling narcotics into Thailand, and Thailand denied that it had any involvement with either the SSA or trafficking and instead blamed the Burmese-backed Wa militia for the flow of narcotics. Another aggravating factor was the number of Shan refugees flowing into Thailand to escape Wa offensives. In a step toward reconciliation, Thai foreign minister Surakiart Sarathai accepted an invitation from the Burmese foreign minister, Win Aung, to visit Burma for talks scheduled for May. By April, however, tensions were still building as the Burmese military reinforced its border positions. The foreign ministers' meeting did little to placate either side. Fighting erupted again, with Thai troops winning a four-day battle to recapture territory that had been seized by the United Wa State Army. Twenty Wa fighters were killed. Burma continued to reinforce its border and further inflamed the situation by bombarding an agricultural research facility across the Thai border.

Tensions eased at the end of May, when it was announced that Thailand's prime minister, Thaksin Shinawatra, would visit Burma in June in the hope of patching up relations between the two states. The parties agreed to cooperate to clamp down on the drug trade and to address border problems. This agreement lead to a deescalation of the conflict and a reopening of border checkpoints between the two countries.

References

CIA World Fact Book. 2002. http://cia.gov/cia/publications/factbook/.

The Europa World Year Book. 2002. London: Europa Publications Limited.

Keesing's Record of World Events: K44000, K44058, K44126, K44155.

3.64 North Korea–South Korea: Naval Incidents November 2001–July 2002

Following the cease-fire that unofficially ended the Korean War of 1950–1953, a roughly demarcated maritime border was established (*see* conflict 3.9). Known as the Northern Limit Line (NLL), the maritime border was enforced by the U.S.-led United Nations Command Armistice Committee (UNCMAC). North Korean fishing vessels, often escorted by North Korean naval patrol vessels, frequently violated this border, leading to a naval battle between the two Koreas in 1999, in which more than 100 North Korean sailors lost their lives and six North Korean naval vessels were lost or seriously damaged. South Korea only reported light injuries on its side (*see* conflict 3.59).

On November 27, 2001, an exchange of fire was reported between the borders of North Korea and South Korea. No casualties were reported.

A naval battle involving North Korean and South Korean ships occurred on June 29, 2002, and lasted approximately twenty-five minutes. South Korea reported four navy personnel killed, one missing, and twenty-two injured, and the loss of its frigate *Chamsuri 357*. North Korea eventually conceded that four of its sailors were killed, although South Korean estimates at the time placed the number closer to thirty. One North Korean vessel, which had also been seriously damaged in the 1999 conflict, was towed away from the scene on fire.

A mere eight days after the battle, on July 7, 2002, North Korea accused South Korea of violating its territorial waters, which South Korea strongly denied. North Korea also demanded that South Korea notify it before conducting a salvage operation because the North Koreans considered the vessel to have sunk in their territorial waters. South Korea denied this claim and warned that, if any further incidents of this type occurred, the response would be swift and violent and that the North Korean military would suffer the consequences.

In the weeks leading up to the battle, especially the two days before, North Korea had repeatedly violated the disputed border as a way to test South Korean responses. The battle occurred at the same time that South Korea was co-hosting the 2002 Soccer World Cup, fueling further speculation on motives.

South Korean navy vessels logged the activation of North Korea's antiship missile radar guiding systems, indicating the possibility of significant escalation, perhaps to a limited war involving missiles and coastal bombardment. Such an escalation may have meant not only a setback for peace and reunification efforts but also the possibility of U.S. and Chinese involvement. As it was, the United States was reported to be considering supplying South Korea with unmanned air vehicles (UAVs) to assist in its surveillance of North Korea.

South Korea issued a strong statement calling for North Korea to apologize, punish those responsible, and agree to steps to ensure that such crises did not happen again. North Korea responded with equally strong rhetoric and sought to place the blame on the South Koreans and the Americans. On July 25, 2002, however, North Korea issued an apology expressing regret and calling for a renewal of dialogue. This offer was received with mixed reaction in South Korea, but the official response was an acceptance of the apology and an agreement to recommence talks to be scheduled for August 2–4, 2002.

Observers speculated that China had influenced North Korea to issue the apology because of the sharp turnaround in North Korean policy. China and North Korea's penchant for secrecy makes such a claim difficult to confirm.

Beyond the damage inflicted on one of its naval vessels and the loss of several sailors, North Korea also lost aid from South Korea in the form of a cancelled shipment of 300,000 tons of surplus rice, a deal to set up a mobile phone service, and the opportunity for talks with the United States over security arrangements. After North Korea issued its formal apology, however, both South Korea and the United States stated their interest in again conducting formal talks.

References

Agence France-Presse. June 29, 30, 2002; July 9, 15, 2002. Downloaded from www.factiva.com July 1, 2003.

Associated Press Newswires. June 30, 2002; July 4, 5, 25, 2003. Downloaded from www.factiva.com July 1, 2003.

Associated Press Online. July 10, 2002. Downloaded from www.factiva.com July 1, 2003.

BBC. Monitoring Asia Pacific—Political. July 8, 2002. Downloaded from www.factiva.com July 1, 2003.

Boutilier, J. A. 2002. "Barometer Falling: Conflict and Cooperation in Asian Seas." *Asia-Pacific Defence Reporter* (Australia) 28, No. 7 (September/October): 40–42.

Dong-A Ilbo. (South Korea). June 30, 2002. Downloaded from www.factiva.com July 1, 2003.

The Economist July 4, 2002. "The Dead Are Not the Only Casualties."

Forecast International Press Release. July 2, 2002. Downloaded from www.factiva.com July 1, 2003.

The Independent (London). July 6, 2002. Downloaded from www.factiva.com July 1, 2003.

Korea Herald. July 5, 2002. Downloaded from www.factiva.com July 1, 2003.

Korea Times. June 20, 29, 2002. Downloaded from www.factiva.com July 1, 2003.

Kyodo News. (Japan). July 6, 30, 2002. Downloaded from www.factiva.com July 1, 2003.

New York Times. June 30, 2002. Downloaded from www.factiva.com July 1, 2003.

Organization of Asia-Pacific News Agencies. June 30, 2002. Downloaded from www.factiva.com July 1, 2003.

Reuters News Service. July 1, 2, 3, 7, 8, 9, 10, 26, 30, 2002. Downloaded from www.factiva.com July 1, 2003.

3.65 Japan–North Korea: Spy Ship Incident December 2001

On December 21, 2001, a Japanese Coast Guard vessel approached an unidentified fishing vessel and ordered it to stop. Following a tip-off by U.S. reconnaissance satellite information, supplied by the U.S. military, an airplane had spotted the fishing boat about 90 kilometers off the southwestern Japanese island of Amami-Oshima. The intruding vessel not only failed to stop but also ignored a warning shot. The Japanese Coast Guard vessel sprayed the bow with machine-gun fire, setting it ablaze. The intruding vessel continued its western path toward China pursued by twenty-seven Japanese ships and fourteen aircraft before four Japanese Coast Guard vessels intercepted and cornered it six hours later. As the Japanese drew close, the vessel in question opened fire using submachine guns, wounding two Japanese sailors.

It was subsequently reported that the vessel had also fired Soviet-era RPG-7 rockets, normally used as anti-tank weapons, and that two of these rockets had flown over Japanese vessel before harmlessly landing in the sea. The Japanese vessel then returned fire using machine guns, which quickly sank the other vessel. There was some suggestion that her sailors scuttled the ship to avoid her capture; one sailor reported he saw a flash about two minutes before the vessel sunk, an account borne out by video footage of the encounter. Two survivors clung to life preservers for two hours in the rough seas, but the waves and concerns the survivors would resist rescue efforts prevented their rescue. Some suggested that the survivors might have killed themselves to avoid capture. By December 24, 2001, two bodies had been recovered, believed to be part of an estimated fifteen-member crew. It was noted that the lifejackets and other items had Korean characters printed on them.

According to the Japanese Defense Agency, Japan had monitored radio communication between the sunken vessel and North Korea during the incident, bolstering claims the vessel was North Korean in origin. Sources from the agency reported the conversation they monitored led them to believe the vessel may have carried the stimulant drug methamphetamine, a substance known to have been imported into Japan from North Korea as a source of hard currency, something North Korea seriously lacks amid economic sanctions and trade embargoes.

On December 26, 2001, North Korea broke its silence, denying any involvement with or responsibility for the vessel and condemning Japan for launching a smear campaign for no reason. Only about ninety pieces of debris had been found by December 26, but nothing concrete linked the vessel to North Korea, prompting the Japanese government to consider a salvage operation of the vessel, which lay 100 meters below the surface. Complicating this option, however, was that the vessel lay in waters the Chinese government considered part of its economic exclusion zone (EEZ), which the Japanese did not question. China had already expressed concern over the incident, especially with regard to the use of arms to sink the vessel. As time passed, more evidence was amassed creating a strong case for the vessel's North Korean origin.

This incident followed two similar incidents in March 1999, when the Japanese Coast Guard fired warning shots at North Korean vessels and pursued them out of Japanese waters but were unable to apprehend them. A meeting reportedly occurred between Japan and North Korea sometime between late December to mid-January. Secrecy surrounded the event, and the details are sketchy, but no progress was reported. Japan successfully salvaged the vessel on September 11, 2002. It was determined to be of North Korean origin. Japan paid China 150 million yen as compensation for damage and disruption to fishing.

References

Associated Press Newswires. December 22, 2001; January 10, 25, 2002. Downloaded from www.factiva.com July 21, 2003.

BBC Monitoring Asia Pacific. December 28, 2002. Downloaded from www.factiva.com July 21, 2003.

Dow Jones International News. December 23, 24, 27, 2001. Downloaded from www.factiva.com July 21, 2003.

Keesing's Record of World Events: 44512.

Kyodo News. (Japan). December 26, 2001. Downloaded from www.factiva.com July 21, 2003.

New York Times. December 26, 2001; September 12, 2002. Downloaded from www.factiva.com July 21, 2003.

Reuters News Service. December 24, 2001. Downloaded from www.factiva.com July 21, 2003.

Valencia, M. J. January 10, 2002. "Japan's Rights and Wrongs in the 'Fishing Boat' Incident." Japan Times Online: http://www.japantimes.com/cgi-bin/getarticle.pl5?eo20020110a1.htm.

Van Dyke, J. M. Undated. "Military Ships and Planes Operating in the EEZ of Another Country." William S. Richardson School of Law, University of Hawaii at Manoa. http://www.hawaii.edu/elp/publications/faculty/TokyoPaperFinal.doc (accessed May 24, 2004).

Washington Post. December 23, 2001. Downloaded from www.factiva.com July 21, 2003.

Asia: Southwest Asia

List of Conflicts

4.1 India: Civil War, Independence, and Partition 207
1945–1948

4.2 Pakistan–India: Postpartition Separatism, First Kashmir War, and India-Pakistan Rivalry 207
October 1947–January 1949

4.3 India–Hyderabad: Postpartition Separatist Violence and Secession Attempt 208
July–September 1948

4.4 Afghanistan–Pakistan: Postindependence Pathan Border Conflict 208
August 1949

4.5 Afghanistan–Pakistan: The Pathan Territorial Conflict 209
June–October 1950

4.6 China–Tibet: Tibetan Autonomy Dispute 209
October 1950–May 1951

4.7 China–Tibet: Incorporation Struggle 210
March 1956–September 1965

4.8 India–Pakistan: Postpartition Border Tension and the Surma River Incidents 210
March 1958–September 1959

4.9 China–Nepal: Boundary Dispute 211
June 1959–July 1960

4.10 China–India: Sino-Indian Antagonism and the McMahon Line Boundary Dispute 211
August 1959–February 1960

4.11 Afghanistan–Pakistan: Boundary Dispute and Pathan Conflict 211
September 1960–May 1963

4.12 India–Portugal: Anti-Portuguese Territorial Dispute in Goa 212
December 1961

4.13 Nepal–India: Pro-Democratic Rebellion and Border Incidents 212
April–November 1962

4.14 India–China: Sino-Indian Wars and McMahon Line Border Dispute 212
October–November 1962

4.15 China–USSR: Territorial Dispute over Damansky Island 213
March 1963–September 1969

4.16 India–Pakistan: Border Skirmishes 213
1965–1970

4.17 India–Pakistan: Territorial Rivalry and the Second Kashmir War 214
August–September 1965

4.18 China–India: Sino-Indian Wars and McMahon Line Border Incidents 214
September 1965

4.19 Bangladesh–Pakistan: Secessionist Warfare and the Bangladesh War of Independence 215
March 1971–February 1974

4.20 Bangladesh: Postindependence Territorial Dispute and the Chittagong Hill Tracts Conflict 215
1975–Ongoing

4.21 China–India: Territorial Dispute and McMahon Line Border Incidents 216
October 1975

4.22 Bangladesh–India: Postcoup Tensions and Border Incidents 216
April 1976

4.23 Pakistan–Afghanistan: Pro-Monarchist Revolt and the Peshawar Rebellion 217
March–July 1979

4.24 Bangladesh–India: Boundary Dispute and Border Incidents 217
November 1979

4.25 USSR–Afghanistan: Soviet Invasion and the Afghan Civil War 218
December 1979–Ongoing

4.26 Pakistan–India: Regional Rivalry, Border Incidents, and India-Pakistan Wars 219
July 1981–August 1982

4.27 Sri Lanka: Communal Violence, Separatist Fighting, and Tamil-Sinhalese Conflict 219
July 1982–Ongoing

4.28 India–Bangladesh: Boundary Dispute and Border Conflict 221
December 1983–June 1984

4.29 **India–Pakistan: Territorial Dispute, India-Pakistan Rivalry, and the Siachin Glacier Dispute** 221
April 1984–September 1985

4.30 **India–Bangladesh: Boundary Disputes and the Muhuri River Incidents** 222
February–April 1986

4.31 **India–Pakistan: Territorial Dispute, Siachin Glacier/Kashmir Conflict, and India–Pakistan Rivalry** 222
Late 1986–Ongoing

4.32 **Maldives: Attempted Coup and Invasion** 223
November 1988

4.33 **Kyrgyzstan: Uzbek and Kyrgyzis Ethnic Conflict and Post–Soviet Violence** 223
June 1990

4.34 **Tajikistan: Post–Soviet Strife and Ethnic-Based Civil War** 224
April 1992–June 1997

4.35 **Nepal: Intervention and Maoist Guerrilla Insurgency** 225
Mid-1998–September 1999

4.36 **India–Bangladesh: Kushita Border Incident** 225
April–August 1999

4.37 **Uzbekistan–Kyrgyzstan/Tajikistan: Border Insurgency** 225
August 1999–September 2000

4.38 **Bangladesh–India: Border Incident and Seizure of Perdiwah** 226
April–July 2001

4.39 **United States–Afghanistan: Post–September 11 "War on Terrorism," Al Qaeda Terrorist Links, and Terrorist Containment** 227
September–December 2001

Countries in the Region

Countries included in this region are:

- Afghanistan
- Bangladesh
- Bhutan
- India
- Kazakhstan
- Kyrgyzstan
- Maldives
- Mongolia
- Nepal
- Pakistan
- Sri Lanka
- Tajikistan
- Turkmenistan
- Uzbekistan

Regional Overview

In early 1947 Britain decided that the time had come to end its rule of India, which at the time included what is now India, Pakistan, and Bangladesh. Pakistan became a separate entity from India under the provisions of the Indian Independence Act, which went into effect on August 15, 1947, and Bangladesh gained its independence from Pakistan in 1971.

The countries of the region have several different forms of government. The Republic of India is a federal republic, governed under a constitution and incorporating various features of the political systems of the United Kingdom, the United States, and other democracies. The Islamic Republic of Pakistan remained a republic until 1999, when General Pervez Musharraf took over in a military coup. Constitutional government was restored in 2002, although Musharraf remained president. The Democratic Socialist Republic of Sri Lanka has a popularly elected president and parliament. Nepal is a constitutional monarchy. The constitution, which was adopted in 1990, ended thirty years of absolute monarchy, in which the king dominated Nepalese politics and all political parties were banned.

The people of Southwest Asia practice a number of religions. For example, Pakistan is 97 percent Muslim; India is 81 percent Hindu, and the rest of the population is more Muslim than Buddhist; and Sri Lanka is 70 percent Buddhist, with a Hindu minority. The majority of Nepalese practice the official religion of Hinduism, but Buddhism is also important within the country.

India has the world's second largest population and is a country of incredible diversity, which is manifested in religious, linguistic, regional, ethnic, and social differences, including caste. A caste is a social class to which a person belongs at birth and which is ranked against other castes, typically on a continuum of perceived purity and pollution. Since independence, the importance of caste in India has declined. It is officially outlawed, but still plays a role in social life, especially when it comes to arranging marriages. Because of the Indian population's diversity, many predicted that democracy would not survive there and that coexistence among the people could happen only under authoritarian or military rule. To the surprise of many, that prediction has not come true, and today India is the world's largest democracy.

The economies of the region are primarily agricultural. In Pakistan nearly 50 percent of the population is employed in agriculture, and in Nepal it provides a livelihood for 79 percent of the population. The United Nations classifies Nepal as one of the least developed countries in the world, which can be attributed to its landlocked geography, rugged terrain, lack of natural resources, and poor infrastructure.

A defining characteristic of Southwest Asia's conflict environment is the ongoing nuclear rivalry between India and Pakistan. India received extensive military aid, especially from the Soviet Union, but many of its weapons systems, including some of the most advanced, such as missiles, are manufactured in India. The country exploded its first nuclear device in 1974, leading to an arms race with neighboring Pakistan. Twenty-four years later, India set off five more nuclear devices and declared itself a "nuclear weapons state." Within weeks, Pakistan responded with its own nuclear tests. The United States imposed economic sanctions against both countries.

Map 6. Southwest Asia

Concern about the nuclear arsenals of both countries has prompted international mediation in the conflict between the two countries over the territory of Kashmir, as a full-scale war between the two countries would have extremely serious global consequences.

Overview of Conflict

Since 1945 Southwest Asia has witnessed many interstate and civil wars. The current conflicts in the region are not new contenders; rather, they are protracted conflicts with long histories. They have lasted through the cold war period and into the twenty-first century.

Postcolonial nation building in Southwest Asia has occurred at the expense of ethnic and other minority groups, which has resulted in a number of intractable and continuing insurgencies. Ethnic groups have fought against other ethnic groups, and ethnic groups have fought the state over their identities and access to resources and to political power. At the root of these violent secessionist movements are economic deprivation, political alienation, and a sense of injustice. For example, the primary internal conflict that has beset Sri Lanka since its independence from Great Britain in 1948 centers on Tamil demands for a separate state in the north and east of the country. The type of democracy the British introduced in Sri Lanka resulted in a majority system in which the Sinhalese would always have political control. The Tamil minority's demands for both official recognition of their language and the establishment of a separate Tamil state under a federal system led to violent riots and heavy loss of life. The Sri Lankan government's refusal to make even minor concessions resulted in the Tamil adopting an even harder line.

The ethnic conflict, which gave rise to a separatist war, has claimed more than 60,000 lives, more than half of whom were civilians. In the 1980s the Tamil Tigers initiated a full-scale guerrilla war against the army. During the early 1980s the Indian government was very supportive of the Tamil movement, but changed its position toward the end of the 1980s. The civil war became an international conflict when India sent in 42,000 troops to northeast Sri Lanka in response to a request by the Sri Lankan government in 1987. A truce negotiated with the Tamil Tigers in 2001 led to a formal cease-fire, brokered by Norway and signed in February 2002. Peace talks began the following September.

Bengali nationalism, and the repression with which it was countered, resulted in civil war and the dismemberment of Pakistan. Pakistan formerly consisted of two regions—West Pakistan and East Pakistan—separated by more than 1,600 kilometers of India. Despite being the largest ethnic group in East Pakistan, the Bengalis were economically and politically marginalized and far removed geographically from West Pakistan, the nucleus of the country. East Pakistan declared its independence on March 26, 1971, causing a civil war that ended when India came to the aid of the new nation of Bangladesh. Despite this development, Pakistan continued to ignore the cultural, religious, ethnic and regional diversity, and the inequality that existed between these groups. The most recent challenge was the Sindh-Mohajir clash, which involved rival religious groups.

Intrareligious conflict between Sunnis and Shiites is a problem in Pakistan. The Pakistani constitution requires that laws be consistent with Islam and imposes some elements of Koranic law on Muslims and religious minorities. The government has little patience or care for religious minorities, and, although it condemns sectarian violence, the government has on occasion failed to intervene in violence directed at minority religious groups. The worst religious violence was directed against the country's Shiite minority, which continues to be disproportionate victims of individual and mass killings.

The enormity of the Indian Subcontinent means that there exists within it a vast array of conflicting groups. Violent conflicts in India that continue today include religious clashes between Hindus and Muslims; independence movements for Kashmir and Nagaland; ethnic conflict, particularly in the northeast between tribal groups and immigrant populations; caste violence and massacres; and agrarian and class conflicts. India has recently been experiencing attacks on religious minorities in many states. The worst took place in Gujarat where Hindus attacked Muslims in early 2002, leaving more than 2,000 dead and creating more than 100,000 refugees. The government failed to punish the participants of these attacks and various others around the country. This inaction against the agitators may encourage further acts of a similar nature.

Nepal, the poorest country in Asia, remained in a feudal condition throughout the twentieth century and also suffers from internal conflict. The civil war in Nepal is primarily fought over ideology. The Maoist insurgency, an armed uprising by Maoist extremists, began in 1996 and by January 2003 had claimed an estimated 5,000 lives. Their objectives are to oust the monarchy and establish a Socialist state. The popularity of communism and Maoist movements in Nepal comes from their association with antifeudalism, antipoverty politics, and democratization in a country with a tradition of autocratic rule. While the government struggles to contain the insurgency, the rebel forces remain in control of large areas of the western highlands. With its rugged terrain and dense forests, this area is favorable for guerrilla warfare. In 2001 the government declared a state of emergency, which gave more power to the army and resulted in the curtailment of civil liberties and brutal retaliatory fighting.

The rivalry between India and Pakistan, which began in 1947, has resulted in four wars—fought in 1947–1948, 1965, 1971, and 1999—and a large number of border disputes. The two countries' competing claims for Kashmir have been a major issue of contention for more than half a century, causing three of the four wars. In Kashmir, a Hindu ruler held sway over a Muslim majority in a country that was geographically and economically tied to West Pakistan. The ruler signed over Kashmir to India in 1947, but Pakistan refused to accept the act. Most Kashmiris are unsatisfied with Indian rule and have a closer affinity with Muslim Pakistan. The Muslim Kashmiris launched a strong secessionist insurgency against India in the 1980s that continues today. The periodic escalations of violence initiated by the separatist movement put a serious strain on relations between India and Pakistan. Fighting between Indian security forces and Muslim separatists in Kashmir escalated in 2001. India blamed Pakistan for supporting Kashmir-based militants who staged an attack on the Indian Parliament in December 2001, a claim Pakistan denies. By 2002 the two countries had amassed an estimated 1 million troops along their shared border. Intense international diplomacy helped to defuse the situation and restore Indian and Pakistani diplomatic ties.

In the 1980s Pakistan was dominated by events occurring in neighboring Afghanistan, where the 1979 Soviet invasion resulted in the flight of more than 3 million people into Pakistan. This huge number of Afghanis, the majority of whom were Pashtuns, added complications to the complex political environment in Pakistan, where Pashtuns were already an important ethnic minority. Their increased numbers intensified the Pashtun nationalist movement and posed an added threat to Pakistan's political and territorial integrity.

Pakistan served as a primary conduit for U.S. aid to the Afghan resistance, resulting in large amounts of U.S. aid to Pakistan as well. A similar situation presented itself following the September 11, 2001, terrorist attacks on the United States, which were linked to Osama bin

Laden. The United States ended its sanctions against Pakistan and sought its help in defeating the Taliban government of Afghanistan that had harbored bin Laden while he planned his attacks on America.

Conflict Management

The United States has adopted the role of mediator between India and Pakistan on a number of occasions. The United Nations mediated a truce between the two countries over the territory of Kashmir in 1949. Indian, U.S., and various European governments have expressed concern over the conflict situation in Nepal; however, no international initiatives to resolve or manage the conflict have been attempted. The only international involvement has come from nongovernmental organizations involved in activities such as human rights monitoring and humanitarian assistance. Norway was successful in mediating a cease-fire in the Sri Lankan civil war.

4.1 India: Civil War, Independence, and Partition 1945–1948

India's struggle for independence from Britain first escalated in 1942, when the Hindu-dominated National Congress Party launched its "Quit India" campaign of civil disobedience aimed at establishing an independent Indian state. India's Muslim population, represented by the Muslim League, laid claim to its own independent state. Although the campaign was interrupted by World War II, the demands for India's independence did not dissipate.

At the conclusion of the war, civil unrest, guerrilla warfare, and mutinies by Indian troops intensified. Police and British troops struggled to maintain order. Mahatma Mohandas Gandhi, who had been leading the nationalist movement since 1915, emerged as a major figure in the postwar negotiations leading to independence. Violence continued through 1946 and 1947 as leaders tried to create a political settlement that was amenable to both the Hindu and Muslim factions. A political solution was ultimately found, revolving around the partition of the Subcontinent into separate Muslim and Hindu states, Pakistan in the west, India in the center, and East Pakistan (later Bangladesh) in the east. The India Independence Act of 1947 specified August 15 as the date of transfer of power from Britain to the newly independent states of India and Pakistan. Burma and Ceylon (later Sri Lanka) also became independent at this time.

No outside attempts at mediation were made, and the fighting and violence associated with the independence struggle were at times savage. Deeply opposed to partition, Gandhi was assassinated in 1948 by a Hindu fanatic who objected to his tolerance for Muslims. Although estimates vary, it is believed that as many as 1 million people died during the conflict. Many of these deaths were the result of the partition, which caused perhaps one of the greatest forced migrations in history. Some 12 million people fled their homes—Muslims leaving India for Pakistan, and Hindus and Sikhs flooding into India from Pakistan. Intercommunal massacres were widespread, as in the use of the so-called "trains of death," in which entire trainloads of refugees were slaughtered and sent on their way with only the train engineer alive. Britain was criticized for not intervening to prevent the bloodshed. The partition of the Subcontinent resulted in persistent boundary problems that have led to wars, border conflicts, and separatist violence (*see* conflicts 4.2; 4.3; 4.8; 4.16; 4.17; 4.22; 4.24; 4.26; 4.28; 4.31; 4.36; 4.38).

References

Barnds, W. J. 1972. *India, Pakistan, and the Great Powers.* London: Pall Mall.

Blinkenberg, L. 1972. *India-Pakistan: The History of Unsolved Conflicts.* Copenhagen: Munksgaard.

Brines, R. 1968. *The Indo-Pakistani Conflict.* London: Pall Mall.

Butterworth, R. L. 1978. *Moderation from Management: International Organizations and Peace.* Pittsburgh: University of Pittsburgh Center for International Studies.

Choudhury, G. 1968. *Pakistan's Relations with India, 1947–1966.* New York: Praeger.

Hodson, H. 1985. *The Great Divide: Britain, India, Pakistan.* New York: Oxford University Press.

Lamb, A. 1967. *The Kashmir Problem: A Historical Survey.* New York: Columbia University Press.

Menon, V. 1961. *The Story of the Integration of the Indian States.* 3d edition. Bombay: Orient Longman.

Ramazani, P. 1978. *Sikkim: The Story of Its Integration with India.* New Delhi: Cosmo.

Tillema, H. K. 1991. *International Armed Conflict Since 1945: A Bibliographic Handbook of Wars and Military Interventions.* Boulder: Westview.

4.2 Pakistan–India: Postpartition Separatism, First Kashmir War, and India–Pakistan Rivalry October 1947–January 1949

After the 1947 partition of India, the status of Kashmir and Jammu became particularly troublesome. India and Pakistan have contested control over the territory in a series of wars.

Although Kashmir and Jammu had been predominantly Muslim since the late fourteenth century, Britain had installed a Hindu prince there in the mid-1800s. The first Kashmir war had its roots in the territory's thorny postpartition decision of whether to cede to Pakistan or

India. In early October 1947 Kashmir's Muslims sought to preempt a decision by staging a revolt in the city of Punch. Deserters from the Kashmir state security force and tribesmen invading from Pakistan soon joined the rebels.

By the end of the month the combined rebel force was nearing the state capital of Srinagar. In a transparent gambit to gain India's protection from the approaching rebels, the maharaja of Kashmir announced on October 27 that Kashmir would cede to India. Pakistan protested. Lord Mountbatten, the governor-general of India, responded by declaring that a plebiscite would be held on the territory's future status once the invaders had been repulsed and law and order restored.

On December 22, 1947, Prime Minister Jawaharlal Nehru of India claimed Pakistan was actively aiding the rebels and demanded that such assistance cease. Pakistan did not reply, and the UN Security Council took up the matter on January 1, 1948, dispatching a UN investigating committee to the region. It recommended on August 13, 1948, that a cease-fire be implemented, that all invading forces be withdrawn, and that India and Pakistan begin negotiations on the fate of Kashmir.

Further UN mediation efforts secured a cease-fire on December 31, 1948. Neither side had gained any battlefield dominance, and the state was divided into two zones of control. In subsequent years, protracted negotiations were held over the issue of a plebiscite in Kashmir. A series of UN negotiators sought to mediate the dispute, among them Sir Owen Simon, an Australian High Court judge; Frank P. Graham, an American university professor; and Gunnar Jarring of Sweden. They had little success.

India announced in 1956 that a plebiscite could not be held until all forces controlled by Pakistan were withdrawn from Kashmir. On November 17, 1956, the Kashmir Constituent Assembly adopted a resolution incorporating Kashmir into India. This declaration was rejected by Pakistan. The issue returned to the Security Council on January 11, 1962, and, with Anglo-American backing, the respective heads of government held a series of talks. The status of Kashmir remained unresolved, and on August 5, 1965, full-scale war once again broke out (*see* conflict 4.17).

The fighting between India and Pakistan was always intense, and more than 3,000 people died during the 1947–1949 conflict. The United Nations achieved an end to the fighting, but the political issues were never resolved; most of the thirty mediations and twelve negotiations were unsuccessful. Control over the territory still remains a contentious issue between India and Pakistan and has been at the root of subsequent conflicts between the two rivals (*see* conflicts 4.8; 4.16; 4.17; 4.26; 4.29; 4.31).

References

Appadorai, A. 1981. *The Domestic Roots of India's Foreign Policy, 1947–1972.* Delhi: Oxford University Press.

Blinkenberg, L. 1972. *India-Pakistan: The History of Unsolved Conflicts.* Copenhagen: Munksgaard.

Brines, R. 1968. *The Indo-Pakistani Conflict.* London: Pall Mall.

Choudhury, G. 1968. *Pakistan's Relations with India, 1947–1966.* New York: Praeger.

Lamb, A. 1967. *The Kashmir Problem: A Historical Survey.* New York: Columbia University Press.

Tillema, H.K. 1991. *International Armed Conflict Since 1945: A Bibliographic Handbook of Wars and Military Interventions.* Boulder: Westview.

4.3 India–Hyderabad: Postpartition Separatist Violence and Secession Attempt July–September 1948

The 1947 partition of the Subcontinent allowed a number of states to choose whether they wished to be part of India or Pakistan. Despite Indian pressure, the state of Hyderabad, in south-central India, chose to cede to neither India nor Pakistan. In 1948 Hyderabad, whose internal security forces possessed insufficient resources to retain control, was racked by communal violence resulting in thousands of deaths. India viewed the situation as a threat to its own internal security, especially after the unrest spilled into the neighboring Indian state of Madras.

Sir Mirza Mohammad Ismail, a former *dewan* (the equivalent of a prime minister) of Hyderabad, attempted to mediate the conflict in July and August, but failed, and India invaded on September 11, 1948. After intense fighting, India established control over the state on September 24. Hyderabad was formally incorporated into India in 1949. Approximately 800 Indian soldiers were killed during the two weeks of fighting, as were more than 1,000 nonmilitary personnel.

References

Appadorai, A. 1981. *The Domestic Roots of India's Foreign Policy, 1947–1972.* Delhi: Oxford University Press.

Leonard, K.I. 1978. *Social History of an Indian Caste: The Kayasths of Hyderabad.* Berkeley and Los Angeles: University of California Press.

Menon, V. 1961. *The Story of the Integration of the Indian States.* 3d edition. Bombay: Orient Longman.

Tillema, H.K. 1991. *International Armed Conflict Since 1945: A Bibliographic Handbook of Wars and Military Interventions.* Boulder: Westview.

4.4 Afghanistan–Pakistan: Postindependence Pathan Border Conflict August 1949

The status of the territory between Afghanistan and what was to become Pakistan had been in dispute since the late nineteenth century, when Britain imposed a boundary to include territory inhabited by a major Afghani tribe. Afghanistan intensified its claims on the region after Pakistan gained its independence and then began to promote separatist sentiment in the area.

In June 1949 a Pakistani aircraft bombed an Afghan base, causing some casualties. In protesting the attack, Afghanistan also accused Pakistan of intervening in its internal affairs. A number of minor border incidents occurred during 1950, including an alleged crossing into Pakistan by Afghan tribesmen and regular troops on September 30. The Afghan government denied official involvement, claiming that the force consisted solely of tribesmen operating within Pakistan.

An offer to mediate the conflict from U.S. ambassador-at-large Philip C. Jessup was not taken up, and a similar attempt by the shah of Iran was also unsuccessful. The dispute intensified in 1955 when Afghanistan mobilized its forces along the disputed border. Turkish prime minister Adnan Menderes succeeded in restoring diplomatic relations between the two states when negotiations broke down in December 1956.

About seventy people were killed during the course of the conflict, and the dispute has strained relations between Afghanistan and Pakistan ever since (*see* conflicts 4.5; 4.11; 4.23).

References

Day, A., ed. 1987. *Border and Territorial Disputes.* 2d edition. Burnt Mill, Harlow (Essex), England: Longman.

Tillema, H.K. 1991. *International Armed Conflict Since 1945: A Bibliographic Handbook of Wars and Military Interventions.* Boulder: Westview.

4.5 Afghanistan–Pakistan: The Pathan Territorial Conflict
June–October 1950

The Pathan conflict was the continuation of a previous dispute over territory that the British had given to Pakistan at Afghanistan's expense. The territory contained Pushtun (Pathan) tribes people, a major Afghani tribe. Afghanistan began agitating for the establishment of an independent Pathanistan in the disputed territory, and a series of armed clashes resulted. Incidents occurred in June, and then on September 30, 1950, a large force of Afghan tribesmen supported by regular Afghan troops invaded the disputed territory. They were pushed back by October 5, after attacks by the Pakistan air force. Afghanistan withdrew its troops early on in the invasion.

The shah of Iran tried to mediate early on, without much success. Later mediations by Saudi Arabia in 1955 and Prime Minister Adnan Menderes of Turkey in 1956 also failed to resolve the issues. In all, more than 100 people were killed during the fighting. Relations between the two countries were never friendly, and Pakistan allowed Afghan mujahideen (also known as mujahadeen or mujahedin) rebels to operate from its territory during Afghanistan's civil war (*see* conflict 4.25).

References

Day, A., ed. 1987. *Border and Territorial Disputes.* 2d edition. Burnt Mill, Harlow (Essex), England: Longman.

Donelan, M.D., and M.J. Grieve. 1973. *International Disputes: Case Histories, 1945–1970.* New York: St. Martin's.

Naumkin, V.V., ed. 1994. *Central Asia and Transcaucasia: Ethnicity and Conflict.* Westport, Conn.: Greenwood.

Tillema, H.K. 1991. *International Armed Conflict Since 1945: A Bibliographic Handbook of Wars and Military Interventions.* Boulder: Westview.

4.6 China–Tibet: Tibetan Autonomy Dispute
October 1950–May 1951

Tibet enjoyed independence from the seventh century until the eighteenth century, when the Manchu incorporated the area into China. China lost control over Tibet after the collapse of the Qing Dynasty in 1911. As a consequence, Britain and Tibet agreed on a new territorial boundary at the Simla Conference (1913–1914). This boundary remarcation, based on the McMahon Line, pushed Indian frontiers forward at Tibet's expense. Tibet successfully fought off a Chinese expedition in 1918, was left alone during World War II, and enjoyed an independent existence without widespread international recognition. With the victory of the Communists in China's civil war in 1949 (*see* conflict 3.1), the Tibetan government, fearing that China would reassert its claims to the region, began tripartite talks with the Chinese ambassador to New Delhi and Prime Minister Jawaharlal Nehru of India.

While negotiations were under way, however, the People's Liberation Army (PLA) invaded Tibet on October 7, 1950. China occupied Lhasa in March 1951, but Tibetan tribesmen violently resisted Chinese attempts to establish control in outlying areas. India protested the invasion but stopped short of intervening militarily. Tibet requested international assistance and protested to the United Nations. The General Assembly deferred consideration of the issue pending a continuance of negotiations between Tibet and China.

Negotiations in Beijing resulted in the Agreement on Measures for the Peaceful Liberation of Tibet (Seventeen Articles Agreement), signed on May 23, 1951. The agreement provided for limited autonomy for Tibet, but for all intents and purposes it had been absorbed into China. Tibet was ruled as a military occupation until annexation in 1965. About 2,000 people were killed in the invasion and subsequent crackdown, and the conflict poisoned relations between India and China for years to come.

References

Ginsburg, G., and M. Mathos. 1964. *Communist China and Tibet: The First Dozen Years.* The Hague: M. Nijhoff.

Richardson, H. 1984. *Tibet and Its History.* 2d edition. Boulder: Shambhala.

Shakabpa, T. 1967. *Tibet: A Political History.* New Haven: Yale University Press.

Tillema, H.K. 1991. *International Armed Conflict Since 1945: A Bibliographic Handbook of Wars and Military Interventions.* Boulder: Westview.

Walt van Praag, M.C. van. 1987. *The Status of Tibet: History, Rights, and Prospects in International Law.* Boulder: Westview.

4.7 China–Tibet: Incorporation Struggle March 1956–September 1965

After China invaded Tibet in 1950 (*see* conflict 4.6), Tibetans continued to agitate for autonomy. In February 1956 a guerrilla movement began in eastern Tibet escalating to a full-scale revolt by March. A period of brutal repression by Chinese forces ensued. Revolts continued to surface periodically, and by 1959 virtually the whole country was involved in a full-fledged guerrilla war. The Chinese moved in more than 200,000 troops. The Dalai Lama, whom Tibetans regard as both a king and a god, failed to reach a concessional agreement with Chinese authorities, and the full-scale conflict that broke out in March 1959 forced him and 100,000 Tibetans to flee to India. China soon crushed the revolt, killing thousands in reprisals and repressive measures. Persistent Tibetan resistance continued until 1965.

The attempt to put down the revolt led indirectly to armed conflict with India in 1959 (*see* conflict 4.10) and provoked incidents on the unmarked Tibetan-Nepali border when Chinese troops pursued rebel Tibetan tribesmen into Nepal territory (*see* conflict 4.9). No attempts at peaceful conflict management were undertaken, and the conflict cost approximately 100,000 lives. As many as 40,000 Chinese soldiers were killed in the fighting.

Chinese authorities have sought to suppress Tibetan culture and religion since the time of the revolt; they also instituted a campaign of Chinese resettlement in Tibet in order to dilute resistance to the authorities. The Dalai Lama is still campaigning for Tibetan independence.

References

Ginsburg, G., and M. Mathos. 1964. *Communist China and Tibet: The First Dozen Years.* The Hague: M. Nijhoff.

Richardson, H. 1984. *Tibet and Its History.* 2d edition. Boulder: Shambhala.

Shakabpa, T. 1967. *Tibet: A Political History.* New Haven: Yale University Press.

Tillema, H.K. 1991. *International Armed Conflict Since 1945: A Bibliographic Handbook of Wars and Military Interventions.* Boulder: Westview.

Walt van Praag, M.C. van. 1987. *The Status of Tibet: History, Rights, and Prospects in International Law.* Boulder: Westview.

4.8 India–Pakistan: Postpartition Border Tension and the Surma River Incidents March 1958–September 1959

Tremendous strains were produced by the 1947 partition of the Subcontinent and the ensuing secession of a primarily Muslim Pakistan from Hindu-dominated India (*see* conflict 4.2). The period of open conflict from March 1958 to September 1959 grew out of these postpartition tensions.

Border smuggling across the Surma River, which separates India from East Pakistan (now Bangladesh), precipitated a number of skirmishes involving small-arms fire between Pakistani and Indian patrols. The conflict escalated in early June 1958 when India began a series of cross-border raids. Pakistani troops began attacking Indian positions across the border in August.

Cross-border raids continued until a cease-fire was declared on August 26, 1958. At least twenty Indian and Pakistani military personnel were killed during the conflict. Senior officials from both countries, including Prime Minister Jawaharlal Nehru of India and President Muhammad Ayub Khan of Pakistan, met nine times before the issue was settled in January 1960. Ongoing tensions between the two states, however, led to conflict again in 1965 (*see* conflict 4.17).

References

Appadorai, A. 1981. *The Domestic Roots of India's Foreign Policy, 1947–1972.* Delhi: Oxford University Press.

Blinkenberg, L. 1972. *India-Pakistan: The History of Unsolved Conflicts.* Copenhagen: Munksgaard.

Brines, R. 1968. *The Indo-Pakistani Conflict.* London: Pall Mall.

Choudhury, G. 1968. *Pakistan's Relations with India, 1947–1966.* New York: Praeger.

Jacques, K. 2000. *Bangladesh, India, and Pakistan: International Relations and Regional Tensions in South Asia.* New York: St. Martin's.

Tillema, H.K. 1991. *International Armed Conflict Since 1945: A Bibliographic Handbook of Wars and Military Interventions.* Boulder: Westview.

4.9 China–Nepal: Boundary Dispute
June 1959–July 1960

The border between China and Nepal had never been officially demarcated, which led to this dispute. Following China's invasion of Tibet, Chinese forces made numerous sorties into Nepalese territory in pursuit of Tibetan rebels. A number of serious border incidents were reported from April to October 1959. On October 29 China and Nepal began negotiations on the border issue, and agreement was reached on March 22, 1960.

Chinese border violations continued, however, and Nepal began massing troops in the area, as did China. A major clash occurred on June 30, 1960, resulting in casualties. Nepal protested, and China agreed to pull back its troops. In October 1960 both sides agreed to officially demarcate the border. They signed a border pact in October 1961 thereby avoiding a major border war.

References

Day, A.R., and M.W. Doyle, eds. 1986. *Escalation and Intervention: Multilateral Security and Its Alternatives.* Boulder: Westview.

Tillema, H.K. 1991. *International Armed Conflict Since 1945: A Bibliographic Handbook of Wars and Military Interventions.* Boulder: Westview.

4.10 China–India: Sino-Indian Antagonism and the McMahon Line Boundary Dispute
August 1959–February 1960

China lost control of Tibet after the collapse of the Qing Dynasty in 1911. As a consequence, Britain and Tibet agreed on a new territorial boundary at the Simla Conference (1913–1914). This boundary remarcation, based on the McMahon Line, pushed Indian frontiers forward at Tibet's expense. The Communists disputed the validity of the boundary when they came to power in China in 1949 (*see* conflict 3.1).

Following China's invasion of Tibet in 1950–1951 and the exile of the Dalai Lama to India, the issue became a source of real contention (*see* conflicts 4.6; 4.7). China claimed India was interfering in Tibet's internal affairs by giving Tibetan nationalist rebels bases from which to launch attacks against occupying Chinese forces. China began moving large numbers of troops to the border areas.

On August 25, 1959, a Chinese force attacked Indian positions and captured the border post of Lonju. On October 21 a Chinese force took an Indian patrol hostage. At least twenty-five soldiers were killed during this conflict. In an attempt to ease tensions, Chinese premier Chou En-lai and Indian prime minister Jawaharlal Nehru met in New Delhi for a series of negotiations about the disputed territory. The talks were soon abandoned. The dispute abated somewhat in the months that followed, only to reemerge in 1962 in a much more serious confrontation (*see* conflict 4.14).

References

Chakravarti, P.C. 1971. *The Evolution of India's Northern Borders.* New York: Asia Publishing.

Day, A., ed. 1987. *Border and Territorial Disputes.* 2d edition. Burnt Mill, Harlow (Essex), England: Longman.

Hoffman, S. 1990. *India and the China Crisis.* Berkeley and Los Angeles: University of California Press.

Maxwell, N. 1972. *India's China War.* Garden City, N.Y.: Doubleday.

Rowland, J. 1967. *A History of Sino-Indian Relations.* Princeton, N.J.: Van Nostrand.

Tillema, H.K. 1991. *International Armed Conflict Since 1945: A Bibliographic Handbook of Wars and Military Interventions.* Boulder: Westview.

Vertzberger, Y. 1984. *Misperception in Foreign Policy Making: The Sino-Indian Conflict, 1959–1962.* Boulder: Westview.

4.11 Afghanistan–Pakistan: Boundary Dispute and Pathan Conflict
September 1960–May 1963

Pakistan and Afghanistan had already fought twice over this disputed boundary on the eastern side of their common border (*see* conflicts 4.4; 4.5). Because it was inhabited by an Afghan tribe, the Pathan (or Pushtu), Afghanistan refused to accept the internationally recognized border, demanding that the area either be integrated into Afghanistan or established as an autonomous Pathanistan.

Tensions rose dramatically in March 1960, when the Soviet Union openly declared support for Afghanistan's position. Starting in September, both Pakistan and Afghanistan made mutual allegations of border transgressions, with Pakistan protesting to Afghanistan about the country's mistreatment of Pakistani nationals living there.

Military actions increased in March 1961, and intermittent fighting continued for two years. Pakistan used its air force to bomb supposed arms distribution points, and cross-border raids became more serious. The Soviet Union began sending arms to Afghanistan, and the Afghan government stepped up its program of fomenting rebellion among the Pathan tribes people. The situation was extremely tense.

With the shah of Iran mediating and a change of government in Afghanistan, the parties reached a settlement on May 30, 1963. The border between the two countries reopened on July 20. In all, approximately thirty fatalities were recorded, but the two countries had narrowly avoided all-out war.

References

Day, A., ed. 1987. *Border and Territorial Disputes.* 2d edition. Burnt Mill, Harlow (Essex), England: Longman.

Donelan, M.D., and M.J. Grieve. 1973. *International Disputes: Case Histories, 1945–1970.* New York: St. Martin's.

Naumkin, V.V., ed. 1994. *Central Asia and Transcaucasia: Ethnicity and Conflict.* Westport, Conn.: Greenwood.

Tillema, H.K. 1991. *International Armed Conflict Since 1945: A Bibliographic Handbook of Wars and Military Interventions.* Boulder: Westview.

4.12 India–Portugal: Anti-Portuguese Territorial Dispute in Goa December 1961

Portugal had occupied a number of ports on the Indian coast since 1505. Many had been relinquished, but at the time of Indian independence in 1948, Portugal still had control over Goa, an economically valuable colony, and a few other smaller territories. India sought to take possession of the protectorates, but Portugal refused. India responded by smuggling in agitators to begin a passive resistance campaign in 1955, but the Portuguese authorities brutally suppressed this movement.

In 1961 the Indian government passed legislation annexing the territories. Both sides strengthened their military forces in the region during a stand-off period. On December 11, 1961, Indian prime minister Jawaharlal Nehru formally demanded that Portugal withdraw from Goa, and on December 15 the first minor border incidents between Portuguese and Indian troops occurred. Portugal appealed to the United Nations, but the Security Council was unable to deal with the conflict.

India launched a full-scale invasion of Goa on December 17, and after brief fighting Portugal surrendered the territory the following day. All the territories were subsequently incorporated into India. About seventy people were killed in the fighting, including two Indian and two Portuguese soldiers. Bitterness between the two states over the conflict continued until the 1974 coup in Lisbon, when Portugal dropped all its claims to the territories.

References

Day, A., ed. 1987. *Border and Territorial Disputes.* 2d edition. Burnt Mill, Harlow (Essex), England: Longman.

Rao, R. 1963. *Portuguese Rule in Goa, 1510–1961.* New York: Asia Publishing.

Rubinoff, A. 1971. *India's Use of Force in Goa.* Bombay: Popular Prakashan.

Tillema, H.K. 1991. *International Armed Conflict Since 1945: A Bibliographic Handbook of Wars and Military Interventions.* Boulder: Westview.

4.13 Nepal–India: Pro-Democratic Rebellion and Border Incidents April–November 1962

In December 1960 the king of Nepal dissolved the country's first democratically elected government. Nepalese rebels led by General Subarna Sumsher began a guerrilla campaign in an effort to restore democratic government. The rebellion spread to areas bordering with India, and Nepal accused India of organizing the rebellion. In fact, a number of Nepalese opposition groups were in exile in India, and from there they had mounted a vicious propaganda campaign.

The conflict escalated after Nepal made several agreements with China, including the building of a road from Nepal to Tibet. India regarded the road as a threat, as Chinese troops could be supplied all the way to the Indian border. By June 1962 the rebellion had become a full-scale uprising, and a number of border incidents occurred as Nepalese troops pursued rebels into Indian territory. China then announced it would defend Nepal if India invaded.

Events in Nepal were overtaken by the Sino-Indian war (*see* conflict 4.14), and the conflict lapsed completely in 1963. The rebellion diminished and was over by April 1963. Approximately thirty-five people were killed during the fighting. No serious attempts at peaceful conflict management took place.

References

Rose, L.E., and M.W. Fisher. 1970. *The Politics of Nepal: Persistence and Change in an Asian Monarchy.* Ithaca, N.Y.: Cornell University Press.

Rose, L.E., and J.T. Scholz. 1980. *Nepal: Profile of a Himalayan Kingdom.* Boulder: Westview.

Tillema, H.K. 1991. *International Armed Conflict Since 1945: A Bibliographic Handbook of Wars and Military Interventions.* Boulder: Westview.

Tyagi, S. 1974. *Indo-Nepalese Relations, 1858–1914.* Delhi: D.K. Publishing.

4.14 India–China: Sino–Indian Wars and McMahon Line Border Dispute October–November 1962

The armed incidents of October and November 1962 were a continuation of the ongoing border dispute between India and China over the McMahon Line (*see* conflict 4.10). Negotiations had proved fruitless, largely owing to Indian intransigence. India reinforced outposts in the area in early 1962, hoping to cut off Chinese supply lines. Numerous incidents occurred, and China also moved to reinforce its troops in the area. Determined to compel a settlement, China attacked in full force on October 20,

1962, and Indian forces retreated. The United States extended military aid to India, while China used its position of strength to propose a settlement. China declared a cease-fire on November 21 and withdrew across the border. India still refused Chinese offers.

Negotiations were held in Colombo under the auspices of the prime minister of Ceylon, Sirimavo Bandaranaike, the widow of Solomon Bandaranaike, the Ceylonese premier, who had been assassinated in 1959. Participants included representatives from Burma, Cambodia, Ceylon, Egypt, Ghana, and Indonesia. The Colombo conference led to a package aimed at resolving the dispute, which China and India accepted on January 28, 1963. It was not implemented, however, because of differing interpretations of each party's obligations under the package. China lost more than 1,000 troops during the fighting, and India lost 2,000. The issues involved were not fully settled until the 1990s and thus remained a source of contention between the two states for many years (*see* conflicts 4.18; 4.21).

References

Chakravarti, P.C. 1971. *The Evolution of India's Northern Borders.* New York: Asia Publishing.

Day, A., ed. 1987. *Border and Territorial Disputes.* 2d edition. Burnt Mill, Harlow (Essex), England: Longman.

Hoffman, S. 1990. *India and the China Crisis.* Berkeley and Los Angeles: University of California Press.

Maxwell, N. 1972. *India's China War.* Garden City, N.Y.: Doubleday.

Rowland, J. 1967. *A History of Sino-Indian Relations.* Princeton, N.J.: Van Nostrand.

Tillema, H.K. 1991. *International Armed Conflict Since 1945: A Bibliographic Handbook of Wars and Military Interventions.* Boulder: Westview.

Vertzberger, Y. 1984. *Misperception in Foreign Policy Making: The Sino-Indian Conflict, 1959–1962.* Boulder: Westview.

4.15 China–USSR: Territorial Dispute over Damansky Island
March 1963–September 1969

A series of treaties concluded between the Chinese and Russian governments between 1600 and 1900 ceded vast tracts of land on both sides of Mongolia to Russia. When Sino-Soviet relations began to deteriorate in 1960 over ideological differences, China reopened the issue of sovereignty over land ceded under the treaties. In March 1963 an official Chinese statement defined them as "Chinese territories taken by imperialism." In September 1964 both countries issued statements alleging border violations and involvement in their counterpart's internal affairs in the Idi region (also Ili) of Xinjiang (also Xingjian). Bilateral negotiations over the boundary problems commenced in February 1964, but were not fruitful and were therefore suspended in May without any progress being made.

A number of diplomatic exchanges took place in the ensuing years, but, with the advent of the Cultural Revolution in China in 1966, tensions increased. In January and February 1967 the Soviet embassy in Beijing was besieged for more than two weeks by protesters inflamed by the Cultural Revolution and the developing conflict. These unruly demonstrations were followed by a massive buildup of Chinese and Soviet forces along the border. The threat eased on February 21, when Chinese forces withdrew.

In the late 1960s a major point of tension was Damansky Island in the Ussuri River. Armed clashes occurred on the island in March 1969, after a Chinese patrol ambushed a Soviet patrol. An initial engagement took place on March 1–2, and intense fighting recurred on March 15, when both sides returned with reinforcements. Intermittent clashes continued on the island for the next few months.

On March 29 the Soviet Union issued a note reaffirming its claim to Damansky Island and called for the Chinese government to resume negotiations. Eventually, tensions eased and the dispute lapsed. It was thought that as many as 3,000 Soviet and Chinese troops were killed during the fighting, which was at times intense. The issues remained unresolved until 1991, when the Soviet Union collapsed. The new Russian government has taken steps to begin talks over the disputed territories.

References

An, T. 1973. *The Sino-Soviet Territorial Dispute.* Philadelphia: Westminster.

Borisov, O., and B. Koloskov. 1975. *Soviet-Chinese Relations, 1945–1970.* Bloomington: Indiana University Press.

Day, A., ed. 1987. *Border and Territorial Disputes.* 2d edition. Burnt Mill, Harlow (Essex), England: Longman.

Tillema, H.K. 1991. *International Armed Conflict Since 1945: A Bibliographic Handbook of Wars and Military Interventions.* Boulder: Westview.

4.16 India–Pakistan: Border Skirmishes
1965–1970

Following the partition of the Subcontinent in 1947, India and Pakistan immediately went to war over the disputed territory of Kashmir and Jammu. Relations had been hostile since then, and armed conflict erupted again in 1958–1959 and yet again in August 1965 (*see* conflicts 4.8; 4.17).

The period from late 1965 to 1970 saw an intensification of the conflicts between India and Pakistan, with frequent border incidents. Clashes occurred regularly in

Kashmir, the Rann of Kutch, and along the West Pakistan border. Despite a number of attempts at mediation, relations between the two sides did not improve. In all, it is estimated that 300 Indian and Pakistani military personnel were killed during these incidents. Four more wars broke out after this: 1971–1974, 1981–1982, 1984–1985, and 1986–Ongoing (*see* conflicts 4.19; 4.26; 4.29; 4.31).

References

Appadorai, A. 1981. *The Domestic Roots of India's Foreign Policy, 1947–1972.* Delhi: Oxford University Press.

Blinkenberg, L. 1972. *India-Pakistan: The History of Unsolved Conflicts.* Copenhagen: Munksgaard.

Brines, R. 1968. *The Indo-Pakistani Conflict.* London: Pall Mall.

Choudhury, G. 1968. *Pakistan's Relations with India, 1947–1966.* New York: Praeger.

Jacques, K. 2000. *Bangladesh, India, and Pakistan: International Relations and Regional Tensions in South Asia.* New York: St. Martin's.

Lamb, A. 1967. *The Kashmir Problem: A Historical Survey.* New York: Columbia University Press.

Tillema, H.K. 1991. *International Armed Conflict Since 1945: A Bibliographic Handbook of Wars and Military Interventions.* Boulder: Westview.

4.17 India–Pakistan: Territorial Rivalry and the Second Kashmir War
August–September 1965

India and Pakistan had been bitter rivals since the 1947 partition of the Subcontinent, with war breaking out almost immediately over the status of Jammu and Kashmir. After intense fighting, the territory was divided between the two countries in 1949, and a cease-fire line was drawn (*see* conflict 4.2).

The second Kashmir war began in August 1965, when large numbers of Pakistani irregulars began infiltrating India-controlled Kashmir. India responded by invading and capturing areas of Pakistan-controlled Kashmir. War broke out when Pakistan counterattacked across the 1949 cease-fire line.

The war took a major turn when India attacked West Pakistan across a wide front. The fighting was fierce, and India made significant territorial gains in the early stages. Intense UN mediation efforts secured a cease-fire in late September 1965, and the world organization then supervised troop withdrawals. More than 7,000 Indian and Pakistani troops were killed in this conflict, and the issues in the dispute remained unresolved. Since 1990 more than 20,000 people have been killed in Kashmir. Fighting between the two states recurred in 1971–1974, 1981–1982, 1984–1985, and 1986 (*see* conflicts 4.19; 4.26; 4.29; 4.30).

References

Appadorai, A. 1981. *The Domestic Roots of India's Foreign Policy, 1947–1972.* Delhi: Oxford University Press.

Blinkenberg, L. 1972. *India-Pakistan: The History of Unsolved Conflicts.* Copenhagen: Munksgaard.

Brines, R. 1968. *The Indo-Pakistani Conflict.* London: Pall Mall.

Choudhury, G. 1968. *Pakistan's Relations with India, 1947–1966.* New York: Praeger.

Lamb, A. 1967. *The Kashmir Problem: A Historical Survey.* New York: Columbia University Press.

Tillema, H.K. 1991. *International Armed Conflict Since 1945: A Bibliographic Handbook of Wars and Military Interventions.* Boulder: Westview.

4.18 China–India: Sino–Indian Wars and McMahon Line Border Incidents
September 1965

Sino–Indian relations had been hostile since China's invasion of Tibet in 1950, just a year after the Communists came to power in Beijing (*see* conflict 4.6). China disputed the McMahon Line, which demarcated the Tibetan-India border in 1914. From 1956 to 1958 India was seen to be supporting Tibetan rebels during Tibet's guerrilla war against the Chinese; furthermore, the Dalai Lama, whom the Tibetans revere as a god and king, chose exile in India, which did little to soothe Sino–Indian relations. Fighting erupted again in 1959–1960 and again in 1962, resulting in a humiliating military defeat for India (*see* conflicts 4.10; 4.14).

Embroiled in a war with Pakistan, India was irked by China's support for Pakistan's territorial ambitions. Mutual recriminations ensued about border violations and intimidating troop maneuvers. India asserted that on September 19, 1965, Chinese border guards had abducted and killed three Indian policemen. India also accused China of kidnapping three-man border patrols in Ladakh and Sikkim on September 26.

At the same time, China began to shell Indian positions on the border of Sikkim; India responded in kind. Neither side made any serious attempts to settle the conflict peacefully, but the fighting did ease after this time. About ten people were killed in the incidents. Armed conflict broke out again between the two states in 1975 (*see* conflict 4.21).

References

Chakravarti, P.C. 1971. *The Evolution of India's Northern Borders.* New York: Asia Publishing.

Day, A., ed. 1987. *Border and Territorial Disputes.* 2d edition. Burnt Mill, Harlow (Essex), England: Longman.

Hoffman, S. 1990. *India and the China Crisis.* Berkeley and Los Angeles: University of California Press.

Maxwell, N. 1972. *India's China War.* Garden City, N.Y.: Doubleday.

Rowland, J. 1967. *A History of Sino-Indian Relations.* Princeton, N.J.: Van Nostrand.

Tillema, H.K. 1991. *International Armed Conflict Since 1945: A Bibliographic Handbook of Wars and Military Interventions.* Boulder: Westview.

Vertzberger, Y. 1984. *Misperception in Foreign Policy Making: The Sino-Indian Conflict, 1959–1962.* Boulder: Westview.

4.19 Bangladesh–Pakistan: Secessionist Warfare and the Bangladesh War of Independence March 1971–February 1974

In addition to creating two new nations, the partition of the Indian Subcontinent in 1947 led to the creation of two separate provinces for Pakistan, one northwest of India (West Pakistan) and one east of India (East Pakistan) (*see* conflict 4.1). Over time, East Pakistan grew to begrudge West Pakistan's control of the central government. This resentment was fueled by the eastern province's geographical isolation in addition to its powerful feelings of Bengali separatism.

Accordingly, in the late 1960s the Awami League, formed by Sheik Mujibar Rahman, began to agitate for separation. The Awami League overwhelmingly won the 1970 elections to the national assembly. But on March 1 West Pakistani authorities postponed the inaugural sitting of the assembly. Large demonstrations and riots followed, bringing cruelly repressive action from the Pakistani military. More than 10 million refugees flooded into India, where some received arms and training and returned to East Pakistan (Bangladesh) to fight government forces.

Starting in April 1971, Pakistani troops conducted raids against Bengali sanctuaries in India, bringing some Indian retaliation. In November 1971 a large Indian force occupied border areas of East Pakistan, provoking a Pakistani mobilization on the West Pakistani border with the Punjab. India subsequently invaded West Pakistan on November 21, and East Pakistan on December 3. Pakistani forces in East Pakistan surrendered on December 17, and Bengali nationalists proclaimed the Republic of Bangladesh.

A cease-fire was announced in West Pakistan the next day, although skirmishes continued in some areas until 1974. Perhaps as many as 1 million Bengalis were killed in the fighting and associated violence and dislocation. Civilians were often the target of attacks, and reprisals and ethnic violence were rife. Nearly 8,000 West Pakistan troops are thought to have been killed during the conflict, along with 2,000 to 3,000 Indian troops.

References

Ahmed, M. 1978. *Bangladesh: Constitutional Quest for Autonomy, 1950–1971.* Wiesbaden: Steiner.

Appadorai, A. 1981. *The Domestic Roots of India's Foreign Policy, 1947–1972.* Delhi: Oxford University Press.

Choudhury, G. 1974. *The Last Days of United Pakistan.* London: C. Hurst.

Jackson, R.V. 1975. *South Asian Crisis: India-Pakistan-Bangladesh.* London: Chatto and Windus.

Jacques, K. 2000. *Bangladesh, India, and Pakistan: International Relations and Regional Tensions in South Asia.* New York: St. Martin's.

Jagdev Singh. 1988. *The Dismemberment of Pakistan: 1971 Indo-Pak War.* New Delhi: Lancer International.

Palit, D.K. 1972. *The Lightning Campaign: The Indo-Pakistan War, 1971.* Salisbury, England: Compton.

Rizvi, H. 1981. *Internal Strife and External Intervention: India's Role in the Civil War in East Pakistan/Bangladesh.* Lahore: Progressive Publishers.

Sisson, R., and L.E. Rose. 1990. *War and Secession: Pakistan, India, and the Creation of Bangladesh.* Berkeley and Los Angeles: University of California Press.

Tillema, H.K. 1991. *International Armed Conflict Since 1945: A Bibliographic Handbook of Wars and Military Interventions.* Boulder: Westview.

4.20 Bangladesh: Postindependence Territorial Dispute and the Chittagong Hill Tracts Conflict 1975–Ongoing

Inhabited by 600,000 Buddhist tribal people, the Chittagong Hill Tracts in eastern Bangladesh were originally administered separately from the rest of India by the British, and strict laws prevented outsiders from settling there. Just after the war for independence, the new Bangladesh government abolished the area's special status and encouraged Bengalis to settle there. To fight the moves, tribal leaders set up an association, the Chittagong Hill Tracts People's Solidarity Association (JSS).

The JSS formed a military wing known as the Shanti Bahini, which in the mid-1970s began attacking army outposts and Bengali villagers. Hundreds of people died in these notoriously brutal attacks. A ruthless campaign of repression ensued. India supported the insurgents from an early stage, and there were frequent cross-border incidents. Despite British counterinsurgency training for Bangladeshi forces, the fighting continued into the 1990s, by which time at least 300,000 Bengalis had settled in the Hill Tracts.

Limited autonomy was granted to the Hill Tracts in 1992. The parties held regular peace talks, but the negotiations failed to resolve the conflict. Low-level fighting continued intermittently until the end of 1995. In 1995,

2,000 tribal insurgents were operating in the Hill Tracts, and Bangladesh as a whole was in a state of civil unrest and political instability. More than 3,500 people had died in the fighting, and 50,000 refugees were encamped in the Indian state of Tripura.

In December 1997 a peace agreement with the Shanti Bahini rebels ended twenty-two years of insurgency and armed conflict. The agreement allowed for amnesty provisions, rebel disarmament, and greater control of the Hill Tracts by district councils. The Shanti Bahini rebels officially surrendered their arms at a ceremony in February 1998. Despite this progress, many of the issues that characterized the conflict remain unresolved, including adverse living conditions and encroachments by Bengali settlers in tribal areas.

References

Ahmed, M. 1978. *Bangladesh: Constitutional Quest for Autonomy, 1950–1971.* Wiesbaden: Steiner.

Brogan, P. 1989. *World Conflicts: Why and Where They Are Happening.* London: Bloomsbury.

Day, A., ed. 1987. *Border and Territorial Disputes.* 2d edition. Burnt Mill, Harlow (Essex), England: Longman.

Gurr, T., M. Marshall, and D. Khosla. 2000. *Peace and Conflict 2001: A Global Survey of Conflicts, Self-Determination Movements, and Democracy.* College Park: Center for International Development and Conflict Management, University of Maryland.

Jacques, K. 2000. *Bangladesh, India, and Pakistan: International Relations and Regional Tensions in South Asia.* New York: St. Martin's.

Reuters Online: 41964, 42271.

Sen Gupta, J. 1974. *History of the Freedom Movement in Bangladesh, 1943–1973.* Calcutta: Naya Prokash.

Sisson, R., and L.E. Rose. 1990. *War and Secession: Pakistan, India, and the Creation of Bangladesh.* Berkeley and Los Angeles: University of California Press.

4.21 China–India: Territorial Dispute and McMahon Line Border Incidents October 1975

Sino-Indian relations had been hostile since China's invasion of Tibet in 1950, just a year after the Communists came to power in Beijing (*see* conflicts 3.1; 4.6). Chinese Communists disputed the McMahon Line, which demarcated the Tibetan-India frontier in 1914. Relations between China and India deteriorated in 1956, when India supported Tibetan guerrillas in their war against the Chinese (*see* conflict 4.7). Matters worsened when India gave sanctuary to the Dalai Lama, whom the Tibetans revere as a god and a king. By the time this particular conflict erupted, China and India had already clashed three times over this disputed area (called the Arunachal Pradesh): in 1959–1960, in 1962, and in 1965 (*see* conflicts 4.10; 4.14; 4.18).

On October 20, 1975, a serious border skirmish occurred when four Indian soldiers were killed in what the Indians described as an ambush by Chinese troops thirty-five miles east of Bhutan. China denied these allegations on October 22, stating that the Indian troops had intruded into Tibet and, when told to withdraw, had opened fire on a Chinese civilian border post. The bodies of the Indian soldiers were returned on October 28, and no further hostilities in relation to the incident occurred. Eventually the dispute simply lapsed altogether, with no attempts at peaceful conflict management. Relations returned to their normal state of antagonism.

References

Chakravarti, P.C. 1971. *The Evolution of India's Northern Borders.* New York: Asia Publishing.

Day, A., ed. 1987. *Border and Territorial Disputes.* 2d edition. Burnt Mill, Harlow (Essex), England: Longman.

Hoffman, S. 1990. *India and the China Crisis.* Berkeley and Los Angeles: University of California Press.

Maxwell, N. 1972. *India's China War.* Garden City, N.Y.: Doubleday.

Rowland, J. 1967. *A History of Sino-Indian Relations.* Princeton, N.J.: Van Nostrand.

Tillema, H.K. 1991. *International Armed Conflict Since 1945: A Bibliographic Handbook of Wars and Military Interventions.* Boulder: Westview.

Vertzberger, Y. 1984. *Misperception in Foreign Policy Making: The Sino-Indian Conflict, 1959–1962.* Boulder: Westview.

4.22 Bangladesh–India: Postcoup Tensions and Border Incidents April 1976

Relations between India and Bangladesh had been cool ever since Bangladesh gained its independence from Pakistan in an extremely bloody war from 1971 to 1974 (*see* conflict 4.19). The strains can be partly explained by the border itself, which had been hastily and arbitrarily drawn during the 1947 partition. In addition, the terrain allowed easy passage for guerrillas, bandits, and refugees intent on crossing the border, and this often led to incidents. India had already been accused of supporting Chittagong Hill Tracts rebels in their insurgency against the Bangladeshi government (*see* conflict 4.20).

Tensions between India and Bangladesh were especially high in 1976 over allegations of Indian involvement in a 1975 military coup in which Sheik Mujibar Rahman, president and founder of Bangladesh, was assassinated, and nine members of his family were killed, including his wife, three sons, and a brother. Border incidents involving

Bangladesh guerrillas and police had already been reported in Meghalaya, an Indian state on Bangladesh's northeastern border. The guerrillas had apparently attacked from the Indian side of the border. Negotiations on the incidents failed to produce any solution, and, in April, Indian and Bangladeshi forces clashed four times, resulting in a number of casualties. Captured Bangladeshi guerrillas admitted to being trained in India. No other peaceful conflict-management activities took place, and the conflict quickly abated. Relations remained cool, however, and fighting broke out again in 1979, 1983–1984, and 1986 (*see* conflicts 4.24; 4.28; 4.30).

References

Ahmed, M. 1978. *Bangladesh: Constitutional Quest for Autonomy, 1950–1971.* Wiesbaden: Steiner.

Choudhury, G. 1974. *The Last Days of United Pakistan.* London: C. Hurst.

Day, A., ed. 1987. *Border and Territorial Disputes.* 2d edition. Burnt Mill, Harlow (Essex), England: Longman.

Jackson, R.V. 1975. *South Asian Crisis: India-Pakistan-Bangladesh.* London: Chatto and Windus.

Jacques, K. 2000. *Bangladesh, India, and Pakistan: International Relations and Regional Tensions in South Asia.* New York: St. Martin's.

Jagdev Singh. 1988. *The Dismemberment of Pakistan: 1971 Indo-Pak War.* New Delhi: Lancer International.

Sisson, R., and L.E. Rose. 1990. *War and Secession: Pakistan, India, and the Creation of Bangladesh.* Berkeley and Los Angeles: University of California Press.

4.23 Pakistan–Afghanistan: Pro-Monarchist Revolt and the Peshawar Rebellion March–July 1979

Afghanistan and Pakistan had been rivals since the 1940s, skirmishing a number of times over territorial issues. Afghanistan's last king, Mohammad Zahir Shah, was deposed in a 1973 military coup that led to the establishment of a pro-Soviet regime. In early 1979 rebel Muslim organizations based in Peshawar, the northwest frontier province of Pakistan, declared war on the Kabul government. Pakistan's intent was to restore the monarchy, and troops immediately began cross-border raids. The conflict was complicated by an internal rebellion that broke out in the Afghan city of Herat, near the border with Iran. Government forces quashed the Herat rebellion at the cost of 5,000 lives. The border with Iran was closed as a result.

Using Pakistani territory as sanctuary from April to July 1979, rebels continued their cross-border raids in an attempt to restore the monarchy. Government troops responded with their own regular cross-border attacks on Pakistan. There were allegations of Soviet aid to the Afghan government, while Pakistan was accused of actively aiding the rebels. Pakistan stated its desire to restore normal relations with Afghanistan, and on June 25 Indian prime minister Morarji Ranchhodji Desai offered to mediate. The president of Pakistan and the Afghan deputy foreign minister conducted talks July 1–3, resulting in an agreement on refugees and the need for further high-level talks. The dispute abated, but later in 1979 Afghanistan itself plunged into civil war and was invaded by the Soviet Union (*see* conflict 4.25).

References

Bhasin, V. 1984. *Soviet Intervention in Afghanistan: Its Background and Implications.* New Delhi: S. Chand.

Naumkin, V.V., ed. 1994. *Central Asia and Transcaucasia: Ethnicity and Conflict.* Westport, Conn.: Greenwood.

Tillema, H.K. 1991. *International Armed Conflict Since 1945: A Bibliographic Handbook of Wars and Military Interventions.* Boulder: Westview.

4.24 Bangladesh–India: Boundary Dispute and Border Incidents November 1979

The borders defining India, Pakistan, and Bangladesh had been the source of disputes ever since the Subcontinent was partitioned in 1947 (*see* conflicts 4.1; 4.2; 4.8; 4.16; 4.17; 4.22). These border disputes erupted into conflict once again in November 1979, and firefights between border troops took place almost daily. Border strains were aggravated by the constantly shifting course of the Muhuri River, which formed the border between India and Bangladesh. India placed spurs on the riverbank in an effort to prevent flooding, and Bangladesh protested that they caused erosion on its side. Spurs are a type of reinforcing construction that prevent erosion of the riverbank, but building up on one side of the riverbank can lead to greater erosion on the other side and change the course of the river.

Combined with other questions of border demarcation, the dispute might have escalated into more serious confrontation. As it was, the question was resolved in negotiations in late October and November, and the firefights abated. Relations remained cool, however, and armed conflict broke out again in 1983 (*see* conflict 4.28).

References

Ahmed, M. 1978. *Bangladesh: Constitutional Quest for Autonomy, 1950–1971.* Wiesbaden: Steiner.

Choudhury, G. 1974. *The Last Days of United Pakistan.* London: C. Hurst.

Day, A., ed. 1987. *Border and Territorial Disputes.* 2d edition. Burnt Mill, Harlow (Essex), England: Longman.

Jackson, R.V. 1975. *South Asian Crisis: India-Pakistan-Bangladesh.* London: Chatto and Windus.

Jagdev Singh. 1988. *The Dismemberment of Pakistan: 1971 Indo-Pak War*. New Delhi: Lancer International.

Sisson, R., and L.E. Rose. 1990. *War and Secession: Pakistan, India, and the Creation of Bangladesh*. Berkeley and Los Angeles: University of California Press.

4.25 USSR–Afghanistan: Soviet Invasion and the Afghan Civil War December 1979–Ongoing

A low-level civil war broke out in Afghanistan in 1973, after Lieutenant General Sardar Mohammad Daoud Khan deposed the last Afghan king, Mohammad Zahir Shah, in a military coup and proclaimed a republic. The new regime quickly aligned itself with the Soviet Union, provoking violent resistance from traditional tribal and other elements. Daoud was assassinated in a 1978 coup, and President Hafizullah Amin was killed in a Soviet-backed 1979 coup and replaced by the pro-Soviet Babrak Karmal.

The new regime proved unable to contain the growing civil war, despite massive Soviet aid. In an attempt to halt the fighting and rebuild the Kabul government, the Soviets moved massive numbers of troops and heavy weaponry into Afghanistan. Mujahideen rebel factions continued to resist the Soviet and Afghan armies for the next ten years in a particularly brutal war that often singled out civilians for reprisal attacks. The rebels received substantial aid from the United States and Pakistan. Cross-border raids into Pakistan and Iran by Afghan and Soviet forces continued throughout the 1980s, and Pakistani troops occasionally entered Afghanistan in support of mujahideen units.

In May 1985 rebel groups controlling large sections of the Afghan countryside formed the Islamic Alliance of Afghan Holy Warriors. The alliance elicited financial support and volunteer fighters from other Islamic states. By the mid-1980s Soviet forces were taking huge losses, and the war was becoming increasingly unpopular with the Soviet public. In 1986 the United Nations began negotiating a Soviet withdrawal from Afghanistan, which began in stages in 1988 and was completed in 1989. The Soviets continued to support the Kabul regime, however, even attacking rebel bases by air from the USSR. Approximately 15,000 Soviet soldiers died during the invasion and 37,000 were wounded.

Beginning in 1990 the Kabul regime became less able to resist the rebel advance, and it collapsed completely in 1992. The rebel alliance had by this time split into various factions that then engaged in a bloody battle for control of Kabul. By 1993 Afghanistan was engulfed in warfare far more intense than any previous fighting, with hundreds being killed every day in Kabul. At least three main factions were involved. The most important were the radical fundamentalist Taliban movement and the forces led by Gulbuddin Hekmatyar, a coalition of local mujahideen warlords centered around Jalabad. But no one side was able to defeat another, so the fighting surged back and forth across Afghanistan into late 1995. By December intense fighting was once again centered on Kabul. With the end of the cold war, however, no major powers seemed interested in intervening in the conflict. The Islamic Conference Organization (ICO), Pakistan, the United Nations, and Iran all made intense mediation efforts beginning in 1992, but peace was elusive, and no breakthroughs were reported.

The Taliban (Islamic students) had emerged as a new political movement in late 1994. Formed of Afghans raised in exile and trained in ultra-conservative Islamic seminaries in Pakistan, this movement sparked the resentment of Pasthun tribes about the corruption of the former mujahideen leaders and the domination of the government by non-Pasthuns. With very little fighting, the Taliban took control over the southern part of the country within a few months, disarming commanders and reestablishing law and order, and applying a strict interpretation of Islamic law. In September 1996 the Taliban captured Kabul and installed their version of Islamic government. The Taliban's restrictive policies, especially concerning women, played a role in preventing most states from recognizing them as the new government of Afghanistan, despite their control of the capital and about 90 percent of the country's territory and population. Strong opposition to the Taliban centered in the northern part of the country as well as in Kabul, and heavy fighting continued in the north.

In the course of the conflict, the regional context became even more polarized. The advance of the militant Taliban Islamic force, aided by Pakistan and Saudi Arabia, alarmed Russia, Central Asia, and Iran. Their fears were bolstered by evidence of serious spillover effects, including armed clashes, in Iran, Tajikistan, and Uzbekistan. Iran believed, with many others in the region, that the United States was allied with Pakistan and Saudi Arabia in an effort to encircle and contain the country, a charge strenuously denied by the U.S. State Department. The Northern Alliance was backed by Iran, Russia, Tajikistan, and Uzbekistan. Pakistan backed the Taliban and was accused of providing troops, weapons, and military expertise to the regime.

The war experience transformed Afghan society in many ways. Since 1973 approximately 1.5 million people have died in the fighting—most of them civilians. Gross violations of human rights occurred, and the country's infrastructure was completely destroyed. The Soviets lost approximately 15,000 military personnel, and Afghan troop losses were two to three times greater. A severe militarization of society was conducted, and half the population experienced forced migration as a result. The displacement of people occurred along ethnic lines, further increasing ethnic polarization.

Numerous peace initiatives failed to find any lasting solution to the conflict. International sanctions against the Taliban weakened the regime but did not lessen its grip on Afghan society until the United States attacked it in 2001 (*see* conflict 4.39). The Taliban are still active in some parts of Afghanistan.

References

Anwar, R. 1988. *The Tragedy of Afghanistan: A First-Hand Account.* Translated by K. Hasan. New York: Verso.

Arnold, A. 1985. *Afghanistan: The Soviet Invasion in Perspective.* Stanford, Calif.: Hoover.

Bhasin, V. 1984. *Soviet Intervention in Afghanistan: Its Background and Implications.* New Delhi: S. Chand.

Bradsher, H. 1985. *Afghanistan and the Soviet Union.* Expanded edition. Durham, N.C.: Duke University Press.

European Platform for Conflict Prevention and Transformation. 2002. "Afghanistan—Endless War in a Fragmented Society": http://www.euconflict.org/euconflict/guides/surveys.htm (March 3, 2002).

Ghaus, A.S. 1988. *The Fall of Afghanistan: An Insider's Account.* Washington, D.C.: Pergamon-Brassey's.

Gurr, T., M. Marshall, and D. Khosla. 2000. *Peace and Conflict 2001: A Global Survey of Conflicts, Self-Determination Movements, and Democracy.* College Park: Center for International Development and Conflict Management, University of Maryland.

Hammond, T. 1984. *Red Flag Over Afghanistan: The Communist Coup, the Soviet Invasion, and the Consequences.* Boulder: Westview.

Tillema, H.K. 1991. *International Armed Conflict Since 1945: A Bibliographic Handbook of Wars and Military Interventions.* Boulder: Westview.

4.26 Pakistan–India: Regional Rivalry, Border Incidents, and India–Pakistan Wars
July 1981–August 1982

Pakistan and India had been rivals since the 1947 partition and the first Kashmir war (*see* conflicts 4.1; 4.2). Relations were typically hostile, and many unresolved disputes led to armed conflict in 1958–1959 and again in 1965–1970 (*see* conflicts 4.8; 4.16; 4.17). Each side distrusted the other, and both were committed to maintaining strong military positions.

After the Soviet Union invaded Afghanistan in 1979, relations between Pakistan and India temporarily improved, but they deteriorated again in 1980 when each nation took steps to strengthen its armed forces. Tensions increased when India expressed concern that Pakistan was planning to develop nuclear weapons capability, which Pakistan denied. The United States was also renewing its military aid to Pakistan in 1981. During June 1981 each country agreed it had a right to acquire arms for its own security and reiterated its commitment to the principles of nonalignment. However, India and Pakistan continued their mutual allegations of military buildups, including the acquisition of nuclear weapons.

In the week beginning July 7, 1981, India alleged that ten Pakistani and four Indian soldiers had been killed in an exchange of fire near the Punch sector of the cease-fire line in Kashmir, and that Pakistan had deployed 350,000 troops along the Indian border. Pakistan's Foreign Ministry denied the troop movements. Hostilities in the disputed area of Jammu and Kashmir were very intense in November 1981, with numerous armed incidents. Both sides began expelling each other's diplomats and repatriating each other's nationals. Tensions were high, and observers feared an outbreak of war.

On December 24, 1981, India formally invited Pakistani representatives to preliminary discussions, which resulted in a proposal for a permanent joint commission and a possible friendship treaty. After further negotiations in May and June 1982, both sides declared that an understanding had been reached and bilateral discussions would continue on August 11 in Islamabad. The incidents stopped after this period, and relations were normalized for the time being. About fifteen fatalities resulted from the actual fighting. The issues in dispute remained unresolved, however, and armed conflicts occurred in 1984–1985 and 1986 (*see* conflicts 4.29; 4.30).

References

Appadorai, A. 1981. *The Domestic Roots of India's Foreign Policy, 1947–1972.* Delhi: Oxford University Press.

Blinkenberg, L. 1972. *India-Pakistan: The History of Unsolved Conflicts.* Copenhagen: Munksgaard.

Brines, R. 1968. *The Indo-Pakistani Conflict.* London: Pall Mall.

Jacques, K. 2000. *Bangladesh, India, and Pakistan: International Relations and Regional Tensions in South Asia.* New York: St. Martin's.

Tillema, H.K. 1991. *International Armed Conflict Since 1945: A Bibliographic Handbook of Wars and Military Interventions.* Boulder: Westview.

4.27 Sri Lanka: Communal Violence, Separatist Fighting, and the Tamil–Sinhalese Conflict
July 1982–Ongoing

Tensions had always existed between Sri Lanka's Buddhist Sinhalese population, comprising more than 70 percent of the country's total population, and the Hindu Tamil minority in the northern part of the island. The period following independence in 1948 had been relatively peaceful, but, after outbreaks of communal violence, a separatist movement of sorts had arisen among the Tamils. As the government responded with widespread repression, the movement grew quickly. In July 1982 a Tamil group calling itself the Liberation Tigers of Tamil Eelam (LTTE), led by Vellupillai Prabhakaran, began a low-level campaign of political violence against the regime.

The conflict escalated in July 1983, when Tamil guerrillas ambushed and killed thirteen soldiers in the Jaffna district. This incident sparked massive communal violence and revenge attacks by government troops, which left more than 400 people dead and underscored the issue of the Tamil minority's political future. The government declared a state of emergency, banning all expressions of separatism, and outlawing a number of Tamil political parties. After Indian mediation in August 1983, the Sri Lankan government called for an all-party roundtable conference to deal with the problem in January 1984. Largely unsuccessful, it was dissolved in December 1984.

By this stage, the LTTE had formed itself into a fanatical, well-disciplined guerrilla army, and the north was in a virtual state of all-out war. The Tigers also began to campaign abroad, and as a result, Tamils from the south Indian state of Tamil Nadu began to agitate and attempted to aid the Sri Lankan Tamils, sending men and supplies in boats. Despite numerous mediations, negotiations, and all-party conferences, the war persisted until July 1987. The violence was intense, with continuous bombings, revenge attacks, and military clashes between guerrillas and government forces. Civilians were more often than not the target of attacks. Despite numerous government offensives in Jaffna, government troops were unable to defeat the Tamil separatists.

In July 1987 India and Sri Lanka signed an agreement that supposedly settled the Tamil issue and included the deployment of thousands of Indian troops as peacekeepers in Tamil areas. With the LTTE's initial acceptance, the plan was proceeding relatively well, until twelve Tamil Tigers committed suicide while in Indian custody. Their deaths provoked a wave of reprisal killings and a major Indian offensive on Tamil strongholds. Despite initial Indian successes and renewed offensives, the war continued, and the Indian troops began to take heavy losses.

Meanwhile, the violence intensified when a banned leftist Sinhalese organization, the Janatha Vimukthi Peramuna (JVP) or People's Liberation Front, staged a comeback by initiating a terrorist campaign against the government and the Tamils. Up to 1,000 people a month were being killed as a result of the 1989 JVP campaign. Earlier that year, Indian troops began to withdraw from Sri Lanka because of rising losses and pressure from the new president, Ranasinghe Premadasa. Mutual accusations led to tension between the two countries and the threat of actual hostilities, but diplomatic moves defused the crisis, and the withdrawal continued. The last Indian troops left Sri Lanka in March 1990. At least 1,000 Indian soldiers had been killed since their deployment in July 1987.

Soon after the Indian withdrawal, peace initiatives were abandoned and all-out war resumed. On May 1, 1993, a Tamil rebel assassinated President Premadasa. Despite numerous government offensives from 1990 to 1994, neither side was able to get the upper hand. At least 100,000 people had died in the conflict, many of them civilians killed in massacres and revenge attacks. In early 1995 peace talks between the government and the LTTE led to optimism that a negotiated settlement could be found, and a period of relative calm set in. Tamil intransigence, however, caused the peace process to break down in May, and the war intensified, especially on the Tamil side, which launched several major suicide bomb attacks on the capital, Colombo. The government responded with an all-out offensive in July in which 2,500 people were killed and about 6,000 wounded. In November 1995 government forces surrounded and laid siege to the Tamil stronghold of Jaffna, capturing the town in December. The fall of Jaffna was a serious setback to the LTTE, but they continued to fight on from the jungle.

A peace proposal drafted in 1995 granting regional autonomy to Tamil-controlled areas was stymied by opposition within both the majority-Sinhala and minority-Tamil communities. Radical elements targeted moderates on both sides with violence for collaborating with the enemy, which left little prospect for peace initiatives to arise from the warring groups. The LTTE abruptly pulled out of peace talks on three occasions since 1987, the most recent in 1996 when Tamil Tigers violated a truce by killing twelve sailors in a strike on the Sri Lankan navy.

Serious fighting continued, and it seemed that no places or persons were secure from military or terrorist attack. In December 1999 President Chandrika Kumaratunga of Sri Lanka was blinded in one eye in an attempted assassination by a suicide bomber, and at least thirty-four people were killed in two explosions. Less than a month later, thirteen people were killed when another suicide bomber blew herself up in front of the office of Prime Minister Sirimavo Bandaranaike. In late 2000 countrywide elections failed to provide the necessary majority for pro-autonomy politicians hoping to defuse the protracted conflict. Kumaratunga, eager to pursue peace, said in November 2000 that she was open to talks with the LTTE but would not stop military operations against the rebels. The government proceeded cautiously in establishing a basis for peace talks with the LTTE. Both sides upheld a mutual ceasefire declared in February 2002. The government and the LTTE entered a new round of negotiations in September 2002, with the Norwegian government mediating. Both parties expressed desire for peace and reconciliation.

References

Braun, D. 1983. *The Indian Ocean: Region of Conflict or "Peace Zone"?* London: C. Hurst.

Brogan, P. 1989. *World Conflicts: Why and Where They Are Happening.* London: Bloomsbury.

Gurr, T., M. Marshall, and D. Khosla. 2000. *Peace and Conflict 2001: A Global Survey of Conflicts, Self-Determination Movements, and Democracy*. College Park: Center for International Development and Conflict Management, University of Maryland.

Manogaran, C. 1987. *Ethnic Conflict and Reconciliation in Sri Lanka*. Honolulu: University of Hawaii Press.

Muni, S.D. 1993. *Pangs of Proximity: India and Sri Lanka's Ethnic Crisis*. Oslo: PRIO; New Delhi and Newbury Park, Calif.: Sage.

O'Ballance, E. 1989. *The Cyanide War: Tamil Insurrection in Sri Lanka, 1973–1988*. Washington, D.C.: Brassey's.

Reuters Alert Net. 2001. "Sri Lanka." http://www.alertnet.org/thefacts/countryprofiles/ 220170?version=1 (February 25, 2002).

Schwarz, W. 1975. *The Tamils of Sri Lanka*. Minority Rights Group Report #25. London: Minority Rights Group.

Vanniasingham, S. 1988. *Sri Lanka: The Conflict Within*. New Delhi: Lancer.

Wilson, A. J. 1988. *The Break-Up of Sri Lanka: The Sinhalese-Tamil Conflict*. Honolulu: University of Hawaii Press.

4.28 India–Bangladesh: Boundary Dispute and Border Conflict
December 1983–June 1984

The 1947 partition of the Subcontinent left many borders unclear and in dispute (*see* conflict 4.1). In fact, relations between India and Bangladesh had been characterized by border control and demarcation disputes ever since Bangladesh's independence in 1974 (*see* conflicts 4.19; 4.22; 4.24). One such dispute had erupted into armed conflict in 1979, and relations between the two states were further strained by Indian support for Bangladeshi rebels in the Chittagong Hill Tracts (*see* conflict 4.20).

In December 1983 and January 1984, several people were killed in serious border incidents. The second incident involved an incursion into Bangladeshi territory by Indian security forces.

At the same time, India attempted to construct a barbed-wire fence along their mutual border to prevent illegal immigration. Bangladesh protested this move, and, when construction of the fence began in April 1984, a Bangladeshi border guard was killed. There were no attempts at peaceful conflict management throughout the dispute, but it eventually lapsed and normal relations resumed.

References

Ahmed, M. 1978. *Bangladesh: Constitutional Quest for Autonomy, 1950–1971*. Wiesbaden: Steiner.

Choudhury, G. 1974. *The Last Days of United Pakistan*. London: C. Hurst.

Day, A., ed. 1987. *Border and Territorial Disputes*. 2d edition. Burnt Mill, Harlow (Essex), England: Longman.

Jackson, R.V. 1975. *South Asian Crisis: India-Pakistan-Bangladesh*. London: Chatto and Windus.

Jagdev Singh. 1988. *The Dismemberment of Pakistan: 1971 Indo-Pak War*. New Delhi: Lancer International.

Sisson, R., and L.E. Rose. 1990. *War and Secession: Pakistan, India, and the Creation of Bangladesh*. Berkeley and Los Angeles: University of California Press.

4.29 India–Pakistan: Territorial Dispute, India–Pakistan Rivalry, and the Siachin Glacier Dispute
April 1984–September 1985

India and Pakistan had been adversaries since the 1947 partition of the Subcontinent, which displaced approximately 12 million people and resulted in intercommunal massacres of an estimated 300,000 people (*see* conflicts 4.1; 4.2). Disputed boundaries appear to have been the principal reason for the series of armed conflicts that followed.

This particular conflict concerned the Siachin Glacier, which is in the Karakorum Range in northern Jammu and Kashmir—in the northernmost reaches of undemarcated territory along the India-Pakistan border. Because it was so inhospitable, the region had been left undemarcated after the 1947 partition, as neither side thought it likely to become a matter of contention. Nevertheless, in early 1984 Indian troops occupied the northern end of the glacier and in April opened fire on a Pakistani helicopter. In June the Pakistanis launched an attack in an unsuccessful attempt to dislodge the Indian contingent.

Intermittent fighting followed, with several further Pakistani attempts to dislodge the Indian force. Perhaps as many as 100 soldiers were killed in the conflict. The dispute lapsed after September 1985. Although the two states undertook several negotiations, the issue was never resolved and remains in contention. Incidents continued in the area throughout the late 1980s and early 1990s, but in 1986 the locus of conflict between the two states returned to Kashmir (*see* conflict 4.31).

References

Appadorai, A. 1981. *The Domestic Roots of India's Foreign Policy, 1947–1972*. Delhi: Oxford University Press.

Blinkenberg, L. 1972. *India-Pakistan: The History of Unsolved Conflicts*. Copenhagen: Munksgaard.

Brines, R. 1968. *The Indo-Pakistani Conflict*. London: Pall Mall.

Tillema, H.K. 1991. *International Armed Conflict Since 1945: A Bibliographic Handbook of Wars and Military Interventions*. Boulder: Westview.

4.30 India–Bangladesh: Boundary Disputes and the Muhuri River Incidents February–April 1986

Relations between India and its neighbors had been strained ever since the 1947 partition of the Subcontinent (*see* conflict 4.1). Ill-defined borders between India and Bangladesh were a constant source of friction, and armed conflict had broken out in 1976 (*see* conflict 4.22). Each side accused the other of harboring rebels. In March and April 1986 a number of skirmishes erupted along the India-Bangladesh border, especially in the disputed Muhuri River area.

Following a two-day meeting between Indian and Bangladeshi officials to discuss border issues, Indian border personnel fired across the Muhuri River on April 9, killing two members of the Bangladesh Rifles. On April 22 forces stationed on both sides of the river withdrew to a "second line of defense," thereby vacating forward offensive positions. No other conflict-management attempts were made, and the dispute eventually lapsed, although border tensions remained.

References

Ahmed, M. 1978. *Bangladesh: Constitutional Quest for Autonomy, 1950–1971.* Wiesbaden: Steiner.

Choudhury, G. 1974. *The Last Days of United Pakistan.* London: C. Hurst.

Day, A., ed. 1987. *Border and Territorial Disputes.* 2d edition. Burnt Mill, Harlow (Essex), England: Longman.

Jackson, R.V. 1975. *South Asian Crisis: India-Pakistan-Bangladesh.* London: Chatto and Windus.

Jacques, K. 2000. *Bangladesh, India, and Pakistan: International Relations and Regional Tensions in South Asia.* New York: St. Martin's.

Jagdev Singh. 1988. *The Dismemberment of Pakistan: 1971 Indo-Pak War.* New Delhi: Lancer International.

Sisson, R., and L.E. Rose. 1990. *War and Secession: Pakistan, India, and the Creation of Bangladesh.* Berkeley and Los Angeles: University of California Press.

4.31 India–Pakistan: Territorial Dispute, Siachin Glacier/Kashmir Conflict, and India–Pakistan Rivalry Late 1986–Ongoing

Indian and Pakistani rivalry extends back to the 1947 partition of the Subcontinent, which left the borders between the two states ill-defined and therefore open to dispute (*see* conflict 4.1). The conflict over Kashmir and Jammu began in 1947, and the two states had gone to war since then on a number of occasions (*see* conflicts 4.2; 4.17). This conflict was preceded by fighting in the Siachin Glacier region in 1984–1985, Indian allegations of Pakistan involvement in Sikh extremist violence, and a number of border incidents (*see* conflict 4.29). Tensions were high at the end of 1985.

Although clashes took place in several different border areas, the main fighting was concentrated in the disputed Siachin Glacier, which is in the northernmost reaches of undemarcated territory along the India-Pakistan border—the Karakorum Range in northern Jammu and Kashmir. Both sides began massing troops on their borders in December 1986, and particularly violent clashes occurred in September 1987 and May 1989. Tensions between the two countries were further heightened by massive unrest in Kashmir in January 1990 and the outbreak of a serious Muslim separatist insurgency. The unrest caused both sides to mobilize for war, and many suspected that both India and Pakistan were preparing nuclear devices. Forceful intervention by the United States, including threats, caused both sides to pull back, and a major war was narrowly averted.

Incidents and intermittent fighting continued into the 1990s, especially in the Siachin border areas and in Kashmir and Jammu. The fighting in Kashmir claimed as many as 20,000 lives between 1989 and 1995 and was highlighted in the international media in 1994 when several Western hostages were taken by separatist rebels. Although India and Pakistan engaged in periodic negotiations, the issues in conflict remain unresolved.

Fresh fighting erupted in September 1997 over Kashmir's independence, and the two sides traded artillery fire. In May 1998 fears of an arms race in South Asia were raised when India carried out five underground nuclear tests. In response, Pakistan conducted its own tests two weeks later. The West, led by the United States, imposed economic sanctions on Pakistan, spinning the country into an economic crisis. Relations between Pakistan and India were very strained, but in June Pakistan announced a unilateral moratorium on nuclear testing, and the two countries resumed negotiations for a treaty.

In talks in February 1999 both sides agreed on steps to reduce the risk of an accidental escalation of hostilities and to wind down regional tension. Relations between the two neighbors collapsed in May 1999, however, when India launched air strikes and ground assaults against what it said were Pakistan-backed infiltrators in Indian-held Kashmir. Pakistan denied it was providing army support to guerrillas. In July, after a series of successful Indian assaults and international pressure to defuse the confrontation, the two countries agreed on the withdrawal of the militants. The Pakistani army's unwavering support for armed struggle in Kashmir contributed to an October 1999 coup in Pakistan, and in November tensions rose again as Pakistan reiterated its support for the Kashmir conflict and clashed with Indian troops.

In 2000 an Indian initiative attempted to end a decade of bloodshed in Kashmir by holding the first-ever face-to-face talks with the pro-Pakistan Hizbul mujahideen (also known as mujahadeen or mujahedin) militant group. The talks collapsed after a deadline to involve Pakistan in the talks was ignored. The Hizbul mujahideen reiterated that New Delhi must accept three-way talks, including Pakistan, to resolve the fifty-three-year-old Kashmir dispute. Despite periodic negotiations between Pakistan and India, the issues in the conflict remain unresolved. It is estimated that 30,000 people have died since the revolt broke out.

References

Appadorai, A. 1981. *The Domestic Roots of India's Foreign Policy, 1947–1972.* Delhi: Oxford University Press.

Blinkenberg, L. 1972. *India-Pakistan: The History of Unsolved Conflicts.* Copenhagen: Munksgaard.

Brines, R. 1968. *The Indo-Pakistani Conflict.* London: Pall Mall.

Gurr, T., M. Marshall, and D. Khosla. 2000. *Peace and Conflict 2001: A Global Survey of Conflicts, Self-Determination Movements, and Democracy.* College Park: Center for International Development and Conflict Management, University of Maryland.

Jacques, K. 2000. *Bangladesh, India, and Pakistan: International Relations and Regional Tensions in South Asia.* New York: St. Martin's.

Lamb, A. 1967. *The Kashmir Problem: A Historical Survey.* New York: Columbia University Press.

Tillema, H.K. 1991. *International Armed Conflict Since 1945: A Bibliographic Handbook of Wars and Military Interventions.* Boulder: Westview.

U.S. Agency for International Development, Asia and the Near East. 2002. "India." Country Overviews: http://www.usaid.gov/regions/ane/newpages/one_pagers/india01a.htm (February 25, 2002).

4.32 Maldives: Attempted Coup and Invasion
November 1988

The Maldives, a small group of islands off the southwest coast of Sri Lanka, gained independence from Britain in 1965. For most of the period following independence, it led a peaceful existence, but on November 3, 1988, some 150 Maldivian insurgents attacked the presidential palace and other government buildings in Male, the Maldives' capital, in an attempted coup. The attackers had arrived by boat from Sri Lanka and were headed by dissident Sri Lankan-based Maldivians led by Abdullah Luthufi and Sagar Ahmed Nasir. The remainder were Sri Lankan Tamil separatists recruited as mercenaries. About twenty people were killed in the fighting, which was fairly intense while the coup attempt was in progress.

The coup attempt was put down without further bloodshed by November 4 with the help of some 300 Indian paratroopers invited in by the Maldivian government. By November 8, 160 people had been rounded up and arrested, and many received long prison terms. The Indian paratroopers returned home a year later. Neither party attempted any peaceful conflict management during the conflict.

References

Babbage, R., and A.D. Gordon. 1992. *India's Strategic Future: Regional, State, or Global Power?* Auckland: Oxford University Press.

Braun, D. 1983. *The Indian Ocean: Region of Conflict or "Peace Zone"?* London: C. Hurst.

Manogaran, C. 1987. *Ethnic Conflict and Reconciliation in Sri Lanka.* Honolulu: University of Hawaii Press.

Ostheimer, J.N. 1975. *The Politics of the West Indian Ocean Islands.* New York: Praeger.

4.33 Kyrgyzstan: Uzbek and Kyrgyzis Ethnic Conflict and Post–Soviet Violence
June 1990

With the disintegration of the Soviet Union, ethnic-based animosities (some going back a millennium) began to resurface in many of the former republics, particularly in the Caucasus and central Asia. This particular conflict began on June 4, 1990, in the Kyrgyz city of Osh in the central Asian republic of Kyrgyzstan. Initially a dispute between ethnic Uzbeks and Kyrgyzis concerning the use of farmland for housing, the conflict soon turned into general ethnic-based violence in the form of riots, pogroms, clashes, and attacks on interior ministry buildings.

The conflict took on an international character and threatened to turn into a full-scale interrepublican armed conflict when up to 15,000 Uzbeks armed with makeshift weapons attempted to cross from Uzbekistan into southern Kyrgyzstan. Gangs of Kyrgyzis, similarly armed, were reported to be massing on their side of the border. The conflict eased after both states declared a state of emergency and closed the border. No peaceful conflict-management attempts were made during the conflict, and after two weeks of violence, it was estimated that nearly 600 people had lost their lives. Animosities remained high for some years, and the problem of ethnic-based violence remains unresolved in the region.

References

Allison, R. 1993. *Military Forces in the Soviet Successor States: An Analysis of the Military Policies, Force Dispositions, and Evolving Threat Perceptions of the Former Soviet States.* Adelphi Papers #280. London: Brassey's.

Colton, T.J., and R. Legvold, eds. 1992. *After the Soviet Union: From Empire to Nations.* New York: Norton.

Duncan, W.R., and G.P. Holman Jr. 1994. *Ethnic Nationalism and Regional Conflict: The Former Soviet Union and Yugoslavia*. Boulder: Westview.

King, R.R. 1973. *Minorities Under Communism*. Cambridge: Harvard University Press.

Maclean, F. 1992. *All the Russias*. New York: Smithmark.

Rupesinghe, K., P. King, and O. Vorkunova, eds. 1992. *Ethnicity and Conflict in a Post-Communist World: The Soviet Union, Eastern Europe, and China*. New York: St. Martin's.

Szajkowski, B. 1993. *Encyclopaedia of Conflicts, Disputes, and Flashpoints in Eastern Europe, Russia, and the Successor States*. Harlow (Essex), England: Longman.

Szporluk, R., ed. 1994. *National Identity and Ethnicity in Russia and the New States of Russia*. Armonk, N.Y.: M.E. Sharpe.

4.34 Tajikistan: Post–Soviet Strife and Ethnic-Based Civil War April 1992–June 1997

After the disintegration of the Soviet Union and the independence of Tajikistan in September 1991, violent conflict broke out in Tajikistan's capital, Dushanbe, between heavily armed supporters of President Rakhman Nabiyev's regime and its pro-Islamic opponents. The independence agreement had included Russian promises to protect Tajikistan, and Russia still maintained significant forces in the country. Negotiations and intervention by the forces of the Commonwealth of Independent States (CIS), the alliance of former Soviet republics, and Komitet Gosudarstvenoi Bezopasnosti (KGB), the Soviet security intelligence bureau—now known as the Federal Service of Security of Russia—resulted in the formation of a coalition government.

Fighting broke out again in the south, however, and was suppressed only with the aid of Russian interior ministry troops. A cease-fire, negotiated in late July, soon failed. Opposition forces ousted President Nabiyev in September, but the new government was unable to prevent further bloodshed. Alarmed by the military success of Islamic forces, Russia and central Asian states sent reinforcements to the region bordering Afghanistan. Rebels were receiving arms, supplies, and some fighters from inside Afghanistan, and Iran is also thought to have been involved in a similar fashion.

In October 1992 the government lost control over the southern provinces of Kulyab and Kurgan-Tyube (Qurghonteppa), these being held by pro-Nabiyev supporters. The rebels advanced toward Dushanbe and briefly took control of the capital before government forces drove them out. As Dushanbe was under siege, the coalition government resigned and a new government took over. A brief cease-fire came into effect in November but was overtaken by disturbances beginning in early December.

The conflict escalated in March 1993, when Russian/CIS troops were deployed along the Afghan border to prevent Afghan fighters from infiltrating and joining the rebels. The rebels themselves established bases just inside Afghanistan and launched a series of strikes resulting in high Russian fatalities, which escalated the conflict further and provoked serious strains between Moscow and Kabul. This pattern of warfare continued throughout 1994 and 1995, and Russian fatalities continued to mount. The United Nations made some attempts at peaceful conflict management, but they were largely ineffectual. Troops of the interior ministry tried unsuccessfully to keep the peace and mediate. The fighting was intense, and it is estimated that as many as 50,000 people were killed, 600,000 were displaced, and another 300,000 were forced to flee to Afghanistan and Russia.

In September 1993 a cease-fire was agreed to at talks in Iran, and in 1994 a UN-sponsored peace process started. The civil war continued sporadically until the Peace and Reconciliation Accord was signed in June 1997, as part of the United Nations' ongoing peace efforts. The peace process included integration of opposition leaders into the Tajik government, and came to a formal close with presidential elections in November 1999 and parliamentary elections in February 2000.

Although the United Tajik Opposition (UTO) is reported to have failed to comply with its promised disarmament, no evidence exists of a concerted UTO challenge to the central regime. Various armed groups continue to operate in the capital city of Dushanbe and in parts of the Karategin Valley. A "third force," concentrated in the north and claiming to represent the rights of ethnic Uzbeks in the region, complicated the conflict in November 1998 by launching an armed rebellion in which more than 200 soldiers, rebels, and civilians died. A government crackdown in early 2000 curtailed the activities of these types of groups, who continue to remain largely outside government control.

In February 2000 Tajikistan's southern neighbor, Afghanistan, continued to be a base of international terrorism, a scene of civil conflict, and the source of a constant flow of narcotics transiting through Tajikistan to Russian and European markets, leaving widespread crime, corruption, and economic and social distortions in its wake. The war in Tajikistan has devastated its economy, leaving it dependent on food aid.

References

Allison, R. 1993. *Military Forces in the Soviet Successor States: An Analysis of the Military Policies, Force Dispositions, and Evolving Threat Perceptions of the Former Soviet States*. Adelphi Papers #280. London: Brassey's.

Colton, T.J., and R. Legvold, eds. 1992. *After the Soviet Union: From Empire to Nations*. New York: Norton.

Duncan, W.R., and G.P. Holman Jr. 1994. *Ethnic Nationalism and Regional Conflict: The Former Soviet Union and Yugoslavia*. Boulder: Westview.

Gurr, T., M. Marshall, and D. Khosla. 2000. *Peace and Conflict 2001: A Global Survey of Conflicts, Self-Determination Movements, and Democracy*. College Park: Center for International Development and Conflict Management, University of Maryland.

Maclean, F. 1992. *All the Russias*. New York: Smithmark.

Reuters Alert Net Online. 2002. "Tajikistan" Country Profile. http://www.alertnet.org/thefacts/countryprofiles/ (accessed February 23, 2002).

Rupesinghe, K., P. King, and O. Vorkunova, eds. 1992. *Ethnicity and Conflict in a Post-Communist World: The Soviet Union, Eastern Europe, and China*. New York: St. Martin's.

Szajkowski, B. 1993. *Encyclopaedia of Conflicts, Disputes, and Flashpoints in Eastern Europe, Russia, and the Successor States*. Harlow (Essex), England: Longman.

Szporluk, R., ed. 1994. *National Identity and Ethnicity in Russia and the New States of Russia*. Armonk, N.Y.: M.E. Sharpe.

U.S. Agency for International Development. 2002. "Tajikistan." http://www.usaid.gov/regions/europe_eurasia/car/tjpage.html (accessed February 22, 2002).

4.35 Nepal: Intervention and Maoist Guerrilla Insurgency Mid-1998–September 1999

Despite the restoration of democracy in Nepal in 1990, the country remains in a state of political instability. The distribution of resources is unequal and exploitative; corruption and severe poverty are widespread. In response to the dire situation, the Nepal Communist Party [Maoist] in 1996 organized a "people's war" against the government. Their demands for reform were ignored, and the government suppressed their cultural and political activities. Consequently, the Maoists began a violent rebel insurgency that has claimed the lives of at least 1,600 people.

In 1998 the Nepalese government claimed that India was sheltering the Maoist guerrillas conducting the insurgency. A dispute arose over the issue, but in September 1999 India and Nepal signed an agreement in which India said it would give no shelter to Maoist guerrillas. In return, Nepal agreed to curb the activities of Pakistan's Inter-Service Intelligence (ISI) agency operating from inside Nepal across its 1,800 kilometer border with India.

References

Keesing's Record of World Events: K43151.

Luitel, S.P. October 11, 2001. "The Maoist People's War and Human Rights in Nepal." Asia Folk School Online: http://asiafolkschoolonline.ahrchk.net/mainfile/php/article/15/ (accessed February 21, 2002).

4.36 India–Bangladesh: Kushita Border Incident April–August 1999

Since gaining independence from Pakistan in 1971, Bangladesh has been involved in a number of disputes with India—in 1976, 1979, 1983, and 1986 (*see* conflicts 4.22; 4.24; 4.28; 4.30). At the heart of these conflicts is the arbitrary nature of border demarcation and the flow of refugees, bandits, and insurgents between the two countries.

The 1999 conflict was sparked by an incident in April during which Indian Border Security Force troops (BSF) allegedly fired upon a Bangladeshi attempting an illegal border crossing. In response the Bangladeshi Rifles (BDR), engaged their Indian counterparts, prompting a fierce gun battle. Nine deaths and approximately sixty injuries were reported. Each side protested the other's actions and claimed compensation from the other at a peace conference on April 21. The situation subsequently deescalated, and neither side continued to push the issue.

Border tensions rose again when Bangladesh protested the erection of a defensive structure near the border that the Indians claimed to be a drainage canal, and serious violence erupted in August. A three-day gun battle erupted after a dispute between Bangladeshi and Indian farmers at the border town of Belonia, near the Muhurichar area. The battle, which resulted in a number of deaths, was eventually halted by telephone communication between BSF and BDR officers. Subsequent to the skirmish, the parties reached agreements regarding the farming rights of Indians in the region, which had caused the initial clash. Indian and Bangladeshi officials also agreed to protocols for reducing the likelihood of escalation in future situations.

References

Keesing's Record of World Events: K42888, K42398, K43102.

Reuters Online. 1999.

4.37 Uzbekistan–Kyrgyzstan/Tajikistan: Border Insurgency August 1999–September 2000

In recent years Islamic unrest has been growing in Central Asia. In Uzbekistan the campaign against the Muslim rebels intensified after February 1999, when a series of bombs exploded near government buildings in Tashkent, killing sixteen people. The government blamed the

Islamic Movement of Uzbekistan (IMU). It is reported that there may be nearly a dozen armed Islamic groups in addition to the IMU and that their support is growing. The IMU is also accused of kidnappings and armed incursions that took place in August 1999 along Uzbekistan's and Kyrgyzstan's common border and in August 2000 along the country's border with Tajikistan. The rebels were demanding a corridor to Uzbekistan where they planned to oust President Islam Karimov and establish an Islamic state.

In response, the government committed substantial military resources, including bombing raids, against suspected IMU hideouts in Kyrgyzstan, killing a number of Kyrgyz civilians. The Kyrgyz army resisted further attempts by the guerrillas and prevented new rebel groups from crossing the border. Four Uzbek fighter aircraft bombed Tajikistan's remote northern territories "by mistake" to help Kyrgyzstan flush out a number of rebels operating near the border, confirming that Kyrgyzstan had asked for Uzbek help against the Islamic rebels. The Uzbek ambassador was summoned by the Tajik government to account for the incident. At the end of August high-level representatives from Kazakhstan, Kyrgyzstan, Tajikistan, and Uzbekistan met to discuss the threat of the "international terrorists" and stated that they are united in their determination to wipe out the "bloodthirsty criminals" holding hostages in Kyrgyzstan.

In September 1999 the four countries tried to isolate the militants in the mountains and prevent them from breaking through into the Ferghana Valley in Uzbekistan. Tajikistan and Uzbekistan sent additional units and armored vehicles to their borders with Kyrgyzstan to prevent the rebels from escaping, and Uzbek aircraft bombed a Kyrgyz village. Sporadic skirmishes between the invaders and government troops were reported. In early October 1999 Uzbekistan bombed regions near Tajikistan's border with Kyrgyzstan. The Tajik government sent a note of protest to the Uzbek government, claiming that the bombing did "not comply with the fundamental principles of mutual understanding and good-neighborliness between the two states."

In early August 2000 further border incursions occurred. It was reported that Islamic rebel forces had crossed into Uzbekistan and Kyrgyzstan from Afghanistan via Tajikistan. The fighters included Uzbeks, Tajiks, Arabs, Pakistanis, Russians, and Chechens. It was alleged that the rebels were financed by "international terrorist organizations," including Osama bin Laden, and that IMU members led the troops. Fighting occurred between Uzbek and Kyrgyz troops and the rebels, resulting in the deaths of up to fifty rebels and a number of troops. Central Asian leaders convened on August 20 to discuss the fighting. The presidents of Kazakhstan, Kyrgyzstan, Tajikistan, and Uzbekistan issued a joint statement of readiness to cooperate in the fight against "terrorism," but made it clear that they opposed preventive air strikes against the territory of other independent states. At the end of August, President Karimov announced that China had agreed to provide military aid to Uzbekistan to fight the rebels. It had been reported that the IMU included Uighur separatist militants from China's non-Western Xinjian autonomous region.

In September 2000 fighting between the rebel Islamic forces and Kyrgyz government troops continued at the southern border with Tajikistan. The Defense Ministry claimed it was in full control of the regions bordering Tajikistan and Uzbekistan, but a three-hour battle occurred the night of September 24–25 near the Kyrgyz-Tajik border.

References

Agency WPS Defense and Security. www.wps.ru/en/products/pp/military/index.html.

College of Behavioral and Social Sciences, University of Maryland. "Minorities at Risk." Now accessed through the Center for International Development and Conflict Management, University of Maryland, College Park. http://www.cidcm.umd.edu/project.asp?id=17; http://www.bsos.umd.edu/cidcm/mar/uzbektaj.htm.

The Economist. August 26, 1999.

Interfax Russian News. www.interfax-news.com/.

Keesing's Record of World Events: K43705, K43753, K43099–100.

Lobe, J. 2001. "Uzbekistan: Regional Conflict Profile." Foreign Policy in Focus Online: http://www.fpif.org/selfdetermination/conflicts/uzbek.html (February 22, 2002).

4.38 Bangladesh–India: Border Incident and Seizure of Perdiwah April–July 2001

Arbitrary border delineation and associated concerns regarding refugee and guerrilla movements have been a constant source of dispute between India and Bangladesh ever since the latter's independence from Pakistan in 1974 and have resulted in violence on a number of occasions. The most notable was a 1976 conflict sparked by suspected Indian involvement in the Bangladeshi coup of 1975 and causing several border clashes (*see* conflict 4.22). Flare-ups have also occurred in 1979, 1983, 1986, and 1999 (*see* conflicts 4.24; 4.28; 4.30; 4.36).

The worst conflagration between these neighbors since 1976 took place in April 2001, when an intense battle broke out between Indian Border Security Force troops and the Bangladeshi Rifles (BDR). The battle was apparently initiated by the Bangladeshi seizure of the Indian village of Perdiwah and resulted in the deaths of sixteen Indian troops and three members of the BDR. The situation was further inflamed by the mutilation of some of the Indian dead. Bangladesh expressed regret at the incident but denied that its troops had entered into India; rather, Bangladesh claimed it had simply been repelling an Indian attack on a BDR outpost. Eventually, India admitted to the possibility that its troops may have mistakenly strayed across the border. Despite the intensity of the initial flare-up, the conflict was quickly contained, and official talks that took place in New Delhi from July 2 to July 4 enabled a return to normalcy.

References

Keesing's Record of World Events: K44107, K44262.

The Europa World Year Book. 2002. London: Europa Publications Limited.

4.39 United States–Afghanistan: Post–September 11 "War on Terrorism," Al Qaeda Terrorist Links, and Terrorist Containment September–December 2001

Although not as directly involved in the Afghan Civil War (1979–Ongoing) as was the Soviet Union, the United States did play a major role, joining Pakistan in helping to arm and train the mujahideen fighters who had taken up arms against the Afghan government and its Soviet backers (*see* conflict 4.25). This support ended with the Soviet withdrawal in 1989, however, leaving the militant Islamic mujahideen to fight on without U.S. aid and creating considerable feelings of resentment among the largely Arab population. In some quarters, anti-American sentiment grew, spurred on by the continuing U.S. presence in Saudi Arabia after the 1990–1991 Gulf War. The United States is also unpopular because of its support for Israel. For Osama bin Laden, this resentment was strong enough to prompt the formation of the al Qaeda (the Base) terrorist organization with intentions to campaign against U.S. interests and interference. Well-funded and well-organized, al Qaeda launched attacks against the World Trade Center in February 1993, U.S. embassies in Kenya and Tanzania in August 1998, and the USS *Cole* in October 2000. In response, the United States launched air strikes against targets in the Sudan where bin Laden was based, and subsequently imposed harsh sanctions on Afghanistan's Taliban rulers, when intelligence suggested that bin Laden was sheltering in that country.

These terrorist attacks and the extent of U.S. retaliation paled in comparison to the events of September 11, 2001, when hijacked planes were flown into both of New York City's World Trade Center towers, which then collapsed, and the Pentagon, just outside of Washington, D.C. A fourth plane crashed in a Pennsylvania field after passengers apparently overwhelmed their hijackers. The resulting loss of life—approximately 3,000—and the symbolic nature of the attacks were unprecedented in American history. The U.S. government held Osama bin Laden and his al Qaeda terrorist network responsible.

In speeches following the events of September 11, U.S. President George W. Bush was quick to establish that the attacks were an act of war, rather than crimes, and Congress moved to increase military expenditures in preparation for a response. The targets of this new war were to be those who committed acts of terror and those who harbored them. America's allies responded in kind, with NATO taking the unprecedented step of invoking Article 5 of its Constitution, under which an attack on one member is deemed an attack on all. NATO's action gave weight to the definition of the attacks as an act of war requiring self-defense, rather than a criminal act requiring prosecution. The UN Security Council also condemned the attacks. Nevertheless, these events also prompted a major criminal investigation, which resulted in hundreds of detainments and the freezing of many financial accounts. It also fixed the blame on al Qaeda, which had not explicitly claimed responsibility. Al Qaeda was in turn quickly tied to the Taliban leadership of Afghanistan, where bin Laden was based. Although little explicit evidence was released to support U.S. leaders' growing suspicions, Pakistani president Pervez Musharraf came under diplomatic pressure to renounce the Taliban leadership and assist the United States. Some Pakistani factions were fiercely opposed to Musharraf's actions, but he soon sent a Pakistani delegation to meet with the Taliban to negotiate the handing over of bin Laden. Mullah Omar, the Taliban leader, made it clear that such an event would occur only if the Taliban could be provided with the proof America had gathered against him. This process of demand and counterdemand was repeated several times with equally unproductive results, resulting in criticism of America's unwillingness to undertake any sort of productive negotiations before launching its reprisals.

As a consequence of this impasse, the United States continued a massive buildup in the region in preparation for military action which began with British and U.S. airstrikes on October 7, 2001. This direct action was coupled with more indirect support and encouragement of opposition forces within Afghanistan, most notably the Northern Alliance, in their efforts to overthrow the Taliban. The removal of the Taliban led to a certain blurring of American goals as it became clear that doing so had become an integral part of America's plans for undermining al Qaeda.

Taliban forces were unable to resist the combined assault of opposition fighters and U.S. bombing, and by November the Northern Alliance had made massive inroads, seizing Kabul and Mazar-i-Sharif. The insertion of American ground troops began a month after the initial bombings and, by December, opposition forces and U.S.

troops controlled almost all of Afghanistan, and the Taliban had been routed.

This aspect of the operation, which had come to be seen as vital for undermining a terrorist breeding ground, was deemed to be a great success. Meanwhile, the battle against al Qaeda itself continued. Numerous major figures within the organization escaped the fall of the Taliban. Many were believed to be pinned down in the Tora Bora mountain region near the border with Pakistan, but few were ultimately found.

America's vulnerability to terrorism was further demonstrated by the apprehension of Richard Reid, the so called "shoe bomber," who was overcome by cabin staff while attempting to set off explosives hidden in his shoe on a flight from Paris to Miami.

The conflict in Afghanistan ended with the fall of the Taliban regime and the subsequent appointment of Hamid Karzai as chairman of the Afghan Interim Authority (AIA) on December 22, 2001. This interim authority was charged with the responsibility of conducting a nationwide Loya Jirga (Grand Assembly) in June 2002. The delegates cast secret ballots and elected Karzai president of the Transitional Islamic State of Afghanistan (TISA). A second national Loya Jirga had the responsibility to finalize the makings of a constitution over an eighteen-month period and hold nationwide elections over a twenty-four-month period. Occasional political violence and ongoing counterterrorist measures still occur but the conflict is essentially over. Afghanistan must now address the potentially destabilizing effects of poverty, a weak infrastructure, and post-conflict issues, such as the removal of landmines.

Estimates place the death toll in the Afghanistan conflict at anywhere between 20,000 and 43,000 fatalities.

References:

Bancroft-Hinchey, T. 2001. "Afghanistan Reborn." PRAVDA: http://english.pravda.ru/diplomatic/2001/12/07/23117.html (accessed December 7, 2001).

CIA Factbook. 2003. www.cia.gov/cia/publications/factbook.

The Europa World Year Book. 2002. London: Europa Publications Limited.

Keesing's Record of World Events: K44333–K44338, K44343, K44344, K44391–K44394, K44448–K44449, K44496, K44503–K44505.

Europe

List of Conflicts

5.1 Greece: Antimonarchist Communist Insurgency and Civil War 236
1945–1949

5.2 Albania–United Kingdom: Corfu Channel Dispute 237
May 1946–December 1949

5.3 Yugoslavia–United States: Cold War Air Incidents 237
August 1946

5.4 USSR–Yugoslavia: Ideological Rift 238
Early 1948–December 1954

5.5 USSR–The Western Allies: The Berlin Airlift Crisis 238
June 1948–May 1949

5.6 Italy–Yugoslavia: Cold War and Trieste Territorial Dispute 239
March 1952–October 1954

5.7 Cyprus–United Kingdom: Intercommunal Violence and the Enosis Movement 239
April 1955–February 1959

5.8 USSR–Poland: Polish October 240
October 1956

5.9 USSR–Hungary: Anti-Communist Revolt, Soviet Invasion, and the Hungarian Uprising of 1956 240
October–December 1956

5.10 USSR–United States: Cold War Dispute and the Berlin Wall 241
July–November 1961

5.11 Cyprus: Intercommunal Violence and Civil War 242
December 1963–November 1967

5.12 USSR–Czechoslovakia: Liberalization Movement, the Prague Spring, and Soviet Military Invasion 242
August 1968

5.13 Iceland–United Kingdom, West Germany, and Denmark: The Cod War 243
November 1971–June 1976

5.14 Cyprus: Communal Violence, Turkish-Greek Invasions, and Partition 244
January 1974–June 1978

5.15 Poland: Internal Crisis, Solidarity Labor Movement, and the Declaration of Martial Law 244
December 1981–February 1982

5.16 Turkey–Greece: Regional Rivalry and Naval Incidents 245
March 1984–January 1988

5.17 Georgia–South Ossetia: Abkhazia Secession War 245
March 1989–Ongoing

5.18 Yugoslavia: Ethnic and Religious Warfare and the Balkans Civil War 246
Mid-1989–November 2000

5.19 USSR–Lithuania: Post-Soviet Independence Crisis 248
March 1990–Late 1991

5.20 Azerbaijan–Armenia: Nagorno-Karabakh Conflict 248
August 1990–Ongoing

5.21 Gagauzia/Dniester–Moldova: Post-Soviet Strife and Gagauzia's Struggle for Autonomy 249
October 1990–July 1992

5.22 USSR–Latvia: Post-Soviet Independence Crisis 250
January 1991

5.23 Macedonia: Civil War, Incursion, and NATO/EU Involvement 251
January 1991–Ongoing

5.24 Russia–Chechnya: Post-Soviet Strife, Separatist Fighting, Chechen and Caucasus Conflicts 252
October 1992–Ongoing

5.25 Cyprus: Ethnic-Based Tensions and Partition Incidents 253
April 1993

5.26 Greece–Albania: Border Tensions 253
April 1994

5.27 Cyprus: Partition Incidents 254
June 1996–Ongoing

5.28 Yugoslavia–Kosovo: Kosovo Conflict and Civil War 254
October 1997–Ongoing

5.29 Russia–Republic of Dagestan: The Dagestan Independence Dispute 255
May 1999

5.30 Russia–Georgia: Chechen Separatism 255
August 2000–Ongoing

Map 7. Europe

See Map 7A for the easternmost parts of the Europe region not shown here, including Armenia, Azerbaijan, Georgia, and other Caucasus republics of the Russian Federation.

Countries in the Region

Countries included in this region are:

- Albania
- Andorra
- Armenia
- Austria
- Azerbaijan
- Belarus
- Belgium
- Bosnia and Herzegovina
- Bulgaria
- Croatia
- Cyprus
- Czech Republic
- Denmark
- Estonia
- Finland
- France
- Georgia
- Germany
- Greece

Map 7A. The Caucasus

The breakup of the Soviet Union led to unprecedented internal instability in Russia as nationalist, ethnic, and religious groups strived for autonomy or expansion. Several of these conflicts, including the Russia–Chechnya war, have occurred in the Caucasus region (*see* conflicts 5.17; 5.20; 5.24; 5.29; and 5.30).

- Greenland
- Hungary
- Iceland
- Ireland
- Italy
- Latvia
- Liechtenstein
- Lithuania
- Luxembourg
- Macedonia, Former Yugoslav Republic of
- Malta
- Moldova
- Monaco
- Netherlands, The
- Norway
- Poland
- Portugal
- Romania
- Russian Federation (including the Caucasus region comprising Chechnya, North Ossetia, Dagestan, Ingushetia, Kabardino-Balkaria, and Karachay-Cherkessia)
- San Marino
- Slovakia
- Slovenia
- Spain
- Sweden
- Switzerland
- Turkey
- Ukraine
- United Kingdom
- Vatican, The
- Yugoslavia, Federal Republic of (now Serbia and Montenegro)

Regional Overview

Since 1945 Europe has been relatively peaceful in that no interstate wars have been fought between the countries of Western Europe. This development is significant, considering that in the first half of the twentieth century the whole of Europe was embroiled in war on two occasions, World War I (1914–1918) and World War II (1939–1945). The integration of European countries first under the European Economic Community (EEC) and then the European Union (EU) has contributed to the preservation of peace between formerly warring nations.

In the post–cold war period, which began with the breakup of the Soviet Union in 1991, the number of violent conflicts in the region increased dramatically, but some intrastate conflicts *had* occurred in Europe prior to this period. In Greece, a Communist resistance group seeking a socialist state fought a civil war against the promonarchists from 1945 to 1949, when the monarchy was reestablished. The civil war in Greece claimed an estimated 160,000 lives. In 1956 a brief but intense civil war was fought in Hungary against the USSR and Communist domination, resulting in the deaths of 20,000 people, mostly civilians.

In addition, ETA, as the Basque Fatherland and Liberty guerrilla group is known, continues to wage an urban guerrilla movement against the Spanish government. The separatist guerrilla campaigns are responsible for approximately 800 deaths. The organization's goal is independence for the Basque region of northern Spain and southwestern France.

The breakup of Yugoslavia resulted in one of the most serious conflicts of the post–cold war period. The international community became involved in the region as the conflict threatened European security and challenged the Western belief that the end of communism would result in stability. Conflict resolution in the Balkans took the form of multiparty mediation. The United States, the EU, the UN, and a joint EU/UN effort attempted to mediate, and former U.S. president Jimmy Carter made a private individual effort. In the end, it took the use of force by NATO to weaken the Serbs, resulting in a mutually painful stalemate, before the United States could mediate successfully in the conflict.

Overview of Conflict

The most powerful force in modern European history is nationalism, which has been at the same time both unifying and divisive. The horrors of World War II showed the potentially disastrous results of nationalism and demonstrated the need for cooperation and integration to maintain peace. During the war the German leader, Adolf Hitler, attempted the systematic extermination of the Jewish people, which resulted in more than 6 million deaths.

The next significant conflict to dominate the world stage was the cold war, an ideological battle between the Communist USSR and the democratic, capitalist United States. The cold war was particularly nerve-racking because the two protagonists were nuclear powers. Instead of confronting each other in a direct war, the two

Map 8. Soviet expansion in Europe, 1939–1991

The Berlin airlift crisis of 1948–1949 was the first of several cold war incidents to chill the relationship between the Soviet Union and the United States following World War II. At the time of the crisis, the Soviet Union had already extended its control over much of East Central Europe.

countries carried on a nuclear arms race, in which both nations amassed thousands of nuclear warheads. Europe was divided into two camps. Eastern Europe became a client of the USSR, controlled by the threat of Soviet military intervention, while Western Europe sought and welcomed American involvement. The battle lines in Europe were so clearly drawn that both sides knew that the slightest trespass could result in total war. By 1949 West and East German governments had been organized, finalizing the division of the continent.

Stability did not necessarily equal prosperity; Communist suppression froze Eastern Europe politically and economically, whereas the American protective umbrella allowed the nations of Western Europe to prosper and develop closer integration. The creation of the North Atlantic Treaty Organization (NATO) in 1949 was further evidence of Western Europe's dependence on the United States.

From the 1960s to the 1980s, strict conformity to the Communist system in the USSR discouraged economic innovation and punished dissent. Consequently, the economy stagnated. Despite its weak economy, the Soviet Union continued to increase its military strength and to act more assertively around the world, invading Afghanistan in 1979 (*see* conflict 4.24).

In 1989 nationalist and democratic protests in Eastern Europe escalated rapidly into revolutions that swept the Communists from power. That year, in a dramatic expression of the new order, the Berlin Wall, which had divided East Germany and West Germany, was dismantled. The collapse of communism from 1989 to 1991 led not only to the reunification of Germany in 1990 but also the collapse of the Soviet Union into fifteen separate republics, each with its own dominant ethnic group. Bosnia and Herzegovina, with a more diverse array of ethnic groups, became the site of violent ethnic conflict after it declared independence from Yugoslavia in 1992.

The seeds of the conflict had been planted at the end of World War I, when Bosnia and Herzegovina and the provinces of Croatia, Slovenia, and Carniola united with Serbia and Montenegro to form the country of the Serbs, Croats, and Slovenes, later renamed Yugoslavia. This new country consisted of several ethnic groups, but strict Communist control kept internal conflicts in check. After communism collapsed, a struggle for power began. In the early 1990s some of the republics began to demand more autonomy, while the government, dominated by Serbs, wanted to increase centralization and Serbian influence. Ethnic conflict and resentment against the Serb population led the republics of Bosnia and Herzegovina, Croatia, Macedonia, and Slovenia to secede. Serbia opposed the secessions, and in Croatia and Bosnia, where there were large Serb minorities, violent conflict broke out. The bloodshed did not end until 1996, after the United Nations endorsed military intervention and policing by NATO forces. Nationalist disputes also brought about an end to Czechoslovakia, but its 1993 separation into the Czech Republic and Slovakia was achieved peacefully.

Several violent conflicts between ethnic groups remain unresolved. In Russia, the conflict with Chechnya remains a serious issue. Chechnya is a small country situated in the North Caucasus on the southernmost border of the Russian Federation's western territory. After the collapse of the USSR, the Muslim population of Chechnya wanted independence. A successful coup against the Communist government of Checheno-Ingushetia was carried out in 1994. Chechenya declared its independence, but Russia rejected the claim. This resulted in a separatist war in the years 1994–1996, which was renewed in 1999 with the Russian armed forces occupying and bombing Chechnya. An estimated 80,000 have died in the conflict so far.

These problems could be overcome if states were prepared to grant a degree of autonomy to ethnic groups or to ensure that the government protects minority rights. That possibility will become more likely as Eastern Europe's governments become more familiar with the political nuances that are essential for democracy. In addition, a regard for human and group rights is a condition for receiving Western aid and for admission to the Western network of international organizations and into the EU itself.

Conflict Management

In an effort to avoid future devastating wars, after World War II the countries of Western Europe, especially France and Germany, agreed to an industrial scheme that provided a measure of economic integration. The European Coal and Steel Community was formed in 1950, but its purpose was not only economic but also political—the beginning of European unity. Since then, Europe has looked to two organizations, the European Union (EU) and the Organization for Security and Cooperation in Europe (OSCE), to solve problems and avoid conflict.

European Union

Primarily a vehicle for continued economic integration, the European Economic Community (EEC) and European Community (EC) officially became the European Union (EU) after the signing of the Treaty on European Union or Maastricht Treaty in 1993. "In November 1993, the European Community became one of the three 'pillars' that made up the new European Union" (McCormick 1999). The EU has evolved to encompass defense issues and security responsibilities in its regional sphere. The Treaty on European Union sets out the EU's obligations toward peaceful conflict settlement (Article J.1):

> to safeguard the common values, fundamental interests, and independence of the Union;
>
> to strengthen the security of the Union and its Member States in all ways;

> to preserve peace and strengthen international security, in accordance with the principles of the United Nations Charter as well as the principles of the Helsinki Final Act and the objectives of the Paris Charter;
>
> to promote international cooperation; and
>
> to develop and consolidate democracy and the rule of law, respect for human rights, and fundamental freedoms (Barbour 1996).

The EU is a structurally complex organization, but its organs have well-defined responsibilities for handling conflicts. Conflict management can be placed on the agendas of the European Commission, the Council of the European Union, the European Parliament, and the European Court of Justice, although those actually involved in management efforts are usually specially appointed bodies. In the initial stages of a conflict, the Council of Ministers provides a forum for discussions and negotiation based on "compromise, bargaining, and diplomacy" (McCormick 1999). The council is the most powerful of the EU organs. The power to initiate proposals remains the bureaucratic domain of the commission, and decision-making is carried out only by the Council of Ministers. The parliament functions in much the same way as any elected government institution, but it has limited legal and policymaking powers. The secretariat-general does not match the high profile role afforded the office in the UN. The secretariat is basically a bureaucratic body acting in support of the Council of Ministers (McCormick 1999).

The presidency of the Council of Ministers is more akin to the organizational role of the UN secretary-general, although it is a position held by a country, not a person. The holder of the presidency "mediates and bargains, and is responsible for promoting cooperation among member states. . . . Holding the presidency allows a member state to convene meetings and launch initiatives on issues of national interest, to try and bring those issues to the top of the EU agenda, and to earn prestige and credibility, assuming it does a good job" (McCormick 1999). The European Court of Justice performs a mostly legislative and interpretative function, but, unlike the International Court of Justice (ICJ), its decisions are binding (McCormick 1999).

EU membership is smaller and more regionally homogenous than the OSCE making it easier for the organization to take decisive action (Sutterlin 1995). The EU has twenty-five members and is generally considered to have a resource-rich membership, despite the addition of eight former Communist bloc countries. The EU, however, does not have peacekeeping capabilities or a standing army of its own, relying on its membership to provide it with the necessary forces and matériel. Instead, the EU has cooperated extensively with the UN and has also mobilized small mediation missions.

The European Community Monitoring Mission (ECMM) was established specifically as a preventive mechanism in Yugoslavia in July 1991 (*see* conflict 5.23). After a series of successful diplomatic initiatives by the ECMM in Yugoslavia, a cease-fire was reached and the EU set about monitoring troop withdrawals. An initial EU mission of 150 personnel entered the area to fulfill this role (Ramsbotham and Woodhouse 1999).

When the International Conference on the Former Yugoslavia (ICFY) was convened in London on August 26–28, 1992, among the parties attending were foreign ministers from most European states, the UN secretary-general, and the president of the Council of Ministers of the EU. The EU president and the UN secretary-general acted as co-chairs in the initial conference. The ICFY created a steering committee co-chaired by the UN secretary-general's personal envoy, Cyrus Vance of the United States, and the European Community mediator, Lord David Owen (United Nations 1996). Owen succeeded Lord Carrington as the European Community mediator, and Thorvald Stoltenberg took over from Vance in May 1993. In June 1995 Carl Bildt (Sweden) succeeded Owen. Altogether, these co-chairs mediated on sixty-three occasions.

The ICFY was a useful mechanism for the parties during the conflict. It was a well-utilized forum for discussion between the parties and helped to negotiate a cease-fire agreement in Croatia on March 29, 1994, and to formulate prospective implementation plans. Among other notable achievements, the ICFY recommended:

> the preventive deployment of UNPROFOR [United Nations Protective Force] in the former Yugoslav Republic of Macedonia; negotiated joint understandings between the Governments of the Republic of Croatia and the Federal Republic of Yugoslavia [Serbia and Montenegro]; provided a framework for addressing humanitarian issues; negotiated confidence-building measures; defused tensions involving ethnic and national communities and minorities; and sponsored efforts looking towards reconstruction and economic development in the area (United Nations 1996).

Vance and Owen were able to persuade the parties to agree on a series of peaceful settlements over the period from January to March 1993, culminating in the Vance-Owen Peace Plan on March 25, 1993. The plan set out measures to expand the UN peacekeeping role in Bosnia and Herzegovina, allowing the creation of a demilitarized zone, a cease-fire and monitoring of borders, restoration of economic and political infrastructures, and a separation of hostile forces. The ICFY was discontinued after January 31, 1996.

In 1991 EU observers were also deployed alongside OSCE observers in Croatia. At the same time, EU representatives were drawing up a joint UN/EU initiative, preparing for the deployment of UNPROFOR

(McCoubrey and White 1995). The EU has assisted in the management of only a handful of regional conflicts, mediating most extensively in the Yugoslavian civil war in the Balkans. With the recent inclusion of Cyprus among its member states, the EU may be able to take a stronger role in managing and resolving the problem of Cyprus's ongoing partition.

Organization for Security and Cooperation

Originally created as a "functional" security regime, the Conference on Security and Cooperation in Europe (CSCE) was developed from November 1972 to August 1975. The Paris summit meeting of 1990 transformed the CSCE from a conference-based functional organization to a structured "cooperative" regional organization. At the 1994 Budapest summit the evolution of the CSCE was formally acknowledged, and the name was changed to the Organization for Security and Cooperation in Europe (OSCE).

The CSCE initially operated as a forum for consultation, dialogue, and negotiation between the East and West until the collapse of the East-West divisions. "From 1975 to 1990, the CSCE, as its name implied, functioned as a series of conferences and meetings where new commitments were negotiated and their implementation reviewed. The Paris summit meeting in 1990 marked the beginning of institutionalization aimed at meeting the challenges presented by the post–Cold War period" (OSCE Internet 1997). At this time, the organization's "constant emphasis on dialogue rather than confrontation provided the European security community with a forum for creative debate" and, in part, contributed to the introduction of broader confidence and security-building measures (CSBM) (Ramsbotham and Woodhouse 1999). Clearly, this open environment for discussion and the freer exchange of information during CSBMs provided a positive political atmosphere for the sweeping Soviet reforms of the 1980s (Woodhouse 1999). Dubbed "the child of détente," the organization could not have been established without the cooperation of the Soviet Union and the United States and has since provided a bridge between the East-West ideological divide (Birnbaum and Peters 1990).

The OSCE organization operates under four main principles:

1. It was established as a "negotiation framework of equals," allowing smaller member states to raise issues that may conflict with former East or West alignments and their respective superpower;
2. It has "comprehensiveness" in its regional membership—it includes the United States—and in the range of issues it is willing to address;
3. It works on a principle of "cooperative bias" where issues are addressed with the cooperative management of intergovernmental and intersystemic relations; and
4. It provides "continuity," regulating member state behavior in procedural and legalistic terms under the Helsinki Final Act, 1975, and the Helsinki Document, 1992 (Birnbaum and Peters 1990).

OSCE members, fifty-five in total, pledge to refrain from the threat or use of force, to promote cooperation and the peaceful settlement of conflicts, and to respect human rights and the self-determination of peoples. "As a regional arrangement under Chapter VII of the Charter of the United Nations, the OSCE has been established as a primary instrument in the OSCE region for early warning, conflict prevention and crisis management in Europe" (OSCE Internet 1997). The obligations of members were carried to extraordinary lengths when the connection was made stronger between the respect for human rights and general security and cooperation. Despite the acknowledgment of sovereignty, nonintervention in internal affairs, and the territorial integrity of states, the OSCE established "that a country systematically violating the fundamental liberties of its own citizens could not be internationally trusted and should even be considered as a potential threat to other countries" (OSCE Internet 1997).

The OSCE's limitations stem from a lack of membership cohesiveness; consensus decision-making procedures; and a lack of military personnel, experience, command structures, and equipment. In addition, it lacks clearly defined operating procedures providing interorganizational cooperation with firm foundations. OSCE conflict management is authorized on a basis of consensus, and the organization's results are a reflection of its disparate membership. With fifty-five member states, the OSCE has the broadest geographic base of all of the regional organizations, and the resulting lack of cohesion makes it difficult for the organization to achieve consensual collective decisions. OSCE action in Yugoslavia is an example (Sutterlin 1995). The organization relies on its members for experienced personnel and equipment. Having no military force or expertise in organizing and commanding a military force, the OSCE can only "elaborate norms of good behavior, insert itself as a mediator, and find out facts on which other institutions, including the Security Council and NATO, could act if action was required" (Farer 1993).

The OSCE has engaged in a number of conflict management strategies, dispatching its first fact-finding mission to Georgia in October 1992 (Greco 1997) and carrying on eleven long-term missions and observer missions. Although the OSCE has not performed independent peacekeeping missions, its cooperative relationship with UN peacekeeping missions is well-documented (Burci 1997). In addition, the OSCE established a Conflict Prevention Center (CPC), which is charged with supporting CSBMs implemented by the OSCE Council. "CSBMs typically include limitations on military maneuvers, advance notification of such maneuvers, exchanges of maneuvers, military-to-military contacts, and exchange of information about force structures, weapons acquisitions, and the import or export of military hardware" (Auton 1998). This role has expanded to include conflict reduction and prevention, with the CPC performing an early warning function for the OSCE high commissioner for the protection of minorities (Sutterlin 1995).

References

Auton, G.P. 1998. "Multilateral Security Regimes: The Politics of CFE and CSBMs." Chapter 8 of *The Promise and Reality of European Security Co-operation—States, Interests, and Institutions.* McKenzie, M.M., and P.H. Loedel, eds. Westport, Conn.: Praeger, 139–156.

Barbour, P., ed. 1996. *The European Union Handbook.* Chicago: Fitzroy Dearborn.

Birnbaum, K.E., and I. Peters. 1990. "The CSCE: A Reassessment of its Role in the 1980's." *Review of International Studies* 16: 305–319.

Burci, G. 1997. "Division of Labour Between the UN and the OSCE in Connection with Peacekeeping." Chapter 11 of *The OSCE in the Maintenance of Peace and Security—Conflict Prevention, Crisis Management and Peaceful Settlement of Disputes.* Bothe, M., N. Ronzitti, and A. Rosas, eds. The Hague, Netherlands: Kluwer Law International, 289–313.

Farer, T.J. 1993. "The Role of Regional Collective Security Arrangements." In *Collective Security in a Changing World.* Weiss, T.G., ed. Boulder: Lynne Rienner, 153–186.

Greco, E. 1997. "Third Party Peacekeeping and the Interaction Between Russia and the OSCE in the CIS Area." Chapter 10 of *The OSCE in the Maintenance of Peace and Security—Conflict Prevention, Crisis Management and Peaceful Settlement of Disputes.* Bothe, M., N. Ronzitti, and A. Rosas, eds. The Hague, Netherlands: Kluwer Law International, 267–288.

McCormick, J. 1999. *Understanding the European Union—A Concise Introduction.* London: Macmillan.

McCoubrey, H., and N.D. White. 1995. *International Organisations and Civil Wars.* Aldershot (Hants), England: Dartmouth Publishing.

Miall, H., O. Ramsbotham, and T. Woodhouse. 1999. *Contemporary Conflict Resolution—The Prevention, Management and Transformation of Deadly Conflicts.* Malden, Mass.: Polity Press, published by Blackwell Publishers.

OSCE Internet. 1997. http://www.osceprag.cz/.

Ramsbotham, O., and T. Woodhouse. 1999. *Encyclopedia of International Peacekeeping Operations.* Santa Barbara: Calif.: ABC-CLIO.

Sutterlin, J.S. 1995. "The Potential of Regional Organizations." Chapter 7 of *The United Nations and the Maintenance of International Security—A Challenge To Be Met.* Sutterlin, J.S., ed. Westport, Conn.: Praeger, 93–111.

United Nations. 1996. *The Blue Helmets: A Review of United Nations Peacekeeping.* 3d edition. New York: UN Department of Public Information.

5.1 Greece: Antimonarchist Communist Insurgency and Civil War 1945–1949

Civil war erupted in Greece after the Axis powers were defeated in 1945. The Communist resistance in Greece, composed of the National Liberation Front (EAM) and the National Popular Liberation Army (ELAS), declared a provisional government and, with violence, attempted to prevent the return of the Greek government-in-exile led by King George II. With the aid of British troops, forces loyal to the government defeated the EAM and ELAS in Athens and restored the government under the Varkiya agreement. The agreement stipulated that a plebiscite would be used to determine whether the king should return.

The plebiscite was decided in the affirmative, and the king returned on September 27, 1946. Days after his return, the Communists resumed guerrilla warfare with the aid of the new Communist governments of Albania, Bulgaria, and Yugoslavia. From 1947 the conflict expanded to include areas of these three countries, as the Greek government launched attacks on rebel sanctuaries. Cross-border bombing raids and ground operations were common, and a number of foreign troops were killed.

Britain scaled down its military support for the Greek government in 1947, but the United States immediately picked up the slack with large-scale military assistance—equipment, training, and military advisers.

Yugoslavia withdrew its support for the rebels in 1949 because of disagreements with the rest of the Soviet bloc. Without Yugoslav support, the rebels were unable to sustain operations, and the conflict ended in 1950 with their defeat.

More than 158,000 people lost their lives in this conflict, many of them civilians; foreign forces suffered no more than 200 fatalities. Although the United Nations attempted to mediate in November 1948, both sides showed an unwillingness to settle their differences peacefully. Even the Soviet Union could not use its influence to bring about a dialogue.

References

Butterworth, R.L. 1978. *Moderation from Management: International Organizations and Peace.* Pittsburgh: University of Pittsburgh, Center for International Studies.

Close, D.H., ed. 1993. *The Greek Civil War, 1943–1950: Studies of Polarization.* London: Routledge.

Kousoulas, D. 1965. *Revolution and Defeat: The Story of the Greek Communist Party.* New York: Oxford University Press.

O'Ballance, E. 1966. *The Greek Civil War, 1944–1949.* New York: Praeger.

Tillema, H.K. 1991. *International Armed Conflict Since 1945: A Bibliographic Handbook of Wars and Military Interventions.* Boulder: Westview.

Woodhouse, C. 1976. *The Struggle for Greece, 1941–1949*. London: Hart-Davis, MacGibbon.

5.2 Albania–United Kingdom: Corfu Channel Dispute May 1946–December 1949

The ships of many different nations sailed through the Corfu Channel until May 1946, when Albania began to complain about Greek vessels entering Albanian territorial waters and committing threatening actions. On May 15 Albanian shore batteries fired upon two British battle cruisers as they passed through Albanian waters. The shots missed, and the British troops did not return fire. The UK lodged a formal protest with the Albanian government over the incident, claiming that the right of innocent passage in the Corfu Channel was protected under international law because the channel was used for connecting traffic between two bodies of international water.

The Albanian government acknowledged that the incident was unfortunate and that the British cruisers had been mistaken for Greek ships. Albania issued a warning to all vessels planning to pass through the Corfu Channel that they should give the Albanians prior notice. The UK declared that it would give no prior notice of its vessels passing through the channel and that if UK cruisers were fired upon again they would retaliate.

On October 22, 1946, a UK destroyer was heavily damaged in the Corfu Channel by a floating mine, which killed forty-four crew members and badly injured forty-two others. Britain informed Albania that the UK navy would sweep the channel for mines. Albania lodged a formal protest with the UK and the UN secretary-general, claiming that the mine-sweeping operation was a violation of its territorial waters. Albania proposed the establishment of a joint commission to determine which area of the channel would be regarded as "free" for international navigation. Over November 12–13, 1946, the UK navy completed its unauthorized mine-sweep of the Corfu Channel. Albania lodged another formal protest with the UN secretary-general, saying that the UK had violated its territorial sovereignty. Britain countered by claiming that Albania had laid or allowed another party to lay mines in international waters after the International Mine Clearance Board had completed its operations in 1944 and 1945.

Britain brought the dispute to the UN Security Council on January 10, 1947. On February 27 the Security Council set up a three-member subcommittee to investigate the matter. The subcommittee made its report on March 12, announcing that its findings were inconclusive. One of the subcommittee members, Poland, did not find that Albania was at fault in the laying of mines, and the USSR vetoed the resolution that declared Albania the responsible party. At the request of the UK, the matter was referred to the International Court of Justice (ICJ) on April 9, 1947.

The ICJ made three decisions on the issue of the Corfu Channel: (1) that the ICJ, not Albania, had jurisdiction over the Corfu Channel (March 25, 1948); (2) that Albania was responsible for the mine explosion on October 22, 1946, even though the Albanian government may have been unaware of the planting of the mines; that the UK had a right to send naval vessels through the channel without first giving prior notice in peacetime; and that the UK mine sweep of the channel had been conducted illegally and therefore violated Albania's sovereignty (April 9, 1949); and (3) that Albania owed the UK £843,947 in reparation for the damage to the vessel.

Albania refused to accept the terms of the third and final ICJ decision and, to date, the reparations have not been paid.

References

Allsebrook, M. 1986. *Prototypes of Peacemaking: The First Forty Years of the United Nations*. Harlow (Essex) England: Longman Group UK Limited.

Brecher, M., J. Wilkenfeld, and S. Moser. 1988. *Crises in the Twentieth Century*. New York: Pergamon.

Butterworth, R.L. 1976. *Managing Interstate Conflict, 1945–1974*. Pittsburgh: Center for International Studies, University of Pittsburgh.

Fretter, J.M. 2001. *Effective Mediation in International Disputes: A Comparative Analysis of Mediation by the United Nations and Regional Organizations 1945–1995*. Doctoral dissertation, Vol. II: Appendices. University of Canterbury, Christchurch, New Zealand.

Tillema, H.K. 1991. *International Armed Conflict Since 1945: A Bibliographic Handbook of Wars and Military Interventions*. Boulder: Westview.

5.3 Yugoslavia–United States: Cold War Air Incidents August 1946

This conflict was rooted in the growing postwar rift between the Allies, with the Soviet Union (and its new satellite regimes in Central and Eastern Europe) facing off against the Western powers—Britain, France, and the United States, all over Europe.

These cold war tensions boiled over on August 9, 1946, when an American C-47 transport plane on a flight from Vienna to Udine was shot down by Yugoslav fighter planes over Slovenia. On August 19 the United States alleged a second attack along the same route. Yugoslav authorities detained the captured crew from the two aircraft. Yugoslavia countered protests from the U.S. government by accusing the United States of making unauthorized flights over Yugoslav territory. On August 21 the United States delivered an ultimatum to Yugoslavia demanding the release of all detained crew within forty-eight hours or the United States would place the matter before the UN Security Council.

Yugoslavia complied with the ultimatum on August 22 and gave assurances there would be no repeat of the air incidents. Although no fighting occurred between U.S. and Yugoslav troops, the context of the conflict had made the potential for escalation very high. The United States engaged in a number of similar incidents with the Soviet Union in the 1950s (*see* conflicts 3.8; 3.11).

References

Bartlett, C.J. 1994. *The Global Conflict: The International Rivalry of Great Powers, 1880–1990.* 2d edition. London: Longman.

Cimbala, S.J., and S.R. Waldman, eds. 1992. *Controlling and Ending Conflict: Issues Before and After the Cold War.* New York: Greenwood.

Gablentz, O.M. van der. 1964. *The Berlin Question in Its Relations to World Politics, 1944–1963.* Munich: Oldenbourg.

Rabel, R.G. 1988. *Between East and West: Trieste, the United States and the Cold War, 1941–1954.* Durham, N.C.: Duke University Press.

5.4 USSR–Yugoslavia: Ideological Rift Early 1948–December 1954

In 1948 a Communist Information Bureau (Cominform) resolution expelled Yugoslavia from the world Communist movement. This split resulted from growing friction between the approach of the Stalinist interstate system and Yugoslavia's leader Marshal Tito. Tito, who was born Josip Broz, was not adhering to the dictates issued by the Communist authorities in Moscow, and the ideological tensions between the USSR and Yugoslavia reached new levels in 1951. Yugoslavia complained about Soviet efforts to interfere with its internal politics, and in November 1951 Yugoslavia made a formal complaint to the United Nations, citing USSR aggression. Yugoslavia cited a blockade, the severing of communications, the blatant violation of mutual treaties, and Soviet troop movements along Yugoslavia's border, as evidence of Soviet aggression.

The UN General Assembly passed a resolution on December 14, 1951, calling for the parties to settle their dispute peacefully according to the terms of the UN Charter. The ideological rift was never fully resolved, however, and Yugoslavia remained on the periphery of Eastern Europe's Communist states, in relative isolation, after its expulsion from Cominform.

References

Allsebrook, M. 1986. *Prototypes of Peacemaking: The First Forty Years of the United Nations.* Harlow (Essex) England: Longman Group UK Limited.

Brecher, M., J. Wilkenfeld, and S. Moser. 1988. *Crises in the Twentieth Century.* New York: Pergamon.

Butterworth, R.L. 1976. *Managing Interstate Conflict, 1945–1974.* Pittsburgh: Center for International Studies, University of Pittsburgh.

Fretter, J.M. 2001. *Effective Mediation in International Disputes: A Comparative Analysis of Mediation by the United Nations and Regional Organizations 1945–1995.* Doctoral dissertation, Vol. II: Appendices. University of Canterbury, Christchurch, New Zealand.

5.5 USSR–The Western Allies: The Berlin Airlift Crisis June 1948–May 1949

In the wake of World War II, Berlin, which lay inside East German territory, was partitioned among the four World War II victors and allies—France, Great Britain, the United States, and the Soviet Union. The three Western allies were accorded designated access corridors through East Germany to Berlin. As cold war strains mounted between the United States and the USSR, Berlin's status took on additional meaning, becoming the focus of the emerging East-West conflict. The Soviet Union began to limit Western access to Berlin.

The conflict escalated on June 18, 1948, when the Western powers announced a currency reform, which applied to their respective sectors of occupation in Germany, including Berlin. On June 23 the Soviet Union announced its own currency reform, which it said would apply to the Soviet sector of Germany and the whole of Berlin. Then, on June 23–24, Soviet authorities imposed an air and land blockade of Berlin. The United States responded on June 28 with a daring airlift to break the blockade, sending U.S. supply planes into Berlin in the face of intense intimidation by Soviet jet fighters.

On July 1 the Soviet Union suspended its cooperation with the Western powers in the governance of Berlin. An offer from the UN secretary-general to mediate was declined, and an attempt to initiate multilateral negotiations failed. At this point Berlin was divided into East and West sectors with completely separate administrations.

The blockade was eventually lifted following negotiations between Philip C. Jessup, the U.S. ambassador at large, and the Soviet UN representative, M. Malik. Although no hostilities occurred, the intimidating use of jet fighters by the Soviet Union and the potential for escalation inherent in the strained superpower relations, made the Berlin crisis extremely serious. This crisis led to the formation of the North Atlantic Treaty Organization (NATO) in 1948, a Western military alliance devoted to safeguarding the Atlantic community against the Soviet bloc. Berlin remained the focus of cold war conflict for a number of years.

References

Gablentz, O.M. van der. 1964. *The Berlin Question in Its Relations to World Politics, 1944–1963*. Munich: Oldenbourg.

Heidelmeyer, W., and G. Hindrichs, eds. 1963. *Documents on Berlin, 1943–1963*. 2d edition. Munich: Oldenbourg.

Keesing's Research Report. 1973. *Germany and Eastern Europe Since 1945: From the Potsdam Agreement to Chancellor Brandt's "Ostpolitik."* New York: Scribner's.

McInnes, E. 1960. *The Shaping of Postwar Germany*. London: Dent.

Smith, J.E. 1963. *The Defense of Berlin*. Baltimore: Johns Hopkins University Press.

Tanter, R. 1974. *Modeling and Managing International Conflicts: The Berlin Crisis*. Beverly Hills: Sage.

Tillema, H.K. 1991. *International Armed Conflict Since 1945: A Bibliographic Handbook of Wars and Military Interventions*. Boulder: Westview.

5.6 Italy–Yugoslavia: Cold War and Trieste Territorial Dispute March 1952–October 1954

After World War I and the dissolution of the Austro-Hungarian Empire, Italy was awarded the port of Trieste at the head of the Adriatic Sea. During World War II an Allied force made up of U.S. and British troops and Yugoslav guerrillas took Trieste, and both Italy and Yugoslavia laid claim to the region after the war.

Beginning in 1947 the United Nations sought to resolve the conflicting claims to Trieste, and on March 20, 1948, the world organization produced the Tripartite Declaration. The declaration, signed by Britain, France, and the United States on March 20, recommended the return of the city and its surrounding territory to Italy. Yugoslavia rejected the declaration and proposed in February 1952 that Trieste be placed under a joint Italian-Yugoslav administration.

Italy reaffirmed its support of the Tripartite Declaration in 1953. In August of that year, in response to Yugoslavia's hints of a forcible annexation of the area, Italy sent a naval force into the region and positioned troops on the Yugoslav border. These military movements greatly aggravated tensions, setting into motion intensive diplomatic efforts to avert a crisis.

On October 8, 1953, the Western allies announced their impending withdrawal from Trieste in keeping with the terms of the declaration. Yugoslavia responded that it would view any Italian movement into Trieste as an act of aggression and respond militarily. On November 4 riots broke out in Trieste; 6 people died and 162 were injured. British troops were deployed to quell the disturbances.

A five-power conference, with delegates from Britain, France, Italy, the United States, and Yugoslavia, was convened on November 13, 1953, with the purpose of resolving the territorial dispute. Eleven months later, on October 6, 1954, the conference participants issued a memorandum of understanding to the effect that Italy and Yugoslavia would both govern Trieste on the basis of redrawn boundaries. Only intense U.S. and British efforts to mediate the dispute averted war.

References

Day, A., ed. 1987. *Border and Territorial Disputes*. 2d edition. Burnt Mill, Harlow (Essex), England: Longman.

Novak, B. 1970. *Trieste, 1941–1954: The Ethnic, Political, and Ideological Struggle*. Chicago: University of Chicago Press.

Rabel, R.G. 1988. *Between East and West: Trieste, the United States and the Cold War, 1941–1954*. Durham, N.C.: Duke University Press.

Tillema, H.K. 1991. *International Armed Conflict Since 1945: A Bibliographic Handbook of Wars and Military Interventions*. Boulder: Westview.

5.7 Cyprus–United Kingdom: Intercommunal Violence and the Enosis Movement April 1955–February 1959

Cyprus, populated by a Greek majority and Turkish minority, came under British control in the nineteenth century. It was subsequently annexed in 1914 and made a crown colony in 1925. After World War II the Greek majority began to agitate for enosis, or union with Greece. Britain declared that it would never relinquish the island, despite its lack of economic or strategic value. In April 1955 the National Organization of Cypriot Fighters (EOKA) initiated a terror campaign aimed at both British and Turkish targets. Assassination and sabotage were the main tactics. Britain deployed 40,000 troops to quell the disturbances. Frequent Turkish retaliatory attacks followed, and, in the most serious fighting between the two ethnic communities in 1958, 115 people were killed.

Starting in 1957 a political solution was sought through negotiations and multilateral conferences among Britain, Greece, Turkey, and the United Nations. The parties reached an agreement in February 1959, and Cyprus was granted independence in 1960. Approximately 100 British soldiers and more than 500 civilians died as a result of the violence. This conflict was the precursor to more serious conflicts in 1963 and 1974, when Greece and Turkey went to war over events on the island (*see* conflicts 5.11; 5.14).

References

Adams, T.W., and A.J. Cottrell. 1968. *Cyprus Between East and West*. Baltimore: Johns Hopkins University Press.

Bitsios, D. 1975. *Cyprus: The Vulnerable Republic.* Thessalonike: Institute for Balkan Studies.

Chandler, G. 1959. *The Divided Land: An Anglo-Greek Tragedy.* London: Macmillan.

Crawley, N. 1978. *The Cyprus Revolt: An Account of the Struggle for Union with Greece.* Boston: Allen and Unwin.

Denktash, R. 1982. *The Cyprus Triangle.* Boston: Allen and Unwin.

Ehrlich, T. 1974. *Cyprus, 1958–1967.* London: Oxford University Press.

Foley, C., and W. Scobie. 1975. *The Struggle for Cyprus.* Stanford, Calif.: Hoover.

Hare, A.P. 1974. *Cyprus—Conflict and Its Resolution.* Cape Town: University of Cape Town.

Hart, P.T. 1990. *Two NATO Allies at the Threshold of War: Cyprus, A Firsthand Account of Crisis Management, 1965–1968.* Durham, N.C.: Duke University Press.

Tillema, H.K. 1991. *International Armed Conflict Since 1945: A Bibliographic Handbook of Wars and Military Interventions.* Boulder: Westview.

5.8 USSR–Poland: Polish October October 1956

Poland was incorporated into the Soviet sphere of influence after World War II and belonged to the Warsaw Pact, the Soviet-led military alliance of Communist states set up as a countermeasure to NATO. Following the death of Joseph Stalin in 1953, Poland felt the first effects of "de-Stalinization" in the Poznan workers' demonstration on June 28, 1956. The government sent the Polish army to put down the demonstration, which had evolved into a riot. Hundreds were killed or wounded. The riot caused the Polish Communist Party to split into two factions: the Natolin faction, which upheld the traditional Stalinist line, and the "evolutionists," who sought political liberalization under the leadership of Wladyslaw Gomulka. He was a former member of the Politburo who had been purged in 1948, because he had been accused of following the example of Marshal Tito of Yugoslavia.

When Gomulka returned to power in Poland in October 1956, he undertook a program of moderate reforms, including the democratization of Communist Party management. The Soviet Union feared the contagious effect of such open dissent on the other Warsaw Pact countries—Albania, Bulgaria, Czechoslovakia, East Germany, Poland, and Romania. Moscow's response to Gomulka's appointment was swift, and a delegation was sent to attend the Polish Warsaw Party Plenum on October 17, 1956. The uninvited delegation arrived in Warsaw on October 19 and included top Soviet Politburo members such as Nikita Khrushchev, Lazar Kaganovich, Anastas Mikoyan, and Vyacheslav Molotov. At the same time, Gomulka alleged that Soviet troops had breached treaty agreements with Poland and were marching from bases near Wroclaw toward Warsaw. Reportedly, Gomulka threatened to broadcast news of these Soviet troop movements knowing that it would cause internal strife and protests. The Soviets continued to apply political pressure in this manner, alerting seven Soviet divisions to patrol the Polish border with East Germany. Khrushchev backed down and ordered all troop movements to cease when he was assured that Warsaw had control of the situation and that there would be no anti-Soviet demonstrations. The show of Soviet strength and willingness to act in Poland was enough to ensure that the new Polish leadership did not overstep the bounds of "acceptable communism."

A compromise was reached in a bilateral meeting held between the new Polish leadership, the Polish United Workers' Party, and the Soviet Politburo Central Committee delegation on October 22, 1956. Gomulka was elected to the position of first secretary of the Polish Communist Party. His party was allowed to formulate the "Polish Road to Socialism," but it was agreed that Soviet troops could remain in Poland so long as they did not interfere in Poland's internal affairs and could not move from their bases without prior consent from the Polish government. Poland was basically granted limited autonomy, but the USSR remained effectively in control. It is likely that a desire to maintain the semblance of Soviet bloc unity and the fact that China had openly supported the Polish position contributed to the peaceful settlement of the conflict.

References

Brecher, M., J. Wilkenfeld, and S. Moser. 1988. *Crises in the Twentieth Century.* New York: Pergamon.

Brzezinski, Z. 1967. *The Soviet Bloc: Unity and Conflict.* Cambridge: Harvard University Press.

Butterworth, R.L. 1976. *Managing Interstate Conflict, 1945–1974.* Pittsburgh: Center for International Studies, University of Pittsburgh.

5.9 USSR–Hungary: Anti-Communist Revolt, Soviet Invasion, and the Hungarian Uprising of 1956 October–December 1956

Hungary was incorporated into the Soviet sphere of influence after World War II and belonged to the Warsaw Pact, the Soviet-led military alliance of Communist states set up as a countermeasure to the North Atlantic Treaty Organization (NATO). Following the death of Joseph Stalin in 1953, the Hungarian leadership split into two factions: those under Premier Imre Nagy, who favored a program of liberalization, and those who favored a continuation of authoritarian Communist policies led by Mutyas Rakosi.

Nagy was forced to relinquish the premiership in a leadership struggle in 1955. In October 1956 riots broke out all over Hungary calling for his return. When central intelligence forces loyal to the Stalinist premier Erno Gero fired on protesters, the crisis escalated and Gero was forced to resign from office. Nagy was returned to power on a wave of popular support. Anti-Communist protests developed into open revolt.

The Soviet Union feared the effect of such open dissent on the other Warsaw Pact countries—Albania, Bulgaria, Czechoslovakia, East Germany, Poland, and Romania. Nagy negotiated a cease-fire on October 28, and the Soviets withdrew from Budapest. Unrest continued, however, and on November 1 Nagy announced Hungary's withdrawal from the Warsaw Pact. On November 4 Soviet forces launched a massive attack on Budapest with 200,000 troops, 2,500 tanks, and armored cars.

The Hungarian revolt ended on November 14 when it became clear that no outside help was likely. Nagy was executed, approximately 3,000 civilians were killed during the uprising, and hundreds of thousands of Hungarians fled the country. At no time did either side attempt to settle the conflict peacefully. A similar conflict occurred in Czechoslovakia in 1968, in which Hungarian troops were involved as part of the Warsaw Pact invasion force, and in Poland in 1981 (*see* conflicts 5.12; 5.15).

References

Barber, N. 1974. *Seven Days of Freedom: The Hungarian Uprising, 1956*. New York: Stein and Day.

Barta, I., contr. 1975. *A History of Hungary*. Edited by E. Pamlényi. Translated by L. Boros. London: Collet's.

Heinrich, H.G. 1986. *Hungary: Politics, Economics, and Society*. Boulder: Lynne Rienner.

Kiraly, B.K., and P. Jonas, eds. 1978. *The Hungarian Revolution of 1956 in Retrospect*. New York: Columbia University Press.

Kovacs, I., ed. 1958. *Facts About Hungary: The Fight for Freedom*. Written by M. Bizottsag. New York: Hungarian Committee.

Lasky, M.J., ed. 1957. *The Hungarian Revolution: A White Book*. New York: Praeger.

Lomax, W. 1976. *Hungary 1956*. London: Allen and Busby.

Mikes, G. 1957. *The Hungarian Revolution*. London: André Deutsch.

Molnar, M. 1971. *Budapest, 1956: A History of the Hungarian Revolution*. Translated by J. Ford. London: Allen and Unwin.

Tillema, H.K. 1991. *International Armed Conflict Since 1945: A Bibliographic Handbook of Wars and Military Interventions*. Boulder: Westview.

5.10 USSR–United States: Cold War Dispute and the Berlin Wall July–November 1961

The events of July to November 1961 have their roots in the postwar division of Germany—and the city of Berlin—into four sectors, with the Eastern sector dominated by the Soviet Union. The airlift crisis of 1948–1949 served as a precursor to this conflict (*see* conflict 5.5). Berlin's exceptional status, hundreds of miles into the Soviet zone of occupation, was the source of some friction between the Soviet Union and the Western powers (Britain, France, and the United States). The friction escalated into an all-out crisis when the Soviet government sought to incorporate Berlin's Western sectors into a demilitarized "free city." A summit meeting between U.S. president John F. Kennedy and Soviet premier Nikita S. Khrushchev in June 1961 failed to guarantee Western access to West Berlin, and the East Germans responded by hastily constructing a wall between East Berlin and West Berlin. The Berlin Wall became one of the most powerful symbols of the cold war.

On June 28, 1961, East Germany announced restrictions on Western air traffic. These were ultimately not enforced, but they further strained East-West relations. The NATO allies warned of dire consequences if their access to West Berlin was impeded. On July 7, and again on August 4, restrictions were placed on East Germans working in West Berlin in an attempt to stem the flow of refugees to the West. The Western powers protested these restrictions.

On August 13, 1961, the border between East and West Berlin was closed, and the Berlin Wall more fully erected on August 17 and 18. In the ensuing days massive U.S. troop reinforcements arrived in Berlin, and patrols were set up in the no-man's land around the wall. The saber-rattling continued over the next few weeks and included a resumption of nuclear weapons testing by both superpowers in November 1961. Neither side attempted to settle the conflict by dialogue. Although no actual fighting took place, the conflict fueled tensions that eventually produced the 1962 Cuban Missile Crisis (*see* conflict 2.17).

References

Gablentz, O.M. van der. 1964. *The Berlin Question in Its Relations to World Politics, 1944–1963*. Munich: Oldenbourg.

Heidelmeyer, W., and G. Hindrichs, eds. 1963. *Documents on Berlin, 1943–1963*. 2d edition. Munich: Oldenbourg.

Keesing's Research Report. 1973. *Germany and Eastern Europe Since 1945: From the Potsdam Agreement to Chancellor Brandt's "Ostpolitik."* New York: Scribner's.

McInnes, E. 1960. *The Shaping of Postwar Germany*. London: Dent.

Smith, J.E. 1963. *The Defense of Berlin.* Baltimore: Johns Hopkins University Press.

Tanter, R. 1974. *Modeling and Managing International Conflicts: The Berlin Crisis.* Beverly Hills: Sage.

Tillema, H.K. 1991. *International Armed Conflict Since 1945: A Bibliographic Handbook of Wars and Military Interventions.* Boulder: Westview.

5.11 Cyprus: Intercommunal Violence and Civil War
December 1963–November 1967

Cyprus gained independence in 1960 following a violent campaign against British rule (*see* conflict 5.7). The majority population of Cyprus was Greek and the minority Turkish, and both groups looked to their respective homelands for support. Following independence, the parties began negotiations on drafting a constitution that addressed the island's intercommunal difficulties. These problems were not resolved, and the strains produced frequent intercommunal violence. The violence erupted into civil war in December 1963, following an incident between Greek Cypriot police and Turkish Cypriot citizens. Despite British efforts to broker a cease-fire, the fighting continued to escalate throughout 1964.

Units of the Turkish navy took up positions off the coast of Cyprus in December 1963, and the Greek government alleged that a Turkish invasion was imminent. The North Atlantic Treaty Organization (NATO) proposed that a peacekeeping force be sent to the island, but both parties rejected the suggestion. On March 4, 1964, the United Nations authorized the UN Peacekeeping Force in Cyprus (UNFICYP), and such a force is still there.

The UN force failed to halt the violence, and major incidents continued throughout 1964, including the bombing of Greek Cypriot targets by the Turkish air force on August 9, 1964. A cease-fire was declared the following day, and, although outbreaks of violence were frequent, moves were made toward finding a peaceful settlement to the dispute.

A series of bilateral talks between the two communities over the subsequent six years produced little progress. Foreign military involvement (apart from the UN peacekeeping forces) in the Cypriot war ended in December 1967, when the United States was able to secure the withdrawal of Greek and Turkish forces stationed on Cyprus. The withdrawal was completed in mid-February 1968. In all, about 1,000 people were killed during the course of the conflict, many of them civilians. The issue of the relationship of the two communities was never resolved, and in 1974 violence once again overtook the island, in this case, leading to a Turkish invasion (*see* conflict 5.14).

References

Adams, T.W., and A.J. Cottrell. 1968. *Cyprus Between East and West.* Baltimore: Johns Hopkins University Press.

Bitsios, D. 1975. *Cyprus: The Vulnerable Republic.* Thessalonike: Institute for Balkan Studies.

Crawley, N. 1978. *The Cyprus Revolt: An Account of the Struggle for Union with Greece.* Boston: Allen and Unwin.

Denktash, R. 1982. *The Cyprus Triangle.* Boston: Allen and Unwin.

Ehrlich, T. 1974. *Cyprus, 1958–1967.* London: Oxford University Press.

Hare, A.P. 1974. *Cyprus—Conflict and Its Resolution.* Cape Town: University of Cape Town.

Hart, P.T. 1990. *Two NATO Allies at the Threshold of War: Cyprus, A Firsthand Account of Crisis Management, 1965–1968.* Durham, N.C.: Duke University Press.

Tillema, H.K. 1991. *International Armed Conflict Since 1945: A Bibliographic Handbook of Wars and Military Interventions.* Boulder: Westview.

5.12 USSR–Czechoslovakia: Liberalization Movement, the Prague Spring, and Soviet Military Invasion
August 1968

Liberated by Soviet forces during World War II, Czechoslovakia was ruled by a Communist regime from 1948 to 1989. In January 1968, however, a democratic reform movement spread explosively through the country. The country's longtime Stalinist leader, Antonin Novotny, was deposed as general secretary of the Czech Communist Party and replaced by Alexander Dubček, who immediately announced a reform program aimed at lifting restrictions imposed by the party on Czechoslovakia's economic and public life, including censorship.

The Soviet Union and its Warsaw Pact allies, Bulgaria, East Germany, Hungary, and Poland, demanded an end to Czechoslovakia's liberalization efforts. When the Dubček regime pressed on with the reform program, Warsaw Pact armies invaded on August 18, 1968, detaining Dubček and his closest aides. Protesters—mostly students and workers—clashed with Warsaw Pact troops, and many protestors were killed. Although Czech citizens called for and expected Western intervention, none was forthcoming. Foreign troops withdrew in September and October after a new government had been installed and the protest movement crushed.

Soviet military forces left a permanent military presence in Czechoslovakia. The initial clashes and the following crackdown left nearly 1,000 dead. The Soviet Union had already shown a willingness to intervene directly in East European states, as it had in Hungary in 1956, and it intervened again in Poland in 1980 (*see* conflicts 5.9; 5.15).

References

Dawisha, K. 1984. *The Kremlin and the Prague Spring.* Berkeley and Los Angeles: University of California Press.

Hodnett, G., and P.J. Potichnyj. 1976. *The Ukraine and the Czechoslovak Crisis.* Occasional Paper #6. Canberra: Department of Political Science, Australian National University.

James, R.R. 1969. *The Czechoslovak Crisis, 1968.* London: Weidenfeld and Nicolson.

Littell, R. 1969. *The Czech Black Book.* Prepared by the Institute of History, Czechoslovak Academy of Sciences. New York: Praeger.

Randle, M. 1968. *Support Czechoslovakia.* London: Housemans.

Remington, R. 1969. *Winter in Prague: Documents on Czechoslovak Communism in Crisis.* Cambridge: Press.

Roberts, A. 1969. *Czechoslovakia 1968.* London: Chatto and Windus.

Schwartz, H. 1969. *Prague's 200 Days: The Struggle for Democracy in Czechoslovakia.* New York: Praeger.

Skilling, H.G. 1976. *Czechoslovakia's Interrupted Revolution.* Princeton, N.J.: Princeton University Press.

Tillema, H.K. 1991. *International Armed Conflict Since 1945: A Bibliographic Handbook of Wars and Military Interventions.* Boulder: Westview.

5.13 Iceland–United Kingdom, West Germany, and Denmark: The Cod War November 1971–June 1976

The United Nations and the International Court of Justice (ICJ) were both involved in managing this dispute over territorial waters around Iceland. This dispute was one of several between Iceland and other nations regarding fishing rights in Icelandic waters.

On November 28, 1971, Iceland declared that it would extend its fishing zone from 12 miles to 50 miles off-shore as of September 1, 1972. Iceland and the United Kingdom conducted negotiations, but no agreement was reached over UK fishing rights in the area. In March 1972 the UK referred the matter to the ICJ for a decision. West Germany lodged a similar case against Iceland with the ICJ in August 1972. The ICJ ruled against Iceland on August 18, 1972, but Iceland ignored the ruling and proceeded to extend its territorial waters to 50 miles on September 2.

Iceland vigorously defended the extended territorial waters. Its gunboats fired at fishing trawlers that dared to enter the waters, reportedly including Danish, German, and UK vessels. In protest, the UK shipping union implemented a boycott of Icelandic ships and, in November 1972, Denmark, the UK, and West Germany lodged a combined protest to the ICJ over Iceland's extension of its territorial waters. Iceland refused to acknowledge that the ICJ had any jurisdiction in the dispute, but agreed to engage in negotiations with the UK.

Clashes continued to occur in the disputed zone into 1973, and the UK sent naval vessels into the area to protect the fishing boats. Although no vessel was attacked, there were reports of ships being rammed. Iceland refused to allow UK naval vessels access to their naval bases, and Iceland also called for the North Atlantic Treaty Organization (NATO) to intervene and order the removal of the UK vessels. NATO referred the dispute to the UN secretary-general, but the secretary-general's actions were limited to the sending a letter of condemnation to both parties. Further UN discussion of the matter was limited to a meeting of the UN Committee on Peaceful Uses of the Seabed. The committee prepared the matter for discussion at a later meeting of the UN Law of the Sea Conference.

When Britain increased the number of its forces in the region in October 1973, Iceland threatened to sever diplomatic relations with the UK. That same month Iceland and the UK agreed to enter into negotiations to work out a peaceful solution, and in November the negotiations proved successful. The parties agreed that Iceland could extend its territorial waters 50 miles off-shore so long as certain areas could be set aside for the sole use of UK fishing fleets.

The dispute resumed along similar lines on July 15, 1975, when Iceland announced that it was going to extend its territorial waters a further 200 miles off-shore, effective October 15. During November Icelandic gunboats threatened any foreign vessels encroaching on the new territorial zone. To safeguard British vessels in the area, the UK dispatched frigates to the disputed waters. Iceland's foreign minister initiated negotiations with the UK in the hope of avoiding a further escalation of the crisis. The two nations' foreign ministers met in December 1975, and their prime ministers met in January 1976. Neither of these meetings produced any progress toward a full peaceful settlement, and Iceland severed diplomatic relations with Britain on February 18. UK naval vessels remained in the area to protect fishing boats during the crisis.

On June 1, 1976, an interim agreement between Iceland and the UK was reached in Oslo, granting British vessels fishing rights within the 200-mile zone, but limiting the number of trawlers operating in a day to twenty-four.

The UN Security Council discussed the matter from June 2 to December 11, 1975. Another round of talks between the disputants was held over the same period under UN auspices. NATO and the Nordic Council also conducted talks on the economic and military impact of Icelandic territorial expansion.

References

Allsebrook, M. 1986. *Prototypes of Peacemaking: The First Forty Years of the United Nations.* Harlow (Essex) England: Longman Group UK Limited.

Brecher, M., J. Wilkenfeld, and S. Moser. 1988. *Crises in the Twentieth Century*. New York: Pergamon.

Butterworth, R.L. 1976. *Managing Interstate Conflict, 1945–1974*. Pittsburgh: Center for International Studies, University of Pittsburgh.

Fretter, J.M. 2001. *Effective Mediation in International Disputes: A Comparative Analysis of Mediation by the United Nations and Regional Organizations 1945–1995*. Doctoral dissertation, Vol. II: Appendices. University of Canterbury, Christchurch, New Zealand.

5.14 Cyprus: Communal Violence, Turkish–Greek Invasions, and Partition January 1974–June 1978

Cyprus gained independence from Britain in 1960 following a violent campaign (*see* conflict 5.7). The issue of the relationship between the majority Greek Cypriot population and the minority Turkish Cypriot population was never resolved, however, and led to massive communal violence in 1963 (*see* conflict 5.11). Although UN troops were stationed on the island to keep the peace between the two communities, tensions remained high.

After disputes with the national guard, dominated by Greek army officers, Archbishop Makarios, the Cypriot president, was overthrown in a military coup on July 15, 1974. Installed in his place was Nikoi Giorgiades Sampson, a former terrorist who had fought against the British for the Greek National Organization of Cypriot Fighters (EOKA). This provoked alarm among the Turkish Cypriot community, some of whom began fleeing the country with the aid of British soldiers. Others began arming themselves, and Turkey and Greece quickly mobilized as the conflict escalated.

Five days after the coup, on July 20, a Turkish invasion force landed in Cyprus and, after fierce fighting, had gained control of the north by the end of August. Almost simultaneously, a Greek force landed, assisting the local Greek militia in halting the Turkish advance. A U.S.-mediated cease-fire failed, but the parties signed a British-mediated cease-fire July 30, 1974. Cyprus had effectively been partitioned by this point. President Makarios returned to head the official Cypriot government in the southern part of the island. A Turkish Cypriot federated state was established in the northern third of the island under the leadership of Rauf Denktash.

A period of protracted negotiations sponsored by the United Nations was initiated in an effort to find a political solution to reunify Cyprus, but without much success. More than 5,000 people lost their lives in the conflict, including 1,000 Turkish troops. Despite the presence of UN troops, tensions between the two countries remained high, and incidents were not uncommon. The civil war also heightened the rivalry between Greece and Turkey, leading to a clash in 1984 (*see* conflict 5.16).

References

Adams, T.W., and A.J. Cottrell. 1968. *Cyprus Between East and West*. Baltimore: Johns Hopkins University Press.

Bitsios, D. 1975. *Cyprus: The Vulnerable Republic*. Thessalonike: Institute for Balkan Studies.

Central Intelligence Agency. *The World Factbook—Cyprus*. 2002. http://www.cia.gov/cia/publications/factbook/geos/cy.html (March 9, 2002).

Crawley, N. 1978. *The Cyprus Revolt: An Account of the Struggle for Union With Greece*. Boston: Allen and Unwin.

Denktash, R. 1982. *The Cyprus Triangle*. Boston: Allen and Unwin.

Ehrlich, T. 1974. *Cyprus, 1958–1967*. London: Oxford University Press.

Foley, C., and W. Scobie. 1975. *The Struggle for Cyprus*. Stanford, Calif.: Hoover.

Hare, A.P. 1974. *Cyprus—Conflict and Its Resolution*. Cape Town: University of Cape Town.

Hart, P.T. 1990. *Two NATO Allies at the Threshold of War: Cyprus, A Firsthand Account of Crisis Management, 1965–1968*. Durham, N.C.: Institute for the Study of Diplomacy, Duke University Press.

Reuters Alert Net. 2001. "Cyprus" Country Profile. http://www.alertnet.org/thefacts/countryprofiles/ (March 9, 2002).

———. 2001. "Turkey" Country Profile: http://www.alertnet.org/thefacts/countryprofiles/ (March 9, 2002).

Tillema, H.K. 1991. *International Armed Conflict Since 1945: A Bibliographic Handbook of Wars and Military Interventions*. Boulder: Westview.

U.S. Agency for International Development. 2002. "Cyprus: Regional Overview." http://www.usaid.gov/country/ee/cy/ (March 9, 2002).

5.15 Poland: Internal Crisis, Solidarity Labor Movement, and the Declaration of Martial Law December 1981–February 1982

Poland had been part of the Soviet sphere of influence since the end of World War II. By the early 1980s, however, internal demands for economic liberalization and greater political freedom were creating fissures in the monolithic Soviet bloc. This was particularly evident in Poland, where Lech Walesa, a Gdansk shipyard worker, had founded the Solidarity labor union. The Soviet Union had amply demonstrated its views on internal dissension with its military invasions of Hungary in 1956 and Czechoslovakia in 1968 (*see* conflicts 5.9; 5.12).

This particular conflict began in December 1981, when General Wojciech Jaruzelski, apparently fearing a Soviet invasion, ordered a preemptive military crackdown. Claiming that Solidarity had plans to overthrow the government, Jaruzelski declared martial law and ordered the arrests of thousands of Poles, including Walesa and other Solidarity leaders. Strikes and demonstrations were brutally suppressed.

Although there was little indication at the time of Soviet collusion in the crisis, subsequent evidence reveals the Soviet Union's deep involvement in preparing for and implementing the crackdown. Once discovered, this complicity provoked a crisis in NATO-Soviet relations and heightened tensions in Europe. Eventually, however, the crisis dissipated. Martial law was lifted in December 1982, a month after Walesa was released from prison. No attempts at peaceful conflict management were made during the conflict. Walesa was awarded the 1983 Nobel Peace Prize and in 1990 elected president of Poland.

References

Bartlett, C.J. 1994. *The Global Conflict: The International Rivalry of Great Powers, 1880–1990.* 2d edition. London: Longman.

Brzezinski, Z. 1967. *The Soviet Bloc: Unity and Conflict.* Cambridge: Harvard University Press.

Cimbala, S.J., and S.R. Waldman, eds. 1992. *Controlling and Ending Conflict: Issues Before and After the Cold War.* New York: Greenwood.

Kaplan, S. ed. 1981. *Diplomacy of Power: Soviet Armed Forces as a Political Instrument.* Washington, D.C.: Brookings.

Simes, D.K. 1977. *Détente and Conflict: Soviet Foreign Policy, 1972–1977.* Beverly Hills: Sage.

5.16 Turkey–Greece: Regional Rivalry and Naval Incidents March 1984–January 1988

Turkey and Greece had been rivals in the region for some time, and conflict had erupted between the two countries between 1974 and 1978 over Cyprus (*see* conflict 5.14). Relations had been cool ever since. In March 1984 Greece protested an incident in which Turkish destroyers had fired on a Greek destroyer in the Aegean Sea. Greece placed its forces on alert, withdrew from North Atlantic Treaty Organization (NATO) exercises, and protested U.S. efforts to rearm Turkey.

Tensions remained high throughout 1985 and 1986, with numerous incidents, including airspace violations, territorial waters violations, and an exchange of fire on the Thracian border. Greece announced its intention to rearm in view of the threat posed by Turkey. Threats were exchanged, and a border incident in the Thracian area left two Turkish infantrymen and one Greek soldier dead. The conflict threatened to escalate to all-out war. Relations were normalized in January 1988, however, after bilateral negotiations and mediation by NATO. The underlying rivalry between the two had not been addressed, however, and the basic relationship between the two countries remained sour.

References

Adams, T.W., and A.J. Cottrell. 1968. *Cyprus Between East and West.* Baltimore: Johns Hopkins University Press.

Crawley, N. 1978. *The Cyprus Revolt: An Account of the Struggle for Union With Greece.* Boston: Allen and Unwin.

Denktash, R. 1982. *The Cyprus Triangle.* Boston: Allen and Unwin.

Hare, A.P. 1974. *Cyprus—Conflict and Its Resolution.* Cape Town: University of Cape Town.

Polyviou, P. 1975. *Cyprus: The Tragedy and the Challenge.* Washington, D.C.: American Hellenic Institute.

Volkan, V.D., and N. Itzkowitz. 1994. *Turks and Greeks: Neighbours in Conflict.* Huntingdon, England: Eothen.

Wilson, A. 1979. *The Aegean Dispute.* Adelphi Papers #155. London: IISS.

5.17 Georgia–South Ossetia: Abkhazia Secession War March 1989–Ongoing

In March 1989 thousands of ethnic Abkhazians began demonstrating for secession from Georgia, then part of the disintegrating Soviet Union. They further demanded the reinstatement of Abkhazia, which is in northwestern Georgia, as a full union republic, a status it had briefly held in the 1920s. Abkhazia's ethnic Georgian population staged a counter-rally, however, which led to intercommunal clashes and further demonstrations. The leadership of Georgia declared Abkhazian separatist demands unconstitutional. Meanwhile, Georgian nationalists themselves were leading a massive campaign for Georgian independence, resulting in brutal repression by Soviet troops in the capital, Tbilisi. In July 1989 serious ethnic-based violence broke out in Abkhazia. Fighting among armed gangs caused dozens of deaths, and Russian Interior Ministry troops were brought in to restore order.

In October 1989 South Ossetia, which lies in northern Georgia and is ethnically closer to Russia than Georgia, began to make similar secessionist demands. It wanted to be elevated to the status of Autonomous Soviet Socialist Republic (ASSR). Separatists set up the Popular Front of South Ossetia, and police reinforcements were drafted to deal with the resulting demonstrations. Violence broke out in November when thousands of ethnic Georgians arrived in South Ossetia to protest the Ossetians' autonomy demands. At the same time, Georgia made further moves toward full independence from the old Soviet Union. South Ossetia declared itself a fully independent republic in September 1990, a move repudiated by Georgia. The violence intensified in December 1990 and

January 1991, and a state of emergency was declared, followed by an economic blockade of the region by Georgian militants. By March 1991 Georgia was entrenched in a state of virtual war, and Georgia and Russia agreed to cooperate in an attempt to restore order.

Meanwhile, four months of violent confrontation in Tbilisi escalated into full-scale armed conflict in December 1991. President Zviad Gamsakhurdia fled, and a military government was formed. In March 1992 Eduard Shevardnadze, the former Soviet foreign minister, agreed to head an interim government and was later elected president. Fighting continued, however, with Gamsakhurdia supporters holding positions in Abkhazia and elsewhere. These clashes continued until 1994, when the government forces routed Gamsakhurdian forces.

Abkhazia declared its independence from Georgia in July 1992, provoking a crisis that grew into all-out armed conflict by August. Fighting persisted into 1994, despite several cease-fire agreements; a cease-fire appeared to hold in South Ossetia after June. In 1994 Abkhazian rebels ousted Georgian forces, who were forced into a humiliating withdrawal. Numerous mediations, negotiations, and multiparty talks went on throughout the conflict, especially by Russia, but with little success. At various times the conflict threatened to spread, with North Ossetians attempting to aid the South Ossetian separatists, rebel Abkhazians receiving arms and support from the Confederation of Caucasian Mountain People, and Russian troops aiding both the rebels and Georgian government forces at various times. Once the conflict began in earnest in 1992, the fighting was intense. More than 5,000 people have been killed in the conflict, most of these from late 1992 onward.

The fighting died down significantly after 1995, when Georgia and Russia signed a military agreement under which Russia agreed to retain military bases in Georgia. Russia also pledged to aid Georgia in its attempts to reunify Abkhazia and South Ossetia with the Georgian state. Continuing political instability and unrest within Georgia led to an attempt on President Shevardnadze's life on August 29, 1995, and the assassination of several other government officials.

In May 1998 Abkhazians drove ethnic Georgians out of disputed territories. The Georgian government chose not to respond militarily to the provocation at that time. A cease-fire was signed on May 30, but no peace accord was formulated. Abkhazia currently enjoys a de facto autonomy, which Georgia's regime tolerates but does not accept. The standoff remains unsettled, and the suspension of hostilities tenuous. Few Georgians remain in Abkhazia, despite accounting for 50 percent of the population prior to the conflict. Currently, more than 300,000 people, mostly Georgians, are refugees from the region.

References

Allison, R. 1993. *Military Forces in the Soviet Successor States: An Analysis of the Military Policies, Force Dispositions, and Evolving Threat Perceptions of the Former Soviet States.* Adelphi Papers #280. London: Brassey's.

Colton, T.J., and R. Legvold, eds. 1992. *After the Soviet Union: From Empire to Nations.* New York: Norton.

Duncan, W.R., and G.P. Holman Jr. 1994. *Ethnic Nationalism and Regional Conflict: The Former Soviet Union and Yugoslavia.* Boulder: Westview.

Gurr, T., M. Marshall, and D. Khosla. 2000. *Peace and Conflict 2001: A Global Survey of Conflicts, Self-Determination Movements, and Democracy.* College Park: Center for International Development and Conflict Management, University of Maryland.

King, R.R. 1973. *Minorities Under Communism.* Cambridge: Harvard University Press.

Maclean, F. 1992. *All the Russias.* New York: Smithmark.

Parker, K., A. Heindel, and A. Branch. 2000. "Armed Conflict in the World Today: A Country by Country Review." Humanitarian Law Project: http://www.hri.ca/doccenter/docs/cpr/armedconflict2000.shtml# (March 20, 2002).

Rupesinghe, K., P. King, and O. Vorkunova, eds. 1992. *Ethnicity and Conflict in a Post-Communist World: The Soviet Union, Eastern Europe, and China.* New York: St. Martin's.

Szajkowski, B. 1993. *Encyclopaedia of Conflicts, Disputes, and Flashpoints in Eastern Europe, Russia, and the Successor States.* Harlow (Essex), England: Longman.

Szporluk, R., ed. 1994. *National Identity and Ethnicity in Russia and the New States of Russia.* Armonk, N.Y.: M.E. Sharpe.

5.18 Yugoslavia: Ethnic and Religious Warfare and the Balkans Civil War Mid-1989–November 2000

Yugoslavia was originally a federation of relatively autonomous republics—Bosnia-Herzegovina, Croatia, Macedonia, Montenegro, Serbia, and Slovenia—dating back to the end of World War I. In 1989, as the Soviet Union began to collapse, the republics voiced their mistrust of Serbia, accusing the powerful republic of imposing its own rule on other regions under the guise of concern for the federation. By mid-1989, many of the republics had made moves toward secession, provoking violent incidents to initiate the process. Secessionist movements gained further momentum with Slovenia's declaration of independence in July 1990.

Ethnic fighting broke out in September 1990, between Orthodox Serbs and Bosnian Muslims in Bosnia, and between Serbs and Catholic Croats in Croatia. Serbian enclaves in Croatia declared themselves independent, provoking further unrest. In January 1991 a major confrontation developed between the Croatian government and the Serb-dominated Yugoslav National Army (JNA) after the latter tried to disarm Croatian republican armed forces and militia. The conflict escalated in March when the JNA was used to put down Croat-Serb violence within Croatia itself. The Serbian republic threatened to arm Serbs living in Croatia if the Croatian authorities did not protect them from attacks by Croat paramilitary groups. The JNA came into direct conflict with Croatian forces in April and May 1991 after the JNA deployed further into Croatia to prevent fighting between Serb separatists and Croatian authorities.

In June 1991 the republics of Slovenia and Croatia both declared independence. This provoked intense fighting in both republics between the JNA and the republican forces, with hundreds of fatalities. By July 1991 Yugoslavia was in a state of complete civil war, and by September the fighting had spread to the ports and to Bosnia. By this time, the JNA was openly identified with Serb nationalist forces. In November 1991, after Croat offensives, the fighting also spread to Serbia.

The war threatened to expand in June 1991, when, after JNA airspace violations, Austria dispatched hundreds of troops to border areas. Hungary did the same in September. From late 1991 the European Community (EC)—now called the European Union (EU)—imposed trade and arms sanctions on the protagonists in an attempt to end the conflict, while the United Nations sent more peacekeeping forces to the region at the beginning of 1992. The EC member states, and many other countries, accorded international recognition to Croatia and Slovenia in January 1992 and to Bosnia-Herzegovina in April 1992.

Fighting intensified in Bosnia from March 1992, and a siege of Sarajevo, the Bosnian capital, began in April. From mid-1992 the fighting in the region tended to center on the Muslim-dominated Bosnian republic, with the Serbs and the Croats making significant territorial gains. In May 1992 Bosnia's Serbian population declared itself independent, further complicating the situation.

Throughout the conflict, intense efforts were made at finding a diplomatic solution, with mediations by the EC, the UN, Russia, the Conference on Security and Cooperation in Europe (CSCE)—now the Organization for Security and Cooperation in Europe (OSCE)—and other parties. Although dozens of cease-fires were signed and numerous settlements announced, the fighting continued, and none of the outstanding issues were resolved. Even North Atlantic Treaty Organization (NATO) air strikes failed to deter the parties from fighting. By the end of 1994, about 25,000 fatalities had occurred. Many of the deaths were civilians who were the victims of massacres, concentration camps, and other atrocities. The term "ethnic cleansing" came into use during 1992 to describe the policy of enforcing ethnically homogenous geographical zones by any means, but usually by extreme violence. No side appeared to have any significant advantage or any will to settle peacefully.

The conflict in Bosnia was particularly brutal and inhumane, including systematic rape in addition to ethnic cleansing. In July 1995 a massacre of Muslim civilians took place in Srebrenica, the UN "safe area," after it was captured by the Bosnian Serbs. Bosnian-Serb political and military leaders have been indicted by the International War Crimes Tribunal in the Hague on related charges. The bodies of 12,000 civilians and soldiers are believed to be in mass graves in the region.

The war in Bosnia ended with the 1996 Dayton accords and NATO enforcement of a de facto separation of ethnic enclaves. The agreement has been criticized as legitimizing Serb aggression in contravention of international law and as solidifying Serb and Croatian hegemony in the region. A force of 60,000 NATO soldiers subsequently replaced the UN peacekeepers' three-year mission.

Bosnia is currently governed by three co-presidents—a Muslim, a Croat, and a Serb. It remains ethnically segregated because of the vitality of Serb and Croatian mini-states on the border that oppose integration and continue to prevent the return of refugees. As a result of ethnic cleansing, tens of thousands of people are living in houses that do not belong to them. Under the agreement, displaced people may reclaim their homes or receive compensation. Up to 3 million refugees have been attempting to return home in the face of fierce resistance. House-burning to thwart their return has been common. At least 250,000 people have died in the conflict. The Bosnian-Croat mini-state of Herceg-Bosnia continues to act separately from the Bosnian government, sharing its currency with Croatia as well as its ruling party and state symbols.

No major incidents have occurred in Croatia since the 1995 Croat offensive against Serbs in the Krajina region. During that incident, the Croatian army recaptured West Slavonia and Krajina. The almost 200,000 Serbs who fled the area have been prevented from returning, and villages have been burned. The bulk of refugees are Serbs from Slavonia. The International War Crimes Tribunal issued an arrest warrant for Croatian-Serb leader Milan Martic for ordering the bombardment of civilians in Zagreb during the 1995 fighting.

In November 1995 the Croatian government and local Serbs signed the Basic Agreement, under which the 150,000 Serbs in East Slavonia, a Serb-held enclave administered by the UN, were to relinquish control of the area to the government under the supervision of 5,000 UN peacekeepers. As a part of the Dayton Agreement, to which Croatia is a party, the 120,000 Serbs in the area were promised the right to return to homes they lost in other parts of Croatia or to compensation. The government has actively discouraged their efforts to reintegrate into Croatian society.

References

Akhavan, P., and R. Howse, eds. 1995. *Yugoslavia, the Former and Future: Reflections by Scholars from the Region.* Washington, D.C.: Brookings; Geneva: United Nations Research Institute for Social Development.

Bennett, C. 1995. *Yugoslavia's Bloody Collapse: Causes, Course, and Consequences.* New York: New York University Press.

Burg, S.L. 1983. *Conflict and Cohesion in Socialist Yugoslavia: Political Decision-Making Since 1966.* Princeton, N.J.: Princeton University Press.

Cohen, L.J., and P. Warwick. 1983. *Political Cohesion in a Fragile Mosaic: The Yugoslav Experience.* Boulder: Westview.

Colton, T.J., and R. Legvold, eds. 1992. *After the Soviet Union: From Empire to Nations.* New York: Norton.

Denitch, B. 1990. *Limits and Possibilities: The Crisis of Yugoslav Socialism and State Socialist Systems.* Minneapolis: University of Minnesota Press.

Donia, R.J., and J.V.A. Fine Jr. 1994. *Bosnia and Hercegovina: A Tradition Betrayed.* New York: Columbia University Press.

Glenny, M. 1993. *The Fall of Yugoslavia: Third Balkan War.* New York: Penguin.

Gow, J. 1992. *Legitimacy and the Military: The Yugoslav Crisis.* London: Pinter.

Gurr, T., M. Marshall, and D. Khosla. 2000. *Peace and Conflict 2001: A Global Survey of Conflicts, Self-Determination Movements, and Democracy.* College Park: Center for International Development and Conflict Management, University of Maryland.

Parker, K., A. Heindel, and A. Branch. 2000. "Armed Conflict in the World Today: A Country by Country Review." Humanitarian Law Project: http://www.hri.ca/doccenter/docs/cpr/armedconflict2000.shtml# (March 20, 2002).

5.19 USSR–Lithuania: Post-Soviet Independence Crisis March 1990–Late 1991

Lithuania had been an independent nation at various times before 1945. The liberalization of Soviet society under Mikhail Gorbachev saw Lithuanian nationalism take on new life in the late 1980s. Conflict between Lithuania and Russia was precipitated by Lithuania's unilateral declaration of independence on March 11, 1990, and its call for the removal of Soviet troops from Lithuanian soil. Moscow's reaction was hostile, declaring the independence declaration unlawful. The Soviet authorities then began to apply intense political, economic, and military pressure on Lithuania.

In March the Soviet Union initiated provocative military moves, such as driving armored convoys through Vilnius, Lithuania's capital. At the same time the Soviet Congress passed laws and declarations against Lithuanian independence. In April an intense economic blockade of the Baltic republic began, cutting off vital supplies such as oil and foodstuffs. The crisis continued throughout 1990 with little international support for Lithuania and fruitless efforts at negotiations. The parties rejected an offer of mediation by French president François Mitterrand and German chancellor Helmut Kohl on April 2, 1990.

In January 1991 the Soviet military cracked down on Lithuania, seizing important facilities and attempting to round up Lithuanian deserters. There were eighteen fatalities in the violence, most of them civilians crushed by tanks as they passively resisted Soviet attempts to seize important buildings. Beginning in May 1991, Soviet OMON forces (Otryad Militsii Osobogo Naznacheniya)—the so-called Black Berets, who were special-purpose militia detachments subordinate to the Soviet Ministry of Internal Affairs—made several attacks on Lithuanian customs control points on the Soviet-Lithuanian border, resulting in ten more fatalities. By the end of 1991 the conflict had died down somewhat, although Soviet troops remained in Lithuania. A number of unsuccessful negotiations took place in May 1992. Lithuania gradually gained international recognition, and Russia withdrew its troops in the following years.

References

Allison, R. 1993. *Military Forces in the Soviet Successor States: An Analysis of the Military Policies, Force Dispositions, and Evolving Threat Perceptions of the Former Soviet States.* Adelphi Papers #280. London: Brassey's.

Colton, T.J., and R. Legvold, eds. 1992. *After the Soviet Union: From Empire to Nations.* New York: Norton.

Duncan, W.R., and G.P. Holman Jr. 1994. *Ethnic Nationalism and Regional Conflict: The Former Soviet Union and Yugoslavia.* Boulder: Westview.

King, R.R. 1973. *Minorities Under Communism.* Cambridge: Harvard University Press.

Maclean, F. 1992. *All the Russias.* New York: Smithmark.

Szajkowski, B. 1993. *Encyclopaedia of Conflicts, Disputes, and Flashpoints in Eastern Europe, Russia, and the Successor States.* Harlow (Essex), England: Longman.

Szporluk, R., ed. 1994. *National Identity and Ethnicity in Russia and the New States of Russia.* Armonk, N.Y.: M.E. Sharpe.

5.20 Azerbaijan–Armenia: Nagorno–Karabakh Conflict August 1990–Ongoing

This conflict erupted in August 1990, when Armenia declared its independence from a disintegrating Soviet Union and laid claim to Nagorno-Karabakh, an ethnically Armenian and largely Christian enclave, in the neighboring Soviet republic of Azerbaijan. The Azeris themselves are Turkic-speaking Shiite Muslims. Fighting broke out when Azeri and Soviet troops attempted to disarm Armenian militias in the enclave. Incidents occurred along the Azeri-Armenian border and within Nagorno-Karabakh until the violence underwent a serious escalation in April 1991, when Armenia accused Soviet troops of siding with Azeri forces. Despite a Soviet-negotiated cease-fire, ethnic-based violence continued along the border. Nearly 800 people had been killed in the conflict by this stage.

In September 1991 Nagorno-Karabakh declared its independence, with full Armenian support for the declaration. Azerbaijan responded by proclaiming direct presidential rule over the enclave. After the Soviet Union disbanded on December 26, all-out war started when Armenian forces invaded Nagorno-Karabakh in January 1992. By May Armenian forces controlled the entire enclave. But an Azeri counteroffensive in June began to reverse some of the losses. By this time, many hundreds were being killed every month. The war continued without letup for the next two years, and neither side was able to totally defeat the other. A cease-fire was signed in May 1994, but it eventually broke down. Fighting continued intermittently, as did peace talks, throughout 1995.

A wider regional conflict loomed in May 1992, when Turkey threatened to invade on the side of the Azeris, who had declared Azerbaijan's independence from the Soviet Union. The Commonwealth of Independent States (CIS), the alliance of former Soviet republics, responded by saying its troops would defend Armenia in the event of Turkish military involvement. Given the specter of a wider Muslim-Christian conflict, a number of mediations were proffered, especially by Russia and Turkey. Despite many cease-fires, the conflict-management attempts failed. By the end of 1995 it was estimated that 20,000 people had been killed and 1 million displaced. The war destabilized both states, which began to suffer serious civil unrest and political turmoil. Azerbaijan withstood a number of serious rebellions and coup attempts from 1993 to 1995.

A 1994 cease-fire led to a 1997 stalemate and resulted in de facto autonomy for the region (and a declaration of independence) that Azerbaijan has not accepted. Negotiations were spearheaded by the Organization for Security and Cooperation in Europe (OSCE) Minsk Group, made up of high-level representatives from Azerbaijan, Armenia, France, Russia, and the United States.

In April 1997 clashes between Azerbaijan and Armenia broke out in two locations along the frontier. Sporadic fighting continued into May, but casualties were unclear. Armenia retained control of territory, linking it to Nagorno-Karabakh, while Azerbaijan (with support from Turkey) maintained an oil embargo and partial blockade of Armenia. Clashes between Armenian and Azerbaijani troops broke out again in February 1998 and June 1999. Four rounds of face-to-face negotiations took place between President Robert Kocharyan of Armenia and President Heydar Aliyev of Azerbaijan in July and August 1999. These were followed by five further dialogues between them in 2000.

Despite these efforts, hostilities continued with sporadic fighting between Azerbaijani and Armenian troops. Although a truce has been in place for several years now, there has been no troop disengagement, no political settlement, and no end to Azerbaijan's trade and energy embargo on Armenia. The prospects for political settlement remain unclear. It would seem that the key to any future peace efforts is control over Caspian oil—the economic opportunities it presents are crucial to future relations between the Armenians and the Azerbaijanis. The conflict has created an estimated 1 million refugees.

References

Allison, R. 1993. *Military Forces in the Soviet Successor States: An Analysis of the Military Policies, Force Dispositions, and Evolving Threat Perceptions of the Former Soviet States.* Adelphi Papers #280. London: Brassey's.

Azer Press. 2000. Reuters, November 21, 2000.

Colton, T. J., and R. Legvold, eds. 1992. *After the Soviet Union: From Empire to Nations.* New York: Norton.

Duncan, W.R., and G.P. Holman Jr. 1994. *Ethnic Nationalism and Regional Conflict: The Former Soviet Union and Yugoslavia.* Boulder: Westview.

Gunter, M.M. 1986. *Pursuing the Just Cause of Their People: A Study of Contemporary Armenian Terrorism.* New York: Greenwood.

Gurr, T., M. Marshall, and D. Khosla. 2000. *Peace and Conflict 2001: A Global Survey of Conflicts, Self-Determination Movements, and Democracy.* College Park: Center for International Development and Conflict Management, University of Maryland.

Keesing's Record of World Events: K41612, K41660, K43032, K43079, K43032, K43121, K43166.

King, R.R. 1973. *Minorities Under Communism.* Cambridge: Harvard University Press.

Maclean, F. 1992. *All the Russias.* New York: Smithmark.

Rupesinghe, K., P. King, and O. Vorkunova, eds. 1992. *Ethnicity and Conflict in a Post-Communist World: The Soviet Union, Eastern Europe, and China.* New York: St. Martin's.

Szajkowski, B. 1993. *Encyclopaedia of Conflicts, Disputes, and Flashpoints in Eastern Europe, Russia, and the Successor States.* Harlow (Essex), England: Longman.

Szporluk, R., ed. 1994. *National Identity and Ethnicity in Russia and the New States of Russia.* Armonk, N.Y.: M.E. Sharpe.

5.21 Gagauzia/Dniester–Moldova: Post–Soviet Strife and Gagauzia's Struggle for Autonomy October 1990–July 1992

With the disintegration of the Soviet Union in the early 1990s, ethnic minorities throughout the former Soviet republics began to agitate for secession. This conflict began in Moldova, which is on the western fringes of the former Soviet Union, near Romania. About 65 percent of the country's population are Romanian-speaking ethnic Moldovans; another 25 percent are Ukrainians and Russians; and a small, Turkic-speaking Gagauz minority lives in the south. Given their strong ethnic and linguistic ties to Romania, the Moldovans were considering union with that country. Feeling oppressed by the Moldovan majority, the Gagauz called elections for their own leadership in October 1990, and Moldova tried to forcibly prevent these moves. Violence broke out when USSR Interior Ministry troops were brought in to calm the situation.

Matters worsened in November 1990, when the largely Russian-Ukrainian slice of eastern Moldova also declared independence as the "Trans-Dniester Republic." Fearing Moldovan attempts to quell the region's moves toward autonomy, the separatists organized armed resistance. Fighting broke out when Moldovan units tried to retake control of the town of Dubossary. After diplomatic intervention by Soviet leader Mikhail Gorbachev, some calm returned to the republic in December 1990.

When Moldova declared its own independence in August 1991, the Dniester region asked to remain part of Russia. In September Dniester reaffirmed its independence and began to assemble its own armed forces. The Gagauzia region made similar moves in December. Fighting broke out again in Dniester and continued sporadically until March 1992, when fighting began in earnest. Russian Cossacks arrived in Dniester to fight on the side of the Russian minority, while Moldova received significant Romanian support. Meanwhile, Ukraine mobilized its border forces to prevent Cossack infiltration and defend its internal security.

Russia and the Conference on Security and Cooperation in Europe (CSCE)—now the Organization for Security and Cooperation in Europe (OSCE)—made intense diplomatic efforts in April 1992 to end the conflict, but the skirmishes continued. In May the conflict intensified, as heavy weapons came into use, and organized military units were deployed. Negotiations were unsuccessful. Moldova declared war on Russia in June after the former Soviet 14th Army, stationed in Dniester, began to intervene on the side of the separatist forces. The potential for a major regional conflict was high.

A peace accord was signed in July 1992 and began to take hold in August. A joint Russian, Moldovan, and Dniester peacekeeping force was deployed; negotiations began; militias were disbanded; the 14th Army began to pull out; and the cease-fire was respected. Although no serious violence occurred for the rest of the year, there were problems in the negotiations over the Soviet 14th Army's withdrawal. The fighting had ended, but tensions remained. Negotiations over the withdrawal of the 14th Army and over political and constitutional arrangements continued for the next three to four years with only minor breakthroughs. Military conflict has not resumed. More than 800 people were killed during the course of the fighting.

References

Allison, R. 1993. *Military Forces in the Soviet Successor States: An Analysis of the Military Policies, Force Dispositions, and Evolving Threat Perceptions of the Former Soviet States.* Adelphi Papers #280. London: Brassey's.

Colton, T. J., and R. Legvold, eds. 1992. *After the Soviet Union: From Empire to Nations.* New York: Norton.

Duncan, W.R., and G.P. Holman Jr. 1994. *Ethnic Nationalism and Regional Conflict: The Former Soviet Union and Yugoslavia.* Boulder: Westview.

King, R.R. 1973. *Minorities Under Communism.* Cambridge: Harvard University Press.

Maclean, F. 1992. *All the Russias.* New York: Smithmark.

Rupesinghe, K., P. King, and O. Vorkunova, eds. 1992. *Ethnicity and Conflict in a Post-Communist World: The Soviet Union, Eastern Europe, and China.* New York: St. Martin's.

Szajkowski, B. 1993. *Encyclopaedia of Conflicts, Disputes, and Flashpoints in Eastern Europe, Russia, and the Successor States.* Harlow (Essex), England: Longman.

Szporluk, R., ed. 1994. *National Identity and Ethnicity in Russia and the New States of Russia.* Armonk, N.Y.: M.E. Sharpe.

5.22 USSR–Latvia: Post-Soviet Independence Crisis January 1991

Like the other Baltic states, Estonia and Lithuania, Latvia had been independent at various times before 1945. The liberalization of the Soviet Union under Mikhail Gorbachev saw a resurgence of Latvian nationalism in the late 1980s and early 1990s. In a case almost identical to Lithuania's independence crisis (*see* conflict 5.19), Latvia also experienced a crackdown by Soviet troops. Moves toward independence and calls for the removal of Soviet troops from Latvian soil had been building in previous weeks.

In early January 1991 Soviet troops attempted to enforce conscription and round up deserters. An assault on the Latvian interior ministry resulted in a gun battle between Soviet troops and Latvian police. Other violent incidents occurred when Soviet troops tried to disperse demonstrators. In all, four people were killed and a number injured. Worldwide condemnation of the crackdown eventually led to Soviet capitulation. Latvian independence soon followed, and Soviet troops were gradually withdrawn. At no time during the conflict did either side attempt to solve the conflict peacefully.

References

Allison, R. 1993. *Military Forces in the Soviet Successor States: An Analysis of the Military Policies, Force Dispositions, and Evolving Threat Perceptions of the*

Former Soviet States. Adelphi Papers #280. London: Brassey's.

Colton, T.J., and R. Legvold, eds. 1992. *After the Soviet Union: From Empire to Nations.* New York: Norton.

Duncan, W.R., and G.P. Holman Jr. 1994. *Ethnic Nationalism and Regional Conflict: The Former Soviet Union and Yugoslavia.* Boulder: Westview.

Maclean, F. 1992. *All the Russias.* New York: Smithmark.

Szajkowski, B. 1993. *Encyclopaedia of Conflicts, Disputes, and Flashpoints in Eastern Europe, Russia, and the Successor States.* Harlow (Essex), England: Longman.

Szporluk, R., ed. 1994. *National Identity and Ethnicity in Russia and the New States of Russia.* Armonk, N.Y.: M.E. Sharpe.

5.23 Macedonia: Civil War, Incursion, and NATO/EU Involvement January 1991–Ongoing

Macedonia was one of several formerly autonomous states adopted into the Federation of Yugoslavia in 1929. This arrangement lasted until January 1991, when, with the Eastern bloc having collapsed and the Balkans erupting into violence, Macedonia declared itself a republic, and lawmakers set about preparing a new constitution (*see* conflict 5.18). The new document, however, established Macedonia as a homeland for Macedonian Slavs alone, marginalizing the ethnic Albanian community that makes up more than a fifth of the country's population. The constitution was indicative of a reactionary sentiment toward Albanian nationalism that had been developing among the Slav population since the early 1980s and was to be a source of conflict in the following years. During this postindependence period, Macedonia experienced numerous Albanian protests throughout the 1990s and was subjected to cross-border incursions from the Albanian-dominated Serbian city of Kosovo.

In late February 2001 a demarcation seeking to more firmly establish the Yugoslavian-Macedonian border triggered clashes with Kosovo-based National Liberation Army (NLA) rebels around the village of Tanusevci, resulting in at least one death. The rebels briefly gained control of the village at the start of March, killing at least three Macedonian officials before withdrawing. When further fighting broke out, the Macedonian government began to move in its heavy artillery, having rejected initial offers of assistance from the North Atlantic Treaty Organization (NATO). The UN was quick to express its concern at these developments, and the implications for the region, as did the United States and European Union (EU).

Some softening of positions were seen when Macedonia's foreign minister, Srjan Kerim, met with EU delegates and promised reforms for ethnic Albanians. Javier Solana, the EU high representative for foreign and security affairs, also met with moderate Albanians during this time. Although UN Security Council Resolution No. 1345 condemned rebel actions, and a twenty-four-hour deadline was given for NLA withdrawal, the situation deteriorated to the point that Macedonian troops were preparing for a major offensive. Efforts were made to address Albanian concerns in April, with Macedonian president Boris Trajovski establishing an interethnic commission to consider Albanian constitutional concerns and the issue of ethnic discrimination. This was followed by a month-long détente that was shattered when eight security force troops were ambushed and killed. This incident sparked a wave of anti-Albanian riots among the Slav population.

The efforts of the newly elected and optimistically named "Government of National Unity," which brought together the main Slav and Albanian parties in coalition, also failed to provide a lasting solution. Likewise, NATO-prompted offers of amnesty and a call for a forty-eight-hour cease-fire proved unsuccessful, and other efforts at this time, such as those by the OSCE, were equally ineffective. During this period, the Macedonian government had rejected calls to declare martial law or to declare outright war on the NLA, but the situation had worsened to the point that NATO began openly discussing the possibility of committing Western troops to the conflict. Indeed, NATO troops played a major role in a subsequent cease-fire broached by Solana, helping to escort NLA fighters away from the town of Aracinove. This action prompted fierce protest among sectors of the Macedonian population and political hierarchy, who had come to perceive the West as unduly supportive of the NLA.

The major Western powers led the attempts to manage the conflict, and talks were held, both by EU envoy François Léotard and U.S. envoy James Pardew, which resulted in a brief truce, and by Solana and NATO secretary-general Lord Robertson, whose crisis mission brokered a cease-fire. Sporadic fighting continued, however, until the Macedonian government, under heavy pressure from the EU and United States, declared a unilateral cease-fire on August 12, 2001. The declaration was followed by a formal peace agreement pledging acknowledgment of the Albanian language and promising a raft of initiatives to improve Albanian education and involvement in government. All major parties signed the peace agreement, with the notable exception of the NLA. NLA leader Ali Ahmeti did, however, sign an agreement to disarm shortly thereafter, which in turn prompted a more moderate approach from the government, and future flare-ups in the conflict met with a restrained response. "Essential Harvest," a NATO operation established to manage the disarmament of the NLA, was activated on August 22. On September 24, the Macedonian legislature officially acknowledged its acceptance of the cease-fire. This development was soon followed by a NATO commitment to long-term involvement in the region, under the mission title "Amber Fox"—and by the announcement that the NLA would be formally dissolved. By this point, some 55,000 refugees had returned home, but 97,000 remained displaced.

In October 2001 several political concerns were evident as hard-liners tried to undermine the peace process. Western pressure eventually led to the approval of the constitutional reform package on November 16. The approved reforms satisfied Albanian demands for greater recognition of their culture and enabled greater access to Macedonia's political system. NATO maintained a presence in the region in the following months, extending its mission twice upon request, even though the conflict had largely subsided.

References

Keesing's Record of World Events: K44019, K44075, K44114, K44166, K44232, K44271, K44360, K44415, K44464, K44529.

The Europa World Year Book. 2002. London: Europa Publications Limited.

5.24 Russia–Chechnya: Post–Soviet Strife, Separatist Fighting, Chechen, and Caucasus Conflicts October 1992–Ongoing

The breakup of the Soviet Union led to unprecedented internal instability in Russia, as nationalist groups emerged almost daily. Law and order broke down in many parts of the country, and ethnic animosities came to the fore. This conflict began as ethnic violence between the Ingush, a Muslim people who had lived in North Ossetia since the time of Stalin, and the largely Christian North Ossetians. About 300 people were killed in ethnic attacks, and both sides claim atrocities. Approximately 50,000 people were displaced as a result of the fighting.

Russia responded by sending in 3,000 elite troops to the area, and the conflict threatened to spread when neighboring Chechnya demanded that the Russian troops withdraw from its borders or face retaliation. Chechen forces then gathered on the border. Despite an agreement for both Chechnya and Russia to withdraw its troops from the border areas, the situation remained tense. Chechnya had designs on forming an extended state by uniting with the Ingush area of North Ossetia.

At this point the center of conflict in the Caucasus moved to Chechnya, which had defied Moscow since declaring independence in October 1991. Russia tried to declare a state of emergency in the region in late 1991 because of the increasing lawlessness of Chechen gunmen and bandits, but had been forced into a humiliating retreat when President Dzhokhar M. Dudayev's forces blocked the airport to prevent the arrival of Russian troops. From this time Russia began to actively support Chechen opposition parties.

In mid-October 1991 the Russian-backed Chechen opposition attacked President Dudayev's forces in an effort to topple him. When this failed, Russia sent in warplanes and threatened to invade. Russia undertook a huge troop buildup in late November and issued an ultimatum. On December 10, 1994, Russian forces invaded Chechnya, and a bloody war ensued. The fighting was intense, with hundreds of fatalities on both sides. Russian forces took the capital, Grozny, in February 1995. A number of belated attempts at negotiation between Dudayev and Russian president Boris Yeltsin had failed to prevent the invasion by Russian forces.

Throughout 1995 the two sides held numerous peace talks under the auspices of the Organization for Security and Cooperation in Europe (OSCE) in Grozny. Largely unsuccessful, these talks often broke down completely. The fighting continued unabated, with separatist forces launching attacks from mountain bases. Chechen rebels twice invaded Russian territory and took Russian civilians as hostages, leading to heavy loss of life. For its part, Russian forces were unable to defeat the Chechens and by the end of 1995 had suffered more than 2,000 fatalities; the Chechen rebels had lost as many as 11,000 men.

In early 1996 Russian aircraft killed Dudayev in a carefully planned surprise attack. The war ended in a standoff in 1996, much to Russia's embarrassment. The Russian army fully withdrew on January 5, 1997, following an August 1996 agreement granting Chechnya autonomy and establishing it as a free economic zone, with its final political status to be resolved before December 31, 2000. More than 50,000 civilians had died in the war. In May 1997 Yeltsin and the Chechen president, Aslan Maskhadov, signed a peace treaty in which Russia pledged never to use force or threaten the use of force in relations between the Russian Federation and the Republic of Chechnya. Even so, skirmishes were reported along the Russian–Chechen border in 1997, and a series of kidnappings and killings occurred in June 1998 in retaliation for the nonimplementation of the agreement.

After Chechnya's presidential election in January 1998, negotiations were hindered further by Russia's refusal to recognize or negotiate with the elected president. Condemnation by the international community failed to alter Russia's stance. Attempts by Chechen guerrillas to extend their control into the neighboring province of Dagestan in August 1999 rekindled serious warfare that had been suspended in the 1996 standoff and created more than 30,000 refugees. The Russian military pushed the rebels back into Chechnya after severe fighting. Atrocities by Russian troops were reported in the town of Alkhan-Yurt in December, including looting, burning of houses, and the massacre of twenty-two civilians who attempted to protect their property. Subsequently, several bombings of apartment buildings in Russia killed around 300 people.

In 2000 Russian forces took control of Grozny, which had been under heavy bombardment since the previous

October and left in ruins. The rebels suffered huge casualties. This incident sparked a long, drawn-out guerrilla war that resulted in further loss of life. The renewed fighting created an estimated 250,000 refugees. President Vladimir Putin of Russia announced that he would permanently station 23,000 troops in Grozny. The United Nations recommended that Russia be suspended from the Council of Europe, in the face of alleged human rights abuses. The conflict continues, even though Russia has announced its desire to seek a peaceful political solution to the conflict.

Forced to retreat from urban areas, the rebel fighters continue guerrilla tactics and terrorist attacks against civilians and authorities. Russian forces occupy relatively flat terrain in northern areas and rely on a strong military presence to contain and subdue Chechen militants in mountain strongholds. Numerous small skirmishes have occurred. Attacks on Russian troops in Ingushetia have produced fears of a widening conflict, and Russia now accuses both Afghanistan and Saudi Arabia of arming the Chechen groups.

References

Allison, R. 1993. *Military Forces in the Soviet Successor States: An Analysis of the Military Policies, Force Dispositions, and Evolving Threat Perceptions of the Former Soviet States.* Adelphi Papers #280. London: Brassey's.

Colton, T. J., and R. Legvold, eds. 1992. *After the Soviet Union: From Empire to Nations.* New York: Norton.

Duncan, W.R., and G.P. Holman Jr. 1994. *Ethnic Nationalism and Regional Conflict: The Former Soviet Union and Yugoslavia.* Boulder: Westview.

Gurr, T., M. Marshall, and D. Khosla. 2000. *Peace and Conflict 2001: A Global Survey of Conflicts, Self-Determination Movements, and Democracy.* College Park: Center for International Development and Conflict Management, University of Maryland.

King, R.R. 1973. *Minorities Under Communism.* Cambridge: Harvard University Press.

Maclean, F. 1992. *All the Russias.* New York: Smithmark.

Parker, K., A. Heindel, and A. Branch. 2000. "Armed Conflict in the World Today: A Country by Country Review." Humanitarian Law Project: http://www.hri.ca/doccenter/docs/cpr/armedconflict2000.shtml# (March 20, 2002).

Rupesinghe, K., P. King, and O. Vorkunova, eds. 1992. *Ethnicity and Conflict in a Post-Communist World: The Soviet Union, Eastern Europe, and China.* New York: St. Martin's.

5.25 Cyprus: Ethnic-Based Tensions and Partition Incidents April 1993

The problem of Cyprus remained unresolved in the 1990s despite years of UN-sponsored talks on the island state's constitutional arrangements. Even with the presence of UN peacekeepers, strains persisted between the two communities—the majority Greeks and the minority Turks (*see* conflicts 5.11; 5.14). In April 1993, two armed incidents raised tensions in Cyprus. On April 8 a Greek Cypriot conscript was shot dead in the UN-controlled buffer zone in Nicosia. A few days later Greek Cypriots fired on Turkish Cypriot border posts.

Tensions rose higher in late April, when a Greek Cypriot gunboat fired on a Turkish freighter in the Mediterranean, wounding two on board. There were no attempts to peacefully settle the conflict, but strains eased in May, and the dispute lapsed. Given the history of violent conflict on Cyprus, these incidents were cause for serious international concern.

References

Adams, T.W., and A. J. Cottrell. 1968. *Cyprus Between East and West.* Baltimore: Johns Hopkins University Press.

Bitsios, D. 1975. *Cyprus: The Vulnerable Republic.* Thessalonike: Institute for Balkan Studies.

Crawley, N. 1978. *The Cyprus Revolt: An Account of the Struggle for Union with Greece.* Boston: Allen and Unwin.

Denktash, R. 1982. *The Cyprus Triangle.* Boston: Allen and Unwin.

Ehrlich, T. 1974. *Cyprus, 1958–1967.* London: Oxford University Press.

Foley, C., and W. Scobie. 1975. *The Struggle for Cyprus.* Stanford, Calif.: Hoover.

Hare, A.P. 1974. *Cyprus—Conflict and Its Resolution.* Cape Town: University of Cape Town.

Hart, P.T. 1990. *Two NATO Allies at the Threshold of War: Cyprus, A Firsthand Account of Crisis Management, 1965–1968.* Durham, N.C.: Institute for the Study of Diplomacy, Duke University Press.

Tillema, H.K. 1991. *International Armed Conflict Since 1945: A Bibliographic Handbook of Wars and Military Interventions.* Boulder: Westview.

5.26 Greece–Albania: Border Tensions April 1994

The root of this conflict lay in the northern Ipiros region of southern Albania, where, according to Greece, up to 200,000 ethnic Greeks lived. The Albanian government feared Greek designs on the territory and countered that there were no more than 90,000 ethnic Greeks residing there. On April 10, 1994, in a training camp near the border, two Albanian soldiers were killed by masked raiders said to be wearing Greek army uniforms. A vicious diplomatic dispute ensued, and troops were reinforced along border areas.

The foreign ministers of both countries met in Zurich in early May in an effort to calm the situation, and, although no specific agreements were made, the fighting eased after this. The basic issue presented by Albania's large and increasingly nationalistic Greek minority was not resolved. This conflict had potential for a much more serious armed confrontation given the violent civil war in the Balkans.

References

Sword, K., ed. 1991. *The Times's Guide to Eastern Europe: Inside the Other Europe.* London: Times Books.

Szajkowski, B. 1993. *Encyclopaedia of Conflicts, Disputes, and Flashpoints in Eastern Europe, Russia, and the Successor States.* Harlow (Essex), England: Longman.

Woodward, S.L. 1995. *Balkan Tragedy: Chaos and Dissolution After the Cold War.* Washington, D.C.: Brookings.

Zametica, J. 1992. *The Yugoslav Conflict: An Analysis of the Causes of the Yugoslav War, the Policies of the Republic, and the Regional and International Implications of the Conflict.* Adelphi Papers #270. London: Brassey's.

5.27 Cyprus: Partition Incidents June 1996–Ongoing

The situation in Cyprus is a war of national liberation in exercise of the right to self-determination. Since the Turkish army invaded Cyprus in 1974 (*see* conflict 5.14), a buffer zone dividing the island into Greek and Turkish halves has been patrolled by United Nations peacekeepers. The Turks declared a Turkish Republic of Northern Cyprus (TRNC) in 1983, which is not recognized by any state except Turkey.

In August 1996 Turkish forces shot and killed two demonstrators and wounded several UN peacekeeping troops and a number of civilians in two separate incidents at the buffer zone. Two rounds of direct talks took place under UN sponsorship during the summer of 1997, but TRNC leader Rauf Denktash withdrew after the European Union (EU) and the Cypriot government began accession talks. Turkey's official acceptance as a candidate for EU membership smoothed the way for discussions to resume in December 1999. A third round occurred in June 2000. The UN favors a peace plan based on a bi-communal, bi-zonal federation. Denkash wants recognition of the TRNC and a confederation between two sovereign states.

At the end of January 1999, Cyprus decided against deployment of long-range missiles and began considering the purchase of short-range missiles that would not be capable of reaching Turkey's air space. Improving Cypriot missile systems to include long-range missile capability would have heightened Turkey's threat perceptions and escalated the existing conflict over partition. A 1999 resolution by the UN Security Council, extending the mandate of the peacekeeping force, requires, for the first time, the approval of both the government of the Republic of Cyprus and the TRNC. The TRNC now claims that by requiring their consent to the deployment, the UN has recognized its sovereignty, but the UN denies this assertion. UN-led talks on the status of Cyprus resumed in December 1999, to prepare the ground for meaningful negotiations leading to a comprehensive settlement. Both sides publicly support a settlement either based on a federation (Greek Cypriot position) or confederation (Turkish Cypriot position).

Fueled by distrust and misunderstanding, Cyprus continued to experience the strain of deep political and socioeconomic division between its ethnic communities. The United States supports the UN secretary-general's efforts to facilitate a comprehensive settlement, although little progress has been made and partition continued into 2000. Turkish troops numbering around 30,000 remain on the island's northern third to protect the Turkish Cypriot minority. The UN peacekeepers number 1,230.

Reference

Parker, K., A. Heindel, and A. Branch. 2000. "Armed Conflict in the World Today: A Country by Country Review." Humanitarian Law Project: http://www.hri.ca/doccenter/docs/cpr/armedconflict2000.shtml# (March 20, 2002).

5.28 Yugoslavia–Kosovo: Kosovo Conflict and Civil War October 1997–Ongoing

The situation in Kosovo is a civil war with a possible claim to self-determination by ethnic Albanians, with extensive involvement by the North Atlantic Treaty Organization (NATO). Ninety percent of the population of Kosovo, a region presently under the political domination of the Federal Republic of Yugoslavia, is ethnically Albanian. Although not the original inhabitants of the region, the Kosovars (ethnic Albanians) had long been settled in their present area.

Kosovo remained relatively autonomous until Yugoslavia revoked that status in 1990 after an unofficial sovereignty referendum. The Democratic League of Kosovo subsequently declared independence and established a parallel government headed by Ibrahim Rugova. Beatings, arrests, house searches, fraudulent trials, and killings began to escalate, and Yugoslav authorities arrested more than 500 political opponents between 1991 and 1997. Because of the stalemate over the determination of the status of Kosovo, some Kosovars formed the Kosovo Liberation Army (KLA), the stated purpose of which is to achieve independence through military means. A smaller military group, the National Movement for the Liberation of Kosovo (NMLK), has also been operating. Throughout 1997 tensions rose, and strikes and other political resistance activities took place. Police attacked 500 students in October, and about thirty-five political killings occurred throughout 1997.

In March 1998 the KLA began a large-scale military action, bringing about 38 percent of Kosovo under its control by July. The Yugoslav army began counterattacks, reportedly massacring civilians in several towns. In early August Yugoslav forces leveled six villages, and by the end of the month had retaken much of the land the KLA had gained. Sporadic fighting continued throughout the fall of 1998, but a cease-fire agreement was signed in October. Under threat of NATO bombings, the Federal Republic of Yugoslavia agreed to talks that the Contact Group (Britain, France, Germany, Italy, Russia, and the United States) arranged for in February 1999 in Rambouillet, France. Although the parties reached a tentative agreement for limited autonomy and a UN peacekeeping force, they did not provide for Kosovars to vote to determine their political status, which the KLA faction considered a major requirement.

Responding to claims that Serbian forces were engaging in ethnic cleansing, in March 1999 NATO began bombing Kosovo and Serbia in an attempt to drive Serbian troops from the area. After the bombing began, further atrocities and expulsions were reported, and 800,000 ethnic Albanians fled to neighboring Albania and Macedonia. After eleven weeks of bombing, Serbia withdrew, and NATO ground troops moved in. At that time, more than 11,000 people had allegedly been killed, but this estimate remained unconfirmed. By October 1999 more than 2,000 bodies had been found at 195 mass grave sites. Critics of the air war claim that the alliance exaggerated the stories of atrocities to justify the bombing at the expense of unprotected civilians in Kosovo. The legality of the bombing has also been challenged as NATO went forward without UN authorization. Additional concerns have been raised because of the use of weaponry containing depleted uranium.

NATO/UN forces continue to monitor and enforce a transitional regime in Kosovo. Disputed sovereignty issues have not been resolved. Since the war ended, ethnic Albanians killed hundreds of Serbs in reprisal attacks, despite the presence of 45,000 NATO troops. With the departure of the Serbian troops, 240,000 Serbs fled the region, and only 30,000 remained. Many of the Kosovans (Kosovars as well as Romani, and other ethnic groups) returned, including nearly 30,000 between January and May 2000. Ongoing confrontations between ethnic Serbs and Kosovar Albanians in Kosovo proper, and between ethnic Albanian insurgents and the Yugoslavian Army in border regions, continue to challenge the postwar settlement.

Incidents against Serbs by Kosovars rose in 2000 and included land mine attacks and bombs. There are also difficulties with ethnic Turks. The October 2000 electoral ouster of Slobadan Milošević and subsequent election of moderates in Kosovo may signal opportunities for defusing regional tensions.

References

Gurr, T., M. Marshall, and D. Khosla. 2000. *Peace and Conflict 2001: A Global Survey of Conflicts, Self-Determination Movements, and Democracy*. College Park: Center for International Development and Conflict Management, University of Maryland.

Parker, K., A. Heindel, and A. Branch. 2000. "Armed Conflict in the World Today: A Country by Country Review." Humanitarian Law Project: http://www.hri.ca/doccenter/docs/cpr/armedconflict2000.shtml# (March 20, 2002).

5.29 Russia–Republic of Dagestan: The Dagestan Independence Dispute May 1999

Dagestan is an autonomous republic within the Russian Federation. It is populated by more than thirty distinct ethnic groups and, because of fierce intergroup competition over scarce resources and power, a multitude of different but interrelated conflicts are taking place. The spillover of instability from neighboring Chechnya, a proliferation of radical Islam, and violent crime contribute further to intergroup rivalry.

This particular conflict involved fundamentalist Islamic groups, in particular the "Sharia Batalillone," that oppose Russian control of Dagestan and want independence. In the capital city, Makhadkala, gunmen stormed a municipal building that had been invaded earlier by civilians, raising the Islamic flag. The invasion resulted in two deaths. In response to these actions, the Chechen Foreign Ministry offered to negotiate a peaceful solution. On May 23, 1999, a resolution was reached between the Muslim gunmen and regional officials. This particular conflict was resolved peacefully through diplomacy, but the underlying issues regarding independence and recognition for Dagestan remain unresolved.

References

Goryania, A. Translated by Jones, R. 2003. "How Many Regions Does Russia Need?" Rosbalt News Agency, June 23, 2003.

Kraev, V. 2001. "A 'Second Front' Against Russia Can Be Organised in the Caucacus." Rosbalt News Agency, October 6, 2001.

Staroverov, A. 2001. "Azerbaijan in Anticipation of Crises." Rosbalt News Agency, August 21, 2001.

5.30 Russia–Georgia: Chechen Separatism August 2000–Ongoing

This conflict is an extension of the Russian-Chechen separatist conflict that, by virtue of the Chechen rebels operating out of bases in northern Georgia, has internationalized to include Georgia. Georgia has accused Russia of bombing villages in its northern Pankisi Gorge, a charge Russia denies. Russia in turn, has accused Georgia of not taking sufficient measures to remove Chechen rebels ensconced in the gorge from which they have been launching attacks against Russia since 2000.

One interesting aspect of this conflict is that Russia has denied it even exists, saying that their planes have never crossed the Russian-Georgian border or bombed the Pankisi Gorge. Several eyewitness accounts, including those by credible Organization for Security and Cooperation in Europe (OSCE) observers monitoring the border, however, have reported unidentified jets flying from the direction of Russia into Georgia as well as flares and the sound of detonations from villages claiming to have been bombed. It seems almost certain from the many sources reporting this conflict that Russia has indeed bombed the Pankisi region repeatedly since 2000.

This conflict was further internationalized when the United States announced that the ongoing "war on terrorism" would be extended to Georgia after Georgian authorities admitted that there were members of al Qaeda hiding and operating in the Pankisi Gorge with the Chechen rebels. To this end the United States sent some 200 military advisers and trainers to school the Georgian military in antiterrorism warfare. This move unsettled the Russians, who undoubtedly would rather not have had the U.S. military so close to their border. The United States affirmed that its troops would be deployed only in a training, advising, and supervisory role and not in direct engagement themselves.

This conflict escalated significantly during August 2002 with several incidents. On August 4 Georgian border guards claimed that Russian SU-25 fighter-bombers returning from Chechnya had bombed them, a claim Russia denied. That same day Russia announced it may seek UN approval to bomb Chechen rebels in the Pankisi Gorge, to which Georgia responded by saying that any attack would be in contravention of international law. On August 6 Georgia refused to hand over thirteen captured Chechen rebels to Russian authorities despite a direct request from Russian president Vladimir Putin to Georgian president Eduard Shevardnadze. On August 8 Georgia again escalated the conflict by disallowing any Russian airplanes, including civilian flights, to cross Georgian airspace between the hours of 6:00 a.m. and 2:00 a.m., effectively dealing a blow to the Russian aviation industry. The greatest escalation occurred on August 23, when Russia carried out a forty-minute bombing raid on the Pankisi Gorge village of Bukhrebi, killing at least one civilian and injuring several others. Although Russia again denied the attack, it was widely confirmed, even by the OSCE, which said attacks were carried out by unidentified war planes, but the OSCE could not officially confirm that the planes were Russian. The raids generated rebuke from several quarters, including the United States. Under diplomatic pressure, Russia agreed on August 28 to launch a joint probe with Georgia into the bombing, but the probe was later called off when Russia demanded to be shown evidence that the bombing had occurred.

On August 30 Georgia began a 1,000-troop sweep of the Pankisi Gorge region, led by many of the troops that had recently been trained by the United States. This sweep had been much publicized, however, and Russia accused Georgia of merely pushing the rebels back across the border into Russia rather than capturing or killing them. Georgia considered that its campaign was effective and invited Russia to send military observers.

Following further skirmishes in mid-September between the Russians and the Chechen rebels, Russia announced that it might seek UN approval to bomb known rebel strongholds in the Pankisi Gorge. An angered Georgia announced that doing so would violate international law. This theme was repeated when Russia announced it was planning to bomb the Pankisi Gorge in late September, to which Georgia responded by saying it was going to place surface-to-air missiles on its Russian border with orders to fire on any Russian planes violating Georgian airspace. This exchange was the first time that Russia and Georgia had directly threatened each other and represented a further escalation of the crisis.

A diplomatic breakthrough occurred on October 6, 2002, at a summit meeting of twelve former Soviet republics in Moldova's capital, Chisinau, where it was announced that a meeting between Putin and Shevardnadze had resulted in an agreement not to escalate the conflict and plans for cooperative measures, including joint border patrols and information sharing, to deal with the Chechen rebel situation. This meeting and its subsequent agreements effectively meant an end to the conflict between Russia and Georgia, and relations have since normalized.

Despite the resolution of the conflict at an interstate level, armed conflict between the Chechen separatists and the Russian government continued. Chechen separatist rebels were blamed for several attacks on Russian helicopters in late 2002 as well as the seizure of 800 hostages in a Moscow theater in October 2002. The hostage crisis ended when Russian troops stormed the building, resulting in approximately 150 deaths, including all the rebels. In late December 2002, eighty people died in a suicide bombing at the headquarters of the Chechen administration. Even after a referendum on a new constitution, Chechen separatists continue to commit suicide bombings: at Znamenskoye on May 16, 2003, causing sixty-one fatalities; at Iliskhan-Yurt, causing thirty fatalities; and at a military hospital in Mozdok in August 2003, causing fifty fatalities. The region remains unstable as the separatist's continue their struggle for total independence.

References

Agence France-Presse. 2002. February 27; May 20; July 29, 30; August 7, 23, 24; September 4, 5, 12; October 10. www.factiva.com (downloaded July 8, 2003).

Associated Press Newswires. 2002. February 27; May 14; August 3, 23, 25; September 7, 8, 17, 23; October 8; November 5. www.factiva.com (downloaded July 8, 2003).

Financial Times. 2002. August 24. www.factiva.com (downloaded July 8, 2003).

Gurr, T., M. Marshall, and D. Khosla. 2000. *Peace and Conflict 2001: A Global Survey of Conflicts, Self-Determination Movements, and Democracy*. College Park: Center for International Development and Conflict Management, University of Maryland.

Hill, F. 2003. "Putin and Bush in Common Cause? Russia's View of the Terrorist Threat After September 11." *Brookings Review* 20 (summer 2002): 33–36.

Keesing's Record of World Events: 44466, 44579, 44630, 44686, 44749, 44915, 44951, 44952, 44998, 45047, 45050.

KOSIMO Conflict Barometer. 2003. Heidelberg Institute on International Conflict Research, University of Heidelberg. *12th Annual Conflict Analysis*. 2d revised edition. January 23. www.hiik.de/en/barometer2003/Conflict_Barometer_2003.pdf.

Reuters News Service. 2002. February 12; August 4, 20. www.factiva.com (downloaded July 8, 2003).

The Times. 2002. September 14. www.factiva.com (downloaded July 8, 2003).

Ware, R.B., E. Kisriev, W.J. Patzelt, and U. Roericht. 2003. "Political Islam in Dagestan. *Europe-Asia Studies* 55 (March): 287–304.

Xinhau News Agency. 2002. August 23, 26, 28. www.factiva.com (downloaded July 8, 2003).

Middle East

List of Conflicts

6.1 France–Levant (Syria/Lebanon): Independence Crisis 265
1945–December 1946

6.2 USSR–Iran: Pro-Communist Campaign of Secession and Azerbaijan/Kurdistan Crisis 265
August 1945–October 1947

6.3 Israel: British Decolonization, Arab–Israeli Territorial Dispute, and War of Independence 266
May 1948–January 1949

6.4 Syria–Lebanon: Syrian Exiles Dispute 266
May–August 1949

6.5 Syria–Israel: Lake Tiberias/Huleh Resource Dispute 267
April–May 1951

6.6 Egypt–United Kingdom: Suez Canal Zone Sovereignty Dispute 268
January 1952–January 1956

6.7 Saudi Arabia–Oman/United Kingdom: The Buraymī Oasis Resource Dispute 268
August 1952–October 1955

6.8 Israel–Jordan: West Bank Border Conflict 269
January 1953–December 1954

6.9 Turkey–Syria: Border Incidents 269
March 1955–1957

6.10 Syria–Israel: Lake Tiberias Dispute 270
October–December 1955

6.11 Yemen–United Kingdom: Aden Conflict 270
1956–1960

6.12 Israel–Jordan: Mt. Scopus Conflict 271
July 1956–January 1958

6.13 Egypt–United Kingdom/France: Sovereignty Dispute and Suez War 271
October–November 1956

6.14 Israel–Syria: Arab-Israeli Territorial Dispute over the Golan Heights 272
July 1957–February 1958

6.15 Egypt–Sudan: Postindependence Territorial Dispute 272
February 1958

6.16 Lebanon: Internal Strife and the First Lebanese Civil War 273
May 1958–June 1959

6.17 Syria–Iraq: Syrian-Backed Putsch, Government Suppression, and Mosul Revolt 273
March–April 1959

6.18 Kurds–Iraq: Kurdish Secession Attempt 274
March 1961–1966

6.19 Iraq–Kuwait: Territorial Dispute and the Kuwaiti Independence Crisis 274
June 1961–February 1962

6.20 Syria–Israel: Arab–Israeli Territorial Dispute over Lake Tiberias 275
February 1962–August 1963

6.21 North Yemen: Civil War and Royalist Rebellion 275
September 1962–October 1967

6.22 Syria–Israel: Arab–Israeli Dispute and Border Incidents 276
June 1964–July 1966

6.23 Israel–Jordan: Arab–Israeli Dispute and Border Incidents 276
December 1964–April 1966

6.24 Lebanon–Israel: Arab–Israeli Dispute and the Hoûla Raids 277
October 1965

6.25 Israel–Arab States: The Six-Day War 277
June 1967

6.26 Iraq–Kurds: Kurdish Struggle for Autonomy 278
October 1968–March 1970

6.27 North Yemen–Saudi Arabia: Border Conflict 278
November 1969–January 1970

6.28 The PLO–Jordan: Coup Attempt 278
February 1970–August 1971

6.29 Iraq–Iran: Border Tensions and the Shatt al-Arab Waterway Dispute 279
1971

6.30 North Yemen–South Yemen: Anti-Communist Insurgency and Border Conflict 279
October 1971–October 1972

6.31 Iran–United Arab Emirates: Tunb Islands Territorial Dispute 280
November 1971

6.32 Oman–South Yemen: Antigovernment Insurgency and Dhofar Rebellion 280
1972–August 1974

6.33 Iran–Iraq: Territorial Dispute and Border War 281
January 1972–February 1975

6.34 Syria/PLO–Israel: PLO Raids, Retaliatory Air Strikes, and the Golan Heights Conflict 281
March 1972–January 1973

6.35 Iraq–Kuwait: Territorial Dispute and Border Incidents 282
March 1973–July 1975

6.36 Israel–Egypt and Syria: Arab–Israeli Territorial Dispute, Arab–Israeli Wars, and the Yom Kippur War 282
October 1973

6.37 Kurds–Iraq: Attempted Secession and the Kurdish Rebellion 283
March 1974–July 1975

6.38 Israel–Lebanon: Arab Infiltrators and Cross-Border Attacks 283
April 1974–July 1975

6.39 Lebanon: Internal Strife, Communal Violence, and the Second Lebanese Civil War 284
February 1975–Late 1992

6.40 Syria–Iraq: Resource Dispute over the Euphrates River 284
April–Late 1975

6.41 Iran: Internal Strife, Orthodox Muslim Backlash, Iranian Civil War, and Islamic Revolution 285
1976–1980

6.42 Kurds–Iraq: Kurdish Separatist Insurgency and Kurdish Autonomy 286
May 1976–Ongoing

6.43 Israel–Lebanon: Arab–Israeli Tensions, Christian–Muslim Factional Fighting, and Border Incidents 287
Mid–Late 1977

6.44 Egypt–Libya: Regional Tensions and Border War 287
July–September 1977

6.45 Israel–Lebanon/PLO: Arab–Israeli Tensions, PLO Incursions, and Israeli Invasion of Southern Lebanon 288
March–June 1978

6.46 North Yemen–South Yemen: Border War 289
February 1979–February 1980

6.47 Israel–Syria: Arab–Israeli Tensions and Air Incidents 289
June 1979–February 1980

6.48 Saudi Arabia–North Yemen: Covert Military Aid and Border Conflict 290
August 1979–March 1980

6.49 Iran–United States: Anti-American Sentiment, Islamic Revolution, and Hostage Crisis 290
November 1979–January 1981

6.50 Iran–Iraq: Regional Rivalry, Territorial Dispute, and the Iran–Iraq War 291
February 1980–1989

6.51 Libya–United States: Regional Instability and Air Incidents 291
August 1981

6.52 Israel–Lebanon: Israeli Invasion of Lebanon 292
Early 1982–Mid-1983

6.53 Israel–Lebanon: Arab–Israeli Hostilities, Muslim–Christian Factional Fighting, and the Security Zone 293
Mid-1983–Ongoing

6.54 Kurds–Turkey: Kurdish Secession Struggle 293
August 1984–Ongoing

6.55 United States–Libya: International Terrorism Fears and Naval Incidents 295
January–April 1986

6.56 Qatar–Bahrain: Sovereignty Dispute and the Hawar Islands Dispute 295
April 1986

6.57 United States–Libya: Rabat Chemical Plant Tensions and Mediterranean Air Incident 295
January 1989

6.58 Iraq–Kuwait/Coalition Forces: Territorial Dispute, Iraqi Expansionism, and the Gulf War 296
August 1990–May 1991

6.59 Iran–United Arab Emirates/Egypt: Abu Musa and Tunb Islands Territorial Dispute 297
April 1992

6.60 Saudi Arabia–Qatar: Post–Gulf War Tensions and Border Incidents 297
September–October 1992

6.61 Egypt–Sudan: Territorial/Resource Dispute and Halaib Dispute 297
December 1992

6.62 Iraq–Coalition Forces: Post–Gulf War Incidents 298
December 1992–July 1993

6.63 Yemen: Unification Difficulties and Yemen Civil War 298
November 1993–July 1994

6.64 Iraq–Coalition Forces: Post–Gulf War Tensions and Kuwaiti Border Incidents 299
October 1994

6.65 Saudi Arabia–Yemen: Post–Gulf War Border Conflict 299
December 1994

6.66 Iran–Iraq: Regional Rivalry and Border Incidents 300
September 1997

6.67 Israel–Syria: Border Clashes 300
February 2001–Ongoing

Map 9. The Middle East

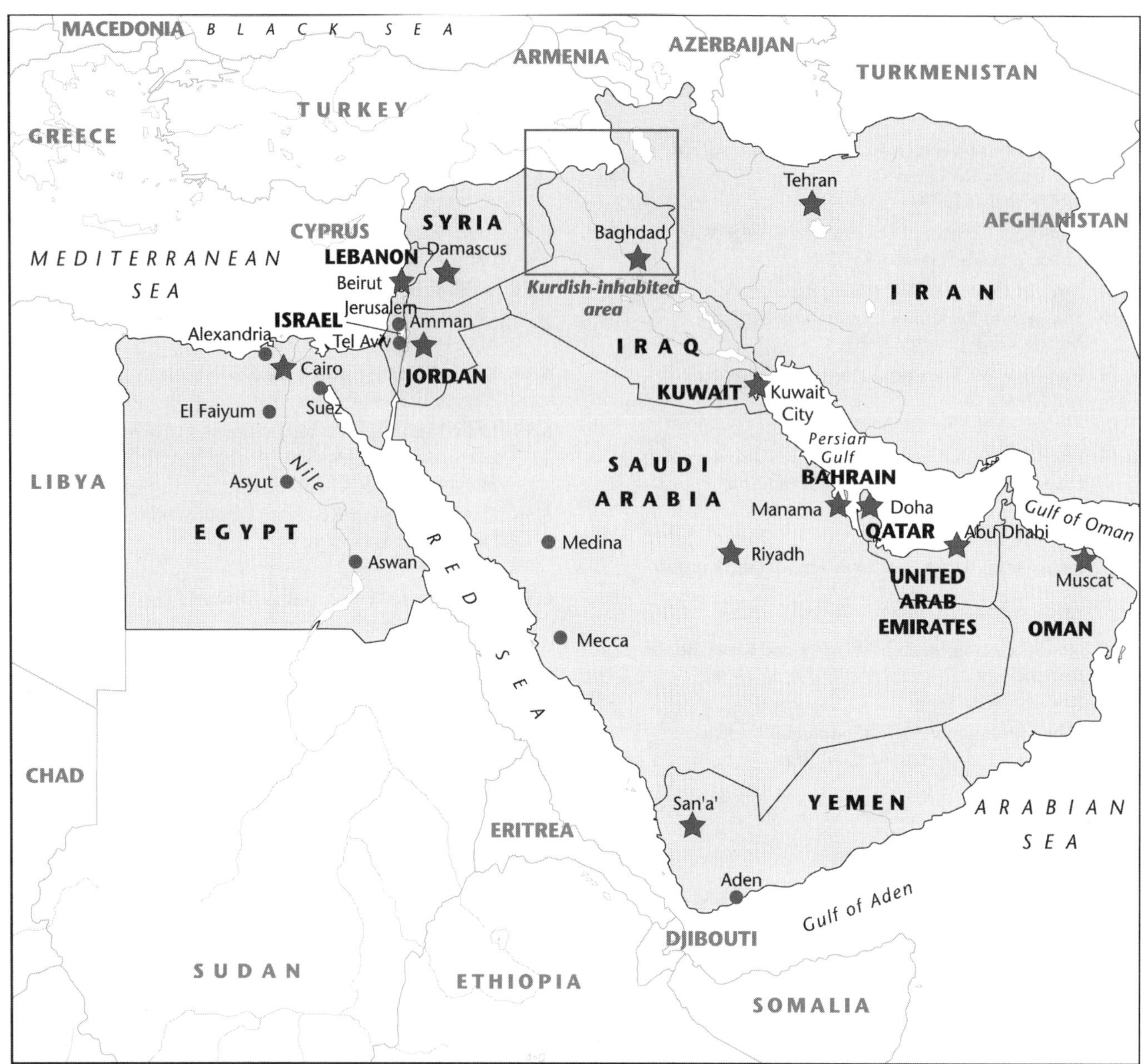

The Kurds have tried since 1920 to secede from the countries they inhabit—Turkey, Iran, and Iraq. The attempted secession from Iraq of 1961 to 1966 ended with a twelve-point plan designed to improve conditions for the Kurds, but their struggle for independence continues to the present day (*see* conflicts 6.18; 6.42; 6.54).

Countries in the Region

Countries included in this region are:

- Bahrain
- Egypt
- Iran
- Iraq
- Israel
- Jordan
- Kuwait
- Lebanon
- Oman
- Palestine
- Qatar
- Saudi Arabia
- Syria
- United Arab Emirates
- Yemen

Regional Overview

Arabs make up the majority of the people of the Middle East, accounting for almost the entire populations of Egypt, Jordan, Lebanon, Syria, the states of the Arabian Peninsula, and for 75 percent of the population of Iraq. Kurds are the next largest ethnic group, numbering at least 26 million. They reside in Iran, Iraq, Syria, and Turkey, as well as in several of the former republics of the USSR. The largest concentration of Kurds is in Turkey, where they constitute 19 percent of the population. Despite their numbers, Kurds have been denied the right to

Map 10. Israel and Occupied Territories

Source: Steven W. Hook and John Spanier, *American Foreign Policy Since World War II,* 16th edition (Washington, D.C.: CQ Press, 2004), 281.

statehood and remain a persecuted minority. Under Saddam Hussein's regime in Iraq, they suffered from "ethnic cleansing," in which an estimated 200,000 were slaughtered toward the end of the Iran–Iraq war (*see* conflict 6.50).

The world's three great monotheistic religions: Judaism, Christianity, and Islam, began in the Middle East. Islam predominates, with more than 90 percent of the area's population. Christians form the next largest group, with about 4 percent of the population, and Jews make up about 2 percent. Almost all Middle Eastern Jews live in Israel.

The carving up of the Middle East by the colonial powers, Britain and France, in the late nineteenth century, led to the creation of artificial states based on the colonial powers' strategic interests and scant regard for the needs and demographic realities of those who had to live within their borders. Consequently, these borders have been highly contested, resulting in numerous disputes in the region since 1945—for example, Egypt and Libya (*see* conflict 6.44), Iraq and Kuwait (*see* conflicts 6.19; 6.35), and Qatar and Bahrain (*see* conflict 6.56).

Disputes in the Middle East also involve the former colonial powers. The Suez Crisis of 1956 is an example of the British and French attempting to maintain their influence in the region. The British and French collaborated with Israelis and bombed Egyptian targets, and their troops occupied Port Said and Port Faud.

Cold war rivalry between the United States and the Soviet Union had a significant influence on the nature of conflict in the Middle East, which has about 65 percent of the world's oil reserves and therefore has global strategic importance. For four decades, the Middle East, like other parts of the world, was used as a theater to play out USSR and U.S. ambitions. Political revolutions in the 1950s resulted in centrally planned governments modeled on the Soviet Union imposed on the economies of Egypt, Iraq, South Yemen, and Syria. The Soviet Union became the main supplier of weapons to these countries. Beginning in the 1950s other pro-Western countries such as Iran, Israel, Jordan, and Turkey received financial or technical aid and military supplies from the West.

By the end of the twentieth century, most regions in the world were making or had made a transition from military to civil rule. The Middle East remained an exception to this pattern of democratization. Many studies suggest that democratic or multiparty states engage in less conflict than nondemocratic states and that, when conflict does occur, the chances of successful resolution are higher. At present, the political systems in many states in the Middle East are far from democratic. Israel is the only parliamentary democracy. Both Oman and Saudi Arabia are monarchic states where political parties are banned. In Saudi Arabia, there is no suffrage. In Oman only 6 percent of the population, who are chosen by the government, are allowed to vote. Kuwait has a nominal constitutional monarchy, where suffrage is limited to 10 percent of the male population. Jordan has a constitutional monarchy.

The Arab–Israeli conflict is a dominant and enduring feature of the Middle East. At a fundamental level the Arab–Israeli conflict is a battle between two peoples over one land—the Holy Land. Resolution of this conflict is problematic because of the incompatibility of the two cultures. Following the departure of the British in 1948, the UN decided that partition of Palestine into Arab and Jewish areas was the best solution. The Jews accepted this proposal, but the Arabs rejected it as a violation of their right to self-determination. Violence erupted and soon turned into full-scale civil war. In early 1948 Jewish guerrilla forces began terrorist attacks on Arab communities, forcing much of the Arab population to flee. When Israel was declared an independent Jewish state upon British withdrawal, forces from neighboring Arab countries joined the war against Israel (*see* conflict 6.3). By the end of fighting in 1949, Israel had substantially increased the size of its territory beyond the area granted to it by the UN partition. Israel further expanded its territory in the Six-Day War of 1967 (*see* conflict 6.25). In October 1974 the Arab League (AL) recognized the Palestine Liberation Organization (PLO) as the legitimate representative of the Palestinian people.

Another cause of conflict in the Middle East is the reassertion of religious fundamentalism. With the onslaught of modernization, which began in the 1960s, some nations in the region became more secular. Islam exerted less influence on social conduct, and religious practice was gradually relegated from the public sphere to the private. One of the most visible effects of these developments was the increase in gender equality. In the late 1960s, however, the rise of Islamic fundamentalism in some countries began to reverse these changes.

In the 1970s Muslims in many countries began to seek, often violently, the revival of Islamic law in both government and society. Various explanations are offered for this "Islamic revival," but many scholars of the region explain it as a rebellion against the influence of the West and modernization. At one time, people believed that social, cultural, and economic modernization would lead to a decline in religion. To the contrary, these factors have contributed to religious revival—and, in particular, the rise of fundamentalism. Modernization has caused a severe disruption in the traditional sources of identity, authority, and community, creating a vacuum, which can be filled by religious, often fundamentalist, groups. At present, Iran and Saudi Arabia adhere strictly to Islamic values. Until 2001 Afghanistan was the most adherent to Islamic law and the Koran, but this changed when a Western alliance moved into Afghanistan to remove the Taliban rulers from power because of their support of al Qaeda, a network of terrorists. Under the new government, the laws regarding adherence to the Koran have been relaxed.

A number of other factors contributed to the rise in Islamic fundamentalism, including the failure of most Middle Eastern governments to deliver on ambitious promises made after independence. The populations became unhappy with the undemocratic and unrepresentative regimes in power in most Middle Eastern states; the lack of progress on major regional issues such as the Arab-Israeli conflict; the growing gap between rich and poor; and widespread poverty caused by war, inflation, and unemployment. Islamic fundamentalists, however, rarely offered viable solutions to correct these conditions. It is widely believed in the Middle East that the corrupt governments of the region survive because the West needs them to ensure a steady supply of oil. These beliefs have caused considerable anti-Western sentiment among the people and have led them to distrust their governments. Islamic fundamentalism is a reaction against the secularism, materialism, and moral corruption they see coming from the West. Many have concluded that Islam is the answer to these problems, and they support the rise of Islamic fundamentalist groups for this reason. Others, however, want to replace their corrupt leaders with representative governments that serve the needs of the people.

The success of the 1979 revolution in Iran led to the establishment of the world's first Islamic republic based on rule by the Shiite clergy. During the 1960s and 1970s Iran's ruler, Muhammad Reza Shah Pahlevi, attempted to modernize Iran at great speed and with harsh measures against those who opposed him. The shah was toppled from power by a coalition of religious and political forces. The revolution emphasized martyrdom in the service of the higher cause of moral and political reform. The explicit message of the revolution was to return Iran to a period of harmony and religious strength, which existed before the secular government of the shahs. Although Muslims in the rest of the world do not necessarily agree with the religious and political agenda of the Iranian revolutionaries, they have been inspired by the revolution as proof that a fundamentalist Islamic revival can take place and can involve a whole society.

In neighboring Iraq, dictator Saddam Hussein feared that the Iranian revolution would prompt Iraqi Shiites, the majority group in his country, to rebel. Using a border dispute as a pretext, Hussein invaded southwestern Iran in September 1980 (*see* conflict 6.50). The war was incredibly costly, with more than 1 million casualties and no significant political or territorial gains for either country. The war ended in 1988 with the acceptance of a UN ceasefire. The Iran–Iraq war had a destabilizing impact on the region. It was a battle by Iraq to prove its prowess and become the region's leading power. But the war severely weakened the Iraqi economy, and Saddam Hussein became deeply unpopular. To divert attention from domestic problems and punish neighboring Kuwait for participating in depressing the price of oil, Hussein directed his forces to invade and annex Kuwait in August 1990 (*see* conflict 6.58). The Western response was Desert Storm, in which an international coalition, led by the United States, with contributions by thirty other countries, including ten Arab nations, defeated Iraq with an air attack followed by a brief ground war. By the end of February 1991, the coalition had defeated Iraqi forces. Saddam Hussein remained in power, however, and Iraq existed as a pariah state with draconian sanctions placed on it by the UN.

In *The Clash of Civilizations*, Samuel Huntington predicted that the next major conflict would not be between nations but civilizations. The eight civilizations he mentions are Western, Islam, Latin American, Confucianism, Hinduism, Japanese, African, and Salvic Orthodox. His thesis appears to be true of the conflict that was ignited when airliners were crashed into the twin towers of the World Trade Center in New York and the Pentagon, killing more than 3,000 people on September 11, 2001. This attack was launched by Osama bin Laden and his al Qaeda network. At the time they were based in Afghanistan, sheltered by the Islamic fundamentalist regime of the Taliban. This act of terrorism, unprecedented in U.S. history, led to a retaliatory and punitive war on Afghanistan by the United States and its allies.

The U.S.-led war on terrorism was used once again by the West to launch a war on Iraq (*see* pp. xxi and 6). The United States and Britain claimed that Iraq possessed weapons of mass destruction, which could fall into the hands of terrorists. After a swift initial victory, a resistance movement made up of Hussein supporters and outside forces began attacking coalition forces. The insurgents then began to direct their attacks against Iraqis who were seen as cooperating with U.S. forces. Young men lining up to join the Iraqi army or police were particular targets. As of yet no conclusive evidence of weapons of mass destruction has been found, but, after a nine-month manhunt, Saddam Hussein was captured.

The wars launched by Western coalitions have strained their relationships with many countries in the Middle East. Despite the acknowledged brutality of Saddam Hussein's regime, many in the so-called Arab street saw the war to remove him as humiliating and a way for America to protect its oil interests in the Middle East. The Israeli–Palestinian conflict continues to destabilize the area. The political alignment of the two sides pits the West (particularly the United States) against the Arab nations of the region. The growing threat of terrorism, and the further rise of Islamic fundamentalism through this, also challenges the future peace of the region.

The lack of resources other than mineral deposits may be the next problem the region faces. As these resources decline, the countries of the Middle East will need to look to other areas for income. Geography, especially limited water reserves, will make this enterprise difficult. Water is already the cause of political contention.

Conflict persists over access to the waters of the Euphrates River, which rises in Turkey and flows across northeastern Syria before entering Iraq. All three countries depend on the river for irrigation and hydroelectric power. In 1984 Turkey built two large dams on the Euphrates, substantially reducing the amount of water available to Syria for power generation. A dam in Syria further reduced Iraq's water supply. The situation nearly led to a war between Iraq and Syria in 1975 (*see* conflict 6.40). From the late 1980s to the 1990s droughts in Ethiopia reduced the flow of the Nile, Egypt's only source of water. Rapid growth in Egypt's population over the same period compounded the water shortage. Indeed, the population of the Middle East, which tripled between 1950 and 1994, makes access to water a frequent source of tension and conflict. The politicized nature of water is evident in the action of the Israeli government, which gave Israeli settlers permission to drill new water wells in the West Bank, but denied Palestinian residents the same right. Any peace agreement between Arabs and Israelis that results in full or partial surrender of Israeli authority over this area will also have to address the issue of control over water supplies.

Overview of Conflict

Since 1945, the Middle East has suffered from violent internal, interstate, and regional conflicts, as well as the involvement of powers from outside the region. Regional interstate conflicts have occurred between Arab states and Israel, Arab states and other Arab states, and Arab states and Iran.

Civil conflicts have been fought in Iraq, Jordan, Lebanon, Syria, and Yemen. The civil war in Lebanon from 1978 to 1990 was the most prolonged. Lebanon became the battleground in which the wider Arab–Israeli conflict was fought, with the involvement of Iran, Israel, Syria, the West, and the UN. During the era between independence from the French in 1946 and the 1970s, Lebanon was viewed as a model of postcolonial success. It was the wealthiest state in the region, had a relatively free and open society, and was an area of peace in a region fraught with violence. One problem was that cooperation between the economically dominant Maronite Christians and the majority Muslims was always fragile. Full-scale civil war broke out in Lebanon in April 1975, with fighting between many different factions: Christians fought against Muslims, and Sunni Muslims fought against Shiites, and each side supported its own private army (*see* conflict 6.39). As the fighting persisted, Palestinian forces joined predominantly leftist Muslim factions. Israel launched Operation Litani, with the intention of driving the PLO out of Lebanon (*see* conflict 6.45).

As the Arab–Israeli conflict continued without a meaningful peace settlement, the Palestinians began a movement known as the intifada. In 1987 a series of demonstrations, strikes, and riots against Israeli rule started in the Gaza Strip and spread throughout the occupied territories. Another intifada began in 2001 and continues today. These intifada consist of violent strikes against civilians, and one of the main tools has been the suicide bomber. The primary targets of suicide bombers tend to be crowded buses carrying Israelis. In the current intifada female suicide bombers were used for the first time.

Conflict Management

Attempts at peacemaking in the Middle East since 1945 have been largely unsuccessful. Israel and a few Arab nations have reached peace agreements. For example, in the 1978 Camp David Accords, mediated by U.S. president Jimmy Carter, Israel returned the Sinai Peninsula to Egypt, and the resulting peace treaty between Egypt and Israel of March 1979 removed Egypt from the Arab–Israeli conflict, and Jordan and Israel signed a peace agreement in 1994. Regional powers were successful in bringing an end to the civil war in Lebanon. Three different Arab actors participated: the Arab League, the governments of Saudi Arabia and Syria, and a commission involving the kings of Morocco and Saudi Arabia and the prince of Algeria. A significant development in conflict resolution in the region was the Israel–Palestine Peace Accord, which was conceived in 1993, after extensive secret meetings between the two parties, facilitated by Norway, followed by a Declaration of Principles signed in Oslo the same year. The Palestinians, led by Yasser Arafat, ultimately rejected the plan.

The Arab League, formerly the League of Arab States, was established under the Alexandria Protocol, October 7, 1944. The organization's purposes and operations were specified later in the Pact of the League of Arab States, signed March 22, 1945. The objectives of the organization regarding conflict management are stated in Article 2 of the pact. The AL's conflict management experience has mainly concerned conflicts of a territorial nature. Over the period from 1945 to 1995, the AL conducted mediation in fifteen conflicts, making just over forty mediation attempts on its own and two cooperative mediation attempts with the UN and the African Union (AU) in Somalia's civil war.

Characteristically, the conflicts addressed occurred in the Middle East, and, "with the exception of Iraq's descent on Kuwait, the life of the Arab League has coincided with the absence of open war between any of its member states" (Farer 1993). The organization generally handled conflicts involving a member state as a disputant, with the exception of Somalia's civil war (May 1988–1995). The organization has even inducted a new member as a way to achieve the peaceful settlement of a conflict. For example, extraordinary maneuvering by the Arab League in the Kuwaiti independence crisis (June 1961–February 1962) helped to avoid a potentially serious conflict (*see* conflict 6.19). On June 25, 1961, Iraq announced claims to the entire territory of Kuwait. Although Kuwait was not an AL member, many of the members were concerned about the potential for serious conflict. After discussion indicated to the Arab League that Kuwait was in favor of replacing British occupying forces with an AL force, Kuwait was brought into the league. Iraq eventually relaxed its claims over the territory and reluctantly acknowledged Kuwaiti claims to independence (Merrills 1991).

The Arab League's strengths can be attributed to membership homogeneity and ample financial and military resources, but, despite its successful action on Kuwait, a low level of regional solidarity has effectively countered this. "A major reason for the relative ineffectiveness of the Arab League has been the deep division of opinion in the membership on major issues of policy" (Merrills 1991). Membership division has sometimes proved crippling for the organization. During North Yemen's civil war (September 1962–October 1967), the Arab League Council found that it was unable to discuss the conflict in its own forum because of the divergent views of its members (*see* conflict 6.21). Divided membership seriously undermined perceptions of the league's impartiality. Subsequent mediation by the AL secretary-general and the chairman of the council was fruitless. It is interesting to note that the only "regional outcast" from AL membership, Israel, has been involved in seventeen conflicts over the period from 1945 to 1995 (Nye 1971; Ramsbotham and Woodhouse 1999). Shared hostility toward Israel has been effective in unifying Arab League members (Goodspeed 1967).

In general, the weaknesses of the Arab League stem from:

1. Consensus decision making: Decisions in the Arab League Council must be unanimous, and achieving consensus on conflict management has proved difficult. Consensus has not been forthcoming even over the AL's position on Israel (Goodspeed 1967).

2. No obligation to refer conflicts: Under conditions in the pact, member states are under no obligation to refer conflicts to the Arab League Council for management. Despite the council's decisions being binding, it is possible that the council will not even vote on how to manage a conflict (Merrills 1991).

3. Lack of regional solidarity: The Arab League has a small, geographically and linguistically homogenous membership. Despite membership homogeneity and a shared cultural history, the AL has frequently been divided over conflict issues. See, for example, conflict 6.17, Syria–Iraq: The Mosul Revolt (March–April 1959), and conflict 6.21, North Yemen: The Royalist Rebellion (September 1962–October 1967).

4. Lack of financial support: The difficulty is not that the organization does not have ample resources among its members; rather, it is the lack of consensus that forces the organization to curb conflict management operations (Nye 1971; Sutterlin 1995). Some members' reluctance to pay their membership dues has hampered the AL, with the United Arab Republics (UAR) often in arrears.

The Arab League has used observer and fact-finding missions and has even attempted to initiate peacekeeping, but successful conflict management has been minimal. Of the fifteen conflicts involving AL mediation, the league has only been influential in aiding resolution in five conflicts.

References

Farer, T.J. 1993. "The Role of Regional Collective Security Arrangements." In *Collective Security in a Changing World.* A World Peace Foundation Study. Weiss, T.G., ed. Boulder: Lynne Rienner, 153–186.

Goodspeed, S.S. 1967. *The Nature and Function of International Organisation.* Oxford, England: Oxford University Press.

Huntington, S.P. 1996. *The Clash of Civilizations and the Remaking of World Order.* New York : Simon and Schuster.

Merrills, J.G. 1991. *International Dispute Settlement.* 2d edition. Cambridge, England: Grotius Publications.

Nye, J.S. Jr. 1971. *Peace in Parts: Integration and Conflict in Regional Organization.* Perspectives on International Relations Series. Written under the auspices of the Center for International Affairs at Harvard University. Boston: Little, Brown.

Ramsbotham, O., and T. Woodhouse. 1999. *Encyclopedia of International Peacekeeping Operations.* Santa Barbara: Calif.: ABC-CLIO.

Sutterlin, J.S. 1995. "The Potential of Regional Organizations." Chapter 7 of *The United Nations and the Maintenance of International Security—A Challenge to Be Met.* Sutterlin, J.S., ed. Westport, Conn.: Praeger, 93–111.

6.1 France–Levant (Syria/Lebanon): Independence Crisis 1945–December 1946

Syria was once part of the Ottoman Empire's vast Arab lands, but World War I (1914–1918) brought about both the empire's collapse and Turkey's defeat alongside that of its allies, Germany and Austria. The Treaty of Versailles (1919) redrew the map of Europe and the Middle East, granting France a mandate to rule Turkey's former holding, the Levant. France subdivided the Levant to create Lebanon and Syria and continued French presence in the territories until after World War II.

By the end of the war, an independence movement had developed. A campaign of civil disruption began, and a formal protest was lodged with the United Nations against France. French troops were attacked.

Britain sought to persuade France in the strongest terms to grant independence to Syria and Lebanon. Indeed, British troops had been in Damascus since 1941; their mission was to dispossess France's collaborationist Vichy regime. When the French shelled Damascus in May 1945 in an effort to quell rioting, the British responded by threatening to occupy Syria unless the French withdrew. The French acceded in December 1946.

No formal attempts at peaceful conflict management took place during the fighting, which left more than 200 dead. To this day, Syria does not fully recognize Lebanon as an independent state. It has intervened in Lebanese affairs on a number of occasions, and thousands of its troops are still stationed on Lebanese territory (*see* conflicts 6.4; 6.16; 6.39).

References

Bar-Simon-Tov, Y. 1983. *Linkage Politics in the Middle East: Syria Between Domestic and External Conflict, 1961–1970.* Boulder: Westview.

Brogan, P. 1989. *World Conflicts: Why and Where They Are Happening.* London: Bloomsbury.

Cobban, H. 1985. *The Making of Modern Lebanon.* Boulder: Westview.

Evron, Y. 1987. *War and Intervention in Lebanon: The Israeli-Syrian Deterrence Dialogue.* Baltimore: Johns Hopkins University Press.

Kedourie, E. 1992. *Politics in the Middle East.* Oxford: Oxford University Press.

Petran, T. 1972. *Syria.* New York: Praeger.

Rabinovich, I. 1985. *The War for Lebanon, 1970–1985.* Revised edition. Ithaca, N.Y.: Cornell University Press.

Shehadi, N., and D.H. Mills, eds. 1988. *Lebanon: A History of Conflict and Consensus.* London: I.B. Tauris.

Tillema, H.K. 1991. *International Armed Conflict Since 1945: A Bibliographic Handbook of Wars and Military Interventions.* Boulder: Westview.

6.2 USSR–Iran: Pro-Communist Campaign of Secession and Azerbaijan/Kurdistan Crisis August 1945–October 1947

During World War II both Britain and the Soviet Union had stationed troops in Persia (Iran), later to be joined by U.S. troops. The United States withdrew its forces toward the end of 1945, as did Britain in February 1946, in compliance with the terms of the Tripartite Treaty signed on January 29, 1942. The Soviets remained in Azerbaijan and Iranian Kurdistan, however, actively fostering pro-Communist movements. These movements launched a violent campaign to secede from Iran. The Democratic Party of Azerbaijan declared independence from Iran in December 1945, and the Democratic Party of Kurdistan did the same in January 1946. Soviet troops actively supported the rebels, and the Soviet Union sent supplies to the rebelling Communist parties.

Iran, with the assistance of the United States, placed the issue before the UN Security Council, which considered it in March 1946. With the Soviet Union absent, the Security Council ordered both Iran and the Soviet Union to report to it before April 3, 1946. They were to outline the status of bilateral negotiations that had commenced on February 19. On April 4 the Soviet Union announced it would withdraw its troops within five to six weeks in exchange for oil concessions. Accordingly, Soviet troops were withdrawn by May 9, and Iran quickly put down the pro-Communist rebellions in both Azerbaijan and Kurdistan. About 2,000 people lost their lives in the disturbances. Apart from the intervention of the UN Security Council, no other outside efforts at peaceful conflict management were attempted.

References

Day, A., ed. 1987. *Border and Territorial Disputes*. 2d edition. Burnt Mill, Harlow (Essex), England: Longman.

Fatemi, F.S. 1980. *The USSR in Iran*. South Brunswick, N.J.: A.S. Barnes.

Lenczowski, G. 1968. *Russia and the West in Iran, 1918–1948*. New York: Greenwood.

Tillema, H.K. 1991. *International Armed Conflict Since 1945: A Bibliographic Handbook of Wars and Military Interventions*. Boulder: Westview.

6.3 Israel: British Decolonization, Arab–Israeli Territorial Dispute, and War of Independence May 1948–January 1949

Tensions in Palestine between Jews and Arabs became increasingly violent during the 1930s, following the influx of European Jews fleeing Nazi persecution. After World War II and disclosures of the Holocaust, Jews stepped up their campaign for an independent Jewish state in Palestine, using both political pressure and terrorist tactics. Britain, which had held a mandate over the territory since the collapse of the Ottoman Empire, was finding it difficult to control the escalation of violence and referred the problem to the United Nations in 1947. A United Nations Special Committee on Palestine (UNSCOP) recommended the partition of Palestine into Jewish and Arab states. The Arab states rejected the plan totally; the Jews accepted it; and the British announced that they would evacuate regardless of whether the UN was ready to administer the territory.

Palestinians and Jews began preparing for war, and fighting broke out even before the end of the British mandate on May 15, 1948. The day before, Israel proclaimed itself a state. As the British withdrew, Jews and Palestinians fought for control of the ports and cities the British had left behind, and Egypt, Iraq, Lebanon, Syria, Transjordan, and other Arab forces in support of Palestinian statehood invaded Israel. The war proceeded intermittently throughout the next eight months, punctuated by two truces. After initial Arab advances, Israeli forces took the initiative—reclaiming all Jewish areas lost, and then, at the cessation of hostilities, gaining control over all Palestine except the West Bank, the Golan Heights, and the Gaza Strip. The Arab Legion also held parts of Jerusalem.

During the conflict, the UN mediator for Palestine, Count Bernadotte, and his successor, Ralph Bunche, made several attempts at mediation. These attempts were often successful in attaining cease-fire agreements that lasted for varying periods. Hostilities ended on January 7, 1949. A series of armistice negotiations were held under UN auspices from January 6 to April 13, 1949, and agreements were signed with all the Arab nations involved in the war.

Fighting was intense for most of the war, with Jewish fatalities estimated at 6,000, including 2,000 civilians, while nearly 8,000 Arab troops lost their lives. The war displaced nearly 800,000 Arabs. They and their descendants, the Palestinians, became the center of much Arab-Israeli conflict in later years, as did the establishment of Israel itself and its borders (*see* conflicts 6.5; 6.8; 6.10; 6.12; 6.14; 6.20; 6.22; 6.23; 6.24; 6.25; 6.34; 6.36; 6.38; 6.43; 6.45; 6.47; 6.52; 6.53; 6.67).

References

Bailey, S. 1990. *Four Arab-Israeli Wars and the Peace Process*. New York: St. Martin's.

Davis, L., E. Rozeman, and J.Z. Rubin, eds. 1988. *Myths and Facts 1989: A Concise Record of the Arab-Israeli Conflict*. Washington, D.C.: Near East Report.

Gainsborough, J.R. 1986. *The Arab-Israeli Conflict: A Politico-Legal Analysis*. Aldershot (Hants), England: Gower.

Gilbert, M. 1993. *Atlas of the Arab-Israeli Conflict*. New York: Macmillan.

Herzog, C. 1984. *The Arab-Israeli Wars: War and Peace in the Middle East from the War of Independence to Lebanon*. Revised edition. London: Arms and Armour.

Kadi, L.S. 1973. *The Arab-Israeli Conflict: The Peaceful Proposals, 1948–1972*. Beirut: Palestine Research Center.

Kurzman, D. 1970. *Genesis 1948: The First Arab-Israeli War*. New York: World Publishing.

Lorch, N. 1968. *Israel's War of Independence, 1947–1949*. 2d revised edition. Hartford: Hartmore House.

Pappe, I. 1992. *The Making of the Arab-Israeli Conflict, 1947–1951*. London: I.B. Tauris.

Tillema, H.K. 1991. *International Armed Conflict Since 1945: A Bibliographic Handbook of Wars and Military Interventions*. Boulder: Westview.

6.4 Syria–Lebanon: Syrian Exiles Dispute May–August 1949

After World War I, the French-administered provinces (villayet) of the old Ottoman Empire were set up as two territories under the League of Nations: Syria and Lebanon. In 1943 Lebanon and Syria were both made self-governing territories. Syria did not gain full independence from France until April 17, 1946 (*see* conflict 6.1). Lebanon proclaimed its independence on November 26, 1941, but full independence did not eventuate until all French troops were evacuated in 1946. During this time, before independence, nationalist movements actively sought to implement their separatist demands: Maronites wanted to establish a separate Christian homeland within Lebanon, and the Syrian Socialist National Party or Parti Populaire Syrien (PPS) advocated the creation of a pan-Syrian state, a union of Cyprus, Iraq, Jordan, Kuwait,

Lebanon, Palestine, and Syria, as a single state. Antun Sa'ada, who formed the PPS in 1932, was forced into exile in 1938 after the French authorities actively suppressed his organization. In 1947 Sa'ada returned to Beirut, Lebanon's capital.

On several occasions just prior to May 1949, Syrian exiles based in Lebanon had attempted to overthrow the Syrian government, which was under the leadership of Khalid al-Azm. Many Syrians were disillusioned with their government, which faced allegations of corruption and was generally seen to be ineffective in solving Syria's growing social and economic problems. Syria's defeat in the Israeli war of independence (May 1948–January 1949) only served to strengthen this underlying dissatisfaction (*see* conflict 6.3). On March 30, 1949, in a military coup d'état, Husni al-Za'im seized power in Syria. Following this change in power, several cross-border incidents occurred involving Lebanese-based Syrian opposition to the new regime.

To deal with exiles that were causing problems for Syrian troops on the border, Syria sent four soldiers across the border into Lebanon. The soldiers killed four Lebanese civilians in the course of their mission and were promptly arrested and faced trial in Lebanon. Whether the deaths were deliberate or accidental was not reported. Syria objected strongly to the soldiers being tried in Lebanon and requested that they be returned to Syria for trial. At the same time, Husni al-Za'im was actively encouraging Sa'ada to attack the Lebanese government and supplied him with enough small arms to make this possible.

With the Lebanese government refusing to return the soldiers, Syria ceased all food shipments to Lebanon. This action effectively undermined the economic stability of both nations. In addition, Syria threatened to invade Lebanon, and Lebanon asked Egypt to mediate.

Egypt conducted a series of mediation attempts from early May to May 26, 1949, but achieved only partial success, as Lebanon reported further border incidents and Syrian troop movements contrary to their developing agreement. In early July Sa'ada's forces attacked a Lebanese police station near the Syrian border. Both Lebanon and Syria then requested arbitration by Egypt and Saudi Arabia. A decision was reached that Lebanon must relinquish the Syrian soldiers to allow them to be tried in Syria. Lebanon abided by the decision, but the issue of troop maneuvers along the border remained unresolved. Antagonism remained high as Syria repeatedly intimidated Lebanon with verbal threats and minor border provocations. By July 6, however, Husni al-Za'im had done an about-face and ordered the capture and delivery of Antun Sa'ada to Lebanese authorities. Sa'ada was later executed in Lebanon. Only one Syrian soldier was killed as a result of this conflict. Although the conflict was largely resolved in June when Lebanon followed the arbitration decision, border tensions did not dissipate until August 1949, when another Syrian coup d'état ousted Husni al-Za'im from power.

References

Butterworth R.L. 1978. *Moderation from Management: International Organizations and Peace*. Pittsburgh: University of Pittsburgh Center for International Studies.

Malone, J.J. 1973. *The Arab Lands of Western Asia*. Englewood Cliffs, N.J.: Prentice Hall.

Meo, L. 1965. *Lebanon–Improbable Nation: A Study in Political Development*. Bloomington: Indiana University Press.

Seale, P. 1965. *The Struggle for Syria: A Study of Post-War Arab Politics, 1945–1958*. New York: Oxford University Press.

Tillema, H.K. 1991. *International Armed Conflict Since 1945: A Bibliographic Handbook of Wars and Military Interventions*. Boulder: Westview.

6.5 Syria–Israel: Lake Tiberias/Huleh Resource Dispute April–May 1951

The Israeli–Syrian armistice following Israel's war of independence left the opposing sides facing each other around Lake Tiberias. Various disputes over the use of the lake erupted into military confrontation in 1951 after Israel declared its intention to reclaim a marshy area near the lake, called the Hula swamp. In March 1951 Syrian and Israeli troops started exchanging fire. The conflict escalated, however, when Syria attacked the border town of El-Hammu on April 4. Israel retaliated the following day. Attacks and counterattacks continued throughout April, and on May 2 Syria captured the Israeli outpost of Tel Mutillah. Israel responded with a series of attacks the same day, and serious fighting continued until May 5. The conflict abated quickly, however, and the fighting was over by May 9.

The United States and the United Nations both tried to mediate an end to the conflict. The UN Security Council managed to secure a cease-fire, and then at negotiations held at Lake Success, got Syria and Israel to settle many of the issues in dispute. There were approximately 100 fatalities on both sides, and the conflict was the start of many more such encounters in the following decades (*see* conflicts 6.10; 6.14; 6.20; 6.22; 6.34; 6.67).

References

Bailey, S. 1990. *Four Arab-Israeli Wars and the Peace Process*. New York: St. Martin's.

Bar-Yaacov, N. 1967. *The Israel-Syrian Armistice: Problems of Implementation, 1949–1966*. Jerusalem: Magnes.

Cobban, H. 1991. *The Superpowers and the Syrian-Israeli Conflict*. New York: Praeger.

Davis, L., E. Rozeman, and J.Z. Rubin, eds. 1988. *Myths and Facts 1989: A Concise Record of the Arab-Israeli Conflict*. Washington, D.C.: Near East Report.

Herzog, C. 1984. *The Arab-Israeli Wars: War and Peace in the Middle East from the War of Independence to Lebanon.* Revised edition. London: Arms and Armour.

Kadi, L.S. 1973. *The Arab-Israeli Conflict: The Peaceful Proposals, 1948–1972.* Beirut: Palestine Research Center.

Pappe, I. 1992. *The Making of the Arab-Israeli Conflict, 1947–1951.* London: I.B. Tauris.

Safran, N. 1969. *From War to War: The Arab-Israeli Confrontation.* New York: Pegasus.

6.6 Egypt–United Kingdom: Suez Canal Zone Sovereignty Dispute January 1952–January 1956

In 1869 a company owned by Britain and France was granted a ninety-nine-year concession to construct the Suez Canal and operate it. Great Britain gained control of the territory surrounding the canal in a 1936 treaty with Egypt. Britain then stationed forces in the area. In an attempt to regain sovereignty, the Egyptian parliament overturned the treaty in 1951 and sought to have British forces removed. Rioting broke out, and British troops and installations were attacked.

The dispute intensified when the nationalistic Gamal Abdel Nasser became president of Egypt in July 1952, with the stated aim of removing all colonial influence from his country. Britain and Egypt began negotiations and agreed to a partial British withdrawal from the Sudan and from around the Suez Canal, but Britain refused to withdraw completely. Nasser's rhetoric heated up on February 24, 1953, when he threatened to attack the Canal Zone if any British troops remained after the withdrawal. Britain suspended further talks.

Between March and May 1953, the United States sought to mediate, but the parties were not amenable to American involvement. Incidents of violence and terrorist attacks became more prevalent, and Egypt attempted to cut off the Canal Zone on May 15. Britain set in place a naval patrol of the canal in response. Violence continued throughout 1953, and on February 14, 1954, Egypt refused to cooperate further at any level with Britain and the United States. Under U.S. diplomatic pressure, Britain agreed on July 28, 1954, to withdraw for the sake of Middle East stability, but reserved the right to return within seven years in the advent of war. The withdrawal was completed on June 13, 1956. About 25 British soldiers and 1,000 Egyptians were killed during the conflict. The issue was not entirely resolved, however, and a much more serious conflict broke out in October 1956 (*see* conflict 6.13).

References

Beauré, A. 1969. *The Suez Expedition.* London: Faber.

Bowie, R.R. 1974. *Suez 1956.* London: Oxford University Press.

Carlton, D. 1989. *Britain and the Suez Crisis.* Oxford: B. Blackwell.

Eden, A. 1968. *The Suez Crisis of 1956.* Boston: Beacon Press.

Epstein, L.D. 1964. *British Politics in the Suez Crisis.* London: Pall Mall.

Fullick, R., and G. Powell. 1979. *Suez: The Double War.* London: Hamish Hamilton.

Kunz, D.B. 1991. *The Economic Diplomacy of the Suez Crisis.* Chapel Hill: University of North Carolina Press.

Kyle, K. 1991. *Suez.* New York: St. Martin's.

Lauterpacht, E. 1960. *The Suez Canal Settlement.* London: Stevens.

6.7 Saudi Arabia–Oman/United Kingdom: The Buraymī Oasis Resource Dispute August 1952–October 1955

When the World War I victors divided up the Arabian Peninsula among themselves, they left some of the borders a little indistinct, including those between Oman and Saudi Arabia. As a consequence, in the late 1940s, when Omani engineers began oil exploration around the Buraymī Oasis, Saudi Arabia responded by claiming sovereignty over the region.

Negotiations between the Saudi government and Britain, which was representing Oman, proceeded from August 1949 to February 1952. When Saudi Arabia could not secure sovereignty through these negotiations, it sent a small force in August 1952 to occupy the oasis. Oman mobilized a force to take it back, but the intervention of the U.S. ambassador to Saudi Arabia led to a stand-still agreement between the parties on October 26, 1952.

Following unauthorized movements by Saudi forces, Britain notified Saudi Arabia on April 2, 1953, that it reserved the right of complete freedom of action because it viewed Saudi actions as a nullification of the stand-still agreement. British and Omani forces subsequently blockaded the Buraymī Oasis. In October 1955 they forcibly occupied it, which resulted in a number of fatalities.

Although negotiations had resumed in October 1953, and continued intermittently until 1975, they were, on the whole, unsuccessful. A 1954–1955 attempt at arbitration failed. The Arab League (AL) also made a number of recommendations on November 16, 1955, urging the parties to return to arbitration and withdraw forces from the Buraymī region. The AL proposed that an international body administer the area during the time of arbitration. It was recognized that the AL was firmly in support of Oman against foreign elements, although its proposals merely echoed former resolutions and had no effect in furthering the dispute's resolution. The league did not engage in mediation in this dispute.

UN mediation was equally unsuccessful in finding resolution. While visiting Saudi Arabia in January 1959, the

UN secretary-general was informed of the Saudi dispute with the UK over the border arrangement. He proceeded to mediate the issues in dispute between Saudi Arabia and the UK, after the Saudis requested it and the UK agreed to it. Meetings were held in New York with representatives from both sides beginning in September 1959. In August 1960 both parties agreed to a visitation by the secretary-general's special representative, Herbert de Ribbing, so that he could investigate the matter further. Although no settlement was achieved, the UN secretary-general's intervention was instrumental in preventing further diplomatic escalation. On January 16, 1963, the UK and Saudi Arabia resumed diplomatic relations and discussions on Buraymī under the supervision of the secretary-general. The dispute persisted but without any military engagements.

In spring 1975 Saudi Arabia and Oman agreed to a settlement that returned Buraymī to Oman in exchange for land with oil-producing potential that also provided Saudi Arabia with a corridor to the sea.

References

Abir, M. 1974. *Oil, Power, and Politics: Conflict in Arabia, the Red Sea, and the Gulf.* London: F. Cass.

Dawisha, A. 1980. *Saudi Arabia's Search for Security.* Adelphi Papers #158. London: IISS.

Halliday, F. 1974. *Arabia Without Sultans: A Political Survey of Instability in the Arab World.* New York: Random House.

Lackner, H. 1978. *A House Built on Sand: A Political Economy of Saudi Arabia.* London: Ithaca Press.

Peterson, J. 1978. *Oman in the Twentieth Century: Political Foundations of an Emerging State.* London: Croom Helm.

Pieragostini, K. 1991. *Britain, Aden and South Arabia: Abandon and Empire.* Basingstoke (Hants), England: Macmillan.

Price, D. 1975. *Oman: Insurgency and Development.* London: Institute for the Study of Conflict.

Townsend, J. 1977. *Oman: The Making of a Modern State.* London: Croom Helm.

6.8 Israel–Jordan: West Bank Border Conflict January 1953–December 1954

Following Israel's war of independence, Jordan annexed Palestinian land on the West Bank of the Jordan River, where many Palestinian refugees were living. Despite the presence of UN peacekeepers, border incidents began almost immediately owing primarily to Arab infiltrators. Israel responded by ordering commando teams into Jordan.

The conflict escalated seriously in October 1953, when an Israeli commando raid on the Jordanian village of Qibya led to more than sixty civilian casualties. Thirteen months later, in November 1954, a Jordanian patrol exchanged fire with Israeli troops at Battir.

In all, 125 people were killed during the conflict. The United Nations made several largely unsuccessful attempts to mediate. These border difficulties presaged more serious conflicts (*see* conflicts 6.12; 6.23).

References

Al Madfai, M.R. 1993. *Jordan, the United States, and the Middle East Peace Process, 1974–1991.* Cambridge: Cambridge University Press.

Bailey, S. 1990. *Four Arab-Israeli Wars and the Peace Process.* New York: St. Martin's.

Davis, L., E. Rozeman, and J.Z. Rubin, eds. 1988. *Myths and Facts 1989: A Concise Record of the Arab-Israeli Conflict.* Washington, D.C.: Near East Report.

Herzog, C. 1984. *The Arab-Israeli Wars: War and Peace in the Middle East from the War of Independence to Lebanon.* Revised edition. London: Arms and Armour.

Kadi, L.S. 1973. *The Arab-Israeli Conflict: The Peaceful Proposals, 1948–1972.* Beirut: Palestine Research Center.

Pappe, I. 1992. *The Making of the Arab-Israeli Conflict, 1947–1951.* London: I.B. Tauris.

Safran, N. 1969. *From War to War: The Arab-Israeli Confrontation.* New York: Pegasus.

Tillema, H.K. 1991. *International Armed Conflict Since 1945: A Bibliographic Handbook of Wars and Military Interventions.* Boulder: Westview.

6.9 Turkey–Syria: Border Incidents March 1955–1957

Against the backdrop of the cold war, this dispute was precipitated by a Soviet–Egyptian military pact and the conclusion of a Syrian–Soviet arms deal, which generated a crisis atmosphere in the region. Strains between Turkey and Syria increased when Syria became sympathetic to the pan-Arabist policies of Egyptian president Gamal Abdel Nasser and began obtaining arms from the Soviet Union. A close ally of the United States, Turkey viewed these developments with disquiet and suspicion, and, with U.S. support, moved troops to the Syrian border. Both sides viewed each other with increasing hostility, and a number of fatal border incidents occurred.

The crisis escalated in September 1957, when the Soviet Union accused the United States of inciting Turkey to invade Syria. The United States responded by stating that any attack on Turkish territory would bring U.S. retaliation on Soviet territory. Rejecting an offer by King Saud ibn Abdul Aziz of Saudi Arabia to mediate, Syria made an appeal to the United Nations on October 15, citing Turkish border violations. In November the dispute de-escalated, having amounted to little more than superpower saber-rattling, although about twenty people were killed in border incidents during the conflict.

References

Bar-Simon-Tov, Y. 1983. *Linkage Politics in the Middle East: Syria Between Domestic and External Conflict, 1961–1970.* Boulder: Westview.

Kedourie, E. 1992. *Politics in the Middle East.* Oxford: Oxford University Press.

Laqueur, W. 1974. *Confrontation: The Middle East and World Politics.* London: Wildwood House.

Petran, T. 1972. *Syria.* New York: Praeger.

Robins, P. 1991. *Turkey and the Middle East.* London: Pinter.

Seale, P. 1965. *The Struggle for Syria: A Study of Post-War Arab Politics, 1945–1958.* New York: Oxford University Press.

Tillema, H.K. 1991. *International Armed Conflict Since 1945: A Bibliographic Handbook of Wars and Military Interventions.* Boulder: Westview.

6.10 Syria–Israel: Lake Tiberias Dispute October–December 1955

Lake Tiberias, also called the Sea of Galilee and Lake Kinneret, was a continuing source of friction between Israel and Syria. Israel claimed it as a matter of right, while Syria had occupied positions near the eastern shore following Israel's war of independence (*see* conflict 6.3). Various incidents took place throughout the 1950s, most involving fishing disputes. Occasionally, Syrian troops would shell Israeli positions.

In October 1955 these minor border incidents gave way to an Israeli commando attack on Syrian border positions in order to silence the artillery. A larger raid followed in mid-December, also in an attempt to eliminate the artillery batteries. Six Israeli soldiers and fifty Syrian military personnel and civilians died in the conflict.

Major General Arthur Burns of the UN Truce Supervision Organization (UNTSO) tried, unsuccessfully, to mediate a settlement. The conflict abated slowly after this, although the lack of progress on settling the underlying issues led to further armed disputes in following years (*see* conflicts 6.14; 6.20; 6.22; 6.25; 6.34; 6.36; 6.47; 6.67).

References

Bailey, S. 1990. *Four Arab-Israeli Wars and the Peace Process.* New York: St. Martin's.

Bar-Yaacov, N. 1967. *The Israel-Syrian Armistice: Problems of Implementation, 1949–1966.* Jerusalem: Magnes.

Cobban, H. 1991. *The Superpowers and the Syrian-Israeli Conflict.* New York: Praeger.

Davis, L., E. Rozeman, and J.Z. Rubin, eds. 1988. *Myths and Facts 1989: A Concise Record of the Arab-Israeli Conflict.* Washington, D.C.: Near East Report.

Herzog, C. 1984. *The Arab-Israeli Wars: War and Peace in the Middle East from the War of Independence to Lebanon.* Revised edition. London: Arms and Armour.

Kadi, L.S. 1973. *The Arab-Israeli Conflict: The Peaceful Proposals, 1948–1972.* Beirut: Palestine Research Center.

Pappe, I. 1992. *The Making of the Arab-Israeli Conflict, 1947–1951.* London: I.B. Tauris.

Safran, N. 1969. *From War to War: The Arab-Israeli Confrontation.* New York: Pegasus.

6.11 Yemen–United Kingdom: Aden Conflict 1956–1960

The series of border clashes between British forces based in Aden and Yemeni troops that occurred between 1956 and 1960 had its origins some years earlier in British efforts to influence tribal leaders in the region. The British had created a buffer zone around the port city of Aden. The local rulers retained autonomy but were subject to British control over their external relations and relations among the rulers themselves.

In the period after 1948 Britain sought to withdraw from the area surrounding Aden while maintaining indefinite control over the port itself. Yemen, to the north, set about to thwart British aspirations in Aden by turning sentiments against the British through a campaign of agitation among the local population. Yemeni raiding parties also crossed into southern Saudi Arabia, resulting in frequent border clashes in 1956 and 1957. British troops and the Royal Air Force (RAF) often pursued Yemeni attackers across the border into Yemen itself. The dispute became part of wider regional and global politics following alliances Yemen formed with Egypt and Saudi Arabia in 1956 and with the Soviet Union in 1957. Britain cut back its military and air operations starting in February 1959.

In January 1958 U.S.-brokered negotiations between Britain and Yemen failed to produce any definite solution to the conflict. Military clashes lapsed in 1958, and Yemen extended its claim to the entire region, including the port of Aden. Approximately 1,000 people were killed in the conflict, including about 40 British soldiers and airmen. Aden was again dragged into war in 1962, when civil war engulfed Yemen and dragged Egypt and Saudi Arabia in with it (*see* conflict 6.21).

References

Gavin, R. 1975. *Aden Under British Rule, 1839–1967.* New York: Barnes and Noble.

Pieragostini, K. 1991. *Britain, Aden and South Arabia: Abandon and Empire.* Basingstoke (Hants), England: Macmillan.

Reilly, B. 1960. *Aden and the Yemen.* London: HMSO.

Tillema, H.K. 1991. *International Armed Conflict Since 1945: A Bibliographic Handbook of Wars and Military Interventions.* Boulder: Westview.

Townsend, J. 1977. *Oman: The Making of a Modern State.* London: Croom Helm.

Wenner, M. 1967. *Modern Yemen, 1918–1966.* Baltimore: Johns Hopkins University Press.

6.12 Israel–Jordan: Mt. Scopus Conflict July 1956–January 1958

The series of armed clashes between Israel and Jordan from 1956 to 1958 were part of the wider Arab–Israeli conflict concerning the area of Mt. Scopus, which is near Jerusalem on the Jordanian West Bank. Jordanian troops had occupied the West Bank during Israel's war of independence, and Jordan's toleration of Arab infiltrators into the new Jewish state was the source of armed conflict in 1953 (*see* conflict 6.8).

The first armed clash was initiated on July 24, 1956, when Jordanian forces occupied a house on Mt. Scopus and began firing on Israeli border positions. On July 27 Israel launched retaliatory artillery strikes at various points along the border and launched ground operations on August 2. Further fighting on September 10 resulted in a number of Israeli fatalities. A series of retaliatory raids were launched, culminating in a major battle at Qalgulya in Jordan on October 10, 1956.

A second conflict occurred on Mt. Scopus in July 1957, when Israeli farmers began moving onto land in the disputed area. Jordanian forces attacked the farmers and the Israeli soldiers guarding them on August 22, provoking further fighting. A third incident occurred on Mt. Scopus on May 26, 1958, when an Israeli border patrol crossed over into Jordan, where it engaged a Jordanian army unit. Fatalities occurred on both sides. Approximately 200 people died during the conflict, and throughout UN peacekeepers under Major General Arthur Burns and UN Secretary-General Dag Hammarskjöld attempted to mediate. They had some successes in this effort, and the referral of the conflict to the UN Security Council also resulted in some short-term agreements.

References

Al Madfai, M.R. 1993. *Jordan, the United States, and the Middle East Peace Process, 1974–1991.* Cambridge: Cambridge University Press.

Bailey, S. 1990. *Four Arab-Israeli Wars and the Peace Process.* New York: St. Martin's.

Davis, L., E. Rozeman, and J.Z. Rubin, eds. 1988. *Myths and Facts 1989: A Concise Record of the Arab-Israeli Conflict.* Washington, D.C.: Near East Report.

Herzog, C. 1984. *The Arab-Israeli Wars: War and Peace in the Middle East from the War of Independence to Lebanon.* Revised edition. London: Arms and Armour.

Kadi, L.S. 1973. *The Arab-Israeli Conflict: The Peaceful Proposals, 1948–1972.* Beirut: Palestine Research Center.

Pappe, I. 1992. *The Making of the Arab-Israeli Conflict, 1947–1951.* London: I.B. Tauris.

Safran, N. 1969. *From War to War: The Arab-Israeli Confrontation.* New York: Pegasus.

Tillema, H.K. 1991. *International Armed Conflict Since 1945: A Bibliographic Handbook of Wars and Military Interventions.* Boulder: Westview.

6.13 Egypt–United Kingdom/France: Sovereignty Dispute and Suez War October–November 1956

The war over the Suez Canal was precipitated by Egyptian president Gamal Abdel Nasser's nationalization of the Suez Canal, thus appropriating it from its Anglo-French owners. In addition, Israel was concerned about the Arab states' failure to pursue a long-term peace treaty, the growing number of terrorist attacks, and Nasser's aggressive foreign policy in the region.

Britain and France formed a secret agreement with Israel under which British and French forces would occupy the Canal Zone following an Israeli invasion of the Sinai. The Israeli invasion began on October 29, 1956, and the Israeli Defense Forces (IDF) quickly seized the whole peninsula, destroying most of Egypt's tanks and heavy weaponry in the process. On October 30 the British and French governments called for a halt to the fighting and requested permission from Egypt to station troops in the Canal Zone, ostensibly to safeguard shipping. Egypt refused, and on October 31 Britain and France began an air offensive against Egyptian bases, virtually wiping out the Egyptian air force. British and French troops landed in the Canal Zone on November 5.

The United States and the Soviet Union opposed the military actions against Egypt from the outset. The United States threatened economic reprisals, and the Soviet Union offered to send troops to Egypt and Syria if the British and French forces did not withdraw. The military plan was a fiasco. British and French forces declared a cease-fire on November 6 and started to withdraw. Under great pressure from the United States, Israel also started a pull out from the Sinai. To separate the Israelis and the Egyptians, the UN sent a peacekeeping force, which began to move into the Sinai on November 15. By March 1957 Israel had relinquished most of the territory it had gained in the invasion.

More than 6,000 military personnel were killed during the conflict, including 20 British and 10 French soldiers. Although the UN Security Council moved quickly to resolve the conflict, it met with little success. Only the heavy-handed approach of the superpowers had any effect. Relations between Israel and Egypt remained tense, and the two states went to war again in 1967 and 1973 (*see* conflicts 6.25; 6.36).

References

Beauré, A. 1969. *The Suez Expedition.* London: Faber.

Bowie, R.R. 1974. *Suez 1956.* London: Oxford University Press.

Browne, H. 1971. *Suez and Sinai.* London: Longman.

Carlton, D. 1989. *Britain and the Suez Crisis.* Oxford: B. Blackwell.

Eden, A. 1968. *The Suez Crisis of 1956.* Boston: Beacon Press.

Epstein, L.D. 1964. *British Politics in the Suez Crisis.* London: Pall Mall.

Fitzsimons, M.A. 1957. *The Suez Crisis and the Containment Policy.* Indianapolis: Bobbs-Merrill.

Freiberger, S.Z. 1992. *Dawn over Suez: The Rise of American Power in the Middle East.* Chicago: I.R. Dee.

Fullick, R., and G. Powell. 1979. *Suez: The Double War.* London: Hamish Hamilton.

Kostiner, J. 1984. *The Struggle for South Yemen.* London: Croom Helm.

Kunz, D.B. 1991. *The Economic Diplomacy of the Suez Crisis.* Chapel Hill: University of North Carolina Press.

Lauterpacht, E. 1960. *The Suez Canal Settlement.* London: Stevens.

Louis, W.R., and E.R.J. Owen, eds. 1989. *Suez 1956: The Crisis and Its Consequences.* Oxford: Clarendon.

Tillema, H.K. 1991. *International Armed Conflict Since 1945: A Bibliographic Handbook of Wars and Military Interventions.* Boulder: Westview.

6.14 Israel–Syria: Arab–Israeli Territorial Dispute over the Golan Heights July 1957–February 1958

Following the Israeli war of independence, Israeli and Syrian forces faced off periodically over the Golan Heights. In July 1957 Syrian troops launched an assault on Israeli border positions on the Golan Heights. Israeli troops responded in kind, and an intense firefight ensued.

Intermittent skirmishes continued into 1958, when the conflict subsided somewhat. UN mediation efforts failed. Although only three deaths occurred, the potential for escalation was always high given the strategic importance of the Golan Heights. Other conflicts over the Golan Heights occurred between 1964 and 1966 and 1972 and 1973 (*see* conflicts 6.22; 6.34).

References

Bailey, S. 1990. *Four Arab-Israeli Wars and the Peace Process.* New York: St. Martin's.

Bar-Yaacov, N. 1967. *The Israel-Syrian Armistice: Problems of Implementation, 1949–1966.* Jerusalem: Magnes.

Cobban, H. 1991. *The Superpowers and the Syrian-Israeli Conflict.* New York: Praeger.

Davis, L., E. Rozeman, and J.Z. Rubin, eds. 1988. *Myths and Facts 1989: A Concise Record of the Arab-Israeli Conflict.* Washington, D.C.: Near East Report.

Herzog, C. 1984. *The Arab-Israeli Wars: War and Peace in the Middle East from the War of Independence to Lebanon.* Revised edition. London: Arms and Armour.

Kadi, L.S. 1973. *The Arab-Israeli Conflict: The Peaceful Proposals, 1948–1972.* Beirut: Palestine Research Center.

Pappe, I. 1992. *The Making of the Arab-Israeli Conflict, 1947–1951.* London: I.B. Tauris.

Safran, N. 1969. *From War to War: The Arab-Israeli Confrontation.* New York: Pegasus.

Tillema, H.K. 1991. *International Armed Conflict Since 1945: A Bibliographic Handbook of Wars and Military Interventions.* Boulder: Westview.

6.15 Egypt–Sudan: Postindependence Territorial Dispute February 1958

Egypt had a long-standing claim to parts of northern Sudan based on an 1899 agreement under which the 22d parallel was to form the Egypt-Sudan border. This issue came to a head shortly after Sudan became independent from Britain in 1956.

On February 9, 1958, Sudanese army units were stationed in the border area after reports of Egyptian troop movements in the region. Against Sudanese wishes, Egyptian officials then sought to move into the area in an attempt to hold a plebiscite. Sudan registered a protest with the UN Security Council.

Following negotiations between President Gamal Abdel Nasser of Egypt and the Sudanese foreign minister, and mediation by the UN Security Council, the conflict was largely settled. Egypt moved its forces back to the existing frontier and did not press its claim. The dispute erupted into armed conflict again in 1992, when Egypt reasserted its claim to the territory (*see* conflict 6.61).

References

Day, A., ed. 1987. *Border and Territorial Disputes.* 2d edition. Burnt Mill, Harlow (Essex), England: Longman.

Drysdale, A., and G.H. Blake. 1985. *The Middle East and North Africa: A Political Geography.* New York: Oxford University Press.

Harris, L.C., ed. 1988. *Egypt: Internal Challenges and Regional Stability.* London: Routledge and Kegan Paul.

Long, D.E., and B. Reich, eds. 1980. *The Government and Politics of the Middle East and North Africa.* Boulder: Westview.

McDermott, A. 1988. *Egypt from Nasser to Mubarak: A Flawed Revolution.* London: Croom Helm.

6.16 Lebanon: Internal Strife and the First Lebanese Civil War May 1958–June 1959

Lebanon was originally part of the Levant, territory given to France by the League of Nations following the breakup of the Ottoman Empire at the end of World War I. The French partitioned this territory into Syria and Lebanon in 1947. Lebanon was populated primarily by Maronite Christians in addition to three Muslim sects: Druze, Sunni, and Shiite. Large numbers of Palestinian refugees also came to live in Lebanon following Israel's war of independence.

Since the 1920s Lebanon had elected its government representatives on a confessional basis, meaning that the seats were divided proportionately among the various religious groups. This system was achieved through the constitution, which left power largely with each religious community. In June 1957 President Camille Chamoun, a Maronite Christian, attempted to preserve his position by manipulating elections. Opponents organized demonstrations, and, after the assassination of the editor of an opposition newspaper in May 1958, full-scale civil war broke out between several heavily armed religious and political factions.

The Lebanese army avoided taking a direct part in the war, but Syria, which had claimed Lebanon as its own territory ever since the French partition, was accused of supporting opposition violence. Lebanon closed its border with Syria on May 13, 1958. The United States intervened on President Chamoun's request on July 15, when a battalion of marines landed at Beirut. The conflict subsided as U.S. marines took up strategic positions, and the U.S. forces were able to withdraw in October. More than 1,300 people were killed during the conflict, which heralded a much deadlier civil war in 1975, when the national pact broke down completely (*see* conflict 6.39). The 1958–1959 conflict was referred to the Arab League and the United Nations in June 1958, with no success.

References

Alamuddin, N. 1993. *Turmoil: The Druzes, Lebanon, and the Arab-Israeli Conflict.* London: Quartet.

Cobban, H. 1985. *The Making of Modern Lebanon.* Boulder: Westview.

Deeb, M. 1980. *The Lebanese Civil War.* New York: Praeger.

Evron, Y. 1987. *War and Intervention in Lebanon: The Israeli-Syrian Deterrence Dialogue.* Baltimore: Johns Hopkins University Press.

Gilmour, D. 1984. *Lebanon: The Fractured Country.* New York: St. Martin's.

Khalidi, W. 1983. *Conflict and Violence in Lebanon: Confrontation in the Middle East.* Cambridge: Center for International Affairs, Harvard University.

MacDowell, D. 1986. *Lebanon: A Conflict of Minorities.* London: Minority Rights Group.

Meo, L. 1965. *Lebanon—Improbable Nation: A Study in Political Development.* Bloomington: Indiana University Press.

Odeh, B.J. 1985. *Lebanon: Dynamic of Conflict.* London: Zed.

Qubain, F. 1961. *Crisis in Lebanon.* Washington, D.C.: Middle East Institute Press.

Shehadi, N., and D.H. Mills, eds. 1988. *Lebanon: A History of Conflict and Consensus.* London: I.B. Tauris.

Tillema, H.K. 1991. *International Armed Conflict Since 1945: A Bibliographic Handbook of Wars and Military Interventions.* Boulder: Westview.

6.17 Syria–Iraq: Syrian-Backed Putsch, Government Suppression, and Mosul Revolt March–April 1959

Having come to power in 1958 through a military coup that ousted King Faisal II, Abdel Karim Kassem served as Iraq's prime minister and head until 1963, when he was deposed by a military coup and killed. His opposition to the pan-Arabist movement did not endear him to neighboring Syria, then part of Egyptian president Gamal Abdel Nasser's United Arab Republic.

Syria had been fomenting opposition to Kassem's regime for some time, supplying large amounts of military hardware to units of the Iraqi army stationed in the Mosul region and led by Colonel Abdel Wahab Shawaf, an Arab nationalist. The so-called Mosul Revolt was ostensibly an abortive military coup designed to overthrow Kassem and his Communist supporters. Shawaf's forces seized control of Mosul in March 1959, but failed to link with his supporters in Baghdad. Kassem was able to remain in command, and he ordered the Iraqi air force to attack the rebel units in and around Mosul. Shawaf was killed.

Once Mosul was recaptured, Kassem allowed Communist forces to go on a rampage of revenge killings. Some of the rebels sought refuge in Syria, which led to a number of border clashes between Iraqi and Syrian forces. The Iraqi air force bombed Syrian villages thought to be rebel sanctuaries. Eventually, the dispute lapsed. In all, 2,000 people were killed in the fighting. An Arab League attempt to mediate a peaceful settlement ended in failure.

References

Bar-Simon-Tov, Y. 1983. *Linkage Politics in the Middle East: Syria Between Domestic and External Conflict, 1961–1970.* Boulder: Westview.

Kedourie, E. 1992. *Politics in the Middle East.* Oxford: Oxford University Press.

Kienle, E. 1990. *Bath vs. Bath: The Conflict Between Syria and Iraq, 1968–1989*. London: I.B. Tauris.

Petran, T. 1972. *Syria*. New York: Praeger.

Seale, P. 1965. *The Struggle for Syria: A Study of Post-War Arab Politics, 1945–1958*. New York: Oxford University Press.

Shwardran, B. 1960. *The Power Struggle in Iraq*. New York: Council for Middle Eastern Affairs.

Tillema, H.K. 1991. *International Armed Conflict Since 1945: A Bibliographic Handbook of Wars and Military Interventions*. Boulder: Westview.

6.18 Kurds–Iraq: Kurdish Secession Attempt March 1961–1966

A Sunni Muslim tribe of non-Arab stock, the Kurds live in a mountainous plateau region comprising parts of Turkey, Iran, and Iraq. Never united under one government, the Kurds have nevertheless agitated for secession from the three countries they inhabit.

In the mid-1940s the Kurds staged an uprising in northern Iraq with Soviet support, but the revolt failed. The Kurdish leader, Mullah Mustafa Barazani, survived and was living in exile in the Soviet Union, waiting for another opportunity to lead a secessionist revolt. When a pardon from the new government of Abdel Karim Kassem allowed him to return to Iraq in 1958, Barazani immediately took up control of the Kurdish Democratic Party (KDP).

Following years of indirect conflict with the government, open warfare broke out between Kurdish rebels under Barazani and the Iraqi army in March 1961. By October the rebels controlled one-third of the country. Iraqi troops immediately counterattacked, and intermittent guerrilla warfare continued for much of the next decade.

At the war's outset, Turkey frequently alleged Iraqi violations of its sovereignty because of Iraqi operations along its border. Turkey was temporarily drawn into the war in August 1962, when the Iraqi air force attacked Turkish border positions and a village. An Iraqi plane was subsequently shot down over Turkey, and Iraq quickly backed down to avoid stepped-up Turkish involvement. During a major Iraqi offensive against the Kurds in June 1963, Syria contributed a force of 5,000 combat troops and aircraft to the Iraqis. Heavy bombing raids, however, failed to suppress the Kurdish guerrilla movement.

In 1965 and 1966 Iraq intensified its efforts to defeat the Kurds, and its operations once again involved sorties into Turkey and Iran. In June 1966 the Kurds and the Iraqi government agreed on a twelve-point plan aimed at improving conditions for Kurds. Fighting continued for the next four years, however, and it was only after the Iraqi government reaffirmed the twelve-point plan in January 1970 that the negotiations leading to an armistice agreement made any progress. The armistice was signed on March 11, 1970. Approximately 10,000 people were killed during the conflict.

References

Arfa, H. 1966. *The Kurds: A Historical and Political Study*. London: Oxford University Press.

Chliand, G., ed. 1993. *A People Without a Country: The Kurds and Kurdistan*. New York: Olive Branch.

Entessaur, N. 1992. *Kurdish Ethnonationalism*. Boulder: Lynn Rienner.

Ghareeb, E. 1981. *The Kurdish Question in Iraq*. Syracuse, N.Y.: Syracuse University Press.

Jawad, S. 1981. *Iraq and the Kurdish Question, 1958–1970*. London: Ithaca Press.

Kreyenbroek, P.G., and S. Sperl, eds. 1992. *The Kurds: A Contemporary Overview*. London: Routledge.

O'Ballance, E. 1973. *The Kurdish Revolt: 1961–1970*. Hamden, Conn.: Archon.

Pelletière, S. 1984. *The Kurds: An Unstable Element in the Gulf*. Boulder: Westview.

Short, M., and A. McDermott. 1985. *The Kurds*. London: Minority Rights Group.

6.19 Iraq–Kuwait: Territorial Dispute and the Kuwaiti Independence Crisis June 1961–February 1962

Kuwait had been a part of the Ottoman Empire's massive Arab land holdings during the nineteenth century. When Kuwait declared its independence in 1899, it sought and gained British protection in exchange for British control over its foreign affairs. Kuwait gained full independence from Britain on June 19, 1961.

On June 25, 1961, Iraqi prime minister Abdel Karim Kassem declared that all Kuwait was in fact part of Iraq's Basra province—a claim Iraqi president Saddam Hussein would repeat in 1990. Kassem also expressed Iraq's intention to incorporate Kuwait. Britain, which under the independence agreement with Kuwait promised to defend the small state, positioned troops close to the Iraqi border. Tensions were extremely high.

In July 1961 Kuwait was elected into the Arab League, which passed a resolution requiring that the British force in Kuwait be replaced by league troops. These troops began to arrive on September 10, and by October 19 the British forces had been withdrawn.

Kassem did not reassert his claims to Kuwait, and the threat dissipated. The Arab League force was disbanded by February 1962. This conflict was later to prove an ominous precursor to much deadlier disputes: from 1973 to 1975 and again in 1990–1991. Although no fatalities occurred in the early 1960s incident, the strains and subsequent armed disputes made this a potentially serious conflict (*see* conflicts 6.35; 6.58).

References

Assiri, A. 1990. *Kuwait's Foreign Policy: City-State in World Politics.* Boulder: Westview.

Butterworth, R.L. 1976. *Managing Interstate Conflict, 1945–1974.* Pittsburgh: Center for International Studies, University of Pittsburgh.

Dann, U. 1969. *Iraq Under Qassem: A Political History, 1958–1963.* New York: Praeger.

Day, A., ed. 1987. *Border and Territorial Disputes.* 2d edition. Burnt Mill, Harlow (Essex), England: Longman.

Marr, P. 1985. *The Modern History of Iraq.* Boulder: Westview.

Martin, L. 1984. *The Unstable Gulf: Threats from Within.* Lexington, Mass.: Lexington Books.

Tillema, H.K. 1991. *International Armed Conflict Since 1945: A Bibliographic Handbook of Wars and Military Interventions.* Boulder: Westview.

6.20 Syria–Israel: Arab–Israeli Territorial Dispute over Lake Tiberias
February 1962–August 1963

Since the Israeli war of independence in 1948 and 1949, Syrian and Israeli troops had frequently clashed along their common border (*see* conflicts 6.5; 6.10; 6.14). In 1962 the strains were especially severe at Lake Tiberias (Kinneret), which Israel controlled. Israel claimed the area on the basis of British maps, but Syria controlled strategic positions on the eastern shore. There were frequent incidents involving Syrian fishermen who did not get Israeli permission for their activities.

Syrian artillery pieces on the eastern shore shelled Israeli positions and patrol boats in February and March 1962, leading to a retaliatory Israeli attack on Syrian gun positions March 16–17. Four fatalities were reported. In August 1963 General Odd Bull of the UN Truce Supervision Organization tried to settle the issue through mediation but was only partially successful.

References

Bailey, S. 1990. *Four Arab-Israeli Wars and the Peace Process.* New York: St. Martin's.

Bar-Yaacov, N. 1967. *The Israel-Syrian Armistice: Problems of Implementation, 1949–1966.* Jerusalem: Magnes.

Cobban, H. 1991. *The Superpowers and the Syrian-Israeli Conflict.* New York: Praeger.

Davis, L., E. Rozeman, and J.Z. Rubin, eds. 1988. *Myths and Facts 1989: A Concise Record of the Arab-Israeli Conflict.* Washington, D.C.: Near East Report.

Herzog, C. 1984. *The Arab-Israeli Wars: War and Peace in the Middle East from the War of Independence to Lebanon.* Revised edition. London: Arms and Armour.

Kadi, L.S. 1973. *The Arab-Israeli Conflict: The Peaceful Proposals, 1948–1972.* Beirut: Palestine Research Center.

Pappe, I. 1992. *The Making of the Arab-Israeli Conflict, 1947–1951.* London: I.B. Tauris.

Safran, N. 1969. *From War to War: The Arab-Israeli Confrontation.* New York: Pegasus.

Tillema, H.K. 1991. *International Armed Conflict Since 1945: A Bibliographic Handbook of Wars and Military Interventions.* Boulder: Westview.

6.21 North Yemen: Civil War and Royalist Rebellion
September 1962–October 1967

At the end of the nineteenth century, the British divided Yemen into North Yemen and South Yemen (the Aden Protectorate) for administrative purposes. Britain retained Aden as a protectorate, but North Yemen was ruled by a series of imams. Imam Saif al-Islam Ahmad, who had held power in North Yemen since 1948, died on September 18, 1962, and his son Muhammad al-Badr claimed to be his legitimate successor. He was deposed in a military coup September 26.

The deposed al-Badr sought to regain power through arms, and civil war ensued between the deposed royalists and the newly established republican government. The war was internationalized from October 1962, when Egyptian troops moved into North Yemen in support of the republicans. Jordan and Saudi Arabia entered on the side of the royalists, and Egyptian air force units stationed in North Yemen intermittently raided Saudi Arabia between November 1962 and May 1967.

A UN observer unit arrived in July 1963. Britain was also involved from October 1962, when the civil war spilled into Britain's protectorates around Aden (South Yemen). The National Front for the Liberation of South Yemen and occasional cross-border sorties by republican Yemeni troops resulted in the British Royal Air Force (RAF) undertaking containment actions to secure Aden's borders. An RAF raid into North Yemen in March 1964 was the sole action involving British forces north of the border. Ground forces saw action in Aden from April 1964 following a rebellion against British rule.

The UN observer unit withdrew from North Yemen in September 1964, and by the end of that year the royalists were restricted to a small region adjoining the border with Saudi Arabia. Egyptian forces also began to withdraw. The withdrawal was completed by October 1967, when the royalists had been weakened to the point where they no longer posed a threat to the republican government. It is estimated that more than 100,000 people were killed in the war, most of them civilian. Egypt and Saudi Arabia lost 1,000 troops each.

Both the UN and the Arab League (AL) tried to solve the conflict peacefully in the early stages of the war but were ineffective, leading to a long, drawn-out conflict. The AL was inhibited by internal rifts, and direct negotiations proved unsuccessful. Indeed, the end of the war did not end the civil strife in the region, with conflicts occurring in 1969, 1971, 1972, 1979, 1993, and 1994 (*see* conflicts 6.27; 6.30; 6.32; 6.46; 6.48; 6.63; 6.65).

References

Badeeb, S. 1986. *The Saudi-Egyptian Conflict over North Yemen, 1962–1970.* Boulder: Westview/American-Arab Affairs Council.

Bidwell, R. 1983. *The Two Yemens.* New York: Longman.

Ismael, T.Y., and J. Ismael. 1986. *The People's Democratic Republic of Yemen: Politics, Economics, and Society—The Politics of Socialist Transformation.* Boulder: Lynne Rienner.

Kostiner, J. 1984. *The Struggle for South Yemen.* London: Croom Helm.

O'Ballance, E. 1971. *The War in the Yemen.* Hamden, Conn.: Archon.

Peterson, J. 1981. *Conflict in the Yemens and Superpower Involvement.* Washington, D.C.: Center for Contemporary Arab Studies, Georgetown University.

Stookey, R. 1978. *Yemen: The Politics of the Yemen Arab Republic.* Boulder: Westview.

Wenner, M. 1967. *Modern Yemen, 1918–1966.* Baltimore: Johns Hopkins University Press.

6.22 Syria–Israel: Arab–Israeli Dispute and Border Incidents June 1964–July 1966

Following the Israeli war of independence in 1948 (*see* conflict 6.3), relations between Israel and Syria remained hostile, and their forces were frequently embroiled in firefights. Armed conflicts had already taken place in 1951, 1955, 1957–1958, and 1962–1963—all of which had the potential to escalate into war (*see* conflicts 6.5; 6.10; 6.14; 6.20).

Beginning in June 1963 Syria began to shell Israeli positions in northern Israel from its strategically valuable position on the Golan Heights. Israel responded by launching an air strike on Syrian territory. Syrian shelling continued throughout 1964, with Israel responding in kind. It was reported that twenty-five people were killed during this conflict, and Syria and Israel were soon at war again in 1967 during the Six-Day War, when Israel captured the Golan Heights (*see* conflict 6.25).

References

Bailey, S. 1990. *Four Arab-Israeli Wars and the Peace Process.* New York: St. Martin's.

Bar-Yaacov, N. 1967. *The Israel-Syrian Armistice: Problems of Implementation, 1949–1966.* Jerusalem: Magnes.

Cobban, H. 1991. *The Superpowers and the Syrian-Israeli Conflict.* New York: Praeger.

Davis, L., E. Rozeman, and J.Z. Rubin, eds. 1988. *Myths and Facts 1989: A Concise Record of the Arab-Israeli Conflict.* Washington, D.C.: Near East Report.

Herzog, C. 1984. *The Arab-Israeli Wars: War and Peace in the Middle East from the War of Independence to Lebanon.* Revised edition. London: Arms and Armour.

Kadi, L.S. 1973. *The Arab-Israeli Conflict: The Peaceful Proposals, 1948–1972.* Beirut: Palestine Research Center.

Safran, N. 1969. *From War to War: The Arab-Israeli Confrontation.* New York: Pegasus.

Tillema, H.K. 1991. *International Armed Conflict Since 1945: A Bibliographic Handbook of Wars and Military Interventions.* Boulder: Westview.

6.23 Israel–Jordan: Arab–Israeli Dispute and Border Incidents December 1964–April 1966

Following the Israeli war of independence of 1948–1949 (*see* conflict 6.3), relations between Israel and Jordan were strained. Armed conflicts had already broken out twice, from 1953 to 1954 and 1956 to 1958 (*see* conflicts 6.8; 6.12). The large numbers of Palestinian refugees encamped in Jordan and the Palestinian guerrillas who launched attacks into Israel from Jordanian territory made matters worse.

In December 1964 Israeli and Jordanian troops clashed in Jerusalem. These hostilities were followed by a number of artillery duels and guerrilla attacks by Palestinian nationalists, which continued throughout 1965. Occasionally, both sides would engage in cross-border raids. Dozens of people were killed in the conflict, and only one relatively minor attempt at conflict management took place. The incidents made the volatile region more unstable than before and fueled the possibility of another war in the region. About fifty people were killed in the incidents. Eventually, the fighting ended, and Israel and Jordan did not battle each other directly until the Six-Day War in 1967 (*see* conflict 6.25).

References

Al Madfai, M.R. 1993. *Jordan, the United States, and the Middle East Peace Process, 1974–1991.* Cambridge: Cambridge University Press.

Bailey, S. 1990. *Four Arab-Israeli Wars and the Peace Process.* New York: St. Martin's.

Davis, L., E. Rozeman, and J.Z. Rubin, eds. 1988. *Myths and Facts 1989: A Concise Record of the Arab-Israeli Conflict.* Washington, D.C.: Near East Report.

Herzog, C. 1984. *The Arab-Israeli Wars: War and Peace in the Middle East from the War of Independence to Lebanon.* Revised edition. London: Arms and Armour.

Kadi, L.S. 1973. *The Arab-Israeli Conflict: The Peaceful Proposals, 1948–1972.* Beirut: Palestine Research Center.

Safran, N. 1969. *From War to War: The Arab-Israeli Confrontation.* New York: Pegasus.

6.24 Lebanon–Israel: Arab–Israeli Dispute and the Hoûla Raids October 1965

Lebanon had joined other Arab states in fighting Israel in the 1948 war of independence (*see* conflict 6.3). Many Palestinian refugees had fled to Lebanon after the war, providing a fertile recruitment ground for Palestinian nationalist organizations like the Palestine Liberation Organization (PLO). Although Israeli Defense Forces (IDF) had frequently skirmished with Syria and Jordan during the 1950s and early 1960s, the Israeli–Lebanese border was generally quiet.

In the mid-1960s, however, relations between the two states became strained when the PLO set up guerrilla bases in southern Lebanon with the tacit compliance of the Lebanese government. IDF border guards detected frequent Palestinian sorties into Israeli territory, and on October 29, 1965, an Israeli force staged a retaliatory raid on Hoûla and Meiss ej Jabal in southern Lebanon. There was one fatality, and the dispute eventually lapsed. This pattern of PLO infiltration and Israeli retaliation was to characterize Israeli–Lebanese relations for the next two decades, with armed incidents in 1974–1975, 1977, 1978, 1982–1983, and again later in 1983 (*see* conflicts 6.38; 6.43; 6.45; 6.52; 6.53).

References

Bailey, S. 1990. *Four Arab-Israeli Wars and the Peace Process.* New York: St. Martin's.

Brynen, R. 1990. *Sanctuary and Survival: The PLO in Lebanon.* Boulder: Westview.

Davis, L., E. Rozeman, and J. Z. Rubin, eds. 1988. *Myths and Facts 1989: A Concise Record of the Arab-Israeli Conflict.* Washington, D.C.: Near East Report.

Gabriel, R. 1984. *Operation Peace for Galilee: The Israeli-PLO War in Lebanon.* New York: Hill and Wang.

Hamizrachi, B. 1988. *The Emergence of the South Lebanon Security Belt: Major Saad Haddad and the Ties with Israel, 1975–1978.* New York: Praeger.

Herzog, C. 1984. *The Arab-Israeli Wars: War and Peace in the Middle East from the War of Independence to Lebanon.* Revised edition. London: Arms and Armour.

Kadi, L. S. 1973. *The Arab-Israeli Conflict: The Peaceful Proposals, 1948–1972.* Beirut: Palestine Research Center.

Safran, N. 1969. *From War to War: The Arab-Israeli Confrontation.* New York: Pegasus.

Tillema, H. K. 1991. *International Armed Conflict Since 1945: A Bibliographic Handbook of Wars and Military Interventions.* Boulder: Westview.

6.25 Israel–Arab States: The Six-Day War June 1967

Relations between Israel and its Arab neighbors had been strained since Israel gained its independence in 1948 (*see* conflict 6.3). The situation was especially difficult in 1967. From its militarily advantageous position on the Golan Heights, Syria would often shell Israeli villages in northern Galilee. The Palestine Liberation Organization (PLO) had begun raiding Israel from its camps in Jordan, Lebanon, and Syria, and all three states had announced plans to divert the Jordan River and thus deprive Israel of two-thirds of its water. Tensions escalated dramatically when Egypt closed the Straits of Tiran to Israeli shipping, cutting off Israel's access to the Red Sea. Egypt then demanded that UN peacekeeping forces be withdrawn from the Sinai, announcing the time had come to destroy Israel. All sides mobilized their forces.

Attempts were made to settle the conflict peacefully, but these failed. Israel was dismayed when both the United States and France declined to supply military aid. On June 5, 1967, the Israeli Air Force attacked Egyptian, Iraqi, Jordanian, and Syrian air bases in a surprise attack, destroying Arab air forces almost entirely. With complete air superiority, Israeli ground forces invaded the Sinai, reaching the Suez Canal in four days. Although Jordan had attacked the Jewish state, Israeli ground forces had occupied the West Bank, Gaza, and the Old City of Jerusalem by June 7. Two days later, on June 9, Israel stormed the Golan Heights, capturing it in two days.

The fighting was intense throughout the war: Israel lost 700 troops, and Arab casualties approached 25,000. UN mediation efforts were totally unsuccessful. Egypt and Syria attempted to regain lost territory in the 1973 Yom Kippur War (*see* conflict 6.36).

References

Al Madfai, M. R. 1993. *Jordan, the United States, and the Middle East Peace Process, 1974–1991.* Cambridge: Cambridge University Press.

Bailey, S. 1990. *Four Arab-Israeli Wars and the Peace Process.* New York: St. Martin's.

Davis, L., E. Rozeman, and J. Z. Rubin, eds. 1988. *Myths and Facts 1989: A Concise Record of the Arab-Israeli Conflict.* Washington, D.C.: Near East Report.

Gilbert, M. 1993. *Atlas of the Arab-Israeli Conflict.* New York: Macmillan.

Herzog, C. 1984. *The Arab-Israeli Wars: War and Peace in the Middle East from the War of Independence to Lebanon.* Revised edition. London: Arms and Armour.

Kadi, L. S. 1973. *The Arab-Israeli Conflict: The Peaceful Proposals, 1948–1972.* Beirut: Palestine Research Center.

Kosut, H. 1968. *Israel and the Arabs: The June 1967 War.* New York: Facts on File.

Laqueur, W. 1969. *The Road to War: The Origin and Aftermath of the Arab-Israeli Conflict, 1967–1968.* Harmondsworth (Middlesex), England: Penguin.

Safran, N. 1969. *From War to War: The Arab-Israeli Confrontation.* New York: Pegasus.

Tillema, H.K. 1991. *International Armed Conflict Since 1945: A Bibliographic Handbook of Wars and Military Interventions.* Boulder: Westview.

6.26 Iraq–Kurds: Kurdish Struggle for Autonomy
October 1968–March 1970

The Kurds are non-Arab tribespeople who inhabit the mountainous plateau region shared by Iran, Iraq, and Turkey. They have been fighting for an independent Kurdistan since the end of World War I, when the Treaty of Sèvres granted them autonomous status. The terms were never implemented, and Kurdish rebels under Mullah Mustafa Barazani began a guerrilla war against Iraq for an independent Kurdistan in the early 1960s (*see* conflict 6.18). The twelve-point program signed in 1966 had led to a cessation of fighting, but in 1968 strenuous government efforts to quell Kurdish rebel activity again led to serious fighting. The Iraqi government committed massive human rights violations against the Kurdish population, and Barazani sent communications to the United Nations alleging Iraqi genocide. Given the Kurds' lack of international standing, however, the United Nations did not take up their cause.

The fighting continued until January 1970, when the Iraqi government reaffirmed the twelve-point program. Following further negotiations, an armistice agreement was signed and the war proclaimed over. The Kurds were given almost complete autonomy in a new peace agreement, but Iraqi failures to fully implement the agreement led to continuing resentment among the Kurds. Fighting broke out again in 1974. More than 2,000 people were killed between 1968 and 1970, most of them Kurdish villagers slaughtered by Iraqi troops (*see* conflict 6.37).

References

Arfa, H. 1966. *The Kurds: A Historical and Political Study.* London: Oxford University Press.

Entessaur, N. 1992. *Kurdish Ethnonationalism.* Boulder: Lynne Rienner.

Ghareeb, E. 1981. *The Kurdish Question in Iraq.* Syracuse, N.Y.: Syracuse University Press.

Jawad, S. 1981. *Iraq and the Kurdish Question, 1958–1970.* London: Ithaca Press.

Kreyenbroek, P.G., and S. Sperl, eds. 1992. *The Kurds: A Contemporary Overview.* London: Routledge.

O'Ballance, E. 1973. *The Kurdish Revolt: 1961–1970.* Hamden, Conn.: Archon.

Pelletière, S. 1984. *The Kurds: An Unstable Element in the Gulf.* Boulder: Westview.

Short, M., and A. McDermott. 1985. *The Kurds.* London: Minority Rights Group.

6.27 North Yemen–Saudi Arabia: Border Conflict
November 1969–October 1970

Following the civil war in North Yemen (1962–1967), Saudi Arabia continued to support the defeated royalists in the hope that the imamate would be restored (*see* conflict 6.21). As a consequence, its relations with the republican government in North Yemen were quite strained.

In September 1969 North Yemeni troops captured the royalist stronghold of Sada. Two months later, royalists attempted to recapture the town with the support of Saudi troops. From November 1969 to October 1970, North Yemeni aircraft launched retaliatory strikes against Saudi positions. North Yemen also alleged Saudi air strikes on its territory. Although no attempts were made to manage the conflict peacefully, the dispute abated. Saudi Arabia did, however, become involved in subsequent wars between North and South Yemen in 1971–1972 and 1979–1980 (*see* conflicts 6.30; 6.46). The two Yemens were unified following a civil war in the early 1990s (*see* conflict 6.63).

References

Badeeb, S. 1986. *The Saudi-Egyptian Conflict over North Yemen, 1962–1970.* Boulder: Westview/American-Arab Affairs Council.

Bidwell, R. 1983. *The Two Yemens.* New York: Longman.

Ismael, T.Y., and J. Ismael. 1986. *The People's Democratic Republic of Yemen: Politics, Economics, and Society—The Politics of Socialist Transformation.* Boulder: Lynne Rienner.

Kostiner, J. 1984. *The Struggle for South Yemen.* London: Croom Helm.

O'Ballance, E. 1971. *The War in the Yemen.* Hamden, Conn.: Archon.

Peterson, J. 1981. *Conflict in the Yemens and Superpower Involvement.* Washington, D.C.: Center for Contemporary Arab Studies, Georgetown University.

Stookey, R. 1978. *Yemen: The Politics of the Yemen Arab Republic.* Boulder: Westview.

Wenner, M. 1967. *Modern Yemen, 1918–1966.* Baltimore: Johns Hopkins University Press.

6.28 The PLO–Jordan: Coup Attempt
February 1970–August 1971

Following the Six-Day War of 1967 (*see* conflict 6.25), the Palestine Liberation Organization (PLO) began to use Jordan as a base for operations against Israel. Israel regularly responded with retaliatory raids into that country. Seeking to deescalate its conflict with Israel, Jordan began to suppress PLO activities in mid-1970, which led to strains between PLO and Jordanian troops.

In a bold move, the PLO attempted to depose King Hussein of Jordan in September 1970. A fierce battle was fought between the PLO and Jordanian troops near Amman on September 17, escalating when Syrian troops intervened on the side of the PLO. Jordan launched retaliatory raids against Syria on September 20; Syrian troops were expelled from Jordan by September 23. On September 27 the PLO moved its forces out of Jordanian cities.

Lingering PLO activities in the towns brought continuing government actions against PLO bases, and the PLO was driven out of Jordan by July 1971. More than 2,000 people were killed in the conflict, including 100 Syrian troops. Numerous attempts at conflict management took place during the fighting, but they achieved only temporary solutions. The PLO later established itself in southern Lebanon and continued to launch attacks against Israel. This situation changed with the 1982 Israeli invasion, which among other things secured the PLO's deportation from Lebanon (*see* conflict 6.52). Relations between Israel and Jordan continued to be volatile.

References

Bailey, C. 1984. *Jordan's Palestinian Challenge, 1948–1983: A Political History.* Boulder: Westview.

Becker, J. 1984. *The PLO: The Rise and Fall of the Palestine Liberation Organization.* New York: St. Martin's.

Brynen, R. 1990. *Sanctuary and Survival: The PLO in Lebanon.* Boulder: Westview.

Cobban, H. 1983. *The Palestinian Liberation Organisation.* Cambridge: Cambridge University Press.

Cooley, J. 1973. *Green March, Black September: The Story of the Palestinian Arabs.* London: F. Cass.

Miller, A.D. 1983. *The PLO and the Politics of Survival.* New York: Praeger.

Nassar, J.R. 1991. *The PLO: From Armed Struggle to the Declaration of Independence.* New York: Praeger.

6.29 Iraq–Iran: Border Tensions and the Shatt al-Arab Waterway Dispute 1971

Iran and Iraq have had a long-standing border dispute over the Shatt al-Arab Waterway, which runs into the Persian Gulf and serves both the Iraqi port of Basra and the Iranian port of Abadan. Numerous negotiations have failed to resolve their conflicting claims.

In 1970–1971 this long-running dispute began to heat up because of two Iranian gambits: first, Iran lent covert support to a Kurdish rebellion in Iraq (*see* conflict 6.26); second, it occupied the Tunb Islands in the Persian Gulf, which are claimed by Iraq and the United Arab Emirates (*see* conflict 6.31). Iraq broke off diplomatic relations with Iran over the incident and, in October 1971, forcibly expelled 11,000 Iranians from Iraq. War appeared imminent, but by the end of the year the strains had eased somewhat, although the issues remained unresolved. Armed conflict broke out again in early 1972 (*see* conflict 6.33).

References

Abdulghani, J. 1984. *Iraq and Iran: The Years of Crisis.* Baltimore: Johns Hopkins University Press.

Cordesman, A.H. 1987. *The Iran-Iraq War and Western Security, 1984–1987: Strategic Implications and Policy Options.* London: Jane's.

Dannreuther, R. 1992. *The Gulf Conflict: A Political and Strategic Analysis.* Adelphi Papers #264. London: Brassey's.

Grummon, S.R. 1982. *The Iran-Iraq War: Islam Embattled.* Washington Papers #92. New York: CSIS/Praeger.

Hiro, D. 1991. *The Longest War: The Iran-Iraq Military Conflict.* New York: Routledge.

Khadduri, M. 1988. *The Gulf War: The Origins and Implications of the Iraq-Iran Conflict.* New York: Oxford University Press.

King, R. 1987. *The Iran-Iraq War: The Political Implications.* Adelphi Papers #219. London: IISS.

Tillema, H.K. 1991. *International Armed Conflict Since 1945: A Bibliographic Handbook of Wars and Military Interventions.* Boulder: Westview.

6.30 North Yemen–South Yemen: Anti-Communist Insurgency and Border Conflict October 1971–October 1972

When Britain withdrew from Aden in 1967, the protectorate renamed itself the People's Democratic Republic of Yemen (South Yemen) and allied itself with the Soviet Union. North Yemen had been an independent imamate since 1918, and, after civil strife from 1962 to 1967 and conflict with Saudi Arabia in 1969, the country allied itself to Saudi Arabia (*see* conflicts 6.21; 6.27).

The rebel organization, the Front for the Liberation of South Yemen, had been actively seeking the overthrow of the South Yemeni government for a number of years. It was supported in this aim by Saudi Arabia and North Yemen, both of which were hostile to the Communist regime. Starting in October 1971 South Yemen attempted to repress opposition to the government by pursuing insurgents across the border into North Yemen. Rebel activities continued throughout 1972, however, and North Yemeni troops actively aided the rebels.

In October 1972 South Yemeni troops invaded North Yemen border areas. The Arab League immediately sought to mediate between the parties, and a cease-fire was agreed to on October 19. It was reported that 200 people were killed during the fighting, including between 40 and 50 North and South Yemeni regular troops. Tensions remained high between the two states, and a war broke out again in 1979 (*see* conflict 6.46). North and South Yemen were unified following a civil war in the early 1990s (*see* conflict 6.63).

References

Bidwell, R. 1983. *The Two Yemens.* New York: Longman.

Halliday, F. 1990. *Revolution and Foreign Policy: The Case of South Yemen, 1967–1987.* New York: Cambridge University Press.

Ismael, T. Y., and J. Ismael. 1986. *The People's Democratic Republic of Yemen: Politics, Economics, and Society—The Politics of Socialist Transformation.* Boulder: Lynne Rienner.

Kostiner, J. 1984. *The Struggle for South Yemen.* London: Croom Helm.

O'Ballance, E. 1971. *The War in the Yemen.* Hamden, Conn.: Archon.

Peterson, J. 1981. *Conflict in the Yemens and Superpower Involvement.* Washington, D.C.: Center for Contemporary Arab Studies, Georgetown University.

Stookey, R. 1978. *Yemen: The Politics of the Yemen Arab Republic.* Boulder: Westview.

———. 1982. *South Yemen: Marxist Republic in Arabia.* Boulder: Westview.

Tillema, H.K. 1991. *International Armed Conflict Since 1945: A Bibliographic Handbook of Wars and Military Interventions.* Boulder: Westview.

Wenner, M. 1967. *Modern Yemen, 1918–1966.* Baltimore: Johns Hopkins University Press.

6.31 Iran–United Arab Emirates: Tunb Islands Territorial Dispute November 1971

Britain granted independence to Bahrain and the United Arab Emirates (UAE) in 1971. Bahrain passed the transition to independence without incident but, on the day before the UAE was to become independent, Iran forcibly seized the islands of Abu Musa and the Tunbs, which are strategically situated at the entrance to the Persian Gulf in the Strait of Hormuz. The islands were originally ruled by individual emirates, which had been controlled by Great Britain since the nineteenth century; Iran and Iraq also laid claim to the islands.

A number of policemen and Iranian soldiers were killed in the fighting. Britain did not press the point, however, and the conflict eventually lapsed, although Iraq and other countries considered Iran's move as a threat to regional security. The islands became the focus of further conflict in 1992 (*see* conflict 6.59).

References

Abdullah, M. 1978. *The United Arab Emirates: A Modern History.* London: Croom Helm.

Abir, M. 1974. *Oil, Power, and Politics: Conflict in Arabia, the Red Sea, and the Gulf.* London: F. Cass.

Alkim, H.H. 1989. *The Foreign Policy of the United Arab Emirates.* London: Saqi.

Amirahmadi, H., and N. Entessar, eds. 1993. *Iran and the Arab World.* New York: St. Martin's.

Day, A., ed. 1987. *Border and Territorial Disputes.* 2d edition. Burnt Mill, Harlow (Essex), England: Longman.

Heard-Bey, F. 1982. *From Trucial States to United Arab Emirates: A Society in Transition.* New York: Longman.

6.32 Oman–South Yemen: Antigovernment Insurgency and Dhofar Rebellion 1972–August 1974

The rebel province of Dhofar in the south of Oman had long been a problem for the Omani government. With the aid of British forces, Oman launched numerous counterinsurgency operations against the Dhofari rebels in the years preceding this conflict. In 1970 Sultan Said bin Timur was deposed by his son, Sultan Qabus bin Said. The new sultan subsequently invited Dhofari rebels to work with the government in a national development program. The rebels refused and continued to agitate against the government.

In February 1972 the rebels formed the Popular Front for the Liberation of Oman and the Arab Gulf (PFLOAG) and, with the support of South Yemen, launched a leftist guerrilla campaign against the Omani government.

In early May 1972 the Omani government began attacking PFLOAG camps and positions within South Yemen. South Yemen retaliated with artillery strikes on Omani positions. At Oman's request, Iran sent large numbers of troops in December 1973, to help drive out the rebels. By late 1974 the Dhofari had largely been defeated, and the conflict with South Yemen gradually abated. In January 1975, after the main rebellion was over, Jordanian troops arrived to help keep the peace. About 2,000 people were killed in the rebellion, including 500 Iranian troops, 20 British troops, and 6 or more South Yemeni regulars. Saudi Arabia made some efforts to mediate, but these attempts were largely unsuccessful.

References

Bidwell, R. 1983. *The Two Yemens.* New York: Longman.

Halliday, F. 1990. *Revolution and Foreign Policy: The Case of South Yemen, 1967–1987.* New York: Cambridge University Press.

Ismael, T. Y., and J. Ismael. 1986. *The People's Democratic Republic of Yemen: Politics, Economics, and Society—*

The Politics of Socialist Transformation. Boulder: Lynne Rienner.

Kostiner, J. 1984. *The Struggle for South Yemen.* London: Croom Helm.

O'Ballance, E. 1971. *The War in the Yemen.* Hamden, Conn.: Archon.

Peterson, J. 1981. *Conflict in the Yemens and Superpower Involvement.* Washington, D.C.: Center for Contemporary Arab Studies, Georgetown University.

Stookey, R. 1978. *Yemen: The Politics of the Yemen Arab Republic.* Boulder: Westview.

———. 1982. *South Yemen: Marxist Republic in Arabia.* Boulder: Westview.

Tillema, H.K. 1991. *International Armed Conflict Since 1945: A Bibliographic Handbook of Wars and Military Interventions.* Boulder: Westview.

Wenner, M. 1967. *Modern Yemen, 1918–1966.* Baltimore: Johns Hopkins University Press.

6.33 Iran–Iraq: Territorial Dispute and Border War
January 1972–February 1975

Relations between Iran and Iraq were strained following Iran's seizure of the Tunb islands in the Strait of Hormuz, and matters worsened after Iraq forcibly expelled 11,000 Iranians in 1971 (*see* conflicts 6.29; 6.31). Iran and Iraq also had a long-standing dispute over the ownership of the Shatt al-Arab Waterway, which was crucial for shipping for both states. These tensions eventually erupted into armed conflict.

Iran commenced artillery attacks and cross-border raids on Iraq in January 1972. Numerous border incidents and low-intensity fighting continued until February 1974, when Iraq began a ground offensive in an attempt to seize full control of various disputed areas. Iran launched a counteroffensive in March. Sporadic artillery exchanges and raids persisted until February 1975 despite a UN-arranged cease-fire.

Iraq formally acceded to Iranian claims in March 1975, in return for Iran's pledge to halt support for Kurdish rebels within Iraq. The 1975 border agreement remarcated the boundary so that it went down the middle of the Shatt al-Arab Waterway, giving both sides joint access. About 1,000 Iraqi and Iranian military personnel died in the sometimes intense fighting. Peaceful conflict management was not pursued, and a bloody and protracted war broke out in 1980 (*see* conflict 6.50).

References

Abdulghani, J. 1984. *Iraq and Iran: The Years of Crisis.* Baltimore: Johns Hopkins University Press.

Cordesman, A.H. 1987. *The Iran-Iraq War and Western Security, 1984–1987: Strategic Implications and Policy Options.* London: Jane's.

Dannreuther, R. 1992. *The Gulf Conflict: A Political and Strategic Analysis.* Adelphi Papers #264. London: Brassey's.

Grummon, S.R. 1982. *The Iran-Iraq War: Islam Embattled.* Washington Papers #92. New York: CSIS/Praeger.

Hiro, D. 1991. *The Longest War: The Iran-Iraq Military Conflict.* New York: Routledge.

Khadduri, M. 1988. *The Gulf War: The Origins and Implications of the Iraq-Iran Conflict.* New York: Oxford University Press.

King, R. 1987. *The Iran-Iraq War: The Political Implications.* Adelphi Papers #219. London: IISS.

Tillema, H.K. 1991. *International Armed Conflict Since 1945: A Bibliographic Handbook of Wars and Military Interventions.* Boulder: Westview.

6.34 Syria/PLO–Israel: PLO Raids, Retaliatory Air Strikes, and the Golan Heights Conflict
March 1972–January 1973

Since its war of independence in 1948, Israel's relations with its Arab neighbors were tense (*see* conflict 6.3). In 1972 Israel's relations with Syria were particularly strained because several years earlier Israel had wrested the strategically valuable Golan Heights from Syria during the Six-Day War (*see* conflict 6.25). For its part, Syria began lending heavy support to the Palestine Liberation Organization (PLO), especially following the PLO's expulsion from Jordan in 1971 (*see* conflict 6.28).

In early 1972 Palestinian guerrillas began to launch attacks on Israeli positions on the Golan Heights from within Syrian territory and with Syrian support. In March Israel responded with retaliatory air attacks, drawing reprisals from the Syrian Air Force. Intermittent attacks continued in the ensuing months, finally diminishing in January 1973. About 200 people are thought to have been killed during the fighting, and this conflict proved to be the precursor to the 1973 war, when Syria and Egypt attacked Israel on the High Holy Day of Yom Kippur (*see* conflict 6.36).

References

Bailey, S. 1990. *Four Arab-Israeli Wars and the Peace Process.* New York: St. Martin's.

Cobban, H. 1991. *The Superpowers and the Syrian-Israeli Conflict.* New York: Praeger.

Davis, L., E. Rozeman, and J.Z. Rubin, eds. 1988. *Myths and Facts 1989: A Concise Record of the Arab-Israeli Conflict.* Washington, D.C.: Near East Report.

Herzog, C. 1984. *The Arab-Israeli Wars: War and Peace in the Middle East from the War of Independence to Lebanon.* Revised edition. London: Arms and Armour.

Khadduri, M. 1988. *The Gulf War: The Origins and Implications of the Iraq-Iran Conflict.* New York: Oxford University Press.

Tillema, H.K. 1991. *International Armed Conflict Since 1945: A Bibliographic Handbook of Wars and Military Interventions.* Boulder: Westview.

6.35 Iraq–Kuwait: Territorial Dispute and Border Incidents March 1973–July 1975

Kuwait, long a part of the Ottoman Empire's massive Arab land holdings, declared itself independent in 1899. In 1914 the British agreed to protect Kuwait in exchange for control over its foreign policy. When the protectorate expired in June 1961, Kuwait became fully independent, whereupon Iraq announced its claim to the territory. A serious conflict ensued. An Arab League force was deployed in Kuwait to deter Iraqi attack following the conflict.

On March 20, 1973, Iraqi forces captured Kuwaiti border posts at Sametah. Saudi troops were once again deployed but did not engage Iraqi forces. With the acquiescence of both parties, Yasser Arafat, leader of the Palestine Liberation Organization (PLO), mediated the dispute and managed to secure an Iraqi withdrawal in early April. Two Iraqis died at Sametah, and the conflict was partially settled. Iraqi claims to Kuwait never completely lapsed, and in 1990 Iraq launched a full-scale invasion of Kuwait, starting the Gulf War (*see* conflict 6.58).

References

Assiri, A. 1990. *Kuwait's Foreign Policy: City-State in World Politics.* Boulder: Westview.

Butterworth, R.L. 1976. *Managing Interstate Conflict, 1945–1974.* Pittsburgh: Center for International Studies, University of Pittsburgh.

Day, A., ed. 1987. *Border and Territorial Disputes.* 2d edition. Burnt Mill, Harlow (Essex), England: Longman.

Marr, P. 1985. *The Modern History of Iraq.* Boulder: Westview.

Martin, L. 1984. *The Unstable Gulf: Threats from Within.* Lexington, Mass.: Lexington Books.

Tillema, H.K. 1991. *International Armed Conflict Since 1945: A Bibliographic Handbook of Wars and Military Interventions.* Boulder: Westview.

6.36 Israel–Egypt and Syria: Arab–Israeli Territorial Dispute, Arab–Israeli Wars, and the Yom Kippur War October 1973

Israel's relations with its Arab neighbors had been strained since its 1948 war of independence (*see* conflict 6.3). These strains resulted in armed conflict on a number of occasions, the most serious being the Six-Day War in 1967, when Israel attacked Egypt, Jordan, and Syria in a preemptive strike (*see* conflict 6.25). During this campaign Israel gained control of the Sinai Peninsula from Egypt and wrested the Golan Heights from Syria. In 1973 President Anwar al-Sadat of Egypt indicated his intentions of winning back the Sinai by war, but Israel considered this threat to be a bluff.

On October 6, 1973, Egypt and Syria launched simultaneous offensives into Israeli-occupied Sinai and the Golan Heights on the Jewish High Holy Day of Yom Kippur. Israel responded with air attacks against Syrian and Egyptian positions. By October 11 Israeli troops had regained the Golan Heights in fierce fighting and advanced into Syrian territory, drawing Jordan, Kuwait, Morocco, and Saudi Arabia into the conflict in defense of Syria. On October 14, Israel launched an offensive on the Sinai, crossing the Suez Canal. Algerian, Kuwaiti, and Tunisian forces came to the aid of Egypt. The Israeli offensive continued, and by October 20 Israel had consolidated its position around the Suez Canal and had a large part of the Egyptian army completely surrounded.

After frantic efforts by the United Nations and the United States to stop the fighting, a cease-fire was declared on October 22, but fighting continued for a number of days, and a military stand-off between the belligerents continued until February 1979. Israel unilaterally withdrew from Syrian territory, back to its former positions on the Golan Heights in June 1974.

More than 10,000 soldiers lost their lives in this conflict, including 5,000 Egyptians, 3,000 Israelis, 3,000 Syrians, and 200 Iraqis. After the fighting stopped, strenuous attempts were made at conflict management, which in 1979, under the good offices of U.S. president Jimmy Carter, produced the Camp David Accords between Egypt and Israel. Relations with Israel's other neighbors continued to be tense, however, and there were numerous subsequent cases of militarized hostilities (*see* conflicts 6.38; 6.43; 6.45; 6.47; 6.52; 6.53; 6.67).

References

Al Madfai, M.R. 1993. *Jordan, the United States, and the Middle East Peace Process, 1974–1991.* Cambridge: Cambridge University Press.

Allen, D., and A. Pijpers, eds. 1984. *European Foreign Policy Making and the Arab-Israeli Conflict.* The Hague: M. Nijhoff.

Bailey, C. 1984. *Jordan's Palestinian Challenge, 1948–1983: A Political History.* Boulder: Westview.

Davis, L., E. Rozeman, and J.Z. Rubin, eds. 1988. *Myths and Facts 1989: A Concise Record of the Arab-Israeli Conflict.* Washington, D.C.: Near East Report.

Gilbert, M. 1993. *Atlas of the Arab-Israeli Conflict.* New York: Macmillan.

Golan, G. 1977. *Yom Kippur and After: The Soviet Union and the Middle East Crisis.* Cambridge: Cambridge University Press.

Herzog, C. 1975. *The War of Atonement, October 1973.* Boston: Little, Brown.

———. 1984. *The Arab-Israeli Wars: War and Peace in the Middle East from the War of Independence to Lebanon.* Revised edition. London: Arms and Armour.

Insight Team of the London Sunday *Times.* 1974. *The Yom Kippur War.* Garden City, N.Y.: Doubleday.

6.37 Kurds–Iraq: Attempted Secession and the Kurdish Rebellion March 1974–July 1975

Kurds are a non-Arab tribe inhabiting an extensive mountainous plateau region that includes parts of Iran, Iraq, and Turkey. The Kurds have been fighting unsuccessfully for an independent state since the end of World War I, when they were granted an autonomous state by the Treaty of Sèvres (1920). The treaty's terms were never implemented.

Like Turkey and Iran, Iraq has suppressed the Kurds' many secessionist revolts, and this led to clashes from 1961 to 1966 and again from 1968 to 1970 (*see* conflicts 6.18; 6.26). In the period leading up to March 1974, the Kurds were particularly dissatisfied with the implementation of the 1970 agreement, which had ended the most recent revolt.

The Kurdish rebellion resumed under the leadership of Mullah Mustafa Barazani. Fighting broke out on March 12, 1974, and Iran provided the rebels with arms and assistance. In the face of cruel Iraqi repression, Kurdish leaders appealed to the United Nations and accused Iraq of genocide. As in the past, the United Nations pointed to the Kurds' status as a stateless people and took no action. The Kurds were driven close to the Iranian border, resulting in frequent border violations by Iraqi forces. Iran began to shell Iraqi positions in retaliation.

A March 1975 agreement resolved a territorial dispute between Iraq and Iran on the condition that Iran cease its support for the Kurds. Without Iranian support, the Kurds could not withstand Iraq's advances. Iraq quickly quelled the rebellion, proclaiming an amnesty for Kurds who surrendered by April 1, 1975. More than 3,000 people were killed during the rebellion, many of them civilians. Barazani fled into exile in Iran. The Kurds returned to armed conflict in 1976 (*see* conflict 6.42).

References

Arfa, H. 1966. *The Kurds: A Historical and Political Study.* London: Oxford University Press.

Chliand, G., ed. 1993. *A People Without a Country: The Kurds and Kurdistan.* New York: Olive Branch.

Entessaur, N. 1992. *Kurdish Ethnonationalism.* Boulder: Lynne Rienner.

Ghareeb, E. 1981. *The Kurdish Question in Iraq.* Syracuse, N.Y.: Syracuse University Press.

Jawad, S. 1981. *Iraq and the Kurdish Question, 1958–1970.* London: Ithaca Press.

Kreyenbroek, P.G., and S. Sperl, eds. 1992. *The Kurds: A Contemporary Overview.* London: Routledge.

O'Ballance, E. 1973. *The Kurdish Revolt: 1961–1970.* Hamden, Conn.: Archon.

Pelletière, S. 1984. *The Kurds: An Unstable Element in the Gulf.* Boulder: Westview.

Short, M., and A. McDermott. 1985. *The Kurds.* London: Minority Rights Group.

6.38 Israel–Lebanon: Arab Infiltrators and Cross-Border Attacks April 1974–July 1975

Following the Israeli war of independence in 1948, many Palestinian refugees settled in southern Lebanon (*see* conflict 6.3). After Jordan expelled the Palestine Liberation Organization (PLO) in 1971 (*see* conflict 6.28), the PLO moved its headquarters to Lebanon. From there, the PLO sent infiltrators across the border into Israel to attack civilian and military targets. These attacks led to border tensions.

This conflict started in April 1974, when Arab terrorists based in southern Lebanon crossed into Israel and massacred eighteen Israelis in the northern town of Qiryat Shemona. The Israelis responded by raiding several villages in southern Lebanon and by threatening Lebanon with massive retaliation if it allowed terrorists to operate from its territory. Similar terrorist attacks in May and June led to massive bombing raids on Palestinian camps in Lebanon, and to naval attacks on Lebanese ports from where infiltrators launched amphibious assaults.

This pattern of conflict continued until July 1975, when Israel became involved in the Lebanese civil war on the side of Christian militias (*see* conflict 6.39). In December 1974 relations between Israel and Lebanon deteriorated further when Israeli planes attacked Palestinian targets on the outskirts of Beirut. Several hundred people were killed during the conflict, and the only two conflict-management attempts, one by the UN Security Council and another joint mediation by French and Romanian diplomats, failed. This conflict was a precursor to armed conflict involving both states in 1977, 1978, 1979, 1982, and 1983 (*see* conflicts 6.43; 6.45; 6.47; 6.52; 6.53).

References

Bailey, S. 1990. *Four Arab-Israeli Wars and the Peace Process.* New York: St. Martin's.

Ben Rafael, E. 1987. *Israel-Palestine: A Guerrilla Conflict in International Politics.* New York: Greenwood.

Brynen, R. 1990. *Sanctuary and Survival: The PLO in Lebanon.* Boulder: Westview.

Davis, L., E. Rozeman, and J.Z. Rubin, eds. 1988. *Myths and Facts 1989: A Concise Record of the Arab-Israeli Conflict.* Washington, D.C.: Near East Report.

Gabriel, R. 1984. *Operation Peace for Galilee: The Israeli-PLO War in Lebanon.* New York: Hill and Wang.

Hamizrachi, B. 1988. *The Emergence of the South Lebanon Security Belt: Major Saad Haddad and the Ties with Israel, 1975–1978.* New York: Praeger.

Herzog, C. 1984. *The Arab-Israeli Wars: War and Peace in the Middle East from the War of Independence to Lebanon.* Revised edition. London: Arms and Armour.

6.39 Lebanon: Internal Strife, Communal Violence, and the Second Lebanese Civil War February 1975–Late 1992

Lebanon was originally part of Syria, and together they formed the Levant states, long a part of the Ottoman Empire. After World War I France was awarded the territory and immediately partitioned the area into two independent states, which were administered under the French mandate until 1941. Under the 1943 national pact, all Lebanese political positions were divided among the country's many religious communities—a confessional system—among them the Christian Maronites and the Muslim Sunni and Druze sects, with Christians holding the majority. Lebanon's delicately balanced civil society began to change in 1948, however, when Israel's war of independence sent droves of Palestinians northward (*see* conflict 6.3).

In 1958 Lebanon was plunged into its first civil war when the national pact broke down with the help of a Syrian-aided revolt against the government's policies; U.S. marines briefly intervened (*see* conflict 6.16). Following the first civil war, an uneasy peace existed among Lebanon's confessional communities. By the 1970s, however, Muslims had become the majority and were agitating for a greater share of political power. Fighting broke out once again when members of the conservative Christian Phalange militia massacred twenty-five Palestinians. Heavily armed leftist Muslim factions retaliated, and by the end of the year full-scale civil war was under way, as each side tried to gain control of Beirut.

By May 1975 the government had collapsed, and in March 1976 the Lebanese army split into Christian and Muslim units. In June 1976 up to 15,000 Syrian troops intervened on the side of the Maronites to fight the Palestinians, and a cease-fire was declared. Syria then occupied much of southern Lebanon and the Bekaa Valley, acting as a buffer between the combatants.

Approximately 60,000 people lost their lives in the 1975–1976 civil war. Sporadic fighting continued in Lebanon until 1992, with several serious outbreaks of violence (*see* conflicts 6.43; 6.45; 6.52; 6.53). Although more than 100 attempts were made at peaceful conflict management, few succeeded, and none has produced a lasting solution to the conflict. In 1992 a number of limited peace agreements among various factions brought the major fighting to an end, although small outbreaks of violence erupted periodically. In 1992 Hezbollah (Party of God) was still attacking Israel from southern Lebanon, while Israel attempted to maintain the area as a security zone. Israel also continued to support Christian militias in the area.

References

Alamuddin, N. 1993. *Turmoil: The Druzes, Lebanon, and the Arab-Israeli Conflict.* London: Quartet.

Cobban, H. 1985. *The Making of Modern Lebanon.* Boulder: Westview.

Deeb, M. 1980. *The Lebanese Civil War.* New York: Praeger.

Evron, Y. 1987. *War and Intervention in Lebanon: The Israeli-Syrian Deterrence Dialogue.* Baltimore: Johns Hopkins University Press.

Gilmour, D. 1984. *Lebanon: The Fractured Country.* New York: St. Martin's.

Khalidi, W. 1983. *Conflict and Violence in Lebanon: Confrontation in the Middle East.* Cambridge: Center for International Affairs, Harvard University.

MacDowell, D. 1986. *Lebanon: A Conflict of Minorities.* London: Minority Rights Group.

Rabinovich, I. 1985. *The War for Lebanon, 1970–1985.* Revised edition. Ithaca, N.Y.: Cornell University Press.

Shehadi, N., and D.H. Mills, eds. 1988. *Lebanon: A History of Conflict and Consensus.* London: I.B. Tauris.

Tillema, H.K. 1991. *International Armed Conflict Since 1945: A Bibliographic Handbook of Wars and Military Interventions.* Boulder: Westview.

6.40 Syria–Iraq: Resource Dispute over the Euphrates River April–Late 1975

Syria and Iraq clashed often, and in 1959 fighting erupted when Syria backed the Mosul Revolt in an effort to unseat the Iraqi government (*see* conflict 6.17). In the months leading up to the April 1975 conflict, each side was waging a propaganda war against the other. Their relations began to worsen in early April in a dispute over the use of water from the Euphrates.

Requesting an emergency meeting of Arab League (AL) foreign ministers, Iraq claimed Syria was diverting excessive amounts of water from the dam, thus endangering the livelihoods of Iraqi farmers. The dispute intensified when Syria closed its airspace to Iraq, broke off diplomatic relations, and threatened to bomb the Tabqa Dam. An AL meeting on April 22, 1975, established a technical committee to mediate the dispute, but the mediation failed when Syria withdrew. A further mediation by Saudi Arabia on May 3 also ended inconclusively, but another attempt in June produced a limited agreement over water allocation, without solving the basic conflict. Relations did not improve, and minor border clashes occurred. The propaganda war continued, but eventually the conflict lapsed.

References

Beschorner, N. 1992. *Water and Instability in the Middle East.* Adelphi Papers #273. London: Brassey's.

Day, A., ed. 1987. *Border and Territorial Disputes.* 2d edition. Burnt Mill, Harlow (Essex), England: Longman.

Khadduri, M. 1969. *Republican Iraq: A Study in Iraqi Politics Since the Revolution of 1958.* New York: Oxford University Press.

Kienle, E. 1990. *Bath vs. Bath: The Conflict Between Syria and Iraq, 1968–1989.* London: I. B. Tauris.

Marr, P. 1985. *The Modern History of Iraq.* Boulder: Westview.

Seale, P. 1965. *The Struggle for Syria: A Study of Post-War Arab Politics, 1945–1958.* New York: Oxford University Press.

Tillema, H. K. 1991. *International Armed Conflict Since 1945: A Bibliographic Handbook of Wars and Military Interventions.* Boulder: Westview.

6.41 Iran: Internal Strife, Orthodox Muslim Backlash, Iranian Civil War, and Islamic Revolution 1976–1980

In 1954 strong monarchist factions in Iran, with powerful Western backing, ousted Muhammad Mossadeq, a militant nationalist who had forced Muhammad Reza Shah Pahlevi to flee from Iran a year earlier. The shah was returned to power and quickly instituted a pro-Western modernization program. At the same time, however, the regime's repressive acts alienated both the progressive and traditional factions in the country, so that by the mid-1970s Iran was beset with intense civil and political unrest. There were frequent allegations of human rights abuses, including torture and politically motivated killings. Members of the Tudeh Party, the banned Communist party, were especially targeted for state repression.

In March 1975 the shah decreed Iran to be a one-party state. By 1976 the country was in a state of widespread civil disorder, as opposition groups and government forces stepped up their violent methods. It was alleged that extremist outside groups and regimes—among them the Palestine Liberation Organization (PLO) and Libya's Muammar Qaddafi—were providing support and military aid for some of the opposition groups.

The unrest was caused mainly by Shiite Muslim clerics opposed to the shah's reform program and the emancipation of women. But the civil disturbances could also be traced to the actions of "Islamic Marxists." By the end of 1977, the Union of National Front Forces was formed to fight the shah's dictatorship and to work for its replacement by a constitutional monarchy. The violence continued throughout 1978, escalating in August with the declaration of martial law and the imposition of curfews.

Although the shah appointed a so-called government of reconciliation, Iran's internal situation worsened. Powerful opposition was being voiced by the militantly conservative followers of Ayatollah Ruhollah Khomeini, who was living in exile in Paris. Despite the continuing violence, the United States continued to back the shah, and on September 14, 1979, sent military aid in the form of aircraft and missiles. On December 29, 1979, the U.S. government was reported to have issued contingency orders for an aircraft carrier task force to move into waters near Iran in the event of anarchy and to discourage Soviet involvement in the conflict. Allegations continued in 1979 of Libyan and PLO military aid to Iranian Muslim groups.

On January 16, 1979, popular opposition forced the shah into exile, as his regime had become untenable. On February 1 Khomeini returned to Iran after a sixteen-year exile. He denounced foreign involvement in Iran and established an Islamic republic. Recognition of the new regime came soon afterward. Iran broke off relations with Israel, and Khomeini began to agitate for worldwide Islamic revolution.

Unrest continued in the wake of reforms of the armed forces, imprisonment and execution of the shah's supporters, and the strict enforcement of Islamic law. In November 1979 militant Islamic revolutionaries seized the U.S. embassy in Tehran, taking sixty-six embassy personnel hostage, demanding that the shah, who was in the United States for medical treatment, be returned to stand trial. The revolutionaries held fifty-two of the hostages for more than a year. Following the shah's death from cancer in 1980, negotiations succeeded in gaining their release.

After the revolution, which, together with the civil war, caused the deaths of nearly 4,000 people, Iran took up a devastating and costly war with Iraq over the Shatt al-Arab Waterway (*see* conflict 6.50). Lasting nine years, the Iran-Iraq War nearly depleted the country's oil reserves and cost more than 1.5 million lives altogether. Iranian civil society in the meantime was wracked with political violence and unrest.

References

Amirahmadi, H., and N. Entessar, eds. 1993. *Iran and the Arab World.* New York: St. Martin's.

Butterworth, C. E., and I. W. Zartman, eds. 1992. *Political Islam.* Newbury Park, Calif.: Sage.

Hashim, A. 1995. *The Crisis of the Iranian State: Domestic, Foreign, and Security Policies in Post-Khomeini Iran.* Oxford: Oxford University Press.

Ramazani, R.K. 1986. *Revolutionary Iran: Challenge and Response in the Middle East.* Baltimore: Johns Hopkins University Press.

Rosen, B., ed. 1985. *Iran Since the Revolution: Internal Dynamics, Regional Conflict and the Superpowers.* New York: Columbia University Press.

Sick, G. 1985. *All Fall Down: America's Tragic Encounter with Iran.* New York: Random House.

Taheri, A. 1988. *Nest of Spies: America's Journey to Disaster in Iran.* New York: Pantheon.

Yodaf, A. 1984. *The Soviet Union and Revolutionary Iran.* London: Croom Helm.

Zabih, S. 1988. *The Iranian Military in Revolution and War.* London: Routledge.

Zakaria, R. 1989. *The Struggle Within Islam: The Conflict Between Religion and Politics.* London: Penguin.

6.42 Kurds–Iraq: Kurdish Separatist Insurgency and Kurdish Autonomy May 1976–Ongoing

Kurds are a non-Arab tribe inhabiting a mountainous plateau region comprising parts of Iran, Iraq, and Turkey. Their fight for an independent Kurdistan began just after World War I, when the Treaty of Sèvres (1920) granted them autonomous status. The treaty's terms were never carried out. A number of conflicts have arisen from their struggle, most notably from 1961 to 1966, 1968 to 1970, and 1974 to 1975 (*see* conflicts 6.18; 6.26; 6.37).

In May 1976 Kurds attacked Iraqi forces. The fighting was precipitated by government plans to forcibly move Kurds from their mountainous home in northern Iraq, replace them with Arabs, and relocate the Kurds in southern Iraq. Despite a 1975 agreement giving Kurdistan limited autonomy, Iraqi implementation of the accord was not marked by speed, and persistent government atrocities further intensified the fighting and fueled Kurdish separatism. The Kurdistan Democratic Party (KDP) and the Patriotic Union of Kurdistan (PUK) were the two main Kurdish resistance organizations.

The conflict was internationalized from an early stage. It was revealed in April 1978 that the Soviet Union was providing arms and aid to the Kurds; in the 1980s Syria and Libya supplied arms to the Kurds via Iran. In June 1978 the fighting spread to Turkey, and in 1979 Turkey and Iraq agreed to join forces to quash Kurdish separatism. The collapse of the Iranian army following the Islamic revolution in Iran allowed the Kurds to cross into that country for supplies, arms, and refuge. In June 1979 Iraq bombed Kurdish villages in Iran, prompting a formal protest from Iran.

The outbreak of the Iran–Iraq War in 1980 (*see* conflict 6.50) took some pressure off the Kurds, and, when Iran invaded northern Iraq in 1983, Kurds linked up with dissident Shiite groups to assist Iranian Revolutionary Guards in consolidating their hold on captured territory. This forced Iraq to come to an agreement with the PUK, but the agreement broke down in late 1984. From 1987 the Kurds made large gains with Iran's help and controlled enough territory to be able to threaten important Iraqi economic and strategic targets. Immediately following the July 1988 cease-fire with Iran, Iraq went on a brutal offensive against the Kurds, often using poison gas in attacks on their villages. A chemical attack on Halabja in 1988 reportedly killed between 4,000 and 7,000 civilians. Later information on the Kurdish genocide revealed a far more brutal result. In the early 1990s, 857 file cartons kept by the Iraqi secret police were discovered. The files described Iraq's policy of genocide. Casualty estimates now range between 200,000 and 300,000 for the period from 1976 to 1992.

The 1990 Gulf War was also advantageous to the Kurds (*see* conflict 6.58). After Iraq's defeat in 1991 by coalition forces, the Kurds mounted a massive rebellion in the north, but, without allied support, it soon faltered. The fighting was brutal, forcing the coalition to establish "safe havens" for the Kurds. A number of negotiations between Iraq and the Kurds at this time were largely unsuccessful. In mid-1992 the Kurds held elections, and by the end of that year Kurdistan had achieved a degree of autonomy, although the conflict was far from resolved.

In 1993 and 1994 the Kurds were torn by infighting, which continued into 1995 despite intense diplomatic efforts to mediate a cease-fire. Hundreds of fatalities occurred in the internecine warfare, which greatly hampered efforts to build a viable Kurdish administration in Iraqi Kurdistan. Kurds continued to face attacks by the Iraqi military, and the situation was complicated by regular Turkish incursions into northern Iraq pursuing rebels from the Kurdish Worker's Party (Partiya Karkeren Kurdistan). The PKK, later called the Kurdish Freedom and Democracy Congress (KADEK), was fighting an insurgency in Turkey. The violence continued into 1995 despite continued attempts to mediate a cease-fire.

In August 1996, following the collapse of a U.S.-sponsored peace agreement, fighting broke out between the Patriotic Union of Kurdistan and the Kurdistan Democratic Party. The KDP gained control of all three Kurdish provinces by September 1996. In early September the United States launched "Operation Desert Strike" against Iraq in retaliation for Iraqi intervention in the conflict between the Kurdish factions. Drawing back from full-scale military confrontation, U.S. officials then made a fresh attempt to mediate between the warring Kurds. It is alleged that at this stage Iran was supporting the PUK and Iraq the KDP.

By October 1996 the PUK had regained much of the territory it had lost in the previous fighting through a series of attacks and counterattacks. A fragile truce was mediated by the United States in late October, as allegations emerged of growing Iranian involvement and fears of renewed Iraqi intervention. Turkey also made mediation efforts. The

United States held a second round of peace talks in November 1996. In mid-September 1998 the United States mediated a peace agreement that the PUK and the KDP signed. The agreement set up a timetable for resolving their remaining differences. Although tensions remain, the parties continue in their bid to normalize relations.

Throughout the conflict, the fighting was often intense. More than 300,000 people were killed, many of them civilians. The Kurds resorted to terrorism, while the Iraqis used torture, deportations, executions, and poison gas extensively.

References

Arfa, H. 1966. *The Kurds: A Historical and Political Study.* London: Oxford University Press.

Chliand, G., ed. 1993. *A People Without a Country: The Kurds and Kurdistan.* New York: Olive Branch.

Entessaur, N. 1992. *Kurdish Ethnonationalism.* Boulder: Lynne Rienner.

Ghareeb, E. 1981. *The Kurdish Question in Iraq.* Syracuse, N.Y.: Syracuse University Press.

Jawad, S. 1981. *Iraq and the Kurdish Question, 1958–1970.* London: Ithaca Press.

Keesing's Record of World Events: K41246, K41296–97, K41343, K41393, K42526.

Kreyenbroek, P.G., and S. Sperl, eds. 1992. *The Kurds: A Contemporary Overview.* London: Routledge.

O'Ballance, E. 1973. *The Kurdish Revolt: 1961–1970.* Hamden, Conn.: Archon.

Pelletière, S. 1984. *The Kurds: An Unstable Element in the Gulf.* Boulder: Westview.

Short, M., and A. McDermott. 1985. *The Kurds.* London: Minority Rights Group.

White, M. 2004. "Secondary Wars and Atrocities of the Twentieth Century." *20th Century Atlas—Alphabetical List of War, Massacre, Tyranny, and Genocide.* http://users.erols.com/mwhite28/warstat3.htm#Kurdistan2 (accessed May 24, 2004).

6.43 Israel–Lebanon: Arab–Israeli Tensions, Christian–Muslim Factional Fighting, and Border Incidents Mid–Late 1977

Israel had been attacked on numerous occasions by Palestinian guerrillas operating from southern Lebanon. These attacks had provoked armed conflict between Israel and Lebanon in 1965 and 1974–1975 (*see* conflicts 6.24; 6.38). The situation was complicated by Lebanon's 1975–1976 civil war (*see* conflict 6.39). Although a cease-fire had been declared, and Syrian forces occupied southern Lebanon, the situation was still volatile. Israel was closely aligned with Christian militias based in the south.

Israel objected both to the proximity of 30,000 Syrian troops and to the failure to implement the third stage of the July 1977 peace agreement. This stage was supposed to include the withdrawal of Palestinian guerrillas from the southern border areas and their replacement by Lebanese troops. Israel demanded a wider-scale withdrawal of Palestinians than previously agreed to and demanded that its border gates, "the good fence," be kept open so that Lebanese civilians had access to medical treatment, employment, and free movement into Israel.

In October and November 1977 Lebanese Muslim factions and Israeli-backed Christian militias clashed several times. On November 6 Yasser Arafat, the leader of the Palestine Liberation Organization (PLO), rejected Israeli demands, stating there would be no Palestinian withdrawal, particularly if Christian forces remained. Further cross-border incidents occurred in November, including air strikes by Lebanon. Israeli forces retaliated, attacking villages and refugee camps.

Talks in Beirut between the U.S. ambassador and the Lebanese and Syrian presidents took place in November 1977, creating some pressure for a reactivation of the cease-fire, and Lebanon released a statement that it was doing all it could to deal with rebel incursions from its territory into Israel. No other peaceful conflict-management attempts were made during the conflict, and it gradually abated. Approximately fifty people were killed in the fighting. Further armed conflicts occurred in 1978, 1979–1980, 1982–1983, and 1983–1995 (*see* conflicts 6.45; 6.47; 6.52; 6.53).

References

Bailey, S. 1990. *Four Arab-Israeli Wars and the Peace Process.* New York: St. Martin's.

Ben Rafael, E. 1987. *Israel-Palestine: A Guerrilla Conflict in International Politics.* New York: Greenwood.

Brynen, R. 1990. *Sanctuary and Survival: The PLO in Lebanon.* Boulder: Westview.

Davis, L., E. Rozeman, and J.Z. Rubin, eds. 1988. *Myths and Facts 1989: A Concise Record of the Arab-Israeli Conflict.* Washington, D.C.: Near East Report.

Gabriel, R. 1984. *Operation Peace for Galilee: The Israeli-PLO War in Lebanon.* New York: Hill and Wang.

Hamizrachi, B. 1988. *The Emergence of the South Lebanon Security Belt: Major Saad Haddad and the Ties with Israel, 1975–1978.* New York: Praeger.

Herzog, C. 1984. *The Arab-Israeli Wars: War and Peace in the Middle East from the War of Independence to Lebanon.* Revised edition. London: Arms and Armour.

6.44 Egypt–Libya: Regional Tensions and Border War July–September 1977

Relations between Egypt and Libya had been strained since 1973 when, in the wake of the Yom Kippur War (*see* conflict 6.36), Egypt sought closer ties with the West, alienating its hard-line Arab allies. The enmity between Colonel Muammar Qaddafi of Libya and President Anwar al-Sadat of Egypt was characterized by unceasing accusations of sabotage and propaganda mixed with periodic troop buildups along their common border. From July 12 to July 17, 1977, the two nations traded accusations of starting hostilities along the border area. Exchanges of fire escalated into heavy fighting involving tanks and aircraft, after Egyptian troops crossed the border to clash with Libyan troops on July 21.

Hostilities continued despite Yasser Arafat's mediation efforts on July 21, which he initiated after heavy attacks on Libyan targets. On July 22 Egyptian troops were recalled from the border area, having "taught Libya a lesson," but the following day Egyptian aircraft based in Sudan attacked Libyan targets. Arafat's mediation efforts, aided by the Arab League, secured a cease-fire on July 24, ending the heavy Egyptian air strikes. Troops remained mobilized on both sides of the border, however, and Qaddafi and Sadat carried on the propaganda war.

The Arab League, Arafat, and Sheikh al-Sabah of Kuwait proposed a peace formula on July 27, 1977, which Egypt immediately accepted. Arab efforts to consolidate the cease-fire through talks with Qaddafi continued into August, and, on August 28 talks mediated by Arafat achieved a settlement ending the conflict. By September 1977 all troops had withdrawn from the border area, and by October bilateral relations between Libya and Egypt had improved significantly. Approximately 300 fatalities resulted from the fighting.

References

Cooley, J. 1982. *Libyan Sandstorm.* New York: Holt, Rinehart, and Winston.

Tillema, H.K. 1991. *International Armed Conflict Since 1945: A Bibliographic Handbook of Wars and Military Interventions.* Boulder: Westview.

6.45 Israel–Lebanon/PLO: Arab–Israeli Tensions, PLO Incursions, and Israeli Invasion of Southern Lebanon March–June 1978

Following Israel's war of independence in 1948, Palestinian refugees flooded into Lebanon (*see* conflict 6.3). From here, Palestinian guerrillas could regularly launch attacks on northern Israeli settlements. Israel's efforts to halt these attacks had resulted in numerous conflicts with Lebanon—in 1965, 1974–1975, and 1977 (*see* conflicts 6.24; 6.38; 6.43). Meanwhile, peace efforts were continuing to be made, although the Palestine Liberation Organization (PLO) was apparently determined to demonstrate that any settlement would have to include and accommodate the Palestinians.

A serious deterioration in Middle East relations occurred in March 1978, when a major Palestinian guerrilla raid provoked an Israeli invasion of southern Lebanon. On March 11 members of the Al Fatah faction of the PLO attacked northern Israel, causing many civilian fatalities. On March 12 the prime minister of Lebanon declared his country was not responsible for the incident.

Hostilities escalated on March 14–15 when Israel launched a major invasion of southern Lebanon by land, sea, and air, despite warnings of the consequences to Middle East peace. Israel stated that the operation was a preventive action in that eliminating Palestinian bases in southern Lebanon would help to establish security against further PLO attacks. Although Israel overwhelmed Palestinian positions, the PLO was able to withstand the attack and saved many of its forces by evacuating the border area before the invasion.

Israel achieved its military objective by March 15, but stressed that it required guarantees that south Lebanon remain free from Palestinian guerrillas before it could withdraw. Within days it was claimed that Israel had cleared a six-mile security belt along the border that was free of guerrillas. PLO counterattacks were continuing, however, and there still loomed the threat of Arab support for Lebanon against Israel and the Christian militia.

On March 18 Israel pushed farther north, past the security zone and well into Lebanon—its aim was the complete eradication of the PLO from Lebanon. The UN Security Council immediately called for Israel's withdrawal from Lebanon and the deployment of UN forces in the area. The international community widely condemned Israel's action. After separate requests by Israel and Lebanon to the UN Security Council in March, a resolution was passed to carry out a two-stage operation for a cease-fire, Israeli withdrawal, and UN monitoring of the area. The cease-fire was accepted by Israel, but not by the PLO, which demanded unconditional Israeli withdrawal.

The UN Interim Force in Lebanon (UNIFIL) began arriving on March 22, but fighting continued, and UN troops came under fire. Israel began withdrawing soon after, but radical Arab guerrillas infiltrated UNIFIL areas and began low-level attacks against Israel. The conflict abated somewhat after this time. As many as 1,500 people were killed in the conflict, many of them civilians. This conflict was the precursor to a more serious invasion of Lebanon in 1982 (*see* conflict 6.52).

References

Bailey, S. 1990. *Four Arab-Israeli Wars and the Peace Process.* New York: St. Martin's.

Ben Rafael, E. 1987. *Israel-Palestine: A Guerrilla Conflict in International Politics.* New York: Greenwood.

Brynen, R. 1990. *Sanctuary and Survival: The PLO in Lebanon.* Boulder: Westview.

Davis, L., E. Rozeman, and J. Z. Rubin, eds. 1988. *Myths and Facts 1989: A Concise Record of the Arab-Israeli Conflict.* Washington, D.C.: Near East Report.

Gabriel, R. 1984. *Operation Peace for Galilee: The Israeli-PLO War in Lebanon.* New York: Hill and Wang.

Hamizrachi, B. 1988. *The Emergence of the South Lebanon Security Belt: Major Saad Haddad and the Ties with Israel, 1975–1978.* New York: Praeger.

Herzog, C. 1984. *The Arab-Israeli Wars: War and Peace in the Middle East from the War of Independence to Lebanon.* Revised edition. London: Arms and Armour.

6.46 North Yemen–South Yemen: Border War February 1979–February 1980

South Yemen gained its independence from Britain in 1967 and in 1970 became the Arab world's only Marxist state. More than 300,000 South Yemenis fled north after independence, provoking two decades of strains and hostilities between the Marxist state and its more moderate northern neighbor, North Yemen.

In February 1979 North Yemeni troops invaded South Yemen, and a North Yemeni dissident group called the National Democratic Front (NDF) staged a simultaneous invasion of North Yemen with the help of South Yemeni regulars. The fighting was intense, and Saudi Arabia placed its troops on full alert. Concern over the possible spread of the conflict to other Arab states led to intense mediation efforts in March 1979. Combined with other conflict-management activities, these efforts resulted in the cessation of hostilities and the withdrawal of troops. By February 1980 many of the issues were resolved, and some progress was made toward unifying the two countries. About 150 fatalities resulted from the fighting. Eventually, after lengthy negotiations, complete unification was achieved in 1990, although a bloody civil war erupted in 1993 (*see* conflict 6.63).

References

Bidwell, R. 1983. *The Two Yemens.* New York: Longman.

Halliday, F. 1990. *Revolution and Foreign Policy: The Case of South Yemen, 1967–1987.* New York: Cambridge University Press.

Ismael, T. Y., and J. Ismael. 1986. *The People's Democratic Republic of Yemen: Politics, Economics, and Society—The Politics of Socialist Transformation.* Boulder: Lynne Rienner.

Kostiner, J. 1984. *The Struggle for South Yemen.* London: Croom Helm.

Peterson, J. 1981. *Conflict in the Yemens and Superpower Involvement.* Washington, D.C.: Center for Contemporary Arab Studies, Georgetown University.

Stookey, R. 1978. *Yemen: The Politics of the Yemen Arab Republic.* Boulder: Westview.

———. 1982. *South Yemen: Marxist Republic in Arabia.* Boulder: Westview.

Wenner, M. 1967. *Modern Yemen, 1918–1966.* Baltimore: Johns Hopkins University Press.

6.47 Israel–Syria: Arab–Israeli Tensions and Air Incidents June 1979–February 1980

Israel and Lebanon had engaged in numerous armed conflicts since 1948, when Israel declared its independence (*see* conflict 6.3). Israel made frequent incursions into Lebanese territory to attack the Palestinian camps that harbored Palestine Liberation Organization (PLO) guerrillas responsible for attacks on northern Israel. Because of Syria's significant military presence in Lebanon, especially in the Bekaa Valley, it came under mounting pressure to protect Muslim civilians—both Palestinian and Lebanese. At the same time, Syrian president Hafez al-Assad was facing a number of serious domestic challenges to his authority.

The Syrian Air Force therefore engaged Israeli jet fighters over southern Lebanese air space on June 27, 1979. The following day, Israel described its raids as "legitimate national self-defense" and said that the clash with Syria would not alter its policy of preemptive strikes on Palestinian targets in Lebanon. Israeli raids continued throughout July and August, intensifying in their effect and damage. A UN cease-fire on August 26 was immediately violated by both sides.

After a period of little Israeli activity in the first three weeks of September 1979, Israeli warplanes again clashed with Syrian planes on September 24, south of Beirut. Tension was also heightened by border clashes in southern Lebanon on September 21. Later that month, the United States announced a major diplomatic initiative to find a peaceful solution to the crisis in Lebanon through consultations with Middle East and European countries and the eight nations contributing to the UN Interim Forces in Lebanon (UNIFIL).

On October 4, 1979, the PLO announced a unilateral cease-fire in Lebanon, but Israel ignored it. Hostilities continued through to the end of 1979 and early 1980, and by February 8, 1980, Israel had put its forces on the Lebanese border on full alert. Approximately forty fatalities resulted from the clashes. The U.S. diplomatic initiative was largely ineffectual, and a major war in Lebanon broke out in 1982 after Israel invaded the country (*see* conflict 6.52).

References

Bailey, C. 1984. *Jordan's Palestinian Challenge, 1948–1983: A Political History.* Boulder: Westview.

Cobban, H. 1991. *The Superpowers and the Syrian-Israeli Conflict.* New York: Praeger.

Hamizrachi, B. 1988. *The Emergence of the South Lebanon Security Belt: Major Saad Haddad and the Ties with Israel, 1975–1978.* New York: Praeger.

Herzog, C. 1984. *The Arab-Israeli Wars: War and Peace in the Middle East from the War of Independence to Lebanon.* Revised edition. London: Arms and Armour.

Tillema, H.K. 1991. *International Armed Conflict Since 1945: A Bibliographic Handbook of Wars and Military Interventions.* Boulder: Westview.

6.48 Saudi Arabia–North Yemen: Covert Military Aid and Border Conflict August 1979–March 1980

Saudi Arabia established diplomatic relations with South Yemen, known as the People's Democratic Republic of Yemen (PDRY) in 1976. Prior to this, Saudi Arabia had actively supported efforts to overthrow the Marxist regime in Aden, backing the South Yemeni rebel groups, in particular the Front for the Liberation of South Yemen (FLOSY). Saudi hostility took on a more discreet guise after 1976, with support given to dissident factions within the ruling Yemeni Socialist Party (YSP) in the form of covert aid.

On August 30, 1979, President Ali Abdullah Saleh of North Yemen, the Yemen Arab Republic (YAR), applied to the Soviet Union for weapons assistance. Soon after the YAR delegation visited Moscow, a large shipment of weapons and ammunition arrived on a Soviet vessel at the port of Hodeida. Later in 1979, there were reports of sizable shipments from the Soviet Union to North Yemen, including about 10 MiH-21 and 100 T-55 tanks and 100 military personnel. Having the Soviet Union as one of North Yemen's main arms suppliers clearly conflicted with Saudi Arabia's foreign policy objectives, which included containing and limiting the spread of Marxist ideologies in the region. Saudi Arabia retaliated in December 1979 by withdrawing approximately $300 billion (U.S.) in military and economic aid to North Yemen.

On March 19, 1980, the YAR conceded to the government of Saudi Arabia, agreeing to receive no more Soviet military aid and to steadily remove Soviet troops from the territory. Saudi foreign policy came to include opposition to the unification of the two Yemens, mainly because it feared that the YSP would dominate the government of a new unified Yemen and provide a launchpad for more radical groups to gain a foothold. After the unification of North and South Yemen in early 1990, Saudi Arabia increased its covert aid to various Yemeni groups opposed to the YSP.

References

Altapedia. 2004. *A–Z of Countries: Yemen and Saudi Arabia.* Holland Park West, Queensland, Australia: Latimer Clarke Corporation. http://www.atlapedia.com/online/countries/ (accessed February 17, 2004).

Keesing's Contemporary Archives. 1979–1981: 30197–30201; 30746–30747.

Kjeilen, T., ed. 2004. *Encyclopaedia of the Orient.* LexicOrient: http://i-cias.com/e.o/saleh_a.htm (accessed February 17, 2004).

U.S. Library of Congress. 2004. *Country Studies–Regional Security: Saudi Arabia.* http://countrystudies.us/saudi-arabia/58.htm (accessed February 17, 2004).

6.49 Iran–United States: Anti-American Sentiment, Islamic Revolution, and Hostage Crisis November 1979–January 1981

After the Ayatollah Khomeini's Islamic revolution of February 1979, anti-Western, especially anti-American, sentiment grew in Iran. The United States had been closely aligned with the recently ousted Muhammad Reza Shah Pahlevi, who had headed a brutally repressive regime. Wanted in Iran for trial as a criminal, the shah lived in exile until his death from cancer in July 1980. Despite Iran's repeated threats and appeals to the United States to deny asylum to the former shah, the United States admitted him on humanitarian grounds on October 22, 1979, for medical treatment. The Iranian government officially protested to the United States in October, demanding the shah's extradition.

On November 4, 1979, with anti-American fervor at a fever pitch, armed Iranian "students" invaded and occupied the U.S. embassy in Tehran. The gunmen held the embassy personnel hostage and demanded the extradition of the shah. On November 6 the U.S. government stated that it would not accede to the demands, despite Iranian government support for the students.

Repeated U.S. and UN demands for the unconditional release of the hostages brought no response from Iran, which instead accused the embassy staff of espionage. Iran also warned against any attempts to rescue them. Some hostages were released in November 1979, and there were many unsuccessful mediation attempts during this time. The United States retaliated with economic and financial pressure, as well as the expulsion of Iranian students. American and British warships began maneuvers in the Arabian Sea, south of Iran, in a provocative display of force; diplomatic relations were severed. Attempts at negotiation were hampered by factional struggles within the Iranian government.

On April 24, 1980, the United States launched an abortive military operation to free the hostages, which failed when the rescue helicopters crashed in the desert. Iran interpreted this as a hostile action, and tensions were high. The shah's death in July 1980 did nothing to defuse the crisis. After intense secret mediation by

Algeria, an agreement providing for the hostages' release was reached in January 1981 to coincide with the swearing in of a new U.S. president, Ronald Reagan. Relations with the United States remained tense, however, and the United States stepped up its support for Iraq, a bitter enemy of Iran.

References

Amirahmadi, H., and N. Entessar, eds. 1992. *Reconstruction and Regional Diplomacy in the Persian Gulf.* London and New York: Routledge.

Butterworth, C.E., and I.W. Zartman, eds. 1992. *Political Islam.* Newbury Park, Calif.: Sage.

Christopher, W., and P. Kreisberg, eds. 1985. *American Hostages in Iran: The Conduct of a Crisis.* New Haven: Yale University Press.

Hashim, A. 1995. *The Crisis of the Iranian State: Domestic, Foreign, and Security Policies in Post-Khomeini Iran.* Oxford: Oxford University Press.

Ramazani, R.K. 1986. *Revolutionary Iran: Challenge and Response in the Middle East.* Baltimore: Johns Hopkins University Press.

Rosen, B., ed. 1985. *Iran Since the Revolution: Internal Dynamics, Regional Conflict, and the Superpowers.* New York: Columbia University Press.

Sick, G. 1985. *All Fall Down: America's Tragic Encounter With Iran.* New York: Random House.

Taheri, A. 1988. *Nest of Spies: America's Journey to Disaster in Iran.* New York: Pantheon.

6.50 Iran–Iraq: Regional Rivalry, Territorial Dispute, and the Iran–Iraq War
February 1980–1989

Iran and Iraq remained rivals following years of conflict over the Shatt al-Arab Waterway, which flows into the Persian Gulf, in the southern border area between the two states. It served ports from both countries and was crucial to shipping. Armed conflict had broken out in 1971 and 1972–1975, although an agreement in 1975 had seemed to resolve the issue (*see* conflicts 6.29; 6.33). Iranian support for Kurdish rebels in Iraq, and the overthrow of the shah in Iran had raised tensions in 1979. Iraq was highly suspicious of the Ayatollah Khomeini of Iran and still had designs on the Shatt al-Arab.

In February 1980 Iraq repudiated the 1975 border agreement and invaded the Shatt al-Arab region in force. At first it seemed that Iraq would win easily, but Iran held on and launched its own counteroffensive in 1981. A lengthy war of attrition followed, with Iran using lightly trained Revolutionary Guards and Iraq resorting to chemical weapons, which brought worldwide condemnation. Although neither side was able to gain an advantage, each still believed it could win. The fighting spread to the Gulf waters in 1984, with frequent attacks on oil facilities and shipping. The United States sent a naval task force to the region to protect Western oil interests, but, because of Soviet interest in the region, did not get actively involved in the conflict, despite numerous attacks and incidents.

In the late 1980s Iran appeared to be getting the upper hand, largely because it was prepared to sacrifice greater numbers of troops. Various breakthroughs occurred, but in the end, the Iraqis could not be dislodged. Both sides attacked civilians, firing Scud missiles randomly into each other's cities in an attempt to demoralize the other. The war took such a toll on both countries that conflict-management efforts, largely by the United Nations, produced a cease-fire and partial settlement by 1989, although the underlying issues were never fully resolved.

It is estimated that more than 1 million people lost their lives in this war, and both economies sustained billions of dollars of damage. Iran lost approximately 400,000 troops in the war, and Iraq lost nearly 200,000. It was the most violent war since Vietnam and by far the most costly conventional war since the Korean War.

References

Abdulghani, J. 1984. *Iraq and Iran: The Years of Crisis.* Baltimore: Johns Hopkins University Press.

Cordesman, A.H. 1987. *The Iran-Iraq War and Western Security, 1984–1987: Strategic Implications and Policy Options.* London: Jane's.

Dannreuther, R. 1992. *The Gulf Conflict: A Political and Strategic Analysis.* Adelphi Papers #264. London: Brassey's.

Eknes, A. 1989. *From Scandal to Success: The United Nations and the Iran-Iraq War, 1980–1988.* Working Paper #406. Oslo: Norwegian Institute of International Affairs.

Hiro, D. 1991. *The Longest War: The Iran-Iraq Military Conflict.* New York: Routledge.

Khadduri, M. 1988. *The Gulf War: The Origins and Implications of the Iraq-Iran Conflict.* New York: Oxford University Press.

King, R. 1987. *The Iran-Iraq War: The Political Implications.* Adelphi Papers #219. London: IISS.

O'Ballance, E. 1988. *The Gulf War.* London: Brassey's.

6.51 Libya–United States: Regional Instability and Air Incidents
August 1981

The attitude of the U.S. government toward Libya hardened with the accession of Ronald Reagan to the U.S. presidency in 1980. The Reagan administration claimed Colonel Muammar Qaddafi's regime was not only destabilizing the region but also promoting international terrorism. Libya, for its part, engaged in hostile anti-American propaganda. U.S.-Libyan relations deteriorated rapidly in mid-1981 amid hostile diplomatic moves and mutual recriminations.

Provocative U.S. naval maneuvers in the Gulf of Sidra, which Libya claimed as territorial waters, produced a number of incidents, the most serious of which was a jet fighter clash on August 19, 1981, in which two Libyan Su-22 jet fighters were shot down. Incidents and recriminations continued after this point, but the dispute gradually abated. There were no attempts at peaceful conflict management, and fighting broke out again in 1986 and 1989 (*see* conflicts 6.55; 6.57).

References

Davis, B.L. 1990. *Qaddafi, Terrorism, and the Origins of the U.S. Attack on Libya.* New York: Praeger.

Haley, P.E. 1984. *Qaddafi and the United States Since 1969.* New York: Praeger.

Martin, L. 1984. *The Unstable Gulf: Threats from Within.* Lexington, Mass.: Lexington Books.

Sicker, M. 1987. *The Making of a Pariah State: The Adventurist Politics of Muammar Qaddafi.* New York: Praeger.

Simons, G.L. 1993. *Libya: The Struggle for Survival.* New York: St. Martin's.

St. John, R.B. 1987. *Qaddafi's World Design: Libyan Foreign Policy, 1969–1987.* London: Atlantic Highlands.

6.52 Israel–Lebanon: Israeli Invasion of Lebanon Early 1982–Mid-1983

Following Israel's war of independence in 1948, Palestinian refugees flooded into southern Lebanon (*see* conflict 6.3). From there, Palestinian guerrillas, mainly from the Palestine Liberation Organization (PLO), launched attacks into northern Israel. Lebanon's intractable civil strife appeared to add to Israel's disquiet about its northern borders (*see* conflicts 6.16; 6.39). In any event, the PLO's presence in Lebanon and persistent cross-border attacks led to armed border conflicts in 1965, 1974–1975, 1977, and 1978, and air incidents in 1979–1980 (*see* conflicts 6.24; 6.38; 6.43; 6.45; 6.47).

The escalation of cross-border Israeli-PLO and Israeli-Syrian engagements in the north from late 1980 to July 1981 led to increasing strains in the area. Syria's deployment of antiaircraft missile batteries in the Bekaa Valley also caused a potentially explosive situation. Intense diplomatic efforts defused the situation by procuring a cease-fire. Southern Lebanon remained relatively stable from July 1981 to April 1982, when cease-fire violations led to Israeli air strikes, an increase in tensions during May, and Israeli troop concentrations in the area.

In an operation code-named "Peace for Galilee," Israel launched an invasion of Lebanon on June 6, 1982, with the stated intention of eliminating the military threat posed by the PLO to Israel's northern borders. Israeli forces stormed through Lebanon, reaching the outskirts of Beirut four days later. By June 14 Israeli forces had completely encircled the Lebanese capital, trapping large numbers of PLO and Syrian troops. During its advance, Israel had destroyed Syrian surface-to-air missile batteries in the Bekaa Valley and engaged in aerial battles with the Syrian Air Force, in which hundreds of Syrian planes are thought to have been shot down. Diplomatic efforts failed to stop the fighting, although they did succeed in averting a wider Israeli–Syrian war.

Israeli forces gradually tightened their grip on Beirut, laying siege to the trapped PLO and Syrian forces. On June 13 Israel announced its demands for a peace plan, saying it would invade West Beirut, where the PLO was cornered, unless the PLO left Lebanon along with the Syrian troops. Owing to intense U.S. diplomatic efforts and continued Israeli pressure, the plan was accepted in late June. The evacuation of PLO and Syrian forces from Beirut began on August 21 and was completed by September 1, 1982. Playing a peacekeeping role, U.S., French, and Italian forces moved into Beirut as part of the security plan.

Israeli troops entered West Beirut following the September 14 assassination of Lebanese president-elect Bashir Gemayel, in which Syria was believed to be involved. Two days later, Lebanese Christian troops entered the Sabra and Shatila refugee camps, massacring hundreds of Palestinian refugees. Israeli troops were accused of complicity in the massacres, and the resulting uproar eventually led to the resignation of the Israeli defense minister Ariel Sharon. Intense U.S. diplomatic activity brought about direct Israeli-Lebanese negotiations, and Israel began troop withdrawals in September 1983, despite continued violence, attacks on the peacekeeping forces, deadlocks in negotiations, breakdowns in cease-fires, and at times, escalations in hostilities.

Lebanon fell into heavy factional fighting after the Israeli withdrawal. Tensions remained high in southern Lebanon, with recurring cross-border incidents as Israel attempted to establish a security zone. The fighting was intense throughout the conflict, and as many as 100,000 people were killed in the fighting, many of them civilians. Israel lost nearly 800 troops.

References

Alamuddin, N. 1993. *Turmoil: The Druzes, Lebanon, and the Arab-Israeli Conflict.* London: Quartet.

Bailey, S. 1990. *Four Arab-Israeli Wars and the Peace Process.* New York: St. Martin's.

Ben Rafael, E. 1987. *Israel-Palestine: A Guerrilla Conflict in International Politics.* New York: Greenwood.

Brynen, R. 1990. *Sanctuary and Survival: The PLO in Lebanon.* Boulder: Westview.

Davis, L., E. Rozeman, and J.Z. Rubin, eds. 1988. *Myths and Facts 1989: A Concise Record of the Arab-Israeli Conflict.* Washington, D.C.: Near East Report.

Gabriel, R. 1984. *Operation Peace for Galilee: The Israeli-PLO War in Lebanon.* New York: Hill and Wang.

Gilbert, M. 1993. *Atlas of the Arab-Israeli Conflict.* York: Macmillan.

Hamizrachi, B. 1988. *The Emergence of the South Lebanon Security Belt: Major Saad Haddad and the Ties with Israel, 1975–1978.* New York: Praeger.

Herzog, C. 1984. *The Arab-Israeli Wars: War and Peace in the Middle East from the War of Independence to Lebanon.* Revised edition. London: Arms and Armour.

Schiff, Z., and E. Yaari. 1984. *Israel's Lebanon War.* Edited and translated by I. Friedman. New York: Simon and Schuster.

6.53 Israel–Lebanon: Arab–Israeli Hostilities, Muslim–Christian Factional Fighting, and the Security Zone Mid-1983–Ongoing

Although this conflict was part of the almost continuous Arab–Israeli hostilities dating back to 1948, its immediate precursor was Israel's 1982 invasion of Lebanon (*see* conflict 6.52), during which the Jewish state set up a "security zone" in southern Lebanon to protect its northern borders from infiltrators and cross-border raids. Israel further buttressed the zone by giving military support to the South Lebanon Army (SLA), a Christian faction, including air power, tanks, and Israeli Defense Force (IDF) troops. The SLA tried to counter the actions of extreme Muslim factions, such as Hezbollah and Amal (Lebanese Resistance Detachments), and the Palestine Liberation Organization (PLO)—groups that were active among the local Shiite population.

The minority Lebanese Shiites initially welcomed the Israeli occupation because it countered PLO power in the area. (Although it is a secular organization, the PLO's majority is Sunni Muslims.) But the Shiites grew to resent the increasingly repressive Israeli occupation and began to support radical Muslim factions. From this time on, a growing cycle of violence ensued. This typically involved armed attacks on Israeli and SLA forces, which then retaliated against Shiite villages with raids and air attacks, followed by further revenge attacks on Israeli/SLA forces.

At various times the IDF mounted large-scale operations that moved troops into southern Lebanon to improve security. Such actions led to the mobilization of Syrian forces and, on several occasions, Lebanese army regulars fired on Israeli positions. As a result of the fighting, an estimated 3,000 to 4,000 people were killed and more than 300,000 Lebanese became refugees. At this point, no active measures were undertaken to resolve the conflict peacefully. In early 1996 the IDF mounted a massive military operation to clear the security zone of Hezbollah fighters, causing heavy loss of life and displacing many people. The operation also caused massive infrastructural damage, as many Lebanese targets were attacked in an apparent effort to force the Lebanese government to exert pressure on Hezbollah.

Several major changes to Lebanese politics occurred at the end of 1998. Emile Lahoud, a reformist general, was elected president in November. Prime Minister Rafik Hariri declined to serve under him, and veteran politician and economist Selim al-Hoss was appointed in his place. The change of government in Israel in July 1999 opened new prospects for peace. Israel's new leader, Ehud Barak, had promised a withdrawal from southern Lebanon in his election campaign. In March 2000 Israel agreed to withdraw from southern Lebanon before July. Then, in a surprise result, former prime minister Hariri returned to power in the September 2000 elections.

References

Alamuddin, N. 1993. *Turmoil: The Druzes, Lebanon, and the Arab-Israeli Conflict.* London: Quartet.

Brynen, R. 1990. *Sanctuary and Survival: The PLO in Lebanon.* Boulder: Westview.

Davis, L., E. Rozeman, and J.Z. Rubin, eds. 1988. *Myths and Facts 1989: A Concise Record of the Arab-Israeli Conflict.* Washington, D.C.: Near East Report.

Deeb, M. 1980. *The Lebanese Civil War.* New York: Praeger.

Gabriel, R. 1984. *Operation Peace for Galilee: The Israeli-PLO War in Lebanon.* New York: Hill and Wang.

Hamizrachi, B. 1988. *The Emergence of the South Lebanon Security Belt: Major Saad Haddad and the Ties with Israel, 1975–1978.* New York: Praeger.

Herzog, C. 1984. *The Arab-Israeli Wars: War and Peace in the Middle East from the War of Independence to Lebanon.* Revised edition. London: Arms and Armour.

Reuters Alert Net. 2001. "Lebanon." Country Profile: http://www.alertnet.org/thefacts/countryprofiles/220170?version=1 (March 20, 2002).

Schiff, Z., and E. Yaari. 1984. *Israel's Lebanon War.* Edited and translated by I. Friedman. New York: Simon and Schuster.

6.54 Kurds–Turkey: Kurdish Secession Struggle August 1984–Ongoing

Kurds had longed for an independent homeland since before the turn of the twentieth century. Iranian Kurdistan had had a brief period of self-rule in 1945, but Iraqi Kurds had been fighting for independence since 1961. The causes of this conflict lay in Turkish oppression of its Kurdish population and the eruption of long-term nationalistic agitation into violence. For many years, Kurdish language and culture had been suppressed and Kurdish organizations banned. In August 1984 the

Partiya Karkeren Kurdistan (PKK)—Kurdish Worker's Party, later called Kurdish Freedom and Democracy Congress (KADEK)—the Kurds' primary nationalist organization that the Turkish government had banned, launched attacks on government and civilian targets.

In September 1984 Turkish troops pursued PKK rebels into Iraqi territory, provoking a storm of protest from Iraq. The PKK began serious guerrilla war in 1985, smuggling weapons and fighters into Turkey via Iraq and Syria. It launched attacks from Syria on a number of occasions. Iran also suffered from Turkish troop incursions and at various times Greek-Cyprus and Syria were thought to be aiding the Kurds. The fighting was intense, and by the end of 1988 more than 3,000 people had died as a result of the conflict. Many of the casualties were civilians, killed by the PKK for being tacit government supporters or by government troops for being potential PKK supporters. Brutal reprisals by government troops on civilian Kurds gave the PKK many new supporters.

From March 1990 the Kurdish insurgency in Turkey's southeastern provinces escalated into a mass nationalist uprising. Thousands of people were killed in the government counterattack. In August 1991 and March 1992 Turkish forces made major incursions into Iraq in pursuit of PKK guerrillas, provoking Iraqi protests. The war escalated even further in 1992. In September more than 200 PKK and government soldiers were killed in a twelve-hour battle, and in October and November a Turkish campaign into northern Iraq led to the threat of Turkey imposing a security zone in the area. Several thousand were reported to have been killed in this operation.

The PKK also operated in mainland Europe, where many Kurdish refugees had found asylum. Here they attacked Turkish embassies and businesses, often in well-coordinated campaigns across several countries. To this point, more than 14,000 people had been killed in the conflict, many of them civilians. Neither side initiated or accepted any serious attempts at peaceful conflict management, convinced as they were of ultimate victory: the Kurds were not prepared to lay down their arms, and the Turkish government was not prepared to offer autonomy.

Turkish forces renewed the offensive against the PKK in April and September 1996 with massive air and ground operations against PKK bases. Hundreds of PKK members were killed. In March 1997 approximately 50,000 Turkish troops targeted PKK rebels with camps in northern Iraq. During the offensive, forces loyal to the Kurdistan Democratic Party (KDP) of Iraq aided the Turkish military. In May 1997 another offensive, "Operation Sledgehammer," was launched and continued until June with total fatalities on both sides reportedly in the thousands. The Turks, again with KDP support, launched a fresh anti-Kurdish offensive in September 1997, resulting in additional casualties. Further offensives and heavy fighting took place in March and May 1998. On August 28, 1998, the leader of the PKK, Abdullah Ocalan, declared a unilateral cease-fire.

In October 1998 the Turkish government warned Syria against supporting Kurdish separatist demands, and relations between the two countries became tense. In talks held October 19–21 Syria agreed not to support the PKK. Further troubles arose in November when Turkey engaged in a diplomatic disagreement with Italy over Ocalan's extradition. Violence followed Ocalan's arrest in March 1999, including the death of thirteen in an arson attack. Fighting continued between the PKK and the KDP despite Ocalan's call in April for a temporary cease-fire and a peaceful solution to the conflict.

In June 1999 Ocalan received the death sentence, and the announcement resulted in further violence. In July the PKK ceased violence, and the Turkish government rejected Ocalan's appeal, which then went to the European Court of Human Rights. On March 12, 2003, the court declared that Ocalan had not received a fair trial. In the meantime, Turkey commuted his sentence to life in prison. Throughout 2000 the PKK continued to call for peace and supported a political approach to the conflict. Nevertheless, in August 2000, the Turkish government launched another series of attacks on Kurdish positions in northern Iraq resulting in further casualties.

References

Arfa, H. 1966. *The Kurds: A Historical and Political Study.* London: Oxford University Press.

BBC. 2000. "Ocalan: Which Way Now?" http://news.bbc.co.uk/1/hi/world/europe/535312.stm. November 21, 2000.

BBC. 2003. "Ocalan File: Timeline." http://news.bbc.co.uk/1/hi/world/europe/281302.stm. March 12, 2003.

Chliand, G., ed. 1993. *A People Without a Country: The Kurds and Kurdistan.* New York: Olive Branch.

Entessaur, N. 1992. *Kurdish Ethnonationalism.* Boulder: Lynne Rienner.

Keesing's Record of World Events: K41060, K41294, K41651, K41652, K41703, K41877, K42229, K42458, K42574, K42635, K42911, K43031, K43078, K43715.

Kreyenbroek, P. G., and S. Sperl, eds. 1992. *The Kurds: A Contemporary Overview.* London: Routledge.

Mango, A. 1994. *Turkey: The Challenge of a New Role.* Westport, Conn.: Praeger.

Pelletière, S. 1984. *The Kurds: An Unstable Element in the Gulf.* Boulder: Westview.

Robins, P. 1991. *Turkey and the Middle East.* London: Pinter.

Short, M., and A. McDermott. 1985. *The Kurds.* London: Minority Rights Group.

6.55 United States–Libya: International Terrorism Fears and Naval Incidents January–April 1986

Relations between Libya and the United States were tense in the months leading up to January 1986 (*see* conflict 6.51). The Reagan administration was concerned about Libyan support for international terrorism and determined to curtail these activities by any means. Libya, meanwhile, engaged in inflammatory statements accusing the United States of terrorism and destabilization. Reports in November 1985 claimed that President Ronald Reagan had authorized a covert operation by the Central Intelligence Agency (CIA) against Colonel Muammar Qaddafi's regime.

On December 27, 1985, gunmen attacked the Rome and Vienna international airports, killing twenty people. The United States blamed the Abu Nidal Palestinian group and Libyan government support for the attacks. In January 1986, as a direct result of these attacks, the United States sent naval forces to positions off the Libyan coast to perform maneuvers. At the same time, it imposed a set of economic sanctions on Libya. In response, Qaddafi placed Libyan forces on full alert.

U.S. naval maneuvers to the north of the Gulf of Sidra in January 1986 produced several confrontations with Libyan forces, although no shots were fired until March 24, when both sides attacked each other's ships, planes, and shore batteries. Between 50 and 100 people were killed in the fighting. Following bomb explosions on April 2 on a TWA aircraft and on April 5 in a West Berlin nightclub, speculation rose about a possible U.S. attack on Libya. On April 15 U.S. aircraft mounted air strikes on Tripoli and Benghazi that killed nearly 150 people. Libya responded with a botched attack on a U.S. Coast Guard station on the Italian island of Lampedusa in the southern Mediterranean and revenge attacks on U.S. and British targets worldwide. International responses were mixed, with a hostile reaction from the Arab world. Neither side attempted to settle the conflict using peaceful methods, but over the next two years strains eased somewhat. The basic issues remained unresolved, however, and another serious armed confrontation occurred in 1989 (*see* conflict 6.57).

References

Davis, B.L. 1990. *Qaddafi, Terrorism, and the Origins of the U.S. Attack on Libya.* New York: Praeger.

Haley, P.E. 1984. *Qaddafi and the United States Since 1969.* New York: Praeger.

Martin, L. 1984. *The Unstable Gulf: Threats from Within.* Lexington, Mass.: Lexington Books.

Sicker, M. 1987. *The Making of a Pariah State: The Adventurist Politics of Muammar Qaddafi.* New York: Praeger.

Simons, G.L. 1993. *Libya: The Struggle for Survival.* New York: St. Martin's.

St. John, R.B. 1987. *Qaddafi's World Design: Libyan Foreign Policy, 1969–1987.* London: Atlantic Highlands.

6.56 Qatar–Bahrain: Sovereignty Dispute and the Hawar Islands Dispute April 1986

The Hawar Islands are situated only 2.4 kilometers off the coast of Qatar but are owned by Bahrain. Both countries had claimed them, however, and the disagreement had escalated into conflict on a number of occasions when Bahrain attempted to search for oil on the islands. Mediation by Saudi Arabia in the 1970s failed to find a solution.

The conflict escalated seriously in late 1985, when Bahrain began to erect military and coast guard installations on the islands and its accompanying reefs. On April 26, 1986, Qatari troops invaded the island of Fash al-Dibal and occupied it in an attempt to stop the work. After mediation by leaders of Oman, Saudi Arabia, and the United Arab Emirates on April 27, the parties reached an agreement providing for the withdrawal of Qatar's troops and the destruction of the installations. The agreement did not, however, deal with all the outstanding issues. Negotiations also took place in August, and Prince Sultan ibn Abdul Aziz, the Saudi defense minister, made a further mediation attempt in October but without success. Although there were no fatalities, the two states had come close to all-out war.

References

Abir, M. 1974. *Oil, Power, and Politics: Conflict in Arabia, the Red Sea, and the Gulf.* London: F. Cass.

Cyrsal, J. 1990. *Oil and Politics in the Gulf: Rulers and Merchants in Kuwait and Qatar.* Cambridge: Cambridge University Press.

Day, A., ed. 1987. *Border and Territorial Disputes.* 2d edition. Burnt Mill, Harlow (Essex), England: Longman.

Halliday, F. 1974. *Arabia Without Sultans: A Political Survey of Instability in the Arab World.* New York: Random House.

6.57 United States–Libya: Rabat Chemical Plant Tensions and Mediterranean Air Incident January 1989

This conflict was the most serious confrontation between the United States and Libya since the 1986 Tripoli bombings (*see* conflict 6.55). Libya was accused of supporting worldwide terrorism, and the United States was actively seeking to confront and destabilize the regime. This confrontation was the culmination of tensions over the construction of a suspected Libyan chemical weapons plant at Rabat, 60 kilometers south of Tripoli. The United States again conducted naval maneuvers in the area, provoking confrontations with Libyan forces.

On January 4, 1989, two U.S. planes shot down two Libyan jets over the Mediterranean, and tensions rose dramatically. Although the dispute was referred to the U.N. Security Council, January 6 through 11, 1989, nothing was achieved, and the conflict gradually faded after that. Eventually, U.S. concerns moved elsewhere, most notably to Saudi Arabia following Iraq's invasion of Kuwait.

References

Davis, B.L. 1990. *Qaddafi, Terrorism, and the Origins of the U.S. Attack on Libya.* New York: Praeger.

Haley, P.E. 1984. *Qaddafi and the United States Since 1969.* New York: Praeger.

Martin, L. 1984. *The Unstable Gulf: Threats from Within.* Lexington, Mass.: Lexington Books.

Sicker, M. 1987. *The Making of a Pariah State: The Adventurist Politics of Muammar Qaddafi.* New York: Praeger.

Simons, G.L. 1993. *Libya: The Struggle for Survival.* New York: St. Martin's.

St. John, R.B. 1987. *Qaddafi's World Design: Libyan Foreign Policy, 1969–1987.* London: Atlantic Highlands.

6.58 Iraq–Kuwait/Coalition Forces: Territorial Dispute, Iraqi Expansionism, and the Gulf War August 1990–May 1991

In early August 1990 the Iraqi army invaded Kuwait, taking the oil sheikdom's small army by complete surprise. Within days, Iraq had occupied the country, and by the end of the month it had absorbed Kuwait into its own territorial administration. Prior to the invasion, Iraq had accused Kuwait of overproduction that drove down oil prices, but Iraqi debts to Kuwait and claims on Kuwaiti oil fields also played a role in the attack. Furthermore, Iraq had long claimed that Kuwait was part of Iraq, going back to Kuwaiti independence and before (*see* conflict 6.19). Following the invasion, there was a vicious crackdown on anti-Iraq elements in Kuwait and a troop buildup on the Kuwait-Saudi Arabia border.

Iraq's actions brought immediate worldwide condemnation, the imposition of sanctions, and the start of a massive buildup of troops in Saudi Arabia and surrounding states. Advanced industrial nations feared Iraqi designs on Saudi Arabia. With Kuwait occupied, Iraq controlled a significant portion of the world's oil production. Despite numerous mediations and negotiations, the situation remained quite tense. An anti-Iraq coalition made up of the United States, a number of European states, and some Arab states began to take shape. On November 29, 1990, the United Nations passed a resolution authorizing the use of force to compel Iraq to withdraw and set January 15, 1991, as the deadline for compliance.

On January 16, despite frantic last-minute diplomatic maneuvering by Russia, a massive allied bombing campaign of Iraqi positions began. Iraq responded with Scud missile attacks on Saudi Arabia and Israel in an attempt to draw Israel into the war and produce a wider regional conflict. This failed to occur, and within days the U.S.-led coalition had complete air superiority. The coalition fought off a small Iraqi invasion of Saudi Arabia on January 29 and on February 24 launched a full-scale ground invasion of Kuwait. Iraqi resistance was weak, and within days the Iraqis surrendered unconditionally. A formal cease-fire was declared on March 3, 1991.

In the wake of the Iraqi defeat, the Shiite community in the south and the Kurds in the north mounted large-scale rebellions, but without foreign assistance they soon faltered and began to suffer brutal reprisals. The coalition forces continued to occupy southern Iraq until May 1991, and in the north they set up safe havens for the Kurds. These lines of contact between the coalition forces and the Iraqi army produced tensions that occasionally flared into armed confrontation.

The number of fatalities was estimated at between 50,000 and 100,000; 200 coalition soldiers were killed. After the conflict Iraq continued to defy the United States and the United Nations, prompting continued UN sanctions and military presence in the Gulf region (*see* conflicts 6.62; 6.64).

References

Dannreuther, R. 1992. *The Gulf Conflict: A Political and Strategic Analysis.* Adelphi Papers #264. London: Brassey's.

Kettle, T.J., and S. Dowrick. 1991. *After the Gulf War: For Peace in the Middle East.* Leichhardt, New South Wales, Australia: Pluto Press.

Renshon, S.A. 1993. *The Political Psychology of the Gulf War: Leaders, Publics, and the Process of Conflict.* Pittsburgh: University of Pittsburgh Press.

Saikal, A., and R. King. 1991. *The Gulf Crisis: Testing a New World Order.* Working Paper #233. Canberra: Strategic and Defence Studies Center, Australian National University.

Tillema, H.K. 1991. *International Armed Conflict Since 1945: A Bibliographic Handbook of Wars and Military Interventions.* Boulder: Westview.

Wood, J. 1992. *Mobilization: The Gulf War in Retrospective.* Working Paper #250. Canberra: Strategic and Defence Studies Center, Australian National University.

6.59 Iran–United Arab Emirates/Egypt: Abu Musa and Tunb Islands Territorial Dispute
April 1992

The conflict over the Abu Musa and Tunb islands in the Persian Gulf had simmered between Iran and the United Arab Emirates (UAE) for years. In 1971 Iran seized the smaller Tunb islands despite competing ownership claims (*see* conflict 6.31). In April 1992 Iran invaded and seized the island of Abu Musa and in August declared an air-exclusion zone over the area, threatening to shoot down any foreign planes. Many nations in the region condemned the invasion, which they saw as a threat to shipping lanes and their own security because of the islands' strategic location in the Gulf.

The conflict had potential for escalation when Russia announced it would defend the UAE in the event of any aggression. Mediation and negotiation in September 1992 failed to resolve the crisis, and pressures increased again when Iran installed pads for Silkworm surface-to-surface missiles on the islands. By late 1992, however, Iran was beginning to make peace moves in an attempt to repair relations with the UAE. The dispute remains unresolved and the source of potential future conflict.

References

Abdullah, M. 1978. *The United Arab Emirates: A Modern History.* London: Croom Helm.

Abir, M. 1974. *Oil, Power, and Politics: Conflict in Arabia, the Red Sea, and the Gulf.* London: F. Cass.

Alkim, H.H. 1989. *The Foreign Policy of the United Arab Emirates.* London: Saqi.

Amirahmadi, H., and N. Entessar, eds. 1993. *Iran and the Arab World.* New York: St. Martin's.

Day, A., ed. 1987. *Border and Territorial Disputes.* 2d edition. Burnt Mill, Harlow (Essex), England: Longman.

Hashim, A. 1995. *The Crisis of the Iranian State: Domestic, Foreign, and Security Policies in Post-Khomeini Iran.* Oxford: Oxford University Press.

Ramazani, R.K. 1986. *Revolutionary Iran: Challenge and Response in the Middle East.* Baltimore: Johns Hopkins University Press.

6.60 Saudi Arabia–Qatar: Post–Gulf War Tensions and Border Incidents
September–October 1992

In the months leading up to this conflict, relations between Saudi Arabia and Qatar became strained primarily because Qatar had signed agreements with Iran, which had refused to join the anti-Iraq coalition in the Gulf War (*see* conflict 6.58). Qatar was also alarmed by Saudi preparations for building military installations on its side of the border.

The increased tension led to an incident on September 30, 1992, which caused three fatalities. Qatar claimed Saudi troops had attacked one of its border posts. As a result, Qatar suspended a 1965 border agreement with Saudi Arabia. Pressures mounted in October when Qatar claimed that Saudi forces had launched further attacks. Iran expressed support for Qatar, and Qatar withdrew from the joint Persian Gulf security force. Tensions eased after frantic mediation attempts by other Arab states, including Egypt, Kuwait, Morocco, Oman, and the United Arab Emirates. Direct talks then resulted in an agreement to withdraw forces and renew friendship.

References

Abir, M. 1974. *Oil, Power, and Politics: Conflict in Arabia, the Red Sea, and the Gulf.* London: F. Cass.

Cyrsal, J. 1990. *Oil and Politics in the Gulf: Rulers and Merchants in Kuwait and Qatar.* Cambridge: Cambridge University Press.

Day, A., ed. 1987. *Border and Territorial Disputes.* 2d edition. Burnt Mill, Harlow (Essex), England: Longman.

Halliday, F. 1974. *Arabia Without Sultans: A Political Survey of Instability in the Arab World.* New York: Random House.

6.61 Egypt–Sudan: Territorial/Resource Dispute and Halaib Dispute
December 1992

Relations between Egypt and Sudan had been tense since Sudan's adoption of a more militant style of Islamic fundamentalist government. Egypt was trying to contain a deadly fundamentalist rebellion at home. The Halaib, a largely empty desert triangle on the border between Egypt and Sudan, was potentially rich in oil and minerals and had been a source of friction and conflict since before the turn of the century. An incident took place on the border in April 1991, and on December 9, 1992, Sudan accused Egypt of increasing its troop strength in the area. Sudan lodged a complaint with the United Nations that Egypt had invaded Sudanese territory with more than 600 troops. Egypt continued to build up its troops in the area until by February 1993 it had more 2,000 troops stationed there.

Both sides claimed the other had training camps for dissidents and was engaging in destabilizing tactics. Tensions were raised in April and May 1993 when Sudan said it would mobilize to counter Egyptian provocation. An all-out border war was feared. Some negotiations were broached, and the fighting eased after this time. But the issues of border demarcation and Sudanese support for Islamic fundamentalist forces remained unresolved, leaving room for future conflict.

References

Day, A., ed. 1987. *Border and Territorial Disputes.* 2d edition. Burnt Mill, Harlow (Essex), England: Longman.

Drysdale, A., and G.H. Blake. 1985. *The Middle East and North Africa: A Political Geography.* New York: Oxford University Press.

Harris, L.C., ed. 1988. *Egypt: Internal Challenges and Regional Stability.* London: Routledge and Kegan Paul.

Long, D.E., and B. Reich, eds. 1980. *The Government and Politics of the Middle East and North Africa.* Boulder: Westview.

McDermott, A. 1988. *Egypt from Nasser to Mubarak: A Flawed Revolution.* London: Croom Helm.

6.62 Iraq–Coalition Forces: Post–Gulf War Incidents December 1992–July 1993

Following Iraq's defeat in the Gulf War in February 1991, coalition forces established air-exclusion or "no fly" zones and safe havens for the Kurds (*see* conflict 6.58). Iraq responded to this imposition on its sovereignty with a series of provocations. In April 1991 the UN Security Council passed Resolution 688, demanding that Iraqi leader Saddam Hussein end the repression of the Kurds and Iraqi civilians. The Iraqi military continued bombing and strafing attacks against the Shiite Muslims in southern Iraq during 1991. By 1992 it appeared obvious that Saddam Hussein was not going to comply with the UN resolution. In December 1992 Iraqi planes entered the no-fly zone, and, in a confrontation with coalition jet fighters, an Iraqi MiG-25 was shot down. In response to the downing of the aircraft, Iraq installed antiaircraft missiles inside the exclusion zone, but was forced to remove them in January 1993 following coalition threats. Also in January Iraqi troops invaded Kuwaiti territory in an attempt to retrieve weapons.

The coalition, made up of four UN allies—France, Russia, the United Kingdom, and the United States, agreed on January 6, 1993, to enforce UNSCR 688. On January 13, 114 coalition jet fighters attacked missile sites and air defense systems in southern Iraq after Iraqi officials banned UN flights carrying weapons inspectors. Later in January another MiG was shot down, and forty cruise missiles were launched at the Iraqi nuclear weapons facility at Zafaraniych. Further armed incidents took place until July. The most serious of these was a missile attack on Iraqi intelligence headquarters in Baghdad after an Iraqi plot to assassinate former U.S. president George H.W. Bush was uncovered. Typically, Iraqi provocations led to swift retaliation by coalition forces.

Although the number of fatalities was relatively low throughout the conflict, tensions were high. Despite many negotiations between senior UN officials and Tariq Aziz, the Iraqi foreign minister, little was resolved. After July the conflict subsided somewhat, until another crisis was precipitated in October 1994 (*see* conflict 6.64).

References

Dannreuther, R. 1992. *The Gulf Conflict: A Political and Strategic Analysis.* Adelphi Papers #264. London: Brassey's.

Global Security. 2004. "Operation Southern Watch": http://www.globalsecurity.org/military/ops/southern_watch.htm.

Kettle, T.J., and S. Dowrick. 1991. *After the Gulf War: For Peace in the Middle East.* Leichhardt, New South Wales, Australia: Pluto Press.

Miller, J., and L. Mylroie. 1990. *Saddam Hussein and the Crisis in the Gulf.* New York: Times Books.

Renshon, S.A. 1993. *The Political Psychology of the Gulf War: Leaders, Publics, and the Process of Conflict.* Pittsburgh: University of Pittsburgh Press.

Saikal, A., and R. King. 1991. *The Gulf Crisis: Testing a New World Order.* Working Paper #233. Canberra: Strategic and Defence Studies Center, Australian National University.

Wood, J. 1992. *Mobilization: The Gulf War in Retrospective.* Working Paper #250. Canberra: Strategic and Defence Studies Center, Australian National University.

6.63 Yemen: Unification Difficulties and Yemen Civil War November 1993–July 1994

Yemen was originally two separate states, and both experienced civil conflict. Since the 1960s North Yemen and South Yemen also had several violent clashes, which drew international intervention (*see* conflicts 6.21; 6.30; 6.32; 6.46). Talks aimed at unifying the two states began in the 1980s, proving successful toward the end of the decade. But the unification process was plagued with difficulties: the armies and police forces of both sides were never fully integrated, and the respective leaders, President Ali Abdullah Saleh in the north and Vice President Ali Salem al-Beidh in the south, maintained a turbulent relationship. These problems, plus the discovery of oil deposits in the south, which would have made seceding an economically viable option, led to a serious breakdown in north-south relations in 1993.

The crisis began with the vice president's failure to take up his government post in Sanaa, the northern capital. As the feud developed, both sides began to move troops into position in November 1993, and a number of armed clashes occurred. The conflict escalated in January 1994, with the political killings of southern leaders. The first serious clashes between the two armies erupted in February, but frantic mediation by Middle East leaders led to a cease-fire and the beginnings of a settlement. An uneasy peace took hold in March. In late April, however, fighting began in earnest with large-scale battles leaving hundreds dead. The south formally seceded on May 21, receiving a measure of support for their cause from the United Arab Emirates and Saudi Arabia, traditional allies of the south. But the south was losing ground, and in July Aden fell to northern forces, and southern leaders were forced to flee. The war was over; it was a complete northern victory.

The conflict caused thousands of fatalities, and, despite many mediation attempts by Middle Eastern nations and the United States, these failed to reunite the two estranged leaders. Yemen remained united at the end of 1995 and was rebuilding. Exiled southern leaders had formed no serious opposition movement, and the regime seemed secure. With the secessionist conflict ended, Saudi Arabia and Yemen agreed to border delimitation in 2000.

References

Bidwell, R. 1983. *The Two Yemens.* New York: Longman.

Central Intelligence Agency. *World Factbook.* Yemen: http://www.cia.gov/cia/publications/factbook/geos/ym.html.

Halliday, F. 1990. *Revolution and Foreign Policy: The Case of South Yemen, 1967–1987.* New York: Cambridge University Press.

Ismael, T. Y., and J. Ismael. 1986. *The People's Democratic Republic of Yemen: Politics, Economics, and Society—The Politics of Socialist Transformation.* Boulder: Lynne Rienner.

Kostiner, J. 1984. *The Struggle for South Yemen.* London: Croom Helm.

O'Ballance, E. 1971. *The War in the Yemen.* Hamden, Conn.: Archon.

Peterson, J. 1981. *Conflict in the Yemens and Superpower Involvement.* Washington, D.C.: Center for Contemporary Arab Studies, Georgetown University.

Stookey, R. 1978. *Yemen: The Politics of the Yemen Arab Republic.* Boulder: Westview.

———. 1982. *South Yemen: Marxist Republic in Arabia.* Boulder: Westview.

Wenner, M. 1967. *Modern Yemen, 1918–1966.* Baltimore: Johns Hopkins University Press.

6.64 Iraq–Coalition Forces: Post–Gulf War Tensions and Kuwaiti Border Incidents October 1994

Following its defeat in the Gulf War and confrontation with the coalition forces—France, Russia, the United Kingdom, and the United States—in 1991 and 1993 (*see* conflicts 6.58; 6.62), Iraq provoked a major crisis with the prospect of war in October 1994, when it massed 80,000 troops on the Kuwaiti border in an apparently hostile move. The coalition forces responded by sending massive numbers of troops, aircraft, and a naval task force to the area.

The tension remained extremely high for several weeks, but mediation by Andrei Kosirev, the Russian foreign minister, eventually led to Iraq's official recognition of Kuwait in November 1994. The troops were withdrawn, and the conflict abated. Although no shots were fired, a return to all-out war was a clear possibility given Iraq leader Saddam Hussein's unpredictability and the U.S.-led coalition's determination to contain him (*see* conflict 4.39).

References

Dannreuther, R. 1992. *The Gulf Conflict: A Political and Strategic Analysis.* Adelphi Papers #264. London: Brassey's.

Kettle, T. J., and S. Dowrick. 1991. *After the Gulf War: For Peace in the Middle East.* Leichhardt, New South Wales, Australia: Pluto Press.

Miller, J., and L. Mylroie. 1990. *Saddam Hussein and the Crisis in the Gulf.* New York: Times Books.

Renshon, S. A. 1993. *The Political Psychology of the Gulf War: Leaders, Publics, and the Process of Conflict.* Pittsburgh: University of Pittsburgh Press.

Saikal, A., and R. King. 1991. *The Gulf Crisis: Testing a New World Order.* Working Paper #233. Canberra: Strategic and Defence Studies Center, Australian National University.

Wood, J. 1992. *Mobilization: The Gulf War in Retrospective.* Working Paper #250. Canberra: Strategic and Defence Studies Center, Australian National University.

6.65 Saudi Arabia–Yemen: Post–Gulf War Border Conflict December 1994

Some ill-defined border areas between Saudi Arabia and Yemen had been a source of some friction between the two countries (*see* conflicts 6.27; 6.48). Yemen's support for Iraq during the Gulf War (1990–1991) further exacerbated these tensions (*see* conflict 6.58). A dispute over potentially oil-rich territory led to strains in March 1992, but no military confrontation. Oil exploration had been suspended, and several rounds of unsuccessful negotiations followed.

In early December 1994, however, Yemen accused Saudi Arabia of erecting observation posts and building roads in the disputed areas. On December 7 a clash between border troops left three Yemeni officers dead. Although tensions remained high for a while, the dispute lapsed, with both sides deciding to engage in negotiations rather than violent confrontation.

References

Bidwell, R. 1983. *The Two Yemens.* New York: Longman.

Ismael, T. Y., and J. Ismael. 1986. *The People's Democratic Republic of Yemen: Politics, Economics, and Society—The Politics of Socialist Transformation.* Boulder: Lynne Rienner.

Kostiner, J. 1984. *The Struggle for South Yemen.* London: Croom Helm.

O'Ballance, E. 1971. *The War in the Yemen.* Hamden, Conn.: Archon.

Stookey, R. 1978. *Yemen: The Politics of the Yemen Arab Republic.* Boulder: Westview.

6.66 Iran–Iraq: Regional Rivalry and Border Incidents September 1997

In September 1997, eight Iranian warplanes launched an air attack against targets inside Iraq, allegedly in response to cross-border incursions and terrorist activities by an Iraq-based Iranian opposition group, the Mujahedeen-e Khalq. No casualties occurred.

Mujahedeen-e Khalq uses Iraq as a base from which to attack Iran and has several camps equipped with tanks, heavy guns, and helicopter gunships near the border. The group advocates the armed overthrow of the clergy-dominated government in Tehran. Mujahedeen-e Khalq had intensified its cross-border raids and attacks inside Iran in the year preceding the attack. Iraq protested to the United Nations over the attacks, claiming Iran had violated "no-fly zones." According to the Council on Foreign Relations, Mujahedeen-e Khalq is still active and "was added to the U.S. State Department's list of foreign terrorist groups in 1997 and to the European Union's terrorist list in 2002 because its attacks have often killed civilians." The *New York Times* reported that many Iranians view the organization "as toxic, if not more so, than the ruling clerics." Iran and Iraq fought a ruinous war from 1980 to 1989, and relations between the two countries remain tense (*see* conflict 6.50).

References

Council on Foreign Relations. http://cfrterrorism.org/home/; http://cfrterrorism.org/groups/mujahedeen2.html#Q14.

Dow Jones News. September 29, 1997.

Reuters Online. September 29, 1997.

6.67 Israel–Syria: Border Clashes February 2001–Ongoing

This conflict originated from clashes between Israel and the militant Islamic group Hezbollah that Israel believes is controlled by Syria (*see* conflicts 6.52; 6.53). Hezbollah considers the Shebaa Farms region to be part of Lebanese territory and is trying to liberate it. Israel, however, considers the area, which it took from the Syrians along with other parts of the Golan Heights during the 1967 Six-Day War (*see* conflict 6.25), to be its territory. On February 16, 2001, Hezbollah guerrillas entered Israel near the Golan Heights and attacked an Israeli military outpost at the Shebaa Farms with anti-tank missiles, killing one Israeli soldier and injuring two others. Israeli forces responded with mortar fire but did not cause any casualties because the guerrillas retreated back across the border to Syria. Following this attack, on April 15 Israeli warplanes bombed a Syrian radar station located in Lebanon, killing three Syrian soldiers and wounding four others.

Hezbollah forces again attacked the Shebaa Farms on June 29, 2001, injuring two Israeli soldiers. Israel responded by bombing another Syrian radar station in Lebanon on July 1, wounding three Syrian and one Lebanese soldier. A three-week period of sporadic exchanges between Hezbollah forces and the Israeli Defense Force (IDF) began on October 3. It followed the by now familiar pattern of Hezbollah attacks on the Shebaa Farms and IDF reprisal attacks on Hezbollah positions in southern Lebanon, notably against the near-by border town of Kfar Shouba. Another set of attacks and counterattacks occurred in January 2002, and in April almost daily exchanges took place, with Israel asserting that both Syria and Iran shared some of the responsibility—Syria for giving what Israel considered to be tacit approval to attack and Iran for its influence and urging on of Hezbollah forces.

As the fighting continued, U.S. secretary of state Colin Powell met with Syrian president Bashar Assad to find a way to peace and to relay an Israeli warning regarding the daily strikes against the Shebaa Farms in northern Israel. During his trip Powell had also met with Israeli prime minister Ariel Sharon and Yasser Arafat, leader of the Palestine Liberation Organization. After almost two weeks of calm, Hezbollah again attacked Israeli positions in the Shebaa Farms, and again Israel responded with artillery fire.

On June 10, 2002, as a good-will gesture Israel released Mohammed Ali al-Barzawi, a Hezbollah captive who had been in prison for fifteen years. A new wave of border clashes began on August 29 around the Shebaa Farms with more Israeli retaliatory strikes against Hezbollah positions in Lebanon. One Israeli soldier was reported dead. Israeli soldiers attacked two Syrian soldiers attempting to infiltrate the Golan Heights area January 10, 2003, killing one and capturing another. An hour later Syria responded by opening fire on Israeli forces. Apparently hoping to avoid escalating the crisis further, Israel did not respond and later turned over the dead and the captured Syrian soldiers to the United Nations for transfer to Syria. Both sides accused the other of initiating the hostilities.

References

Asher Kaufman, A. "Who Owns the Shebaa Farms? Chronicle of a Territorial Dispute." *Middle East Journal* 56 (autumn 2002): 576–597.

"Chronology." *Middle East Journal* 56 (spring 2002): 297–322.

Keesing's Record of World Events: 44026, 44130, 44283, 45216.

Lee, R. A. 2002. *New and Recent Wars and Conflicts of the World.* http://www.historyguy.com/current_conflicts/index.htm (accessed April 30, 2003).

United Press International. October 3, 2001; April 2, 8, 10, 22, 25, 26, 2002; June 10, 2002; August 29, 2002. www.infotrac.com (downloaded June 26, 2003).

Xinhau News Agency. July 1, 2001; January 23, 2002; April 22, 2002. www.infotrac.com (downloaded June 26, 2003).

Appendix A
Countries and Their Regions

This is an alphabetical list of all the countries and the regions in which they appear. Each regional section also has a complete list of its countries.

Country	Region
Afghanistan	Southwest Asia
Albania	Europe
Algeria	Africa
American Samoa	East Asia and the Pacific
Andorra	Europe
Angola	Africa
Antigua and Barbuda	Americas
Argentina	Americas
Armenia	Europe
Aruba	Americas
Australia	East Asia and the Pacific
Austria	Europe
Azerbaijan	Europe
Bahamas	Americas
Bahrain	Middle East
Bangladesh	Southwest Asia
Barbados	Americas
Belarus	Europe
Belgium	Europe
Belize	Americas
Benin	Africa
Bermuda	Americas
Bhutan	Southwest Asia
Bolivia	Americas
Bosnia and Herzegovina	Europe
Botswana	Africa
Brazil	Americas
Brunei	East Asia and the Pacific
Bulgaria	Europe
Burkina Faso	Africa
Burma (Myanmar)	East Asia and the Pacific
Burundi	Africa
Cambodia (Kampuchea)	East Asia and the Pacific
Cameroon	Africa
Canada	Americas
Cape Verde	Africa
Central African Republic	Africa
Chad	Africa
Chile	Americas
China (including Hong Kong, Macau, and Tibet)	East Asia and the Pacific
Colombia	Americas
Comoros	Africa
Congo	Africa
Cook Islands	East Asia and the Pacific
Costa Rica	Americas
Croatia	Europe
Cuba	Americas
Cyprus	Europe
Czech Republic	Europe
Democratic Republic of the Congo	Africa
Denmark	Europe
Djibouti	Africa
Dominica	Americas
Dominican Republic	Americas
East Timor	East Asia and the Pacific
Ecuador	Americas
Egypt	Middle East
El Salvador	Americas
Equatorial Guinea	Africa
Eritrea	Africa
Estonia	Europe
Ethiopia	Africa
Falkland Islands	Americas
Federated States of Micronesia	East Asia and the Pacific
Fiji	East Asia and the Pacific
Finland	Europe
France	Europe
French Guiana	Americas
Gabon	Africa
Gambia	Africa
Georgia	Europe
Germany	Europe
Ghana	Africa

Country	Region
Greece	Europe
Grenada	Americas
Guatemala	Americas
Guinea	Africa
Guinea-Bissau	Africa
Guyana	Americas
Haiti	Americas
Honduras	Americas
Hungary	Europe
Iceland	Europe
India	Southwest Asia
Indonesia	East Asia and the Pacific
Iran	Middle East
Iraq	Middle East
Ireland	Europe
Israel	Middle East
Italy	Europe
Ivory Coast	Africa
Jamaica	Americas
Japan	East Asia and the Pacific
Jordan	Middle East
Kazakhstan	Southwest Asia
Kenya	Africa
Kiribati	East Asia and the Pacific
Kuwait	Middle East
Kyrgyzstan	Southwest Asia
Laos	East Asia and the Pacific
Latvia	Europe
Lebanon	Middle East
Lesotho	Africa
Liberia	Africa
Libya	Africa
Liechtenstein	Europe
Lithuania	Europe
Luxembourg	Europe
Macedonia, Former Yugoslav Republic of	Europe
Madagascar	Africa
Malawi	Africa
Malaysia	East Asia and the Pacific
Maldives	Southwest Asia
Mali	Africa
Malta	Europe
Marshall Islands	East Asia and the Pacific
Mauritania	Africa
Mauritius	Africa
Mexico	Americas
Moldova	Europe
Monaco	Europe
Mongolia	Southwest Asia
Montserrat	Americas
Morocco	Africa
Mozambique	Africa
Namibia	Africa
Nauru	East Asia and the Pacific
Nepal	Southwest Asia
Netherlands, The	Europe
New Zealand	East Asia and the Pacific
Nicaragua	Americas
Niger	Africa
Nigeria	Africa
Niue	East Asia and the Pacific
North Korea (Democratic People's Republic of Korea)	East Asia and the Pacific
Norway	Europe
Oman	Middle East
Pakistan	Southwest Asia
Palau	East Asia and the Pacific
Palestine	Middle East
Panama	Americas
Papua New Guinea	East Asia and the Pacific
Paraguay	Americas
Peru	Americas
Philippines, The	East Asia and the Pacific
Poland	Europe
Portugal	Europe
Puerto Rico	Americas
Qatar	Middle East
Romania	Europe
Russian Federation (including the Caucasus region comprising Chechnya, Dagestan, Ingushetia, Kabardino-Balkaria, Karachay-Cherkessia, and North Ossetia)	Europe
Rwanda	Africa
Saint Kitts and Nevis	Americas
Saint Lucia	Americas
Saint Vincent and the Grenadines	Americas
Samoa	East Asia and the Pacific
San Marino	Europe
São Tomé and Principe	Africa
Saudi Arabia	Middle East
Senegal	Africa

Country	Region
Seychelles	Africa
Sierra Leone	Africa
Singapore	East Asia and the Pacific
Slovakia	Europe
Slovenia	Europe
Solomon Islands	East Asia and the Pacific
Somalia	Africa
South Africa	Africa
South Korea (Republic of Korea)	East Asia and the Pacific
Spain	Europe
Spratly Islands	East Asia and the Pacific
Sri Lanka	Southwest Asia
Sudan	Africa
Suriname	Americas
Swaziland	Africa
Sweden	Europe
Switzerland	Europe
Syria	Middle East
Taiwan	East Asia and the Pacific
Tajikistan	Southwest Asia
Tanzania	Africa
Thailand	East Asia and the Pacific
Togo	Africa
Tokelau	East Asia and the Pacific
Tonga	East Asia and the Pacific
Trinidad and Tobago	Americas
Tunisia	Africa
Turkey	Europe
Turkmenistan	Southwest Asia
Tuvalu	East Asia and the Pacific
Uganda	Africa
Ukraine	Europe
United Arab Emirates	Middle East
United Kingdom	Europe
United States of America	Americas
Uruguay	Americas
Uzbekistan	Southwest Asia
Vanuatu	East Asia and the Pacific
Vatican, The	Europe
Venezuela	Americas
Vietnam	East Asia and the Pacific
Virgin Islands	Americas
Western Sahara	Africa
Yemen	Middle East
Yugoslavia, Federal Republic of (now Serbia and Montenegro)	Europe
Zambia	Africa
Zimbabwe	Africa

Appendix B
Chronology of Regional Conflicts

The chronological order of conflicts has been determined first by start date and then by length of conflict, with more general dates (for example, 1945) preceding more specific ones (for example, August 1945).

Placement of conflicts with "Early," "Mid-," or "Late" in their start and/or end dates is based on surrounding conflicts that include months.

Dates	Conflict	Conflict Number	Page
1945–1948	India: Civil War, Independence, and Partition	4.1	207
1945–1949	China: Civil War	3.1	163
1945–1949	Greece: Antimonarchist Communist Insurgency and Civil War	5.1	236
1945–December 1946	France–Levant (Syria/Lebanon): Independence Crisis	6.1	265
August 1945–October 1947	USSR–Iran: Pro-Communist Campaign of Secession and Azerbaijan/Kurdistan Crisis	6.2	265
Late 1945–November 1949	The Netherlands–The Dutch East Indies: Indonesian Nationalism and War of Independence	3.2	164
December 1945–July 1954	France–Indochina: Independence Struggle	3.3	165
May 1946–December 1949	Albania–United Kingdom: Corfu Channel Dispute	5.2	237
August 1946	Yugoslavia–United States: Cold War Air Incidents	5.3	237
Early 1947–December 1951	Dominican Republic–Haiti/Cuba: Regional Aggression	2.1	123
March–August 1947	Madagascar–France: Nationalist Rebellion	1.1	60
October 1947–January 1949	Pakistan–India: Postpartition Separatism, First Kashmir War, and India-Pakistan Rivalry	4.2	207
Early 1948–December 1954	USSR–Yugoslavia: Ideological Rift	5.4	238
March–April 1948	Costa Rica: Anticorruption Military Insurgency and Civil War	2.2	125
May 1948–January 1949	Israel: British Decolonization, Arab–Israeli Territorial Dispute, and War of Independence	6.3	266
June 1948–May 1949	USSR–The Western Allies: The Berlin Airlift Crisis	5.5	238
June 1948–July 1960	United Kingdom–Malaya and Singapore: Anti-British Communist Insurgency and the Malayan Emergency	3.4	165
July–September 1948	India–Hyderabad: Postpartition Separatist Violence and Secession Attempt	4.3	208
August 1948–1954	Burma: Kuomintang/People's Liberation Army Cross-Border Conflict	3.5	166
December 1948–February 1949	Nicaragua–Costa Rica: Border Conflict	2.3	125
January 1949–Ongoing	Burma (Myanmar): Karen Separatist Insurgency and Civil War	3.6	167
May–August 1949	Syria–Lebanon: Syrian Exiles Dispute	6.4	266
July 1949–December 1950	Eritrea–Ethiopia: Eritrean Nationalism and Agitation for Independence	1.2	60
August 1949	Afghanistan–Pakistan: Postindependence Pathan Border Conflict	4.4	208

Africa = 1.1–1.97, Americas = 2.1–2.45, Asia: East Asia and the Pacific = 3.1–3.65, Asia: Southwest Asia = 4.1–4.39, Europe = 5.1–5.30, Middle East = 6.1–6.67.

Dates	Conflict	Conflict Number	Page
October 1949–June 1953	China–Taiwan: Communist-Nationalist Conflict in the Straits of Formosa	3.7	168
April–October 1950	United States–USSR: Cold War Air Incidents	3.8	168
June–October 1950	Afghanistan–Pakistan: The Pathan Territorial Conflict	4.5	209
June 1950–July 1953	United States–North Korea: Cold War Territorial Dispute and the Korean War	3.9	169
October 1950–May 1951	China–Tibet: Tibetan Autonomy Dispute	4.6	209
April–May 1951	Syria–Israel: Lake Tiberias/Huleh Resource Dispute	6.5	267
January 1952–January 1956	Egypt–United Kingdom: Suez Canal Zone Sovereignty Dispute	6.6	268
January 1952–March 1956	Tunisia: Tunisian Independence and African Nationalism	1.3	61
March 1952–October 1954	Italy–Yugoslavia: Cold War and Trieste Territorial Dispute	5.6	239
July–August 1952	China–Portugal: The Macao Territorial Conflict	3.10	169
July 1952–August 1993	Argentina–Chile: The Beagle Channel Border Dispute	2.4	126
August 1952–October 1955	Saudi Arabia–Oman/United Kingdom: The Buraymī Oasis Resource Dispute	6.7	268
August 1952–December 1963	Kenya–United Kingdom: Anticolonial Tribal Uprising and Mau Mau Revolt	1.4	61
October 1952–July 1956	USSR–United States: Cold War Air Incidents	3.11	170
January 1953–December 1954	Israel–Jordan: West Bank Border Conflict	6.8	269
Early 1953–May 1975	Cambodia–Siam (Thailand): Border Conflict and the Occupation of the Temple of Preah Vhear	3.12	170
April 1954–April 1955	China–United States/Taiwan: The Quemoy Confrontation	3.13	171
June 1954–Ongoing	Guatemala: Civil War and Insurgency	2.5	128
November 1954–March 1962	Algeria: The Fight for Independence	1.5	62
January 1955	Nicaragua–Costa Rica: Exiles Invasion Attempt	2.6	129
March 1955–1957	Turkey–Syria: Border Incidents	6.9	269
April 1955–February 1959	Cyprus–United Kingdom: Intercommunal Violence and the Enosis Movement	5.7	239
October–December 1955	Syria–Israel: Lake Tiberias Dispute	6.10	270
1956–1960	Yemen–United Kingdom: Aden Conflict	6.11	270
February 1956–January 1962	Dominican Republic–Cuba/Venezuela: Dominican Republic Aggression and Exiles Conflict	2.7	129
March 1956–September 1965	China–Tibet: Incorporation Struggle	4.7	210
June–August 1956	Taiwan–South Vietnam: The Paracel Islands Dispute	3.14	172
July 1956–January 1958	Israel–Jordan: Mt. Scopus Conflict	6.12	271
October 1956	USSR–Poland: Polish October	5.8	240
October–November 1956	Egypt–United Kingdom/France: Sovereignty Dispute and Suez War	6.13	271
October–December 1956	USSR–Hungary: Anti-Communist Revolt, Soviet Invasion, and the Hungarian Uprising of 1956	5.9	240
December 1956–January 1959	Cuba: Communist Revolution and Cuban Civil War	2.8	131
April–June 1957	Nicaragua–Honduras: Boundary Dispute and Mocoran Seizure	2.9	131
July 1957–February 1958	Israel–Syria: Arab–Israeli Territorial Dispute over the Golan Heights	6.14	272
November 1957–April 1958	Morocco–Spain: Postindependence Autonomy and the Sahara Conflict	1.6	62
1958–May 1959	Panama: Cuban-Backed Invasion and Panama Revolutionaries Conflict	2.10	132
February 1958	Egypt–Sudan: Postindependence Territorial Dispute	6.15	272

Africa = 1.1–1.97, Americas = 2.1–2.45, Asia: East Asia and the Pacific = 3.1–3.65, Asia: Southwest Asia = 4.1–4.39, Europe = 5.1–5.30, Middle East = 6.1–6.67.

Dates	Conflict	Conflict Number	Page
February–May 1958	France–Tunisia: Postindependence Autonomy and Military Bases Conflict	1.7	63
March 1958–September 1959	India–Pakistan: Postpartition Border Tension and the Surma River Incidents	4.8	210
May 1958–June 1959	Lebanon: Internal Strife and the First Lebanese Civil War	6.16	273
July–December 1958	China–United States/Taiwan: Communist-Nationalist Territorial Dispute and Bombardment of the Quemoy Islands	3.15	172
December 1958–September 1959	Guatemala–Mexico: Mexican Shrimp Boat Incident	2.11	132
December 1958–1962	Laos: Political Anarchy and the First Laotian Civil War	3.16	173
February–August 1959	France–Tunisia: French–Algerian Border Incidents	1.8	63
Early 1959–December 1961	Paraguay–Argentina: Paraguayan Exiles Conflict	2.12	133
March–April 1959	Syria–Iraq: Syrian-Backed Putsch, Government Suppression, and Mosul Revolt	6.17	273
June 1959–July 1960	China–Nepal: Boundary Dispute	4.9	211
August 1959	Cuba–Haiti: Cuban-Sponsored Military Invasion and Haitian Exiles Conflict	2.13	133
August 1959–February 1960	China–India: Sino-Indian Antagonism and the McMahon Line Boundary Dispute	4.10	211
Mid-1960–February 1963	Mauritania–Mali: Hodh Region Conflict	1.9	63
July 1960–Mid-1964	Congo (Zaire): Secession, Anarchy, Civil War, and the Belgian Congo Crisis	1.10	64
September 1960–May 1963	Afghanistan–Pakistan: Boundary Dispute and Pathan Conflict	4.11	211
December 1960–May 1975	North Vietnam–South Vietnam/United States: Communist Vietcong Insurgency, Anti-Communist U.S. Military Intervention, and Civil War	3.17	173
1961–July 1975	The African Territories–Portugal: African Nationalism and Independence Struggle	1.11	65
March 1961–1966	Kurds–Iraq: Kurdish Secession Attempt	6.18	274
April–May 1961	United States–Cuba: Anti-Castro Military Invasion—The Bay of Pigs	2.14	134
June 1961–February 1962	Iraq–Kuwait: Territorial Dispute and the Kuwaiti Independence Crisis	6.19	274
July–September 1961	Tunisia–France: Postindependence Autonomy Dispute in Bizerte	1.12	65
July–November 1961	USSR–United States: Cold War Dispute and the Berlin Wall	5.10	241
December 1961	India–Portugal: Anti-Portuguese Territorial Dispute in Goa	4.12	212
1962–November 1965	Indonesia–Malaysia: Separatist Civil Disturbances and the Borneo Conflict	3.18	174
January–August 1962	Indonesia–The Netherlands: West Irian Administration Dispute and Separatist Insurgency	3.19	175
February 1962–August 1963	Syria–Israel: Arab–Israeli Territorial Dispute over Lake Tiberias	6.20	275
February 1962–June 1970	Venezuela–Guyana (UK): Essequibo River Dispute	2.15	134
March–December 1962	China–Taiwan: CCP-KMT Territorial Dispute and Invasion Threat	3.20	175
March 1962–1964	Chile–Bolivia: Lauca River Dam Dispute	2.16	135
April–November 1962	Nepal–India: Pro-Democratic Rebellion and Border Incidents	4.13	212
September–November 1962	United States–USSR: Cold War Dispute and the Cuban Missile Crisis	2.17	136

Africa = 1.1–1.97, Americas = 2.1–2.45, Asia: East Asia and the Pacific = 3.1–3.65, Asia: Southwest Asia = 4.1–4.39, Europe = 5.1–5.30, Middle East = 6.1–6.67.

Dates	Conflict	Conflict Number	Page
September 1962–October 1967	North Yemen: Civil War and Royalist Rebellion	6.21	275
October–November 1962	India–China: Sino-Indian Wars and McMahon Line Border Dispute	4.14	212
November 1962–September 1967	Somalia–Kenya/Ethiopia: Somali Expansionism and Separatist Insurgency	1.13	66
March 1963–September 1969	China–USSR: Territorial Dispute over Damansky Island	4.15	213
April–September 1963	Haiti–Dominican Republic: Exiles Asylum and Invasion Attempt	2.18	137
September 1963–March 1972	Sudan: Southern Separatism, Anya-Nya Terrorism, and the First Sudan Civil War	1.14	66
October 1963–February 1964	Morocco–Algeria: Territorial Dispute and the Tindouf War	1.15	67
November 1963–May 1967	Cuba–Venezuela: Terrrorism and Invasion Attempt	2.19	138
December 1963–June 1965	Niger–Dahomey (Benin): Lete Island Dispute	1.16	68
December 1963–November 1967	Cyprus: Intercommunal Violence and Civil War	5.11	242
January–March 1964	Somalia–Ethiopia: Somali Expansionism, Separatist Guerrilla Fighting, and the First Ogaden War	1.17	68
January–April 1964	Panama–United States: Sovereignty Dispute and the Flag Riots	2.20	139
January 1964–January 1965	Rwanda–Burundi: Postindependence Ethnic Violence Between the Hutu and Tutsi	1.18	69
February 1964	France–Gabon: Military Putsch, French Military Intervention, and Aubame's Coup	1.19	69
March–December 1964	South Vietnam–Cambodia: Anti-Vietminh Cross-Border Raids	3.21	176
April 1964–December 1966	North Vietnam–Laos: Political Anarchy and the Second Laotian Civil War	3.22	176
June 1964–June 1966	Ghana–Upper Volta: Ghanaian Border Dispute	1.20	69
June 1964–July 1966	Syria–Israel: Arab–Israeli Dispute and Border Incidents	6.22	276
August 1964–May 1975	North Vietnam–The United States: The Vietnam War	3.23	177
December 1964–April 1966	Israel–Jordan: Arab–Israeli Dispute and Border Incidents	6.23	276
1965–1970	India–Pakistan: Border Skirmishes	4.16	213
1965–May 1993	Eritrea–Ethiopia: Eritrean Nationalism and War of Secession	1.21	70
1965–Ongoing	Irian Jaya–Indonesia: Territorial Dispute and Secession Insurgency	3.24	178
1965–Ongoing	Colombia: Banditry and Leftist Guerrilla Insurgency	2.21	139
January–May 1965	Ghana–Togo: Ghanaian Expansionism and Border Incidents	1.22	71
February–March 1965	Uganda–Congo (Zaire): Rebel Activity and Border Incidents	1.23	71
April 1965–September 1966	United States–Dominican Republic: Civil War, U.S. Military Intervention, and the Constitutionalist Rebellion	2.22	140
Mid-1965–March 1968	North Korea–South Korea: Cold War Dispute and Border Incidents	3.25	179
August–September 1965	India–Pakistan: Territorial Rivalry and the Second Kashmir War	4.17	214
September 1965	China–India: Sino-Indian Wars and McMahon Line Border Incidents	4.18	214
October 1965	Lebanon–Israel: Arab–Israeli Dispute and the Hoûla Raids	6.24	277
November 1965–1972	Chad–Sudan: Internal Strife, Sudanese Intervention, and First Chad Civil War	1.24	71
1966–March 1990	Namibia: Violent Insurrection, War, and Independence Struggle	1.25	72
March–April 1966	Ivory Coast–Guinea: Coup Plot	1.26	72
October–November 1966	Ghana–Guinea: Nkrumah's Ouster and Postcoup Tensions	1.27	73

Africa = 1.1–1.97, Americas = 2.1–2.45, Asia: East Asia and the Pacific = 3.1–3.65, Asia: Southwest Asia = 4.1–4.39, Europe = 5.1–5.30, Middle East = 6.1–6.67.

Dates	Conflict	Conflict Number	Page
November 1966–July 1970	Bolivia: Cuban-Assisted Guerrilla Insurgency	2.23	141
1967–January 1980	Rhodesia: African Nationalism, Guerrilla Warfare, and Zimbabwe's Struggle for Independence	1.28	73
February–September 1967	Guinea–Ivory Coast: Regional Rivalry and Hostage Crisis	1.29	74
June 1967	Israel–Arab States: The Six-Day War	6.25	277
July 1967–January 1970	Nigeria–Biafra: Ethnic and Regional Rivalries, Secession Attempt, and the Biafran Civil War	1.30	74
August 1967–April 1968	Congo (Zaire)–Rwanda: Regional Instability and the Mercenaries Dispute	1.31	75
January–December 1968	North Korea–United States: USS *Pueblo* Seizure	3.26	179
August 1968	USSR–Czechoslovakia: Liberalization Movement, the Prague Spring, and Soviet Military Invasion	5.12	242
October 1968–March 1970	Iraq–Kurds: Kurdish Struggle for Autonomy	6.26	278
January–November 1969	China–Burma: Tribal Conflicts and Border Incidents	3.27	180
July 1969	El Salvador–Honduras: The "Football War" Border Dispute	2.24	141
August 1969–November 1970	Guyana–Suriname: New River Triangle Border Dispute	2.25	142
November 1969–October 1970	North Yemen–Saudi Arabia: Border Conflict	6.27	278
January 1970–April 1975	Cambodia (Kampuchea)–South Vietnam/United States: U.S. Bombing Campaign and Vietnam War	3.28	180
January 1970–Ongoing	Mindanao–The Philippines: Communal Violence, Land Disputes, and Muslim Secessionist Insurgency	3.29	181
February 1970–August 1971	The PLO–Jordan: Coup Attempt	6.28	278
November 1970	Guinea–Portugal: PAIGC Guerrilla Warfare and the Conakry Raids	1.32	75
1971	Iraq–Iran: Border Tensions and the Shatt al-Arab Waterway Dispute	6.29	279
January 1971–October 1972	Uganda–Tanzania: Postcoup Border Clashes	1.33	75
March 1971–February 1974	Bangladesh–Pakistan: Secessionist Warfare and the Bangladesh War of Independence	4.19	215
October 1971–October 1972	North Yemen–South Yemen: Anti-Communist Insurgency and Border Conflict	6.30	279
November 1971	Iran–United Arab Emirates: Tunb Islands Territorial Dispute	6.31	280
November 1971–June 1976	Iceland–United Kingdom, West Germany, and Denmark: The Cod War	5.13	243
1972–August 1974	Oman–South Yemen: Antigovernment Insurgency and Dhofar Rebellion	6.32	280
January 1972–February 1975	Iran–Iraq: Territorial Dispute and Border War	6.33	281
March 1972–January 1973	Syria/PLO–Israel: PLO Raids, Retaliatory Air Strikes, and the Golan Heights Conflict	6.34	281
June–November 1972	Equatorial Guinea–Gabon: Territorial Dispute over the Corisco Bay Islands	1.34	76
Mid-1972–1985	Ethiopia–Somalia: Somali Expansionism, Territorial Dispute, and the Second Ogaden War	1.35	76
March 1973–July 1975	Iraq–Kuwait: Territorial Dispute and Border Incidents	6.35	282
October 1973	Israel–Egypt and Syria: Arab–Israeli Territorial Dispute, Arab–Israeli Wars, and the Yom Kippur War	6.36	282
January 1974	South Vietnam–China: Territorial Dispute and the Paracel Islands	3.30	182
January 1974–June 1978	Cyprus: Communal Violence, Turkish–Greek Invasions, and Partition	5.14	244
March 1974–July 1975	Kurds–Iraq: Attempted Secession and the Kurdish Rebellion	6.37	283
April 1974–July 1975	Israel–Lebanon: Arab Infiltrators and Cross-Border Attacks	6.38	283

Africa = 1.1–1.97, Americas = 2.1–2.45, Asia: East Asia and the Pacific = 3.1–3.65, Asia: Southwest Asia = 4.1–4.39, Europe = 5.1–5.30, Middle East = 6.1–6.67.

Dates	Conflict	Conflict Number	Page
October 1974–Ongoing	Morocco–Mauritania: Saharan Nationalism, Territorial Dispute, and the Western Saharan Conflict	1.36	77
December 1974–June 1975	Mali–Upper Volta (Burkina Faso): Territorial and Resource Dispute	1.37	77
1975–Ongoing	Angola–South Africa: Guerrilla Warfare in Namibia, Intervention, and Angolan Civil War	1.38	78
1975–Ongoing	Bangladesh: Postindependence Territorial Dispute and the Chittagong Hill Tracts Conflict	4.20	215
February–July 1975	North Korea–South Korea: Demilitarized Zone and Invasion Threat	3.31	182
February 1975–Late 1992	Lebanon: Internal Strife, Communal Violence, and the Second Lebanese Civil War	6.39	284
April–Late 1975	Syria–Iraq: Resource Dispute over the Euphrates River	6.40	284
May 1975	Cambodia (Kampuchea)–United States: Post–Vietnam War Tensions and the *Mayaguez* Incident	3.32	183
June 1975–January 1976	Laos–Thailand: Postrevolution Exodus and Border Incidents	3.33	183
October 1975	China–India: Territorial Dispute and McMahon Line Border Incidents	4.21	216
October 1975–May 2002	East Timor–Indonesia: Independence Struggle	3.34	184
November 1975–February 1976	Zaire–Angola: Rebel Activity and Border War	1.39	79
December 1975–February 1976	Cambodia (Kampuchea)–Thailand: Refugee Influx, Regional Tensions, and Border Skirmishes	3.35	185
1976–1980	Iran: Internal Strife, Orthodox Muslim Backlash, Iranian Civil War, and Islamic Revolution	6.41	285
1976–October 1992	Mozambique–South Africa: African Nationalism, Intervention, and Civil War	1.40	80
February–August 1976	Uganda–Kenya: Amin Provocations and Border Incidents	1.41	81
April 1976	Bangladesh–India: Postcoup Tensions and Border Incidents	4.22	216
May 1976–Ongoing	Kurds–Iraq: Kurdish Separatist Insurgency and Kurdish Autonomy	6.42	286
June 1976–November 1979	Chad–Libya: Guerrilla Warfare, Factional Fighting, and Libyan Annexation of the Aozou Strip	1.42	81
July 1976–October 1980	El Salvador–Honduras: Territorial Dispute and Border Incidents	2.26	142
November–December 1976	Thailand–Cambodia (Kampuchea): Refugee Influx, Regional Instability, and Khmer Rouge Border Incidents	3.36	185
January 1977–October 1978	Cambodia (Kampuchea)–Thailand: Refugee Influx, Regional Instability, and Khmer Rouge Border Incidents	3.37	186
January 1977–Late 1992	El Salvador: Civil Conflict and the Salvadoran Civil War	2.27	143
March–May 1977	Zaire–Angola: Internal Dissension, Regional Instability, and the First Invasion of Shaba	1.43	82
June 1977–January 1978	Ecuador–Peru: Regional Rivalry, Territorial Dispute, and the Amazon/Marañón Waterway Incidents	2.28	143
Mid–Late 1977	Israel–Lebanon: Arab–Israeli Tensions, Christian–Muslim Factional Fighting, and Border Incidents	6.43	287
July–September 1977	Egypt–Libya: Regional Tensions and Border War	6.44	287
October 1977	Nicaragua–Costa Rica: Regional Rivalry and Border Incidents	2.29	144
January 1978–June 1982	Chad: Internal Strife, Foreign Intervention, and the Second Chad Civil War	1.44	83
March–June 1978	Israel–Lebanon/PLO: Arab–Israeli Tensions, PLO Incursions, and Israeli Invasion of Southern Lebanon	6.45	288

Africa = 1.1–1.97, Americas = 2.1–2.45, Asia: East Asia and the Pacific = 3.1–3.65, Asia: Southwest Asia = 4.1–4.39, Europe = 5.1–5.30, Middle East = 6.1–6.67.

Dates	Conflict	Conflict Number	Page
May 1978	Zaire–Angola: Regional Instability, Congolese Dissension, and the Second Invasion of Shaba	1.45	83
September–December 1978	Nicaragua–Costa Rica: Regional Rivalry, Cross-Border Raids, and Border Incidents	2.30	144
October 1978–May 1979	Tanzania–Uganda: Cross-Border Raids, Tanzanian Invasion, and Ouster of the Amin Regime	1.46	84
January 1979–Ongoing	Cambodia (Kampuchea)–Vietnam: Border Fighting, Vietnamese Invasion, and the Cambodian Civil War	3.38	187
January 1979–June 1982	China–Vietnam: Regional Rivalry and Border War	3.39	188
February 1979–February 1980	North Yemen–South Yemen: Border War	6.46	289
March–July 1979	Pakistan–Afghanistan: Pro-Monarchist Revolt and the Peshawar Rebellion	4.23	217
June–October 1979	Morocco–Algeria: Western Saharan Nationalism and Border Conflict	1.47	85
June 1979–February 1980	Israel–Syria: Arab–Israeli Tensions and Air Incidents	6.47	289
August 1979–March 1980	Saudi Arabia–North Yemen: Covert Military Aid and Border Conflict	6.48	290
November 1979	Bangladesh–India: Boundary Dispute and Border Incidents	4.24	217
November 1979–January 1981	Iran–United States: Anti-American Sentiment, Islamic Revolution, and Hostage Crisis	6.49	290
December 1979–October 1980	Cambodia (Kampuchea)–Thailand: Khmer Rouge Insurgency and Border Conflict	3.40	188
December 1979–Ongoing	USSR–Afghanistan: Soviet Invasion and the Afghan Civil War	4.25	218
January 1980–February 1994	Honduras–Nicaragua: Right-Wing Insurgency and the Contra War	2.31	145
February 1980–1989	Iran–Iraq: Regional Rivalry, Territorial Dispute, and the Iran–Iraq War	6.50	291
May–September 1980	Espiritu Santo–Vanuatu (The New Hebrides): Secession Attempt	3.41	189
January–April 1981	Ecuador–Peru: Territorial Dispute and Border War	2.32	145
May–July 1981	Cameroon–Nigeria: Border Incident	1.48	85
July 1981–August 1982	Pakistan–India: Regional Rivalry, Border Incidents, and India–Pakistan Wars	4.26	219
August 1981	Libya–United States: Regional Instability and Air Incidents	6.51	291
December 1981–February 1982	Poland: Internal Crisis, Solidarity Labor Movement, and the Declaration of Martial Law	5.15	244
December 1981–1994	Uganda: Civil War	1.49	86
Early 1982–Mid-1983	Israel–Lebanon: Israeli Invasion of Lebanon	6.52	292
February–September 1982	Zaire–Zambia: Lake Mweru Dispute	1.50	86
April–June 1982	United Kingdom–Argentina: Sovereignty Dispute and the Falklands War	2.33	146
May 1982–October 1984	Indonesia–Papua New Guinea (PNG): Secessionist Warfare, Border Incidents, and the Irian Jaya Dispute	3.42	189
June 1982	Laos–Thailand: Territorial Dispute and Border Incidents	3.43	190
Mid-1982–Ongoing	Libya–Chad: Political Instability, Rebel Fighting, Foreign Intervention, and the Third Chad Civil War	1.51	87
July 1982–Ongoing	Sri Lanka: Communal Violence, Separatist Fighting, and Tamil–Sinhalese Conflict	4.27	219
August–October 1982	Ghana–Togo: Territorial Dispute and Border Incidents	1.52	88
September 1982–January 1983	Guatemala–Mexico: Regional Instability, Guatemalan Civil War, and Border Incidents	2.34	147

Africa = 1.1–1.97, Americas = 2.1–2.45, Asia: East Asia and the Pacific = 3.1–3.65, Asia: Southwest Asia = 4.1–4.39, Europe = 5.1–5.30, Middle East = 6.1–6.67.

Dates	Conflict	Conflict Number	Page
December 1982	South Africa–Lesotho: Guerrilla Insurgency Fears and Anti-ANC Raid	1.53	88
January 1983–Ongoing	Sudan: Secessionist Fighting, Civil War, and the Second Sudan Civil War	1.54	89
February–March 1983	Liberia–Sierra Leone: Doe Regime Tensions	1.55	90
April 1983	China–Vietnam: Regional Rivalry and Border Conflict	3.44	190
April–July 1983	Chad–Nigeria: Boundary/Resources Dispute and the Lake Chad Conflict	1.56	90
Mid-1983–Ongoing	Israel–Lebanon: Arab–Israeli Hostilities, Muslim–Christian Factional Fighting, and the Security Zone	6.53	293
September 1983–January 1984	Zaire–Zambia: Regional Tensions, Deportations, and Border Dispute	1.57	91
October–December 1983	United States–Grenada: Anti-Communist Military Invasion	2.35	147
December 1983–June 1984	India–Bangladesh: Boundary Dispute and Border Conflict	4.28	221
January 1984	Ecuador–Peru: Regional Rivalry, Territorial Dispute, and Border Conflict	2.36	148
January 1984–March 1987	Vietnam–China: Regional Rivalry and Border Conflict	3.45	190
March 1984	Burma–Thailand: Karen Separatist Insurgency, Counterinsurgency Raids, and Border Incidents	3.46	191
March 1984–January 1988	Turkey–Greece: Regional Rivalry and Naval Incidents	5.16	245
April 1984	Guatemala–Mexico: Regional Instability, Guatemalan Civil War, and Border Incident	2.37	148
April 1984–September 1985	India–Pakistan: Territorial Dispute, India–Pakistan Rivalry, and the Siachin Glacier Dispute	4.29	221
June 1984–December 1988	Thailand–Laos: Boundary Dispute and Border War	3.47	191
August 1984–Ongoing	Kurds–Turkey: Kurdish Secession Struggle	6.54	293
October 1984–May 1986	South Africa–Botswana: African Nationalism and Anti-ANC Raids	1.58	91
November 1984	North Korea–South Korea: Cold War Border Incidents	3.48	192
November 1984	Zaire: Internal Dissent and the Third Invasion of Shaba	1.59	92
May–June 1985	Nicaragua–Costa Rica: Regional Rivalry and Border Incidents	2.38	148
June 1985	Zaire: Internal Strife, the Fourth Invasion of Shaba, and the Collapse of the Mobutu Regime	1.60	92
December 1985–January 1986	Mali–Burkina Faso: Territorial/Resource Dispute and Border War	1.61	92
January–April 1986	United States–Libya: International Terrorism Fears and Naval Incidents	6.55	295
February–April 1986	India–Bangladesh: Boundary Disputes and the Muhuri River Incidents	4.30	222
April 1986	Nicaragua–Costa Rica: Regional Rivalry and Border Incidents	2.39	149
April 1986	Qatar–Bahrain: Sovereignty Dispute and the Hawar Islands Dispute	6.56	295
July 1986–December 1992	Suriname: Guerrilla Insurgency	2.40	149
September 1986	Togo–Ghana: Regional Rivalry and Coup Attempt	1.62	93
Late 1986–Ongoing	India–Pakistan: Territorial Dispute, Siachin Glacier/Kashmir Conflict, and India–Pakistan Rivalry	4.31	222
January 1987	Zaire–People's Republic of Congo: Regional Instability and Border Incident	1.63	93
February 1987–April 1988	Ethiopia–Somalia: Somali Expansionism and the Third Odagen War	1.64	94

Africa = 1.1–1.97, Americas = 2.1–2.45, Asia: East Asia and the Pacific = 3.1–3.65, Asia: Southwest Asia = 4.1–4.39, Europe = 5.1–5.30, Middle East = 6.1–6.67.

Dates	Conflict	Conflict Number	Page
April 1987	South Africa–Zambia: African Nationalism, Insurgency Fears, and Anti-ANC Raid	1.65	94
September 1987–July 1988	People's Republic of Congo: Civil Unrest and Army Rebellion	1.66	95
December 1987	Uganda–Kenya: Ugandan Civil War, Refugee Influx, and Border Conflict	1.67	95
March 1988	Vietnam–China: Regional Rivalry, Sovereignty Dispute, and the Spratly Islands Dispute	3.49	192
May 1988–Ongoing	Somalia: Clan-Based Violence and the Somalian Civil War	1.68	95
August 1988–Ongoing	Burundi: Tribe-Based Communal Violence and the Hutu Conflict	1.69	97
October 1988–Ongoing	Bougainville–Papua New Guinea: Separatist Insurgency and Secession Attempt	3.50	192
November 1988	Maldives: Attempted Coup and Invasion	4.32	223
January 1989	United States–Libya: Rabat Chemical Plant Tensions and Mediterranean Air Incident	6.57	295
March 1989	Uganda–Kenya: Border Conflict	1.70	98
March 1989–Ongoing	Georgia–South Ossetia: Abkhazia Secession War	5.17	245
April 1989–January 1990	Mauritania–Senegal: Ethnic Violence and Border Incidents	1.71	98
Mid-1989–November 2000	Yugoslavia: Ethnic and Religious Warfare and the Balkans Civil War	5.18	246
December 1989	United States–Panama: U.S. Anti-Noriega Military Invasion	2.41	150
December 1989–Ongoing	Liberia: Civil War	1.72	98
March 1990–Late 1991	USSR–Lithuania: Post-Soviet Independence Crisis	5.19	248
April–May 1990	Guinea-Bissau–Senegal: Border Conflict	1.73	100
May 1990–October 1994	Tuareg–Niger: Confrontation and Reprisals	1.74	100
June 1990	Kyrgyzstan: Uzbek and Kyrgyzis Ethnic Conflict and Post–Soviet Violence	4.33	223
Mid-1990–Ongoing	Senegal: The Casamance Rebellion	1.75	100
June 1990–Ongoing	Tuareg–Mali: Sahel Pastoralist Rebellion and Military Coup	1.76	102
August 1990–May 1991	Iraq–Kuwait/Coalition Forces: Territorial Dispute, Iraqi Expansionism, and the Gulf War	6.58	296
August 1990–Ongoing	Azerbaijan–Armenia: Nagorno–Karabakh Conflict	5.20	248
September 1990–Ongoing	Rwanda: Tribal Conflict, Genocide, and Exiles Invasion	1.77	102
October 1990–July 1992	Gagauzia/Dniester–Moldova: Post–Soviet Strife and Gagauzia's Struggle for Autonomy	5.21	249
January 1991	USSR–Latvia: Post–Soviet Independence Crisis	5.22	250
January 1991–Ongoing	Macedonia: Civil War, Incursion and NATO/EU Involvement	5.23	251
March 1991–Ongoing	Liberia–Sierra Leone: Intervention, Destabilization, and the Sierra Leone Civil War	1.78	104
November 1991–July 1993	Djibouti: Ethnic-Based Violence and Civil War	1.79	105
December 1991	Burma (Myanmar)–Bangladesh: Rohingya Muslim Rebellion and Border Incidents	3.51	193
April 1992	Iran–United Arab Emirates/Egypt: Abu Musa and Tunb Islands Territorial Dispute	6.59	297
April 1992–June 1997	Tajikistan: Post-Soviet Strife and Ethnic-Based Civil War	4.34	224
May 1992	North Korea–South Korea: Historical Enmity and Border Incident	3.52	194
September–October 1992	Saudi Arabia–Qatar: Post–Gulf War Tensions and Border Incidents	6.60	297

Africa = 1.1–1.97, Americas = 2.1–2.45, Asia: East Asia and the Pacific = 3.1–3.65, Asia: Southwest Asia = 4.1–4.39, Europe = 5.1–5.30, Middle East = 6.1–6.67.

Dates	Conflict	Conflict Number	Page
October 1992–Ongoing	Russia–Chechnya: Post–Soviet Strife, Separatist Fighting, Chechen and Caucasus Conflicts	5.24	252
December 1992	Egypt–Sudan: Territorial/Resource Dispute and Halaib Dispute	6.61	297
December 1992–July 1993	Iraq–Coalition Forces: Post–Gulf War Incidents	6.62	298
March–September 1993	Burma (Myanmar)–Bangladesh: Border Incidents	3.53	194
April 1993	Cyprus: Ethnic-Based Tensions and Partition Incidents	5.25	253
November 1993–July 1994	Yemen: Unification Difficulties and Yemen Civil War	6.63	298
December 1993–March 1994	Nigeria–Cameroon: Territorial Dispute and the Diamond and Djabane Islands Dispute	1.80	105
January–February 1994	Ghana–Togo: Border Incidents	1.81	106
April 1994	Greece–Albania: Border Tensions	5.26	253
May–August 1994	Burma (Myanmar)–Bangladesh: Border Incidents	3.54	194
September 1994	United States–Haiti: U.S. Military Invasion and Aristide's Return from Exile	2.42	150
October 1994	Iraq–Coalition Forces: Post–Gulf War Tensions and Kuwaiti Border Incidents	6.64	299
November 1994	Taiwan–China: Nationalist-Communist Dispute and Shelling Incident	3.55	195
December 1994	Saudi Arabia–Yemen: Post–Gulf War Border Conflict	6.65	299
January–February 1995	China–The Philippines: Territorial Dispute and the Paracel and Spratly Islands Incidents	3.56	195
January–March 1995	Ecuador–Peru: Regional Rivalry and Cenepa Headwaters Confrontation	2.43	151
January 1995–October 1998	Ecuador–Peru: Condor Mountain Territorial Dispute	2.44	151
March 1995	Taiwan–Vietnam: Territorial Dispute and Spratly Islands Clash	3.57	196
May 1995–Ongoing	Uganda: Intervention and Democratic Movements	1.82	106
August 1995	Belize–Guatemala: Postindependence Territorial Dispute and Border Incidents	2.45	152
September 1995–Ongoing	Federal Republic of Grande Comoros: Coup Attempt and Anjouan and Moheli Independence	1.83	107
November 1995–October 1998	Eritrea–Yemen: Invasion of the Hunish Islands	1.84	108
January 1996–August 1999	China–Taiwan: Rivalry and Military Tensions	3.58	196
June 1996–Ongoing	Cyprus: Partition Incidents	5.27	254
September 1996–November 2000	North Korea–South Korea: Continuing Rivalry	3.59	197
October 1996–Ongoing	Congo: Independence Movements	1.85	109
November 1996–July 1998	Uganda–Kenya: Ethnic Cross-Border Clashes	1.86	109
December 1996–April 1999	Niger: Diffa Border Insurgency	1.87	110
April 1997–July 1999	China–The Philippines: Spratly Islands Incident	3.60	198
May 1997–Late 2000	Congo–Brazzaville: Democratic Struggle	1.88	110
September 1997	Iran–Iraq: Regional Rivalry and Border Incidents	6.66	300
October 1997–Ongoing	Yugoslavia–Kosovo: Kosovo Conflict and Civil War	5.28	254
Early 1998–December 2000	Djibouti: Intervention and Djibouti Civil War	1.89	110
May 1998–March 1999	Lesotho: Intervention and Military Factions	1.90	111
May 1998–June 1999	Eritrea–Ethiopia: Yirga Triangle Territorial Dispute	1.91	111
June 1998–January 2000	Guinea-Bissau: Military Factions	1.92	112
Mid-1998–September 1999	Nepal: Intervention and Maoist Guerrilla Insurgency	4.35	225
October 1998–January 1999	Ethiopia–Kenya: Ethnic Border Clashes	1.93	113
April–August 1999	India–Bangladesh: Kushita Border Incident	4.36	225

Africa = 1.1–1.97, Americas = 2.1–2.45, Asia: East Asia and the Pacific = 3.1–3.65, Asia: Southwest Asia = 4.1–4.39, Europe = 5.1–5.30, Middle East = 6.1–6.67.

Dates	Conflict	Conflict Number	Page
May 1999	Russia–Republic of Dagestan: The Dagestan Independence Dispute	5.29	255
August 1999–September 2000	Uzbekistan–Kyrgyzstan/Tajikistan: Border Insurgency	4.37	225
September 1999–April 2001	Liberia–Guinea: Border Dispute	1.94	113
September 1999–Ongoing	Ivory Coast: Civil War	1.95	114
October 1999	Vietnam–The Philippines: Spratly Islands Firing Incident	3.61	198
August–September 2000	Thailand–Laos: Mekong River Territories	3.62	199
August 2000–Ongoing	Russia–Georgia: Chechen Separatism	5.30	255
February 2001–Ongoing	Israel–Syria: Border Clashes	6.67	300
March–May 2001	Thailand–Burma: Internal Civil Strife, Militia Activities, and Border Skirmishes	3.63	199
April–July 2001	Bangladesh–India: Border Incident and Seizure of Perdiwah	4.38	226
Mid-2001–December 2002	Central African Republic–Chad: Attempted Coup, Foreign Intervention, and Territorial Occupation	1.96	115
September–December 2001	United States–Afghanistan: Post–September 11 "War on Terrorism," Al Qaeda Terrorist Links, and Terrorist Containment	4.39	227
November 2001	Angola–Zambia: Civil Strife and Border Skirmishes	1.97	116
November 2001–July 2002	North Korea–South Korea: Naval Incidents	3.64	200
December 2001	Japan–North Korea: Spy Ship Incident	3.65	201

Africa = 1.1–1.97, Americas = 2.1–2.45, Asia: East Asia and the Pacific = 3.1–3.65, Asia: Southwest Asia = 4.1–4.39, Europe = 5.1–5.30, Middle East = 6.1–6.67.

Appendix C
Organization Factsheets

United Nations (UN)

Sphere of Influence: Global.

Establishment: The United Nations was established in 1945 at the San Francisco Conference. The UN Charter was signed on June 26, 1945. The charter became effective on October 24, 1945. On April 18, 1946, the League of Nations officially transferred its buildings, assets, and responsibilities to the United Nations.

Concerns of the Organization: The supreme purpose of the United Nations is stated in the preamble to the charter and repeated throughout; it remains the foremost obligation of its members, that is:

> To maintain international peace and security, and to that end: to take effective collective measures for the prevention and removal of threats to the peace, and for the suppression of acts of aggression or other breaches of the peace and to bring about by peaceful methods, and in conformity with the principles of justice and international law, adjustment or settlement of international disputes or situations which might lead to a breach of the peace.

Stated Obligations Toward the Peaceful Settlement of Conflict: The UN Charter details the organization's approach to dispute management in Chapter VI: Pacific Settlement of Disputes.

> Article 33: The parties to a dispute, the continuance of which is likely to endanger the maintenance of international peace and security, shall first of all, seek a solution by negotiation, enquiry, mediation, conciliation, arbitration, judicial settlement, resort to regional agencies or arrangements, or other peaceful means of their own choice.

The Security Council shall, when it deems necessary, call upon the parties to settle their dispute by such means.

> Article 34: The Security Council may investigate any dispute, or any situation which might lead to international friction or give rise to a dispute, in order to determine whether the continuance of the dispute or situation is likely to endanger the maintenance of international peace and security.

> Article 35: Any Member of the United Nations may bring any dispute, or any situation of the nature referred to in Article 34, to the attention of the Security Council or of the General Assembly.

A state which is not a Member of the United Nations may bring to the attention of the Security Council or of the General Assembly any dispute to which it is a party if it accepts in advance, for the purposes of the dispute, the obligations of pacific settlement provided in the present Charter.

The proceedings of the General Assembly in respect of matters brought to its attention under this Article will be subject to the provisions of Articles 11 and 12.

> Article 36: The Security Council may, at any stage of a dispute of the nature referred to in Article 33, or of a situation of like nature, recommend appropriate procedures or method of adjustment.

The Security Council should take into consideration any procedures for the settlement of the dispute which have already been adopted by the parties.

In making recommendations under this Article the Security Council should also take into consideration that legal disputes should as a general rule be referred by the parties to the International Court of Justice in accordance with the provisions of the statute of the Court.

> Article 37: Should the parties to a dispute of the nature referred to in Article 33 fail to settle it by the means indicated in that Article, they shall refer it to the Security Council.

If the Security Council deems that the continuance of the dispute is in fact likely to endanger the maintenance of international peace and security, it shall decide whether to take action under Article 36 or to recommend such terms of settlement as it may consider appropriate.

> Article 38: Without prejudice to the provisions of Articles 33 to 37, the Security Council may, if all the parties to any disputes request, make recommendations to the parties with a view to a pacific settlement of the dispute.

Structural Hierarchy: The structural hierarchy consists of the Security Council, secretary-general, General Assembly, and Court on Conciliation and Arbitration.

Membership: 191 members (as of April 2004). The member states and the dates on which they joined the organization are listed below. Vatican City is now the only undisputed nation that is not a member.

Afghanistan	November 19, 1946
Albania	December 14, 1955
Algeria	October 8, 1962
Andorra	July 28, 1993
Angola	December 1, 1976
Antigua and Barbuda	November 11, 1981
Argentina	October 24, 1945
Armenia	March 2, 1992
Australia	November 1, 1945
Austria	December 14, 1955
Azerbaijan	March 9, 1992
Bahamas, The	September 18, 1973
Bahrain	September 21, 1971
Bangladesh	September 17, 1974
Barbados	December 9, 1966
Belarus (formerly Byelorussian S.S.R.)	October 24, 1945
Belgium	December 27, 1945
Belize	September 25, 1981
Benin (formerly Dahomey)	September 20, 1960
Bhutan	September 21, 1971
Bolivia	November 14, 1945
Bosnia and Herzegovina	May 22, 1992
Botswana	October 17, 1966
Brazil	October 24, 1945
Brunei Darussalam	September 21, 1984
Bulgaria	December 14, 1955
Burkina Faso (formerly Upper Volta)	September 20, 1960
Burundi	September 18, 1962
Cambodia	December 14, 1955
Cameroon	September 20, 1960
Canada	November 9, 1945
Cape Verde	September 16, 1975
Central African Republic	September 20, 1960
Chad	September 20, 1960
Chile	October 24, 1945
China	October 24, 1945
Colombia	November 5, 1945
Comoros	November 12, 1975
Congo (formerly Middle Congo, Congo/Brazzaville)	September 20, 1960
Costa Rica	November 2, 1945
Côte d'Ivoire (formerly Ivory Coast)	September 20, 1960
Croatia	May 22, 1992
Cuba	October 24, 1945
Cyprus	September 20, 1960
Czech Republic	January 19, 1993
Democratic People's Republic of Korea (North Korea)	September 17, 1991
Democratic Republic of the Congo (formerly Congo Free State, Belgian Congo, Congo/Leopoldville, Congo/Kinshasa, Zaire)	September 20, 1960
Denmark	October 24, 1945
Djibouti	September 20, 1977
Dominica	December 18, 1978
Dominican Republic	October 24, 1945
East Timor	September 27, 2002
Ecuador	October 24, 1945
El Salvador	October 24, 1945
Equatorial Guinea	November 12, 1968
Eritrea	May 28, 1993
Estonia	September 17, 1991
Ethiopia	November 13, 1945
Fiji	October 13, 1970
Finland	December 14, 1955
France	October 24, 1945
Gabon	September 20, 1960
Gambia	September 21, 1965
Georgia	July 31, 1992
Germany (formerly East and West Germany)	September 18, 1973
Ghana	March 8, 1957
Greece	October 25, 1945
Grenada	September 17, 1974
Guatemala	November 21, 1945
Guinea	December 12, 1958
Guinea-Bissau	September 17, 1974
Guyana	September 20, 1966
Haiti	December 17, 1945
Hungary	December 14, 1955
Iceland	November 19, 1946
India	October 30, 1945
Indonesia	September 28, 1950
Iran (Islamic Republic of Iran)	October 24, 1945
Iraq	December 21, 1945
Ireland	December 14, 1955
Israel	May 11, 1949
Italy	December 14, 1955
Jamaica	September 18, 1962
Japan	December 18, 1956
Jordan	December 14, 1955
Kazakhstan	March 2, 1992
Kenya	December 16, 1963
Kiribati	September 14, 1999
Kuwait	May 14, 1963
Kyrgyzstan	March 2, 1992
Laos (formerly Lao People's Democratic Republic)	December 14, 1955
Latvia	September 17, 1991
Lebanon	October 24, 1945
Lesotho	October 17, 1966
Liberia	November 2, 1945
Libya	December 14, 1955
Liechtenstein	September 18, 1990
Lithuania	September 17, 1991

Luxembourg	October 24, 1945
Macedonia The Former Yugoslav Republic of	April 8, 1993
Madagascar	September 20, 1960
Malawi	December 1, 1964
Malaysia (formerly Malaya)	September 17, 1957
Maldives	September 21, 1965
Mali	September 28, 1960
Malta	December 1, 1964
Marshall Islands	September 17, 1991
Mauritania	October 7, 1961
Mauritius	April 24, 1968
Mexico	November 7, 1945
Micronesia (Federated States of Micronesia)	September 17, 1991
Monaco	May 28, 1993
Mongolia	October 27, 1961
Morocco	November 12, 1956
Mozambique	September 16, 1975
Myanmar (formerly Burma)	April 19, 1948
Namibia	April 23, 1990
Nauru	September 14, 1999
Nepal	December 14, 1955
Netherlands, The	December 10, 1945
New Zealand	October 24, 1945
Nicaragua	October 24, 1945
Niger	September 20, 1960
Nigeria	October 7, 1960
North Korea	September 17, 1991
Norway	November 27, 1945
Oman	October 7, 1971
Pakistan	September 30, 1947
Palau	December 15, 1994
Panama	November 13, 1945
Papua New Guinea	October 10, 1975
Paraguay	October 24, 1945
Peru	October 31, 1945
Philippines, The	October 24, 1945
Poland	October 24, 1945
Portugal	December 14, 1955
Qatar	September 21, 1971
Republic of Korea (South Korea)	September 17, 1991
Republic of Moldova	March 2, 1992
Romania	December 14, 1955
Russian Federation (formerly Union of Soviet Socialist Republics)	October 24, 1945
Rwanda	September 18, 1962
Saint Kitts and Nevis	September 23, 1983
Saint Lucia	September 18, 1979
Saint Vincent and the Grenadines	September 16, 1980
Samoa (formerly Western Samoa)	December 15, 1976
San Marino	March 2, 1992
São Tomé and Príncipe	September 16, 1975
Saudi Arabia	October 24, 1945
Senegal	September 28, 1960
Serbia and Montenegro (as of February 4, 2003; formerly admitted as Yugoslavia, October 24, 1945; Federal Republic of Yugoslavia readmitted in 2000)	November 1, 2000
Seychelles	September 21, 1976
Sierra Leone	September 27, 1961
Singapore	September 21, 1965
Slovakia	January 19, 1993
Slovenia	May 22, 1992
Solomon Islands	September 19, 1978
Somalia	September 20, 1960
South Africa	November 7, 1945
South Korea	September 17, 1991
Spain	December 14, 1955
Sri Lanka (formerly Ceylon)	December 14, 1955
Sudan, The	November 12, 1956
Suriname	December 4, 1975
Swaziland	September 24, 1968
Sweden	November 19, 1946
Switzerland	September 10, 2002
Syria	October 24, 1945
Tajikistan	March 2, 1992
Tanzania, United Republic of (formerly United Republic of Tanganyika and Zanzibar)	December 14, 1961
Thailand	December 16, 1946
Togo	September 20, 1960
Tonga	September 14, 1999
Trinidad and Tobago	September 18, 1962
Tunisia	November 12, 1956
Turkey	October 24, 1945
Turkmenistan	March 2, 1992
Tuvalu	September 5, 2000
Uganda	October 25, 1962
Ukraine (formerly Ukrainian S.S.R)	October 24, 1945
United Arab Emirates	December 9, 1971
United Kingdom of Great Britain and Northern Ireland	October 24, 1945
United States of America	October 24, 1945
Uruguay	December 18, 1945
Uzbekistan	March 2, 1992
Vanuatu	September 15, 1981
Venezuela	November 15, 1945
Vietnam	September 20, 1977
Yemen (formerly Aden and Sana/North and South Yemen)	September 30, 1947
Zambia	December 1, 1964
Zimbabwe	August 25, 1980

Observer status is granted to the Holy See and the Palestine Liberation Organization (PLO).

Organs Responsible for Handling Conflict: The organs responsible for handling conflict are the Security

Council, secretary-general, General Assembly, and Court on Conciliation and Arbitration. The Security Council, the main decision-making body, handles dispute referrals and authorizes the initiation of UN management. When the Security Council is unable to reach a decision, the secretary-general is able to intervene on his own initiative. On rare occasions, when the use of vetoes has hamstrung Security Council action, the General Assembly has voted to initiate dispute management (for example, conflict 6.14). The Court on Conciliation and Arbitration makes recommendations but has not been used extensively.

Secretaries-General

October 24, 1945–January 29, 1946	Sir Gladwyn Jebb (UK) (acting)
February 2, 1946–April 7, 1953	Trygve Lie (Norway)
April 10, 1953–September 18, 1961	Dag Hammerskjöld (Sweden)
November 3, 1961–December 31, 1971	U Thant (Burma) (acting to November 30, 1962)
January 1, 1972–December 31, 1981	Kurt Waldheim (Austria)
January 1, 1982–December 31, 1991	Javier Pérez de Cuéllar (Peru)
January 1, 1992–December 31, 1996	Boutros Boutros-Ghali (Egypt)
January 1, 1997–	Kofi Annan (Ghana)

Presidents of the General Assembly

January 10, 1946–September 16, 1947	Paul-Henri Spaak (Belgium)
September 16, 1947–April 16, 1948	Oswaldo Aranha (Brazil)
April 16, 1948–September 21, 1948	José Arce (Argentina)
September 21, 1948–September 20, 1949	Herbert Vere Evatt (Australia)
September 20, 1949–September 19, 1950	Carlos Peña Romulo (Philippines)
September 19, 1950–November 6, 1951	Nasrollah Entezam (Iran)
November 6, 1951–October 14, 1952	Luis Padilla Nervo (Mexico)
October 14, 1952–September 15, 1953	Lester B. Pearson (Canada)
September 15, 1953–September 21, 1954	Vijaya Lakshmi Pandit (India)
September 21, 1954–September 20, 1955	Eelco Nicolaas van Kleffens (Netherlands)
September 20, 1955–November 1, 1956	José Maza (Chile)
November 1, 1956–November 12, 1956	Rudecindo Ortega Masson (Chile)
November 12, 1956–September 17, 1957	Prince Wan Waithayakon (Thailand)
September 17, 1957–September 16, 1958	Sir Leslie Munro (New Zealand)
September 16, 1958–September 15, 1959	Charles Habib Malik (Lebanon)
September 15, 1959–September 20, 1960	Víctor Andrés Belaúnde (Peru)
September 20, 1960–September 20, 1961	Frederick Henry Boland (Ireland)
September 20, 1961–September 18, 1962	Mongi Slim (Tunisia)
September 18, 1962–September 17, 1963	Sir Mohammad Zafrulla Khan (Pakistan)
September 17, 1963–December 1, 1964	Carlos Sosa Rodríguez (Venezuela)
December 1, 1964–September 21, 1965	Alex Quaison-Sackey (Ghana)
September 21, 1965–September 20, 1966	Amintore Fanfani (Italy)
September 20, 1966–September 19, 1967	Abdul Rahman Pazhwak (Afghanistan)
September 19, 1967–September 24, 1968	Corneliu Manescu (Romania)
September 24, 1968–April 17, 1969	Emilio Arenales Catalán (Guatemala)
September 16, 1969–September 15, 1970	Angie Brooks (Liberia) (from April 27, 1970, Angie Brooks-Randolph)
September 15, 1970–September 21, 1971	Edvard Hambro (Norway)
September 21, 1971–September 19, 1972	Adam Malik (Indonesia)
September 19, 1972–September 18, 1973	Stanislaw Trepczynski (Poland)
September 18, 1973–September 17, 1974	Leopoldo Benites Vinueza (Ecuador)
September 17, 1974–September 16, 1975	Abdelaziz Bouteflika (Algeria)
September 16, 1975–September 21, 1976	Gaston Thorn (Luxembourg)
September 21, 1976–September 20, 1977	Hamilton Shirley Amerasinghe (Sri Lanka)
September 20, 1977–September 19, 1978	Lazar Mojsov (Yugoslavia)
September 19, 1978–September 18, 1979	Indalecio Liévano Aguirre (Colombia)
September 18, 1979–September 16, 1980	Salim Ahmed Salim (Tanzania)
September 16, 1980–September 15, 1981	Rüdiger von Wechmar (W. Germany)
September 15, 1981–September 21, 1982	Ismat T. Kittani (Iraq)

September 21, 1982–September 20, 1983	Imre Hollai (Hungary)
September 20, 1983–September 18, 1984	Jorge Illueca (Panama)
September 18, 1984–September 17, 1985	Paul J. F. Lusaka (Zambia)
September 17, 1985–September 16, 1986	Jaime de Piniés (Spain)
September 16, 1986–September 15, 1987	Humayun Rasheed Chowdhury (Bangladesh)
September 15, 1987–September 20, 1988	Peter Florin (E. Germany)
September 20, 1988–September 19, 1989	Dante Caputo (Argentina)
September 19, 1989–September 18, 1990	Joseph Nanven Garba (Nigeria)
September 18, 1990–September 17, 1991	Guido de Marco (Malta)
September 17, 1991–September 15, 1992	Samir S. Shihabi (Saudi Arabia)
September 15, 1992–September 21, 1993	Stoyan Ganev (Bulgaria)
September 21, 1993–September 20, 1994	Samuel R. Insanally (Guyana)
September 20, 1994–September 19, 1995	Amara Essy (Ivory Coast)
September 19, 1995–September 17, 1996	Diogo Freitas do Amaral (Portugal)
September 17, 1996–September 16, 1997	Razali Ismail (Malaysia)
September 16, 1997–September 9, 1998	Hennadii Udovenko (Ukraine)
September 9, 1998–September 14, 1999	Didier Opertti Badan (Uruguay)
September 14, 1999–September 5, 2000	Theo-Ben Gurirab (Namibia)
September 5, 2000–September 12, 2001	Harri Holkeri (Finland)
September 12, 2001–September 10, 2002	Han Seung Soo (South Korea)
September 10, 2002–September 16, 2003	January Kavan (Czech Republic)
September 16, 2003–	Julyian Hunte (Saint Lucia)

United Nations High Commissioners for Refugees

January 1, 1951–July 8, 1956	Gerrit J. van Heuven Goedhart (Netherlands)
January 1, 1957– December 31, 1960	Auguste R. Lindt (Switzerland)
January 1, 1961–December 31, 1965	Felix Schnyder (Switzerland)
January 1, 1966–December 31, 1977	Sadruddin Aga Khan (Iran)
January 1, 1978–December 31, 1985	Poul Hartling (Denmark)
January 1, 1986–December 31, 1989	Jean-Pierre Hocké (Switzerland)
January 1, 1990–November 1990	Thorvald Stoltenberg (Norway)
January 1, 1991–December 31, 2000	Sadako Ogata (Japan)
January 1, 2001–	Rudolphus "Ruud" Lubbers (Netherlands)

United Nations High Commissioners for Human Rights

April 5, 1994–March 15, 1997	José Ayala Lasso (Ecuador)
March 15, 1997–September 12, 1997	Ralph Zacklin (UK) (interim)
September 12, 1997– September 12, 2002	Mary Robinson (Ireland)
September 12, 2002–July 19, 2003	Sérgio Vieira de Mello (Brazil)
June 2, 2003–	Bertie Ramcharan (Guyana)(acting for Mello to July 19, 2003)

Composition Strengths and Homogeneity: Strength exists in the organization's enormous resource base and leverage garnered from the organization's truly international status. UN membership lacks homogeneity due to its universal nature and its globally and ethnically diverse composition. Its membership is disparate and often divided along lines of ideology and economic wealth.

Major Regional Organizations

AFRICA

African Union (AU)

Sphere of Influence: Regional—Pan African.

Establishment: The Organization of African Unity (OAU) was established May 25, 1963, in Addis Ababa, after some six years of maturation (Wallerstein 1966). The OAU changed its name to the African Union (AU) on July 9, 2002.

Concerns of the Organization: The African Union is concerned with the political, economic, social, and cultural development of the region. Political objectives have taken priority, however, and aim: "to support movements to end colonial and white-minority governments in Africa; to provide intra-African conflict resolution; to unite in support of common positions in the United Nations, North-South Conferences, and other international fora; and to support the ideological concept of Pan Africanism" (Taylor 1984).

Stated Obligations Toward the Peaceful Settlement of Conflict: The preamble of the Charter of the Organization of African Unity reaffirms the aims and obligations stated in the UN Charter regarding the "peaceful and positive cooperation among States."

Article 3 (4) states that the member states declare their adherence to the principle of: "peaceful settlement of disputes by negotiation, mediation, conciliation or arbitration."

Article 19 states "Member States pledge to settle all disputes among themselves by peaceful means and, to this end decide to establish a Commission of Mediation, Conciliation and Arbitration." (Andemicael 1976).

Structural Hierarchy: The structural hierarchy of the OAU consisted of: Assembly of Heads of State and Government; Council of Ministers; Commission of Mediation, Conciliation and Arbitration (Arbitration Commission); general secretariat; secretary-general (administrative role only); and specialized commissions.

The structural hierarchy of the AU consists of: Assembly; Executive Council; Commission; Permanent Representatives' Committee; Peace and Security Council (PSC); Pan-African Parliament; Economic, Social and Cultural Council (ECOSOCC); Court of Justice; specialized technical committees; financial institutions (African Central bank, African Monetary Fund, African Investment Bank); AU Commission; Portfolios include: PEACE AND SECURITY (Conflict Prevention, Management and Resolution, and Combating Terrorism).

Membership: 53 members.

Algeria	1963
Angola	1975
Benin	1963
Botswana	1966
Burkina Faso	1963
Burundi	1963
Cameroon	1963
Cape Verde	1975
Central African Republic	1963
Chad	1963
Comoros	1975
Congo (cap. Brazzaville)	1963
Congo (cap. Kinshasa) (Zanzibar 1966–1971; Zaire 1971–1997)	1963
Congo (cap. Léopoldville)	1963
Djibouti	1977
Egypt	1963
Equatorial Guinea	1968
Eritrea	1993
Ethiopia	1963
Gabon	1966
Gambia	1965
Ghana	1966
Guinea	1966
Ivory Coast	1966
Kenya	1966
Lesotho	1966
Liberia	1966
Libya	1966
Madagascar	1966
Malawi	1964
Mali	1966
Mauritania	1966
Mauritius	1968
Morocco (Withdrew in 1984.)	1966
Mozambique	1975
Namibia	1990
Niger	1963
Nigeria	1963
Rwanda	1963
Saharan Arab Democratic Republic	1982
São Tomé and Príncipe	1975
Senegal	1963
Seychelles	1976
Sierra Leone	1963
Somalia	1963
South Africa	1994
Sudan	1963
Swaziland	1968
Tanzania	1963
Togo	1963
Tunisia	1963
Uganda	1963
Zambia	1963
Zimbabwe	1980

Organs Responsible for Handling Conflict: As the OAU: Assembly of Heads of State and Government; Council of Ministers; Commission of Mediation, Conciliation and Arbitration. The OAU's secretary-general performs an administrative role in comparison to the more active mediation roles of the UN and OAS secretaries-general (Merrills 1991).

As the AU: Peace and Security Council (PSC)–By Decision AHG/December 160 (xxxvii) of the Summit of Lusaka, July 2001, a decision was made for the creation within the African Union of the Peace and Security Council. The Protocol establishing the PSC is in the process of ratification. The AU Commission's portfolios include: Peace and Security (Conflict Prevention, Management and Resolution, and Combating Terrorism).

Secretaries-General

1964–1972	Diallo Telli (Guinea)
1972–1974	Nzo Ekangaki (Cameroon)
1974–1978	William Eteki (Cameroon)
1978–1984	Edem Kodjo (Togo)
1984–1985	Peter Onu (Nigeria)
1985–1989	Ide Oumarou (Niger)
1989–2001	Salim Ahmed Salim (Tanzania)
2001–2002	Amara Essy (Ivory Coast)

Chairmen

1972–1973	Hassan II (Morocco)
1973–1974	Yakubu Gowon (Nigeria)
1974–1975	Muhammad Siyad Barrah (Somalia)
1975–1976	Idi Amin (Uganda)
1976–1977	Sir Seewoosagur Ramgoolam (Mauritius)
1977–1978	Omar Bongo (Gabon)
1978–1979	Gaafar Nimeiry (Sudan)
1979–1980	William R. Tolbert Jr. (Liberia)
1980–1981	Siaka Stevens (Sierra Leone)
1981–1983	Daniel arap Moi (Kenya)
1983–1984	Mengistu Haile Mariam (Ethiopia)
1984–1985	Julyius Nyerere (Tanzania)
1985–1986	Abdou Diouf (Senegal) (1st time)
1986–1987	Denis Sassou-Nguesso (Congo)
1987–1988	Kenneth Kaunda (Zambia)
1988–1989	Moussa Traoré (Mali)
1989–1990	Hosni Mubarak (Egypt) (1st time)
1990–1991	Yoweri Museveni (Uganda)
1991–1992	Ibrahim Babangida (Nigeria)
1992–1993	Abdou Diouf (Senegal) (2d time)
1993–1994	Hosni Mubarak (Egypt) (2d time)
1994–1995	Zine al-Abidine Ben Ali (Tunisia)
1995–1996	Meles Zenawi (Ethiopia)
1996–1997	Paul Biya (Cameroon)
1997–1998	Robert Mugabe (Zimbabwe)
1998–1999	Blaise Compaoré (Burkina Faso)
1999–2000	Abdelaziz Bouteflika (Algeria)
2000–2001	Gnassingbe Eyadéma (Togo)
2001–2002	Frederick Chiluba (Zambia)
2002–2002	Levy Mwanawasa (Zambia)
2002–2003	Thabo Mbeki (South Africa)
2003–present	Joaquim Chissano (Mozambique)

Chairmen of the Commission

2002–2003	Amara Essy (Ivory Coast) (interim)
2003–present	Alpha Oumar Konaré (Mali)

Composition Strengths and Homogeneity: The AU has very loose organizational obligations and ensures that its members place a greater emphasis on moral obligations rather than on the organization's legal provisos. The assembly has "no power to enforce decisions or to expel members for non-compliance," and one of its greatest weaknesses comes from the fact that the organization pays the utmost respect to maintain member state sovereignty (Merrills 1991).

Economic Community of West African States (ECOWAS)

Sphere of Influence: Regional—Africa, predominantly West Africa.

Establishment: "The idea for a West African community goes back to President William Tubman of Liberia, who made the call in 1964. An agreement was signed between Ivory Coast, Guinea, Liberia, and Sierra Leone in February 1965, but came to nothing. In April 1972 General [Yakubu] Gowon of Nigeria and General [Gnassingbe] Eyadema of Togo relaunched the idea, drew up proposals, and toured twelve countries, soliciting their plan from July to August 1973. A meeting was then called at Lomé, Togo, from December 10 to December 15, 1973, which studied a draft treaty. The draft was further examined at a meeting of experts and jurists in Accra in January 1974 and by a ministerial meeting in Monrovia in January 1975. Fifteen West African countries signed the treaty for an Economic Community of West African States (Treaty of Lagos) on May 28, 1975. The protocols launching ECOWAS were signed in Lomé on November 5, 1976.

"In July 1993 the parties signed a revised ECOWAS treaty designed to accelerate economic integration and to increase political cooperation. ECOWAS has been designated one of the five regional pillars of the African Economic Community (AEC). Together with COMESA [Common Market for Eastern and Southern Africa], ECCAS [Economic Community of Central African States], IGAD [Intergovernmental Authority on Development], and SADC [Southern African Development Community], ECOWAS signed the Protocol on Relations between the AEC and Regional Economic Communities (RECs) in February 1998" (ECOWAS 2004).

Concerns of the Organization: The Economic Community of West African States is concerned with the control and management of conflicts, the promotion of cooperation and security, and the furtherance of political and economic development.

Stated Obligations Toward the Peaceful Settlement of Conflict: The revised treaty of 1993, which was to extend economic and political cooperation among member states, designates the achievement of a common market and a single currency as economic objectives, while in the political sphere it provides for a West African parliament, an economic and social council, and an ECOWAS court of justice to replace the existing tribunal and enforce community decisions. The treaty also formally assigned the community with the responsibility of preventing and settling regional conflicts.

Structural Hierarchy: The structural hierarchy consists of the Authority of Heads of State and Government (as a conference); the Council of Ministers; the Community Tribunal; the ECOWAS Parliament and Executive Secretariat, and six specialized commissions, one of which is the Commission for Political, Judicial and Legal Affairs, Regional Security, and Immigration.

Membership: 15 members.

Benin	1975
Burkina Faso	1975

Cape Verde	1977
Gambia	1975
Ghana	1975
Guinea	1975
Guinea-Bissau	1975
Ivory Coast	1975
Liberia	1975
Mali	1975
Mauritania (Announced withdrawal in December 1999.)	1975
Niger	1975
Nigeria	1975
Senegal	1975
Sierra Leone	1975
Togo	1975

Organs Responsible for Handling Conflict: The organs responsible for handling conflict are the Mechanism for Conflict Prevention, Management and Resolution, Peace and Security and its subgroups. The ECOWAS Summit of December 1999 agreed on the protocol that established the mechanism, which also has a Council of Elders and a Security and Mediation Council. The ten members of the latter are the foreign ministers of Benin, Gambia, Ghana, Guinea, Ivory Coast, Liberia, Mali (chair), Nigeria, Senegal, and Togo.

Executive Secretaries

January 1977–1985	Aboubakar Diaby Ouattara (Ivory Coast)
1985–1989	Momodu Munu (Sierra Leone)
1989–1993	Abass Bundu (Sierra Leone)
1993–1997	Edouard Benjamin (Guinea)
September 1997–February 6, 2002	Lansana Kouyate (Guinea)
February 6, 2002–	Mohamed Ibn Chambas (Ghana)

Chairmen

1977–1978	Gnassingbe Eyadema (Togo) (1st time)
1978–1979	Olusegun Obasanjo (Nigeria)
1979–1980	Léopold Sédar Senghor (Senegal)
1980–1981	Gnassingbe Eyadema (Togo) (2d time)
1981–1982	Siaka Stevens (Sierra Leone)
1982–1983	Mathieu Kérékou (Benin)
1983–1984	Ahmed Sékou Touré (Guinea)
1984–1985	Lansana Conté (Guinea)
1985–August 27, 1985	Mohammadu Buhari (Nigeria)
August 27, 1985–1989	Ibrahim Babangida (Nigeria)
1989–1990	Sir Dawda Jawara (Gambia) (1st time)
1990–1991	Blaise Compaoré (Burkina Faso)
1991–1992	Sir Dawda Jawara (Gambia) (2d time)
1992–1993	Abdou Diouf (Senegal)
1993–1994	Nicéphore Soglo (Benin)
1994–July 27, 1996	Jerry John Rawlings (Ghana)
June 8, 1998	Sani Abacha (Nigeria)
June 9, 1998–1999	Abdulsalami Abubakar (Nigeria)
1999	Gnassingbe Eyadema (Togo) (3d time)
1999–December 21, 2001	Alpha Oumar Konaré (Mali)
December 21, 2001–January 31, 2003	Abdoulaye Wade (Senegal)
January 31, 2003–	John Agyekum Kufuor (Ghana)

Composition Strengths and Homogeneity: ECOWAS has a resource-poor membership but is regionally homogenous and becoming more active in regional conflict management.

AMERICAS

Organization of American States (OAS)

Sphere of Influence: Regional—Central and South America.

Establishment: The Organization of American States was established with the signing of the Charter of the Organization of American States and the Inter-American Treaty for the Peaceful Settlement of Disputes in Bogota, Colombia, in April 1948. Initial conferences had aimed to "establish a system of continental security for the American states," with the 1947 Inter-American Treaty of Reciprocal Assistance (Rio Pact), focusing on a collective security arrangement to deal with internal and external threats (Taylor 1984). The eventual Inter-American Treaty for the Peaceful Settlement of Disputes established some mechanisms for dispute resolution, through arbitration, and a legal framework for operations.

Concerns of the Organization: The Organization of American States is concerned with maintaining regional security primarily by taking diplomatic measures rather than engaging in military enforcement. It is also concerned with human rights and economic and social development.

Stated Obligations Toward the Peaceful Settlement of Conflict: The charter of the Organization of American States, Chapter V, "Pacific Settlement of Disputes," states in Article 24, that "International disputes between Member States shall be submitted to the peaceful procedures set forth in this Charter" (OAS Charter).

Structural Hierarchy: The structural hierarchy consists of the General Assembly, the Permanent Council, the Meeting of Consultation of Ministers of Foreign Affairs, four specialist councils/commissions, General Secretariat, secretary-general (administrative role only until 1985), and six specialized portfolios.

Membership: 35 members.

Antigua and Barbuda	1981
Argentina	1948
The Bahamas	1982
Barbados	1967
Belize	1991
Bolivia	1948
Brazil	1948
Canada	1990
Chile	1948
Colombia	1948
Costa Rica	1948
Cuba	1948
(Cuba was excluded from the OAS in 1962.)	
Dominica	1979
Dominican Republic	1948
Ecuador	1948
El Salvador	1948
Grenada	1975
Guatemala	1948
Guyana	1991
Haiti	1948
Honduras	1948
Jamaica	1969
Mexico	1948
Nicaragua	1948
Panama	1948
Paraguay	1948
Peru	1948
Saint Kitts and Nevis	1984
Saint Lucia	1979
Saint Vincent and the Grenadines	1981
Suriname	1977
Trinidad and Tobago	1967
United States of America	1948
Uruguay	1948
Venezuela	1948

Organs Responsible for Handling Conflict: The organs responsible for handling conflict are the Permanent Council, secretary general, and the Inter-American Committee on Peaceful Settlement. The original role of the secretary-general, specified in Article 116 of the OAS Charter was limited to administrative duties. The Protocol of Cartagena de Indias (1985), Article 116, expanded the role of the secretary-general. One of the position's duties now is to notify the assembly or council of "any matter which in his opinion might threaten the peace and security of the hemisphere or the development of Member States" (Merrills 1991).

Secretaries-General

1954–1955	Carlos Guillermo Davila (Chile)
1956–1968	José A. Mora (Uruguay)
1968–1975	Galo Plaza Lasso (Ecuador)
1975–1984	Alejandro Orfila (Argentina)
1984–1994	João Baena Soares (Brazil)
1994	Christopher Thomas (Trinidad and Tobago)
March 27, 1994–present	César Gaviria Trujillo (Colombia)

Assistant Secretaries-General

November 1989–June 1995	Christopher R. Thomas (Trinidad and Tobago)
June 1995–present	Christopher R. Thomas (Trinidad and Tobago)

Composition Strengths and Homogeneity: The OAS has resource strength with U.S. support and an active secretary-general exercising good offices and mediation in dispute management.

ASIA: EAST ASIA AND THE PACIFIC

Association of Southeast Asian Nations (ASEAN)

Sphere of Influence: Regional—Southeast Asia.

Establishment: The Association of Southeast Asian Nations was established August 8, 1967, at the foreign ministers' meeting in Bangkok, Thailand. The ministers were from Indonesia, Malaysia, the Philippines, Singapore, and Thailand. Brunei was admitted in January 1984. The Association of Southeast Asia, consisting of Malaysia, the Philippines, and Thailand was in existence from 1961 to 1962.

Concerns of the Organization: ASEAN is concerned primarily with economic matters, although regional security issues have grown in importance. Security was a major motivation for the founding states in 1967, but it was not addressed as such. "It was contemplated in practical terms as a by-product of institutionalised regional reconciliation. To that end, the five founding governments hoped in time to attract to their ranks all of the states of South-East Asia" (Leifer 1989).

Stated Obligations Toward the Peaceful Settlement of Conflict: ASEAN's obligations toward the peaceful settlement of disputes are set out in four of the organization's documents.

1. The ASEAN Declaration (Bangkok Declaration), signed in Thailand on August 8, 1967, states that the aims and purposes of the association shall be "To promote regional peace and stability through abiding respect for justice and the rule of law in the relationship among countries of the region and adherence to the principles of the United Nations Charter."
2. The Zone of Peace, Freedom, and Neutrality Declaration, was signed in Malaysia on November 27, 1971. Member states are "dedicated to the maintenance of peace, freedom and independence unimpaired...."
3. ASEAN's provisions for the peaceful settlement of disputes are contained within the articles of Chapter IV in the Treaty of Amity and Cooperation in Southeast Asia, signed in Indonesia on February 24, 1976.

> Article 13: The High Contracting Parties shall have the determination and good faith to prevent disputes from arising. In case disputes on matters directly affecting them shall refrain from the threat or use of force and shall at all times settle such disputes among themselves through friendly negotiations.
>
> Article 14: To settle disputes through regional processes, the High Contracting Parties shall constitute, as a continuing body, a High Council comprising a Representative at ministerial level from each of the High Contracting Parties to take cognisance of the existence of disputes or situations likely to disturb regional peace and harmony.
>
> Article 15: In the event no solution is reached through direct negotiations, the High Council shall take cognisance of the dispute or the situation and shall recommend to the parties in dispute appropriate means of settlement such as good offices, mediation, inquiry or conciliation. The High Council may however offer its good offices, or upon agreement of the parties in dispute, constitute itself into a committee of mediation, inquiry or conciliation. When deemed necessary, the High Council shall recommend appropriate measures for the prevention of a deterioration of the dispute or the situation.
>
> Article 16: The foregoing provision of this chapter shall not apply to a dispute unless all the parties to the dispute agree to their application to that dispute. However, this shall not preclude the other High Contracting Parties not party to the dispute from offering all possible assistance to settle the said dispute. Parties to the dispute should be well disposed towards such offers of assistance.
>
> Article 17: Nothing in this Treaty shall preclude recourse to the modes of peaceful settlement contained in Article 33 (1) of the Charter of the United Nations. The High Contracting Parties which are parties to a dispute should be encouraged to take initiatives to solve it by friendly negotiations before resorting to the other procedures provided for in the Charter of the United Nations.

The fourth document, the Declaration of ASEAN Concord, was signed in Indonesia on February 24, 1976. Principle 6, ratified in this document states that "Member states, in the spirit of ASEAN solidarity, shall rely exclusively on peaceful processes in the settlement of intra-regional differences." In the stated political goals of the organization, members are to seek the "settlement of intra-regional disputes by peaceful means as soon as possible."

Rodolfo C. Severino Jr., secretary-general of ASEAN, commented on the organization's regional objectives at a ASEAN–UNESCO symposium on cooperative peace, entitled "Co-operative Peace in Southeast Asia," held in Jakarta, September 11, 1998. In an address to the symposium, Severino said:

> ASEAN is founded on the universal principles of regional co-operation [in] ASEAN's founding document, the Bangkok Declaration of 1967.... Peaceful co-operation does not come about automatically as a function of regional organization. It evolves and flourishes in a certain environment. Toward this end, the ASEAN Concord of 1976 says that "Member states shall strive, individually and collectively, to create conditions conducive to the promotion of peaceful co-operation among the nations of Southeast Asia on the basis of mutual respect and mutual benefit." Co-operative peace in Southeast Asia aims to promote regional resilience based on the specific principles embodied in the 1976 Treaty of Amity and Co-operation in Southeast Asia. These principles include: (a) mutual respect for the independence, sovereignty, equality, territorial integrity and national identity of all nations; (b) the right of every State to lead its national existence free from external interference, subversion or coercion; (c) non-interference in the internal affairs of one another; (d) settlement of differences or disputes by peaceful means; (e) renunciation of the threat or use of force; and (f) effective co-operation among themselves.

Structural Hierarchy: The structural hierarchy consists of Heads of Government Summit Meetings; ASEAN Ministerial Meeting (AMM); ASEAN Economic Minister (AEM); Sectoral Ministers Meeting; other noneconomic ministerial meetings; Joint Ministerial Meeting (JMM); secretary-general; ASEAN Standing Committee (ASC); Senior Officials Meeting (SOM); Senior Economic Officials Meeting (SEOM); other ASEAN senior officials meeting; Joint Consultative Meeting (JCM); ASEAN National Secretariats; ASEAN Committees in Third Countries; and ASEAN Secretariat.

Membership: 10 members.

Brunei	1984
Cambodia	1999
Indonesia	1967
Laos	1995
Malaysia	1967
Myanmar (Burma)	1995
Philippines	1967
Singapore	1967
Thailand	1967
Vietnam	1995

Observer status is granted to Papua New Guinea.

Organs Responsible for Handling Conflict: Dispute management is discussed at various ministerial meetings and foreign ministers can be sent to mediate disputes as official organization representatives. ASEAN's secretary-general has not been utilized the same way as the UN secretary-general. ASEAN is only beginning to take its position as a regional dispute manager and will probably evolve into a more defined role, as it becomes more active.

Secretaries-General

June 7, 1976–February 18, 1978	Hartono Dharsono (Indonesia)
February 19, 1978–July 1, 1978	Umarjadi Njotowijono (Indonesia)
July 10, 1978–July 1, 1980	Datuk Ali bin Abdullah (Malaysia)
July 1, 1980–July 1, 1982	Narciso G. Reyes (Philippines)
July 18, 1982–July 16, 1984	Chan Kai Yau (Singapore)
July 16, 1984–July 16, 1986	Phan Wannamethee (Thailand)
July 16, 1986–July 16, 1989	Roderick Yong (Brunei)
July 17, 1989–January 1, 1993	Rusli Noor (Indonesia)
January 1, 1993–January 5, 1998	Datuk Ajit Singh (Malaysia)
January 5, 1998–January 6, 2003	Rodolfo C. Severino (Philippines)
January 6, 2003–	Ong Keng Yong (Singapore)

Composition Strengths and Homogeneity: ASEAN has some regional solidarity but was only able to act symbolically in the China–Vietnam border war as its members were divided over how seriously to take Chinese actions (*see* conflict 3.39). The resource-rich membership lacks strong unity in security issues involving member states.

Pacific Islands Forum (PIF)

Sphere of Influence: Regional—Pacific, South Pacific, Oceania.

Establishment: An earlier version of the Pacific Islands Forum, the South Pacific Forum (SPF), was established August 5, 1971. In 1999 the Heads of Government South Pacific Forum meeting decided that the forum would change its name to more accurately reflect the membership of the present-day forum. The organization became the Pacific Islands Forum (PIF) on October 27, 2000. "Sixteen countries from the Pacific region that come together every year to discuss issues that impact on the Pacific community. The Pacific Islands Forum has evolved into the only regional grouping of Pacific nations with the scope to discuss, develop and implement strategies that enhance the security, governance and sustainable development of its membership. It also provides a collective voice for the region in wider international settings" (New Zealand Ministry of Foreign Affairs and Trade 2004).

Concerns of the Organization: Since 1971 the Pacific Islands Forum has provided member nations with the opportunity to express their joint political views and cooperate in areas of political and economic concern.

Stated Obligations Toward the Peaceful Settlement of Conflict: The Thirty-third Pacific Islands Forum Communiqué (August 15-17, 2002) resulted in the Baketawa Declaration. This declaration launched the forum's first ever observer mission (Forum Elections Observer Mission), which was established to observe the 2001 Solomon Islands elections and to support the implementation of a democratic process. This action "signals an increasingly proactive role by the Forum in maintaining peace and stability in the region" (New Zealand Ministry of Foreign Affairs and Trade 2003).

Structural Hierarchy: The structural hierarchy of the Pacific Islands Forum includes the heads of government of all the independent and self-governing Pacific Island countries, Australia, and New Zealand. Forum heads of government meet in one member country for several days each year. Leaders and delegates deal with matters brought to their attention by the forum secretariat, forum committees, forum ministers' meetings, and regional organizations. A leaders' retreat provides the opportunity for private discussion, and the conclusions of the heads of government meeting are published in a communiqué.

The Pacific Islands Forum Secretariat undertakes programs and activities that support, or implement, decisions by the forum leaders. The secretariat gives policy advice and technical assistance on development and economic issues, promotes the forum's positions and interests in international forums, and helps members to improve their trade and investment performances. The Forum Secretariat chairs the Council of Regional Organisations in the Pacific (CROP), and operates four trade offices in Auckland, Beijing, Sydney, and Tokyo (New Zealand Ministry of Foreign Affairs and Trade 2004).

Membership: 16 members.

Australia	August 5, 1971
Cook Islands	August 5, 1971
Fiji	August 5, 1971
Kiribati	August 29, 1979
Marshall Islands	May 29, 1987
Micronesia, Federated States of	May 29, 1979
Nauru	August 5, 1971
New Zealand	August 5, 1971
Niue	July 1, 1975
Palau	September 3, 1995
Papua New Guinea	March 20, 1974
Samoa (formerly Western Samoa)	August 5, 1971
Solomon Islands	September 16, 1980
Tonga	August 5, 1971
Tuvalu	September 16, 1980
Vanuatu	July 14, 1980

New Caledonia and East Timor have forum observer status.

Forum Dialogue Partners
Canada
China, People's Republic of
European Union France
India
Indonesia
Japan
Korea
Malaysia
Philippines
United Kingdom
United States of America

Secretaries-General

September 1988–January 1, 1992	Henry Faati Naisali (Tuvalu)
January 1, 1992–January 1998	Ieremia T. Tabai (Kiribati)
February 1998–January 16, 2004	W. Noel Levi (Papua New Guinea)
January 16, 2004–	Greg Urwin (Australia)

Directors of the South Pacific Bureau for Economic Cooperation

November 1972–1980	Mahe Tupouniua (Tonga) (1st time)
1980–1982	Gabriel Gris (Papua New Guinea)
1982–January 1983	John Sheppard (acting) (Australia)
January 1983–January 1, 1986	Mahe Tupouniua (Tonga) (2d time)
January 1, 1986–September 1988	Henry Faati Naisali (Tuvalau)

Composition Strengths and Homogeneity: Membership is regionally homogenous but geographically dispersed, covering an oceanic area that comprises approximately 18 percent of the globe.

EUROPE

European Union (EU)

Sphere of Influence: Regional—Europe.

Establishment: The European Community became the European Union on November 1, 1993, in the Treaty on European Union or Maastricht Treaty.

Concerns of the Organization: The European Union began as primarily a vehicle for continued economic integration in the European Economic Community (EEC) and European Community (EC). The European Union (EU) has evolved to encompass defense issues and security responsibilities in its regional sphere.

Stated Obligations Toward the Peaceful Settlement of Conflict: The EU's obligations to peaceful dispute settlement are stated in the Treaty on European Union, Title V–Provisions on a Common Foreign and Security Policy, Article J.

> Article J.1: (2) The objectives of the common foreign and security policy shall be:
>
> - to safeguard the common values, fundamental interests and independence of the Union;
> - to strengthen the security of the Union and its Member States in all ways;
> - to preserve peace and strengthen international security, in accordance with the principles of the United Nations Charter as well as the principles of the Helsinki Final Act and the objectives of the Paris Charter;
> - to promote international co-operation;
> - to develop and consolidate democracy and the rule of law, respect for human rights and fundamental freedoms (Barbour 1996).

Structural Hierarchy: The structural hierarchy consists of the European Commission, Council of the European Union, European Parliament, and Court of Justice. Various other organs make decisions on economic matters, for example, the Economic and Social Committee and the Committee of Regions.

Membership: 25 members.

Austria	January 1, 1995
Belgium	January 1, 1958
Cyprus	May 1, 2004
Czech Republic	May 1, 2004
Denmark	January 1, 1973
Estonia	May 1, 2004
Finland	January 1, 1995
France	January 1, 1958
Germany, Federal Republic of	January 1, 1958
Greece	January 1, 1981
Hungary	May 1, 2004
Ireland	January 1, 1973
Italy	January 1, 1958
Latvia	May 1, 2004
Lithuania	May 1, 2004
Luxembourg	January 1, 1958
Malta	May 1, 2004
The Netherlands	January 1, 1958
Poland	May 1, 2004
Portugal	January 1, 1986
Slovakia	May 1, 2004
Slovenia	May 1, 2004
Spain	January 1, 1986
Sweden	January 1, 1995
United Kingdom	January 1, 1973

Greenland, which joined as part of Denmark, was never recognized as a separate member; withdrew February 1, 1985.

Organs Responsible for Handling Conflict: The organs responsible for handling conflict are the European Commission, Court of Justice (legal disputes only), and specially appointed committees or mediators.

Composition Strengths and Homogeneity: The European Union is a structurally complex organization, but organs have well-defined responsibilities with regard to handling disputes. It has strong regional homogeneity and a resource-rich membership.

Presidency of the European Council

July 1, 1987–December 31, 1987	Denmark
January 1, 1988–June 30, 1988	West Germany
July 1, 1988–December 31, 1988	Greece
January 1, 1989–June 30, 1989	Spain
July 1, 1989–December 31, 1989	France
January 1, 1990–June 30, 1990	Ireland
July 1, 1990–December 31, 1990	Italy
January 1, 1991–June 30, 1991	Luxembourg
July 1, 1991–December 31, 1991	Netherlands
January 1, 1992–June 30, 1992	Portugal
July 1, 1992–December 31, 1992	United Kingdom
January 1, 1993–June 30, 1993	Denmark
July 1, 1993–December 31, 1993	Belgium
January 1, 1994–June 30, 1994	Greece
July 1, 1994–December 31, 1994	Germany
January 1, 1995–June 30, 1995	France
July 1, 1995–December 31, 1995	Spain
January 1, 1996–June 30, 1996	Italy
July 1, 1996–December 31, 1996	Ireland
January 1, 1997–June 30, 1997	Netherlands
July 1, 1997–December 31, 1997	Luxembourg
January 1, 1998–June 30, 1998	United Kingdom
July 1, 1998–December 31, 1998	Austria
January 1, 1999–June 30, 1999	Germany
July 1, 1999–December 31, 1999	Finland
January 1, 2000–June 30, 2000	Portugal
July 1, 2000–December 31, 2000	France
January 1, 2001–June 30, 2001	Sweden
July 1, 2001–December 31, 2001	Belgium
January 1, 2002–June 30, 2002	Spain
July 1, 2002–December 31, 2002	Denmark
January 1, 2003–June 30, 2003	Greece
July 1, 2003–December 31, 2003	Italy
January 1, 2004–June 30, 2004	Ireland
July 1, 2004–	Netherlands

Presidents of the European Commission

January 31, 1958–June 30, 1967	Walter Hallstein (West Germany)
July 1, 1967–July 1, 1970	Jean Max Georges Rey (Belgium)
July 2, 1970–March 22, 1972	Franco Maria Malfatti (Italy)
March 22, 1972–January 5, 1973	Sicco Leendert Mansholt (Netherlands)
January 9, 1973–January 5, 1977	François–Xavier Ortoli (France)
January 11, 1977–January 5, 1981	Roy Harris Jenkins (United Kingdom)
January 12, 1981–January 5, 1985	Gaston Thorn (Luxembourg)
January 5, 1985–January 5, 1995	Jacques Lucien Jean Delors (France)
January 24, 1995–July 14, 1999	Jacques Santer (Luxembourg)
July 14, 1999–September 15, 1999	Manuel Marín (Spain) (acting)
September 15, 1999–	Romano Prodi (Italy)

Organization of Security and Cooperation in Europe (OSCE)

Sphere of Influence: Regional—Pan European (from Vancouver to Vladisvostok); Northern Hemisphere.

Establishment: The Conference on Security and Cooperation in Europe (CSCE) developed as a forum for consultation over the period from November 1972 to August 1975. The name changed to the Organization of Security and Cooperation in Europe at the Budapest Summit in 1994. The Paris Summit (1990) had transformed the CSCE from the form of a consultative process to an organization with permanent structure and institutions.

June 25, 1973	Conference on Security and Cooperation in Europe (CSCE)
August 1, 1975	Helsinki Final Act signed
November 21, 1990	Charter of Paris for a new Europe signed
January 1, 1995	Organization for Security and Cooperation in Europe (OSCE)

Concerns of the Organization: The Organization for Security and Cooperation in Europe is concerned with the control and management of conflicts. It attempts to promote cooperation and security and further political and economic development.

Stated Obligations Toward the Peaceful Settlement of Conflict: The stated obligations of the organization are: "(1) To consolidate common values and build societies; (2) To prevent local conflicts, restore stability and bring peace to war-torn areas; (3) To overcome real and perceived security deficits and to avoid the creation of new divisions by promoting a co-operative system of security" (Organization of Security and Cooperation in Europe 1997).

Structural Hierarchy: The structural hierarchy consists of the Secretariat, secretary-general, Chairman in Office, Heads of State or Government Summits, Ministerial Council, Senior Council, Permanent Council, Forum for Security Co-operation, Parliamentary Assembly, and Court on Conciliation and Arbitration.

Membership: 55 members.

Albania	June 19, 1991
Andorra	April 25, 1996
Armenia	January 30, 1992
Austria	June 25, 1973
Azerbaijan	January 30, 1992
Belarus	January 30, 1992
Belgium	June 25, 1973
Bosnia and Herzegovina	April 30, 1992
Bulgaria	June 25, 1973
Canada	June 25, 1973
Croatia	March 24, 1992
Cyprus	June 25, 1973
Czech Republic	January 1, 1993
Denmark	June 25, 1973
Estonia	September 10, 1991
Finland	June 25, 1973
France	June 25, 1973
Georgia	March 24, 1992
Germany	June 25, 1973
Greece	June 25, 1973
Holy See	June 25, 1973
Hungary	June 25, 1973
Iceland	June 25, 1973
Ireland	June 25, 1973
Italy	June 25, 1973
Kazakhstan	January 30, 1992
Kyrgyzstan	January 30, 1992
Latvia	September 10, 1991
Liechtenstein	June 25, 1973
Lithuania	September 10, 1991
Luxembourg	June 25, 1973
Macedonia	October 12, 1995
Malta	June 25, 1973
Moldova	January 30, 1992
Monaco	June 25, 1973
Netherlands	June 25, 1973
Norway	June 25, 1973
Poland	June 25, 1973
Portugal	June 25, 1973
Romania	June 25, 1973
Russian Federation	June 25, 1973
San Marino	June 25, 1973
Serbia and Montenegro	November 10, 2000
Slovak Republic	January 1, 1993
Slovenia	March 24, 1992
Spain	June 25, 1973
Sweden	June 25, 1973
Switzerland	June 25, 1973
Tajikistan	January 30, 1992
Turkey	June 25, 1973
Turkmenistan	January 30, 1992
Ukraine	January 30, 1992
United Kingdom	June 25, 1973
United States of America	June 25, 1973
Uzbekistan	January 30, 1992

Organs Responsible for Handling Conflict: The organs responsible for handling conflict are the secretary-general, chairman in office, and the Court on Conciliation and Arbitration. The OSCE has established eleven long-term operations and several observer missions to deal with disputes.

Secretaries-General

June 15, 1993–June 15, 1996	Wilhelm Höynck (Germany)
June 15, 1996–June 15, 1999	Giancarlo Aragona (Italy)
June 15, 1999–	Ján Kubis (Slovakia)

Chairmen-in-Office

June 1991–December 31, 1991	Hans-Dietrich Genscher (Germany)
January 1, 1992–July 2, 1992	Jirí Dienstbier (Czechoslovakia)
July 2, 1992–December 31, 1992	Jozef Moravcik (Czechoslovakia)

January 1, 1993–December 31, 1993	Margaretha af Ugglas (Sweden)
January 1, 1994–May 11, 1994	Beniamino Andreatta (Italy)
May 11, 1994–December 31, 1994	Antonio Martino (Italy)
January 1, 1995–December 31, 1995	László Kovács (Hungary)
January 1, 1996–December 31, 1996	Flavio Cotti (Switzerland)
January 1, 1997–December 31, 1997	Niels Helveg Petersen (Denmark)
January 1, 1998–December 31, 1998	Bronislaw Geremek (Poland)
January 1, 1999–December 31, 1999	Knut Vollebáek (Norway)
January 1, 2000–February 4, 2000	Wolfgang Schússel (Austria)
February 4, 2000–December 31, 2000	Benita Ferrero-Waldner (Austria)
January 1, 2001–December 31, 2001	Mircea Geoana (Romania)
January 1, 2002–April 6, 2002	Jaime Gama (Portugal)
April 6, 2002–December 31, 2002	Antônio Martins da Cruz (Portugal)
January 1, 2003–December 3, 2003	Jakob "Jaap" Gijsbert de Hoop Scheffer (Netherlands)
December 3, 2003–December 31, 2003	Ben Bot (Netherlands)
January 1, 2004–	Solomon Passy (Bulgaria)

Composition Strengths and Homogeneity: The OSCE is resource-rich and relatively homogenous in composition. The organization has had few noticeable deficiencies to date.

MIDDLE EAST

Arab League (AL)

Sphere of Influence: Regional—Middle East, North Africa.

Establishment: The Arab League, formerly the League of Arab States, was established under the Alexandria Protocol, October 7, 1944. The organization's purposes and operations were specified later in the Pact of the League of Arab States, signed March 22, 1945.

Concerns of the Organization: The concerns of the Arab League are regional security, cooperation, and economic development.

Stated Obligations Toward the Peaceful Settlement of Conflict: The Pact of the League of Arab States specifically refers to the organization's responsibility to mediate and the members' obligations with regard to settlement of disputes.

> Article 2: The League has as its purpose the strengthening of the relations between the member states; the co-ordination of their policies in order to achieve co-operation between them and to safeguard their independence and sovereignty; and a general concern with the affairs and interests of the Arab countries. . . .
>
> Article 5: Any resort to force in order to resolve disputes arising between two or more member states of the League is prohibited. If there should arise among them a difference which does not concern a state's independence, sovereignty or territorial integrity, and if the parties to the dispute have recourse to the Council for the settlement of this difference, the decision of the Council shall be enforceable and obligatory. . . . The Council shall mediate in all differences which threaten to lead to war between two member states, or a member state and a third state, with a view to bringing about their reconciliation. Decisions of arbitration and mediation shall be taken by majority vote" (Macdonald 1965).

Structural Hierarchy: The structural hierarchy consists of the Political Council, General Secretariat, secretary-general, Joint Defence Council, Economic Council, Arab League Council, Advisory Panel, and permanent committees.

Membership: 21 members.

Algeria	1962
Bahrain	1971
Comoros	1993
Djibouti	1977
Egypt	1945
(Suspended from 1979 to 1989.)	
Iraq	1945
Jordan	1945
Kuwait	1961
Lebanon	1945
Libya	1953
Mauritania	1973
Morocco	1958
Oman	1971
Palestine Liberation Organization	1976
Qatar	1971
Saudi Arabia	1945
Somalia	1974
Sudan	1956
Syria	1945
Tunisia	1958
United Arab Emirates	1971
Yemen (Aden)	1945
Yemen (Sana)	1967

(Yemen [Aden] and Yemen [Sana] united in 1990.)

Organs Responsible for Handling Conflict: The organs responsible for handling conflict are the secretary-general and specially created committees or missions to facilitate and mediate the resolution of disputes.

Secretaries-General
The names of the Arab League secretaries-general can be translated into English with slight variations. The alternate spellings are in brackets.

1945–1952	Abdel Rahman Azzam [Abdul-Razzaq Azzam] (Egypt)
1952–1972	Abdel Khaliq Hassuna [Abdul-Khaleq Hassouna] (Egypt)
1972–1979	Mahmoud Riad [Mahmoud Riyadh] (Egypt)
1979–1990	Chedli Klebi [Chedi Klibi] (Tunisia)
1990–1991	Assad al-Assad (Lebanon)
1991–	Esmat Abdel Meguid [Dr. Ahmad Esmat Abdul-Maguid] (Egypt)

Composition Strengths and Homogeneity: The members of the Arab League are territorially concentrated. Although the league is territorially homogeneous, including only states from its region, it conspicuously lacks the involvement of three important actors in the area, Iran, Israel, and Turkey (Farer 1993). The membership is resource-rich.

Other Major Organizations

North Atlantic Treaty Organization (NATO)

Sphere of Influence: Regional—Links the security of North America to Europe.

Establishment: The North Atlantic Treaty Organization was established on April 4, 1949, by the foreign ministers of the North Atlantic Alliance as a defense, political, and military alliance of independent countries promoted through mutual cooperation and consultation in political, military, economic, and scientific fields in accordance with the UN Charter.

NATO has nineteen members. The twelve original members (1949) are Belgium, Canada, Denmark, France, Iceland, Italy, Luxembourg, the Netherlands, Norway, Portugal, United Kingdom, and the United States. The other members are Czech Republic (joined 1999), Germany (1955), Greece (1952), Hungary (1999), Poland (1999), Spain (1982), and Turkey (1952).

Organization of the Islamic Conference (OIC)

Sphere of Influence: Global—Links Muslim peoples and states around the globe.

Establishment: The Organization of the Islamic Conference was established September 22–25, 1969.

The Organization of the Islamic Conference seeks "to promote Islamic solidarity through economic, social, cultural cooperation, and political affairs, working towards peace and security for members based on justice and safeguarding the dignity, independence and rights of all Muslim peoples."

The organization has fifty-seven members: Afghanistan, Albania, Algeria, Azerbaijan, Bahrain, Bangladesh, Benin, Brunei, Burkina Faso, Cameroon, Chad, Comoros, Djibouti, Egypt, Gabon, Gambia, Guinea, Guinea-Bissau, Guyana, Indonesia, Iran, Iraq, Ivory Coast, Jordan, Kazakhstan, Kuwait, Kyrgyzstan, Lebanon, Libya, Malaysia, Maldives, Mali, Mauritania, Morocco, Mozambique, Niger, Nigeria, Oman, Pakistan, Qatar, Saudi Arabia, Senegal, Sierra Leone, Somalia, Sudan, Suriname, Syria, Tajikistan, Togo, Tunisia, Turkey, Turkmenistan, Uganda, United Arab Emirates, Uzbekistan, Yemen, and the Palestine Liberation Organization.

Four other entities enjoy observer status in the organization: Bosnia and Herzegovina, Central African Republic, Moro National Liberation Front (Philippines), and the "Turkish Republic of Northern Cyprus."

British Commonwealth

Sphere of Influence: Global. An intergovernmental organization linking former colonies of the British Empire.

Establishment: Originally founded through the Imperial Conference in 1926, the group was a free association of sovereign independent states evolving from the British Empire, equal in status and united through a common allegiance to the Crown. The British Commonwealth was formally established by the Statute of Westminster on December 31, 1931. In 1949 the Commonwealth evolved to include republics within the Commonwealth of Nations.

The organization work toward cooperation, consultation, and mutual assistance to safeguard the human rights, democracy, and rule of law of its members. The Commonwealth, coordinated by the Commonwealth Secretariat, possesses UN observer status. The Commonwealth Heads of Government meeting (CHOGOM) is a biannual conference for coordinating Commonwealth discussions and negotiations. The Queen is recognized as the symbolic head of the Commonwealth. Total membership of the Commonwealth consists of thirty-three republics and twenty-one monarchies, sixteen of which are Queen's realms.

The Commonwealth has fifty-one members. The eight original members are denoted with an asterisk: Antigua and Barbuda 1981; Australia 1931*; Bahamas 1973; Bangladesh 1971; Barbados 1966; Belize 1981; Botswana 1966; Brunei 1984; Cameroon 1995; Canada 1931*; Cyprus 1961; Dominica 1978; Fiji 1970 (withdrew 1987, rejoined 1997 as the Fiji Islands); Gambia 1965; Ghana 1957; Grenada 1974; Guyana 1966; India 1947*; Ireland 1931 (withdrew 1948); Jamaica 1962; Kenya 1963; Kiribati 1979; Lesotho 1966; Malawi 1964; Malaysia 1957 (joined as Malaya, became Malaysia in 1963); Maldives

1982; Malta 1964; Mauritius 1968; Mozambique 1995; Namibia 1990; New Zealand 1931*; Nigeria 1960 (suspended since 1995); Pakistan 1947* (withdrew 1972, rejoined 1989); Papua New Guinea 1975; Saint Kitts and Nevis 1983; Saint Lucia 1979; Saint Vincent and the Grenadines 1979; Samoa 1970 (was Western Samoa until 1997); Seychelles 1976; Sierra Leone 1961; Singapore 1965; Solomon Islands 1978; South Africa* (withdrew 1961, rejoined 1994); Sri Lanka 1948* (joined as Ceylon, became Sri Lanka 1972); Swaziland 1968; Tanzania 1961 (joined as Tanganyika, became Tanzania in 1964); Tonga 1970; Trinidad and Tobago 1962; Uganda 1962; United Kingdom 1931*, Vanuatu 1980; Zambia 1964; and Zimbabwe 1980.

The Commonwealth also has two special members: Nauru 1968 and Tuvalu 1978. In addition to Commonwealth member states are twenty-three United Kingdom Overseas Territories and Associated States that belong by settlement, conquest, or annexation to the British, Australian, or New Zealand Crown.

The thirteen associated with the United Kingdom are Anguilla, Bermuda, British Antarctic Territory, British Indian Ocean Territory, British Virgin Islands, Cayman Islands, Falkland Islands, Gibraltar, Montserrat, Pitcairn Islands, St. Helena and Dependencies, South Georgia and South Sandwich Islands, Turks and Caicos Islands.

The six Australian External Territories are Ashmore and Cartier Islands, Australian Antarctic, Christmas Island, Cocos Islands, Coral Sea Islands, and Heard and McDonald Islands.

The two New Zealand Dependent Territories are the Ross Dependency and Tokelau Islands

The two New Zealand Associated States are Cook Islands and Niue.

The Red Cross (ICRC and IFRCS)

Sphere of Influence: Global. Independent of governments and international or regional organizations.

Establishment: The International Committee of the Red Cross (ICRC) was founded in Geneva, Switzerland, in February 1863 to provide humanitarian aid in wartime, and was extended through the establishment of the International Federation of Red Cross and Red Crescent Societies (IFRCS) on May 5, 1919, (formally known as the League of Red Cross and Red Crescent Societies–LORCS) to provide peacetime humanitarian aid.

The International Red Cross and Red Crescent Movement (ICRM), established in 1928, is the International Movement of 163 National Societies through which the activities of the ICRC and IFRCS are promoted.

The Red Cross seeks to help all victims of war, internal violence, armed conflict, refugees, and displaced people; to organize, coordinate, and direct international relief actions; to protect, assist, and help them to regain autonomy and assist with development programs; and to promote compliance with international humanitarian law.

Worldwide there are 181 IFRCS members: Afghanistan, Albania, Algeria, Andorra, Angola, Antigua and Barbuda, Argentina, Armenia, Australia, Austria, Azerbaijan, Bahamas, Bahrain, Bangladesh, Barbados, Belarus, Belgium, Belize, Benin, Bolivia, Bosnia and Herzegovina, Botswana, Brazil, Brunei, Bulgaria, Burkina Faso, Burma, Burundi, Cambodia, Cameroon, Canada, Cape Verde, Central African Republic, Chad, Chile, China, Colombia, Democratic Republic of Congo, Republic of the Congo, Cook Islands, Costa Rica, Croatia, Cuba, Czech Republic, Denmark, Djibouti, Dominica, Dominican Republic, Ecuador, Egypt, El Salvador, Equatorial Guinea, Estonia, Ethiopia, Fiji, Finland, France, Gabon, Gambia, Georgia, Germany, Ghana, Greece, Grenada, Guatemala, Guinea, Guinea-Bissau, Guyana, Haiti, Honduras, Hungary, Iceland, India, Indonesia, Iran, Iraq, Ireland, Italy, Ivory Coast, Jamaica, Japan, Jordan, Kazakhstan, Kenya, Kiribati, North Korea, South Korea, Kuwait, Kyrgyzstan, Laos, Latvia, Lebanon, Lesotho, Liberia, Libya, Liechtenstein, Lithuania, Luxembourg, the Former Yugoslav Republic of Macedonia, Madagascar, Malawi, Malaysia, Mali, Malta, Mauritania, Mauritius, Mexico, Micronesia, Moldova, Monaco, Mongolia, Morocco, Mozambique, Namibia, Nepal, the Netherlands, New Zealand, Nicaragua, Niger, Nigeria, Norway, Pakistan, Panama, Papua New Guinea, Palau, Paraguay, Peru, Philippines, Poland, Portugal, Qatar, Romania, Russia, Rwanda, Saint Kitts and Nevis, Saint Lucia, Saint Vincent and the Grenadines, Samoa, San Marino, São Tomé and Príncipe, Saudi Arabia, Senegal, Seychelles, Sierra Leone, Singapore, Slovakia, Slovenia, Solomon Islands, Somalia, South Africa, Spain, Sri Lanka, Sudan, Suriname, Swaziland, Sweden, Switzerland, Syria, Tajikistan, Tanzania, Thailand, Togo, Tonga, Trinidad and Tobago, Tunisia, Turkey, Turkmenistan, Uganda, Ukraine, United Arab Emirates, United Kingdom, United States, Uruguay, Uzbekistan, Vanuatu, Venezuela, Vietnam, Yemen, Yugoslavia, Zambia, and Zimbabwe.

The organization has six observer nations Comoros, East Timor, Eritrea, Israel, Palestine, and Tuvalu.

The Vatican

Sphere of Influence: Global. Government of the Roman Catholic Church.

Establishment: Vatican City was established as a fully independent sovereign state on February 11, 1929.

The pope (Roman pontiff) exercises sovereignty and has absolute legislative, executive, and judicial powers of the Roman Catholic Church. The pope is assisted by a hierarchy of advisors and representatives through the Sacred College of Cardinals and the Synod of Bishops in charge of Roman Catholic congregations around the world. The Holy See, or government of the Roman Catholic Church, is represented by a commission appointed by the pope and represents the church's diplomatic relations with foreign countries. Through the Holy See the Vatican has permanent observer status at the UN.

Reference Sources

Web Sites

African Union: www.africa-union.org
Arab League: www.arableagueonline.org/arableague/index_en.jsp
Association of Southeast Asian Nations: www.aseansec.org/home.htm
British Commonwealth: www.thecommonwealth.org/HomePage.asp?NodeID=20593
Economic Community of West African States: www.ecowas.int
European Union: www.europa.eu.int
North Atlantic Treaty Organization: www.nato.int
Organization of American States: www.oas.org
Organization for Security and Cooperation in Europe: www.osce.org
Organization of the Islamic Conference: www.oic-oci.org
Pacific Islands Forum: www.forumsec.org.fj
The Red Cross (ICRC and IFRCS): www.IFRC.org
United Nations: www.un.org
The Vatican: www.vatican.va

References

Andemicael, B. 1976. *The OAU and the UN—Relations Between the Organisation of African Unity and the United Nations.* A UNITAR Regional Study No. 2, United Nations Institute for Training and Research. New York: Africana.

Barbour, P., ed. 1996. *The European Union Handbook.* Chicago: Fitzroy Dearborn.

Economic Community of West African States (ECOWAS). 2004. www.ecowas.int.

Farer, T. J. 1993. "The Role of Regional Collective Security Arrangements." *Collective Security in a Changing World.* Weiss, T. G., ed. Boulder: Lynne Rienner, 153–186.

Haynes, E. 1998. http://haynese.winthrop.edu/mlas/Secretaries.html (April 6, 1998).

Leifer, M. 1989. *ASEAN and the Security of South-East Asia.* London: Routledge.

Macdonald, R. W. 1965. *The League of Arab States—A Study in the Dynamics of Regional Organization.* Princeton, N.J.: Princeton University Press.

Merrills, J. G. 1991. *International Dispute Settlement.* 2d edition. Cambridge, England: Grotius.

New Zealand Ministry of Foreign Affairs and Trade. 2003, 2004.

Organization of American States. 2003. www.oas.org.

Organization of Security and Cooperation in Europe. 1997. www.osce.org.

Taylor, P. 1984. *Nonstate Actors in International Politics: From Transregional to Substate Organizations.* Boulder: Westview.

UN Press Release. ORG/1190 (December 15, 1994)–Updated June 19, 1998.

Wallerstein, I. 1966. "The Early Years of the OAU: The Search for Organisational Pre-eminence." *International Organisation.* 20, No. 4 (autumn): 774–787.

References

AFRICA

Amate, C. O. C. 1986. *Inside the OAU.* New York: St. Martin's.

Andemicael, B. 1972. *Peaceful Settlement Among African States: Roles of the United Nations and the Organization of African Unity.* New York: UNITAR.

———. 1976. *The OAU and the UN: Relations Between the Organization of African Unity and the United Nations.* UNITAR Regional Study No. 2, United Nations Institute for Training and Research. New York: Africana Publishing Company.

Bennett, A. 1998. "Somalia, Bosnia, and Haiti: What Went Right, What Went Wrong?" Chapter 6 of *Collective Conflict Management and Changing World Politics.* Lepgold, J., and T. G. Weiss, eds. Albany: State University of New York Press, 133–155.

Boatena, E.A. 1978. *A Political Geography of Africa.* Cambridge: Cambridge University Press.

Bozzoli, B., ed. 1987. *Class, Community, and Conflict: South African Perspectives.* Johannesburg: Ravan.

Brown, M. 1979. *Madagascar Rediscovered: A History from Early Times to Independence.* Hamden, Conn.: Archon.

Cervenka, Z. 1969. *The Organization of African Unity and Its Charter.* New York: Praeger.

Chan, S., and V. Jabri, eds. 1993. *Mediation in Southern Africa.* London: Macmillan.

Clapham, C. 1998. "Rwanda: The Perils of Peacemaking." *Journal of Peace Research* 35, No. 2: 193–210.

Coker, C. 1985. *NATO, the Warsaw Pact, and Africa.* New York: St. Martin's.

———. 1987. *South Africa's Security Dilemmas.* New York: Praeger.

Damis, J. 1983. *Conflict in North West Africa.* Stanford, Calif.: Hoover.

Delarue, J. 1994. *L'OAS contre de Gaulle.* Paris: Fayard.

Deng, F., ed. 1991. *Conflict Management in Africa.* Washington, D.C.: Brookings.

Doob, L. W. 1970. *Resolving Conflict in Africa: The Fermeda Workshop.* New Haven: Yale University Press.

El-Ayouty, Y., and I. W. Zartman, eds. 1984. *The OAU After Twenty Years.* New York: Praeger.

Harbeson, J., and D. Rothchild, eds. 1991. *Africa in World Politics.* Boulder: Westview.

Holt, D., 1994, "United Nations Angola Verification Mission II." Chapter 17 of *Building International Community: Cooperating for Peace Case Studies.* Clements, K., and R. Ward, eds. St. Leonards, NSW, Australia: Allen and Unwin, in association with the Peace Research Centre, Research School of Pacific and Asian Studies, Australian National University, Canberra, ACT, Australia, 302–310.

Jabri, V. 1990. *Mediating Conflict: Decision-Making and Western Intervention in Namibia.* Manchester: Manchester University Press.

Keller, E. J., and D. S. Rothchild, eds. 1987. *Afro-Marxist Regimes: Ideology and Public Policy.* Boulder: Lynne Rienner.

Khadiagala, G. M. 1998. "Prospects for a Division of Labour: African Regional Organisations in Conflict Prevention." Chapter 8 of *Early Warning and Conflict Prevention: Limitations and Possibilities.* Van Walraven, K., ed. The Hague, Boston: Kluwer Law International, 131–148.

Kobak, D. 1997. "Rwanda: Never Again?" Chapter 5 of *Breaking the Cycle: A Framework for Conflict Intervention.* Von Lipsey, R., ed. New York: St. Martin's, 149–171.

Lendon, B. 1994. "Somalia: International Intervention in a Failed State." Chapter 3 of *Building International Community: Cooperating for Peace Case Studies.* Clements, K., and R. Ward, eds. St. Leonards, NSW, Australia: Allen and Unwin, in association with the Peace Research Centre, Research School of Pacific and Asian Studies, Australian National University, Canberra, ACT, Australia, 104–139.

Leys, C., J. S. Saul, and S. Brown. 1995. *Namibia's Liberation Struggle: The Two-Edged Sword.* London: J. Currey.

Madden, J. 1994. "Namibia: A Lesson for Success." Chapter 12 of *Building International Community: Cooperating for Peace Case Studies.* Clements, K., and R. Ward, eds. St. Leonards, NSW, Australia: Allen and Unwin, in association with the Peace Research Centre, Research School of Pacific and Asian Studies, Australian National University, Canberra, ACT, Australia, 255–260.

Makinda, S. 1982. *Kenya's Role in the Somali-Ethiopian Conflict.* Working Paper #55. Canberra: Center for Strategic and Defence Studies, Australian National University.

Morris, M. S. L. 1974. *Armed Conflict in Southern Africa: A Survey of Regional Terrorisms from Their Beginnings to the Present, With a Comprehensive Examination of the Portuguese Position.* Cape Town: J. Spence.

Mungazi, D. A. 1992. *Colonial Policy and Conflict in Zimbabwe: A Study of Cultures in Collision, 1890–1979.* New York: Crane, Russak.

Naidoo, P. 1992. *Le Rona Re Batho: An Account of the 1982 Masera Massacre.* Verulam, South Africa: P. Naidoo.

Nyhamar, T. 1997. "Rationality Explanations: The Case of Kissinger's Decision to Supply Arms to Angola." *Cooperation and Conflict* 32, No. 2: 181–205.

Odom, T. 1988. *Dragon Operations: Hostage Rescues in the Congo, 1964–1965.* Leavenworth, Kan.: Combat Studies Institute, U.S. Army Command and General Staff College.

Ojo, O. J. C. B., D. K. Orwa, and C. M. B. Utete. 1985. *African International Relations.* London and New York: Longman.

Oliver, A. 1997. "The Somalia Syndrome." Chapter 4 of *Breaking the Cycle: A Framework for Conflict Intervention.* Von Lipsey, R., ed. New York: St. Martin's, 119–148.

Oluo, S. L. O. 1982. *Conflict Management of the OAU in Intra-African Conflicts, 1963–1980.* Ann Arbor, Mich.: University Microfilms International.

Onwuka, R. I., and T. M. Shaw, eds. 1989. *Africa in World Politics: Into the 1990s.* New York: St. Martin's.

Ottaway, M. 1991. "Mediation in a Transitional Conflict: Eritrea." Zartman, I. W., ed. *Resolving Regional Conflicts: International Perspectives. Annals of the American Academy of Political and Social Science* 518 (November): 69–81.

Patman, R. 1996. *Disarmament in a Failed State: The Experience of the UN in Somalia.* Working Paper #162. Canberra: Australian National University Research School of Pacific Studies, Peace Research Centre, 1–39.

Rothchild, D., and C. Hartzell. 1991. "Great and Medium Power Mediations: Angola." Zartman, I. W., ed. *Resolving Regional Conflicts: International Perspectives, Annals of the American Academy of Political and Social Science* 518 (November): 39–57.

Selassie, B. 1980. *Conflict and Intervention in the Horn of Africa.* New York: Monthly Review Press.

Shaw, T. M., S. J. MacLean, and K. Orr. 1998. "Peace-Building and African Organisations: Towards Subcontracting or a New and Sustainable Division of Labour?" Chapter 9 of *Early Warning and Conflict Prevention: Limitations and Possibilities.* Van Walraven, K., ed. The Hague, Boston: Kluwer Law International, 149–161.

Smith, S. 1990. *Front-line Africa: The Right to a Future: An Oxfam Report on Conflict and Poverty in South Africa.* Oxford: Oxfam.

Steadman, S. J. 1991. *Peacemaking in Civil War: International Mediation in Zimbabwe, 1974–1980.* Boulder: Lynne Rienner.

Stockholm International Peace Research Institute (SIPRI). 1976. *Southern Africa: The Escalation of a Conflict: A Politico-Military Study.* New York: Praeger.

Touval, S. 1972. *The Boundary Politics of Independent Africa.* Cambridge: Harvard University Press.

University of London, Center for African Studies. 1972. *Conflicts in Africa.* Adelphi Papers #93. London: IISS.

Vansina, J. 1990. *Paths in the Rainforests: Toward a History of Political Tradition in Equatorial Africa.* London: J. Currey.

Wight, J. L. 1989. *Libya, Chad, and the Central Sahara.* Totowa, N.J.: Barnes and Noble.

Wild, P. B., 1971. "The Organisation of African Unity and the Algerian-Moroccan Border Conflict: A Study of New Machinery for Peacekeeping and for the Peaceful Settlement of Disputes Among African States." *Regional International Organisations/Structures and Functions.* Tharp, R. A., ed. New York: St. Martin's, 182–199.

Wilson, A. 1991. *The Challenge Road: Women and the Eritrean Revolution.* London: Earthscan.

Windrich, E. 1992. *The Cold War Guerrilla: Jonas Savimbi, the U.S. Media, and the Angolan War.* New York: Greenwood.

Woodward, P., and M. Forthsyth, eds. 1994. *Conflict and Peace in the Horn of Africa: Federalism and Its Alternatives.* Aldershot (Hants), England: Dartmouth.

Woronoff, J. 1970. *Organization of African Unity.* Metuchen, N.J.: Scarecrow.

Zartman, I. W. 1989. *Ripe for Resolution: Conflict and Intervention in Africa.* Updated edition. New York: Oxford University Press.

———. 1999. "Mediation by Regional Organisations: The Organisation of African Unity (OAU) in Chad and Congo." Chapter 5 of *Studies in International Mediation: Essays in Honor of Jeffrey Z. Rubin.* Bercovitch, J., ed. New York: Palgrave MacMillan.

———., ed. 1993. *Europe and Africa: The New Phase.* Boulder: Lynne Rienner.

Zewde, B. 1991. *A History of Modern Ethiopia, 1855–1974.* London: J. Currey.

THE AMERICAS

Bagley, B., ed. 1987. *Contadora and the Diplomacy of Peace in Central America.* Boulder: Westview.

Bennett, A. 1998. "Somalia, Bosnia, and Haiti: What Went Right, What Went Wrong?" Chapter 6 of *Collective Conflict Management and Changing World Politics.* Lepgold, J., and T. G. Weiss, eds. Albany: State University of New York Press, 133–155.

Brown, J., and W. P. Snyder, eds. 1985. *The Regionalization of Warfare: The Falklands/Malvinas Islands, Lebanon, and the Iran-Iraq Conflicts.* New Brunswick, N.J.: Transactions.

Central Office of Information Reference Division. 1982. *The Falkland Islands: The Facts.* London: HMSO.

Coleman, K. M., and G. C. Herring. 1985. *The Central American Crisis: Sources of Conflict and the Failure of U.S. Policy.* Wilmington, Del.: Scholarly Resources.

Dominguez, J. I. 1989. *To Make a World Safe for Revolution: Cuba's Foreign Policy.* Cambridge: Harvard University Press.

Dreier, J. C. 1962. *The Organization of American States and the Hemisphere Crisis.* New York: Harper and Row.

Dunkerley, J. 1985. *The Long War: Dictatorship and Revolution in El Salvador.* New York and London: Verso.

———. 1988. *Power in the Isthmus: A Political History of Modern Central America.* New York and London: Verso.

English, A. 1984. *Armed Forces of Latin America.* London: Jane's.

Franks, O. 1983. "Falkland Island Review: Report of a Committee of Privy Councilors." London: Falkland Islands Review Committee/HMSO.

Freedman, L. 1988. *Britain and the Falklands War.* Oxford: B. Blackwell.

Gamba, V. 1987. *The Falklands/Malvinas War: A Model for North-South Crisis Prevention.* Boston: Allen and Unwin.

Goldblat, J., and V. Millan. 1983. *The Falklands/Malvinas Conflict: A Spur to Arms Build-Up.* Solna, Sweden: SIPRI.

Gopal, M. M. 1992. *Politics, Race, and Youth in Guyana.* San Francisco: Mellen Research University Press.

Halebsky, S., R. Hernandez, and J. M. Kirk, eds. 1990. *Transformation and Struggle: Cuba Faces the 1990s.* New York: Praeger.

Hastings, M., and S. Jenkins. 1983. *The Battle for the Falklands.* London: Michael Joseph.

Horowitz, I. L. 1993. *The Conscience of Worms and the Cowardice of Lions: Cuban Politics and Culture in an American Context.* University of Miami Lectures, North-South Center, Coral Gables, Florida. New Brunswick, N.J.: Transaction.

———., ed. 1978. *Castro's Cuba in the 1970s.* 3d edition. New Brunswick, N.J.: Transaction.

Karol, K. S. 1970. *Guerrillas in Power: The Course of the Cuban Revolution.* Translated by A. Pomerans. New York: Hill and Wang.

Kirk, J. M. 1989. *Between God and the Party: Religion and Politics in Revolutionary Cuba.* Gainesville: University of Florida Press.

Kornbluh, P. 1987. *Nicaragua: the Price of Intervention: Reagan's Wars Against the Sandinistas.* Washington, D.C.: Institute for Policy Studies.

Lernoux, P. 1982. *Cry of the People: The Struggle for Human Rights in Latin America: The Catholic Church in Conflict with U.S. Policy.* Harmondsworth (Middlesex), England: Penguin.

Levin, A. L. 1974. *The Organization of American States and the United Nations: Relations in the Peace and Security Field.* A United Nations Institute for Training and Research (UNITAR) Regional Study, Peaceful Settlement No. 7, No. 4. New York: UNITAR.

Levine, D. H. 1981. *Religion and Politics in Latin America: The Catholic Church in Venezuela and Colombia.* Princeton, N.J.: Princeton University Press.

Lopes, C. 1987. *Guinea-Bissau: From Liberation Struggle to Independent Statehood.* Translated by Michael Wolfers. Boulder: Westview.

Lowenthal, A. F. 1987. *Partners in Conflict: The United States and Latin America.* Baltimore: Johns Hopkins University Press.

McClintock, M. 1985. *The American Connection.* London: Zed.

Medin, T. 1990. *Cuba: The Shaping of Revolutionary Consciousness.* Boulder: Lynne Rienner.

Middlebrook, M. 1985. *Operation Corporate: The Falklands War, 1982.* London: Viking.

Morley, M. T. T. 1987. *Imperial State and Revolution: The U.S. and Cuba, 1952–1986.* Cambridge: Cambridge University Press.

Moro, R. 1989. *The History of the South Atlantic Conflict: The War for the Malvinas.* New York: Praeger.

Mujal-Leon, E. M. 1989. *European Socialism and the Conflict in Central America.* Washington Papers #138. New York: CSIS/Praeger.

Munck, R. 1984. *Revolutionary Trends in Latin America.* Montreal: Centre for Developing Area Studies, McGill University.

Pastor, R. 1987. *Condemned to Repetition: The United States and Nicaragua.* Princeton, N.J.: Princeton University Press.

Pear, R., and E. E. Larson. 1983. *The Falkland Islands Dispute in International Law and Politics: A Documentary Source Book.* London: Oceana.

Purcell, S. K. 1992. *Cuba at the Turning Point: A Conference Report, 1992.* New York: Americas Society.

Rabkin, R. P. 1991. *Cuban Politics: The Revolutionary Experiment.* New York: Praeger.

Ropp, S. C., and J. A. Morris. 1984. *Central America: Crisis and Adaptation.* Albuquerque: University of New Mexico Press.

Sater, W. F. 1990. *Chile and the United States: Empires in Conflict.* Athens: University of Georgia Press.

Schulz, D. E., ed. 1994. *Cuba and the Future.* Westport, Conn.: Greenwood.

Shearman, P. 1987. *The Soviet Union and Cuba.* London: Routledge and Kegan Paul.

Simon, J. 1988. *Guatemala: Eternal Spring, Eternal Tyranny.* New York: Norton.

Slater, J. 1965. *A Revaluation of Collective Security: The OAS in Action.* Columbus: Ohio State University Press.

———. 1970. *Intervention and Negotiation: The United States and the Dominican Revolution.* New York: Harper and Row.

Somoza, A. 1980. *Nicaragua Betrayed.* As told to Jack Cox. Boston: Western Islands.

Spinner, T. J. 1984. *A Political and Social History of Guyana, 1945–1983.* Boulder: Westview.

Stockwell, J. 1978. *In Search of Enemies: A CIA Story.* New York: Norton.

Stoll, D. 1993. *Between Two Armies in the Ixil Towns of Guatemala.* New York: Columbia University Press.

Stuart, D. 1994. "United Nations Involvement in the Peace Process in El Salvador." Chapter 13 of *Building International Community: Cooperating for Peace Case Studies.* Clements, K., and R. Ward, eds. St. Leonards, NSW, Australia: Allen and Unwin, in association with the Peace Research Centre, Research School of Pacific and Asian Studies, Australian National University, Canberra, ACT, Australia, 261–272.

Stubbs, J. 1989. *Cuba: The Test of Time.* London: Latin America Bureau.

Turner, R. 1987. *Nicaragua v. United States: A Look at the Facts.* Washington, D.C.: Pergamon-Brassey's.

Vaky, V. P. and H. Muñoz. 1993. *The Future of the Organization of American States: Essays.* New York: Twentieth Century Fund Press.

Vanderlaan, M. 1986. *Revolution and Foreign Policy in Nicaragua.* Boulder: Westview.

Vasques, C., and M. Garcia y Griego. 1983. *Mexican-U.S. Relations: Conflict and Convergence.* Los Angeles: UCLA Latin American Center Publications.

Welch, R. E. 1985. *Response to Revolution: The United States and the Cuban Revolution, 1959–1961.* Chapel Hill: University of North Carolina Press.

Windsor, P. 1983. "Diplomatic Dimensions of the Falkland Crisis." *Millennium: Journal of International Studies* 12, No. 1 (spring): 88–96.

Wydem, P. 1980. *Bay of Pigs: The Untold Story*. New York: Simon and Schuster.

Wyndham, H. 1994. "The Falklands: Failure of a Mission." Chapter 9 of *Building International Community: Cooperating for Peace Case Studies*. Clements, K., and R. Ward, eds. St. Leonards, NSW, Australia: Allen and Unwin, in association with the Peace Research Centre, Research School of Pacific and Asian Studies, Australian National University, Canberra, ACT, Australia, 229–242.

ASIA: EAST ASIA AND THE PACIFIC

Acharya, A. 1993. *Third World Conflicts and International Order After the Cold War*. Working Paper #134. Canberra: Peace Research Center, Australian National University.

———. 1994. "Cambodia, The United Nations and the Problems of Peace," *Pacific Review* 7, No. 3: 297–307.

Aijmer, G., ed. 1984. *Leadership on the China Coast*. London: Curzon.

Alley, R. 1994. "The United Nations and the Asia Pacific: An Overview." *Pacific Review* 7, No. 3: 245–260.

———. 1998. *The United Nations in Southeast Asia and the South Pacific*. International Political Economy Series. London: Macmillan.

Amnesty International. 1985. *East Timor: Violations of Human Rights: Extrajudicial Executions, "Disappearances," Torture, and Political Imprisonment, 1975–1984*. London: Amnesty International.

Aung San Suu Kyi. 1995. *Freedom from Fear, and Other Writings*. Edited with an introduction by Michael Aris. Revised edition. New Delhi and New York: Penguin.

Ayoob, M., ed. 1986. *Regional Security in the Third World: Case Studies from South East Asia and the Middle East*. London: Croom Helm.

Chandler, D. P. 1992. *Brother Number One: A Political Biography of Pol Pot*. Boulder: Westview.

Clements, K. P., ed. 1993. *Peace and Security in the Asia Pacific Region: Post–Cold War Problems and Prospects*. Palmerston North, New Zealand: Dunmore.

Crawford, J. A. B. 1996. *In the Field for Peace: New Zealand's Contribution to International Peace-Support Operations—1950–1995*. New Zealand: New Zealand Defence Force.

Doyle, M. W., I. Johnstone, and R. C. Orr, eds. 1997. *Keeping the Peace: Multidimensional UN Operations in Cambodia and El Salvador*. Cambridge: International Peace Academy, Cambridge University Press.

Elliot, D. W. P. 1981. *The Third Indochina Conflict*. Boulder: Westview.

Grinter, L. E., and Y. W. Kihl, eds. 1987. *East Asian Conflict Zones: Prospects for Regional Stability and Deescalation*. New York: St. Martin's.

Herr, R. A. 1994. "The United Nations and the South Pacific." *Pacific Review* 7, No. 3: 261–269.

Jackson, K., ed. 1989. *Cambodia, 1975–1978: Rendezvous with Death*. Princeton, N.J.: Princeton University Press.

Kemish, I. 1994. "Managing Potential Conflict in the South China Sea." Chapter 8 of *Building International Community: Cooperating for Peace Case Studies*. Clements, K., and R. Ward, eds. St. Leonards, NSW, Australia: Allen and Unwin, in association with the Peace Research Centre, Research School of Pacific and Asian Studies, Australian National University, Canberra, ACT, Australia, 222–228.

Khong, Y. F. 1997. "ASEAN and the Southeast Asian Security Complex." Chapter 14 of *Regional Orders: Building Security in a New World*. Lake, D. A., and P. M. Morgan, eds. University Park: Pennsylvania State University Press, 318–339.

Kiernan, B. 1985. *How Pol Pot Came to Power: A History of Communism in Kampuchea, 1930–1975*. London: Verso.

Kiljunen, K., ed. 1984. *Kampuchea: Decade of the Genocide: Report of a Finnish Inquiry Commission*. London: Zed.

Klintworth, G. 1989. *The Vietnamese Achievement in Kampuchea*. Working Paper #181. Canberra: Strategic and Defence Studies Center, Australian National University.

———. 1989. *Vietnam's Intervention in Cambodia in International Law*. Canberra: AGPS.

———. 1990. *Vietnam's Withdrawal from Cambodia: Regional Issues and Realignments*. Working Paper #64. Canberra: Strategic and Defence Studies Center, Australian National University.

Kolko, G. 1986. *Vietnam: Anatomy of a War 1940–1975*. London: Allen and Unwin.

Langley, G. 1992. *A Decade of Dissent: Vietnam and the Conflict on the Australian Home Front*. North Sydney: Allen and Unwin.

Leifer, M. 1980. *Conflict and Regional Order in South East Asia*. Adelphi Papers #162. London: IISS.

———. 1989. *ASEAN and the Security of South-East Asia*. London: Routledge.

Lintner, B. 1990. *Outrage: Burma's Struggle for Democracy*. 2d edition. London: White Lotus.

Lithgow, S. 1994. "Cambodia." Chapter 1 of *Building International Community: Cooperating for Peace Case Studies*. Clements, K., and R. Ward, eds. St. Leonards, NSW, Australia: Allen and Unwin, in association with the Peace Research Centre, Research School of Pacific and Asian Studies, Australian National University, Canberra, ACT, Australia, 27–57.

Lockhart, G. 1985. *"Strike in the South, Clear in the North": The "Problem of Kampuchea" and the Roots of Vietnamese Strategy There*. Clayton (Victoria), Australia: Monash University.

Low, A. D. 1987. *The Sino-Soviet Confrontation Since Mao Zedong: Dispute, Detente, or Conflict?* Boulder: Social Science Monographs.

Lu, C. 1986. *The Sino-Indian Border Dispute: A Legal Study*. New York: Greenwood.

Maung, M. 1991. *The Burma Road to Poverty*. New York: Praeger.

Maung Maung, G. 1983. *Burmese Political Values: The Socio-Political Roots of Authoritarianism*. New York: Praeger.

Maung Maung, U. 1980. *From Sangha to Laity: Nationalist Movements of Burma, 1920–1940*. New Delhi: Manohar.

McDougall, H., and J. Want. 1985. "Burma in 1984: Political Stasis or Political Renewal?" *Asian Survey* 25 (February): 241–248, 789.

Millar, T. B., ed. 1983. *International Security in the South-East Asia and South–West Pacific Region.* St. Lucia, Australia: University of Queensland Press.

Mobbed, I. W., and D. P. Chandler. 1995. *The Khmers.* Oxford: B. Blackwell.

Nair, K. K. 1984. *ASEAN-Indochina Relations Since 1979: The Politics of Accommodation.* Working Paper #30. Canberra: Strategic and Defence Studies Center, Australian National University.

———. 1984. *ASEAN-Indonesia Relations Since 1975: The Politics of Accommodation.* Canberra Papers on Strategy and Defence, No. 30. Canberra, Australia: Strategic and Defence Studies Centre, Research School of Pacific Studies, Australian National University.

Neemia, U. F. 1986. *Cooperation and Conflict: Costs, Benefits, and National Interests in Pacific Regional Cooperation.* Suva, Fiji: Institute of Pacific Studies, University of the South Pacific.

Nguyen-Vo, T. H. 1992. *Khmer-Viet Relations and the Third Indochina Conflict.* Jefferson, N.C.: McFarland.

Project Maje. 1992. *Deadly Enterprises: A Burma-India Situation Report.* December. Cranford, N.J.: Project Maje.

Ranjit Singh, D. 1984. *Brunei, 1839–1983: The Problems of Political Survival.* Singapore and New York: Oxford University Press.

Richardson, H. 1984. *Tibet and Its History.* 2d edition. Boulder: Shambhala.

Ross, R. 1988. *The Indochina Tangle: China's Vietnam Policy, 1975–1979.* New York: Columbia University Press.

Sakamoto, Y. 1988. *Asia, Militarization, and Regional Conflict.* New York: Zed.

Scalapino, R. A., S. Sato, and J. Wanandi, eds. 1986. *Internal and External Security Issues in Asia.* Berkeley: Institute of East Asian Studies, University of California.

Segal, G. 1985. *Defending China.* New York: Oxford University Press.

Snitwongse, K. 1991. *South East Asia Beyond a Cambodian Settlement: Conflict or Cooperation?* Working Paper #223. Canberra: Strategic and Defence Studies Center, Australian National University.

Steinberg, D. I. 1981. *Burma's Road Toward Development: Growth and Ideology Under Military Rule.* Boulder: Westview.

Sum, Ngai-Ling. 1996. "The Newly Industrial Countries (NICs) and Competing Strategies of East Asian Regionalism." Chapter 7 of *Regionalism and World Order.* Gamble, A., and A. Payne, eds. London: Macmillan, 207–245.

Summers, H. 1985. *Vietnam War Almanac.* New York: Facts on File.

Taylor, R. H. 1983. *An Undeveloped State: The Study of Modern Burma's Politics.* London: Department of Economics and Political Studies, School of Oriental and African Studies, University of London.

Tinker, H., ed. 1984. *Burma: The Struggle for Independence, 1944–1948: Documents from Official and Private Sources.* London: HMSO.

Turley, W. 1986. *The Second Indochina War: A Short Political and Military History, 1954–1975.* Boulder: Westview.

Vickery, M. 1984. *Cambodia, 1975–1982.* Boston: South End.

Wah, C. K. 1995. "ASEAN: Consolidation and Institutional Change." *Pacific Review* 8, No. 3: 424–439.

Young, M. B. 1991. *The Vietnam Wars, 1945–1990.* New York: HarperCollins.

Zakaria, H. A. 1984. *War and Conflict Studies in Malaysia: The State of the Art.* Working Paper #76. Canberra: Strategic and Defence Studies Center, Australian National University.

Zheng, Y. 1994. "Perforated Sovereignty: Provincial Dynamism and China's Foreign Trade." *Pacific Review* 7, No. 3: 309–321.

ASIA: SOUTHWEST ASIA

Bradnock, R. W. 1990. *India's Foreign Policy Since 1971.* London: Royal Institute of International Affairs; New York: Council of Foreign Relations Press.

Bretherton, D. 1997. *A Mediation Process for Sri Lanka.* Working Paper #168. Canberra: Australian National University Research School of Pacific Studies, Peace Research Centre, 1–26.

Crossette, B. 1993. *India: Facing the Twenty-first Century.* Bloomington: Indiana University Press.

International Commission of Jurists Secretariat. 1972. *The Events in East Pakistan, 1971: A Legal Study.* Geneva: International Commission of Jurists Secretariat.

Maley, W. 1994. "Peacemaking Diplomacy: United Nations Good Offices in Afghanistan." Chapter 11 of *Building International Community: Cooperating for Peace Case Studies.* Clements, K., and R. Ward, eds. St. Leonards, NSW, Australia: Allen and Unwin, in association with the Peace Research Centre, Research School of Pacific and Asian Studies, Australian National University, Canberra, ACT, Australia, 250–254.

Ray, H. 1983. *China's Strategy in Nepal.* New Delhi: Radiant Publishers.

Tucker, K. K. 1997. "Enfranchisement Wanted: Tajikistan. Chapter 10 of *Breaking the Cycle: A Framework for Conflict Intervention.* Von Lipsey, R., ed. New York: St. Martin's, 249–267.

Volk, F. 1994. "Kashmir: The Problem of United Nations Peacekeeping Contributing to Political 'Stasis.' " Chapter 16 of *Building International Community: Cooperating for Peace Case Studies.* Clements, K., and R. Ward, eds. St. Leonards, NSW, Australia: Allen and Unwin, in association with the Peace Research Centre, Research School of Pacific and Asian Studies, Australian National University, Canberra, ACT, Australia, 288–301.

Yasmeen, S. 1987. *India and Pakistan: Why the Latest Exercise in Brinkmanship?* Working Paper #125. Canberra: Strategic and Defence Studies Center, Australian National University.

EUROPE

Allison, R. 1988. *The Soviet Union and the Strategy of Non-Alignment in the Third World.* Cambridge: Cambridge University Press.

Allison, R., and P. Williams. 1990. *Superpower Competition and Crisis Prevention in the Third World.* Cambridge: Cambridge University Press.

Antola, E. 1989. "The CSCS as a Collaborative Order." Chapter 4 of *The Processes of International Negotiations*. Mautner-Markhof, F., ed. Boulder: Westview Press, 43–53.

Archer, C. 1994. *Organising Europe: The Institutions of Integration*. 2d edition. London: Edward Arnold.

Atiyas, N. B. 1995. "Mediating Regional Conflicts and Negotiating Flexibility: Peace Efforts in Bosnia-Herzegovina." *Annals of the American Academy of Political and Social Science* 542 (November): 185–201.

Bennett, A. 1998 "Somalia, Bosnia, and Haiti: What Went Right, What Went Wrong?" Chapter 6 of *Collective Conflict Management and Changing World Politics*. Lepgold, J., and T. G. Weiss, eds. Albany: State University of New York Press, 133–155.

Bothe, M., N. Ronzitti, and A. Rosas, eds. 1997. *The OSCE in the Maintenance of Peace and Security: Conflict Prevention, Crisis Management and Peaceful Settlement of Disputes*. The Hague, Netherlands: Kluwer Law International.

Burg, S. L. 1995. "The International Community and the Yugoslav Crisis." Chapter 9 of *International Organizations and Ethnic Conflict*. Esman, M. J., and S. Telhami, eds. Ithaca, N.Y.: Cornell University Press, 235–271.

Cohen, L. J. 1995. *Broken Bonds: Yugoslavia's Disintegration and Balkan Politics in Transition*. 2d edition. Boulder: Westview.

Denitch, B. 1994. *Ethnic Nationalism: The Tragic Death of Yugoslavia*. Minneapolis: University of Minnesota Press.

Dewar, M. 1984. *Brush Fire Wars: Minor Campaigns of the British Army Since 1945*. New York: St. Martin's.

Dinan, D., ed. 1998. *Encyclopedia of the European Union*. Boulder: Lynne Rienner.

Eknes, Å. 1995. "The United Nations' Predicament in the Former Yugoslavia." Chapter 7 of *The United Nations and Civil Wars*. Weiss, T. G., ed. Boulder: Lynne Rienner, 109–126.

European Union Encyclopedia and Directory, The. 1996. 2d edition. London: Europa Publications.

Eyal, J. 1993. *Europe and Yugoslavia: Lessons From a Failure*. Whitehall Paper #19. London: Royal United Services Institute for Defence Studies.

Freeman, J. 1991. *Security and the CSCE Process: The Stockholm Conference and Beyond*. New York: St. Martin's.

Griffiths, S. I. 1993. *Nationalism and Ethnic Conflict: Threats to European Security*. Oxford: Oxford University Press.

Hong, Ki-Joon. 1997. *The CSCE Security Regime Formation: An Asian Perspective*. London: Macmillan Press Ltd.

Institute for European Studies. 1993. *Interethnic Conflict and War in the Former Yugoslavia*. Working Paper #140. Canberra: Australian National University.

Jørgensen, K. E., ed. 1997. *European Approaches to Crisis Management*. The Hague, Netherlands: Kluwer Law International.

Khan, R. M. 1991. *Untying the Afghan Knot: Negotiation and Soviet Withdrawal*. Institute for the Study of Diplomacy. Durham, N.C.: Duke University Press.

Leach, R. 2000. *Europe: A Concise Encyclopedia of the European Union from Aachen to Zollverein*. 3d edition. London: Profile Books.

MacKenzie, K. 1983. "Greece and Turkey: Disarray on NATO's Southern Flank." *Conflict Studies* No. 154. London: Institute for the Study of Conflict.

MacQueen, N. 1983. "Ireland and the United Nations Peacekeeping Force in Cyprus." *Review of International Studies* 9, No. 2 (April): 95–108.

Magas, B. 1993. *The Destruction of Yugoslavia: Tracking the Breakup, 1980–1992*. London: Verso.

Markides, K. 1977. *The Rise and Fall of the Cyprus Republic*. New Haven, Conn.: Yale University Press.

McKenzie, M. M., and P. H. Loedel, eds. 1998. *The Promise and Reality of European Security Co-operation: States, Interests, and Institutions*. Westport, Conn.: Praeger.

Miall, H., ed. 1994. *Redefining Europe: New Patterns of Conflict and Cooperation*. New York: Pinter.

Mojzes, P. 1994. *The Yugoslavian Inferno: Ethnoreligious Warfare in the Balkans*. New York: Continuum.

Morris, D. 1994. "Keeping but Not Making Peace: The UN Peacekeeping Force in Cyprus." Chapter 14 of *Building International Community: Cooperating for Peace Case Studies*. Clements, K., and R. Ward, eds. St. Leonards, NSW, Australia: Allen and Unwin, in association with the Peace Research Centre, Research School of Pacific and Asian Studies, Australian National University, Canberra, ACT, Australia, 273–279.

Nelsen, B. F., and A. Stubb, eds. 1998. *The European Union: Readings on the Theory and Practice of European Integration*. 2d edition. Boulder: Lynne Rienner.

Nilson, H. R. 1997. "Nordic Regionalisation: On How Transborder Regions Work and Why They Don't Work." *Conflict and Cooperation* 32, No. 4: 399–426.

Oleser, A. 1995. *Islam and Politics in Afghanistan*. Richmond (Surrey), England: Curzon.

Pajic, Z. 1993. *Violation of Fundamental Rights in the Former Yugoslavia*. Occasional Paper #2. London: David Davies Memorial Institute of International Studies.

Parker, M. 1997. "Anatomy of a Conflict: Chechnya." Chapter 11 of *Breaking the Cycle: A Framework for Conflict Intervention*. Von Lipsey, R., ed. New York: St. Martin's: 269–282.

Patrick, R. A., J. H. Bater, and R. Preston, eds. 1976. *Political Geography and the Cyprus Conflict, 1963–1971*. Publication Series #4. Waterloo, Ontario: Department of Geography, Faculty of Environmental Studies, University of Waterloo.

Ramcharan, B. G., ed. 1997. *The International Conference on the Former Yugoslavia: Official Papers—Vol. 2*. The Hague, Netherlands: Kluwer Law International.

Ramet, S. P. 1992. *Nationalism and Federalism in Yugoslavia, 1962–1991*. 2d edition. Bloomington: Indiana University Press.

Ramet, S. P., and L. S. Adamovich, eds. 1995. *Beyond Yugoslavia: Politics, Economics, and Culture in a Shattered Community*. Boulder: Westview.

Ronen, D. 1994. *The Origins of Ethnic Conflict: Lessons from Yugoslavia*. Working Paper #155. Australian National University Research School of Pacific Studies, Peace Research Centre, Canberra: 1–56.

Rossow, R. 1956. "The Battle of Azerbaijan, 1946." *Middle East Journal* 10 (winter): 17–32.

Roy, O. 1991. *The Lessons of the Soviet-Afghan War*. Adelphi Papers #259. London: Brassey's.

Rubinstein, A. Z. 1988. *Moscow's Third World Strategy*. Princeton, N.J.: Princeton University Press.

Rusinow, D., ed. 1988. *Yugoslavia: A Fractured Federalism.* Washington, D.C.: Wilson Center Press.

Salem, N., ed. 1992. *Cyprus: A Regional Conflict and Its Resolution.* New York: St. Martin's.

Sandole, D. J. D. 1995. "Changing Ideologies in the Conference on Security and Cooperation in Europe." *Annals of the American Academy of Political and Social Science* 542 (November): 131–147.

Schake, K. N. 1997. "The Breakup of Yugoslavia." Chapter 3 of *Breaking the Cycle: A Framework for Conflict Intervention.* Von Lipsey, R., ed. New York: St. Martin's: 95–117.

Schmid, A. P. 1985. *Soviet Military Interventions Since 1945.* With case studies by E. Berends. New Brunswick, N.J.: Transaction.

Sena, C. 1986. *Afghanistan: Politics, Economics, and Society: Revolution, Resistance, Intervention.* Boulder: Lynne Rienner.

Simecka, M. 1984. *The Restoration of Order: The Normalization of Czechoslovakia, 1969–1976.* Translated by A. G. Brain. London: Verso.

Sloss, L., and M. Scott Davis, eds. 1986. *A Game of High Stakes: Lessons Learned in Negotiating With the Soviet Union.* Cambridge, Mass.: Ballinger.

Stern, L. M. 1977. *The Wrong Horse: The Politics of Intervention and Failure of American Diplomacy.* New York: Times Books.

Suda, Z. 1969. *The Czechoslovak Socialist Republic.* Baltimore: Johns Hopkins University Press.

Sugar, P., P. Harak, and T. Frank. 1990. *A History of Hungary.* Bloomington: Indiana University Press.

Svitak, I. 1971. *The Czechoslovak Experiment, 1968–1969.* New York: Columbia University Press.

t'Hart, P., E. Stern, and B. Sundelius. 1998. "Crisis Management: An Agenda for Research and Training in Europe." *Cooperation and Conflict* 33, No. 2: 207–224.

Tigrid, P. 1971. *Why Dubcek Fell.* London: MacDonald and Company.

Toma, P. A. 1988. *Socialist Authority: The Hungarian Experience.* New York: Praeger.

Toma, P. A., and I. Volyges. 1977. *Politics in Hungary.* San Francisco: W. H. Freeman.

Urban, M. 1989. *War in Afghanistan.* New York: St. Martin's.

Valenta, J. 1979. *Soviet Intervention in Czechoslovakia, 1968: Anatomy of a Decision.* Baltimore: Johns Hopkins University Press.

Valents, J. 1989. *Gorbachev's New Thinking and Third World Conflicts.* New York: Transaction.

Vali, F. 1961. *Rift and Revolt in Hungary: Nationalism Versus Communism.* Cambridge: Harvard University Press.

Vanezis, P. 1977. *Cyprus: The Unfinished Agony.* London: Abelard-Schuman.

Warnes, K. 1994. *Developing More Effective Regional Peacemaking Structures: Western European Intercession in the Yugoslav Conflict (1990–1993).* Working Paper #153. Canberra: Australian National University Research School of Pacific Studies, Peace Research Centre, 1–45.

Webb, K., V. Koutrakou, and M. Walters. 1996. "The Yugoslavian Conflict, European Mediation, and the Contingency Model: A Critical Perspective." Chapter 8 of *Resolving International Conflicts: The Theory and Practice of Mediation.* Bercovitch, J., ed. Boulder: Lynne Rienner, 171–189.

Webber, M. 1996. "Coping with Anarchy: Ethnic Conflict and International Organizations in the Former Soviet Union." *International Relations* 13, No. 1 (April): 1–27.

Weiss, T. G., and M. A. Kessler. 1990. "Moscow's UN Policy." *Foreign Policy* 79 (summer): 94–112.

Whelan, J. G. 1983. *Soviet Diplomacy and Negotiating Behavior.* Boulder: Westview.

White, S. 1992. "Towards a Post Soviet Politics?" Chapter 1 of *Developments in Soviet and Post-Soviet Politics.* 2d edition. White, S., A. Pravda, and Z. Gitelman, eds. London: Macmillan, 1–21.

Willerton, J. P. 1992. *Patronage and Politics in the USSR.* Cambridge: Cambridge University Press.

Wilson, D. 1979. *Tito's Yugoslavia.* Cambridge: Cambridge University Press.

Wilson, M. 1994. "The Balkans." Chapter 4 of *Building International Community: Cooperating for Peace Case Studies.* Clements, K., and R. Ward, eds. St. Leonards, NSW, Australia: Allen and Unwin, in association with the Peace Research Centre, Research School of Pacific and Asian Studies, Australian National University, Canberra, ACT, Australia, 140–162.

MIDDLE EAST

Agha, H., and A. S. Khalidi. 1995. *Syria and Iran: Rivalry and Cooperation.* New York: Council on Foreign Relations Press for the Royal Institute of International Affairs.

Albin, C. 1997. "Negotiating Intractable Conflicts: On the Future of Jerusalem." *Cooperation and Conflict* 32, No. 1: 29–77.

Anderson, R., R. F. Seibert, and J. G. Wagner. 1990. *Politics and Change in the Middle East: Sources of Conflict and Accommodation.* Englewood Cliffs, N.J.: Prentice Hall.

Aronoff, M. J. 1989. *Israeli Visions and Division: Cultural Change and Political Conflict.* New Brunswick, N.J.: Transaction.

Aronson, S. 1978. *Conflict and Bargaining in the Middle East: An Israeli Perspective.* Baltimore: Johns Hopkins University Press.

Ayoob, M. 1981. *Defusing the Middle East Time Bomb: A State for the Palestinians.* Working Paper #35. Canberra: Strategic and Defence Studies Center, Australian National University.

———., ed. 1986. *Regional Security in the Third World: Case Studies From South East Asia and the Middle East.* London: Croom Helm.

Baker, R. W. 1990. *Sadat and After: Struggles for Egypt's Political Soul.* Cambridge: Harvard University Press.

Barnett, M. N. 1992. *Confronting the Costs of War: Military Power, State, and Society in Egypt and Israel.* Princeton, N.J.: Princeton University Press.

Bell, C. 1986. *Politics, Diplomacy, and Islam: Four Case Studies.* Canberra Studies in World Affairs #21. Canberra: International Relations, Research School of Pacific Studies, Australian National University.

Ben-Dor, G., and D. B. Dewitt, eds. 1987. *Conflict Management in the Middle East.* Lexington, Mass.: Lexington Books.

Bercovitch, J. 1997. "Conflict Management and the Oslo Experience: Assessing the Success of Israeli-Palestinian Peacemaking." *International Negotiation* 2: 217–235.

Boulding, E. 1994. *Building Peace in the Middle East: Challenges for States and Civil Society.* Boulder: Lynne Rienner.

Brown, L. C. 1984. *International Politics and the Middle East: Old Rules, Dangerous Game.* London: I. B. Tauris.

Butterworth, C. E., and I. W. Zartman, eds. 1992. *Political Islam.* Newbury Park, Calif.: Sage.

Capitanchik, D. B. 1991. *The Middle East: Conflict and Stability.* Oxford: B. Blackwell.

Cohen, R. I., ed. 1990. *Culture and Conflict in Egyptian-Israeli Relations: A Dialogue of the Deaf.* Bloomington: Indiana University Press.

Dawisha, A., and I. W. Zartman, eds. 1988. *Beyond Coercion: The Durability of the Arab State.* London: Croom Helm.

Dowty, A. 1984. *Middle East Crisis: U.S. Decision-Making in 1958, 1970, and 1973.* Berkeley and Los Angeles: University of California Press.

Fahmy, I. 1983. *Negotiating for Peace in the Middle East.* London: Croom Helm.

Farah, N. R. 1986. *Religious Strife in Egypt: Crisis and Ideological Conflict in the 1970s.* New York: Gordon and Breach Science Publishers.

Feste, K. A. 1991. *Plans for Peace: Negotiation and the Arab-Israeli Conflict.* New York: Greenwood.

Fischer, S. 1994. *Securing Peace in the Middle East.* Cambridge: MIT Press.

Freidlander, M. A. 1983. *Sadat and Begin: The Domestic Politics of Peacemaking.* Boulder: Westview.

Gause, F. 1990. *Saudi-Yemeni Relations: Domestic Structures and Foreign Policies.* New York: Columbia University Press.

George, A. L. 1993. *Bridging the Gap: Theory and Practice in Foreign Policy.* Washington, D.C.: U.S. Institute for Peace Press.

Golan, G. 1992. *Moscow and the Middle East: New Thinking on Regional Conflict.* London: Pinter.

Groom, A. J. R., E. Newman, and P. Taylor. 1996. *Burdensome Victory: The United Nations and Iraq.* Working Paper #163. Canberra: Australian National University Research School of Pacific Studies, Peace Research Centre: 1–34.

Heller, M., and S. Nusseibeh. 1991. *No Trumpets, No Drums: A Two-State Settlement of the Israeli-Palestinian Conflict.* New York: Hill and Wang.

Hollis, R. 1993. *Gulf Security: No Consensus.* Whitehall Paper #20. London: Royal United Services Institute for Defence Studies.

Hopwood, D. 1991. *Egypt, Politics, and Society, 1945–1990.* 3d edition. London: HarperCollins Academic.

Jackson, E. I. 1983. *Middle East Mission: The Story of a Major Bid for Peace in the Time of Nasser and Ben-Gurion.* New York: Norton.

Jansen, J. J. G. 1986. *The Neglected Duty: The Creed of Sadat's Assassins and Islamic Resurgence in the Middle East.* New York: Macmillan.

Kamil, M. I. 1986. *The Camp David Accords: A Testimony.* Boston: Routledge and Kegan Paul.

Kaufman, E., S. Abed, and R. L. Rothstein, eds. 1993. *Democracy, Peace, and the Israeli-Palestinian Conflict.* Boulder: Lynne Rienner.

Kellerman, B., and J. Z. Rubin, eds. 1988. *Leadership and Negotiation in the Middle East.* New York: Praeger.

Kelman, H. C. 1995. "In Practice: Contributions of an Unofficial Conflict Resolution Effort to the Israeli-Palestinian Breakthrough." *Negotiation Journal* 11, No. 1: 19–27.

Kimmerling, B. 1979. *A Conceptual Framework for the Analysis of Behaviour in a Territorial Conflict: The Generalization of the Israeli Case.* Jerusalem Papers on Peace Problems #25. Jerusalem: Leonard Davis Institute for International Relations, Hebrew University.

Kriesberg, L. 1992. *International Conflict Resolution: The US–USSR and Middle East Cases.* New Haven, Conn.: Yale University Press.

Lackner, H. 1985. *P. D. R. Yemen: Outpost of Socialist Development.* London: Ithaca Press.

Lapidoth, R. E., and M. Hirsch. 1992. *The Arab-Israel Conflict and Its Resolution: Selected Documents.* Boston: M. Nijhoff.

Lesh, A. M., and MA. Tessler. 1989. *Israel, Egypt, and the Palestinians: From Camp David to Intifada.* Bloomington: Indiana University Press.

Lissak, M., ed. 1984. *Israeli Society and Its Defence Establishment: The Social and Political Impact of a Protracted Violent Conflict.* London: F. Cass.

Little, D., J. Kelsay, and A. A. Sucedina. 1988. *Human Rights and the Conflict of Cultures: West and Islamic Perspectives on Religious Liberty.* Columbia: University of South Carolina Press.

Litwak, R. 1981. *Sources of Inter-State Conflict.* Vol. 2 of *Security in the Persian Gulf.* Aldershot (Hants), England: IISS/Gower.

Lucas, W. S. 1991. *Divided We Stand: Britain, the United States, and the Suez Crisis.* London: Hodder and Stoughton.

Lukacs, Y., ed. 1984. *Documents on the Israel-Palestine Conflict, 1967–1983.* Cambridge: Cambridge University Press.

———. 1992. *The Israeli-Palestinian Conflict: A Documentary Record.* Cambridge: Cambridge University Press.

Mackinlay, J. 1989. *The Peacemakers: An Assessment of Peacemaking Operations at the Arab-Israel Interface.* London: Unwin Hyman.

Mango, A. 1994. *Turkey: The Challenge of a New Role.* Westport, Conn.: Praeger.

Middle East Contemporary Survey. Annual 1976/1977 .

Mor, B. D. 1993. *Decision and Interaction in Crisis: A Model of International Crisis Behavior.* Westport, Conn.: Praeger.

Oded, A. 1987. *Africa and the Middle East Conflict.* Boulder: Lynne Rienner.

Parker, R. B. 1993. *The Politics of Miscalculation in the Middle East.* Bloomington: Indiana University Press.

Peters, J. 1984. *From Time Immemorial: The Origins of the Arab-Jewish Conflict over Palestine.* New York: Harper and Row.

Pogany, I. S. 1984. *The Security Council and the Arab-Israeli Conflict.* New York: St. Martin's.

Quandt, W. B. 1977. *Decade of Decisions: American Policy Toward the Arab-Israeli Conflict, 1967–1976.* Berkeley and Los Angeles: University of California Press.

———. 1986. *Camp David: Peacemaking and Politics.* Washington, D.C.: Brookings.

———. 1988. *The Middle East: Ten Years at Camp David.* Washington, D.C.: Brookings.

———. 1993. *Peace Process: American Diplomacy and the Arab-Israeli Conflict Since 1967.* Washington, D.C.: Brookings.

Rakisits, C. 1994. "The Gulf Crisis: Failure of Preventive Diplomacy." Chapter 2 of *Building International Community: Cooperating for Peace Case Studies.* Clements, K., and R. Ward, eds. St. Leonards, NSW, Australia: Allen and Unwin, in association with the Peace Research Centre, Research School of Pacific and Asian Studies, Australian National University, Canberra, ACT, Australia, 58–103.

Rasmussen, J. L., and R. B. Oakley. 1992. *Conflict Resolution in the Middle East: Simulating a Diplomatic Negotiation Between Israel and Syria.* Washington, D.C.: U.S. Institute of Peace Press.

Roth, S. J., ed. 1988. *The Impact of the Six-Day War: A Twenty-Year Assessment.* Basingstoke (Hants), England: Macmillan.

Rubin, B. 1990. *Islamic Fundamentalism in Egyptian Politics.* New York: St. Martin's.

Rubin, J., ed. 1981. *Dynamics of Third-Party Intervention: Kissinger in the Middle East.* New York: Praeger.

Rubinstein, A. Z., ed. 1991. *The Arab-Israeli Conflict: Perspectives.* 2d edition. New York: HarperCollins.

Safty, A. 1992. *From Camp David to the Gulf: Negotiations, Language and Propaganda, and War.* Montreal, N.Y.: Black Rose Books.

Sandler, S., and H. Frisch. 1984. *Israel, the Palestinians, and the West Bank: A Study in Intercommunal Conflict.* Lexington, Mass.: Lexington Books.

Saunders, H. 1985. *The Other Walls: The Politics of the Arab-Israeli Peace Process.* Washington, D.C.: American Enterprise Institute for Public Policy Research.

Schiff, Z. 1993. *Peace and Security: Israel's Minimal Security Requirements in Negotiations with Syria.* Washington, D.C.: Washington Institute for Near East Policy.

Sirriyeh, H. 1989. *Lebanon: Dimensions of Conflict.* London: Brassey's.

Skeet, I. 1992. *Oman: Politics and Development.* New York: St. Martin's.

Smith, C. D. 1992. *Palestine and the Arab-Israeli Conflict.* 2d edition. New York: St. Martin's.

Smolansky, O. M., and B. M. Smolansky. 1991. *The USSR and Iraq: The Soviet Quest for Influence.* Durham, N.C.: Duke University Press.

Spiegel, S. L. 1992. *Conflict Management in the Middle East.* Boulder: Westview.

———., ed. 1992. *The Arab-Israeli Search for Peace.* Boulder: Lynne Rienner.

Talhami, G. H. 1992. *Palestine and Egyptian National Identity.* New York: Praeger.

Tibi, B. 1993. *Conflict and War in the Middle East, 1967–1991: Regional Dynamic and the Superpowers.* New York: St. Martin's.

Touval, S. 1982. *The Peace-Brokers: Mediators in the Arab-Israeli Conflict, 1948–1979.* Princeton, N.J.: Princeton University Press.

Tripp, C., ed. 1984. *Regional Security in the Middle East.* Aldershot (Hants), England: Gower.

Troen, S. I., and M. Shemesh. 1990. *The Suez-Sinai Crisis, 1956: Retrospective and Reappraisal.* New York: Columbia University Press.

Wilson, K. M., ed. 1983. *Imperialism and Nationalism in the Middle East: The Anglo-Egyptian Experience, 1882–1982.* London: Mansell.

Witty, C. 1980. *Mediation and Society: Conflict Management in Lebanon.* New York: Academic Press.

Index

Abdallah, Ahmed, 107
Abdul Aziz, Sultan ibn, 269
Abkhazia, 18
  Georgia–South Ossetia, Abkhazia (March 1989–), 245–246
Abu Musa Island, 280, 297
Abu Nidal, 295
Aden, Haji, 96
Aden conflict (1956–1960), 270–271
Aden Protectorate. *See* South Yemen
ADF. *See* Allied Democratic Front
ADFL. *See* Alliance of Democratic Forces for the Liberation of Congo-Democratic Republic of the Congo
Adjudication, 27
Afghan Interim Authority (AIA), 228
Afghanistan
  Afghanistan–Pakistan (August 1949), 208–209; (June–October 1950), 209; (September 1960–May 1963), 211–212; (March–July 1979), 217
  Pathan conflict (June–October 1950), 209; (September 1960–May 1963), 211–212
  Peshawar rebellion (March–July 1979), 217
  Tajikistan (April 1992–June 1997), 224–225
  U.S.–Afghanistan (September–December 2001), 227–228
  USSR–Afghanistan (December 1979–), 218–219
Africa. *See also specific countries*
  central, 57, 65, 75, 86, 111
  characteristics of conflicts, 46
  conflict management, 57–60
  conflicts, overview of, 56–57
  country list, alphabetical, 303–305
  Horn of, 56
  international conflicts, 9
  maps
    Africa in 1945, 55
    Africa today, 54
  nationalism
    African territories–Portugal (1961–July 1975), 65
    Algeria (November 1954–March 1962), 62
    Mozambique–South Africa (1976–October 1992), 80–81
    Rhodesia (Zimbabwe) (1967–January 1980), 73–74
    South Africa–Botswana (October 1984–May 1986), 91–92
    South Africa–Zambia (April 1987), 94
    Tunisia (January 1952–March 1956), 61
  overview, 54–56
African corps, 58, 84
African National Congress (ANC), 10, 73, 80
  anti-ANC raids (December 1982), 88–89; (October 1984–May 1986), 91–92; (April 1987), 94
African territories–Portugal (1961–July 1975), 65
African Union (AU), 12, 15, 28, 40, 45, 69, 104, 114, 122, 264
  chairmen, list of, 323
  composition strengths and homogeneity, 323
  concerns of, 321
  establishment of, 57–59, 321
  membership of, 322
  observer mission, 18
  organs for handling conflict, 322
  secretaries-general, list of, 322
  sphere of influence, 321
  stated obligations of, 322
  structural hierarchy, 322
Agent Orange, 11, 159
Agreement on Measures for the Peaceful Liberation of Tibet (Seventeen Articles Agreement), 209
Ahmeti, Ali, 251
AIA. *See* Afghan Interim Authority
Aidid, Mohammed Farah, 96
Air incidents
  cold war
    U.S.–USSR (April–October 1950), 168–169; (October 1952–July 1956), 170
    U.S.–Yugoslavia (August 1946), 237–238
  Israel–Syria (June 1979–February 1980), 289–290
  U.S.–Libya (August 1981), 291–292; (January 1989), 295–296
Airlift, Berlin (June 1948–May 1949), 238–239
AL. *See* Arab League
Albania
  Albania–United Kingdom (May 1946–December 1949), 237
  Greece–Albania (April 1994), 253–254
Albright, Madeleine K., 16, 197
Al Fatah, 288
Algeria
  Algeria–Morocco (October 1963–February 1964), 67; (June–October 1979), 85
  France–Algeria (November 1954–March 1962), 62
  Tindouf war (October 1963–February 1964), 67
  Western Saharan conflict (October 1974–), 77
  Yom Kippur War (October 1973–), 282–283
Alliance of Democratic Forces for the Liberation of Congo-Democratic Republic of the Congo (ADFL), 109
Allied Democratic Front (ADF), 106
ALN. *See* National Liberation Army
Al Qaeda, 227–228
Amal (Lebanese Resistance Detachments), 293
Americas
  characteristics of conflicts, 46
  conflict management, 121–123
  conflict, overview of, 120–121
  country list, alphabetical, 303–305
  map, 119
  regional overview, 118–120
Amin, Hafizullah, 218
Amin, Idi
  ouster (October 1978–May 1979), 84–85

Amin, Idi—*continued*
post-Amin civil war (December 1981–1994), 86
Uganda-Kenya (February–August 1976), 81
Amity Agreement, 129
ANAD. *See* Non-Aggression and Defense Aid Agreement
Anarchy. *See also* Civil conflicts/wars
Belgian Congo (July 1960–mid-1964), 64–65
Laos (December 1958–1962), 175; (April 1964–May 1975), 176–177
ANC. *See* African National Congress
Anga, Pierre, 95
Angola
African territories–Portugal (1961–July 1975), 65
Angola–South Africa (1975–), 78–79
Angola–Zambia (November 2001), 116
civil war (1975–), 78–79
invasions of Shaba (March–May 1977), 82–83; (May 1978), 83–84
rebel activity (November 1975–February 1976), 79–80
Zaire–Angola (November 1975–February 1976), 79–80; (March–May 1977), 82–83; (May 1978), 83–84
Annan, Kofi, 16
Antigovernment insurgencies. *See also* Insurgencies
Costa Rica–Nicaragua (December 1948–February 1949), 125
Oman–South Yemen (1972–August 1974), 280–281
Anya-Nya (September 1963–March 1972), 66–67
Anya-Nya II, 67, 89
Aoba, 189
AOL. *See* Army of Liberation for the Sahara
Aozou strip, Libyan annexation of (June 1976–November 1979), 81–82
Apodeti. *See* Associacão da Populaca Democratica de Timor
Aptidon, Hassan Gouled, 105, 110
Aquino, Corazon, 198
Arab–Israeli conflicts. *See also specific countries and parties*
air incidents
Israel–Syria (June 1979–February 1980), 289–290
border incidents
Israel–Jordan (December 1964–April 1966), 276–277
Israel–Lebanon (mid-late 1977), 287
Syria–Israel (October–December 1955), 270; (June 1964–July 1966), 276
cross-border attacks
Israel–Lebanon (April 1974–July 1975), 283–284
Hoûla raids (October 1965), 277
Israel (May 1948–January 1949), 266
Israel–Arab states (June 1967), 277–278
Israel–Egypt (October 1973), 282–283
Israel–Jordan (January 1953–December 1954), 269
Israel–Lebanon (March–June 1978), 288–289; (early 1982–mid-1983), 292–293
Six-Day war (June 1967), 277–278
territorial disputes
Israel (May 1948–January 1949), 266
Israel–Jordan (July 1956–January 1958), 271
Israel–Syria (July 1957–February 1958), 272
Syria–Israel (February 1962–August 1963), 275
Yom Kippur War (October 1973), 282–283
Arab League (AL), 28, 39–43, 45, 58, 84, 122, 262, 264, 268, 273, 274–275, 279, 282, 284, 288
composition strengths and homogeneity, 332
concerns of, 331
establishment of, 331
fact-finding missions, 18
membership of, 331
peacekeeping, 21
secretaries-general, list of, 332
sphere of influence, 331
stated obligations of, 331
structural hierarchy, 331
Arab Legion, 266
Arab states. *See also* Arab–Israeli conflicts
Israel–Arab states (June 1967), 277–278
Six-Day war (June 1967), 277–278
Arafat, Yasser, 6, 264, 282, 287–288, 300
Arana Osorio, Manuel, 128
arap Moi, Daniel, 85, 95
Arbitration, 26–27
conflicts managed by, 13–15, 57
effectiveness, 29
international, 26–27
Arevalo, Juan José, 125
Argentina
Argentina–Chile (July 1952–August 1993), 126–128
Beagle Channel dispute (July 1952–August 1993), 126–128
Paraguay–Argentina (early 1959–December 1961), 133
United Kingdom–Argentina (April–June 1982), 146–147
Arias, Gilberto, 132
Arias, Roberto, 132
Aristide, Jean-Bertrand, 150–151
Armenia
Azerbaijan–Armenia (August 1990–), 248–249
Army of Liberation for the Sahara (AOL), 62
Army rebellions
People's Republic of the Congo (September 1987–July 1988), 95
Arnault, Jean, 128
ASEAN. *See* Association of Southeast Asian Nations
Asia. *See* East Asia/Pacific; Southwest Asia; *specific countries*
Assad, Bashar, 300
Associacão da Populaca Democratica de Timor (Apodeti), 184
Association of Southeast Asian Nations (ASEAN), 45, 189, 198–199
composition strengths and homogeneity, 327
concerns of, 325
establishment of, 160–162, 325
membership of, 327
organs for handling conflict, 327
secretaries-general, list of, 327
sphere of influence, 325
stated obligations of, 326
structural hierarchy, 326
AU. *See* African Union
Aubaume, Jean-Hilaire, 69
Australia
anti-British Communist insurgencies (June 1948–July 1960), 165–166
Borneo conflict (1962–November 1965), 174–175
Korean War (June 1950–July 1953), 169
Vietnam War (December 1960–May 1975), 173–174
Autonomy disputes
Aden conflict (1956–1960), 270–271
Gagauz struggle (October 1990–July 1992), 249–250
Iraq–Kurds (October 1968–March 1970), 278
postindependence
France–Tunisia (February–May 1958), 63; (July–September 1961), 65–66
Spain–Morocco (November 1957–April 1958), 62
Russia–Dagestan (May 1999), 255
Awami League, 215
Azerbaijan
Azerbaijan–Armenia (August 1990–), 248–249
Azerbaijan crisis (August 1945–October 1947), 265–266
Azeris, 248–249
Aziz, Tariq, 298

Badr, Muhammad al-, 275
Bahrain, Qatar–Bahrain (April 1986), 295
Bakary, Djibo, 68
Balaguer, Joaquín, 130
Balkans conflict (mid-1989–November 2000), 246–248
Macedonia (January 1991–), 251–252
summary, 246–248
Bandaranaike, Sirimavo, 213, 220

Bandaranaike, Solomon, 213
Banditry
Colombia (1965–), 139–140
Bangladesh. *See also* East Pakistan
Bangladesh–India (April 1976), 216–217; (April–July 2001), 226–227
Burma–Bangladesh (December 1991), 193–194; (March–September 1993), 194; (May–August 1994), 194–195
Chittagong Hill Tracts conflict (1975–), 215–216
India–Bangladesh (November 1979), 217–218; (December 1983–June 1984), 221; (February–April 1986), 222; (April–August 1999), 225
Muhuri River incidents (February–April 1986), 222
Pakistan–Bangladesh (March 1971–February 1974), 215
Bangladesh Rifles, 222
Ban Than island, 196
Barazani, Mullah Mustafa, 274, 278, 283
Bargaining and negotiation, 16
Barre, Muhammad Siad, 94, 95–96
Batista y Zaldívar, Fulgencio, 129, 131
Bavaria, 170
Beagle Channel dispute (July 1952–August 1993), 126–128
Bech-Friis, Johan, 171
Bédié, Henri Konan, 114
Beidh, Ali Salem al-, 41
Belgian Congo (Congo, Zaire). *See also* Congo; Zaire
civil war (July 1960–mid-1964), 64–65
Belgium
Belgian Congo (July 1960–mid-1964), 64–65
Korean War (June 1950–July 1953), 169
Belí River, 92
Belize
Belize–Guatemala (August 1995), 152
Benin. *See* Dahomey
Benoit, Pedro Bartolene, 140
Bering Strait, 170
Berlin airlift (June 1948–May 1949), 238–239
Berlin Wall (July–November 1961), 241–242
Bernadotte, Count, 266
Biafra
Nigeria–Biafra (July 1967–January 1970), 74–75
bin Laden, Osama, 227
Bishop, Maurice, 147
Bizerte conflict (July–September 1961), 65–66
Black African Christians, 5
"Black Berets." *See* Otryad Militsii Osobogo Naznacheniya
Blackshirts, 181
Bokassa, Jean-Bédel, 80
Bolivia
Chile–Bolivia (March 1962–1964), 135–136
guerrilla insurgency (November 1966–July 1970), 141
Bombing campaigns
Cambodia–South Vietnam (January 1970–April 1975), 180–181
Border conflicts. *See also* Cross-border conflicts
Algeria–Morocco (June–October 1979), 85
Argentina–Chile (July 1952–August 1993), 126–128
Belize–Guatemala (August 1995), 152
Cambodia–Siam (Thailand) (early 1953–May 1975), 170–171; (December 1979–October 1980), 188–189
China–India (August 1959–February 1960), 211
China–Vietnam (April 1983), 190
Ecuador–Peru (January 1984), 148; (January–March 1995), 151
Guinea-Bissau–Senegal (April 1990–May 1990), 100
India–Bangladesh (December 1983–June 1984), 221
Niger–Dahomey (Benin) (December 1963–June 1965), 68
North Yemen–Saudi Arabia (November 1969–January 1970), 278
North Yemen–South Yemen (October 1971–October 1972), 279–280
Saudi Arabia–North Yemen (August 1979–March 1980), 290–291
Saudi Arabia–Yemen (December 1994), 299–300
Thailand–Burma (March–May 2001), 199–200
Uganda–Kenya (December 1987), 95; (March 1989), 98
Vietnam–China (January 1984–March 1987), 190–191
Border crises
North Korea–South Korea (February–July 1975), 182–183
Border disputes. *See also* Territorial disputes
Angola–Zambia (November 2001), 116
Beagle Channel (July 1952–August 1993), 126–128
Chad–Nigeria (April–July 1983), 90–91
China–Nepal (June 1959–July 1960), 211
Diamond Islands (December 1993–March 1994), 105–106
El Salvador–Honduras (July 1969), 141–142
Eritrea–Ethiopia (May 1998–June 1999), 111–112
Ethiopia–Kenya (October 1998–January 1999), 113
football war (July 1969), 141–142
Ghana–Upper Volta (June 1964–June 1966), 69–70
Honduras–Nicaragua (April–June 1957), 131–132
India–Bangladesh (November 1979), 217–218; (July 1981–August 1982), 219; (December 1983–June 1984), 221
Lake Chad conflict (April–July 1983), 90–91
Liberia–Guinea (September 1999–April 2001), 113–114
Mauritania–Mali (mid-1960–February 1963), 63–64
McMahon Line (August 1959–February 1960), 211; (October–November 1962), 212–213
Mekong River (August–September 2000), 199
New River Triangle (August 1969–November 1970), 142
Nigeria–Cameroon (December 1993–March 1994), 105–106
Pakistan–Afghanistan (September 1960–May 1963), 211–212
Thailand–Laos (June 1984–December 1988), 191–192; (August–September 2000), 199
Zaire–Zambia (February–September 1982), 86–87
Border incidents
Arab–Israeli
Israel–Jordan (December 1964–April 1966), 276–277
Israel–Lebanon (April 1974–July 1975), 283–284; (mid-late 1977), 287
Syria–Israel (October–December 1955), 270; (June 1964–July 1966), 276
Bangladesh–India (April 1976), 216–217; (April–July 2001), 226–227
Belize–Guatemala (August 1995), 152
Burma–Bangladesh (December 1991), 193–194; (March–September 1993), 194; (May–August 1994), 194–195
Burma–Thailand (March 1984), 191
Cambodia–Thailand (December 1975–February 1976), 185; (January 1977–October 1978), 186–187
Cambodia–Vietnam (January 1979–), 187–188
Cameroon–Nigeria (May–July 1981), 85–86
China–Burma (January–November 1969), 180
China–India (October 1975), 216
Congo–Uganda (February–March 1965), 71
Costa Rica–Nicaragua (December 1948–February 1949), 125
Ecuador–Peru (June 1977–January 1978), 143–144
El Salvador–Honduras (July 1976–October 1980), 142–143
France–Tunisia (February–August 1959), 63
Ghana–Togo (January–May 1965), 71; (August–October 1982), 88; (January–February 1994), 106
Guatemala–Mexico (September 1982–January 1983), 147
India–Bangladesh (November 1979), 217–218; (April–August 1999), 225
Indonesia–Papua New Guinea (May 1982–October 1984), 189–190
Iraq–Iran (September 1997), 300
Israel–Jordan (January 1953–December 1954), 269
Israel–Syria (February 2001–), 300–301
Laos–Thailand (June 1975–January 1976), 183–184; (June 1982), 190
McMahon Line (September 1965), 214–215
Muhuri River (February–April 1986), 222
Nepal–India (April–November 1962), 212
Nicaragua–Costa Rica (October 1977), 144; (September–December 1978), 144–145; (May–June 1985), 148–149; (April 1986), 149

Border incidents—*continued*
Niger, Diffa border insurgency (December 1996–April 1999), 110
North Korea–South Korea (mid-1965–March 1968), 179; (November 1984), 192; (May 1992), 194
Pakistan–India (July 1981–August 1982), 219
Saudi Arabia–Qatar (September–October 1992), 297
Thailand–Cambodia (November–December 1976), 185–186
Turkey–Syria (March 1955–1957), 269–270
Uganda–Kenya (February–August 1976), 81
Uganda–Tanzania (1971–October 1972), 75–76
Uzbekistan–Kyrgyzstan/Tajikistan (August 1999–September 2000), 225–226
Zaire–People's Republic of the Congo (January 1987), 93–94
Border/resources disputes. *See also* Border disputes
Chad–Nigeria (April–July 1983), 90–91
Border tensions
Greece–Albania (April 1994), 253–254
India–East Pakistan (March 1958–September 1959), 210
Iraq–Coalition forces (October 1994), 299
Iraq–Iran (1971), 279
North Korea–South Korea (September 1996–November 2000), 197–198
Border war
China–Vietnam (February 1979–June 1982), 188
Ecuador–Peru (January–April 1981), 145–146
Egypt–Libya (July–September 1977), 287–288
Iran–Iraq (January 1972–February 1975), 281
Mali–Burkina Faso (December 1985–January 1986), 92–93
North Yemen–South Yemen (February 1979–February 1980), 289
Thailand–Laos (June 1984–December 1988), 191–192
Zaire–Angola (November 1975–February 1976), 79–80
Borneo conflict (1962–November 1965), 174–175
Bosch, Juan, 137
Bosnia
ethnic and religious warfare (mid-1989–November 2000), 246–248
Bosnia-Herzegovina, 5, 246–247
Botswana
South Africa–Botswana (October 1984–May 1986), 91–92
Bougainville
Bougainville–Papua New Guinea (October 1988–), 192–193
Bougainville Revolutionary Army (BRA), 156, 160, 193
Boundary disputes. *See* Border disputes; Territorial disputes
Bourguiba, Habib, 61
Boutros-Ghali, Boutros, 22, 43, 108, 161
Bozize, Francois, 115
BRA. *See* Bougainville Revolutionary Army
Brazzaville
Congo–Brazzaville (May 1997–late-2000), 110
Britain. *See* United Kingdom
British Commonwealth, 332–333
establishment of, 332
sphere of influence, 332
Brunswijk, Ronnie, 149
Bulgaria, 236, 240, 241, 242
Bull, Odd, 275
Bunche, Ralph, 266
Bunker, Ellsworth, 175
Burkina Faso. *See also* Upper Volta
Mali–Burkina Faso (December 1985–January 1986), 92–93
Burma
Burma–Bangladesh (December 1991), 193–194; (March–September 1993), 194; (May–August 1994), 194–195
Burma–Thailand (March 1984), 191
China–Burma (January–November 1969), 180
civil war (January 1949–), 167–168
Karen separatist insurgency (March 1984), 191
KMT–PLA cross-border conflict (August 1948–1954), 166
Rohingya Muslim rebellion (December 1991), 193–194
Thailand–Burma (March–May 2001), 199–200
Burns, Arthur, 270, 271
Burundi
Hutu conflict (August 1988–), 97–98
Rwanda–Burundi (January 1964–January 1965), 69
Bush, George H. W., 150, 298
Bush, George W., 227
Bush Negroes, 150
Bustamente y Rivero, José Luis, 142

Calderón, Rafael Angel, 125
Calí drug cartel, 140
Cambodia
Borneo conflict (1962–November 1963), 174–175
Cambodia–South Vietnam (January 1970–April 1975), 180–181
Cambodia–Thailand (December 1975–February 1976), 185; (January 1977–October 1978), 186–187; (December 1979–October 1980), 188–189
Cambodia–Vietnam (January 1979–), 187–188
France–French Indochina (December 1945–July 1954), 165
Khmer Rouge border incidents (November–December 1976), 185–186; (January 1977–October 1978), 186–187
Mayaguez incident (May 1975), 183
South Vietnam–Cambodia (March–December 1964), 176
Thailand–Cambodia (November–December 1976), 185–186
U.S.–Cambodia (May 1975), 183
Vietnam War (December 1960–May 1975), 173–174
post–Vietnam War tensions (May 1975), 183
Cameroon
Cameroon–Nigeria (May–July 1981), 85–86
Nigeria–Cameroon (December 1993–March 1994), 105–106
Canada, 4, 8, 140, 162
Korean War (June 1950–July 1953), 169
Cape Verde Islands (1961–July 1975), 65
Caribbean Pact, 125
Carter, Jimmy, 16, 57, 89, 151, 231, 264, 282
Casamance rebellion (mid-1990–), 100–101
Castillo Armas, Carlos, 128
Castro, Fidel, 118, 131, 138, 141
U.S.–Cuba (April–May 1961), 134
Catholic Croats, 246
Caucasus conflict (October 1992–), 252–253
map, 231
CCP. *See* Chinese Communist Party
CEAO. *See* West African Economic Community
CEMAC. *See* Economic and Monetary Community of the Central African States
Central African Republic
Central African Republic–Chad (mid-2001–December 2002), 115–116
Sudan (September 1963–March 1972), 66–67
Central America, 5, 120, 122, 123, 125, 128, 144, 148
Central Intelligence Agency (CIA), 128, 134, 145, 295
Ceylon (Sri Lanka), 207, 213
Tamil conflict (July 1982–), 219–221
Chad
Central African Republic–Chad (mid-2001–December 2002), 115–116
Chad–Libya (June 1976–November 1979), 81–82; (mid-1982–), 87–88
Chad–Nigeria (April–July 1983), 90–91
civil war (November 1965–1972), 71–72; (January 1978–June 1982), 83; (mid-1982–), 87–88
Lake Chad conflict (April–July 1983), 90–91
Chamoun, Camille, 273
Chechens, 8, 226, 252
Chechnya, 5, 16, 18, 21, 231, 233
Chechen separatism (August 2000–), 255–257
Chechen war (October 1992–), 252–253
Russia–Georgia (August 2000–), 255–257
Chiang, Kai-shek, 163–164, 168, 196
Chile
Argentina–Chile (July 1952–August 1993), 126–128

Beagle Channel dispute (July 1952–August 1993), 126–128
Chile–Bolivia (March 1962–1964), 135–136
China
bombardment of Quemoy (April 1954–April 1955), 171–172; (July–December 1958), 172–173
China–Burma (January–November 1969), 180
China–India (October 1975), 216
China–Nepal (June 1959–July 1960), 211
China–The Philippines (January–February 1995), 195–196; (April 1997–July 1999), 198
China–Portugal (July–August 1952), 169–170
China–Taiwan (October 1949–June 1953), 168; (March–December 1962), 175–176; (January 1996–August 1999), 196–197
China–Tibet (October 1950–May 1951), 209–210
China–USSR (March 1963–September 1969), 213
China–Vietnam (February 1979–June 1982), 188
civil war (1945–1949), 163–164
Cultural Revolution, 213
KMT–PLA (August 1948–1954), 166
Korean War (June 1950–July 1953), 169
Macao conflict (July–August 1952), 169–170
McMahon Line border dispute (August 1959–February 1960), 211; (October–November 1962), 212–213
McMahon Line border incidents (September 1965), 214–215
Paracel Islands dispute (January–February 1995), 195–196
South Vietnam–China (January 1974), 182
Spratly Islands (March 1988), 192; (January–February 1995), 195–196; (April 1997–July 1999), 198
Taiwan–China (April 1954–April 1955), 171–172; (November 1994), 195
Tibet–China (March 1956–September 1965), 210
U.S.–North Korea (June 1950–July 1953), 169
Ussuri River conflict (March 1963–September 1969), 213
U.S./Taiwan–China (July–December 1958), 172–173
Vietnam–China (January 1984–March 1987), 190–191; (March 1988), 192
Chinese Communist Party (CCP), 163, 167
KMT–CCP (October 1949–June 1953), 168; (April 1954–April 1955), 171–172; (July–December 1958), 172–173; (March–December 1962), 175–176
Chittagong Hill Tracts conflict (1975–), 215–216
Chittagong Hill Tracts People's Solidarity Association (JSS), 215
Chou En-lai, 211
Christian–Muslim factional fighting
Israel–Lebanon (mid-late 1977), 287
Chronology of regional conflicts, 306–316
CIA. *See* Central Intelligence Agency
CIS. *See* Commonwealth of Independent States
Civil conflicts/wars
Afghanistan (December 1979–), 218–219
Angola (1975–), 78–79
Angola–Zambia (November 2001), 116
Belgian Congo (July 1960–mid-1964), 64–65
Biafra (July 1967–January 1970), 74–75
Burma (January 1949–), 167–168
Cambodia–Vietnam (January 1979–), 187–188
Chad (November 1965–1972), 71–72; (January 1978–June 1982), 83; (mid-1982–), 87–88
China (1945–1949), 163–164
Congo (July 1960–mid-1964), 64–65; (October 1996–), 109
Congo–Brazzaville (May 1997–late-2000), 110
Costa Rica (March–April 1948), 125
Cuba (December 1956–January 1959), 131
Cyprus (December 1963–November 1967), 241
Djibouti (November 1991–July 1993), 105; (early 1998–December 2000), 110–111
Dominican Republic (April 1965–September 1966), 140–141
El Salvador (January 1977–end of 1992), 143
Greece (1945–1949), 236–237
Guatemala (June 1954–), 128–129; (September 1982–January 1983), 147; (April 1984), 148
India (1945–1948), 207
Indonesia–Malaysia (1962–November 1965), 174–175
Iran (1976–1980), 285–286
Ivory Coast (September 1999–), 114–115
Laos (December 1958–1962), 175; (April 1964–May 1975), 176–177
Lebanon (May 1958–June 1959), 273; (February 1975–late 1992), 284
Liberia (December 1989–), 98–100
Macedonia (January 1991–), 251–252
Mozambique–South Africa (1976–October 1992), 80–81
North Yemen (September 1962–October 1967), 275–276
North Yemen–Saudi Arabia (November 1969–October 1970), 278
People's Republic of the Congo (September 1987–July 1988), 95
Sierra Leone (March 1991–), 104–105
Somalia (May 1988–), 95–97
Sudan (September 1963–March 1972), 66–67; (January 1983–), 89–90
Tajikistan (April 1992–June 1997), 224–225
Thailand–Burma (March–May 2001), 199–200
Uganda (December 1981–1994), 86; (December 1987), 95
USSR–Afghanistan (December 1979–), 218–219
Vietnam (December 1960–May 1975), 173–174
Yemen (November 1993–July 1994), 298–299
Yugoslavia–Kosovo (October 1997–), 254–255
Clan-based violence
Somalia (May 1988–), 95–97
Clinton, Bill, 197
Cod War (November 1971–June 1976), 243–244
Cold war
air incidents
U.S.–USSR (April–October 1950), 168–169; (October 1952–July 1956), 170
U.S.–Yugoslavia (August 1946), 237–238
Berlin airlift crisis (June 1948–May 1949), 238–239
border incidents
North Korea–South Korea (mid-1965–March 1968), 179; (February–July 1975), 182–183; (November 1984), 192
territorial disputes
Italy–Yugoslavia (March 1952–October 1954), 239
U.S.–North Korea (June 1950–July 1953), 169
Turkey–Syria (March 1955–1957), 269–270
U.S.–USSR (July–November 1961), 241–242; (September–November 1962), 136–137
Colombia
Korean War (June 1950–July 1953), 169
leftist guerrilla insurgencies (1965–), 139–140
Colonialism. *See* Decolonization
Combo, Ayouba, 107
Commonwealth of Independent States (CIS), 44
Communal violence
Burundi (August 1988–), 97–98
Cyprus (January 1974–June 1978), 244
Lebanon (February 1975–late 1992), 284
Mindanao–The Philippines (January 1970–), 181–182
Sri Lanka (July 1982–), 219–221
Communism
anti-Communist insurgencies or revolts
Hungary–USSR (October–December 1956), 240–241
North Yemen–South Yemen (October 1971–October 1972), 279–280
USSR–Poland (October 1956), 240
anti-Communist U.S. military intervention
U.S.–Grenada (October–December 1983), 147–148
Vietnam War (December 1960–May 1975), 173–174
Communist insurgencies
Cambodia–Siam (Thailand) (early 1953–May 1975), 170–171
Greece (1945–1949), 236–237
United Kingdom–Malaya (June 1948–July 1960), 165–166
USSR–Iran (August 1945–October 1947), 265–266
Communist–Nationalist disputes
Taiwan–China (November 1994), 195

Communist Party of Malaya, 165–166
Communist revolutions
China (1945–1949), 163–164
Cuba (December 1956–January 1959), 131
Community of Portuguese-Speaking Countries (CPLP), 112
Comoros
attempted coup (September 1995–), 107–108
Conakry raids (November 1970), 75
Conciliation, 25
Condor Mountain dispute (January 1995–October 1998), 151–152
Confederation of Caucasian Mountain People, 246
Conference on Security and Cooperation in Europe (CSCE), 235, 247, 250
Conflict
definition of, 3–4
ethnic, 5
forums for airing issues, 24–25
interstate, 7
regions of, 45–46
Conflict control, 13
Conflict management
approaches to, 13–14
choices, 14–15
effectiveness, 31
legal, 25–26
need for, 11–12
patterns of, 28–31
peaceful, 18–22
political, 28
responsibilities, roles and constraints, 34–38
Conflict prevention, 13
Congo. *See also* Democratic Republic of the Congo; People's Republic of the Congo; Zaire
Belgian Congo (July 1960–mid-1964), 64–65
Congo–Brazzaville (May 1997–late-2000), 110
Congo–Rwanda (August 1967–April 1968), 75
Congo–Uganda (February–March 1965), 71
dissension (May 1978), 83–84
independence movements (October 1996–), 109
mercenaries dispute (August 1967–April 1968), 75
Congolese National Liberation Front (FLNC), 82, 84
Contadora Group, 18, 122, 149
Contra war (January 1980–February 1994), 145
Corfu Channel dispute (May 1946–December 1949), 237
Corisco Bay islands dispute (June–November 1972), 76
Costa Rica
civil war (March–April 1948), 125
Costa Rica–Nicaragua (December 1948–February 1949), 125
Nicaragua–Costa Rica (January 1955), 129; (October 1977), 144; (September–December 1978), 144–145; (May–June 1985), 148–149; (April 1986), 149
Counceil de l'Entente (CDE), 68
Countries and their regions, alphabetical list, 303–305
Coups. *See also* Putsches
attempted
Central African Republic–Chad (mid-2001–December 2002), 115–116
Comoros (September 1995–), 107–108
Jordan (February 1970–August 1971), 278–279
Maldives (November 1988), 223
PLO–Jordan (February 1970–August 1971), 278–279
Togo–Ghana (September 1986), 93
Aubame's coup (February 1964), 69
Guinea–Ivory Coast (March–April 1966), 72–73
Mali–Tuareg (June 1990–), 102
postcoup tensions
Bangladesh–India (April 1976), 216–217
Ghana–Guinea (October–November 1966), 73
Uganda–Tanzania (1971–October 1972), 75–76
CPLP. *See* Community of Portuguese-Speaking Countries
Crimean War, 26
Crises
Azerbaijan (August 1945–October 1947), 265–266
Berlin airlift (June 1948–May 1949), 238–239
Buraymī Oasis (August 1952–October 1955), 268–269
Congo (July 1960–mid-1964), 64–65
Cuban Missile Crisis (September–November 1962), 136–137
France–Levant (1945–December 1946), 265
hostage
Guinea–Ivory Coast (February–September 1967), 74
U.S.–Iran (November 1979–January 1981), 290
Kuwait (June 1961–February 1962), 274–275
North Korea–South Korea (February–July 1975), 182–183
post–Soviet independence
USSR–Latvia (January 1991), 250–251
USSR–Lithuania (March 1990–late 1991), 248
Suez (October–November 1956), 271–272
Trieste (March 1952–October 1954), 239
Croatia, 5, 18, 21, 233–234, 246–247
Bosnia (mid-1989–November 2000), 246–248
Crocker, Chester, 72
Cross-border conflicts
KMT–PLA (August 1948–1954), 166
Macedonia (January 1991–), 251–252
Uganda–Kenya (November 1996–July 1998), 109–110
Cross-border raids
Israel–Lebanon (April 1974–July 1975), 283–284
Nicaragua–Costa Rica (September–December 1978), 144–145
South Vietnam–Cambodia (March–December 1964), 176
Syria–Israel (October–December 1955), 270
Syria–Lebanon (May–August 1949), 266–267
Tanzania–Uganda (October 1978–May 1979), 84–85
CSCE. *See* Conference on Security and Cooperation in Europe
Cuba
Bay of Pigs (April–May 1961), 134
Bolivia (November 1966–July 1970), 141
civil war (December 1956–January 1959), 131
Cuba–Haiti (August 1959), 133–134
Cuba–Venezuela (November 1963–May 1967), 138–139
Dominican Republic–Cuba/Venezuela (February 1956–January 1962), 129–131
Dominican Republic–Haiti/Cuba (early 1947–December 1951), 123–125
Ogaden war (mid-1972–1985), 76–77
Panama (1958–May 1959), 132
Tindouf war, participation in (October 1963–February 1964), 67
U.S.–Cuba (April–May 1961), 134
U.S.–Grenada (October–December 1983), 147–148
Cuban Missile Crisis (September–November 1962), 136–137
Cyprus
civil war (December 1963–November 1967), 241
enosis movement (April 1955–February 1959), 239–240
ethnic-based tensions (April 1993), 253
partition (January 1974–June 1978), 244
partition incidents (June 1996–), 254
Czechoslovakia
USSR–Czechoslovakia (August 1968), 241–242
Czech Republic. *See* Czechoslovakia

Daddah, Moktar Ould, 64
Dagestan, 252
Russia–Dagestan (May 1999), 255
Dahomey
Niger–Dahomey (Benin) (December 1963–June 1965), 68
Dalai Lama, 210–211, 214, 216
Damansky Island, 213
Daoud Khan, Sardar Mohammad, 218
Dayton accord, 30, 247
Déby, Idriss, 87, 115
Decolonization, 5, 54–55
Algeria (November 1954–March 1962), 62
Israel (May 1948–January 1949), 266

Mau Mau revolt (August 1952–December 1963), 61
Defamouth, Jean-Jacques, 115
Democracy
Congo–Brazzaville (May 1997–late-2000), 110
Nepal–India (April–November 1962), 212
Democratic Front of Renewal (FDR), 110
Democratic Kampuchea, 185, 186, 187. *See also* Cambodia
Democratic Party of Azerbaijan, 265
Democratic Party of Kurdistan, 265
Democratic Republic of the Congo (formerly Zaire), 56–57, 65, 71, 92, 93, 97, 103, 106–107, 109
Dénard, Bob, 107
Denmark
Iceland–United Kingdom, West Germany, Denmark (November 1971–June 1976), 243–244
Deportations
Zaire–Zambia (September 1983–January 1984), 91
Desai, Morarji Ranchhodji, 217
Destabilization. *See also* Political instability; Regional instability
Liberia–Sierra Leone (March 1991–), 104–105
d'Estaing, Valéry Giscard, 84
Dhofar rebellion (1972–August 1974), 280–281
Diamond Islands (December 1993–March 1994), 105–106
Diffa border insurgency (December 1996–April 1999), 110
Diola tribe, 101
Diori, Hamani, 68
Diplomacy
bargaining and negotiation, 16
forums for airing conflict issues, 24–25
good offices, 22–24
international organizations, 24–25
mediation, 16–17
observer and fact-finding missions, 17–18
peacekeeping, 18–22
shuttle diplomacy, 22–24
traditional, 15–16
Disobedience, civil
India (1945–1948), 207
Dissension
Congo (May 1978), 83–84
Djabane Islands, 105
Djibouti
civil war (November 1991–July 1993), 105; (early 1998–December 2000), 110–111
Djohar, Said Mohammed, 107
Dniester
Gagauzia/Dniester–Moldova (October 1990–July 1992), 249/250
Doe, Samuel K., 90
regime tensions (February–March 1983), 90
Dominican Republic
civil war (April 1965–September 1966), 140–141
Dominican Republic–Cuba/Venezuela (February 1956–January 1962), 129–131
Dominican Republic–Haiti/Cuba (early 1947–December 1951), 123–125
exiles conflict (February 1956–January 1962), 129–131
Haiti–Dominican Republic (April–September 1963), 137–138
U.S.–Dominican Republic (April 1965–September 1966), 140–141
dos Santos, José Eduardo, 116
Doudou, Emile Boga, 114
DPK. *See* Democratic Party of Kurdistan
Drugs
Calí drug cartel, 140
Dubcek, Alexander, 242
Dudayev, Dzhokhar M., 252
Dutch East Indies (Indonesia). *See also* Indonesia
Netherlands–Dutch East Indies (1945–November 1949), 164–165
Duvalier, François "Papa Doc," 133, 137
EAM. *See* National Liberation Front
East Asia/Pacific. *See also specific countries*
characteristics of conflicts, 46
conflict management, 160–163
conflicts, overview of, 157–160
country list, alphabetical, 303–305
maps
Indochina, 157
region, 156
regional overview, 155–157
East Central Europe. *See specific countries*
Eastern Europe. *See specific countries*
East Germany
Berlin airlift crisis (June 1948–May 1949), 238–239
Berlin Wall (July–November 1961), 241–242
East Pakistan (Bangladesh). *See also* Bangladesh
India–East Pakistan (March 1958–September 1959), 210
East Timor
East Timor–Indonesia (October 1975–May 2002), 184–185
EC. *See* European Community
ECOMOG. *See* ECOWAS Monitoring Group
Economic and Monetary Community of the Central African States (CEMAC), 115
Economic Community of West African States (ECOWAS), 30, 43, 99, 112, 113, 114
chairmen, list of, 324
composition strengths and homogeneity, 324
concerns of, 323
establishment of, 59, 323
executive secretaries, list of, 324
membership of, 323
organs for handling conflict, 324
stated obligations of, 323
structural hierarchy, 323
ECOWAS. *See* Economic Community of West African States
ECOWAS Monitoring Group (ECOMOG), 99, 112
Ecuador
Ecuador–Peru (June 1977–January 1978), 143–144; (January–April 1981), 145–146; (January 1984), 148; (January–March 1995), 151; (January 1995–October 1998), 151–152
Panama revolutionaries conflict (1958–May 1959), 132
EDF. *See* Eritrean Democratic Front
Egypt
Aden conflict (1956–1960), 270–271
Egypt–Libya (July–September 1977), 287–288
Egypt–Sudan (February 1958), 272; (December 1992), 297–298
Egypt–United Kingdom (January 1952–January 1956), 268
Egypt–United Kingdom, France (October–November 1956), 271–272
Halaib dispute (December 1992), 297–298
Israel (May 1948–January 1949), 266
Israel–Arab states (June 1967), 277–278
Israel–Egypt (October 1973), 282–283
North Yemen (September 1962–October 1967), 275–276
Six-Day war (June 1967), 277–278
Suez crisis (October–November 1956), 271–272
Yom Kippur War (October 1973), 282–283
Ejército de Liberación Nacional (ELN), 139
ELAS. *See* National Popular Liberation Army
Election controversies
Lesotho (May 1998–March 1999), 111
ELF. *See* Eritrean Liberation Front
ELN. *See* Ejército de Liberación Nacional
El Salvador
civil war (January 1977–end of 1992), 143
El Salvador–Honduras (July 1969), 141–142; (July 1976–October 1980), 142–143
football war (July 1969), 141–142
San José plan, 142
Enosis movement (April 1955–February 1959), 239–240
EOKA. *See* National Organization of Cypriot Fighters

Equatorial Guinea–Gabon (June–November 1972), 76
Eritrea
  Eritrea–Ethiopia (July 1949–December 1950), 60–61; (1965–May 1993), 70–71; (May 1998–June 1999), 111–112
  Eritrea–Yemen (November 1995–October 1998), 108–109
Eritrean Democratic Front (EDF), 70
Eritrean Liberation Front (ELF), 70
Espiritu Santo
  Vanuatu–Espiritu Santo (May–September 1980), 189
Essequibo River dispute (February 1962–June 1970), 134–135
Estrada, Joseph, 198
Ethiopia
  Eritrea–Ethiopia (July 1949–December 1950), 60–61; (1965–May 1993), 70–71; (May 1998–June 1999), 111–112
  Ethiopia–Kenya (October 1998–January 1999), 113
  Ethiopia–Somalia (mid-1972–1985), 76–77
  Korean War (June 1950–July 1953), 169
  Ogaden war (January–March 1964), 68–69; (mid-1972–1985), 76–77; (February 1987–April 1988), 94
  Somalia–Ethiopia (January–March 1964), 68–69
  Somalia–Kenya (November 1962–September 1967), 66
Ethnic conflicts, 5. *See also* Tribal conflicts
  Azerbaijan–Armenia (August 1990–), 248–249
  Bosnia (mid-1989–November 2000), 246–248
  Bougainville–Papua New Guinea (October 1988–), 192–193
  Cyprus (April 1993), 253
  Djibouti (November 1991–July 1993), 105
  Ethiopia–Kenya (October 1998–January 1999), 113
  Georgia–South Ossetia, Abkhazia (March 1989–), 245–246
  Kyrgyzstan (June 1990), 223–224
  Mauritania–Senegal (April 1989–January 1990), 98
  Mindanao–The Philippines (January 1970–), 181–182
  Moldova (October 1990–July 1992), 249–250
  Nigeria–Biafra (July 1967–January 1970), 74–75
  Russia–Chechnya (October 1992–), 252–253
  Rwanda (September 1990–), 102–104
  Rwanda–Burundi (January 1964–January 1965), 69
  Somalia (May 1988–), 95–97
  Sudan (January 1983–), 89–90
  Tajikistan (April 1992–June 1997), 224–225
  Uganda–Kenya (November 1996–July 1998), 109–110
  USSR–Lithuania (March 1990–late 1991), 248
EU. *See* European Union
Euphrates dispute (April–late 1975), 284–285
Europe
  characteristics of conflicts, 46
  conflict management, 233–236
  conflicts, overview of, 231–233
  country list, alphabetical, 230–231, 303–305
  maps
    the Caucasus, 231
    modern Europe, 230
    Soviet expansion, 232
  regional overview, 231
  Soviet expansion in, 232
European Community (EC), 18, 45, 146, 233, 234, 247. *See also* European Union
European Union (EU), 15, 18, 28, 146, 162, 231
  composition strengths and homogeneity, 329
  concerns of, 328
  establishment of, 233–235, 328
  Macedonia (January 1991–), 251–252
  membership of, 329
  organs for handling conflict, 329
  presidents of European Commission, list of, 329
  presidents of European Council, list of, 329
  sphere of influence, 328
  stated obligations of, 328
  structural hierarchy, 328
Exiles conflicts
  Cuba–Haiti (August 1959), 133–134
  Dominican Republic–Cuba/Venezuela (February 1956–January 1962), 129–131
  Haiti–Dominican Republic (April–September 1963), 137–138
  Laos (June 1975–January 1976), 183–184
  Paraguay–Argentina (early 1959–December 1961), 133
  Syria–Lebanon (May–August 1949), 266–267
Expansionism
  Ghana–Togo (January–May 1965), 71
  Iraq–Coalition forces (August 1990–May 1991), 296
  Somali
    Ethiopia–Somalia (mid-1972–1985), 76–77; (February 1987–April 1988), 94
    Somalia–Ethiopia (January–March 1964), 68–69; (1987–1988), 94
    Somalia–Kenya (November 1962–September 1967), 66
Eyadéma, Gnassingbé, 59, 93

Facio, Gauzalo, 23–24, 144
Fact-finding missions, 16–17
Factional fighting
  Chad–Libya (June 1976–November 1979), 81–82
  Israel–Lebanon (mid-late 1977), 287
Falklands war (April–June 1982), 146–147
FAN. *See* Forces armées du nord
FAO. *See* Food and Agriculture Organization; Nicaraguan Broad Opposition Front
FAR. *See* Rebel Armed Forces
Farabundo Martí National Liberation Front (FMLN), 143
FARC. *See* Fuerzas Armadas Revolucionarias Colombianas
Faso, Burkino, 114
FAT. *See* Forces armées tchadiennes
Fatalities, 10
FDA. *See* Federal Democratic Army
FDR. *See* Democratic Front of Renewal
Federal Democratic Army (FDA), 106
Federal Republic of Grande Comoros. *See* Comoros
Federation of Malaysia. *See also* Malaya
  Indonesia–Malaysia (1962–November 1965), 174–175
Figueres Ferrer, José, 125
Fishing disputes, 8, 74, 76, 105, 185, 198
  Iceland–United Kingdom, West Germany, Denmark (November 1971–June 1976), 243–244
  Mexican shrimp boat incident (December 1958–September 1959), 132–133
FLAA. *See* Liberation Front of Air and Azawad
Flag riots (January–April 1964), 139
FLN. *See* National Liberation Front
FLNC. *See* Congolese National Liberation Front
FMLN. *See* Farabundo Martí National Liberation Front
FNLA. *See* Frente Nacional de Libertação de Angola
Food and Agriculture Organization (FAO), 28
Football war (July 1969), 141–142
Forces armées du nord (FAN), 83, 87
Forces armées tchadiennes (FAT), 83
Foreign intervention. *See* Intervention; Military intervention
Formosa. *See* Taiwan
France
  Berlin airlift (June 1948–May 1949), 238–239
  Chad (January 1978–June 1982), 83
  Comoros (September 1995–), 107–108
  Egypt–United Kingdom, France (October–November 1956), 271–272
  France–Algeria (November 1954–March 1962), 62
  France–French Indochina (December 1945–July 1954), 165
  France–Gabon (February 1964), 69
  France–Indochina (December 1945–July 1954), 165
  France–Levant (1945–December 1946), 265
  France–Madagascar (March–August 1947), 60
  France–Tunisia (February–May 1958), 63; (February–August 1959), 63; (July–September 1961), 65–66
  Ivory Coast (September 1999–), 114–115

Korean War (June 1950–July 1953), 169
military bases conflict (February–May 1958), 63
Sahara conflict (November 1957–April 1958), 62
Tripartite Declaration, 239
Tunisia (January 1952–March 1956), 61
USSR–Western allies (June 1948–May 1949), 238–239
Free Cambodia. *See* Khmer Issarak
"Free Khmers," 186
Free Lao. *See* Lao Issara
Frelimo. *See* Mozambique Liberation Front
French–Algerian war (November 1954–March 1962), 62
France–Tunisia (February–August 1959), 63
French–Indochina war (December 1945–July 1954), 165
Frente Nacional de Libertação de Angola (FNLA), 78, 82
Frente Popular para la Liberatión de Saguia el-Hamra y Rio de Oro. *See* Polisario Front
Frente Revolutionario de Este Timor Independente (Fretilin), 184–185
Frente Sandinista de Libertación Nacional (FSLN), 145
Fretilin. *See* Frente Revolutionario de Este Timor Independente
FROLINAT. *See* Front de libération nationale du Tchad
Front de libération nationale du Tchad (FROLINAT), 81, 83
Front for the Liberation of South Yemen, 275, 279, 290
Front for the Restoration of Unity and Democracy (FRUD), 105, 110
FRUD. *See* Front for the Restoration of Unity and Democracy
FSLN. *See* Sandinista National Liberation Front
Fuerzas Armadas Revolucionarias Colombianas (FARC), 139–140
Fulanis, 101

Gabon
Aubame's coup (February 1964), 69
Equatorial Guinea–Gabon (June–November 1972), 76
France–Gabon (February 1964), 69
Gagauzia/Dniester–Moldova (October 1990–July 1992), 249–250
Gamsakhurdia, Zviad, 246
Gandhi, Mohandas, 207
Garang, John, 89
Gaulle, Charles de, 62
Gaza, 263, 266, 277
Gbagbo, Laurent, 114
Gemayel, Bashir, 292
Genocidal conflicts
Iraq–Kurds (October 1968–March 1970), 278; (May 1976–), 286–287
Kurds–Iraq (March 1974–July 1975), 283
Rwanda (September 1990–), 102–104
George II, 236
Georgia
Georgia–South Ossetia, Abkhazia (March 1989–), 245–246
Russia–Georgia (August 2000–), 255–257
Gero, Erno, 241
Ghana
Ghana–Guinea (October–November 1966), 73
Ghana–Togo (January–May 1965), 71; (August–October 1982), 88; (January–February 1994), 106
Ghana–Upper Volta (June 1964–June 1966), 69–70
Togo–Ghana (September 1986), 93
Goa conflict (December 1961), 212
Godoy, Hector Garcia, 140
Golan Heights conflicts
Israel–Syria (July 1957–February 1958), 272; (March 1972–January 1973), 281–282; (February 2001–), 300–301
Six-Day war (June 1967), 277–278
Yom Kippur War (October 1973), 282–283
Gomulka, Wladyslaw, 240
Gorbachev, Mikhail, 248, 250
Gowon, Yakubu, 59, 74
Graham, Frank P., 208
Great Britain. *See* United Kingdom
Greece
civil war (1945–1949), 236–237
Cyprus (December 1963–November 1967), 241; (January 1974–June 1978), 244
Greece–Albania (April 1994), 253–254
Korean War (June 1950–July 1953), 169
Turkey–Greece (March 1984–January 1988), 245
Grenada
U.S.–Grenada (October–December 1983), 147–148
Guardia, Ernesto de la, 132
Guatemala
Belize–Guatemala (August 1995), 152
civil war (June 1954–), 128–129; (September 1982–January 1983), 147; (April 1984), 148
Guatemala–Mexico (December 1958–September 1959), 132–133; (September 1982–January 1983), 147
Panama (1958–May 1959), 132
Guatemalan National Revolutionary Unity (URNG), 147
Guei, Robert, 114
Guelleh, Ismael Omar, 111
Guerrilla wars
Bolivia (November 1966–July 1970), 141
Chad–Libya (June 1976–November 1979), 81–82
Colombia (1965–), 139–140
Guinea–Portugal (November 1970), 75
Karen separatist insurgency (January 1949–), 167–168
Namibia (1975–), 78–79
Rhodesia (Zimbabwe) (1967–January 1980), 73–74
Somalia–Ethiopia (January–March 1964), 68–69
South Africa–Lesotho (December 1982), 88–89
Suriname (July 1986–December 1992), 149–150
Tibet–China (March 1956–September 1965), 210
Uzbekistan–Kyrgyzstan/Tajikistan (August 1999–September 2000), 225–226
Guevara, Ché, 141
Guinea
Conakry raids (November 1970), 75
coup plot (March–April 1966), 72–73
Ghana–Guinea (October–November 1966), 73
Guinea–Ivory Coast (March–April 1966), 72–73; (February–September 1967), 74
Guinea–Portugal (November 1970), 75
hostage crisis (February–September 1967), 74
Liberia–Guinea (September 1999–April 2001), 113–114
postcoup tensions (October–November 1966), 73
Guinea-Bissau
African territories–Portugal (1961–July 1975), 65
Guinea-Bissau–Senegal (April 1990–May 1990), 100
Guinea–Portugal (November 1970), 75
military factions (June 1998–January 2000), 112–113
Gulf war (August 1990–May 1991), 296
post–Gulf war conflicts
Iraq–Coalition forces (December 1992–July 1993), 298; (October 1994), 299
Saudi Arabia–Qatar (September–October 1992), 297
Saudi Arabia–Yemen (December 1994), 299–300
GUNT (Transitional Government of National Unity), 87
Guyana
Guyana–Suriname (August 1969–November 1970), 142
Venezuela–Guyana (U.K.) (February 1962–June 1970), 134–135

Habré, Hissène, 83, 87
Habyarimana, Juvénal, 102
Hague Convention for the Pacific Settlement of International Disputes, 26
Haig, Alexander, 146
Haile Mariam, Mengistu, 94
Haile Selassie, 60, 67, 70
Hainan Island, 168
Haiti
Cuba–Haiti (August 1959), 133–134
Dominican Republic–Haiti/Cuba (early 1947–December 1951), 123–125

Haiti—*continued*
- Haiti–Dominican Republic (April–September 1963), 137–138
- reinstallation of Aristide (September 1994), 150–151
- U.S.–Haiti (September 1994), 150–151

Halaib dispute (December 1992), 297–298
Hammarskjöld, Dag, 35, 42, 63, 66, 171, 271
Harrington, Lord, 73
Hassan II, 84
Hawar Islands (April 1986), 295
Hekmatyar, Gulbuddin, 218
Hezbollah (Party of God), 284, 293, 300
Hirsi, Mohammed Said, 96
Historical enmity. *See* Rivalries
Ho Chi Minh, 159, 165, 174
Hodh region conflict (mid-1960–February 1963), 63–64
"Holy Spirit," 86
Honduras
- contra war (January 1980–February 1994), 145
- El Salvador–Honduras (July 1969), 141–142; (July 1976–October 1980), 142–143
- football war (July 1969), 141–142
- Honduras–Nicaragua (April–June 1957), 131–132
- Mocoran seizure (April–June 1957), 131–132
- San José plan, 142

Horn of Africa, 56
Hostage crises
- Guinea–Ivory Coast (February–September 1967), 74
- U.S.–Iran (November 1979–January 1981), 290

Hostility, 3
Hoûla raids (October 1965), 277
Houphouët-Boigny, Félix, 93
Hula swamp, 267
Humberto Mejia, Oscar, 128
Hungarian uprising of 1956, 240–241
Hungary
- Hungary–USSR (October–December 1956), 240–241

Hunish Islands, invasion of (November 1995–October 1998), 108–109
Hussein I, 279
Hussein, Saddam, 6, 13, 262–263, 274, 298
Hutuland, 97
Hutus
- Congo (October 1996–), 109
- Hutu conflict (August 1988–), 97–98
- Rwanda (September 1990–), 102–104
- Rwanda–Burundi (January 1964–January 1965), 69

Hyderabad (July–September 1948), 208

IAPC. *See* Inter-American Peace Committee
ICAO. *See* International Civil Aviation Organization
Iceland
- Iceland–United Kingdom, West Germany, Denmark (November 1971–June 1976), 243–244

ICO. *See* Islamic Conference Organization
ICRC. *See* Red Cross
ICRM. *See* International Red Cross and Red Crescent Movement
IDF. *See* Israeli Defense Forces
IFRCS. *See* Red Cross
IGOs. *See* Intergovernmental organizations
ILO. *See* International Labor Organization
IMU. *See* Islamic Movement of Uzbekistan
Incidents. *See also* Air incidents; Border incidents
- naval
  - Japan–North Korea (December 2001), 201–202
  - North Korea–South Korea (November 2001–July 2002), 200–201
  - North Korea–U.S. (January–December 1968), 179–180
  - Turkey–Greece (March 1984–January 1988), 245
  - U.S.–Libya (January–April 1986), 295
  - USS *Pueblo* seizure (January–December 1968), 179–180
- post–Gulf war
  - Iraq–Coalition forces (December 1992–July 1993), 298
- shelling
  - Ghana–Togo (January–February 1994), 106
  - Taiwan–China (November 1994), 195

Incorporation struggles
- China–Tibet (October 1950–May 1951), 209–210
- Tibet–China (March 1956–September 1965), 210

Independence. *See also* Autonomy disputes; Secession conflicts
- postindependence disputes
  - Bangladesh (1975–), 215–216
  - Belize–Guatemala (August 1995), 152
  - Egypt–Sudan (February 1958), 272
  - France–Tunisia (February–May 1958), 63; (July–September 1961), 65–66
  - Pakistan–Afghanistan (August 1949), 208–209
  - Rwanda–Burundi (January 1964–January 1965), 69
  - Spain–Morocco (November 1957–April 1958), 62
- struggles for
  - African territories–Portugal (1961–July 1975), 65
  - Congo (October 1996–), 109
  - East Timor–Indonesia (October 1975–May 2002), 184–185
  - Eritrea–Ethiopia (July 1949–December 1950), 60–61
- wars of
  - Bangladesh (March 1971–February 1974), 215
  - France–Algeria (November 1954–March 1962), 62
  - France–French Indochina (December 1945–July 1954), 165
  - India (1945–1948), 207
  - Israel (May 1948–January 1949), 266
  - Netherlands–Dutch East Indies (1945–November 1949), 164–165
  - Rhodesia (1967–January 1980), 73–74
  - South West Africa (1966–March 1990), 72
  - Tunisia (January 1952–March 1956), 61
  - United Kingdom–Malaya (June 1948–July 1960), 165–166

Independence crises
- France–Levant (1945–December 1946), 265
- Kuwait (June 1961–February 1962), 274–275
- post-Soviet
  - USSR–Latvia (January 1991), 250–251
  - USSR–Lithuania (March 1990–late 1991), 248

India
- Bangladesh (1975–), 215–216
- Bangladesh–India (April 1976), 216–217; (April–July 2001), 226–227
- China–India (October 1975), 216
- civil war (1945–1948), 207
- Goa conflict (December 1961), 212
- India–Bangladesh (November 1979), 217–218; (December 1983–June 1984), 221; (February–April 1986), 222; (April–August 1999), 225
- India–Pakistan (October 1947–January 1949), 207–208; (1965–1970), 213–214; (August–September 1965), 214; (July 1981–August 1982), 219; (April 1984–September 1985), 221; (1986–), 222–223
- India–Portugal (December 1961), 212
- Kashmir wars (August–September 1965), 214
- Maldives (November 1988), 223
- Muhuri River incidents (February–April 1986), 222
- Nepal–India (April–November 1962), 212
- Pakistan–Bangladesh (March 1971–February 1974), 215
- postpartition conflicts
  - India–East Pakistan (March 1958–September 1959), 210
  - India–Hyderabad (July–September 1948), 208
  - India–Pakistan (October 1947–January 1949), 207–208
- Siachin Glacier dispute (April 1984–September 1985), 221
- Siachin Glacier/Kashmir conflict (1986–), 222–223
- Sino-Indian wars
  - McMahon Line border dispute (August 1959–February 1960), 211; (October–November 1962), 212–213
  - McMahon Line border incidents (September 1965), 214–215
- Surma River incidents (March 1958–September 1959), 210
- war of independence (1945–1948), 207

India Independence Act of 1947, 207

Indochina, 5, 7, 159, 171
  France–French Indochina (December 1945–July 1954), 165
  U.S.–Vietnam (December 1960–May 1975), 173–174
Indonesia
  Borneo conflict (1962–November 1965), 174–175
  East Timor–Indonesia (October 1975–May 2002), 184–185
  Indonesia–Malaysia (1962–November 1965), 174–175
  Indonesia–Papua New Guinea (May 1982–October 1984), 189–190
  Irian Jaya–Indonesia (1965–), 178–179
  Netherlands–Dutch East Indies (1945–November 1949), 164–165
  Netherlands–Indonesia (January–August 1962), 175
  West Irian conflict (January–August 1962), 175
Ingush area (North Ossetia), 252
Ingushetia, 233, 253
Inquiry, 25
Insurgencies
  Communist
    Cambodia–Siam (Thailand) (early 1953–May 1975), 170–171
    Greece (1945–1949), 236–237
    Nepal (mid-1998–September 1999), 225
    United Kingdom–Malaya (June 1948–July 1960), 165–166
  Costa Rica (March–April 1948), 125
  Costa Rica–Nicaragua (December 1948–February 1949), 125
  guerrilla
    Bolivia (November 1966–July 1970), 141
    Colombia (1965–), 139–140
    South Africa–Lesotho (December 1982), 88–89
    Suriname (July 1986–December 1992), 149–150
    Uzbekistan–Kyrgyzstan/Tajikistan (August 1999–September 2000), 225–226
  Honduras–Nicaragua (January 1980–February 1994), 145
  Karen separatist (January 1949–), 167–168; (March 1984), 191
  Khmer Rouge (December 1979–October 1980), 188–189
  leftist
    Colombia (1965–), 139–140
    Guatemala (June 1954–), 128–129
  North Yemen–South Yemen (October 1971–October 1972), 279–280
  Oman–South Yemen (1972–August 1974), 280–281
  separatist
    Bougainville–Papua New Guinea (October 1988–), 192–193
    Kurdish (May 1976–), 286–287; (August 1984–), 293–294
    Netherlands–Indonesia (January–August 1962), 175
    Somalia–Kenya (November 1962–September 1967), 66
Inter-American Peace Committee (IAPC), 129
Intercommunal violence
  Cyprus (April 1955–February 1959), 239–240; (December 1963–November 1967), 241
Internal strife
  Chad (November 1965–1972), 71–72; (January 1978–June 1982), 83
  Iran (1976–1980), 285–286
  Lebanon (February 1975–late 1992), 284
  Zaire (November 1984), 92; (June 1985), 92
  Zaire–Angola (March–May 1977), 82–83
International arbitration, 26–27
International Civil Aviation Organization (ICAO), 28
International Committee of the Red Cross. *See* Red Cross
International conflict. *See also specific conflicts*
  characteristics of, 8
  definition of, 3–4
  dispute outcomes, 11
  duration of disputes, 9
  fatalities, 10
  incidence of by geopolitical region, 9
  internationalized civil conflict, 7–8
  issue complexity, 10
  nature of, 3–12
  patterns, 8–11
  types of, 7–8
International conflict management
  approaches to, 39–40
  need for, 11–12
  understanding of, 13–33
International Court of Justice (ICJ), 14, 20, 35, 58, 72, 77, 87, 93, 106, 121, 126, 132, 136, 142, 171, 234, 237, 243
International Federation of Red Cross and Red Crescent Societies. *See* Red Cross
Internationalized civil conflict, 7–8
International Labor Organization (ILO), 28
International law
  limitations of, 27–28
International organizations, 24–25. *See also specific organizations*
  conflicts managed by, 41–43
  definition, 38
  effectiveness, 40
  mediation outcomes, 31
  as mediators, 16–17
  origins and functions, 43–45
International Red Cross and Red Crescent Movement (ICRM), 333
International Telecommunication Union (ITU), 28
Interstate conflicts, 7
Intervention. *See also* Military intervention
  Angola (1975–), 78–79
  Chad (January 1978–June 1982), 83
  Chad–Libya (mid-1982–), 87–88
  Chad–Sudan (November 1965–1972), 71–72
  Djibouti civil war (early 1998–December 2000), 110–111
  Liberia–Sierra Leone (March 1991–), 104–105
  Mozambique–South Africa (1976–October 1992), 80–81
  Nepal (mid-1998–September 1999), 225
  Uganda (May 1995–), 106–107
Invasions. *See also* Military invasions
  China–Taiwan (March–December 1962), 175–176
  Cuba–Panama (1958–May 1959), 132
  Cuba–Venezuela (November 1963–May 1967), 138–139
  Cyprus (January 1974–June 1978), 244
  Dominican Republic–Cuba/Venezuela (February 1956–January 1962), 129–131
  Dominican Republic–Haiti/Cuba (early 1947–December 1951), 123–125
  East Timor (1975), 184–185
  Haiti–Dominican Republic (April–September 1963), 137–138
  Hunish Islands (November 1995–October 1998), 108–109
  Israel–Lebanon (March–June 1978), 288–289
  Maldives (November 1988), 223
  Nicaragua–Costa Rica (January 1955), 129
  Rwanda (September 1990–), 102–104
  Shaba (March–May 1977), 82–83; (May 1978), 83–84; (November 1984), 92; (June 1985), 92
  U.S.–Grenada (October–December 1983), 147–148
  USSR–Afghanistan (December 1979–), 218–219
Iran
  civil war (1976–1980), 285–286
  Iran–Iraq (January 1972–February 1975), 281; (February 1980–1989), 291
  Iran–United Arab Emirates (November 1971), 280; (April 1992), 297
  Iraq–Iran (1971), 279; (September 1997), 300
  Islamic revolution (1976–1980), 285–286
  Kurdish areas, 274, 278, 279, 281, 283, 286, 291
  Tunb islands dispute (November 1971), 280; (April 1992), 297
  U.S.–Iran (November 1979–January 1981), 290
  USSR–Iran (August 1945–October 1947), 265–266
Iran–Iraq War (February 1980–1989), 291
Iraq
  Euphrates dispute (April–late 1975), 284–285
  Gulf war (August 1990–May 1991), 296
  Iran–Iraq (January 1972–February 1975), 281; (February 1980–1989), 291
  Iraq–Coalition forces (August 1990–May 1991), 296; (December 1992–July 1993), 298; (October 1994), 299; (2003), 6, 263

Iraq—*continued*
Iraq–Iran (1971), 279; (September 1997), 300
Iraq–Kurds (October 1968–March 1970), 278; (May 1976–), 286–287
Iraq–Kuwait (June 1961–February 1962), 274–275; (March 1973–July 1975), 282
Israel (May 1948–January 1949), 266
Kurds, 28, 30, 260, 274, 278, 283, 286–287, 293–294, 296, 298
Kurds–Iraq (March 1961–1966), 274; (March 1974–July 1975), 283
Mosul Revolt (March–April 1959), 273–274
Six-Day war (June 1967), 277–278
Syria–Iraq (March–April 1959), 273–274; (April–late 1975), 284–285
12-point program, 278
Irian Jaya. *See also* West Irian
Indonesia–Papua New Guinea (Mary 1982–October 1984), 189–190
Irian Jaya–Indonesia (1965–), 178–179
Ironsi, Aguiyi, 74
Islam Ahmad, Saif al-, 275
Islamic Alliance of Afghan Holy Warriors, 218
Islamic Conference Organization (ICO), 181, 218
Islamic law (Shari'a), 89, 218, 262, 285
Islamic Marxists, 285
Islamic Movement of Uzbekistan (IMU), 226
Islamic revolution
Iran (1976–1980), 285–286
U.S.–Iran hostage crisis (November 1979–January 1981), 290
Islas Malvinas, 146
Ismail, Mirza, 208
Israel
air strikes (March 1972–January 1973), 281–282
Egypt–United Kingdom, France (October–November 1956), 271–272
Israel–Arab states (June 1967), 277–278
Israel–Egypt (October 1973), 282–283
Israel–Jordan (January 1953–December 1954), 269; (July 1956–January 1958), 271; (December 1964–April 1966), 276–277
Israel–Lebanon (April 1974–July 1975), 283–284; (mid-late 1977), 287; (March–June 1978), 288–289; (early 1982–mid-1983), 292–293; (mid-1983–), 293
Israel–Syria (July 1957–February 1958), 272; (June 1979–February 1980), 289–290; (February 2001–), 300–301
Lebanon (February 1975–late 1992), 284
Lebanon–Israel (October 1965), 277
Mt. Scopus conflict (July 1956–January 1958), 271
occupied territories, map, 261
Six-Day war (June 1967), 277–278
Suez crisis (October–November 1956), 271–272
Syria–Israel (April–May 1951), 267–268; (February 1962–August 1963), 275; (June 1964–July 1966), 276; (March 1972–January 1973), 281–282
war of independence (May 1948–January 1949), 266
West Bank (January 1953–December 1954), 269
Yom Kippur War (October 1973), 282–283
Israeli Defense Forces (IDF)
Hoûla raids (October 1965), 277
Israel–Syria (February 2001–), 300–301
Suez crisis (October–November 1956), 271–272
Issas, 105
Italy
Italy–Yugoslavia (March 1952–October 1954), 239
Trieste crisis (March 1952–October 1954), 239
ITU. *See* International Telecommunication Union
Ivory Coast
civil war (September 1999–), 114–115
Guinea–Ivory Coast (March–April 1966), 72–73; (February–September 1967), 74

Janatha Vimukthi Peramuna (People's Liberation Front) (JVP), 220
Japan
Japan–North Korea (December 2001), 201–202
Jarring, Gunnar, 208
Jaruzelski, Wojciech, 244–245
Jawanization, 184
Jessup, Philip C., 209, 238
Jews. *See* Israel
JFFL. *See* Joint Forces for the Liberation of Liberia
Johnson, Lyndon, 177
Johnson, Roosevelt, 99
Johnson, Yormie, 99
Joint Forces for the Liberation of Liberia (JFFL), 113–114
Jordan
attempted coup (February 1970–August 1971), 278–279
Israel (May 1948–January 1949), 266
Israel–Arab states (June 1967), 277–278
Israel–Jordan (January 1953–December 1954), 269; (July 1956–January 1958), 271; (December 1964–April 1966), 276–277
Mt. Scopus conflict (July 1956–January 1958), 271
PLO–Jordan (February 1970–August 1971), 278–279
Six-Day war (June 1967), 277–278
West Bank (January 1953–December 1954), 269
Yom Kippur War (October 1973), 282–283
Jordan River. *See* West Bank
JSS. *See* Chittagong Hill Tracts People's Solidarity Association

Kabardino-Balkaria, 231
Kabila, Laurent, 71, 92, 103, 109
Kachins, 180
Kamchatka Peninsula, 170
Kampuchea. *See* Cambodia
Karachay-Cherkessia, 231
Karamojong, 109
Karen National Unity (KNU), 167
Karen separatist insurgencies (January 1949–), 167–168; (March 1984), 191
Karimov, Islam, 226
Karmal, Babrak, 218
Karzai, Hamin, 228
Kasavubu, Joseph, 64
Kashmir
Kashmir wars (October 1947–January 1949), 207–208; (August–September 1965), 214
Siachin Glacier/Kashmir conflict (1986–), 222–223
UN Kashmir Commission, 34
Kassem, Abdel Karim, 273, 274
Katanga. *See* Shaba
Kaunda, Kenneth, 87, 91, 95
KDP. *See* Kurdish Democratic Party
Keita, Drissa, 93
Keiti, Modibo, 64
Kennedy, John F., 136, 241
Kenya
Ethiopia–Kenya (October 1998–January 1999), 113
Kenya–United Kingdom (August 1952–December 1963), 61
Mau Mau revolt (August 1952–December 1963), 61
Somalia–Kenya (November 1962–September 1967), 66
Uganda–Kenya (February–August 1976), 81; (December 1987), 95; (March 1989), 98; (November 1996–July 1998), 109–110
Kenyatta, Jomo, 81
Kerim, Srjan, 251
KGB, 224
Khan, Muhammad Ayub, 210
Khmer Issarak (Free Cambodia), 165
Khmer Rouge, 11, 158, 181, 185, 186, 187, 188, 190, 191
border incidents
Cambodia–Thailand (January 1977–October 1978), 186–187
Thailand–Cambodia (November–December 1976), 185–186
insurgency (December 1979–October 1980), 188–189
Khomeini, Ruhollah, 285, 291
Khun Sa, 199
Kim Il Sung, 182

KLA. *See* Kosovo Liberation Army
KMT. *See* Kuomintang
KNU. *See* Karen National Unity
Kohl, Helmut, 248
Kolela, Bernard, 110
Kolingba, André, 115
Korea. *See also* North Korea; South Korea
cold war air incidents (April–October 1950), 168–169
Korean War (June 1950–July 1953), 169
Kosirev, Andrei, 299
Kosovo
Yugoslavia–Kosovo (October 1997–), 254–255
Kosovo Liberation Army (KLA), 254
Kosygin, Aleksei, 173
Kuomintang (KMT), 163, 166, 167, 168, 171, 172, 196
China (1945–1949), 163–164
KMT–CCP (October 1949–June 1953), 168; (April 1954–April 1955), 171–172; (July–December 1958), 172–173; (March–December 1962), 175–176
KMT–PLA (August 1948–1954), 166
Kurdish Democratic Party (KDP), 274
Kurdish Worker's Party (PKK), 286, 294
Kurdistan, 265, 278, 283, 286, 293, 294
Kurds
Iraq–Kurds (October 1968–March 1970), 278; (May 1976–), 286–287
Kurds–Iraq (March 1961–1966), 274; (March 1974–July 1975), 283
Kurds–Turkey (August 1984–), 293–294
Kushita border incident (April–August 1999), 225
Kuwait
Gulf war (August 1990–May 1991), 296
Iraq–Coalition forces (August 1990–May 1991), 296; (December 1992–July 1993), 298; (October 1994), 299
Iraq–Kuwait (June 1961–February 1962), 274–275; (March 1973–July 1975), 282
Yom Kippur War (October 1973), 282–283
Kyrgyzstan (June 1990), 223–224
Uzbekistan–Kyrgyzstan/Tajikistan (August 1999–September 2000), 225–226

Labor turmoil
Poland (December 1981–February 1982), 244–245
Lake Chad conflict (April–July 1983), 90–91
Lake Kinneret. *See* Lake Tiberias dispute
Lake Mweru border dispute (February–September 1982), 86–87
Lake Tiberias disputes (April–May 1951), 267–268; (October–December 1955), 270; (February 1962–August 1963), 275
Land disputes. *See* Territorial disputes
Lao Issara (Free Lao), 165
Laos
civil war (December 1958–1962), 175; (April 1964–May 1975), 176–177
France–French Indochina (December 1945–July 1954), 165
Laos–North Vietnam (April 1964–May 1975), 176–177
Laos–Thailand (June 1975–January 1976), 183–184; (June 1982), 190
Thailand–Laos (June 1984–December 1988), 191–192; (August–September 2000), 199
Vietnam War (December 1960–May 1975), 173–174
Latin America. *See specific countries*
Latvia
cold war air incidents (April–October 1950), 168–169
USSR–Latvia (January 1991), 250–251
Lauca River dam dispute (March 1962–1964), 135–136
Law
international, 27–28
sources for arbitration, 26–27
LCD. *See* Lesotho Congress for Democracy
League of Nations, 26, 27, 34, 72, 159, 266, 273
Lebanon
civil war (May 1958–June 1959), 273; (February 1975–late 1992), 284
France–Levant (1945–December 1946), 265
Hoûla raids (October 1965), 277
Israel (May 1948–January 1949), 266
Israel–Lebanon (April 1974–July 1975), 283–284; (mid-late 1977), 287; (March–June 1978), 288–289; (early 1982–mid-1983), 292–293; (mid-1983–), 293
Lebanon–Israel (October 1965), 277
security zone (mid-1983–), 293
Syria–Lebanon (May–August 1949), 266–267
Lee Teng Hui, 196
Leftist insurgencies
Colombia (1965–), 139–140
Guatemala (June 1954–), 128–129
Lekwana, Alice, 86
Leoni, Raúl, 135
Léotard, François, 251
Lesotho
intervention and military factions (May 1998–March 1999), 111
South Africa–Lesotho (December 1982), 88–89
Lesotho Congress for Democracy (LCD), 111
Lesotho Liberation Army (LLA), 88–89
Lete Island dispute
December 1963–June 1965, 68
Letsie III, 111
Levant
France–Levant (1945–December 1946), 265
Liberalization. *See also* Independence
"Prague Spring" (August 1968), 241–242
Liberation Front of Air and Azawad (FLAA), 100
Liberation Tigers of Tamil Eelam (LTTE), 220
Liberia
civil war (December 1989–), 98–100
Doe regime tensions (February–March 1983), 90
Liberia–Guinea (September 1999–April 2001), 113–114
Liberia–Sierra Leone (February–March 1983), 90; (March 1991–), 104–105
Libya
Chad (January 1978–June 1982), 83
Chad–Libya (June 1976–November 1979), 81–82; (mid-1982–), 87–88
Egypt–Libya (July–September 1977), 287–288
U.S.–Libya (August 1981), 291–292; (January–April 1986), 295; (January 1989), 295–296
Li Mi, 166
Lissouba, Pascal, 110
Lithuania
USSR–Lithuania (March 1990–late 1991), 248
LLA. *See* Lesotho Liberation Army
Lord's Resistance Army (LRA), 106
LRA. *See* Lord's Resistance Army
LTTE. *See* Liberation Tigers of Tamil Eelam
Lumumba, Patrice, 64
Luthufi, Abdullah, 223
Luxembourg, 169, 231

Macao conflict (July–August 1952), 169–170
MacArthur, Douglas, 169
Macedonia, 6, 18, 231, 233, 234, 246, 255
civil war (January 1991–), 251–252
Machel, Samora Moïses, 80
Madagascar
France–Madagascar (March–August 1947), 60
Madingos, 101
Maga, Coutoucou Hubert, 68
Maghreb Union, 98
Mahdi, Sadiq al-, 67, 89
Makarios, 244
Malakula, 189

Malawi, 11, 53, 55, 80, 94
Malaya (Malaysia and Singapore)
United Kingdom–Malaya (June 1948–July 1960), 165–166
Malayan emergency (June 1948–July 1960), 165–166
Malayan People's Anti-British Army (MPABA), 165–166
Malaysia. *See* Federation of Malaysia; Malaya
Maldives
attempted coup (November 1988), 223
Mali
Mali–Burkina Faso (December 1985–January 1986), 92–93
Mali–Tuareg (June 1990–), 102
Mali–Upper Volta (December 1974–June 1975), 77–78
Mauritania–Mali (mid-1960–February 1963), 63–64
Malloum, Félix, 81, 83
Mandela, Nelson, 6, 57, 91, 94, 97, 111
Mané, Ansumane, 112
Mao Zedong, 163, 168
Maps
Africa in 1945, 55
Africa today, 54
Americas, 119
the Caucasus, 231
East Asia/Pacific, 156
Europe, modern, 230
Indochina, 157
Israel and occupied territories, 261
Middle East region, 260
Southwest Asia, 206
Soviet expansion in Europe, 232
Marakwet, 109
Maronites, 266, 284
Marshall, George C., 164
Martial law
Poland (December 1981–February 1982), 244–245
Marxists
Islamic, 285
Mau Mau revolt (August 1952–December 1963), 61
Mauritania, 53, 77, 98
Mauritania–Mali (mid-1960–February 1963), 63–64
Mauritania–Senegal (April 1989–January 1990), 98
Morocco–Mauritania (October 1974–), 77
Western Saharan conflict (October 1974–), 77
Mayaguez incident (May 1975), 183
Mbeki, Thabo, 114
Mboumosa, Eteki, 23, 81
Mbumba, Nathanael, 82, 84
McMahon Line border dispute (August 1959–February 1960), 211; (October–November 1962), 212–213; (September 1965), 214–215; (October 1975), 216
MDRM. *See* Mouvement Démocratique de la Rénovation Malagalese
Mediation, 16–17
outcomes, 31
Mediators, 16–17
Mekong River islands dispute (August–September 2000), 199
Menderes, Adnan, 209
Mendez Montenegro, Julio César, 128
Meo refugees, 183
Mexico
Guatemala–Mexico (December 1958–September 1959), 132–133; (September 1982–January 1983), 147; (April 1984), 148
MFDC. *See* Movement of Democratic Forces of Casamance
Middle Congo. *See* People's Republic of the Congo
Middle East. *See also* Arab–Israeli conflicts; *specific countries*
characteristics of conflicts, 46
conflict management, 263–265
conflicts, overview of, 263
country list, alphabetical, 260, 303–305
international conflicts, 9
map
Israel and occupied territories, 261
region, 260
regional overview, 260–263
MILF. *See* Moro Islamic Liberation Front
Militarized disputes, 8
France–Tunisia (February–May 1958), 63
Mali–Tuareg (June 1990–), 102
U.S.–Grenada (October–December 1983), 147–148
Military factions
Guinea-Bissau (June 1998–January 2000), 112–113
Military insurgencies
Costa Rica (March–April 1948), 125
Military intervention. *See also* Intervention
Central African Republic–Chad (mid-2001–December 2002), 115–116
France–Gabon (February 1964), 69
Ivory Coast (September 1999–), 114–115
Lesotho (May 1998–March 1999), 111
U.S.–Dominican Republic (April 1965–September 1966), 140–141
U.S.–Vietnam (December 1960–May 1975), 173–174
Military invasions. *See also* Invasions
Cuba–Haiti (August 1959), 133–134
Israel–Lebanon (early 1982–mid-1983), 292–293
U.S.–Cuba (April–May 1961), 134
U.S.–Grenada (October–December 1983), 147–148
U.S.–Haiti (September 1994), 150–151
U.S.–Panama (December 1989), 150
USSR–Czechoslovakia (August 1968), 241–242
Military Observers Ecuador–Peru (MOMEP), 151
Military occupations
China–Tibet (October 1950–May 1951), 209–210
Military putsches. *See also* Coups; Putsches
France–Gabon (February 1964), 69
Mindanao
Mindanao–The Philippines (January 1970–), 181–182
Mischief Reef, 195, 198
Mitterrand, François, 248
MJP. *See* Movement for Justice and Peace
M19 guerrilla group, 139–140
MNLF. *See* Moro National Liberation Front
Mobutu, Joseph Désiré, 64–65
Mobutu Sésé Séko, 40, 64–65, 69, 71, 75, 76, 79, 80, 82, 83–84, 87, 91, 92, 102, 109
Corisco Bay islands dispute (June–November 1972), 76
Lake Mweru border dispute (February–September 1982), 86–87
mercenaries dispute (August 1967–April 1968), 75
Mocoran seizure (April–June 1957), 131–132
Mohammed, Ali, 96
Moldova
Gagauz struggle for autonomy (October 1990–July 1992), 249–250
Molina, Rafael Leónidas Trujillo, 123, 129, 137
MOMEP. *See* Military Observers Ecuador–Peru
Monarchism
Afghanistan–Pakistan (March–July 1979), 217
Greece (1945–1949), 236–237
Montt, Efran Rios, 128
Morocco
Algeria–Morocco (October 1963–February 1964), 67; (June–October 1979), 85
Mauritania–Mali (mid-1960–February 1963), 63–64
Morocco–Mauritania (October 1974–), 77
Sahara conflict (November 1957–April 1958), 62
Spain–Morocco (November 1957–April 1958), 62
Tindouf war (October 1963–February 1964), 67
Western Saharan conflict (October 1974–), 77
Yom Kippur War (October 1973), 282–283
Moro Islamic Liberation Front (MILF), 181
Moro National Liberation Front (MNLF), 181
Moros, 158, 181
Mosisili, Bethuel Pakalitha, 111
Mossadeq, Muhammad, 285
Mosul Revolt (March–April 1959), 273–274

Mountbatten, Lord, 208
Mouvement Démocratique de la Rénovation Malagalese (MDRM), 60
Movement for Justice and Peace (MJP), 114
Movement of Democratic Forces of Casamance (MFDC), 100
Movimento Popular de Libertação de Angola (MPLA), 7, 78, 79, 82, 84
Mozambique, 4–5, 10, 11, 53, 54, 56, 65, 73, 80, 91, 94
  African territories–Portugal (1961–July 1975), 65
  Mozambique–South Africa (1976–October 1992), 80–81
Mozambique Liberation Front (Frelimo), 80
Mozambique National Resistance Movement (Renamo), 80
MPABA. *See* Malayan People's Anti-British Army
MPCI. *See* Patriotic Movement of the Ivory Coast
MPIGO. *See* Popular Ivorian Movement for the Far West
MPLA. *See* Movimento Popular de Libertação de Angola
MPS. *See* Patriotic Salvation Movement
Mt. Scopus conflict (July 1956–January 1958), 271
Muhuri River incidents (February–April 1986), 222
Mujahedeen-e Khalq, 300
Mujahideen, 209, 223
Mullah Omar, 227
Museveni, Yoweri, 86, 95, 106
Musharraf, Pervez, 227
Muslim League, 207
Muslims
  Arabic, 5, 9, 67
  Bosnian, 246
  Iran (1976–1980), 285–286
  Israel–Lebanon (mid-late 1977), 287; (mid-1983–), 293
  Mindanao–The Philippines (January 1970–), 181–182
  Rohingya rebellion (December 1991), 193–194
  Shiite, 7, 206, 248, 262, 271, 285, 286, 293, 296, 298
  Sunni, 263, 273, 274, 284, 293
Mutinies
  Guinea–Bissau (June 1998–January 2000), 112–113
Muzorewa, Abel, 73
Myanmar. *See* Burma

Nabiyev, Rakhman, 224
Nagorno–Karabakh conflict (August 1990–), 248–249
Nagriamel movement, 189
Nagy, Imre, 240, 241
Nairobi Accords, 107
NALU. *See* National Army for the Liberation of Uganda
Namibia
  guerrilla warfare (1975–), 78–79
  war of independence (1966–March 1990), 72
Nanri island, 168
Nasir, Sagar Ahmed, 223
Nasser, Gamal Abdel, 268, 269, 271, 272, 273
National Army for the Liberation of Uganda (NALU), 106
National Army of North Borneo (TMKU), 174–175
National Congress Party, 207
National Democratic Alliance (NDA), 106
National Democratic Front (NDF), 289
National Front for the Liberation of South Yemen, 275
Nationalism
  African
    African territories–Portugal (1961–July 1975), 65
    Algeria (November 1954–March 1962), 62
    Eritrea–Ethiopia (July 1949–December 1950), 60–61; (1965–May 1993), 70–71
    France–Madagascar (March–August 1947), 60
    Morocco–Mauritania (October 1974–), 77
    Mozambique–South Africa (1976–October 1992), 80–81
    Netherlands–Dutch East Indies (1945–November 1949), 164–165
    Rhodesia (Zimbabwe) (1967–January 1980), 73–74
    South Africa–Botswana (October 1984–May 1986), 91–92
    South Africa–Zambia (April 1987), 94
    Tunisia (January 1952–March 1956), 61
    Western Sahara (June–October 1979), 85
  Asian
    China–Taiwan (January 1996–August 1999), 196–197
    Taiwan–China (November 1994), 195
Nationalists. *See* Kuomintang (KMT)
National Liberation Army (ALN), 62, 251
National Liberation Army (NLA), 251
National Liberation Front (EAM), 236
National Liberation Front (FLN), 62, 138
National Movement for the Liberation of Kosovo (NMLK), 254
National Organization of Cypriot Fighters (EOKA), 239, 244
National organizations
  leaders of as mediators, 16–17. *See also specific leaders and organizations*
National Patriotic Front of Liberia (NPFL), 98, 104–105
National Popular Liberation Army (ELAS), 236
National Resistance Army (NRA), 86
National Resistance Council (NRC), 86
NATO. *See* North Atlantic Treaty Organization
Naval incidents
  Japan–North Korea (December 2001), 201–202
  North Korea–South Korea (November 2001–July 2002), 200–201
  North Korea–U.S. (January–December 1968), 179–180
  Turkey–Greece (March 1984–January 1988), 245
  U.S.–Libya (January–April 1986), 295
  USS *Pueblo* seizure (January–December 1968), 179–180
NDA. *See* National Democratic Alliance
NDF. *See* National Democratic Front
Nehru, Jawaharlal, 208, 209, 210, 211, 212
Neo-Déstour Party, 61
Nepal
  anti-Chinese guerrilla warfare (March 1956–September 1965), 210
  China–Nepal (June 1959–July 1960), 211
  Maoist guerrilla insurgency (mid-1998–September 1999), 225
  Nepal–India (April–November 1962), 212
The Netherlands
  Korean War (June 1950–July 1953), 169
  Netherlands–Dutch East Indies (1945–November 1949), 164–165
  Netherlands–Indonesia (January–August 1962), 175
Neto, António Agostinho, 82
Neutrality laws, 13
New River Triangle border dispute (August 1969–November 1970), 142
"New villages," 166
New Zealand
  anti-British Communist insurgencies (June 1948–July 1960), 165–166
  Borneo conflict (1962–November 1965), 174–175
  Korean War (June 1950–July 1953), 169
  Vietnam War (December 1960–May 1975), 173–174
Ngouabi, Marien, 76
Nicaragua
  contra war (January 1980–February 1994), 145
  Costa Rica (March–April 1948), 125
  Costa Rica–Nicaragua (December 1948–February 1949), 125
  Honduras–Nicaragua (April–June 1957), 131–132
  Mocoran seizure (April–June 1957), 131–132
  Nicaragua–Costa Rica (January 1955), 129; (October 1977), 144; (September–December 1978), 144–145; (May–June 1985), 148–149; (April 1986), 149
Nicaraguan Broad Opposition Front (FAO), 144
Niger
  Diffa border insurgency (December 1996–April 1999), 110
  Niger–Dahomey (Benin) (December 1963–June 1965), 68
  Niger–Tuaregs (May 1990–October 1994), 100
Nigeria
  Cameroon–Nigeria (May–July 1981), 85–86
  Chad–Nigeria (April–July 1983), 90–91
  Ivory Coast (September 1999–), 114–115
  Lake Chad conflict (April–July 1983), 90–91
  Nigeria–Biafra (July 1967–January 1970), 74–75
  Nigeria–Cameroon (December 1993–March 1994), 105–106

Nimley, David, 99
Ninth October Movement, 106
Nkomati accord, 80, 91
Nkrumah, Kwame, 69, 71, 73
NLA. *See* National Liberation Army
NLL. *See* Northern Limit Line
NMLK. *See* National Movement for the Liberation of Kosovo
Nol, Lon, 181, 186
Non-Aggression and Defense Aid Agreement (ANAD), 93
Noriega, Manuel Antonio, 150
North America. *See specific countries*
North Atlantic Treaty Organization (NATO), 28, 38, 41, 233, 238, 240, 242, 243, 245, 247, 332
  establishment of, 332
  Macedonia (January 1991–), 251–252
  sphere of influence, 332
  Yugoslavia–Kosovo (October 1997–), 254–255
Northern Ireland, 8
Northern Limit Line (NLL), 200
North Korea
  Japan–North Korea (December 2001), 201–202
  North Korea–South Korea (mid-1965–March 1968), 179; (February–July 1975), 182–183; (November 1984), 192; (May 1992), 194; (September 1996–November 2000), 197–198; (November 2001–July 2002), 200–201
  North Korea–U.S. (January–December 1968), 179–180
  U.S.–North Korea (June 1950–July 1953), 169
North Ossetia, 231, 252
North Vietnam. *See* Socialist Republic of Vietnam
North Yemen
  civil war (September 1962–October 1967), 275–276
  North Yemen–Saudi Arabia (November 1969–October 1970), 278
  North Yemen–South Yemen (October 1971–October 1972), 279–280; (February 1979–February 1980), 289
  Saudi Arabia–North Yemen (August 1979–March 1980), 290–291
  Yemen (November 1993–July 1994), 298–299
Novotny, Antonin, 242
NPFL. *See* National Patriotic Front of Liberia
NRA. *See* National Resistance Army
NRC. *See* National Resistance Council
Nu, U, 171
Nuba people, 89
Nuclear weapons, 12, 13, 136, 182, 204, 219, 241, 298
Nujoma, Sam, 72
Numeiry, Gaafar Mohammed, 89

OAS. *See* Organization of American States
OAU. *See* Organization of African Unity
Obote, A. Milton, 75, 81, 84, 86
Observer missions, 16–17
Ogaden wars (January–March 1964), 68–69; (mid-1972–1985), 76–77; (February 1987–April 1988), 94
OIC. *See* Organization of the Islamic Conference
Oil
  Buraymi crisis (August 1952–October 1955), 268–269
  Corisco Bay islands dispute (June–November 1972), 76
  Halaib dispute (December 1992), 297–298
  Lake Chad (April–July 1983), 90–91
  Oman–Saudi Arabia (August 1952–October 1955), 268–269
Ojukwa, Chukwuemeka Odumegwu, 74
Okello, Bazilio, 86
OLF. *See* Oromo Liberation Front
Oman
  Buraymi crisis (August 1952–October 1955), 268–269
  Dhofar rebellion (1972–August 1974), 280–281
  Oman–Saudi Arabia (August 1952–October 1955), 268–269
  Oman–South Yemen (1972–August 1974), 280–281
OMON. *See* Otryad Militsii Osobogo Naznacheniya
Ona, Francis, 193
Ongoing conflicts
  Afghanistan (December 1979–), 218–219
  Angola–South Africa (1975–), 78–79
  Azerbaijan–Armenia (August 1990–), 248–249
  Bangladesh (1975–), 215–216
  Bougainville–Papua New Guinea (October 1988–), 192–193
  Burma (January 1949–), 167–168
  Burundi (August 1988–), 97–98
  Cambodia–Vietnam (January 1979–), 187–188
  Casamance rebellion (mid-1990–), 100–101
  Caucasus (October 1992–), 252–253
  Chad–Libya (mid-1982–), 87–88
  Chechen war (October 1992–), 252–253
  Chittagong Hill Tracts (1975–), 215–216
  Colombia (1965–), 139–140
  Comoros (September 1995–), 107–108
  Congo (October 1996–), 109
  Cyprus (June 1996–), 254
  Georgia–South Ossetia, Abkhazia (March 1989–), 245–246
  Guatemala (June 1954–), 128–129
  Hutu conflict (August 1988–), 97–98
  India–Pakistan wars (1986–), 222–223
  Iraq–Kurds (May 1976–), 286–287
  Irian Jaya–Indonesia (1965–), 178–179
  Israel–Lebanon (mid-1983–), 293
  Israel–Syria (February 2001–), 300–301
  Ivory Coast (September 1999–), 114–115
  Karen separatist insurgency (January 1949–), 167–168
  Kurds–Turkey (August 1984–), 293–294
  Liberia (December 1989–), 98–100
  Liberia–Sierra Leone (March 1991–), 104–105
  Macedonia (January 1991–), 251–252
  Mali–Tuareg (June 1990–), 102
  Mindanao–The Philippines (January 1970–), 181–182
  Morocco–Mauritania (October 1974–), 77
  Nagorno–Karabakh (August 1990–), 248–249
  Russia–Chechnya, the Caucasus (October 1992–), 252–253
  Russia–Georgia (August 2000–), 255–257
  Rwanda (September 1990–), 102–104
  Sahel rebellion (June 1990–), 102
  Senegal (mid-1990–), 100–101
  Siachin Glacier/Kashmir conflict (1986–), 222–223
  Sierra Leone (March 1991–), 104–105
  Somalia (May 1988–), 95–97
  Sri Lanka (July 1982–), 219–221
  Sudan (January 1983–), 89–90
  Tamil conflict (July 1982–), 219–221
  Uganda (May 1995–), 106–107
  Western Sahara (October 1974–), 77
  Yugoslavia–Kosovo (October 1997–), 254–255
Operation Dove, 84
OPM. *See* Organisasi Papua Mendeka
Organisasi Papua Mendeka (OPM), 178
Organization for Security and Cooperation in Europe (OSCE), 18, 28, 233, 247, 249, 250, 252, 256, 329–331
  chairmen-in-office, list of, 330
  composition strengths and homogeneity, 331
  concerns of, 330
  establishment of, 235–236, 329
  membership of, 330
  organs for handling conflict, 330
  secretaries-general, list of, 330
  sphere of influence, 329
  stated obligations of, 330
  structural hierarchy, 330
Organization of African Unity (OAU), 55, 57–59, 66, 70, 71, 73, 74, 78, 80, 81, 82, 83, 84, 85, 91, 93, 95, 97, 98, 102, 106, 108, 112, 113, 115
Organization of American States (OAS), 12, 17, 28, 39, 42, 45, 125, 127, 129, 132–133, 135, 137–138, 140–142, 144–146
  assistant secretaries-general, list of, 325
  composition strengths and homogeneity, 325
  concerns of, 324

establishment of, 121–123, 324
limitations of, 123
mediations, 145
membership of, 325
organs for handling conflict, 325
secretaries-general, list of, 325
sphere of influence, 324
stated obligations of, 325
structural hierarchy, 122, 325
Organization of the Islamic Conference (OIC), 332
establishment of, 332
sphere of influence, 332
Oromo Liberation Front (OLF), 113
OSCE. *See* Organization for Security and Cooperation in Europe
Otryad Militsii Osobogo Naznacheniya (OMON) ("Black Berets"), 248
Oueddei, Goukouni, 83, 87
Oumarou, Ide, 93
Owen, Lord David, 17, 29, 234

Pacific Islands Forum (PIF), 327–328
composition strengths and homogeneity, 328
concerns of, 327
directors of South Pacific Bureau for Economic Cooperation, 328
establishment of, 162–163, 327
forum dialogue partners, 328
membership of, 328
secretaries-general, list of, 328
sphere of influence, 327
stated obligations of, 327
structural hierarchy, 327
Pacific region. *See* East Asia/Pacific; *specific countries*
Pahlevi, Muhammad Reza Shah, 262, 285, 290
PAIGC. *See* Partido Africano da Indepêndencia de Guinée Cabo Verde
Pakistan
Afghanistan–Pakistan (June–October 1950), 209; (March–July 1979), 217
India–Pakistan wars (October 1947–January 1949), 207–208; (August–September 1965), 214; (1965–1970), 213–214; (July 1981–August 1982), 219; (April 1984–September 1985), 221; (1986–), 222–223
Kashmir wars (August–September 1965), 214
Pakistan–Afghanistan (August 1949), 208–209; (September 1960–May 1963), 211–212
Pakistan–Bangladesh (March 1971–February 1974), 215
Siachin Glacier dispute (April 1984–September 1985), 221
Siachin Glacier/Kashmir conflict (1986–), 222–223
Palestine
Israel (May 1948–January 1949), 266
U.N. partition of 1947, 266
Palestine Liberation Organization (PLO), 16, 18, 37, 262, 283, 285, 287, 300
incursions (January 1953–December 1954), 269; (March–June 1978), 288–289
Israel–Lebanon (early 1982–mid-1983), 292–293; (mid-1983–), 293
Israel–Syria (June 1979–February 1980), 289–290
Lebanon–Israel (October 1965), 277
PLO–Jordan (February 1970–August 1971), 278–279
raids (March 1972–January 1973), 281–282
Palestinians, 21, 263–264, 266, 284, 287, 288
Palmer, R. V., 166
Panama, 11, 118, 120, 125, 131, 144, 149
flag riots (January–April 1964), 139
revolutionaries conflict (1958–May 1959), 132
U.S.–Panama (January–April 1964), 139; (December 1989), 150
Pan American (airline), 73
Panguna mine, 193
Papal nuncio, 74, 125
Papua New Guinea
Bougainville–Papua New Guinea (October 1988–), 192–193
Indonesia–Papua New Guinea (Mary 1982–October 1984), 189–190
Irian Jaya–Indonesia (1965–), 178–179
Paracel Islands
China–The Philippines (January–February 1995), 195–196
territorial dispute (June–August 1956), 172
Paraguay
Paraguay–Argentina (early 1959–December 1961), 133
Pardew, James, 251
Paris Peace Accords, 181
Partido Africano da Indepêndencia de Guinée Cabo Verde (PAIGC), 75
Partido Democratico (PCU), 184
Partitions
Cyprus, 235, 253; (January 1974–June 1978), 244; (June 1996–), 254
Hyderabad (July–September 1948), 208
India–East Pakistan (March 1958–September 1959), 210
India–Pakistan (October 1947–January 1949), 207–208
Levant, 273
Palestine, 261–262, 266
Subcontinent of Asia, 5, 167, 207–208, 210, 213–216, 219, 221–222
Vietnam, 156, 165
Western Sahara (October 1974–), 77
Party of God. *See* Hezbollah
Pastoral tribes
Sahel rebellion (June 1990–), 102
Sahel separatism (May 1990–October 1994), 100
Patassé, Ange-Félix, 115
Pathan conflicts
June–October 1950, 209
September 1960–May 1963, 211–212
Pathanistan, 209, 211
Pathet Lao, 155, 159, 173, 176, 183, 190
Patriotic Movement of the Ivory Coast (MPCI), 114
Patriotic Salvation Movement (MPS), 87
Patriotic Union of Kurdistan (PUK), 286
PCIJ. *See* Permanent Court of International Justice
PDU. *See* Partido Democratico
Peace for Galilee, 292
Peacekeeping, 18–22
People's Democratic Republic of Yemen (South Yemen), 76, 279, 290
People's Liberation Army (PLA), 166, 209
China–Tibet (October 1950–May 1951), 209–210
KMT–PLA (August 1948–1954), 166
People's Republic of China. *See* China
People's Republic of Kampuchea (PRK), 188–189
People's Republic of the Congo. *See also* Congo
army rebellion (September 1987–July 1988), 95
civil unrest (September 1987–July 1988), 95
Zaire–People's Republic of the Congo (January 1987), 93–94
Peralta Azurdia, Enrique, 128
Perdiwah, seizure of (April–July 2001), 226–227
Permanent Court of International Justice (PCJ), 27
Persia. *See* Iran
Persian Gulf
Gulf war (August 1990–May 1991), 296
post–Gulf war conflicts
Iraq–Coalition forces (December 1992–July 1993), 298; (October 1994), 299
Saudi Arabia–Qatar (September–October 1992), 297
Saudi Arabia–Yemen (December 1994), 299–300
Tunb islands dispute (November 1971), 280
Peru
Ecuador–Peru (June 1977–January 1978), 143–144; (January–April 1981), 145–146; (January 1984), 148; (January–March 1995), 151; (January 1995–October 1998), 151–152
Panama revolutionaries conflict (1958–May 1959), 132
Peshawar rebellion (March–July 1979), 217
PFLOAG. *See* Popular Front for the Liberation of Oman and the Arab Gulf

The Philippines
Borneo conflict (1962–November 1965), 174–175
China–The Philippines (January–February 1995), 195–196; (April 1997–July 1999), 198
Korean War (June 1950–July 1953), 169
Mindanao–The Philippines (January 1970–), 181–182
Paracel and Spratly Islands dispute (January–February 1995), 195–196
Spratly Islands (April 1997–July 1999), 198
Vietnam–The Philippines (October 1999), 198–199
Vietnam War (December 1960–May 1975), 173–174
Picado Michalski, Teodoro, 125
PIF. *See* Pacific Islands Forum
Piracy
Mayaguez incident (May 1975), 183
PKK. *See* Kurdish Worker's Party
PLA. *See* People's Liberation Army
PLO. *See* Palestine Liberation Organization
PNG. *See* Papua New Guinea
Pointe-Noire Peace Agreement, 110
Poland
labor turmoil, martial law (December 1981–February 1982), 244–245
USSR–Poland (October 1956), 240
Police actions
Netherlands–Dutch East Indies (1945–November 1949), 164–165
Polisario Front (Frente Popular para la Liberatión de Saguia el-Hamra y Rio de Oro), 85
Political anarchy
Laos (December 1958–1962), 175; (April 1964–May 1975), 176–177
Political incidents, 8
Political instability
Chad–Libya (mid-1982–), 87–88
Georgia–South Ossetia, Abkhazia (March 1989–), 245–246
Uganda–Kenya (March 1989), 98
Pol Pot, 158, 187
Pope. *See* Papal nuncio
Popular Front for the Liberation of Oman and the Arab Gulf (PFLOAG), 280
Popular Front of South Ossetia, 245
Popular Ivorian Movement for the Far West (MPIGO), 114
Portugal
African territories–Portugal (1961–July 1975), 65
China–Portugal (July–August 1952), 169–170
East Timor–Indonesia (October 1975–May 2002), 184–185
Goa conflict (December 1961), 212
Guinea–Portugal (November 1970), 75
India–Portugal (December 1961), 212
Macao conflict (July–August 1952), 169–170
Powell, Colin, 300
POWs. *See* Prisoners of war
Prabhakaran, Vellupillai, 220
Prague Spring (August 1968), 241–242
Pramoj, Kukrit, 185
Premadasa, Ranasinghe, 220
Prisoners of war, 13, 77
PRK. *See* People's Republic of Kampuchea
Proxy wars, 7, 157, 160
PUK. *See* Patriotic Union of Kurdistan
Pushtu. *See* Pathan conflicts
Putsches. *See also* Coups
France–Gabon (February 1964), 69
Iraq (March–April 1959), 273–274

Qaddafi, Muammar, 82, 285, 288, 291, 295
Qatar
Qatar–Bahrain (April 1986), 295
Saudi Arabia–Qatar (September–October 1992), 297
Quemoy, bombardment of, (April 1954–April 1955), 171–172; (July–December 1958) , 172–173
Quiros, Daniel Oduber, 144
Quit India campaign, 207

Rabat chemical plant tensions (January 1989), 295–296
RAF. *See* Royal Air Force
Rahman, Mujibar, 215, 216
Rakosi, Muryas, 241
Ramos, Fidel, 198
Reagan, Ronald, 128, 143, 145, 147, 290, 291, 295
Rebel Armed Forces (FAR), 128
Rebellions
Casamance (mid-1990–), 100–101
Dhofar (1972–August 1974), 280–281
Dominican Republic (April 1965–September 1966), 140–141
France–Madagascar (March–August 1947), 60
Kurds (March 1974–July 1975), 283
Nepal–India (April–November 1962), 212
North Yemen (September 1962–October 1967), 275–276
People's Republic of the Congo (September 1987–July 1988), 95
Peshawar (March–July 1979), 217
Rohingya Muslim (December 1991), 193–194
Sahel (June 1990–), 102
Rebels
Angola (November 1975–February 1976), 79–80
Chad–Libya (mid-1982–), 87–88
Congo (Zaire)–Uganda (February–March 1965), 71
Costa Rica–Nicaragua (December 1948–February 1949), 125
Nicaragua–Costa Rica (January 1955), 129
Rwanda (September 1990–), 102–104
Reconstruction costs
emergency aid, 12
Red Army, 163
Red Cross (ICRC and IFRCS), 184, 333
establishment of, 333
sphere of influence, 333
Referrals, 24–25
Refugees, 55–56
Angola–South Africa (1975–), 78–79
Angola–Zambia (November 2001), 116
Burundi (August 1988–), 97–98
Cambodia–Thailand (December 1975–February 1976), 185; (January 1977–October 1978), 186–187
Congo-Brazzaville (May 1997–late-2000), 110
Eritrea–Ethiopia (May 1998–June 1999), 111–112
Ethiopia–Kenya (October 1998–January 1999), 113
Georgia–South Ossetia, Abkhazia (March 1989–), 245–246
Laos–Thailand (June 1975–January 1976), 183–184
Liberia–Guinea (September 1999–April 2001), 113–114
Liberia–Sierra Leone (March 1991–), 104–105
Rwanda (September 1990–), 102–104
Senegal (mid-1990–), 100–101
Thailand–Cambodia (November–December 1976), 185–186
Uganda (May 1995–), 106–107
Uganda–Kenya (December 1987), 95
Western Saharan conflict (October 1974–), 77
Zaire–Zambia (February–September 1982), 86–87
Regional aggression. *See also* Regional rivalries
Dominican Republic–Cuba/Venezuela (February 1956–January 1962), 129–131
Dominican Republic–Haiti/Cuba (early 1947–December 1951), 123–125
Regional conflicts. *See also* Regional rivalries
chronology of, 306–316
geopolitical regions, 45–46
Regional instability
Cambodia–Thailand (January 1977–October 1978), 186–187
Congo (October 1996–), 109
Congo–Rwanda (August 1967–April 1968), 75
Guatemala–Mexico (September 1982–January 1983), 147; (April 1984), 148
Thailand–Cambodia (November–December 1976), 185–186

Uganda (May 1995–), 106–107
U.S.–Libya (August 1981), 291–292
Zaire–Angola (March–May 1977), 82–83; (May 1978), 83–84
Zaire–People's Republic of the Congo (January 1987), 93–94
Regional organizations, 28, 321–334
conflict management outcomes, 31
cooperation and complementarity, 41–43
differences from UN, 38–43
as forum for airing conflict issues, 24–26
limitations of, 28
mediation outcomes, 31
as mediators, 16–17, 39–41
as observers and fact-finders, 17–18
origins and functions, 43–45
peacekeeping missions, 18–22
Regional rivalries
Argentina–Chile (July 1952–August 1993), 126–128
Cambodia–Siam (Thailand) (early 1953–May 1975), 170–171
China–Vietnam (February 1979–June 1982), 188; (April 1983), 190
Ecuador–Peru (June 1977–January 1978), 143–144; (January 1984), 148; (January–March 1995), 151
Guinea–Ivory Coast (February–September 1967), 74
India–Pakistan (1965–1970), 213–214; (July 1981–August 1982), 219
Iran–Iraq (February 1980–1989), 291
Nicaragua–Costa Rica (October 1977), 144; (September–December 1978), 144–145; (May–June 1985), 148–149; (April 1986), 149
Nigeria–Biafra (July 1967–January 1970), 74–75
Togo–Ghana (September 1986), 93
Turkey–Greece (March 1984–January 1988), 245
Vietnam–China (January 1984–March 1987), 190–191; (March 1988), 192
Regional tensions
Cambodia–Thailand (December 1975–February 1976), 185
Egypt–Libya (July–September 1977), 287–288
Zaire–Zambia (September 1983–January 1984), 91
Religious warfare
Bosnia (mid-1989–November 2000), 246–248
Renamo. *See* Mozambique National Resistance Movement
Republic of South Africa
Angola–South Africa (1975–), 78–79
anti-ANC raids (December 1982), 88–89; (October 1984–May 1986), 91–92
Korean War (June 1950–July 1953), 169
Mozambique–South Africa (1976–October 1992), 80–81
South Africa–Botswana (October 1984–May 1986), 91–92
South Africa–Lesotho (December 1982), 88–89
South Africa–Zambia (April 1987), 94
Republic of Vanuatu
Vanuatu–Espiritu Santo (May–September 1980), 189
Republic of Vietnam (South Vietnam)
Cambodia–South Vietnam (January 1970–April 1975), 180–181
Paracel Islands dispute (January 1974), 182
South Vietnam–Cambodia (March–December 1964), 176
South Vietnam–China (January 1974), 182
Taiwan–South Vietnam (June–August 1956), 172
U.S.–Vietnam (August 1964–May 1975), 177–178
Vietnam War (August 1964–May 1975), 177–178
Resource disputes. *See also* Border disputes; *specific resources*
Euphrates (April–late 1975), 284–285
Revolutionary United Front (RUF), 104
Revolutions
Afghanistan–Pakistan (March–July 1979), 217
Cuba (December 1956–January 1959), 131
Hungary–USSR (October–December 1956), 240–241
Mosul Revolt (March–April 1959), 273–274
Rhodesia (Zimbabwe) (1967–January 1980), 73–74
Right-wing insurgencies
Honduras–Nicaragua (January 1980–February 1994), 145
Riots
flag riots (January–April 1964), 139
Rivalries. *See also specific rivals*
ethnic. *See also* Ethnic conflicts
Nigeria–Biafra (July 1967–January 1970), 74–75
nationalist
China–Taiwan (January 1996–August 1999), 196–197
North Korea–South Korea (May 1992), 194; (September 1996–November 2000), 197–198
regional. *See* Regional rivalries
Robertson, Lord, 251
Rohingya Muslim rebellion (December 1991), 193–194
Romania, 6, 231, 240, 241, 248, 249
Royal Air Force (RAF), 61, 270, 275
Royalist rebellions
North Yemen (September 1962–October 1967), 275–276
RPF. *See* Rwandan Patriotic Front
Rugova, Ibrahim, 254
Russia
Chechen war (October 1992–), 252–253
Russia–Dagestan (May 1999), 255
Russia–Georgia (August 2000–), 255–257
Tajikistan (April 1992–June 1997), 224–225
Rwanda
Congo–Rwanda (August 1967–April 1968), 75
Rwanda–Burundi (January 1964–January 1965), 69
tribal conflict (September 1990–), 102–104
Rwandan Patriotic Front (RPF), 102–104

Sabah, 155, 174
Sabah, Sheikh al-, 288
Sabajo, Thomas, 150
Sadat, Anwar el-, 282, 288
SADC. *See* South African Development Community
SADF. *See* South African Defence Forces
Sahara
Morocco–Mauritania (October 1974–), 77
Sahara conflict (November 1957–April 1958), 62
Sahel
pastoralist rebellion (June 1990–), 102
pastoralist separatism (May 1990–October 1994), 100
Said, Qabus bin, 280
Saleh, Ali Abdullah, 290, 298
Samore, Cardinal, 127
Sampson, Nikoi Giorgiades, 244
Samrin, Heng, 187, 188, 190
Sandinista National Liberation Front (FSLN), 145
Sandinistas, 120, 144, 145
Sandino, Augusto César, 145
San José plan, 142
Sankoh, Foday, 104
SANU. *See* Sudan Africa National Union
Sâo Tome and Principe
African territories–Portugal (1961–July 1975), 65
Sarawak, 155, 174
Sarawak Advanced Youth's Association (SAYA), 174
Sarawak United People's Party (SUPP), 145
Sassou-Nguesso, Denis, 110
Saudi Arabia
Aden conflict (1956–1960), 270–271
Euphrates dispute (April–late 1975), 284–285
Gulf war (August 1990–May 1991), 296
North Yemen (September 1962–October 1967), 275–276
North Yemen–Saudi Arabia (November 1969–October 1970), 278
Oman–Saudi Arabia (August 1952–October 1955), 268–269
Saudi Arabia–North Yemen (August 1979–March 1980), 290–291
Saudi Arabia–Qatar (September–October 1992), 297
Saudi Arabia–Yemen (December 1994), 299–300
Yom Kippur War (October 1973), 282–283
Saud ibn Abdul Aziz, 269
Savimbi, Jonas, 79

Sawaba Party, 68
Sawyer, Amos, 99
SAYA. *See* Sarawak Advanced Youth's Association
Sea of Galilee. *See* Lake Tiberias dispute
Sea of Japan, 170, 179, 197
Secession conflicts
attempted secessions
Kurds–Iraq (March 1961–1966), 274; (March 1974–July 1975), 283
Nigeria–Biafra (July 1967–January 1970), 74–75
Belgian Congo (July 1960–mid-1964), 64–65
Casamance rebellion (mid-1990-), 100–101
Eritrea–Ethiopia (1965–May 1993), 70–71
Indonesia–Papua New Guinea (May 1982–October 1984), 189–190
Irian Jaya–Indonesia (1965-), 178–179
Mindanao–The Philippines (January 1970-), 181–182
Pakistan–Bangladesh (March 1971–February 1974), 215
Senegal (mid-1990-), 100–101
Sudan (January 1983-), 89–90
USSR–Iran (August 1945–October 1947), 265–266
Vanuatu–Espiritu Santo (May–September 1980), 189
Secret Army Organization (SAO), 62
Security Council. *See* United Nations
Sékou Touré, Ahmed, 72, 90
Senegal
Casamance rebellion (mid-1990–), 100–101
Guinea-Bissau–Senegal (April 1990–May 1990), 100
Mauritania–Senegal (April 1989–January 1990), 98
Separatism
Chechen (August 2000–), 255–257
Georgia–South Ossetia, Abkhazia (March 1989–), 245–246
Indonesia–Malaysia (1962–November 1965), 174–175
insurgencies
Bougainville–Papua New Guinea (October 1988–), 192–193
Karen (January 1949–), 167–168; (March 1984), 191
Kurdish (May 1976–), 286–287; (August 1984–), 293–294
Netherlands–Indonesia (January–August 1962), 175
Somalia–Kenya (November 1962–September 1967), 66
Thailand–Burma (March–May 2001), 199–200
Katanga (July 1960–mid-1964), 64–65
postpartition India
India–Pakistan (October 1947–January 1949), 207–208
violence (July–September 1948), 208
Russia–Chechnya, the Caucasus (October 1992–), 252–253
Sahel pastoralist (May 1990–October 1994), 100
Somalia–Ethiopia (January–March 1964), 68–69
Sudan (September 1963–March 1972), 66–67
September 11, 2001, attacks, 5–7, 227–228
Serbia, 18, 231, 233, 234, 246, 247, 255
Shaba
invasions of (March–May 1977), 82–83; (May 1978), 83–84; (November 1984), 92; (June 1985), 92
separatism (July 1960–mid-1964), 64–65
Shah, Mohammad Zahir, 217, 218
Shans, 180
Shan State Army (SSA), 199
Shanti Bahini, 215, 216
Shari'a, 89
Sharon, Ariel, 292, 300
Shatt al Arab Waterway, 279
Shelling incidents
Taiwan–China (November 1994), 195
Shevardnadze, Eduard, 246, 256
Shiite Muslims, 248, 298
Azeris, 248–249
Shuttle diplomacy, 22–24
Siachin Glacier dispute (April 1984–September 1985), 10, 221
Siachin Glacier/Kashmir conflict (1986–), 222–223
Siam (Thailand). *See also* Thailand
Cambodia–Siam (early 1953–May 1975), 170–171
Sierra Leone
civil war (March 1991–), 104–105
Liberia (December 1989–), 98–100
Liberia–Sierra Leone (February–March 1983), 90; (March 1991–), 104–105
Sihanouk, Norodom, 181, 187
Simla Conference, 209, 211
Simon, Owen, 208
Sinai, 264, 271, 277, 282
Singapore. *See* Malaya
Sinhalese, 205, 219–220
Sino–Indian wars
McMahon Line border disputes (August 1959–February 1960), 211; (October–November 1962), 212–213; (September 1965), 214–215
Six-Day war (June 1967), 277–278
SLA. *See* South Lebanon Army; Surinamese Liberation Army
SLORC. *See* State Law and Order Restoration Council
Slovak Republic. *See* Czechoslovakia
Slovenia, 231, 233, 237, 246–247
Smith, Ian, 73
SNM. *See* Somali National Movement
Socialist Republic of Vietnam (North Vietnam)
Laos (December 1958–1962), 175
Laos–North Vietnam (April 1964–May 1975), 176–177
U.S.–Vietnam (August 1964–May 1975), 177–178
Vietnam War (August 1964–May 1975), 177–178
Soglo, Christophe, 68
Solana, Javier, 251
Somalia
civil war (May 1988–), 95–97
expansionism
Ethiopia–Somalia (February 1987–April 1988), 94; (mid-1972–1985), 76–77
Somalia–Ethiopia (January–March 1964), 68–69
Somalia–Kenya (November 1962–September 1967), 66
Ogaden wars (January–March 1964), 68–69; (mid-1972–1985), 76–77; (February 1987–April 1988), 94
Somaliland, 60, 70, 96, 110
Somali National Movement (SNM), 94, 95
Somoza Debayle, Anastasio, 144
Souphanouvong, 176
South Africa. *See* Republic of South Africa
South African Defence Forces (SADF), 94
South African Development Community (SADC), 111
South China Sea
Paracel Islands (June–August 1956), 172
Southeast Asia. *See* East Asia/Pacific
Southern Africa. *See specific countries*
South Korea
North Korea–South Korea (mid-1965–March 1968), 179; (February–July 1975), 182–183; (November 1984), 192; (May 1992), 194; (September 1996–November 2000), 197–198; (November 2001–July 2002), 200–201
U.S.–North Korea (June 1950–July 1953), 169
Vietnam War (August 1964–May 1975), 177–178
South Lebanon Army (SLA), 293
South Ossetia
Georgia–South Ossetia, Abkhazia (March 1989–), 245–246
South Pacific Forum. *See* Pacific Islands Forum
South Vietnam. *See* Republic of Vietnam
South West Africa (Namibia). *See also* Namibia
war of independence (1966–March 1990), 72
South West Africa People's Organization (SWAPO), 13, 72, 78
Southwest Asia. *See also specific countries*
characteristics of conflicts, 46
conflict management, 207
conflicts, overview of, 205–207
country list, alphabetical, 204, 303–305
map, 206
regional overview, 204–205

South Yemen
North Yemen–South Yemen (October 1971–October 1972), 279–280; (February 1979–February 1980), 289
Oman–South Yemen (1972–August 1974), 280–281
Yemen (November 1993–July 1994), 298–299
Souvanna Phouma, 176
Sovereignty disputes
Egypt–United Kingdom (January 1952–January 1956), 268
Egypt–United Kingdom, France (October–November 1956), 271–272
Falklands war (April–June 1982), 146–147
Hawar Islands (April 1986), 295
Qatar–Bahrain (April 1986), 295
Spratly Islands disputes (March 1988), 192; (April 1997–July 1999), 198
United Kingdom–Argentina (April–June 1982), 146–147
U.S.–Panama (January–April 1964), 139
Vietnam–China (March 1988), 192
Soviet Union. *See* Union of Soviet Socialist Republics (USSR)
Spain, 6, 8, 76–77, 118, 159, 231
Spain–Morocco (November 1957–April 1958), 62
SPF. *See* Pacific Islands Forum
SPLA. *See* Sudan People's Liberation Army
Spratly Islands, 11, 14, 29, 155, 182, 192
China–The Philippines (January–February 1995), 195–196; (April 1997–July 1999), 198
Taiwan–South Vietnam (June–August 1956), 172
Taiwan–Vietnam (March 1995), 196
Vietnam–China (March 1988), 192
Vietnam–The Philippines (October 1999), 198–199
Spy ship incident (December 2001), 201–202
Sri Lanka, 204–207, 223
Tamil conflict (July 1982–), 219–221
SSA. *See* Shan State Army
State Law and Order Restoration Council (SLORC), 167, 195
State mediation, 16–17
Sudan
Chad–Sudan (November 1965–1972), 71–72
civil war (January 1983–), 89–90
Egypt–Sudan (February 1958), 272; (December 1992), 297–298
Halaib dispute (December 1992), 297–298
Ogaden war (January–March 1964), 68–69
Sudan Africa National Union (SANU), 67
Sudan People's Liberation Army (SPLA), 89–90, 106
Suez Canal, 9, 268, 271, 277
Canal Zone dispute (January 1952–January 1956), 268
Yom Kippur War (October 1973), 282–283
Suez Canal (Company), 268, 271
Suez crisis (October–November 1956), 271–272
Sukarno, Ahmed, 164, 174
Sunni Muslims, 263, 293
SUPP. *See* Sarawak United People's Party
Suriname
guerrilla insurgency (July 1986–December 1992), 149–150
Guyana–Suriname (August 1969–November 1970), 142
Surinamese Liberation Army (SLA), 149–150
Surma River incidents (March 1958–September 1959), 210
SWAPO. *See* South West Africa People's Organization
Syria
Euphrates dispute (April–late 1975), 284–285
France–Levant (1945–December 1946), 265
Israel (May 1948–January 1949), 266
Israel–Arab states (June 1967), 277–278
Israel–Lebanon (early 1982–mid-1983), 292–293
Israel–Syria (July 1957–February 1958), 272; (June 1979–February 1980), 289–290; (February 2001–), 300–301
Lebanon (February 1975–late 1992), 284
PLO–Jordan (February 1970–August 1971), 278–279
Six-Day war (June 1967), 277–278
Syria–Iraq (March–April 1959), 273–274; (April–late 1975), 284–285
Syria–Israel (April–May 1951), 267–268; (February 1962–August 1963), 275; (June 1964–July 1966), 276; (March 1972–January 1973), 281–282
Syria–Lebanon (May–August 1949), 266–267
Turkey–Syria (March 1955–1957), 269–270
Yom Kippur War (October 1973), 282–283

Tachen islands, 171
Taiwan
China (1945–1949), 163–164
China–Taiwan (October 1949–June 1953), 168; (March–December 1962), 175–176; (January 1996–August 1999), 196–197
Spratly Islands clash (March 1995), 196
Taiwan–China (April 1954–April 1955), 171–172; (November 1994), 195
Taiwan–South Vietnam (June–August 1956), 172
Taiwan–Vietnam (March 1995), 196
U.S./Taiwan–China (July–December 1958), 172–173
Taiwan strait (October 1949–June 1953), 168
Tajikistan
civil war (April 1992–June 1997), 224–225
Uzbekistan–Kyrgyzstan/Tajikistan (August 1999–September 2000), 225–226
Taliban movement, 207, 218–219, 262–263
U.S.–Afghanistan (September–December 2001), 227–228
Tam, In, 185
Tamil conflict (July 1982–), 219–221
Tanna, 189
Tanzania, 11, 18, 40–41, 53, 55, 73, 80, 94, 102–103, 227
Tanzania–Uganda (October 1978–May 1979), 84–85
Uganda (December 1981–1994), 86
Uganda–Tanzania (1971–October 1972), 75–76
Zaire (November 1984), 92; (June 1985), 92
Taylor, Charles, 98–99
Temple of Preal Vihear, occupation of, 170–171
Territorial disputes. *See also* Border disputes
Afghanistan–Pakistan (June–October 1950), 209
Albania–United Kingdom (May 1946–December 1949), 237
Algeria–Morocco (October 1963–February 1964), 67
Arab–Israeli
Golan Heights conflict (July 1957–February 1958), 272
Israel (May 1948–January 1949), 266
Israel–Jordan (July 1956–January 1958), 271
Israel–Syria (July 1957–February 1958), 272
Syria–Israel (February 1962–August 1963), 275
Argentina–Chile (July 1952–August 1993), 126–128
Beagle Channel (July 1952–August 1993), 126–128
Cameroon–Nigeria (May–July 1981), 85–86
Chile–Bolivia (March 1962–1964), 135–136
China–The Philippines (January–February 1995), 195–196
China–Taiwan (October 1949–June 1953), 168; (March–December 1962), 175–176
China–USSR (March 1963–September 1969), 213
cold war
Italy–Yugoslavia (March 1952–October 1954), 239
U.S.–North Korea (June 1950–July 1953), 169
Condor Mountain region (January 1995–October 1998), 151–152
Corfu Channel dispute (May 1946–December 1949), 237
Corisco Bay islands dispute (June–November 1972), 76
Ecuador–Peru (June 1977–January 1978), 143–144; (January–April 1981), 145–146; (January 1984), 148; (January 1995–October 1998), 151–152
El Salvador–Honduras (July 1976–October 1980), 142–143
Equatorial Guinea–Gabon (June–November 1972), 76
Eritrea–Ethiopia (May 1998–June 1999), 111–112
Essequibo River dispute (February 1962–June 1970), 134–135
Ethiopia–Somalia (mid-1972–1985), 76–77
Ghana–Togo (August–October 1982), 88
Guatemala–Mexico (December 1958–September 1959), 132–133
Gulf war (August 1990–May 1991), 296

Territorial disputes—*continued*
India–Pakistan (1965–1970), 213–214; (August–September 1965), 214; (April 1984–September 1985), 221; (1986–), 222–223
India–Portugal (December 1961), 212
Iran–Iraq (January 1972–February 1975), 281
Iran–Iraq War (February 1980–1989), 291
Iran–United Arab Emirates (November 1971), 280; (April 1992), 297
Iraq–Coalition forces (August 1990–May 1991), 296
Iraq–Iran (1971), 279
Iraq–Kuwait (June 1961–February 1962), 274–275; (March 1973–July 1975), 282
Irian Jaya–Indonesia (1965–), 178–179
KMT–CCP (October 1949–June 1953), 168; (April 1954–April 1955), 171–172; (July–December 1958), 172–173; (March–December 1962), 175–176
Laos–Thailand (June 1982), 190
Lauca River dam dispute (March 1962–1964), 135–136
Liberia–Guinea (September 1999–April 2001), 113–114
Macao conflict (July–August 1952), 169–170
McMahon Line (October 1975), 216
Mekong River (August–September 2000), 199
Mexican shrimp boat incident (December 1958–September 1959), 132–133
Mindanao–The Philippines (January 1970–), 181–182
Paracel Islands (June–August 1956), 172; (January–February 1995), 195–196
postindependence
Bangladesh (1975–), 215–216
Belize–Guatemala (August 1995), 152
Chittagong Hill Tracts conflict (1975–), 215–216
Egypt–Sudan (February 1958), 272
Pakistan–Afghanistan (August 1949), 208–209
Siachin Glacier (April 1984–September 1985), 221
Siachin Glacier/Kashmir conflict (1986–), 222–223
South Vietnam–China (January 1974), 182
Spratly Islands (January–February 1995), 195–196; (March 1995), 196; (April 1997–July 1999), 198
Taiwan–China (April 1954–April 1955), 171–172
Taiwan–South Vietnam (June–August 1956), 172
Taiwan–Vietnam (March 1995), 196
Thailand–Laos (August–September 2000), 199
Tunb islands (November 1971), 280; (April 1992), 297
Venezuela–Guyana (U.K.) (February 1962–June 1970), 134–135
Yirga Triangle dispute (May 1998–June 1999), 111–112
Territorial occupation
Central African Republic–Chad (mid-2001–December 2002), 115–116
Territorial/resource disputes
Egypt/Sudan (December 1992), 297–298
Halaib (December 1992), 297–298
Mali–Burkina Faso (December 1985–January 1986), 92–93
Mali–Upper Volta (December 1974–June 1975), 77–78
Oman–Saudi Arabia (August 1952–October 1955), 268–269
Syria–Israel (April–May 1951), 267–268
Terrorism
Anya-Nya (September 1963–March 1972), 66–67
Mujahedeen-e Khalq, 300
post–September 11, 5–7
U.S.–Afghanistan (September–December 2001), 227–228
U.S.–Libya (January–April 1986), 295
Uzbekistan–Kyrgyzstan/Tajikistan (August 1999–September 2000), 225–226
Thailand
Borneo conflict (1962–November 1965), 174–175
Burma–Thailand (March 1984), 191
Cambodia–Siam (early 1953–May 1975), 170–171
Cambodia–Thailand (December 1975–February 1976), 185; (January 1977–October 1978), 186–187; (December 1979–October 1980), 188–189
Khmer Rouge border incidents (November–December 1976), 185–186; (January 1977–October 1978), 186–187
Korean War (June 1950–July 1953), 169
Laos–Thailand (June 1975–January 1976), 183–184; (June 1982), 190
Mayaguez incident (May 1975), 183
Thailand–Burma (March–May 2001), 199–200
Thailand–Cambodia (November–December 1976), 185–186
Thailand–Laos (June 1984–December 1988), 191–192; (August–September 2000), 199
Vietnam War (December 1960–May 1975), 173–174
Thant, U, 74, 135, 171, 173, 175, 177
Third-party intervention. *See* Intervention; Military intervention
Tibet, 155
Agreement on Measures for the Peaceful Liberation of Tibet (Seventeen Articles Agreement), 209
China–Tibet (October 1950–May 1951), 209–210
McMahon Line dispute (August 1959–February 1960), 211; (October–November 1962), 212–213; (September 1965), 214–215; (October 1975), 216
Tibet–China (March 1956–September 1965), 210
Timur, Said bin, 280
Tindemans, Léo, 84
Tindouf war (October 1963–February 1964), 67
TISA (Transitional Islamic State of Afghanistan). *See* Afghanistan
TMKU. *See* National Army of North Borneo
Togo
attempted coup (September 1986), 93
Ghana–Togo (January–May 1965), 71; (August–October 1982), 88; (January–February 1994), 106
Togo–Ghana (September 1986), 93
Tolbert, William Richard, 74
Tombolbaye, Ngarta, 71
Toruno, Roldolfo, 128
Touré, Sékou, 72, 90
Trajovski, Boris, 251
Trans-Dniester Republic, 250
Transitional Government of National Unity. *See* GUNT
Transitional Islamic State of Afghanistan (TISA). *See* Afghanistan
Transjordan, 266
Tribal conflicts
Burundi (August 1988–), 97–98
China–Burma (January–November 1969), 180
Hutu conflict (August 1988–), 97–98
Mau Mau revolt (August 1952–December 1963), 61
Rwanda (September 1990–), 102–104
Somalia (May 1988–), 95–97
Trieste crisis (March 1952–October 1954), 239
Tripartite Declaration, 239
Tripartite Treaty, 265
TRNC. *See* Turkish Republic of Northern Cyprus
Trujillo. *See* Molina, Rafael Leónidas Trujillo
Tuareg
Mali–Tuareg (June 1990–), 102
Niger–Tuaregs (May 1990–October 1994), 100
Tucayana Amazonicas, 150
Tudeh Party, 285
Tunb islands disputes (November 1971), 280; (April 1992), 297
Tunisia
Bizerte conflict (July–September 1961), 65–66
France–Tunisia (February–May 1958), 63; (February–August 1959), 63; (July–September 1961), 65–66
military bases conflict (February–May 1958), 63
war of independence (January 1952–March 1956), 61
Yom Kippur War (October 1973), 282–283
Turkey, 4, 6–7, 23, 209, 231, 239, 249, 254, 263, 274, 278, 283, 286, 328
Cyprus (December 1963–November 1967), 241; (January 1974–June 1978), 244
Korean War (June 1950–July 1953), 169
Kurds, 28, 30, 260, 293–294
Kurds–Turkey (August 1984–), 293–294
Turkey–Greece (March 1984–January 1988), 245
Turkey–Syria (March 1955–1957), 269–270

Turkish Republic of Northern Cyprus (TRNC), 254
Tutsiland, 97
Tutsis, 97, 109
  Rwanda (September 1990–), 102–104
  Rwanda–Burundi (January 1964–January 1965), 69

U.A.E. *See* United Arab Emirates
Uganda
  Amin ouster (October 1978–May 1979), 84–85
  civil wars (December 1981–1994), 86; (December 1987), 95
  Congo–Uganda (February–March 1965), 71
  intervention and democratic movements (May 1995–), 106–107
  Tanzania–Uganda (October 1978–May 1979), 84–85
  Uganda–Kenya (February–August 1976), 81; (December 1987), 95; (March 1989), 98; (November 1996–July 1998), 109–110
  Uganda–Tanzania (1971–October 1972), 75–76
Ugandan National Liberation Front (UNLF), 85–86
Ugandan People's Defense Forces (UPDF), 106
Ugandan People's Democratic Army (UPDA), 86
Uganda Patriotic Movement (UPM), 86
Ukrainians, 6, 8, 250
Ulate Blanco, Otilio, 125
ULIMO. *See* United Liberation Movement of Liberia for Democracy
UN. *See* United Nations
UNAR. *See* Union Nationale Rwandaise
UNCI. *See* United Nations Commission for Indonesia
UNCMAC. *See* United Nations Command Armistice Committee
UNFICYP. *See* United Nations Peace-keeping Force in Cyprus
UNHCR. *See* United Nations High Commission for Refugees
União Nacional para a Independência Total de Angola (UNITA), 116
Unification difficulties
  Yemen (November 1993–July 1994), 298–299
UNIFIL. *See* United Nations Interim Force in Lebanon
Union Africaine et Malgache (UAM), 68
Union for the Total Independence of Angola (UNITA), 78
Union Nationale Rwandaise (UNAR), 69
Union of Angolan People (UPA), 65
Union of National Front Forces, 285
Union of Soviet Socialist Republics (USSR), 95, 157, 162, 171, 180, 233, 237, 260. *See also* Russia
  Aden conflict (1956–1960), 270–271
  Berlin airlift (June 1948–May 1949), 238–239
  China–USSR (March 1963–September 1969), 213
  cold war, 4–5, 8–9, 56, 123, 168, 170, 173, 231–232, 238, 241, 261
    USSR–Poland (October 1956), 240
    U.S.–USSR (October 1952–July 1956), 170; (July–November 1961), 241–242; (September–November 1962), 136–137
  Cuban Missile Crisis (September–November 1962), 136–137
  expansion in Europe, 232
  Hungary–USSR (October–December 1956), 240–241
  Ogaden war (mid-1972–1985), 76–77
  Pathan conflict (September 1960–May 1963), 211–212
  Poland (December 1981–February 1982), 244–245
  post–Soviet conflicts
    Azerbaijan–Armenia (August 1990–), 248–249
    Georgia–South Ossetia, Abkhazia (March 1989–), 245–246
    Kyrgystan (June 1990), 223–224
    Moldova (October 1990–July 1992), 249–250
    Nagorno-Karabakh conflict (August 1990–), 248–249
    Russia–Chechnya, the Caucasus (October 1992–), 252–253
    Tajikistan (April 1992–June 1997), 224–225
    USSR–Latvia (January 1991), 250–251
    USSR–Lithuania (March 1990–late 1991), 248
  Suez crisis (October–November 1956), 271–272
  U.S.–Grenada (October–November 1983), 147–148
  USSR–Afghanistan (December 1979–), 218–219
  USSR–Czechoslovakia (August 1968), 241–242
  USSR–Hungary (October–December 1956), 240–241
  USSR–Iran (August 1945–October 1947), 265–266
  USSR–Latvia (January 1991), 250–251
  USSR–Western allies (June 1948–May 1949), 238–239
  USSR–Yugoslavia (early 1948–December 1954), 238
  Ussuri River conflict (March 1963–September 1969), 213
  U.S.–USSR (April–October 1950), 168–169
UNITA. *See* União Nacional para a Independência Total de Angola; Union for the Total Independence of Angola
United Arab Emirates
  Iran–United Arab Emirates (November 1971), 280; (April 1992), 297
  Tunb islands dispute (November 1971), 280; (April 1992), 297
United Fruit, 128
United Kingdom
  Aden conflict (1956–1960), 270–271
  Albania–United Kingdom (May 1946–December 1949), 237
  Berlin airlift (June 1948–May 1949), 238–239
  Borneo (1962–November 1965), 174–175
  Chittagong Hill Tracts conflict (1975–), 215–216
  Cyprus (December 1963–November 1967), 241
  Egypt–United Kingdom (January 1952–January 1956), 268
  Egypt–United Kingdom, France (October–November 1956), 271–272
  Falklands war (April–June 1982), 146–147
  Greece (1945–1949), 236–237
  Iceland–United Kingdom, West Germany, Denmark (November 1971–June 1976), 243–244
  India (1945–1948), 207
  Israel (May 1948–January 1949), 266
  Kenya–United Kingdom (August 1952–December 1963), 61
  Korean War (June 1950–July 1953), 169
  Mau Mau revolt (August 1952–December 1963), 61
  North Yemen (September 1962–October 1967), 275–276
  Trieste crisis (March 1952–October 1954), 239
  Tripartite Declaration, 239
  United Kingdom–Argentina (April–June 1982), 146–147
  United Kingdom–Malaya (June 1948–July 1960), 165–166
  USSR–Western allies (June 1948–May 1949), 238–239
  Venezuela–Guyana (U.K.) (February 1962–June 1970), 134–135
  Yemen–United Kingdom (1956–1960), 270–271
United Liberation Movement of Liberia for Democracy (ULIMO), 99
United Nations (UN). *See also specific disputes*
  commissioners for human rights, list of, 320
  commissioners for refugees, list of, 320
  concerns of, 317
  constraints on, 36–38
  differences from regional organizations, 38–43
  establishment of, 15, 26, 317
  fact-finding missions, 16–17
  as forum for airing conflict issues, 24–26
  General Assembly presidents, list of, 320
  involvement in disputes, 16–17, 31
  limitations of, 38
  mediation outcomes, 31
  membership of, 318
  organs for handling conflict, 319
  peacekeeping, 18–22
  primary objective of, 34
  referral to, 24–25
  secretaries-general, list of, 320
  secretary-general, responsibilities of, 35–36
  Security Council
    handling conflict, 319
    primary responsibilities, 35
  strengths of, 320
  structural hierarchy, 317
United Nations Charter, 34, 234
  stated obligations toward peaceful settlements, 317
United Nations Command Armistice Committee (UNCMAC), 200
United Nations Commission for Indonesia (UNCI), 164
United Nations High Commission for Refugees (UNHCR), 112
United Nations Interim Force in Lebanon (UNIFIL), 21, 40, 288, 289
United Nations Kashmir Commission, 34
United Nations Operation in the Congo (UNOC), 20, 64
United Nations Peace-keeping Force in Cyprus (UNFICYP), 242

United Nations Special Committee on Palestine (UNSCOP), 266
United Nations Truce Supervision Organization (UNTSO), 270, 275
United Somali Congress (USC), 96
United States
Aden conflict (1956–1960), 270–271
Bay of Pigs (April–May 1961), 134
Berlin airlift (June 1948–May 1949), 238–239
Cambodia–South Vietnam (January 1970–April 1975), 180–181
cold war
U.S.–USSR (October 1952–July 1956), 170; (July–November 1961), 241–242; (September–November 1962), 136–137
contra war (January 1980–February 1994), 145
Cuban Missile Crisis (September–November 1962), 136–137
flag riots (January–April 1964), 139
Gulf war (August 1990–May 1991), 296
Haitian exiles conflict (August 1959), 133–134
Iraq–Coalition forces (August 1990–May 1991), 296; (2003), 6, 263
Ivory Coast (September 1999–), 114–115
Korean War (June 1950–July 1953), 169
Lebanon (May 1958–June 1959), 273
Mayaguez incident (May 1975), 183
North Korea–U.S. (January–December 1968), 179–180
Rabat chemical plant tensions (January 1989), 295–296
Reagan administration, 128, 143, 145, 291, 295
Sahara conflict (November 1957–April 1958), 62
Somalia (May 1988–), 95–97
Suez crisis (October–November 1956), 271–272
Trieste crisis (March 1952–October 1954), 239
Tripartite Declaration, 239
U.S.–Afghanistan (September–December 2001), 227–228
U.S.–Cuba (April–May 1961), 134
U.S.–Dominican Republic (April 1965–September 1966), 140–141
U.S.–Grenada (October–December 1983), 147–148
U.S.–Haiti (September 1994), 150–151
U.S.–Iran hostage crisis (November 1979–January 1981), 290
U.S.–Libya (August 1981), 291–292; (January–April 1986), 295; (January 1989), 295–296
U.S.–North Korea (June 1950–July 1953), 169
U.S.–Panama (January–April 1964), 139; (December 1989), 150
USS *Pueblo* seizure (January–December 1968), 179–180
U.S./Taiwan–China (July–December 1958), 172–173
U.S.–USSR (April–October 1950), 168–169
U.S.–Vietnam (December 1960–May 1975), 173–174
U.S.–Yugoslavia (August 1946), 237–238
USSR–Western allies (June 1948–May 1949), 238–239
Vietnam War (December 1960–May 1975), 173–174
post–Vietnam War tensions (May 1975), 183
Yom Kippur War (October 1973), 282–283
Universal Postal Union (UPU), 28
UNLF. *See* Ugandan National Liberation Front
UNOC. *See* United Nations Operation in the Congo
UNSCOP. *See* United Nations Special Committee on Palestine
UPA. *See* Union of Angolan People
UPDA. *See* Ugandan People's Democratic Army
UPDF. *See* Ugandan People's Defense Forces
UPM. *See* Uganda Patriotic Movement
Upper Volta (Burkina Faso)
Ghana–Upper Volta (June 1964–June 1966), 69–70
Mali–Upper Volta (December 1974–June 1975), 77–78
UPU. *See* Universal Postal Union
URNG. *See* Guatemalan National Revolutionary Unity
USC. *See* United Somali Congress
USS *Pueblo* seizure (January–December 1968), 179–180
USSR. *See* Union of Soviet Socialist Republics
Ussuri River conflict (March 1963–September 1969), 213
Uzbekistan–Kyrgyzstan/Tajikistan (August 1999–September 2000), 225–226

Vance, Cyrus, 17, 29, 234
Vanuatu. *See* Republic of Vanuatu
Varkiya agreement, 236
The Vatican, 333
Venezuela
Cuba–Venezuela (November 1963–May 1967), 138–139
Dominican Republic–Cuba/Venezuela (February 1956–January 1962), 129–131
Nicaragua–Costa Rica (September–December 1978), 144–145
Venezuela–Guyana (U.K.) (February 1962–June 1970), 134–135
Vieira, Joao Bernardo, 112
Vietcong, 173–174, 176, 180
Vietminh, 157, 159, 165, 171
South Vietnam–Cambodia (March–December 1964), 176
Vietnam. *See also* Republic of Vietnam; Socialist Republic of Vietnam
Cambodia–Vietnam (January 1979–), 187–188
China–Vietnam (February 1979–June 1982), 188; (April 1983), 190
civil war (December 1960–May 1975), 173–174
France–French Indochina (December 1945–July 1954), 165
Spratly Islands disputes (March 1988), 192; (March 1995), 196; (April 1997–July 1999), 198
Taiwan–Vietnam (March 1995), 196
U.S.–Vietnam (August 1964–May 1975), 177–178
Vietnam–China (January 1984–March 1987), 190–191; (March 1988), 192
Vietnam–The Philippines (October 1999), 198–199
Vietnam War (August 1964–May 1975), 177–178
Gulf of Tonkin incident, 173
Mayaguez incident (May 1975), 183
Paris Peace Accords, 181
Tet offensive, 173–174
U.S. bombing campaign (January 1970–April 1975), 180–181
Violence
communal
Lebanon (February 1975–late 1992), 284
Mindanao–The Philippines (January 1970–), 181–182
Sri Lanka (July 1982–), 219–221
definition, 3
intercommunal
Cyprus (April 1955–February 1959), 239–240; (December 1963–November 1967), 241
South West Africa (1966–March 1990), 72
Vladivostok, 170

Wade, Abdoulaye, 114
Waldheim, Kurt, 35, 177–178, 183, 189
Walesa, Lech, 244–245
War on terrorism. *See* Terrorism
Warsaw Pact, 240, 241, 242
Wars of independence
Algeria (November 1954–March 1962), 62
Bangladesh (March 1971–February 1974), 215
France–French Indochina (December 1945–July 1954), 165
India (1945–1948), 207
Israel (May 1948–January 1949), 266
Netherlands–Dutch East Indies (1945–November 1949), 164–165
Rhodesia (Zimbabwe) (1967–January 1980), 73–74
South West Africa (1966–March 1990), 72
Tunisia (January 1952–March 1956), 61
United Kingdom–Malaya (June 1948–July 1960), 165–166
Water
Euphrates dispute (April–late 1975), 284–285
Mali–Burkina Faso (December 1985–January 1986), 92–93
West African Economic Community (CEAO), 93
West Bank
Israel–Jordan (January 1953–December 1954), 269
Mt. Scopus conflict (July 1956–January 1958), 271
Six-Day war (June 1967), 277–278
Western allies. *See* Coalition forces
Western Sahara (October 1974–), 77
Algeria–Morocco (June–October 1979), 85
summary, 77

West Germany
Iceland–United Kingdom, West Germany, Denmark (November 1971–June 1976), 243–244
West Irian (Irian Jaya), 178–179
Indonesia–Papua New Guinea (May 1982–October 1984), 189–190
Irian Jaya–Indonesia (1965–), 178–179
West Irian conflict (January–August 1962), 175
West New Guinea (Irian Jaya). *See* West Irian
West Nile Bank Front (WNBF), 106
West Pakistan. *See* Pakistan
WHO. *See* World Health Organization
Win Aung, 199
WNBF. *See* West Nile Bank Front
Worker's Self-Defense Movement, 139
World Cup, 121, 141, 200
World Health Organization (WHO), 28

Xanana, 184

Yameogo, Maurice, 68
YANSA. *See* Yunnan Anti-Communist and National Salvation Army
Ydigoras Fuentes, Miguel, 128
Yeltsin, Boris, 252
Yemen. *See also* North Yemen; South Yemen
Aden conflict (1956–1960), 270–271
civil war (November 1993–July 1994), 298–299
Eritrea–Yemen (November 1995–October 1998), 108–109
Saudi Arabia–Yemen (December 1994), 299–300
Yemen–United Kingdom (1956–1960), 270–271
Yhombi-Opango, Joachim, 95
Yirga Triangle dispute (May 1998–June 1999), 111–112
Yom Kippur War (October 1973), 282–283
Yugoslavia, 5, 9, 12, 18, 29, 31, 37, 42–44, 231, 233–237, 240, 251
Bosnia (mid-1989–November 2000), 246–248
Italy–Yugoslavia (March 1952–October 1954), 239
Trieste crisis (March 1952–October 1954), 239
USSR–Yugoslavia (early 1948–December 1954), 238
Yugoslavia–Kosovo (October 1997–), 254–255
Yugoslav National Army (JNA), 246
Yunnan Anti-Communist and National Salvation Army (YANSA), 166
Yuri Island, 170

Zaire. *See also* Congo; Democratic Republic of the Congo; People's Republic of the Congo
Belgian Congo (July 1960–mid-1964), 64–65
invasions of Shaba (June 1985), 92; (March–May 1977), 82–83; (May 1978), 83–84; (November 1984), 92
Lake Mweru border dispute (February–September 1982), 86–87
Uganda (December 1981–1994), 86
Zaire–Angola (November 1975–February 1976), 79–80; (March–May 1977), 82–83; (May 1978), 83–84
Zaire–People's Republic of the Congo (January 1987), 93–94
Zaire–Zambia (February–September 1982), 86–87; (September 1983–January 1984), 91
Zambia, 7, 8, 10, 12, 40, 53, 65, 72–73, 78, 80, 88, 115
Angola–Zambia (November 2001), 116
Lake Mweru border dispute (February–September 1982), 86–87
South Africa–Zambia (April 1987), 94
Zaire–Zambia (February–September 1982), 86–87; (September 1983–January 1984), 91
ZANU. *See* Zimbabwe African National Union
ZAPO. *See* Zimbabwe African People's Organization
ZAPU. *See* Zimbabwe African People's Union
Zimbabwe (1967–January 1980), 73–74
Zimbabwe African National Union (ZANU), 73, 80
Zimbabwe African People's Organization (ZAPO), 73
Zimbabwe African People's Union (ZAPU), 7

ARCTIC OCEAN
GREENLAND
Beaufort Sea
Baffin Bay
Chukchi Sea
Arctic Circle
Bering Strait
ALASKA
RUSSIA
Davis Strait
Denmark Strait
ICELAND
Norweg
Hudson Bay
Bering Sea
Gulf of Alaska
CANADA
IRELAND
Aleutian Islands
Newfoundland
NORTH
ATLANTIC
OCEAN
PORTUGAL
UNITED STATES OF AMERICA
Bermuda
MOROCCO
Canary Islands
Virgin Is.
Barbuda
Antigua
Montserrat
St. Kitts & Nevis
Guadeloupe
Dominica
Martinique
St. Lucia
Barbados
St. Vincent & the Grenadines
Bahamas
Gulf of Mexico
WESTERN SAHARA
Tropic of Cancer
MEXICO
Andros Is.
Turks & Caicos Is.
Hawaiian Islands
WEST INDIES
CUBA
Great Inagua
JAMAICA
HAITI
DOMINICAN REPUBLIC
PUERTO RICO
MAURITANIA
BELIZE
Cape Verde
SENEGAL
GAMBIA
GUINEA-BISSAU
GUINEA
SIERRA LEONE
LIBERIA
GUATEMALA
EL SALVADOR
HONDURAS
NICARAGUA
Grenada
Tobago
Trinidad
Aruba
Netherlands Antilles
COSTA RICA
PANAMA
VENEZUELA
GUYANA
SURINAME
FRENCH GUIANA
Galapagos Islands
COLOMBIA
POLYNESIA
Equator
ECUADOR
Kiritimati
Line Islands
Gilbert Is.
Kiribati
Phoenix Is.
PERU
Îs Marquises
BRAZIL
Tokelau
Tuvalu
Wallis & Futuna
French Polynesia
Samoa
American Samoa
Fiji
Cook Is.
Tahiti
Îs.de la Société
Îs. Tuamotu
SOUTH
ATLANTI
Tonga
Niue
Îs. Tubuai
Îs. Gambier
BOLIVIA
Tropic of Capricorn
PARAGUAY
OCEAN
CHILE
PACIFIC
OCEAN
URUGUAY
North I.
ARGENTINA
NEW ZEALAND
South I.
FALKLAND/MALVINAS ISLANDS
South Georgia
Antarctic Circle